AMERICAN CONSTITUTIONAL DEVELOPMENT

Volume II

The Rights of Persons

Richard S. Randall
New York University

New York   San Francisco   Boston
London   Toronto   Sydney   Tokyo   Singapore   Madrid
Mexico City   Munich   Paris   Cape Town   Hong Kong   Montreal

To the memory of Judge Eugene H. Nickerson,
a great civil libertarian and remarkable human being

Vice President/ Publisher: Priscilla McGeehon
Executive Editor : Eric Stano
Senior Marketing Manager: Megan Galvin-Fak
Production Manager: Denise Phillip
Project Coordination, Text Design, and Electronic Page Makeup: WestWords, Inc.
Cover Designer/Manager: John Callahan
Cover Image: Courtesy Corbis
Photo Researcher: Photosearch, Inc.
Manufacturing Buyer: Al Dorsey
Printer and Binder: Hamilton Printing Company
Cover Printer: Coral Graphics

For permission to use copyrighted material, grateful acknowledgment is made to the copyright holders on p. 655, which is hereby made part of this copyright page.

Library of Congress Cataloging-in-Publication Data

Randall, Richard S.
  American constitutional development / Richard S. Randall.
     p. cm.
Includes bibliographical references and index.
  ISBN 0-8013-2021-6
1. Constitutional history—United States. l. Title.
  KF4541 .R36 2002
  342.73'029—dc21   2001050440

Please visit our website at http://www.ablongman.com

ISBN 0-801-32021-6

10 9 8 7 6 5 4 3 2   —HT—05 04 03

BRIEF CONTENTS

DETAILED CONTENTS

PREFACE

Combining text and edited cases, this book deals with the Supreme Court's most important decisions on individual rights and the conflicts from which they have arisen. It is organized in three parts corresponding to the great trinity of values in American civil liberties: freedom, due process, and equality. Decisions of the Court are seen as presenting not simply questions of law and doctrine but also issues of political, social, moral, and cultural consequence.

Volume I of *American Constitutional Development: The Powers of Government* dealt with three constitutional regimes: the Formative, occupied with the question of union and ending with the Civil War; the Middle, which oversaw the new political economy of industrial capitalism and the ascent of the United States from transcontinental to world power; and the Modern, arising from the New Deal crisis and the Great Depression. Constitutional civil liberties are almost entirely the work of the last. Along with new empowerment of the national government and of the president within it, the elaboration of constitutionally guaranteed rights characterizes the Modern Constitution. Civil liberties cases have accounted for half the work of the Supreme Court during the last 70 years. They have led to a social revolution in race relations, an unparalleled freedom in communications, a right of privacy, an almost totally secularized state, an extensive revision of criminal justice procedures, and greater fairness in representation. On liberties and rights, the constitutional life of the nation today is as different from that of the Middle Constitution a century ago as that regime was from the Founding Constitution a century before that.

This volume deals with these and other developments of civil liberties. The cases discussed and chosen for excerpt not only present important matters of law and doctrine, but issues in public life as well. As in Volume I, a low-level, relatively nonintrusive analysis is used to ask the same kinds of questions of the Court's work that we ask about other institutional performance and policy-making in American government.

The text assumes that conflict and its adjustment or resolution lie at the heart of politics and government action and that all authoritative results—policies, programs, executive and administrative actions, statutes, judicial decisions, and constitutions themselves—have distributive effect, allocating gains, losses, benefits, and costs to those with immediate interests at stake and, eventually, to others as well.

The Constitution and interpretations of what it permits, requires, or forbids is the most authoritative allocator of all. The disputes in many of the Supreme Court's great civil liberties cases began in nonjudicial arenas and, receiving provisional resolution there, were cast or recast in legal terms by actors or parties defeated or dissatisfied. In the immediate, the Court distributes rights and obligations by granting or denying the former and imposing or providing release from the latter. These fungible legal values are transformed into the gains and losses by which we measure the "scarce" resources of our world—wealth, power, status, security, expressive freedom, and the hegemony of moral preferences—at stake in the fundamental or underlying conflict. With the imprimatur of constitutional authority, the Court's settlements, final or provisional as they may be, have shaped American civil liberties.

It is important for students to see that civil liberties compete with different ends and interests that may be worthy or unworthy. These may include the nation's security, crime control, civil peace, moral hegemony of the majority, the administration and enforcement of bias, and the like. A civil liberty may also clash with other liberties or rights, for example, freedom of the press with privacy or fair trial; free exercise of religion with the separation of church and state; freedom from race discrimination with freedom from "reverse discrimination."

The competition of ends, the resolution of conflict, and the distribution of gains and losses are analytic points that can be applied to almost any political phenomena. Civil liberties should be no exception. In this book, as in its companion volume, I have tried to take a step or two away from the law school orientation that often constricts undergraduate liberal arts instruction in constitutional law, and return, at least modestly, to government and politics.

Certain topics receive somewhat greater attention than they do in most other books. The media, now in perpetual revolution, is one. As the politically critical "fourth estate" yet also one economic interest among many, they have come to dominate our culture and intrude upon the functions of different institutions from political parties to the family.

A separate chapter, "Privacy and Public Morality," deals with conflicts over moral preferences and "ways of life," sometimes made worse by our natural social diversity and the media age in which we live. These struggles, often symbolic in their distributive effect, have unusual emotional valance for large numbers of persons, and are certain to receive greater attention from the Supreme Court.

Immigration and the assimilation of diverse peoples have been vital in American economic and social life and will surely remain so. A separate chapter deals with this development and its constitutional engagement in questions of alienage and citizenship.

Discrimination based on gender, age, sexual orientation, and class are also dealt with in a separate chapter.

Cases are placed at the ends of chapters and include almost all of those generally agreed to be "landmark" or chief secondary decisions in doctrinal development and political significance. They are edited to allow students to grasp the issues before the Court, the Court's analysis and reasoning and, where present and of note, disagreement among the justices. Their arrangement is the order in which they are taken up in the text, but they can be assigned selectively, in any order.

A number of sidebars discuss matters of interest not easily incorporated in their detail in the narrative of the text. These include biographical or jurisprudential sketches of major figures and background on cases like *Dennis v. United States, RAV v. St. Paul,* and *Bush v. Gore.* Others deal with civil liberties "events" like the Scopes evolution trial, the Nazi threat to march in Skokie, Ill., and the jailing of a *New York Times* reporter in the murder trial of "Doctor X." Still others examine civil liberties conditions, including the use of treason and antiterror prosecutions, the demographics of death row, and the right to have offspring.

Each chapter is followed by a bibliography of recent leading works for reference or further reading. An extensive supplementary bibliography at the end of the book goes beyond these sources and includes works in all areas of civil liberties and civil rights.

Several appendices provide additional information and help. These include a scheme for case briefing with a developmental emphasis, a guide for doing legal research in the library and on the Internet, a line biography of the justices from Jay to Breyer, and a list of the justices by "historic" Courts.

Cases have been edited with readability in mind. Most footnotes and citational references beyond case names, have been omitted. In a few instances, I have summarized precedential lists or references that have been cut, in brackets. Verbal excesses or flourishes, such as "It is my opinion in the case before us today," have been eliminated, as have decorative Latin phrases or pure legalisms that add nothing to meaning. Where it made sense, the names of the parties to the case have been substituted for "respondent," "petitioner," "plaintiff in error," and the like. In a very few instances, I have taken the liberty of inserting a much needed comma. Any substituted words or punctuation are in editor's brackets.

For each case, questions dealing with political or doctrinal matters have been inserted before the Opinion of the Court, to serve as guide to reading or a basis for discussion. In most cases, essential facts are given in the opinion; where not, a brief statement of them appears before the opinion.

I have tried to remain sensitive to the problem that confronts every casebook author or editor, that of not saying too much or too little. Each of the cases excerpted is discussed, at least briefly, in the chapter text. A sharp student, reading only the text, would have a good sense of the importance of the case in constitutional development, but would probably not fully understand how the Court reached its decision nor many of the issues the justices debated. For that, there is no substitute for reading the opinion(s).

Though this book and Volume I are the work of one person who bears all responsibility for errors and shortcomings, they have profited greatly from the suggestions and comments of many others. I would particularly like to thank Danny M. Adkison, Oklahoma State University; Christopher R. Banks, University of Akron; William A. Blomquist, Indiana University— Purdue University Indianapolis; Robert C. Bradley, Illinois State University; Richard A. Brisbin, Jr., West Virginia University; John Fliter, Kansas State University; Tracey Gladstone-Sovell, University of Wisconsin—River Falls; Barbara Luck Graham, University of Missouri—St. Louis; Michael J. Horan, University of Wyoming; Mark Landis, Hofstra University; Paul Lermack, Bradley University; Timothy C. Luther, California Baptist University; Sam W. McKinstry, East Tennessee State University; Mark C. Miller, Clark University; Kathleen M. Moore, University of Connecticut; C. Scott Peters, University of Louisville; Richard M. Pious, Barnard College; Steven Puro, St. Louis University; and Paul Wice, Drew University, who read all or part of the manuscript of Volumes I and II.

I would like to thank, as well, various editors at Longman, including Pam Gordon, Peter Glovin, Eric Stano, Anita Castro, Brian Van Buren, and Christine Maisano, and also Pat McCutcheon and Julie Hollist, production and copy editors at WestWords. Thanks are also due Maria Constantinescu, whose able help as a graduate assistant was especially valuable at several points. They have contributed importantly to this book at various stages and with whom it has been a pleasure to work.

Richard S. Randall

THE CONSTITUTION OF THE UNITED STATES

Preamble

We the People of the United States, in Order to form a more perfect Union, establish Justice, insure domestic Tranquility, provide for the common defence, promote the general Welfare, and secure the blessings of Liberty to ourselves and our Posterity, do ordain and establish this Constitution for the United States of America.

Article One

Section 1. All legislative powers herein granted shall be vested in a Congress of the United States, which shall consist of a Senate and House of Representatives.

Section 2. The House of Representatives shall be composed of members chosen every second year by the people of the several States, and the electors in each State shall have the qualifications requisite for electors of the most numerous branch of the State legislature.

No Person shall be a Representative who shall not have attained to the age of twenty five years, and been seven years a citizen of the United States, and who shall not, when elected, be an inhabitant of that State in which he shall be chosen.

Representatives and direct taxes shall be apportioned among the several States which may be included within this Union, according to their respective numbers, which shall be determined by adding to the whole number of free persons, including those bound to service for a term of years, and excluding Indians not taxed, three fifths of all other persons. The actual enumeration shall be made within three years after the first meeting of the Congress of the United States, and within every subsequent term of ten years, in such manner as they shall by law direct. The number of Representatives shall not exceed one for every thirty thousand, but each State shall have at least one Rep-

resentative; and until such enumeration shall be made, the State of New Hampshire shall be entitled to choose three, Massachusetts eight, Rhode Island and Providence Plantations one, Connecticut five, New York six, New Jersey four, Pennsylvania eight, Delaware one, Maryland six, Virginia ten, North Carolina five, South Carolina five and Georgia three.

When vacancies happen in the Representation from any State, the executive authority thereof shall issue writs of election to fill such vacancies.

The House of Representatives shall choose their Speaker and other officers; and shall have the sole power of Impeachment.

Section 3. The Senate of the United States shall be composed of two Senators from each State, chosen by the legislature thereof, for six years; and each Senator shall have one Vote.

Immediately after they shall be assembled in consequence of the first election, they shall be divided as equally as may be into three classes. The seats of the Senators of the first class shall be vacated at the expiration of the second year, of the second class at the expiration of the fourth year, and of the third class at the expiration of the sixth year, so that one third may be chosen every second year; and if vacancies happen by resignation, or otherwise, during the recess of the legislature of any State, the executive thereof may make temporary appointments until the next meeting of the legislature, which shall then fill such vacancies.

No person shall be a Senator who shall not have attained to the age of thirty years, and been nine years a citizen of the United States, and who shall not, when elected, be an inhabitant of that State for which he shall be chosen.

The Vice-President of the United States shall be President of the Senate, but shall have no vote, unless they be equally divided.

The Senate shall choose their other officers, and also a President pro tempore, in the absence of the

Vice-President, or when he shall exercise the office of President of the United States.

The Senate shall have the sole power to try all impeachments. When sitting for that purpose, they shall be on oath or affirmation. When the President of the United States is tried, the Chief Justice shall preside: And no Person shall be convicted without the concurrence of two thirds of the members present.

Judgment in cases of impeachment shall not extend further than to removal from office, and disqualification to hold and enjoy any office of honor, trust or profit under the United States: but the party convicted shall nevertheless be liable and subject to indictment, trial, judgment and punishment, according to law.

Section 4.   The times, places and manner of holding elections for Senators and Representatives, shall be prescribed in each State by the legislature thereof; but the Congress may at any time by law make or alter such regulations, except as to the places of choosing Senators.

The Congress shall assemble at least once in every year, and such meeting shall be on the first Monday in December, unless they shall by law appoint a different day.

Section 5.   Each house shall be the judge of the elections, returns and qualifications of its own members, and a majority of each shall constitute a quorum to do business; but a smaller number may adjourn from day to day, and may be authorized to compel the attendance of absent members, in such manner, and under such penalties as each house may provide.

Each house may determine the rules of its proceedings, punish its members for disorderly behavior, and, with the concurrence of two-thirds, expel a member.

Each house shall keep a journal of its proceedings, and from time to time publish the same, excepting such parts as may in their judgment require secrecy; and the yeas and nays of the members of either house on any question shall, at the desire of one fifth of those present, be entered on the journal.

Neither house, during the session of Congress, shall, without the consent of the other, adjourn for more than three days, nor to any other place than that in which the two Houses shall be sitting.

Section 6.   The Senators and Representatives shall receive a compensation for their services, to be ascertained by law, and paid out of the Treasury of the United States. They shall in all cases, except treason, felony and breach of the peace, be privileged from arrest during their attendance at the session of their respective houses, and in going to and returning from the same; and for any speech or debate in either house, they shall not be questioned in any other place.

No Senator or Representative shall, during the time for which he was elected, be appointed to any civil office under the authority of the United States which shall have been created, or the emoluments whereof shall have been increased during such time; and no person holding any office under the United States, shall be a member of either house during his continuance in office.

Section 7.   All bills for raising revenue shall originate in the House of Representatives; but the Senate may propose or concur with amendments as on other bills.

Every bill which shall have passed the House of Representatives and the Senate, shall, before it become a law, be presented to the President of the United States; If he approve he shall sign it, but if not he shall return it, with his objections to that house in which it shall have originated, who shall enter the objections at large on their journal, and proceed to reconsider it. If after such reconsideration two thirds of that house shall agree to pass the bill, it shall be sent, together with the objections, to the other house, by which it shall likewise be reconsidered, and if approved by two thirds of that house, it shall become a law. But in all such cases the votes of both houses shall be determined by yeas and nays, and the names of the persons voting for and against the bill shall be entered on the journal of each house respectively. If any bill shall not be returned by the President within ten days (Sundays excepted) after it shall have been presented to him, the same shall be a law, in like manner as if he had signed it, unless the Congress by their adjournment prevent its return, in which case it shall not be a law.

Every order, resolution, or vote to which the concurrence of the Senate and House of Representatives may be necessary (except on a question of adjournment) shall be presented to the President of the United States; and before the same shall take effect, shall be approved by him, or being disapproved by him, shall be repassed by two thirds of the Senate and House of Representatives, according to the rules and limitations prescribed in the case of a bill.

Section 8.   The Congress shall have power to lay and collect taxes, duties, imposts and excises, to pay the debts and provide for the common defence and general welfare of the United States; but all duties, imposts and excises shall be uniform throughout the United States;

To borrow money on the credit of the United States;

To regulate commerce with foreign nations, and among the several States, and with the Indian tribes;

To establish an uniform rule of naturalization, and uniform Laws on the subject of bankruptcies throughout the United States;

To coin money, regulate the value thereof, and of foreign coin, and fix the standard of weights and measures;

To provide for the punishment of counterfeiting the securities and current Coin of the United States;

To establish post-offices and post-roads;

To promote the progress of science and useful arts, by securing for limited times to authors and inventors the exclusive right to their respective writings and discoveries;

To constitute tribunals inferior to the Supreme Court;

To define and punish piracies and felonies committed on the high seas, and offenses against the law of nations;

To declare war, grant letters of marque and reprisal, and make rules concerning captures on land and water;

To raise and support armies, but no appropriation of money to that use shall be for a longer term than two years;

To provide and maintain a navy;

To make rules for the government and regulation of the land and naval forces;

To provide for calling forth the militia to execute the laws of the union, suppress insurrections and repel invasions;

To provide for organizing, arming, and disciplining, the militia, and for governing such part of them as may be employed in the service of the United States, reserving to the States respectively, the appointment of the officers, and the authority of training the militia according to the discipline prescribed by Congress;

To exercise exclusive legislation in all cases whatsoever, over such district (not exceeding ten miles square) as may, by cession of particular States, and the acceptance of Congress, become the seat of the Government of the United States, and to exercise like authority over all places purchased by the consent of the legislature of the State in which the same shall be, for the erection of forts, magazines, arsenals, dockyards, and other needful Buildings; and

To make all laws which shall be necessary and proper for carrying into execution the foregoing powers, and all other powers vested by this Constitution in the Government of the United States, or in any department or officer thereof.

Section 9. The migration or importation of such persons as any of the States now existing shall think proper to admit, shall not be prohibited by the Congress prior to the Year one thousand eight hundred and eight, but a tax or duty may be imposed on such importation, not exceeding ten dollars for each person.

The privilege of the writ of habeas corpus shall not be suspended, unless when in cases of rebellion or invasion the public safety may require it.

No bill of attainder or ex post facto law shall be passed.

No capitation, or other direct tax shall be laid, unless in proportion to the census or enumeration herein before directed to be taken.

No tax or duty shall be laid on articles exported from any State.

No preference shall be given by any regulation of commerce or revenue to the ports of one State over those of another: nor shall vessels bound to, or from, one State, be obliged to enter, clear, or pay duties in another.

No money shall be drawn from the Treasury, but in consequence of appropriations made by law; and a regular statement and account of the receipts and expenditures of all public money shall be published from time to time.

No title of nobility shall be granted by the United States; and no person holding any office of profit or trust under them, shall, without the consent of the Congress, accept of any present, emolument, office, or title, of any kind whatever, from any king, prince or foreign State.

Section 10. No State shall enter into any treaty, alliance, or confederation; grant letters of marque and reprisal; coin money; emit bills of credit; make anything but gold and silver coin a tender in payment of debts; pass any bill of attainder, ex post facto law, or law impairing the obligation of contracts, or grant any title of nobility.

No State shall, without the consent of the Congress, lay any imposts or duties on imports or exports, except what may be absolutely necessary for executing it's inspection laws: and the net produce of all duties and imposts, laid by any State on imports or exports, shall be for the use of the Treasury of the United States; and all such laws shall be subject to the revision and control of the Congress.

No State shall, without the consent of Congress, lay any duty of tonnage, keep troops, or ships of war in time of peace, enter into any agreement or compact with another State, or with a foreign power, or engage in war, unless actually invaded, or in such imminent danger as will not admit of delay.

Article Two

Section 1. The executive power shall be vested in a President of the United States of America. He shall hold his office during the term of four years, and, together with the Vice-President chosen for the same term, be elected, as follows:

Each State shall appoint, in such manner as the legislature thereof may direct, a number of electors, equal to the whole number of Senators and Representatives to which the State may be entitled in the Congress: but no Senator or Representative, or person holding an office of trust or profit under the United States, shall be appointed an elector.

The electors shall meet in their respective States, and vote by ballot for two persons, of whom one at least shall not lie an inhabitant of the same State with themselves. And they shall make a list of all the persons voted for, and of the number of votes for each; which list they shall sign and certify, and transmit sealed to the seat of the government of the United States, directed to the President of the Senate. The President of the Senate shall, in the presence of the Senate and House of Representatives, open all the certificates, and the votes shall then be counted. The person having the greatest number of votes shall be the President, if such number be a majority of the whole number of electors appointed; and if there be more than one who have such majority, and have an equal number of votes, then the House of Representatives shall immediately choose by ballot one of them for President; and if no person have a majority, then from the five highest on the list the said House shall in like manner choose the President. But in choosing the President, the votes shall be taken by States, the representation from each State having one vote; a quorum for this purpose shall consist of a member or members from two thirds of

the States, and a majority of all the States shall be necessary to a choice. In every case, after the choice of the President, the person having the greatest number of votes of the electors shall be the Vice-President. But if there should remain two or more who have equal votes, the Senate shall choose from them by ballot the Vice-President.

The Congress may determine the time of choosing the electors, and the day on which they shall give their votes; which day shall be the same throughout the United States.

No person except a natural born citizen, or a citizen of the United States, at the time of the adoption of this Constitution, shall be eligible to the office of President; neither shall any person be eligible to that office who shall not have attained to the age of thirty five years, and been fourteen years a resident within the United States.

In case of the removal of the President from office, or of his death, resignation, or inability to discharge the powers and duties of the said office, the same shall devolve on the Vice-President, and the Congress may by law provide for the case of removal, death, resignation or inability, both of the President and Vice-President, declaring what officer shall then act as President, and such officer shall act accordingly, until the disability be removed, or a President shall be elected.

The President shall, at stated times, receive for his services, a compensation, which shall neither be increased nor diminished during the period for which he shall have been elected, and he shall not receive within that period any other emolument from the United States, or any of them.

Before he enter on the execution of his office, he shall take the following oath or affirmation:

"I do solemnly swear (or affirm) that I will faithfully execute the office of President of the United States, and will to the best of my ability, preserve, protect and defend the Constitution of the United States."

Section 2. The President shall be Commander-in-Chief of the Army and Navy of the United States, and of the militia of the several States, when called into the actual service of the United States; he may require the opinion, in writing, of the principal officer in each of the executive departments, upon any subject relating to the duties of their respective offices, and he shall have power to grant reprieves and pardons for offenses against the United States, except in cases of impeachment.

He shall have power, by and with the advice and consent of the Senate, to make treaties, provided two thirds of the Senators present concur; and he shall nominate, and by and with the advice and consent of the Senate, shall appoint ambassadors, other public ministers and consuls, judges of the Supreme Court, and all other officers of the United States, whose appointments are not herein otherwise provided for, and which shall be established by law: but the Congress may by law vest the appointment of such inferior officers, as they think proper, in the President alone, in the courts of law, or in the heads of departments.

The President shall have power to fill up all vacancies that may happen during the recess of the Senate, by granting commissions which shall expire at the end of their next session.

Section 3. He shall from time to time give to the Congress information of the State of the Union, and recommend to their consideration such measures as he shall judge necessary and expedient; he may, on extraordinary occasions, convene both houses, or either of them, and in case of disagreement between them, with respect to the time of adjournment, he may adjourn them to such time as he shall think proper; he shall receive ambassadors and other public ministers; he shall take care that the laws be faithfully executed, and shall commission all the officers of the United States.

Section 4. The President, Vice-President and all civil officers of the United States, shall be removed from office on impeachment for, and conviction of, treason, bribery, or other high crimes and misdemeanors.

Article Three

Section 1. The judicial power of the United States, shall be vested in one Supreme Court, and in such inferior courts as the Congress may from time to time ordain and establish. The judges, both of the supreme and inferior courts, shall hold their offices during good behavior, and shall, at stated times, receive for their services, a compensation, which shall not be diminished during their continuance in office.

Section 2. The judicial power shall extend to all cases, in law and equity, arising under this Constitution, the laws of the United States, and treaties made, or which shall be made, under their authority; to all cases affecting ambassadors, other public ministers and consuls; to all cases of admiralty and maritime jurisdiction; to controversies to which the United States shall be a party; to controversies between two or more States; between a State and citizens of another State; between citizens of different States; between citizens of the same State claiming lands under grants of different States, and between a State, or the citizens thereof, and foreign States, citizens or subjects.

In all cases affecting ambassadors, other public ministers and consuls, and those in which a State shall be party, the Supreme Court shall have original jurisdiction. In all the other cases before mentioned, the Supreme Court shall have appellate jurisdiction, both as to law and fact, with such exceptions, and under such regulations as the Congress shall make.

Trial of all crimes, except in cases of impeachment, shall be by jury; and such trial shall be held in the State where the said crimes shall have been committed; but when not committed within any State, the trial shall be at such place or places as the Congress may by law have directed.

Section 3. Treason against the United States, shall consist only in levying war against them, or in adhering to their enemies, giving them aid and comfort. No person shall be convicted of treason unless on the testimony of two witnesses to the same overt act, or on confession in open court.

The Congress shall have power to declare the punishment of treason, but no attainder of treason shall work corruption of blood, or forfeiture except during the life of the person attainted.

Article Four

Section 1. Full faith and credit shall be given in each State to the public acts, records, and judicial proceedings of every other State. And the Congress may by general laws prescribe the manner in which such acts, records and proceedings shall be proved, and the effect thereof.

Section 2. The citizens of each State shall be entitled to all privileges and immunities of citizens in the several States.

A person charged in any State with treason, felony, or other crime, who shall flee from justice, and be found in another State, shall on demand of the executive authority of the State from which he fled, be delivered up, to be removed to the State having jurisdiction of the crime.

No person held to service or labor in one State, under the laws thereof, escaping into another, shall, in consequence of any law or regulation therein, be discharged from such service or labor, But shall be delivered up on claim of the party to whom such service or labor may be due.

Section 3. New States may be admitted by the Congress into this Union; but no new States shall be formed or erected within the jurisdiction of any other State; nor any State be formed by the junction of two or more States, or parts of States, without the consent of the legislatures of the States concerned as well as of the Congress.

The Congress shall have power to dispose of and make all needful rules and regulations respecting the territory or other property belonging to the United States; and nothing in this Constitution shall be so construed as to prejudice any claims of the United States, or of any particular State.

Section 4. The United States shall guarantee to every State in this Union a republican form of government, and shall protect each of them against invasion; and on application of the legislature, or of the executive (when the legislature cannot be convened) against domestic violence.

Article Five

The Congress, whenever two thirds of both houses shall deem it necessary, shall propose amendments to this Constitution, or, on the application of the Legislatures of two thirds of the several States, shall call a convention for proposing amendments, which, in either case, shall be valid to all intents and purposes, as part of this Constitution, when ratified by the Legislatures of three fourths of the several States, or by conventions in three fourths thereof, as the one or the other mode of ratification may be proposed by the Congress; provided that no amendment which may be made prior to the Year One thousand eight hundred and eight shall in any manner affect the first and fourth Clauses in the Ninth Section of the first Article; and that no State, without its consent, shall be deprived of it's equal suffrage in the Senate.

Article Six

All debts contracted and engagements entered into, before the adoption of this Constitution, shall be as valid against the United States under this Constitution, as under the Confederation.

This Constitution, and the laws of the United States which shall be made in pursuance thereof; and all treaties made, or which shall be made, under the authority of the United States, shall be the supreme law of the land; and the judges in every State shall be bound thereby, anything in the Constitution or laws of any State to the contrary notwithstanding.

The Senators and Representatives before mentioned, and the members of the several State Legislatures, and all executive and judicial officers, both of the United States and of the several States, shall be bound by oath or affirmation, to support this Constitution; but no religious test shall ever be required as a qualification to any office or public trust under the United States.

Article Seven

The ratification of the Conventions of nine States, shall be sufficient for the establishment of this Constitution between the States so ratifying the same.

Done in Convention by the unanimous consent of the States present the seventeenth day of September in the year of our Lord one thousand seven hundred and eighty-seven and of the Independence of the United States of America the twelfth, in witness whereof we have hereunto subscribed our Names,

George Washington,	*President and Deputy from Virginia*
New Hampshire:	*John Langdon* *Nicholas Gilman*
Massachustts:	*Nathaniel Gorham* *Rufus King*
Connecticut:	*William Samuel Johnson* *Roger Sherman*
New York:	*Alexander Hamilton*
New Jersey:	*William Livingston* *David Brearley* *William Paterson* *Jonathan Dayton*

Pennsylvana:

Benjamin Franklin
Thomas Mifflin
Robert Morris
George Clymer
Thomas FitzSimons
Jared Ingersoll
James Wilson
Gouverneur Morris

Delaware:

George Read
Gunning Bedford, Jr.
John Dickinson
Richard Bassett
Jacob Broom

Maryland:

James McHenry
Daniel of St. Thomas Jenifer
Daniel Carroll

Virginia:

John Blair
James Madison, Jr.

North Carolina:

William Blount
Richard. Dobbs Spaight
Hugh Williamson

South Carolina:

John Rutledge
Charles Cotesworth Pinckney
Charles Pinckney
Pierce Butler

Georgia:

William Few
Abraham Baldwin

(Signed September 17, 1787)

Amendment I

(Amendments I–X were ratified December 15, 1791)

Congress shall make no law respecting an establishment of religion, or prohibiting the free exercise thereof; or abridging the freedom of speech, or of the press; or the right of the people peaceably to assemble, and to petition the government for a redress of grievances.

Amendment II

A well regulated militia, being necessary to the security of a free State, the right of the people to keep and bear arms, shall not be infringed.

Amendment III

No soldier shall, in time of peace be quartered in any house, without the consent of the owner, nor in time of war, but in a manner to be prescribed by law.

Amendment IV

The right of the people to be secure in their persons, houses, papers, and effects, against unreasonable searches and seizures, shall not be violated, and no warrants shall issue, but upon probable cause, supported by Oath or affirmation, and particularly describing the place to be searched, and the persons or things to be seized.

Amendment V

No person shall be held to answer for a capital, or otherwise infamous crime, unless on a presentment or indictment of a Grand Jury, except in cases arising in the land or naval forces, or in the militia, when in actual service in time of war or public danger; nor shall any person be subject for the same offence to be twice put in jeopardy of life or limb; nor shall be compelled in any criminal case to be a witness against himself, nor be deprived of life, liberty, or property, without due process of law; nor shall private property be taken for public use, without just compensation.

Amendment VI

In all criminal prosecutions, the accused shall enjoy the right to a speedy and public trial, by an impartial jury of the State and district wherein the crime shall have been committed, which district shall have been previously ascertained by law, and to be informed of the nature and cause of the accusation; to be confronted with the witnesses against him; to have compulsory process for obtaining witnesses in his favor, and to have the assistance of counsel for his defence.

Amendment VII

In suits at common law, where the value in controversy shall exceed twenty dollars, the right of trial by jury shall be preserved, and no fact tried by a jury, shall be otherwise re-examined in any court of the United States, than according to the rules of the common law.

Amendment VIII

Excessive bail shall not lie required, nor excessive fines imposed, nor cruel and unusual punishments inflicted.

Amendment IX

The enumeration in the Constitution, of certain rights, shall not be construed to deny or disparage others retained by the people.

Amendment X

The powers not delegated to the United States by the Constitution, nor prohibited by it to the States, are reserved to the States respectively, or to the people.

Amendment XI

(Ratified January 8, 1798)

The judicial power of the United States shall not be construed to extend to any suit in law or equity, commenced or prosecuted against one of the United States by Citizens of another State, or by citizens or subjects of any foreign State.

Amendment XII

(Ratified September 25, 1804)

The electors shall meet in their respective States, and vote by ballot for President and Vice-President, one of whom, at least, shall not be an inhabitant of the same State with themselves; they shall name in their ballots the person voted for as President, and in distinct ballots the person voted for as Vice-President, and they shall make distinct lists of all persons voted for as President, and of all persons voted for as Vice-President and of the number of votes for each, which lists they shall sign and certify, and transmit sealed to the seat of the Government of the United States, directed to the President of the Senate; The President of the Senate shall, in the presence of the Senate and House of Representatives, open all the certificates and the votes shall then be counted; the person having the greatest number of votes for President, shall be the President, if such number be a majority of the whole number of Electors appointed; and if no person have such majority, then from the persons having the highest numbers not exceeding three on the list of those voted for as President, the House of Representatives shall choose immediately, by ballot, the President. But in choosing the President, the votes shall be taken by States, the representation from each State having one vote; a quorum for this purpose shall consist of a member or members from two-thirds of the States, and a majority of all the States shall be necessary to a choice. And if the House of Representatives shall not choose a President whenever the right of choice shall devolve upon them, before the fourth day of March next following, then the Vice-President shall act as President, as in the case of the death or other constitutional disability of the President. The person having the greatest number of votes as Vice-President, shall be the Vice-President, if such number be a majority of the whole number of Electors appointed, and if no person have a majority, then from the two highest numbers on the list, the Senate shall choose the Vice-President; a quorum for the purpose shall consist of two-thirds of the whole number of Senators, and a majority of the whole number shall be necessary to a choice. But no person constitutionally ineligible to the office of President shall be eligible to that of Vice-President of the United States.

Amendment XIII

(Ratified December 18, 1865)

Section 1. Neither slavery nor involuntary servitude, except as a punishment for crime whereof the party shall have been duly convicted, shall exist within the United States, or any place subject to their jurisdiction.

Section 2. Congress shall have power to enforce this Amendment by appropriate legislation.

Amendment XIV

(Ratified July 28, 1868)

Section 1. All persons born or naturalized in the United States, and subject to the jurisdiction thereof, are citizens of the United States and of the State wherein they reside. No State shall make or enforce any law which shall abridge the privileges or immunities of citizens of the United States; nor shall any State deprive any person of life, liberty, or property, without due process of law; nor deny to any person within its jurisdiction the equal protection of the laws.

Section 2. Representatives shall be apportioned among the several States according to their respective numbers, counting the whole number of persons in each State, excluding Indians not taxed. But when the right to vote at any election for the choice of Electors for President and Vice-President of the United States, Representatives in Congress, the executive and judicial officers of a State, or the members of the Legislature thereof, is denied to any of the male inhabitants of such State, being twenty-one years of age, and citizens of the United States, or in any way abridged, except for participation in rebellion, or other crime, the basis of representation therein shall be reduced in the proportion which the number of such male citizens shall bear to the whole number of male citizens twenty-one years of age in such State.

Section 3. No person shall be a Senator or Representative in Congress, or elector of President and Vice-President, or hold any office, civil or military, under the United States, or under any State, who, having previously taken an oath, as a member of Congress, or as an officer of the United States, or as a member of any State legislature, or as an executive or judicial officer of any State, to support the Constitution of the United States, shall have engaged in insurrection or rebellion against the same, or given aid or comfort to the enemies thereof. But Congress may by a vote of two-thirds of each House, remove such disability.

Section 4. The validity of the public debt of the United States, authorized by law, including debts incurred for payment of pensions and bounties for services in suppressing insurrection or rebellion, shall not be questioned. But neither the United States nor any State shall assume or pay any debt or obligation incurred in aid of insurrection or rebellion against the United States, or any claim for the loss or emancipation of any slave; but all such debts, obligations and claims shall be held illegal and void.

Section 5. The Congress shall have power to enforce, by appropriate legislation, the provisions of this Amendment.

Amendment XV

(Ratified March 30, 1870)

Section 1. The right of citizens of the United States to vote shall not be denied or abridged by the United States or by any State on account of race, color, or previous condition of servitude.

Section 2. The Congress shall have power to enforce this Amendment by appropriate legislation.

Amendment XVI

(Ratified February 25, 1913)

The Congress shall have power to lay and collect taxes on incomes, from whatever source derived, without apportionment among the several States and without regard to any census or enumeration.

Amendment XVII

(Ratified May 31, 1913)

The Senate of the United States shall be composed of two senators from each State, elected by the people thereof, for six years; and each Senator shall have one vote. The electors in each State shall have the qualifications requisite for electors of the most numerous branch of the State legislature.

When vacancies happen in the representation of any State in the Senate, the executive authority of such State shall issue writs of election to fill such vacancies: Provided, That the legislature of any State may empower the executive thereof to make temporary appointments until the people fill the vacancies by election as the legislature may direct.

This amendment shall not be so construed as to affect the election or term of any senator chosen before it becomes valid as part of the Constitution.

Amendment XVIII

(Ratified January 29, 1919)

Section 1. After one year from the ratification of this Amendment, the manufacture, sale, or transportation of intoxicating liquors within, the importation thereof into, or the exportation thereof from the United States and all territory subject to the jurisdiction thereof for beverage purposes is hereby prohibited.

Section 2. The Congress and the several States shall have concurrent power to enforce this Amendment by appropriate legislation.

Section 3. This Amendment shall be inoperative unless it shall have been ratified as an amendment to the Constitution by the legislatures of the several States, as provided in the Constitution, within seven years from the date of the submission hereof to the States by Congress.

Amendment XIX

(Ratified August 26, 1920)

The right of citizens of the United States to vote shall not be denied or abridged by the United States or by any States on account of sex.

The Congress shall have power by appropriate legislation to enforce the provisions of this Amendment.

Amendment XX

(Ratified February 6, 1933)

Section 1. The terms of the President and Vice-President shall end at noon on the twentieth day of January, and the terms of Senators and Representatives at noon on the third day of January, of the years in which such terms would have ended if this Amendment had not been ratified; and the terms of their successors shall then begin.

Section 2. The Congress shall assemble at least once in every year, and such meeting shall begin at noon on the third day of January, unless they shall by law appoint a different day.

Section 3. If, at the time fixed for the beginning of the term of the President, the President-elect shall have died, the Vice-President-elect shall become President. If a President shall not have been chosen before the time fixed for the beginning of his term, or if the President-elect shall have failed to qualify, then the Vice-President-elect shall act as President until a President shall have qualified; and the Congress may by law provide for the case wherein neither a President-elect nor a Vice-President-elect shall have qualified, declaring who shall then act as President, or the manner in which one who is to act shall be selected, and such person shall act accordingly until a President or Vice-President shall have qualified.

Section 4. The Congress may by law provide for the case of the death of any of the persons from whom the House of Representatives may choose a President whenever the right of choice shall have devolved upon them, and for the case of the death of any of the persons from whom the Senate may choose a Vice-President whenever the right of choice shall have devolved upon them.

Section 5. Sections 1 and 2 shall take effect on the 15th day of October following the ratification of this Amendment.

Section 6. This Amendment shall be inoperative unless it shall have been ratified as an amendment to the Constitution by the legislatures of three-fourths of the several States within seven years from the date of its submission.

Amendment XXI

(Ratified December 5, 1933)

Section 1. The eighteenth article of amendment to the Constitution of the United States is hereby repealed.

Section 2. The transportation or importation into any State, Territory, or possession of the United States for delivery or use therein of intoxicating liquors, in violation of the laws thereof, is hereby prohibited.

Section 3. The Amendment shall be inoperative unless it shall have been ratified as an amendment to the Constitution by conventions in the several States, as provided in the Constitution, within seven years from the date of the submission hereof to the States by the Congress.

Amendment XXII

(Ratified February 26, 1951)

Section 1. No person shall be elected to the office of the President more than twice, and no person who has held the office of President, or acted as President for more than two years of a term to which some other person was elected President shall be elected to the office of the President more than once. But this Amendment shall not apply to any person holding the office of President when this Amendment was proposed by the Congress, and shall not prevent any person who May be holding the office of President, or acting as President, during the term within which this Amendment becomes operative from holding the office of President or acting as President during the remainder of such term.

Section 2. This Amendment shall be inoperative unless it shall have been ratified as an amendment to the Constitution by the legislatures of three-fourths of the several States within seven years from the date of its submission to the States by the Congress.

Amendment XXIII

(Ratified June 16, 1960)

Section 1. The District constituting the seat of government of the United States shall appoint in such manner as the Congress may direct:

A number of electors of President and Vice-President equal to the whole number of Senators and Representatives in Congress to which the District would be entitled if it were a State, but in no event more than the least populous State; they shall be in addition to those appointed by the States, but they shall be considered, for the purposes of the election of President and Vice-President, to be electors appointed by a State; and they shall meet in the district and perform such duties as provided by the twelfth Amendment of amendment.

Section 2. The Congress shall have power to enforce this Amendment by appropriate legislation.

Amendment XXIV

(Ratified February 4, 1964)

Section 1. The right of citizens of the United States to vote in any primary or other election for President or Vice-President, for electors for President or Vice-President, or for Senator or Representative in Congress, shall not be denied or abridged by the United States or any State by reason of failure to pay any poll tax or other tax.

Section 2. The Congress shall have power to enforce this Amendment by appropriate legislation.

Amendment XXV

(Ratified February 10, 1967)

Section 1. In case of the removal of the President from office or of his death or resignation, the Vice-President shall become President.

Section 2. Whenever there is a vacancy in the office of the Vice-President, the President shall nominate a Vice-President who shall take office upon confirmation by a majority vote of both Houses of Congress.

Section 3. Whenever the President transmits to the President pro tempore of the Senate and the Speaker of the House of Representatives his written declaration that he is unable to discharge the powers and duties of his office, and until he transmits to them a written declaration to the contrary, such powers and duties shall be discharged by the Vice-President as Acting President.

Section 4. Whenever the Vice-President and a majority of either the principal officers of the executive departments or of such other body as Congress may by law provide, transmit to the President pro tempore of the Senate and the Speaker of the House of Representatives their written declaration that the President is unable to discharge the powers and duties of his office, the Vice-President shall immediately assume the powers and duties of the office as Acting President.

Thereafter, when the President transmits to the President pro tempore of the Senate and the Speaker of the House of Representatives his written declaration that no inability exists, he shall resume the powers and duties of his office unless the Vice-President and a majority of either the principal officers of the executive department or of such other body as Congress may by law provide, transmit within four day to the President pro tempore of the Senate and the Speaker of the House of Representatives their written declaration that the President is unable to discharge the powers and duties of his office. Thereupon Congress shall decide the issue, assembling within forty-eight hours for that purpose if not in session. If the Congress, within twenty-one days after receipt of the latter written declaration, or, if Congress is not in session, within twenty-one days after Congress is required to assemble, determines by two-thirds vote of both Houses that the President is unable to discharge the powers and duties of his office, the Vice-President shall continue to discharge the same as Acting President; otherwise, the President shall resume the powers and duties of his office.

Amendment XXVI

(Ratified July 1, 1971)

Section 1. The right of citizens of the United States, who are eighteen years of age or older, to vote shall not be denied or abridged by the United States or by any State on account of age.

Section 2. The Congress shall have power to enforce this Amendment by appropriate legislation.

Amendment XXVII

(Ratified May 7, 1992)

No law, varying the compensation for the services of the Senators and Representatives, shall take effect, until an election of Representatives shall have intervened.

I

A NATION OF RIGHTS

1

CIVIL LIBERTIES IN THE UNITED STATES

Civil Liberties as Public Philosophy

Perhaps no aspect of the American political experience has greater salience than civil liberties. The nation itself was "conceived in liberty," as Lincoln would later say at Gettysburg. The Declaration of Independence explained its collective political act as a claim to individual rights—"life, liberty, and the pursuit of happiness"—that were fundamentally personal, received from a higher source, and inalienable by government. Eleven years later, in 1787, the Framers of the Constitution concluded its elegant and explanatory Preamble with the ringing aim of securing "the blessings of liberty to ourselves and our posterity."

The circumstances of America's emergence as a new nation made liberty, in the words of the historian Peter Gay, "an American specialty." Regard for individual rights and freedom has become a kind of civil religion, having many attributes of a belief system rooted in an otherworldly source. With an almost spiritual reverence, we have come to expect a scripture—the Bill of Rights—interpreted by high priests—the

justices of the Supreme Court—to guide us to realization of ordained liberties. One observer has described Americans as preferring, "Liberty over authority, freedom over responsibility, rights over duties . . . [F]rom the days of [Roger] Williams and [John] Wise [early colonial religious dissenters] . . . Americans have talked about practically nothing else but liberty. Not the good man, but the free man has been the measure of all things . . . not national glory but individual liberty has been the object of political authority and the test of its worth."*

This faith has been encompassing and ill-defined enough to embrace the idea of equality, even though equality may at times present obstacles for liberty, as liberty does for equality. The ideal of equality also had formal dedication in the birth of American nationhood, the Declaration of Independence proclaiming in its opening paragraph that "All men are created equal."

---

* Clinton Rossiter, *Conservatism in America: The Thankless Persuasion*, 2nd ed., (New York: Vintage Books, 1962), 72.

An egalitarian principle is well established in American beliefs, but the equality that has flourished is equality before the law and equality of opportunity, each readily fused with ideas of individual liberty and freedom. It has not been equality of economic condition. As the sociologist Daniel Bell observed, "In the United States, the tension between equality and liberty, which framed the great philosophical debates in Europe, was dissolved by an individualism which encompassed both. Equality meant a personal identity, free of arbitrary class distinctions."*

As an idea or ideal, democracy itself tends to be seen as an equality of individual rights—a belief that all persons have a right to share in their government—rather than a way for collective action in the name of the majority. Despite clear commitment to the structures and principles of democratic government, Americans have retained an ambivalence about authority and fear about the uses to which it may be put. This has led a British student of American political ideas to observe that "the force of democracy in America . . . can often be seen as a negative technique, by which the populace can prevent the misuse of power by politicians and interests."†

In the American mind, individual rights and liberties have traditionally been protections against government and thus limits on public power and an important part of constitutionalism itself. This liberty is sometimes phrased as "negative," as freedom *from* interference, harassment, or oppression by authority. In contrast, "positive" liberty refers to realization of certain rights or aspects of equality *through* government action. It assumes that inequalities of circumstance and condition, such as those resulting from poverty, deficiencies in education, the effects of racism, or physical handicap, need to be redressed if those who suffer them are to have

true liberty. The chief instrument for doing this is government through assistance or regulation. Negative liberty, on the other hand, though looking to government for order and security, is traditionally skeptical of its intervention in the sphere of personal rights and freedoms.

Reconciling negative and positive liberty presents the same difficulties, logically and empirically, as reconciling liberty and equality, because the negative liberty of some persons may clash with the positive liberty of others and vice versa. As we will see in this book, the American tradition of civil liberty has overwhelmingly focused on negative liberty, underwritten by uncertainty about government. Nonetheless, in the last half-century positive liberty, with its sensitivity to inequality, has come to occupy a modest though important place in the American ideology of rights.

Civil Liberties as Legal Right and Practice

Individual rights and liberties are well established as a matter of general belief and public philosophy. In this book, we will be chiefly concerned with how this ideological commitment is translated into law, that is, into defined, enforceable rights and how these rights have been exercised. Rights are set out in ordinary law and in the constitutions of the national and state governments. They are given specific meaning usually by courts in cases coming before them. These decisions and particularly those appealed to higher courts, including the United States Supreme Court, form the legal or constitutional doctrine of individual rights.

Two disparate facts stand out in this development and in the American experience with individual rights and liberties. First, when practice is compared with ideal, at least as ideal is expressed in general but vague philosophical commitment, practice has often fallen short, sometimes woefully so. Second, when the United States is compared with other nations, especially other large nations, its record on realizing civil liberties has often been exceptional. Even saying this, the growth of civil liberties, as one historian

---

* Daniel Bell, "The End of American Exceptionalism," in Nathan Glazer and Irving Kristol, eds., *The American Commonwealth—1976,* (New York: Basic Books, 1976), 209.
† Michael Foley, *American Political Ideas,* (Manchester and New York: Manchester University Press, 1991), 82.

has observed, "is not the story of linear progress or simply a series of Supreme Court decisions, but a highly uneven and bitterly contested part of the story of American freedom."*

Declarations and inventories of civil liberties, systematically stated in "bills of rights" attached to the federal and all state constitutions, were in place earlier in the United States than any other country and have served as models for others around the world. Freedom of the press, indispensable to all politically open societies, has long had a lofty place in American political life, from reaction to the censorious Sedition Act of 1798 that cost the Federalists the election of 1800 to the Pentagon Papers controversy of the 1970s. Religious freedom and the separation of church and state were realized earlier and more thoroughly in the United States than anywhere else. Individual liberty has combined with social mobility and economic opportunity to attract persons from all parts of the world. Voting with their feet, millions of immigrants have left their native lands to come to the United States. For as long as the United States has been a nation, lines have formed outside its doors. Few of those who entered changed their minds, and few native-born Americans have emigrated. This is striking testimony to comparative freedom.

No society is perfect; nations are populated with and governed by human beings, not angels. Even in open, free societies, these imperfect creatures can be mean-spirited, unfair, intolerant, and oppressive. Even as a bastion and an asylum of freedom, the United States has had its darker side and its share of ill-liberal self-contradictions and failures. Slavery and the history of racial discrimination is one. Mal-treatment of American Indians, intolerant nativism, the Red Scare after World War I, forcible internment of Japanese-American citizens in World War II, and witch-hunting McCarthyism in the early Cold War are a few others.

Perhaps other nations or societies over the last 200 years could have realized greater individual rights than the United States. But the historical record of other societies inspires little confidence. The moral distance between proclaimed values and actual practice in the United States, chasm-like at times, is hardly ground for cynicism or for scaling back the effort to achieve those values. Lincoln spoke exactly to this point on the eve of the Civil War in describing the high ideals of the Declaration of Independence as "[A] maxim for free society, which should be familiar to all, and revered by all; constantly looked to, constantly labored for, and even though never perfectly attained, constantly approximated . . ."*

Civil Liberties as Conflict and Contest

We can easily appreciate the value of individual rights and how hard it may be to get and keep them when they are threatened by arbitrary, discriminatory, oppressive, or simply careless government action. Yet, viewed another way, individual rights and their exercise may threaten government in what it is charged to do, for example, safeguarding national security, maintaining order, and protecting against crime. They may also threaten strong interests of the community or nation, reflecting preferences of a majority, at times a large majority, for whom democratic government acts. In other words, if individual freedom and rights were never threatening, they would not be controversial. They would not need elaborate protection and would not be the subject of our civil religion.

Morally, the "easy" civil liberties case is one in which individual right clashes with arbitrary, discriminatory, oppressive, or short-sighted government action. But where government has acted to effect vital collective ends, "right" and "wrong" may be much less clear. For example, freedom

---

* Eric Foner, *The Story of American Freedom*, (New York: W. W. Norton, 1998), xvii.

* John G. Nicolay and John Hay, eds., *Complete Works of Abraham Lincoln*, vol. II, (Lincoln Memorial Library, 1894), 236.

of the press may clash with national security; freedom of speech with public order; separation of church and state with the quality of education; the rights of criminal defendants with efforts to punish and deter crime; freedom of economic opportunity and the protection of property with the health and safety of others.

More confounding, one civil liberty or individual right may conflict with another. Freedom of the press may interfere with privacy or fair trial, freedom of speech with the right of others to move about or have quiet, and free exercise of religion with the separation of church and state. Efforts to overcome the effects of racial discrimination may create "reverse" discrimination by limiting the freedom and opportunity of those who have not discriminated.

Civil liberties disputes, then, are not always clear-cut matters of freedom or oppression, fairness or unfairness, equal treatment or discrimination. In civil liberties cases there are two or more sides and, as in other disputes, a wide range of values may be at stake. The outcome of the conflict, whether advancing or restricting a civil liberty, distributes costs and benefits. Who gains and who loses and what is gained and lost are questions we may ask about the resolution of civil liberties disputes as we ask them about tax and spending matters or any decisions or policies of government.

This is clearer if we look at civil liberties conflict in its most familiar form and the one we focus on in this book—the legal dispute between parties in court. When a judicial tribunal, say, the United States Supreme Court, settles a civil liberties dispute, the immediate and formal distributions (gains and losses) are *rights* and their corresponding costs, *obligations*. As an allocated civil liberty, a right is a legally enforceable claim for use against governmental and sometimes nongovernmental parties to be free from certain obstacles. An obligation is a liability requiring its bearer to not interfere with someone's exercise of a right. A right is a civil liberties benefit and, if exercised, a power; an obligation is a civil liberties cost and, if discharged, a disability. Winning a le-

gal right to speak in a public park in violation of a local ordinance requiring a permit to do so, for example, obliges government, including local police, not to interfere. Similarly, not winning the right relieves government of that obligation.

A right declared may not be immediately exercised by those who win it. It then becomes stored value, like a bond or insurance. A declared obligation, when not called upon for discharge, is stored liability. In a lifetime, a person may exercise only a small fraction of his or her declared and stored rights and, in some areas, such as the criminal law, may never need to exercise any at all.

If the person claiming a right should lose, the legal distribution is negative and is a cost or a *right-denial*. The benefit distributed goes to the government as *obligation-avoidance*. If a court upholds a local ordinance barring sound trucks from amplifying messages above certain decibel levels on public streets after 1 a.m., for example, it has denied a right to a would-be user and removed an obligation from local government, which is now free to ticket or arrest the user. Similarly, in a criminal case, conviction denies the defendant (depending on the crime) full right to life, liberty, or property and removes from government the obligation (depending on the crime) to refrain from taking his or her life, liberty, or property.

As legal distributions, rights conferred or denied and obligations imposed or avoided are highly fungible. They may be readily converted, voluntarily or otherwise, into gains or deprivations of more basic values at stake in the conflict. (See "Basic Values at Stake in Civil Liberties Conflict.")

Some of these values—opportunities to communicate and associate with others, engage in expressive behavior, gain access to intelligence, advocate or communicate ideas, for example, tend to be distributed mainly as libertarian benefits and nonlibertarian costs. Others—national security, public safety, health, or morality, political orthodoxy, and exclusion of others, tend to be mainly libertarian costs and nonlibertarian

Basic Values at Stake in Civil Liberties Conflict

Civil liberties cases are conflicts between the claim of a right by a private interest and an action of government or, less often, an action of another private interest. Many different values—desired ends or resources—may be at stake in these conflicts. In resolving the issues they raise, court decisions distribute values by bestowing or withholding rights and obligations. These fungible legal categories of awarded benefits and imposed costs are eventually transformed into gains and losses of nonlegal values or resources that underlay the conflict. Analytically, these may include any of the following.

I. **Wealth**
   A. Property (material assets, income, goods and services)
   B. Opportunity (enterprise, employment)
II. **Well-being** (physical and psychological safety and security)
   A. Individual (life, health, protection)
   B. Collective and indivisible (national security, public order, economic and ecological prosperity)
III. **Power** (participation in, influence on, access to authoritative decisions: office-holding, lobbying, voting)
IV. **Expression** (intellectual, associational, emotional, and physical opportunities to communicate)
V. **Beliefs** (political, social, religious, moral, aesthetic, lifestyle ideas and sentiments "in force")
VI. **Status** (individual or group respect, identification)
VII. **Intelligence** (information, enlightenment)
VIII. **Privacy** (autonomy, seclusion)

---

gains. Still other values—privacy, promotion of religion or religious institutions, economic gain, jobs, status, power, and well-being—may be distributed as either libertarian or nonlibertarian benefits or costs.

Material values, central to most other conflicts, are apt to be less prominent in civil liberties disputes. If present, they tend to be associated with the government or nonlibertarian interest, though sometimes the libertarian side, as in a pornography case, for example, may be driven by underlying material concerns. With few exceptions, such as civil rights conflict over jobs or other economic opportunities, civil liberties cases are not usually about material gains and losses. In some cases, such as those over school prayers, material values may be absent entirely.

The general lack of material concerns is a distinguishing feature of civil liberties disputes and makes their resolution or management more problematic. Money and wealth, the common denominators of so many other conflicts in which their fungible quality and ready quantification

can ease settlements, are much less ready for compromising civil liberties disputes. The issues in many civil liberties disputes have mainly symbolic consequence for one or both parties and for interested "bystanders." In these disputes, the chief issue is often whose moral precepts, political beliefs, aesthetic preferences, or normative view of the world will be "in force" or at least prevail over opposing or competing ones.

For example, conflicts over First Amendment rights—freedoms of speech, press, association, religious exercise, and church-state separation—usually have wide symbolic consequence. Disputes over abortion, pornography, homosexual rights, capital punishment, and suicide also have wide symbolic meaning for many persons far removed from the cases. Even laws and policies with clear instrumental purpose, such as restricting a speaker for reasons of traffic control or curbing a religious practice in the interest of public health, may be seen by some as approving or disapproving certain religious, moral, or political beliefs or as creating status differences derived from having or not having one's ideas or

Footnote Four

In 1938, the Supreme Court was in the early stages of a dramatic transition, perhaps the most important in its history. Its great battle with President Franklin Roosevelt's New Deal had ended the year before in judicial capitulation when Justice Owen Roberts "switched sides." Dominated by four laissez-faire-minded justices—the Four Horsemen, as they came to be called—the Court had scuttled some of the New Deal's most important programs that had been designed to lift the nation from the Great Depression. By narrow votes, the Court had repeatedly struck down efforts of Congress and state legislatures to impose new regulations on business and economic markets. The Court's critics, of whom there were many, said the justices, under the guise of discovering constitutional curbs, were actually ruling on the expedience of the New Deal laws and substituting their own political judgments for that of elected representatives.

With Roberts's change of heart and Roosevelt's first appointments to the Court in 1937 and 1938, it was clear that the new "Roosevelt" Court-in-the-making would move down a very different constitutional path from its predecessor in reviewing legislative action. On April 25, it decided *United*

Harlan Fiske Stone

States v. Carolene Products, in which Justice Harlan Stone, writing for a majority of six, upheld a federal law banning interstate shipment of "filled" milk, in this instance milk from which butter fat had been replaced by coconut oil. The decision, unremarkable by today's standards, was like several others the new Court had begun to make. In contrast to the anti-New Deal decisions, Stone expressly deferred to the Congress's debatable finding that such milk

---

ideals "in force." Loyalty oaths, for example, though having a formal instrumental purpose of protecting the government against subversion, were almost entirely symbolic in meaning for both supporters and opponents.

Such conflicts bring with them high emotional investment that makes resolution or settlement more difficult. Competing notions of what is good and bad, true and untrue, beautiful and ugly, are apt to be more directly contradictory and mutually exclusive than competing positions over material values. Norms of compromise, reciprocity, and fair play may fail to perform their circumscribing tasks. In the extreme case, many persons who would not condone violence or risk their lives or freedom in disputes over, say, taxation and spending, might be readier to

do so in defense of importantly held beliefs or first principles.

The Primacy of Courts

Individual rights are formidable in American law and politics because they usually have constitutional status. Though rights can be and sometimes are created by legislation most are part of the highest law of the realm. As that law, constitutions create the basic structure and procedures of government and delegate powers among its parts. Not only is government limited by these provisions, it is forever after responsible to the higher authority. This is the essence of the venerable phrase "government of laws not men" and the embodiment of

was injurious to health. In economic regulations, constitutionality would be presumed if the law rested on "some rational basis within the knowledge and experience legislature." Such statements of a more self-restrained judicial review were becoming common for the new Court.

But Stone, who would later become chief justice, went further and, doing so, made *Carolene Products* a remarkable case and a symbol for the Court moving between two eras. The new deference to legislative judgment would not be general. In Footnote Four to his opinion, little noticed at the time but to become the most celebrated aside in the Court's history, he indicated there would be a narrower presumption of constitutionality, that is, a wider judicial scrutiny, when a law dealt with personal rights as opposed to those of property. The reason was that those affected by such laws—individuals and "insular minorities," such as racial, religious, or ethnic groups—could not as easily defend their interests through the ordinary ways of politics like voting, association, and lobbying.

Stone's note assumed that business and economic interests and the majority itself had ready access to "the political processes which can ordinarily be expected to bring about repeal of undesirable legislation." The remedy for a bad law lay in the elected and representative institutions of democratic government, not in the courts exercising a close, activist review. But where individuals or insular groups were affected adversely by a law, the Court would not simply presume constitutionality but would recognize that in the conflict between individual rights and strong or prejudicial majority interests, the "political processes" playing field might not be level.

Though only a tentative statement, Footnote Four provided the theoretical basis for a post-New Deal judicial intervention on behalf of individual liberties and rights and, eventually, for an important standard in applying equal protection of the law. Stone's note was also a new job description for the Court as it retreated from one venue to work in another. Cases presenting issues of individual rights and freedoms, which accounted for less than 5 percent of the Court's work before 1938, came to occupy more than half its docket in later years, a division of labor familiar to students of the Court today. The new activism, reaching its zenith during the Warren Court, has accounted for many of the Court's most dramatic and controversial decisions.

Justice Lewis Powell was undoubtedly correct some 40 years later in calling the Footnote Four "perhaps the most far-sighted dictum in our modern judicial heritage."

*"Carolene Products Revisited," 82 *Columbia Law Review* 1087, 1088 (1982).

---

the American tradition of higher law. The Constitution may be changed in its basic writ by amendment, but it is a difficult road not often taken, requiring approval of two-thirds of each house of Congress and three-quarters of the legislatures of the 50 states. In more than two centuries it has been changed only 18 times, resulting in 27 amendments.

Because constitutions are laws, appeals to rights protected by them are legal claims and are handled by courts. Civil liberties cases are decided by judges and, if appealed far enough, by the nine justices of the United States Supreme Court. Starting with the Court's basic decision in *Marbury v. Madison* in 1803, we have come to accept the right and responsibility of courts to exercise judicial review—the power to declare that a challenged law or action of government is constitutional or unconstitutional. In doing this at the highest level in hundreds of cases, the Supreme Court has elaborated the rights and liberties of the Constitution. Though its decisions and declarations may sometimes be evaded, they remain, like the Constitution they interpret, the highest law of the land.

There is good reason why courts and the Supreme Court especially have been accorded this extraordinary power. Except for a few provisions, the text of the Constitution, including the Bill of Rights and the Civil War Amendments, is phrased in general terms. On freedom of speech, for example, it merely says "Congress shall make no law . . . abridging the freedom of speech." This general and indeterminate rule, applied in hundreds of cases with highly specific facts, has called for interpretation and elaboration. As institutions, courts are designed to apply law through regularized procedures in discrete disputes between adversary parties. In this, they are particularly well suited to decide the specific bounds of constitutional rights.

Beyond this, courts are more removed from the beaten political path, from the power and influence of public opinion and majority rule than are legislatures and executives. In a dispute between an individual and government, the playing field is more likely to be level in the judicial arena than anywhere else. Because courts are at some distance from politics and public opinion, their decisions may sometimes be unpopular. If that unpopularity is deep or widespread, the legitimacy of those decisions may be questioned spurring attempts to overcome them through constitutional amendment or actions that are nullifying, evading, or noncomplying.

The Supreme Court's power of judicial review and the life appointments of its members, who are not directly accountable to anyone, has produced continuous debate about the Court's role as arbiter of the highest law. How aggressive or self-restrained should it be? How much discretion should it exercise in deciding what the Constitution requires or permits? To what extent should it take distributive consequences into account in reaching a decision?

Some students of the Court argue that despite the generalities and ambiguities in the Constitution, justices should use their training to reflect carefully and fairly on the text of the document and the intent of its Framers to discover what is largely already there. When they fail to do this, they act without legitimate guidelines and read their own preferences into the Constitution, becoming a kind of a nonelected super legislature. Critics of this view argue that because the Constitution is so brief and, at so many points, indeterminate or just silent, justices must often go beyond text and original intent and cannot avoid a large element of discretion. This interpretative "slack" opens the way to "necessary and desirable constructions which have allowed the Constitution to remain a living entity of acceptable meanings and applications."*

There is probably no correct answer in this debate, which has been going on almost as long as we have had the Constitution, and many students of the Court would take positions somewhere between the two sides. We will see the issue reflected in many decisions included in this book, especially when justices disagree on where the boundaries of rights and liberties should be drawn. Their explanations for granting or denying a right, imposing or lifting an obligation, may often be cast as how much activism they believe the role of judicial reviewer allows and how much self-restraint it requires.

The Supreme Court and the American Judiciary

Litigation—a legal case—is a formalized way of settling a dispute between two or more parties who may be individuals, groups, organizations, or agencies of government. Cases start in a trial court or other tribunal said to have original jurisdiction. Such courts apply legal principles to specific facts in the disputes before them. The finder of fact may be a jury or simply the presiding judge. If the side losing at trial believes an error in the application of law has been made, it may appeal to a higher court. In appellate review no witnesses are called, no new evidence is introduced, and normally no new questions may be raised. (Because of the double jeopardy provision of the Fifth Amendment, acquittals of defendants in criminal cases may not be appealed by the government.)

The American judicial system is a complex arrangement of courts—federal and state, trial and appellate, general and specialized—in which justices, judges, and magistrates hear a great range of legal disputes. At the summit is the United States Supreme Court. With few exceptions, cases coming before it have passed through two lower courts. (See Figure 1.1.)

---

* Foley, 205.

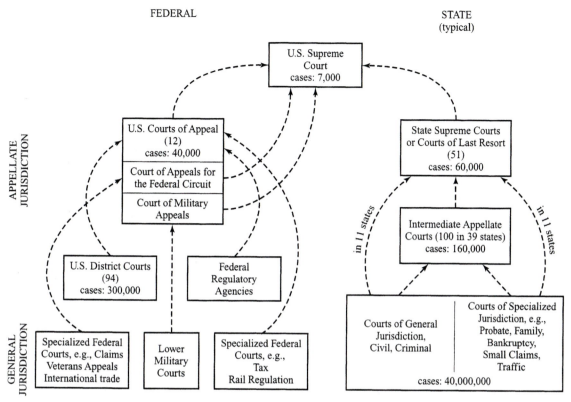

Figure 1.1 The American Judicial System, Lines of Appeal, Annual number of Cases.

At the base of the federal judiciary are 94 District Courts, at least one in each state, the District of Columbia, and four American territories. These are trial courts of general jurisdiction empowered to hear civil and criminal cases. With few exceptions, cases are heard by a single judge, but the number of judges assigned to a district court depends on its workload. The court for the Southern District of New York, for example, the largest district court, has 28. Jurisdiction is limited to cases raising a "federal question"—an issue arising under federal laws, treaties, or the Constitution—or in which there is diversity of citizenship (opposing parties living in different states) and the monetary claim is above a fixed amount. The district courts dispose of about 300,000 cases a year.

Decisions may be appealed to 12 Federal Courts of Appeal. Eleven are organized region-ally into circuits of three or more states. The twelfth is in Washington, D.C. Their size varies, ranging from six judges in the First Circuit (Maine, New Hampshire, Massachusetts, Rhode Island, and Puerto Rico) to twenty-eight in the Ninth Circuit (Washington State, Oregon, California, Montana, Idaho, Nevada, Arizona, Alaska, and Hawaii). Normally appeals are heard by rotating panels of three judges, though exceptional cases may come before the court's entire roster of judges sitting *en banc*. The Courts of Appeal dispose of about 40,000 cases a year, including appeals of rulings from federal regulatory agencies. Losing parties may petition the United States Supreme Court for review.

The federal judiciary also has several specialized trial and appellate tribunals. These include bankruptcy courts, which operate within the district court system; the United States Tax Court, hearing appeals from rulings of the Internal Revenue Service; the United States Court of Federal Claims, hearing monetary claims against the U.S. government; the United States Court of Military Appeals, hearing appeals from military courts martial; the United States Court of Veterans Appeals, hearing cases from the Board of Veterans Appeals in the Veterans Administration; the United States Court of International Trade, hearing cases arising under trade and import laws; and the Court of Appeals for the Federal Circuit, having jurisdiction over patent, trademark, and copyright disputes and hearing appeals from several of the specialized courts. Losing parties may petition the United States Supreme Court for review.

State court systems vary with no two exactly alike. All, however, have trial courts of general jurisdiction, though in some states criminal cases are heard in separate courts. All states also have different specialized trial courts, typically dealing with probate, family, tax, small claims, and traffic matters. It is in these lower state courts, general and specialized, that most of the judicial work of the country is done. The exact number of cases disposed of annually is not known, but it is probably nearly 40,000,000, heard by more than 30,000 judges.

In most states, cases disposed of by lower courts can be appealed to an intermediate level appellate court, as in the federal system. All states have an appellate court of last resort, usually called the Supreme Court, though in New York and Maryland it is the Court of Appeals. Texas and Oklahoma also maintain a Court of Criminal Appeals as the court of last resort for criminal cases. Eleven of the less populated states—Maine, Mississippi, Montana, Nebraska, Nevada, New Hampshire, Rhode Island, South Dakota, Vermont, West Virginia, and Wyoming—do not have intermediate appellate courts. In these states, trial decisions may be appealed directly to the state supreme court. Intermediate state appellate courts dispose of about 160,000 cases a year, those of last resort, about 60,000. The jurisdiction of state courts is governed by state law, but gener-

ally, unless limited by subject matter, may include any question of law—statutory, common, administrative, or constitutional—that the federal Constitution or Congress has not reserved exclusively for federal courts.

The United States Supreme Court is the ultimate American court of last resort. Though more than 99 percent of its work is appellate, it does have limited original jurisdiction in which it is the court of first and only resort. This jurisdiction, set out in Article III-2 of the Constitution, includes cases involving ambassadors and those in which a state is a party, (usually against another state over a disputed boundary or water rights.) An exercise of original jurisdiction does not mean a trial is held in the Court—the justices would hardly have time for that. Instead, the case is assigned to a Special Master, often a retired judge appointed by the Court, who hears it and files a report with the Court, which it usually accepts but is free to reject or modify. Cases under the Court's original jurisdiction seldom number more than four or five a year. The Court has had fewer than 200 in its history.

Though all other cases before the Court are informally called "appeals," there are actually three routes to Supreme Court appellate review: appeal, certification, and certiorari. Cases in the first group, "on appeal," are those in which a lower court has declared a law to violate the federal Constitution or in which a state court has upheld a state law challenged as violating the federal Constitution. Congress, using power to change the Supreme Court's appellate jurisdiction, had once made review of such cases mandatory. But the justices often sidestepped the requirement by summarily affirming the lower court's decision without opinion or, in state cases, dismissing appeals "for want of a substantial federal question." In 1988, at the Court's urging, Congress officially made the "on appeal" what it had nearly already become, discretionary. The only exceptions are cases arising under statutes, such as the Voting Rights Act, in which Congress has required that disputes first heard by special three-judge district courts have mandatory appeal directly to the Supreme Court.

The Supreme Court's conference room. Every other week during the Court's term, the justices meet Wednesday afternoons to discuss appeals they have heard and to decide cases. They also meet all day Friday to decide which petitions for review they will grant and to do other business. The meetings are completely closed, and the Chief Justice presides. No clerks or secretaries are present.

In certification the request for review comes not from one of the parties but from one of the federal Court of Appeals, in a pending case. The presiding judges interrupt the case to seek clarification of a question of federal law by "certifying" it to the Supreme Court. It is a seldom exercised appellate route, and the Court is not obliged to accept such requests.

Most of the nearly 8,000 cases the Court is asked to hear each year arrive by the third route, the petition for a writ of certiorari, in which the losing party in the court below asks for review. For the Court the matter is entirely discretionary. It takes a case up by granting the writ, literally from the Latin, "to be informed."

The Court today has near complete control of its appellate docket. This is important because it allows it to choose from a wide range of cases petitioned and thus set its own agenda of issues and questions.

In a typical year, the Supreme Court accepts fewer than 150 of the cases for review, about a sixth of those from the federal Courts of Appeal and 1 in 50 from state courts of last resort. The chance of the Supreme Court eventually being asked to hear a case filed in an American court is about 1 in 6,000. Though this is but a small window on the body of judicial work of the country, the cases the Court does hear include many raising important political, legal, and constitutional issues.

Exactly what kinds of cases is the Court likely to accept for review? Here, it has supplied a partial answer in the formal guidelines in its Rule 10 governing certiorari petitions:

A petition . . . will be granted only for compelling reasons. The following, although neither controlling nor fully measuring the Court's discretion, indicate the character of the reasons the Court considers:

(a) a United States court of appeals has entered a decision in conflict with the decision of another United States court of appeals on the same important matter; has decided an important federal question in a way that conflicts with a decision by a state court of last resort; or has so far departed from the accepted and usual course of judicial proceedings, or sanctioned such a departure by a lower court, as to call for an exercise of this Court's supervisory power;

(b) a state court of last resort has decided an important federal question in a way that conflicts with the decision of another state court of last resort or of a United States court of appeals;

(c) a state court or a United States court of appeals has decided an important question of federal law that has not been, but should be, settled by this Court, or has decided an important federal question in a way that conflicts with relevant decisions of this Court.

Other considerations also come into play. For example, the Court accepts nearly three-quarters of appeals brought on behalf of the federal government by the Solicitor General, the Justice Department's chief litigating officer. This proportion shows the public importance of many cases to which the United States is a party. Cases in which many "outside" but interested parties have filed *amicus curiae*—"friend of the court"—briefs are more likely to be accepted by the Court than others. As with the Solicitor General's appeals, these briefs, representing interests beyond the immediate parties to the case, often reflect the public importance of issues presented in the cases.* Finally, there is little doubt that the political ideology and personal preferences of individual justices play a role in the Court's selection of cases.

If the Court refuses to hear a case, the decision of the court below, whether federal or state, is final. However, there can be no legal inference from the Court's refusal of review that it has affirmed or looked with favor on the lower court's decision. State supreme court cases that do not raise a question of federal law are not reviewable by the Supreme Court. In those, decisions of the state court on matters of state law and the state constitution are final.

The Supreme Court at Work

Of the 8,000 or so cases the Supreme Court is asked to hear in a given year, only about 125 are accepted for full argument and review. These have been winnowed by the justices and their law clerks. Should four or more justices vote to hear a case, it is put on the Court's review schedule. A handful of other cases, usually about inconsequential issues or little more than simple error correction, may be dealt with summarily, that is, without full dress review. These decisions are *per curiam*—"by the Court"—with unsigned opinions offering little elaboration. Though fully binding on the parties, they have little value as precedent.

If a case is scheduled for full review, the appealing party (appellant or petitioner) must submit a legal brief of the case in 45 days, after which the opposing party (appellee or respondent) has 30 days to file a reply brief. These documents, along with the opinion of the lower court from which the case was appealed, are the Court's main review materials. The briefs must be submitted in 40 copies and not exceed 50 pages. The Court requires the briefs to include a description of the issues presented for review; citation of statutes, ordinances, treaties, or constitutional provisions relevant to the case; a factual statement of the case; a detailed argument from points of fact and law; and a conclusion stating the relief sought. Briefs may also contain important supportive factual material.

At this stage, *amicus curiae* briefs may be received from interest groups and other organizations who, as outside third parties, are concerned less with the fate of the adversaries than legal and constitutional issues and how the Court's decision might affect their members. In most cases no *amicus* briefs are filed.

Once the justices have had time to review the briefs, the case is scheduled for oral argument before the full Court in the Court's courtroom. This part of the case is open to the public, and counsel for each side is given 30 minutes, though in exceptional cases more time may be allowed. What starts as a presentation (simply reading a written statement aloud is discouraged) is often quickly transformed into a colloquy, with the justices interrupting, sometimes peppering counsel with questions and comments.

Later the same week, the case and others recently argued are discussed in a conference of all nine justices. A nonbinding vote is taken to

---

* See Gregory A. Caldeira and John R. Wright, "Organized Interests and Agenda Setting in the U.S. Supreme Court," *American Political Science Review* 82 (1988), 1,109–1,127.

Decisions of the Supreme Court are formally signed by those justices who have voted in favor. Here Justice Clarence Thomas affixes his signature in the Court's conference room. From left are Justices David Souter, Antonin Scalia, Sandra Day O'Connor, John Paul Stevens, Byron White, Chief Justice William Rehnquist, and Justice Anthony Kennedy.

reach a preliminary disposition. The case is then assigned to one of the justices who, if the Court has not been unanimous, has voted with the majority, for writing the Opinion of the Court stating and explaining the decision reached.

When the justice has written a draft of the opinion, it is circulated among the other justices, who may make suggestions or even raise objections. The original draft may then be modified and recirculated. This stage may take several weeks, even months, and include negotiations over points of law or explanation. Occasionally, a justice may change his or her vote; on rare occasions in a close case, this may change the majority to a minority and vice-versa. Only after the final draft has been circulated and it has the signatures of a majority of the justices does it become the Opinion of the Court in a decided case.

A justice who has voted with the majority on disposition, but who does not fully agree with the majority's reasoning or believes a point needs further elaboration, may write a concurring opinion. A justice who disagrees with the majority's decision may write a dissenting opinion. Occasionally, the Court may be so fragmented that though there is a majority to decide the case, there is none supporting one line of reasoning for the decision. In these instances, the Opinion of the Court rests on a simple plurality. Such opinions have less force as precedents; fortunately, they are few. Should the Court be divided 4-4 because a justice has been absent or there is a temporary vacancy, the case remains undecided and the decision of the lower court stands. The Court will not decide a case with fewer than seven justices participating.

The final step is public announcement of the decision on one of the Court's "opinion days," scheduled weekly or biweekly during the latter half of its term. These are held in the Court's courtroom with the parties, the press, and interested members of the public (who usually include many Washington tourists) in attendance. The justice who has written the Opinion of the Court usually gives a brief summary, perhaps including an excerpt, rather than reading the entirety. Justices writing concurring or dissenting opinions may do likewise with their positions.

A decision by the Court affirms or reverses the decision of the court below. In some cases, the Court "remands," that is, sends the case back to the lower court with instructions on continuing further.

The traditional October Term of the Court, starting the first Monday of October, now runs the full year, with a summer recess starting in late June or early July. During the working part of the term, the justices alternate between two weeks of hearing oral arguments and conference discussion and two weeks of reading briefs, case research, and opinion-writing. Oral arguments are heard Mondays through Wednesdays, with the Court usually tackling 12 cases a week.

Conferences are held Wednesday afternoons and all day Friday. They are presided over by the chief justice, who first briefly summarizes each case argued that week and states his views on how it should be decided. In turn, each associate justice in order of seniority is given time to comment as each case is discussed. If the chief justice is in the majority after a vote has been taken, he has responsibility for assigning the opinion to an associate justice or retaining it himself. Should he be in the minority, the most senior associate in the majority assigns the opinion. The conferences are strictly closed; no one other than the nine justices is even allowed in the room. There is no public record of their deliberations.

The work of the law clerks is vital to the Court's operations. Several clerk positions—four in recent years—are assigned to each justice, who hires the clerks to fill them, usually for one term of the Court. Most clerks are recent graduates with distinguished academic records at leading law schools. These talented persons become the justices' "right arms" in the research and analysis of cases. They do most of the first reading of the several thousand certiorari petitions, summarizing them and making recommendations. Of cases scheduled for review, the clerks often do research on the questions of law. Some justices entrust their clerks to prepare drafts of opinions, confining their role to supervision and final editing. Even justices writing opinions alone usually rely heavily on their clerks for research and editorial assistance.

The Court is a collegial body; its decisions are collective efforts and the procedures that lead to them call for the participation of all nine members. Yet, for the most part the justices work with a great deal of independence and in isolation from one another. Each has his or her suite of offices and a staff composed of law clerks and secretaries. By the time the justices reach conference discussion, for example, most have already made up their minds about the cases on the table, and it is unlikely that a great deal of persuasion will take place. As Justice Lewis Powell once observed, "For the most part, perhaps as much as 90 percent of our total time, we function as nine small, independent law firms."*

The Locus of Rights and Liberties

Most Americans think of the Bill of Rights—the first 10 amendments to the Constitution—as the repository of individual liberties. This is mainly but not completely correct. These amendments do contain our chief statement of rights, but important protections lie elsewhere as well. The original, unamended Constitution contains several. Article I-9, for example, forbids the national government from suspending the writ of habeas corpus except in cases of rebellion, invasion, or need to maintain public safety. It also bars Congress from enacting bills of attainder or ex post facto laws. Article I-10 forbids states from passing such laws. Article III requires that all federal criminal trials be by jury and be held in the state where the crime was committed. One of the most detailed clauses of the Constitution, Article III-2, defines the crime of treason, limiting it only to the making of war against the United States or "adhering to its enemies, giving aid and comfort." Conviction requires the testimony of two witnesses to the same act or confession in open court. Article VI forbids religious tests as qualification for holding office in the federal government.

Rights are also set out in amendments other than the Bill of Rights. After the Civil War, the

---

* Lewis F. Powell, Jr., "What the Justices Are Saying . . . ," *American Bar Association Journal* 62 (1976), 1,454.

Thirteenth Amendment outlawed slavery and peonage (the forced working off of debts); the Fourteenth barred states from abridging the privileges and immunities of the citizens of the United States, from depriving anyone of life, liberty, or property without due process of law, and from denying anyone the equal protection of the laws; and the Fifteenth barred denial of the right to vote because of race or past condition of slavery. In 1920, the Nineteenth Amendment gave women the right to vote. The Twenty-fourth, in 1964, barred use of poll taxes to deny anyone the right to vote. The Twenty-sixth Amendment, seven years later, guaranteed the right to vote to anyone age 18 or older.

Extensive rights are also found in the constitutions of the states, each of which has a bill of rights, usually paralleling but sometimes going beyond the federal version. These inventories are limits on state and local power.

Finally, rights may be created by statute as hundreds have been in the enactments of Congress, state legislatures, and law-making bodies of local government. For example, the federal Voting Rights Act of 1965, aimed at the discriminatory use of literacy tests, declares that "no voting qualifications or prerequisites" can be used to deny anyone the right to vote because of race. The Civil Rights Act of 1964 guarantees equal access to specified public accommodations. In military conscription laws, Congress has created a "conscientious objector" exemption for those qualifying as pacifists. The National Bail Reform Act of 1966 allows most persons awaiting trial on noncapital charges release on their own recognizance or unsecured bonds. The Federal Rules of Civil Procedure, enacted by Congress with advice of the federal judiciary, governs the conduct of federal criminal trials and provides scores of trial, pretrial, and posttrial rights for accused persons. These and other statutory rights may be altered, amended, or withdrawn by legislation because they are not constitutional requirements.

In the federal Bill of Rights, only the first eight amendments declare substantive rights. The Ninth simply states that the listing of rights in the first eight does not mean there are not "others retained by the people." The Tenth is less a statement of liberty than a distribution of power. It declares that powers the Constitution neither gives to the federal government nor denies to the states are reserved "to the states respectively, or to the people." For many years it was a matter of sharp debate, not over the rights of persons but those of states and whether state powers were independent limits on the national government. Today, the amendment is considered by many to be largely a truism, that powers not surrendered are retained, and a concluding tidiness telling us where powers unaccounted for reside.

The First Amendment contains protections for the freedoms of speech, press, assembly, and religious worship, and a provision forbidding governmental establishment of religion. The Second and Third deal with the right to bear arms and protection against quartering of troops in private homes. The Fourth sets out rights against arbitrary searches, seizures, and arrest. The Fifth guarantees certain criminal justice rights including indictment by grand jury, protections against double jeopardy and forced self-incrimination; the right to be justly compensated for property taken for public use; and the all-important right not to be deprived of "life, liberty, or property without due process of law." The Sixth and Seventh set out different trial rights, including that of a speedy and public proceeding before an impartial jury. The Eighth protects against imposing excessive bail or cruel and unusual punishments.

Genesis of the Bill of Rights

The Constitution the Framers drafted at Philadelphia and sent to state ratifying conventions in the fall of 1787 did not contain a systematic statement of individual liberties—a bill of rights. Omission was not from indifference or opposition to rights; some rights, as already noted, were included in various sections of the Constitution. Instead, most Framers believed that because the new national government they were proposing would have only enumerated and thus limited powers, further guarantees were not needed.

Modern Americans, accustomed to much more active government and to large inventories of rights, might take issue with such optimism, but there is little doubt that most Framers genuinely believed the proposition.

Omission of a statement of rights was seized upon by opponents of the Constitution, the Anti-Federalists, during the ratification debates. Their criticism made enough headway that James Madison, the most important of the Framers and now the Constitution's "campaign manager," admitted the error and pledged that adding a bill of rights would be one of the new government's first tasks after ratification.

With that government in place in 1789, Madison, who had been elected to the House of Representatives, took the lead in preparing the first amendments. More than 200 suggestions dealing with nearly 100 matters had been forwarded by the state ratifying conventions. Some had little to do with individual rights and were mainly aimed at removing powers from the new central government in the interest of states rights. A few, such as objection to barring religious tests for federal office because it might allow Jews or "infidels" to take over the government, were motivated by bigotry rather than an interest in liberty.

Though many among both Federalists and Anti-Federalists in Congress were genuinely concerned about individual rights, the motives of others were complex and positions taken not always straightforward. Some Federalists who still believed a statement of rights was unnecessary supported the amendments out of moral obligation. Some Anti-Federalists were in favor because they saw the amendments as one more way to tie down central power on behalf of the states. Many Federalists were in favor because they thought rights amendments would head off pressures for another constitutional convention. A few Anti-Federalists were opposed because they thought defeat of amendments would have the opposite effect.

It was understood that the rights being proposed would be held only against the new federal government. Checks on the states were not needed because state constitutions had their own bills of rights. Still, at one point in the debate it was proposed that the rights be guaranteed against both levels of government. This was voted down. The phrase that introduces the First Amendment and thus the entire Bill of Rights "Congress shall made no law . . ." also makes clear which government was being addressed.

In all, Congress sent 12 proposed amendments to the states for ratification. Two, dealing with adjustments in Congressional representation and limits on the pay of members of Congress and not having to do with rights, failed to gain approval. Ratification of the others, now the first 10 amendments or the Bill of Rights, was completed on December 15, 1791.

Like the Constitution of which they were now a part, they are nondoctrinaire. There is no talk of natural rights, no lofty or abstract statements of freedom and liberty as there were in the Declaration of Independence. Instead, rights are confined to concrete statements of settled and traditional protections. They are more the expression of lawyers than philosophers. This characteristic has made specific application easier but has sometimes left doubt about full meaning in changing times.

Nationalization of the Bill of Rights

Many contemporaries of the day played down the Bill of Rights as simply a restatement of the obvious. In fact, the amendments had little immediate effect beyond declaration. The chief reason was that the federal or central government passed few laws and had few policies that intruded upon individual rights. Then as now, most government action affecting individual behavior directly and thus individual rights was that of state authority. Most criminal law, for example, was of state and local creation.

Yet it was only a matter of time before applicability of the Bill of Rights to the states would become an issue. It came before the Supreme Court for the first time in 1833 in a case brought by John Barron, owner of a wharf in Baltimore. Harbor improvements by the city had left the water around his wharf shallower, making it less accessible to shipping and thus less valuable as property. This, he argued, was a "taking" of his property for a public purpose for which he was entitled to "just compensation" required by the Fifth Amendment. The Supreme Court's response in *Barron v. Baltimore,* the last constitutional opinion written by Chief Justice John Marshall, was negative. Marshall held, on sound historical grounds, that the Bill of Rights was not intended to apply as a protection against the actions of state governments or, as in this case, their chartered municipalities.

There the issue remained until the Civil War and the ratification of the Fourteenth Amendment in 1868 three years after the war's end. Reflecting what the war had been fought about, the amendment placed three important limits on state power in the name of individual rights, each of which would have been politically unthinkable in the antebellum period. In its so-called privileges and immunities clause, it declared that "no state shall make or enforce any law which shall abridge the privileges and immunities of citizens of the United States." Nor could any state deprive anyone of "life, liberty, or property without due process of law," the same wording found in the due process clause in the Fifth Amendment. In a third clause, states were forbidden to "deny to any person within their jurisdiction the equal protection of the laws."

In the 30 years that followed, the Supreme Court gave a narrow interpretation to each of the clauses. In the Slaughterhouse Cases in 1873, a group of New Orleans butchers argued that Louisiana's grant of a virtual monopoly to the operator of one slaughterhouse violated their privilege to be an otherwise lawful business. But the Court held that the "privileges and immunities of citizens of the United States" referred only to those of national as opposed to state citizenship. The former were few and had to do with a person's relationship to federal government, such as the right to vote in a federal

election or to travel to the seat of the national government.

In 1896, in *Plessy v. Ferguson,* the Court formulated the "separate but equal" doctrine to give a limited cast to the equal protection clause, allowing Southern states to segregate the races as long as the separated facilities were equal.

It was the middle or due process clause of the amendment that became the vehicle for a new claim that some or all the rights in the Bill of Rights were held against the states. The issue came to the Court in *Hurtado v. California* in 1884 (p. 36), in which the appellant, convicted of murder, argued that he had not been indicted by a grand jury required by the Fifth Amendment. California law permitted indictments by "information," in which a prosecutor puts preliminary evidence against the accused before a judge rather than a grand jury to gauge whether it is enough to warrant trial. Hurtado's lawyer reasoned that grand jury indictment was required by due process of law, also in the Fifth Amendment, and concluded, as John Barron could not, that it was thus required by the same clause in the Fourteenth Amendment. The claim was ingenious but failed in the end. The Supreme Court held that because indictment by information was a procedure in long use it did not violate due process and, further, that the framers of the Bill of Rights would not have engaged in the redundancy of mentioning grand jury and due process rights separately if they meant the one to comprehend the other.

But might there be rights in the Bill of Rights that could be considered part of due process and thus be limits on the states? Thirteen years later in *Chicago, Burlington, & Quincy Railroad v. Chicago,* the Court's answer was a qualified yes. The case, however, like *Barron v. Baltimore,* was over a property right rather than one of criminal procedure. The plaintiff railroad disputed the amount it was paid for property taken by the city through eminent domain for street improvements. The city's payment, it argued, fell short of "just compensation" required by the Fifth Amendment when property is seized for public purposes. The Court agreed, saying that without such compensation "almost all other rights become worthless," and held due process to have been violated by the city's modest payment. It was the first time a right of the Bill of Rights had been applied to state action or, to put it differently, was "incorporated" into the Fourteenth Amendment's due process clause.

This nationalization was not immediately extended. In the next few years, the Court twice rejected claims that certain criminal justice rights applied. In *Maxwell v. Dow*, 1900, a robbery case, it held that trial by a traditional 12-person jury, the practice in the federal courts, was not required by due process (the defendant had been convicted by a jury of eight under a Utah law). In *Twining v. New Jersey*, 1908, it ruled the Fifth Amendment's protection against self-incrimination was not part of due process either. The trial judge in the case had told the jury they could take the defendant's failure to testify into account in determining his guilt or innocence. Though the Supreme Court's ruling was negative, it did say that "fundamental and inalienable" rights in the Bill of Rights might be incorporated, though no hint was given about which ones they might be.

That statement first came in *Gitlow v. New York*, 1925, in the Court's review of a communist criminal anarchy conviction for distributing a pamphlet calling for the forcible overthrow of the government and capitalist system. Though upholding the conviction, the Court accepted the general argument of Gitlow's famed defense attorney Clarence Darrow, that freedom of speech and press in the First Amendment was also part of "liberty" protected by the due process clause. "For present purposes," wrote Justice Edward Sanford, "we do assume that freedom of speech and of the press... are among the fundamental personal rights and 'liberties' protected by the due process clause of the Fourteenth Amendment from impairment by the states." [268 U.S. 652 at 666]

Because the Court upheld Gitlow's conviction, this important avowal was officially only a dictum—a nonbinding observation not vital to

the outcome of the case. Six years later in *Near v. Minnesota*, the Court had a chance to actually base a decision on this new doctrine. It held Minnesota's "gag" law that allowed the state to shut down a weekly newspaper for publishing defamatory material, was an unconstitutional prior restraint, violating freedom of the press in the First Amendment. "It is no longer open to doubt," said Chief Justice Hughes for a Court divided 5-4, "that the liberty of the press... is within the liberty safeguarded by the due process clause of the Fourteenth Amendment from incursion by state action." [283 U.S. 697 at 706]

The door of incorporation, opened the smallest crack in *Chicago, Burlington*, was now ajar, yet the Court had not said what other provisions of the Bill of Rights might be part of due process or why. Those questions began to receive answers in *Palko v. Connecticut* in 1937 (p. 38). A criminal defendant convicted of second degree murder and sentenced to life imprisonment was retried because of an error made against the state and then convicted of first degree murder, a capital offense. Faced with the argument that the second trial violated the double jeopardy provision of the Fifth Amendment, Justice Benjamin Cardozo formulated the Court's standard for incorporation. A right was part of due process not because it was in the Bill of Rights, but because it was part of "the very essence of a scheme of ordered liberty... principles of justices so rooted in the traditions and conscience of our people as to be ranked fundamental."

Palko fashioned the doctrine of selective incorporation by which different provisions in the Bill of Rights came to be applied to the states through the Fourteenth Amendment's due process clause on a case-by-case basis. In the years immediately following, a group of justices led by Hugo Black, who had joined the Court the year the case was decided, argued for full absorption of the Bill of Rights into due process and, by that, for a uniform set of rights limiting both levels of government. Though not all historians agree with him, Black argued that this was what

Incorporation of the Bill of Rights into the Due Process Clause of the Fourteenth Amendment

First Amendment

Freedom of speech	*Gitlow v. New York* (1925)
Freedom of the press	*Near v. Minnesota* (1931)
Freedom of assembly	*DeJonge v. Oregon* (1937)
Freedom of petition	*Hague v. C.I.O.* (1939)
Free exercise of religion	*Cantwell v. Connecticut* (1940)
Separation of church and state	*Everson v. Board of Education* (1947)
Freedom of association	*N.A.A.C.P. v. Alabama* (1958)

Fourth Amendment

Protection against unreasonable searches and seizures	*Wolf v. Colorado* (1949)
Exclusion of illegally seized evidence	*Mapp v. Ohio* (1961)

Fifth Amendment

Just compensation	*Chicago, Burlington & Quincy Railway v. Chicago* (1897)
Privilege against self-incrimination	*Malloy v. Hogan* (1964)
Protection against double jeopardy	*Benton v. Maryland* (1969)

Sixth Amendment

Counsel (capital cases)	*Powell v. Alabama* (1932)
Public trial	*In re Oliver* (1948)
Notice of charges	*Cole v. Arkansas* (1948)
Counsel (felonies)	*Gideon v. Wainwright* (1963)
Confrontation of witnesses	*Pointer v. Texas* (1965)
Impartial jury	*Parker v. Gladden* (1966)
Speedy trial	*Klopfer v. North Carolina* (1967)
Compulsory process for obtaining witnesses	*Washington v. Texas* (1967)
Jury trial	*Duncan v. Louisiana* (1968)
Counsel (misdemeanors)	*Argersinger v. Hamlin* (1972)

Eighth Amendment

Protection against cruel and unusual punishments	*Robinson v. California* (1962)

the framers of the Fourteenth Amendment had intended. The doctrine of total incorporation, as this approach became known, reached its crest in *Adamson v. California,* 1947. There it was embraced by four justices dissenting from the majority's decision to uphold a conviction in which the trial judge, as in *Twining v. New Jersey,* had commented adversely about the defendant's failure to testify.

Though Black was never successful in persuading a majority of the Court to accept total incorporation, in the long run it did not matter. Using Cardozo's guidelines in *Palko,* the Court continued selectively to hold provisions in the Bill of Rights to be part of due process of law and thus apply them to the states. The development was accelerated during the Warren Court, 1953–1969, when 11 rights, mainly dealing with criminal justice, were incorporated. Today, all but a handful of the rights apply to the states. (See "Incorporation of the Bill of Rights into the Due Process Clause of the Fourteenth Amendment.")

Different views on incorporation, reflecting debate among the justices near the end of Warren's tenure, were set out in *Duncan v. Louisiana* in 1968 (p. 41). The case, holding that the Sixth Amendment's provision for a jury trial is required by due process even for petty criminal offenses, was one of the Court's last incorporating decisions and offers one of its fullest discussions of the issue.

Remaining not incorporated are the Second Amendment's right to bear arms, the Third's protection against the quartering of soldiers in private houses in peacetime without consent of the owners, the Fifth's right not to be criminally tried unless indicted by a grand jury, and the Seventh's right to a jury trial in civil cases. Incorporation of these remaining provisions appears unlikely. Indictment by information, for example, the issue in *Hurtado,* is seen by many students of civil liberties as giving as much, perhaps more, protection against weakly supported prosecutions as indictment by grand jury. Similarly, requiring states to use juries in all civil cases would vastly increase judicial operating costs and slow litigation, without necessarily enhancing the fairness of decisions reached.

Due process of law continues to be both more and less extensive than the Bill of Rights. If its net does not catch all provisions of the first eight amendments, it does reach many other rights— aspects of privacy, for example—not among those specifically set out in the Bill of Rights.

Near total selective incorporation has expanded applicability of the Bill of Rights and created a minimum uniform standard of protection for which Black had argued. State governments cannot ignore rules of liberty and equality that bind the federal. The chief drawback in this development is the degrading of one of the federal system's important advantages: the opportunity for states to experiment. Many students of civil liberties, however, see this cost worth the benefit gained from nationalization— recognition that the rights incorporated are basic to ordered liberty and not reducible by any level of government.

FURTHER READING

A Nation of Rights and Liberties

Abernathy, Glenn M., and Barbara A. Perry, *Civil Liberties Under the Constitution* (1993)

Abraham, Henry J., and Barbara A. Perry, *Freedom and the Court,* 7th ed. (1998)

Amar, Akhil Reed, *The Bill of Rights: Creation and Reconstruction* (1998)

———, and Alan Hirsch, *For the People: What the Constitution Really Says about Your Rights* (1998)

Baer, Judith A., *Equality under the Constitution: Reclaiming the Fourteenth Amendment* (1983)

Barnett, Randy E., ed., *The Rights Retained by the People: The History and Means of the Ninth Amendment* (1989)

———, *The Structure of Liberty: Justice and the Rule of Law* (1998)

Bigel, Alan I., *The Supreme Court on Emergency Powers, Foreign Affairs, and the Protection of Civil Liberties, 1935–1975* (1986)

Brigham, John, *Civil Liberties and American Democracy* (1984)

Campbell, Colton C., and John F. Stack, eds., *Congress and the Politics of Emerging Rights* (2001)

Casper, Jonathan, *The Politics of Civil Liberties* (1972)

Cohen, William, Murray Schwartz, and DeAnne Sobul, *The Bill of Rights: A Source Book* (1976)

Cortner, Richard C., *The Supreme Court and Civil Liberties Policy* (1975)

DeRosa, Marshall, *The Ninth Amendment and the Politics of Creative Jurisprudence: Disparaging the Fundamental Right of Popular Control* (1996)

Dorsen, Norman, *Frontiers of Civil Liberties* (1968)

———, *The Evolving Constitution: Essays on the Bill of Rights and the United States Supreme Court* (1987)

Dworkin, Ronald, *Taking Rights Seriously* (1977)

Epp, Charles, *The Rights Revolution: Lawyers, Activists, and Supreme Courts in Comparative Perspective* (1998)

Epstein, Richard A., *Principles for a Free Society: Reconciling Individual Liberty with the Common Good* (1998)

Finkelman, Paul, and Stephen E. Gottlieb, eds., *Toward a Usable Past: Liberty under State Constitutions* (1991)

Foley, Michael, *American Political Ideas* (1991)

Foner, Eric, *The Story of American Freedom* (1998)

Gardner, James A., ed., *State Expansion of Federal Constitutional Liberties: Individual Rights in a Dual Constitutional System* (1999)

Glendon, Mary Ann, *Rights Talk* (1991)

George, Robert P., *Making Men Moral: Civil Liberties and Public Morality* (1993)

Goldman, Roger L., *Individual Rights: The Universal Challenge: 1791–1991, Bicentennial Celebration of the Bill of Rights* (1991)

Goldwin, Robert A., and William A. Schambra, eds., *How Does the Constitution Secure Rights?* (1985)

Gottlieb, Stephen E., *Morality Imposed: The Rehnquist Court and Liberty in America* (2000)

Hensley, Thomas R., Christopher E. Smith, and Joyce A. Baugh, *The Changing Supreme Court: Constitutional Rights and Liberties* (1997)

Hickok, Eugene W., Gary L. McDowell, and Philip J. Costopoulos, eds., *Our Peculiar Security: The Written Constitution and Limited Government* (1993)

Katz, Ellis, and G. Alan Tarr, eds., *Federalism and Rights* (1996)

Keller, Robert H., ed., *In Honor of Justice Douglas: A Symposium on Individual Freedom and the Government* (1979)

Kommers, Donald P., *Liberty and Community in American Constitutional Law: Continuing Tensions* (1986)

Landynski, Jacob W., *Individual Rights and Public Police in the New Supreme Court* (1982)

Massey, Calivin R., *Silent Rights: the Ninth Amendment and the Constitution's Unenumerated Rights* (1995)

McClellan, James, *Liberty, Order, and Justice: An Introduction to the Constitutional Principles of America Government* (1999)

Moore, Wayne D., *Constitutional Rights and Powers of the People* (1996)

Morgan, Richard E., *The Law and Politics of Civil Rights and Liberties* (1985)

Phelps, Glenn A., and Robert A. Poirier, eds., *Contemporary Debates on Civil Liberties: The Enduring Questions* (1985)

Powe, Lucas A., Jr., *The Warren Court and American Politics* (2000)

Renstrom, Peter, *Constitutional Rights Sourcebook* (1999)

Saari, David J., *Too Much Liberty? Perspectives on Freedom and the American Dream* (1995)

Scheingold, Stuart A., *The Politics of Rights* (1974)

Schlam, Lawrence, *The Bill of Rights: Fundamental Freedom* (1981)

Schwartz, Bernard, *The Great Rights of Mankind: A History of the American Bill of Rights* (1992)

Shaw, Stephen K., *The Ninth Amendment: Preservation of the Constitutional Mind* (1990)

Stephens, Otis H., and John M. Scheb, *American Civil Liberties* (1999)

Tushnet, Mark V., ed., *The Warren Court in Historical Perspective* (1993)

Walker, Samuel, *The Rights Revolution: Rights and Community in Modern American* (1998)

Watson, Bradley C. S., *Civil Rights and the Paradox of Liberal Democracy* (1999)

———, *Courts and the Culture Wars* (2002)

Wills, Gary, *A Necessary Evil: A History of American Distrust of Government* (1999)

The Supreme Court and the American Judiciary

Barrow, Deborah J., Gary Zuk, and George S. Gryski, *The Federal Judiciary and Institutional Change* (1996)

Baum, Lawrence, *The Supreme Court*, 7th ed. (2000)

Gates, John B., and Charles A. Johnson, eds., *The American Courts: A Critical Assessment* (1991)

Howard, J. Woodford, Jr., *Courts of Appeals in the Federal Judicial System* (1981)

Kuersten, Ashlyn K., and Donald R. Songer, *Decisions of the United States Courts of Appeal* (2001)

Maltzman, Forest, Paul J. Wahlbeck, and James Spriggs, *Crafting Law on the Supreme Court: The Collegial Game* (2000)

Marshall, Thomas, *Public Opinion and the Supreme Court* (1989)

O'Brien, David M., *Storm Center: The Supreme Court in American Politics*, 3rd ed. (1993)

Pacelle, Richard L., Jr., *Transformation of the Supreme Court's Agenda* (1991)

Perry, H. W., Jr., *Deciding to Decide: Agenda Setting in the United States Supreme Court* (1991)

Provine, Doris Marie, *Case Selection in the United States Supreme Court* (1980)

Radcliffe, James E., *The Case-or-Controversy Provision* (1978)

Rehnquist, William H., *The Supreme Court: How It Was, How It Is* (1987)

Rowland, C. K., and Robert A. Carp, *Politics and Judgment in Federal District Courts* (1996)

Songer, Donald R., Reginald S. Sheehan, and Susan B. Haire, *Continuity and Change in the United States Courts of Appeal* (2000)

van Geel, T. R., *Understanding Supreme Court Opinions* (1991)

Walker, Thomas G., and Lee Epstein, *The Supreme Court of the United States: An Introduction* (1992)

Wasby, Stephen L., *The Supreme Court in the Federal Judicial System* (1993)

Origins of the Bill of Rights

Goldwin, Robert A., *From Parchment to Power: How James Madison Used the Bill of Rights to Save the Constitution* (1997)

Hickok, Eugene W., ed., *The Bill of Rights: Original Meaning Current Understanding* (1991)

Levy, Leonard W., *Origins of the Bill of Rights* (1999)

Rutland, Robert A., *Birth of the Bill of Rights, 1776–1791* (1955)

Veit, Helen E., Kenneth R. Bowling, and Charles Bangs Bickford, *Creating the Bill of Rights: The Documentary Record from the First Federal Congress* (1991)

The Bill of Rights and the States

Berger, Raoul, *Government by Judiciary: Transformation of the Fourteenth Amendment* (1977)

———, *The Fourteenth Amendment and the Bill of Rights* (1989)

Cortner, Richard C., *The Supreme Court and the Second Bill of Rights* (1981)

Curtis, Michael Kent, *No State Shall Abridge: The Fourteenth Amendment and the Bill of Rights* (1990)

Levy, Leonard W., *Introduction to the Fourteenth Amendment and the Bill of Rights: Incorporation Theory* (1970)

Lewis, Frederick P., *The Dilemma of the Congressional Power to Enforce the Fourteenth Amendment* (1980)

———, *The Nationalization of Liberty* (1990)

Magee, James J., *Mr. Justice Black: Absolutist on the Court* (1980)

Nelson, Michael, *The Fourteenth Amendment: From Political Principle to Judicial Doctrine* (1988)

Yarborough, Tinsley E., *Mr. Justice Black and His Critics* (1998)

Additional worked listed in General and Supplementary Bibliography.

CASES

Hurtado v. California

110 U.S. 516 (1884), 7-1
Opinion of the Court: Matthews (Blatchford, Bradley, Gray, Miller, Waite, Woods)
Dissenting: Harlan
Not participating: Field

Joseph Hurtado was convicted of murdering his wife's lover and sentenced to death. He had not been indicted by a grand jury as required in the federal courts and those of many states. Instead, he had been charged through a process called an information, *allowed under California law, in which the prosecutor presents evidence to a judge rather than to a grand jury to determine whether it is strong enough to bring a criminal charge.*

Is the Court's reasoning in this case based on the words of the Constitution, history, pragmatic considerations, or what? On what view of the Constitution does Harlan base his dissent? As a result of this decision how can due process of law be described? How can constitutionally required due process be described?

Matthews, for the Court:

It is claimed on behalf of [Hurtado] that the conviction and sentence are void, on the ground that they are repugnant to that clause of the Fourteenth . . . Amendment . . . which is in these words: "Nor shall any State deprive any person of life, liberty, or property without due process of law."

The proposition of law we are asked to affirm is that an indictment or presentment by a grand jury, as known to the common law of England, is essential to that "due process of law," when applied to prosecutions for felonies, which is secured and guaranteed by this provision of the Constitution of the United States, and which, accordingly, it is forbidden to the States respectively to dispense with in the administration of criminal law. . . .

The Constitution of the United States was ordained . . . by descendants of Englishmen, who inherited the traditions of English law and history; but it was made for an undefined and expanding future, and for a people gathered and to be gathered from many nations and of many tongues. And while we take just pride in the principles and institutions of the common law, we are not to forget that, in lands where other systems of jurisprudence prevail, the ideas and processes of civil justice are also not unknown. Due process of law, in spite of the absolutism of continental governments, is not alien to that code which survived the Roman Empire as the foundation of modern civilization in Europe, and which has given us [a] fundamental maxim of distributive justice. . . . There is nothing in Magna Carta, rightly construed as a broad charter of public right and law, which ought to exclude the best ideas of all systems and of every age, and as it was the characteristic principle of the common law to draw its inspiration from every fountain of justice, we are not to assume that the sources of its supply have been exhausted. On the contrary, we should expect that the new and various experiences of our own situation and system will mould and shape it into new and not less useful forms. . . .

We are to construe this phrase in the Fourteenth Amendment by the *usus loquendi* of the Constitution itself. The same words are contained in the Fifth Amendment. That article makes specific and express provision for perpetuating the institution of the grand jury so far as relates to prosecutions for the more aggravated crimes under the laws of the United States. It declares that: No person shall be held to answer for a capital or otherwise infamous crime, unless on a presentment or indictment of a grand jury, except in cases arising in the land or naval forces, or in the militia when in actual service in time of war or public danger; nor shall any person be subject for the same offense to be twice put in jeopardy of life or limb; nor shall he be compelled in any criminal case to be witness against himself. [It then immediately adds:] or be deprived of life, liberty, or property, without due process of law.

According to a recognized canon of interpretation especially applicable to formal and solemn instruments of constitutional law, we are forbidden to assume, without clear reason to the contrary, that any part of this most important amendment is superfluous. The natural and obvious inference is that, in the sense of the Constitution, "due process of law" was not meant or intended to include, *ex vi termini*, the institution and procedure of a grand jury in any case. The conclusion is equally irresistible that, when the same phrase was employed in the Fourteenth Amendment to restrain the action of the States, it was used in the same sense and with no greater extent, and that, if in the adoption of that amendment it had been part of its purpose to perpetuate the institution of the grand jury in all the States, it would have embodied, as did the Fifth Amendment, express declarations to that effect. Due process of law in the latter refers to that law of the land which derives its authority from the legislative powers conferred upon Congress by the Constitution of the United States, exercised within the limits therein prescribed and interpreted according to the principles of the common law. In the Fourteenth Amendment, by parity of reason, it refers to that law of the land in each State which derives its authority from the inherent and reserved powers of the State . . .

Tried by these principles, we are unable to say that the substitution for a presentment or indictment by a grand jury of the proceeding by information, after examination and commitment by a magistrate, certifying to the probable guilt of the defendant, with the right on his part to the aid of counsel, and to the cross-examination of the witnesses produced for the prosecution, is not due process of law. It is, as we have seen, an ancient proceeding at common law, which might include every case of an offense of less grade than a felony, except misprision of treason, and in every circumstance of its administration, as authorized by the statute of California, it carefully considers and guards the substantial interest of the prisoner. It is merely a preliminary proceeding, and can result in no final judgment except as the consequence of a regular judicial trial, conducted precisely as in cases of indictments . . .

Harlan, dissenting:

. . . I omit further citations of authorities, which are numerous, to prove that, according to the settled usages and modes of proceeding existing under the common and statute law of England at the settlement of this country, information in capital cases was not consistent with the "law of the land," or with "due process of law." Such was the understanding of the patriotic men who established free institutions upon this continent. Almost the identical words of Magna Carta were incorporated into most of the State Constitutions before the adoption of our national Constitution. When they declared, in substance, that no person should be deprived of life, liberty, or property except by the judgment of his peers or the law of the land, they intended to assert his right to the same guaranties that were given in the mother country by the great charter and the laws passed in furtherance of its fundamental principles. . . .

But it is said that the framers of the Constitution did not suppose that due process of law necessarily required for a capital offense the institution and procedure of a grand jury, else the would not, in the same amendment, prohibiting the deprivation of life, liberty, or property, without due process of law, have made specific and express provision for a grand jury where the crime is capital or otherwise infamous; therefore, it is argued, the requirement by the Fourteenth Amendment of due process of law in all proceedings involving life, liberty, and property, without specific reference to grand juries in any case whatever, was not intended as a restriction upon the power which it is claimed the States previously had, so far as the express restrictions of the national Constitution are concerned, to dispense altogether with grand juries.

This line of argument, it seems to me, would lead to results which are inconsistent with the vital principles of republican government. If the presence in the Fifth Amendment of a specific provision for grand juries in capital cases, alongside the provision for due process of law in proceedings involving life, liberty, or property, is held to prove that "due process of law" did not, in the judgment of the framers of the Constitution, necessarily require a grand jury in capital cases, inexorable logic would require it to be, likewise, held that the right not to be put twice in jeopardy of life and limb for the same offense, nor compelled in a criminal case to testify against one's self—rights and immunities also specifically recognized in the Fifth Amendment—were not protected by that due process of law required by the settled us-

ages and proceedings existing under the common and statute law of England at the settlement of this country. More than that, other amendments of the Constitution proposed at the same time, expressly recognize the right of persons to just compensation for private property taken for public use; their right, when accused of crime, to be informed of the nature and cause of the accusation against them, and to a speedy and public trial, by an impartial jury of the State and district wherein the crime was committed; to be confronted by the witnesses against them, and to have compulsory process for obtaining witnesses in their favor. Will it be claimed that these rights were not secured by the "law of the land" or by "due process of law," as declared and established at the foundation of our government? Are they to be excluded from the enumeration of the fundamental principles of liberty and justice, and, therefore, not embraced by "due process of law"? If the argument of my brethren be sound, those rights—although universally recognized at the establishment of our institutions as secured by that due process of law which for centuries had been the foundation of Anglo-Saxon liberty—were not deemed by our fathers as essential in the due process of law prescribed by our Constitution; because—such seems to be the argument—had they been regarded as involved in due process of law, they would not have been specifically and expressly provided for, but left to the protection given by the general clause forbidding the deprivation of life, liberty, or property without due process of law. Further, the reasoning of the opinion indubitably leads to the conclusion that, but for the specific provisions made in the Constitution for the security of the personal rights enumerated, the general inhibition against deprivation of life, liberty, and property without due process of law would not have prevented Congress from enacting a statute in derogation of each of them . . .

Palko v. Connecticut

302 U.S. 319 (1937), 8-1
Opinion of the Court: Cardozo (Black, Brandeis, Hughes, McReynolds, Roberts, Stone, Sutherland)
Dissenting: Butler

Background facts are stated in the opinion.
Does Cardozo clarify which rights in the Bill of Rights apply to the states? How can it be determined which rights are

"fundamental" and which are not? As a result of this decision, how would you support a claim in a future case that a right in the Bill of Rights was applicable to the states? In Cardozo's reasoning, is due process a larger or smaller repository of rights than the Bill of Rights? Was it unfair of Connecticut to retry Palko?

Cardozo, for the Court:

A statute of Connecticut permitting appeals in criminal cases to be taken by the state is challenged by [Palko] as an infringement of the Fourteenth Amendment of the Constitution of the United States. Whether the challenge should be upheld is now to be determined.

[Palko] was indicted . . . for murder in the first degree. A jury found him guilty of murder in the second degree, and he was sentenced to confinement in the state prison for life. Thereafter, the State of Connecticut . . . gave notice of appeal to the Supreme Court of Errors [which] reversed the judgment and ordered a new trial. . . . It found that there had been error of law to the prejudice of the state (1) in excluding testimony as to a confession by defendant; (2) in excluding testimony upon cross-examination of defendant to impeach his credibility, and (3) in the instructions to the jury as to the difference between first and second degree murder.

. . . [Palko] was brought to trial again. Before a jury was impaneled and also at later stages of the case, he made the objection that the effect of the new trial was to place him twice in jeopardy for the same offense, and, in so doing, to violate the Fourteenth Amendment of the Constitution of the United States. Upon the overruling of the objection, the trial proceeded. The jury returned a verdict of murder in the first degree, and the court sentenced [Palko] to the punishment of death. . . . The case is here upon appeal.

1. The execution of the sentence will not deprive [Palko] of his life without the process of law assured to him by the Fourteenth Amendment of the Federal Constitution.

The argument for [Palko] is that whatever is forbidden by the Fifth Amendment is forbidden by the Fourteenth also. The Fifth Amendment, which is not directed to the states, but solely to the federal government, creates immunity from double jeopardy. No person shall be "subject for the same offense to be twice put in jeopardy of life or limb." The Fourteenth Amendment ordains, "nor shall any State deprive any person of life, liberty, or property, without due process of law." To retry a defendant, though under one in-

dictment and only one, subjects him, it is said, to double jeopardy in violation of the Fifth Amendment if the prosecution is one on behalf of the United States. From this the consequence is said to follow that there is a denial of life or liberty without due process of law, if the prosecution is one on behalf of the People of a State. . . .

We have said that . . . the Fourteenth Amendment is to be taken as embodying the prohibitions of the Fifth. [Palko's] thesis is even broader. Whatever would be a violation of the original bill of rights (Amendments I to VIII) if done by the federal government is now equally unlawful by force of the Fourteenth Amendment if done by a state. There is no such general rule.

The Fifth Amendment provides, among other things, that no person shall be held to answer for a capital or otherwise infamous crime unless on presentment or indictment of a grand jury. This court has held that, in prosecutions by a state, presentment or indictment by a grand jury may give way to informations at the instance of a public officer. *Hurtado v. California*, 1884. The Fifth Amendment provides also that no person shall be compelled in any criminal case to be a witness against himself. This court has said that, in prosecutions by a state, the exemption will fail if the state elects to end it. *Twining v. New Jersey*, 1908. The Sixth Amendment calls for a jury trial in criminal cases, and the Seventh for a jury trial in civil cases at common law where the value in controversy shall exceed twenty dollars. This court has ruled that consistently with those amendments trial by jury may be modified by a state or abolished altogether.

On the other hand, the due process clause of the Fourteenth Amendment may make it unlawful for a state to abridge by its statutes the freedom of speech which the First Amendment safeguards against encroachment by the Congress, or the like freedom of the press, or the free exercise of religion, or the right of peaceable assembly, without which speech would be unduly trammeled, or the right of one accused of crime to the benefit of counsel. In these and other situations, immunities that are valid as against the federal government by force of the specific pledges of particular amendments have been found to be implicit in the concept of ordered liberty, and thus, through the Fourteenth Amendment, become valid as against the states.

The line of division may seem to be wavering and broken if there is a hasty catalogue of the cases on the one side and the other. Reflection and analysis will induce a different view. There emerges the perception of a rationalizing principle which gives to discrete instances a proper order and coherence. The right to trial by jury and the immunity from prosecution except as the result of an indictment may have value and importance. Even so, they are not of the very essence of a scheme of ordered liberty. To abolish them is not to violate a "principle of justice so rooted in the traditions and conscience of our people as to be ranked as fundamental." Few would be so narrow or provincial as to maintain that a fair and enlightened system of justice would be impossible without them. What is true of jury trials and indictments is true also, as the cases show, of the immunity from compulsory self-incrimination. *Twining v. New Jersey.* This too might be lost, and justice still be done. Indeed, today, as in the past, there are students of our penal system who look upon the immunity as a mischief, rather than a benefit, and who would limit its scope, or destroy it altogether. No doubt there would remain the need to give protection against torture, physical or mental. Justice, however, would not perish if the accused were subject to a duty to respond to orderly inquiry. The exclusion of these immunities and privileges from the privileges and immunities protected against the action of the states has not been arbitrary or casual. It has been dictated by a study and appreciation of the meaning, the essential implications, of liberty itself.

We reach a different plane of social and moral values when we pass to the privileges and immunities that have been taken over from the earlier articles of the federal bill of rights and brought within the Fourteenth Amendment by a process of absorption. These, in their origin, were effective against the federal government alone. If the Fourteenth Amendment has absorbed them, the process of absorption has had its source in the belief that neither liberty nor Justice would exist if they were sacrificed. *Twining v. New Jersey.* This is true, for illustration, of freedom of thought, and speech. Of that freedom one may say that it is the matrix, the indispensable condition, of nearly every other form of freedom. With rare aberrations, a pervasive recognition of that truth can be traced in our history, political and legal. So it has come about that the domain of liberty, withdrawn by the Fourteenth Amendment from encroachment by the states, has been enlarged by latter-day judgments to include liberty of the mind as well as liberty of action. The extension became, indeed, a logical imperative when once it was recognized, as long ago it was, that liberty is something more than exemption from physical restraint, and that, even in the field of substantive rights and duties, the legislative judgment, if oppressive and arbitrary, may be overridden by the courts. Fundamental too in the concept of due process, and so in that of liberty, is the thought that condemnation shall be rendered only after trial. The hearing, moreover, must be a real one, not a sham or a pretense. For that reason, ignorant defendants in a capital case were held to have been condemned unlawfully when in truth, though not in form, they were refused the aid of counsel. The decision did not turn upon the fact that the benefit of counsel would have been guaranteed to the defendants by the provisions of the Sixth Amendment if they had been prosecuted in a federal court. The decision turned upon the fact that, in the particular situation laid before us in the evidence, the benefit of counsel was essential to the substance of a hearing.

Our survey of the cases serves, we think, to justify the statement that the dividing line between them, if not unfaltering throughout its course, has been true for the most part to a unifying principle. On which side of the line the case made out by [Palko] has appropriate location must be the next inquiry, and the final one. Is that kind of double jeopardy to which the statute has subjected him a hardship so acute and shocking that our polity will not endure it? Does it violate those "fundamental principles of liberty and justice which lie at the base of all our civil and political institutions"? The answer surely must be "no." What the answer would have to be if the state were permitted after a trial free from error to try the accused over again or to bring another case against him, we have no occasion to consider. We deal with the statute before us, and no other. The state is not attempting to wear the accused out by a multitude of cases with accumulated trials. It asks no more than this, that the case against him shall go on until there shall be a trial free from the corrosion of substantial legal error. This is not cruelty at all, nor even vexation in any immoderate degree. If the trial had been infected with error adverse to the accused, there might have been review at his instance, and as often as necessary to purge the vicious taint. A reciprocal privilege, subject at all times to the discretion of the presiding judge, has now been granted to the state. There is here no seismic innovation. The edifice of justice stands, its symmetry, to many, greater than before.

2. The conviction of [Palko] is not in derogation of any privileges or immunities that belong to him as a citizen of the United States.

The judgment is affirmed.

Duncan v. Louisiana

391 U.S. 145 (1968), 7-2
Opinion of the Court: White (Brennan, Marshall, Warren, C.J.)
Concurring: Black, Douglas, Fortas
Dissenting: Harlan, Stewart

Background facts are stated in the opinion.

Which view of the case is most persuasive, White's, Black's, or Harlan's? Is the majority of the Court still battling here over selective as opposed to total incorporation of the Bill of Rights? Why are considerations of federalism important to Harlan? How does Black answer them? Would Black be willing to have the Court define liberty and due process under the Fourteenth Amendment?

White, for the Court:
Appellant, Gary Duncan, was convicted of simple battery in the Twenty-fifth Judicial District Court of Louisiana. Under Louisiana law, simple battery is a misdemeanor, punishable by a maximum of two years' imprisonment and a $300 fine. [He] sought trial by jury, but, because the Louisiana Constitution grants jury trials only in cases in which capital punishment or imprisonment at hard labor may be imposed, the trial judge denied the request. [He] was convicted and sentenced to serve 60 days in the parish prison and pay a fine of $10. . . . [He] sought review in this Court, alleging that the Sixth and Fourteenth Amendments to the United States Constitution secure the right to jury trial in state criminal prosecutions where a sentence as long as two years may be imposed. . . .

[Duncan] was 19 years of age when tried. While driving on Highway 23 in Plaquemines Parish on October 18, 1966, he saw two younger cousins engaged in a conversation by the side of the road with four white boys. Knowing his cousins, Negroes who had recently transferred to a formerly all-white high school, had reported the occurrence of racial incidents at the school, Duncan stopped the car, got out, and approached the six boys. At trial, the white boys and a white onlooker testified, as did appellant and his cousins. The testimony was in dispute on many points,

but the witnesses agreed that appellant and the white boys spoke to each other, that appellant encouraged his cousins to break off the encounter and enter his car, and that appellant was about to enter the car himself for the purpose of driving away with his cousins. The whites testified that, just before getting in the car, appellant slapped Herman Landry, one of the white boys, on the elbow. The Negroes testified that appellant had not slapped Landry, but had merely touched him. The trial judge concluded that the State had proved beyond a reasonable doubt that Duncan had committed simple battery, and found him guilty . . .

The test for determining whether a right extended by the Fifth and Sixth Amendments with respect to federal criminal proceedings is also protected against state action by the Fourteenth Amendment has been phrased in a variety of ways in the opinions of this Court. The question has been asked whether a right is among those "fundamental principles of liberty and justice which lie at the base of all our civil and political institutions," and whether it is "a fundamental right, essential to a fair trial." The claim before us is that the right to trial by jury guaranteed by the Sixth Amendment meets these tests. The position of Louisiana, on the other hand, is that the Constitution imposes upon the States no duty to give a jury trial in any criminal case, regardless of the seriousness of the crime or the size of the punishment which may be imposed. Because we believe that trial by jury in criminal cases is fundamental to the American scheme of justice, we hold that the Fourteenth Amendment guarantees a right of jury trial in all criminal cases which—were they to be tried in a federal court—would come within the Sixth Amendment's guarantee. Since we consider the appeal before us to be such a case, we hold that the Constitution was violated when appellant's demand for jury trial was refused.

The history of trial by jury in criminal cases has been frequently told. It is sufficient for present purposes to say that, by the time our Constitution was written, jury trial in criminal cases had been in existence in England for several centuries and carried impressive credentials traced by many to Magna Carta. Its preservation and proper operation as a protection against arbitrary rule were among the major objectives of the revolutionary settlement which was expressed in the Declaration and Bill of Rights of 1689. . . .

Jury trial came to America with English colonists, and received strong support from them. Royal interference with the jury trial was deeply resented. Among the resolutions adopted by the First Congress of the American Colonies (the Stamp Act Congress) on October 19, 1765—resolutions deemed by their authors to state "the most essential rights and liberties of the colonists"—was the declaration "That trial by jury is the inherent and invaluable right of every British subject in these colonies."

The First Continental Congress, in the resolve of October 14, 1774, objected to trials before judges dependent upon the Crown alone for their salaries and to trials in England for alleged crimes committed in the colonies . . .

The Declaration of Independence stated solemn objections to the King's making "Judges dependent on his Will alone, for the tenure of their offices, and the amount and payment of their salaries," to his "depriving us in many cases, of the benefits of Trial by Jury," and to his "transporting us beyond Seas to be tried for pretended offenses." The Constitution itself, in Art. III, § 2, commanded: "The Trial of all Crimes, except in Cases of Impeachment, shall be by Jury, and such Trial shall be held in the State where the said Crimes shall have been committed."

Objections to the Constitution because of the absence of a bill of rights were met by the immediate submission and adoption of the Bill of Rights. Included was the Sixth Amendment which, among other things, provided: "In all criminal prosecutions, the accused shall enjoy the right to a speedy and public trial, by an impartial jury of the State and district wherein the crime shall have been committed."

The constitutions adopted by the original States guaranteed jury trial. Also, the constitution of every State entering the Union thereafter in one form or another protected the right to jury trial in criminal cases.

Even such skeletal history is impressive support for considering the right to jury trial in criminal cases to be fundamental to our system of justice . . .

We are aware of prior cases in this Court in which the prevailing opinion contains statements contrary to our holding today that the right to jury trial in serious criminal cases is a fundamental right, and hence must be recognized by the States as part of their obligation to extend due process of law to all persons within their jurisdiction. Louisiana relies especially on *Maxwell v. Dow,* (1900); *Palko v. Connecticut,* (1937), and *Snyder v. Massachusetts,* (1934). None of these cases, however, dealt with a State which had purported to dispense entirely with a jury trial in serious

criminal cases. *Maxwell* held that no provision of the Bill of Rights applied to the States—a position long since repudiated—and that the Due Process Clause of the Fourteenth Amendment did not prevent a State from trying a defendant for a noncapital offense with fewer than 12 men on the jury. It did not deal with a case in which no jury at all had been provided. In neither *Palko* nor *Snyder* was jury trial actually at issue, although both cases contain important dicta asserting that the right to jury trial is not essential to ordered liberty and may be dispensed with by the States regardless of the Sixth and Fourteenth Amendments. These observations, though weighty and respectable, are nevertheless dicta, unsupported by holdings in this Court that a State may refuse a defendant's demand for a jury trial when he is charged with a serious crime . . . Respectfully, we reject the prior dicta regarding jury trial in criminal cases.

The guarantees of jury trial in the Federal and State Constitutions reflect a profound judgment about the way in which law should be enforced and justice administered. A right to jury trial is granted to criminal defendants in order to prevent oppression by the Government. Those who wrote our constitutions knew from history and experience that it was necessary to protect against unfounded criminal charges brought to eliminate enemies and against judges too responsive to the voice of higher authority. The framers of the constitutions strove to create an independent judiciary, but insisted upon further protection against arbitrary action. Providing an accused with the right to be tried by a jury of his peers gave him an inestimable safeguard against the corrupt or overzealous prosecutor and against the compliant, biased, or eccentric judge. If the defendant preferred the common sense judgment of a jury to the more tutored but perhaps less sympathetic reaction of the single judge, he was to have it. Beyond this, the jury trial provisions in the Federal and State Constitutions reflect a fundamental decision about the exercise of official power—a reluctance to entrust plenary powers over the life and liberty of the citizen to one judge or to a group of judges. Fear of unchecked power, so typical of our State and Federal Governments in other respects, found expression in the criminal law in this insistence upon community participation in the determination of guilt or innocence. The deep commitment of the Nation to the right of jury trial in serious criminal cases as a defense against arbitrary law enforcement qualifies for protection under the Due Process Clause of the Fourteenth Amendment, and must therefore be respected by the States.

Black, concurring:

The Court today holds that the right to trial by jury guaranteed defendants in criminal cases in federal courts by Art. III of the United States Constitution and by the Sixth Amendment is also guaranteed by the Fourteenth Amendment to defendants tried in state courts. With this holding I agree for reasons given by the Court. I also agree because of reasons given in my dissent in *Adamson v. California*. In that dissent, I took the position, contrary to the holding in *Twining v. New Jersey,* that the Fourteenth Amendment made all of the provisions of the Bill of Rights applicable to the States. . . .

. . . I am very happy to support this selective process through which our Court has, since the Adamson case, held most of the specific Bill of Rights protections applicable to the States to the same extent they are applicable to the Federal Government. Among these are the right to trial by jury decided today, the right against compelled self-incrimination, the right to counsel, the right to compulsory process for witnesses, the right to confront witnesses, the right to a speedy and public trial, and the right to be free from unreasonable searches and seizures. . . .

. . . I believe as strongly as ever that the Fourteenth Amendment was intended to make the Bill of Rights applicable to the States. I have been willing to support the selective incorporation doctrine, however, as an alternative, although perhaps less historically supportable than complete incorporation. The selective incorporation process, if used properly, does limit the Supreme Court in the Fourteenth Amendment field to specific Bill of Rights' protections only and keeps judges from roaming at will in their own notions of what policies outside the Bill of Rights are desirable and what are not. And, most importantly for me, the selective incorporation process has the virtue of having already worked to make most of the Bill of Rights' protections applicable to the States.

Harlan, dissenting:

. . . The question before us is not whether jury trial is an ancient institution, which it is; nor whether it plays a significant role in the administration of criminal Justice, which it does; nor whether it will endure, which

it shall. The question in this case is whether the State of Louisiana, which provides trial by jury for all felonies, is prohibited by the Constitution from trying charges of simple battery to the court alone. In my view, the answer to that question, mandated alike by our constitutional history and by the longer history of trial by jury, is clearly "no."

The States have always borne primary responsibility for operating the machinery of criminal justice within their borders, and adapting it to their particular circumstances. In exercising this responsibility, each State is compelled to conform its procedures to the requirements of the Federal Constitution. The Due Process Clause of the Fourteenth Amendment requires that those procedures be fundamentally fair in all respects. It does not, in my view, impose or encourage nationwide uniformity for its own sake; it does not command adherence to forms that happen to be old, and it does not impose on the States the rules that may be in force in the federal courts except where such rules are also found to be essential to basic fairness.

The Court's approach to this case is an uneasy and illogical compromise among the views of various Justices on how the Due Process Clause should be interpreted. The Court does not say that those who framed the Fourteenth Amendment intended to make the Sixth Amendment applicable to the States. And the Court concedes that it finds nothing unfair about the procedure by which the present appellant was tried. Nevertheless, the Court reverses his conviction: it holds, for some reason not apparent to me, that the Due Process Clause incorporates the particular clause of the Sixth Amendment that requires trial by jury in federal criminal cases—including, as I read its opinion, the sometimes trivial accompanying baggage of judicial interpretation in federal contexts. I have raised my voice many times before against the Court's continuing undiscriminating insistence upon fastening on the States federal notions of criminal justice, and I must do so again in this instance. With all respect, the Court's approach and its reading of history are altogether topsy-turvy. . . .

. . . The first section of the Fourteenth Amendment was meant neither to incorporate, nor to be limited to, the specific guarantees of the first eight Amendments. The overwhelming historical evidence . . . demonstrates . . . that the Congressmen and state legislators who wrote, debated, and ratified the Fourteenth Amendment did not think they were "incorporating" the Bill of Rights the very breadth and generality of the Amendment's provisions suggest that its authors did not suppose that the Nation would always be limited to mid-19th century conceptions of "liberty" and "due process of law," but that the increasing experience and evolving conscience of the American people would add new "intermediate premises." In short, neither history nor sense supports using the Fourteenth Amendment to put the States in a constitutional straitjacket with respect to their own development in the administration of criminal or civil law.

Although I therefore fundamentally disagree with the total incorporation view of the Fourteenth Amendment, it seems to me that such a position does at least have the virtue, lacking in the Court's selective incorporation approach, of internal consistency: we look to the Bill of Rights, word for word, clause for clause, precedent for precedent because, it is said, the men who wrote the Amendment wanted it that way. For those who do not accept this "history," a different source of "intermediate premises" must be found. The Bill of Rights is not necessarily irrelevant to the search for guidance in interpreting the Fourteenth Amendment, but the reason for and the nature of its relevance must be articulated.

Apart from the approach taken by the absolute incorporationists, I can see only one method of analysis that has any internal logic. That is to start with the words "liberty" and "due process of law" and attempt to define them in a way that accords with American traditions and our system of government. This approach, involving a much more discriminating process of adjudication than does "incorporation," is, albeit difficult, the one that was followed throughout the 19th and most of the present century. It entails a "gradual process of judicial inclusion and exclusion, seeking, with due recognition of constitutional tolerance for state experimentation and disparity, to ascertain those "immutable principles . . . of free government which no member of the Union may disregard." . . .

II

COMMUNIC
AND BEI

2

RELIGION: FREEDOM FOR, FREEDOM FROM

Religion is commonly a set of beliefs and practices that offer a spiritual understanding of the universe and one's place in it, usually, but not always, transcending the known and material world. It often includes an object of devotion and moral prescriptions for one's own behavior. Religious beliefs may have high emotional valence and occupy an important place in the personality. Turned outward, beliefs can generate great energy in the world of human events, from consolation and selfless work in relief of human suffering to intolerance and even murderous aggression toward those holding different beliefs or none at all. For these reasons, religion has often had a problematic relationship to secular and political authority.

"We are a religious people," Justice William O. Douglas said of Americans in a 1952 decision that released children from the public schools so that they might get religious instruction in their churches or synagogues. (*Zorach v. Clauson*) Sweeping as this generalization may be, there is no underestimating the aggregate effect of religion on American culture and values. Religious beliefs were important in the founding of the colonies. Like the ancient Hebrews, the Pilgrims and Puritans built communities in a Promised Land to escape religious persecution. Quakers in Pennsylvania and Roman Catholics in Maryland sought religious havens. A legacy of religious dissent helped seed the religious pluralism and religious freedom that has distinguished American society.

Religious faith and commitment has usually taken traditional forms, but from time to time evangelical fervor has asserted itself against the supposed apathy of the "older" churches or the growing secularization in public and private life. This happened in the Great Awakening of the 1730s, the Second Great Awakening in the late eighteenth and early nineteenth centuries, the revivalism of Billy Sunday at the turn of the twentieth century, and the renewal of biblical fundamentalism in our own time. Evangelical or not, religious beliefs have sometimes brought great moral force to public issues. Many American social movements, including those of abolition, temperance, women's suffrage, civil rights in the 1960s, and the present-day right-to-life, have been motivated in part by religious beliefs. It is not surprising that falling church membership and church attendance, so marked in modern industrial societies, have been less conspicuous in the United States.

De Toqueville observed that, "Americans rightly think their patriotism is a sort of religion strengthened by practical service." Indeed, a spiritual or quasi-religious view has helped shape a sense of American national identity. Generations of Americans have found it easy to believe their country occupies a special place in the providential scheme of things, giving it a mission in a darker world. Elements of this view are evident in the Puritan John Winthrop's vision of a "City on a Hill," and Jefferson's transcendent assertions in the Declaration of Independence. They appear again in the belief in a national "manifest destiny" during the antebellum period, in Lincoln's reassurance that the fallen of Gettysburg "shall not have died in vain," Woodrow Wilson's ideal of making the world safe for democracy in a "war to end wars," and the casting of the Cold War as a struggle against the godless Communism of an "evil empire." All show an unmistakable religiosity in the approach to human affairs and conflict.

The United States was the first modern Western nation founded by Protestants rather than Catholics, and Protestantism was the dominant American religious sensibility until well into the twentieth century. Its defiance of tradition, suspicion of hierarchy, emphasis on individualism and congregational democracy were well suited to settling a new world. That task put a premium on innovation, enterprise, self-reliance, and social mobility. It was easy for Protestants to assume that their values were, or should be, the values of American culture generally. The United States has never had a state church, but for much of its history its government and politics were pervasively influenced by what legal historian Mark DeWolfe Howe called a "de facto Protestant establishment."

Yet, even at its peak, Protestant dominance could not deny the force of religious pluralism. From the start, religion in the United States has been that of many churches housing believers with many differing creeds. These have included Presbyterians, Congregationalists, Episcopalians, Baptists, Methodists, Lutherans, and Quakers, besides Roman Catholics, Jews, Orthodox Catholics, Moslems, and many lesser Protestant denominations. The nation has also spawned many new and breakaway sects, including the Shakers, Mormons, Unitarians, Seventh Day Adventists, Christian Scientists, Jehovah's Witnesses, and the Nation of Islam. Proliferation of denominations and groups produced an American religious diversity rivaling that of ethnicity and race.

American religious groups differ importantly in their history, social characteristics, values, and practices. Because religion is seldom limited simply to private spiritual experience or individually held ethical convictions, religious diversity is potentially a source of social and political conflict. Some religious teachings carry implicit political directives while others may encourage dispositional tendencies in worshippers leading them to partisan stands on public issues. American churches and their members have not differed markedly from secular groups in trying to enlist public authority to reach preferred ends. Dominant or ascendant denominations have sometimes been able to infuse local, state, or national public policy with sectarian values. Such success marked the de facto Protestant establishment for many years. Today it may hold for the "Christian majority" or the "Judeo-Christian tradition."

Conflicts produced by religious differences have not been as pervasive as those over wealth or economic status. But because religious conflicts are often about moral values and absolute beliefs, they are likely to run deeper and prove harder to compromise. Many of these clashes are about whose views and values should prevail in public life and public policy.

In this chapter, we look at the two great constitutional elements of American religious pluralism: the First Amendment's bar to governmental establishment of religion and its protection of religious exercise and practice. The first, which enjoins favoritism, is a recognition of religious diversity and the guarantee of a secular state. The second, paralleling freedoms of speech and press also in the Amendment, limits government's power to interfere or burden religious practice, yet weighs that protection against a believer's obligation to obey laws that apply to everyone else.

Church and State

State churches were a fixture of most eighteenth-century European nations. The Roman Catholic Church was established in France, Spain, the Italian states, and much of the rest of the Continent. The Protestant Anglican Church was established in England. Formal institutional ties between church and state allowed public policies to reflect church interests. They also permitted state power to be used against other denominations especially those having an independent or dissident bent. Except for Rhode Island, New Jersey, Pennsylvania, and Delaware, all the American colonies had established churches: the Anglican in New York and in four Southern colonies and the Congregationalist in Massachusetts. This eighteenth-century colonial establishment rarely led to the aggressive persecution or political disablement of outsiders often found in Europe, but full recognition of religious pluralism that would later set the United States apart among nations had not yet taken root.

In 1789, when the first Congress debated the proposed Bill of Rights as the first amendments to the new federal Constitution, religion got prime attention. The establishment clause is the opening provision, requiring that Congress "make no law respecting an establishment of religion." It is the constitutional basis for separating church and state.

Religion is mentioned in one other place in the Constitution, Article VI-3 forbidding religious oaths for holding office in the new central government. Unlike that provision's exactness the establishment clause is general and ambiguous, reflecting the wide range of views evident in the Congressional debates. It is impossible to say exactly what its framers intended. Did the clause merely bar preferential treatment among denominations, for example, or did it prevent any government support of religion, even if neutral among denominations? Nor did its framers define an "establishment of religion" or what constituted "a law respecting" it.

One thing clearly not intended was that the Bill of Rights should apply to the states. As earlier noted, James Madison's proposal that the two religion provisions should restrict the states, was easily rejected. States were left to deal with religion undisturbed by the Constitution. Not until the 1940s were the religion provisions of the First Amendment held to apply to the states.

When the Bill of Rights was ratified in 1791, formal religious establishment was alive in some states but not thriving. The emphasis on secularism and rational tolerance of the eighteenth century's Enlightenment had taken a toll. So had the Revolution. Anti-British sentiment was turned against preferential treatment for American affiliates of the Church of England. By the end of the war, Anglicanism had been disestablished and American Anglicans renamed themselves Episcopalians. Vestiges of formal religious influence remained in a few states. Pennsylvania and Maryland and the new states of Vermont, Kentucky, and Tennessee, for example, required a belief in God as a condition for holding public office. Massachusetts authorized towns and villages to hire Protestant teachers of "piety, religion, and morality." Connecticut used a portion of its tax revenue to support Congregationalism, exempting dissenting Christian sects from the levy. But by the 1830s, even these traces had largely disappeared. This was not because of the federal establishment clause, which did not yet apply to the states, but because of the steady growth of religious tolerance and separatism, reinforced by the demands of economic and territorial expansion that would only be impeded by discrimination and strife.

The death of eighteenth-century-style formal establishment did not lead to a completely secularized government or public life. A general de facto Protestant influence prevailed in many areas until well into the twentieth century. As public schools were founded, they often had a markedly Protestant cast including daily prayers or readings from the King James Bible. In urban areas with large immigrant populations, this dismayed many Irish and German Catholics, who pressed for the creation of Roman Catholic parochial schools.

In almost all areas, Christian holidays were officially recognized. Many communities passed Sunday closing laws, and a few made blasphemy a punishable offense. Spurred by the revivalism of the late nineteenth and early twentieth century, Protestant fundamentalists in some Western states and many rural areas got laws passed against drinking, gambling, and teaching of evolution. Aimed at countering the perceived pagan forces of modern life, these actions did not violate the establishment clause because it was yet inapplicable to state or local government. Many state constitutions had establishment clauses of their own, but these were assumed to bar only English-style institutional establishment, that is, an official state church. They did not call for complete divorce of religion and government or a muting of religious influence on public life.

De facto Protestant establishment lanquished in the first half of the twentieth century. Growing secularization of modern life, influence of new ideas like those of Darwin and Freud, and the advance of science all challenged the certainty with which traditional religious beliefs were held. Growing numbers of non-Protestants disputed the prevailing church-state relationship, some demanding that it be severed, others that they be included in supportive or preferential laws and policies. Finally, in the 1940s, the Supreme Court, which until then had heard almost no church-state cases because few federal laws raised establishment questions, applied the two religion clauses of the First Amendment to the states.

In *Cantwell v. Connecticut*, 1940, discussed in the next section, it held the free exercise right to be part of due process in the Fourteenth Amendment and thus a limit on state power. In *Everson v. Board of Education*, 1947(p. 73), it did the same with the establishment clause, offering its first definitive statement on the separation of church and state. A local taxpayer challenged the inclusion of parochial school students in New Jersey's scheme to reimburse parents for their children's bus fares to and from school. Reviewing the background of the establishment clause, the Court concluded that it called for government to be neutral not simply among religious denominations but also between religion and nonreligion. Speaking for the Court, Justice Hugo Black accepted Jefferson's oft-quoted view that the clause erected a "wall of separation" between church and state.

Despite this strongly separatist conclusion, Black and four other justices upheld the bus fare payments. They saw the New Jersey law primarily benefiting parents and students rather than church schools or religious education, thus not breaching the establishment bar. The decision set out a general rule of separation without finding fault with incidental or indirect benefits to religion or religious schools that might be conferred by general public policies or public spending. It opened the door to scores of cases in which the Court was asked to raise or lower the "wall of separation." Its construction has often proved uneven as decisions have drawn doctrinal battle lines between separationist views favoring a high wall and those of accommodation, favoring a lower one.

Financial Aid to Religion and Religious Schools

Material or financial benefits bestowed by government range from outright grants and subsidies to exemptions from obligations generally imposed. The last includes the one of the oldest, most common, and financially most important public benefits received by religion—exemption of churches and religious organizations from income and property taxes. This special treatment is older than the republic itself, and the Congressional framers of the Bill of Rights did not intend to dis-

Who Are the True Believers?

Disputes within church congregations or between local congregations and higher church authority are not uncommon and sometimes find their way into courts, but the American judiciary may not declare which party is correct in matters of religious doctrine. To do so would violate both religion clauses of the First Amendment—the establishment clause in ruling for the winner, the free exercise clause in ruling against the loser.

The Supreme Court's earliest case of intrachurch conflict was *Watson v. Jones*, 1871, and it was formative. It grew out of a dispute within a congregation over who owned the local church's real and personal property. On the eve of the Civil War, the Walnut Street Presbyterian Church in Louisville, Kentucky, had split over a resolution condemning slavery. Each side argued that it was the one faithful to Presbyterian tenets and thus the rightful possessor of the local church.

Because the Bill of Rights did not yet apply to the states, the dispute did not raise a First Amendment question. But the Court's handling of it set out a principle for deciding twentieth-century cases of separation of church and state. As a government body, it studiously avoided examining Presbyterian doctrine, analyzing instead the denomination's organizational scheme to discover who in it had authority to settle such disputes. In this instance, and those of other hierarchically organized churches, like the Roman Catholic, the Court held it was the higher church authority. In congregationally organized religious bodies, such as Baptist and Jewish, the deciding authority would be the majority of the congregation.

The principle of not being drawn into interpreting church doctrine was dramatically reaffirmed 80 years later on First Amendment grounds in the Cold War-era case of *Kedroff v. St. Nicholas Cathedral*, 1952. A factional dispute developed in a Russian Orthodox congregation in New York City between a group loyal to the Patriarch of Moscow as head of the world Russian Orthodox Church and a breakaway group asserting the Patriarch was under Communist control and could not represent the true faith. When each side claimed entitlement to the valuable church property in Manhattan, a sympathetic New York legislature declared the anti-Communist dissidents to be the owners. The Supreme Court followed its *Watson* approach of sidestepping religious doctrine. It held that organizationally the Moscow hierarchy of the church was the traditional governing authority and, as such, had power to settle internal disputes. Because the First Amendment's establishment clause by then applied to the states, the act of the New York legislature was unconstitutional.

The civil rights movement in the South in the 1960s gave rise to a number of intrachurch disputes over integration. In *Presbyterian Church v. Mary Elizabeth Blue Hull Memorial Church*, 1969, the issue—whether two local churches could withdraw from the general church yet retain the local church property—turned on whether the general church was adhering to the faith and doctrine it had when the local churches affiliated with it. The Supreme Court ruled the judiciary could not inquire into ecclesiastical fidelity. As a hierarchically organized church, that issue could be resolved only by the highest church authority. The ruling, like *Kedroff*, in effect, let one of the parties decide its own case. The Court thought it preferable to judicial intervention.

These decisions do not mean that "neutral" principles of property law cannot be applied to intrachurch disputes, but such rules can be used to resolve only purely secular aspects of those disputes. (*Jones v. Wolf*, 1979) "The law," the Court said in *Watson v. Jones*, "knows no heresy, and is committed to the support of no dogma, the establishment of no sect." [13 Wall. 679 at 728]

turb it. Yet its subsidizing effect and cost to the public is obvious. For every exemption, remaining taxpayers must pay higher rates if the same amount of revenue is to be raised.

The issue came before the Supreme Court in *Walz v. Tax Commissioner*, 1970, (p. 81) in which a property-owning taxpayer in New York disputed the state's releasing churches from property levies. Though the Court conceded the special treatment bestowed economic benefits on religious institutions, it saw government "entanglement" with religion being much greater were church

From Backcountry to the Court

Hugo Lafayette Black served on the Supreme Court 34 years and a month, the fourth longest tenure of any justice. From his appointment in 1937, his career spanned the period from the New Deal to the beginning of the Burger Court. That period saw unprecedented development of civil liberties in almost all areas, and Black, often as not, was its intellectual leader.

That he would have a shaping effect on twentieth-century constitutional law could not have easily been predicted from his early career or the controversy that surrounded his appointment.

Black was born in the rural Alabama hill country that lies between Birmingham and the Georgia border, in 1886. His father was a small-town storekeeper in Clay County, and Black had a country boy's youth, marked by an early fascination with local courts and politics. When the traveling circuit court came to Ashland, the county seat, young Hugo was usually in attendance, observing the performance and strategies of the lawyers who argued before it. Though an ardent reader, his formal education was spotty. Instead of finishing high school, he managed to enroll in a medical studies program, completing its two-year course in one. But drawn back to the early love of courts, he entered University of Alabama law school in 1904. After graduating, he set up law practice in Ashland, across the street from the courthouse. When his law office was destroyed in a fire the next year, he decided to try to establish himself in the big city—Birmingham.

Black proved not only an able trial lawyer, becoming expert in personal injury cases, but also an avid joiner and civic activist befitting an ambitious young attorney new in town. His membership in one organization, however, the Ku Klux Klan, though lasting only three years, would come back to haunt him.

It is not surprising that he found his way to politics. He was appointed a part-time police court judge in 1911, and in 1914 won election as the metropolitan county prosecutor, an office in which he efficiently cleared a long-overcrowded docket. In 1926, as a populist candidate espousing economic justice for the disadvantaged, he entered a crowded Democratic Senate field and, in an upset, won the party's nomination. He was an able "down-home" campaigner who did not hesitate to use his native musical ability to warm up

crowds with country music at the piano or on the fiddle and harmonica, or to challenge the best local checkers and dominoes players in games he had learned well around the Ashland courthouse.

In the Senate, Black used the resources of the Library of Congress in what became lifelong reading and research program that gave him the liberal arts education he had missed as a youth. His reelection in 1932, during the worst of the Great Depression, coincided with Franklin Roosevelt's great presidential victory. The populist senator found a natural home in the New Deal that Roosevelt initiated and became one of its legislative captains.

When Roosevelt had his first chance to appoint a Justice to the Supreme Court, to replace the retiring anti-New Dealer Willis Van Devanter in 1937, he nominated Black. Politically, the choice appeared to make sense, but the nominee had meager judicial experience and was not distinguished as a lawyer. Black was easily confirmed by the Senate, but before he was to take his seat, newspapers discovered his earlier membership in the Klan. The disclosure generated a public storm and calls from liberal critics for his resignation. In a bold and unusual move, Black made a national radio address to plead his case, becoming one of the first public figures to use the medium to speak to the mass audience.

He explained that many ambitious young business and professional men in the South joined the organization as they might join the Rotary or Chamber of Commerce, not because they subscribed to its ideological ends but to make valuable acquaintances. He strongly denied any racial or religious bigotry, an assertion that was consistently borne out in his votes and opinions on the Court. Though the controversy did not immediately die down, the address very likely saved his career.

Black came to the Court a liberal activist but also a reactive opponent of judicial discretion. He had seen the latter used by anti-New Deal justices to give the Constitution a laissez-faire gloss that allowed them to strike down important social and economic programs. Black reconciled these two positions by embracing a literalist reading of the Constitution and a determination to search for historical intent where the text did not yield clear meaning. In this, he helped move the post-New Deal Court away from a close, almost supervisory review of government's tax and commerce powers and to take greater interest in individual liberties and rights, a change that has marked the Court's work ever since.

This led to one of Black's chief constitutional projects—nationalizing of the Bill of Rights so that its protections would be limits on state as well as federal government. This was to be done by incorporating all its protections into the due process clause of the Fourteenth Amendment. Black's historical research convinced him that this was exactly what the post-Civil War framers of the amendment had intended. Though he could not persuade a majority of his fellow justices to embrace "total incorporation," the Court eventually, on a selective case-by-case basis, incorporated nearly all those rights, thus largely ending up where Black had begun and giving the nation a more or less uniform set of individual rights.

Black's literal interpretation of the opening command of the First Amendment, "Congress shall make no law..." led him to take a near-absolute position on its speech, press, and religion provisions. In reading its establishment clause, in *Everson v. Board of Education* he persuaded the Court to adopt a Jeffersonian "high wall" view of the separation of church and state. This led, in turn, to his controversial ruling against school prayers in *Engel v. Vitale.* "No law" meant exactly that, zero tolerance for religion in the classroom.

His similarly absolute positions on speech and press freedoms led him to oppose government suppression of politically subversive speech, obscenity, and the use of defamation laws against the press, in decisions hardly less controversial than his school

prayers opinion. He was a consistent critic of the "balancing" approach to First Amendment questions that required a weighing the freedoms against other values. In early years on the Court, Black often expressed these views in dissents, but later, especially during the Warren period, they were apt to be majority views.

Black's literalism also led him to oppose creation or recognition of rights he could not find in the Constitution's text or intent of the Framers. During the Warren years he refused to join in reading a right to marital privacy into the Constitution in *Griswold v. Connecticut* and in extending free speech protection to picketing and other symbolic or demonstrative acts he thought to be behavior rather than "speech." This led some critics to say that the later Black had grown conservative. But Black and his defenders argued that he had been consistent throughout, insisting that what was in the Constitution be given fullest, even absolute effect but refusing to use judicial discretion to create new rights. Black carried with him at all times a well-thumbed vest-pocket copy of the Constitution, almost as a symbol of its everyday applied sufficiency.

Black's simple but well-worked-out constitutional jurisprudence was all the more effective because of his personal qualities as a justice and his place on the Court. His opinions were usually models of clarity and logical reasoning, backed by solid research. As a colleague, he could be a wily and tenacious defender of his positions. After Chief Justice Stone's death in 1946, Black was the most senior Justice for the next 25 years. This meant that he exercised some of the chief justice's powers when the seat was empty during transitions between chiefs, of which there were three in Black's tenure. As the Court's most senior associate justice, he also had power to assign majority opinions whenever he was in the majority and the chief justice was not.

Black was deeply saddened by the unexpected death of his wife of 30 years, Josephine Foster, in 1951. Six years later, at 72, he married his long-time personal secretary, Elizabeth DeMerritte. Though friends and clerks said the justice was less hard-driving and more relaxed in later years, he remained a vigorous force on the Court as well as an avid tennis player until well into his eighties. He resigned from the Court after suffering a debilitating stroke in 1971. He died a week later and was buried in Arlington National Cemetery, a copy of his beloved Constitution with him in a vest pocket.

property to be taxed. Taxation could open the door to such matters as market valuations, liens, foreclosures, rate appeals, and the like. The Court was also persuaded that the exemption was secular in purpose and that its primary effect was not to advance religion. It was more like those given to hospitals, libraries, colleges, and other private and nonprofit associations that perform charitable or otherwise publicly valuable services. In *Walz,* the Court refused to deliver what would have been a crushing financial blow for many local churches. It was a victory for an accommodation, one so uniformly and popularly well settled that it seemed almost part of the political landscape.

"Active" financial aid is constitutionally more problematic. The chief issue here is aid for the operations of parochial schools, which are mainly Roman Catholic and Lutheran. When the school-age population boomed in the 1960s, school costs rose sharply. Many states, particularly in the Northeast and Midwest in which there are large Roman Catholic populations, looked for ways to relieve the financial strain on parochial schools. Accommodationists argued that the schools educated a sizable fraction of the school population—more than a sixth at the elementary level and more than a tenth at the secondary. Should they close, great new burdens would fall on the public schools and thus on taxpayers. Moreover, parents of parochial students paid twice—public taxes and private tuition—and thus helped to subsidize public schools from which they received no benefit. Separationists countered that whatever Protestant bias once existed in the public schools it had long since disappeared. The tax-paying public was not obliged to subsidize the promotion of religious tenets and values.

In *Board of Education v. Allen,* 1968, its first state aid case after *Everson,* the Court upheld the constitutionality of a New York scheme that called for local school boards to lend textbooks bought with public money to all students including those in parochial schools. Because none of the books could be on a religious subject, a majority of the justices held the law had only secular purpose.

Though acknowledging that religious schools gave religious instruction, they found no evidence the books on secular subjects had the effect of advancing religion. The Court thus reiterated the "child benefit" theory it had used in *Everson.*

Far more extensive "parochiad" came before the Court in the companion cases of *Lemon v. Kurtzman* (p. 85) and *Early v. DeCenso* from Pennsylvania and Rhode Island, in 1971. Each state had enacted a program to give fractional salary support for teachers of secular subjects in parochial schools. Pennsylvania also reimbursed the schools for textbooks and other instructional materials on secular subjects. Conceding the need for a more definitive approach to modern establishment questions, the Court pulled together elements of its *Allen* and *Walz* decisions into a new three-part test. To be constitutional, public benefits or aid affecting parochial schools must be secular in purpose, have a primary effect that neither advanced nor inhibited religion, and did not foster "excessive entanglement" with religion.

Programs in the two cases were found wanting on the third element. Each would call for continuous monitoring of teaching to make sure that religion and religious values did not enter instruction. The average parochial school teacher, being a "dedicated religious person, teaching in a school affiliated with his or her faith and operated to inculcate its tenets," would find it hard to remain "religiously neutral."

In the years since, the Court has used the purpose, effect, and entanglement criteria to review a wide range of government programs aimed at giving some degree of aid or relief to financially pressed religious schools. Its decisions have yielded mixed results and several leave questions about the workability of the *Lemon* test. Here it is possible only to briefly summarize this work.

Though reaffirming the validity of secular textbook loans to parochial school students, the Court has struck down loans of other instructional materials, such as recording and laboratory equipment (*Meek v. Pittenger,* 1975), and the financing of field trips planned and supervised by school authorities (*Wolman v. Walter,* 1977). Other programs violating establishment principles include those subsidizing school maintenance and repairs (*Committee for Public Education and Religious Liberty v. Nyquist,* 1973); the costs of administering state-mandated tests and record keeping (*Levitt v. Committee for Public Education and Religious Liberty,* 1973); and the payment of parochial school teachers to teach secular subjects after school hours on school premises (*Grand Rapids School District v. Ball,* 1985).

In these separationist rulings, the public aid failed the *Lemon* test. The Court was not persuaded benefits would not advance religious education or avoid excessive administrative entanglement of public and parochial authorities. Where programs had built-in monitoring arrangements to insure aid not be used for religious purposes, the Court was apt to see those safeguards as increasing the chance of entanglement. In several rulings it spoke of the "political divisiveness" of the programs, but stopped short of elevating that concern to a *Lemon* criterion. All this has left little room for direct aid to primary and secondary parochial schools, which the Court has described as "pervasively sectarian."

The Court has tended to take an accommodationist stand where the religious-affiliated schools are colleges and universities rather than those at elementary and secondary levels. It concluded that college and graduate education, organized around disciplines, limits opportunities for sectarian influence and that college students, presumably more sophisticated than younger persons, are less susceptible to religious indoctrination. Accordingly, in *Tilton v. Richardson,* 1971, decided the same day as *Lemon,* it upheld eligibility of church-affiliated colleges and universities for federal construction grants for buildings in which only secular subjects would be taught. In later cases, issuance of state revenue bonds for construction at private religious colleges where the buildings were not to be used for sectarian purposes was upheld (*Hunt v. McNair,* 1973), as were direct state per-student grants to church-affiliated colleges equal to 15 percent of

the per-student amount that the state spent in the public college system (*Roemer v. Board of Public Works,* 1976).

Would establishment be violated if a public school district was created for students of a religious sect? This unusual situation came about when New York state allowed the Satmar, a strict Orthodox Jewish sect of 8,500 in Orange County who operated their own schools, to incorporate itself as a public school district. It did this so that handicapped students could receive state services on school premises rather than being sent to "outside" public schools where it was said they were ridiculed. But in *Board of Education of Kiryas Joel Village School v. Grumet,* 1994, the Court ruled the incorporation unconstitutional as creating a "fusion of government and religious functions."

The Court has been willing to uphold eligibility of parochial school students for publicly funded disability benefits given to public school students. In *Zobrest v. Catalina Foothills School District,* 1993, it ruled that a deaf student attending a Roman Catholic high school could be given a publicly funded sign-language interpreter. Benefits to handicapped children, it said, were distributed neutrally and did not advance or promote religion or religious education.

In 1997, the Justices made a small but important retreat on publicly funded services in parochial schools. Earlier, in *Aguilar v. Felton* and *School District of Grand Rapids v. Ball,* both in 1985, it had struck down New York and Michigan programs in which public school teachers and counselors entered parochial schools to give remedial education to disadvantaged children. After these decisions, New York retained its program by leasing vans at a cost of more than $100 million and using them as mobile units that could be parked on public streets outside parochial schools. In dramatic turnaround in *Agostini v. Felton* (p. 88), the Court, 5-4, overruled the 1985 decisions. Justice O'Connor, speaking for the majority, said the Court had erred in concluding that full-time public employees teaching in parochial schools would necessarily advance religion.

The Court has also tended to take a more accommodationist stand where immediate beneficiaries of public aid are religious persons—students or their parents—rather than religious schools. Using the child benefit theory of *Everson,* it has observed that money "saved" in such circumstances was not apt to be used to advance religion or produce excessive entanglement. Though direct reimbursement of parents for parochial school tuition or granting them a tax credit for such tuition were held invalid in *Committee for Public and Religious Liberty v. Nyquist,* the Court retreated from this position without overruling the decision a decade later. In *Mueller v. Allen,* it upheld a Minnesota law that allowed a state income tax deduction for tuition, textbook, or transportation expenses paid by parents of children in public or private elementary and secondary schools. *Nyquist* was distinguished in that the tuition reimbursements and tax credit there went only to parents of children in private schools. The Court largely ignored the fact that children attending public schools paid no tuition and had few textbook expenses. Operationally, the deduction mainly benefited parents who sent their children to private schools, most of which were Roman Catholic or Lutheran.

In the late 1990s, poor performance of many public inner-city schools in urban areas gave rise to experiments with educational vouchers, notably in Milwaukee and Cleveland. These initiatives, which gave public stipends to parents of children to pay tuition at private schools of their choice, were generally opposed by public school interests, including the powerful teachers unions, as undermining or abandoning the public schools. Support came from an unusual alliance of minority groups, the parochial school lobby, and conservatives who believed the long-run answer to poor public schools lay in competition and other market forces. The vouchers also raised a formidable establishment clause issue because in most areas where they were tried or proposed, nearly all private schools were religious. If those schools were excluded from a voucher pro-

gram, the program's effect would be miniscule. If they were included, large underwriting sums of public money could be channeled to them through the voucher payments of parents taking their children out of the public schools.

Doubt about constitutionality was removed by the Supreme Court in *Zelman v. Simmons-Harris,* (p. 92) decided on the final day of its 2001–2002 term. Divided 5-4, the Court upheld Cleveland's six-year-old voucher program in which 3,700 of its 75,000 students, all from low-income families, used stipends of up to $2,250 to attend private schools. About 95 percent of them attended religious schools, almost all of which were Roman Catholic. Extending its child benefit theory further than it had ever before, the Court emphasized that the program was enacted for a valid secular purpose and was "neutral in all respects toward religion." The dissenters, focusing on the program's effect, argued that it violated settled constitutional lines separating church and state.

The controversial ruling may have momentous consequences for the architecture of the wall of separation and for secondary education. It will no doubt spur wider experimentation with vouchers which, in turn, will subsidize many religious schools, as well as encourage creation of new secular private schools. Supporters believe that offering choice to "clients" will have the same effect that allowing private carriers to compete with the Postal Service had in delivering mail and packages—vastly improved service. Critics voice concern about accountability of the private schools and the possibility of religious indoctrination. Whatever the effect of vouchers on secondary education however, the Court's decision significantly lowers the wall separating church and state, at least as it is measured by effect, if not design.

Religion and the Public Schools

Official endorsement or support of religious tenets or practices in public institutions and places, sometimes called "public religion," has raised as many establishment questions as public aid to religious institutions. Historically, public presence of religion was taken for granted and evident in such matters as official observance of the Christian Christmas, Easter, and Good Friday holidays, restriction of commercial activity on Sunday, the motto "In God We Trust" on coinage, and the opening of legislative sessions with prayers.

Perhaps nowhere was a "basic piety" more well settled than in the public schools. The original Protestant bent was gradually modified to meet Catholic concerns, but what survived had an unmistakably Christian emphasis. In time, this preference appeared more and more at odds with the growing recognition of religious pluralism and the legitimacy of nonreligion. The Court's call in *Everson* for a "wall" of separation between church and state meant that government neutrality must be more than a simple even-handedness among Christian denominations or the inclusion of Judaism as one of the "three great faiths."

Public school establishment questions arise in three contexts: the saying of prayers and other devotionals, the influence of religious ideas on instruction, and the use of school facilities and resources by churches and religious groups.

Two early "released time" cases heard shortly after *Everson* reflect the basic tension between accommodation and strict separation. In the first, an Illinois program permitted students to get weekly religious instruction in their school during the school day from clergy chosen by a local interfaith council. Students choosing not to take part were given a study period. In *Illinois ex. rel. McCollum v. Board of Education,* 1948, the Court held the program to violate the establishment clause, citing the release of students from their legal obligation to receive secular education during the school day, on condition they attend religious classes.

Four years later, in *Zorach v. Clausen,* the Court partly retreated. It upheld a New York City program that allowed students to be released one hour a week to receive religious instruction in their churches or synagogues. Though compulsory school attendance was compromised, the distinguishing fact was the removal of religious instruction from school premises.

Prayers and Other Devotionals. At the time of *Everson,* a brief prayer or reading from the Bible, along with pledge of national allegiance and salute of the flag were common if not universal opening exercises in public schools throughout the country. Many Christians took the validity (and desirability) of these rituals for granted. Though parents of non-Christian students sometimes objected to the practice, the Supreme Court did not hear a challenge until *Engel v. Vitale,* the school prayers case, in 1962.

Partly in response to *Everson's* emphasis on government neutrality among religious denominations, the New York State Board of Regents, the general supervisory authority for public schools in the state, drafted a nondenominational prayer to be said in place of more traditional ones. The brief, 22-word offering, which invoked "Almighty God" but was not otherwise identified with the tenets of an organized faith, was opposed by the parents of several students as not representing their religious beliefs and practices. In an important extension of the wall of separation, seven justices spoken for by Black held the prayer unconstitutional, saying it was not the role of public officials "to compose official prayers . . . to be recited as part of a religious program carried on by government." It did not matter that the prayer was nondenominational or participation in it voluntary.

The following year in *Abington School District v. Schempp* (p. 77) and *Murray v. Curlett,* heard together, the Court extended the establishment bar to passages from the Bible. It agreed with the petitioners, Unitarian parents who objected to certain literal passages and an atheist parent objecting to the emphasis placed on belief. By calling for the Biblical reading, the state had abandoned the neutrality toward religion the Constitution now required. Nothing in the decision, the Court was careful to add, prevented study of the Bible as

Madalyn E. Murray and her two sons, William, left, and Garth, leaving the U.S. Supreme Court after oral argument in *Murray v. Curlett* in which Murray successfully challenged Bible reading in the Baltimore school that William attended. Murray, an atheist and anti-religious activist, disappeared in 1996 and was officially declared a missing person. William had disavowed his mother's beliefs several years earlier.

history or literature. Nor was the religious majority denied the right to exercise its religious freedom, merely the right to use the "mechanism of the state to practice its beliefs." Though the prayer and Bible-reading cases were decided before *Lemon v. Kurtzman*, the emphasis on purpose and effect anticipates the three-part test the Court eventually devised.

Seldom have two decisions generated more popular criticism and greater negative response from elected officials. This has led to widespread classroom evasion of their writ and to periodic proposals in Congress to amend the Constitution. The Court has nonetheless held steadfastly to its position that government programs or practices giving support, even tacit, to religious beliefs or views in public elementary and secondary schools are unconstitutional. In contrast to the dissenting justices who would have sustained some devotional presence in the schools because of wide and long-standing practice, the majority stressed the impressionability of school-age children and their vulnerability to religious indoctrination having state endorsement.

In the aftermath of *Engel* and *Abington School District*, many states and local school districts looked for ways to keep some kind of religious or spiritual moment in public schools. A Kentucky program requiring a copy of the Ten Commandments, privately paid for, be posted on the wall of each classroom was struck down in *Stone v. Graham*, 1980. Applying the *Lemon* test, the Court held the posting "plainly religious" and without secular legislative purpose. A small-print notation at the bottom of each posting apparently to give the Commandments a secular effect as part of "the fundamental legal code of Western Civilization and the common law of the United States" was held a mere subterfuge.

A more common legislative response to *Engel* and *Abington School District* was the adoption of a daily moment of silence, introduced in 23 states. Alabama's called for a minute-long period "that should be observed for meditation" but later the legislature said the moment was also "for meditation or voluntary prayer." Challenged in *Wallace v. Jaffree*, 1985, this elaboration proved fatal. Yet the decision left open the possibility that a moment of silence might be sustained if it were not cast as an opportunity for prayer. Such a program from New Jersey, held invalid by a lower court, reached the Court in *Karcher v. May,* 1987, but a majority of the justices sidestepped the constitutional issue, holding that the appellants as former but not current members of the state legislature lacked standing to maintain the appeal.

Given the high wall of separation erected by the prayer and Bible-reading decisions and reinforced in *Stone* and *Wallace,* it was inevitable that other devotional exercises in the public schools would come under constitutional attack. In *Lee v. Weisman,* 1992, for example, the Court was asked to rule on an invocation and benediction by a rabbi at a junior high school graduation, attendance at which was voluntary. In ruling the practice unconstitutional, five Justices held that a state may not "exact religious conformity from a student as a price for attending his or her own graduation."

The Court's stand against any prayers associated with the public schools was carried a step further in *Santa Fe Independent School District v. Doe,* 2000 (p. 105), in which it ruled public prayers before a high school football game, a tradition in many communities, unconstitutional. By permitting and encouraging student-led prayers over a public address system, the school endorsed religion. The Court also saw an element of coercion. Though attendance at the games was voluntary for most students it was not for some, namely the players, band members, and cheerleaders. The challenge to the prayers had been brought by two students and their families, who were allowed to remain anonymous as "Doe" to protect them from harassment.

Religion and the Curriculum. Devotionals have not been the only presence of religious influence in the public schools. When modern science challenged traditional religious explanations of the world and the place of human beings in it, some state legislatures tried to defend Biblical literalism by controlling what could be taught about human origin in public schools. This led to one of the most celebrated trials in American history,

the prosecution and conviction in 1925 of John T. Scopes, a high school biology teacher in Tennessee for teaching Darwin's theory of evolution in violation of state law. (See "Adam and Eve and Darwin.")

Though several other states, mainly in the South, also had antievolution laws, the statutes were rarely enforced. When the issue finally reached the Supreme Court 40 years after Scopes's trial, it was in a case brought by rather than against a teacher. Susan Epperson, a high school biology instructor in Arkansas, contended that the state's antievolution law put her in fear of criminal prosecution if she adopted a textbook containing a chapter on evolution. In *Epperson v. Arkansas,* 1968, in a rare show of unanimity on an establishment issue, the Court voided the statute, which was defended half-heartedly by the state's attorney general, as having the purpose of furthering religious beliefs. The state had failed to maintain neutrality between religion and nonreligion.

Despite this decision, fundamentalist revivalism in the 1970s and 1980s led several Southern states to require traditional religious views on the origin of life be given "equal time" or at least a substantial hearing in biology courses. Typical of these laws was Louisiana's Balanced Treatment for Creation Science and Evolution Science in Public School Instruction Act. Though not outlawing evolutionary theory as older statutes had, it called for teaching theories of creationism whenever evolution was taught. In *Edwards v. Aguillard,* 1987 (p. 98), the Supreme Court, rejecting a claim that the law promoted academic freedom, ruled that its language and legislative history showed an intention to promote particular religious beliefs. Several Justices noted that the study of religious beliefs and texts would be permissible in history, literature, or other courses as long as the purpose or effect was not to advance religion.

Access to Public School Facilities and Resources. In the McCollum released time case, the Supreme Court had held public school classrooms could not be used for religious instruction. This basic separationist principle remains intact, but in several later cases raising access questions, the

Adam and Eve and Darwin

In July 1925, John T. Scopes, a 24-year-old high school biology teacher in Dayton, Tennessee, was prosecuted for violating a state law that barred the teaching of "anything that denies the story of the divine creation of man as taught in the Bible, and to teach instead that man has descended from a lower order of animals." The Monkey Trial, as the 12-day proceeding came to be known, seemed to pit science against religion, modernity against tradition, cosmopolitan sophistication against the simplicity of small-town values. For many, it was a battle of enlightenment against ignorance.

The trial featured two giants of American politics and law, William Jennings Bryan and Clarence Darrow, as the chief prosecutor and defense attorney. Bryan, now 66, was a former secretary of state and three times the Democratic nominee for president. An eloquent spokesman for religious fundamentalism, he volunteered his services to Dayton. Darrow, a lifelong agnostic, was the leading criminal lawyer of his time, a legendary defender of unpopular and underdog clients.

The case was contrived from the start. The Tennessee law, similar to later ones in several other Southern states, had been passed in 1923, partly the result of a nationwide campaign led by Bryan against the teaching of evolution. Its enactment prompted the newly formed American Civil Liberties Union to issue a statement that appeared in many Tennessee newspapers: "We are looking for a Tennessee teacher who is willing to accept our services in testing this law in the courts."

It did not have to wait long. A group of civic boosters in the small town of Dayton, 30 miles north of Chattanooga in the southeast corner of the state, hatched a scheme "to put Dayton on the map." They persuaded Scopes, who had come to Dayton only the year before, to violate the statute and the local prosecutor to indict him for doing so. They could not have imagined their plan would produce the "trial of the century" and, in its epic battle of ideas, help shape America's culture wars for years to come.

By the time it began in humid July weather in the large courtroom of Dayton's small courthouse, the trial was already a media event. Newspaper reporters descended on the tiny town like bees to clover. The one local hotel had to turn many away. National magazines sent correspondents, and Chicago radio station WGN set up to broadcast the proceeding, the first trial to be covered on radio. H. L. Mencken, the urbane, cynical journalist and literary critic who arrived with "a typewriter and five bottles of scotch," was prepared for a field day.

The judge, John T. Raulston, served on the Tennessee circuit court for the area. Up for reelection the next year, he basked in the attention, making

Opposing counsel. Clarence Darrow, left, and William Jennings Bryan are side-by-side at this moment in the 1926 Dayton, Tenn., "Monkey Trial." Darrow later called Bryan to the witness stand in the sweltering courtroom to interrogate him on the Biblical version of creation.

sure the media, especially WGN, were well accommodated in the courtroom. The circus was on.

Darrow's legal strategy was to get Raulston to rule the antievolution law unconstitutional or, failing that, to have Scopes convicted so the case could be taken to a higher court. His larger aim was to strike a blow at the repression of ideas and at religious fundamentalism itself. In seeking a conviction, Bryan hoped to make an equally strong statement affirming the Biblical version of creation against crackpot atheistic science.

Raulston did not strike down the law and later refused to allow submission of scientific evidence of organic evolution, including testimony from several Darwinian biologists (all Christians) whom Darrow had brought to Dayton. Scopes himself was all but forgotten as Bryan and Darrow sparred. Politically, the giants were not that far apart—Darrow had readily supported Bryan in his presidential campaigns—but on religion they were separated by an unbridgeable gulf.

Outside the courtroom, the small town's streets were filled with the curious from nearby towns and with members of religious groups. Preachers preached on street corners, and occasionally the voice of a self-proclaimed rationalist could be heard in dissent. Largely absent were the big-spending tourists the civic boosters had hoped to attract. Much, of course, was made of apes. In his dispatches for the Baltimore *Sun*, Mencken dubbed the locals "primates." A man with a pet chimpanzee who did tricks was a featured daily attraction. Another entrepreneur brought in a gorilla in a freight car. When the beast sized up the gawking *homo sapiens,* it cowered in a corner.

With the exclusion of scientific evidence, the trial seemed headed for an anticlimactic conclusion. But then Darrow made a daring and unorthodox move—he summoned Bryan himself to the witness stand as a qualified expert witness on the Bible. Against advice, Bryan accepted the call. One of the most formidable speakers in American politics and a lifelong student of the Bible, the Great Commoner saw an opportunity to make a case for the greatest cause of his life.

The courtroom confrontation of Bryan and Darrow has become fixed in American memory. Starting slowly, Darrow led Bryan into simple "village atheist" kinds of questions about Genesis. Did he think the sun was made on the fourth day? That

Joshua made it stand still? That the whale swallowed Jonah? Bryan's spirited affirmation that he believed in those and other "miracles" in the Bible impressed and cheered the local audience many of whom now saw Darrow as the Anti-Christ, but it played much less well across the country. Bryan visibly wilted in the heat but continued the dogged exchange, maintaining his belief in the literal truth of the Bible. Though three years younger than Darrow, he now seemed to many an old man whose time had passed.

After the testimony, Darrow's final ploy was to forego a summation speech, thereby denying Bryan opportunity to make his closing argument for the prosecution. Bryan had worked for a week preparing a forceful defense of the fundamentalist interpretation of creation and a critique of evolutionary theory that was more intricate than that reflected in his answers on the witness stand. Darrow, the champion of free exchange of ideas, had "gagged" his opponent.

The trial ended with Scopes's conviction and fine of $100, which surprised no one. Eventually, on appeal, the Tennessee Supreme Court overturned the conviction on a technicality—the fine had been set by the judge rather than the jury—but refused to hold the antievolution law unconstitutional.

Bryan remained in Dayton for a few days after the trial, speaking and preaching to adoring audiences. The Sunday following, he took an afternoon nap and died in his sleep. When the iconoclast Mencken learned of his death, he quipped that God had hurled a thunderbolt at Darrow, missed, and hit Bryan instead. For many others, however, the exhausted Bryan had died a martyr.

Legally and constitutionally, the trial and appeal settled little. Yet, as the historian Edward J. Larson concluded in his study of the trial *Summer for the Gods,* the issues raised "endure precisely because they embody the characteristically American struggle between individual liberty and majoritarian democracy, and cast it in the timeless debate over science and religion."

Religious fundamentalism did not die with Bryan. It remains alive and well and able to give a more sophisticated account of itself than it was 80 years ago. Nor has scientifically triumphant evolutionary theory been without its amendments and scientific critics. Constitutionally, however, religious views may no longer control or inspire a public school curriculum or even give much hint of their presence.

Court has had to weigh establishment strictures against free speech claims. In these it has taken a more accommodationist position.

In *Widmar v. Vincent,* 1981, for example, it found that the University of Missouri's denial of meeting rooms to a student religious group violated the students' freedom of speech. By opening its facilities to other groups but excluding a religious one the state school had based its denial on the content of speech. Applying the *Lemon* test, the Court rejected the university's establishment clause defense. Permitting access would not be motivated by a religious purpose or create excessive entanglement, nor would equal access confer state approval or benefit religion more than incidentally.

In 1984, Congress passed the Equal Access Act requiring that all public schools having "limited open forum" policies not discriminate among student groups on the religious, political, or philosophical content of their meetings. The law was challenged on establishment grounds by a secondary school in *Board of Education of Westside Community School v. Mergens* in 1990. Refusing to make a distinction between university and secondary schools that it had embraced in other establishment clause cases, the Court held the law not to have a primary effect of advancing religion.

The equal access right to secondary school facilities was unanimously reaffirmed two years later in *Lamb's Chapel v. Center Moriches Union Free School District.* An evangelical church was denied after-hours use of school rooms for a lecture series on how the media affected Christian family values. In permitting after-hours use of school property by social, civic, recreational, and political groups, but excluding those whose purpose was religious, the local school board violated the First Amendment's protection of speech.

This analysis was carried further in *Good News Club v. Milford Central School* in 2001 (p. 100). Though civic, social, and education groups used its building after hours, the school refused permission to a private Christian organization for children ages 6 to 12. It contended the club's activities—singing songs, Bible lessons, scripture

memorization, and praying—were the equivalent of religious worship and not the discussion-type activity in *Lamb's Chapel.* A majority of the Court disagreed and held that refusing permission was "viewpoint discrimination," denying freedom of speech. There was no establishment violation because the club's meetings would not be mistaken for school endorsement of religion. Allowing the club to meet on school grounds would, the Court said, "ensure, not threaten, neutrality toward religion."

Equal access had taken a different and more controversial turn in *Rosenberger v. University of Virginia,* 1995, in which the issue was not use of school buildings but school funds. The university maintained a student activities fund, paid for by a $14 fee charged to all full-time students. Student groups that filed constitutions and statements showing they were independent of the university could get support from the fund. Excluded were groups whose activity "primarily promotes or manifests a particular belief in or about a deity or an ultimate reality." The case arose after an undergraduate group was denied money to print a newspaper urging Christians to live "according to the faith they proclaim" and "consider what a personal relationship with Jesus Christ means." Divided more sharply than in earlier access cases, the Court held that exclusion by being based on content, violated freedom of speech. Neutrality between religion and nonreligion would not be compromised by making the religious group eligible for money on the same basis as other groups. But exclusion, the Court said, would undermine neutrality by fostering a bias against religion. Four dissenting justices saw the decision as one approving the use of public money for the "direct subsidization" of basic religious activities, forbidden by the establishment clause.

Other Church-State Relations

American public life and institutions are affected by a range of laws and public practices that were once part of an accepted interplay of religion and government but which are called to question by a modern wall of separation doctrine. Because many existed when the Bill of Rights was adopted, they cannot be said to have been unacceptable to the framers of the establishment clause.

For example, Sunday closing laws, dating to early colonial times and until recently still be found in many communities, originally had clear religious purpose. By reducing commercial activity on the Christian Sabbath, they honored the day, made it easier for Christians to attend church, and limited distractions from worship and other religious activity. These laws first came before the Supreme Court in 1961 in *McGowan v. Maryland* and three companion cases (*Two Guys from Harrison-Allentown, Inc. v. McGinley, Braunfeld v. Brown,* and *Gallagher v. Crown Kosher Super Market*). In sustaining the laws the Court held that they had lost their religious character and now had a secular purpose of providing one day of relative quiet. But the Court made it clear that if such laws were again to have explicit religious purpose they would violate the modern requirements of the establishment clause. Today most Sunday closing laws have been repealed or limited to the sale of liquor.

Religious displays on public property or paid for by public money, usually during the Christmas holiday season and usually depicting the Nativity, survived a modern challenge in *Lynch v. Donnelly,* 1984. City officials in Pawtucket, Rhode Island, had contributed a crèche or nativity scene to a Christmas tableau that included a Santa Claus and reindeer and other nonreligious displays, in a park owned by a nonprofit organization. Citing the long history of Christmas celebrations in the country, a majority of five Justices concluded that most onlookers would probably not see the crèche as a public endorsement of religion and found no government intent to further religion. Using an historical analysis rather than a strict application of the *Lemon* test, the Court observed that Christmas and its attendant displays had become a nonsectarian national holiday.

Five years later, another divided Court found contextual reasons to justify a partial retreat from this accommodationist position. During the Christmas and Chanukah holiday season, officials in Allegheny County, Pennsylvania, erected a crèche standing alone on the main staircase of the county courthouse in Pittsburgh. A Jewish menorah was displayed outside another county building with other symbols of the holiday season, including a Christmas tree. In *County of Allegheny v. American Civil Liberties Union,* 1989, a majority of the Court ruled that the crèche standing alone in prominent display sent "an unmistakable message that [the government] supports and promotes . . . the crèche's message," thus violating the establishment clause; the menorah, as part of a display of many symbols, did not. The decision suggests that the constitutional line for public religious holiday displays may, for better or worse, be drawn through the details of location and setting.

Another long-standing conjunction of religion and government is the practice in Congress and in most state legislatures of opening sessions with a prayer, usually by a minister, priest, or rabbi. The practice in Nebraska, in which a Presbyterian minister was hired to lead an opening prayer, was challenged by one of the legislators in *Marsh v. Chambers,* 1983. Upholding the practice, the Court all but ignored the *Lemon* test. It cited tradition and the intent of the first Congress that drafted the First Amendment that "In light of the unambiguous and unbroken history of more than 200 years, there can be no doubt that . . . the opening of legislative sessions with a prayer has become part of the fabric of society." [463 U.S. 783 at 792] As such it was not a promotion or establishment of religion.

Presumably this approach would sustain such other long-standing "mixings" of religion and state as White House prayer breakfasts, the annual presidential lighting of a White House Christmas tree, the rendition of Christmas carols on government property or with government support, and, not least, the declaration "In God We Trust" on American coins. The Supreme Court is correct in saying that the Founders of the nation would not have found these matters to "establish" religion. But it is also true, as the justices observed in *Marsh,* that history alone "cannot justify contemporary violations of the establishment clause." Wisely perhaps, the Court has not heard challenges in these matters.

Not all establishment issues engage the validity of old practices. In *Larkin v. Grendel's Den,* 1982, for example, the Court held a Massachusetts statute that gave churches and schools power to veto liquor license applications for businesses within 500 feet of their buildings, unconstitutional as it applied to churches. Even if the law had a secular purpose and an effect of promoting quiet and stability in certain neighborhoods, which the Court did not concede, it created an excessive entanglement of church and state. States may regulate areas near churches, schools, hospitals, and other institutions, including the denying of liquor licenses, but may not delegate that power to a church.

Nor may a state grant a sales tax exemption to publications of a "religious faith that consist wholly of writing promulgating the teaching of the faith and books that consist wholly of writings sacred to a religious faith." Though there was no majority opinion *in Texas Monthly v. Bullock,* 1989, five Justices held the regulation in Texas to violate the establishment clause because only churches and religious organizations were given the release.

Free Exercise of Religion

The establishment clause forbids government sponsorship of religion or favoring one denomination over another. It requires government neutrality but not hostility. The free exercise clause is the other side of the same constitutional coin. It forbids government interference with religion or with religious beliefs and practices. It calls for accommodation of religion, but not its preferential treatment. At times the clauses may be mutually antagonistic; effect given to one may violate the other.

Free exercise issues range from outright government discrimination at one extreme (actual persecution has been rare in American history) to the operation of general laws and policies having incidental effects on religious practices. Two questions are central: Does a person or group have the right to follow religious practices called for by their beliefs but forbidden by law? Can a person or group be excused from obligations that are contrary to their religious beliefs?

Freedom to believe, as opposed to acting on beliefs, brooks no government interference. In that sense, belief is the only absolute constitutional freedom. No confessions of faith may be demanded, and no one may be punished for having "wrong" beliefs. But actions are another matter. The Court made this distinction clear in the first free exercise case it heard, *Reynolds v. United States,* 1878 (p. 109). The defendant, a Mormon living in the Utah Territory, had been convicted of polygamy, a practice then called for by Mormon tenets "where circumstances would admit." Anticipating its eventual statehood and fully aware of local Mormon dominance, Congress outlawed polygamy in the territory, thus bringing its marriage law into conformity with public morality in all other legal jurisdictions. The Court sustained Reynolds's conviction, holding the law to be a regulation of practice not belief. A person may not excusably violate a generally applicable criminal statute on the plea that his or her act was called for by religious belief. The case can also be read as one in which the moral values of the majority (an overwhelming majority in this instance) were imposed on a minority religion. Every state then, as now, had antipolygamy laws.

The Court's wariness about secular authority deciding the truth or falsity of beliefs, so evident in the intrachurch disputes, as we have seen, was the source of its ruling in the mail fraud prosecution *United States v. Ballard,* 1944. The defendants, Edna and Donald Ballard, had solicited donations through the mail, claiming they had been given secrets to healing many diseases from Saint Germain (who died in 1040). The Court held that a jury could not be asked to decide the truth or falsity of the Ballards' beliefs, that is, whether the supposed events on which they relied really happened. But because the crime of fraud requires knowing or calculated misrepresentation, the jury could presumably consider the question of sincerity, that is whether the beliefs were honestly held.

Public Order

Reynolds left unanswered whether any religiously motivated acts or practices would be exempt from generally applied regulations. As long as the free exercise clause limited only federal power, the issue seldom arose because few acts of Congress affected religious exercise. After the Court held the clause to apply to the states in *Cantwell v. Connecticut* in 1940, its docket changed dramatically. In the next decade, it heard more than a dozen cases dealing with the effect of state or local public order laws on religious acts, especially the seeking of converts and donations. Most arose from application of local laws to Jehovah's Witnesses for whom aggressive preaching and proselytization is an article of faith. Most were decided by "time, place, and manner" freedom of speech principles (discussed in the next chapter), but because government regulations had restricted religious practice, the Court also dealt with whether free exercise rights were violated.

In *Cantwell* it struck down a statute that permitted state officials to issue licenses for the solicitation of money where the "cause is a religious one." The law, it said, gave government discretionary authority to decide what was religious and what was not. In succeeding cases, almost all of which included both free exercise and free speech claims, the Court struck down a variety state and local laws and actions. These included the licensing of bookselling (*Jones v. Opelika*, 1943), a tax on the canvassing or solicitation of orders (*Murdock v. Pennsylvania*, 1943), a bar to door-to-door solicita-

tion or distribution of literature where the homeowner had not given permission (*Martin v. Struthers*, 1943), arrests in response to complaints about proselytization on Sundays (*Douglas v. City Jeanette*, 1943), a bar to the distribution of religious literature in a private company town (*Marsh v. Alabama*, 1946), denial of the use of a public park for a religious meeting (*Niemotko v. Maryland*, 1951), and a bar to Jehovah's Witnesses from using a public park for religious services where permission had been given to those of other denominations (*Fowler v. Rhode Island*, 1953).

Two cases from this period make clear the principles on which order laws can be upheld against free exercise claims. In *Cox v. New Hampshire*, 1941, the Court sustained a "time, place, and manner" parade law against Jehovah's Witnesses who had marched without a permit, because the law left officials little discretion in whether a license should or should not be issued. In *Prince v. Massachusetts*, 1944, a state law barring underage children from selling newspapers or periodicals on the streets after certain hours was upheld as applied to a nine-year-old child distributing religious literature with her adult guardian. Though the law would undoubtedly have been struck down if applied to adults, the Court held that free exercise must bow to the state's interest in the health and safety of children. In the later case of *Heffron v. International Society for Krishna Consciousness*, 1981, the Court reaffirmed its stand behind neutral time, place, and manner restrictions by upholding a state fair regulation that solicitation and pamphlet distribution be confined to one location on the fairgrounds.

Patriotic Ritual

Some Jehovah's Witnesses have interpreted salute of a national flag as paying homage to a graven image and thus a mortal sin in the Biblical tenets of their faith. In 1936, two Witness children of Walter Gobitis were expelled from their public school for refusing to participate in a

Walter Gobitis and his two children, William and Lillian, were the principles in the first flag salute case, *Minersville School District v. Gobitis* in 1940.

daily salute. The ritual, including the following recitation: "I pledge allegiance to my flag and to the Republic for which it stands, one nation indivisible, with liberty and justice for all," was used in most schools. When a challenge to their expulsions reached the Supreme Court in *Minersville School District v. Gobitis,* 1940, World War II had begun in Europe and American entry seemed not far off. The Court voted 8-1 to sustain the expulsions. For the majority, Justice Frankfurter argued that because national unity was needed for national security, it was reasonable for a local school board to use the salute as a means to that end. The decision, overturning lower court victories for Gobitis, met with wide criticism in the press and legal community.

Three years later, the Court took the matter up again in *West Virginia Board of Education v. Barnette* (p. 111) and reversed *Gobitis,* 6-3. This unusually quick about-face was partly attributable to the arrival of two new justices, Robert Jackson and Wiley Rutledge. But three others in the *Gobitis* majority—Hugo Black, William O. Douglas, and Frank Murphy—perhaps responding to the criti-

cism, simply changed their minds. In striking down the state's requirement of a compulsory salute, the Court went beyond the free exercise question to base its decision on broader issues of personal liberty including freedom of speech. Jackson put the matter eloquently for the majority in one of the most oft-quoted passages in the annals of the Court's opinions: "If there is any fixed star in our Constitutional constellation, it is that no official, high or petty, can prescribe what shall be orthodox in politics, nationalism, religion or other matters of opinion or force citizens to confess by word or act their faith therein."

Justice Frankfurter's dissenting opinion, a paean to judicial self-restraint, was hardly less eloquent: "As a member of this Court I can not justify writing my private notions of policy into the Constitution, no matter how deeply I may cherish them . . . I cannot . . . believe that the 'liberty' secured by the due process clause gives this Court the authority to deny to the state of West Virginia the attainment of . . . a legitimate legislative end, namely the promotion of good citizenship, by employment of the means here chosen."

The view of the *Barnette* majority became a main building block for the Court in developing an expansive constitutional theory of First Amendment protection of the rights of conscience and expression.

A similar "right to silence" issue was presented by *Wooley v. Maynard,* 1973, in which a Jehovah's Witness had taped over New Hampshire's state motto "Live Free or Die" on his auto license plate because it expressed an idea repugnant to his religious beliefs. Though he did not hide the plate numbers, he was convicted under the state law making it a misdemeanor to obscure a license plate. The Supreme Court overturned, invoking free speech and well as free exercise principles. The First Amendment includes the right to speak freely and the right not to speak at all. Here, without a compelling reason, the state had required each driver to carry an official message that was not ideologically neutral.

Military Service

A pledge to "support and defend the Constitution and the laws of the United States against all enemies, foreign and domestic," is a condition for resident aliens becoming citizens. This was interpreted by the Naturalization Service (now the Immigration and Naturalization Service) to call for a willingness to bear arms. When the Supreme Court first dealt with denial of citizenship to religious pacifists in *United States v. Schwimmer,* 1929, and *United States v. MacIntosh,* 1931, it sustained the interpretation, only later to reverse itself in the post-World War II case of *Girouard v. United States,* 1946. It held the oath did not expressly require a pledge to bear arms and so a religious pacifist could in good faith pledge to defend the Constitution and the nation.

Religious pacifism meets a formidable challenge, however, in military conscription. Military drafts were in effect during the Civil War, World Wars I and II, and through most of the Cold War period including the Korean and Vietnam conflicts. All conscription statutes have had "conscientious objector" exemptions and have usually called for those granted the status to perform some form of alternate service. The exemption in the Selective Service Act of 1917 was limited to objectors who belonged to "well recognized" religious sects or organizations. The draft law enacted in 1940, a year before American entry into World War II, broadened the exemption to include objectors whose pacifism came from "religious training and belief." Most religious conscientious objectors (C.O.'s) were Jehovah's Witnesses, Quakers, or Mennonites. After the war, Congress clarified the exemption to require that an objector's pacifism relate to belief in "a Supreme Being" and not be based on "essentially political, sociological, or philosophical views or a merely personal moral code."

The limits of this provision were constitutionally challenged in several cases arising during the Vietnam conflict. In *United States v. Seeger,* 1965, the Court held that a C.O. classification was wrongly denied to a religious pacifist who did not admit to believing in a Supreme Being. The requirement was satisfied if the applicant's belief occupied a place in his life "parallel to that filled by the God of those admittedly qualifying for the exemption." [380 U.S. 163 at 166]

In the Military Service Act of 1967, Congress removed the requirement of belief in a Supreme Being, but did not recognize nonreligious pacifism. That issue came up in *Welsh v. United States,* 1970, where a C.O. classification had been denied an applicant whose opposition to war was not based on religious beliefs at all but on moral and ethical grounds rooted in philosophical and sociological considerations. Though seeming to contradict the plain words of the statute and Congress's intent, the Court ruled the exemption to apply. Purely secular moral views, it said, could be held so strongly as to be "religious" in the meaning of the statute. Because basing a benefit strictly on religious grounds would probably violate establishment principles, the Court's judicial "surgery" may have been necessary to save the C.O. exemption.

The logical progression of the C.O. issue—to selective pacifism—came in *Gillette v. United*

States, a year after *Welsh,* and forced the Court to address both religion clauses. C.O. status had been denied an applicant who argued that his religious beliefs called for refusal to bear arms in "unjust" wars, which he believed the Vietnam conflict to be. Rejecting this claim the Court held the draft law, authorizing exemptions for men "conscientiously opposed to war in any form," ruled out selective conscientious objection. The law did not violate the establishment clause merely because it benefited applicants whose religious beliefs led them to oppose all wars. Nor did it violate the free exercise clause since it did not discriminate against C.O. applicants who had religious objection to all wars. Concluding that Congress had acted reasonably and neutrally in creating the exemption, the Court refused to make selective conscientious objection a constitutional right.

In a later case, *Johnson v. Robison,* 1974, denial of veterans education benefits to conscientious objectors who had been called on to perform alternative service was held to place only a slight burden on religious freedom and so not to violate a free exercise right.

Economic Benefits: Eligibility

Religious practices can conflict with many government rules and regulations that have general application. When enforcement places a direct or indirect economic burden on those holding particular religious tenets, does the free exercise right call for a release from imposed legal obligation?

When the question first came up in the Sunday closing law case of *Braunfeld v. Brown,* 1961, a majority of the Court held that an Orthodox Jew who closed his business on Saturday to observe the Sabbath could be forced to close on Sunday also, even though being closed two days a week was an obvious economic disadvantage. No free exercise violation occurred because the law did not interfere with observance of the Saturday Sabbath nor did his religious beliefs call for being open on Sunday. The decision did not prevent state or local Sunday closing laws from providing exemptions for those whose Sabbath is not Sunday, but that was a matter of legislative discretion not constitutional requirement.

The hardship imposed on Sabbatarians by *Braunfeld* apparently weighed heavily on several of the justices, for in *Sherbert v. Verner* (p. 115), two years later, the Court took a different position. A Seventh Day Adventist had been denied state unemployment benefits in South Carolina after she refused jobs that called for work on Saturday, her Sabbath. Speaking for a majority of seven, Justice William Brennan, who had dissented in *Braunfeld,* held that a regulation economically burdening the exercise of religion, even though incidentally and for a secular purpose, could be sustained only if it was in pursuit of a "compelling" government interest and was the least restrictive means possible. South Carolina's interest in guarding against fraudulent claims did not meet that test. *Braunfeld* was distinguished on these grounds and so not overruled.

The Court then used the *Sherbert* test to uphold free exercise rights against other regulations. It overturned a ruling denying unemployment benefits to a Jehovah's Witness who, after being transferred by his manufacturer-employer to work on making tank turrets, quit because his religious beliefs forbade making weapons of war. (*Thomas v. Review Board of Indiana Employment Security Division,* 1981) It disallowed denial of benefits to a Seventh Day Adventist who had been fired from her job for refusing to work on Saturday even though she had become an Adventist after her employment began. (*Hobbie v. Florida Unemployment Appeals Compensation Commission,* 1987) And still later, it held that a state could not deny benefits to a Christian who for religious reasons refused to work on Sundays, simply because he was not a member of an organized church. (*Frazee v. Illinois Department of Employment Security,* 1989)

The federal tax code, which gives a tax exempt status to private colleges and universities, disallows it if racial discrimination is practiced. In *Bob Jones University v. United States,* 1983, the Court used the *Sherbert* test to uphold denial of the status to a religious-affiliated university that contended its racially discriminatory admissions policy rested on religious tenets. The government's interest in ending race discrimination in education was compelling and thus overrode the free exercise claim. The Court added that loss of the tax exempt status would not prevent the private school from following its religious tenets.

It is noteworthy that the reciprocal of the issue in *Sherbert*—the granting of an affirmative right not to work on one's Sabbath—creates a conflict between the free exercise and establishment clauses. Connecticut's requirement that private employers accommodate any employee who refused to work on his or her Sabbath, was struck down in *Estate of Thornton v. Caldor*, 1985, as having a primary effect of advancing religion, thus violating the Establishment Clause. There was no right, the Court said, to force others to conform to one's religious necessities.

By 1990, as cases in the next section show, members of the Court were having second thoughts about the reach and implications of the *Sherbert* rules. In *Employment Division, Oregon Department of Human Resources v. Smith* (p. 118), a majority of the Justices retreated from the compelling interest criterion. Oregon had denied unemployment benefits to two counselors fired from their jobs at a drug and alcohol abuse clinic for using peyote, a hallucinogenic drug illegal under state law. The plaintiffs, members of the Native American Church, which believes peyote to be a sacramental substance, argued that their ingestion at a religious ceremony was in accord with church tenets. The Supreme Court, 6-3, upheld the state, ruling that free exercise rights did not prevent it from administering "generally applicable" regulations—here denial of benefits to those fired for criminal acts—that have only unintended and "incidental" effects on religious practices. The decision thus narrowed *Sherbert*, which was distinguished on the ground that South Carolina's denial was not based on unemployment resulting from criminal behavior.

In direct response to *Smith* and to the lobbying of many religious groups, Congress enacted the Religious Freedom Restoration Act (RFRA) in 1993. A main provision barred burdening of religious freedom unless it furthered a "compelling government interest" and was the least restrictive means. In effect, the law restored and codified the *Sherbert* test. In 1997, in *City of Boerne v. Flores* the Supreme Court declared this provision of the RFRA unconstitutional (p. 124) thus reinforcing its position in *Smith*.

Economic Obligations: Exemption

Claims of free exercise have clashed with state and federal laws imposing generally applicable material obligations, most notably taxes. In these instances, the Court has tended to accord less protection than in *Sherbert*, the justices indicating concern about opening the door to religious-based civic avoidance.

In *United States v. Lee*, 1982, for example, it held that Amish employers must pay social security taxes for their Amish employees even though the Amish believe payment of such taxes a sin and Congress had exempted self-employed Amish from such taxes. Infringement on religious freedom was justified by an "overriding government interest" in maintaining a system of retirement and disability insurance.

In other cases, the Court has held free exercise rights not to be violated by various government actions. These include requirement that a religious group comply with the federal minimum wage law (*Tony and Susan Alamo Foundation v. Secretary of Labor*, 1985); issuance of social security numbers to persons despite their religious objections (*Bowen v. Roy*, 1986); an I.R.S. ruling that contributions paid to the Church of Scientology in return for religious training were not tax deductible (*Hernandez v. Internal Revenue Service*, 1989); a California sales tax as applied to the sale of religious materials (*Jimmy Swaggert Ministries v. Board of Equalization*, 1990); and an I.R.S. ruling that parents' support of their sons while the sons served as missionaries for their church was not tax deductible (*Davis v. United States*, 1990).

In these cases, the Court did not consider the burdens imposed by government substantial. More important, however, was the weight accorded the government's fiscal or administrative interest and that the laws, regulations, and rulings had a generally applicable purpose, not directed at religion.

Compulsory Education

All states have compulsory school attendance laws, typically requiring schooling through the tenth grade or age 16. Though the Supreme Court had ruled in *Pierce v. Society of Sisters,* 1925, that states could not make attending public schools mandatory, private schools must meet basic education standards and their students are subject to laws setting out a minimum number of years of schooling.

Education beyond the eighth grade conflicts with the religious beliefs of the Old Order of Amish, a fundamentalist branch of the Mennonite Church, whose members live mainly in a few simple, self-contained rural communities in Pennsylvania and states of the Midwest. Descended from German and Swiss Anabaptists, the Amish have generally been hard-working, law-abiding farmers, austerely opposed to the use of automobiles, electricity, and most other modern conveniences and technology. Trying to remain separate from the world, they see advanced secular education as lessening the chance of salvation for those exposed to it. The Amish run their own schools through grade eight, and most states had worked out an uneasy accommodation with them. But when Wisconsin tried to enforce its requirement that all children in the state remain in school until age 16, it produced a much-publicized legal conflict that reached the Supreme Court as *Wisconsin v. Yoder* (p. 122) in 1971.

In it, the Court ruled the Amish were entitled to a release from the state requirement. Finding their entire way of life including beliefs about extended secular education to be religious, it held the state law placed a substantial burden on free exercise rights. Thus Wisconsin would need to have a compelling reason not to grant an exemp-

tion. Because most Amish children spend their entire lives in Amish communities, it had failed to carry this burden of proof. The Court's emphasis on the Amish living in settled, self-contained communities and sharing deep religious convictions "intimately related to daily living" suggests the decision may be better understood anthropologically than jurisprudentially. The Court no doubt realized that the generous exception it was creating would apply to few, if any, others.

Other Free Exercise Questions

Religious pluralism and the sheer diversity of religious beliefs and practices offer many other points of ready conflict with public or community interests asserted by government. In *Goldman v. Weinberger,* 1986, for example, the Court upheld the Air Force's uniform dress code that kept a captain who was also an Orthodox Jewish rabbi from wearing a yarmulke (a small religious skull cap) called for by his faith. Noting that military life afforded less individual autonomy than civilian, five justices held the dress code to be part of the Air Force's mission to "foster instinctive obedience, unity, commitment, and esprit de corps." In an unusual dissent, Justice Brennan urged Congress, which has constitutional authority to make rules for the military, to correct the "wrong" of the decision. Congress did so the following year, creating a statutory right for members of the armed forces "to wear an item of religious apparel while in uniform" as long as it was "neat and conservative" and did not interfere with military duties.

The Court has given substantial deference to decisions of prison administrators. In *O'Lone v. Estate of Shabazz,* 1987, it upheld regulations for work outside the prison that prevented Muslim prisoners from attending Friday prayers called for by their faith. Noting that the prison had accommodated other Muslim worship practices, including dietary restrictions, the Court found the work rules reasonably related to security.

The Court moved yet further from the *Sherbert* test in *Lyng v. Northwest Indian Cemetery Protec-*

tion Association, 1988. It upheld the federal government's right to build roads and permit logging on publicly owned forest land that was also an Indian burial site held sacred by several Native American tribes. The Court said these operations imposed only an incidental burden on the practice of religious beliefs, not enough to support a constitutional claim to limit the government in conducting its internal affairs.

Despite these rulings against free exercise claims, the Court continues to look closely at any government regulation burdening religious practice. In *Church of Lukumi Babalu Aye v. City of Hialeah*, 1993, for example, it found that an ordinance banning animal sacrifice was aimed specifically at a local branch of the Santerian faith, whose members ritually killed animals in religious ceremony. Instead of being neutral, the law was an attack on specific religious practices.

The Religious Freedom Restoration Act

In 1993, Congress passed the Religious Freedom Restoration Act (RFRA), largely in response to the Court's decision in *Employment Division, Oregon Department of Human Resources v. Smith*, 1990, discussed earlier. Its stated purpose was "to restore the compelling interest test as set forth in *Sherbert v. Verner* and *Wisconsin v. Yoder* and to guarantee its application in all cases in which free exercise of religion is substantially burdened." Even with regulations having general applicability, such burden would be permissible only if it furthered a "compelling government interest and is the least restrictive means for doing so." Though the RFRA had wide support in both parties and among most religious groups, it was opposed by state and local authorities who believed it would encourage claims for exemptions from neutrally designed laws applicable to everyone else.

Unsurprisingly, a challenge soon developed. The City of Boerne, Texas, had denied a local Roman Catholic church a permit to replace its church building, because the structure was in a designated historic district that the city wanted to keep largely unchanged. Contending that the existing structure was no longer large enough to house all parishioners, the church appealed the decision under the RFRA.

In *City of Boerne v. Flores*, 1997 (p. 124), the Supreme Court did not dwell on whether the city's interest was "compelling" or whether denial of the permit was a least restrictive means. Instead, it held 6-3 the RFRA itself unconstitutional as beyond Congress's legislative power. Congress could neither narrow a right in the Bill of Rights nor enlarge one, as it had done here, by simple act of legislation. To do so, would change the Constitution without going through the amending process. In trying to "restore" an earlier constitutional interpretation of the Court, it had usurped the Court's own authority to interpret the Constitution established in *Marbury v. Madison*. Such authority, the Court said, includes power to define limits of the free exercise clause.

The decision in *Boerne* reaffirms the Court's retreat from *Sherbert* and its determination to hold its institutional ground against opposition from an elected coequal branch. In religion decisions, whether striking out school prayers or, as here, supporting neutral but less than compelling government regulations, that ground may often spark popular opposition.

FURTHER READING

Religion in American Society and Polity

Adams, Arlin M., and Charles J. Emmerich, *A Nation Dedicated to Religious Liberty: The Constitutional Heritage of the Religion Clauses* (1990)

Ahlstrom, Sidney E., *A Religious History of the American People* (1972)

Berman, Harold J., *Faith and Order: The Reconciliation of Law and Religion* (1993)

Carter, Leif, *An Introduction to Constitutional Interpretation: Cases in Law and Religion* (1991)

Carter, Stephen, *The Culture of Disbelief* (1993)

Choper, Jesse, *Securing Religious Liberty: Principles for Judicial Interpretation of the Religion Clauses* (1995)

Currey, Thomas J., *The First Amendment Freedoms: Church and State in America to the Passage of the First Amendment* (1986)

Eidsmoe, John, *Christianity and the Constitution: The Faith of Our Founding Fathers* (1987)

Firmage, Edwin Brown, and Richard Collin Mangrum, *Zion in the Courts: A Legal History of the Church of Jesus Christ of Latter-Day Saints, 1830–1900* (1988)

George, Robert P., *The Clash of Orthodoxies: Law, Religion, and Morality in Crisis* (2001)

Greenawalt, Kent, *Religious Convictions and Political Choice* (1988)

Herberg, Will, *Protestant, Catholic, Jew: An Essay in American Religious Sociology* (1960)

Howe, Mark deWolfe, *The Garden and the Wilderness: Religion and Government in American Constitutional History* (1965)

Ivers, Gregg, *Redefining the First Freedom* (1993)

Kurland, Phillip, *Religion and the Law* (1962)

———, *Church and State: The Supreme Court and the First Amendment* (1975)

Lee, Francis Graham, *Church-State Relations* (2002)

Malbin, Michael, *Religion and Politics: Intentions of the Authors of the First Amendment* (1978)

Marty, Martin E., *A Nation of Believers* (1976)

———, *Pilgrims in Their Own Land: 500 Years of Religion in America* (1984)

Miller, William Lee, *The First Liberty: Religion and the American Republic* (1985)

Monsma, Stephen V., *When Sacred and Secular Mix* (1996)

Monsma, Stephen V., and J. Christopher Soper, *Equal Treatment of Religion in a Pluralistic Society* (1998)

Morgan, Richard E., *The Supreme Court and Religion* (1972)

Mazur, Eric Michael, *The Americanization of Religious Minorities: Confronting the Constitutional Order* (1999)

Noonan, John T., *The Lustre of Our Country: The American Experience of Religious Freedom* (1998)

Pfeffer, *God, Caesar, and the Constitution* (1975)

Richards, David A. J., *Toleration and the Constitution* (1975)

Rosenblum, Nancy L., *Obligations of Citizenship and Demands of Faith: Religious Accommodation in Pluralist Democracy* (2000)

Sandoz, Ellis, *A Government of Laws: Political Theory, Religion, and the American Founding* (1990)

Spinner-Halev, Jeff, *Surviving Diversity: Religion and Democratic Citizenship* (2000)

Stokes, Anson Phelps, *Church and State in the United States*, 3 vols. (1950)

Weber, Paul J., ed., *Equal Separation: Understanding the Religion Clauses of the First Amendment* (1990)

Wilcox, Clyde, *God's Warriors: The Christian Right in Twentieth Century America* (1993)

Wills, Garry, *Under God* (1990)

Church and State

Alley, Robert, *The Supreme Court on Church and State* (1988)

Cord, Robert L., *Separation of Church and State: Historical Fact and Current Fiction* (1982)

Dolbeare, Kenneth M., and Phillip E. Hammond, *The School Prayers Decisions: From Court Policy to Local Practice* (1971)

Eldredge, Niles, *The Monkey Business: A Scientist Looks at Creationism* (1992)

Feldman, Stephen, *Please Don't Wish Me a Merry Christmas: A Critical History of the Separation of Church and State* (1997)

Gedicks, Frederick Mark, *The Rhetoric of Church and State* (1995)

Hutcheson, Richard G., Jr., *God in the White House: How Religion Has Changed the Modern Presidency* (1989)

Ivers, Gregg, *To Build a Wall: American Jews and the Separation of Church and State* (1995)

Jelen, Ted G., *To Serve God and Mammon: Church-State Relations in American Politics* (2000)

Keynes, Edward, and Randall K. Miller, *The Court vs. Congress: Prayer, Busing, and Abortion* (1989)

Levy, Leonard, *The Establishment Clause: Religion and the First Amendment* (1986)

Morgan, Richard E., *The Politics of Religious Conflict: Church and State in America* (1980)

Muir, William K., *Prayer in the Public Schools: Law and Attitude Change* (1967)

Pfeffer, Leo, *Religion, State, and the Burger Court* (1985)

Ravitch, Frank S., *School Prayer and Discrimination* (1999)

Sorouf, Frank J., *The Wall of Separation: The Constitutional Politics of Church and State* (1976)

Sullivan, Winnifred Fallers, *Paying the Words Extra: Religious Discourse in the Supreme Court of the United States* (1995)

Swanson, Wayne R., *The Christ Child Goes to Court* (1990)

Weber, Paul J., and Dennis A. Gilber, *Private Churches and Public Money: Church-Government Fiscal Relations* (1981)

Religious Freedom

Evans, Bette, *Interpreting the Free Exercise of Religion* (1997)

Guliuzza, Frank, *Over the Wall: Protecting Religious Expression in the Public Square* (2000)

Hostetler, John A., *Amish Society,* 4th ed. (1993)

Kelly, Dean M., ed., *Government Intervention in Religious Affairs* (1982)

Peters, Shawn Francis, *Judging Jehovah's Witnesses: Religious Persecution and the Dawn of the Rights Revolution* (2000)

Pfeffer, Leo, *God, Caesar, and the Constitution* (1975)

Sheffer, Martin S., *God versus Caesar: Belief, Worship, and Proselytization under the First Amendment* (1999)

Smith, Steven, *Foreordained Failure: The Quest for a Constitutional Principle of Religious Freedom* (1995)

On Leading Cases

Larson, Edward, *Summer for the Gods: The Scopes Trial and America's Continuing Debate over Science and Religion* (1997)

Long, Carolyn N., *Religious Freedom and Indian Rights: The Case of* Oregon v. Smith (2000)

Manwaring, David, *Render unto Caesar: The Flag Salute Controversy* (1962)

Additional works are included in the General and Supplementary Bibliography.

CASES

Everson v. Board of Education

330 U.S. 1 (1947), 5-4

Opinion of the Court: Black (Douglas, Murphy, Reed, Vinson)

Dissenting: Burton, Frankfurter, Jackson, Rutledge

Does this decision widen or narrow the separation of church and state? Is Justice Black's rhetoric consistent with his holding? Who are the beneficiaries of the state's program in his view? Do the dissenters dispute this?

Black, for the Court:

A New Jersey statute authorizes its local school districts to make rules and contracts for the transportation of children to and from schools. The appellee, a township board of education, acting pursuant to this statute, authorized reimbursement to parents of money expended by them for the bus transportation of their children on regular busses operated by the public transportation system. Part of this money was for the payment of transportation of some children in the community to Catholic parochial schools. These church schools give their students, in addition to secular education, regular religious instruction conforming to the religious tenets and modes of worship of the Catholic Faith. The superintendent of these schools is a Catholic priest.

[Everson], in his capacity as a district taxpayer, filed suit in a state court challenging the right of the Board to reimburse parents of parochial school students. He contended that the statute and the resolution passed pursuant to it violated both the State and the Federal Constitutions. . . .

. . . The only contention here is that the state statute and the resolution, insofar as they authorized reimbursement to parents of children attending parochial schools, violate the Federal Constitution in these two respects, which to some extent overlap. First. They authorize the State to take by taxation the private property of some and bestow it upon others to be used for their own private purposes. This, it is alleged, violates the due process clause of the Fourteenth Amendment. Second. The statute and the resolution forced inhabitants to pay taxes to help support and maintain schools which are dedicated to, and which regularly teach, the Catholic Faith. This is alleged to be a use of state power to support church schools contrary to the prohibition of the First Amendment which the Fourteenth Amendment made applicable to the states.

First. . . . It is much too late to argue that legislation intended to facilitate the opportunity of children to get a secular education serves no public purpose. The same thing is no less true of legislation to reimburse needy parents, or all parents, for payment of the fares of their children so that they can ride in public busses to and from schools, rather than run the risk of traffic and other hazards incident to walking or "hitchhiking." . . .

Second. The New Jersey statute is challenged as a "law respecting an establishment of religion." The First Amendment, as made applicable to the states by the Fourteenth commands that a state "shall make no law respecting an establishment of religion, or prohibiting the free exercise thereof . . . 'Whether this New Jersey law is one respecting an "establishment of religion" requires an understanding of the meaning of that language, particularly with respect to the imposition of taxes. . . .

A large proportion of the early settlers of this country came here from Europe to escape the bondage of laws which compelled them to support and attend government-favored churches. The centuries immediately before and contemporaneous with the colonization of America had been filled with turmoil, civil strife and persecutions, generated in large part by established sects determined to maintain their absolute political and religious supremacy. . . . In efforts to force loyalty to whatever religious group happened to be on top and in league with the government of a particular time and place, men and women had been fined, cast in jail, cruelly tortured, and killed. Among the offenses for which these punishments had been inflicted were such things as speaking disrespectfully of the views of ministers of government-established churches, non-attendance at those churches, expressions of nonbelief in their doctrines, and failure to pay taxes and tithes to support them.

These practices of the old world were transplanted to, and began to thrive in, the soil of the new America. The very charters granted by the English Crown to the individuals and companies designated to make the laws which would control the destinies of the colonials authorized these individuals and companies to erect religious establishments which all, whether believers or nonbelievers, would be required to support and attend. An exercise of this authority was accompanied by a repetition of many of the old-world practices and persecutions. Catholics found themselves hounded and proscribed because of their faith; Quakers who followed their conscience went to jail; Baptists were peculiarly obnoxious to certain dominant Protestant sects; men and women of varied faiths who happened to be in a minority in a particular locality were persecuted because they steadfastly persisted in worshiping God only as their own consciences dictated. And all of these dissenters were compelled to pay tithes and taxes to support government-sponsored churches whose ministers preached inflammatory sermons designed to strengthen and consolidate the established faith by generating a burning hatred against dissenters.

These practices became so commonplace as to shock the freedom-loving colonials into a feeling of abhorrence. The imposition of taxes to pay ministers' salaries and to build and maintain churches and church property aroused their indignation. It was these feelings which found expression in the First Amendment. No one locality and no one group throughout the Colonies can rightly be given entire credit for having aroused the sentiment that culminated in adoption of the Bill of Rights' provisions embracing religious liberty. But Virginia, where the established church had achieved a dominant influence in political affairs and where many excesses attracted wide public attention, provided a great stimulus and able leadership for the movement. The people there, as elsewhere, reached the conviction that individual religious liberty could be achieved best under a government which was stripped of all power to tax, to support, or otherwise to assist any or all religions, or to interfere with the beliefs of any religious individual or group.

The movement toward this end reached its dramatic climax in Virginia in 1785–86 when the Virginia legislative body was about to renew Virginia's tax levy for the support of the established church. Thomas Jefferson and James Madison led the fight against this tax. Madison wrote his great Memorial and Remonstrance against the law. In it, he eloquently argued that a true religion did not need the support of law; that no person, either believer or nonbeliever, should be taxed to support a religious institution of any kind; that the best interest of a society required that the minds of men always be wholly free, and that cruel persecutions were the inevitable result of government-established religions. Madison's Remonstrance received strong support throughout Virginia, and the Assembly postponed consideration of the proposed tax measure until its next session. When the proposal came up for consideration at that session, it not only died in committee, but the Assembly enacted the famous "Virginia Bill for Religious Liberty" originally written by Thomas Jefferson. The preamble to that Bill stated, among other things, that

Almighty God hath created the mind free; that all attempts to influence it by temporal punishments or burthens, or by civil incapacitations, tend only to beget habits of hypocrisy and meanness, and are a departure from the plan of the Holy author of our religion, who being Lord both of body and mind, yet chose not to propagate it by coercions on either . . . ; that to compel a man to furnish contributions of money for the propagation of opinions which he disbelieves is sinful and tyrannical; that even the forcing him to support this or that teacher of his own religious persuasion is depriving him of the comfortable liberty of giving his contributions to the particular pastor whose morals he would make his pattern. . . .

And the statute itself enacted, "That no man shall be compelled to frequent or support any religious worship, place, or ministry whatsoever, nor shall be enforced, restrained, molested, or burthened in his body or goods, nor shall otherwise suffer on account of his religious opinions or belief." . . .

This Court has previously recognized that the provisions of the First Amendment, in the drafting and adoption of which Madison and Jefferson played such leading roles, had the same objective, and were intended to provide the same protection against governmental intrusion on religious liberty as the Virginia statute. Prior to the adoption of the Fourteenth Amendment, the First Amendment did not apply as a restraint against the states. Most of them did soon provide similar constitutional protections for religious liberty. But some states persisted for about half a century in imposing restraints upon the free exercise of religion and in discriminating against particular religious groups. In recent years, so far as the provision against the establishment of a religion is concerned, the question has most frequently arisen in connection with proposed state aid to church schools and efforts to carry on religious teachings in the public schools in accordance with the tenets of a particular sect . . .

The meaning and scope of the First Amendment, preventing establishment of religion or prohibiting the free exercise thereof, in the light of its history and the evils it was designed forever to suppress, have been several times elaborated by the decisions of this Court prior to the application of the First Amendment to the states by the Fourteenth. The broad meaning given the Amendment by these earlier cases has been accepted by this Court in its decisions concerning an individual's religious freedom rendered since the Fourteenth Amendment was interpreted to make the prohibitions of the First applicable to state action abridging religious freedom. There is every reason to give the same application and broad interpretation to the "establishment of religion" clause. The interrelation of these complementary clauses was well summarized . . . *Watson v. Jones:*

The structure of our government has, for the preservation of civil liberty, rescued the temporal institutions from religious interference. On the other hand, it has secured religious liberty from the invasion of the civil authority.

The "establishment of religion" clause of the First Amendment means at least this: neither a state nor the Federal Government can set up a church. Neither can pass laws which aid one religion, aid all religions, or prefer one religion over another. Neither can force nor influence a person to go to or to remain away from church against his will or force him to profess a belief or disbelief in any religion. No person can be punished for entertaining or professing religious beliefs or disbeliefs, for church attendance or non-attendance. No tax in any amount, large or small, can be levied to support any religious activities or institutions, whatever they may be called, or whatever form they may adopt to teach or practice religion. Neither a state nor the Federal Government can, openly or secretly, participate in the affairs of any religious organizations or groups, and vice versa. In the words of Jefferson, the clause against establishment of religion by law was intended to erect "a wall of separation between church and State." *Reynolds v. United States.*

We must consider the New Jersey statute in accordance with the foregoing limitations imposed by the First Amendment. But we must not strike that state statute down if it is within the State's constitutional power, even though it approaches the verge of that power. New Jersey cannot, consistently with the "establishment of religion" clause of the First Amendment, contribute tax raised funds to the support of an institution which teaches the tenets and faith of any church. On the other hand, other language of the amendment commands that New Jersey cannot hamper its citizens in the free exercise of their own religion. Consequently, it cannot exclude individual Catholics, Lutherans, Mohammedans, Baptists, Jews, Methodists, Nonbelievers, Presbyterians, or the members of any other faith, because of their faith, or lack of it, from receiving the benefits of public welfare legislation. While we do not mean to intimate that a state could not provide transportation only to children attending public schools, we must be careful, in protecting the citizens of New Jersey against state-established churches, to be sure that we do not inadvertently prohibit New Jersey from extending its general state law benefits to all its citizens without regard to their religious belief.

Measured by these standards, we cannot say that the First Amendment prohibits New Jersey from spending tax-raised funds to pay the bus fares of parochial school pupils as a part of a general program under which it pays the fares of pupils attending public and other schools. It is undoubtedly true that children are helped to get to church schools. There is even a possibility that some of the children might not be sent to the church schools if the parents were compelled to pay their children's bus fares out of their own pockets when transportation to a public school would have been paid for by the State. The same possibility exists where the state requires a local transit company to provide reduced fares to school children, including those attending parochial schools, or where a municipally owned transportation system undertakes to carry all school children free of charge. Moreover, state-paid policemen, detailed to protect children going to and from church schools from the very real hazards of traffic, would serve much the same purpose and accomplish much the same result as state provisions intended to guarantee free transportation of a kind which the state deems to be best for the school children's welfare. And parents might refuse to risk their children to the serious danger of traffic accidents going to and from parochial schools the approaches to which were not protected by policemen. Similarly, parents might be reluctant to permit their children to attend schools which the state had cut off from such general government services as ordinary police and fire protection, connections for sewage disposal, public highways and sidewalks. Of course, cutting off church schools from these services so separate and so indisputably marked off from the religious function would make it far more difficult for the schools to operate. But such is obviously not the purpose of the First Amendment. That Amendment requires the state to be a neutral in its relations with groups of religious believers and nonbelievers; it does not require the state to be their adversary. State power is no more to be used so as to handicap religions than it is to favor them.

This Court has said that parents may, in the discharge of their duty under state compulsory education laws, send their children to a religious, rather than a public, school if the school meets the secular educational requirements which the state has power to impose. It appears that these parochial schools meet New Jersey's requirements. The State contributes no money to the schools. It does not support them. Its legislation, as applied, does no more than provide a general program to help parents get their children, regardless of their religion, safely and expeditiously to and from accredited schools.

The First Amendment has erected a wall between church and state. That wall must be kept high and impregnable. We could not approve the slightest breach. New Jersey has not breached it here.

Jackson, dissenting:

. . . The Township of Ewing is not furnishing transportation to the children in any form; it is not operating school busses itself, or contracting for their operation, and it is not performing any public service of any kind with this taxpayer's money. All school children are left to ride as ordinary paying passengers on the regular busses operated by the public transportation system. What the Township does, and what the taxpayer complains of, is, at stated intervals, to reimburse parents for the fares paid, provided the children attend either public schools or Catholic Church schools. This expenditure of tax funds has no possible effect on the child's safety or expedition in transit. As passengers on the public busses, they travel as fast, and no faster, and are as safe, and no safer, since their parents are reimbursed, as before.

In addition to thus assuming a type of service that does not exist, the Court also insists that we must close our eyes to a discrimination which does exist. The resolution which authorizes disbursement of this taxpayer's money limits reimbursement to those who attend public schools and Catholic schools. That is the way the Act is applied to this taxpayer.

The New Jersey Act in question makes the character of the school, not the needs of the children, determine the eligibility of parents to reimbursement. The Act permits payment for transportation to parochial schools or public schools, but prohibits it to private schools operated in whole or in part for profit. Children often are sent to private schools because their parents feel that they require more individual instruction than public schools can provide, or because they are backward or defective, and need special attention. If all children of the state were objects of impartial solicitude, no reason is obvious for denying transportation reimbursement to students of this class, for these often are as needy and as worthy as those who go to public or parochial schools. . . .

It seems to me that the basic fallacy in the Court's reasoning, which accounts for its failure to apply the principles it avows, is in ignoring the essentially religious test by which beneficiaries of this expenditure are selected. A policeman protects a Catholic, of course,—but not because he is a Catholic; it is because he is a man, and a member of our society. The fireman protects the Church school—but not because it is a Church school; it is because it is property, part of the assets of our society. Neither the fireman nor the policeman has to ask before he renders aid, "is this man or building identified with the Catholic Church?" But, before these school authorities draw a check to reimburse for a student's fare, they must ask just that question, and, if the school is a Catholic one, they may render aid because it is such, while if it is of any other faith or is run for profit, the help must be withheld. . . .

Rutledge dissenting:

No one conscious of religious values can be unsympathetic toward the burden which our constitutional separation puts on parents who desire religious instruction mixed with secular for their children. They pay taxes for others' children's education; at the same time, the added cost of instruction for their own. Nor can one happily see benefits denied to children which others receive because, in conscience, they, or their parents for them, desire a different kind of training others do not demand.

But if those feelings should prevail, there would be an end to our historic constitutional policy and command. No more unjust or discriminatory, in fact, is it to deny attendants at religious schools the cost of their transportation than it is to deny them tuitions, sustenance for their teachers, or any other educational expense which others receive at public cost. . . .

Short treatment will dispose of what remains. Whatever might be said of some other application of New Jersey's statute, the one made here has no semblance of bearing as a safety measure or, indeed, for securing expeditious conveyance. The transportation supplied is by public conveyance, subject to all the hazards and delays of the highway and the streets incurred by the public generally in going about its multifarious business. . . .

Abington School District v. Schempp

374 U.S. 203 (1963), 8-1
Opinion of the Court: Black (Brennan, Clark, Douglas, Goldberg, Harlan, Warren, White)
Dissenting: Stewart

Here, for the first time, the Court weighs the validity of using the Bible in public school devotionals. Pennsylvania required that "at least ten verses from the Holy Bible shall be read without comment, at the opening of each public school on each school day." A child could be excused from the devotional on written request from a parent. The case was heard with the companion case, Murray v. Curlett, *where a Baltimore school rule required a reading without comment of "a chapter in the Holy Bible and/or the use of the Lord's Prayer." The Schempps were Unitarians who objected to some "doctrines purveyed by a literal reading of the Bible." The Murrays were atheists who objected to a teaching that a belief in God is the "source of all moral and spiritual values." A lower federal court held the Pennsylvania practice unconstitutional, but Maryland's was sustained in the state courts.*

Does this decision place religion at a "state-created disadvantage," as Justice Stewart argues in dissent? Why doesn't an exemption from taking part in the devotional make it constitutional? Would prayers or Bible-reading in the public schools be constitutional if no one objected and there was no evidence of coercion? Would a school board policy that required the daily recitation of the same prayer used to open sessions of Congress be constitutional? How high can the wall of separation of church and state be built before government becomes hostile to religion?

Clark, for the Court:

. . . The wholesome "neutrality" of which this Court's cases speak thus stems from a recognition of the teachings of history that powerful sects or groups might bring about a fusion of governmental and religious functions or a concert or dependency of one upon the other to the end that official support of the State or Federal Government would be placed behind the tenets of one or of all orthodoxies. This the Establishment Clause prohibits. And a further reason for neutrality is found in the Free Exercise Clause, which recognizes the value of religious training, teaching and observance and, more particularly, the right of every person to freely choose his own course with reference thereto, free of any compulsion from the state. This the Free Exercise Clause guarantees. Thus, as we have seen, the two clauses may overlap. As we have indicated, the Establishment Clause has been directly considered by this Court eight times in the past score of years and, with only one Justice dissenting on the point, it has consistently held that the clause withdrew all legislative power respecting religious belief or the expression thereof. The test may be stated as follows: what are the purpose and the primary effect of the enactment? If either is the advancement or inhibition of religion, then the enactment exceeds the scope of legislative power as circumscribed by the Constitution. That is to say that, to withstand the strictures of the Establishment Clause, there must be a secular legislative purpose and a primary effect that neither advances nor inhibits religion. The Free Exercise Clause, likewise considered many times here, withdraws from legislative power, state and federal, the exertion of any restraint on the free exercise of religion. Its purpose is to secure religious liberty in the individual by prohibiting any invasions thereof by civil authority. Hence, it is necessary in a free exercise case for one to show the coercive effect of the enactment as it operates against him in the practice of his religion. The distinction between the two clauses is apparent—a violation of the Free Exercise Clause is predicated on coercion, while the Establishment Clause violation need not be so attended.

Applying the Establishment Clause principles to the cases at bar, we find that the States are requiring the selection and reading at the opening of the school day of verses from the Holy Bible and the recitation of the Lord's Prayer by the students in unison. These exercises are prescribed as part of the curricular activities of students who are required by law to attend school. They are held in the school buildings under the supervision and with the participation of teachers employed in those schools. None of these factors, other than compulsory school attendance, was present in the program upheld in *Zorach v. Clauson*. The trial court in [*Schempp*] has found that such an opening exercise is a religious ceremony, and was intended by the State to be so. We agree with the trial court's finding as to the religious character of the exercises. Given that finding, the exercises and the law requiring them are in violation of the Establishment Clause.

There is no such specific finding as to the religious character of the exercises in [*Murray*], and the State contends (as does the State in *Schempp*) that the pro-

gram is an effort to extend its benefits to all public school children without regard to their religious belief. Included within its secular purposes, it says, are the promotion of moral values, the contradiction to the materialistic trends of our times, the perpetuation of our institutions and the teaching of literature. The case came up on demurrer, of course, to a petition which alleged that the uniform practice under the rule had been to read from the King James version of the Bible, and that the exercise was sectarian. The short answer, therefore, is that the religious character of the exercise was admitted by the State. But even if its purpose is not strictly religious, it is sought to be accomplished through readings, without comment, from the Bible. Surely the place of the Bible as an instrument of religion cannot be gainsaid, and the State's recognition of the pervading religious character of the ceremony is evident from the rule's specific permission of the alternative use of the Catholic Douay version, as well as the recent amendment permitting nonattendance at the exercises. None of these factors is consistent with the contention that the Bible is here used either as an instrument for nonreligious moral inspiration or as a reference for the teaching of secular subjects.

The conclusion follows that, in both cases, the laws require religious exercises, and such exercises are being conducted in direct violation of the rights of the [Schempps] and [Murrays]. Nor are these required exercises mitigated by the fact that individual students may absent themselves upon parental request, for that fact furnishes no defense to a claim of unconstitutionality under the Establishment Clause. Further, it is no defense to urge that the religious practices here may be relatively minor encroachments on the First Amendment. The breach of neutrality that is today a trickling stream may all too soon become a raging torrent and, in the words of Madison, "it is proper to take alarm at the first experiment on our liberties."

It is insisted that, unless these religious exercises are permitted, a "religion of secularism" is established in the schools. We agree, of course, that the State may not establish a "religion of secularism" in the sense of affirmatively opposing or showing hostility to religion, thus "preferring those who believe in no religion over those who do believe." We do not agree, however, that this decision in any sense has that effect. In addition, it might well be said that one's education is not complete without a study of comparative religion or the history of religion and its relationship to the advancement of civilization. It certainly may be said that the Bible is worthy of study for its literary and historic qualities. Nothing we have said here indicates that such study of the Bible or of religion, when presented objectively as part of a secular program of education, may not be effected consistently with the First Amendment. But the exercises here do not fall into those categories. They are religious exercises, required by the States in violation of the command of the First Amendment that the Government maintain strict neutrality, neither aiding nor opposing religion.

Finally, we cannot accept that the concept of neutrality, which does not permit a State to require a religious exercise even with the consent of the majority of those affected, collides with the majority's right to free exercise of religion. While the Free Exercise Clause clearly prohibits the use of state action to deny the rights of free exercise to anyone, it has never meant that a majority could use the machinery of the State to practice its beliefs. Such a contention was effectively answered by Mr. Justice Jackson for the Court in *West Virginia Board of Education v. Barnette*

The very purpose of a Bill of Rights was to withdraw certain subjects from the vicissitudes of political controversy, to place them beyond the reach of majorities and officials, and to establish them as legal principles to be applied by the courts. One's right to . . . freedom of worship . . . and other fundamental rights may not be submitted to vote; they depend on the outcome of no elections.

The place of religion in our society is an exalted one, achieved through a long tradition of reliance on the home, the church and the inviolable citadel of the individual heart and mind. We have come to recognize through bitter experience that it is not within the power of government to invade that citadel, whether its purpose or effect be to aid or oppose, to advance or retard. In the relationship between man and religion, the State is firmly committed to a position of neutrality. Though the application of that rule requires interpretation of a delicate sort, the rule itself is clearly and concisely stated in the words of the First Amendment. Applying that rule to the facts of these cases, we affirm the judgment in [*Schempp*] In [*Murray*], the judgment is reversed, and the cause remanded to the Maryland Court of Appeals for further proceedings consistent with this opinion.

Brennan, concurring:

. . . A too literal quest for the advice of the Founding Fathers upon the issues of these cases seems to me futile and misdirected for several reasons: first, on our precise problem, the historical record is, at best, ambiguous, and statements can readily be found to support either side of the proposition. The ambiguity of history is understandable if we recall the nature of the problems uppermost in the thinking of the statesmen who fashioned the religious guarantees; they were concerned with far more flagrant intrusions of government into the realm of religion than any that our century has witnessed. While it is clear to me that the Framers meant the Establishment Clause to prohibit more than the creation of an established federal church such as existed in England, I have no doubt that, in their preoccupation with the imminent question of established churches, they gave no distinct consideration to the particular question whether the clause also forbade devotional exercises in public institutions.

Second, the structure of American education has greatly changed since the First Amendment was adopted. In the context of our modern emphasis upon public education available to all citizens, any views of the eighteenth century as to whether the exercises at bar are an "establishment" offer little aid to decision. Education, as the Framers knew it, was in the main confined to private schools more often than not under strictly sectarian supervision. Only gradually did control of education pass largely to public officials. It would, therefore, hardly be significant if the fact was that the nearly universal devotional exercises in the schools of the young Republic did not provoke criticism; even today, religious ceremonies in church supported private schools are constitutionally unobjectionable. Third, our religious composition makes us a vastly more diverse people than were our forefathers. They knew differences chiefly among Protestant sects. Today, the Nation is far more heterogeneous religiously, including as it does substantial minorities not only of Catholics and Jews but as well of those who worship according to no version of the Bible and those who worship no God at all. In the face of such profound changes, practices which may have been objectionable to no one in the time of Jefferson and Madison may today be highly offensive to many persons, the deeply devout and the nonbelievers alike.

Whatever Jefferson or Madison would have thought of Bible reading or the recital of the Lord's Prayer in what few public schools existed in their day, our use of the history of their time must limit itself to broad purposes, not specific practices. By such a standard, I am persuaded, as is the Court, that the devotional exercises carried on in the Baltimore and Abington schools offend the First Amendment because they sufficiently threaten in our day those substantive evils the fear of which called forth the Establishment Clause of the First Amendment. It is "a constitution we are expounding," and our interpretation of the First Amendment must necessarily be responsive to the much more highly charged nature of religious questions in contemporary society.

Stewart, dissenting:

I think the records in the two cases before us are so fundamentally deficient as to make impossible an informed or responsible determination of the constitutional issues presented. Specifically, I cannot agree that, on these records, we can say that the Establishment Clause has necessarily been violated. But I think there exist serious questions under both that provision and the Free Exercise Clause—insofar as each is imbedded in the Fourteenth Amendment—which require the remand of these cases for the taking of additional evidence. . . .

. . . For there is involved in these cases a substantial free exercise claim on the part of those who affirmatively desire to have their children's school day open with the reading of passages from the Bible. . . .

It might also be argued that parents who want their children exposed to religious influences can adequately fulfill that wish off school property and outside school time. With all its surface persuasiveness, however, this argument seriously misconceives the basic constitutional justification for permitting the exercises at issue in these cases. For a compulsory state educational system so structures a child's life that, if religious exercises are held to be an impermissible activity in schools, religion is placed at an artificial and state-created disadvantage. Viewed in this light, permission of such exercises for those who want them is necessary if the schools are truly to be neutral in the matter of religion. And a refusal to permit religious exercises thus is seen not as the realization of state neutrality, but rather as the establishment of a religion of secularism, or, at the least, as government support of the beliefs of those who think that religious exercises should be conducted only in private. . . .

. . . [I]t is important to stress that, strictly speaking, what is at issue here is a privilege, rather than a right. In other words, the question presented is not whether exercises such as those at issue here are constitutionally compelled, but rather whether they are constitutionally invalid. And that issue, in my view, turns on the question of coercion.

It is clear that the dangers of coercion involved in the holding of religious exercises in a school room differ qualitatively from those presented by the use of similar exercises or affirmations in ceremonies attended by adults. Even as to children, however, the duty laid upon government in connection with religious exercises in the public schools is that of refraining from so structuring the school environment as to put any kind of pressure on a child to participate in those exercises; it is not that of providing an atmosphere in which children are kept scrupulously insulated from any awareness that some of their fellows may want to open the school day with prayer, or of the fact that there exist in our pluralistic society differences of religious belief. . . .

Viewed in this light, it seems to me clear that the records in both of the cases before us are wholly inadequate to support an informed or responsible decision. Both cases involve provisions which explicitly permit any student who wishes, to be excused from participation in the exercises. There is no evidence in either case as to whether there would exist any coercion of any kind upon a student who did not want to participate. No evidence at all was adduced in the Murray case, because it was decided upon a demurrer. All that we have in that case, therefore, is the conclusory language of a pleading. While such conclusory allegations are acceptable for procedural purposes, I think that the nature of the constitutional problem involved here clearly demands that no decision be made except upon evidence. In the Schempp case, the record shows no more than a subjective prophecy by a parent of what he thought would happen if a request were made to be excused from participation in the exercises under the amended statute. No such request was ever made, and there is no evidence whatever as to what might or would actually happen, nor of what administrative arrangements the school actually might or could make to free from pressure of any kind those who do not want to participate in the exercises. . . .

What our Constitution indispensably protects is the freedom of each of us, be he Jew or Agnostic, Christian or Atheist, Buddhist or Freethinker, to believe or disbelieve, to worship or not worship, to pray or keep silent, according to his own conscience, uncoerced and unrestrained by government. It is conceivable that these school boards, or even all school boards, might eventually find it impossible to administer a system of religious exercises during school hours in such a way as to meet this constitutional standard—in such a way as completely to free from any kind of official coercion those who do not affirmatively want to participate. But I think we must not assume that school boards so lack the qualities of inventiveness and good will as to make impossible the achievement of that goal.

Walz v. Tax Commission

397 U.S. 664 (1970), 7-1
Opinion of the Court: Burger (Black, Stewart, White, Marshall)
Concurring: Brennan, Harlan
Dissenting: Douglas

What are the various grounds on which this decision rests? Are some more important than others? Does the fact that a policy is of long-standing justify its continuation? Its constitutionality? What would "excessive entanglement" of church and state look like? What effect would removing the property tax exemption have? Does this practical consideration enter into Chief Justice Burger's reasoning?

Burger, for the Court:
[Walz], owner of real estate in Richmond County, New York, sought an injunction in the New York courts to prevent the New York City Tax Commission from granting property tax exemptions to religious organizations for religious properties used solely for religious worship. The exemption from state taxes is authorized by Art. 16, § 1, of the New York Constitution, which provides in relevant part:

> Exemptions from taxation may be granted only by general laws. Exemptions may be altered or repealed except those exempting real or personal property used exclusively for religious, educational or charitable purposes as defined by law and owned by any corporation or association organized or conducted exclusively for one or more of such purposes and not operating for profit.

The essence of [Walz's] contention was that the New York City Tax Commission's grant of an exemption to church property indirectly requires [Walz] to make a contribution to religious bodies, and thereby violates provisions prohibiting establishment of religion under the First Amendment which, under the Fourteenth Amendment, is binding on the States. . . .

The Establishment and Free Exercise Clauses of the First Amendment are not the most precisely drawn

portions of the Constitution. The sweep of the absolute prohibitions in the Religion Clauses may have been calculated, but the purpose was to state an objective, not to write a statute. In attempting to articulate the scope of the two Religion Clauses, the Court's opinions reflect the limitations inherent in formulating general principles on a case by-case basis. The considerable internal inconsistency in the opinions of the Court derives from what, in retrospect, may have been too sweeping utterances on aspects of these clauses that seemed clear in relation to the particular cases, but have limited meaning as general principles.

The Court has struggled to find a neutral course between the two Religion Clauses, both of which are cast in absolute terms, and either of which, if expanded to a logical extreme, would tend to clash with the other. . . .

The course of constitutional neutrality in this area cannot be an absolutely straight line; rigidity could well defeat the basic purpose of these provisions, which is to insure that no religion be sponsored or favored, none commanded, and none inhibited. The general principle deducible from the First Amendment and all that has been said by the Court is this: that we will not tolerate either governmentally established religion or governmental interference with religion. Short of those expressly proscribed governmental acts, there is room for play in the joints productive of a benevolent neutrality which will permit religious exercise to exist without sponsorship and without interference.

Each value judgment under the Religion Clauses must therefore turn on whether particular acts in question are intended to establish or interfere with religious beliefs and practices or have the effect of doing so. Adherence to the policy of neutrality that derives from an accommodation of the Establishment and Free Exercise Clauses has prevented the kind of involvement that would tip the balance toward government control of churches or governmental restraint on religious practice.

Adherents of particular faiths and individual churches frequently take strong positions on public issues, including, as this case reveals in the several briefs amici, vigorous advocacy of legal or constitutional positions. Of course, churches, as much as secular bodies and private citizens, have that right. No perfect or absolute separation is really possible; the very existence of the Religion Clauses is an involvement of sorts—one that seeks to mark boundaries to avoid excessive entanglement.

The hazards of placing too much weight on a few words or phrases of the Court is abundantly illustrated within the pages of the Court's opinion in *Everson v. Board of Education.* Mr. Justice Black, writing for the Court's majority, said the First Amendment "means at least this: neither a state nor the Federal Government can . . . pass laws which aid one religion, aid all religions, or prefer one religion over another."

Yet he had no difficulty in holding that:

> Measured by these standards, we cannot say that the First Amendment prohibits New Jersey from spending tax raised funds to pay the bus fares of parochial school pupils as a part of a general program under which it pays the fares of pupils attending public and other schools. *It is undoubtedly true that children are helped to get to church schools. There is even a possibility that some of the children might not be sent to the church schools if the parents were compelled to pay their children's bus fares out of their own pockets.* (emphasis added.) . . .

The Court did not regard such "aid" to schools teaching a particular religious faith as any more a violation of the Establishment Clause than providing "state-paid policemen, detailed to protect children . . . [at the schools] from the very real hazards of traffic. . . ."

Mr. Justice Jackson, in perplexed dissent in *Everson,* noted that "the undertones of the opinion, advocating complete and uncompromising separation . . . seem utterly discordant with its conclusion." . . .

Perhaps so. One can sympathize with Mr. Justice Jackson's logical analysis but agree with the Court's eminently sensible and realistic application of the language of the Establishment Clause. In *Everson,* the Court declined to construe the Religion Clauses with a literalness that would undermine the ultimate constitutional objective as illuminated by history. Surely, bus transportation and police protection to pupils who receive religious instruction "aid" that particular religion to maintain schools that plainly tend to assure future adherents to a particular faith by having control of their total education at an early age. No religious body that maintains schools would deny this as an affirmative, if not dominant, policy of church schools. But if, as in *Everson,* buses can be provided to carry and policemen to protect church school pupils, we fail to see how a broader range of police and fire protection given equally to all churches, along with nonprofit hospitals, art galleries, and libraries receiving the same tax exemption, is different for purposes of the Religion Clauses.

Similarly, making textbooks available to pupils in parochial schools in common with public schools was surely an "aid" to the sponsoring churches, because it relieved those churches of an enormous aggregate cost for those books. Supplying of costly teaching materials was not seen either as manifesting a legislative purpose to aid or as having a primary effect of aid contravening the First Amendment. In so holding, the Court was heeding both its own prior decisions and our religious tradition. Mr. Justice Douglas, in *Zorach v. Clauson,* after recalling that we "are a religious people whose institutions presuppose a Supreme Being," went on to say:

> We make room for as wide a variety of beliefs and creeds as the spiritual needs of man deem necessary. . . . *When the state encourages religious instruction . . . it follows the best of our traditions.* For it then respects the religious nature of our people and accommodates the public service to their spiritual needs. (emphasis added.)

With all the risks inherent in programs that bring about administrative relationships between public education bodies and church-sponsored schools, we have been able to chart a course that preserved the autonomy and freedom of religious bodies while avoiding any semblance of established religion. This is a "tightrope," and one we have successfully traversed.

The legislative purpose of the property tax exemption is neither the advancement nor the inhibition of religion; it is neither sponsorship nor hostility. New York, in common with the other States, has determined that certain entities that exist in a harmonious relationship to the community at large, and that foster its "moral or mental improvement," should not be inhibited in their activities by property taxation or the hazard of loss of those properties for nonpayment of taxes. It has not singled out one particular church or religious group, or even churches as such; rather, it has granted exemption to all houses of religious worship within a broad class of property owned by nonprofit, quasi-public corporations which include hospitals, libraries, playgrounds, scientific, professional, historical, and patriotic groups. The State has an affirmative policy that considers these groups as beneficial and stabilizing influences in community life and finds this classification useful, desirable, and in the public interest. Qualification for tax exemption is not perpetual or immutable; some tax exempt groups lose that status when their activities take them outside the classification and new entities can come into being and qualify for exemption.

Governments have not always been tolerant of religious activity, and hostility toward religion has taken many shapes and forms economic, political, and sometimes harshly oppressive. Grants of exemption historically reflect the concern of authors of constitutions and statutes as to the latent dangers inherent in the imposition of property taxes; exemption constitutes a reasonable and balanced attempt to guard against those dangers. The limits of permissible state accommodation to religion are by no means coextensive with the noninterference mandated by the Free Exercise Clause. To equate the two would be to deny a national heritage with roots in the Revolution itself. We cannot read New York's statute as attempting to establish religion; it is simply sparing the exercise of religion from the burden of property taxation levied on private profit institutions.

We find it unnecessary to justify the tax exemption on the social welfare services or "good works" that some churches perform for parishioners and others—family counseling, aid to the elderly and the infirm, and to children. Churches vary substantially in the scope of such services; programs expand or contract according to resources and need. As public-sponsored programs enlarge, private aid from the church sector may diminish. The extent of social services may vary, depending on whether the church serves an urban or rural, a rich or poor constituency. To give emphasis to so variable an aspect of the work of religious bodies would introduce an element of governmental evaluation and standards as to the worth of particular social welfare programs, thus producing a kind of continuing day-to-day relationship which the policy of neutrality seeks to minimize. Hence, the use of a social welfare yardstick as a significant element to qualify for tax exemption could conceivably give rise to confrontations that could escalate to constitutional dimensions.

Determining that the legislative purpose of tax exemption is not aimed at establishing, sponsoring, or supporting religion does not end the inquiry, however. We must also be sure that the end result—the

effect—is not an excessive government entanglement with religion. The test is inescapably one of degree. Either course, taxation of churches or exemption, occasions some degree of involvement with religion. Elimination of exemption would tend to expand the involvement of government by giving rise to tax valuation of church property, tax liens, tax foreclosures, and the direct confrontations and conflicts that follow in the train of those legal processes.

Granting tax exemptions to churches necessarily operates to afford an indirect economic benefit, and also gives rise to some, but yet a lesser, involvement than taxing them. In analyzing either alternative, the questions are whether the involvement is excessive and whether it is a continuing one calling for official and continuing surveillance leading to an impermissible degree of entanglement. Obviously a direct money subsidy would be a relationship pregnant with involvement and, as with most governmental grant programs, could encompass sustained and detailed administrative relationships for enforcement of statutory or administrative standards, but that is not this case. The hazards of churches supporting government are hardly less in their potential than the hazards of government supporting churches; each relationship carries some involvement, rather than the desired insulation and separation. We cannot ignore the instances in history when church support of government led to the kind of involvement we seek to avoid.

The grant of a tax exemption is not sponsorship, since the government does not transfer part of its revenue to churches, but simply abstains from demanding that the church support the state. No one has ever suggested that tax exemption has converted libraries, art galleries, or hospitals into arms of the state or put employees "on the public payroll." There is no genuine nexus between tax exemption and establishment of religion. As Mr. Justice Holmes commented in a related context, "a page of history is worth a volume of logic." The exemption creates only a minimal and remote involvement between church and state, and far less than taxation of churches. It restricts the fiscal relationship between church and state, and tends to complement and reinforce the desired separation insulating each from the other.

Separation in this context cannot mean absence of all contact; the complexities of modern life inevitably produce some contact, and the fire and police protection received by houses of religious worship are no more than incidental benefits accorded all persons or institutions within a State's boundaries, along with many other exempt organizations. [Walz] has not established even an arguable quantitative correlation between the payment of an ad valorem property tax and the receipt of these municipal benefits.

All of the 50 States provide for tax exemption of places of worship, most of them doing so by constitutional guarantees. For so long as federal income taxes have had any potential impact on churches—over 75 years—religious organizations have been expressly exempt from the tax. Such treatment is an "aid" to churches no more and no less in principle than the real estate tax exemption granted by States. Few concepts are more deeply embedded in the fabric of our national life, beginning with pre-Revolutionary colonial times, than for the government to exercise at the very least this kind of benevolent neutrality toward churches and religious exercise generally so long as none was favored over others and none suffered interference.

It is significant that Congress, from its earliest days, has viewed the Religion Clauses of the Constitution as authorizing statutory real estate tax exemption to religious bodies. . . .

It is obviously correct that no one acquires a vested or protected right in violation of the Constitution by long use, even when that span of time covers our entire national existence, and indeed predates it. Yet an unbroken practice of according the exemption to churches, openly and by affirmative state action, not covertly or by state inaction, is not something to be lightly cast aside. . . .

Nothing in this national attitude toward religious tolerance and two centuries of uninterrupted freedom from taxation has given the remotest sign of leading to an established church or religion, and, on the contrary, it has operated affirmatively to help guarantee the free exercise of all forms of religious belief. Thus, it is hardly useful to suggest that tax exemption is but the "foot in the door" or the "nose of the camel in the tent" leading to an established church. If tax exemption can be seen as this first step toward "establishment" of religion, as Mr. Justice Douglas fears, the second step has been long in coming. Any move that realistically "establishes" a church or tends to do so can be dealt with "while this Court sits." . . .

Douglas, dissenting:

. . . Churches perform some functions that a State would constitutionally be empowered to perform. I refer to nonsectarian social welfare operations such as the care of orphaned children and the destitute and people who are sick. A tax exemption to agencies performing those functions would therefore be as constitutionally proper as the grant of direct subsidies to them. Under the First Amendment, a State may not, however, provide worship if private groups fail to do so. . . .

That is a major difference between churches, on the one hand, and the rest of the nonprofit organizations, on the other. Government could provide or finance operas, hospitals, historical societies, and all the rest because they represent social welfare programs within the reach of the police power. In contrast, government may not provide or finance worship because of the Establishment Clause any more than it may single out "atheistic" or "agnostic" centers or groups and create or finance them.

The Brookings Institution, writing in 1933, before the application of the Establishment Clause of the First Amendment to the States, said about tax exemptions of religious groups:

> Tax exemption, no matter what its form, is essentially a government grant or subsidy. Such grants would seem to be justified only if the purpose for which they are made is one for which the legislative body *would be equally willing to make* a direct appropriation from public funds equal to the amount of the exemption. This test would not be met except in the case where the exemption is granted to encourage certain activities of private interests which, if not thus performed, would have to be assumed by the government at an expenditure at least as great as the value of the exemption. (emphasis added.)

Since 1947, when the Establishment Clause was made applicable to the States, that report would have to state that the exemption would be justified only where "the legislative body could make" an appropriation for the cause.

On the record of this case, the church qua nonprofit, charitable organization is intertwined with the church qua church. A church may use the same facilities, resources, and personnel in carrying out both its secular and its sectarian activities. The two are unitary, and, on the present record, have not been separated one from the other. . . .

Whether a particular church seeking an exemption for its welfare work could constitutionally pass muster would depend on the special facts. The assumption is that the church is a purely private institution, promoting a sectarian cause. The creed, teaching, and beliefs of one may be undesirable or even repulsive to others. Its sectarian faith sets it apart from all others, and makes it difficult to equate its constituency with the general public. The extent that its facilities are open to all may only indicate the nature of its proselytism. Yet, though a church covers up its religious symbols in welfare work, its welfare activities may merely be a phase of sectarian activity. I have said enough to indicate the nature of this tax exemption problem.

Direct financial aid to churches or tax exemptions to the church qua church is not, in my view, even arguably permitted. Sectarian causes are certainly not anti-public, and many would rate their own church, or perhaps all churches, as the highest form of welfare. The difficulty is that sectarian causes must remain in the private domain, not subject to public control or subsidy. That seems to me to be the requirement of the Establishment Clause. . . .

If believers are entitled to public financial support, so are nonbelievers. A believer and nonbeliever under the present law are treated differently because of the articles of their faith. Believers are doubtless comforted that the cause of religion is being fostered by this legislation. Yet one of the mandates of the First Amendment is to promote a viable, pluralistic society and to keep government neutral, not only between sects, but also between believers and nonbelievers. The present involvement of government in religion may seem de minimis. But it is, I fear, a long step down the Establishment path. Perhaps I have been misinformed. But as I have read the Constitution and its philosophy, I gathered that independence was the price of liberty.

I conclude that this tax exemption is unconstitutional.

Lemon v. Kurtzman

403 U.S. 602 (1971), 8-0
Opinion of the Court: Burger (Black, Blackmunn, Brennan, Douglas, Harlan, Stewart, White)
Not Participating: Marshall

In this case and its companion, Earley v. DiCenso, *the Court reviewed Pennsylvania and Rhode Island programs to aid church-related schools. The vote in* Earley *was 8-1, with Justice Marshall joining the Opinion of the Court and Justice White dissenting.*

What test has the Court developed here for determining whether there is a violation of the establishment clause? Is this decision consistent with Walz? *(p. 81) Who would gain or lose and what would they gain or lose if sectarian schools were to close for financial reasons? Do parents who pay tuition and send their children to sectarian schools, in effect, subsidize the public schools?*

Burger, for the Court:

These two appeals raise questions as to Pennsylvania and Rhode Island statutes providing state aid to church-related elementary and secondary schools. Both statutes are challenged as violative of the Establishment and Free Exercise Clauses of the First Amendment and the Due Process Clause of the Fourteenth Amendment.

Pennsylvania has adopted a statutory program that provides financial support to nonpublic elementary and secondary schools by way of reimbursement for the cost of teachers' salaries, textbooks, and instructional materials in specified secular subjects. Rhode Island has adopted a statute under which the State pays directly to teachers in nonpublic elementary schools a supplement of 15% of their annual salary. Under each statute, state aid has been given to church-related educational institutions. We hold that both statutes are unconstitutional. . . .

In *Everson v. Board of Education,* this Court upheld a state statute that reimbursed the parents of parochial school children for bus transportation expenses. There, Mr. Justice Black, writing for the majority, suggested that the decision carried to "the verge" of forbidden territory under the Religion Clauses. Candor compels acknowledgment, moreover, that we can only dimly perceive the lines of demarcation in this extraordinarily sensitive area of constitutional law.

The language of the Religion Clauses of the First Amendment is, at best, opaque, particularly when compared with other portions of the Amendment. Its authors did not simply prohibit the establishment of a state church or a state religion, an area history shows they regarded as very important and fraught with great dangers. Instead, they commanded that there should be "no law respecting an establishment of religion." A law may be one "respecting" the forbidden objective while falling short of its total realization. A law "respecting" the proscribed result, that is, the establishment of religion, is not always easily identifiable as one violative of the Clause. A given law might not establish a state religion, but nevertheless be one "respecting" that end in the sense of being a step that could lead to such establishment, and hence offend the First Amendment.

In the absence of precisely stated constitutional prohibitions, we must draw lines with reference to the three main evils against which the Establishment Clause was intended to afford protection: "sponsorship, financial support, and active involvement of the sovereign in religious activity."

Every analysis in this area must begin with consideration of the cumulative criteria developed by the Court over many years. Three such tests may be gleaned from our cases. First, the statute must have a secular legislative purpose; second, its principal or primary effect must be one that neither advances nor inhibits religion, (*Board of Education v. Allen,* 1968) finally, the statute must not foster "an excessive government entanglement with religion."

Inquiry into the legislative purposes of the Pennsylvania and Rhode Island statutes affords no basis for a conclusion that the legislative intent was to advance religion. On the contrary, the statutes themselves clearly state that they are intended to enhance the quality of the secular education in all schools covered by the compulsory attendance laws. There is no reason to believe the legislatures meant anything else. A State always has a legitimate concern for maintaining minimum standards in all schools it allows to operate. As in *Allen,* we find nothing here that undermines the stated legislative intent; it must therefore be accorded appropriate deference.

In *Allen,* the Court acknowledged that secular and religious teachings were not necessarily so intertwined that secular textbooks furnished to students by the State were, in fact, instrumental in the teaching of religion. The legislatures of Rhode Island and Pennsylvania have concluded that secular and religious education are identifiable and separable. In the abstract, we have no quarrel with this conclusion.

The two legislatures, however, have also recognized that church-related elementary and secondary schools have a significant religious mission, and that a substantial portion of their activities is religiously oriented. They have therefore sought to create statutory restrictions designed to guarantee the separation between secular and religious educational functions, and to ensure that State financial aid supports only the former. All these provisions are precautions taken in candid recognition that these programs approached, even

if they did not intrude upon, the forbidden areas under the Religion Clauses. We need not decide whether these legislative precautions restrict the principal or primary effect of the programs to the point where they do not offend the Religion Clauses, for we conclude that the cumulative impact of the entire relationship arising under the statutes in each State involves excessive entanglement between government and religion.

In *Walz v. Tax Commission,* the Court upheld state tax exemptions for real property owned by religious organizations and used for religious worship. That holding, however, tended to confine, rather than enlarge, the area of permissible state involvement with religious institutions by calling for close scrutiny of the degree of entanglement involved in the relationship. The objective is to prevent, as far as possible, the intrusion of either into the precincts of the other. . . .

In order to determine whether the government entanglement with religion is excessive, we must examine the character and purposes of the institutions that are benefited, the nature of the aid that the State provides, and the resulting relationship between the government and the religious authority. Mr. Justice Harlan, in a separate opinion in *Walz,* echoed the classic warning as to "programs, whose very nature is apt to entangle the state in details of administration. . . ." Here we find that both statutes foster an impermissible degree of entanglement.

(a) Rhode Island program

The District Court made extensive findings on the grave potential for excessive entanglement that inheres in the religious character and purpose of the Roman Catholic elementary schools of Rhode Island, to date the sole beneficiaries of the Rhode Island Salary Supplement Act.

The church schools involved in the program are located close to parish churches. This understandably permits convenient access for religious exercises, since instruction in faith and morals is part of the total educational process. The school buildings contain identifying religious symbols such as crosses on the exterior and crucifixes, and religious paintings and statues either in the classrooms or hallways. Although only approximately 30 minutes a day are devoted to direct religious instruction, there are religiously oriented extracurricular activities. Approximately two-thirds of the teachers in these schools are nuns of various religious orders. Their dedicated efforts provide an atmosphere in which religious instruction and religious vocations are natural and proper parts of life in such schools. Indeed, as the District Court found, the role of teaching nuns in enhancing the religious atmosphere has led the parochial school authorities to attempt to maintain a one-to-one ratio between nuns and lay teachers in all schools, rather than to permit some to be staffed almost entirely by lay teachers. . . .

The substantial religious character of these church-related schools gives rise to entangling church-state relationships of the kind the Religion Clauses sought to avoid. Although the District Court found that concern for religious values did not inevitably or necessarily intrude into the content of secular subjects, the considerable religious activities of these schools led the legislature to provide for careful governmental controls and surveillance by state authorities in order to ensure that state aid supports only secular education. . . .

There is another area of entanglement in the Rhode Island program that gives concern. The statute excludes teachers employed by nonpublic schools whose average per-pupil expenditures on secular education equal or exceed the comparable figures for public schools. In the event that the total expenditures of an otherwise eligible school exceed this norm, the program requires the government to examine the school's records in order to determine how much of the total expenditures is attributable to secular education and how much to religious activity. This kind of state inspection and evaluation of the religious content of a religious organization is fraught with the sort of entanglement that the Constitution forbids. It is a relationship pregnant with dangers of excessive government direction of church schools, and hence of churches. The Court noted "the hazards of government supporting churches" in *Walz v. Tax Commission,* and we cannot ignore here the danger that pervasive modern governmental power will ultimately intrude on religion and thus conflict with the Religion Clauses.

(b) Pennsylvania program

The Pennsylvania statute also provides state aid to church-related schools for teachers' salaries. The complaint describes an educational system that is very similar to the one existing in Rhode Island. According to the allegations, the church-related elementary and secondary schools are controlled by religious organizations, have the purpose of propagating and promoting a particular religious faith, and conduct their operations to fulfill that purpose. Since this complaint was dismissed for failure to state a claim for relief, we must accept these allegations as true for purposes of our review.

As we noted earlier, the very restrictions and surveillance necessary to ensure that teachers play a strictly nonideological role give rise to entanglements between church and state. The Pennsylvania statute, like that of Rhode Island, fosters this kind of relationship. Reimbursement is not only limited to courses offered in the public schools and materials approved by state officials, but the statute excludes "any subject matter expressing religious teaching, or the morals or forms of worship of any sect." In addition, schools seeking reimbursement must maintain accounting procedures that require the State to establish the cost of the secular, as distinguished from the religious, instruction.

The Pennsylvania statute, moreover, has the further defect of providing state financial aid directly to the church-related school. This factor distinguishes both *Everson* and *Allen,* for, in both those cases, the Court was careful to point out that state aid was provided to the student and his parents—not to the church-related school. . . .

A broader base of entanglement of yet a different character is presented by the divisive political potential of these state programs. In a community where such a large number of pupils are served by church-related schools, it can be assumed that state assistance will entail considerable political activity. Partisans of parochial schools, understandably concerned with rising costs and sincerely dedicated to both the religious and secular educational missions of their schools, will inevitably champion this cause and promote political action to achieve their goals. Those who oppose state aid, whether for constitutional, religious, or fiscal reasons, will inevitably respond and employ all of the usual political campaign techniques to prevail. Candidates will be forced to declare, and voters to choose. It would be unrealistic to ignore the fact that many people confronted with issues of this kind will find their votes aligned with their faith. . . .

In *Walz,* it was argued that a tax exemption for places of religious worship would prove to be the first step in an inevitable progression leading to the establishment of state churches and state religion. That claim could not stand up against more than 200 years of virtually universal practice imbedded in our colonial experience and continuing into the present.

The progression argument, however, is more persuasive here. We have no long history of state aid to church-related educational institutions comparable to 200 years of tax exemption for churches. Indeed, the state programs before us today represent something of an innovation. We have already noted that modern governmental programs have self-perpetuating and self-expanding propensities. These internal pressures are only enhanced when the schemes involve institutions whose legitimate needs are growing and whose interests have substantial political support. Nor can we fail to see that, in constitutional adjudication, some steps which, when taken, were thought to approach "the verge" have become the platform for yet further steps. A certain momentum develops in constitutional theory, and it can be a "downhill thrust" easily set in motion but difficult to retard or stop. Development by momentum is not invariably bad; indeed, it is the way the common law has grown, but it is a force to be recognized and reckoned with. The dangers are increased by the difficulty of perceiving in advance exactly where the "verge" of the precipice lies. As well as constituting an independent evil against which the Religion Clauses were intended to protect, involvement or entanglement between government and religion serves as a warning signal.

Finally, nothing we have said can be construed to disparage the role of church-related elementary and secondary schools in our national life. Their contribution has been and is enormous. Nor do we ignore their economic plight in a period of rising costs and expanding need. Taxpayers generally have been spared vast sums by the maintenance of these educational institutions by religious organizations, largely by the gifts of faithful adherents.

The merit and benefits of these schools, however, are not the issue before us in these cases. The sole question is whether state aid to these schools can be squared with the dictates of the Religion Clauses. Under our system, the choice has been made that government is to be entirely excluded from the area of religious instruction, and churches excluded from the affairs of government. The Constitution decrees that religion must be a private matter for the individual, the family, and the institutions of private choice,

and that, while some involvement and entanglement are inevitable, lines must be drawn.

Agostini v. Felton

521 U.S. 203 (1997), 5-4
Opinion of the Court: O'Connor (Kennedy, Rehnquist, Scalia, Thomas)
Dissenting: Breyer, Ginsburg, Souter, Stevens

In Aguilar v. Felton, *1985, the Court held a New York City program that sent public school teachers into parochial schools to provide remedial instruction for disadvantaged students under Title I of the Elementary and Secondary Education Act of 1965, to create an "excessive entanglement" of church and state. Enjoined from sending teachers into the schools, the city continued to provide the remedial services to parochial school students but in mobile units, usually parked on the street outside. The expense of this arrangement and the fact that several justices in later cases indicated* Aguilar *should be reconsidered resulted in the filing and eventual appeal of the present case.*

How was the Lemon test used in this case? Does the Court's decision significantly lower the wall of separation between church and state? Does it infringe upon "the rights of dissenters and non-believers," as a critical editorial in the Washington Post *asserted? What is the effect of the Court reversing a decision handed down only a dozen years before?*

O'Connor, for the Court:

. . . In order to evaluate whether *Aguilar v. Felton* has been eroded by our subsequent Establishment Clause cases, it is necessary to understand the rationale upon which *Aguilar,* as well as its companion case, *School Dist. of Grand Rapids v. Ball,* rested.

In *Ball,* the Court evaluated two programs implemented by the School District of Grand Rapids, Michigan. The district's Shared Time program, the one most analogous to Title I, provided remedial and "enrichment" classes, at public expense, to students attending nonpublic schools. The classes were taught during regular school hours by publicly employed teachers, using materials purchased with public funds, on the premises of nonpublic schools. The Shared Time courses were in subjects designed to supplement the "core curriculum" of the nonpublic schools. Of the 41 nonpublic schools eligible for the program, 40 were "'pervasively sectarian'" in character—that is, "the purpos[e] of [those] schools [was] to advance their particular religions." . . .

. . . Distilled to essentials, the Court's conclusion that the Shared Time program in *Ball* had the impermissible effect of advancing religion rested on three assumptions: (i) any public employee who works on the premises of a religious school is presumed to inculcate religion in her work; (ii) the presence of public employees on private school premises creates a symbolic union between church and state; and (iii) any and all public aid that directly aids the educational function of religious schools impermissibly finances religious indoctrination, even if the aid reaches such schools as a consequence of private decisionmaking. Additionally, in *Aguilar* there was a fourth assumption: that New York City's Title I program necessitated an excessive government entanglement with religion because public employees who teach on the premises of religious schools must be closely monitored to ensure that they do not inculcate religion.

Our more recent cases have undermined the assumptions upon which *Ball* and *Aguilar* relied. To be sure, the general principles we use to evaluate whether government aid violates the Establishment Clause have not changed since *Aguilar* was decided. . . .

As we have repeatedly recognized, government inculcation of religious beliefs has the impermissible effect of advancing religion. Our cases subsequent to *Aguilar* have, however, modified in two significant respects the approach we use to assess indoctrination.

. . . First, we have abandoned the presumption erected in *Meek* [v. *Pittenger*] and *Ball* that the placement of public employees on parochial school grounds inevitably results in the impermissible effect of state sponsored indoctrination or constitutes a symbolic union between government and religion. In *Zobrest v. Catalina Foothills School Dist.* we examined whether the IDEA [Individuals with Disabilities Education Act] was constitutional as applied to a deaf student who sought to bring his state employed sign language interpreter with him to his Roman Catholic high school. We held that this was permissible, expressly disavowing the notion that "the Establishment Clause [laid] down [an] absolute bar to the placing of a public employee in a sectarian school. . . . Such a flat rule, smacking of antiquated notions of 'taint,' would indeed exalt form over substance." Ibid. We refused to presume that a publicly employed interpreter would be pressured by the pervasively sectarian surroundings to inculcate religion by "add[ing] to

[or] subtract[ing] from" the lectures translated. Ibid. In the absence of evidence to the contrary, we assumed instead that the interpreter would dutifully discharge her responsibilities as a full time public employee and comply with the ethical guidelines of her profession by accurately translating what was said. Because the only government aid in *Zobrest* was the interpreter, who was herself not inculcating any religious messages, no government indoctrination took place and we were able to conclude that "the provision of such assistance [was] not barred by the Establishment Clause." *Zobrest* therefore expressly rejected the notion—relied on in *Ball* and *Aguilar*—that, solely because of her presence on private school property, a public employee will be presumed to inculcate religion in the students. *Zobrest* also implicitly repudiated another assumption on which *Ball* and *Aguilar* turned: that the presence of a public employee on private school property creates an impermissible "symbolic link" between government and religion. . . .

Second, we have departed from the rule relied on in *Ball* that all government aid that directly aids the educational function of religious schools is invalid. In *Witters v. Washington Dept. of Servs. for Blind* we held that the Establishment Clause did not bar a State from issuing a vocational tuition grant to a blind person who wished to use the grant to attend a Christian college and become a pastor, missionary, or youth director. Even though the grant recipient clearly would use the money to obtain religious education, we observed that the tuition grants were "'made available generally without regard to the sectarian nonsectarian, or public nonpublic nature of the institution benefited.'" The grants were disbursed directly to students, who then used the money to pay for tuition at the educational institution of their choice. In our view, this transaction was no different from a State's issuing a paycheck to one of its employees, knowing that the employee would donate part or all of the check to a religious institution. In both situations, any money that ultimately went to religious institutions did so "only as a result of the genuinely independent and private choices of" individuals. . . .

Zobrest and *Witters* make clear that, under current law, the Shared Time program in *Ball* and New York City's Title I program in *Aguilar* will not, as a matter of law, be deemed to have the effect of advancing religion through indoctrination. Indeed, each of the premises upon which we relied in *Ball* to reach a contrary conclusion is no longer valid. First, there is no reason to presume that, simply because she enters a parochial school classroom, a full time public employee such as a Title I teacher will depart from her assigned duties and instructions and embark on religious indoctrination, any more than there was a reason in *Zobrest* to think an interpreter would inculcate religion by altering her translation of classroom lectures. Certainly, no evidence has ever shown that any New York City Title I instructor teaching on parochial school premises attempted to inculcate religion in students. . . .

. . . *Zobrest* also repudiates *Ball's* assumption that the presence of Title I teachers in parochial school classrooms will, without more, create the impression of a "symbolic union" between church and state. . . .

What is most fatal to the argument that New York City's Title I program directly subsidizes religion is that it applies with equal force when those services are provided off campus, and *Aguilar* implied that providing the services off campus is entirely consistent with the Establishment Clause. Justice Souter resists the impulse to upset this implication, contending that it can be justified on the ground that Title I services are "less likely to supplant some of what would otherwise go on inside [the sectarian schools] and to subsidize what remains" when those services are offered off campus. But Justice Souter does not explain why a sectarian school would not have the same incentive to "make patently significant cut backs" in its curriculum no matter where Title I services are offered, since the school would ostensibly be excused from having to provide the Title I type services itself. Because the incentive is the same either way, we find no logical basis upon which to conclude that Title I services are an impermissible subsidy of religion when offered on campus, but not when offered off campus. Accordingly, contrary to our conclusion in *Aguilar*, placing full time employees on parochial school campuses does not as a matter of law have the impermissible effect of advancing religion through indoctrination. . . .

We turn now to *Aguilar's* conclusion that New York City's Title I program resulted in an excessive entanglement between church and state. Whether a government aid program results in such an entanglement has consistently been an aspect of our Establishment Clause analysis. . . .

Not all entanglements, of course, have the effect of advancing or inhibiting religion. Interaction between church and state is inevitable, and we have always tolerated some level of involvement between the two.

Entanglement must be "excessive" before it runs afoul of the Establishment Clause. . . .

To summarize, New York City's Title I program does not run afoul of any of three primary criteria we currently use to evaluate whether government aid has the effect of advancing religion: it does not result in governmental indoctrination; define its recipients by reference to religion; or create an excessive entanglement. We therefore hold that a federally funded program providing supplemental, remedial instruction to disadvantaged children on a neutral basis is not invalid under the Establishment Clause when such instruction is given on the premises of sectarian schools by government employees pursuant to a program containing safeguards such as those present here. The same considerations that justify this holding require us to conclude that this carefully constrained program also cannot reasonably be viewed as an endorsement of religion. . . . Accordingly, we must acknowledge that *Aguilar*, as well as the portion of *Ball* addressing Grand Rapids' Shared Time program, are no longer good law. . . .

Souter, dissenting:

. . . I believe *Aguilar* was a correct and sensible decision, and my only reservation about its opinion is that the emphasis on the excessive entanglement produced by monitoring religious instructional content obscured those facts that independently called for the application of two central tenets of Establishment Clause jurisprudence. The State is forbidden to subsidize religion directly and is just as surely forbidden to act in any way that could reasonably be viewed as religious endorsement. . . .

. . . [T]he flat ban on subsidization antedates the Bill of Rights and has been an unwavering rule in Establishment Clause cases, qualified only by the conclusion two Terms ago that state exactions from college students are not the sort of public revenues subject to the ban. The rule expresses the hard lesson learned over and over again in the American past and in the experiences of the countries from which we have come, that religions supported by governments are compromised just as surely as the religious freedom of dissenters is burdened when the government supports religion. "When the government favors a particular religion or sect, the disadvantage to all others is obvious, but even the favored religion may fear being 'taint[ed] . . . with corrosive secularism.' The favored religion may be compromised as political figures reshape the religion's beliefs for their own purposes; it may be reformed as government largesse brings government regulation." *Lee v. Weisman.* The ban against state endorsement of religion addresses the same historical lessons. Governmental approval of religion tends to reinforce the religious message (at least in the short run) and . . . carry a message of exclusion to those of less favored views. The human tendency, of course, is to forget the hard lessons, and to overlook the history of governmental partnership with religion when a cause is worthy, and bureaucrats have programs. That tendency to forget is the reason for having the Establishment Clause (along with the Constitution's other structural and libertarian guarantees), in the hope of stopping the corrosion before it starts.

These principles were violated by the programs at issue in *Aguilar* and *Ball,* as a consequence of several significant features common to both Title I, as implemented in New York City before *Aguilar,* and the Grand Rapids Shared Time program: each provided classes on the premises of the religious schools, covering a wide range of subjects including some at the core of primary and secondary education, like reading and mathematics; while their services were termed "supplemental," the programs and their instructors necessarily assumed responsibility for teaching subjects that the religious schools would otherwise have been obligated to provide, the public employees carrying out the programs had broad responsibilities involving the exercise of considerable discretion, while the programs offered aid to nonpublic school students generally (and Title I went to public school students as well), participation by religious school students in each program was extensive and, finally, aid under Title I and Shared Time flowed directly to the schools in the form of classes and programs, as distinct from indirect aid that reaches schools only as a result of independent private choice. . . .

What, therefore, was significant in *Aguilar* and *Ball* about the placement of state paid teachers into the physical and social settings of the religious schools was not only the consequent temptation of some of those teachers to reflect the schools' religious missions in the rhetoric of their instruction, with a resulting need for monitoring and the certainty of entanglement. What was so remarkable was that the schemes in issue assumed a teaching responsibility indistinguishable from the responsibility of the schools themselves. The obligation of primary and secondary schools to teach reading necessarily extends to teaching those who are

having a hard time at it, and the same is true of math. Calling some classes remedial does not distinguish their subjects from the schools' basic subjects, however inadequately the schools may have been addressing them.

What was true of the Title I scheme as struck down in *Aguilar* will be just as true when New York reverts to the old practices with the Court's approval after today. There is simply no line that can be drawn between the instruction paid for at taxpayers' expense and the instruction in any subject that is not identified as formally religious. While it would be an obvious sham, say, to channel cash to religious schools to be credited only against the expense of "secular" instruction, the line between "supplemental" and general education is likewise impossible to draw. If a State may constitutionally enter the schools to teach in the manner in question, it must in constitutional principle be free to assume, or assume payment for, the entire cost of instruction provided in any ostensibly secular subject in any religious school. . . .

It may be objected that there is some subsidy in remedial education even when it takes place off the religious premises, some subsidy, that is, even in the way New York City has administered the Title I program after *Aguilar.* In these circumstances, too, what the State does, the religious school need not do; the schools save money and the program makes it easier for them to survive and concentrate their resources on their religious objectives. . . . [B]ut if [this argument] is not thought strong enough to bar even off premises aid in teaching the basics to religious school pupils (an issue not before the Court in *Aguilar* or today), it does nothing to undermine the sense of drawing a line between remedial teaching on and off premises. The off premises teaching is arguably less likely to open the door to relieving religious schools of their responsibilities for secular subjects simply because these schools are less likely (and presumably legally unable) to dispense with those subjects from their curriculums or to make patently significant cut backs in basic teaching within the schools to offset the outside instruction; if the aid is delivered outside of the schools, it is less likely to supplant some of what would otherwise go on inside them and to subsidize what remains. . . . [T]he difference in the degree of reasonably perceptible endorsement is substantial. Sharing the teaching responsibilities within a school having religious objectives is far more likely to telegraph approval of the school's mission than keeping the State's distance would do.... When, moreover, the aid goes overwhelmingly to one religious denomination, minimal contact between state and church is the less likely to feed the resentment of other religions that would like access to public money for their own worthy projects.

In sum, if a line is to be drawn short of barring all state aid to religious schools for teaching standard subjects, the *Aguilar-Ball* line was a sensible one capable of principled adherence. It is no less sound, and no less necessary, today....

Finally, instead of aid that comes to the religious school indirectly in the sense that its distribution results from private decisionmaking, a public educational agency distributes Title I aid in the form of programs and services directly to the religious schools. In *Zobrest* and *Witters*, it was fair to say that individual students were themselves applicants for individual benefits on a scale that could not amount to a systemic supplement. But under Title I, a local educational agency... may receive federal funding by proposing programs approved to serve individual students who meet the criteria of need, which it then uses to provide such programs at the religious schools, students eligible for such programs may not apply directly for Title I funds. The aid, accordingly, is not even formally aid to the individual students (and even formally individual aid must be seen as aid to a school system when so many individuals receive it that it becomes a significant feature of the system).

In sum, nothing since *Ball* and *Aguilar* and before this case has eroded the distinction between "direct and substantial" and "indirect and incidental." That principled line is being breached only here and now.

The Court notes that aid programs providing benefits solely to religious groups may be constitutionally suspect, while aid allocated under neutral, secular criteria is less likely to have the effect of advancing religion. The opinion then says that *Ball* and *Aguilar* "gave this consideration no weight," ibid., and accordingly conflict with a number of decisions. But what exactly the Court thinks *Ball* and *Aguilar* inadequately considered is not clear, given that evenhandedness is a necessary but not a sufficient condition for an aid program to satisfy constitutional scrutiny. Title I services are available to all eligible children regardless whether they go to religious or public schools, but... that fact does not define the reach of the Establishment Clause. If a scheme of government aid results in support for religion in some substantial degree, or in endorsement of its value, the formal neutrality of the scheme does

not render the Establishment Clause helpless or the holdings in *Aguilar* and *Ball* inapposite....

.... [T]he object of Title I is worthy without doubt, and the cost of compliance is high. In the short run there is much that is genuinely unfortunate about the administration of the scheme under *Aguilar's* rule. But constitutional lines have to be drawn, and on one side of every one of them is an otherwise sympathetic case that provokes impatience with the Constitution and with the line. But constitutional lines are the price of constitutional government.

Zelman v. Simmons-Harris

U.S. 536 (2002), 5-4
Opinion of the Court: Rehnquist (Kennedy, O'Connor, Scalia, Thomas)
Dissenting: Breyer, Ginsburg, Souter, Stevens

Does the Court's decision depart from its earlier line of cases on public aid or is it consistent with them? Has the Court now given more weight to "purpose" and less to "effect" in its establishment clause analysis or has it read "effect" out of the analysis altogether? To what extent does this decision support or not support extending public aid to other religious programs that do valuable work such as charity, social services, and the operation of hospitals? The poor performance of many inner-city schools is one of the most intractable problems in American community life. Is that enough to justify some lowering of the wall of separation to allow experimenting with a new solution? This case has enormous distributive consequences. Who gains and loses what?

Rehnquist, for the Court:

The State of Ohio has established a pilot program designed to provide educational choices to families with children who reside in the Cleveland City School District. The question presented is whether this program offends the Establishment Clause of the United States Constitution. We hold that it does not.

There are more than 75,000 children enrolled in the Cleveland City School District. The majority of these children are from low-income and minority families. Few of these families enjoy the means to send their children to any school other than an inner-city public school. For more than a generation, however, Cleveland's public schools have been among the worst performing public schools in the Nation. In 1995, a Federal District Court declared a "crisis of magnitude" and placed the entire Cleveland school district under state control. Shortly thereafter, the state auditor found that Cleveland's public schools were in the midst of a "crisis that is perhaps unprecedented in the history of American education." The district had failed to meet any of the 18 state standards for minimal acceptable performance. . . .

It is against this backdrop that Ohio enacted, among other initiatives, its Pilot Project Scholarship Program. The program provides financial assistance to families in any Ohio school district that is or has been "under federal court order requiring supervision and operational management of the district by the state superintendent." Cleveland is the only Ohio school district to fall within that category.

The program provides two basic kinds of assistance to parents of children in a covered district: . . . tuition aid for students in kindergarten through third grade, expanding each year through eighth grade, to attend a participating public or private school of their parent's choosing, and . . . tutorial aid for students who choose to remain enrolled in public school.

The tuition aid portion of the program is designed to provide educational choices to parents who reside in a covered district. Any private school, whether religious or nonreligious, may participate in the program and accept program students so long as the school is located within the boundaries of a covered district and meets statewide educational standards. . . . Any public school located in a school district adjacent to the covered district may also participate in the program. Adjacent public schools are eligible to receive a $2,250 tuition grant for each program student accepted in addition to the full amount of per-pupil state funding attributable to each additional student. . . .

Tuition aid is distributed to parents according to financial need. . . . Where tuition aid is spent depends solely upon where parents who receive tuition aid choose to enroll their child. . . .

The tutorial aid portion of the program provides tutorial assistance through grants to any student in a covered district who chooses to remain in public school. Parents arrange for registered tutors to provide assistance to their children and then submit bills for those services to the State for payment. . . .

The program has been in operation within the Cleveland City School District since the 1996–1997 school year. In the 1999–2000 school year, 56 private schools participated in the program, 46 (or 82%) of which had a religious affiliation. None of the public

schools in districts adjacent to Cleveland have elected to participate. More than 3,700 students participated in the scholarship program, most of whom (96%) enrolled in religiously affiliated schools. Sixty percent of these students were from families at or below the poverty line. In the 1998–1999 school year, approximately 1,400 Cleveland public school students received tutorial aid . . . .

The Establishment Clause of the First Amendment, applied to the States through the Fourteenth Amendment, prevents a State from enacting laws that have the "purpose" or "effect" of advancing or inhibiting religion. . . . There is no dispute that the program challenged here was enacted for the valid secular purpose of providing educational assistance to poor children in a demonstrably failing public school system. Thus, the question presented is whether the Ohio program nonetheless has the forbidden "effect" of advancing or inhibiting religion.

To answer that question, our decisions have drawn a consistent distinction between government programs that provide aid directly to religious schools, and programs of true private choice, in which government aid reaches religious schools only as a result of the genuine and independent choices of private individuals. While our jurisprudence with respect to the constitutionality of direct aid programs has "changed significantly" over the past two decades, our jurisprudence with respect to true private choice programs has remained consistent and unbroken. Three times we have confronted Establishment Clause challenges to neutral government programs that provide aid directly to a broad class of individuals, who, in turn, direct the aid to religious schools or institutions of their own choosing. Three times we have rejected such challenges.

In *Mueller v. Allen,* we rejected an Establishment Clause challenge to a Minnesota program authorizing tax deductions for various educational expenses, including private school tuition costs, even though the great majority of the program's beneficiaries (96%) were parents of children in religious schools. . . . We thus found it irrelevant to the constitutional inquiry that the vast majority of beneficiaries were parents of children in religious schools. . . .

In *Witters v. Washington Department of Services for the Blind,* we used identical reasoning to reject an Establishment Clause challenge to a vocational scholarship program that provided tuition aid to a student studying at a religious institution to become a pastor. . . . Our holding thus rested not on whether few or many recipients chose to expend government aid at a religious school but, rather, on whether recipients generally were empowered to direct the aid to schools or institutions of their own choosing.

Finally, in *Zobrest v. Catalina Foothills School District,* we applied *Mueller* and *Witters* to reject an Establishment Clause challenge to a federal program that permitted sign-language interpreters to assist deaf children enrolled in religious schools. Reviewing our earlier decisions, we stated that "government programs that neutrally provide benefits to a broad class of citizens defined without reference to religion are not readily subject to an Establishment Clause challenge." Looking once again to the challenged program as a whole, we observed that the program "distributes benefits neutrally to any child qualifying as 'disabled.'" Its "primary beneficiaries," we said, were "disabled children, not sectarian schools." . . .

Mueller, Witters, and *Zobrest* thus make clear that where a government aid program is neutral with respect to religion, and provides assistance directly to a broad class of citizens who, in turn, direct government aid to religious schools wholly as a result of their own genuine and independent private choice, the program is not readily subject to challenge under the Establishment Clause. A program that shares these features permits government aid to reach religious institutions only by way of the deliberate choices of numerous individual recipients. The incidental advancement of a religious mission, or the perceived endorsement of a religious message, is reasonably attributable to the individual recipient, not to the government, whose role ends with the disbursement of benefits. . . .

We believe that the program challenged here is a program of true private choice, consistent with *Mueller, Witters,* and *Zobrest,* and thus constitutional. As was true in those cases, the Ohio program is neutral in all respects toward religion. It is part of a general and multifaceted undertaking by the State of Ohio to provide educational opportunities to the children of a failed school district. It confers educational assistance directly to a broad class of individuals defined without reference to religion, *i.e.,* any parent of a school-age child who resides in the Cleveland City School District. The program permits the participation of *all* schools within the district, religious or nonreligious. Adjacent public schools also may participate and have a financial incentive to do so. Program ben-

efits are available to participating families on neutral terms, with no reference to religion. The only preference stated anywhere in the program is a preference for low-income families, who receive greater assistance and are given priority for admission at participating schools. . . .

Respondents suggest that even without a financial incentive for parents to choose a religious school, the program creates a "public perception that the State is endorsing religious practices and beliefs." But we have repeatedly recognized that no reasonable observer would think a neutral program of private choice, where state aid reaches religious schools solely as a result of the numerous independent decisions of private individuals, carries with it the *imprimatur* of government endorsement. The argument is particularly misplaced here since "the reasonable observer in the endorsement inquiry must be deemed aware" of the "history and context" underlying a challenged program. Any objective observer familiar with the full history and context of the Ohio program would reasonably view it as one aspect of a broader undertaking to assist poor children in failed schools, not as an endorsement of religious schooling in general.

There also is no evidence that the program fails to provide genuine opportunities for Cleveland parents to select secular educational options for their school-age children. Cleveland schoolchildren enjoy a range of educational choices: They may remain in public school as before, remain in public school with publicly funded tutoring aid, obtain a scholarship and choose a religious school, obtain a scholarship and choose a nonreligious private school, enroll in a community school, or enroll in a magnet school. That 46 of the 56 private schools now participating in the program are religious schools does not condemn it as a violation of the Establishment Clause. The Establishment Clause question is whether Ohio is coercing parents into sending their children to religious schools, and that question must be answered by evaluating *all* options Ohio provides Cleveland schoolchildren, only one of which is to obtain a program scholarship and then choose a religious school . . . .

Respondents finally claim that we should look to *Committee for Public Ed. & Religious Liberty v. Nyquist,* to decide these cases. We disagree for two reasons. First, the program in *Nyquist* was quite different from the program challenged here. *Nyquist* involved a New York program that gave a package of benefits exclusively to private schools and the parents of private school enrollees. Although the program was enacted for ostensibly secular purposes, we found that its "function" was "*unmistakably* to provide desired financial support for nonpublic, sectarian institutions." Its genesis, we said, was that private religious schools faced "increasingly grave fiscal problems." The program thus provided direct money grants to religious schools. It provided tax benefits "unrelated to the amount of money actually expended by any parent on tuition," ensuring a windfall to parents of children in religious schools. It similarly provided tuition reimbursements designed explicitly to "offe[r] ... an incentive to parents to send their children to sectarian schools." Indeed, the program flatly prohibited the participation of any public school, or parent of any public school enrollee. Ohio's program shares none of these features.

Second, were there any doubt that the program challenged in *Nyquist* is far removed from the program challenged here, we expressly reserved judgment with respect to "a case involving some form of public assistance (*e.g.*, scholarships) made available generally without regard to the sectarian-nonsectarian, or public-nonpublic nature of the institution benefited." That, of course, is the very question now before us, and it has since been answered, first in *Mueller*, then in *Witters*, and again in *Zobrest*, To the extent the scope of *Nyquist* has remained an open question in light of these later decisions, we now hold that *Nyquist* does not govern neutral educational assistance programs that, like the program here, offer aid directly to a broad class of individual recipients defined without regard to religion.

In sum, the Ohio program is entirely neutral with respect to religion. It provides benefits directly to a wide spectrum of individuals, defined only by financial need and residence in a particular school district. It permits such individuals to exercise genuine choice among options public and private, secular and religious. The program is therefore a program of true private choice. In keeping with an unbroken line of decisions rejecting challenges to similar programs, we hold that the program does not offend the Establishment Clause. . . .

O'Connor, concurring:

. . . I write separately for two reasons. First, although the Court takes an important step, I do not believe that today's decision, when considered in light of other longstanding government programs that impact religious organizations and our prior Establishment Clause jurisprudence, marks a dramatic break from the past. Second, given the emphasis the Court places on verifying that parents of voucher students in religious schools have exercised "true private choice," I think it is worth elaborating on the Court's conclusion that this inquiry should consider all reasonable educational alternatives to religious schools that are available to parents. To do otherwise is to ignore how the educational system in Cleveland actually functions. . . .

. . . Even if one assumes that all voucher students came from low-income families and that each voucher student used up the entire $2,250 voucher, at most $8.2 million of public funds flowed to religious schools under the voucher program in 1999–2000. . . .

Although $8.2 million is no small sum, it pales in comparison to the amount of funds that federal, state, and local governments already provide religious institutions. Religious organizations may qualify for exemptions from the federal corporate income tax, the corporate income tax in many States, and property taxes in all 50 States, and clergy qualify for a federal tax break on income used for housing expenses. In addition, the Federal Government provides individuals, corporations, trusts, and estates a tax deduction for charitable contributions to qualified religious groups. Finally, the Federal Government and certain state governments provide tax credits for educational expenses, many of which are spent on education at religious schools. . . .

Thomas, concurring:

. . . Despite this Court's observation nearly 50 years ago in *Brown v. Board of Education,* that "it is doubtful that any child may reasonably be expected to succeed in life if he is denied the opportunity of an education," urban children have been forced into a system that continually fails them. . . . Besieged by escalating financial problems and declining academic achievement, the Cleveland City School District was in the midst of an academic emergency when Ohio enacted its scholarship program.

The dissents and respondents wish to invoke the Establishment Clause . . . to constrain a State's neutral efforts to provide greater educational opportunity for underprivileged minority students. Today's decision properly upholds the program as constitutional, and I join it in full. . . .

Although one of the purposes of public schools was to promote democracy and a more egalitarian culture, failing urban public schools disproportionately affect minority children most in need of educational opportunity. At the time of Reconstruction, blacks considered public education "a matter of personal liberation and a necessary function of a free society." Today, however, the promise of public school education has failed poor inner-city blacks. While in theory providing education to everyone, the quality of public schools varies significantly across districts. Just as blacks supported public education during Reconstruction, many blacks and other minorities now support school choice programs because they provide the greatest educational opportunities for their children in struggling communities. Opponents of the program raise formalistic concerns about the Establishment Clause but ignore the core purposes of the Fourteenth Amendment.

While the romanticized ideal of universal public education resonates with the cognoscenti who oppose vouchers, poor urban families just want the best education for their children, who will certainly need it to function in our high-tech and advanced society. . . .

Justice Breyer, dissenting:

. . . I believe that the Establishment Clause concern for protecting the Nation's social fabric from religious conflict poses an overriding obstacle to the implementation of this well-intentioned school voucher program. And by explaining the nature of the concern, I hope to demonstrate why, in my view, "parental choice" cannot significantly alleviate the constitutional problem. . . .

In a society as religiously diverse as ours, the Court has recognized that we must rely on the Religion Clauses of the First Amendment to protect against religious strife, particularly when what is at issue is an area as central to religious belief as the shaping, through primary education, of the next generation's minds and spirits. . . .

. . . In a society composed of many different religious creeds, I fear that this present departure from the Court's earlier understanding risks creating a form of religiously based conflict potentially harmful to the Nation's social fabric. Because I believe the Establishment Clause was written in part to avoid this kind of conflict, and for reasons set forth by Justice Souter and Justice Stevens, I respectfully dissent.

Souter, dissenting:

The Court's majority holds that the Establishment Clause is no bar to Ohio's payment of tuition at private religious elementary and middle schools under a scheme that systematically provides tax money to support the schools' religious missions. The occasion for the legislation thus upheld is the condition of public education in the city of Cleveland. The record indicates that the schools are failing to serve their objective, and the vouchers in issue here are said to be needed to provide adequate alternatives to them. If there were an excuse for giving short shrift to the Establishment Clause, it would probably apply here. But there is no excuse. Constitutional limitations are placed on government to preserve constitutional values in hard cases, like these. "[C]onstitutional lines have to be drawn, and on one side of every one of them is an otherwise sympathetic case that provokes impatience with the Constitution and with the line. But constitutional lines are the price of constitutional government." *Agostini v. Felton* . . . .

. . . In the city of Cleveland the overwhelming proportion of large appropriations for voucher money must be spent on religious schools if it is to be spent at all, and will be spent in amounts that cover almost all of tuition. The money will thus pay for eligible students' instruction not only in secular subjects but in religion as well, in schools that can fairly be characterized as founded to teach religious doctrine and to imbue teaching in all subjects with a religious dimension. . . .

Consider first the criterion of neutrality. As recently as two Terms ago, a majority of the Court recognized that neutrality conceived of as evenhandedness toward aid recipients had never been treated as alone sufficient to satisfy the Establishment Clause. But at least in its limited significance, formal neutrality seemed to serve some purpose. Today, however, the majority employs the neutrality criterion in a way that renders it impossible to understand.

Neutrality in this sense refers, of course, to evenhandedness in setting eligibility as between potential religious and secular recipients of public money. Thus, for example, the aid scheme in *Witters* provided an eligible recipient with a scholarship to be used at any institution within a practically unlimited universe of schools; it did not tend to provide more or less aid depending on which one the scholarship recipient chose, and there was no indication that the maximum scholarship amount would be insufficient at secular schools. Neither did any condition of Zobrest's interpreter's subsidy favor religious education.

In order to apply the neutrality test, then, it makes sense to focus on a category of aid that may be directed to religious as well as secular schools, and ask whether the scheme favors a religious direction. Here, one would ask whether the voucher provisions, allowing for as much as $2,250 toward private school tuition (or a grant to a public school in an adjacent district), were written in a way that skewed the scheme toward benefiting religious schools.

This, however, is not what the majority asks. The majority looks not to the provisions for tuition vouchers, but to every provision for educational opportunity: "The program permits the participation of *all* schools within the district, [as well as public schools in adjacent districts], religious or nonreligious." The majority then finds confirmation that "participation of *all* schools" satisfies neutrality by noting that the better part of total state educational expenditure goes to public schools, thus showing there is no favor of religion.

The illogic is patent. If regular, public schools (which can get no voucher payments) "participate" in a voucher scheme with schools that can, and public expenditure is still predominantly on public schools, then the majority's reasoning would find neutrality in a scheme of vouchers available for private tuition in districts with no secular private schools at all. "Neutrality" as the majority employs the term is, literally, verbal and nothing more. . . .

The majority addresses the issue of choice the same way it addresses neutrality, by asking whether recipients or potential recipients of voucher aid have a choice of public schools among secular alternatives to religious schools. Again, however, the majority asks the wrong question and misapplies the criterion. The majority has confused choice in spending scholarships with choice from the entire menu of possible educational placements, most of them open to anyone willing to attend a public school. . . . The majority now has transformed this question about private choice in channeling aid into a question about selecting from examples of state spending (on education) including direct spending on magnet and community public schools that goes through no private hands and could never reach a religious school under any circumstance. When the choice test is transformed from where to spend the money to where to go to school, it is cut loose from its very purpose. . . .

Justice Stevens, dissenting:

Is a law that authorizes the use of public funds to pay for the indoctrination of thousands of grammar school children in particular religious faiths a "law respecting an establishment of religion" within the meaning of the First Amendment? In answering that question, I think we should ignore three factual matters that are discussed at length by my colleagues.

First, the severe educational crisis that confronted the Cleveland City School District when Ohio enacted its voucher program is not a matter that should affect our appraisal of its constitutionality. In the 1999–2000 school year, that program provided relief to less than five percent of the students enrolled in the district's schools. The solution to the disastrous conditions that prevented over 90 percent of the student body from meeting basic proficiency standards obviously required massive improvements unrelated to the voucher program. Of course, the emergency may have given some families a powerful motivation to leave the public school system and accept religious indoctrination that they would otherwise have avoided, but that is not a valid reason for upholding the program.

Second, the wide range of choices that have been made available to students *within the public school system* has no bearing on the question whether the State may pay the tuition for students who wish to reject public education entirely and attend private schools that will provide them with a sectarian education. The fact that the vast majority of the voucher recipients who have entirely rejected public education receive religious indoctrination at state expense does, however, support the claim that the law is one "respecting an establishment of religion." The State may choose to divide up its public schools into a dozen different options and label them magnet schools, community schools, or whatever else it decides to call them, but the State is still required to provide a public education and it is the State's decision to fund private school education over and above its traditional obligation that is at issue in these cases.

Third, the voluntary character of the private choice to prefer a parochial education over an education in the public school system seems to me quite irrelevant to the question whether the government's choice to pay for religious indoctrination is constitutionally permissible. Today, however, the Court seems to have decided that the mere fact that a family that cannot afford a private education wants its children educated in a parochial school is a sufficient justification for this use of public funds. . . .

Edwards v. Aguillard

482 U.S. 578 (1987), 7-2
Opinion of the Court: Brennan (Blackmun, Marshall, O'Connor, Powell, Stevens, White)
Dissenting: Scalia, Rehnquist

How does the Court determine that the curricular content at issue in this case is religious? Has the Court been able to avoid deciding that creation science is not good science? Is Justice Scalia's criticism valid? How has the Lemon test been applied? Should legislative motivation, the examination of which the Court has forsworn in many previous cases, be assessed to determine a law's constitutionality? How can it be known for certain?

Brennan, for the Court:
The question for decision is whether Louisiana's "Balanced Treatment for Creation-Science and Evolution-Science in Public School Instruction" Act (Creationism Act), is facially invalid as violative of the Establishment Clause of the First Amendment.

The Creationism Act forbids the teaching of the theory of evolution in public schools unless accompanied by instruction in "creation science." No school is required to teach evolution or creation science. If either is taught, however, the other must also be taught. Ibid. The theories of evolution and creation science are statutorily defined as "the scientific evidences for [creation or evolution] and inferences from those scientific evidences."

Appellees, who include parents of children attending Louisiana public schools, Louisiana teachers, and religious leaders, challenged the constitutionality of the Act in District Court, seeking an injunction and declaratory relief. Appellants, Louisiana officials charged with implementing the Act, defended on the ground that the purpose of the Act is to protect a legitimate secular interest, namely, academic freedom.

The Establishment Clause forbids the enactment of any law "respecting an establishment of religion." The Court has applied a three-pronged test to determine whether legislation comports with the Establishment Clause. First, the legislature must have adopted the law

with a secular purpose. Second, the statute's principal or primary effect must be one that neither advances nor inhibits religion. Third, the statute must not result in an excessive entanglement of government with religion. *Lemon v. Kurtzman* State action violates the Establishment Clause if it fails to satisfy any of these prongs. . . .

[I]n employing the three-pronged Lemon test, we must do so mindful of the particular concerns that arise in the context of public elementary and secondary schools. We now turn to the evaluation of the Act under the Lemon test.

Lemon's first prong focuses on the purpose that animated adoption of the Act. . . . A governmental intention to promote religion is clear when the State enacts a law to serve a religious purpose. . . . In this case, appellants have identified no clear secular purpose for the Louisiana Act.

True, the Act's stated purpose is to protect academic freedom. This phrase might, in common parlance, be understood as referring to enhancing the freedom of teachers to teach what they will. The Court of Appeals, however, correctly concluded that the Act was not designed to further that goal. We find no merit in the State's argument that the legislature may not [have] use[d] the terms "academic freedom" in the correct legal sense. They might have [had] in mind, instead, a basic concept of fairness; teaching all of the evidence.

Even if "academic freedom" is read to mean "teaching all of the evidence" with respect to the origin of human beings, the Act does not further this purpose. The goal of providing a more comprehensive science curriculum is not furthered either by outlawing the teaching of evolution or by requiring teaching of creation science.

While the Court is normally deferential to a State's articulation of a secular purpose, it is required that the statement of such purpose be sincere, and not a sham. . . .

It is clear from the legislative history that the purpose of the legislative sponsor, Senator Bill Keith, was to narrow the science curriculum. During the legislative hearings, Senator Keith stated: "My preference would be that neither [creationism nor evolution] be taught." Such a ban on teaching does not promote— indeed, it undermines—the provision of a comprehensive scientific education.

It is equally clear that requiring schools to teach creation science with evolution does not advance academic freedom. The Act does not grant teachers a flexibility that they did not already possess to supplant the present science curriculum with the presentation of theories, besides evolution, about the origin of life. Indeed, the Court of Appeals found that no law prohibited Louisiana public school teachers from teaching any scientific theory. . . .

Furthermore, the goal of basic "fairness" is hardly furthered by the Act's discriminatory preference for the teaching of creation science and against the teaching of evolution. While requiring that curriculum guides be developed for creation science, the Act says nothing of comparable guides for evolution. Similarly, resource services are supplied for creation science, but not for evolution. Only "creation scientists" can serve on the panel that supplies the resource services. The Act forbids school boards to discriminate against anyone who "chooses to be a creation scientist" or to teach "creationism," but fails to protect those who choose to teach evolution or any other non-creation-science theory, or who refuse to teach creation science.

If the Louisiana Legislature's purpose was solely to maximize the comprehensiveness and effectiveness of science instruction, it would have encouraged the teaching of all scientific theories about the origins of humankind. But under the Act's requirements, teachers who were once free to teach any and all facets of this subject are now unable to do so. Moreover, the Act fails even to ensure that creation science will be taught, but instead requires the teaching of this theory only when the theory of evolution is taught. Thus we agree with the Court of Appeals' conclusion that the Act does not serve to protect academic freedom, but has the distinctly different purpose of discrediting "evolution by counterbalancing its teaching at every turn with the teaching of creationism. . . ."

. . . The legislative history documents that the Act's primary purpose was to change the science curriculum of public schools in order to provide persuasive advantage to a particular religious doctrine that rejects the factual basis of evolution in its entirety. . . .

The Louisiana Creationism Act advances a religious doctrine by requiring either the banishment of the theory of evolution from public school classrooms or the presentation of a religious viewpoint that rejects evolution in its entirety. The Act violates the Establishment Clause of the First Amendment because it seeks to employ the symbolic and financial support of government to achieve a religious purpose. The judgment of the Court of Appeals therefore is affirmed.

Scalia, dissenting:

Even if I agreed with the questionable premise that legislation can be invalidated under the Establishment Clause on the basis of its motivation alone, without regard to its effects, I would still find no justification for today's decision. The Louisiana legislators who passed the "Balanced Treatment for Creation-Science and Evolution-Science Act," each of whom had sworn to support the Constitution, were well aware of the potential Establishment Clause problems, and considered that aspect of the legislation with great care. After seven hearings and several months of study, resulting in substantial revision of the original proposal, they approved the Act overwhelmingly, and specifically articulated the secular purpose they meant it to serve. Although the record contains abundant evidence of the sincerity of that purpose (the only issue pertinent to this case), the Court today holds, essentially on the basis of "its visceral knowledge regarding what must have motivated the legislators," that the members of the Louisiana Legislature knowingly violated their oaths and then lied about it. I dissent. Had requirements of the Balanced Treatment Act that are not apparent on its face been clarified by an interpretation of the Louisiana Supreme Court, or by the manner of its implementation, the Act might well be found unconstitutional; but the question of its constitutionality cannot rightly be disposed of on the gallop, by impugning the motives of its supporters.

This case arrives here in the following posture: the Louisiana Supreme Court has never been given an opportunity to interpret the Balanced Treatment Act, State officials have never attempted to implement it, and it has never been the subject of a full evidentiary hearing. We can only guess at its meaning. We know that it forbids instruction in either "creation science" or "evolution science" without instruction in the other, but the parties are sharply divided over what creation science consists of. Appellants insist that it is a collection of educationally valuable scientific data that has been censored from classrooms by an embarrassed scientific establishment. Appellees insist it is not science at all, but thinly veiled religious doctrine. Both interpretations of the intended meaning of that phrase find considerable support in the legislative history.

At least at this stage in the litigation, it is plain to me that we must accept appellants' view of what the statute means. . . . "Creation science" is unquestionably a "term of art," and thus, under Louisiana law, is "to be interpreted according to [its] received meaning and acceptation with the learned in the art, trade or profession to which [it] refer[s]." The only evidence in the record of the "received meaning and acceptation" of "creation science" is found in five affidavits filed by appellants. In those affidavits, two scientists, a philosopher, a theologian, and an educator, all of whom claim extensive knowledge of creation science, swear that it is essentially a collection of scientific data supporting the theory that the physical universe and life within it appeared suddenly, and have not changed substantially since appearing. These experts insist that creation science is a strictly scientific concept that can be presented without religious reference. At this point, then, we must assume that the Balanced Treatment Act does not require the presentation of religious doctrine.

Nothing in today's opinion is plainly to the contrary, but what the statute means and what it requires are of rather little concern to the Court. Like the Court of Appeals, the Court finds it necessary to consider only the motives of the legislators who supported the Balanced Treatment Act. After examining the statute, its legislative history, and its historical and social context, the Court holds that the Louisiana Legislature acted without "a secular legislative purpose," and that the Act therefore fails the "purpose" prong of the three-part test set forth in *Lemon v. Kurtzman.* I doubt whether that "purpose" requirement of *Lemon* is a proper interpretation of the Constitution; but even if it were, I could not agree with the Court's assessment that the requirement was not satisfied here. . . .

. . . [T]he Balanced Treatment Act did not fly through the Louisiana Legislature on wings of fundamentalist religious fervor—which would be unlikely, in any event, since only a small minority of the State's citizens belong to fundamentalist religious denominations. . . .

. . . Our task is not to judge the debate about teaching the origins of life, but to ascertain what the members of the Louisiana Legislature believed. The vast majority of them voted to approve a bill which explicitly stated a secular purpose; what is crucial is not their wisdom in believing that purpose would be achieved by the bill, but their sincerity in believing it would be. . . . We have no way of knowing, of course, how many legislators believed the testimony of Senator Keith and his witnesses. But in the absence of evidence to the contrary, we have to assume that many of them did. Given that assumption, the Court today

plainly errs in holding that the Louisiana Legislature passed the Balanced Treatment Act for exclusively religious purposes. . . .

. . . The people of Louisiana, including those who are Christian fundamentalists, are quite entitled, as a secular matter, to have whatever scientific evidence there may be against evolution presented in their schools, just as Mr. Scopes was entitled to present whatever scientific evidence there was for it. Perhaps what the Louisiana Legislature has done is unconstitutional because there is no such evidence, and the scheme they have established will amount to no more than a presentation of the Book of Genesis. But we cannot say that on the evidence before us in this summary judgment context, which includes ample uncontradicted testimony that "creation science" is a body of scientific knowledge, rather than revealed belief. Infinitely less can we say (or should we say) that the scientific evidence for evolution is so conclusive that no one could be gullible enough to believe that there is any real scientific evidence to the contrary, so that the legislation's stated purpose must be a lie. Yet that illiberal judgment, that Scopes-in-reverse, is ultimately the basis on which the Court's facile rejection of the Louisiana Legislature's purpose must rest. . . .

In the past, we have attempted to justify our embarrassing Establishment Clause jurisprudence on the ground that it "sacrifices clarity and predictability for flexibility." One commentator has aptly characterized this as "a euphemism . . . for . . . the absence of any principled rationale." I think it time that we sacrifice some "flexibility" for "clarity and predictability." Abandoning *Lemon's* purpose test—a test which exacerbates the tension between the Free Exercise and Establishment Clauses, has no basis in the language or history of the Amendment, and, as today's decision shows, has wonderfully flexible consequences—would be a good place to start.

Good News Club v. Milford Central School

533 U.S. 98 (2001), 6-3
Opinion of the Court: Thomas (Breyer, in part; Kennedy, O'Connor, Rehnquist, Scalia, in part)
Concurring: Breyer, in part; Scalia, in part
Dissenting: Ginsburg, Stevens, Souter

How did the Milford Central School violate the free speech rights of the Good News Club? Was the violation justified by the school's concern that accommodating the Club's activities would violate the establishment clause? Did the restriction placed on the club's speech discriminate on the basis of viewpoint? Was it reasonable in light of the purpose served by the forum? Has the Lemon test been strengthened, weakened, or disregarded in this decision? Why has the Court been more accommodationist about access to public school facilities and some forms of public financial aid than about expressions of religion in the classroom?

Thomas, for the Court:

This case presents two questions. The first question is whether Milford Central School violated the free speech rights of the Good News Club when it excluded the Club from meeting after hours at the school. The second question is whether any such violation is justified by Milford's concern that permitting the Club's activities would violate the Establishment Clause. We conclude that Milford's restriction violates the Club's free speech rights and that no Establishment Clause concern justifies that violation.

The State of New York authorizes local school boards to adopt regulations governing the use of their school facilities. In particular, N.Y. Educ. Law §414 enumerates several purposes for which local boards may open their schools to public use. In 1992, respondent Milford Central School (Milford) enacted a community use policy adopting seven of §414's purposes for which its building could be used after school. Two of the stated purposes are relevant here. First, district residents may use the school for "instruction in any branch of education, learning or the arts." Second, the school is available for "social, civic and recreational meetings and entertainment events, and other uses pertaining to the welfare of the community, provided that such uses shall be nonexclusive and shall be opened to the general public."

Stephen and Darleen Fournier reside within Milford's district and therefore are eligible to use the school's facilities as long as their proposed use is approved by the school. Together they are sponsors of the local Good News Club, a private Christian organization for children ages 6 to 12. Pursuant to Milford's policy, in September 1996 the Fourniers submitted a request to Dr. Robert McGruder, interim superintendent of the district, in which they sought permission to hold the Club's weekly afterschool meetings in the school cafeteria. The next month, McGruder formally denied the Fourniers' request on the ground that the proposed use-to have "a fun time of

singing songs, hearing a Bible lesson and memorizing scripture," was "the equivalent of religious worship." According to McGruder, the community use policy, which prohibits use "by any individual or organization for religious purposes," foreclosed the Club's activities. . . .

The standards that we apply to determine whether a State has unconstitutionally excluded a private speaker from use of a public forum depend on the nature of the forum. . . .

When the State establishes a limited public forum, the State is not required to and does not allow persons to engage in every type of speech. The State may be justified "in reserving [its forum] for certain groups or for the discussion of certain topics." The State's power to restrict speech, however, is not without limits. The restriction must not discriminate against speech on the basis of viewpoint, and the restriction must be "reasonable in light of the purpose served by the forum."

Applying this test, we first address whether the exclusion constituted viewpoint discrimination. We are guided in our analysis by two of our prior opinions, *Lamb's Chapel* [*v. Center Moriches Unioin Free School District*] and *Rosenberger* [*v. University of Virginia*]. In *Lamb's Chapel,* we held that a school district violated the Free Speech Clause of the First Amendment when it excluded a private group from presenting films at the school based solely on the films' discussions of family values from a religious perspective. Likewise, in *Rosenberger,* we held that a university's refusal to fund a student publication because the publication addressed issues from a religious perspective violated the Free Speech Clause. Concluding that Milford's exclusion of the Good News Club based on its religious nature is indistinguishable from the exclusions in these cases, we hold that the exclusion constitutes viewpoint discrimination. Because the restriction is viewpoint discriminatory, we need not decide whether it is unreasonable in light of the purposes served by the forum.

Milford has opened its limited public forum to activities that serve a variety of purposes, including events "pertaining to the welfare of the community." Milford interprets its policy to permit discussions of subjects such as child rearing, and of "the development of character and morals from a religious perspective." For example, this policy would allow someone to use Aesop's Fables to teach children moral values. Additionally, a group could sponsor a debate on whether there should be a constitutional amendment to permit prayer in public schools. . . . In short, any group that "promote[s] the moral and character development of children" is eligible to use the school building.

Just as there is no question that teaching morals and character development to children is a permissible purpose under Milford's policy, it is clear that the Club teaches morals and character development to children. . . . Nonetheless, because Milford found the Club's activities to be religious in nature—"the equivalent of religious instruction itself," it excluded the Club from use of its facilities. . . .

We disagree that something that is "quintessentially religious" or "decidedly religious in nature" cannot also be characterized properly as the teaching of morals and character development from a particular viewpoint. . . . that matters for purposes of the Free Speech Clause is that we can see no logical difference in kind between the invocation of Christianity by the Club and the invocation of teamwork, loyalty, or patriotism by other associations to provide a foundation for their lessons. . . . [W]e reaffirm our holdings in *Lamb's Chapel* and *Rosenberger* that speech discussing otherwise permissible subjects cannot be excluded from a limited public forum on the ground that the subject is discussed from a religious viewpoint. Thus, we conclude that Milford's exclusion of the Club from use of the school, pursuant to its community use policy, constitutes impermissible viewpoint discrimination.

Milford argues that, even if its restriction constitutes viewpoint discrimination, its interest in not violating the Establishment Clause outweighs the Club's interest in gaining equal access to the school's facilities. In other words, according to Milford, its restriction was required to avoid violating the Establishment Clause. We disagree. . . .

We rejected Establishment Clause defenses similar to Milford's in two previous free speech cases, *Lamb's Chapel* and *Widmar* [*v. Vincent*]. In particular, in *Lamb's Chapel*, we explained that "[t]he showing of th[e] film series would not have been during school hours, would not have been sponsored by the school, and would have been open to the public, not just to church members." Accordingly, we found that "there would have been no realistic danger that the community would think that the District was endorsing religion or any particular creed." Likewise, in *Widmar*, where the university's forum was already available to other groups, this Court concluded that there was no Establishment Clause problem.

The Establishment Clause defense fares no better in this case. As in *Lamb's Chapel*, the Club's meetings were held after school hours, not sponsored by the school, and open to any student who obtained parental consent, not just to Club members. As in *Widmar*, Milford made its forum available to other organizations. The Club's activities are materially indistinguishable from those in *Lamb's Chapel* and *Widmar*. Thus, Milford's reliance on the Establishment Clause is unavailing. Milford attempts to distinguish *Lamb's Chapel* and *Widmar* by emphasizing that Milford's policy involves elementary school children. According to Milford, children will perceive that the school is endorsing the Club and will feel coercive pressure to participate, because the Club's activities take place on school grounds, even though they occur during nonschool hours. This argument is unpersuasive.

First, we have held that "a significant factor in upholding governmental programs in the face of Establishment Clause attack is their neutrality towards religion." . . . The Good News Club seeks nothing more than to be treated neutrally and given access to speak about the same topics as are other groups. . .

Second, to the extent we consider whether the community would feel coercive pressure to engage in the Club's activities, the relevant community would be the parents, not the elementary school children. It is the parents who choose whether their children will attend the Good News Club meetings. . . . Milford does not suggest that the parents of elementary school children would be confused about whether the school was endorsing religion. Nor do we believe that such an argument could be reasonably advanced.

Third, whatever significance we may have assigned in the Establishment Clause context to the suggestion that elementary school children are more impressionable than adults, we have never extended our Establishment Clause jurisprudence to foreclose private religious conduct during nonschool hours merely because it takes place on school premises where elementary school children may be present. . . .

Fourth, even if we were to consider the possible misperceptions by schoolchildren in deciding whether Milford's permitting the Club's activities would violate the Establishment Clause, the facts of this case simply do not support Milford's conclusion. There is no evidence that young children are permitted to loiter outside classrooms after the schoolday has ended. . . . The meetings were held in a combined high school resource room and middle school special education room, not in an elementary school classroom. The instructors are not schoolteachers. And the children in the group are not all the same age as in the normal classroom setting; their ages range from 6 to 12. In sum, these circumstances simply do not support the theory that small children would perceive endorsement here.

Finally, even if we were to inquire into the minds of schoolchildren in this case, we cannot say the danger that children would misperceive the endorsement of religion is any greater than the danger that they would perceive a hostility toward the religious viewpoint if the Club were excluded from the public forum. This concern is particularly acute given the reality that Milford's building is not used only for elementary school children. . . . Any bystander could conceivably be aware of the school's use policy and its exclusion of the Good News Club, and could suffer as much from viewpoint discrimination as elementary school children could suffer from perceived endorsement. . . .

We are not convinced that there is any significance in this case to the possibility that elementary school children may witness the Good News Club's activities on school premises, and therefore we can find no reason to depart from our holdings in *Lamb's Chapel* and *Widmar*. Accordingly, we conclude that permitting the Club to meet on the school's premises would not have violated the Establishment Clause.

When Milford denied the Good News Club access to the school's limited public forum on the ground that the Club was religious in nature, it discriminated against the Club because of its religious viewpoint in violation of the Free Speech Clause of the First Amendment. Because Milford has not raised a valid Establishment Clause claim, we do not address the question whether such a claim could excuse Milford's viewpoint discrimination. . . .

Scalia, concurring:

. . . First, I join Part IV of the Court's opinion, regarding the Establishment Clause issue, with the understanding that its consideration of coercive pressure, and perceptions of endorsement, "to the extent" that the law makes such factors relevant, is consistent with the belief that in this case that extent is zero. . . . What is at play here is not coercion, but the compulsion of ideas—and the private right to exert and receive that compulsion (or to have one's children receive it) is protected by the Free Speech and Free Exercise Clauses. . . .

As to endorsement, I have previously written that "[r]eligious expression cannot violate the Establish-

ment Clause where it (1) is purely private and (2) occurs in a traditional or designated public forum, publicly announced and open to all on equal terms." . . .

Second . . . [r]espondent has opened its facilities to any "us[e] pertaining to the welfare of the community, provided that such us[e] shall be nonexclusive and shall be opened to the general public." Shaping the moral and character development of children certainly "pertain[s] to the welfare of the community." Thus, respondent has agreed that groups engaged in the endeavor of developing character may use its forum.

. . . When the Club attempted to teach Biblical-based moral values, however, it was excluded because its activities "d[id] not involve merely a religious perspective on the secular subject of morality" and because "it [was] clear from the conduct of the meetings that the Good News Club goes far beyond merely stating its viewpoint."

From no other group does respondent require the sterility of speech that it demands of petitioners. . . . The Club may only discuss morals and character, and cannot give its reasons why they should be fostered-because God wants and expects it, because it will make the Club members "saintly" people, and because it emulates Jesus Christ. . . . This is blatant viewpoint discrimination. Just as calls to character based on patriotism will go unanswered if the listeners do not believe their country is good and just, calls to moral behavior based on God's will are useless if the listeners do not believe that God exists. . . .

Stevens, dissenting:

The Milford Central School has invited the public to use its facilities for educational and recreational purposes, but not for "religious purposes." Speech for "religious purposes" may reasonably be understood to encompass three different categories. First, there is religious speech that is simply speech about a particular topic from a religious point of view. The film in *Lamb's Chapel v. Center Moriches Union Free School Dist.* illustrates this category. . . . Second, there is religious speech that amounts to worship, or its equivalent. Our decision in *Widmar v. Vincent* concerned such speech. Third, there is an intermediate category that is aimed principally at proselytizing or inculcating belief in a particular religious faith. . . .

[W]hile a public entity may not censor speech about an authorized topic based on the point of view expressed by the speaker, it has broad discretion to "preserve the property under its control for the use to which it is lawfully dedicated."... The novel question that this case presents concerns the constitutionality of a public school's attempt to limit the scope of a public forum it has created. More specifically, the question is whether a school can, consistently with the First Amendment, create a limited public forum that admits the first type of religious speech without allowing the other two.

Distinguishing speech from a religious viewpoint, on the one hand, from religious proselytizing, on the other, is comparable to distinguishing meetings to discuss political issues from meetings whose principal purpose is to recruit new members to join a political organization.... Such recruiting meetings may introduce divisiveness and tend to separate young children into cliques that undermine the school's educational mission.

School officials may reasonably believe that evangelical meetings designed to convert children to a particular religious faith pose the same risk. And, just as a school may allow meetings to discuss current events from a political perspective without also allowing organized political recruitment, so too can a school allow discussion of topics such as moral development from a religious (or nonreligious) perspective without thereby opening its forum to religious proselytizing or worship....

The particular limitation of the forum at issue in this case is one that prohibits the use of the school's facilities for "religious purposes." It is clear that, by "religious purposes," the school district did not intend to exclude all speech from a religious point of view.... In other words, the school sought to allow the first type of religious speech while excluding the second and third types. As long as this is done in an even handed manner, I see no constitutional violation in such an effort. The line between the various categories of religious speech may be difficult to draw, but I think that the distinctions are valid, and that a school, particularly an elementary school, must be permitted to draw them....

[R]egardless of whether the Good News Club's activities amount to "worship," it does seem clear, based on the facts in the record, that the school district correctly classified those activities as falling within the third category of religious speech and therefore beyond the scope of the school's limited public forum. In short, I am persuaded that the school district could (and did) permissibly exclude from its limited public forum proselytizing religious speech that does not rise to the level of actual worship....

Souter, dissenting:

... The sole question ... [is] ... whether, in refusing to allow Good News's intended use, Milford was misapplying its unchallenged restriction in a way that amounted to imposing a viewpoint-based restriction on what could be said or done by a group entitled to use the forum for an educational, civic, or other permitted purpose....

Good News's classes open and close with prayer. In a sample lesson considered by the District Court, children are instructed that "[t]he Bible tells us how we can have our sins forgiven by receiving the Lord Jesus Christ. It tells us how to live to please Him.... If you have received the Lord Jesus as your Saviour from sin, you belong to God's special group—His family.".…

While Good News's program utilizes songs and games, the heart of the meeting is the "challenge" and "invitation," which are repeated at various times throughout the lesson. During the challenge, "saved" children who "already believe in the Lord Jesus as their Savior" are challenged to "'stop and ask God for the strength and the "want"... to obey Him.'".... During the invitation, the teacher "invites" the "unsaved" children "'to trust the Lord Jesus to be your Savior from sin,'" and "'receiv[e] [him] as your Savior from sin.'"....

It is beyond question that Good News intends to use the public school premises not for the mere discussion of a subject from a particular, Christian point of view, but for an evangelical service of worship calling children to commit themselves in an act of Christian conversion....

This Court has accepted the independent obligation to obey the Establishment Clause as sufficiently compelling to satisfy strict scrutiny under the First Amendment.... Milford's actions would offend the Establishment Clause if they carried the message of endorsing religion under the circumstances, as viewed by a reasonable observer. The majority concludes that such an endorsement effect is out of the question in Milford's case, because the context here is "materially indistinguishable" from the facts in *Lamb's Chapel* and *Widmar*. In fact, the majority is in no position to say that, for the principal grounds on which we based our Establishment Clause holdings in those cases are clearly absent here.

In *Widmar*, we held that the Establishment Clause did not bar a religious student group from using a public university's meeting space for worship as well as discussion. As for the reasonable observers who might perceive government endorsement of religion, we pointed out that the forum was used by university students, who "are, of course, young adults," and, as such, "are less impressionable than younger students and should be able to appreciate that the University's policy is one of neutrality toward religion." To the same effect, we remarked that the "large number of groups meeting on campus" negated "any reasonable inference of University support from the mere fact of a campus meeting place.". . .

Lamb's Chapel involved an evening film series on child-rearing open to the general public (and, given the subject matter, directed at an adult audience). There, school property "had repeatedly been used by a wide variety of private organizations," and we could say with some assurance that "[u]nder these circumstances. . . . there would have been no realistic danger that the community would think that the District was endorsing religion or any particular creed. . . ."

What we know about this case looks very little like *Widmar* or *Lamb's Chapel*. The cohort addressed by Good News is not university students with relative maturity, or even high school pupils, but elementary school children as young as six. . . . Nor is Milford's limited forum anything like the sites for wide-ranging intellectual exchange that were home to the challenged activities in *Widmar* and *Lamb's Chapel*. . . .

The timing and format of Good News's gatherings, on the other hand, may well affirmatively suggest the imprimatur of officialdom in the minds of the young children. The club is open solely to elementary students, only four outside groups have been identified as meeting in the school, and Good News is, seemingly, the only one whose instruction follows immediately on the conclusion of the official school day. . . .

. . . [T]here is a good case that Good News's exercises blur the line between public classroom instruction and private religious indoctrination, leaving a reasonable elementary school pupil unable to appreciate that the former instruction is the business of the school while the latter evangelism is not. . . .

Santa Fe Independent School District v. Doe

530 U.S. 290 (2000), 6-3
Opinion of the Court: Stevens (Breyer, Ginsburg, Kennedy, O'Connor, Souter)
Dissenting: Rehnquist, Scalia, Thomas

Are the prayers in this case "private speech endorsing religion" as Chief Justice Rehnquist phrases it in dissent, and therefore protected by the free exercise clause or are they "government speech endorsing religion" and therefore forbidden by the establishment clause? Does this decision allow a small number of persons to control what a large number want to do? Is this an inevitable effect of having an establishment clause and a wall of separation between church and state or does it represent secular hostility toward public religious expression? Compare the policy struck down in this case with that sustained in Walz, *(p. 81) In which was government more involved? Which benefited religion more?*

Stevens, for the Court:

Prior to 1995, the Santa Fe High School student who occupied the school's elective office of student council chaplain delivered a prayer over the public address system before each varsity football game for the entire season. This practice, along with others, was challenged in District Court as a violation of the Establishment Clause of the First Amendment. While these proceedings were pending in the District Court, the school district adopted a different policy that permits, but does not require, prayer initiated and led by a student at all home games. The District Court entered an order modifying that policy to permit only nonsectarian, nonproselytizing prayer. The Court of Appeals held that, even as modified by the District Court, the football prayer policy was invalid. . . .

The Santa Fe Independent School District (District) is a political subdivision of the State of Texas, responsible for the education of more than 4,000 students in a small community in the southern part of the State. . . . Respondents are two sets of current or former students and their respective mothers. One family is Mormon and the other is Catholic. The District Court permitted respondents (Does) to litigate anonymously to protect them from intimidation or harassment. . . .

. . . In *Lee v. Weisman* we held that a prayer delivered by a rabbi at a middle school graduation ceremony violated that Clause. Although this case involves student prayer at a different type of school function, our analysis is properly guided by the principles that we endorsed in *Lee*. . . .

In this case the District first argues that this principle is inapplicable to its October policy because the messages are private student speech, not public speech. It reminds us that "there is a crucial difference between government speech endorsing religion, which the Establishment Clause forbids, and private speech endorsing religion, which the Free Speech and Free Exercise Clauses protect." *Board of Ed. of Westside Community Schools (Dist. 66) v. Mergens.* We certainly

Sign outside a church in Santa Fe, Texas, reflects a local response to the Supreme Court's decision on student-led prayer at high school football games.

agree with that distinction, but we are not persuaded that the pregame invocations should be regarded as "private speech."

These invocations are authorized by a government policy and take place on government property at government-sponsored school-related events. Of course, not every message delivered under such circumstances is the government's own. . . .

The District has attempted to disentangle itself from the religious messages by developing the two-step student election process. The text of the October policy, however, exposes the extent of the school's entanglement. The elections take place at all only because the school "board has chosen to permit students to deliver a brief invocation and/or message." The elections thus "shall" be conducted "by the high school student council" and "[u]pon advice and direction of the high school principal." The decision whether to deliver a message is first made by majority vote of the entire student body, followed by a choice of the speaker in a separate, similar majority election. Even though the particular words used by the speaker are not determined by those votes, the policy mandates that the "statement or invocation" be "consistent with the goals and purposes of this policy," which are "to solemnize the event, to promote good sports-

manship and student safety, and to establish the appropriate environment for the competition."

In addition to involving the school in the selection of the speaker, the policy, by its terms, invites and encourages religious messages. The policy itself states that the purpose of the message is "to solemnize the event." A religious message is the most obvious method of solemnizing an event. Moreover, the requirements that the message "promote good citizenship" and "establish the appropriate environment for competition" further narrow the types of message deemed appropriate, suggesting that a solemn, yet nonreligious, message, such as commentary on United States foreign policy, would be prohibited. Indeed, the only type of message that is expressly endorsed in the text is an "invocation"—a term that primarily describes an appeal for divine assistance. In fact, as used in the past at Santa Fe High School, an "invocation" has always entailed a focused religious message. Thus, the expressed purposes of the policy encourage the selection of a religious message, and that is precisely how the students understand the policy. The results of the elections described in the parties' stipulation make it clear that the students understood that the central question before them was whether prayer should be a part of the pregame ceremony. We recognize the important role that public worship plays in many communities, as well as the sincere desire to include public prayer as a part of various occasions so as to mark those occasions' significance. But such religious activity in public schools, as elsewhere, must comport with the First Amendment.

The actual or perceived endorsement of the message, moreover, is established by factors beyond just the text of the policy. Once the student speaker is selected and the message composed, the invocation is then delivered to a large audience assembled as part of a regularly scheduled, school-sponsored function conducted on school property. . . .

In this context the members of the listening audience must perceive the pregame message as a public expression of the views of the majority of the student body delivered with the approval of the school administration. In cases involving state participation in a religious activity, one of the relevant questions is "whether an objective observer, acquainted with the text, legislative history, and implementation of the statute, would perceive it as a state endorsement of prayer in public schools." *Wallace* [v. *Jaffree*] Regardless of the listener's support for, or objection to, the message, an objective Santa Fe High School student will unquestionably perceive the inevitable pregame prayer as stamped with her school's seal of approval. . . .

School sponsorship of a religious message is impermissible because it sends the ancillary message to members of the audience who are nonadherants "that they are outsiders, not full members of the political community, and an accompanying message to adherants that they are insiders, favored members of the political community." *Lynch v. Donnelly*. The delivery of such a message–over the school's public address system, by a speaker representing the student body, under the supervision of school faculty, and pursuant to a school policy that explicitly and implicitly encourages public prayer—is not properly characterized as "private" speech.

The District next argues that its football policy is distinguishable from the graduation prayer in *Lee* because it does not coerce students to participate in religious observances. Its argument has two parts: first, that there is no impermissible government coercion because the pregame messages are the product of student choices; and second, that there is really no coercion at all because attendance at an extracurricular event, unlike a graduation ceremony, is voluntary. . . .

One of the purposes served by the Establishment Clause is to remove debate over this kind of issue

from governmental supervision or control. We explained in *Lee* that the "preservation and transmission of religious beliefs and worship is a responsibility and a choice committed to the private sphere." The two student elections authorized by the policy, coupled with the debates that presumably must precede each, impermissibly invade that private sphere. The election mechanism, when considered in light of the history in which the policy in question evolved, reflects a device the District put in place that determines whether religious messages will be delivered at home football games. The mechanism encourages divisiveness along religious lines in a public school setting, a result at odds with the Establishment Clause. Although it is true that the ultimate choice of student speaker is "attributable to the students," the District's decision to hold the constitutionally problematic election is clearly "a choice attributable to the State."

The District further argues that attendance at the commencement ceremonies at issue in *Lee* "differs dramatically" from attendance at high school football games, which it contends "are of no more than passing interest to many students" and are "decidedly extracurricular," thus dissipating any coercion. Attendance at a high school football game, unlike showing up for class, is certainly not required in order to receive a diploma. Moreover, we may assume that the District is correct in arguing that the informal pressure to attend an athletic event is not as strong as a senior's desire to attend her own graduation ceremony. . . .

Even if we regard every high school student's decision to attend a home football game as purely voluntary, we are nevertheless persuaded that the delivery of a pregame prayer has the improper effect of coercing those present to participate in an act of religious worship. . . .

The Religion Clauses of the First Amendment prevent the government from making any law respecting the establishment of religion or prohibiting the free exercise thereof. By no means do these commands impose a prohibition on all religious activity in our public schools. Indeed, the common purpose of the Religion Clauses "is to secure religious liberty." Thus, nothing in the Constitution as interpreted by this Court prohibits any public school student from voluntarily praying at any time before, during, or after the schoolday. But the religious liberty protected by the Constitution is abridged when the State affirmatively sponsors the particular religious practice of prayer. . . .

The District ... asks us to pretend that we do not recognize what every Santa Fe High School student understands clearly—that this policy is about prayer. The District further asks us to accept what is obviously untrue: that these messages are necessary to "solemnize" a football game and that this single-student, year-long position is essential to the protection of student speech. We refuse to turn a blind eye to the context in which this policy arose, and that context quells any doubt that this policy was implemented with the purpose of endorsing school prayer....

Rehnquist, dissenting:

The Court distorts existing precedent to conclude that the school district's student-message program is invalid on its face under the Establishment Clause. But even more disturbing than its holding is the tone of the Court's opinion; it bristles with hostility to all things religious in public life. Neither the holding nor the tone of the opinion is faithful to the meaning of the Establishment Clause, when it is recalled that George Washington himself, at the request of the very Congress which passed the Bill of Rights, proclaimed a day of "public thanksgiving and prayer, to be observed by acknowledging with grateful hearts the many and signal favors of Almighty God."

We do not learn until late in the Court's opinion that respondents in this case challenged the district's student-message program at football games before it had been put into practice. As the Court explained in *United States v. Salerno*, the fact that a policy might "operate unconstitutionally under some conceivable set of circumstances is insufficient to render it wholly invalid." While there is an exception to this principle in the First Amendment overbreadth context because of our concern that people may refrain from speech out of fear of prosecution, there is no similar justification for Establishment Clause cases. No speech will be "chilled" by the existence of a government policy that might unconstitutionally endorse religion over nonreligion. Therefore, the question is not whether the district's policy may be applied in violation of the Establishment Clause, but whether it inevitably will be....

... [T]he district's student-message policy should not be invalidated on its face. The Court applies *Lemon* and holds that the "policy is invalid on its face because it establishes an improper majoritarian election on religion, and unquestionably has the purpose and creates the perception of encouraging the delivery of prayer at a series of important school events." The Court's reliance on each of these conclusions misses the mark.

First, the Court misconstrues the nature of the "majoritarian election" permitted by the policy as being an election on "prayer" and "religion." To the contrary, the election permitted by the policy is a two-fold process whereby students vote first on whether to have a student speaker before football games at all, and second, if the students vote to have such a speaker, on who that speaker will be. It is conceivable that the election could become one in which student candidates campaign on platforms that focus on whether or not they will pray if elected. It is also conceivable that the election could lead to a Christian prayer before 90 percent of the football games. If, upon implementation, the policy operated in this fashion, we would have a record before us to review whether the policy, as applied, violated the Establishment Clause or unduly suppressed minority viewpoints. But it is possible that the students might vote not to have a pregame speaker, in which case there would be no threat of a constitutional violation. It is also possible that the election would not focus on prayer, but on public speaking ability or social popularity. And if student campaigning did begin to focus on prayer, the school might decide to implement reasonable campaign restrictions.

But the Court ignores these possibilities by holding that merely granting the student body the power to elect a speaker that may choose to pray, "regardless of the students' ultimate use of it, is not acceptable." The Court so holds despite that any speech that may occur as a result of the election process here would be private, not government, speech. The elected student, not the government, would choose what to say. Support for the Court's holding cannot be found in any of our cases. And it essentially invalidates all student elections. A newly elected student body president, or even a newly elected prom king or queen, could use opportunities for public speaking to say prayers. Under the Court's view, the mere grant of power to the students to vote for such offices, in light of the fear that those elected might publicly pray, violates the Establishment Clause.

Second, with respect to the policy's purpose, the Court holds that "the simple enactment of this policy, with the purpose and perception of school endorsement of student prayer, was a constitutional violation." But the policy itself has plausible secular purposes: "[T]o solemnize the event, to promote good sportsmanship and student safety, and to establish the appropriate environment for the competition." Where a governmental body "expresses a plausible secular purpose" for an enactment, "courts should generally defer to that stated intent." The Court grants no deference to—and appears openly hostile toward—the policy's stated purposes, and wastes no time in concluding that they are a sham.

For example, the Court dismisses the secular purpose of solemnization by claiming that it "invites and encourages religious messages." The Court so concludes based on its rather strange view that a "religious message is the most obvious means of solemnizing an event." But it is easy to think of solemn messages that are not religious in nature, for example urging that a game be fought fairly. And sporting events often begin with a solemn rendition of our national anthem, with its concluding verse "And this be our motto: 'In God is our trust.'" Under the Court's logic, a public school that sponsors the singing of the national anthem before football games violates the Establishment Clause....

The Court also relies on our decision in *Lee v. Weisman*, to support its conclusion. In *Lee*, we concluded that the content of the speech at issue, a graduation prayer given by a rabbi, was "directed and controlled" by a school official. In other words, at issue in *Lee* was government speech. Here, by contrast, the potential speech at issue, if the policy had been allowed to proceed, would be a message or invocation selected or created by a student. That is, if there were speech at issue here, it would be private speech. The "crucial difference between government speech endorsing religion, which the Establishment Clause forbids, and private speech endorsing religion, which the Free Speech and Free Exercise Clauses protect," applies with particular force to the question of endorsement....

Finally, the Court seems to demand that a government policy be completely neutral as to content or be considered one that endorses religion. This is undoubtedly a new requirement, as our Establishment Clause jurisprudence simply does not mandate "content neutrality." That concept is found in our First Amendment speech cases and is used as a guide for determining when we apply strict scrutiny. For example, we look to "content neutrality" in reviewing loudness restrictions imposed on speech in public forums. The Court seems to think that the fact that the policy is not content neutral somehow controls the Establishment Clause inquiry.

But even our speech jurisprudence would not require that all public school actions with respect to student speech be content neutral.... Schools do not violate the First Amendment every time they restrict student speech to certain categories....

The policy at issue here may be applied in an unconstitutional manner, but it will be time enough to invalidate it if that is found to be the case....

Reynolds v. United States

98 U.S. 145 (1879), 9-0
Opinion of the Court: Waite (Bradley, Clifford, Field, Harlan, Hunt, Miller, Strong, Swayne)

In 1862, exercising its power to enact territorial legislation, Congress passed an antipolygamy law that applied to the Utah Territory. The territory had been settled largely by Mormons, and the law was clearly directed at the Mormon religious practice of plural marriage. In a test case, George Reynolds, secretary to the Mormon leader Brigham Young, took a second wife with the church's approval and was convicted in a territorial court of violating the federal law. He was fined $500 and sentenced to two years in prison.

Is this a case of the majority's morals being imposed on a minority or a case of not exempting someone from obeying the criminal law? If the criminal law can apply to some acts that genuinely pursue religious beliefs, are there any limits to what religious acts duly enacted laws can make criminal? Who gains and loses and what is gained or lost as a result of this decision?

Waite, for the Court:
... [Reynolds] proved that, at the time of his alleged second marriage, he was, and for many years before had been, a member of the Church of Jesus Christ of Latter-Day Saints, commonly called the Mormon Church, and a believer in its doctrines; that it was an accepted doctrine of that church

> that it was the duty of male members of said church, circumstances permitting, to practise polygamy; ... that this duty was enjoined by different books which the members of said church believed to be of divine origin, and, among others, the Holy Bible, and also that the members of the church believed that the practice of polygamy was directly enjoined upon the male members thereof by the Almighty God, in a revelation to Joseph Smith, the founder and prophet of said church; that the failing or refusing to practise polygamy by such male members of said church, when circumstances would admit, would be punished, and that the penalty for such failure and refusal would be damnation in the life to come....

... The inquiry is not as to the power of Congress to prescribe criminal laws for the Territories, but as to the guilt of one who knowingly violates a law which has been properly enacted if he entertains a religious belief that the law is wrong.

Congress cannot pass a law for the government of the Territories which shall prohibit the free exercise of religion. The first amendment to the Constitution expressly forbids such legislation. Religious freedom is guaranteed everywhere throughout the United States, so far as congressional interference is concerned. The question to be determined is, whether the law now under consideration comes within this prohibition.

The word "religion" is not defined in the Constitution. We must go elsewhere, therefore, to ascertain its meaning, and nowhere more appropriately, we think, than to the history of the times in the midst of which the provision was adopted. The precise point of the inquiry is what is the religious freedom which has been guaranteed.

Before the adoption of the Constitution, attempts were made in some of the colonies and States to legislate not only in respect to the establishment of religion, but in respect to its doctrines and precepts as well. The people were taxed, against their will, for the support of religion, and sometimes for the support of particular sects to whose tenets they could not and did not subscribe. Punishments were prescribed for a failure to attend upon public worship, and sometimes for entertaining heretical opinions. The controversy upon this general subject was animated in many of the States, but seemed at last to culminate in Virginia. In 1784, the House of Delegates of that State, having under consideration "a bill establishing provision for teachers of the Christian religion," postponed it until the next session, and directed that the bill should be published and distributed, and that the people be requested "to signify their opinion respecting the adoption of such a bill at the next session of assembly."

This brought out a determined opposition. Amongst others, Mr. Madison prepared a "Memorial and Remonstrance," which was widely circulated and signed, and in which he demonstrated "that religion, or the duty we owe the Creator," was not within the cognizance of civil government. At the next session, the proposed bill was not only defeated, but another, "for establishing religious freedom," drafted by Mr. Jefferson, was passed. In the preamble of this act religious freedom is defined, and, after a recital "that to suffer the civil magistrate to intrude his powers into the field of opinion, and to restrain the profession or propagation of principles on supposition of their ill tendency is a dangerous fallacy which at once destroys all religious liberty," it is declared "that it is time enough for the rightful purposes of civil government for its officers to interfere when principles break out into overt acts against peace and good order." In these two sentences is found the true distinction between what properly belongs to the church and what to the State.

In a little more than a year after the passage of this statute, the convention met which prepared the Constitution of the United States. Of this convention, Mr. Jefferson was not a member, he being then absent as minister to France. As soon as he saw the draft of the Constitution proposed for adoption, he, in a letter to a friend, expressed his disappointment at the absence of an express declaration insuring the freedom of religion, but was willing to accept it as it was, trusting that the good sense and honest intentions of the people would bring about the necessary alterations. Five of the States, while adopting the Constitution, proposed amendments. Three—New Hampshire, New York, and Virginia—included in one form or another a declaration of religious freedom in the changes they desired to have made, as did also North Carolina, where the convention at first declined to ratify the Constitution until the proposed amendments were acted upon. Accordingly, at the first session of the first Congress, the amendment now under consideration was proposed with others by Mr. Madison. It met the views of the advocates of religious freedom, and was adopted. Mr. Jefferson afterwards, in reply to an address to him by a committee of the Danbury Baptist Association, took occasion to say:

> Believing with you that religion is a matter which lies solely between man and his God; that he owes account to none other for his faith or his worship; that the legislative powers of the government reach actions only, and not opinions— I contemplate with sovereign reverence that act of the whole American people which declared that their legislature should "make no law respecting an establishment of religion or prohibiting the free exercise thereof," thus building a wall of separation between church and State. Adhering to this expression of the supreme will of the nation in behalf of the rights of conscience, I shall see with sincere satisfaction the progress of

those sentiments which tend to restore man to all his natural rights, convinced he has no natural right in opposition to his social duties.

Coming as this does from an acknowledged leader of the advocates of the measure, it may be accepted almost as an authoritative declaration of the scope and effect of the amendment thus secured. Congress was deprived of all legislative power over mere opinion, but was left free to reach actions which were in violation of social duties or subversive of good order.

Polygamy has always been odious among the northern and western nations of Europe, and, until the establishment of the Mormon Church, was almost exclusively a feature of the life of Asiatic and of African people. . . .

. . . [I]t is impossible to believe that the constitutional guaranty of religious freedom was intended to prohibit legislation in respect to this most important feature of social life. Marriage, while from its very nature a sacred obligation, is nevertheless, in most civilized nations, a civil contract, and usually regulated by law. Upon it society may be said to be built, and out of its fruits spring social relations and social obligations and duties with which government is necessarily required to deal. . . .

In our opinion, the statute immediately under consideration is within the legislative power of Congress. It is constitutional and valid as prescribing a rule of action for all those residing in the Territories, and in places over which the United States have exclusive control. This being so, the only question which remains is whether those who make polygamy a part of their religion are excepted from the operation of the statute. If they are, then those who do not make polygamy a part of their religious belief may be found guilty and punished, while those who do, must be acquitted and go free. This would be introducing a new element into criminal law. Laws are made for the government of actions, and while they cannot interfere with mere religious belief and opinions, they may with practices. . . .

So here, as a law of the organization of society under the exclusive dominion of the United States, it is provided that plural marriages shall not be allowed. Can a man excuse his practices to the contrary because of his religious belief? To permit this would be to make the professed doctrines of religious belief superior to the law of the land, and, in effect, to permit every citizen to become a law unto himself. Government could exist only in name under such circumstances.

A criminal intent is generally an element of crime, but every man is presumed to intend the necessary and legitimate consequences of what he knowingly does. Here, the accused knew he had been once married, and that his first wife was living. He also knew that his second marriage was forbidden by law. When, therefore, he married the second time, he is presumed to have intended to break the law. And the breaking of the law is the crime. Every act necessary to constitute the crime was knowingly done, and the crime was therefore knowingly committed. Ignorance of a fact may sometimes be taken as evidence of a want of criminal intent, but not ignorance of the law. The only defence of the accused in this case is his belief that the law ought not to have been enacted. It matters not that his belief was a part of his professed religion; it was still belief, and belief only. . . .

West Virginia State Board of Education v. Barnette

319 U.S. 624 (1943), 6-3
Opinion of the Court: Jackson (Black, Douglas, Murphy, Rutledge, Stone)
Dissenting: Frankfurter, Reed, Roberts

What test does Justice Jackson use to decide this case? How do he and Frankfurter differ on the role of the Supreme Court in the kind of question presented here? Why do the children in this case win only an exemption from a classroom exercise but those in Abington School District v. Schempp *(p. 77) won the right to have the exercise stopped? How is the government's interest characterized? Is it significant that the Court's conclusions in this case came after the tide of battle in World War II had turned in both Europe and the Pacific, rather than two or three years earlier when the nation's security was in greater doubt?*

Jackson, for the Court:

Following the decision by this Court on June 3, 1940, in *Minersville School District v. Gobitis*, the West Virginia legislature amended its statutes to require all schools therein to conduct courses of instruction in history, civics, and in the Constitutions of the United States and of the State "for the purpose of teaching, fostering and perpetuating the ideals, principles and spirit of Americanism, and increasing the knowledge of the organization and machinery of the government." . . .

The Board of Education . . . adopted a resolution containing recitals taken largely from the Court's Go-bitis opinion and ordering that the salute to the flag become "a regular part of the program of activities in the public schools," that all teachers and pupils shall be required to participate in the salute honoring the Nation represented by the Flag; provided, however, that refusal to salute the Flag be regarded as an act of insubordination, and shall be dealt with accordingly.

The resolution originally required the "commonly accepted salute to the Flag," which it defined. Objections to the salute as "being too much like Hitler's" were raised.... Some modification appears to have been made in deference to these objections, but no concession was made to Jehovah's Witnesses. What is now required is the "stiff-arm" salute, the saluter to keep the right hand raised with palm turned up while the following is repeated: "I pledge allegiance to the Flag of the United States of America and to the Republic for which it stands; one Nation, indivisible, with liberty and justice for all."

Failure to conform is "insubordination," dealt with by expulsion. Readmission is denied by statute until compliance. Meanwhile, the expelled child is "unlawfully absent," and may be proceeded against as a delinquent. His parents or guardians are liable to prosecution, and, if convicted, are subject to fine not exceeding $50 and Jail term not exceeding thirty days.

Appellees ... brought suit ... to restrain enforcement of these laws and regulations against Jehovah's Witnesses. The Witnesses are an unincorporated body teaching that the obligation imposed by law of God is superior to that of laws enacted by temporal government. Their religious beliefs include a literal version of Exodus, Chapter 20, verses 4 and 5, which says: Thou shalt not make unto thee any graven image, or any likeness of anything that is in heaven above, or that is in the earth beneath, or that is in the water under the earth; thou shalt not bow down thyself to them nor serve them." They consider that the flag is an "image" within this command. For this reason, they refuse to salute it....

The freedom asserted by these appellees does not bring them into collision with rights asserted by any other individual. It is such conflicts which most frequently require intervention of the State to determine where the rights of one end and those of another begin. But the refusal of these persons to participate in the ceremony does not interfere with or deny rights of others to do so. Nor is there any question in this case that their behavior is peaceable and orderly....

... They are not merely made acquainted with the flag salute so that they may be informed as to what it is

or even what it means. The issue here is whether this slow and easily neglected route to aroused loyalties constitutionally may be short-cut by substituting a compulsory salute and slogan. This issue is not prejudiced by the Court's previous holding that, where a State, without compelling attendance, extends college facilities to pupils who voluntarily enroll, it may prescribe military training as part of the course without offense to the Constitution. It was held that those who take advantage of its opportunities may not, on ground of conscience, refuse compliance with such conditions. In the present case, attendance is not optional. That case is also to be distinguished from the present one, because, independently of college privileges or requirements, the State has power to raise militia and impose the duties of service therein upon its citizens....

Nor does the issue ... turn on one's possession of particular religious views or the sincerity with which they are held. While religion supplies appellees' motive for enduring the discomforts of making the issue in this case, many citizens who do not share these religious views hold such a compulsory rite to infringe constitutional liberty of the individual. It is not necessary to inquire whether nonconformist beliefs will exempt from the duty to salute unless we first find power to make the salute a legal duty....

... We examine, rather than assume existence of, this power, and, against this broader definition of issues in this case, reexamine specific grounds assigned for the Gobitis decision.

1. It was said that the flag salute controversy confronted the Court with the problem which Lincoln cast in memorable dilemma: "Must a government of necessity be too *strong* for the liberties of its people, or too *weak* to maintain its own existence?", and that the answer must be in favor of strength....

Government of limited power need not be anemic government. Assurance that rights are secure tends to diminish fear and jealousy of strong government, and, by making us feel safe to live under it, makes for its better support. Without promise of a limiting Bill of Rights, it is doubtful if our Constitution could have mustered enough strength to enable its ratification. To enforce those rights today is not to choose weak government over strong government. It is only to adhere as a means of strength to individual freedom of mind in preference to officially disciplined uniformity for which history indicates a disappointing and disastrous end....

2. It was also considered in the Gobitis case that functions of educational officers in States, counties

and school districts were such that to interfere with their authority "would in effect make us the school board for the country."

The Fourteenth Amendment, as now applied to the States, protects the citizen against the State itself and all of its creatures—Boards of Education not excepted. These have, of course, important, delicate, and highly discretionary functions, but none that they may not perform within the limits of the Bill of Rights. That they are educating the young for citizenship is reason for scrupulous protection of Constitutional freedoms of the individual, if we are not to strangle the free mind at its source and teach youth to discount important principles of our government as mere platitudes. . . .

3. The Gobitis opinion reasoned that this is a field "where courts possess no marked, and certainly no controlling, competence," that it is committed to the legislatures, as well as the courts, to guard cherished liberties, and that it is constitutionally appropriate to fight out the wise use of legislative authority in the forum of public opinion and before legislative assemblies, rather than to transfer such a contest to the judicial arena, since all the "effective means of inducing political changes are left free." . . .

In weighing arguments of the parties, it is important to distinguish between the due process clause of the Fourteenth Amendment as an instrument for transmitting the principles of the First Amendment and those cases in which it is applied for its own sake. The test of legislation which collides with the Fourteenth Amendment, because it also collides with the principles of the First, is much more definite than the test when only the Fourteenth is involved. Much of the vagueness of the due process clause disappears when the specific prohibitions of the First become its standard. The right of a State to regulate, for example, a public utility may well include, so far as the due process test is concerned, power to impose all of the restrictions which a legislature may have a "rational basis" for adopting. But freedoms of speech and of press, of assembly, and of worship may not be infringed on such slender grounds. They are susceptible of restriction only to prevent grave and immediate danger to interests which the State may lawfully protect. It is important to note that, while it is the Fourteenth Amendment which bears directly upon the State, it is the more specific limiting principles of the First Amendment that finally govern this case. . . .

. . . [W]e act in these matters not by authority of our competence, but by force of our commissions. We cannot, because of modest estimates of our competence in such specialties as public education, withhold the judgment that history authenticates as the function of this Court when liberty is infringed.

4. Lastly, and this is the very heart of the Gobitis opinion, it reasons that "National unity is the basis of national security," that the authorities have "the right to select appropriate means for its attainment," and hence reaches the conclusion that such compulsory measures toward "national unity" are constitutional. Upon the verity of this assumption depends our answer in this case.

National unity, as an end which officials may foster by persuasion and example, is not in question. The problem is whether, under our Constitution, compulsion as here employed is a permissible means for its achievement. . . .

Struggles to coerce uniformity of sentiment in support of some end thought essential to their time and country have been waged by many good, as well as by evil, men. Nationalism is a relatively recent phenomenon, but, at other times and places, the ends have been racial or territorial security, support of a dynasty or regime, and particular plans for saving souls. As first and moderate methods to attain unity have failed, those bent on its accomplishment must resort to an ever-increasing severity. As governmental pressure toward unity becomes greater, so strife becomes more bitter as to whose unity it shall be. Probably no deeper division of our people could proceed from any provocation than from finding it necessary to choose what doctrine and whose program public educational officials shall compel youth to unite in embracing. Ultimate futility of such attempts to compel coherence is the lesson of every such effort from the Roman drive to stamp out Christianity as a disturber of its pagan unity, the Inquisition, as a means to religious and dynastic unity, the Siberian exiles as a means to Russian unity, down to the fast failing efforts of our present totalitarian enemies. Those who begin coercive elimination of dissent soon find themselves exterminating dissenters. Compulsory unification of opinion achieves only the unanimity of the graveyard.

It seems trite but necessary to say that the First Amendment to our Constitution was designed to avoid these ends by avoiding these beginnings. There is no mysticism in the American concept of the State or of the nature or origin of its authority. We set up government by consent of the governed, and the Bill of Rights denies those in power any legal opportunity to coerce that consent. Authority here is to be controlled by public opinion, not public opinion by authority.

The case is made difficult not because the principles of its decision are obscure, but because the flag involved is our own. Nevertheless, we apply the limitations of the Constitution with no fear that freedom to be intellectually and spiritually diverse or even contrary will disintegrate the social organization. To believe that patriotism will not flourish if patriotic ceremonies are voluntary and spontaneous, instead of a compulsory routine, is to make an unflattering estimate of the appeal of our institutions to free minds. We can have intellectual individualism and the rich cultural diversities that we owe to exceptional minds only at the price of occasional eccentricity and abnormal attitudes. When they are so harmless to others or to the State as those we deal with here, the price is not too great. But freedom to differ is not limited to things that do not matter much. That would be a mere shadow of freedom. The test of its substance is the right to differ as to things that touch the heart of the existing order.

If there is any fixed star in our constitutional constellation, it is that no official, high or petty, can prescribe what shall be orthodox in politics, nationalism, religion, or other matters of opinion, or force citizens to confess by word or act their faith therein. If there are any circumstances which permit an exception, they do not now occur to us.

We think the action of the local authorities in compelling the flag salute and pledge transcends constitutional limitations on their power, and invades the sphere of intellect and spirit which it is the purpose of the First Amendment to our Constitution to reserve from all official control.

The decision of this Court in *Minersville School District v. Gobitis,* and the holdings of those few per curiam decisions which preceded and foreshadowed it, are overruled, and the judgment enjoining enforcement of the West Virginia Regulation is affirmed.

Frankfurter, dissenting:

One who belongs to the most vilified and persecuted minority in history is not likely to be insensible to the freedoms guaranteed by our Constitution. Were my purely personal attitude relevant, I should wholeheartedly associate myself with the general libertarian views in the Court's opinion, representing, as they do, the thought and action of a lifetime. But, as judges, we are

neither Jew nor Gentile, neither Catholic nor agnostic. We owe equal attachment to the Constitution, and are equally bound by our judicial obligations whether we derive our citizenship from the earliest or the latest immigrants to these shores. As a member of this Court, I am not justified in writing my private notions of policy into the Constitution, no matter how deeply I may cherish them or how mischievous I may deem their disregard. The duty of a judge who must decide which of two claims before the Court shall prevail, that of a State to enact and enforce laws within its general competence or that of an individual to refuse obedience because of the demands of his conscience, is not that of the ordinary person. It can never be emphasized too much that one's own opinion about the wisdom or evil of a law should be excluded altogether when one is doing one's duty on the bench. The only opinion of our own even looking in that direction that is material is our opinion whether legislators could, in reason, have enacted such a law. In the light of all the circumstances, including the history of this question in this Court, it would require more daring than I possess to deny that reasonable legislators could have taken the action which is before us for review. Most unwillingly, therefore, I must differ from my brethren with regard to legislation like this. I cannot bring my mind to believe that the "liberty" secured by the Due Process Clause gives this Court authority to deny to the State of West Virginia the attainment of that which we all recognize as a legitimate legislative end, namely, the promotion of good citizenship, by employment of the means here chosen. . . .

One's conception of the Constitution cannot be severed from one's conception of a judge's function in applying it. The Court has no reason for existence if it merely reflects the pressures of the day. Our system is built on the faith that men set apart for this special function, freed from the influences of immediacy and from the deflections of worldly ambition, will become able to take a view of longer range than the period of responsibility entrusted to Congress and legislatures. We are dealing with matters as to which legislators and voters have conflicting views. Are we as judges to impose our strong convictions on where wisdom lies? That which three years ago had seemed to five successive Courts to lie within permissible areas of legislation is now outlawed by the deciding shift of opinion of two Justices. What reason is there to believe that they or their successors may not have another view a few years hence? Is that which was deemed to be of so fundamental a nature as to be written into the Constitution to endure for all times to be the sport of shifting winds of doctrine? Of course, judicial opinions, even as to questions of constitutionality, are not immutable. As has been true in the past, the Court will from time to time reverse its position. But I believe that never before these Jehovah's Witnesses cases (except for minor deviations subsequently retraced) has this Court overruled decisions so as to restrict the powers of democratic government. Always heretofore it has withdrawn narrow views of legislative authority so as to authorize what formerly it had denied. . . .

Of course, patriotism cannot be enforced by the flag salute. But neither can the liberal spirit be enforced by judicial invalidation of illiberal legislation. Our constant preoccupation with the constitutionality of legislation, rather than with its wisdom, tends to preoccupation of the American mind with a false value. The tendency of focusing attention on constitutionality is to make constitutionality synonymous with wisdom, to regard a law as all right if it is constitutional. Such an attitude is a great enemy of liberalism. Particularly in legislation affecting freedom of thought and freedom of speech, much which should offend a free-spirited society is constitutional. Reliance for the most precious interests of civilization, therefore, must be found outside of their vindication in courts of law. Only a persistent positive translation of the faith of a free society into the convictions and habits and action of a community is the ultimate reliance against unabated temptations to fetter the human spirit.

Sherbert v. Verner

374 U.S. 398 (1963), 7-2
Opinion of the Court: Brennan (Black, Clark, Douglas, Goldberg, Stewart, Warren)
Dissenting: Harlan, White

How does this case represent a conflict between the free exercise and establishment clauses? How would Justice Stewart resolve this conflict? Exactly what is a "compelling government interest"? What might be one that could justify South Carolina's regulation in this case? Can the decision here and those in Reynolds v. United States *(p. 109) and* West Virginia Board of Education v. Barnette *(p. 111) be explained by differences in the importance of the government's interest? In which case(s) is the religious practice most important for the believer? Is that a question courts or students of constitutional law should ask? Does the decision give preference to religious worship over other worthy activities such as refusing Saturday*

work in order to spend time with one's young children? Does it make a difference that free exercise is expressly protected in the Constitution but being an attentive parent is not?

Brennan, for the Court:
[Sherbert], a member of the Seventh-day Adventist Church, was discharged by her South Carolina employer because she would not work on Saturday, the Sabbath Day of her faith. When she was unable to obtain other employment because, from conscientious scruples, she would not take Saturday work, she filed a claim for unemployment compensation benefits under the South Carolina Unemployment Compensation Act. That law provides that, to be eligible for benefits, a claimant must be "able to work and . . . available for work"; and, further, that a claimant is ineligible for benefits "[i]f . . . The has failed, without good cause . . . to accept available suitable work when offered him by the employment office or the employer. . . ."

The appellee Employment Security Commission, in administrative proceedings under the statute, found that [Sherbert's] restriction upon her availability for Saturday work brought her within the provision disqualifying for benefits insured workers who fail, without good cause, to accept "suitable work when offered . . . by the employment office or the employer. . . ."

. . . If . . . the decision of the South Carolina Supreme Court is to withstand [Sherbert's] constitutional challenge, it must be either because her disqualification as a beneficiary represents no infringement by the State of her constitutional rights of free exercise, or because any incidental burden on the free exercise of [Sherbert's] religion may be justified by a "compelling state interest in the regulation of a subject within the State's constitutional power to regulate. . . ." *NAACP v. Button*

We turn first to the question whether the disqualification for benefits imposes any burden on the free exercise of [Sherbert's] religion. We think it is clear that it does. In a sense, the consequences of such a disqualification to religious principles and practices may be only an indirect result of welfare legislation within the State's general competence to enact; it is true that no criminal sanctions directly compel [Sherbert] to work a six-day week. But this is only the beginning, not the end, of our inquiry. For "[i]f the purpose or effect of a law is to impede the observance of one or all religions or is to discriminate invidiously between religions, that law is constitutionally invalid even though the burden may be characterized as being only indirect." *Braunfeld v. Brown* Here, not only is it apparent that [Sherbert's] declared ineligibility for benefits derives solely from the practice of her religion, but the pressure upon her to forego that practice is unmistakable. The ruling forces her to choose between following the precepts of her religion and forfeiting benefits, on the one hand, and abandoning one of the precepts of her religion in order to accept work, on the other hand. Governmental imposition of such a choice puts the same kind of burden upon the free exercise of religion as would a fine imposed against [Sherbert] for her Saturday worship. . . .

We must next consider whether some compelling state interest enforced in the eligibility provisions of the South Carolina statute justifies the substantial infringement of [Sherbert's] First Amendment right. It is basic that no showing merely of a rational relationship to some colorable state interest would suffice; in this highly sensitive constitutional area, "[o]nly the gravest abuses, endangering paramount interests, give occasion for permissible limitation," *Thomas v. Collins* No such abuse or danger has been advanced in the present case. The [Commission] suggest[s] no more than a possibility that the filing of fraudulent claims by unscrupulous claimants feigning religious objections to Saturday work might not only dilute the unemployment compensation fund, but also hinder the scheduling by employers of necessary Saturday work. But that possibility is not apposite here, because no such objection appears to have been made before the South Carolina Supreme Court, and we are unwilling to assess the importance of an asserted state interest without the views of the state court. Nor, if the contention had been made below, would the record appear to sustain it; there is no proof whatever to warrant such fears of malingering or deceit as those which the respondents now advance. Even if consideration of such evidence is not foreclosed by the prohibition against judicial inquiry into the truth or falsity of religious beliefs—a question as to which we intimate no view, since it is not before us—it is highly doubtful whether such evidence would be sufficient to warrant a substantial infringement of religious liberties. For even if the possibility of spurious claims did threaten to dilute the fund and disrupt the scheduling of work, it would plainly be incumbent upon the [Commission] to demonstrate that no alternative forms of regulation would combat such abuses without infringing First Amendment rights.

In these respects, then, the state interest asserted in the present case is wholly dissimilar to the interests

which were found to justify the less direct burden upon religious practices in *Braunfeld v. Brown.* The Court recognized that the Sunday closing law which that decision sustained undoubtedly served "to make the practice of [the Orthodox Jewish merchants'] . . . religious beliefs more expensive." But the statute was nevertheless saved by a countervailing factor which finds no equivalent in the instant case—a strong state interest in providing one uniform day of rest for all workers. That secular objective could be achieved, the Court found, only by declaring Sunday to be that day of rest. Requiring exemptions for Sabbatarians, while theoretically possible, appeared to present an administrative problem of such magnitude, or to afford the exempted class so great a competitive advantage, that such a requirement would have rendered the entire statutory scheme unworkable. In the present case, no such justifications underlie the determination of the state court that [Sherbert's] religion makes her ineligible to receive benefits.

In holding as we do, plainly we are not fostering the "establishment" of the Seventh-day Adventist religion in South Carolina, for the extension of unemployment benefits to Sabbatarians in common with Sunday worshippers reflects nothing more than the governmental obligation of neutrality in the face of religious differences, and does not represent that involvement of religious with secular institutions which it is the object of the Establishment Clause to forestall. Nor does the recognition of the [Sherbert's] right to unemployment benefits under the state statute serve to abridge any other person's religious liberties. Nor do we, by our decision today, declare the existence of a constitutional right to unemployment benefits on the part of all persons whose religious convictions are the cause of their unemployment. This is not a case in which an employee's religious convictions serve to make him a nonproductive member of society. Finally, nothing we say today constrains the States to adopt any particular form or scheme of unemployment compensation. Our holding today is only that South Carolina may not constitutionally apply the eligibility provisions so as to constrain a worker to abandon his religious convictions respecting the day of rest. . . .

Stewart, concurring:

Although fully agreeing with the result which the Court reaches in this case, I cannot join the Court's opinion. This case presents a double-barreled dilemma which, in all candor, I think the Court's opinion has not succeeded in papering over. The dilemma ought to be resolved. . . .

I am convinced that no liberty is more essential to the continued vitality of the free society which our Constitution guarantees than is the religious liberty protected by the Free Exercise Clause explicit in the First Amendment and imbedded in the Fourteenth. And I regret that, on occasion, and specifically in *Braunfeld v. Brown,* supra, the Court has shown what has seemed to me a distressing insensitivity to the appropriate demands of this constitutional guarantee. By contrast, I think that the Court's approach to the Establishment Clause has, on occasion, . . . been not only insensitive but positively wooden, and that the Court has accorded to the Establishment Clause a meaning which neither the words, the history, nor the intention of the authors of that specific constitutional provision even remotely suggests.

But my views as to the correctness of the Court's decisions in these cases are beside the point here. The point is that the decisions are on the books. And the result is that there are many situations where legitimate claims under the Free Exercise Clause will run into head-on collision with the Court's insensitive and sterile construction of the Establishment Clause. The controversy now before us is clearly such a case.

South Carolina would deny unemployment benefits to a mother unavailable for work on Saturdays because she was unable to get a babysitter. Thus, we do not have before us a situation where a State provides unemployment compensation generally, and singles out for disqualification only those persons who are unavailable for work on religious grounds. This is not, in short, a scheme which operates so as to discriminate against religion as such. But the Court nevertheless holds that the State must prefer a religious over a secular ground for being unavailable for work . . .

Yet in cases decided under the Establishment Clause, the Court has decreed otherwise. It has decreed that government must blind itself to the differing religious beliefs and traditions of the people. With all respect, I think it is the Court's duty to face up to the dilemma posed by the conflict between the Free Exercise Clause of the Constitution and the Establishment Clause as interpreted by the Court. It is a duty, I submit, which we owe to the people, the States, and the Nation, and a duty which we owe to ourselves. For so long as the resounding but fallacious fundamentalist rhetoric of some of our Establishment Clause opinions remains on our books, to be disregarded at will, as in the present case, or to be undiscriminatingly invoked, as in the Schempp case, so long will the possibility of consistent and perceptive decision in this most difficult and delicate area of constitutional law be impeded and impaired. And so long, I fear, will the guarantee of true religious freedom in our pluralistic society be uncertain and insecure.

My second difference with the Court's opinion is that I cannot agree that today's decision can stand consistently with *Braunfeld v. Brown.* The Court says that there was a "less direct burden upon religious practices" in that case than in this. With all respect, I think the Court is mistaken, simply as a matter of fact. I think the Braunfeld case was wrongly decided, and should be overruled, and accordingly I concur in the result reached by the Court in the case before us.

Harlan, dissenting:

. . . What the Court is holding is that, if the State chooses to condition unemployment compensation on the applicant's availability for work, it is constitutionally compelled to carve out an exception—and to provide benefits—for those whose unavailability is due to their religious convictions. Such a holding has particular significance in two respects.

First, despite the Court's protestations to the contrary, the decision necessarily overrules *Braunfeld v. Brown.* . . .

Second, the implications of the present decision are far more troublesome than its apparently narrow dimensions would indicate at first glance. The meaning of today's holding . . . is that the State must furnish unemployment benefits to one who is unavailable for work if the unavailability stems from the exercise of religious convictions. The State, in other words, must single out for financial assistance those whose behavior is religiously motivated, even though it denies such assistance to others whose identical behavior (in this case, inability to work on Saturdays) is not religiously motivated.

. . . It has been suggested that such singling out of religious conduct for special treatment may violate the constitutional limitations on state action. My own view, however, is that, at least under the circumstances of this case, it would be a permissible accommodation of religion for the State, if it chose to do so, to create an exception to its eligibility requirements for persons like the [Sherbert]. The constitutional obligation of "neutrality," is not so narrow a channel that the slightest deviation from an absolutely straight course leads to condemnation. . . .

For very much the same reasons, however, I cannot subscribe to the conclusion that the State is constitutionally compelled to carve out an exception to its general rule of eligibility in the present case.

Employment Division, Department of Human Resources of Oregon v. Smith

494 U.S. 872 (1990), 6-3

Opinion of the Court: Scalia (Kennedy, Rehnquist, Stevens, White)
Concurring: O'Connor
Dissenting: Blackmun, Brennan, Marshall

Has Justice Scalia convincingly distinguished Sherbert v. Verner? *(p. 115) What, if anything, is left of it? Is the government interest here more important than in* Sherbert *or did the Court reject the "compelling interest" test? Is this a case of majority intolerance of minority beliefs or of honoring the norms and morality manifest in criminal statutes? Is there any difference between the two? How can this case be reconciled with the next case,* Wisconsin v. Yoder?

Scalia, for the Court:

This case requires us to decide whether the Free Exercise Clause of the First Amendment permits the State of Oregon to include religiously inspired peyote use within the reach of its general criminal prohibition on use of that drug, and thus permits the State to deny unemployment benefits to persons dismissed from their jobs because of such religiously inspired use.

Oregon law prohibits the knowing or intentional possession of a "controlled substance" unless the substance has been prescribed by a medical practitioner. The law defines "controlled substance" as a drug classified in Schedules I through V of the Federal Controlled Substances Act, as modified by the State Board of Pharmacy. Persons who violate this provision by possessing a controlled substance listed on Schedule I are "guilty of a Class B felony." As compiled by the State Board of Pharmacy under its statutory authority, Schedule I contains the drug peyote, a hallucinogen . . .

Respondents Alfred Smith and Galen Black were fired from their jobs with a private drug rehabilitation organization because they ingested peyote for sacramental purposes at a ceremony of the Native American Church, of which both are members. When respondents applied to petitioner Employment Division for unemployment compensation, they were determined to be ineligible for benefits because they had been discharged for work-related "misconduct". . . .

. . . The free exercise of religion means . . . the right to believe and profess whatever religious doctrine one desires. Thus, the First Amendment obviously excludes all "governmental regulation of religious beliefs as such." The government may not compel affirmation of religious belief, punish the expression of religious doctrines it believes to be false, impose special disabilities on the basis of religious views or religious status, or lend its power to one or the other side in controversies over religious authority or dogma.

But the "exercise of religion" often involves not only belief and profession but the performance of (or abstention from) physical acts: assembling with others for a worship service, participating in sacramental use of bread and wine, proselytizing, abstaining from certain foods or certain modes of transportation. It would be true, we think (though no case of ours has involved the point), that a state would be "prohibiting the free exercise [of religion]" if it sought to ban such acts or abstentions only when they are engaged in for religious reasons, or only because of the religious belief that they display. It would doubtless be unconstitutional, for example, to ban the casting of "statues that are to be used for worship purposes," or to prohibit bowing down before a golden calf.

Respondents in the present case, however, seek to carry the meaning of "prohibiting the free exercise [of religion]" one large step further. They contend that their religious motivation for using peyote places them beyond the reach of a criminal law that is not specifically directed at their religious practice, and that is concededly constitutional as applied to those who use the drug for other reasons. They assert, in other words, that "prohibiting the free exercise [of religion]" includes requiring any individual to observe a generally applicable law that requires (or forbids) the performance of an act that his religious belief forbids (or requires). As a textual matter, we do not think the words must be given that meaning. It is no more necessary to regard the collection of a general tax, for example, as "prohibiting the free exercise [of religion]" by those citizens who believe support of organized government to be sinful than it is to regard the same tax as "abridging the freedom . . . of the press" of those publishing companies that must pay the tax as a condition of staying in business. It is a permissible reading of the text, in the one case as in the other, to say that, if prohibiting the exercise of religion (or burdening the activity of printing) is not the object of the tax, but merely the incidental effect of a generally applicable and otherwise valid provision, the First Amendment has not been offended. . . .

Our decisions reveal that the latter reading is the correct one. We have never held that an individual's religious beliefs excuse him from compliance with an otherwise valid law prohibiting conduct that the State is free to regulate. . . .

The only decisions in which we have held that the First Amendment bars application of a neutral, generally applicable law to religiously motivated action have involved not the Free Exercise Clause alone, but the Free Exercise Clause in conjunction with other constitutional protections, such as freedom of speech and of the press. . . .

The present case does not present such a hybrid situation, but a free exercise claim unconnected with any communicative activity or parental right. Respondents urge us to hold, quite simply, that when otherwise prohibitable conduct is accompanied by religious convictions, not only the convictions but the conduct itself must be free from governmental regulation. . . .

Respondents argue that, even though exemption from generally applicable criminal laws need not automatically be extended to religiously motivated actors, at least the claim for a religious exemption must be evaluated under the balancing test set forth in *Sherbert v. Verner.* Under the Sherbert test, governmental actions that substantially burden a religious practice must be justified by a compelling governmental interest. Applying that test, we have, on three occasions, invalidated state unemployment compensation rules that conditioned the availability of benefits upon an applicant's willingness to work under conditions forbidden by his religion. We have never invalidated any governmental action on the basis of the Sherbert test except the denial of unemployment compensation. . . .

Even if we were inclined to breathe into *Sherbert* some life beyond the unemployment compensation field, we would not apply it to require exemptions from a generally applicable criminal law. . . .

. . . We conclude today that the sounder approach, and the approach in accord with the vast majority of our precedents, is to hold the test inapplicable to such challenges. The government's ability to enforce generally applicable prohibitions of socially harmful conduct, like its ability to carry out other aspects of

public policy, "cannot depend on measuring the effects of a governmental action on a religious objector's spiritual development." To make an individual's obligation to obey such a law contingent upon the law's coincidence with his religious beliefs, except where the State's interest is "compelling"—permitting him, by virtue of his beliefs, "to become a law unto himself," *Reynolds v. United States*—contradicts both constitutional tradition and common sense.

The "compelling government interest" requirement seems benign, because it is familiar from other fields. But using it as the standard that must be met before the government may accord different treatment on the basis of race, or before the government may regulate the content of speech, is not remotely comparable to using it for the purpose asserted here. What it produces in those other fields—equality of treatment, and an unrestricted flow of contending speech—are constitutional norms; what it would produce here—a private right to ignore generally applicable laws—is a constitutional anomaly.

Nor is it possible to limit the impact of respondents' proposal by requiring a "compelling state interest" only when the conduct prohibited is "central" to the individual's religion. It is no more appropriate for judges to determine the "centrality" of religious beliefs before applying a "compelling interest" test in the free exercise field than it would be for them to determine the "importance" of ideas before applying the "compelling interest" test in the free speech field. What principle of law or logic can be brought to bear to contradict a believer's assertion that a particular act is "central" to his personal faith? . . .

If the "compelling interest" test is to be applied at all, then, it must be applied across the board, to all actions thought to be religiously commanded. Moreover, if "compelling interest" really means what it says (and watering it down here would subvert its rigor in the other fields where it is applied), many laws will not meet the test. Any society adopting such a system would be courting anarchy, but that danger increases in direct proportion to the society's diversity of religious beliefs, and its determination to coerce or suppress none of them. . . .

Values that are protected against government interference through enshrinement in the Bill of Rights are not thereby banished from the political process. Just as a society that believes in the negative protection accorded to the press by the First Amendment is likely to enact laws that affirmatively foster the dissemination of the printed word, so also a society that believes in the negative protection accorded to religious belief can be expected to be solicitous of that value in its legislation as well. It is therefore not surprising that a number of States have made an exception to their drug laws for sacramental peyote use. But to say that a nondiscriminatory religious practice exemption is permitted, or even that it is desirable, is not to say that it is constitutionally required, and that the appropriate occasions for its creation can be discerned by the courts. It may fairly be said that leaving accommodation to the political process will place at a relative disadvantage those religious practices that are not widely engaged in; but that unavoidable consequence of democratic government must be preferred to a system in which each conscience is a law unto itself or in which judges weigh the social importance of all laws against the centrality of all religious beliefs.

Because respondents' ingestion of peyote was prohibited under Oregon law, and because that prohibition is constitutional, Oregon may, consistent with the Free Exercise Clause, deny respondents unemployment compensation when their dismissal results from use of the drug. The decision of the Oregon Supreme Court is accordingly reversed.

O'Connor, concurring:

...Because the First Amendment does not distinguish between religious belief and religious conduct, conduct motivated by sincere religious belief, like the belief itself, must therefore be at least presumptively protected by the Free Exercise Clause.

The Court today, however, interprets the Clause to permit the government to prohibit, without justification, conduct mandated by an individual's religious beliefs, so long as that prohibition is generally applicable. But a law that prohibits certain conduct—conduct that happens to be an act of worship for someone—manifestly does prohibit that person's free exercise of his religion. A person who is barred from engaging in religiously motivated conduct is barred from freely exercising his religion. Moreover, that person is barred from freely exercising his religion regardless of whether the law prohibits the conduct only when engaged in for religious reasons, only by members of that religion, or by all persons. It is difficult to deny that a law that prohibits religiously motivated conduct, even if the law is generally applicable, does not at least implicate First Amendment concerns. ...

To say that a person's right to free exercise has been burdened, of course, does not mean that he has an absolute right to engage in the conduct. Under

our established First Amendment jurisprudence, we have recognized that the freedom to act, unlike the freedom to believe, cannot be absolute. Instead, we have respected both the First Amendment's express textual mandate and the governmental interest in regulation of conduct by requiring the Government to justify any substantial burden on religiously motivated conduct by a compelling state interest and by means narrowly tailored to achieve that interest. The compelling interest test effectuates the First Amendment's command that religious liberty is an independent liberty, that it occupies a preferred position, and that the Court will not permit encroachments upon this liberty, whether direct or indirect, unless required by clear and compelling governmental interests "of the highest order."

Only an especially important governmental interest pursued by narrowly tailored means can justify exacting a sacrifice of First Amendment freedoms as the price for an equal share of the rights, benefits, and privileges enjoyed by other citizens.

The Court today gives no convincing reason to depart from settled First Amendment jurisprudence. ... The Court's parade of horribles not only fails as a reason for discarding the compelling interest test, it instead demonstrates just the opposite: that courts have been quite capable of applying our free exercise jurisprudence to strike sensible balances between religious liberty and competing state interests.

Finally, the Court today suggests that the disfavoring of minority religions is an "unavoidable consequence" under our system of government, and that accommodation of such religions must be left to the political process. ...

...The compelling interest test reflects the First Amendment's mandate of preserving religious liberty to the fullest extent possible in a pluralistic society. ...

The Court's holding today not only misreads settled First Amendment precedent; it appears to be unnecessary to this case. I would reach the same result applying our established free exercise jurisprudence.

There is no dispute that Oregon's criminal prohibition of peyote places a severe burden on the ability of respondents to freely exercise their religion. Peyote is a sacrament of the Native American Church, and is regarded as vital to respondents' ability to practice their religion. ...

...Under Oregon law, as construed by that State's highest court, members of the Native American Church must choose between carrying out the ritual embodying their religious beliefs and avoidance of criminal prosecution. That choice is, in my view, more than sufficient to trigger First Amendment scrutiny. . . .

. . . [T]he critical question in this case is whether exempting respondents from the State's general criminal prohibition "will unduly interfere with fulfillment of the governmental interest." Although the question is close, I would conclude that uniform application of Oregon's criminal prohibition is "essential to accomplish," its overriding interest in preventing the physical harm caused by the use of a Schedule I controlled substance. Oregon's criminal prohibition represents that State's judgment that the possession and use of controlled substances, even by only one person, is inherently harmful and dangerous. Because the health effects caused by the use of controlled substances exist regardless of the motivation of the user, the use of such substances, even for religious purposes, violates the very purpose of the laws that prohibit them. Moreover, in view of the societal interest in preventing trafficking in controlled substances, uniform application of the criminal prohibition at issue is essential to the effectiveness of Oregon's stated interest in preventing any possession of peyote.

For these reasons, I believe that granting a selective exemption in this case would seriously impair Oregon's compelling interest in prohibiting possession of peyote by its citizens. Under such circumstances, the Free Exercise Clause does not require the State to accommodate respondents' religiously motivated conduct. . . .

Blackmun, dissenting:
This Court over the years painstakingly has developed a consistent and exacting standard to test the constitutionality of a state statute that burdens the free exercise of religion. Such a statute may stand only if the law in general, and the State's refusal to allow a religious exemption in particular, are justified by a compelling interest that cannot be served by less restrictive means.

Until today, I thought this was a settled and inviolate principle of this Court's First Amendment jurisprudence. The majority, however, perfunctorily dismisses it as a "constitutional anomaly." . . .

. . . It is not the State's broad interest in fighting the critical "war on drugs" that must be weighed against respondents' claim, but the State's narrow interest in refusing to make an exception for the religious, ceremonial use of peyote. . . .

The State proclaims an interest in protecting the health and safety of its citizens from the dangers of un-

lawful drugs. It offers, however, no evidence that the religious use of peyote has ever harmed anyone. The factual findings of other courts cast doubt on the State's assumption that religious use of peyote is harmful. . . .

The fact that peyote is classified as a Schedule I controlled substance does not, by itself, show that any and all uses of peyote, in any circumstance, are inherently harmful and dangerous. The Federal Government, which created the classifications of unlawful drugs from which Oregon's drug laws are derived, apparently does not find peyote so dangerous as to preclude an exemption for religious use.

The carefully circumscribed ritual context in which respondents used peyote is far removed from the irresponsible and unrestricted recreational use of unlawful drugs. The Native American Church's internal restrictions on, and supervision of, its members' use of peyote substantially obviate the State's health and safety concerns . . .

The State also seeks to support its refusal to make an exception for religious use of peyote by invoking its interest in abolishing drug trafficking. There is, however, practically no illegal traffic in peyote. . . . Peyote simply is not a popular drug; its distribution for use in religious rituals has nothing to do with the vast and violent traffic in illegal narcotics that plagues this country.

Finally, the State argues that granting an exception for religious peyote use would erode its interest in the uniform, fair, and certain enforcement of its drug laws. The State fears that, if it grants an exemption for religious peyote use, a flood of other claims to religious exemptions will follow. It would then be placed in a dilemma, it says, between allowing a patchwork of exemptions that would hinder its law enforcement efforts, and risking a violation of the Establishment Clause by arbitrarily limiting its religious exemptions. This argument, however, could be made in almost any free exercise case. This Court, however, consistently has rejected similar arguments in past free exercise cases, and it should do so here as well.

The State's apprehension of a flood of other religious claims is purely speculative. Almost half the States, and the Federal Government, have maintained an exemption for religious peyote use for many years, and apparently have not found themselves overwhelmed by claims to other religious exemptions. Allowing an exemption for religious peyote use would not necessarily oblige the State to grant a similar exemption to other religious groups. The unusual circumstances that make the religious use of peyote compatible with the State's interests in health and safety and in preventing drug trafficking would not apply to other religious claims. Some religions, for example, might not restrict drug use to a limited ceremonial context, as does the Native American Church. Some religious claims involve drugs such as marijuana and heroin, in which there is significant illegal traffic, with its attendant greed and violence, so that it would be difficult to grant a religious exemption without seriously compromising law enforcement efforts. That the State might grant an exemption for religious peyote use, but deny other religious claims arising in different circumstances, would not violate the Establishment Clause. Though the State must treat all religions equally, and not favor one over another, this obligation is fulfilled by the uniform application of the "compelling interest" test to all free exercise claims, not by reaching uniform results as to all claims. A showing that religious peyote use does not unduly interfere with the State's interests is "one that probably few other religious groups or sects could make," this does not mean that an exemption limited to peyote use is tantamount to an establishment of religion. . . .

For these reasons, I conclude that Oregon's interest in enforcing its drug laws against religious use of peyote is not sufficiently compelling to outweigh respondents' right to the free exercise of their religion. Since the State could not constitutionally enforce its criminal prohibition against respondents, the interests underlying the State's drug laws cannot justify its denial of unemployment benefits. Absent such justification, the State's regulatory interest in denying benefits for religiously motivated "misconduct," is indistinguishable from the state interests this Court has rejected. . . . The State of Oregon cannot, consistently with the Free Exercise Clause, deny respondents unemployment benefits.

Wisconsin v. Yoder

406 U.S. 205 (1972), 6-1
Opinion of the Court: Burger (Blackmun, Brennan, Marshall, Stewart, White)
Dissenting: Douglas
Not participating: Powell, Rehnquist

Is Wisconsin's interest in educating the young "compelling"? In educating the Amish young, who may number in the thousands or tens of thousands? It is clear what the Amish gain

by this decision. Does society lose anything by it, or are all losses "absorbed" by the Amish? Has the Court given "religion" broader scope and meaning in this case than the concept has in common usage? Does it allow religion to be largely self-defined? How can this case be reconciled with Reynolds v. the United States *(p. 109)? Does the decision extend free exercise rights at the expense of the wall of separation or is it merely a generous accommodation of religious diversity? Was the fact that the Amish are widely acknowledged to be "law-abiding" and "hard-working" citizens a factor in this case? Would this decision be defensible if it were shown that a large number of Amish children leave their communities as adults? Would a community of dedicated atheists or philosophers be permitted to refuse to allow their children to be educated beyond the eighth grade?*

Burger, for the Court:

On petition of the State of Wisconsin, we granted the writ of certiorari in this case to review a decision of the Wisconsin Supreme Court holding that respondents' convictions of violating the State's compulsory school attendance law were invalid under the Free Exercise Clause of the First Amendment. . . .

Respondents Jonas Yoder and Wallace Miller are members of the Old Order Amish religion, and respondent Adin Yutzy is a member of the Conservative Amish Mennonite Church. They and their families are residents of Green County, Wisconsin. Wisconsin's compulsory school attendance law required them to cause their children to attend public or private school until reaching age 16, but the respondents declined to send their children, ages 14 and 15, to public school after they completed the eighth grade. The children were not enrolled in any private school, or within any recognized exception to the compulsory attendance law, and they are conceded to be subject to the Wisconsin statute.

On complaint of the school district administrator for the public schools, respondents were charged, tried, and convicted of violating the compulsory attendance law in Green County Court, and were fined the sum of $5 each. Respondents defended on the ground that the application of the compulsory attendance law violated their rights under the First and Fourteenth Amendments. The trial testimony showed that respondents believed, in accordance with the tenets of Old Order Amish communities generally, that their children's attendance at high school, public or private, was contrary to the Amish religion and way of life. They believed that, by sending their children to high school, they would not only expose themselves to the danger of the censure of the church community, but, as found by the county court, also endanger their own salvation and that of their children. The State stipulated that respondents' religious beliefs were sincere. . . .

We come . . . to the quality of the claims of the respondents concerning the alleged encroachment of Wisconsin's compulsory school attendance statute on their rights and the rights of their children to the free exercise of the religious beliefs they and their forebears have adhered to for almost three centuries. . . .

. . . . [W]e see that the record in this case abundantly supports the claim that the traditional way of life of the Amish is not merely a matter of personal preference, but one of deep religious conviction, shared by an organized group, and intimately related to daily living. . . .

As the society around the Amish has become more populous, urban, industrialized, and complex, particularly in this century, government regulation of human affairs has correspondingly become more detailed and pervasive. The Amish mode of life has thus come into conflict increasingly with requirements of contemporary society exerting a hydraulic insistence on conformity to majoritarian standards. So long as compulsory education laws were confined to eight grades of elementary basic education imparted in a nearby rural schoolhouse, with a large proportion of students of the Amish faith, the Old Order Amish had little basis to fear that school attendance would expose their children to the worldly influence they reject. But modern compulsory secondary education in rural areas is now largely carried on in a consolidated school, often remote from the student's home and alien to his daily home life. As the record so strongly shows, the values and programs of the modern secondary school are in sharp conflict with the fundamental mode of life mandated by the Amish religion; modern laws requiring compulsory secondary education have accordingly engendered great concern and conflict. The conclusion is inescapable that secondary schooling, by exposing Amish children to worldly influences in terms of attitudes, goals, and values contrary to beliefs, and by substantially interfering with the religious development of the Amish child and his integration into the way of life of the Amish faith community at the crucial adolescent stage of development, contravenes the basic religious tenets and practice of the Amish faith, both as to the parent and the child. . . .

We turn, then, to the State's broader contention that its interest in its system of compulsory education is so compelling that even the established religious practices of the Amish must give way. Where fundamental claims of religious freedom are at stake, however, we cannot accept such a sweeping claim; despite its admitted validity in the generality of cases, we must searchingly examine the interests that the State seeks to promote by its requirement for compulsory education to age 16, and the impediment to those objectives that would flow from recognizing the claimed Amish exemption.

The State advances two primary arguments in support of its system of compulsory education. It notes, as Thomas Jefferson pointed out early in our history, that some degree of education is necessary to prepare citizens to participate effectively and intelligently in our open political system if we are to preserve freedom and independence. Further, education prepares individuals to be self-reliant and self-sufficient participants in society. We accept these propositions.

However, the evidence adduced by the Amish in this case is persuasively to the effect that an additional one or two years of formal high school for Amish children in place of their long-established program of informal vocational education would do little to serve those interests. . . .

The State . . . supports its interest in providing an additional one or two years of compulsory high school education to Amish children because of the possibility that some such children will choose to leave the Amish community, and that, if this occurs, they will be ill-equipped for life. The State argues that, if Amish children leave their church, they should not be in the position of making their way in the world without the education available in the one or two additional years the State requires. However, on this record, that argument is highly speculative. There is no specific evidence of the loss of Amish adherents by attrition, nor is there any showing that, upon leaving the Amish community, Amish children, with their practical agricultural training and habits of industry and self-reliance, would become burdens on society because of educational shortcomings. Indeed, this argument of the State appears to rest primarily on the State's mistaken assumption, already noted, that the Amish do not provide any education for their children beyond the eighth grade, but allow them to grow in "ignorance." To the contrary, not only do the Amish accept the necessity for formal schooling through the eighth grade level, but continue to provide what has been characterized by the undisputed testimony of expert educators as an "ideal" vocational education for their children in the adolescent years.

There is nothing in this record to suggest that the Amish qualities of reliability, self-reliance, and dedication to work would fail to find ready markets in today's society. Absent some contrary evidence supporting the State's position, we are unwilling to assume that persons possessing such valuable vocational skills and habits are doomed to become burdens on society should they determine to leave the Amish faith, nor is there any basis in the record to warrant a finding that an additional one or two years of formal school education beyond the eighth grade would serve to eliminate any such problem that might exist. . . .

Finally, the State . . . argues that a decision exempting Amish children from the State's requirement fails to recognize the substantive right of the Amish child to a secondary education, and fails to give due regard to the power of the State as parens patriae to extend the benefit of secondary education to children regardless of the wishes of their parents. . . .

Contrary to the suggestion of the dissenting opinion of Mr. Justice Douglas, our holding today in no degree depends on the assertion of the religious interest of the child, as contrasted with that of the parents. It is the parents who are subject to prosecution here for failing to cause their children to attend school, and it is their right of free exercise, not that of their children, that must determine Wisconsin's power to impose criminal penalties on the parent. The dissent argues that a child who expresses a desire to attend public high school in conflict with the wishes of his parents should not be prevented from doing so. There is no reason for the Court to consider that point, since it is not an issue in the case. The children are not parties to this litigation. The State has at no point tried this case on the theory that respondents were preventing their children from attending school against their expressed desires, and, indeed, the record is to the contrary. The state's position from the outset has been that it is empowered to apply its compulsory attendance law to Amish parents in the same manner as to other parents—that is, without regard to the wishes of the child. That is the claim we reject today. . . .

For the reasons stated we hold, with the Supreme Court of Wisconsin, that the First and Fourteenth Amendments prevent the State from compelling respondents to cause their children to attend formal high school to age 16. . . .

Douglas, dissenting:

. . . The Court's analysis assumes that the only interests at stake in the case are those of the Amish parents, on the one hand, and those of the State, on the other. The difficulty with this approach is that, despite the Court's claim, the parents are seeking to vindicate not only their own free exercise claims, but also those of their high-school-age children.

. . . Where the child is mature enough to express potentially conflicting desires, it would be an invasion of the child's rights to permit such an imposition without canvassing his views. . . . As the child has no other effective forum, it is in this litigation that his rights should be considered. And if an Amish child desires to attend high school, and is mature enough to have that desire respected, the State may well be able to override the parents' religiously motivated objections. . . .

City of Boerne v. Flores

521 U.S. 507 (1997), 6-3
Opinion of the Court: Kennedy (Ginsburg, Rehnquist, Scalia, Stevens, Thomas)
Dissenting: O'Connor, Souter, Breyer

Does Congress have the right to "correct" the Court by making one of the Court's partially abandoned holdings prevailing law? Can it do this if that earlier holding was an interpretation of a constitutional provision? Would that be allowing Congress to interpret the Constitution? Is that unconstitutional? If you agree that Congress changed the meaning of the free exercise clause in the Religious Freedom Restoration Act, was doing so an unconstitutional establishment of religion?

Kennedy, for the Court:

A decision by local zoning authorities to deny a church a building permit was challenged under the Religious Freedom Restoration Act of 1993 (RFRA). The case calls into question the authority of Congress to enact RFRA. We conclude the statute exceeds Congress' power.

Situated on a hill in the city of Boerne, Texas, some 28 miles northwest of San Antonio, is St. Peter Catholic Church. Built in 1923, the church's structure replicates the mission style of the region's earlier history. The church seats about 230 worshippers, a number too small for its growing parish. Some 40 to 60 parishioners cannot be accommodated at some Sunday masses. In order to meet the needs of the congregation the Archbishop of San Antonio gave permission to the parish to plan alterations to enlarge the building.

A few months later, the Boerne City Council passed an ordinance authorizing the city's Historic Landmark Commission to prepare a preservation plan with proposed historic landmarks and districts. Under the ordinance, the Commission must preapprove construction affecting historic landmarks or buildings in a historic district.

Soon afterwards, the Archbishop applied for a building permit so construction to enlarge the church could proceed. City authorities, relying on the ordinance and the designation of a historic district (which, they argued, included the church), denied the application. The Archbishop brought this suit challenging the permit denial. . . .

Congress enacted RFRA in direct response to the Court's decision in *Employment Div., Dept. of Human Resources of Ore. v. Smith.* There we considered a Free Exercise Clause claim brought by members of the Native American Church who were denied unemployment benefits when they lost their jobs because they had used peyote. Their practice was to ingest peyote for sacramental purposes, and they challenged an Oregon statute of general applicability which made use of the drug criminal. In evaluating the claim, we declined to apply the balancing test set forth in *Sherbert v. Verner,* under which we would have asked whether Oregon's prohibition substantially burdened a religious practice and, if it did, whether the burden was justified by a compelling government interest. We stated:

> "[G]overnment's ability to enforce generally applicable prohibitions of socially harmful conduct . . . cannot depend on measuring the effects of a governmental action on a religious objector's spiritual development. To make an individual's obligation to obey such a law contingent upon the law's coincidence with his religious beliefs, except where the State's interest is 'compelling' . . . contradicts both constitutional tradition and common sense." . . . .

. . . *Smith* held that neutral, generally applicable laws may be applied to religious practices even when not supported by a compelling governmental inter-

est. . . . Many [members of Congress] criticized the Court's reasoning, and this disagreement resulted in the passage of RFRA. . . .

. . . . The Act's mandate applies to any "branch, department, agency, instrumentality, and official (or other person acting under color of law) of the United States," as well as to any "State, or . . . subdivision of a State." The Act's universal coverage . . . . "applies to all Federal and State law, and the implementation of that law, whether statutory or otherwise, and whether adopted before or after [RFRA's enactment]." . . .

Congress relied on its Fourteenth Amendment enforcement power in enacting the most far reaching and substantial of RFRA's provisions, those which impose its requirements on the States. . . .

The parties disagree over whether RFRA is a proper exercise of Congress' §5 power "to enforce" by "appropriate legislation" the constitutional guarantee that no State shall deprive any person of "life, liberty, or property, without due process of law" nor deny any person "equal protection of the laws." . . .

Legislation which deters or remedies constitutional violations can fall within the sweep of Congress' enforcement power even if in the process it prohibits conduct which is not itself unconstitutional and intrudes into "legislative spheres of autonomy previously reserved to the States." *Fitzpatrick v. Bitzer.* . . .

It is also true, however, that "[a]s broad as the congressional enforcement power is, it is not unlimited." *Oregon v. Mitchell* . . . .

Congress' power under §5 . . . extends only to "enforc[ing]" the provisions of the Fourteenth Amendment. The Court has described this power as "remedial," *South Carolina v. Katzenbach.* The design of the Amendment and the text of §5 are inconsistent with the suggestion that Congress has the power to decree the substance of the Fourteenth Amendment's restrictions on the States. Legislation which alters the meaning of the Free Exercise Clause cannot be said to be enforcing the Clause. Congress does not enforce a constitutional right by changing what the right is. It has been given the power "to enforce," not the power to determine what constitutes a constitutional violation. Were it not so, what Congress would be enforcing would no longer be, in any meaningful sense, the "provisions of [the Fourteenth Amendment]."

While the line between measures that remedy or prevent unconstitutional actions and measures that make a substantive change in the governing law is not easy to discern, and Congress must have wide latitude in determining where it lies, the distinction exists and must be observed. There must be a congruence and proportionality between the injury to be prevented or remedied and the means adopted to that end. Lacking such a connection, legislation may become substantive in operation and effect. . . .

The design of the Fourteenth Amendment has proved significant also in maintaining the traditional separation of powers between Congress and the Judiciary. The first eight Amendments to the Constitution set forth self-executing prohibitions on governmental action, and this Court has had primary authority to interpret those prohibitions. . . . As enacted, the Fourteenth Amendment confers substantive rights against the States which, like the provisions of the Bill of Rights, are self-executing. The power to interpret the Constitution in a case or controversy remains in the Judiciary.

The remedial and preventive nature of Congress' enforcement power, and the limitation inherent in the power, were confirmed in our earliest cases on the Fourteenth Amendment. In the Civil Rights Cases the Court invalidated sections of the Civil Rights Act of 1875 which prescribed criminal penalties for denying to any person "the full enjoyment of" public accommodations and conveyances, on the grounds that it exceeded Congress' power by seeking to regulate private conduct. The Enforcement Clause, the Court said, did not authorize Congress to pass "general legislation upon the rights of the citizen, but corrective legislation; that is, such as may be necessary and proper for counteracting such laws as the States may adopt or enforce, and which, by the amendment, they are prohibited from making or enforcing. . . .

Any suggestion that Congress has a substantive, non-remedial power under the Fourteenth Amendment is not supported by our case law. . . .

If Congress could define its own powers by altering the Fourteenth Amendment's meaning, no longer would the Constitution be "superior paramount law, unchangeable by ordinary means." It would be "on a level with ordinary legislative acts, and, like other acts, . . . alterable when the legislature shall please to alter it." *Marbury v. Madison.* Under this approach, it is difficult to conceive of a principle that would limit congressional power. Shifting legislative majorities could change the Constitution and effectively circumvent the difficult and detailed amendment process contained in Article V. . . .

Respondent contends that RFRA is a proper exercise of Congress' remedial or preventive power. The Act, it is said, is a reasonable means of protecting the free exercise of religion as defined by *Smith*. . . . If Congress can prohibit laws with discriminatory effects in order to prevent racial discrimination in violation of the Equal Protection Clause, then it can do the same, respondent argues, to promote religious liberty.

While preventive rules are sometimes appropriate remedial measures, there must be a congruence between the means used and the ends to be achieved. The appropriateness of remedial measures must be considered in light of the evil presented. Strong measures appropriate to address one harm may be an unwarranted response to another, lesser one.

A comparison between RFRA and the Voting Rights Act is instructive. In contrast to the record which confronted Congress and the judiciary in the voting rights cases, RFRA's legislative record lacks examples of modern instances of generally applicable laws passed because of religious bigotry. The history of persecution in this country detailed in the hearings mentions no episodes occurring in the past 40 years. . . .

Regardless of the state of the legislative record, RFRA cannot be considered remedial, preventive legislation, if those terms are to have any meaning. RFRA is so out of proportion to a supposed remedial or preventive object that it cannot be understood as responsive to, or designed to prevent, unconstitutional behavior. It appears, instead, to attempt a substantive change in constitutional protections. Preventive measures prohibiting certain types of laws may be appropriate when there is reason to believe that many of the laws affected by the congressional enactment have a significant likelihood of being unconstitutional. . .

RFRA is not so confined. Sweeping coverage ensures its intrusion at every level of government, displacing laws and prohibiting official actions of almost every description and regardless of subject matter. RFRA's restrictions apply to every agency and official of the Federal, State, and local Governments. RFRA applies to all federal and state law, statutory or otherwise, whether adopted before or after its enactment. RFRA has no termination date or termination mechanism. Any law is subject to challenge at any time by any individual who alleges a substantial burden on his or her free exercise of religion. . . .

The stringent test RFRA demands of state laws reflects a lack of proportionality or congruence between the means adopted and the legitimate end to be achieved. If an objector can show a substantial burden on his free exercise, the State must demonstrate a compelling governmental interest and show that the law is the least restrictive means of furthering its interest. Claims that a law substantially burdens someone's exercise of religion will often be difficult to contest. Requiring a State to demonstrate a compelling interest and show that it has adopted the least restrictive means of achieving that interest is the most demanding test known to constitutional law. . . . This is a considerable congressional intrusion into the States' traditional prerogatives and general authority to regulate for the health and welfare of their citizens. . . .

. . . It is a reality of the modern regulatory state that numerous state laws, such as the zoning regulations at issue here, impose a substantial burden on a large class of individuals. When the exercise of religion has been burdened in an incidental way by a law of general application, it does not follow that the persons affected have been burdened any more than other citizens, let alone burdened because of their religious beliefs. In addition, the Act imposes in every case a least restrictive means requirement–a requirement that was not used in the pre-*Smith* jurisprudence RFRA purported to codify—which also indicates that the legislation is broader than is appropriate if the goal is to prevent and remedy constitutional violations.

When Congress acts within its sphere of power and responsibilities, it has not just the right but the duty to make its own informed judgment on the meaning and force of the Constitution. This has been clear from the early days of the Republic. . . . Were it otherwise, we would not afford Congress the presumption of validity its enactments now enjoy.

Our national experience teaches that the Constitution is preserved best when each part of the government respects both the Constitution and the proper actions and determinations of the other branches. When the Court has interpreted the Constitution, it has acted within the province of the Judicial Branch, which embraces the duty to say what the law is. *Marbury v. Madison*. When the political branches of the Government act against the background of a judicial interpretation of the Constitution already issued, it must be understood that in later cases and controversies the Court will treat its precedents with the respect due them under settled principles, including stare decisis, and contrary expectations must be disappointed.

RFRA was designed to control cases and controversies, such as the one before us; but as the provisions of the federal statute here invoked are beyond congressional authority, it is this Court's precedent, not RFRA, which must control.

It is for Congress in the first instance to "determin[e] whether and what legislation is needed to secure the guarantees of the Fourteenth Amendment," and its conclusions are entitled to much deference. Congress' discretion is not unlimited, however, and the courts retain the power, as they have since *Marbury v. Madison*, to determine if Congress has exceeded its authority under the Constitution. Broad as the power of Congress is under the Enforcement Clause of the Fourteenth Amendment, RFRA contradicts vital principles necessary to maintain separation of powers and the federal balance. . . .

Stevens, concurring:

In my opinion, the Religious Freedom Restoration Act of 1993 (RFRA) is a "law respecting an establishment of religion" that violates the First Amendment to the Constitution.

If the historic landmark on the hill in Boerne happened to be a museum or an art gallery owned by an atheist, it would not be eligible for an exemption from the city ordinances that forbid an enlargement of the structure. Because the landmark is owned by the Catholic Church, it is claimed that RFRA gives its owner a federal statutory entitlement to an exemption from a generally applicable, neutral civil law. Whether the Church would actually prevail under the statute or not, the statute has provided the Church with a legal weapon that no atheist or agnostic can obtain. This governmental preference for religion, as opposed to irreligion, is forbidden by the First Amendment.

O'Connor, dissenting:

. . . I agree with the Court that the issue before us is whether the Religious Freedom Restoration Act (RFRA) is a proper exercise of Congress' power to enforce §5 of the Fourteenth Amendment. But as a yardstick for measuring the constitutionality of RFRA, the Court uses its holding in *Employment Div., Dept. of Human Resources of Ore. v. Smith*, the decision that prompted Congress to enact RFRA as a means of more rigorously enforcing the Free Exercise Clause. I remain of the view that *Smith* was wrongly decided, and I would use this case to reexamine the Court's holding there. Therefore, I would direct the parties to brief the question whether *Smith* represents the correct understanding of the Free Exercise Clause and set the case for reargument. If the Court were to correct the misinterpretation of the Free Exercise Clause set forth in *Smith*, it would simultaneously put our First Amendment jurisprudence back on course and allay the legitimate concerns of a majority in Congress who believed that *Smith* improperly restricted religious liberty. We would then be in a position to review RFRA in light of a proper interpretation of the Free Exercise Clause. . . .

3

SPEECH AND ASSEMBLY

The freedoms of speech and press, which follow the religion clauses in the First Amendment, refer together to the right to communicate. They are prominent in the Bill of Rights for good reason.

Communication is not only transmitting information—facts and ideas—it is also the expression of opinions, attitudes, and feelings. Though usually relying on the spoken or written word, communication may use other symbolic means—graphic, electronic, or simply that which is embodied in certain behavior. In conveying meaning, communication is the avenue between the "unlimited" inner world of thought, imagination, and emotion and the outer one of act and event circumscribed by physical limits and social probabilities. In a material sense, communication is more than the first but less than the second. Though not affecting its audience physically or materially, it may do so cognitively or psychologically. Though not action itself, it may lead to acts.

Most communication is probably informative, instructive, even entertaining. But the power to represent—to convey meaning and opinion—can be challenging, even threatening to others, including established political, social, or cultural authority. It is not surprising to find communication a source of conflict and strife in all societies. In the long history of politics and government, disputes about what may be communicated or otherwise symbolized have vied in importance with classic struggles over competing religious beliefs or the distribution of material resources.

A Freedom Slow to Develop

Communicated ideas, opinions, attitudes, and feelings can clash with different interests. Some of the latter are rightfully equated with short-sighted, foolish, or oppressive authority, but others may embody desirable political and social ends, such as national security, public order, privacy and personal reputation, and simple peace and quiet.

Like many other civil liberties, freedom of speech can be traced in a thin line to the Magna Carta, which English nobles who were unhappy with royal policies forced King John to sign in 1215. The "Great Charter" did not mention the freedom specifically, but it seeded constitutional limits on government in the name of individual liberty.

Political liberty and the right to speak freely about government has a checkered history of many advances and setbacks. At first, only royalty and high church officials had anything like a right to speak their minds about the King and regime. For others, criticism might be equated with treason and risk severe penalty. Not until the English Bill of Rights in 1689 was this freedom officially given even to members of Parliament, and then only when in session. Though such limits seem cramped to us, they were directed mainly at two "evils": sedition—criticism of authority assumed to lead to disloyalty and insurrection against the state—and blasphemy. Out of this struggle over political and religious expression the modern Anglo-American freedom of speech emerged.

For a century beginning in 1542, the notorious Court of the Star Chamber, the judicial arm of the King's Privy Council, heard hundreds of sedition cases, most dealing with the new technology of printing and publishing. The Court sat without jury and guilty verdicts often rested on confessions extracted by torture. After it was abolished, common law courts heard sedition cases before juries, but truth, believed more damaging to the government than falsehood, was not permitted as a defense. Not until Fox's Libel Act in 1792 could the jury, rather than judge, decide whether the offending speech was in fact seditious, and find truth in it exonerating.

Suppression of political dissent had its ecclesiastical counterpart in prosecutions for blasphemous libel. In these, with government support the state Church of England could legally suppress heretical opinions and "false teachings."

Seditious and blasphemous libel were limits on free expression in colonial America as well, though tempered perhaps by the greater social and religious diversity and sheer physical space

in the New World. The chief agents of control at first were the royal governors and popular colonial assemblies, but this power soon passed to the courts. In a notable 1735 case, a jury acquitted John Peter Zenger for publishing an attack on the governor of New York accusing him of incompetence and several illegal acts. Accepting truth as a defense (more than half a century before Fox's Libel Act did so in England), the jury ignored the judge's instructions. Though a free speech landmark, the libertarian verdict was more the exception than the rule in colonial sedition cases.

Growing conflict between the colonies and the parent country in the 1760s and 1770s gave open political debate new standing as American revolutionists celebrated dissent and the criticism of English authority. But the root was more pragmatic than principled. The same freedom of speech the revolutionaries used so effectively was only reluctantly accorded to Tory opponents of independence. During and immediately after the Revolution, the average American probably had more freedom to express political opinions than persons in almost any other country, though in both theory and practice it fell well short of the modern concept.

How far Americans had advanced in recognizing a freedom to communicate is evident in the bills of rights that were fixtures in several new state constitutions, beginning with Virginia's in 1776. All included speech and press provisions. The first national constitution, the Articles of Confederation, being little more than a contract of alliance among 13 independent states, did not address individual liberties. The Federal Constitution in 1787, though containing several liberty-protecting provisions, did not mention speech or press freedoms either. Its omission of a formal bill of rights that most state constitutions had became a salient issue in the debate over ratification. The promise of the Constitution's supporters to add protections was important in securing final approval. When the Bill of Rights was proposed as the first 10 amendments, freedoms of speech and press were set out in the first.

It is far from clear what the framers of the Bill of Rights—members of the first Congress—meant by speech and press freedom. The matter has divided historians of civil liberties. One view is that the two freedoms reflected settled law, and thus were aimed mainly at preventing governmental prior restraints on political speech and publication but permitted after-the-fact prosecution for seditious libel. Another holds the freedoms were intended, as well, to prevent punishment for seditious libel, and thus protect any truthful speech critical of government. Whichever the case, it is clear the protections were mainly of "political speech," the communication most likely to have led to government suppression in the past, and were not considered absolute.

Seditious speech became an important issue before the First Amendment was even a decade old. Anticipating war with revolutionary France, which never came, a Federalist majority in Congress in 1798 pushed through laws that became known as the Alien and Sedition Acts. The first aimed to restrict the many French aliens in the country. The second made it a crime to write or speak in such a way as to defame the government or its leaders by bringing them into "contempt or disrepute" or to "excite against them . . . the hatred of the good people of the United States." Hoping to unite the country and silence their more vocal Republican critics, the Federalists badly miscalculated. It was not that the law was particularly harsh—truth was a defense and the finding of malicious intent was left to the jury, not the judge, two provisions more liberal than those in the common law. Rather it was the heavy-handed enforcement that brought grief to its sponsors.

The Adams administration quickly arrested several prominent Republican newspaper editors and a member of Congress. Fifteen were indicted, ten convicted. Eventually, the net was cast more widely and snared many ordinary citizens including, in one instance, a drunk who merely opined that he didn't care if someone fired a cannon through President Adams's ass!

The crackdown met with widespread protest including resolutions of the Virginia and Kentucky legislatures (anonymously written by James Madison and Thomas Jefferson, respectively) denouncing the Sedition Act and its prosecutions. Though advancing a free speech principle, their greater thrust came from the states rights argument that the central government had no delegated power to pass such laws; only the states did.

The sedition prosecutions helped send the Federalists down to a resounding electoral defeat in 1800. The new president, Jefferson, pardoned those convicted under the act, which had expired through its own provisions a day before he took office.

It is tempting to see response to the Sedition Act and eventual Federalist comeuppance as a milestone in the development of free speech. Important as these events were, they did not definitively settle the matter of government control of political speech. The national act had expired, but almost every state had antisedition laws and the offense of seditious libel was included in their common law. These were not challenged by the Republicans and Jefferson. Later when he, himself, came under sharp editorial attack as president, he looked the other way as Federalist editors were prosecuted in state courts.

During the 120 years between the Sedition Act and America's entry into World War I in 1917, relatively few federal or state laws restricted speech or communications. Some exceptions are worth noting. As the debate over slavery intensified in the 1830s, many Southern states, starting with Virginia in 1836, made it a crime to advocate abolition or otherwise challenge slaveholding. When Northern abolitionists flooded the South with antislavery mail, the postmaster general urged his Southern subordinates to intercept the material and deliver it only to those who came forward to ask for it. Eventually, many Southern postmasters simply dumped large quantities of the abolitionist pamphlets.

Given the magnitude and duration of the Civil War and the uncertain loyalty of a minority of Northerners, it is remarkable that Congress enacted no legislation directly aimed at political speech. It did authorize the president to take control of the telegraph system but for reasons of military security. The same concerns also led the government to restrict the privileges of certain war correspondents. By executive order, a few newspapers that published articles thought to interfere with the war effort were denied use of the mail system, though their publication was not affected.

In the rapid industrialization of the late nineteenth and early twentieth century, many states targeted the speech and publications of anarchists, economic radicals, and union activists that urged violent industrial or political change. New York's antisedition law was typical. Enacted after the assassination of President William McKinley by a self-styled anarchist, it made "criminal anarchy" and advocacy of violent overthrow of government punishable offenses. The effect of this law and others like it in peacetime was largely symbolic; prosecutions under them were few.

The relative lack of general legislation aimed at speech between the Sedition Act and World War I did not mean there was much affirmative protection of speech as a legal right. Control of troubling, threatening, or possibly harmful communication was apt to be local and informal. More often than not it was simply effected privately through social pressure or intimidation, sometimes supported by the police. Control by the "custom of the community" was nothing new—it has probably existed in one form or other as long as articulate human beings have lived in organized society, the resulting conformity being a feature of human social life. But without a well-developed legal right to speak freely, there was often no way to check restrictive excesses of the community or local majority.

By World War I, the Supreme Court had heard only a handful of free speech cases. In the best known of these, *Patterson v. Colorado,* 1907, it upheld the contempt conviction of a publisher for articles and cartoons critical of the state's supreme court justices. Justice Oliver Wendell Holmes, writing for a majority of the Court, rejected the argument that truth was a defense and embraced instead a so-called "bad tendency" reasoning. If a class of speech tended to be harmful—here presumably lowering respect for a court in pending cases—the truth of particular statements did not matter. Ironically, this was a position Holmes would recant in the 1920s.

A more developed protection of speech by the courts would need await greater repression by government and a more libertarian outlook from the justices of the highest court. As twentieth-century world war approached, courts had not said much about the freedom's purpose or writ. Was it limited to political speech, that is, to keeping the political processes open and fluid so that the acceptance or rejection of change could be decided through persuasion rather than force, or did it also reach other speech having little or nothing to do with politics? Was its justification based solely on political or social utility or might it also include some notion of self-fulfillment? Did it embrace a right to receive communication? A right not to speak? And what countervailing interests were important enough to justify limits on speech? These were questions the Court would turn to in scores of cases. At the end of another century, it would still be grappling for some of the answers.

Subversion and National Security

Each of three war periods—those of World Wars I and II and the long Cold War with the Soviet Union—placed limits on freedom of speech. Each led to disputes that eventually produced a higher definition of the constitutional right, but the path was anything but straight or easy. Times of external threat and national emergency usually bring with them fears of espionage, subversion, and even overthrow of the government. However justified these concerns may be, their repressive net has invariably snared a wide range of oppositional but harmless expression. Restricting unpopular speech has served symbolic ends as well, strengthening a sense of patriotism, loyalty, and unity. In war or national emergency, governmental restraints have usually had strong support in public opinion and found reinforcement in private, informal acts. In excess, they have led to a hysteria of intolerance.

World Wars I and II

In June 1917, two months after American entry into World War I, Congress passed the Espionage Act to punish spying by foreign agents but cast broadly enough to outlaw a range of subversive or disloyal activities, such as obstruction of military recruitment or causing disobedience in the armed forces. It also empowered the postmaster general to exclude seditious material from the mails. A year later, the Sedition Act of 1918 provided severe penalties for willfully using "disloyal, profane, scurrilous, or abusive language" about the government, the Constitution, flag, or armed forces, or urging slackening of the war effort. Enforcement of this sweeping limit on dissident speech was directed mainly at pacifists, socialists, members of the International Workers of the World (IWW), supporters of Bolshevism in Russia, and a few German-Americans outspoken against the war. Indictments under the two laws ran to the thousands. Among the convicted was Eugene V. Debs, perennial Socialist Party candidate for president, who was sentenced to 10 years for a militant antiwar speech.

Appeals from several convictions reached the Supreme Court early in 1919 after the war had ended. The Court sustained the wartime security acts in every case. In *Schenck v. United States* (p. 162), it upheld a conviction under the espionage law for the mailing of antidraft leaflets to men being inducted into the armed forces. In *Frohwerk v. United States,* it refused to overturn conviction of an editor of a German-language newspaper for publishing articles criticizing the war and questioning the constitutionality of the draft. In *Debs v. United States,* conviction of the socialist leader was upheld. Later in the year, the Court in *Abrams v. United States* upheld Sedition Act convictions of four radicals who had circulated pamphlets calling for a general strike to protest the dispatch of American forces to Russia after the Bolshevik seizure of power. In the Milwaukee *Leader* case, *United States ex. rel. Milwaukee Social Democratic Publishing Co.,* it upheld the postmaster general's exclusion from the mails of a socialist newspaper that had published articles severely critical of war policies.

In each of these cases, the Court rejected the idea that the utterance or publication was constitutionally protected speech. The decisions did nothing to discourage the Attorney General A. Mitchell Palmer from carrying out a series of raids on suspected subversive groups during the winter of 1919–1920. While President Wilson lay paralyzed by a stroke, Palmer's agents arrested and detained several thousand persons, mainly labor agitators and foreign-born radicals said to be plotting widespread disruptions with the help of the Communist government in Russia. When these did not occur, Palmer's excesses were seen for what they were. The so-called Red Scare was over and so were Palmer's ambitions for the Democratic presidential nomination in 1920.

Despite the government's victories before the Court, the Espionage and Sedition Act cases are important in the longer-run development of a constitutional shield for dissident opinion. In the Schenck case, Justice Holmes, writing for the Court, echoed the bad tendency reasoning of his earlier opinion in *Patterson v. Colorado.* In wartime, Schenck's pamphlets would tend to obstruct recruitment, Holmes said. "If the act, its tendency and the intent with which it is done are the same, we perceive no ground for saying that success alone warrants making the act a crime." But Holmes also called attention to context, "The character of every act depends on the circumstances in which it is done." Putting the two principles together, he formulated a rule of proximate causation: "The question in every case is whether the words used are used in such circumstances and are of such nature as to create a clear and present danger that they will bring about the substantive evils that Congress has a right to prevent." Though the justices unanimously concluded that Schenck's pamphlets had created such a danger, the rule, which would become known as the "clear and present danger test," would open a door to protecting speech left shut by the "bad tendency" standard.

The clear and present danger doctrine was better worked out by Holmes in the Abrams case eight months later, but this time in dissent. Stung by civil liberties critics of his *Schenck* holding and disturbed by the government's oppressive actions in the antiradical hysteria, Holmes, joined by Louis Brandeis, argued the government had failed to show that "the surreptitious publishing of a silly leaflet by an unknown man" had any effect on the war effort or presented any "immediate danger." Without such proof, the defendants, sentenced to 15 to 20 years in prison, had as much right to circulate the leaflets "as the government has to publish the Constitution." With characteristic brevity and eloquence, he went still further giving freedom of speech a grand and compelling purpose: the trade in ideas. "The best test of truth is the power of thought to get itself accepted in the competition of the market." Many civil libertarians view the emphasis on immediate cause and on a marketplace of ideas in *Abrams v. New York* as the first true application of the clear and present danger doctrine. The case has taken its place along side *Plessy v. Ferguson* on racial segregation and *Lochner v. New York* on liberty of contract, as ones in which ideas in a powerful dissenting opinion eventually prevailed to vitally change the course of the highest law.

Reluctance of a majority of the Court to accept the clear and present danger test was dramatically evident in two cases appealing convictions under state antisedition laws. During the war and early postwar years, more than 30 states enacted new laws or amended older ones to control subversive speech. In *Gitlow v. New York* (p. 163), 1925,

the Court upheld the state's Criminal Anarchy Act used to convict a radical socialist for publishing the "Left Wing Manifesto" a pamphlet urging proletarian revolution in the United States, by mass strikes and other unlawful acts. The law made such speech—advocacy of illegal overthrow of the government—itself criminal without regard to its effectiveness. Seven justices, in an opinion by Edward Sanford, applied the established "bad tendency" standard, holding it reasonable for a state to proscribe dangerous classes of speech. He argued that the *Schenck* clear and present danger test did not apply because the question was not the linking of words to unlawful acts but simply whether unlawful words had been published. Holmes, again with Brandeis, dissented. Applying the clear and present danger test of his *Abrams* opinion, he argued that a prosecution even under a statute making certain speech unlawful must go beyond the mere fact of its publication and show a link to action.

Though Gitlow's conviction was upheld, another aspect of the case as we have already seen, was to have momentous consequence for the protection of civil liberties. All nine justices agreed that freedom of speech in the First Amendment was part of due process of law and thus could also serve to limit state governments through the due process clause of the Fourteenth Amendment. For the first time a right in the Bill of Rights other than protection of property, was "incorporated" into due process and made applicable to the states.

Brandeis elaborated on Holmes's clear and present danger test in their concurring opinion in *Whitney v. California*, 1927. Charlotte Whitney, a social activist and niece of a former member of the Court, was convicted under the state's Criminal Syndicalism Act that made it a felony to organize a group advocating "unlawful acts of force or violence . . . or terrorism" to bring about industrial or political change. As a member of the Communist Labor Party of California, Whitney had attended a convention of the group that passed resolutions calling for revolutionary

Justices Oliver Wendell Holmes and Louis Brandeis in the late 1920s. After Holmes formulated the clear and present danger test in *Schenck v. United States,* he and Brandeis developed the "free marketplace of ideas" justification for the protection of speech in notable dissenting and concurring opinions in *Abrams v. United States, Gitlow v. New York,* and *Whitney v. California.*

change, though she had personally opposed them. The majority of the Court upheld her conviction on authority of *Gitlow.* Brandeis's concurrence—he voted to sustain the conviction on the technical procedural ground that Whitney's lawyers had not raised the clear and present danger issue in the lower courts—reads more like a dissent. Echoing Holmes's marketplace of ideas concept in *Abrams,* he argued that

> To courageous and self-reliant men with confidence in the power of free and fearless reasoning applied through the processes of popular government, no danger flowing from speech can be deemed clear and present, unless the incidence of the evil apprehended is so imminent that it may befall before there is opportunity for full discussion. If there be time to expose through discussion the falsehood and fallacies, to avert the evil by the processes of education, the remedy to be applied is more speech no enforced silence. Only an emergency can justify repression. [274 U.S. 357 at 377]

The cases from *Schenck* to *Whitney* had all begun during the war or in the brief period of antiradical agitation following it. Repressive acts abated in the 1920s. Though the clear and present danger test had yet to be used to overturn a conviction, it had been eloquently stated and would later become, with its philosophic partner, the free marketplace of ideas, the intellectual centerpiece of an expanding freedom of speech.

In 1931, with several new justices occupying seats, the Court handed down *Near v. Minnesota,* an important decision explored in the next chapter, holding that freedom of the press, like that of speech, was also part of due process and thus protected against both state and national government. It did the same for freedom of assembly in *De Jonge v. Oregon,* in 1937, where it reversed conviction of a Communist under the state's criminal syndicalism law for helping to organize a protest meeting growing out of a labor dispute. In *Herndon v. Lowry,* the same term, it used the clear and present danger test for the first time to reverse a conviction. In this instance, it was of a Communist Party organizer who in distributing pamphlets had been charged under Georgia's law against inciting insurrection.

The national emergency of World War II was greater in magnitude than that of the first war. American engagement, spanning nearly four years, was more than twice as long and required fighting not mainly in one country in Europe but on several continents. Effort on such a scale called for unprecedented mobilization and sacrifice. Nonetheless, with one glaring exception—the internment of Japanese-Americans living on the West Coast, discussed in Chapter 8— the Roosevelt administration showed far greater sensitivity to civil liberties than had President Wilson's. Lessons had been learned from earlier excesses, and Roosevelt's attorney general, Francis Biddle, avoided extensive attacks on dissident speech.

In 1940, more than a year before American entry, Congress updated the 1917 Espionage Act and passed the Alien Registration Act, otherwise known as the Smith Act after its chief sponsor Representative Howard W. Smith of Virginia. Aimed at conspiracies to overthrow the government, the new law empowered the Justice Department to prosecute advocacy or conspiracy to advocate violent overthrow or organization of or membership in a group advocating overthrow. Though the act was to be important in the early Cold War period, its speech provisions produced only two prosecutions during the war.

Few national security cases about speech came to the Supreme Court. In one that did, *Hartzel v. United States,* 1944, a Nazi sympathizer had been convicted under the Espionage Act of mailing pamphlets to members of the armed forces urging an alliance with Germany and occupation of the country by foreign troops. For the first time, the Court applied the clear and present danger test in a national security case to protect speech, holding that as offensive as Hartzel's ideas were, they posed no imminent threat to the country. As we will see in the next section, the Court had already used the test to protect the rights of speakers in several cases not having to do with national security.

By the 1940s, the Roosevelt Court, as it was now sometimes called, was a very different body from the one that had fought the president and Congress over the New Deal economic regulation a few years before. Roosevelt had been able to make eight appointments in less than six years, starting with Hugo Black's in 1937. In average age of the justices, the oldest Court had become one of the youngest. It had already turned much of its attention to civil liberties and civil rights matters, and eventually half its cases were ones raising those issues. The Court's sensitivity to free speech questions contrasted sharply with its jurisprudence during and immediately following World War I. This almost surely discouraged overzealous prosecution and private intimidation of those expressing unpopular or offensive views. Its most dramatic wartime statement of the expanding free speech doctrine came in the second flag salute case, *West Virginia Board of Education v. Barnette,* 1943, discussed in the previous chapter. In it, Justice Robert Jackson eloquently rationalized the right to remain silent during a patriotic ritual as a high philosophical purpose of the First Amendment: freedom from enforced orthodoxy in religion, politics, or any matters of opinion or belief.

The Cold War

Conflict with the Soviet Union began almost as soon as World War II ended and continued until the collapse of that regime four decades later. The antagonism was marked by fighting wars in Korea and Vietnam, and was shadowed almost from the start by presence of nuclear weapons and long-range missile delivery systems on both sides. It remained "cold" in the sense that the two powers avoided direct military conflict with each other that might have led to a third world war. The Cold War was a war, nonetheless, because both countries (and much of the rest of the world allied with one or the other) remained highly mobilized militarily and economically and waged a nonstop ideological battle. That the global struggle was one of two sharply contrasting ways of political life and belief, gave it a quasi-religious fervor that had important consequences for American domestic politics and free speech.

The external threat of Communism, revelations of spying, and the presence of domestic Communists all stirred fears of subversion and infiltration. At turns, this anxiety imperiled the developing and expanding constitutional freedom of speech. Ironically, in its early years at least, the Cold War had a more restrictive or "chilling" effect on that freedom than did either of the century's fighting world wars.

Disturbing international events in the immediate postwar years, including the Soviet takeover of Eastern Europe, the fall of China to Communist forces, Soviet development of the atomic bomb, and war in Korea were paralleled by revelations of spying and possible subversion high in the government. This led to fear that important institutions including labor unions, universities, and the entertainment industry might be ridden with Communists. Immediate targets of this concern were members of the American Communist Party and Communist sympathizers known as "fellow travelers." In its greater reach, the anti-Communist response caste suspicion on the entire American Left, including many liberals who were simply believed to be "soft" on Communism. For its part, the Communist Party, which retained its bent for secrecy, did little in it to ease fears that it was Moscow's pawn and a danger to the country.

The government's response was manifold. The Truman administration set up a loyalty program to check federal employees and dismiss those whose allegiance was in doubt. Between 1947 and 1953 nearly 5 million persons in the government underwent such checks, the scrutiny leading to more than 500 firings and several thousand resignations. In 1950, Congress passed the Internal Security Act, generally known as the McCarran Act, and in 1954, the Communist Control Act. The first declared that "the recent success of Communist methods in other countries, and the nature and control of the world Communist movement itself, present a clear and present danger to the security of the

United States and to the existence of free American institutions." Accordingly, it required "Communist action" and "Communist front" organizations to register with the Subversive Activities Control Board, created by the act. Registration would require the party to disclose its members and sources of financial support. The Communist Control Act went further. Instead of relying on exposure and ostracism, it tried to destroy the Communist Party by removing whatever rights and privileges it had as a political organization.

Congressional investigations were the most dramatic but often least credible response to the Communist internal threat. In the House, the UnAmerican Activities Committee (HUAC) conducted a series of high profile inquiries into alleged Communist influence in the film industry and played an important role in the espionage case against Alger Hiss. Later it abandoned any pretense of legislative purpose, aiming instead, as it said, to "inform American public opinion" through exposure and publicity.

HUAC's Senate counterpart was the Governmental Operations Committee's Subcommittee on Investigation of Communism. From 1953 to 1955, it was chaired by Senator Joseph R. McCarthy, and its wide-ranging, headline-making hearings were irresponsible anti-Communism at its zenith. Witnesses called before the committee were often harassed, denied counsel, not shown evidence against them, nor allowed to confront accusers. Neither McCarthy's committee nor HUAC uncovered many Communists in government nor did they recommend much legislation. But they did leave a trail of smashed careers and fortunes. Worse, the investigations had a severely chilling effect on the freedoms of speech and association. "McCarthyism" lives today as a term for bullying, opportunistic demagoguery, both exploiting and inflating an atmosphere of suspicion and fear.

It was not the congressional investigations nor the new legislation, but the prewar Smith Act that produced the Cold War's most important speech case and drew the line between the

The Battle of Foley Square

It was the quintessential political trial and one of the longest criminal justice proceedings in the annals of American courts. *United States v. Dennis,* the federal government's prosecution of the 11 top leaders of the Communist Party under the Smith Act, began March 1, 1949, and ran nine tumultuous months in the federal district court at Foley Square in downtown Manhattan. Almost daily it commanded front page news coverage. Almost daily, supporters of the defendants demonstrated outside the courthouse, occasionally opposed by counter protesters. Ever present as well was an army of police officers, at times numbering more than 400.

The Smith Act indictments charged the defendants with conspiracy to "organize as the Communist Party of the United States, a society, group, and assembly of persons who teach and advocate the overthrow and destruction of the government of the United States by force and violence, and knowingly and willfully to advocate and teach the duty and necessity of overthrowing and destroying the Government of the United States by force."

In bringing the case, the Truman administration, which had aggressively begun to contain Communism abroad, was aware of its vulnerability to conservative attacks of being lax about Communist influence and subversion at home. Neither the president nor Attorney General Tom Clark (later to be a Supreme Court justice) regarded the party and its 60,000 members as much of a threat to national security. But with the difficult 1948 election looming and polls showing nearly two-thirds of the public in favor of outlawing the party altogether, Clark went ahead with the prosecutions.

The defendants believed, perhaps mistakenly, that they had little or no chance of being acquitted and decided to use the trial as a political forum to attack the capitalist regime and, by doing so, promote class consciousness. Quixotically, they believed their best chance of going free lay in creating mass protests against the trial.

Even before the government presented its case, the defense attorneys had spent more than six weeks unsuccessfully challenging the grand jury system that indicted the defendants. The selection of jurors, they argued, grossly underrepresented ethnic and racial minorities and the working class, a charge essentially accurate at the time but alone not proof of bias against the defendants. The trial jury was more representative. Its foreman was a black homemaker and part-time dressmaker. Other members included two homemakers, a writer, an engineer, two salesmen, and various "workers."

The trial judge was Harold Medina, the son of wealthy Mexican immigrants and educated at elite schools. Appointed to the bench only two years before, this was his first criminal case. He had had a highly successful legal practice and had taught part-time for many years at Columbia Law School. He had also earned a reputation for combativeness and egotism in the courtroom, qualities soon to emerge at Foley Square as he tangled repeatedly with the equally quarrelsome defense attorneys.

The government's case focused less on the specific utterances of the defendants than on proving the Communist Party was organized and maintained to bring about violent overthrow of the government. To do this, it relied heavily on "old" literature, including Marx's *Communist Manifesto,* published a century before, and writings of Lenin and Stalin. Witnesses were brought in to interpret these works and explain how they directed the party. The most important of these was Louis Budenz, an economics professor and former party

First Amendment and national security. In 1948, federal prosecutors indicted the 12 members of the Communist Party's national board for advocating violent overthrow of the government and conspiring to form a group advocating overthrow and being members of such a group. This led to a spectacular nine-month trial and convictions (see "The Battle of Foley Square") and an appeal to the Supreme Court in *Dennis v. United States* in 1950 (p. 166). Reviewing only the constitutionality of the act and not its specific application, a majority of six justices voted to uphold but was divided on a theory for doing so. Four, in an opinion of Chief Justice Fred Vinson, applied a modified version of the clear and present danger test. Acknowledging that Dennis and

official who, having broken with the party, had fashioned a lucrative second career as a professional anti-Communist, lecturing, writing, and testifying in court. Over defense objections, Budenz explained how statements in the party's constitution that appeared to foreswear violent revolution or subversion, were really "Aesopian language," meaning exactly the opposite of what they said.

The defendants' decision to use the trial as a propaganda platform made a legal defense more difficult. Added to this, Medina was severe in disallowing testimony and other evidence that went at all beyond narrow rebuttal of the government's charge that the defendants as members of the Communist Party taught and advocated violence.

After a trial record of more than 5 million words, the case was given to the jury on October 14. Deliberating seven-and-a-half hours, it found all defendants guilty as charged. A week later Medina sentenced 10 of them to five years in prison and a $10,000 fine. The eleventh was given a reduced penalty because of heroic military service in World War II.

During the trial, Medina had grown exasperated with the obstreperous tactics of the five defense lawyers, which he saw as an attempt to provoke a mistrial and discredit the judicial system. He also became convinced they were deliberately trying to impair his health, a matter to which he was particularly sensitive. After sentencing the defendants, he announced that there was "some unfinished business," and charged each of the five attorneys with multiple acts of contempt and imposed fines and jail sentences of up to six months, an unusual if not unprecedented act of judicial retribution.

The case had many ramifications. Followed by "little" Dennis prosecutions of lesser party figures in different cities, it put the party on the run and led to its demise as a viable political entity. The

prison terms worked great hardship on the individual defendants. Four who fled rather than surrender, were caught and given additional time to serve. Many other party members went underground or for years kept themselves inconspicuous.

The defense lawyers appealed their contempt sentences, eventually to the Supreme Court. The convictions were sustained by a divided Court in *Sachar v. United States,* 1952. They had devastating effect on the careers of each of the attorneys.

Judge Medina, reported to have gotten more than 50,000 letters of congratulation, was heralded as a courageous defender of the judicial system and oracle of patriotic virtue. Within two years he was promoted to the federal appellate bench by President Truman. He died in 1990 at 102, having retired just 10 years before.

The convictions of Dennis and his colleagues were sustained on appeal by the Second Circuit Court of Appeals. The United States Supreme Court, reviewing only the constitutionality of the Smith Act, upheld its validity in *Dennis v. United States,* 1950.

Eventually, in *Yates v. United States,* 1957, the Court gave the Smith Act a narrower reading imposing a more rigorous evidentiary requirement for conviction. This effectively ended further prosecution of Communists under it. But by then, American policy of containing world Communism was more secure, an armistice had ended the Korean War, Stalin had died, and a Republican president, Eisenhower, less vulnerable to criticism of being "soft" on domestic Communism, established an early détente with the new Soviet leaders. At home, Senator Joseph McCarthy had passed from the scene, and the Communist Party lay in shambles. The heated political atmosphere that had produced the Dennis case had measurably cooled.

his fellow defendants posed no immediate threat to the government, Vinson embraced a "gravity of the evil discounted by its improbability" standard. It had been developed by Judge Learned Hand in federal Second Circuit Court of Appeals, which had heard the first appeal in the case. If the "evil" were serious enough—here overthrow of the government by a conspiratorial

group virtually directed by the nation's chief international adversary—it mattered less that the danger was yet remote. Thus speech in such circumstances might be restricted, but advocating unlawful ends in other circumstances might find protection. Justices Jackson and Felix Frankfurter, each concurring, largely embraced the government's "bad tendency" theory the Court had sustained in *Gitlow v. New York.* Where conspiratorial speech advocating violent revolution was itself proscribed, the clear and present danger test was inapplicable and should give way to reasonable judgment by Congress balancing free speech and protection of government. In dissent, Justices Black and William O. Douglas applied a "pure" form of the Holmes-Brandeis clear and present danger test. Douglas put the matter epigrammatically: the Communist Party leaders were but "miserable merchants of unwanted ideas. Their wares remain unsold. The fact that their ideas are abhorrent does not make them powerful."

The Dennis decision had predictable effect. In the next few years, the Justice Department got Smith Act indictments against second level and regional party leaders as "little" Dennis trials were held in a dozen cities. From these, there were more than 100 convictions. Hundreds of other party members fearing imprisonment went underground. By the late 1950s, the party was in disarray and a vastly reduced force. Yet from these later Smith Act prosecutions came a

Supreme Court decision that clarified and narrowed the doctrinal bite of *Dennis.* In *Yates v. United States,* 1957, the Court, 6-1, overturned convictions of 14 party leaders in California. The constitutionally of the Smith Act was again affirmed, but its advocacy provisions were held to proscribe only the urging of acts that would lead to forcible overthrow now or some date in the future rather than advocacy of overthrow as an abstract doctrine. Because the trial judge failed to make this distinction clear in instructing the jury, the convictions could not stand. Concurring, Black and Douglas argued that the Smith Act was an unconstitutional infringement on freedom of speech. Though the majority's distinction may seem a fine point, its evidentiary consequences were important. Using the writings and speeches of Communist Party members, it was now much harder for the government to show that they urged specific unlawful acts rather than simply expressing general political beliefs or opinions. Unsurprisingly after *Yates,* no further prosecutions were brought under the advocacy provisions of the Smith Act.

Five of the defendants in *Dennis v. United States,* including Eugene Dennis, second from left, in a police wagon following their convictions in 1949. All eleven defendants, the top leaders of the American Communist Party, were sentenced to prison terms for violating the Smith Act.

In another interpretation of the Smith Act, in *Pennsylvania v. Nelson*, 1956, the Court held state laws aimed at protecting the federal government from subversion were invalid. Overturning conviction of a Communist Party member under a Pennsylvania antisedition law, it held the Smith, McCarran, and Communist Control Acts had occupied the entire field of protecting the federal government from violent overthrow, thus preempting state laws on the matter. Both *Nelson* and *Yates* rest on the Court's interpretation of what Congress intended, not on anything called for by the Constitution. Congress could have amended and clarified its statutes giving them a different meaning from the Court's understanding, but it did not do so.

Important questions of what was and was not protected speech remained. Was the distinction between advocacy in the abstract and that of specific acts limited to a reading of the Smith Act or might it become a constitutional requirement of the First Amendment? Was the urging of unlawful acts in a distant future when circumstances might be more favorable advocacy of specific acts or merely abstract doctrine?

Answers came a dozen years later, near the end of the Warren Court, but in a state prosecution of hate speech rather than a federal national security case. In *Brandenburg v. Ohio*, 1969 (p. 170), the defendant had addressed an outdoor Ku Klux Klan rally at which he called for racial strife and urged that Jews be "sent back to Israel." He had been convicted under that state's criminal syndicalism act making it a felony to advocate "crime, sabotage, violence, or unlawful methods of terrorism as a means of forging industrial or political reform." The Court unanimously reversed the conviction and without invoking the clear and present danger doctrine, went well beyond it. It held that even speech urging specific illegal acts was protected unless "such advocacy is directed to inciting or producing imminent lawless acts and is likely to incite or produce such action." The distinction between mere advocacy and that of immediate illegal action was now elevated to a constitutional requirement. Doing this,

the Court expressly overruled its earlier decision in *Whitney v. California* where the sustained conviction was under a law similar to Ohio's. As far-reaching and clarifying as *Brandenburg* was, it left both the Smith Act and the Dennis case, with its discount of immediacy, intact. *Brandenburg* was not about a well-organized, internationally driven subversive group advocating violent overthrow of the general government during national emergency. Whether *Brandenburg's* generous, far-reaching protection of speech would be sustained under such circumstances remains, even now, problematic.

Freedom of Association

Forming groups and consorting with like-minded others is often critical to effective expression of opinion and communication of ideas. If free speech were not accompanied by some degree of associational freedom, it would be a far lesser right and less important as a conduit for peaceful, persuasive change. Not mentioned in the First Amendment, freedom to associate must be inferred from the Amendment's expressed rights of speech, press, religion, assembly, and petition. Governments, on the other hand, have been keenly aware of the threat that collective activity—especially conspiracy—may pose to internal security. It is not surprising that state antisedition and criminal anarchy acts have taken aim at associative activity as much as at individual speech. The federal Smith Act specifically made it a crime to organize or be a member of a group advocating violent overthrow of the government. The later McCarran and Communist Control Acts also singled out organized activity.

In the early Cold War period, Congress and the Truman administration struck hard at the associative aspects of speech by trying to keep Communists and "fellow travelers" out of the government and important institutions. A provision of the Taft-Hartley labor law, for example, called for union officers to swear they were not members of the Communist Party or any other group that advocated overthrow of the government by force. If they refused, their union would forego the benefits and services of various federal labor laws. The provision was unsuccessfully challenged on First Amendment grounds in *American Communication Association v. Douds,* 1950, by a union that had a record of Communist infiltration. In holding the law to reasonably balance political freedom against the protection of national security from Communist-motivated strikes, the Court drew a distinction between freedom of speech and unfettered associative rights. The second was less sure than the first.

Many states enacted loyalty oath requirements for public employees including teachers. Besides calling for the affirmation of loyalty to the United States, these laws typically required swearing that one was not a member of the Communist Party or other groups advocating violent overthrow of the government. Failure to so affirm usually barred hiring or, if already hired, was ground for dismissal. Though the Supreme Court at first upheld the oath requirements in the early Cold War years finding there was no violation of free speech or constitutional right to public employment, it eventually took a different view of the speech issue. In 1966 in *Elfbrandt v. Russell,* it struck down an oath that simply required swearing to uphold state and federal laws because it would be violated per se if taken by a member of the Communist Party, who would then be open to a perjury indictment. A year later in *Keyisian v. Board of Regents,* the Court invalidated a New York law that made Communist Party membership prima facie evidence of disqualification for public employment. In both cases, the oath requirements failed to distinguish between membership with specific intent to further the organization's unlawful activities and passive status that did not subscribe to such ends.

Earlier, the Court had used a similar distinction to rule on the membership clause of the Smith Act. In the companion cases of *Scales v. United States* and *Noto v. United States,* 1961, it sustained the provision as constitutional but held the act called for proof of "knowing" as opposed

to nominal or passive membership. For the first, the defendant would have had to have worked to further the party's illegal ends. Thus the Court gave the membership provision the same narrow reading it had given the act's advocacy proscription in *Yates.* Applied to the facts of the cases, it sustained the conviction of Scales but overturned Noto's. Though the government was successful in *Scales,* the statutory interpretation and its more demanding evidentiary requirement effectively ended prosecutions under the membership provision.

In *Yates,* the Court had interpreted the third part of the Smith Act, the organizing provision, to refer to acts of founding or re-forming rather than the continuous maintaining of an organization. Because the Communist Party had been last reorganized in 1945, a three-year statute of limitations for bringing the Smith Act charge had already expired at the time of the defendants' indictments in 1951.

In setting up the Subversive Activities Control Board (SACB), the McCarran Act aimed at the exposure of Communist activities rather than outlaw of the party. If the Board found a group to be a "communist-front" or "communist-action" organization, it was required to register with the government and give a full list of its officers and members. These persons were then barred from work in the federal government or in defense plants and from getting U.S. passports. When, to no one's surprise, the Board found the Communist Party to be such a group, the party refused to register. This led to *Communist Party v. SACB,* which reached the Supreme Court in 1961 after years of litigation. The Court sustained the registration requirement, holding that Congress had balanced speech and associative concerns against those of the public interest. "Where the mask of anonymity which an organization's members wear," Justice Frankfurter wrote, "serves the double purpose of protecting them from popular prejudice and of enabling them to cover over a foreign-directed conspiracy [and] infiltrate into other groups," the First Amendment does not bar Congress "from removing that mask." [307 U.S. 1 at 102-103] The Court, however, postponed ruling on the act's enforcement provisions.

When they were addressed in the heyday of the Warren Court, the justices were much less generous to the government. In *Albertson v. SACB*, 1965, for example, the Court held that because members of the Communist Party could, theoretically at least, be criminally prosecuted under the Smith Act, the forced registration and disclosure of members under the McCarren Act would violate the Fifth Amendment's privilege against self-incrimination. Two years later in *United States v. Robel*, it held the barring of party members from defense work was cast too broadly and so violated associational freedom. The grounds were similar to those the Court had used in the Smith Act membership cases: failure to distinguish between active, knowing membership that subscribed to the goals of violent revolution and mere passive membership. In *Aptheker v. United States*, 1964, the Court struck down the passport section of the McCarran Act as a restriction on the right to travel.

Though important elements of associational freedom were shaped by restraints put on federal and state efforts to suppress the Communist Party, the freedom also owes much to civil rights struggles against racial segregation in the 1950s and 1960s. In 1956, Alabama sued to compel the National Association for the Advancement of Colored People (NAACP) to comply with a state law requiring out-of-state organizations doing business in the state to register with the state. It won a lower court order requiring the organization to produce its records including a list of members. The action and the order were transparent attempts to hamper the NAACP in its efforts to desegregate Alabama schools and other public facilities, by inviting harassment of known individual members. The organization supplied most of the information requested but refused to give a list of members, after which it was held in contempt of court and fined $100,000.

On appeal to the Supreme Court in *NAACP v. Alabama*, 1958 (p. 172), the Alabama action was reversed. The Court's decision is notable for two reasons besides its importance to the civil rights movement. It marked the first time it had formally based a decision on a right of association, which it said was a part of the First Amendment despite its absence from the wording. Justice John Marshall Harlan, II, made the connection explicit and applied it to the states, "Effective advocacy of both public and private points of view, particularly controversial ones, is undeniably embraced by group association . . . [F]reedom to engage in association for the advancement of beliefs and ideas is an inseparable aspect of "liberty" assured by the Due Process clause of the Fourteenth Amendment." He then added that a right to association would not be effective without a privacy of that association. Here the state failed to show a need for the membership list strong enough to overcome the right of associational privacy, especially given the NAACP's unrebutted evidence of the likelihood of economic reprisal and physical coercion against known members. In reaching its decision, the Court needed to overrule or distinguish its 1928 decision in *Bryant v. Zimmerman* where it had sustained the conviction of a Ku Klux Klan officer for not complying with a New York law that required certain organizations file membership lists with the state. Harlan reasoned that the New York law was aimed at groups whose acts were known to include unlawful intimidation and violence. Implicit in the saving of *Zimmerman* and in the NAACP decision itself is that associational privacy is not absolute.

The Court soon applied the principles of *NAACP* to other cases arising out the civil rights struggle in Southern states. In *Shelton v. Tucker*, 1960, it struck down an Arkansas law requiring public school teachers to file affidavits listing all organizations to which they had belonged or contributed money in the last five years. Transparency of the law being evident, a teacher who was an NAACP member refused to file the affidavit and was fired. Though the Court conceded that inquiring about associational ties might be a valid part of a state's interest in the competence of its teachers, the Arkansas law was too broad in requiring disclosure of *all* ties including those that might have no bearing on teaching qualifications.

In *NAACP v. Button*, 1963, the Court invalidated a Virginia "ambulance chasing" statute that barred soliciting clients for litigation by anyone not a party to the case or not having financial interest in it. The Court held the restriction to interfere with the NAACP's freedom to associate and to solicit clients and sponsor suits challenging racial discrimination. In the civil rights struggle, Justice William Brennan observed that sponsored litigation might be the only way some persons and groups have to express grievances and seek redress. "For such a group, associating for litigation may be the most effective form of political association."

In *Gibson v. Florida Legislative Investigating Committee*, the same year, issues of associational freedom in the civil rights struggle coalesced with those of Communist subversion. The legislative committee, investigating whether a local chapter of the NAACP had been infiltrated by Communists, cited the chapter president for contempt for refusing to produce membership lists with him when he was called as a witness. Overturning the contempt conviction, the Court distinguished the national security cases, saying they did not hold that "other groups—concededly legitimate—automatically forfeit their rights to privacy of association simply because the general matter of legislative inquiry is Communist subversion or infiltration."

By the mid-1960s, the Warren Court had firmly set out a right of association and associational privacy in civil rights cases where Southern states had blatantly tried to identify members of groups opposing segregation. But there were strong indications that the right was less firmly settled where the issues were subversion and national security. Much of the Court's protection of the right had come after the Com-

munist Party was battered and national concern over its infiltration of government and private institutions had abated. How secure associational freedom would be in a future national emergency in which well-organized dissidents allied with external enemies organize to advocate overthrow of the government remains, like that of their speech, uncertain.

In recent years, the Court has also dealt with freedom of association issues in other contexts. An important one arose where private clubs claimed the right in restricting membership to males. In *Roberts v. United States Jaycees*, 1984, this was struck down in the name of another right, equal protection of the law. This decision and others in gender discrimination cases are taken up in Chapter 9.

Exclusion based on sexual orientation came before the Court in *Boy Scouts of America v. Dale*, 2000 (p. 174). The organization had revoked the membership of an assistant scoutmaster and former Eagle Scout after he publicly acknowledged being gay. The Court held that the Boy Scouts, unlike the Jaycees in *Roberts*, was an "expressive association" that promoted particular views and values including, in this instance, that homosexuality was not acceptable conduct. Though conceding expressive associational freedom was not absolute, the Court said that forcing the Boy Scouts to accept Dale as a member would impair its ability to express its views publicly and privately.

Assembly, Protest, and Public Order

So far, we have dealt mainly with speech and association that may be harmful to the nation's security in time of war or emergency. More common is speech that is unpopular, offensive, or communicates grievances that challenge established policies, conventions, or beliefs within a community—city, town, village, or neighborhood. Tension produced by dissident views at this level is one of the oldest problems faced by the human community because it often vents— or generates—hostile feelings in close quarters. The classic example is the speaker who addresses or harangues an audience of willing or unwilling listeners in a public place. But dissident or unpopular expression may also be that of many persons acting together and include not simply words but also symbols, such as flags and insignia, and acts, such as marches, demonstrations, and picketing. Though local protests by groups create problems for public order that the "pure speech" of a single communicator does not, they can be a vital element in expressing ideas and points of view. Such communication finds specific recognition in the First Amendment's protection of "the right of the people to peaceably assemble, and to petition the government for a redress of grievances."

Unpopular or offensive communication may conflict with many public and community ends, including protection against riot, breach of the peace, obstruction of traffic, damage to property, invasion of privacy, and loss of public tranquillity. The Supreme Court has generally been solicitous of local dissident speech, but as with other protections of the First Amendment, the freedom is not absolute and must be balanced against the public interest. The Court has been particularly concerned that restrictions affecting speech be content-neutral, that is, not aimed at the substance of expression or the identity of speakers or protesters.

Because the conflicts here are usually within a community, most government action has been the local enforcement of state or municipal laws. No appeals from these disputes were heard by the Supreme Court until the 1930s, when the freedoms of speech and assembly were first held applicable to states and local government.

Personal Provocation

Speech that so personally riles or offends that a listener might be led to violent response against the speaker produces a basic human conflict and a threat to public order and safety. The Supreme Court first dealt with this matter in the 1942 case of *Chaplinsky v. New Hampshire* where a Jehovah's Witness had distributed religious literature that attacked other religions, on a street corner. After many complaints, he was led away by a police officer whom he cursed as a "Goddamned racketeer and damned fascist." For these epithets, he was convicted under a state law that made it a crime to call anyone derisive or abusive names in public. The Court unanimously sustained the conviction, Justice Frank Murphy distinguishing protected expression from "certain well-defined and narrowly limited classes of speech . . . of such slight social value as a step to truth that any benefit that may be derived from them is clearly outweighed by the social interest in order and morality." [315 U.S. 568 at 571, 572] Such speech included obscenity, profanity, defamation and, in this case, "insulting or 'fighting words' . . . which by their utterance inflict injury or tend to incite an immediate breach of the peace."

The decision reflected a basic "two-tiered" conception of speech: protected and unprotected. As we shall see here and in the next chapter, the Court has kept this distinction while steadily narrowing the unprotected tier. *Chaplinsky* became synonymous with the "fighting words" doctrine, that some epithets are so powerful they provoke a violent response from a person to whom they are directed and are thus unprotected. Though the Court has retained the doctrine and mentions it regularly as an example of speech outside the First Amendment, it has not used it again to uphold a conviction.

In several cases, for example, it found state and local laws to be too broad or impermissibly vague where they made provocative words punishable. In *Gooding v. Wilson,* 1972, it reversed conviction of a man who yelled at a police officer, "You are a son of a bitch and I'll choke you to death." In *Lewis v. New Orleans,* 1974, "you motherfucking police" was held protected speech. And in *Rosenblatt v. New Jersey,* 1972, the Court reached the same conclusion about the cursing of local school board members and local teachers as "motherfuckers" at an open school board meeting. Considering these and similar decisions, it is doubtful that Chaplinsky's utterance would qualify as unprotected fighting words today.

The Hostile Audience and Riot

The fighting words doctrine dealing with a speaker and a person cursed face-to-face, does not easily apply to the more dangerous and difficult situation where many persons are stirred to anger and possible violence. Such was the case where a defrocked Catholic priest, though urging no specific acts, gave a profascist speech denouncing Jews, blacks, and the Roosevelt administration to a sympathetic audience in a closed auditorium. He was arrested after a large, hostile crowd gathered outside and tried to break into the meeting. In *Terminiello v. Chicago,* 1949, the Supreme Court reversed the conviction but avoided a definitive ruling on whether the speech, under the circumstances, was protected by the First Amendment. Instead, it found the trial judge's instruction to the jury defective in allowing it to find the defendant guilty if his speech had merely stirred anger and controversy. Speaking for a majority of the Court, Justice Douglas took the opportunity to write a paean to the value of provocative speech, one that was almost beside the point in the case but now seems close to the philosophical center of gravity of First Amendment protection.

> [A] function of free speech under our system of government is to invite dispute. It may indeed best serve its high purpose when it induces a condition of unrest, creates dissatisfaction with conditions as they are, or even stirs people to anger. Speech is often provocative and challenging. It may strike at prejudices and preconceptions and have profound unsettling effects as it presses for acceptance of an idea. That is why

freedom of speech, though not absolute . . . is nevertheless protected against censorship or punishment, unless shown likely to produce a clear and present danger of a serious substantive evil that rises far above public inconvenience, annoyance or unrest. [337 U.S. 1 at 4-5]

Two years after *Terminiello,* the Court directly confronted the issue of incitement in *Feiner v. New York* but was divided on whether a clear and present danger of riot or breach of the peace was at hand. In a harangue to a racially mixed crowd on a Syracuse street, Feiner, speaking for the Progressive Party, attacked national and local officials and urged black persons to take up arms and fight for their rights. Some listeners were friendly but many others were not and eventually threatened to remove Feiner, at which point police arrested him for speaking with intent to cause a breach of the peace. The Court applied the clear and present danger test. A majority of six justices upheld the conviction, but their disagreement with the dissenters showed that answers given by the test might be anything but clear and certain, especially when based on an abstract record of what officers at the scene had to face. The case shows the difficulty in drawing a line between not allowing a "heckler's veto" and requiring police to go the brink of disorder before acting.

What of offensive words directed at no one in particular and creating little or no danger of public disorder? The Supreme Court ruled on this point in *Cohen v. California,* 1971, where a young man had walked around the corridors of a Los Angeles courthouse wearing a jacket on the back of which was printed "Fuck the Draft." He was arrested and convicted under a state law making it unlawful to "disturb the peace . . . by offensive conduct." A majority of the justices in an opinion by Justice Harlan held the wearing of the jacket with the message on the back was a form of expression, in this case of political opinion. Absent evidence that it would provoke public disorder, it was protected speech. The message did not qualify as fighting words because it was not personally directed at anyone present. Nor may a state punish political expression because it is offensive to some persons. "One man's vulgarity," Harlan observed, "is another's lyric...Words are often chosen as much for their emotive as their cognitive force."

The Court dealt definitively with so-called symbolic speech—nonverbal communication through expressive acts—in the 1968 case of *United States v. O'Brien* (p. 179), which, like *Cohen,* grew out of anti-Vietnam War protests. It sustained a government regulation that affected expression but was not aimed at expression. O'Brien burned his draft card before onlookers on the steps of a Boston courthouse and was later convicted under a provision of the Selective Service Act making it unlawful to mutilate or destroy a draft card. The Court recognized the communicative purpose of O'Brien's act, but said that expressive conduct does not automatically have full First Amendment protection. Here an important constitutional power of government— the raising and maintaining military forces— might limit such "speech" because the restriction was incidental to the expression and put a bur-

den on it no greater than needed for administering the selective service system.

The flag has been a ready tool for different kinds of protest, especially those against prevailing government policies. As the national symbol, its desecration or unusual use is bound to gain attention. But for many persons, the flag is a revered object and a perceived insult to it is upsetting and offensive. The Court, has found state and federal antidesecration laws an abridgment of symbolic expression not outweighed by a compelling government interest.

In *Spence v. Washington,* 1974, for example, conviction of a student who affixed a peace symbol to a flag he owned and flew it upside down from his apartment window to protest the Vietnam War and the Kent State shootings, was overturned. The same year in *Smith v. Goguen,* the Court struck down a Massachusetts law making it unlawful to treat the flag "contemptuously," as applied to a man who had sewn a small flag to the seat of his pants as a political protest. In overturning conviction of a man who had publicly burned a flag outside the 1984 Republican National Convention in

David P. O'Brien and three other pacifists burning their draft cards outside a Boston courthouse in protest against the Vietnam War.

The Anti-Judge

No justice served on the Court longer—36 years and seven months—nor wrote more opinions or books, and few showed as much sheer intellectual ability or had as much political ambition as William O. Douglas. Yet the record he left behind was mixed, filled with bold and vigorous support for civil liberties in various contexts, yet marred by questionable judicial workmanship, problematic motives, and philosophical vanity.

Born in 1898, Douglas grew up in and around Yakima, Wash., son of a Presbyterian minister who died when young "Bill" was six, leaving the family penniless. A case of childhood polio was nearly fatal and left him with weakened legs that he rehabilitated with strenuous hiking in the hills around Yakima. This youthful rigor made him a lifelong outdoorsman and environmentalist.

He worked his way through Whitman College, at one time sleeping in a tent to save money. As he recounted later in the first of his autobiographical volumes, *Go East, Young Man*, he rode a freight train across the country to New York to attend law school at Columbia, which had given him a scholarship. He graduated second in his class, specializing in corporate law and, in 1925, joined a prestigious Wall Street law firm. After two years, he tired of defending the interests of large businesses and went home to set up practice in Yakima. A year later, he jumped at the chance to return to Columbia to teach law.

It was an environment in which he thrived, and where he gained a reputation as an specialist in corporate bankruptcy and reorganization. He soon left Columbia for Yale where, at 34, he was given the prestigious Sterling Chair of Commercial and Corporate Law. As the New Deal tried to grapple with business failures during the Depression, his authority brought him to the attention of President Franklin Roosevelt who appointed him to the newly created Securities and Exchange Commission in 1934 and made him commission chairman in 1937.

In Washington, Douglas quickly became a member of the administration's inner circle and was often a guest at the president's poker games. When Justice Louis Brandeis retired in 1939, Roosevelt looked for a Westerner to fill the seat and turned to

Douglas though the nominee's reputation had been made mainly in the East. At 41, he was the second youngest justice to take a seat on the highest court (after Joseph Story who was 32 when appointed 125 years earlier).

On the Court he joined other Roosevelt appointees in upholding government power to regulate business and markets and establish basic social welfare programs that were the heart of the New Deal. During the Cold War years, he frequently joined with Justice Hugo Black in defending freedom of speech, often in dissenting opinions. His eloquent dismissal of the threat posed by homegrown Communists in *Dennis v. United States* in 1952 is memorable in this regard.

It was also in these post-World War II years that Douglas's judicial idiosyncrasies became more evident, perhaps the result of roles he saw for himself beyond the Court. Roosevelt had thought about him as his vice-presidential running mate in 1944, but eventually chose Senator Harry Truman. (Roosevelt's death the following year would have made Douglas president.) In June 1948, he flirted with the idea of a late entry to challenge Truman for the Democratic nomination when the latter's November reelection prospects appeared dim.

His judicial and personal style seemed to change. He divorced the first of four wives, and his restlessness on the Court seemed to grow. At Columbia and Yale he had been greatly influenced by legal realism, the iconoclastic school of jurisprudence holding that a judge's value preferences largely preside over his or her formulation of legal principles, the latter being little more than rationalizations for internal positions. In exposing the subjective elements of judging as unavoidable and largely irreducible, realism played down the differences between judging and the decision making of elected officials. It was exactly these differences many post-New Deal judges were struggling to maintain by emphasizing the intellectual, professional, and institutional constraints of the judicial process itself that they believed gave judging and interpreting law an element of objectivity.

Increasingly, Douglas paid less attention to precedent and the doctrinal elements of constitutional law and more to the political results cases were likely to produce and the philosophy on which they were decided. Thus on the Warren Court he could happily support its expansion of First Amendment freedoms, civil rights, the rights of criminal defendants, and review of legislative apportionment. He could depart from the literalist Black, for example, in finding symbolic and demonstrative behavior to be protected speech in *Adderley v. Florida.* It mattered less that a right or freedom be found in constitutional text or intent than that it seem right that it should be there. The paradigmatic Douglas opinion was the controversial *Griswold v. Connecticut* (p. 301, Chapter 5) that read a right of marital privacy into the Constitution. In it, Douglas spoke of "zones," "penumbras," and "emanations" produced by established rights as though those rights could, by themselves or with the help of wise judicial midwifery, spawn other, new rights. The opinion was audacious and innovative. The right it produced was very likely desirable but, as Black pointed out in dissent, that alone did not make it constitutionally required.

As Douglas listened to his own drummer, he cultivated the maverick's role and seemed increasingly distracted by off-Court pursuits. He traveled the world, wrote more than 30 books, and produced hundreds of articles (including a controversial one for *Playboy*) and talks, many eloquently advocating his positions on liberties and rights, ecology, and internationalism. Many of his activities were infused with a self-dramatizing flair that personalized his ideology. Unsurprisingly, he became a larger-than-life hero for many while succeeding in riling others.

His melodramatic last-minute stay of the execution of the atomic spies Julius and Ethel Rosenberg in 1953 led some of his fellow justices and critics to believe he had acted with cynical grandiosity. He had earlier opposed a review of their conviction where he might have had to acknowledge the strength of the government's case, and later voted for such a review only when it appeared that the majority of the Court would not grant it. The eleventh-hour stay, which he knew the full Court would overturn, seemed to many designed to polish his image as a liberal tribune fighting hysteria on behalf of justice.

Douglas's self-confidence in his own views caused him to disdain criticism and even mock his critics. This, his liberal ideology, and activist behavior off the Court led to a vindictive move by congressional conservatives initiated by Representative Gerald Ford, the minority leader of the House, to impeach Douglas, in 1970. For a while the effort picked up support, but was eventually rejected by a House judiciary subcommittee.

In the meantime, Douglas's private life became increasingly unsettled. In a dozen years he had divorced and remarried three times, the last two marriages to college-age women 40 years his junior. As a parent of two children it was said he often seemed distant and demanding, and he was sometimes abusive to his staff. Though a conversationalist of wit and charm, he had few close friends. In December 1974, he suffered a stroke that left him partly paralyzed. He tried to continue on the Court, but intense pain forced him to resign a year later. He died in June 1980 at 81.

Douglas's idea of himself might have been more appropriate were justices Platonic philosopher kings. But, like every justice before and after him, he was not entrusted with one-ninth of the power of one-third of the government because his views were invariably right or infallibly instructive. At best, Douglas conflated his own conscience with that of the nation; at worst, he acted subjectively without much regard for the interpretive conventions that guided most of his black-robed peers. That he did so little to control or even hide his personal preferences and deferred so little to constitutional text and intent, doctrinal precedent, and the cautions of

(Continued)

self-restraint, led the judicial biographer G. Edward White to call him, "the foremost anti-judge of his time."

Douglas's reputation as an eloquent and outspoken champion of individualism and civil liberties survives. But compared with Black, who left important theoretical marks on the development of civil liberties, or Brennan, who was a master civil liberties strategist and an effective persuader within the Court, Douglas's lasting effect on constitutional law is slight despite his energy, intellect and long service.

Dallas to protest Reagan administration policies, in *Texas v. Johnson*, 1987 (p. 181), the majority of the justices searched in vain for a government interest important enough to punish flag desecration. The Court found no evidence the burning had caused a breach of the peace, nor could it separate the state's claim to preserve the flag's integrity as a symbol of nationhood from the state's antipathy to Johnson's message.

The decision produced a public outcry and demands for a constitutional amendment. Within months Congress passed the Flag Protection Act providing that anyone who "knowingly mutilates, defaces, physically defiles, burns, maintains on the floor or ground, or tramples upon any flag," would be guilty of a criminal act. In *Eichman v. United States*, 1990, the Court held the new law unconstitutional because it was based on preserving the flag as a symbol, an interest inseparable from suppressing expression "out of concern for its likely communicative impact." This reasoning appears to make it all but impossible for an antidesecration law to avoid being linked to disapproval of the message conveyed by the desecrator.

Hate Speech

Expression based on hostility toward innate or defining characteristics of others—race, religion, ethnicity, gender, sexual orientation—presents still another problem of balancing free speech against asserted public interests. So-called hate speech is hardly new in human communication, but heightened sensitivity to it in our time is shown by many attempts of government to make it criminal. We saw the Supreme Court set out wide protection for such speech in *Brandenburg v. Ohio* where the speech stopped short of advocating immediate and specific unlawful acts. But what of hostile expression that does not embody protest against government policies, but is intended simply to hurt and demean and is entirely in the form of conduct?

In 1990, two white teenagers in St. Paul, Minn., imitating racist acts of the Ku Klux Klan in the once-segregated South, fashioned a crude wooden cross and set it aflame in the yard of a black family. (See "Mr. Cleary Goes to Washington.") Conviction of one of the teenagers under the city's Bias-Motivated Crime Law was overturned by the Supreme Court in *R.A.V. v. St. Paul*, 1992 (p. 186). The ordinance, which barred use of symbols or objects known to arouse "anger, alarm, or resentment" because of "race, color, creed, religion, or gender," was unconstitutional as a content-based regulation of expressive conduct singling out some kinds of fighting words but not others. The ruling did not bar punishment under laws phrased to proscribe conduct alone, such as those against arson or terrorist acts, which St. Paul had but did not use.

A year later in *Wisconsin v. Mitchell* (p. 190), the Court refused to extend the R.A.V. ruling when it upheld a punishment enhancement law that increased the penalties for crimes motivated by prejudice directed at race, religion, ethnicity, gender, or sexual orientation. The defendant and several other young black men, angered by a scene of whites beating a black person in the film "Mississippi Burning" which they had just seen, singled out a white teenager

Mr. Cleary Goes to Washington

Practicing in St. Paul, Minn., Edward Cleary was not exactly a small-town lawyer. As a part-time public defender, he had handled scores of criminal cases including those of almost every stripe. Yet nothing in his dozen years at the bar prepared him for the extraordinary case of Robert A. Viktora, the anger and passion his crime engendered, and the free speech issues it raised in its journey through the American legal system.

On the night of June 21, 1990, in a mostly white working class neighborhood on St. Paul's east side, a crude cross made from two chair legs and a scrap of terrycloth was planted and set ablaze on the lawn of Russell and Laura Jones, a black couple with five children, who had moved in months earlier. Police arrested two white youths, 17 and 18, who lived on the same street. Though they might have been charged under any of several state or city laws against vandalism, arson, or terrorism, the prosecutor chose the city's new antibias ordinance that made it a crime to place "on public or private property a symbol, object, appellation, characterization, or graffiti, including, but not limited to, a burning cross or Nazi swastika, which one knows or has reasonable grounds to know arouses anger, alarm, or resentment in others on the basis of race, color, creed, religion, or gender."

The older youth pleaded guilty, the younger, Robert Viktora, a self-proclaimed white separatist, denied involvement. Because he was then a juvenile, only his initials—R. A. V.—were used in the proceedings that followed. Two years and a day to the date of the crossburning, the United States Supreme Court unanimously found the ordinance to violate the First Amendment's guarantee of freedom of speech.

Cleary and fellow lawyer, Michael Cromett, represented Viktora throughout. They were part-time contractual attorneys with the Ramsey County Public Defender's Office, and Cleary's first involvement was purely chance. He had simply been "on duty" to represent all indigent juveniles the morning on which the charge against Viktora was filed.

He had little sympathy for his racist client and none at all for the reprehensible act. But he thought the ordinance, in intent and effect, punished speech rather than act and singled out some kinds of abusive speech and fighting words and not others, thus compromising government's obligation of content neutrality. As Justice David Souter was later to restate the matter, the issue was not about "the wisdom of eradicating intolerance [but] . . . about the method of reaching that goal."

When Viktora was convicted, Cleary took the case to the Minnesota Supreme Court, which sustained the verdict. He then asked the U.S. Supreme Court for review, though he did not think there was

Lawyer Edward Cleary returned to his practice in St. Paul, Minn., after presenting oral argument to the Supreme Court in *R.A.V. v. St. Paul*, in December 1991.

much chance in the Court's busy traffic of petitions that the case would be accepted.

In the meantime, Cleary had become an unpopular figure. A life-long liberal Democrat who had represented dozens of black clients as a public defender, he was shunned by many black lawyers and civil rights activists and by many indignant whites, despite his consistent condemnation of the cross-burning as a criminal act. Cleary got many threats and was the object of other harassment, in some instances extending to members of his family. One anonymous caller shouted that he should be burned upon a cross. The ostracism and pressure of the case affected his personal life. He and his partner were accused in the press of using more than $100,000 of the taxpayers' money on case. In fact, no public money was available for the appeal, and the two attorneys donated their time, which, in all, was many hundreds of hours.

When the Supreme Court did grant the petition for review, Cleary with the same dogged determination that had led him to appeal the conviction in the state courts, decided to try the case himself. He had not had much chance to plead constitutional issues before and, of course, had never appeared before the Supreme Court. Needing to sharpen his command of First Amendment law and of how to approach the Court, he looked for advice from established constitutional scholars. Several, not wanting to be involved in an unpopular case, begged off saying they were too busy even to comment on the draft of his brief. Two leading legal scholars who were interested suggested he step aside to allow them or their friends to argue the case. "This is not the Minnesota Supreme Court," one told him, apparently believing Cleary not up to the task.

As the date for oral argument approached, media attention grew intense. There were interviews, requests for more interviews, commentary, and opinion. Few pundits and few of those who regularly covered legal affairs gave Cleary much chance of winning. Some editorials were critical or hostile. In much of its reporting, the media had difficulty making the free speech issue clear and separating it from the act of crossburning.

The case was also a magnet for intervenors. With open permission of the parties, more than 30 organi-

zations, representing a substantial cross-cutting of the political spectrum, filed amicus curiae (friend-of-the-Court) briefs, most supporting St. Paul. Among those on the free speech side were the Association of American Publishers, the American Library Association, the American Jewish Congress, and the far-right Patriots Defense Foundation. Those opposed included the NAACP, the Anti-Defamation League, People for the American Way, the National Lawyers Guild, the U.S. Conference of Mayors, the YWCA, and the conservative law-and-order Criminal Justice Legal Foundation. Though Cleary had support of the Minnesota Civil Liberties Union, the parent ACLU offered little or none, and after the decision, circulated a memorandum critical of it, an ambivalence in marked contrast to its work in the Skokie affair a dozen years earlier. (See "The Nazis and The Free Marketplace of Ideas.")

Instead of plunging directly into the issue of the St. Paul ordinance as would be customary, Cleary opened his half hour of oral argument with an unorthodox statement. He quoted the cautionary words of Sir Thomas More from Robert Bolt's play *A Man for All Seasons,* about good intentions in disregard of law. To his zealous lawyer son-in-law, who has asserted he would cut down every law in England to get after the Devil, More replies

> Oh? And when the last law was down, and the Devil turned round on you—where would you hide, the laws all being flat? . . . If you cut them down . . . d'you really think you could stand upright in the wind that would blow then? Yes, I'd give the Devil benefit of law, for my own safety's sake.

Six months later, on June 22, 1992, the Supreme Court handed down its decision. Though the justices did not totally agree on a theory for their holding, Cleary had won a unanimous 9-0 victory. The decision drew mixed response in the media and in public opinion. In St. Paul it was denounced by the mayor and county attorney and drew angry response from many quarters. Cleary remained something of a persona non grata, still shunned by many former acquaintances. His odyssey, Nat Hentoff, the civil liberties writer, told him, "was a Frank Capra script without the applause at the end."

for his race and beat him unconscious. Mitchell's discussion with his friends about the impending assault was used as evidence of race bias to support doubling his sentence. The Court refused to accept his argument that the heavier sentence was, in effect, punishment based on expression—his beliefs evident in what he said to the others. It held that the First Amendment did not bar evidentiary use of speech to prove elements of a crime including motive or intent.

Group Demonstrations

Protest or provocation by individuals through "pure speech," symbolic speech, or expressive behavior may threaten the peace by inciting a sympathetic audience or provoking a hostile one. Balancing free speech against public order and safety is especially difficult where both speakers and audience are large numbers of persons and communication is through expressive conduct addressing volatile issues. Preventing clashes between groups is one of the oldest and highest responsibilities of local authority. It is also one that invites the favoring or disfavoring of substantive "messages," especially where they address war policies, civil rights, abortion, labor disputes, or other issues producing strong feelings or deep commitment.

In one of its earliest local speech and assembly cases, the Supreme Court set out the basic principle that groups have a right to use public areas, such as streets and parks, for discussion of public issues. In Jersey City, N.J., the mayor, Frank Hague, denied the Congress of Industrial Organizations (CIO), then the nation's second largest labor organization, use of public places for speeches and distribution of union materials because he believed the organization was controlled by Communists. In *Hague v. CIO,* 1939, the Court upheld an injunction against Hague, Justice Owen Roberts observing that streets and parks have "immemorially been held in trust for the use of the public and time out of mind have been used for . . . assembly, communicating thoughts between citizens and discussing public questions." [306 U.S. 496 at 515-516] Their use may be regulated but not arbitrarily denied by authorities because they do not like the ideas discussed.

The 1960s civil rights movement, which made effective use of demonstrations, marches, sit-ins, and other protests, produced several important speech and assembly cases. The most notable was *Edwards v. South Carolina,* 1963 (p. 192), an appeal from breach of the peace convictions. Some 200 black college and high school students holding placards and singing patriotic songs walked peaceably through the grounds of the state capitol in Columbia to protest policies of racial discrimination. After about 45 minutes during which there was no sign of disturbance from a large group of onlookers, the students were told to disperse by police and were arrested when they refused. The Supreme Court held the law under which they were prosecuted to be impermissibly broad in permitting "a state to make criminal the peaceful expression of unpopular views." The convictions were based on evidence, Justice Stewart observed, "which showed no more than that the opinions which they were peaceably expressing were sufficiently opposed to the views of the majority of the community to attract a crowd and necessitate police protection."

Protests at abortion clinics by right-to-life groups have created public order problems where demonstrators block access to the buildings. In *Madsen v. Women's Health Center,* 1994, the Court sustained an injunction that set out a 36-foot buffer zone around a clinic in Melbourne, Fla., from which protesters were barred. It found the restraint to be content-neutral in placing burdens on speech "no more . . . than necessary to serve a significant government interest"—here protecting the right to get lawful medical counseling or services. Three years later in *Schenck v. Pro-Choice Network of Western New York,* the Court, though again upholding a fixed buffer zone around a clinic, vacated an injunction that required a 15-foot "floating" zone around persons or vehicles entering or leaving the clinic. But in the more recent *Hill v. Colorado,* 2000

The Nazis and the Free Marketplace of Ideas

In October 1976, the National Socialist Party of America (NSPA), an American Nazi organization in Chicago, announced that it would stage a march in the Village of Skokie, a suburb north of the city. Its purpose would be to dramatize the group's belief in white power, and racial purity, and expose Jewish influence in American society. The plan was exquisitely mean-spirited. Skokie was chosen because it had a large Jewish population that included many survivors of Hitler's concentration camps and others whose relatives died in the camps.

Frank Collin, NSPA leader, who proved adept at getting media attention, explained in an interview, "I hope they're terrified. I hope they're shocked. Because we're coming to get them again. I don't care if someone's mother or father died in the gas chambers. The unfortunate thing is not that there were six million Jews who died. The unfortunate thing is that there were so many Jewish survivors."* Ironically, Collin, born Cohn, was half-Jewish and his German-born father had actually spent three months in Dachau, compelling testimony, perhaps, to the power of filial conflict that may lurk in the unconscious mind.

What followed was an 18-month legal battle waged by Skokie to keep the Nazis from marching. It occupied the attention of six courts including the U.S. Supreme Court before the free speech issues it raised were settled. The village (with a population of 70,000, more like a city) first got an injunction against the march. It barred anyone from "marching, walking or parading in the uniform of the National Socialist Party ... displaying the swastika ... distributing pamphlets or displaying any materials which incite or promote hatred against persons of any faith or ancestry, race or religion."

To get legal help in fighting the injunction, which operated as a prior restraint, Collin appealed to the Illinois American Civil Liberties Union. Its board of directors voted unanimously to defend the Nazis' right to demonstrate as an exercise of freedom of speech. Unsuccessful in getting the injunction lifted in state courts or a hearing on its merits, an appeal was taken to the U.S. Supreme Court. In *NSPA v. Skokie,* June 1977, the Court held that the injunction either had to be vacated or arguments heard immediately on the merits of the case. If the Village tried to impose a restraint of this kind, the Court said, "It must provide strict procedural safeguards including appellate review." Because it had not, a First Amendment right to freedom of speech was violated. It sent the case back to Illinois courts for further proceeding.

Frank Collin leads American Nazi party members in a well-policed march in Federal Plaza, Chicago.

The Illinois Appellate Court narrowed the injunction by removing the bar to wearing Nazi uniforms and to distributing materials, but retained the ban on swastikas. On appeal, the Illinois Supreme Court struck down the modified injunction, saying that display of the swastika was not "fighting words" but a form of symbolic speech protected by the First Amendment.

In the meantime, Skokie had enacted three ordinances also designed to head off the march. Two simply incorporated the language of the now-defunct injunction against demonstrations in military-style uniforms and the distribution of literature that had racial or religious slurs. The third, phrased as a traffic and safety law, required would-be demonstrators to get a permit 30 days in advance and post liability insurance bonds of $350,000. When Collin applied for but was refused a permit because the NPSA could not post the bonds and Skokie refused to waive the requirement, the ACLU lawyers filed suit in federal district court. In *Smith v. Collin*, early in 1978, that court struck down all three ordinances. The racial slur law was ill-defined because it went beyond "fighting words" to include expression that communicated ideas however reprehensible they might be. The ban on military-type uniforms had no acceptable justification for singling out that kind of symbolic speech. The insurance bond scheme fell as "a drastic restriction of the right of freedom of speech and assembly," because most groups would not be able to meet it. The court also thought that Skokie had applied it arbitrarily because it had been waived for other groups.

Skokie appealed, but the district court's decision was upheld by the Seventh Circuit Court of Appeals. The U.S. Supreme Court refused to grant review, thus letting the district court's finding against the Village stand.

Free to march, Collin announced the event would take place on Hitler's birthday; later he changed it to the first day of Passover. Then, in a final ironic turn, declaring the NSPA's constitutional rights had been vindicated, he moved the march to Federal Plaza in Chicago. On June 23, 1978, in full uniform 20 or so Nazis paraded for 15 minutes under heavy police guard, greeted mainly by hecklers.

Collin soon dropped from sight. Later, he served three years in prison for taking indecent liberties with children. After his release he changed his name again and quit Nazism.

Though the ending was more whimper than bang, the lessons of Skokie endure. A free speech society sometimes makes great demands on its members; it is perhaps the bravest and most forbearing political arrangement human beings have ever willingly entered. In this case, it asked that many persons who had endured much suffering and loss put up with the cruelest and most insulting reminders of it. The Skokie conflict also took a toll of the chief defenders of free speech. About 2,400 members of the Illinois ACLU—more than 30 percent of its entire list—resigned in disgust at its defense of the Nazis' First Amendment rights. Nearly 20 percent of the national organization's 250,000 members either resigned or did not renew their membership. The loss of income and the extensive legal expenses of the Skokie cases forced the Union to lay off employees and suspend some publications. David Goldberger, the Illinois ACLU's chief lawyer in the cases, had abuse heaped on him, much of it from Jews and Jewish groups angry that a fellow Jew could go to such lengths to defend Nazis.

But in the end, the free speech society worked the way it is supposed to work. If, as Justice Holmes said, the test of truth is its acceptance in the competition of the marketplace, then the answer to bad ideas is not suppression or censorship, but better ideas; not less speech but more. In the Skokie conflict, the reprehensible ideas of a handful of political misfits generated a countervailing flood of opinion in the marketplace. Meetings, rallies, interfaith demonstrations, and commemorations took place, many well beyond the Chicago area, to say nothing of perhaps hundreds of thousands of simple discussions. Bonds of sympathy and brotherhood were discovered or renewed. Editorials across the country denounced the NPSA, and the media attention probably acquainted many with the Holocaust who had not known much if anything about it before. The Nazis and everything they stood for were exposed for all to see. The rejection was emphatic; the free marketplace had dealt with a bad idea.

---

* Philippa Strum, *When the Nazis Came to Skokie* (Lawrence, Kans.: University of Kansas Press, 1999), 15. The personal material on Collin in this sidebar is also drawn from Strum's excellent study.

(p. 194), it upheld a state law that limited speech within a 100-foot radius of any "health care facility," passed mainly to allow unharried access to abortion clinics. Specifically, the law barred any demonstrator from approaching within eight feet of anyone entering or leaving without their consent and from distributing literature, making oral protest, or offering counseling. Despite the transparent purpose, the Court held the restrictions to be content-neutral, narrowly tailored, and within the state's power to protect persons who are "often in particularly vulnerable physical and emotional conditions."

Labor Picketing

Picketing by unions is a special case of group protest and has been treated that way by the Supreme Court. Such demonstrations can provide public information about a work dispute but, as a by-product of workplace strife, they are also aimed at economic coercion which, in turn, has sometimes led to violence. Because of its threat to property, almost all labor picketing was illegal or readily subject to restraint through civil action until well into the twentieth century. The Roosevelt Court, reflecting its New Deal orientation, expressly brought peaceful picketing under the protection of the First Amendment in *Thornhill v. Alabama*, 1940, in which it struck down a state law that barred most labor demonstrations. Though the Court acknowledged that freedom to picket was not absolute, Justice Murphy observed that "Every expression of opinion . . . has the potentiality for inducing action in the interests of one rather than another group in society. But the group in power at any moment may not impose penal sanctions on peaceful and truthful discussion of matters of public interest merely on a showing that others may thereby be persuaded to take action inconsistent with its interests." [310 U.S. 88 at 104]

The Court has elaborated another principle of *Thornhill* in several cases since, that speech and its educational aspects do not shield picketing from limited regulation for public ends.

Thus it has not protected labor demonstrations that urge workers to join illegal strikes or pressure employers to interfere with the rights of nonunion workers or enter into illegal restraints of trade. Nor has it protected picketing that is part of a secondary boycott against third parties who deal with the business with whom the pickets have a dispute, or where a union's picketing had led to violence in the past. Justice Frankfurter summarized these developments in *International Brotherhood of Teamsters, Local 695 v. Vogt*, 1957, as having "established a broad field in which a state in enforcing some public policy, whether of its criminal or its civil law, and whether announced by its legislature or its courts, could constitutionally enjoin peaceful picketing aimed at preventing effectuation of that policy." [354 U.S. 284 at 294]

The issue of liability for economic damage caused by demonstrations came to the Court in *NAACP v. Claiborne Hardware*, 1982, where NAACP had led picketing and a boycott of several white merchants to protest discriminatory hiring practices. The Court held that neither the organization nor individual boycotters could be held liable for business losses sustained by the merchants where the boycott and demonstrations had been peaceful.

Because the First Amendment limits only government, picketing in quasi-public areas presents a unique issue. The matter came up in *Amalgamated Food Employees Union v. Logan Valley Plaza*, 1968, where the owner of a private shopping mall near Altoona, Penn., got an injunction barring picketing at a store in the mall. Vacating the order, the Court relied on its 1946 decision in *Marsh v. Alabama*, which affirmed the right to distribute religious literature in a town wholly owned by a private company. In *Logan Valley*, the Court likened the shopping mall to the business district of the company town, a place to which the public had general access and which served as the functional equivalent of the community's business district.

But in *Hudgens v. NLRB*, 1976, another private mall case, a divided Court had second thoughts.

Striking employees of a shoe company warehouse some distance from the mall picketed one of the company's retail stores in the mall. A majority of seven justices sustained the right of the mall owners to bar picketing but were divided on whether the Logan Valley case was overruled or simply distinguished because the pickets in *Hudgens* were not protesting operations of the retail store but conveying information about a dispute outside the mall. The distinction, supported by three justices, coupled with the views of the two dissenters in the case may mean that there is still some First Amendment protection for peaceful labor picketing in quasi-public areas.

Time, Place, and Manner Issues

Besides the conflicts discussed, protection of public order includes a wide range of circumstantial ends. Their pursuit may constrict speech or may be hampered by speech and expressive conduct. These matters have to do with the how, where, and when of communication rather than the who or what. The Court has made it clear that local restrictions on speech that are not content-neutral will be struck down unless they apply to a category of speech unprotected by the First Amendment, such as advocacy of unlawful acts, "fighting words," obscenity, or defamatory expression. Nor will restrictions even incidental to speech be allowed to stand if they excessively burden the flow of ideas and opinion, are not the least restrictive means possible, and other vehicles for communication are not available or difficult to use. At the same time the Court has recognized the legitimacy of local government's protection of public health, safety and tranquillity, as well as privacy, the flow of traffic, the conduct of business and government, and the special needs of the school day. Balancing these interests against freedom of speech is made all the harder by the need to separate the form of communication from its content and the fact that seemingly neutral regulations may sometimes be a pretext for controlling or discouraging unpopular messages and opinions.

The general balancing principle was described by Justice Roberts in *Schneider v. Irvington*, 1939, "Municipal authorities, as trustees for the public, have a duty to keep their communities' streets open and available for movement of people and property, the primary purpose to which streets are dedicated. So long as legislation to this end does not abridge the constitutional liberty of one rightfully upon the street to import information through speech or the distribution of literature, it may lawfully regulate the conduct of those using the streets." [308 U.S. 147 at 160] The principle has been applied to several types of time, place, and manner restrictions.

Permits and Administrative Discretion. In several early cases, the Supreme Court set out the basic rule that laws requiring prior administrative approval before public space could be used for speech or other expressive acts were invalid if they gave officials more than the narrowest discretion. In *Lovell v. Griffin*, 1938, it struck down an ordinance that had no guidelines for the issuance or denial of permits to distribute literature. In contrast, in *Cox v. New Hampshire*, 1940, it recognized the local interest in traffic safety and flow by upholding a permit requirement for marches and parades. The law was drawn precisely enough to keep officials from basing decisions on whether of not they favored the views that would be expressed.

Five years later the Court overturned a contempt conviction of a labor union organizer who spoke to workers without first getting an organizer's permit. In *Thomas v. Collins*, it stressed the high place occupied by speech: "Only the gravest abuses endangering paramount interests give occasion for permissible limitation." [323 U.S. 516 at 530] Advocating unionism was not one of them. Nor in *Kunz v. New York*, 1950, was a previous inflammatory attack on particular religions. The city's denial of a permit to preach in a public place—in this case, a sidewalk—was invalid for not having clear and narrow standards and being a prior restraint based on the anticipated content of speech.

Public Tranquillity. When it first dealt with the matter of speech as excessive noise, the Court found it easy to strike down a local ordinance that barred sound amplification in public places without a permit. In *Saia v. New York,* 1948, a Jehovah's Witness was arrested for using sound equipment after he had been denied a permit to amplify religious talks in a public park because of complaints about the noise. Though recognizing denial was for no other reason than sound volume, it held the ordinance "void on its face" because it gave officials discretion to issue or refuse permits for any reason at all and because it operated as a prior restraint on speech.

But a year later in *Kovacs v. Cooper,* it backed away from this broad ruling in upholding a Trenton, N.J., ordinance that banned sound trucks and amplification equipment emitting "loud and raucous noises." Unlike the law in *Saia,* this was a standard narrow enough to limit discretion of officials, and the ordinance did not require prior permits. The two cases left open whether a flat ban on all sound amplification equipment in public places would be constitutional. Though not returning to that question directly, the Court upheld a New York City ordinance in *Ward v. Rock Against Racism,* 1989, that required groups at a band shell in Central Park to use an amplification system and sound technician provided by the city.

Unwanted sound was an issue in a different setting in *Public Utilities Commission v. Pollak,* 1952, where the Court upheld the right of a private transit company in the District of Columbia to play news, music, and advertisements in its streetcars and buses. Against complaints by riders, it held there was no absolute right of privacy in public places to overcome First Amendment interests.

Restricted Public Places. The Court has used the same principles that it has applied to speech on streets and sidewalks to speech in other public places. In *Edwards v. South Carolina,* we saw its willingness to uphold the right to demonstrate

peacefully on state capitol grounds. Closer to home in *Grace v. United States,* 1983, it held a District of Columbia ordinance that barred picketing, sign-carrying, and leafleting in areas around the U.S. Supreme Court building without stating the need for such restriction, to be an unjustified total suppression of communication in a public place. The Court reiterated the constitutional requirements, "The government may enforce reasonable time, place, and manner regulations as long as the restrictions are content-neutral, are narrowly tailored to serve a significant government interest, and leave open ample alternative channels of communication." [461 U.S. 171 at 195]

Two cases from the 1960s civil rights movement show how difficult weaving a thread of consistency may be. In *Brown v. Louisiana,* 1966, the Court overturned breach of the peace convictions of five black men who stood silently in and refused to leave a whites-only section of a public library. But the same year in *Adderley v. Florida,* it upheld trespass convictions of several civil rights activists who demonstrated in the yard of a county jail in which other activists arrested earlier in the day for trying to integrate a theater were being held. The Court distinguished both *Edwards* and *Brown,* noting the special security problems surrounding a jailhouse and that its grounds were not traditionally open to the public.

It also applied "traditional use" reasoning in *Greer v. Spock,* 1976, to sustain a ban on political speeches and demonstrations at the Fort Dix army base in New Jersey, saying that the function of the base was "to train soldiers, not provide a public forum." Later it upheld National Park Service rules forbidding overnight camping in certain parks, as applied to demonstrators in Lafayette Park across from the White House who wanted to stage a sleep-in to protest national policies on the poor and homeless. In the case, *Clark v. Community for Creative Non-Violence,* 1984, it found the rule to be content-neutral and a reasonable restriction in the interest of protecting park lands and conservation.

Schools are a special case of restricted public space because of the needs of the school day. The Court's most important statement here came in *Tinker v. Des Moines Independent School District* 1969, (p. 198), where school authorities suspended and sent home several students for wearing black armbands to protest Vietnam War policies, in violation of a school rule. Though admitting school administrators had wide authority to maintain order and decorum, it said neither students nor teachers "shed their constitutional rights to freedom of speech and expression at the schoolhouse gate." Noting that the rule against armbands had been adopted only two days before and that the school permitted other political symbols to be worn, it found the ban anything but content-neutral. Nor without evidence of specific disruption could such a ban be justified simply on general fear of disturbance.

Areas surrounding schools were the issue in two decisions in 1972. In the first, *Grayned v. City of Rockford*, the Court upheld an ordinance barring demonstrations near school buildings that disturbed the "peace and good order" of the school session. But in *Police Department of Chicago v. Mosely*, it found an ordinance disallowing picketing within 150 feet of a school during the school day to be invalid because it made an exception for labor picketing. This, the Court said, was regulation by "the message on the picket sign." In allowing demonstrations by some groups, government may not then bar others from assembling or speaking because of what they intend to say.

In other restricted area cases, the Court said that solicitation by religious and other groups could be confined to a designated area at a state fair in *Heffron v. International Society for Krishna Consciousness*, 1981. It noted that traffic and safety concerns may be more pressing at a large temporary event like a fair than on a typical city street. In *International Society for Krishna Consciousness v. Lee*, 1992, it upheld a ban on soliciting money at air terminals. Because terminals are not traditional forums for speech, the ban

need only be reasonable. But in a companion case between the same parties, *Lee v. International Society for Krishna Consciousness*, another airport rule that banned the distribution of literature was held invalid.

Residential Considerations. Drawing a line between protected speech and protected privacy has forced the Court to make fine distinctions. It set out a general rule in the early case of *Martin v. City of Struthers*, 1943, holding unconstitutional an ordinance that barred door-to-door distribution of handbills, circulars, or other advertisements or doorbell ringing to summon residents to receive the material. Though the ordinance was designed to protect the sleep of the many residents of the Ohio industrial town who worked at night, Justice Black wrote that house-to-house distribution was "essential to the poorly financed causes of little people." But the Court partly retreated in *Breard v. City of Alexandria*, 1951, upholding an ordinance barring door-to-door solicitation of magazine subscriptions without permission of the householder. It cited the commercial element in the solicitation to distinguish the case from *Martin*. In *Village of Schaumberg v. Citizens for a Better Environment*, 1980, it held that a municipality's interest in protecting residents against fraud did not justify an ordinance that required door-to-door charity solicitors show that at least 75 percent of money collected was used for charitable purposes.

The Court revisited the door-to-door solicitation issue in *Watchtower Bible and Tract Society v. Village of Stratton*, 2002, in which Jehovah's Witnesses challenged a small Ohio town's ordinance that restricted such canvassing. The law made it a crime for an uninvited canvasser to enter a householder's property to promote or explain any cause without providing identification and getting a permit from the mayor. By an 8-1 vote, the Court invalidated the ordinance, Justice John Paul Stevens observing for the majority that it was "offensive not only to the values protected by the First Amendment, but to the very notion of a free society that in the context of everyday public discourse a citizen must first inform the government of her desire to speak to her neighbors and then obtain a permit to do so." Though the affected interest in this case was a religious group, the Court avoided basing its defense of door-to-door solicitation on free exercise grounds. Because the Stratton ordinance was so broadly cast, the Court's decision is not likely to effect thousands of local laws that regulate door-to-door commercial activity.

Demonstrations singling out a person's home were at issue in *Gregory v. Chicago,* 1969, where about 100 black civil rights activists marched on the sidewalks outside the home of the city's mayor to protest school policies. When a crowd of angry white neighbors grew, police arrested several marchers, who were later found guilty of disorderly conduct. In reversing these convictions for lack of evidence, the Supreme Court affirmed that a peaceful and orderly march is protected by the First Amendment, even though it is a residential neighborhood. But in *Frisby v. Schultz,* 1988, where it had to address the issue more directly, the Court upheld a Brookfield, Wis., ordinance that specifically forbade picketing individual homes. The law was invoked after a group of antiabortion protesters, sometimes as many as 40, had several times picketed the home of a doctor who worked at an abortion clinic. The Court read the ordinance narrowly, to ban only demonstrations "focused" on a particular home and not those in residential neighborhoods generally.

Privately Owned "Public" Property. Several questions have arisen about the right of private owners of "public" property to limit speech on that property and the right of private property owners to use their property for public communication. As with labor picketing, the Supreme Court has wavered on the extent to which the First Amendment protects protests at privately owned malls and shopping centers. In *Lloyd v. Tanner,* 1972, it retreated from its earlier reasoning that a private mall might be the functional equivalent of a business district, to hold that the First Amendment did not protect distribution of handbills—in this instance protesting Vietnam War policies—on the property. In inviting the public to do business with its tenants, the owners did not open the mall "for any and all purposes." The Court added that it had never held that, "an uninvited guest may exercise general rights of free speech on property privately owned and used non-discriminantly for private purpose only." [407 U.S. 551 at 568] However, in *Prune Yard Shopping Center v. Robins,* 1980, where signatures were collected for an anti-Vietnam War petition to Congress, the Court held that a state under its own constitution—in this case California—could give such activity free speech protection even if it were unprotected by the First Amendment.

Homes privately owned have "public" aspects that may be regulated through zoning and other laws that limit use in the name of community health, safety, and aesthetics. Occasionally, such regulations have directly clashed with the speech interests of the property owners. In such cases, the restrictions have gotten close and generally unsympathetic attention from the Court. In *Linmark Associates v. Township of Willingboro,* 1977, for example, it struck down an ordinance that aimed to discourage "white flight" by barring homeowners and realtors from posting "For Sale" or "Sold" signs on front lawns. Because other lawn signs were allowed, the restriction was not content-neutral. More broadly, the Court objected that if the township could restrict dissemination of this information, other localities could suppress facts that reflected poorly on them. In 1994, a local ordinance that barred most lawn signs to reduce "visual clutter" was held unconstitutional as applied to a homeowner who put signs in her front yard opposing the Persian Gulf War. In *City of Ladue v. Gilleo,* the Court said the ordinance almost entirely foreclosed a venerable means of communication that was unique and important.

FURTHER READING

Freedom of Speech in American Society and Polity

Alexander, Larry, ed., *Freedom of Speech* (1999)

Allen, David, and Robert Jensen, eds., *Freeing the First Amendment: Critical Perspectives on Freedom of Expression* (1995)

Baker, C. Edwin, *Human Liberty and Freedom of Speech* (1989)

Berns, Walter, *The First Amendment and the Future of American Democracy* (1976)

Blanchard, Margaret, *Revolutionary Sparks: Freedom of Expression in Modern America* (1992)

Bollinger, Lee C., *Freedom of Speech and Extremist Speech in America* (1986)

———, *Eternally Vigilant: Free Speech in the Modern Era* (2002)

Bosmajian, Haig, *The Freedom Not to Speak* (1999)

Chafee, Zechariah, Jr., *Free Speech in the United States* (1941)

Cox, Archibald, *Freedom of Expression* (1981)

Curtis, Michael Kent, *Free Speech, "The People's Darling Privilege"* (2000)

Easton, Susan, *The Case for the Right to Silence* (1998)

Emerson, Thomas I., *The System of Freedom of Expression* (1970)

———, *Toward a General Theory of the First Amendment* (1967)

Fish, Stanley, *There's No Such Thing as Free Speech, and It's a Good Thing Too* (1994)

Fiss, Owen, *The Irony of Free Speech* (1996)

———, *Liberalism Divided: Freedom of Speech and the Many Uses of State Power* (1996)

Graber, Mark A., *Transforming Free Speech: The Ambiguous Legacy of Civil Libertarianism* (1991)

Hensley, Thomas R., ed., *The Boundaries of Freedom of Expression and Order in American Democracy* (2001)

Ingelhart, Louis E., ed., *Press and Speech Freedoms in America, 1619–1995: A Chronology* (1997)

Kalven, Harry, *A Worthy Tradition: Freedom of Speech in America* (1988)

Krislov, Samuel, *The Supreme Court and Political Freedom* (1968)

Meiklejohn, Alexander, *Political Freedom: The Constitutional Powers of the People* (1960)

———, *Free Speech and Its Relation to Self-Government* (1948)

Rabban, David M., *Free Speech in Its Forgotten Years* (1997)

Schauer, Frederick F., *Free Speech: A Philosophical Enquiry* (1982)

Shiffren, Steven H., *The First Amendment, Democracy and Romance* (1990)

Smolla, Rodney, *Free Speech in an Open Society* (1992)

Sunstein, Cass A., *Democracy and the Problem of Free Speech* (1993)

Van Alstyne, William W., *Interpretations of the First Amendment* (1984)

National Security

Belknap, Michal R., *Coldwar Political Justice: The Smith Act, the Communist Party, and American Civil Liberties* (1977)

Dowell, Eldridge F., *A History of Criminal Syndicalism Laws in the United States* (1939)

Smith, James Morton, *Freedom's Fetters: The Alien and Sedition Laws and American Civil Liberties* (1956)

Taylor, Telford, *Grand Inquest* (1955)

Washburn, Patrick S., *A Question of Sedition* (1986)

Assembly, Protest, and Public Order

Anastaplo, George, *Campus Hate-Speech Codes and Twentieth Century Atrocities* (1997)

Cord, Robert, *Protest, Dissent, and the Supreme Court* (1971)

Delgado, Richard, and Jean Stefancic, *Must We Defend Nazis? Hate Speech, Pornography, and the New First Amendment* (1997)

Dooling, Richard, *Blue Streak: Swearing, Free Speech, and Sexual Harassment* (1996)

Downs, Donald A., *Nazis in Skokie: Freedom, Community, and the First Amendment* (1985)

Goldstein, Robert Justin, *The Flag: The Great 1989–1990 American Flag Desecration Controversy* (1996)

Greenawalt, Kent, *Fighting Words: Individuals, Communities, and Liberties of Speech* (1995)

Heumann, Milton, Thomas Church, with David Redlawsk, eds., *Hate Speech on Campus: Cases, Case Studies, and Commentary* (1997)

Johnson, John W., *The Struggle for Student Rights:* Tinker v. Des Moines *and the 1960's* (1997)

Matsuda, Mari, Charles Lawrence, Richard Delgado, and Kimberle Crenshaw, *Words That Wound: Critical*

Race Theory, Assaultive Speech, and the First Amendment (1993)

Murphy, Paul L., *The Meaning of Freedom of Speech: First Amendment Freedoms from Wilson to FDR* (1972)

O'Neill, Robert M., *Free Speech in the College Community* (1997)

Strum, Philippa, *When the Nazis Came to Skokie: Freedom for the Speech We Hate* (1999)

Walker, Samuel, *Hate Speech: The History of an American Controversy* (1994)

Wolfson, Nicholas, *Hate Speech, Sex Speech, Free Speech* (1997)

Freedom of Association

Abernathy, M. Glenn, *The Right of Assembly and Association* (1981)

Fellman, David, *The Constitutional Right of Association* (1963)

Fiss, Owen, *Civil Rights Injunction* (1978)

Gutman, A., *Freedom of Association* (1998)

Horn, Robert A., *Groups and the Constitution* (1956)

Kalven, Harry, *The Negro and the First Amendment* (1965)

Rice, Charles, Freedom of Association (1962)

Soifer, Aviam, *Law and the Company We Keep* (1995)

On Leading Cases

Cleary, Edward J., *Beyond the Burning Cross: The First Amendment and the Landmark R. A. V. Case* (1994)

Goldstein, Robert Justin, *Flag Burning and Free Speech: The Case of* Texas v. Johnson (2000)

Martin, Charles H., *The Angelo Herndon Case and Southern Justice* (1976)

Polenberg, Richard, *Fighting Faiths: The Abrams Case, the Supreme Court, and Free Speech* (1989)

Additional works are listed in the General and Supplemental Bibliography.

CASES

Schenck v. United States

249 U.S. 47 (1919), 9-0

Opinion of the Court: Holmes (Brandeis, Clark, Day, McKenna, McReynolds, Pitney, Van Devanter, White)

Was Schenck convicted for speaking in violation of the law or for acting in violation? Though the Court upholds the defendant's conviction, how does this decision theoretically expand the protection of speech? Does a "clear and present danger" test draw a practical line between free speech and national security? A desirable line?

Holmes, for the Court:

This is an indictment in three counts. The first charges a conspiracy to violate the Espionage Act of June 15, 1917 by causing and attempting to cause insubordination, &c., in the military and naval forces of the United States, and to obstruct the recruiting and enlistment service of the United States, when the United States was at war with the German Empire, to-wit, that the defendants willfully conspired to have printed and circulated to men who had been called and accepted for military service under the Act of

May 18, 1917, a document set forth and alleged to be calculated to cause such insubordination and obstruction. The count alleges overt acts in pursuance of the conspiracy, ending in the distribution of the document set forth. The second count alleges a conspiracy to commit an offence against the United States, to-wit, to use the mails for the transmission of matter declared to be nonmailable by Title XII, § 2 of the Act of June 15, 1917, to-wit, the above mentioned document, with an averment of the same overt acts. The third count charges an unlawful use of the mails for the transmission of the same matter and otherwise as above. The defendants were found guilty on all the counts. They set up the First Amendment to the Constitution forbidding Congress to make any law abridging the freedom of speech, or of the press, and bringing the case here on that ground have argued some other points also of which we must dispose.

The document in question, upon its first printed side, recited the first section of the Thirteenth Amendment, said that the idea embodied in it was violated by the Conscription Act, and that a conscript is little better than a convict. In impassioned language, it intimated that conscription was despotism in its worst form, and a monstrous wrong against humanity in the interest of

Wall Street's chosen few. It said "Do not submit to intimidation," but in form, at least, confined itself to peaceful measures such as a petition for the repeal of the act. The other and later printed side of the sheet was headed "Assert Your Rights." It stated reasons for alleging that anyone violated the Constitution when he refused to recognize "your right to assert your opposition to the draft," and went on, "If you do not assert and support your rights, you are helping to deny or disparage rights which it is the solemn duty of all citizens and residents of the United States to retain." It described the arguments on the other side as coming from cunning politicians and a mercenary capitalist press, and even silent consent to the conscription law as helping to support an infamous conspiracy. It denied the power to send our citizens away to foreign shores to shoot up the people of other lands, and added that words could not express the condemnation such cold-blooded ruthlessness deserves, &c., &c., winding up, "You must do your share to maintain, support and uphold the rights of the people of this country." Of course, the document would not have been sent unless it had been intended to have some effect, and we do not see what effect it could be expected to have upon persons subject to the draft except to influence them to obstruct the carrying of it out. The defendants do not deny that the jury might find against them on this point.

But it is said, suppose that that was the tendency of this circular, it is protected by the First Amendment to the Constitution. Two of the strongest expressions are said to be quoted respectively from well known public men. It well may be that the prohibition of laws abridging the freedom of speech is not confined to previous restraints, although to prevent them may have been the main purpose. We admit that, in many places and in ordinary times, the defendants, in saying all that was said in the circular, would have been within their constitutional rights. But the character of every act depends upon the circumstances in which it is done. The most stringent protection of free speech would not protect a man in falsely shouting fire in a theatre and causing a panic. It does not even protect a man from an injunction against uttering words that may have all the effect of force. The question in every case is whether the words used are used in such circumstances and are of such a nature as to create a clear and present danger that they will bring about the substantive evils that Congress has a right to prevent. It is a question of proximity and degree. When a nation is at war, many things that might be said in

time of peace are such a hindrance to its effort that their utterance will not be endured so long as men fight, and that no Court could regard them as protected by any constitutional right. It seems to be admitted that, if an actual obstruction of the recruiting service were proved, liability for words that produced that effect might be enforced. The statute of 1917, in §4, punishes conspiracies to obstruct, as well as actual obstruction. If the act (speaking, or circulating a paper), its tendency, and the intent with which it is done are the same, we perceive no ground for saying that success alone warrants making the act a crime. . . .

Gitlow v. New York

268 U.S. 652 (1925), 7-2
Opinion of the Court: Sanford (Butler, McReynolds, Stone, Sutherland, Taft, Van Devanter)
Dissenting: Holmes, Brandeis

What did the New York statute make illegal? Was Gitlow convicted of illegal speech or illegal acts? Did his speech present a "clear and present danger" of violent overthrow of the government? Any danger of violent overthrow? Any danger of any illegal action? In Justice Sanford's reasoning, what did the state need to prove to justify conviction? Is there anything in Sanford's opinion that advances freedom of speech? Is it Justice Holmes's view that undesirable or "bad" ideas are protected only if they are ineffective? Who is to determine whether they are ineffective?

Sanford, for the Court:

Benjamin Gitlow was indicted in the Supreme Court of New York, with three others, for the statutory crime of criminal anarchy. He was separately tried, convicted, and sentenced to imprisonment. . . .

The contention here is that the statute, by its terms and as applied in this case, is repugnant to the due process clause of the Fourteenth Amendment. Its material provisions are:

§160. Criminal anarchy defined. Criminal anarchy is the doctrine that organized government should be overthrown by force or violence, or by assassination of the executive head or of any of the executive officials of government, or by any unlawful means. The advocacy of such doctrine either by word of mouth or writing is a felony. . . .

The following facts were established on the trial by undisputed evidence and admissions: the defendant is a member of the Left Wing Section of the Socialist Party, a dissenting branch or faction of that party formed in opposition to its dominant policy of "moderate Socialism." Membership in both is open to aliens as well as citizens. The Left Wing Section was organized nationally at a conference in New York City in June, 1919, attended by ninety delegates from twenty different States. The conference elected a National Council, of which the defendant was a member, and left to it the adoption of a "Manifesto." This was published in The Revolutionary Age, the official organ of the Left Wing. The defendant was on the board of managers of the paper, and was its business manager. He arranged for the printing of the paper, and took to the printer the manuscript of the first issue which contained the Left Wing Manifesto, and also a Communist Program and a Program of the Left Wing that had been adopted by the conference. Sixteen thousand copies were printed, which were delivered at the premises in New York City used as the office of the Revolutionary Age and the headquarters of the Left Wing, and occupied by the defendant and other officials. These copies were paid for by the defendant, as business manager of the paper. Employees at this office wrapped and mailed out copies of the paper under the defendant's direction, and copies were sold from this office. It was admitted that the defendant signed a card subscribing to the Manifesto and Program of the Left Wing, which all applicants were required to sign before being admitted to membership; that he went to different parts of the State to speak to branches of the Socialist Party about the principles of the Left Wing and advocated their adoption, and that he was responsible for the Manifesto as it appeared, that "he knew of the publication, in a general way, and he knew of its publication afterwards, and is responsible for its circulation."

There was no evidence of any effect resulting from the publication and circulation of the Manifesto. . . .

Extracts from the Manifesto. . . . condemned the dominant "moderate Socialism" for its recognition of the necessity of the democratic parliamentary state; repudiated its policy of introducing Socialism by legislative measures, and advocated, in plain and unequivocal language, the necessity of accomplishing the "Communist Revolution" by a militant and "revolutionary Socialism," based on "the class struggle" and mobilizing the "power of the proletariat in action,"

through mass industrial revolts developing into mass political strikes and "revolutionary mass action," for the purpose of conquering and destroying the parliamentary state and establishing in its place, through a "revolutionary dictatorship of the proletariat," the system of Communist Socialism. The then recent strikes in Seattle and Winnipeg were cited as instances of a development already verging on revolutionary action and suggestive of proletarian dictatorship, in which the strike-workers were "trying to usurp the functions of municipal government," and revolutionary Socialism, it was urged, must use these mass industrial revolts to broaden the strike, make it general and militant, and develop it into mass political strikes and revolutionary mass action for the annihilation of the parliamentary state. . . .

The precise question presented, and the only question which we can consider under this writ of error, then is whether the statute, as construed and applied in this case by the state courts, deprived the defendant of his liberty of expression in violation of the due process clause of the Fourteenth Amendment. . . .

For present purposes, we may and do assume that freedom of speech and of the press which are protected by the First Amendment from abridgment by Congress are among the fundamental personal rights and "liberties" protected by the due process clause of the Fourteenth Amendment from impairment by the States. . . .

It is a fundamental principle, long established, that the freedom of speech and of the press which is secured by the Constitution does not confer an absolute right to speak or publish, without responsibility, whatever one may choose, or an unrestricted and unbridled license that gives immunity for every possible use of language and prevents the punishment of those who abuse this freedom. Reasonably limited, it was said by Story in the passage cited, this freedom is an inestimable privilege in a free government; without such limitation, it might become the scourge of the republic.

That a State in the exercise of its police power may punish those who abuse this freedom by utterances inimical to the public welfare, tending to corrupt public morals, incite to crime, or disturb the public peace, is not open to question. Thus, it was held by this Court in the Fox Case that a State may punish publications advocating and encouraging a breach of its criminal laws; and, in the Gilbert Case, that a State may punish utterances teaching or advocating that its citizens should not assist the United States in prosecuting or carrying on war with its public enemies.

And, for yet more imperative reasons, a State may punish utterances endangering the foundations of organized government and threatening its overthrow by unlawful means. These imperil its own existence as a constitutional State. Freedom of speech and press, said Story does not protect disturbances to the public peace or the attempt to subvert the government. It does not protect publications or teachings which tend to subvert or imperil the government or to impede or hinder it in the performance of its governmental duties. It does not protect publications prompting the overthrow of government by force; the punishment of those who publish articles which tend to destroy organized society being essential to the security of freedom and the stability of the State. And a State may penalize utterances which openly advocate the overthrow of the representative and constitutional form of government of the United States and the several States, by violence or other unlawful means. In short, this freedom does not deprive a State of the primary and essential right of self-preservation, which, so long as human governments endure, they cannot be denied. . . .

By enacting the present statute, the State has determined, through its legislative body, that utterances advocating the overthrow of organized government by force, violence and unlawful means are so inimical to the general welfare and involve such danger of substantive evil that they may be penalized in the exercise of its police power. That determination must be given great weight. Every presumption is to be indulged in favor of the validity of the statute. And the case is to be considered "in the light of the principle that the State is primarily the judge of regulations required in the interest of public safety and welfare;" and that its police statutes may only be declared unconstitutional where they are arbitrary or unreasonable attempts to exercise authority vested in the State in the public interest.

That utterances inciting to the overthrow of organized government by unlawful means present a sufficient danger of substantive evil to bring their punishment within the range of legislative discretion is clear. Such utterances, by their very nature, involve danger to the public peace and to the security of the State. They threaten breaches of the peace, and ultimate revolution. And the immediate danger is none the less real and substantial because the effect of a given utterance cannot be accurately foreseen. The State cannot reasonably be required to measure the danger from every such utterance in the nice balance of a jeweler's scale. A single revolutionary spark may kindle a fire that, smouldering for a time, may burst into a sweeping and destructive conflagration. It cannot be said that the State is acting arbitrarily or unreasonably when, in the exercise of its judgment as to the measures necessary to protect the public peace and safety, it seeks to extinguish the spark without waiting until it has enkindled the flame or blazed into the conflagration. It cannot reasonably be required to defer the adoption of measures for its own peace and safety until the revolutionary utterances lead to actual disturbances of the public peace or imminent and immediate danger of its own destruction; but it may, in the exercise of its judgment, suppress the threatened danger in its incipiency. . . .

We cannot hold that the present statute is an arbitrary or unreasonable exercise of the police power of the State unwarrantably infringing the freedom of speech or press, and we must and do sustain its constitutionality. . . .

Holmes dissenting:

Mr. Justice Brandeis and I are of opinion that this judgment should be reversed. The general principle of free speech, it seems to me, must be taken to be included in the Fourteenth Amendment, in view of the scope that has been given to the word "liberty" as there used, although perhaps it may be accepted with a somewhat larger latitude of interpretation than is allowed to Congress by the sweeping language that governs or ought to govern the laws of the United States. If I am right, then I think that the criterion sanctioned by the full Court in *Schenck v. United States,* applies.

> The question in every case is whether the words used are used in such circumstances and are of such a nature as to create a clear and present danger that they will bring about the substantive evils that [the State] has a right to prevent.

It is true that, in my opinion, this criterion was departed from in *Abrams v. United States,* but the convictions that I expressed in that case are too deep for it to be possible for me as yet to believe that it and

Schaefer v. United States, have settled the law. If what I think the correct test is applied, it is manifest that there was no present danger of an attempt to overthrow the government by force on the part of the admittedly small minority who shared the defendant's views. It is said that this manifesto was more than a theory, that it was an incitement. Every idea is an incitement. It offers itself for belief, and, if believed, it is acted on unless some other belief outweighs it or some failure of energy stifles the movement at its birth. The only difference between the expression of an opinion and an incitement in the narrower sense is the speaker's enthusiasm for the result. Eloquence may set fire to reason. But whatever may be thought of the redundant discourse before us, it had no chance of starting a present conflagration. If, in the long run, the beliefs expressed in proletarian dictatorship are destined to be accepted by the dominant forces of the community, the only meaning of free speech is that they should be given their chance and have their way.

If the publication of this document had been laid as an attempt to induce an uprising against government at once, and not at some indefinite time in the future, it would have presented a different question. The object would have been one with which the law might deal, subject to the doubt whether there was any danger that the publication could produce any result, or in other words, whether it was not futile and too remote from possible consequences. But the indictment alleges the publication, and nothing more.

Dennis v. United States

341 U.S. 494 (1951), 6-2
Opinion of the Court: Vinson (Burton, Minton, Reed)
Concurring: Frankfurter, Jackson
Dissenting: Black, Douglas
Not participating: Clark

*What are the contrasting views of freedom of speech found in the opinions of this case? What has happened to the clear and present danger test? What are the practical differences between "gravity of the evil discounted by its improbability" and the clear and present danger test? Could convictions of the defendants be sustained under an application of the clear and present danger test? How do the justices differ on the danger of violent overthrow of the government? Who should determine whether speech presents such a danger? Congress? The Court? The trial jury? Con-*trast Justice Jackson's skepticism and Justice Douglas's optimism about the inevitable triumph of "truth" if freedom of speech is extended to the defendants. Is Douglas's view supported by historical evidence or is it mainly an article of faith? If an article of faith, does that have value?*

Vinson, for the Court:
Petitioners were indicted in July, 1948, for violation of the conspiracy provisions of the Smith Act during the period of April, 1945, to July, 1948.... We granted certiorari limited to the following two questions: (1) Whether either §2 or §3 of the Smith Act, inherently or as construed and applied in the instant case, violates the First Amendment and other provisions of the Bill of Rights; (2) whether either §2 or §3 of the Act, inherently or as construed and applied in the instant case, violates the First and Fifth Amendments because of indefiniteness.

Sections 2 and 3 of the Smith Act provide as follows:

SEC. 2.(a) It shall be unlawful for any person—

1. to knowingly or willfully advocate, abet, advise, or teach the duty, necessity, desirability, or propriety of overthrowing or destroying any government in the United States by force or violence, or by the assassination of any officer of any such government;
2. with intent to cause the overthrow or destruction of any government in the United States, to print, publish, edit, issue, circulate, sell, distribute, or publicly display any written or printed matter advocating, advising, or teaching the duty, necessity, desirability, or propriety of overthrowing or destroying any government in the United States by force or violence;
3. to organize or help to organize any society, group, or assembly of persons who teach, advocate, or encourage the overthrow or destruction of any government in the United States by force or violence; or to be or become a member of, or affiliate with, any such society, group, or assembly of persons, knowing the purposes thereof. . . .

The indictment charged the petitioners with willfully and knowingly conspiring (1) to organize as the Communist Party of the United States of America a society, group and assembly of persons who teach and advocate the overthrow and destruction of the Government of the United States by force and violence, and (2) knowingly and willfully to advocate and teach the duty and necessity of overthrowing and destroying the Government of the United States by force and violence. The indictment further alleged that §2 of the Smith Act proscribes these acts and that any conspiracy to take such action is a violation of §3 of the Act.

The trial of the case extended over nine months, six of which were devoted to the taking of evidence, resulting in a record of 16,000 pages. Our limited grant of the writ of certiorari has removed from our consideration any question as to the sufficiency of the evidence to support the jury's determination that petitioners are guilty of the offense charged. Whether, on this record, petitioners did, in fact, advocate the overthrow of the Government by force and violence is not before us, and we must base any discussion of this point upon the conclusions stated in the opinion of the Court of Appeals, which treated the issue in great detail. That court held that the record in this case amply supports the necessary finding of the jury that petitioners, the leaders of the Communist Party in this country, were unwilling to work within our framework of democracy, but intended to initiate a violent revolution whenever the propitious occasion appeared. . . .

The obvious purpose of the statute is to protect existing Government not from change by peaceable, lawful and constitutional means, but from change by violence, revolution and terrorism. That it is within the power of the Congress to protect the Government of the United States from armed rebellion is a proposition which requires little discussion. Whatever theoretical merit there may be to the argument that there is a "right" to rebellion against dictatorial governments is without force where the existing structure of the government provides for peaceful and orderly change. We reject any principle of governmental helplessness in the face of preparation for revolution, which principle, carried to its logical conclusion, must lead to anarchy. No one could conceive that it is not within the power of Congress to prohibit acts intended to overthrow the Government by force and violence. The question with which we are concerned here is not whether Congress has such power, but whether the means which it has employed conflict with the First and Fifth Amendments to the Constitution.

One of the bases for the contention that the means which Congress has employed are invalid takes the form of an attack on the face of the statute on the grounds that, by its terms, it prohibits academic discussion of the merits of Marxism-Leninism, that it stifles ideas and is contrary to all concepts of a free speech and a free press. . . .

The very language of the Smith Act negates the interpretation which petitioners would have us impose on that Act. It is directed at advocacy, not discussion. Thus, the trial judge properly charged the jury that they could not convict if they found that petitioners did "no more than pursue peaceful studies and discussions or teaching and advocacy in the realm of ideas." He further charged that it was not unlawful, "to conduct in an American college or university a course explaining the philosophical theories set forth in the books which have been placed in evidence."

Such a charge is in strict accord with the statutory language, and illustrates the meaning to be placed on those words. Congress did not intend to eradicate the free discussion of political theories, to destroy the traditional rights of Americans to discuss and evaluate ideas without fear of governmental sanction. Rather Congress was concerned with the very kind of activity in which the evidence showed these petitioners engaged. . . .

In this case, we are squarely presented with the application of the "clear and present danger" test, and must decide what that phrase imports. We first note that many of the cases in which this Court has reversed convictions by use of this or similar tests have been based on the fact that the interest which the State was attempting to protect was itself too insubstantial to warrant restriction of speech. . . . Overthrow of the Government by force and violence is certainly a substantial enough interest for the Government to limit speech. Indeed, this is the ultimate value of any society, for if a society cannot protect its very structure from armed internal attack, it must follow that no subordinate value can be protected. If, then, this interest may be protected, the literal problem which is presented is what has been meant by the use of the phrase "clear and present danger" of the utterances bringing about the evil within the power of Congress to punish.

Obviously, the words cannot mean that, before the Government may act, it must wait until the putsch is about to be executed, the plans have been laid and the signal is awaited. If Government is aware that a group aiming at its overthrow is attempting to indoctrinate its members and to commit them to a course whereby they will strike when the leaders feel the circumstances permit, action by the Government is required. The argument that there is no need for Government to concern itself, for Government is strong, it possesses ample powers to put down a rebellion, it may defeat the revolution with ease needs no answer. For that is not the question. Certainly an attempt to overthrow the Government by force, even though doomed from the outset because of inadequate numbers or power of the revolutionists, is a sufficient evil for Congress to prevent. The damage which such attempts create both physically and politically to a nation makes it impossible to measure the validity in terms of the probability of success, or the immediacy of a successful attempt. In the instant case, the trial judge charged the jury that they could not convict unless they found that petitioners intended to overthrow the Government "as speedily as circumstances would permit." This does not mean, and could not properly mean, that they would not strike until there was certainty of success. What was meant was that the revolutionists would strike when they thought the time was ripe. We must therefore reject the contention that success or probability of success is the criterion. . . .

Chief Judge Learned Hand, writing for the majority below, interpreted the phrase as follows: "In each case, [courts] must ask whether the gravity of the "evil," discounted by its improbability, justifies such invasion of free speech as is necessary to avoid the danger." We adopt this statement of the rule. As articulated by Chief Judge Hand, it is as succinct and inclusive as any other we might devise at this time. It takes into consideration those factors which we deem relevant, and relates their significances. More we cannot expect from words.

Likewise, we are in accord with the court below, which affirmed the trial court's finding that the requisite danger existed. The mere fact that, from the period 1945 to 1948, petitioners' activities did not result in an attempt to overthrow the Government by force and violence is, of course, no answer to the fact that there was a group that was ready to make the attempt. The formation by petitioners of such a highly organized conspiracy, with rigidly disciplined members subject to call when the leaders, these petitioners, felt that the time had come for action, coupled with the inflammable nature of world conditions, similar uprisings in other countries, and the touch-and-go nature of our relations with countries with whom petitioners were in the very least ideologically attuned, convince us that their convictions were justified on this score. And this analysis disposes of the contention

that a conspiracy to advocate, as distinguished from the advocacy itself, cannot be constitutionally restrained, because it comprises only the preparation. It is the existence of the conspiracy which creates the danger. If the ingredients of the reaction are present, we cannot bind the Government to wait until the catalyst is added. . . .

We hold that §§2(a)(1), 2(a)(3) and 3 of the Smith Act do not inherently, or as construed or applied in the instant case, violate the First Amendment and other provisions of the Bill of Rights, or the First and Fifth Amendments because of indefiniteness. Petitioners intended to overthrow the Government of the United States as speedily as the circumstances would permit. Their conspiracy to organize the Communist Party and to teach and advocate the overthrow of the Government of the United States by force and violence created a "clear and present danger" of an attempt to overthrow the Government by force and violence. They were properly and constitutionally convicted for violation of the Smith Act. The judgments of conviction are affirmed.

Frankfurter, concurring:

. . . Absolute rules would inevitably lead to absolute exceptions, and such exceptions would eventually corrode the rules. The demands of free speech in a democratic society, as well as the interest in national security are better served by candid and informed weighing of the competing interests, within the confines of the judicial process, than by announcing dogmas too inflexible for the non-Euclidian problems to be solved.

But how are competing interests to be assessed? Since they are not subject to quantitative ascertainment, the issue necessarily resolves itself into asking, who is to make the adjustment?—who is to balance the relevant factors and ascertain which interest is in the circumstances to prevail? Full responsibility for the choice cannot be given to the courts. Courts are not representative bodies. They are not designed to be a good reflex of a democratic society. Their judgment is best informed, and therefore most dependable, within narrow limits. Their essential quality is detachment, founded on independence. History teaches that the independence of the judiciary is jeopardized when courts become embroiled in the passions of the day and assume primary responsibility in choosing between competing political, economic and social pressures.

Primary responsibility for adjusting the interests which compete in the situation before us of necessity belongs to the Congress. The nature of the power to be exercised by this Court has been delineated in decisions not charged with the emotional appeal of situations such as that now before us. We are to set aside the judgment of those whose duty it is to legislate only if there is no reasonable basis for it. We are to determine whether a statute is sufficiently definite to meet the constitutional requirements of due process, and whether it respects the safeguards against undue concentration of authority secured by separation of power. . . .

Jackson, concurring:

The authors of the clear and present danger test never applied it to a case like this, nor would I. If applied as it is proposed here, it means that the Communist plotting is protected during its period of incubation; its preliminary stages of organization and preparation are immune from the law; the Government can move only after imminent action is manifest, when it would, of course, be too late. . . .

Of course, it is not always easy to distinguish teaching or advocacy in the sense of incitement from teaching or advocacy in the sense of exposition or explanation. It is a question of fact in each case.

What really is under review here is a conviction of conspiracy, after a trial for conspiracy, on an indictment charging conspiracy, brought under a statute outlawing conspiracy. . . .

The Communist Party realistically is a state within a state, an authoritarian dictatorship within a republic. It demands these freedoms not for its members, but for the organized party. . . .

The law of conspiracy has been the chief means at the Government's disposal to deal with the growing problems created by such organizations. I happen to think it is an awkward and inept remedy, but I find no constitutional authority for taking this weapon from the Government. . . .

Black, dissenting:

At the outset, I want to emphasize what the crime involved in this case is, and what it is not. These petitioners were not charged with an attempt to overthrow the Government. They were not charged with overt acts of any kind designed to overthrow the Government. They were not even charged with saying anything or writing anything designed to overthrow the Govern-

ment. The charge was that they agreed to assemble and to talk and publish certain ideas at a later date: the indictment is that they conspired to organize the Communist Party and to use speech or newspapers and other publications in the future to teach and advocate the forcible overthrow of the Government. No matter how it is worded, this is a virulent form of prior censorship of speech and press, which I believe the First Amendment forbids. I would hold §3 of the Smith Act authorizing this prior restraint unconstitutional on its face and as applied.

But let us assume, contrary to all constitutional ideas of fair criminal procedure, that petitioners, although not indicted for the crime of actual advocacy, may be punished for it. Even on this radical assumption, the other opinions in this case show that the only way to affirm these convictions is to repudiate directly or indirectly the established "clear and present danger" rule. This the Court does in a way which greatly restricts the protections afforded by the First Amendment. The opinions for affirmance indicate that the chief reason for jettisoning the rule is the expressed fear that advocacy of Communist doctrine endangers the safety of the Republic. Undoubtedly a governmental policy of unfettered communication of ideas does entail dangers. To the Founders of this Nation, however, the benefits derived from free expression were worth the risk. They embodied this philosophy in the First Amendment's command that "Congress shall make no law . . . abridging the freedom of speech, or of the press. . . ." I have always believed that the First Amendment is the keystone of our Government, that the freedoms it guarantees provide the best insurance against destruction of all freedom. . . .

. . . I cannot agree that the First Amendment permits us to sustain laws suppressing freedom of speech and press on the basis of Congress' or our own notions of mere "reasonableness." Such a doctrine waters down the First Amendment so that it amounts to little more than an admonition to Congress. The Amendment as so construed is not likely to protect any but those "safe" or orthodox views which rarely need its protection. . . .

Public opinion being what it now is, few will protest the conviction of these Communist petitioners. There is hope, however, that, in calmer times, when present pressures, passions and fears subside, this or some later Court will restore the First Amendment liberties to the high preferred place where they belong in a free society.

Douglas dissenting:

If this were a case where those who claimed protection under the First Amendment were teaching the techniques of sabotage, the assassination of the President, the filching of documents from public files, the planting of bombs, the art of street warfare, and the like, I would have no doubts. The freedom to speak is not absolute; the teaching of methods of terror and other seditious conduct should be beyond the pale along with obscenity and immorality. This case was argued as if those were the facts. The argument imported much seditious conduct into the record. That is easy, and it has popular appeal, for the activities of Communists in plotting and scheming against the free world are common knowledge. But the fact is that no such evidence was introduced at the trial. There is a statute which makes a seditious conspiracy unlawful. Petitioners, however, were not charged with a "conspiracy to overthrow" the Government. They were charged with a conspiracy to form a party and groups and assemblies of people who teach and advocate the overthrow of our Government by force or violence and with a conspiracy to advocate and teach its overthrow by force and violence. It may well be that indoctrination in the techniques of terror to destroy the Government would be indictable under either statute. But the teaching which is condemned here is of a different character.

So far as the present record is concerned, what petitioners did was to organize people to teach and themselves teach the Marxist-Leninist doctrine contained chiefly in four books: Stalin, Foundations of Leninism (1924); Marx and Engels, Manifesto of the Communist Party (1848); Lenin, The State and Revolution (1917); History of the Communist Party of the Soviet Union (B.) (1939). . . .

The vice of treating speech as the equivalent of overt acts of a treasonable or seditious character is emphasized by a concurring opinion, which, by invoking the law of conspiracy, makes speech do service for deeds which are dangerous to society. The doctrine of conspiracy has served divers and oppressive purposes, and, in its broad reach, can be made to do great evil. But never until today has anyone seriously thought that the ancient law of conspiracy could constitutionally be used to turn speech into seditious conduct. Yet that is precisely what is suggested. I repeat that we deal here with speech alone, not with speech plus acts of sabotage or unlawful conduct. Not a single seditious act is charged in the indictment. To make a lawful speech unlawful because two men conceive it is to raise the law of conspiracy to appalling proportions. That course is to make a radical break with the past and to violate one of the cardinal principles of our constitutional scheme. . . .

There comes a time when even speech loses its constitutional immunity. Speech innocuous one year may at another time fan such destructive flames that it must be halted in the interests of the safety of the Republic. That is the meaning of the clear and present danger test. When conditions are so critical that there will be no time to avoid the evil that the speech threatens, it is time to call a halt. Otherwise, free speech which is the strength of the Nation will be the cause of its destruction.

Yet free speech is the rule, not the exception. The restraint to be constitutional must be based on more than fear, on more than passionate opposition against the speech, on more than a revolted dislike for its contents. There must be some immediate injury to society that is likely if speech is allowed. . . .

How it can be said that there is a clear and present danger that this advocacy will succeed is, therefore, a mystery. Some nations less resilient than the United States, where illiteracy is high and where democratic traditions are only budding, might have to take drastic steps and jail these men for merely speaking their creed. But in America, they are miserable merchants of unwanted ideas; their wares remain unsold. The fact that their ideas are abhorrent does not make them powerful. . . .

Brandenburg v. Ohio

395 U.S. 444 (1969), 8-0
Per curiam opinion (Black, Brennan, Douglas, Harlan, Marshall, Stewart, Warren, White)

What must be proved before the Court will sustain convictions for the sort of speech made by Brandenburg? How does the standard differ from the clear and present danger test? Which is more protective of speech? Would Schenck have been convicted under the Court's standard in this case? Gitlow? Dennis? Who gains and who loses as a result of this decision? What is gained and lost?

Per curiam:

The appellant, a leader of a Ku Klux Klan group, was convicted under the Ohio Criminal Syndicalism statute for "advocat[ing] . . . the duty, necessity, or propriety of crime, sabotage, violence, or unlawful methods of terrorism as a means of accomplishing industrial or political reform" and for voluntarily assembl[ing] with any society, group, or assemblage of persons formed to teach or advocate the doctrines of criminal syndicalism.

He was fined $1,000 and sentenced to one to 10 years' imprisonment. The appellant challenged the constitutionality of the criminal syndicalism statute under the First and Fourteenth Amendments to the United States Constitution, but the intermediate appellate court of Ohio affirmed his conviction without opinion. The Supreme Court of Ohio dismissed his appeal sua sponte "for the reason that no substantial constitutional question exists herein." It did not file an opinion or explain its conclusions. Appeal was taken to this Court, and we noted probable jurisdiction. We reverse.

The record shows that a man, identified at trial as the appellant, telephoned an announcer-reporter on the staff of a Cincinnati television station and invited him to come to a Ku Klux Klan "rally" to be held at a farm in Hamilton County. With the cooperation of the organizers, the reporter and a cameraman attended the meeting and filmed the events. Portions of the films were later broadcast on the local station and on a national network.

The prosecution's case rested on the films and on testimony identifying the appellant as the person who communicated with the reporter and who spoke at the rally. The State also introduced into evidence several articles appearing in the film, including a pistol, a rifle, a shotgun, ammunition, a Bible, and a red hood worn by the speaker in the films.

One film showed 12 hooded figures, some of whom carried firearms. They were gathered around a large wooden cross, which they burned. No one was present other than the participants and the newsmen who made the film. Most of the words uttered during the scene were incomprehensible when the film was projected, but scattered phrases could be understood that were derogatory of Negroes and, in one instance, of Jews. Another scene on the same film showed the appellant, in Klan regalia, making a speech. The speech, in full, was as follows:

> This is an organizers' meeting. We have had quite a few members here today which are—we have hundreds, hundreds of members throughout the State of Ohio. I can quote from a newspaper clipping from the Columbus, Ohio, Dispatch, five weeks ago Sunday morning. The Klan has more members in the State of Ohio than does any other organization. We're not a revengent organization, but if our President, our Congress, our Supreme Court, continues to suppress the white, Caucasian race, it's possible that there might have to be some revengeance taken.

> We are marching on Congress July the Fourth, four hundred thousand strong. From there, we are dividing into two groups, one group to march on St. Augustine, Florida, the other group to march into Mississippi. Thank you.

The second film showed six hooded figures one of whom, later identified as the appellant, repeated a speech very similar to that recorded on the first film. The reference to the possibility of "revengeance" was omitted, and one sentence was added: "Personally, I believe the nigger should be returned to Africa, the Jew returned to Israel." Though some of the figures in the films carried weapons, the speaker did not.

The Ohio Criminal Syndicalism Statute was enacted in 1919. From 1917 to 1920, identical or quite similar laws were adopted by 20 States and two territories. In 1927, this Court sustained the constitutionality of California's Criminal Syndicalism Act, the text of which is quite similar to that of the laws of Ohio. *Whitney v. California.* The Court upheld the statute on the ground that, without more, "advocating" violent means to effect political and economic change involves such danger to the security of the State that the State may outlaw it. But Whitney has been thoroughly discredited by later decisions. These later decisions have fashioned the principle that the constitutional guarantees of free speech and free press do not permit a State to forbid or proscribe advocacy of the use of force or of law violation except where such advocacy is directed to inciting or producing imminent lawless action and is likely to incite or produce such action. As we said in *Noto v. United States,* "the mere abstract teaching . . . of the moral propriety or even moral necessity for a resort to force and violence is not the same as preparing a group for violent action and steeling it to such action." A statute which fails to draw this distinction impermissibly intrudes upon the freedoms guaranteed by the First and Fourteenth Amendments. It sweeps within its condemnation speech which our Constitution has immunized from governmental control.

Measured by this test, Ohio's Criminal Syndicalism Act cannot be sustained. The Act punishes persons who "advocate or teach the duty, necessity, or propriety" of violence "as a means of accomplishing industrial or political reform"; or who publish or circulate or display any book or paper containing such advocacy; or who "justify" the commission of violent acts "with intent to exemplify, spread or advocate the propriety of the doctrines of criminal syndicalism"; or who "voluntarily assemble" with a group formed "to teach or advocate the doctrines of criminal syndicalism." Neither the indictment nor the trial judge's instructions to the jury in any way refined the statute's bald definition of the crime in terms of mere advocacy not distinguished from incitement to imminent lawless action.

Accordingly, we are here confronted with a statute which, by its own words and as applied, purports to punish mere advocacy and to forbid, on pain of criminal punishment, assembly with others merely to advocate the described type of action. Such a statute falls within the condemnation of the First and Fourteenth Amendments. The contrary teaching of *Whitney v. California,* cannot be supported, and that decision is therefore overruled.

Douglas, concurring:

. . . I see no place in the regime of the First Amendment for any "clear and present danger" test, whether strict and tight, as some would make it, or free-wheeling, as the Court in Dennis rephrased it.

When one reads the opinions closely and sees when and how the "clear and present danger" test has been applied, great misgivings are aroused. First, the threats were often loud, but always puny, and made serious only by judges so wedded to the status quo that critical analysis made them nervous. Second, the test was so twisted and perverted in Dennis as to make the trial of those teachers of Marxism an all-out political trial which was part and parcel of the cold war that has eroded substantial parts of the First Amendment. . . .

The line between what is permissible and not subject to control and what may be made impermissible and subject to regulation is the line between ideas and overt acts.

The example usually given by those who would punish speech is the case of one who falsely shouts fire in a crowded theatre.

This is, however, a classic case where speech is brigaded with action. They are indeed inseparable, and a prosecution can be launched for the overt acts actually caused. Apart from rare instances of that kind, speech is, I think, immune from prosecution.

Certainly there is no constitutional line between advocacy of abstract ideas . . . and advocacy of political action . . . The quality of advocacy turns on the depth of the conviction, and government has no power to invade that sanctuary of belief and conscience.

National Association for the Advancement of Colored People v. Alabama

357 U.S. 449 (1958), 9-0
Opinion of the Court: Harlan (Black, Brennan, Burton, Clark, Douglas, Frankfurter, Warren, Whittaker)

What is the constitutional basis for a "freedom of association"? What exactly does the freedom protect? Why did Alabama ask the NAACP for the names of its members? Would a state ever have a right to such information?

Harlan, for the Court:

We review from the standpoint of its validity under the Federal Constitution a judgment of civil contempt entered against petitioner, the National Association for the Advancement of Colored People, in the courts of Alabama. The question presented is whether Alabama, consistently with the Due Process Clause of the Fourteenth Amendment, can compel petitioner to reveal to the State's Attorney General the names and addresses of all its Alabama members and agents, without regard to their positions or functions in the Association. The judgment of contempt was based upon petitioner's refusal to comply fully with a court order requiring in part the production of membership lists. . . .

Alabama has a statute, similar to those of many other States, which requires a foreign corporation, except as exempted, to qualify before doing business by filing its corporate charter with the Secretary of State and designating a place of business and an agent to receive service of process. . . . The National Association for the Advancement of Colored People is a nonprofit membership corporation organized under the laws of New York. Its purposes, fostered on a nationwide basis, are those indicated by its name, and it operates through chartered affiliates which are independent unincorporated associations, with membership therein equivalent to membership in petitioner. The first Alabama affiliates were chartered in 1918. Since that time, the aims of the Association have been advanced through activities of its affiliates, and, in 1951, the Association itself opened a regional office in Alabama, at which it employed two supervisory persons and one clerical worker. The Association has never complied with the qualification statute, from which it considered itself exempt.

In 1956, the Attorney General of Alabama brought an equity suit in the State Circuit Court, Montgomery County, to enjoin the Association from conducting further activities within, and to oust it from, the State. . . .

. . . [T]he State moved for the production of a large number of the Association's records and papers, including bank statements, leases, deeds, and records containing the names and addresses of all Alabama "members" and "agents" of the Association. It alleged that all such documents were necessary for adequate preparation for the hearing, in view of petitioner's denial of the conduct of intrastate business within the meaning of the qualification statute. Over petitioner's objections, the court ordered the production of a substantial part of the requested records, including the membership lists . . . , and postponed the hearing on the restraining order to a date later than the time ordered for production. . . .

. . . [P]etitioner produced substantially all the data called for by the production order except its membership lists, as to which it contended that Alabama could not constitutionally compel disclosure, and moved to modify or vacate the contempt judgment, or stay its execution pending appellate review. This motion was denied. While a similar stay application, which was later denied was pending before the Supreme Court of Alabama, the Circuit Court made a further order adjudging petitioner in continuing contempt and increasing the fine already imposed to $100,000. . . .

Effective advocacy of both public and private points of view, particularly controversial ones, is undeniably enhanced by group association, as this Court has more than once recognized by remarking upon the close nexus between the freedoms of speech and assembly. It is beyond debate that freedom to engage in association for the advancement of beliefs and ideas is an inseparable aspect of the "liberty" assured by the Due Process Clause of the Fourteenth Amendment, which embraces freedom of speech. Of course, it is immaterial whether the beliefs sought to be advanced by association pertain to political, economic, religious or cultural matters, and state action which may have the effect of curtailing the freedom to associate is subject to the closest scrutiny.

The fact that Alabama, so far as is relevant to the validity of the contempt judgment presently under review, has taken no direct action, to restrict the right of petitioner's members to associate freely, does not end inquiry into the effect of the production order. In the domain of these indispensable liberties, whether of speech, press, or association, the decisions of this Court recognize that abridgment of such rights, even though unintended, may inevitably follow from varied forms of governmental action. . . .

It is hardly a novel perception that compelled disclosure of affiliation with groups engaged in advocacy may constitute as effective a restraint on freedom of association as the forms of governmental action in the cases above were thought likely to produce upon the particular constitutional rights there involved. This Court has recognized the vital relationship between freedom to associate and privacy in one's associations. . . .

. . . Inviolability of privacy in group association may in many circumstances be indispensable to preservation of freedom of association, particularly where a group espouses dissident beliefs.

We think that the production order, in the respects here drawn in question, must be regarded as entailing the likelihood of a substantial restraint upon the exercise by petitioner's members of their right to freedom of association. Petitioner has made an uncontroverted showing that, on past occasions, revelation of the identity of its rank-and-file members has exposed these members to economic reprisal, loss of employment, threat of physical coercion, and other manifestations of public hostility. Under these circumstances, we think it apparent that compelled disclosure of petitioner's Alabama membership is likely to affect adversely the ability of petitioner and its members to pursue their collective effort to foster beliefs which they admittedly have the right to advocate, in that it may induce members to withdraw from the Association and dissuade others from joining it because of fear of exposure of their beliefs shown through their associations and of the consequences of this exposure.

It is not sufficient to answer, as the State does here, that whatever repressive effect compulsory disclosure of names of petitioner's members may have upon participation by Alabama citizens in petitioner's activities follows not from state action, but from private community pressures. The crucial factor is the interplay of governmental and private action, for it is only after the initial exertion of state power represented by the production order that private action takes hold.

We turn to the final question—whether Alabama has demonstrated an interest in obtaining the disclosures it seeks from petitioner which is sufficient to justify the deterrent effect which we have concluded these disclosures may well have on the free exercise by petitioner's members of their constitutionally protected right of association. Such a " . . . subordinating interest of the State must be compelling." . . .

Whether there was "justification" in this instance turns solely on the substantiality of Alabama's interest in obtaining the membership lists. During the course of a hearing before the Alabama Circuit Court on a motion of petitioner to set aside the production order, the State Attorney General presented at length, under examination by petitioner, the State's reason for requesting the membership lists. The exclusive purpose was to determine whether petitioner was conducting intrastate business in violation of the Alabama foreign corporation registration statute, and the membership lists were expected to help resolve this question. The issues in the litigation commenced by Alabama by its bill in equity were whether the character of petitioner and its activities in Alabama had been such as to make petitioner subject to the registration statute, and whether the extent of petitioner's activities without qualifying suggested its permanent ouster from the State. Without intimating the slightest view upon the merits of these issues, we are unable to perceive that the disclosure of the names of petitioner's rank-and-file members has a substantial bearing on either of them. As matters stand in the state court, petitioner (1) has admitted its presence and conduct of activities in Alabama since 1918; (2) has offered to comply in all respects with the state qualification statute, although preserving its contention that the statute does not apply to it, and (3) has apparently complied satisfactorily with the production order, except for the membership lists, by furnishing the Attorney General with varied business records, its charter and statement of purposes, the names of all of its directors and officers, and with the total number of its Alabama members and the amount of their dues. . . .

We hold that the immunity from state scrutiny of membership lists which the Association claims on behalf of its members is here so related to the right of the members to pursue their lawful private interests privately and to associate freely with others in so do-

ing as to come within the protection of the Fourteenth Amendment. And we conclude that Alabama has fallen short of showing a controlling justification for the deterrent effect on the free enjoyment of the right to associate which disclosure of membership lists is likely to have. Accordingly, the judgment of civil contempt and the $100,000 fine which resulted from petitioner's refusal to comply with the production order in this respect must fall. . . .

Boy Scouts of America v. Dale

530 U.S. 640 (2000), 5-4
Opinion of the Court: Rehnquist (Kennedy, O'Connor, Scalia, Thomas)
Dissenting: Breyer, Ginsburg, Souter, Stevens

On what grounds does the Court allow the Boy Scouts to exclude Dale when in other recent cases it has held that freedom of association does not permit exclusion for reasons of gender? How did the Boy Scouts rationalize their exclusion? What determines whether a group is an "expressive association"? Why should such a group be permitted to exclude certain persons but other groups not? How does Justice Stevens's analysis differ from that of Chief Justice Rehnquist's?

Rehnquist, for the Court:

Petitioners are the Boy Scouts of America and the Monmouth Council, a division of the Boy Scouts of America (collectively, Boy Scouts). The Boy Scouts is a private, not-for-profit organization engaged in instilling its system of values in young people. The Boy Scouts asserts that homosexual conduct is inconsistent with the values it seeks to instill. Respondent is James Dale, a former Eagle Scout whose adult membership in the Boy Scouts was revoked when the Boy Scouts learned that he is an avowed homosexual and gay rights activist. The New Jersey Supreme Court held that New Jersey's public accommodations law requires that the Boy Scouts admit Dale. This case presents the question whether applying New Jersey's public accommodations law in this way violates the Boy Scouts' First Amendment right of expressive association. We hold that it does. . . .

In *Roberts v. United States Jaycees,* we observed that "implicit in the right to engage in activities protected by the First Amendment" is "a corresponding right to associate with others in pursuit of a wide variety of political, social, economic, educational, religious, and cultural ends." This right is crucial in preventing the majority from imposing its views on groups that would rather express other, perhaps unpopular, ideas. . . . Government actions that may unconstitutionally burden this freedom may take many forms, one of which is "intrusion into the internal structure or affairs of an association" like a "regulation that forces the group to accept members it does not desire." Forcing a group to accept certain members may impair the ability of the group to express those views, and only those views, that it intends to express. Thus, "[f]reedom of association . . . plainly presupposes a freedom not to associate." . . .

To determine whether a group is protected by the First Amendment's expressive associational right, we must determine whether the group engages in "expressive association." The First Amendment's protection of expressive association is not reserved for advocacy groups. But to come within its ambit, a group must engage in some form of expression, whether it be public or private. . . .

[T]he general mission of the Boy Scouts is clear: "[T]o instill values in young people." Ibid. The Boy Scouts seeks to instill these values by having its adult leaders spend time with the youth members, instructing and engaging them in activities like camping, archery, and fishing. During the time spent with the youth members, the scoutmasters and assistant scoutmasters inculcate them with the Boy Scouts' values—both expressly and by example. It seems indisputable that an association that seeks to transmit such a system of values engages in expressive activity.

Given that the Boy Scouts engages in expressive activity, we must determine whether the forced inclusion of Dale as an assistant scoutmaster would significantly affect the Boy Scouts' ability to advocate public or private viewpoints. This inquiry necessarily requires us first to explore, to a limited extent, the nature of the Boy Scouts' view of homosexuality.

The values the Boy Scouts seeks to instill are "based on" those listed in the Scout Oath and Law. The Boy Scouts explains that the Scout Oath and Law provide "a positive moral code for living; they are a list of 'do's' rather than 'don'ts.'" The Boy Scouts asserts that homosexual conduct is inconsistent with the values embodied in the Scout Oath and Law, particularly with the values represented by the terms "morally straight" and "clean."

Obviously, the Scout Oath and Law do not expressly mention sexuality or sexual orientation. And the terms "morally straight" and "clean" are by no means self-defining. Different people would attribute to those terms very different meanings. For example, some people may believe that engaging in homosexual conduct is not at odds with being "morally straight" and "clean." And others may believe that engaging in homosexual conduct is contrary to being "morally straight" and "clean." The Boy Scouts says it falls within the latter category. . . .

The Boy Scouts asserts that it "teach[es] that homosexual conduct is not morally straight," and that it does "not want to promote homosexual conduct as a legitimate form of behavior," We accept the Boy Scouts' assertion. We need not inquire further to determine the nature of the Boy Scouts' expression with respect to homosexuality. But because the record before us

James Dale after hearing that the New Jersey Supreme Court had ruled in his favor in his suit against the Boy Scouts. Dale, a former scoutmaster and Eagle Scout, was barred from the Scouts after he announced he was gay. The state court ruling was overturned by the U.S. Supreme Court in *Dale v. Boy Scouts of America*, 2000.

contains written evidence of the Boy Scouts' viewpoint, we look to it as instructive, if only on the question of the sincerity of the professed beliefs.

A 1978 position statement to the Boy Scouts' Executive Committee . . . expresses the Boy Scouts' "official position" with regard to "homosexuality and Scouting". . . .

. . . The Boy Scouts of America is a private, membership organization and leadership therein is a privilege and not a right. We do not believe that homosexuality and leadership in Scouting are appropriate. We will continue to select only those who in our judgment meet our standards and qualifications for leadership."

Thus, at least as of 1978—the year James Dale entered Scouting—the official position of the Boy Scouts was that avowed homosexuals were not to be Scout leaders.

A position statement promulgated by the Boy Scouts in 1991 (after Dale's membership was revoked but before this litigation was filed) also supports its current view: "We believe that homosexual conduct is inconsistent with the requirement in the Scout Oath that a Scout be morally straight and in the Scout Law that a Scout be clean in word and deed, and that homosexuals do not provide a desirable role model for Scouts."

This position statement was redrafted numerous times but its core message remained consistent. For example, a 1993 position statement, the most recent in the record, reads, in part: "The Boy Scouts of America has always reflected the expectations that Scouting families have had for the organization. We do not believe that homosexuals provide a role model consistent with these expectations. Accordingly, we do not allow for the registration of avowed homosexuals as members or as leaders of the BSA."

We must then determine whether Dale's presence as an assistant scoutmaster would significantly burden the Boy Scouts' desire to not "promote homosexual conduct as a legitimate form of behavior." As we give deference to an association's assertions regarding the nature of its expression, we must also give deference to an association's view of what would impair its expression. That is not to say that an expressive association can erect a shield against antidiscrimination laws simply by asserting that mere acceptance of a member from a particular group would impair its message. But here Dale, by his own admission, is one of a group of gay Scouts who have "become leaders in their community and are open

and honest about their sexual orientation." Dale was the copresident of a gay and lesbian organization at college and remains a gay rights activist. Dale's presence in the Boy Scouts would, at the very least, force the organization to send a message, both to the youth members and the world, that the Boy Scouts accepts homosexual conduct as a legitimate form of behavior.

Hurley [*v. Irish-American GLIB*] is illustrative on this point. There we considered whether the application of Massachusetts' public accommodations law to require the organizers of a private St. Patrick's Day parade to include among the marchers an Irish-American gay, lesbian, and bisexual group, GLIB, violated the parade organizers' First Amendment rights. We noted that the parade organizers did not wish to exclude the GLIB members because of their sexual orientations, but because they wanted to march behind a GLIB banner. . . .

Here, we have found that the Boy Scouts believes that homosexual conduct is inconsistent with the values it seeks to instill in its youth members; it will not "promote homosexual conduct as a legitimate form of behavior." As the presence of GLIB in Boston's St. Patrick's Day parade would have interfered with the parade organizers' choice not to propound a particular point of view, the presence of Dale as an assistant scoutmaster would just as surely interfere with the Boy Scout's choice not to propound a point of view contrary to its beliefs. . . .

. . . [T]he Boy Scouts is an expressive association and that the forced inclusion of Dale would significantly affect its expression, we inquire whether the application of New Jersey's public accommodations law to require that the Boy Scouts accept Dale as an assistant scoutmaster runs afoul of the Scouts' freedom of expressive association. We conclude that it does.

State public accommodations laws were originally enacted to prevent discrimination in traditional places of public accommodation—like inns and trains. Over time, the public accommodations laws have expanded to cover more places. New Jersey's statutory definition of "'[a] place of public accommodation'" is extremely broad. The term is said to "include, but not be limited to," a list of over 50 types of places. Many on the list are what one would expect to be places where the public is invited. For example, the statute includes as places of public accommodation taverns, restaurants, retail shops, and public libraries. But the statute also includes places that often may not carry with them open invitations to the public, like summer camps and roof gardens. In this case, the New Jersey Supreme Court went a step further and applied its public accommodations law to a private entity without even attempting to tie the term "place" to a physical location. As the definition of "public accommodation" has expanded from clearly commercial entities, such as restaurants, bars, and hotels, to membership organizations such as the Boy Scouts, the potential for conflict between state public accommodations laws and the First Amendment rights of organizations has increased.

We recognized in cases such as *Roberts*... that States have a compelling interest in eliminating discrimination against women in public accommodations. But in each of these cases we went on to conclude that the enforcement of these statutes would not materially interfere with the ideas that the organization sought to express....

In *Hurley,* we applied traditional First Amendment analysis to hold that the application of the Massachusetts public accommodations law to a parade violated the First Amendment rights of the parade organizers. Although we did not explicitly deem the parade in *Hurley* an expressive association, the analysis we applied there is similar to the analysis we apply here. We have already concluded that a state requirement that the Boy Scouts retain Dale as an assistant scoutmaster would significantly burden the organization's right to oppose or disfavor homosexual conduct. The state interests embodied in New Jersey's public accommodations law do not justify such a severe intrusion on the Boy Scouts' rights to freedom of expressive association. That being the case, we hold that the First Amendment prohibits the State from imposing such a requirement through the application of its public accommodations law.

Justice Stevens' dissent makes much of its observation that the public perception of homosexuality in this country has changed. Indeed, it appears that homosexuality has gained greater societal acceptance. But this is scarcely an argument for denying First Amendment protection to those who refuse to accept these views. The First Amendment protects expression, be it of the popular variety or not. And the fact that an idea may be embraced and advocated by increasing numbers of people is all the more reason to protect the First Amendment rights of those who wish to voice a different view....

We are not, as we must not be, guided by our views of whether the Boy Scouts' teachings with respect to homosexual conduct are right or wrong; public or judicial disapproval of a tenet of an organization's expression does not justify the State's effort to compel the organization to accept members where such acceptance would derogate from the organization's expressive message. "While the law is free to promote all sorts of conduct in place of harmful behavior, it is not free to interfere with speech for no better reason than promoting an approved message or discouraging a disfavored one, however enlightened either purpose may strike the government." *Hurley.*

The judgment of the New Jersey Supreme Court is reversed, and the cause remanded for further proceedings not inconsistent with this opinion.

Stevens, dissenting:
... The majority holds that New Jersey's law violates BSA's right to associate and its right to free speech. But that law does not "impos[e] any serious burdens" on BSA's "collective effort on behalf of [its] shared goals," *Roberts v. United States Jaycees,* nor does it force BSA to communicate any message that it does not wish to endorse. New Jersey's law, therefore, abridges no constitutional right of the Boy Scouts....

BSA's claim finds no support in our cases.... In fact, until today, we have never once found a claimed right to associate in the selection of members to prevail in the face of a State's antidiscrimination law. To the contrary, we have squarely held that a State's antidiscrimination law does not violate a group's right to associate simply because the law conflicts with that group's exclusionary membership policy.

In *Roberts v. United States Jaycees,* we addressed just such a conflict. The Jaycees... claimed that applying the law to it violated its right to associate—in particular its right to maintain its selective membership policy.

We rejected that claim. Cautioning that the right to associate is not "absolute," we held that "[i]nfringements on that right may be justified by regulations adopted to serve compelling state interests, unrelated to the suppression of ideas, that cannot be achieved through means significantly less restrictive of associational freedoms." We found the State's purpose of eliminating discrimination is a compelling state interest that is unrelated to the suppression of ideas....

As in *Jaycees,* we rejected the claim, holding that "the evidence fails to demonstrate that admitting women to Rotary Clubs will affect in any significant way the existing members' ability to carry out their various purposes." . . .

Several principles are made perfectly clear by *Jaycees* and [*Rotary International v.*] *Rotary Club* [*of Duarte*]. First, to prevail on a claim of expressive association in the face of a State's antidiscrimination law, it is not enough simply to engage in some kind of expressive activity. Both the Jaycees and the Rotary Club engaged in expressive activity protected by the First Amendment, yet that fact was not dispositive. Second, it is not enough to adopt an openly avowed exclusionary membership policy. Both the Jaycees and the Rotary Club did that as well. Third, it is not sufficient merely to articulate some connection between the group's expressive activities and its exclusionary policy. . . .

The evidence before this Court makes it exceptionally clear that BSA has, at most, simply adopted an exclusionary membership policy and has no shared goal of disapproving of homosexuality. BSA's mission statement and federal charter say nothing on the matter; its official membership policy is silent; its Scout Oath and Law—and accompanying definitions—are devoid of any view on the topic; its guidance for Scouts and Scoutmasters on sexuality declare that such matters are "not construed to be Scouting's proper area," but are the province of a Scout's parents and pastor; and BSA's posture respecting religion tolerates a wide variety of views on the issue of homosexuality. Moreover, there is simply no evidence that BSA otherwise teaches anything in this area, or that it instructs Scouts on matters involving homosexuality in ways not conveyed in the Boy Scout or Scoutmaster Handbooks. In short, Boy Scouts of America is simply silent on homosexuality. There is no shared goal or collective effort to foster a belief about homosexuality at all—let alone one that is significantly burdened by admitting homosexuals.

As in *Jaycees*, there is "no basis in the record for concluding that admission of [homosexuals] will impede the [Boy Scouts'] ability to engage in [its] protected activities or to disseminate its preferred views" and New Jersey's law "requires no change in [BSA's] creed." And like *Rotary Club*, New Jersey's law "does not require [BSA] to abandon or alter any of" its activities. The evidence relied on by the Court is not to the contrary. . . .

Equally important is BSA's failure to adopt any clear position on homosexuality. BSA's temporary, though ultimately abandoned, view that homosexuality is incompatible with being "morally straight" and "clean" is a far cry from the clear, unequivocal state-

ment necessary to prevail on its claim. Despite the solitary sentences in the 1991 and 1992 policies, the group continued to disclaim any single religious or moral position as a general matter and actively eschewed teaching any lesson on sexuality. It also continued to define "morally straight" and "clean" in the Boy Scout and Scoutmaster Handbooks without any reference to homosexuality. As noted earlier, nothing in our cases suggests that a group can prevail on a right to expressive association if it, effectively, speaks out of both sides of its mouth. A State's antidiscrimination law does not impose a "serious burden" or a "substantial restraint" upon the group's "shared goals" if the group itself is unable to identify its own stance with any clarity. . . .

. . . [T]the majority insists that we must "give deference to an association's assertions regarding the nature of its expression" and "we must also give deference to an association's view of what would impair its expression.". . .

This is an astounding view of the law. I am unaware of any previous instance in which our analysis of the scope of a constitutional right was determined by looking at what a litigant asserts in his or her brief and inquiring no further. It is even more astonishing in the First Amendment area, because, as the majority itself acknowledges, "we are obligated to independently review the factual record." It is an odd form of independent review that consists of deferring entirely to whatever a litigant claims. But the majority insists that our inquiry must be "limited," because "it is not the role of the courts to reject a group's expressed values because they disagree with those values or find them internally inconsistent."

But nothing in our cases calls for this Court to do any such thing. An organization can adopt the message of its choice, and it is not this Court's place to disagree with it. But we must inquire whether the group is, in fact, expressing a message (whatever it may be) and whether that message (if one is expressed) is significantly affected by a State's antidiscrimination law. More critically, that inquiry requires our independent analysis, rather than deference to a group's litigating posture. . . .

There is, of course, a valid concern that a court's independent review may run the risk of paying too little heed to an organization's sincerely held views. But unless one is prepared to turn the right to associate into a free pass out of antidiscrimination laws, an independent inquiry is a necessity. . . .

In this case, no such concern is warranted. It is entirely clear that BSA in fact expresses no clear, unequivocal message burdened by New Jersey's law. . . .

. . . Under the majority's reasoning, an openly gay male is irreversibly affixed with the label "homosexual." That label, even though unseen, communicates a message that permits his exclusion wherever he goes. His openness is the sole and sufficient justification for his ostracism. Though unintended, reliance on such a justification is tantamount to a constitutionally prescribed symbol of inferiority. . . .

That such prejudices are still prevalent and that they have caused serious and tangible harm to countless members of the class New Jersey seeks to protect are established matters of fact that neither the Boy Scouts nor the Court disputes. That harm can only be aggravated by the creation of a constitutional shield for a policy that is itself the product of a habitual way of thinking about strangers. As Justice Brandeis so wisely advised, "we must be ever on our guard, lest we erect our prejudices into legal principles." . . .

United States v. O'Brien

391 U.S. 367 (1968), 7-1
Opinion of the Court: Warren (Black, Brennan, Fortas, Harlan, Stewart, White)
Dissenting: Douglas
Not participating: Marshall

What test does the Court develop for deciding the limits of freedom of speech in cases of this sort? Was O'Brien convicted of speaking or acting? Does this decision mean that symbolic or "expressive" speech has less protection than more conventional forms? The Court uses such terms as "substantial," "incidental," and "essential." Does it make clear what they mean or do they remain vague, general concepts? What does the Court say about legislative motive? How can we be sure that a law is not directed at the content of speech?

Warren, for the Court:

On the morning of March 31, 1966, David Paul O'Brien and three companions burned their Selective Service registration certificates on the steps of the South Boston Courthouse. A sizable crowd, including several agents of the Federal Bureau of Investigation, witnessed the event. Immediately after the burning, members of the crowd began attacking O'Brien and his companions. An FBI agent ushered

O'Brien to safety inside the courthouse. After he was advised of his right to counsel and to silence, O'Brien stated to FBI agents that he had burned his registration certificate because of his beliefs, knowing that he was violating federal law. He produced the charred remains of the certificate, which, with his consent, were photographed.

For this act, O'Brien was indicted, tried, convicted, and sentenced in the United States District Court for the District of Massachusetts. . . .

The indictment upon which he was tried charged that he

> "willfully and knowingly did mutilate, destroy, and change by burning . . . [his] Registration Certificate in violation of Title 50, App. United States Code, Section 462(b)." Section 462(b) is part of the Universal Military Training and Service Act of 1948. Section 462(b)(3), one of six numbered subdivisions of §462(b), was amended by Congress in 1965 . . . so that, at the time O'Brien burned his certificate, an offense was committed by any person, "who forges, alters, knowingly destroys, knowingly mutilates, or in any manner changes any such certificate. . . . "

By the 1965 Amendment, Congress added to §12(b)(3) of the 1948 Act the provision here at issue, subjecting to criminal liability not only one who "forges, alters, or in any manner changes," but also one who "knowingly destroys, [or] knowingly mutilates" a certificate. We note at the outset that the 1965 Amendment plainly does not abridge free speech on its face, and we do not understand O'Brien to argue otherwise. Amended §12(b)(3), on its face, deals with conduct having no connection with speech. It prohibits the knowing destruction of certificates issued by the Selective Service System, and there is nothing necessarily expressive about such conduct. The Amendment does not distinguish between public and private destruction, and it does not punish only destruction engaged in for the purpose of expressing views. A law prohibiting destruction of Selective Service certificates no more abridges free speech on its face than a motor vehicle law prohibiting the destruction of drivers' licenses, or a tax law prohibiting the destruction of books and records.

O'Brien nonetheless argues that the 1965 Amendment is unconstitutional in its application to him, and is unconstitutional as enacted because what he calls the "purpose" of Congress was "to suppress freedom of speech." We consider these arguments separately.

O'Brien first argues that the 1965 Amendment is unconstitutional as applied to him because his act of burning his registration certificate was protected "symbolic speech" within the First Amendment. His argument is that the freedom of expression which the First Amendment guarantees includes all modes of "communication of ideas by conduct," and that his conduct is within this definition because he did it in "demonstration against the war and against the draft."

We cannot accept the view that an apparently limitless variety of conduct can be labeled "speech" whenever the person engaging in the conduct intends thereby to express an idea. However, even on the assumption that the alleged communicative element in O'Brien's conduct is sufficient to bring into play the First Amendment, it does not necessarily follow that the destruction of a registration certificate is constitutionally protected activity. This Court has held that, when "speech" and "nonspeech" elements are combined in the same course of conduct, a sufficiently important governmental interest in regulating the nonspeech element can justify incidental limitations on First Amendment freedoms. To characterize the quality of the governmental interest which must appear, the Court has employed a variety of descriptive terms: compelling; substantial; subordinating; paramount; cogent; strong. Whatever imprecision inheres in these terms, we think it clear that a government regulation is sufficiently justified if it is within the constitutional power of the Government; if it furthers an important or substantial governmental interest; if the governmental interest is unrelated to the suppression of free expression, and if the incidental restriction on alleged First Amendment freedoms is no greater than is essential to the furtherance of that interest. We find that the 1965 Amendment to §12(b)(3) of the Universal Military Training and Service Act meets all of these requirements, and consequently that O'Brien can be constitutionally convicted for violating it.

The constitutional power of Congress to raise and support armies and to make all laws necessary and proper to that end is broad and sweeping. The power of Congress to classify and conscript manpower for military service is "beyond question." Pursuant to this power, Congress may establish a system of registration for individuals liable for training and service, and may require such individuals, within reason, to cooperate in the registration system. The issuance of certificates indicating the registration and eligibility classification of individuals is a legitimate and substantial administrative aid in the functioning of this system. And legislation to insure the continuing availability of issued certificates serves a legitimate and substantial purpose in the system's administration.

O'Brien's argument to the contrary is necessarily premised upon his unrealistic characterization of Selective Service certificates. He essentially adopts the position that such certificates are so many pieces of paper designed to notify registrants of their registration or classification, to be retained or tossed in the wastebasket according to the convenience or taste of the registrant. Once the registrant has received notification, according to this view, there is no reason for him to retain the certificates. O'Brien notes that most of the information on a registration certificate serves no notification purpose at all; the registrant hardly needs to be told his address and physical characteristics. We agree that the registration certificate contains much information of which the registrant needs no notification. This circumstance, however, does not lead to the conclusion that the certificate serves no purpose, but that, like the classification certificate, it serves purposes in addition to initial notification. Many of these purposes would be defeated by the certificates' destruction or mutilation. Among these are:

1. The registration certificate serves as proof that the individual described thereon has registered for the draft. . . .

2. The information supplied on the certificates facilitates communication between registrants and local boards, simplifying the system and benefiting all concerned. To begin with, each certificate bears the address of the registrant's local board, an item unlikely to be committed to memory. Further, each card bears the registrant's Selective Service number, and a registrant who has his number readily available so that he can communicate it to his local board when he supplies or requests information can make simpler the board's task in locating his file. . . .

3. Both certificates carry continual reminders that the registrant must notify his local board of any change of address, and other specified changes in his status. . . .

4. The regulatory scheme involving Selective Service certificates includes clearly valid prohibitions against the alteration, forgery, or similar deceptive misuse of certificates. . . .

The many functions performed by Selective Service certificates establish beyond doubt that Congress has a legitimate and substantial interest in preventing their wanton and unrestrained destruction and assuring their continuing availability by punishing people who knowingly and willfully destroy or mutilate them. And we are unpersuaded that the preexistence of the non-possession regulations in any way negates this interest.

In the absence of a question as to multiple punishment, it has never been suggested that there is anything improper in Congress' providing alternative statutory avenues of prosecution to assure the effective protection of one and the same interest. Here, the preexisting avenue of prosecution was not even statutory. Regulations may be modified or revoked from time to time by administrative discretion. Certainly, the Congress may change or supplement a regulation.

Equally important, a comparison of the regulations with the 1965 Amendment indicates that they protect overlapping but not identical governmental interests, and that they reach somewhat different classes of wrongdoers. The gravamen of the offense defined by the statute is the deliberate rendering of certificates unavailable for the various purposes which they may serve. Whether registrants keep their certificates in their personal possession at all times, as required by the regulations, is of no particular concern under the 1965 Amendment, as long as they do not mutilate or destroy the certificates so as to render them unavailable. . . .

O'Brien finally argues that the 1965 Amendment is unconstitutional as enacted because what he calls the "purpose" of Congress was "to suppress freedom of speech." We reject this argument because under settled principles the purpose of Congress, as O'Brien uses that term, is not a basis for declaring this legislation unconstitutional.

It is a familiar principle of constitutional law that this Court will not strike down an otherwise constitutional statute on the basis of an alleged illicit legislative motive. As the Court long ago stated:

> The decisions of this court from the beginning lend no support whatever to the assumption that the judiciary may restrain the exercise of lawful power on the assumption that a wrongful purpose or motive has caused the power to be exerted.

. . . Inquiries into congressional motives or purposes are a hazardous matter. When the issue is simply the interpretation of legislation, the Court will look to statements by legislators for guidance as to the purpose of the legislature, because the benefit to sound decisionmaking in this circumstance is thought sufficient to risk the possibility of misreading Congress' purpose. It is entirely a different matter when we are asked to void a statute that is, under well settled criteria, constitutional on its face, on the basis of what fewer than a handful of Congressmen said about it. What motivates one legislator to make a speech about a statute is not necessarily what motivates scores of others to enact it, and the stakes are sufficiently high for us to eschew guesswork. We decline to void essentially on the ground that it is unwise legislation which Congress had the undoubted power to enact and which could be reenacted in its exact form if the same or another legislator made a "wiser" speech about it. . . .

Texas v. Johnson

491 U.S. 397 (1989), 5-4
Opinion of the Court: Brennan (Blackmun, Kennedy, Marshall, Scalia)
Dissenting: O'Connor, Rehnquist, Stevens, White

How can this case be distinguished from United States v. O'Brien *(p. 179)? Following Justice Brennan's analysis, would government ever have a strong enough reason to punish flag desecration? What might it be? How do the dissenters differ from Brennan on this point? Why isn't flag-burning the collective equivalent of "fighting words"? Is there any difference between symbolic speech and "pure" speech? If there is, should it affect the ways in which government may regulate or the interests it may defend? Does this case mean that any object, no matter how revered, can be used as a vehicle for symbolic communication? Is nothing sacred or "off limits"? Should anything be? What is gained and lost as a result of this decision?*

Brennan, for the Court:
While the Republican National Convention was taking place in Dallas in 1984, respondent Johnson participated in a political demonstration dubbed the "Republican War Chest Tour." As explained in literature distributed by the demonstrators and in speeches made by them, the purpose of this event was to protest the policies of the Reagan administration and of certain Dallas-based corporations. The demonstrators marched through the Dallas streets, chanting political

slogans and stopping at several corporate locations to stage "die-ins" intended to dramatize the consequences of nuclear war. On several occasions they spray-painted the walls of buildings and overturned potted plants, but Johnson himself took no part in such activities. He did, however, accept an American flag handed to him by a fellow protestor who had taken it from a flagpole outside one of the targeted buildings.

The demonstration ended in front of Dallas City Hall, where Johnson unfurled the American flag, doused it with kerosene, and set it on fire. While the flag burned, the protestors chanted, "America, the red, white, and blue, we spit on you." After the demonstrators dispersed, a witness to the flag burning collected the flag's remains and buried them in his backyard. No one was physically injured or threatened with injury, though several witnesses testified that they had been seriously offended by the flag burning.

Of the approximately 100 demonstrators, Johnson alone was charged with a crime. The only criminal offense with which he was charged was the desecration of a venerated object . . .

Johnson was convicted of flag desecration for burning the flag, rather than for uttering insulting words. This fact somewhat complicates our consid-

Gregory Johnson and his symbol for protest.

eration of his conviction under the First Amendment. We must first determine whether Johnson's burning of the flag constituted expressive conduct, permitting him to invoke the First Amendment in challenging his conviction. If his conduct was expressive, we next decide whether the State's regulation is related to the suppression of free expression. If the State's regulation is not related to expression, then the less stringent standard we announced in *United States v. O'Brien* for regulations of noncommunicative conduct controls. If it is, then we are outside of *O'Brien's* test, and we must ask whether this interest justifies Johnson's conviction under a more demanding standard. A third possibility is that the State's asserted interest is simply not implicated on these facts, and, in that event, the interest drops out of the picture. . . .

In deciding whether particular conduct possesses sufficient communicative elements to bring the First Amendment into play, we have asked whether "[a]n intent to convey a particularized message was present, and [whether] the likelihood was great that the message would be understood by those who viewed it." . . .

The State of Texas conceded for purposes of its oral argument in this case that Johnson's conduct was expressive conduct. . . .

In order to decide whether *O'Brien's* test applies here, therefore, we must decide whether Texas has asserted an interest in support of Johnson's conviction that is unrelated to the suppression of expression. If we find that an interest asserted by the State is simply not implicated on the facts before us, we need not ask whether *O'Brien's* test applies. The State offers two separate interests to justify this conviction: preventing breaches of the peace and preserving the flag as a symbol of nationhood and national unity. We hold that the first interest is not implicated on this record, and that the second is related to the suppression of expression.

Texas claims that its interest in preventing breaches of the peace justifies Johnson's conviction for flag desecration. However, no disturbance of the peace actually occurred or threatened to occur because of Johnson's burning of the flag. Although the State stresses the disruptive behavior of the protestors during their march toward City Hall, it admits that "no actual breach of the peace occurred at the time of the flagburning or in response to the flagburning." The State's emphasis on the protestors' disorderly actions prior to arriving at City Hall is not only somewhat surprising, given that no charges were brought on the basis of this conduct, but it also fails to show that a disturbance of the peace was a likely reaction to Johnson's conduct. The only evidence offered by the State at trial to show the reaction to Johnson's actions was the testimony of several persons who had been seriously offended by the flag burning. The State's position, therefore, amounts to a claim that an audience that takes serious offense at particular expression is necessarily likely to disturb the peace, and that the expression may be prohibited on this basis. . . .

[W]e have not permitted the government to assume that every expression of a provocative idea will incite a riot, but have instead required careful consideration of the actual circumstances surrounding such expression, asking whether the expression "is directed to inciting or producing imminent lawless action and is likely to incite or produce such action." *Brandenburg v. Ohio* To accept Texas' arguments that it need only demonstrate "the potential for a breach of the peace," and that every flag burning necessarily possesses that potential, would be to eviscerate our holding in *Brandenburg*. This we decline to do.

Nor does Johnson's expressive conduct fall within that small class of "fighting words" that are "likely to provoke the average person to retaliation, and thereby cause a breach of the peace." *Chaplinsky v. New Hampshire* No reasonable onlooker would have regarded Johnson's generalized expression of dissatisfaction with the policies of the Federal Government as a direct personal insult or an invitation to exchange fisticuffs.

We thus conclude that the State's interest in maintaining order is not implicated on these facts. . . .

The State also asserts an interest in preserving the flag as a symbol of nationhood and national unity. . . . The State, apparently, is concerned that such conduct will lead people to believe either that the flag does not stand for nationhood and national unity, but instead reflects other, less positive concepts, or that the concepts reflected in the flag do not in fact exist, that is, that we do not enjoy unity as a Nation. These concerns blossom only when a person's treatment of the flag communicates some message, and thus are related "to the suppression of free expression" within the meaning of *O'Brien*. We are thus outside of *O'Brien's* test altogether.

It remains to consider whether the State's interest in preserving the flag as a symbol of nationhood and national unity justifies Johnson's conviction. . . .

. . . The Texas law is thus not aimed at protecting the physical integrity of the flag in all circumstances, but is designed instead to protect it only against impairments that would cause serious offense to others. Texas concedes as much: "Section 42.09(b) reaches only those severe acts of physical abuse of the flag carried out in a way likely to be offensive. The statute mandates intentional or knowing abuse, that is, the kind of mistreatment that is not innocent, but rather is intentionally designed to seriously offend other individuals."

Whether Johnson's treatment of the flag violated Texas law thus depended on the likely communicative impact of his expressive conduct. . . .

. . . Johnson's political expression was restricted because of the content of the message he conveyed. We must therefore subject the State's asserted interest in preserving the special symbolic character of the flag to "the most exacting scrutiny." . . .

. . . According to Texas, if one physically treats the flag in a way that would tend to cast doubt on either the idea that nationhood and national unity are the flag's referents or that national unity actually exists, the message conveyed thereby is a harmful one, and therefore may be prohibited.

If there is a bedrock principle underlying the First Amendment, it is that the government may not prohibit the expression of an idea simply because society finds the idea itself offensive or disagreeable.

We have not recognized an exception to this principle even where our flag has been involved. . . .

We never before have held that the Government may ensure that a symbol be used to express only one view of that symbol or its referents. . . .

. . . To conclude that the government may permit designated symbols to be used to communicate only a limited set of messages would be to enter territory having no discernible or defensible boundaries. Could the government, on this theory, prohibit the burning of state flags? Of copies of the Presidential seal? Of the Constitution? In evaluating these choices under the First Amendment, how would we decide which symbols were sufficiently special to warrant this unique status? To do so, we would be forced to consult our own political preferences, and impose them on the citizenry, in the very way that the First Amendment forbids us to do.

There is, moreover, no indication—either in the text of the Constitution or in our cases interpreting it—that a separate juridical category exists for the

American flag alone. Indeed, we would not be surprised to learn that the persons who framed our Constitution and wrote the Amendment that we now construe were not known for their reverence for the Union Jack. The First Amendment does not guarantee that other concepts virtually sacred to our Nation as a whole—such as the principle that discrimination on the basis of race is odious and destructive—will go unquestioned in the marketplace of ideas. We decline, therefore, to create for the flag an exception to the joust of principles protected by the First Amendment.

It is not the State's ends, but its means, to which we object. It cannot be gainsaid that there is a special place reserved for the flag in this Nation, and thus we do not doubt that the government has a legitimate interest in making efforts to "preserv[e] the national flag as an unalloyed symbol of our country." We reject the suggestion, urged at oral argument by counsel for Johnson, that the government lacks "any state interest whatsoever" in regulating the manner in which the flag may be displayed. Congress has, for example, enacted precatory regulations describing the proper treatment of the flag, and we cast no doubt on the legitimacy of its interest in making such recommendations. . . .

The way to preserve the flag's special role is not to punish those who feel differently about these matters. It is to persuade them that they are wrong. . . .

. . . And, precisely because it is our flag that is involved, one's response to the flag-burner may exploit the uniquely persuasive power of the flag itself. We can imagine no more appropriate response to burning a flag than waving one's own, no better way to counter a flag burner's message than by saluting the flag that burns, no surer means of preserving the dignity even of the flag that burned than by—as one witness here did—according its remains a respectful burial. We do not consecrate the flag by punishing its desecration, for in doing so we dilute the freedom that this cherished emblem represents. . . .

Kennedy, concurring:

I write not to qualify the words Justice Brennan chooses so well, for he says with power all that is necessary to explain our ruling. I join his opinion without reservation, but with a keen sense that this case, like others before us from time to time, exacts its personal toll. . . .

The hard fact is that sometimes we must make decisions we do not like. We make them because they are right, right in the sense that the law and the Constitution, as we see them, compel the result. And so

great is our commitment to the process that, except in the rare case, we do not pause to express distaste for the result, perhaps for fear of undermining a valued principle that dictates the decision. This is one of those rare cases. . . .

I do not believe the Constitution gives us the right to rule as the dissenting Members of the Court urge, however painful this judgment is to announce. Though symbols often are what we ourselves make of them, the flag is constant in expressing beliefs Americans share, beliefs in law and peace and that freedom which sustains the human spirit. The case here today forces recognition of the costs to which those beliefs commit us. It is poignant but fundamental that the flag protects those who hold it in contempt.

For all the record shows, this respondent was not a philosopher and perhaps did not even possess the ability to comprehend how repellent his statements must be to the Republic itself. But whether or not he could appreciate the enormity of the offense he gave, the fact remains that his acts were speech, in both the technical and the fundamental meaning of the Constitution. So I agree with the Court that he must go free.

Rehnquist, dissenting:

In holding this Texas statute unconstitutional, the Court ignores Justice Holmes' familiar aphorism that "a page of history is worth a volume of logic." For more than 200 years, the American flag has occupied a unique position as the symbol of our Nation, a uniqueness that justifies a governmental prohibition against flag burning in the way respondent Johnson did here. . . .

The American flag . . . has come to be the visible symbol embodying our Nation. It does not represent the views of any particular political party, and it does not represent any particular political philosophy. The flag is not simply another "idea" or "point of view" competing for recognition in the marketplace of ideas. Millions and millions of Americans regard it with an almost mystical reverence, regardless of what sort of social, political, or philosophical beliefs they may have. I cannot agree that the First Amendment invalidates the Act of Congress, and the laws of 48 of the 50 States, which make criminal the public burning of the flag. . . .

[T]he public burning of the American flag by Johnson was no essential part of any exposition of ideas, and at the same time it had a tendency to incite a breach of the peace. Johnson was free to make any verbal denunciation of the flag that he wished; indeed, he was free to burn the flag in private. He could publicly burn other symbols of the Government or effigies of political leaders. He did lead a march through the streets of Dallas, and conducted a rally in front of the Dallas City Hall. He engaged in a "die-in" to protest nuclear weapons. He shouted out various slogans during the march, including: "Reagan, Mondale which will it be? Either one means World War III"; "Ronald Reagan, killer of the hour, Perfect example of U.S. power"; and "red, white and blue, we spit on you, you stand for plunder, you will go under." For none of these acts was he arrested or prosecuted; it was only when he proceeded to burn publicly an American flag stolen from its rightful owner that he violated the Texas statute. . . .

. . . The Texas statute deprived Johnson of only one rather inarticulate symbolic form of protest—a form of protest that was profoundly offensive to many—and left him with a full panoply of other symbols and every conceivable form of verbal expression to express his deep disapproval of national policy. Thus, in no way can it be said that Texas is punishing him because his hearers—or any other group of people—were profoundly opposed to the message that he sought to convey. Such opposition is no proper basis for restricting speech or expression under the First Amendment. It was Johnson's use of this particular symbol, and not the idea that he sought to convey by it or by his many other expressions, for which he was punished. . . .

. . . Uncritical extension of constitutional protection to the burning of the flag risks the frustration of the very purpose for which organized governments are instituted. The Court decides that the American flag is just another symbol, about which not only must opinions pro and con be tolerated, but for which the most minimal public respect may not be enjoined. The government may conscript men into the Armed Forces where they must fight and perhaps die for the flag, but the government may not prohibit the public burning of the banner under which they fight. I would uphold the Texas statute as applied in this case.

Stevens, dissenting:

. . . The creation of a federal right to post bulletin boards and graffiti on the Washington Monument might enlarge the market for free expression, but at a cost I would not pay. . . .

. . . The content of [Johnson's] message has no relevance whatsoever to the case. The concept of "dese-

cration" does not turn on the substance of the message the actor intends to convey, but rather on whether those who view the act will take serious offense. Accordingly, one intending to convey a message of respect for the flag by burning it in a public square might nonetheless be guilty of desecration if he knows that others—perhaps simply because they misperceive the intended message—will be seriously offended. Indeed, even if the actor knows that all possible witnesses will understand that he intends to send a message of respect, he might still be guilty of desecration if he also knows that this understanding does not lessen the offense taken by some of those witnesses. Thus, this is not a case in which the fact that "it is the speaker's opinion that gives offense" provides a special "reason for according it constitutional protection." The case has nothing to do with "disagreeable ideas." It involves disagreeable conduct that, in my opinion, diminishes the value of an important national asset.

The Court is therefore quite wrong in blandly asserting that [Johnson] "was prosecuted for his expression of dissatisfaction with the policies of this country, expression situated at the core of our First Amendment values."

[Johnson] was prosecuted because of the method he chose to express his dissatisfaction with those policies. Had he chosen to spraypaint—or perhaps convey with a motion picture projector—his message of dissatisfaction on the facade of the Lincoln Memorial, there would be no question about the power of the Government to prohibit his means of expression. The prohibition would be supported by the legitimate interest in preserving the quality of an important national asset. Though the asset at stake in this case is intangible, given its unique value, the same interest supports a prohibition on the desecration of the American flag. . . .

R.A.V. v. St. Paul

505 U.S. 377 (1992), 9-0
Opinion of the Court: Scalia (Kennedy, Rehnquist, Souter, Thomas)
Concurring: Blackmun, O'Connor, Stevens, White

What fault did the Court find with the St. Paul ordinance? Since R. A. V. could have been prosecuted under several different criminal laws, why do you suppose he was charged under the one at issue in the case? How does Justice White's concurring analysis differ from Justice Scalia's? Are public university "speech codes" that typically forbid face-to-face racial, religious, or sexual insults invalid as a result of this decision? Should preserving dignity or preventing hurt feelings, resentment, or offense be a strong enough government interest to justify limiting freedom of speech? Or does a free speech society require a "thick skin" and willingness to endure disturbing or insulting communication as long as it is simply "communication"? Is it entirely consistent to see ideas and their communication as potentially persuasive enough to justify constitutional protection and yet see them as essentially harmless as long as they remain "words"?

Scalia, for the Court:

In the predawn hours of June 21, 1990, petitioner and several other teenagers allegedly assembled a crudely made cross by taping together broken chair legs. They then allegedly burned the cross inside the fenced yard of a black family that lived across the street from the house where petitioner was staying. Al-

Russell and Laura Jones leaving the U.S. Supreme Court after arguments in *R.A.V. v. St. Paul*, December, 1991. The defendant in the case, Ronald Vicktora, was charged with burning a cross on their front lawn.

though this conduct could have been punished under any of a number of laws, one of the two provisions under which respondent city of St. Paul chose to charge petitioner (then a juvenile) was the St. Paul Bias-Motivated Crime Ordinance, (1990), which provides:

> Whoever places on public or private property a symbol, object, appellation, characterization or graffiti, including, but not limited to, a burning cross or Nazi swastika, which one knows or has reasonable grounds to know arouses anger, alarm or resentment in others on the basis of race, color, creed, religion or gender commits disorderly conduct and shall be guilty of a misdemeanor. . . .

In construing the St. Paul ordinance, we are bound by the construction given to it by the Minnesota court. Accordingly, we accept the Minnesota Supreme Court's authoritative statement that the ordinance reaches only those expressions that constitute "fighting words" within the meaning of *Chaplinsky* [*v. New Hampshire*].

Petitioner and his amici urge us to modify the scope of the *Chaplinsky* formulation, thereby invalidating the ordinance as "substantially overbroad." We find it unnecessary to consider this issue. Assuming, arguendo, that all of the expression reached by the ordinance is proscribable under the "fighting words" doctrine, we nonetheless conclude that the ordinance is facially unconstitutional in that it prohibits otherwise permitted speech solely on the basis of the subjects the speech addresses.

The First Amendment generally prevents government from proscribing speech, or even expressive conduct, because of disapproval of the ideas expressed. Content-based regulations are presumptively invalid. From 1791 to the present, however, our society, like other free but civilized societies, has permitted restrictions upon the content of speech in a few limited areas, which are of such slight social value as a step to truth that any benefit that may be derived from them is clearly outweighed by the social interest in order and morality.

We have recognized that "the freedom of speech" referred to by the First Amendment does not include a freedom to disregard these traditional limitations. Our decisions since the 1960's have narrowed the scope of the traditional categorical exceptions for defamation, and for obscenity, but a limited categorical approach has remained an important part of our First Amendment jurisprudence.

We have sometimes said that these categories of expression are "not within the area of constitutionally protected speech," or that the "protection of the First Amendment does not extend" to them. Such statements must be taken in context, however, and are no more literally true than is the occasionally repeated shorthand characterizing obscenity "as not being speech at all." What they mean is that these areas of speech can, consistently with the First Amendment, be regulated because of their constitutionally proscribable content (obscenity, defamation, etc.)—not that they are categories of speech entirely invisible to the Constitution, so that they may be made the vehicles for content discrimination unrelated to their distinctively proscribable content. Thus, the government may proscribe libel; but it may not make the further content discrimination of proscribing only libel critical of the government. We recently acknowledged this distinction in [*New York v.*] *Ferber*, where, in upholding New York's child pornography law, we expressly recognized that there was no "question here of censoring a particular literary theme. . . ."

Our cases surely do not establish the proposition that the First Amendment imposes no obstacle whatsoever to regulation of particular instances of such proscribable expression, so that the government "may regulate [them] freely." That would mean that a city council could enact an ordinance prohibiting only those legally obscene works that contain criticism of the city government or, indeed, that do not include endorsement of the city government. Such a simplistic, all-or-nothing-at-all approach to First Amendment protection is at odds with common sense and with our jurisprudence as well. It is not true that "fighting words" have at most a "de minimis" expressive content, ibid., or that their content is in all respects "worthless and undeserving of constitutional protection," sometimes they are quite expressive indeed. We have not said that they constitute "no part of the expression of ideas," but only that they constitute "no essential part of any exposition of ideas."

The proposition that a particular instance of speech can be proscribable on the basis of one feature (e.g., obscenity) but not on the basis of another (e.g., opposition to the city government) is commonplace, and has found application in many contexts. We have long held, for example, that nonverbal expressive activity can be banned because of the action

it entails, but not because of the ideas it expresses—so that burning a flag in violation of an ordinance against outdoor fires could be punishable, whereas burning a flag in violation of an ordinance against dishonoring the flag is not. Similarly, we have upheld reasonable "time, place, or manner" restrictions, but only if they are "justified without reference to the content of the regulated speech." And just as the power to proscribe particular speech on the basis of a non-content element (e.g., noise) does not entail the power to proscribe the same speech on the basis of a content element, so also the power to proscribe it on the basis of one content element (e.g., obscenity) does not entail the power to proscribe it on the basis of other content elements.

. . . [T]he exclusion of "fighting words" from the scope of the First Amendment simply means that, for purposes of that Amendment, the unprotected features of the words are, despite their verbal character, essentially a "nonspeech" element of communication. Fighting words are thus analogous to a noisy sound truck: each is . . . a "mode of speech," both can be used to convey an idea; but neither has, in and of itself, a claim upon the First Amendment. As with the sound truck, however, so also with fighting words: the government may not regulate use based on hostility—or favoritism—towards the underlying message expressed. . . .

When the basis for the content discrimination consists entirely of the very reason the entire class of speech at issue is proscribable, no significant danger of idea or viewpoint discrimination exists. Such a reason, having been adjudged neutral enough to support exclusion of the entire class of speech from First Amendment protection, is also neutral enough to form the basis of distinction within the class. To illustrate: a State might choose to prohibit only that obscenity which is the most patently offensive in its prurience—i.e., that which involves the most lascivious displays of sexual activity. But it may not prohibit, for example, only that obscenity which includes offensive political messages. And the Federal Government can criminalize only those threats of violence that are directed against the President . . . But the Federal Government may not criminalize only those threats against the President that mention his policy on aid to inner cities. . . .

Applying these principles to the St. Paul ordinance, we conclude that, even as narrowly construed by the Minnesota Supreme Court, the ordinance is facially unconstitutional. Although the phrase in the ordinance, "arouses anger, alarm or resentment in others," has been limited by the Minnesota Supreme Court's construction to reach only those symbols or displays that amount to "fighting words," the remaining, unmodified terms make clear that the ordinance applies only to "fighting words" that insult, or provoke violence, "on the basis of race, color, creed, religion or gender." Displays containing abusive invective, no matter how vicious or severe, are permissible unless they are addressed to one of the specified disfavored topics. Those who wish to use "fighting words" in connection with other ideas—to express hostility, for example, on the basis of political affiliation, union membership, or homosexuality—are not covered. The First Amendment does not permit St. Paul to impose special prohibitions on those speakers who express views on disfavored subjects. . . .

What we have here, it must be emphasized, is not a prohibition of fighting words that are directed at certain persons or groups (which would be facially valid if it met the requirements of the Equal Protection Clause); but rather, a prohibition of fighting words that contain (as the Minnesota Supreme Court repeatedly emphasized) messages of "bias-motivated" hatred and, in particular, as applied to this case, messages "based on virulent notions of racial supremacy." One must wholeheartedly agree with the Minnesota Supreme Court that "[i]t is the responsibility, even the obligation, of diverse communities to confront such notions in whatever form they appear," ibid., but the manner of that confrontation cannot consist of selective limitations upon speech. St. Paul's brief asserts that a general "fighting words" law would not meet the city's needs, because only a content-specific measure can communicate to minority groups that the "group hatred" aspect of such speech "is not condoned by the majority." The point of the First Amendment is that majority preferences must be expressed in some fashion other than silencing speech on the basis of its content. . . .

. . . St. Paul has not singled out an especially offensive mode of expression—it has not, for example, selected for prohibition only those fighting words that communicate ideas in a threatening (as opposed to a merely obnoxious) manner. Rather, it has proscribed fighting words of whatever manner that communicate messages of racial, gender, or religious intolerance. Selectivity of this sort creates the possibility that the city is seeking to handicap the expression of particular ideas. That possibility would alone be enough to render the ordinance presumptively invalid, but St. Paul's comments and concessions in this case elevate the possibility to a certainty. . . .

Finally, St. Paul and its amici . . . assert that the ordinance helps to ensure the basic human rights of members of groups that have historically been subjected to discrimination, including the right of such group members to live in peace where they wish. We do not doubt that these interests are compelling, and that the ordinance can be said to promote them. But the "danger of censorship" presented by a facially content-based statute requires that that weapon be employed only where it is "necessary to serve the asserted [compelling] interest." . . . The dispositive question in this case, therefore, is whether content discrimination is reasonably necessary to achieve St. Paul's compelling interests; it plainly is not. An ordinance not limited to the favored topics, for example, would have precisely the same beneficial effect. In fact, the only interest distinctively served by the content limitation is that of displaying the city council's special hostility towards the particular biases thus singled out. That is precisely what the First Amendment forbids. . . .

Let there be no mistake about our belief that burning a cross in someone's front yard is reprehensible. But St. Paul has sufficient means at its disposal to prevent such behavior without adding the First Amendment to the fire. . . .

White, concurring:

This case could easily be decided within the contours of established First Amendment law by holding, as petitioner argues, that the St. Paul ordinance is fatally overbroad because it criminalizes not only unprotected expression but expression protected by the First Amendment. . . .

But in the present case, the majority casts aside long-established First Amendment doctrine without the benefit of briefing and adopts an untried theory. . . .

This Court's decisions have plainly stated that expression falling within certain limited categories so lacks the values the First Amendment was designed to protect that the Constitution affords no protection to that expression. . . .

Nevertheless, the majority holds that the First Amendment protects those narrow categories of expression long held to be undeserving of First Amendment protection—at least to the extent that lawmakers may not regulate some fighting words more strictly than others because of their content. The Court announces that such content-based distinctions violate the First Amendment because "the government may not regulate use based on hostility—or favoritism—towards the underlying message expressed." Should the government want to criminalize certain fighting words, the Court now requires it to criminalize all fighting words.

To borrow a phrase, "Such a simplistic, all-or-nothing-at-all approach to First Amendment protection is at odds with common sense, and with our jurisprudence as well." It is inconsistent to hold that the government may proscribe an entire category of speech because the content of that speech is evil, but that the government may not treat a subset of that category differently without violating the First Amendment; the content of the subset is, by definition, worthless and undeserving of constitutional protection.

The majority's observation that fighting words are "quite expressive indeed," is no answer. Fighting words are not a means of exchanging views, rallying supporters, or registering a protest; they are directed against individuals to provoke violence or to inflict injury. Therefore, a ban on all fighting words or on a subset of the fighting words category would restrict only the social evil of hate speech, without creating the danger of driving viewpoints from the marketplace. . . .

Any contribution of this holding to First Amendment jurisprudence is surely a negative one, since it necessarily signals that expressions of violence, such as the message of intimidation and racial hatred conveyed by burning a cross on someone's lawn, are of sufficient value to outweigh the social interest in order and morality that has traditionally placed such fighting words outside the First Amendment. Indeed, by characterizing fighting words as a form of "debate," the majority legitimates hate speech as a form of public discussion.

Furthermore, the Court obscures the line between speech that could be regulated freely on the basis of content (i.e., the narrow categories of expression falling outside the First Amendment) and that which could be regulated on the basis of content only upon a showing of a compelling state interest (i.e., all remaining expression). By placing fighting words, which the Court has long held to be valueless, on at least equal constitutional footing with political discourse and other forms of speech that we have deemed to have the greatest social value, the majority devalues the latter category. . . .

. . . Under the majority's view, a narrowly drawn, content-based ordinance could never pass constitutional muster if the object of that legislation could be accomplished by banning a wider category of speech. This appears to be a general renunciation of strict scrutiny review, a fundamental tool of First Amendment analysis. . . .

Wisconsin v. Mitchell

508 U.S. 476 (1993), 9-0

Opinion of the Court: Rehnquist (Blackmun, Kennedy, O'Connor, Scalia, Souter, Stevens, Thomas, White)

In what way does Mitchell believe his freedom of speech was compromised? Is he punished more severely because he spoke and expressed certain ideas or are his words merely evidence of his motivation? What test does the Court develop to sustain Mitchell's conviction? Is this case consistent with R. A. V. v. St. Paul (p. 186)?

Rehnquist, for the Court:

Respondent Todd Mitchell's sentence for aggravated battery was enhanced because he intentionally selected his victim on account of the victim's race. The question presented in this case is whether this penalty enhancement is prohibited by the First and Fourteenth Amendments. We hold that it is not.

On the evening of October 7, 1989, a group of young black men and boys, including Mitchell, gathered at an apartment complex in Kenosha, Wisconsin. Several members of the group discussed a scene from the motion picture "Mississippi Burning," in which a white man beat a young black boy who was praying. The group moved outside and Mitchell asked them: "'Do you all feel hyped up to move on some white people?'" Shortly thereafter, a young white boy approached the group on the opposite side of the street where they were standing. As the boy walked by, Mitchell said: "'You all want to fuck somebody up? There goes a white boy; go get him.'" Mitchell counted to three and pointed in the boy's direction. The group ran towards the boy, beat him severely, and stole his tennis shoes. The boy was rendered unconscious and remained in a coma for four days.

After a jury trial in the Circuit Court for Kenosha County, Mitchell was convicted of aggravated battery.

Wis. Stat. §§939.05 and 940.19(1m) That offense ordinarily carries a maximum sentence of two years' imprisonment. §§940.19(1m) and 939.50(3)(e). But because the jury found that Mitchell had intentionally selected his victim because of the boy's race, the maximum sentence for Mitchell's offense was increased to seven years under §939.645. That provision enhances the maximum penalty for an offense whenever the defendant "[i]ntentionally selects the person against whom the crime . . . is committed . . . because of the race, religion, color, disability, sexual orientation, national origin or ancestry of that person. . . . " §939.645(1)(b). The Circuit Court sentenced Mitchell to four years' imprisonment for the aggravated battery. . . .

The State argues that the statute does not punish bigoted thought, as the Supreme Court of Wisconsin said, but instead punishes only conduct. While this argument is literally correct, it does not dispose of Mitchell's First Amendment challenge. To be sure, our cases reject the "view that an apparently limitless variety of conduct can be labeled 'speech' whenever the person engaging in the conduct intends thereby to express an idea." *United States v. O'Brien.* Thus, a physical assault is not by any stretch of the imagination expressive conduct protected by the First Amendment. . . .

Traditionally, sentencing judges have considered a wide variety of factors in addition to evidence bearing on guilt in determining what sentence to impose on a convicted defendant. The defendant's motive for committing the offense is one important factor. Thus, in many States the commission of a murder, or other capital offense, for pecuniary gain is a separate aggravating circumstance under the capital sentencing statute.

But it is equally true that a defendant's abstract beliefs, however obnoxious to most people, may not be taken into consideration by a sentencing judge. In *Dawson* [v. *Delaware*], the State introduced evidence at a capital sentencing hearing that the defendant was a member of a white supremacist prison gang. Because "the evidence proved nothing more than [the defendant's] abstract beliefs," we held that its admission violated the defendant's First Amendment rights. In so holding, however, we emphasized that "the Constitution does not erect a per se barrier to the admission of evidence concerning one's beliefs and associations at sentencing simply because those beliefs and associations are protected by the First Amendment." Thus, in *Barclay v. Florida* we allowed the sentencing judge to take into account the defendant's racial animus to-

wards his victim. The evidence in that case showed that the defendant's membership in the Black Liberation Army and desire to provoke a "race war" were related to the murder of a white man for which he was convicted. Because "the elements of racial hatred in [the] murder" were relevant to several aggravating factors, we held that the trial judge permissibly took this evidence into account in sentencing the defendant to death. . . .

Mitchell argues that the Wisconsin penalty enhancement statute is invalid because it punishes the defendant's discriminatory motive, or reason, for acting. But motive plays the same role under the Wisconsin statute as it does under federal and state antidiscrimination laws, which we have previously upheld against constitutional challenge. . . .

Nothing in our decision last Term in *R. A. V.* [v. *St. Paul*] compels a different result here. That case involved a First Amendment challenge to a municipal ordinance prohibiting the use of "'fighting words' that insult, or provoke violence, 'on the basis of race, color, creed, religion or gender.' " Because the ordinance only proscribed a class of "fighting words" deemed particularly offensive by the city—i.e., those "that contain . . . messages of 'bias motivated' hatred,"—we held that it violated the rule against content based discrimination. But whereas the ordinance struck down in *R. A. V.* was explicitly directed at expression (i.e., "speech" or "messages"), the statute in this case is aimed at conduct unprotected by the First Amendment.

Moreover, the Wisconsin statute singles out for enhancement bias inspired conduct because this conduct is thought to inflict greater individual and societal harm. For example, according to the State and its amici, bias motivated crimes are more likely to provoke retaliatory crimes, inflict distinct emotional harms on their victims, and incite community unrest. The State's desire to redress these perceived harms provides an adequate explanation for its penalty enhancement provision over and above mere disagreement with offenders' beliefs or biases. . . .

Finally, there remains to be considered Mitchell's argument that the Wisconsin statute is unconstitutionally overbroad because of its "chilling effect" on free speech. Mitchell argues (and the Wisconsin Supreme Court agreed) that the statute is "overbroad" because evidence of the defendant's prior speech or associations may be used to prove that the defendant intentionally selected his victim on account of the victim's protected status. Consequently, the argument goes, the statute impermissibly chills free expression with respect to such matters by those concerned about the possibility of enhanced sentences if they should in the future commit a criminal offense covered by the statute. We find no merit in this contention.

The sort of chill envisioned here is far more attenuated and unlikely than that contemplated in traditional "overbreadth" cases. We must conjure up a vision of a Wisconsin citizen suppressing his unpopular bigoted opinions for fear that if he later commits an offense covered by the statute, these opinions will be offered at trial to establish that he selected his victim on account of the victim's protected status, thus qualifying him for penalty enhancement. To stay within the realm of rationality, we must surely put to one side minor misdemeanor offenses covered by the statute, such as negligent operation of a motorvehicle; for it is difficult, if not impossible, to conceive of a situation where such offenses would be racially motivated. We are left, then, with the prospect of a citizen suppressing his bigoted beliefs for fear that evidence of such beliefs will be introduced against him at trial if he commits a more serious offense against person or property. This is simply too speculative a hypothesis to support Mitchell's overbreadth claim.

The First Amendment, moreover, does not prohibit the evidentiary use of speech to establish the elements of a crime or to prove motive or intent. Evidence of a defendant's previous declarations or statements is commonly admitted in criminal trials subject to evidentiary rules dealing with relevancy, reliability, and the like. Nearly half a century ago, in *Haupt v. United States,* we rejected a contention similar to that advanced by Mitchell here. Haupt was tried for the offense of treason, which, as defined by the Constitution (Art. III, §3), may depend very much on proof of motive. To prove that the acts in question were committed out of "adherence to the enemy" rather than "parental solicitude," the Government introduced evidence of conversations that had taken place long prior to the indictment, some of which consisted of statements showing Haupt's sympathy with Germany and Hitler and hostility towards the United States. We rejected Haupt's argument that this evidence was improperly admitted. While "[s]uch testimony is to be scrutinized with care to be certain the statements are not expressions of mere lawful and permissible difference of opinion with our own government or

quite proper appreciation of the land of birth," we held that "these statements . . . clearly were admissible on the question of intent and adherence to the enemy."

For the foregoing reasons, we hold that Mitchell's First Amendment rights were not violated by the application of the Wisconsin penalty enhancement provision in sentencing him. The judgment of the Supreme Court of Wisconsin is therefore reversed, and the case is remanded for further proceedings not inconsistent with this opinion.

Edwards v. South Carolina

372 U.S. 229 (1963), 8-1
Opinion of the Court: Stewart (Black, Brennan, Douglas, Goldberg, Harlan II, Warren, White)
Dissenting: Clark

How important was it that the site of the protest in this case was the state capitol grounds? What facts would need to be different to persuade the Court to uphold the convictions of the defendants?

Stewart, for the Court:

The petitioners, 187 in number, were convicted in a magistrate's court in Columbia, South Carolina, of the common law crime of breach of the peace. Their convictions were ultimately affirmed by the South Carolina Supreme Court. . . .

. . . Late in the morning of March 2, 1961, the petitioners, high school and college students of the Negro race, met at the Zion Baptist Church in Columbia. From there, at about noon, they walked in separate groups of about 15 to the South Carolina State House grounds, an area of two city blocks open to the general public. Their purpose was "to submit a protest to the citizens of South Carolina, along with the Legislative Bodies of South Carolina, our feelings and our dissatisfaction with the present condition of discriminatory actions against Negroes in general, and to let them know that we were dissatisfied, and that we would like for the laws which prohibited Negro privileges in this State to be removed."

Already on the State House grounds when the petitioners arrived were 30 or more law enforcement officers, who had advance knowledge that the petitioners were coming. Each group of petitioners entered the grounds through a driveway and parking area known in the record as the "horseshoe." As they entered, they were told by the law enforcement officials that "they had a right, as a citizen, to go through the State House grounds, as any other citizen has, as long as they were peaceful." During the next half hour or 45 minutes, the petitioners, in the same small groups, walked single file or two abreast in an orderly way, through the grounds, each group carrying placards bearing such messages as "I am proud to be a Negro" and "Down with segregation."

During this time, a crowd of some 200 to 300 onlookers had collected in the horseshoe area and on the adjacent sidewalks. There was no evidence to suggest that these onlookers were anything but curious, and no evidence at all of any threatening remarks, hostile gestures, or offensive language on the part of any member of the crowd. The City Manager testified that he recognized some of the onlookers, whom he did not identify, as "possible troublemakers," but his subsequent testimony made clear that nobody among the crowd actually caused or threatened any trouble. There was no obstruction of pedestrian or vehicular traffic within the State House grounds. No vehicle was prevented from entering or leaving the horseshoe area. Although vehicular traffic at a nearby street intersection was slowed down somewhat, an officer was dispatched to keep traffic moving. There were a number of bystanders on the public sidewalks adjacent to the State House grounds, but they all moved on when asked to do so, and there was no impediment of pedestrian traffic. Police protection at the scene was at all times sufficient to meet any foreseeable possibility of disorder.

In the situation and under the circumstances thus described, the police authorities advised the petitioners that they would be arrested if they did not disperse within 15 minutes. Instead of dispersing, the petitioners engaged in what the City Manager described as "boisterous," "loud," and "flamboyant" conduct, which, as his later testimony made clear, consisted of listening to a "religious harangue" by one of their leaders, and loudly singing "The Star Spangled Banner" and other patriotic and religious songs, while stamping their feet and clapping their hands. After 15 minutes had passed, the police arrested the petitioners and marched them off to jail.

Upon this evidence, the state trial court convicted the petitioners of breach of the peace, and imposed sentences ranging from a $10 fine or five days in jail to a $100 fine or 30 days in jail. In affirming the judg-

ments, the Supreme Court of South Carolina said that, under the law of that State, the offense of breach of the peace "is not susceptible of exact definition," but that the "general definition of the offense" is as follows:

> In general terms, a breach of the peace is a violation of public order, a disturbance of the public tranquility, by any act or conduct inciting to violence . . . , it includes any violation of any law enacted to preserve peace and good order. It may consist of an act of violence or an act likely to produce violence. It is not necessary that the peace be actually broken to lay the foundation for a prosecution for this offense. If what is done is unjustifiable and unlawful, tending with sufficient directness to break the peace, no more is required. Nor is actual personal violence an essential element in the offense. . . .
>
> By "peace," as used in the law in this connection, is meant the tranquility enjoyed by citizens of a municipality or community where good order reigns among its members, which is the natural right of all persons in political society.

. . . It has long been established that these First Amendment freedoms are protected by the Fourteenth Amendment from invasion by the States. The circumstances in this case reflect an exercise of these basic constitutional rights in their most pristine and classic form. The petitioners felt aggrieved by laws of South Carolina which allegedly "prohibited Negro privileges in this State." They peaceably assembled at the site of the State Government, and there peaceably expressed their grievances "to the citizens of South Carolina, along with the Legislative Bodies of South Carolina." Not until they were told by police officials that they must disperse on pain of arrest did they do more. Even then, they but sang patriotic and religious songs after one of their leaders had delivered a "religious harangue." There was no violence or threat of violence on their part, or on the part of any member of the crowd watching them. Police protection was "ample."

This, therefore, was a far cry from the situation in *Feiner v. New York*, where two policemen were faced with a crowd which was "pushing, shoving and milling around," where at least one member of the crowd "threatened violence if the police did not act," where "the crowd was pressing closer around petitioner and the officer," and where "the speaker passes the bounds of argument or persuasion and undertakes incitement to riot." And the record is barren of any evidence of "fighting words."

We do not review in this case criminal convictions resulting from the evenhanded application of a precise and narrowly drawn regulatory statute evincing a legislative judgment that certain specific conduct be limited or proscribed. If, for example, the petitioners had been convicted upon evidence that they had violated a law regulating traffic, or had disobeyed a law reasonably limiting the periods during which the State House grounds were open to the public, this would be a different case. These petitioners were convicted of an offense so generalized as to be, in the words of the South Carolina Supreme Court, "not susceptible of exact definition." And they were convicted upon evidence which showed no more than that the opinions which they were peaceably expressing were sufficiently opposed to the views of the majority of the community to attract a crowd and necessitate police protection. . . .

Clark, dissenting:
. . . Beginning, as did the South Carolina courts, with the premise that the petitioners were entitled to assemble and voice their dissatisfaction with segregation, the enlargement of constitutional protection for the conduct here is as fallacious as would be the conclusion that free speech necessarily includes the right to broadcast from a sound truck in the public streets . . .

. . . [I]n *Feiner v. New York,* we upheld a conviction for breach of the peace in a situation no more dangerous than that found here. There, the demonstration was conducted by only one person, and the crowd was limited to approximately 80, as compared with the present lineup of some 200 demonstrators and 300 onlookers. There, the petitioner was "endeavoring to arouse the Negro people against the whites, urging that they rise up in arms and fight for equal rights." Only one person—in a city having an entirely different historical background—was exhorting adults. Here, 200 youthful Negro demonstrators were being aroused to a "fever pitch" before a crowd of some 300 people who undoubtedly were hostile. Perhaps their speech was not so animated, but, in this setting, their actions, their placards reading "You may jail our bodies, but not our souls," and their chanting of "I Shall Not Be Moved," accompanied by stamping feet and clapping

hands, created a much greater danger of riot and disorder. It is my belief that anyone conversant with the almost spontaneous combustion in some Southern communities in such a situation will agree that the City Manager's action may well have averted a major catastrophe.

The gravity of the danger here surely needs no further explication. The imminence of that danger has been emphasized at every stage of this proceeding, from the complaints charging that the demonstrations "tended directly to immediate violence" to the State Supreme Court's affirmance on the authority of *Feiner.* This record, then, shows no steps backward from a standard of "clear and present danger." But to say that the police may not intervene until the riot has occurred is like keeping out the doctor until the patient dies. I cannot subscribe to such a doctrine. . . .

Hill v. Colorado

530 U.S. 703 (2000), 6-3
Opinion of the Court: Stevens (Breyer, Ginsburg, O'Connor, Rehnquist, Souter)
Dissenting: Kennedy, Scalia, Thomas

Is the Colorado law at issue here a time, place, and manner regulation, or is Justice Scalia correct in describing it as a "speech regulation directed against the opponents of abortion"? What interest is the state defending? How does Justice Stevens describe the law and analyze the state's interest? If Scalia is correct, would the law be unconstitutional? Does the law and the Court's decision upholding it leave anti-abortion protesters and "counsellors" adequate means to communicate? Is this decision consistent with R.A.V. v. St. Paul (p. 186) and Edwards v. South Carolina (p. 192)?

Stevens, for the Court:
At issue is the constitutionality of a 1993 Colorado statute that regulates speech-related conduct within 100 feet of the entrance to any health care facility. The specific section of the statute that is challenged, Colo. Rev. Stat. §18—9—122(3) (1999), makes it unlawful within the regulated areas for any person to "knowingly approach" within eight feet of another person, without that person's consent, "for the purpose of passing a leaflet or handbill to, displaying a sign to, or engaging in oral protest, education, or counseling with such other person. . . . " Although the statute prohibits

speakers from approaching unwilling listeners, it does not require a standing speaker to move away from anyone passing by. Nor does it place any restriction on the content of any message that anyone may wish to communicate to anyone else, either inside or outside the regulated areas. It does, however, make it more difficult to give unwanted advice, particularly in the form of a handbill or leaflet, to persons entering or leaving medical facilities.

The question is whether the First Amendment rights of the speaker are abridged by the protection the statute provides for the unwilling listener.

Five months after the statute was enacted, petitioners [sought] . . . an injunction against its enforcement. They stated that . . . they had engaged in "sidewalk counseling" on the public ways and sidewalks within 100 feet of the entrances to facilities where human abortion is practiced or where medical personnel refer women to other facilities for abortions. "Sidewalk counseling" consists of efforts "to educate, counsel, persuade, or inform passersby about abortion and abortion alternatives by means of verbal or written speech, including conversation and/or display of signs and/or distribution of literature." They further alleged that such activities frequently entail being within eight feet of other persons and that their fear of prosecution under the new statute caused them "to be chilled in the exercise of fundamental constitutional rights." . . .

Before confronting the question whether the Colorado statute reflects an acceptable balance between the constitutionally protected rights of law-abiding speakers and the interests of unwilling listeners, it is appropriate to examine the competing interests at stake. A brief review of both sides of the dispute reveals that each has legitimate and important concerns.

The First Amendment interests of petitioners are clear and undisputed. As a preface to their legal challenge, petitioners emphasize three propositions. First, they accurately explain that the areas protected by the statute encompass all the public ways within 100 feet of every entrance to every health care facility everywhere in the State of Colorado. There is no disagreement on this point, even though the legislative history makes it clear that its enactment was primarily motivated by activities in the vicinity of abortion clinics. Second, they correctly state that their leafletting, sign displays, and oral communications are protected by the First Amendment. The fact that the messages conveyed by those communications may be offensive to their recipients does not deprive them of constitutional protection. Third, the public sidewalks, streets, and ways affected by the statute are "quintessential" public forums for free speech. Finally, although there is debate about the magnitude of the statutory impediment to their ability to communicate effectively with persons in the regulated zones, that ability, particularly the ability to distribute leaflets, is unquestionably lessened by this statute.

On the other hand, petitioners do not challenge the legitimacy of the state interests that the statute is intended to serve. It is a traditional exercise of the States' "police powers to protect the health and safety of their citizens." *Medtronic, Inc. v. Lohr.* That interest may justify a special focus on unimpeded access to health care facilities and the avoidance of potential trauma to patients associated with confrontational protests. Moreover, as with every exercise of a State's police powers, rules that provide specific guidance to enforcement authorities serve the interest in evenhanded application of the law. Whether or not those interests justify the particular regulation at issue, they are unquestionably legitimate.

It is also important when conducting this interest analysis to recognize the significant difference between state restrictions on a speaker's right to address a willing audience and those that protect listeners from unwanted communication. This statute deals only with the latter.

The right to free speech, of course, includes the right to attempt to persuade others to change their views, and may not be curtailed simply because the speaker's message may be offensive to his audience. But the protection afforded to offensive messages does not always embrace offensive speech that is so intrusive that the unwilling audience cannot avoid it. . . .

We have . . . recognized that the "right to persuade" . . . is protected by the First Amendment, as well as by federal statutes. Yet we have continued to maintain that "no one has a right to press even 'good' ideas on an unwilling recipient." None of our decisions has minimized the enduring importance of "the right to be free" from persistent "importunity, following and dogging" after an offer to communicate has been declined. While the freedom to communicate is substantial, "the right of every person 'to be let alone' must be placed in the scales with the right of others to communicate." It is that right, as well as the right of "passage without obstruction," that the Colorado statute legitimately seeks to protect. The restrictions imposed by the Colorado statute only apply to communications that interfere with these rights rather than those that involve willing listeners. . . .

. . . First, [the statute] it is not a "regulation of speech." Rather, it is a regulation of the places where some speech may occur. Second, it was not adopted "because of disagreement with the message it conveys." This conclusion is supported not just by the Colorado courts' interpretation of legislative history, but more importantly by the State Supreme Court's unequivocal holding that the statute's "restrictions apply equally to all demonstrators, regardless of viewpoint, and the statutory language makes no reference to the content of the speech." Third, the State's interests in protecting access and privacy, and providing the police with clear guidelines, are unrelated to the content of the demonstrators' speech. As we have repeatedly explained, government regulation of expressive activity is "content neutral" if it is justified without reference to the content of regulated speech. . . .

It is common in the law to examine the content of a communication to determine the speaker's purpose. Whether a particular statement constitutes a threat, blackmail, an agreement to fix prices, a copyright violation, a public offering of securities, or an offer to sell goods often depends on the precise content of the statement. We have never held, or suggested, that it is improper to look at the content of an oral or written statement in order to determine whether a rule of law applies to a course of conduct. With respect to the conduct that is the focus of the Colorado statute, it is unlikely that there would often be any need to know exactly what words were spoken in order to determine whether "sidewalk counselors" are engaging in "oral protest, education, or counseling" rather than pure social or random conversation.

Theoretically, of course, cases may arise in which it is necessary to review the content of the statements made by a person approaching within eight feet of an unwilling listener to determine whether the approach is covered by the statute. But that review need be no more extensive than a determination of whether a general prohibition of "picketing" or "demonstrating" applies to innocuous speech. The regulation of such expressive activities, by definition, does not cover social, random, or other everyday communications. . . .

The Colorado statute's regulation of the location of protests, education, and counseling is easily distinguishable from *Carey* [v. *Brown*]. It places no restrictions on—and clearly does not prohibit—either a particular viewpoint or any subject matter that may be discussed by a speaker. Rather, it simply establishes a minor place restriction on an extremely broad category of communications with unwilling listeners. Instead of drawing distinctions based on the subject that the approaching speaker may wish to address, the statute applies equally to used car salesmen, animal rights activists, fundraisers, environmentalists, and missionaries. Each can attempt to educate unwilling listeners on any subject, but without consent may not approach within eight feet to do so. . . .

With respect to oral statements, the distance certainly can make it more difficult for a speaker to be heard, particularly if the level of background noise is high and other speakers are competing for the pedestrian's attention. Notably, the statute places no limitation on the number of speakers or the noise level, including the use of amplification equipment, although we have upheld such restrictions in past cases. More significantly, this statute does not suffer from the failings that compelled us to reject the "floating buffer zone." Unlike the 15-foot zone in *Schenck* [v. *Pro-Choice Network of Western New York*], this 8-foot zone allows the speaker to communicate at a "normal conversational distance." Additionally, the statute allows the speaker to remain in one place, and other individuals can pass within eight feet of the protester without causing the protester to violate the statute. Finally, here there is a "knowing" requirement that protects speakers "who thought they were keeping pace with the targeted individual" at the proscribed distance from inadvertently violating the statute. . . .

The burden on the ability to distribute handbills is more serious because it seems possible that an 8-foot interval could hinder the ability of a leafletter to deliver handbills to some unwilling recipients. The statute does not, however, prevent a leafletter from simply standing near the path of oncoming pedestrians and proffering his or her material, which the pedestrians can easily accept. And, as in all leafletting situations, pedestrians continue to be free to decline the tender. In *Heffron v. International Soc. for Krishna Consciousness, Inc.*, we upheld a state fair regulation that required a religious organization desiring to distribute literature to conduct that activity only at an assigned location—in that case booths. As in this case, the regulation primarily burdened the distributors' ability to communicate with unwilling readers. We concluded our opinion by emphasizing that the First Amendment protects the right of every citizen to "'reach the minds of willing listeners and to do so there must be opportunity to win their attention.' *Kovacs v. Cooper*. The Colorado statute adequately protects those rights.

Finally, in determining whether a statute is narrowly tailored, we have noted that "[w]e must, of course, take account of the place to which the regulations apply in determining whether these restrictions burden more speech than necessary." *Madsen* [v. *Women's Health Center*]. States and municipalities plainly have a substantial interest in controlling the activity around certain public and private places. For example, we have recognized the special governmental interests surrounding schools, courthouses, polling places, and private homes. Additionally, we previously have noted the unique concerns that surround health care facilities. . . .

Persons who are attempting to enter health care facilities—for any purpose—are often in particularly vulnerable physical and emotional conditions. The State of Colorado has responded to its substantial and legitimate interest in protecting these persons from unwanted encounters, confrontations, and even assaults by enacting an exceedingly modest restriction on the speakers' ability to approach. . . .

Finally, the 8-foot restriction occurs only within 100 feet of a health care facility—the place where the restriction is most needed. The restriction interferes far less with a speaker's ability to communicate than did the total ban on picketing on the sidewalk outside a residence, the restriction of leafletting at a fairground to a booth or the "silence" often required outside a hospital. Special problems that may arise where clinics have particularly wide entrances or are situated within multipurpose office buildings may be worked out as the statute is applied. . . .

Finally, petitioners argue that §18—9—122(3)'s consent requirement is invalid because it imposes an unconstitutional "prior restraint" on speech. We rejected this argument previously in *Schenck* and *Madsen*. Moreover, the restrictions in this case raise an even lesser prior restraint concern than those at issue in *Schenck* and *Madsen* where particular speakers were at times completely banned within certain zones. Under this statute, absolutely no channel of communication is foreclosed. No speaker is silenced. And no message is prohibited. Petitioners are simply wrong when they assert that "[t]he statute compels speakers to obtain consent to speak and it authorizes private citizens to deny petitioners' re-quests to engage in expressive activities." To the contrary, this statute does not provide for a "heckler's veto" but rather allows every speaker to engage freely in any expressive activity communicating all messages and viewpoints subject only to the narrow place requirement imbedded within the "approach" restriction.

Furthermore, our concerns about "prior restraints" relate to restrictions imposed by official censorship. The regulations in this case, however, only apply if the pedestrian does not consent to the approach. Private citizens have always retained the power to decide for themselves what they wish to read, and within limits, what oral messages they want to consider. This statute simply empowers private citizens entering a health care facility with the ability to prevent a speaker, who is within eight feet and advancing, from communicating a message they do not wish to hear. Further, the statute does not authorize the pedestrian to affect any other activity at any other location or relating to any other person. These restrictions thus do not constitute an unlawful prior restraint.

Scalia, dissenting:

The Court today concludes that a regulation requiring speakers on the public thoroughfares bordering medical facilities to speak from a distance of eight feet is "not a 'regulation of speech,'" but "a regulation of the places where some speech may occur," and that a regulation directed to only certain categories of speech (protest, education, and counseling) is not "content-based." For these reasons, it says, the regulation is immune from the exacting scrutiny we apply to content-based suppression of speech in the public forum. The Court then determines that the regulation survives the less rigorous scrutiny afforded content-neutral time, place, and manner restrictions because it is narrowly tailored to serve a government interest—protection of citizens' "right to be let alone"—that has explicitly been disclaimed by the State, probably for the reason that, as a basis for suppressing peaceful private expression, it is patently incompatible with the guarantees of the First Amendment.

None of these remarkable conclusions should come as a surprise. What is before us, after all, is a speech regulation directed against the opponents of abortion, and it therefore enjoys the benefit of the "ad hoc nullification machine" that the Court has set in motion to push aside whatever doctrines of constitutional law stand in the way of that highly favored practice. Having deprived abortion opponents of the political right to persuade the electorate that abortion should be restricted by law, the Court today continues and expands its assault upon their individual right to persuade women contemplating abortion that what they are doing is wrong. Because, like the rest of our abortion jurisprudence, today's decision is in stark contradiction of the constitutional principles we apply in all other contexts, I dissent.

... Whatever may be said about the restrictions on the other types of expressive activity, the regulation as it applies to oral communications is obviously and undeniably content-based. A speaker wishing to approach another for the purpose of communicating any message except one of protest, education, or counseling may do so without first securing the other's consent. Whether a speaker must obtain permission before approaching within eight feet—and whether he will be sent to prison for failing to do so—depends entirely on what he intends to say when he gets there. I have no doubt that this regulation would be deemed content-based in an instant if the case before us involved antiwar protesters, or union members seeking to "educate" the public about the reasons for their strike. "[I]t is," we would say, "the content of the speech that determines whether it is within or without the statute's blunt prohibition," *Carey v. Brown.* But the jurisprudence of this Court has a way of changing when abortion is involved....

... [I]t blinks reality to regard this statute, in its application to oral communications, as anything other than a content-based restriction upon speech in the public forum. As such, it must survive that stringent mode of constitutional analysis our cases refer to as "strict scrutiny," which requires that the restriction be narrowly tailored to serve a compelling state interest. Since the Court does not even attempt to support the regulation under this standard, I shall discuss it only briefly. Suffice it to say that if protecting people from unwelcome communications (the governmental interest the Court posits) is a compelling state interest, the First Amendment is a dead letter. And if . . . forbidding peaceful, nonthreatening, but uninvited speech from a distance closer than eight feet is a "narrowly tailored" means of preventing the obstruction of entrance to medical facilities (the governmental interest the State asserts) narrow tailoring must refer

not to the standards of Versace, but to those of Omar the tentmaker....

... [T]he 8-foot buffer zone attaches to every person on the public way or sidewalk within 100 feet of the entrance of a medical facility, regardless of whether that person is seeking to enter or exit the facility. In fact, the State acknowledged at oral argument that the buffer zone would attach to any person within 100 feet of the entrance door of a skyscraper in which a single doctor occupied an office on the 18th floor. And even with respect to those who are seeking to enter or exit the facilities, the statute does not protect them only from speech that is so intimidating or threatening as to impede access. Rather, it covers all unconsented-to approaches for the purpose of oral protest, education, or counseling (including those made for the purpose of the most peaceful appeals) and, perhaps even more significantly, every approach made for the purposes of leafletting or handbilling, which we have never considered, standing alone, obstructive or unduly intrusive. The sweep of this prohibition is breathtaking....

Those whose concern is for the physical safety and security of clinic patients, workers, and doctors should take no comfort from today's decision. Individuals or groups intent on bullying or frightening women out of an abortion, or doctors out of performing that procedure, will not be deterred by Colorado's statute; bullhorns and screaming from eight feet away will serve their purposes well. But those who would accomplish their moral and religious objectives by peaceful and civil means, by trying to persuade individual women of the rightness of their cause, will be deterred; and that is not a good thing in a democracy. This Court once recognized, as the Framers surely did, that the freedom to speak and persuade is inseparable from, and antecedent to, the survival of self-government. The Court today rotates that essential safety valve on our democracy one-half turn to the right, and no one who seeks safe access to health care facilities in Colorado or elsewhere should feel that her security has by this decision been enhanced....

Does the deck seem stacked? You bet. As I have suggested throughout this opinion, today's decision is not an isolated distortion of our traditional constitutional principles, but is one of many aggressively proabortion novelties announced by the Court in recent years. Today's distortions, however, are particularly blatant. Restrictive views of the First Amendment that have been in dissent since the 1930's suddenly find themselves in the majority. "Uninhibited, robust, and wide open" debate is replaced by the power of the state to protect an unheard-of "right to be let alone" on the public streets. I dissent.

Tinker v. Des Moines Independent Community School District

393 U.S. 503 (1969), 7-2
Opinion of the Court: Fortas (Brennan, Douglas, Marshall, Stewart, Warren, White)
Dissenting: Black, Harlan

Was the school district's policy content neutral? What evidence would be needed for the Court to uphold suspension of the students? How can this case be distinguished from United States v. O'Brien (p. 179)? Does the Court's decision mean that a child's First Amendment rights are coextensive with an adult's? That a student's First Amendment rights at school are coextensive with those outside of school? That symbolic speech has as much protection as "pure" speech?

Fortas, for the Court:
Petitioner John F. Tinker, 15 years old, and petitioner Christopher Eckhardt, 16 years old, attended high schools in Des Moines, Iowa. Petitioner Mary Beth Tinker, John's sister, was a 13-year-old student in junior high school.

In December, 1965, a group of adults and students in Des Moines held a meeting at the Eckhardt home. The group determined to publicize their objections to the hostilities in Vietnam and their support for a truce by wearing black armbands during the holiday season and by fasting on December 16 and New Year's Eve. . . .

The principals of the Des Moines schools became aware of the plan to wear armbands. On December 14, 1965, they met and adopted a policy that any student wearing an armband to school would be asked to remove it, and, if he refused, he would be suspended until he returned without the armband. Petitioners were aware of the regulation that the school authorities adopted.

On December 16, Mary Beth and Christopher wore black armbands to their schools. John Tinker wore his armband the next day. They were all sent home and suspended from school until they would come back without their armbands. They did not return to school until after the planned period for wearing armbands had expired—that is, until after New Year's Day.

The District Court recognized that the wearing of an armband for the purpose of expressing certain views is the type of symbolic act that is within the Free Speech Clause of the First Amendment. . . . [T]he wearing of armbands in the circumstances of this case was entirely divorced from actually or potentially disruptive conduct by those participating in it. It was closely akin to "pure speech" which, we have repeatedly held, is entitled to comprehensive protection under the First Amendment.

First Amendment rights, applied in light of the special characteristics of the school environment, are available to teachers and students. It can hardly be argued that either students or teachers shed their constitutional rights to freedom of speech or expression at the schoolhouse gate. This has been the unmistakable holding of this Court for almost 50 years. This Court, in opinions by Mr. Justice McReynolds, held that the Due Process Clause of the Fourteenth Amendment prevents States from forbidding the teaching of a foreign language to young students. Statutes to this effect, the Court held, unconstitutionally interfere with the liberty of teacher, student, and parent. . . .

The problem posed by the present case does not relate to regulation of the length of skirts or the type of clothing, to hair style, or deportment. It does not concern aggressive, disruptive action or even group demonstrations. Our problem involves direct, primary First Amendment rights akin to "pure speech."

The school officials banned and sought to punish petitioners for a silent, passive expression of opinion, unaccompanied by any disorder or disturbance on the part of petitioners. There is here no evidence whatever of petitioners' interference, actual or nascent, with the schools' work or of collision with the rights of other students to be secure and to be let alone. Accordingly, this case does not concern speech or action that intrudes upon the work of the schools or the rights of other students.

Only a few of the 18,000 students in the school system wore the black armbands. Only five students were suspended for wearing them. There is no indication that the work of the schools or any class was disrupted. Outside the classrooms, a few students made hostile remarks to the children wearing armbands, but there were no threats or acts of violence on school premises.

The District Court concluded that the action of the school authorities was reasonable because it was based upon their fear of a disturbance from the wearing of the armbands. But, in our system, undifferentiated fear or apprehension of disturbance is not enough to overcome the right to freedom of expression. Any departure from absolute regimentation may cause trouble. Any variation from the majority's opinion may inspire fear. Any word spoken, in class, in the lunchroom, or on the campus, that deviates from the views of another person may start an argument or cause a disturbance. But our Constitution says we must take this risk, and our history says that it is this sort of hazardous freedom—this kind of openness—that is the basis of our national strength and of the independence and vigor of Americans who grow up and live in this relatively permissive, often disputatious, society. . . .

On the contrary, the action of the school authorities appears to have been based upon an urgent wish to avoid the controversy which might result from the expression, even by the silent symbol of armbands, of opposition to this Nation's part in the conflagration in Vietnam. It is revealing, in this respect, that the meeting at which the school principals decided to issue the contested regulation was called in response to a student's statement to the journalism teacher in one of the schools that he wanted to write an article on Vietnam and have it published in the school paper. (The student was dissuaded.)

It is also relevant that the school authorities did not purport to prohibit the wearing of all symbols of political or controversial significance. The record shows that students in some of the schools wore buttons relating to national political campaigns, and some even wore the Iron Cross, traditionally a symbol of Nazism. The order prohibiting the wearing of armbands did not extend to these. Instead, a particular symbol—black armbands worn to exhibit opposition to this Nation's involvement in Vietnam—was singled out for prohibition. Clearly, the prohibition of expression of one particular opinion, at least without evidence that it is necessary to avoid material and substantial interference with schoolwork or discipline, is not constitutionally permissible.

In our system, state-operated schools may not be enclaves of totalitarianism. School officials do not possess absolute authority over their students. Students in school, as well as out of school, are "persons" under our Constitution. They are possessed of fundamental rights which the State must respect, just as they themselves must respect their obligations to the State. In our system, students may not be regarded as closed-circuit recipients of only that which the State chooses to communicate. They may not be confined to the expression of those sentiments that are officially approved. In the absence of a specific showing of constitutionally valid reasons to regulate their speech, students are entitled to freedom of expression of their views. . . .

Under our Constitution, free speech is not a right that is given only to be so circumscribed that it exists in principle, but not in fact. Freedom of expression would not truly exist if the right could be exercised only in an area that a benevolent government has provided as a safe haven for crackpots. The Constitution says that Congress (and the States) may not abridge the right to free speech. This provision means what it says. We properly read it to permit reasonable regulation of speech-connected activities in carefully restricted circumstances. But we do not confine the permissible exercise of First Amendment rights to a telephone booth or the four corners of a pamphlet, or to supervised and ordained discussion in a school classroom.

If a regulation were adopted by school officials forbidding discussion of the Vietnam conflict, or the expression by any student of opposition to it anywhere on school property except as part of a prescribed classroom exercise, it would be obvious that the regulation would violate the constitutional rights of students, at least if it could not be justified by a showing that the students' activities would materially and substantially disrupt the work and discipline of the school. In the circumstances of the present case, the prohibition of the silent, passive "witness of the armbands," as one of the children called it, is no less offensive to the Constitution's guarantees. . . .

Black, dissenting:

The Court's holding in this case ushers in what I deem to be an entirely new era in which the power to control pupils by the elected "officials of state supported public schools . . . " in the United States is in ultimate effect transferred to the Supreme Court. . . . Ordered to refrain from wearing the armbands in school by the elected school officials and the teachers vested with state authority to do so, apparently only seven out of the school system's 18,000 pupils deliberately refused to obey the order. . . .

Assuming that the Court is correct in holding that the conduct of wearing armbands for the purpose of conveying political ideas is protected by the First Amendment, the crucial remaining questions are whether students and teachers may use the schools at their whim as a platform for the exercise of free speech—"symbolic" or "pure"—and whether the courts will allocate to themselves the function of deciding how the pupils' school day will be spent. While I have always believed that, under the First and Fourteenth Amendments, neither the State nor the Federal Government has any authority to regulate or censor the content of speech, I have never believed that any person has a right to give speeches or engage in demonstrations where he pleases and when he pleases. This Court has already rejected such a notion. In *Cox v. Louisiana*, for example, the Court clearly stated that the rights of free speech and assembly "do not mean that everyone with opinions or beliefs to express may address a group at any public place and at any time."

While the record does not show that any of these armband students shouted, used profane language, or were violent in any manner, detailed testimony by some of them shows their armbands caused comments, warnings by other students, the poking of fun at them, and a warning by an older football player that other nonprotesting students had better let them alone. There is also evidence that a teacher of mathematics had his lesson period practically "wrecked," chiefly by disputes with Mary Beth Tinker, who wore her armband for her "demonstration." Even a casual reading of the record shows that this armband did divert students' minds from their regular lessons, and that talk, comments, etc., made John Tinker "self-conscious" in attending school with his armband. While the absence of obscene remarks or boisterous and loud disorder perhaps justifies the Court's statement that the few armband students did not actually "disrupt" the classwork, I think the record overwhelmingly shows that the armbands did exactly what the elected school officials and principals foresaw they would, that is, took the students' minds off their classwork and diverted them to thoughts about the highly emotional subject of the Vietnam war. And I repeat that, if the time has come when pupils of state-supported schools, kindergartens, grammar schools, or high schools, can defy and flout orders of school officials to keep their minds on their own schoolwork, it is the beginning of a new revolutionary era of permissiveness in this

country fostered by the judiciary. The next logical step, it appears to me, would be to hold unconstitutional laws that bar pupils under 21 or 18 from voting, or from being elected members of the boards of education. . . .

. . . The truth is that a teacher of kindergarten, grammar school, or high school pupils no more carries into a school with him a complete right to freedom of speech and expression than an anti-Catholic or anti-Semite carries with him a complete freedom of speech and religion into a Catholic church or Jewish synagogue. Nor does a person carry with him into the United States Senate or House, or into the Supreme Court, or any other court, a complete constitutional right to go into those places contrary to their rules and speak his mind on any subject he pleases. It is a myth to say that any person has a constitutional right to say what he pleases, where he pleases, and when he pleases. Our Court has decided precisely the opposite.

In my view, teachers in state-controlled public schools are hired to teach there. Although Mr. Justice McReynolds may have intimated to the contrary in *Meyer v. Nebraska*, certainly a teacher is not paid to go into school and teach subjects the State does not hire him to teach as a part of its selected curriculum. Nor are public school students sent to the schools at public expense to broadcast political or any other views to educate and inform the public. The original idea of schools, which I do not believe is yet abandoned as worthless or out of date, was that children had not yet reached the point of experience and wisdom which enabled them to teach all of their elders. It may be that the Nation has outworn the old-fashioned slogan that "children are to be seen, not heard," but one may, I hope, be permitted to harbor the thought that taxpayers send children to school on the premise that, at their age, they need to learn, not teach. . . .

Change has been said to be truly the law of life, but sometimes the old and the tried and true are worth holding. The schools of this Nation have undoubtedly contributed to giving us tranquility and to making us a more law-abiding people. Uncontrolled and uncontrollable liberty is an enemy to domestic peace. We cannot close our eyes to the fact that some of the country's greatest problems are crimes committed by the youth, too many of school age. School discipline, like parental discipline, is an integral and important part of training our children to be good citizens—to be better citizens. Here a very small number of students have crisply and summarily refused to obey a school order designed to give pupils who want to learn the opportunity to do so. One does not need to be a prophet or the son of a prophet to know that, after the Court's holding today, some students in Iowa schools—and, indeed, in all schools—will be ready, able, and willing to defy their teachers on practically all orders. This is the more unfortunate for the schools since groups of students all over the land are already running loose, conducting break-ins, sit-ins, lie-ins, and smash-ins. Many of these student groups, as is all too familiar to all who read the newspapers and watch the television news programs, have already engaged in rioting, property seizures, and destruction. They have picketed schools to force students not to cross their picket lines, and have too often violently attacked earnest but frightened students who wanted an education that the pickets did not want them to get. Students engaged in such activities are apparently confident that they know far more about how to operate public school systems than do their parents, teachers, and elected school officials. It is no answer to say that the particular students here have not yet reached such high points in their demands to attend classes in order to exercise their political pressures. Turned loose with lawsuits for damages and injunctions against their teachers as they are here, it is nothing but wishful thinking to imagine that young, immature students will not soon believe it is their right to control the schools, rather than the right of the States that collect the taxes to hire the teachers for the benefit of the pupils. . . .

4

THE MEDIA

The Supreme Court has made no theoretical distinctions between the freedoms of speech and press. They are mentioned together in the First Amendment and together they refer to expression and communication. Nonetheless, there are important structural and circumstantial differences between the two. In most "speech" cases in the last chapter, relatively few persons—often only one—communicated often with relatively few others, usually in local, face-to-face encounters. But the "press" in freedom of the press typically refers to communication with many persons, even a mass audience, through "media." Though once referring mainly to newspapers and other printed publications, these vehicles now include radio, television, motion pictures, telegraph, telephone, recordings, and the Internet. Much of the media today is composed of large, resourceful organizations created and conducted for profit. Much of what is communicated is entertainment and "commercial speech"—advertisements and other business communications—rather than communication of ideas and opinions on government or public issues. These characteristics do not dilute First Amendment protection but they generate complex countervailing interests that often differ from those in the speech cases of the last chapter.

The value of press freedom in representative government, especially in a democracy, cannot be overstated. Historically, communications media have been the chief sources of public information about government and its policies and chief vehicles for dissenting views. In a socially diverse society with formidable centrifugal forces, the media are also a chief means by which support for government may be mobilized and a sense of social and political unity affirmed. Justice Lewis Powell put it succinctly,

> An informed public depends on accurate and effective reporting by the news media. No individual can obtain for himself the information needed for the intelligent discharge of his political responsibilities. For most citizens the prospect of personal familiarity with newsworthy events is hopelessly unrealistic. In seeking out the news the press therefore acts as an agent of the public at large. It is the means by which the people receive that free flow of information and ideas essential to intelligent self-government.

[Dissenting opinion in *Saxbe v. Washington Post*, 417 U.S. 843 (1974) at 863]

The media then have a paradoxical double role. They are agents of the public, its eyes and ears, and often its critical voice. They *represent* nearly every bit as much as elected officials. Yet each medium is made up of profit-seeking vehicles with interests of their own. How comfortably public responsibility rides with private venture is of continuing, perhaps endless, concern in a free democratic society.

Freedom for the media may conflict with other important, legitimate ends, including the realization of other rights and liberties. These competing ends seldom include that of keeping public order, so important in cases of the previous chapter, and only slightly more often national security and preservation of government. Media freedom is most likely to be challenged by interests we have not yet considered. These include protecting reputation and privacy, guarding public decency and morality, preventing misrepresentation and fraud, securing the fairness of trials and other proceedings, and the government's need for information confidentially obtained. The cases in this chapter show how the Supreme Court has tried to balance those interests with media freedom, starting with its earliest press decisions almost 75 years ago.

Prior Restraints

Prior restraints are the classic limitation on communication. They were institutionalized in England with the licensing of those who had early printing presses shortly after development of that device in the late fifteenth century, and remained in force until repealed in 1695. By requiring printed material first be approved by authorities, licensing allowed the state and the established church to prevent blasphemous, heretical, seditious or simply hostile publication. When the American Bill of Rights was ratified in 1790, the speech and press clauses were meant to protect against prior restraints as those sanc-

tions were known historically. Historians differ on whether the clauses were intended to go beyond this protection.

Prior restraint is synonymous with "censorship" and averse to a free marketplace of opinion and information. The intended communication does not take place because it is stopped before reaching its audience or the public and so never enters the marketplace at all. The rule against prior restraint does not prevent punishment if speech or publication does harm, but that sanction must be imposed *after* communication takes place, and is usually given effect through a criminal prosecution or civil action.

The procedural differences between prior restraint and later punishment are substantial. Because prior restraints can be imposed by injunction, they are often easier to initiate than criminal prosecutions, which require indictment, arraignment, pretrial motions, and selection of a jury before a trial even starts. As actions in equity, injunctions can be obtained by simple application to a judge sitting without a jury. They may issue on the government's offer of "clear and convincing" proof of harm, a much lighter evidentiary burden than the guilt-beyond-a-reasonable-doubt standard demanded in a prosecution.

One of the Court's earliest and most important free press cases, *Near v. Minnesota*, 1931 (p. 231), dealt directly with the issue of prior restraint. In the 1920s, the Minnesota legislature passed an unusual "gag" law that allowed a "malicious, scandalous, and defamatory newspaper, magazine, or other periodical" to be stopped from further publication by court order. Near, publisher of *The Saturday Press,* a weekly that featured scandal and sensational reporting, alleged that Minneapolis officials, including the mayor and police chief, were working with gangsters and racketeers. Offended officials used the law to enjoin further publication of the paper. When the state supreme court upheld the order, Near appealed to the United States Supreme Court.

Though the gag law did not require publications first be submitted to government censors as English licensing laws had, the Court nonetheless found it an unconstitutional prior restraint. The law suppressed future publication because of the content of past issues. For the Court's majority of five, Chief Justice Charles Evans Hughes held prior restraints were constitutional only in exceptional circumstances where, for example, national security, or controlling incitement to violence, or obscenity were at issue. None of these interests were threatened by Near's publication. The decision was also important for another reason: the Court held freedom of the press in the First Amendment to be part of due process of law and thus a limit on state power through the Fourteenth Amendment. In *Gitlow v. New York*, as we saw in the previous chapter, the Court had already said freedom of speech was part of due process, but because it had upheld Gitlow's conviction on other grounds the point was merely a dictum. *Near v. Minnesota* was thus the first case in which the Court used a nonproperty right in the Bill of Rights to strike down a state law.

National security was the issue in the Pentagon Papers case, 40 years later, in which the federal government tried for the first and only time to suppress publication through injunction. During the Vietnam War, a government scientist disillusioned with American policies, illegally copied and then leaked a 7,000-page classified government study "History of the United States Decision-making Processes on Vietnam Policy"—the Pentagon Papers—to the *New York Times* and *Washington Post*. The document revealed how much secrecy and deception had formed war policy. When the two newspapers began printing it in serialized form, the Justice Department got a temporary restraining order from a federal district judge halting publication. Though the study dealt only with past policies and was thus a "history," the government argued that publishing it would jeopardize present and future war policy. The restraining order was quickly appealed by the newspapers. Because it restricted speech that might be constitutionally protected, the case move rapidly, bypassing the intermediate Court of Appeals and going directly to the Supreme Court. All this occurred within

10 days; the Court decided the case five days after that.

In *New York Times v. United States*, 1971 (p. 235), voting 6-3 and issuing only a three-paragraph per curiam opinion, the Court vacated the restraining order, and the newspapers immediately resumed printing the report. The government, the Court ruled, had not met the "heavy burden" of proof needed to justify a prior restraint. The decision was a blow to censorship, but it also showed deep division among the justices, made worse by the haste with which the case was heard and decided. The per curiam opinion gave little guidance for the future and no sound defense of freedom of the press. Adding to the uncertainty, each of the nine justices wrote an opinion of his own. These ranged from near absolute rejection of all prior restraints, to rejection unless the government could show national security would be endangered, to a willingness to sustain the injunction until issues could be argued more deliberately in the lower courts.

Neither this decision nor *Near* would bar a prosecution if publication violated criminal laws. In the Pentagon Papers matter, the government later indicted Daniel Ellsberg, who had leaked the information, for theft, espionage, and conspiracy. Because no documents were stolen or information given to a foreign power and the "law" violated was not a criminal statute but an executive order setting up the classification scheme, the case against him was weak and eventually collapsed.

Injunctions are not the only devices of prior restraint. Many cities and towns require permits before public space, including streets, can be used for speech or demonstration. As we saw in the previous chapter, these arrangements are constitutional only where clear guidelines leave officials little or no discretion to deny permits because they do not like the "message." Newspapers were subject of a local restriction in *Lakewood v. Plain Dealer Publishing Co.*, 1988, in which the city's mayor had authority to issue permits for sidewalk vending machines. Though conceding the city could regulate vending racks on its

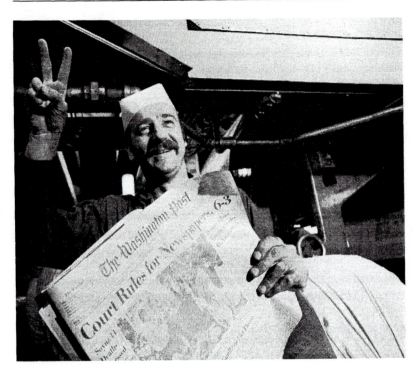

A big victory. The chief of presses at *The Washington Post* celebrates the Supreme Court's decision in *New York Times v. United States,* June 30, 1971. The *Post* and the *Times* immediately resumed their serialized publication of the "Pentagon Papers."

streets, the Court held that the ordinance gave the mayor almost complete discretion and thus raised "a substantial threat of . . . censorship."

Prior restraint licensing systems may be highly structured institutions as they were for many years in the control of movie exhibition. From their earliest days, movies were widely believed to have an "immoral" influence, and many states and cities subjected them to censorship review. Typically, this arrangement required films scheduled for state or local exhibition first be licensed by a government board. Denial of a license meant that the film could not be shown in that jurisdiction, at least not without prescribed editing. Directed at content, these procedures were classic prior restraints. In an early challenge in *Mutual Film Corp. v. Ohio,* 1915, they were sustained, the Supreme Court holding that movies were "a business pure and simple, organized and conducted for profit . . . not to be regarded . . . as part of the press of the country or as organs of public opinion." With this estimate of the medium, not unusual for the time, government was free to reg-

ulate or license movies as though they were simply another item of commerce.

By the 1950s, however, movies were widely recognized as a serious and important medium of communication, and the Supreme Court's expansive free speech doctrine was reaching well beyond "political" ideas and opinion. When the New York State Motion Picture Division refused to license Roberto Rossellini's short film "The Miracle" because it was "sacrilegious," the stage was set for a constitutional challenge. In *Burstyn v. Wilson,* 1952, the Supreme Court invalidated the Division's rejection and, undoing the Mutual Film decision, read movies into the speech and press protections of the First Amendment. As a content-specific standard, "sacrilegious," could not be a reason for barring exhibition. But the Court did not hold prior censorship of the medium unconstitutional, thereby assigning the movies a kind of second-class status within the First Amendment.

For several years, the Court continued to narrow movie censorship, holding such substantive standards as "indecent," "immoral," and "harmful" unconstitutional as criteria for denying exhibition permits. In *Freedman v. Maryland*, 1965, it imposed certain procedural requirements on the censorship boards though, again, stopping short of finding prior review unconstitutional. Boards would need to be prompt in reviewing a film. Should they deny a license, they would need go to court immediately and, once there, carry the burden of proving the film to be outside First Amendment protection rather than the exhibitor or distributor needing to show the film protected. To prevent long trials during which an unlicensed film would be out of the marketplace, the Court also required that judicial determination be prompt. These decisions narrowing the substantive standards of censorship and imposing procedural rigor enervated prior censorship as an institution. Denial of exhibition permits became so hard to sustain that most states and cities with boards of review abandoned them. Maryland's was the last to go in 1981.

Though the postal system is not a substantive medium of speech or press, it is a chief distributor for print communication. Denial of access to the mails, though not preventing publication, curbs circulation. For magazines and other periodicals dependent on subscriptions, such exclusion can be ruinous. The Postal Service has long had power to keep fraudulent and obscene material from the mails. We have already seen that the Supreme Court upheld Congress's wartime extension of it to seditious matter in the 1917 Espionage Act. In World War II, the Postal Service confiscated many foreign periodicals and books thought to be politically suspect. During the early Cold War period, many publications from Communist countries, including the Russian newspapers *Pravda* and *Izvestia*, were intercepted and not delivered. The practice was stopped by presidential order in 1961, but the next year Congress authorized the postmaster general to deliver foreign mailing of "Communist political propaganda" only if the addressee made a request in writing. In *Lamont v. Postmaster General*, 1965, the Supreme Court held this to be an unconstitutional abridgment of the addressee's First Amendment rights.

Communication and expression not protected by the First Amendment can be kept from the mails, but the Supreme Court has been emphatic that the Postal Service has no general powers of censorship. In *Hannegan v. Esquire*, 1946, it unanimously struck down the postmaster general's order withholding a second-class mailing permit from *Esquire*, because he believed the magazine to be "morally improper."

As we have seen, not all prior restraints look alike or operate in the same way. Though the Court has been particularly sensitive to their chief defect—exclusion of communication from the marketplace of ideas—it has not held all prior restraint to be beyond the constitutional pale. Here, as in many other cases we will deal with in the remainder of the chapter, a fully developed theory of press freedom continues to be elusive.

Regulation of the Media as Business

Because of their complex relationship to public authority, particularly as vehicles of information and comment about that authority, the media have been affected by a wide range of laws and government regulations. It is now well settled that freedom of the press does not give media an immunity from laws that apply to business generally. In *Associated Press v. National Labor Relations Board*, 1937, for example, Supreme Court upheld federal nondiscriminatory labor regulations that did not affect news gathering or distribution. Nor are the media exempt from antitrust laws. As Justice Hugo Black put the matter in *Associated Press v. United States*, 1945, "Freedom to publish means freedom for all and not for some. Freedom to publish is guaranteed by the Constitution, but freedom to combine to keep others from publishing is not ... The First Amendment affords not the slightest support for the contention that a combination to restrain trade in

news and views has any constitutional immunity."
[326 U.S. 1 at 20]

Media are subject to nondiscriminatory taxes, but the Court is apt to look closely at a levy to make sure it is not a "deliberate and calculated device . . . to limit the circulation of information." In the 1930s, the Louisiana legislature, controlled by the state's flamboyant populist governor Huey Long, imposed a 2 percent tax on gross advertising receipts of newspapers having weekly circulations of more than 20,000. This meant the tax affected only 13 of 163 newspapers in the state, all but one of which had opposed the Long regime. In *Grosjean v. American Press Co.,* 1936, the Court struck this measure down as a transparent attack on what the newspapers had to say and thus a violation of the First Amendment.

A tax singling out the media may be invalid even if innocent of censorial design. In *Minnesota Star and Tribune Co. v. Minnesota Commissioner of Revenue,* 1983, the Court, though making it clear that media were subject to nondiscriminatory business taxes, nonetheless struck down the state's special "use" tax on newsprint and ink. Though without punitive motive, the levy was aimed at the press and so could not be justified simply by the need to raise revenue. In contrast, in *Leathers v. Medlock,* 1991, the Court upheld extension of the Arkansas sales tax to cable television service though the tax exempted the print media. A tax may discriminate among media as long as it is not content-based or motivated by antipathy to particular ideas or content.

Access of the Media to Trials and Other Work of Government

Reporting judicial proceedings is a special problem for freedom of the press. In democratic society, a watchdog media informs the public about the government's acts, encourages discussion of its policies, and allows popular pressures to be brought back to government. But a trial, whether civil or criminal, is designed to be a calm, deliberative inquiry in which an unbiased finder of fact, judge or jury, reaches a just deci-

sion from carefully examined evidence. It is meant to be free of popular pressures. Constitutionally, civil litigants and criminal defendants are entitled to fair trials as a matter of due process of law under the Fifth and Fourteenth Amendments.

But in the United States, the media have traditionally had wide freedom to cover judicial proceedings. In the case of a crime, this often starts with police investigation and may include reporting every scrap of information about a suspect, who may later become an indicted defendant. For sensational crimes, this can lead to "trial by newspaper" and a prejudging of the defendant that may make it hard to impanel an unbiased jury. Potential for conflict between freedom of the press and fair trial has grown with advancing media technology and the ever-larger audiences that can be reached. Not all free-speech societies allow as much latitude in reporting judicial proceedings. In Great Britain, for example, media are routinely put under restraint about what they may publish about a pending prosecution and later trial.

The Supreme Court reversed a criminal conviction because of prejudicial publicity for the first time in the 1961 case, *Irvin v. Dowd.* The confession of the defendant, who was accused of six murders, had been widely and sensationally reported as had other investigatory details of the case. As a result, more than 400 prospective jurors had to be examined to select a panel of 12. Most of those dismissed had fixed opinions about the defendant's guilt. Eight of the impaneled jurors admitted that it would take evidence to persuade them the defendant was not guilty, thus reversing the burden of proof carried by prosecution and defense. The Court did not address responsibilities of the press or offer guidelines for covering criminal trials, but the circumstances of the case prompted concurring Justice Felix Frankfurter to remark caustically that though "the minds of potential jurors were poisoned, the poisoner is constitutionally protected in plying his trade."

Five years later, in *Sheppard v. Maxwell* (p. 240), the Court heard an appeal from a conviction in

Dr. Sam Sheppard kisses his second wife, Ariane, Sept. 8, 1966, after pleading not guilty in a new trial for the murder of his first wife ten years before. At left is son Samuel Reese Sheppard; at right, attorney F. Lee Bailey. Though acquitted, Sheppard was unable to resume his medical career, fell into alcohol abuse, and died of liver disease in 1970 at age 46.

one of the most widely and sensationally reported crimes and criminal trials in the annals of American justice. From the time that Sam Sheppard, a Cleveland osteopath, first came under police suspicion for the murder of his wife, the media turned the case into what the Court later termed a "carnival." The same atmosphere pervaded the courtroom, which was dominated by the media and its needs. Overturning the conviction as a violation of Sheppard's due process rights, the Court was severely critical of the trial judge. He could have insulated the jury and witnesses, prevented police and prosecutors from releasing leads and gossip, which often turned out to be false, and better controlled the media inside the courtroom.

After the Sheppard decision, many trial judges were more aggressive in protecting defendants and insulating jurors from prejudicial publicity in sensational cases. But in *Nebraska Press Association v. Stuart,* 1976, the Court unanimously held that a "gag" order imposed directly on the media went too far and acted as an unconstitutional prior restraint. For 11 weeks the press had been under a restraining order not to publish a confession and other facts that linked the defendant to the gruesome murders of six members of a family. It did not say all direct restraining orders on the media were forbidden, only that an absolute need for one had not been shown in the case. Remedial steps outlined in *Sheppard,* such as change of venue (relocation of the trial), sequestration of the jurors, and restraining orders on the parties and their lawyers, it said, might have been used to protect neutrality of the trial.

When the Court first dealt with televised trial coverage in *Estes v. Texas,* 1961, a case in which the defendant objected, it found such reporting inherently prejudicial to a fair trial. Returning to the issue in *Chandler v. Florida,* 1981, it concluded that televising did not per se violate the defendant's due process rights. Noting that the medium's equipment was now less cumbersome and distracting, it held that a state might experiment with such coverage.

After *Sheppard,* many judges resorted to closing certain pretrial hearings to the press. Such action was sustained in *Gannett Co. v. DePasquale,* 1979, in which neither prosecutor nor defendant objected to closing a hearing on admissibility of evidence. The majority of the Court held that the Sixth Amendment's guarantee of a public trial was a right of the accused not of the press. But the following year, the Court limited the ruling by holding that a trial itself could not be closed, even if both prosecution and defense agreed otherwise. In *Richmond Newspapers v. Virginia*, 1980, the trial court had granted the defendant's motion to exclude the press because three previous trials on the same charge, murder, could not be brought to verdict. The Court held, as it had not in *Gannett*, that the press and public had First Amendment rights to attend criminal trials, but the justices could not agree on how the right might be limited, if at all.

The *Richmond* theory has been extended in later cases. In *Globe Newspapers v. Superior Court*, 1982, the Court in striking down a Massachusetts law that required closing of the courtroom to the media and public during the testimony of minors who were victims of unlawful sexual acts, held that open proceedings were the rule. Closing would require a showing of reasonable fear of harm to the minor. Access to voir dire proceedings—the pretrial screening of prospective jurors—was held to be a First Amendment right in *Press Enterprise Co. v. Superior Court*, 1984, in which the trial judge had closed all but a few days of a six-week selection. As in *Globe Newspapers*, the Court reaffirmed the "presumption of openness," but did say there might be circumstances in which protection of the privacy rights of prospective jurors was a "compelling interest."

The media cannot be penalized for publishing truthful information lawfully obtained from public records or proceedings, even though the information intruded on individual privacy. In *Cox Broadcasting v. Cohn*, 1975, the Court held a television station not liable for publishing a rape victim's name where the information was from courthouse records open to the public. A similar result was obtained in *Florida Star v. B.J.F.*, 1989, in which a newspaper had gotten the name of a rape victim from a publicly released police report. And in *Landmark Communications v. Virginia*, 1978, those who were not official parties to a judicial disciplinary hearing could not be punished for publishing truthful information about a confidential issue. As the Court said in the *Florida Star* case, "where a newspaper publishes truthful information which it has lawfully gotten, punishment may lawfully imposed, if at all, only where narrowly tailored to a state interest of the highest order." [435 U.S. 829 at 851]

The Court has taken a different approach where restrictions are placed on interviewing prisoners and reporting on jailhouse conditions. In the companion cases of *Pell v. Procunier* and *Saxbe v. Washington Post Co.*, 1974, dealing with the California and federal prison systems, it upheld certain limits on interviews, citing prison security and discipline. And in a 4-3 decision in *Houchins v. KQED*, 1978, it sustained a sheriff's refusal to allow a television station to photograph a section of the county jail where an inmate had committed suicide or interview fellow prisoners. Noting that the jail had monthly tours open to the public, a plurality of the justices held the media did not have access rights greater than those of the public. It distinguished the right of access to information from the right to publish information already obtained.

Access *to* the Media

Because the media are powerful and protected vehicles for gathering and reporting information and giving opinion, should there be rights of access *to* them, where they may have valuable but unreported information or where identified persons have been editorially criticized? In several cases, the Supreme Court has been asked to balance these interests against freedom of the press.

The Need for Information in Public Inquiries

Certain relationships are recognized as privileged by statute or common law in almost every jurisdiction. These include doctor-patient, lawyer-client, pastor-confessor, and husband-wife. Because of

The Newsman and the Accused: the Case of M.A. Farber and "Dr. X"

In late 1975, the *New York Times* published an award-winning series on the mysterious deaths of several patients at an Oradell, N. J. hospital, 10 years before. Written by M. A. Farber, an investigative reporter, the articles suggested the deaths were caused by overdose injections of curare, a muscle-relaxant, deliberately administered by an unnamed "Dr. X." They soon led to the indictment of Dr. Mario Jascalevich, chief of surgery at the hospital, for the murders of five of the patients.

During the trial, the longest in New Jersey's history, the defense asked for Farber's investigative notes and other materials he had gotten in the case including a report of a toxicologist who had since died. It argued that Farber had worked closely with the prosecutor's office in his research. Without requiring the defense be more specific in what it was looking for, the trial judge, William Arnold, issued a broad subpoena on Farber and the *Times* to submit the materials to him so that he could decide whether they were of use to the defense. When the reporter and newspaper refused, Arnold held them each in civil and criminal contempt of court.

On the civil charge, Farber was ordered to jail until he complied with the order; on the criminal, he was sentenced to six months to start after he complied. He was also fined $2,000. The *Times* was fined $100,000 on the criminal charge and $5,000 a day on the civil until it complied. Farber and the *Times* argued that the judge's order violated both the First Amendment and New Jersey's "shield" law that gave journalists a right not to disclose investigatory materials or sources. They asked for a hearing on these questions, but Arnold refused, saying he could not rule on the merits of the arguments until Farber and the *Times* submitted the materials. A petition for a temporary stay of the order was turned down by the New Jersey Supreme Court and, later, by two justices of the U.S. Supreme Court, Byron White and Thurgood Marshall. Each cited the absence of a constitutional right of the press to withhold information needed in an official proceeding.

Still refusing to comply, Farber was confined and the *Times* began to pay its daily fine. In the meantime, the Jascalevich trial continued and two months later ended with the defendant's acquittal. The verdict also ended Farber's open-ended civil sentence—he had served forty days—and the *Times's* civil fine. In all, the newspaper had paid $285,000 in penalties.

On appeal of the contempt charges, the New Jersey Supreme Court sustained Arnold in *In re Farber and the New York Times*, 1978. It relied largely on *Branzberg v. Hayes* and the Watergate decision of *United States v. Nixon*, 1974, in which the U.S. Supreme Court held that the president's right to the confidentiality of taped conversations with subordinates had to yield, at least to a judge's *in camera* examination, where the material was needed in a criminal trial. The New Jersey court also held that the state's shield law, similar to those in 27 other states at the time, violated an accused person's Sixth Amendment right to "have compulsory process for obtaining witnesses in his favor." The United States Supreme Court declined to review the decision. The governor of New Jersey eventually pardoned Farber on the criminal contempt charge and returned $100,000 in fines to the *Times*.

The press's position in cases like *Branzberg* and *In re Farber* has had legislative support reflected in the passage of shield laws. But these laws confer statutory not constitutional rights. Though lower courts have often interpreted these statutes liberally, the number of annual subpoenas issued to journalists for production of notes, increased markedly after *Branzberg* and *Farber*. In the meantime, courts have struggled to prevent journalists from becoming targets of "fishing expeditions" yet not exempt them from the obligations of every citizen to give testimony where justice may require it. As a civil liberties problem, conflict of the press's right to be free of forced disclosures and a criminal defendant's right to a fair trial has no easy or certain resolution.

---

the value accorded confidentiality, the parties in these relationships cannot be forced to reveal what has passed between them. On constitutional grounds the media have claimed the same status for the relationship of reporters to their informants. The interest is not one of intimacy and privacy but that of not inhibiting the giving of information to the press. Protecting confidentiality as part of news gathering, it is argued, is but an extension of protecting publication. The claim to such a privileged relationship can collide, however, with the need to have information in official inquiries.

The Supreme Court first took up the matter in three cases heard together in 1972 in which reporters refused to comply with grand jury orders to disclose certain information they had obtained about criminal matters under investigation. Two dealt with activities of the Black Panthers, a radical group advocating violence as a way of political protest, the third with the making and use of illegal drugs. The Court decided the appeals together in *Branzberg v. Hayes* (p. 242), narrowly holding that journalists do not have a constitutional right to withhold information obtained in confidence when that information is needed for "fair and effective law enforcement." The media have no greater right to hide criminal information than do members of the public.

Response to the decisions led to a proposal in Congress for a national shield law that would protect the confidentiality of sources. But when the media proved divided on the need for such a law, the matter was dropped. This did not keep several states from passing such laws or retaining those already enacted. These statutes vary greatly in who and what they protect and in how they are enforced. Many lower courts have interpreted the federal constitutional issue in *Branzberg* narrowly, partly because of the 5-4 vote and certain reservations expressed by a concurring member of the majority, Justice Powell. They have required government show how the information sought is relevant to a compelling interest and that it has no other way of getting it, all points made in Justice Potter Stewart's *dissenting* opinion in *Branzberg*. Courts have been more apt to impose these requirements in civil cases than in criminal.

In *Cohen v. Cowles Media Co.*, 1991, a case with an unusual twist, the Court partly reaffirmed the *Branzberg* principle. A campaign adviser to a Republican gubernatorial candidate in Minnesota had given damaging information about the Democratic candidate to reporters on condition they not identify him as the source. When they were overruled on this by their editors and Cohen's name was published, he sued the newspapers for breach of an oral contract. The Supreme Court held that the First Amendment did not protect against liability for compensatory damages (he had been fired from his job) if contract law has been broken.

A different conflict between the interests of the media and law enforcement arose in *Zurcher v. The Stanford Daily* in 1978. With a valid search warrant, police in Palo Alto, Calif., entered and searched the offices of *The Stanford Daily*, the day after a riot on the Stanford campus injured several police officers. The paper had printed a photograph of the incident that police believed might identify those who attacked the officers. Echoing its *Branzberg* principle, the Court held that the First Amendment did not give the media rights against a valid search warrant that other citizens did not have. Nor were law enforcement officials obliged first to try to get needed information through subpoena rather than search warrant.

Though newsroom searches are rare, the decision caused a furor in the media and in the ranks of many civil libertarians. This time it led to success in Congress. In the Privacy Protection Act of 1980, searches of journalists' work areas or work products are forbidden excerpt under special circumstances. These include situations where death or injury may be prevented, where needed information may be destroyed, where the subpoena has been ineffective, and where journalists themselves are thought to be party to a crime.

Fairness in Criticism and Opinion

Because of ever-greater concentration of media ownership, the opportunity for a small number of media persons to influence a large number of others may be greater today than ever before. Though most media organs welcome comment and strive for a semblance of fairness in offering points of view, it is probably impossible to represent all voices or be completely even-handed while still playing the role of critic and opinion leader. This has raised a question of whether fairness might be required by law without turning the media into a public utility.

In 1972, the *Miami Herald* published editorials critical of a candidate for the state legislature. He demanded the paper print his reply, under a Florida law that required a newspaper attacking the character or record of a candidate for public office to give free space to answer. The paper refused to do so. In *Miami Herald v. Tornillo,* 1974, the Supreme Court had little difficulty striking down the law as violating the First Amendment by interfering with editorial judgment. Though admitting that fewer newspapers and greater concentration of ownership might cause fewer contrasting views to be represented, the Court believed a legally mandated right of reply would discourage critical commentary.

What holds for newspapers, however, may not necessarily apply to the broadcast media. In the early days of commercial radio, a rush to broadcast resulted in a jamming of the airwaves with stations. Because broadcast frequencies are limited, too many stations using a band could interfere with reception and cause audial chaos. To deal with this, Congress passed the Radio Act of 1927, declaring the airwaves to be property of the United States and not the private stations. It also created and empowered the Federal Radio Commission to license broadcast stations and limit their number to prevent destructive jamming.

These provisions were incorporated into the more comprehensive Federal Communications Act of 1934, setting up the Federal Communications Commission (FCC) as an independent regulatory agency for limited government control of radio and, later, television broadcasting. A would-be broadcaster must apply for a license—five years for a television station, seven for radio—for exclusive use of a particular airwave frequency. Under the law, broadcasters are temporary trustees of the public airwaves, and thus the licenses, which may be renewed, are for "public interest, convenience, and necessity." The Supreme Court sustained this arrangement in

National Broadcasting Co. v. United States, 1943, holding simply that, "The right of free speech does not include . . . the right to use the facilities of radio without a license." [311 U.S. 190 at 225]

The FCC also used its licensing power to challenge the monopoly that broadcasters had on expression of views and opinions over the airwaves. To prevent the broadcasting of one-sided views on issues, it first ruled that stations could not editorialize. When this was strongly opposed by broadcasters, the Commission developed what became known as the Fairness Doctrine. This rule permitted editorials but required that other views also be aired. Where a personal attack or criticism was broadcast, it required a "right of reply."

The doctrine was unsuccessfully challenged in *Red Lion Broadcasting Co. v. FCC,* 1969 (p. 246), in which a broadcaster denied the author of a book opportunity to answer a personal attack. Citing the scarcity of airwave frequencies, the Court distinguished broadcasting from print media. Not only did the Fairness Doctrine help "preserve an uninhibited marketplace of ideas," it was "the right of the viewers and listeners, not the right of the broadcasters, which is paramount."

The FCC has ruled that broadcasters are not obliged to accept editorial advertising—paid announcements of particular views on social or political issues—but if they do, the Fairness Doctrine requires time be given to opposing views. When CBS refused editorial ads from a group wanting to criticize Vietnam War policies, the rule was challenged in *CBS v. Democratic National Committee,* 1973. Basing its decision on statutory rather than First Amendment interpretation, the Court held the Federal Communications Act did not require the agency "mandate a private right of access to the media."

Despite the decision in *Red Lion,* the Fairness Doctrine remained controversial and an object of media complaint. In 1987, the FCC announced it would no longer require overall balance in station programming, but the personal attack and political editorial elements of the doctrine would be retained.

In the Federal Election Campaign Act of 1971, Congress empowered the FCC to revoke licenses where broadcasters repeatedly denied candidates for federal elective office opportunity to buy time for editorial advertising. When CBS and two other national networks refused ads of the Carter-Mondale Presidential Election Committee in October 1979, arguing that the 1980 presidential campaign did not start until January 1980, the FCC ruled in favor of the committee. On appeal, in *CBS v. FCC,* 1981, the Supreme Court sustained the FCC. In contrast to *CBS v. Democratic National Committee,* in which it refused to create a general constitutional right of access, the Court upheld a limited statutory right of the same.

Though broadcast frequencies remain limited in number, recent advances in communications technology and the creation of new media, including cable television, satellites, and the Internet allow more voices to enter the marketplace of ideas and opinion. This has, in turn, reduced the importance of broadcasting access.

Commercial Speech

Though commercial speech does not have exact meaning in the law, it usually refers to information about a product or service offered for profit. Most, but not all, commercial speech is advertising. Because commercial messages were widely distrusted and thought to have less social utility than other communication, courts were slow to give them First Amendment protection. Laws have long regulated certain commercial speech in the public interest. In the Food and Drug Act 1906, for example, Congress barred mislabeled foods, drugs, and liquors from interstate commerce. In the Federal Trade Act of 1914, aimed mainly at unfair business practices, it set up the Federal Trade Commission and empowered it to penalize dishonest advertising. Three other federal agencies—the FCC, the Securities and Exchange Commission, and the U.S. Postal Service—also have power to protect against fraudulent commercial communications.

Even though the great mass of commercial speech was not untruthful or fraudulent, the Supreme Court on first review held it not to be part of freedom of the press. In the 1942 case of *Valentine v. Chrestensen,* an exhibitor of an old navy submarine had been barred under New York City's sanitation code from distributing handbills advertising his attraction. Upholding the code provision, which permitted circulation of political handbills, the Court reasoned that if communication was "purely commercial" it was no different from other forms of business activity and could be regulated accordingly.

For the next 30 years, the *Chrestensen* doctrine kept commercial speech outside the First Amendment. In *Breard v. Alexandria,* 1951, the Court was willing to extend it to door-to-door subscription sales of magazines, a medium clearly within the First Amendment, by upholding an ordinance requiring the householder's permission for such solicitation.

A hint of change came in *Pittsburgh Press v. Commission on Human Relations,* 1973, in which a newspaper challenged a municipal gender discrimination ordinance barring such designations as "male help wanted" and "female help wanted" in its classified employment ads. Though the Court upheld the ordinance, it said, "the exchange of information is as important in the commercial realm as in any other," suggesting there could be First Amendment protection of advertising for lawful ends.

This was exactly the distinction the Court made two years later in *Bigelow v. Virginia,* in which the editor of a Charlottesville weekly had been convicted under a state law barring advertisements for the "procuring of abortion," then illegal in the state. The ad at issue had been bought by a clinic in New York where abortion was legal. In an important retreat from *Chrestensen,* the Court held the ad to be protected speech because it had truthful information "of potential interest and value to a diverse audience" that included not merely women seeking abortion but anyone interested in the abortion issue.

The following year, the Court moved further from *Chrestensen* by holding that commercial speech having no connection with a public issue merited at least a degree of constitutional protection. In *Virginia State Board of Pharmacy v. Virginia Consumers Council*, it struck down a Virginia law that made it illegal to advertise the prices of prescription drugs. Stressing the utility to consumers of the free flow of commercial information, especially prices, the Court said that resources in a free enterprise economy were largely allocated "through numerous private economic decisions. It is a matter of public interest that these decisions . . . be intelligent and well-informed." [425 U.S. 748 at 765] The same reasoning was used in *Linmark Associates v. Willingboro*, 1977, noted in the previous chapter, to strike down a local ordinance barring "Sold" or "For Sale" signs in front of homes.

With the door to protecting commercial speech now opened, the Court moved to strike down a range of long-standing regulations barring or limiting the advertising of professional services. In *Bates v. State Bar of Arizona*, 1977, it invalidated a legally enforceable ethics code under which two lawyers had been censured by the state bar association for advertising their services and fees. The right to convey truthful information about services and fees and the right of those using legal services to have such information outweighed adverse effects on legal professionalism. By undermining bar associations' minimum fee schedules, the decision opened legal practice to greater competition. The Court made it clear, however, that certain professional standards might be enforced over a First Amendment claim. In *Ohralik v. Ohio State Bar Association*, a year after *Bates*, it upheld a disciplinary action against an attorney who had personally solicited clients. The Court distinguished the advertising of fees and services from direct solicitation where the possibility of "fraud, undue influence, or intimidation" is greater.

The Court soon extended protection of commercial speech to cover business spending for expression of views on public questions. At issue was a Massachusetts law that barred corporate election spending to influence voters on issues other than those affecting the business or property of the corporation itself. In *First National Bank v. Bellotti*, 1978, the Court held the law invalid as applied to a bank publicizing its opposition to a proposed constitutional amendment for a graduated income tax. Citing the previous commercial speech decisions, it said it would be an anomaly to protect information about prices and services but not the "political speech" of corporations.

The decision was followed in 1980 by *Consolidated Edison v. New York Public Service Commission* in which the Court, using a similar analysis, sustained a public utility's right to include flyers with its monthly bills discussing controversial public issues, in this instance, expansion of nuclear electrical power.

Finally, the same year in *Central Hudson Gas and Electric v. New York Public Service Commission* (p. 248), the Court announced a four-part test for commercial speech. To be protected, the commercial message must be truthful and not advocate illegal activity. For regulations to be sustained, the government's interest must be legitimate and substantial, the regulations must directly advance that interest, and must be narrowly drawn, being no greater than needed. Applying these criteria, the Court invalidated the commission's order that to save energy, the utility stop advertising to promote the use of electricity. The restriction was greater than necessary to serve the state's interest.

The Court has been more accommodating of restrictions on commercial speech where the advertised goods or services may be harmful. In *Posadas de Puerto Rico Associates v. Tourism Company of Puerto Rico*, 1986, for example, it upheld regulations that barred a legal gambling casino from advertising within the commonwealth but permitted it to advertise for tourists outside Puerto Rico. The regulations satisfied the *Central Hudson* requirements. Even though casino gambling was legal in Puerto Rico, the Court concluded the commonwealth's interest in discouraging excessive gambling by its citizens was "substantial."

In the last 30 years, commercial speech has gone from being a class outside the First Amendment to one having extensive if not full constitutional protection. It is still set apart from noncommercial speech because it must not be false, and the government's regulatory interest need only by "substantial" rather than "compelling." In addition, regulations need only be "no more extensive than necessary" rather than the "least restrictive means" required for noncommercial speech.

Defamation

Defamation is damage to reputation through communication to third parties. If proved, the law recognizes a tort injury—a civil wrong—and may award compensatory and possibly punitive damages to the injured plaintiff. Defamatory words in print are libel, if oral, slander, but with the complexities of modern communications technology the distinction has little utility today.

Historically, defamation could also be a seditious criminal act if the government or its officials were the object of the negative publication. Prosecution could be used, as it was with the Sedition Act of 1798, to inhibit criticism of the government and its officers. Today criminal or seditious libel laws have largely passed from the American legal and political scene. There is little doubt that the Supreme Court would hold such restrictions unconstitutional, short of their application to speech linked to an attempt to overthrow the government.

Civil defamation suits, however, challenge the media's freedom to comment on or criticize the behavior of public officials, nongovernmental public figures, and those who are purely private persons. In each instance, the countervailing interest to freedom of the press is protection of reputation against injury from irresponsible or malicious publication, though not publication arising from open discussion of public issues and personalities. Defamatory damage may include loss of standing in the community, loss of friends, a job, or opportunities.

The truth of a defamatory statement will usually make it legally defensible. But truth may not be easy to prove and where the statement is an opinion, may be beside the point. Whether the defamation was intentional, merely negligent, or completely inadvert, is important in determining liability and the damages that may be awarded. Certain classes of persons under limited circumstances are immune from defamation liability for what they say. These include legislators while engaged in law-making, and judges, lawyers, and witnesses at trial. In these circumstances, insuring the freest flow of information outweighs protection of reputation.

In two early First Amendment cases already discussed, *Near v. Minnesota,* 1931, and *Chaplinsky v. New Hampshire,* 1941, the Supreme Court observed that defamatory speech and certain other communication, such as "fighting words" obscenity, or incitement to crime, were unprotected classes of speech. But the first time the Court ruled on defamation as a constitutional issue was in *New York Times v. Sullivan,* 1964 (p. 251), where it opened the door to limited First Amendment protection for libelous publication. Sullivan, supervisor of police in Montgomery, Ala., sued over a full-page ad published in the *Times* and paid for by civil rights activists. A plea for donations to help fight segregation in the South, the ad described misconduct of police in dealing with students and activists taking part in protests at an Alabama college. Though Sullivan was not mentioned by name, he alleged injury because he was identifiable as the police supervisor. The ad contained several misstatements though most were trivial. Sullivan won the case in the Alabama courts and was awarded $500,000 in damages, very large compensation then by Alabama and national standards. The subtext of the case, of course, was the conflict over civil rights in the South and the generally sympathetic coverage given the civil rights movement by the national media. The large award and the expense of defending similar libel suits—at the time there were more than $5 million in libel claims pending against the *Times* in Alabama—might have inhibited media reporting of the civil rights struggle.

Premature celebration. L.B. Sullivan, second from right, a Montgomery, Ala., city commissioner and supervisor of police, and his attorneys celebrate their libel victory over the *New York Times* in the Alabama Supreme Court, in 1963. The judgment was overturned by the U.S. Supreme Court a year later in the landmark *New York Times v. Sullivan.*

As much a case about civil rights as the First Amendment, it might well have been titled *New York Times v. Alabama.*

Setting aside the judgment, a unanimous Supreme Court in an opinion by Justice William Brennan held that damaging comment about a public official was protected speech even if false unless it was made with "actual malice," defined as knowing falsity or a "reckless disregard" for truth or falsity. Mere negligence—carelessness—would not be enough to establish liability where the comment was about public officials. Three justices—Black, Douglas, and Goldberg—would have gone further and protected all comment about public officials no matter how reckless or malicious.

The *Times* case and those that soon followed cut a wide swath through traditional libel law. The Court quickly expanded the class of persons who would have less protection against false statements. In *Rosenblatt v. Baer,* 1966, for example, it included in "public officials," the supervisor of a county recreation area and in *Monitor Patriot Co. v. Roy,* 1971, a person who was only a candidate for public office, in this instance, the state legislature. In later cases, lower courts included in the public official category almost any government person in a position of "substantial responsibility." This has included tax assessors, school administrators, police officers, social workers, building inspectors, and Internal Revenue Service agents.

The Court soon expanded the public official group to "public figures"—persons in public life but not connected to government. In two cases decided together in 1967, *Associated Press v. Walker* and *Curtis Publishing Co. v. Butts,* the Court held that a retired army general who had repeatedly thrust himself into public controversies as a right-wing activist and a popular long-time University of Georgia football coach were both public figures. As libel plaintiffs, they carried the same heavier burden of proof as public officials. Walker had based his action on inaccuracies in an Associated Press report of his role in a student riot at the University of Mississippi following the appearance of the school's first black student. Butts's case was based on a *Saturday Evening Post* article that falsely stated he had "fixed" a Georgia football game by giving the team's plays to the opposing coach.

Each of the plaintiffs won in the lower courts. On appeal, the Supreme Court reversed Walker's judgment but sustained Butts's and clarified the meaning of the "actual malice" or reckless disregard for the truth. The misinformation in

The Friendly Persuader

Justice William J. Brennan served 34 years on the Supreme Court, 1956 to 1990, longer than all but five other justices. He wrote 1,360 opinions during this tenure, more than any other justice except William O. Douglas. Of these, 450 were Opinions of the Court. In his early years, Brennan was a mainstay of the Warren Court and helped underwrite its activism. In later years, when the Court's center of gravity shifted toward self-restraint, he recast himself as a dissenter. Still, he was often able to pull majorities together for liberal ends, a tribute to his intellectual skills and the personal charm he was able to work on his colleagues. His influence on the Court in the last half of the twentieth century and on American constitutional development, especially in the expansion of civil liberties, was monumental.

One of eight children of Irish immigrant parents who had met in the United States, Brennan was born and raised in Newark, N.J. His father, with little formal education, became a union leader and active in Democratic politics, for a dozen years serving as director of public safety in Newark. Young William, showing little enthusiasm for the hurly-burly world of local politics, excelled academically. He graduated with honors from the University of Pennsylvania and later ranked near the top of his law school class at Harvard. On graduation, he joined a leading New Jersey law firm and soon gained a reputation in labor law. On American entry into World War II, he enlisted and served as assistant to the Under Secretary of the Army, specializing in workforce problems created by war mobilization. Discharged as a colonel, he returned to postwar practice in New Jersey and became a leading member of the bar in working for court reform.

He soon gave up a lucrative career as a private attorney to become a trial judge in one of the new courts he had helped create. His rise in the judiciary was meteoric. Though a life-long Democrat, he was soon appointed to the state supreme court by a Republican governor impressed with his work on judicial reform. Three years later, in 1956, he was named to the U.S. Supreme Court by another Republican executive, Dwight Eisenhower. With the presidential election looming, Eisenhower, im-

---

Walker's case was from an Associated Press stringer's phone report during a fast-breaking news event that gave little time for thorough checking of accuracy. Under these circumstances, the defamatory reporting was not "reckless." In *Butts,* however, the misstatements were in an article prepared well in advance for a weekly magazine and were based on a questionable source that might easily have been checked further.

A public figure need not be someone nationally known. In *Greenbelt Cooperative Publishing Association v. Bresler,* 1970, a local real estate developer who had negotiated a controversial land sale to a municipality was held to be a public figure in the community, at least for that event. In *Time, Inc. v. Pape,* a year later, the Court again indicated that "actual malice" or "reckless disregard" would be a hard burden of proof to carry. It overturned a judgment a police officer had gotten for a *Time* magazine story about police brutality where the misstatements were from a report of the U.S. Civil Rights Commission. The Court held that *Time's* assumption that information in the report was accurate and did not need further checking was "at most an error of judgment" and not a reckless disregard of truth or falsity.

The *New York Times* decision and the cases that followed were new evidence of the Court's

pressed with Brennan's record, also saw political advantage in nominating a Northeastern Roman Catholic Democrat to the Court. In this the president was probably correct, but he later came to regret Brennan's liberalism.

Hardly an area of civil liberties exists in which Brennan has not left an important mark. On freedom of speech and press, he wrote the Court's opinion narrowing the right of public officials to recover defamation damages in *New York Times v. Sullivan* and the Court's opinion revising the obscenity test in *Roth v. United States.* He also spoke for the five-member majority in *Texas v. Johnson,* upholding protection for flag-burning as political protest. He helped lead the way in applying the Fourteenth Amendment's equal protection clause to strike down gender discrimination in *Frontiero v. Richardson* and *Craig v. Boren.* In 1964, in *Malloy v. Hogan* he held the Fifth Amendment's privilege against self-incrimination applicable to the states. In *Edwards v. Aguillard,* his majority opinion declared a Louisiana law requiring the teaching of creative science to be unconstitutional. In a number of cases his opinions for the Court, or in concurrence or dissent, strongly opposed capital punishment and strongly supported affirmative action.

One of his most important opinions was that for the Court in *Baker v. Carr,* holding that the issue of state legislative malapportionment was not a "political question," but one courts could hear. The long-run effect of this decision was the redistricting of scores of unequally apportioned law-making bodies, revitalizing representative government and eventually leading to the one-person, one-vote standard for apportionment.

Concluding that the more conservative Burger Court would take few new initiatives in civil liberties, Brennan wrote a widely influential law review article urging that state supreme court judges, of whom he had once been one, look to their state constitutions as sources of new protections for individual rights.

Brennan's activism was not without its critics and detractors who shuddered at his "radical egalitarianism" in transforming the Constitution, so they said, into a vehicle for social change. Others were dismayed by his insistence that the Constitution's essential meaning was to be found in contemporary values and sensibilities and by the slight weight he seemed to give the Framers' "original understanding." More neutral observers point to the irony of Brennan being a champion of individual rights yet a leading force in many decisions that enlarged the role of government in the life of the governed.

Critics and admirers both agree that his skills as a jurist and his ability to work quietly to build agreement among his fellows made him one of the most successful justices of his time. Though he disliked being called the Court's preeminent "politician," he was exactly that. His pragmatism and ebullient, engaging personality were effectively enlisted in winning interpretation of the Constitution.

Brennan retired from the Court in 1990 after suffering a minor stroke. He died seven years later at age 91.

---

expanding commitment to protecting a "wide open and robust" discussion of public issues and the acts of those in public life. The development was part of the larger one we have already noted, extension of First Amendment protection to communication well beyond "political" speech.

With the end of Warren Court era in the early 1970s, several justices began to express doubts about the reach of the public figure doctrine. An eventual, partial retreat was kindled by *Rosenbloom v. Metromedia,* 1971, in which the Court overturned a damage judgment for a magazine distributor who was arrested in a police crackdown on pornography. He had repeatedly been described as a "smut distributor" by a local radio station. When the magazines were found not obscene, Rosenbloom sued the station for defamation. The Court was deeply divided in the decision. Eight justices produced five separate opinions, but a plurality argued that the public figure rule should be extended to public issues even where the parties were private persons and wanted to remain so.

In *Gertz v. Robert Welch, Inc.,* 1974 (p. 254), the Court backed away from the fractured decision and adopted a position close to that of the case's dissenters. In doing so, it clarified the limits of defamation protection where the plaintiff was a private person. Gertz, an attorney, had been hired by the family of a youth killed by a policeman, to file a civil damages action against the officer. During the trial, an issue of *American Opinion*, an ultraconservative magazine owned by the defendant, claimed Gertz had helped "frame" the policeman, had a criminal record, and was a "Communist fronter." The Supreme Court held that Gertz did not become a public figure simply by being part of a public event. To prevail in a libel action, he need only prove that the false statements were published negligently rather than with malice or reckless disregard for their truth.

The decision braked the public figure doctrine, yet it also set out important protections for the media where the plaintiff was, like Gertz, a private person. The Court said that the common law standard of *strict* liability—liability even where the defamatory publication was entirely accidental, that is, without malice or negligence—in such cases would no longer hold. Liability would need to rest on a standard of fault. Nor would damages simply be presumed once defamation was shown, as they were at common law. All compensatory damages would need rest on proved not presumed injury. Finally, for punitive damages to be awarded, even a private-person plaintiff would need to prove the defendant acted with malice.

The Court wrestled further with the question of who fell into the public figure group. In *Time, Inc. v. Firestone*, 1976, it held that a prominent socialite did not become a public figure in the reporting of her divorce, however evocative her husband's allegations may have been. Private persons become public figures when they thrust themselves "into the forefront of particular public controversies in order to influence the resolution of issues involved." A defendant in a divorce does not meet this test and need only show that misstatements were negligently made. This rule was then applied to two other libel plaintiffs involuntarily thrust into the public's attention. In *Wolston v. Reader's Digest*, 1979, the Court held a person convicted of contempt for refusing to testify before a grand jury investigating Soviet espionage, did not become a public figure because of his conviction. And in *Hutchinson v. Proxmire*, also 1979, a research scientist who received a federal grant was later held up to public ridicule by being given a U.S. Senator's monthly "Golden Fleece Award" for supposed waste of the taxpayers' money. He had not become a public figure, the Court said, simply by being awarded a grant.

A public figure plaintiff, needing to prove malice, is entitled to probe the "state of mind" of the defendant publishers in pretrial discovery proceedings. This was the issue in *Herbert v. Lando*, 1979, in which the defendant producer of the television program *60 Minutes* refused to answer questions about his writing and editing of the program, on the ground that his editorial decisions were protected by the First Amendment. The Supreme Court held they were not.

At common law, an allegation of falsehood was presumed to be true until the defendant proved it otherwise. But in *Philadelphia Newspapers v. Hepps*, 1986, the Supreme Court reversed this burden of proof where the publication dealt with a matter of "public concern." The *Philadelphia Inquirer* had published a story alleging that a certain company had connections to organized crime. In a libel action by its chief stockholder, the Court held that because comment on public matters is at the heart of freedom of speech and press, some "breathing space" was needed even if it meant protection for an occasional falsehood or misstatement.

But in changing another common law rule, the Court has held that statements of opinion do not have "wholesale" protection. In *Milkovich v. Lorain Journal Co.*, 1990, a high school wrestling coach sued over a sports columnist's insinuation that he had perjured himself in an investigation of a brawl that took place during a match. The Constitution, the Court said, does not confer blanket immunity from liability on those who publish opinions any more than it does on those who publish supposed fact.

What then of a statement of "fact" that is not factual at all but a parody? The question arose when a well-known television evangelist sued *Hustler* magazine after it published a satirical "ad" in which he described his first sexual experience as being with his mother in an outhouse while drunk. Though a jury found the ad, which was labeled a parody, not defamatory because no reasonable person would understand it to be a factual account, it nonetheless awarded damages for emotional distress. The Supreme Court in *Hustler Magazine v. Falwell*, 1988 (p. 259), agreeing that the account was not libelous, overturned the damage award. A public figure may not recover for the intentional infliction of emotional distress resulting from publication unless false statements of "fact" are shown to have been made

Larry Flynt, publisher of Hustler magazine, holds the offending "advertisement" lampooning the sex life of television evangelist Jerry Falwell, which produced Falwell's lawsuit, eventually appealed to the Supreme Court in *Falwell v. Hustler Magazine*, 1988.

with malice. In this case, the Court said, the publication was an obvious lampoon, so there were no statements of fact. It reaffirmed the First Amendment's protection of political and social caricature, cartoon, and satire even where they may be "slashing and one-sided," and go beyond "good taste." Vicious attacks on public figures, it said, are not outside the American tradition of political commentary.

A different aspect of personal portrayal arises with the controversial journalistic practice of constructing quotations. In a magazine article about the firing of the director of Freud Archives, extensive interview quotations were used that made him seem shallow and boastful. In bringing suit, he alleged these attributions were not accurate and did not represent what he had said. In *Masson v. New Yorker*, 1991, the Supreme Court held that though the First Amendment protected some editing of attributable quotations beyond grammar and syntax, deliberate changes would amount to malice if they led to a "material change in the meaning of the statement." Whether the contested quotations did or did not, the Court said, were questions of fact for a jury to decide, and it remanded the case to the trial court for further proceedings.

Informational Privacy

"Right to privacy" has a familiar and ringing tone for most Americans and is usually thought to be a basic part of liberty. Yet the idea is amorphous and ill-defined in the law. The right has now been elevated to constitutional status, yet it is mentioned nowhere in the Constitution. Its protection may apply to such presumably autonomous aspects of a person's life as the decision to abort a pregnancy or end one's life, taken up in the next chapter, as well as keeping personal information from the eyes of others, which bear little or no relation to each other. In each instance, it may conflict with valid and important public ends. Yet the right can be seen as vital to a modern civilized society in which government, media, and the public they represent have ever more opportunity to intrude on personal life.

The earliest formulation of a legal right of privacy appeared in an 1890 *Harvard Law Review* article, "The Right to Privacy" written by a young lawyer, Louis D. Brandeis, later to serve with distinction on the Supreme Court, and Samuel D. Warren, his former law partner. In the best tradition of common law synthesis, Warren and Brandeis pieced together many old and recent cases from such disparate areas of the law as defamation, property, and contacts, in which plaintiffs who claimed certain aspects of their personal life had been interfered with by others, had won relief. The authors argued these decisions were based on a common analytic principle they called "the right of privacy" and described it in lofty terms.

> The intensity and complexity of life, attendant upon advancing civilization, have rendered necessary some retreat from the world, and man, under the refining influence of culture, has become more sensitive to publicity, so that solitude and privacy have become more essential to the individual; but modern enterprise and invention have, through invasions upon his privacy, subjected him to mental pain and distress, far greater than could be inflicted by mere bodily injury. [*Harvard Law Review*, 1890, vol. 4, p. 196]

Warren and Brandeis wrote in reaction to the prying journalistic excesses of their day, but they painted the "right" broadly enough to reach other kinds of intrusive behavior. The article became one of the most influential essays in American legal history. Slowly but steadily a right to privacy began to be recognized in court decisions in one state after another. Many state legislatures gave it statutory form. First applied as a rule of tort liability for a civil wrong at private hands, the basic right against intrusion eventually came to limit acts of government as well.

Though as will be noted in the next chapter, an independent right of privacy was not constitutionally recognized until the 1960s, a privacy principle had been an important part of several

rights of the Bill of Rights including the Fourth Amendment's protection against unreasonable searches and seizures, the Fifth's against self-incrimination, the Third's against the peacetime quartering of soldiers in private homes, and the First's right of association as a part of freedom of speech.

The matter of keeping others from seeing, hearing, or knowing personal facts and information first came before the Court in *Time, Inc. v. Hill*, 1967 (p. 261). *Life* magazine had published an article about the opening of a Broadway play, "The Desperate Hours," depicting the ordeal of a family held hostage in their home by escaped convicts. The play and the novel from which it was drawn were based on a real, well-publicized incident that had happened to the Hill family in their home near Philadelphia. The Hills were released unharmed, but the episode was so traumatic that they discouraged all media attention and eventually moved to another state. The *Life* story posed actors in the Hill's former home and linked the play to the family. The story also included several false though not defamatory statements about the Hills. The family sued the publisher under a New York right of privacy statute creating tort liability if a person's name was used for commercial purposes without consent. The Supreme Court overturned a damage award the Hills won in the lower courts. Noting the play's opening was a newsworthy event, as had been the Hills' ordeal itself, the Court applied reasoning it first used in its landmark defamation decision, *New York Times v. Sullivan*, three years before, in dealing with a libel action brought by a public official. There could be no recovery for "false light" statements unless they were made with "actual malice" or in "reckless disregard" for the truth. Thus a privacy plaintiff would have the same burden of proving fault for nondefamatory "false light" statements as a public official or public figure would have for proving defamatory false statements.

The case showed the three-cornered relationship of the individual, the media, and government in privacy tort claims arising from disclosure of personal information. In this, the government may variously be protector of privacy, as New York had been in enacting its right of privacy law, collector of information, or divulger of information.

Some states, for example, have passed laws making it unlawful to publish the names or identities of rape victims. In *Cox Broadcasting Corp. v. Cohn,* 1975, noted earlier, the father of a woman who was killed in a rape sued a television station that had identified her in reporting on a prosecution in the case. The Supreme Court disallowed recovery because the victim's name appeared in the indictment of the criminal suspects. As a public document, the charge was open to anyone, including the media, which had an absolute right to publish its contents under the First Amendment's protection of freedom of the press.

A similar result was reached in *Oklahoma Publishing Co. v. District Court,* in which the Court overturned a lower judicial order that barred publication of the name or photo of an 11 year old who had been charged with murder. Because reporters were allowed to be present during juvenile court hearings, the press had gotten the information lawfully. Publication of truthful information so obtained about a newsworthy event was protected by the First Amendment against claims of privacy (*The Florida Star v. B. J. F.,* 1989), noted earlier. The Court has reaffirmed, however, that a "false light" privacy right may allow recovery against a publisher if the false but nondefamatory statements caused mental anguish and humiliation (*Cantrell v. Forest City Publishing Co.,* 1974).

The triangular interface of government, media, and privacy was at the center of the unusual civil damages case of *Bartnicki v. Vopper,* 2001 (p. 265). The defendant Vopper, a radio talk show host, played a tape of a cell phone conversation between the president of a union representing local high school teachers and the union's chief negotiator in contentious contract negotiations with the school board. The tape was given to Vopper by a third party who intercepted the conversation in violation of the Omnibus Crime Control and Safe Streets Act. Title III of the act bars such interceptions and disclosure of their contents and provided for a civil damage action by anyone whose privacy was compromised. The Supreme Court held the last provision in this instance to violate the First Amendment. Though privacy of communication was an important interest the government could protect, it was outweighed here by the interest that comment on public issues be "uninhibited, robust, and wide-open." Illegal conduct by a third party, though punishable, was not enough reason to leave speech about a matter of public interest unprotected.

Obscenity and Pornography

Pornography is the depiction of transgressive or otherwise offensive sexuality. Obscenity is the legal proscription of pornography. Pornography is largely subjective, but obscenity, as a legal category, is presumably largely objective. Therein lies a great difficulty for both the courts and society. Historically, obscenity, like defamatory expression, has been speech outside the First Amendment. As we have just seen, the Court in its expansive free speech doctrine has given protection to libel and slander under various circumstances. Though obscenity remains totally an outlaw category, the Court's free speech doctrine has affected it even more dramatically than it has defamatory speech. But, unlike the latter, it has come through a progressive narrowing of what the outlaw category contains.

Though we may be amused by the reticence and intolerance of the Victorians and some other generations past, all societies and cultures, past and present, primitive and modern, including our own, have proscribed some representations of sexuality. To be sure, what has been regarded as sexually transgressive—pornographic—has differed substantially from one time and place to another. Pornography that is legally designated as obscene has varied no less.

American legal controls on pornographic expression go back to colonial times. But no court or legislature tried to define obscenity—except through synonymous words like "lewd," "lascivious," and "indecent," themselves begging for definition—until well into the nineteenth century. When American courts finally clarified the bounds of the outlaw speech, they borrowed from the English case *Regina v. Hicklin,* 1868, which dealt with suppression of a pamphlet purporting to describe sexual depravity and immorality in the Roman Catholic clergy. Legal proscription would depend on "whether the tendency of the matter charged as obscenity is to deprave and corrupt those whose minds are open to such immoral influences and into whose hands a publication of this sort may fall." [L.R. 3 Q.B. 360 at 371]

Such finding could be based on isolated passages rather than the work as a whole. Neither intent of the author nor the literary or social merit of the work mattered. The *Hicklin* rule, as it became called, tied obscenity to the *effects* expression *might* have on persons who were particularly susceptible, mainly children, discounted by the improbability of exposure.

The rule prevailed in English and American law for nearly a hundred years, as its deficiencies grew ever more clear. It did little to prevent the prosecution of many late nineteenth- and early twentieth-century works of literary merit. Nor could it be easily reconciled with the growing constitutional interest in the value of nonpolitical speech. Though American courts had heard hundreds, even thousands of obscenity cases by the 1950s, the Supreme Court had given almost no attention to the doctrinal or theoretical aspects of the issue until its *Roth-Alberts* decision in 1957. In two cases decided together, *Roth v. United States* (p. 269), involving unlawful use of the mails and *Alberts v. California,* a state obscenity prosecution, the Court abandoned the *Hicklin* rule and recast the test for obscenity. Holding that obscenity was "utterly without redeeming social importance," it affirmed its exclusion from First Amendment protection. It could be legally proscribed without a showing of clear and present danger of harmful effect or other proof normally required for restricting communication. The important question then was whether a given sexual representation was in the category or not.

The answer, the Court said, was "whether to the average person, applying contemporary community standards, the dominant theme of the material taken as a whole appeals to the prurient interest." This formulation, which became known as the *Roth* test, was an important departure from the *Hicklin* rule. First, the hypothetical referent was not the most vulnerable person in the population but the "average person." Second, that person had to be of the "contemporary community," not from another day or place, a matter the older rule left open. Third, the communication must be judged not by isolated or selected parts but its dominant theme. Finally, its effect or design must be to stimulate "prurient interest" rather than tend to "deprave or corrupt."

Though the Court upheld convictions in *Roth* and *Alberts,* the new test was immediately recognized for what it was: a libertarian rule that would narrow the scope of proscribable sexual expression. Like many legal reformulations, however, it raised almost as many questions as it answered. In an age overtaken by changing social standards and new media technology, *Roth* sent the Supreme Court down a tortuous path of separating constitutionally acceptable sexual materials from those that remained illegal.

The years following *Roth* saw a surge in sexual publications of all sorts and much less restraint in what was portrayed. In response to new popular demands for control, obscenity prosecutions multiplied as well. But when convictions were obtained, as they often were, the new obscenity test encouraged appeals. As a result, much erotic representation—mainly in books, small-circulation periodicals, and movies—came under scrutiny in the higher courts including the Supreme Court. But the agreement among the justices that was evident in the *Roth* formulation became strained and the Court's position fragmented as the test was applied. Dissensus in the decade after *Roth* prompted Justice Harlan to remark that, "The subject of obscenity has produced a variety of views among members of the Court unmatched in any other course of Constitutional adjudication." [*Interstate Circuit, Inc. v. Dallas,* 390 U.S. 676 (1968) at 704-705] In 13 cases with signed opinions between 1957 and 1967, the justices filed 54 separate statements of their views, an average of almost four per case.

Despite this division, the Court managed to make several important changes in the obscenity test. It removed so-called thematic or ideological obscenity from the proscriptive category in *Kingsley International Pictures v. Board of Regents,* 1959. The New York Motion Picture Division had denied a license to *Lady Chatterley's Lover,* based on the D.H. Lawrence novel, because it portrayed adultery as a "desirable, acceptable, and proper pattern of behavior." In reversing, the Court held the state had tried to control advocacy of an idea; portrayal of immoral behavior alone was not obscene even if it were shown in a favorable light. The decision was something of a milestone, since controlling the portrayal of immoral behavior, along with profanity and nudity, had historically been the chief aim of antiobscenity law. More blatant depiction had not generally been at issue because little was produced or circulated.

In *"Memoirs of a Woman of Pleasure" v. Massachusetts,* 1966, the "Fanny Hill" case, the Court held that proscribable expression, besides having prurient appeal, must also be "patently offensive" that is, so offensive on its face as to affront standards of the contemporary community. Republication of John Cleland's 1747 ribald novel was not such a work. A plurality opinion also suggested that sexual material could not be obscene unless it was also "utterly without redeeming social value," a matter mentioned but left in doubt in *Roth.* The social value redemptive element became a requirement of the test rather than simply a description of the non-obscene.

These and other decisions adding requirements to the *Roth* test and narrowing its restrictive reach, led many observers and lower courts to conclude that now only hard-core pornography could meet it. At odds with this interpretation were several other cases in which the Supreme Court seemed to say that obscenity might vary with the circumstances of the communication and the audience for it. The issue emerged dramatically in *Ginzburg v. United States,* 1966, in which a publisher was convicted under an antiobscenity postal statute for mailing issues of two periodicals, *Eros* and *Liaison,* and a book, *The Housewife's Handbook on Selective Promiscuity.* The Court upheld the conviction, not because the materials were obscene—they probably were not under the emerging standard—but because they were presented in a way the Court described as "the sordid business of pandering." It took note of advertisements stressing the lewd rather than redeeming literary aspects of the publications and Ginzburg's attempt to get them postmarked in such places as Intercourse, Pa., and Middlesex, N.J. "Such evidence may support the determination that the material is obscene even though in other contexts the material would escape such condemnation." [383 U.S. 463 at 475-476] As a conditional step back from the hard-core interpretation of the *Roth* test, the ruling incorporated the idea of "variable" obscenity. But the Court refrained from developing the pandering criterion more fully in later cases, and it would be hard to imagine it reaching the same decision in *Ginzburg* today.

The Court has been willing to apply the variable idea, however, to sexual representation directed at what it called deviant groups. In *Mishkin v. New York,* 1966, for example, it rejected a claim that publications depicting homosexuality, fetishism, bondage, and other sadomasochistic acts were not obscene under the *Roth* test because they did not have prurient appeal to the "average person." If the material is "designed for and primarily disseminated to a clearly defined deviant sexual group, rather than the public at large, the

A melodramatic eleventh-hour open letter to the U.S. Supreme Court in a full-page ad in the *New York Times* did not keep publisher Ralph Ginzburg from serving a three-year sentence for using the mails to distribute obscene material.

prurient appeal requirement of the *Roth* test is satisfied if the dominant theme of the material taken as a whole appeals to the prurient interest in sex of the members of that group." [383 U.S. 502 at 508]

Juveniles are another and larger audience for whom the "average person" standard does not apply. Though little pornography is aimed directly at them, shielding young persons is one of the chief aims of the legal control of sexual material. When the Court addressed this problem in *Ginsberg v. New York*, 1968, it again gave the obscenity a variable interpretation. Under a statute barring distribution of material "harmful to minors," defined as persons under 17, a newsdealer had been convicted of selling underage persons "girlie" magazines that were not obscene for general distribution. Using the method adopted in *Mishkin*, the Court held that obscenity "might vary according to the group to which the questionable material is directed." When sexual material was distributed to minors, the prurient appeal to be shown was not to the "average person" but to minors.

In still another variation, this time involving regulatory structure, the Court was willing to give protection to obscene materials possessed in the privacy of the home. In *Stanley v. Georgia*, 1969, possession of a hard-core 8-millimeter film seized in an otherwise lawful police search of a house, was held not a punishable offense because of the countervailing right of privacy. "A state has no business," the Court said, "telling a man, sitting alone in his house, what books he may read or films he may watch." [394 U.S. 557 at 574]

In the 15 years following *Roth*, the formulaic aspects of the obscenity test and the tension between its apparent hard-core notation and the "variable" exceptions offered uncertain guidance to lower courts, legislators, and prosecutors faced with growing demands for control. The Court's determination to narrow the scope of the outlaw category left little choice but to review almost every conviction appealed to it. To many, the Court seemed ever more to resemble the "Supreme Board of Censors" Justice Black had feared it would become after *Kingsley International Pictures*. As a result, whether a given expression was or was not obscene was often uncertain until the Court ruled on it.

The Burger Court was able to marshal a new majority on obscenity question, in 1973, in *Miller v. California* (p. 273), and set about revising important parts of the test. It began by reaffirming the inclusion of patent offensiveness, equating it with hard-core pornography. Such representations included "ultimate sexual acts, normal or perverted, actual or simulated . . . masturbation, excretory functions, and lewd exhibition of genitals."

Addressing the redemptive element, it expressly abandoned "utterly without redeeming social importance" for a new formulation: "whether the work, taken as a whole, lacks serious artistic, literary, political, or scientific value." Since prurient interest, patent offensiveness, and the redemptive element were each a necessary rather than sufficient part of the test, the revision meant that prurient, patently offensive material could be obscene only if it also lacked "serious artistic, literary, political, or scientific value." The new redemptive measure did not so much broaden the obscenity designation as save it. "Utterly without redeeming social importance" had to be abandoned if legal regulation were to be kept at all because almost any sexual material, including hard-core pornography, could be said to have some ideological, educational, psychological, or recreational value.

The Court also clarified "community" of the original *Roth* test. Before *Miller* most lower courts had held that it was the nation itself. That idea was now emphatically rejected. Prurient appeal and patent offensiveness were "essentially questions of fact, and our nation is simply too big and too diverse for the Court to reasonably expect that such standard could be articulated for all 50 States in a single formulation, even assuming the prerequisite consensus exists." The "community standards" to be applied were those of the state or possibly a more locally defined jurisdiction. But variant state or local standards would not apply to the redemptive element—artistic, literary, political, or scientific values, interests protected by the First Amendment—that would continue to be governed by national uniform standards.

By revising the obscenity test and devolving controlling standards to the community, the Court also tried to shift some of the burden of obscenity cases from its own chambers to the lower courts and thus strengthen the role of the fact-finding jury in applying the test. That different juries might reach different conclusions about the same material was "one of the consequences we accept under our jury system."

Devolution of the sort intended by *Miller* is apt to work well where doctrinal requirements are understood and adhered to by actors at lower levels. Just how problematic this might be in determining obscenity was evident in *Jenkins v. Georgia,* a year later, when a jury applying local community standards found the Hollywood film *Carnal Knowledge* obscene even though it fell well short of hard-core pornography. When the state supreme court upheld the verdict, the Court on appeal was forced to rule otherwise. On its own viewing, it found the work not patently offensive and concluded that juries did not have "unbridled discretion" to decide patent offensiveness (or, presumably, any other element) in the obscenity test.

In *Paris Adult Theater v. Slaton,* a companion case to *Miller,* the Court refused to extend the privacy right it had set out in *Stanley v. Georgia* to settings outside the home. It held that a state might bar exhibition of obscene material in a public theater even if the audience was made up entirely of consenting adults.

By affirming the hard-core limitation, *Miller* did little to resolve the doctrinal strain between this elemental idea and the "variable" obscenity the Court had embraced several times before. The latter was used again to avoid the libertarian results of a strict application of the revised *Roth-Miller* test. In *FCC v. Pacifica Foundation,* for example, the Court reviewed FCC sanctions against a New York City radio station that had broadcast a recorded satire on seven "dirty" words—"shit," "piss," "fuck," "motherfucker," "cocksucker," "cunt," and "tits." Conceding the words were not obscene, the Court nonetheless found them "indecent" under a federal statute barring use of either "obscene" or "indecent" language in broadcasting. Citing the ease with which children get access to broadcast material and the medium's inherent intrusiveness into the home, the Court found the words to be "patently offensive" and could be confined to hours when children were not likely to be listening. Vulgar, offensive, and shocking language was not entitled to "absolute constitutional protection under all circumstances."

In another departure, the Court held that a state might legally proscribe photographic or cinematic "sexual conduct"—actual or simulated intercourse, masturbation, bestiality, sadomasochistic acts, or "lewd exhibition of genitals"—of persons under 16, even though such expression might not be obscene under the *Roth-Miller* test. In this step, taken in *New York v. Ferber,* 1982, it widened the area of proscribable sexual material while side-stepping the obscenity test. The Court's distaste for child pornography was evident in its unanimity and its willingness to see regulation applied to the *sale* of such material and thus to limit speech of buyers who were not themselves exploiting children. The Court went still further in *Osborne v. Ohio,* 1990, upholding a ban on the mere possession of child pornography, thus narrowing further the privacy holding of *Stanley v. Georgia.* It stressed the countervailing public interest of protecting children from being exploited in the production of pornography by eliminating the legal market for such material. The First Amendment right to have access to nonobscene material, the Court said, was not substantially abridged.

A question raised but not answered by the Ferber decision was whether depicting sexual acts of children could be banned if no children were involved in creating the material. With advances in computer-imaging technology in the 1990s it became possible to produce "virtual" child pornography—highly realistic images of children in sexual acts without the use of any real children. Congress acted to make such depiction illegal in the Child Pornography Prevention Act of 1996. But in a challenge to its enforcement in *Ashcroft v. Free Speech Coalition,* 2002, (p. 279) the Supreme Court held the law unconstitutionally broad in barring material that was not obscene

under the Roth-Miller standard and not produced by exploiting children.

In a time, place, and manner variation of obscenity control, the Court has approved use of municipal zoning power to regulate the availability of sexual materials. In *Young v. American Mini-Theatres,* 1976, it upheld Detroit's "Anti-Skid-Row" ordinance that barred adult bookstores and movie houses within 500 feet of areas zoned for residential use or 1,000 feet of any two other "regulated" uses. The ordinance defined an adult movie theater as one emphasizing films depicting certain sexual activities or "anatomical areas." Since such content was not necessarily hard-core pornography, the Court had again upheld limited regulation of sexual materials falling short of obscenity under the *Roth-Miller* test.

In response to feminist antipornography efforts, several cities passed ordinances declaring that certain kinds of sexual portrayal of women to be a violation of a woman's civil rights. Typical of these measures was that of Indianapolis barring the portrayal of women as sexually enjoying pain or humiliation or simply being an object of sexual conquest. A woman aggrieved by such portrayal could bring a civil action against the seller, distributor, or publisher, or file a complaint with a local equal opportunity office, which in turn could seek a "cease and desist" order. The offending material did not have to be legally obscene. In *American Booksellers Association v. Hudnut,* 1985, the Supreme Court, without opinion, affirmed a lower federal court ruling that the law discriminated against the content of speech by prescribing an approved view of women and of sexual relationships while silencing nonconforming expression.

New communications technology and marketing have created new points of conflict. To protect children against "dial-a-porn"—access to explicit sexual messages by telephone call—Congress in 1988 empowered the Federal Communications Commission to ban all obscene and "indecent" interstate commercial telephone messages. In *Sable Communications. v. FCC,* 1989, the Court, noting that most callers were adults, struck down the ban on indecent messages, since such speech is not obscene for adults. A more narrowly tailored rule to protect children, such as requiring the use of credit cards, access codes, or scrambling devices, it said, might be valid.

With the protection of children in mind again, Congress passed the Cable Television Consumer Protection and Competition Act of 1992, which included three provisions aimed at sexual portrayal. Two dealt with the "leased channels" that cable companies must reserve for commercial lease to unaffiliated third parties and the "public access" channels that the companies must set aside for public, educational, or governmental purposes in return for permission to install cables under city streets and in other public space. The provisions allowed cable companies to reject programming that showed "sexual or excretory activities or organs in a patently offensive manner." If a company permitted such programming among leased channels, it was required to segregate it to a single channel unless viewers made written requests in advance to have access to it.

In *Denver Area Educational Telecommunications Consortium v. FCC*, 1996, a fragmented Court issuing six opinions upheld allowing the companies to ban indecent programming from leased commercial channels but not from public access ones. Historically, the Court said, cable companies have exercised greater editorial control over commercial than public access channels and those were the channels most watched by children. But it was not willing to allow indecent programming on commercial channels to be segregated and blocked. That would be a substantial burden on adult freedom of speech, particularly because new technology, such as lock boxes and V-chips, offered less restrictive ways of keeping indecent content from children.

In the early days of the Internet, Congress passed the Communications Decency Act in response to complaints about children's access to ready sexual communications. The act barred the "knowing" transmission of obscene or indecent communication that depicted "in terms patently offensive as measured by contemporary community standards, sexual or excretory activities or organs," to anyone under 18. Certain affirmative defenses were provided where "good faith . . . effective actions" were taken to restrict access by minors. In *Reno v. American Civil Liberties Union*, 1997 (p. 276), the Supreme Court, though divided 5-4, held these provisions to violate First Amendment rights. The decision was not surprising given the Court's obscenity doctrine. Not only did the statute define obscenity differently from *Roth-Miller* standards, it failed to say what would be indecent. It also made no provision for protecting material that had redeeming scientific, artistic, or educational value. For the moment at least, the world's ultimate communications medium through which anyone can communicate with anyone else has defied government restriction that would protect minors yet meet First Amendment standards.

FURTHER READING

The Media as the Fourth Estate

Barron, Jerome, *Freedom of the Press for Whom: The Right of Access to Mass Media* (1973)
Bollinger, Lee C., *Images of a Free Press* (1991)
Cortner, Richard C., *The Kingfish and the Constitution: Huey Long, the First Amendment, and the Emergence of Modern Press Freedom in America* (1966)
Daly, John Charles, *The Press and the Courts* (1978)

Flink, Stanley E., *Sentinel under Seige: The Triumphs and Troubles of America's Free Press* (1998)
Haltom, William, *Reporting on the Courts: How the Mass Media Cover Judicial Actions* (1998)
Kelly, Sean, *Access Denied: The Politics of Press Censorship* (1978)
Levy, Leonard W., ed., *Freedom of the Press from Zenger to Jefferson* (1996)

_____, *Emergence of a Free Press* [revised edition of the author's 1960 work *Legacy of Suppression*] (1985)

Lofton, John, *The Press as Guardian of the First Amendment* (1980)

McCoy, Ralph E., *Freedom of the Press: An Annotated Bibliography, Second Supplement, 1978–1992* (1994)

Neuborne, Burt, *Free Speech, Free Markets, Free Choice: An Essay on Commercial Speech* (1987)

_____, *The Fourth Estate and the Constitution* (1991)

Reeves, Richard, *What the People Know: Freedom and the Press* (1999)

Rotunda, Ronald D., *Responding to the Media: the Ethical and Constitutional Parameters* (1994)

Smith, Jeffrey, *Printers and Press Freedom* (1988)

_____, *War and Press Freedom: The Problem of Prerogative Power* (1999)

Wolfson, Nicholas, *Corporate First Amendment Rights and the SEC* (1990)

Yalof, David, and Kenneth Dautrich, *The First Amendment and the Media in the Court of Public Opinion* (2001)

Movies, Broadcasting, and New Media

Carmen, Ira H., *Movies, Censorship, and the Law* (1966)

Carter, T. Barton, *The First Amendment and the Fifth Estate: Regulation of Electronic Mass Media* (1993)

Garry, Patrick, *Scrambling for Protection: The New Media and the First Amendment* (1994)

Krattenmaker, Thomas G., and Lucas A. Powe, *Regulating Broadcast Programming* (1994)

Pool, Ithiel de Sola, *Technologies of Freedom* (1983)

Powe, Lucas A., *American Broadcasting and the First Amendment* (1987)

Randall, Richard S., *Censorship of the Movies: The Social and Political Control of a Mass Medium* (1970)

Defamation

Barendt, Eric M., Laurence Lustgarten, Kenneth Norrie, and Hugh Stephenson, eds., *Libel and the Media: The Chilling Effect* (1997)

Dennis, Everette, and Eli Noam, *The Costs of Libel* (1989)

Forer, Louis G., A Chilling Effect: *The Mounting Threat of Libel and Invasion of Privacy Action to the First Amendment* (1987)

Gillmor, Donald M., *Power, Publicity, and the Abuse of Libel Law* (1992)

Hopkins, W. Wat, *Actual Malice* (1989)

Kane, Peter E., *Errors, Lies, and Libel* (1992)

Rosenberg, Norman L., *Protecting the Best Men: An Interpretive History of the Law of Libel* (1986)

Smolla, Rodney A., *Suing the Press: Libel, the Media, and Power* (1986)

_____, *Jerry Falwell v. Larry Flynt: The First Amendment on Trial* (1990)

_____, *The Law of Defamation* (1999)

Informational Privacy

Bennett, Colin J., and Rebecca Grant, eds., *Visions of Privacy: Policy Choices for the Digital Age* (1999)

Bloustein, Edward J., *Individual and Group Privacy* (1978)

Cate, Fred H., *Privacy in the Information Age* (1997)

Decew, Judith Wagner, *In Pursuit of Privacy: Law, Ethics, and the Rise of Technology* (1997)

Regan, Priscilla M., *Legislating Privacy: Technology, Social Values, and Public Policy* (1995)

Warren, Samuel D., and Louis Brandeis, "The Right to Privacy," *Harvard Law Review* 4 (1890)

Weston, Alan F., Privacy and Freedom (1967)

Obscenity and Pornography

Baird, Robert M., and Stuart E. Rosenbaum, eds., *Pornography: Private Right or Public Menace?* (1998)

Berger, Ronald, *Feminism and Pornography* (1991)

Clor, Harry M., *Obscenity and Public Morality: Censorship in a Liberal Society* (1969)

_____, *Public Morality and Liberal Society: Essays on Decency, Law, and Pornography* (1996)

Copp, David, and Susan Wendell, eds., *Pornography and Censorship* (1983)

Cossman, Brenda, Shannon Bell, Becki Ross, Lisa Gotell, *Bad Attitudes on Trial: Pornography, Feminism, and the Butler Decision* (1997)

Downs, Donald Alexander, *The New Politics of Pornography* (1989)

Friedman, Leon, ed., *Obscenity: The Complete Oral arguments before the Supreme Court in the Major Obscenity Cases* (1983)

Gubar, Susan, *For Adult Use Only: The Dilemmas of Violent Pornography* (1989)

Heins, Margaret, *Sin, Sex, and Blasphemy* (1993)

Hunt, Lynn, ed., *The Invention of Pornography* (1993)

Kobylka, Joseph F., *The Politics of Obscenity: Group Litigation in a Time of Legal Change* (1991)

Hixson, Richard F., *Pornography and the Justices: The Supreme Court and the Intractable Obscenity Problem* (1996)

Itzin, Catherine, ed., *Pornography: Women, Violence, and Civil Liberties* (1993)

MacKinnon, Catherine, *Only Words* (1993)

Randall, Richard S., *Freedom and Taboo: Pornography and the Politics of a Self Divided* (1989)

Rembar, Charles, *The End of Obscenity* (1968)

Saunders, Kevin W., *Violence as Obscenity: Limiting the Media's First Amendment Protection* (1996)

Schauer, Frederick F., *The Law of Obscenity* (1976)

Strossen, Nadine, *Defending Pornography: Free Speech, Sex, and the Fight for Women's Rights* (2000)

Sutherland, Lane, *Obscenity: The Court, the Congress, and the President's Commission* (1985)

Zimring, Franklin E., and Gordon J. Hawkins, *Pornography in a Free Society* (1991)

On Leading Cases

Friendly, Fred, *Minnesota Rag: The Dramatic Story of the Landmark Supreme Court Case That Gave Meaning to Freedom of the Press* (1981)

Gertz, Elmer, *Gertz v. Robert Welch, Inc.: The Story of a Landmark Libel Case* (1992)

Kirby, James, *Fumble: Bear Bryant, Wally Butts, and the Great College Football Scandal* (1986)

Lewis, Anthony, *Make No Law: The Sullivan Case and the First Amendment* (1991)

Rudenstine, David, *The Day the Presses Stopped: A History of the Pentagon Papers Case* (1996)

Shapiro, Martin, *The Pentagon Papers and the Courts* (1972)

Smolla, Rodney A., *Jerry Falwell v. Larry Flynt: The First Amendment on Trial* (1990)

Additional works are listed in General and Supplementary Bibliography.

CASES

Near v. Minnesota

283 U.S. 697 (1931), 5-4

Opinion of the Court: Hughes (Brandeis, Holmes, Roberts, Stone)

Dissenting: Butler, McReynolds, Sutherland, Van Devanter

Why did Minnesota enjoin publication of The Saturday Press *rather than punish publication of past issues? Why does the Court see this distinction as important? In what ways does the decision extend the protection of freedom of speech? What constitutional theory or theories did Chief Justice Hughes develop to decide this case? This was a state case decided on First Amendment grounds. Was there any precedent for limiting what states might do on the basis of rights in the Bill of Rights?*

Hughes, for the Court:

Chapter 285 of the Session Laws of Minnesota for the year 1925 provides for the abatement, as a public nuisance, of a "malicious, scandalous and defamatory newspaper, magazine or other periodical." Section one of the Act is as follows:

> Section 1. Any person who, as an individual, or as a member or employee of a firm, or associa-

tion or organization, or as an officer, director, member or employee of a corporation, shall be engaged in the business of regularly or customarily producing, publishing or circulating, having in possession, selling or giving away

> (a) an obscene, lewd and lascivious newspaper, magazine, or other periodical, or

> (b) a malicious, scandalous and defamatory newspaper, magazine or other periodical,

> is guilty of a nuisance, and all persons guilty of such nuisance may be enjoined, as hereinafter provided....

Section two provides that, whenever any such nuisance is committed or exists, the County Attorney of any county where any such periodical is published or circulated, or, in case of his failure or refusal to proceed upon written request in good faith of a reputable citizen, the Attorney General, or, upon like failure or refusal of the latter, any citizen of the county may maintain an action in the district court of the county in the name of the State to enjoin perpetually the persons committing or maintaining any such nuisance from further committing or maintaining it. Upon such evidence as the court shall deem sufficient, a temporary injunction may be granted....

Jay Near, publisher of *The Saturday Press* in Minneapolis, won one of freedom of speech's great rulings in *Near v. Minnesota*. This only known photograph of Near, a racial and religious bigot who made a career of "exposure" journalism, appeared with his obituary in the Minneapolis *Tribune* in 1936.

Under this statute, clause (b), the County Attorney of Hennepin County brought this action to enjoin the publication of what was described as a "malicious, scandalous and defamatory newspaper, magazine and periodical" known as "The Saturday Press," published by the defendants in the city of Minneapolis. The complaint alleged that the defendants, on September 24, 1927, and on eight subsequent dates in October and November, 1927, published and circulated editions of that periodical which were "largely devoted to malicious, scandalous and defamatory articles" concerning Charles G. Davis, Frank W. Brunskill, the Minneapolis Tribune, the Minneapolis Journal, Melvin C. Passolt, George E. Leach, the Jewish Race, the members of the Grand Jury of Hennepin County impaneled in November, 1927, and then holding office, and other persons . . . [I]t appears from the briefs of both parties that Charles G. Davis was a special law enforcement officer employed by a civic organization, that George E. Leach was Mayor of Minneapolis, that Frank W. Brunskill was its Chief of Police, and that Floyd B. Olson (the relator in this action) was County Attorney.

Without attempting to summarize the contents of the voluminous exhibits attached to the complaint, we deem it sufficient to say that the articles charged in substance that a Jewish gangster was in control of gambling, bootlegging and racketeering in Minneapolis, and that law enforcing officers and agencies were not energetically performing their duties. Most of the charges were directed against the Chief of Police; he was charged with gross neglect of duty, illicit relations with gangsters, and with participation in graft. The County Attorney was charged with knowing the existing conditions and with failure to take adequate measures to remedy them. The Mayor was accused of inefficiency and dereliction. One member of the grand jury was stated to be in sympathy with the gangsters. A special grand jury and a special prosecutor were demanded to deal with the situation in general, and, in particular, to investigate an attempt to assassinate one Guilford, one of the original defendants, who, it appears from the articles, was shot by gangsters after the first issue of the periodical had been published. There is no question but that the articles made serious accusations against the public officers named and others in connection with the prevalence of crimes and the failure to expose and punish them.

At the beginning of the action, on November 22, 1927, and upon the verified complaint, an order was made directing the defendants to show cause why a temporary injunction should not issue and meanwhile forbidding the defendants to publish, circulate or have in their possession any editions of the periodical from September 24, 1927, to November 19, 1927, inclusive, and from publishing, circulating, or having in their possession, "any future editions of said *The Saturday Press*." . . .

This statute, for the suppression as a public nuisance of a newspaper or periodical, is unusual, if not unique, and raises questions of grave importance transcending the local interests involved in the particular action. It is no longer open to doubt that the liberty of the press, and of speech, is within the liberty safeguarded by the due process clause of the Fourteenth Amendment from invasion by state action. . . .

. . . It is thus important to note precisely the purpose and effect of the statute as the state court has construed it.

First. The statute is not aimed at the redress of individual or private wrongs. Remedies for libel remain available and unaffected. The statute . . . is aimed at the distribution of scandalous matter as "detrimental to public morals and to the general welfare," tending "to disturb the peace of the community" and "to provoke assaults and the commission of crime." In order to obtain an injunction to suppress the future publication of the newspaper or periodical, it is not necessary to prove the falsity of the charges that have been made in the publication condemned. . . . It is alleged, and the statute requires the allegation, that the publication was "malicious." But, as in prosecutions for libel, there is no requirement of proof by the State of malice in fact, as distinguished from malice inferred from the mere publication of the defamatory matter. The judgment in this case proceeded upon the mere proof of publication. The statute permits the defense not of the truth alone, but only that the truth was published with good motives and for justifiable ends. It is apparent that, under the statute, the publication is to be regarded as defamatory if it injures reputation, and that it is scandalous if it circulates charges of reprehensible conduct, whether criminal or otherwise, and the publication is thus deemed to invite public reprobation and to constitute a public scandal. . . .

Second. The statute is directed not simply at the circulation of scandalous and defamatory statements with regard to private citizens, but at the continued publication by newspapers and periodicals of charges against public officers of corruption, malfeasance in office, or serious neglect of duty. Such charges, by their very nature, create a public scandal. They are scandalous and defamatory within the meaning of the statute, which has its normal operation in relation to publications dealing prominently and chiefly with the alleged derelictions of public officers.

Third. The object of the statute is not punishment, in the ordinary sense, but suppression of the offending newspaper or periodical. The reason for the enactment, as the state court has said, is that prosecutions to enforce penal statutes for libel do not result in "efficient repression or suppression of the evils of scandal." Describing the business of publication as a public nuisance does not obscure the substance of the proceeding which the statute authorizes. It is the continued publication of scandalous and defamatory matter that constitutes the business and the declared nuisance. In the case of public officers, it is the reiteration of charges of official misconduct, and the fact that the newspaper or periodical is principally devoted to that purpose, that exposes it to suppression. In the present instance, the proof was that nine editions of the newspaper or periodical in question were published on successive dates, and that they were chiefly devoted to charges against public officers and in relation to the prevalence and protection of crime. In such a case, these officers are not left to their ordinary remedy in a suit for libel, or the authorities to a prosecution for criminal libel. Under this statute, a publisher of a newspaper or periodical, undertaking to conduct a campaign to expose and to censure official derelictions, and devoting his publication principally to that purpose, must face not simply the possibility of a verdict against him in a suit or prosecution for libel, but a determination that his newspaper or periodical is a public nuisance to be abated, and that this abatement and suppression will follow unless he is prepared with legal evidence to prove the truth of the charges and also to satisfy the court that, in addition to being true, the matter was published with good motives and for justifiable ends.

This suppression is accomplished by enjoining publication, and that restraint is the object and effect of the statute.

Fourth. The statute not only operates to suppress the offending newspaper or periodical, but to put the publisher under an effective censorship. When a newspaper or periodical is found to be "malicious, scandalous, and defamatory," and is suppressed as such, resumption of publication is punishable as a contempt of court by fine or imprisonment. Thus, where a newspaper or periodical has been suppressed because of the circulation of charges against public officers of official misconduct, it would seem to be clear that the renewal of the publication of such charges would constitute a contempt, and that the judgment would lay a permanent restraint upon the publisher, to escape which he must satisfy the court as to the character of a new publication. Whether he would be permitted again to publish matter deemed to be derogatory to the same or other public officers would depend upon the court's ruling. In the present instance, the judgment restrained the defendants from publishing, circulating, having in their possession, selling or giving away any publication whatsoever which is a malicious, scandalous or defamatory newspaper, as defined by law. . . .

If we cut through mere details of procedure, the operation and effect of the statute, in substance, is that public authorities may bring the owner or publisher of a newspaper or periodical before a judge upon a charge of conducting a business of publishing scandalous and defamatory matter—in particular, that the matter consists of charges against public officers of official dereliction—and, unless the owner or publisher is able and disposed to bring competent evidence to satisfy the judge that the charges are true and are published with good motives and for justifiable ends, his newspaper or periodical is suppressed and further publication is made punishable as a contempt. This is of the essence of censorship. . . .

. . . [I]t is recognized that punishment for the abuse of the liberty accorded to the press is essential to the protection of the public, and that the common law rules that subject the libeler to responsibility for the public offense, as well as for the private injury, are not abolished by the protection extended in our constitutions. The law of criminal libel rests upon that secure foundation. There is also the conceded authority of courts to punish for contempt when publications directly tend to prevent the proper discharge of judicial functions. In the present case, we have no occasion to inquire as to the permissible scope of subsequent punishment. For whatever wrong the appellant has committed or may commit by his publications the State appropriately affords both public and private redress by its libel laws. As has been noted, the statute in question does not deal with punishments; it provides for no punishment, except in case of contempt for violation of the court's order, but for suppression and injunction, that is, for restraint upon publication.

The objection has also been made that the principle as to immunity from previous restraint is stated too broadly, if every such restraint is deemed to be prohibited. That is undoubtedly true; the protection even as to previous restraint is not absolutely unlimited. But the limitation has been recognized only in exceptional cases: "When a nation is at war, many things that might be said in time of peace are such a hindrance to its effort that their utterance will not be endured so long as men fight, and that no Court could regard them as protected by any constitutional right." *Schenck v. United States.* No one would question but that a government might prevent actual obstruction to its recruiting service or the publication of the sailing dates of transports or the number and location of troops. On similar grounds, the primary requirements of decency may be enforced against obscene publications. The security of the community life may be protected against incitements to acts of violence and the overthrow by force of orderly government. . . . These limitations are not applicable here. . . .

. . . [T]he administration of government has become more complex, the opportunities for malfeasance and corruption have multiplied, crime has grown to most serious proportions, and the danger of its protection by unfaithful officials and of the impairment of the fundamental security of life and property by criminal alliances and official neglect, emphasizes the primary need of a vigilant and courageous press, especially in great cities. The fact that the liberty of the press may be abused by miscreant purveyors of scandal does not make any the less necessary the immunity of the press from previous restraint in dealing with official misconduct. Subsequent punishment for such abuses as may exist is the appropriate remedy consistent with constitutional privilege. . . .

For these reasons we hold the statute, so far as it authorized the proceedings in this action under clause (b) of section one, to be an infringement of the liberty of the press guaranteed by the Fourteenth Amendment. . . .

Butler, dissenting:

. . . The Minnesota statute does not operate as a previous restraint on publication within the proper meaning of that phrase. It does not authorize administrative control in advance such as was formerly exercised by the licensers and censors but prescribes a remedy to be enforced by a suit in equity. In this case, there was previous publication made in the course of the business of regularly producing malicious, scandalous and defamatory periodicals. The business and publications unquestionably constitute an abuse of the right of free press. The statute denounces the things done as a nuisance on the ground, as stated by the state supreme court, that they threaten morals, peace and good order. There is no question of the power of the State to denounce such transgressions. The restraint authorized is only in respect of continuing to do what has been duly adjudged to constitute a nuisance. . . .

. . . It is fanciful to suggest similarity between the granting or enforcement of the decree authorized by this statute to prevent further publication of malicious, scandalous and defamatory articles and the previous restraint upon the press by licensers as referred to by Blackstone and described in the history of the times to which he alludes.

The opinion seems to concede that, under clause (a) of the Minnesota law, the business of regularly publishing and circulating an obscene periodical may be enjoined as a nuisance. It is difficult to perceive any distinction, having any relation to constitutionality, between clause (a) and clause (b) under which this action was brought. Both nuisances are offensive to morals, order and good government. As that resulting from lewd publications constitutionally may be enjoined, it is hard to understand why the one resulting from a regular business of malicious defamation may not.

It is well known, as found by the state supreme court, that existing libel laws are inadequate effectively to suppress evils resulting from the kind of business and publications that are shown in this case. The doctrine that measures such as the one before us are invalid because they operate as previous restraints to infringe freedom of press exposes the peace and good order of every community and the business and private affairs of every individual to the constant and protracted false and malicious assaults of any insolvent publisher who may have purpose and sufficient capacity to contrive and put into effect a scheme or program for oppression, blackmail or extortion.

New York Times v. United States

403 U.S. 713 (1971), 6-3
Per curiam opinion (Black, Brennan, Douglas, Marshall, Stewart, White)
Dissenting: Blackmun, Burger, Harlan

Are prior restraints unconstitutional or did the Court in this case merely weigh freedom of the press against government claims and find in favor of the freedom? Does the decision mean that the press can publish documents that jeopardize national security? Was the government's interest that of protecting national security or protecting itself from embarrassment? Are those interests mutually exclusive? Would the government ever be able to justify a prior restraint? Was it necessary for the Supreme Court to hear this case so quickly? The First Amendment says that Congress shall make no law abridging freedom of speech or press. Here the objectionable restriction was not statutory but judicial, in the form of an injunction. Does that make a difference? Should it? This decision distributed wide gains and losses. What did they include?*

Per Curiam Opinion:
We granted certiorari in these cases in which the United States seeks to enjoin the New York Times and the Washington Post from publishing the contents of a classified study entitled "History of U.S. Decision-Making Process on Viet Nam Policy."

"Any system of prior restraints of expression comes to this Court bearing a heavy presumption against its constitutional validity." The Government "thus carries a heavy burden of showing justification for the imposition of such a restraint." The District Court for the Southern District of New York, in the New York Times case, and the District Court for the District of Columbia and the Court of Appeals for the District of Columbia Circuit, in the Washington Post case, held that the Government had not met that burden. We agree.

The judgment of the Court of Appeals for the District of Columbia Circuit is therefore affirmed. The order of the Court of Appeals for the Second Circuit is reversed, and the case is remanded with directions to enter a judgment affirming the judgment of the District Court for the Southern District of New York. The stays entered . . . by the Court are vacated. . . .

Black, concurring:
. . . I believe that every moment's continuance of the injunctions against these newspapers amounts to a flagrant, indefensible, and continuing violation of the First Amendment. . . . In my view, it is unfortunate that some of my Brethren are apparently willing to hold that the publication of news may sometimes be enjoined. Such a holding would make a shambles of the First Amendment.

Our Government was launched in 1789 with the adoption of the Constitution. The Bill of Rights, including the First Amendment, followed in 1791. Now, for the first time in the 182 years since the founding of the Republic, the federal courts are asked to hold that the First Amendment does not mean what it says, but rather means that the Government can halt the publication of current news of vital importance to the people of this country.

In seeking injunctions against these newspapers, and in its presentation to the Court, the Executive Branch seems to have forgotten the essential purpose and history of the First Amendment. . . .

. . . Both the history and language of the First Amendment support the view that the press must be left free to publish news, whatever the source, without censorship, injunctions, or prior restraints.

In the First Amendment, the Founding Fathers gave the free press the protection it must have to fulfill its essential role in our democracy. The press was to serve the governed, not the governors. The Government's power to censor the press was abolished so that the press would remain forever free to censure the Government. The press was protected so that it could bare the secrets of government and inform the people. Only a free and unrestrained press can effectively expose deception in government. And paramount among the responsibilities of a free press is the duty to prevent any part of the government from deceiving the people and sending them off to distant lands to die of foreign fevers and foreign shot and shell. In my view, far from deserving condemnation for their courageous reporting, the New York Times, the Washington Post, and other newspapers should be commended for serving the purpose that the Founding Fathers saw so clearly. In revealing the workings of government that led to the Vietnam war, the newspapers nobly did precisely that which the Founders hoped and trusted they would do. . . .

. . . [W]e are asked to hold that, despite the First Amendment's emphatic command, the Executive Branch, the Congress, and the Judiciary can make laws enjoining publication of current news and abridging freedom of the press in the name of "national security." The Government does not even attempt to rely on any act of Congress. Instead, it makes the bold and dangerously far-reaching contention that the courts should take it upon themselves to "make" a law abridging freedom of the press in the name of equity, presidential power and national security, even when the representatives of the people in Congress have adhered to the command of the First Amendment and refused to make such a law. To find that the President has "inherent power" to halt the publication of news by resort to the courts would wipe out the First Amendment and destroy the fundamental liberty and security of the very people the Government hopes to make "secure." . . .

Douglas, concurring:

. . . It should be noted at the outset that the First Amendment provides that "Congress shall make no law . . . abridging the freedom of speech, or of the press." That leaves, in my view, no room for governmental restraint on the press.

There is, moreover, no statute barring the publication by the press of the material which the Times and the Post seek to use. Title 18 U.S.C. §793(e) provides that "[w]hoever having unauthorized possession of, access to, or control over any document, writing . . . or information relating to the national defense which information the possessor has reason to believe could be used to the injury of the United States or to the advantage of any foreign nation, willfully communicates . . . the same to any person not entitled to receive it . . . [s]hall be fined not more than $10,000 or imprisoned not more than ten years, or both."

The Government suggests that the word "communicates" is broad enough to encompass publication. . . .

The . . . evidence that §793 does not apply to the press is a rejected version of §793. That version read "During any national emergency resulting from a war to which the United States is a party, or from threat of such a war, the President may, by proclamation, declare the existence of such emergency and, by proclamation, prohibit the publishing or communicating of, or the attempting to publish or communicate any information relating to the national defense which, in his judgment, is of such character that it is or might be useful to the enemy." During the debates in the Senate, the First Amendment was specifically cited, and that provision was defeated. . . .

Moreover, the Act of September 23, 1950, in amending 18 U.S.C. §793 states in §1(b) that "Nothing in this Act shall be construed to authorize, require, or establish military or civilian censorship or in any way to limit or infringe upon freedom of the press or of speech as guaranteed by the Constitution of the United States and no regulation shall be promulgated hereunder having that effect."

Thus, Congress has been faithful to the command of the First Amendment in this area.

So any power that the Government possesses must come from its "inherent power." . . .

The Government says that it has inherent powers to go into court and obtain an injunction to protect the national interest, which, in this case, is alleged to be national security. . . .

Near v. Minnesota repudiated that expansive doctrine in no uncertain terms.

The dominant purpose of the First Amendment was to prohibit the widespread practice of governmental suppression of embarrassing information. It is common knowledge that the First Amendment was adopted against the widespread use of the common law of seditious libel to punish the dissemination of material that is embarrassing to the powers-that-be. The present cases will, I think, go down in history as the most dramatic illustration of that principle. A debate of large proportions goes on in the Nation over our posture in Vietnam. That debate antedated the disclosure of the contents of the present documents. The latter are highly relevant to the debate in progress.

Secrecy in government is fundamentally antidemocratic, perpetuating bureaucratic errors. Open debate and discussion of public issues are vital to our national health. On public questions, there should be "uninhibited, robust, and wide-open" debate. . . .

Brennan, concurring:

I write separately in these cases only to emphasize what should be apparent: that our judgments in the present cases may not be taken to indicate the propriety, in the future, of issuing temporary stays and restraining orders to block the publication of material sought to be suppressed by the Government. So far as I can determine, never before has the United States sought to enjoin a newspaper from publishing information in its possession. The relative novelty of the questions presented, the necessary haste with which decisions were reached, the magnitude of the interests asserted, and the fact that all the parties have concentrated their arguments upon the question whether permanent restraints were proper may have justified at least some of the restraints heretofore imposed in these cases. Certainly it is difficult to fault the several courts below for seeking to assure that the issues here involved were preserved for ultimate review by this Court. But even if it be assumed that some of the interim restraints were proper in the two cases before us, that assumption has no bearing upon the propriety of similar judicial action in the future. To begin with, there has now been ample time for reflection and judgment; whatever values there may be in the preservation of novel questions for appellate review may not support any restraints in the future. More important, the First Amendment stands as an absolute bar to the imposition of judicial restraints in circumstances of the kind presented by these cases. . . .

Stewart, concurring:

In the governmental structure created by our Constitution, the Executive is endowed with enormous power in the two related areas of national defense and international relations. This power, largely unchecked by the Legislative and Judicial branches, has been pressed to the very hilt since the advent of the nuclear missile age. For better or for worse, the simple fact is that a President of the United States possesses vastly greater constitutional independence in these two vital areas of power than does, say, a prime minister of a country with a parliamentary form of government.

In the absence of the governmental checks and balances present in other areas of our national life, the only effective restraint upon executive policy and power in the areas of national defense and international affairs may lie in an enlightened citizenry—in an informed and critical public opinion which alone can here protect the values of democratic government. For this reason, it is perhaps here that a press that is alert, aware, and free most vitally serves the basic purpose of the First Amendment. For, without an informed and free press, there cannot be an enlightened people. . . .

I think there can be but one answer to this dilemma, if dilemma it be. The responsibility must be where the power is. If the Constitution gives the Executive a large degree of unshared power in the conduct of foreign affairs and the maintenance of our national defense, then, under the Constitution, the Executive must have the largely unshared duty to determine and preserve the degree of internal security necessary to exercise that power successfully. It is an awesome responsibility, requiring judgment and wisdom of a high order. I should suppose that moral, political, and practical considerations would dictate that a very first principle of that wisdom would be an insistence upon avoiding secrecy for its own sake. For when everything is classified, then nothing is classified, and the system becomes one to be disregarded by the cynical or the careless, and to be manipulated by those intent on self-protection or self-promotion. I should suppose, in short, that the hallmark of a truly effective internal security system would be the maximum possible disclosure, recognizing that secrecy can best be preserved only when credibility is truly maintained. But, be that as it may, it is clear to me that it is the constitutional duty of the Executive—as a matter of sovereign prerogative, and not as a matter of law as the courts know law—through the promulgation and enforcement of executive regulations, to protect the confidentiality necessary to carry

out its responsibilities in the fields of international relations and national defense.

This is not to say that Congress and the courts have
no role to play. Undoubtedly, Congress has the power
to enact specific and appropriate criminal laws to protect government property and preserve government
secrets. Congress has passed such laws, and several of
them are of very colorable relevance to the apparent
circumstances of these cases. And if a criminal prosecution is instituted, it will be the responsibility of the
courts to decide the applicability of the criminal law
under which the charge is brought. Moreover, if Congress should pass a specific law authorizing civil proceedings in this field, the courts would likewise have
the duty to decide the constitutionality of such a law,
as well as its applicability to the facts proved.

But in the cases before us, we are asked neither to
construe specific regulations nor to apply specific laws.
We are asked, instead, to perform a function that the
Constitution gave to the Executive, not the Judiciary.
We are asked, quite simply, to prevent the publication
by two newspapers of material that the Executive
Branch insists should not, in the national interest, be
published. I am convinced that the Executive is correct with respect to some of the documents involved.
But I cannot say that disclosure of any of them will
surely result in direct, immediate, and irreparable
damage to our Nation or its people. That being so,
there can under the First Amendment be but one judicial resolution of the issues before us. I join the judgments of the Court.

White, concurring:

I concur in today's judgments, but only because of the
concededly extraordinary protection against prior restraints enjoyed by the press under our constitutional
system. I do not say that in no circumstances would
the First Amendment permit an injunction against
publishing information about government plans or
operations. Nor, after examining the materials the
Government characterizes as the most sensitive and
destructive, can I deny that revelation of these documents will do substantial damage to public interests.
Indeed, I am confident that their disclosure will have
that result. But I nevertheless agree that the United
States has not satisfied the very heavy burden that it
must meet to warrant an injunction against publication in these cases, at least in the absence of express
and appropriately limited congressional authorization
for prior restraints in circumstances such as these.

... [B]ecause the material poses substantial dangers to national interests, and because of the hazards
of criminal sanctions, a responsible press may choose
never to publish the more sensitive materials. To sustain the Government in these cases would start the
courts down a long and hazardous road that I am not
willing to travel, at least without congressional guidance and direction. . . .

The Criminal Code contains numerous provisions
potentially relevant to these cases. Section 797 makes
it a crime to publish certain photographs or drawings
of military installations. Section 798, also in precise
language, proscribes knowing and willful publication
of any classified information concerning the crypto-
graphic systems or communication intelligence activities of the United States, as well as any information
obtained from communication intelligence operations. If any of the material here at issue is of this nature, the newspapers are presumably now on full
notice of the position of the United States, and must
face the consequences if they publish. I would have
no difficulty in sustaining convictions under these sections on facts that would not justify the intervention
of equity and the imposition of a prior restraint. . . .

. . . I am not, of course, saying that either of
these newspapers has yet committed a crime, or that
either would commit a crime if it published all the
material now in its possession. That matter must
await resolution in the context of a criminal proceeding if one is instituted by the United States. In
that event, the issue of guilt or innocence would be
determined by procedures and standards quite different from those that have purported to govern
these injunctive proceedings.

Marshall, concurring:

It would . . . be utterly inconsistent with the concept
of separation of powers for this Court to use its power
of contempt to prevent behavior that Congress has
specifically declined to prohibit. There would be a
similar damage to the basic concept of these co-equal
branches of Government if, when the Executive
Branch has adequate authority granted by Congress
to protect "national security," it can choose, instead,
to invoke the contempt power of a court to enjoin the
threatened conduct. The Constitution provides that
Congress shall make laws, the President execute laws,
and courts interpret laws. It did not provide for government by injunction in which the courts and the
Executive Branch can "make law" without regard to

the action of Congress. It may be more convenient for the Executive Branch if it need only convince a judge to prohibit conduct, rather than ask the Congress to pass a law, and it may be more convenient to enforce a contempt order than to seek a criminal conviction in a jury trial. Moreover, it may be considered politically wise to get a court to share the responsibility for arresting those who the Executive Branch has probable cause to believe are violating the law. But convenience and political considerations of the moment do not justify a basic departure from the principles of our system of government. . . .

Even if it is determined that the Government could not in good faith bring criminal prosecutions against the New York Times and the Washington Post, it is clear that Congress has specifically rejected passing legislation that would have clearly given the President the power he seeks here and made the current activity of the newspapers unlawful. When Congress specifically declines to make conduct unlawful, it is not for this Court to redecide those issues—to overrule Congress. . . .

Burger, dissenting:

So clear are the constitutional limitations on prior restraint against expression that, from the time of *Near v. Minnesota* we have had little occasion to be concerned with cases involving prior restraints against news reporting on matters of public interest. There is, therefore, little variation among the members of the Court in terms of resistance to prior restraints against publication. Adherence to this basic constitutional principle, however, does not make these cases simple. In these cases, the imperative of a free and unfettered press comes into collision with another imperative, the effective functioning of a complex modern government, and, specifically, the effective exercise of certain constitutional powers of the Executive. Only those who view the First Amendment as an absolute in all circumstances—a view I respect, but reject—can find such cases as these to be simple or easy.

These cases are not simple for another and more immediate reason. We do not know the facts of the cases. No District Judge knew all the facts. No Court of Appeals judge knew all the facts. No member of this Court knows all the facts.

Why are we in this posture, in which only those judges to whom the First Amendment is absolute and permits of no restraint in any circumstances or for any reason, are really in a position to act?

I suggest we are in this posture because these cases have been conducted in unseemly haste. . . . The prompt setting of these cases reflects our universal abhorrence of prior restraint. But prompt judicial action does not mean unjudicial haste.

Here, moreover, the frenetic haste is due in large part to the manner in which the Times proceeded from the date it obtained the purloined documents. It seems reasonably clear now that the haste precluded reasonable and deliberate judicial treatment of these cases, and was not warranted. The precipitate action of this Court aborting trials not yet completed is not the kind of judicial conduct that ought to attend the disposition of a great issue.

The newspapers make a derivative claim under the First Amendment; they denominate this right as the public "right to know"; by implication, the Times asserts a sole trusteeship of that right by virtue of its journalistic "scoop." The right is asserted as an absolute. Of course, the First Amendment right itself is not an absolute, as Justice Holmes so long ago pointed out in his aphorism concerning the right to shout "fire" in a crowded theater if there was no fire. There are other exceptions, some of which Chief Justice Hughes mentioned by way of example in *Near v. Minnesota*. There are no doubt other exceptions no one has had occasion to describe or discuss. Conceivably, such exceptions may be lurking in these cases and, would have been flushed had they been properly considered in the trial courts, free from unwarranted deadlines and frenetic pressures. An issue of this importance should be tried and heard in a judicial atmosphere conducive to thoughtful, reflective deliberation, especially when haste, in terms of hours, is unwarranted in light of the long period the Times, by its own choice, deferred publication.

It is not disputed that the Times has had unauthorized possession of the documents for three to four months, during which it has had its expert analysts studying them, presumably digesting them and preparing the material for publication. During all of this time, the Times, presumably in its capacity as trustee of the public's "right to know," has held up publication for purposes it considered proper, and thus public knowledge was delayed. No doubt this was for a good reason; the analysis of 7,000 pages of complex material drawn from a vastly greater volume of material would inevitably take time, and the writing of good news stories takes time. But why should the United States Government, from whom this information was illegally acquired by someone, along with all the counsel, trial judges, and appellate judges be placed under needless pressure? After these months of deferral, the alleged "right to know" has somehow and suddenly become a right that must be vindicated instanter.

Would it have been unreasonable, since the newspaper could anticipate the Government's objections to release of secret material, to give the Government an opportunity to review the entire collection and determine whether agreement could be reached on publication? Stolen or not, if security was not, in fact, jeopardized, much of the material could no doubt have been declassified, since it spans a period ending in 1968. With such an approach—one that great newspapers have in the past practiced and stated editorially to be the duty of an honorable press—the newspapers and Government might well have narrowed the area of disagreement as to what was and was not publishable, leaving the remainder to be resolved in orderly litigation, if necessary. To me, it is hardly believable that a newspaper long regarded as a great institution in American life would fail to perform one of the basic and simple duties of every citizen with respect to the discovery or possession of stolen property or secret government documents. That duty, I had thought—perhaps naively—was to report forthwith, to responsible public officers. This duty rests on taxi drivers, Justices, and the New York Times. The course followed by the Times, whether so calculated or not, removed any possibility of orderly litigation of the issue. If the action of the judges up to now has been correct, that result is sheer happenstance.

Our grant of the writ of certiorari before final judgment in the Times case aborted the trial in the District Court before it had made a complete record pursuant to the mandate of the Court of Appeals for the Second Circuit.

The consequence of all this melancholy series of events is that we literally do not know what we are acting on. As I see it, we have been forced to deal with litigation concerning rights of great magnitude without an adequate record, and surely without time for adequate treatment either in the prior proceedings or in this Court. It is interesting to note that counsel on both sides, in oral argument before this Court, were frequently unable to respond to questions on factual points. Not surprisingly, they pointed out that they had been working literally "around the clock," and simply were unable to review the documents that give rise to these cases and were not familiar with them. This Court is in no better posture. . . .

I would affirm the Court of Appeals for the Second Circuit and allow the District Court to complete the trial aborted by our grant of certiorari, meanwhile preserving the status quo in the Post case. I would direct that the District Court, on remand, give priority to the Times case to the exclusion of all other business of that court, but I would not set arbitrary deadlines. . . .

Harlan, dissenting:

. . . It is plain to me that the scope of the judicial function in passing upon the activities of the Executive Branch of the Government in the field of foreign affairs is very narrowly restricted. This view is, I think, dictated by the concept of separation of powers upon which our constitutional system rests. . . .

Even if there is some room for the judiciary to override the executive determination, it is plain that the scope of review must be exceedingly narrow. I can see no indication in the opinions of either the District Court or the Court of Appeals in the Post litigation that the conclusions of the Executive were given even the deference owing to an administrative agency, much less that owing to a co-equal branch of the Government operating within the field of its constitutional prerogative.

Blackmun, dissenting:

. . . I hope that damage has not already been done. If, however, damage has been done, and if, with the Court's action today, these newspapers proceed to publish the critical documents and there results therefrom "the death of soldiers, the destruction of alliances, the greatly increased difficulty of negotiation with our enemies, the inability of our diplomats to negotiate," to which list I might add the factors of prolongation of the war and of further delay in the freeing of United States prisoners, then the Nation's people will know where the responsibility for these sad consequences rests.

Sheppard v. Maxwell

384 U.S. 333, (1966), 8-1
Opinion of the Court: Clark (Brennan, Douglas, Fortas, Harlan, Stewart, Warren, White)
Dissenting: Black

What could or should the trial judge have done to keep the proceeding from being adversely affected by media coverage? Did the evidence show merely that the trial was affected by the media or that the affect caused it to be unfair to Sheppard, that is, caused him to be convicted instead of possibly acquitted? Where does the public interest lie in this case?

Clark, for the Court:

This federal habeas corpus application involves the question whether Sheppard was deprived of a fair trial in his state conviction for the second-degree murder of his wife because of the trial judge's failure to protect Sheppard sufficiently from the massive, pervasive and prejudicial publicity that attended his prosecution. . . .

The principle that justice cannot survive behind walls of silence has long been reflected in the "Anglo-American distrust for secret trials." A responsible press has always been regarded as the handmaiden of effective judicial administration, especially in the criminal field. Its function in this regard is documented by an impressive record of service over several centuries. The press does not simply publish information about trials, but guards against the miscarriage of justice by subjecting the police, prosecutors, and judicial processes to extensive public scrutiny and criticism. This Court has, therefore, been unwilling to place any direct limitations on the freedom traditionally exercised by the news media for "[w]hat transpires in the courtroom is public property." . . .

But the Court has also pointed out that "[l]egal trials are not like elections, to be won through the use of the meeting-hall, the radio, and the newspaper." And the Court has insisted that no one be punished for a crime without "a charge fairly made and fairly tried in a public tribunal free of prejudice, passion, excitement, and tyrannical power." . . .

The [trial] court's fundamental error is compounded by the holding that it lacked power to control the publicity about the trial. From the very inception of the proceedings, the judge announced that neither he nor anyone else could restrict prejudicial news accounts. . . .

The carnival atmosphere at trial could easily have been avoided, since the courtroom and courthouse premises are subject to the control of the court. As we stressed in *Estes* [v. *Texas*], the presence of the press at judicial proceedings must be limited when it is apparent that the accused might otherwise be prejudiced or disadvantaged. Bearing in mind the massive pretrial publicity, the judge should have adopted stricter rules governing the use of the courtroom by newsmen, as Sheppard's counsel requested. The number of reporters in the courtroom itself could have been limited at the first sign that their presence would disrupt the trial. They certainly should not have been placed inside the bar. Furthermore, the judge should have more closely regulated the conduct of newsmen in the courtroom. For instance, the judge belatedly asked them not to handle and photograph trial exhibits lying on the counsel table during recesses.

Secondly, the court should have insulated the witnesses. All of the newspapers and radio stations apparently interviewed prospective witnesses at will, and in many instances disclosed their testimony. . . .

Thirdly, the court should have made some effort to control the release of leads, information, and gossip to the press by police officers, witnesses, and the counsel for both sides. Much of the information thus disclosed was inaccurate, leading to groundless rumors and confusion. . . .

Defense counsel immediately brought to the court's attention the tremendous amount of publicity in the Cleveland press that "misrepresented entirely the testimony" in the case. Under such circumstances, the judge should have at least warned the newspapers to check the accuracy of their accounts. And it is obvious that the judge should have further sought to alleviate this problem by imposing control over the statements made to the news media by counsel, witnesses, and especially the Coroner and police officers. . . .

More specifically, the trial court might well have proscribed extrajudicial statements by any lawyer, party, witness, or court official which divulged prejudicial matters, such as the refusal of Sheppard to submit to interrogation or take any lie detector tests; any statement made by Sheppard to officials; the identity of prospective witnesses or their probable testimony; any belief in guilt or innocence; or like statements concerning the merits of the case. Being advised of the great public interest in the case, the mass coverage of the press, and the potential prejudicial impact of publicity, the court could also have requested the appropriate city and county officials to promulgate a regulation with respect to dissemination of information about the case by their employees. In addition, reporters who wrote or broadcast prejudicial stories could have been warned as to the impropriety of publishing material not introduced in the proceedings. The judge was put on notice of such events by defense counsel's complaint about the WHK broadcast on the second day of trial. In this manner, Sheppard's right to a trial free from outside interference would have been given added protection without corresponding curtailment of the news media. Had the judge, the other officers of the court, and the police placed the interest of justice first, the news media would have soon learned to be content with the task of reporting the case as it unfolded in the courtroom—not pieced together from extrajudicial statements.

From the cases coming here, we note that unfair and prejudicial news comment on pending trials has become increasingly prevalent. Due process requires that the accused receive a trial by an impartial jury free from outside influences. Given the pervasiveness of modern communications and the difficulty of effacing prejudicial publicity from the minds of the jurors, the trial courts must take strong measures to ensure that the balance is never weighed against the accused. And appellate tribunals have the duty to make an independent evaluation of the circumstances. Of course, there is nothing that proscribes the press from reporting events that transpire in the courtroom. But where there is a reasonable likelihood that prejudicial news prior to trial will prevent a fair trial, the judge should continue the case until the threat abates, or transfer it to another county not so permeated with publicity. In addition, sequestration of the jury was something the judge should have raised sua sponte with counsel. If publicity during the proceedings threatens the fairness of the trial, a new trial should be ordered. But we must remember that reversals are but palliatives; the cure lies in those remedial measures that will prevent the prejudice at its inception. The courts must take such steps by rule and regulation that will protect their processes from prejudicial outside interferences. Neither prosecutors, counsel for defense, the accused, witnesses, court staff nor enforcement officers coming under the jurisdiction of the court should be permitted to frustrate its function. Collaboration between counsel and the press as to information affecting the fairness of a criminal trial is not only subject to regulation, but is highly censurable, and worthy of disciplinary measures.

Since the state trial judge did not fulfill his duty to protect Sheppard from the inherently prejudicial publicity which saturated the community and to control disruptive influences in the courtroom, we must reverse the denial of the habeas petition. The case is remanded to the District Court with instructions to issue the writ and order that Sheppard be released from custody unless the State puts him to its charges again within a reasonable time.

Branzburg v. Hayes

408 U.S. 665 (1972) 5-4
Opinion of the Court: White (Blackmun, Burger, Powell, Rehnquist)
Dissenting: Brennan, Douglas, Marshall, Stewart

This case was heard and decided with two others, In re Pappas *and* United States v. Caldwell, *dealing with the issue of a journalist's privilege not to disclose sources.*

What is a "journalist's privilege"? Why does the Supreme Court not sustain it? In receiving confidential information, are journalists more like doctors, lawyers, or clergy, who may generally withhold it, or are they more like ordinary lay persons, who must disclose such information if officially called upon to do so? The public interest in this case is complex. How can it be stated?

White, for the Court:

On November 15, 1969, the Courier-Journal carried a story under petitioner's by-line describing in detail his observations of two young residents of Jefferson County synthesizing hashish from marihuana, an activity which, they asserted, earned them about $5,000 in three weeks. The article included a photograph of a pair of hands working above a laboratory table on which was a substance identified by the caption as hashish. The article stated that petitioner had promised not to reveal the identity of the two hashish makers. Petitioner was shortly subpoenaed by the Jefferson County grand jury; he appeared, but refused to identify the individuals he had seen possessing marihuana or the persons he had seen making hashish from marihuana. A state trial court judge ordered petitioner to answer these questions and rejected his contention that the Kentucky reporters' privilege statute, the First Amendment of the United States Constitution, or §§1, 2, and 8 of the Kentucky Constitution authorized his refusal to answer. . . .

The second case involving petitioner Branzburg arose out of his later story published on January 10, 1971, which described in detail the use of drugs in Frankfort, Kentucky. The article reported that, in order to provide a comprehensive survey of the "drug scene" in Frankfort, petitioner had "spent two weeks interviewing several dozen drug users in the capital city," and had seen some of them smoking marihuana. A number of conversations with and observations of several unnamed drug users were recounted. Subpoenaed to appear before a Franklin County grand jury "to testify in the matter of violation of statutes concerning use and sale of drugs," petitioner Branzburg moved to quash the summons; the motion was denied. . . .

In re Pappas originated when petitioner Pappas, a television newsman-photographer working out of the Providence, Rhode Island, office of a New Bedford, Massachusetts, television station, was called to New Bedford on July 30, 1970, to report on civil disorders there which involved fires and other turmoil. He intended to cover a Black Panther news conference at that group's headquarters in a boarded-up store. Petitioner found the streets around the store barricaded, but he ultimately gained entrance to the area and recorded and photographed a prepared statement read by one of the Black Panther leaders at about 3 p.m. He then asked for and received permission to reenter the area. Returning at about 9 o'clock, he was allowed to enter and remain inside Panther headquarters. As a condition of entry, Pappas agreed not to disclose anything he saw or heard inside the store except an anticipated police raid, which Pappas, "on his own," was free to photograph and report as he wished. Pappas stayed inside the headquarters for about three hours, but there was no police raid, and petitioner wrote no story and did not otherwise reveal what had occurred in the store while he was there. Two months later, petitioner was summoned before the Bristol County Grand Jury and appeared, answered questions as to his name, address, employment, and what he had seen and heard outside Panther headquarters, but refused to answer any questions about what had taken place inside headquarters while he was there, claiming that the First Amendment afforded him a privilege to protect confidential informants and their information. A second summons was then served upon him, again directing him to appear before the grand jury and "to give such evidence as he knows relating to any matters which may be inquired of on behalf of the Commonwealth before . . . the Grand Jury.". . .

United States v. Caldwell, arose from subpoenas issued by a federal grand jury in the Northern District of California to respondent Earl Caldwell, a reporter for the New York Times assigned to cover the Black Panther Party and other black militant groups. A subpoena duces tecum was served on respondent on February 2, 1970, ordering him to appear before the grand jury to testify and to bring with him notes and tape recordings of interviews given him for publication by officers and spokesmen of the Black Panther Party concerning the aims, purposes, and activities of that organization. Re-

spondent objected to the scope of this subpoena, and an agreement between his counsel and the Government attorneys resulted in a continuance. A second subpoena, served on March 16, omitted the documentary requirement and simply ordered Caldwell "to appear . . . to testify before the Grand Jury.". . .

Petitioners Branzburg and Pappas and respondent Caldwell press First Amendment claims that may be simply put: that, to gather news, it is often necessary to agree either not to identify the source of information published or to publish only part of the facts revealed, or both; that, if the reporter is nevertheless forced to reveal these confidences to a grand jury, the source so identified and other confidential sources of other reporters will be measurably deterred from furnishing publishable information, all to the detriment of the free flow of information protected by the First Amendment. Although the newsmen in these cases do not claim an absolute privilege against official interrogation in all circumstances, they assert that the reporter should not be forced either to appear or to testify before a grand jury or at trial until and unless sufficient grounds are shown for believing that the reporter possesses information relevant to a crime the grand jury is investigating, that the information the reporter has is unavailable from other sources, and that the need for the information is sufficiently compelling to override the claimed invasion of First Amendment interests occasioned by the disclosure. . . .

We do not question the significance of free speech, press, or assembly to the country's welfare. Nor is it suggested that news gathering does not qualify for First Amendment protection; without some protection for seeking out the news, freedom of the press could be eviscerated. But these cases involve no intrusions upon speech or assembly, no prior restraint or restriction on what the press may publish, and no express or implied command that the press publish what it prefers to withhold. No exaction or tax for the privilege of publishing, and no penalty, civil or criminal, related to the content of published material is at issue here. The use of confidential sources by the press is not forbidden or restricted; reporters remain free to seek news from any source by means within the law. No attempt is made to require the press to publish its sources of information or indiscriminately to disclose them on request.

The sole issue before us is the obligation of reporters to respond to grand jury subpoenas as other citizens do, and to answer questions relevant to an investigation into the commission of crime. . . .

Despite the fact that news gathering may be hampered, the press is regularly excluded from grand jury proceedings, our own conferences, the meetings of other official bodies gathered in executive session, and the meetings of private organizations. Newsmen have no constitutional right of access to the scenes of crime or disaster when the general public is excluded, and they may be prohibited from attending or publishing information about trials if such restrictions re necessary to assure a defendant a fair trial before an impartial tribunal. . . .

It is thus not surprising that the great weight of authority is that newsmen are not exempt from the normal duty of appearing before a grand jury and answering questions relevant to a criminal investigation. At common law, courts consistently refused to recognize the existence of any privilege authorizing a newsman to refuse to reveal confidential information to a grand jury. . . .

The prevailing constitutional view of the newsman's privilege is very much rooted in the ancient role of the grand jury that has the dual function of determining if there is probable cause to believe that a crime has been committed and of protecting citizens against unfounded criminal prosecutions. . . . Because its task is to inquire into the existence of possible criminal conduct and to return only well founded indictments, its investigative powers are necessarily broad. . . .

A number of States have provided newsmen a statutory privilege of varying breadth, but the majority have not done so, and none has been provided by federal statute. Until now, the only testimonial privilege for unofficial witnesses that is rooted in the Federal Constitution is the Fifth Amendment privilege against compelled self-incrimination. We are asked to create another by interpreting the First Amendment to grant newsmen a testimonial privilege that other citizens do not enjoy. This we decline to do. . . .

This conclusion itself involves no restraint on what newspapers may publish or on the type or quality of information reporters may seek to acquire, nor does it threaten the vast bulk of confidential relationships between reporters and their sources. Grand juries address themselves to the issues of whether crimes have been committed and who committed them. Only where news sources themselves are implicated in crime or possess information relevant to the grand jury's task need they or the reporter be concerned about grand jury subpoenas. Nothing before us indicates that a large number or percentage of all confidential news sources falls into either category and would in any way be deterred by our

holding that the Constitution does not, as it never has, exempt the newsman from performing the citizen's normal duty of appearing and furnishing information relevant to the grand jury's task. . . .

The argument that the flow of news will be diminished by compelling reporters to aid the grand jury in a criminal investigation is not irrational, nor are the records before us silent on the matter. But we remain unclear how often and to what extent informers are actually deterred from furnishing information when newsmen are forced to testify before a grand jury. The available data indicate that some newsmen rely a great deal on confidential sources, and that some informants are particularly sensitive to the threat of exposure, and may be silenced if it is held by this Court that, ordinarily, newsmen must testify pursuant to subpoenas, but the evidence fails to demonstrate that there would be a significant constriction of the flow of news to the public if this Court reaffirms the prior common law and constitutional rule regarding the testimonial obligations of newsmen. Estimates of the inhibiting effect of such subpoenas on the willingness of informants to make disclosures to newsmen are widely divergent and to a great extent speculative. . . .

Accepting the fact, however, that an undetermined number of informants not themselves implicated in crime will nevertheless, for whatever reason, refuse to talk to newsmen if they fear identification by a reporter in an official investigation, we cannot accept the argument that the public interest in possible future news about crime from undisclosed, unverified sources must take precedence over the public interest in pursuing and prosecuting those crimes reported to the press by informants and in thus deterring the commission of such crimes in the future. . . .

It is said that currently press subpoenas have multiplied, that mutual distrust and tension between press and officialdom have increased, that reporting styles have changed, and that there is now more need for confidential sources, particularly where the press seeks news about minority cultural and political groups or dissident organizations suspicious of the law and public officials. These developments, even if true, are treacherous grounds for a far-reaching interpretation of the First Amendment fastening a nationwide rule on courts, grand juries, and prosecuting officials everywhere. . . .

The privilege claimed here is conditional, not absolute; given the suggested preliminary showings and compelling need, the reporter would be required to testify. Presumably, such a rule would reduce the instances in which reporters could be required to appear, but predicting in advance when and in what circumstances they could be compelled to do so would be difficult. . . .

We are unwilling to embark the judiciary on a long and difficult journey to such an uncertain destination. The administration of a constitutional newsman's privilege would present practical and conceptual difficulties of a high order. Sooner or later, it would be necessary to define those categories of newsmen who qualified for the privilege, a questionable procedure in light of the traditional doctrine that liberty of the press is the right of the lonely pamphleteer who uses carbon paper or a mimeograph just as much as of the large metropolitan publisher who utilizes the latest photocomposition methods. . . .

In each instance where a reporter is subpoenaed to testify, the courts would also be embroiled in preliminary factual and legal determinations with respect to whether the proper predicate had been laid for the reporter's appearance: Is there probable cause to believe a crime has been committed? Is it likely that the reporter has useful information gained in confidence? Could the grand jury obtain the information elsewhere? Is the official interest sufficient to outweigh the claimed privilege?

Thus, in the end, by considering whether enforcement of a particular law served a "compelling" governmental interest, the courts would be inextricably involved in distinguishing between the value of enforcing different criminal laws. By requiring testimony from a reporter in investigations involving some crimes but not in others, they would be making a value judgment that a legislature had declined to make, since, in each case, the criminal law involved would represent a considered legislative judgment, not constitutionally suspect, of what conduct is liable to criminal prosecution. The task of judges, like other officials outside the legislative branch, is not to make the law, but to uphold it in accordance with their oaths.

At the federal level, Congress has freedom to determine whether a statutory newsman's privilege is necessary and desirable and to fashion standards and rules as narrow or broad as deemed necessary to deal with the evil discerned and, equally important, to refashion those rules as experience from time to time may dictate. There is also merit in leaving state legislatures free, within First Amendment limits, to fashion their own standards in light of the conditions and problems with respect to the relations between law enforcement officials and press in their own areas. It goes without

saying, of course, that we are powerless to bar state courts from responding in their own way and construing their own constitutions so as to recognize a newsman's privilege, either qualified or absolute. . . .

Finally, as we have earlier indicated, news gathering is not without its First Amendment protections, and grand jury investigations, if instituted or conducted other than in good faith, would pose wholly different issues for resolution under the First Amendment. Official harassment of the press undertaken not for purposes of law enforcement, but to disrupt a reporter's relationship with his news sources would have no justification. Grand juries are subject to judicial control and subpoenas to motions to quash. We do not expect courts will forget that grand juries must operate within the limits of the First Amendment as well as the Fifth. . . .

Douglas, dissenting:
Today's decision will impede the wide-open and robust dissemination of ideas and counterthought which a free press both fosters and protects and which is essential to the success of intelligent self-government. Forcing a reporter before a grand jury will have two retarding effects upon the ear and the pen of the press. Fear of exposure will cause dissidents to communicate less openly to trusted reporters. And fear of accountability will cause editors and critics to write with more restrained pens. . . .

A reporter is no better than his source of information. Unless he has a privilege to withhold the identity of his source, he will be the victim of governmental intrigue or aggression. If he can be summoned to testify in secret before a grand jury, his sources will dry up and the attempted exposure, the effort to enlighten the public, will be ended. If what the Court sanctions today becomes settled law, then the reporter's main function in American society will be to pass on to the public the press releases which the various departments of government issue.

It is no answer to reply that the risk that a newsman will divulge one's secrets to the grand jury is no greater than the threat that he will, in any event, inform to the police. Even the most trustworthy reporter may not be able to withstand relentless badgering before a grand jury.

The record in this case is replete with weighty affidavits from responsible newsmen, telling how important is the sanctity of their sources of information. When we deny newsmen that protection, we deprive the people of the information needed to run the affairs of the Nation in an intelligent way. . . .

Today's decision is more than a clog upon news gathering. It is a signal to publishers and editors that they should exercise caution in how they use whatever information they can obtain. Without immunity, they may be summoned to account for their criticism. Entrenched officers have been quick to crash their powers down upon unfriendly commentators.

The intrusion of government into this domain is symptomatic of the disease of this society. As the years pass, the power of government becomes more and more pervasive. It is a power to suffocate both people and causes. Those in power, whatever their politics, want only to perpetuate it. Now that the fences of the law and the tradition that has protected the press are broken down, the people are the victims. The First Amendment, as I read it, was designed precisely to prevent that tragedy. . . .

Stewart, dissenting:

The Court's crabbed view of the First Amendment reflect a disturbing insensitivity to the critical role of an independent press in our society. The question whether a reporter has a constitutional right to a confidential relationship with his source is of first impression here, but the principles that should guide our decision are as basic as any to be found in the Constitution. . . . [T]he Court in these cases holds that a newsman has no First Amendment right to protect his sources when called before a grand jury. The Court thus invites state and federal authorities to undermine the historic independence of the press by attempting to annex the journalistic profession as an investigative arm of government. Not only will this decision impair performance of the press' constitutionally protected functions, but it will, I am convinced, in the long run harm, rather than help, the administration of justice. . . .

The reporter's constitutional right to a confidential relationship with his source stem from the broad societal interest in a full and free flow of information to the public. . . .

It is obvious that informants are necessary to the news-gathering process as we know it today. . . . It is equally obvious that the promise of confidentiality may be a necessary prerequisite to a productive relationship between a newsman and his informants. . . .

Finally, and most important, when governmental officials possess an unchecked power to compel newsmen to disclose information received in confidence, sources will clearly be deterred from giving information, and reporters will clearly be deterred from publishing it, because uncertainty about exercise of the power will lead to "self-censorship." . . .

Posed against the First Amendment's protection of the newsman's confidential relationships in these cases is society's interest in the use of the grand jury to administer justice fairly and effectively. . . . Yet the longstanding rule making every person's evidence available to the grand jury is not absolute. The rule has been limited by the Fifth Amendment, the Fourth Amendment, and the evidentiary privileges of the common law. . . .

Accordingly, when a reporter is asked to appear before a grand jury and reveal confidences, I would hold that the government must (1) show that there is probable cause to believe that the newsman has information that is clearly relevant to a specific probable violation of law; (2) demonstrate that the information sought cannot be obtained by alternative means less destructive of First Amendment rights; and (3) demonstrate a compelling and overriding interest in the information.

This is not to say that a grand jury could not issue a subpoena until such a showing were made, and it is not to say that a newsman would be in any way privileged to ignore any subpoena that was issued. Obviously, before the government's burden to make such a showing were triggered, the reporter would have to move to quash the subpoena, asserting the basis on which he considered the particular relationship a confidential one. . . .

Red Lion Broadcasting Co. v. Federal Communications Commission

395 U.S. 367 (1969), 7-0
Opinion of the Court: White (Black, Brennan, Harlan, Marshall, Stewart, White)
Not participating: Douglas

What is the fairness doctrine? How can such a government rule affecting freedom of the media be constitutionally justified? What is gained and lost by the rule and by upholding it? Does the rule affect program content?

White, for the Court:

The Federal Communications Commission has for many years imposed on radio and television broadcasters the requirement that discussion of public issues be presented on broadcast stations, and that each side of those issues must be given fair coverage.

This is known as the fairness doctrine, which originated very early in the history of broadcasting and has maintained its present outlines for some time. It is an obligation whose content has been defined in a long series of FCC rulings in particular cases, and which is distinct from the statutory requirement of §315 of the Communications Act that equal time be allotted all qualified candidates for public office. . . .

The Red Lion Broadcasting Company is licensed to operate a Pennsylvania radio station, WGCB. On November 27, 1964, WGCB carried a 15-minute broadcast by the Reverend Billy James Hargis as part of a "Christian Crusade" series. A book by Fred J. Cook entitled "Goldwater—Extremist on the Right" was discussed by Hargis, who said that Cook had been fired by a newspaper for making false charges against city officials; that Cook had then worked for a Communist-affiliated publication; that he had defended Alger Hiss and attacked J. Edgar Hoover and the Central Intelligence Agency, and that he had now written a "book to smear and destroy Barry Goldwater." When Cook heard of the broadcast, he concluded that he had been personally attacked and demanded free reply time, which the station refused. After an exchange of letters among Cook, Red Lion, and the FCC, the FCC declared that the Hargis broadcast constituted a personal attack on Cook; that Red Lion had failed to meet its obligation under the fairness doctrine. . . . to send a tape, transcript, or summary of the broadcast to Cook and offer him reply time, and that the station must provide reply time whether or not Cook would pay for it. . . .

The broadcasters challenge the fairness doctrine and its specific manifestations in the personal attack and political editorial rules on conventional First Amendment grounds, alleging that the rules abridge their freedom of speech and press. Their contention is that the First Amendment protects their desire to use their allotted frequencies continuously to broadcast whatever they choose, and to exclude whomever they choose from ever using that frequency. No man may be prevented from saying or publishing what he thinks, or from refusing in his speech or other utterances to give equal weight to the views of his opponents. This right, they say, applies equally to broadcasters. . . .

. . . It would be strange if the First Amendment, aimed at protecting and furthering communications, prevented the Government from making radio communication possible by requiring licenses to broadcast and by limiting the number of licenses so as not to overcrowd the spectrum. . . .

. . . No one has a First Amendment right to a license or to monopolize a radio frequency; to deny a station license because "the public interest" requires it "is not a denial of free speech." . . .

. . . There is nothing in the First Amendment which prevents the Government from requiring a licensee to share his frequency with others and to conduct himself as a proxy or fiduciary with obligations to present those views and voices which are representative of his community and which would otherwise, by necessity, be barred from the airwaves.

This is not to say that the First Amendment is irrelevant to public broadcasting. On the contrary, it has a major role to play, as the Congress itself recognized in §326, which forbids FCC interference with "the right of free speech by means of radio communication." Because of the scarcity of radio frequencies, the Government is permitted to put restraints on licensees in favor of others whose views should be expressed on this unique medium. But the people as a whole retain their interest in free speech by radio and their collective right to have the medium function consistently with the ends and purposes of the First Amendment. It is the right of the viewers and listeners, not the right of the broadcasters, which is paramount. It is the purpose of the First Amendment to preserve an uninhibited marketplace of ideas in which truth will ultimately prevail, rather than to countenance monopolization of that market, whether it be by the Government itself or a private licensee. . . . "[S]peech concerning public affairs is more than self-expression; it is the essence of self-government." It is the right of the public to receive suitable access to social, political, esthetic, moral, and other ideas and experiences which is crucial here. That right may not constitutionally be abridged either by Congress or by the FCC. . . .

Nor can we say that it is inconsistent with the First Amendment goal of producing an informed public capable of conducting its own affairs to require a broadcaster to permit answers to personal attacks occurring in the course of discussing controversial issues, or to require that the political opponents of those endorsed by the station be given a chance to communicate with the public. Otherwise, station owners and a few networks would have unfettered power to make time available only to the highest bidders, to communicate only their own views on public issues, people and candidates, and to permit on the air only those with whom they agreed. There is no sanctuary in the First Amendment for unlimited private censorship operating in a medium not open to all. "Freedom of the press from governmental interference under the First Amendment does not sanction repression of that freedom by private interests." *Associated Press v. United States*. . . .

It is strenuously argued, however, that, if political editorials or personal attacks will trigger an obligation in broadcasters to afford the opportunity for expression to speakers who need not pay for time and whose views are unpalatable to the licensees, then broadcasters will be irresistibly forced to self-censorship, and their coverage of controversial public issues will be eliminated, or at least rendered wholly ineffective. Such a result would indeed be a serious matter, for, should licensees actually eliminate their coverage of controversial issues, the purposes of the doctrine would be stifled.

At this point, however, as the Federal Communications Commission has indicated, that possibility is, at best, speculative. The communications industry, and, in particular, the networks, have taken pains to present controversial issues in the past, and even now they do not assert that they intend to abandon their efforts in this regard. It would be better if the FCC's encouragement were never necessary to induce the broadcasters to meet their responsibility. And if experience with the administration of these doctrines indicates that they have the net effect of reducing, rather than enhancing, the volume and quality of coverage, there will be time enough to reconsider the constitutional implications. The fairness doctrine in the past has had no such overall effect.

. . . [I]f present licensees should suddenly prove timorous, the Commission is not powerless to insist that they give adequate and fair attention to public issues. It does not violate the First Amendment to treat licensees given the privilege of using scarce radio frequencies as proxies for the entire community, obligated to give suitable time and attention to matters of great public concern. To condition the granting or renewal of licenses on a willingness to present representative community views on controversial issues is consistent with the ends and purposes of those constitutional provisions forbidding the abridgment of freedom of speech and freedom of the press. Congress need not stand idly by and permit those with licenses to ignore the problems which beset the people or to exclude from the airways anything but their own views of fundamental questions. . . .

Central Hudson Gas & Electric v. Public Service Commission

447 U.S. 557 (1980), 8-1
Opinion of the Court: Powell (Berger, Marshall, Stuart, White)
Concurring: Brennan, Blackmun, Stevens
Dissenting: Rehnquist

Why does commercial speech have First Amendment protection? What value did the Court see in the utility's ads? What conditions must be met before government may restrict commercial speech? Do they mean that the protection of commercial speech is less than that for noncommercial? How does Justice Rehnquist's view of the constitutional protection for commercial speech differ from that of the majority of the Court?

Powell, for the Court:

This case presents the question whether a regulation of the Public Service Commission of the State of New York violates the First and Fourteenth Amendments because it completely bans promotional advertising by an electrical utility.

In December, 1973, the Commission, appellee here, ordered electric utilities in New York State to cease all advertising that "promot[es] the use of electricity." The order was based on the Commission's finding that "the interconnected utility system in New York State does not have sufficient fuel stocks or sources of supply to continue furnishing all customer demands for the 1973–1974 winter." . . .

The Commission's order explicitly permitted "informational" advertising designed to encourage "shifts of consumption" from peak demand times to periods of low electricity demand. Ibid. (emphasis in original). Informational advertising would not seek to increase aggregate consumption, but would invite a leveling of demand throughout any given 24-hour period. The agency offered to review "specific proposals by the companies for specifically described [advertising] programs that meet these criteria."

When it rejected requests for rehearing . . . the Commission supplemented its rationale for the advertising ban. The agency observed that additional electricity probably would be more expensive to produce than existing output. Because electricity rates in New York were not then based on marginal cost, the Commission feared that additional power would be priced below the actual cost of generation. The additional electricity would be subsidized by all consumers through generally higher rates. The state agency also thought that promotional advertising would give "misleading signals" to the public by appearing to encourage energy consumption at a time when conservation is needed. . . .

The Commission's order restricts only commercial speech, that is, expression related solely to the economic interests of the speaker and its audience. The First Amendment, as applied to the States through the Fourteenth Amendment, protects commercial speech from unwarranted governmental regulation. Commercial expression not only serves the economic interest of the speaker, but also assists consumers and furthers the societal interest in the fullest possible dissemination of information. In applying the First Amendment to this area, we have rejected the "highly paternalistic" view that government has complete power to suppress or regulate commercial speech. . . .

. . . Even when advertising communicates only an incomplete version of the relevant facts, the First Amendment presumes that some accurate information is better than no information at all.

Nevertheless, our decisions have recognized the "common sense" distinction between speech proposing a commercial transaction, which occurs in an area traditionally subject to government regulation, and other varieties of speech. The Constitution therefore accords a lesser protection to commercial speech than to other constitutionally guaranteed expression. The protection available for particular commercial expression turns on the nature both of the expression and of the governmental interests served by its regulation.

The First Amendment's concern for commercial speech is based on the informational function of advertising. Consequently, there can be no constitutional objection to the suppression of commercial messages that do not accurately inform the public about lawful activity. The government may ban forms of communication more likely to deceive the public than to inform it, commercial speech related to illegal activity. . . .

In commercial speech cases . . . a four-part analysis has developed. At the outset, we must determine whether the expression is protected by the First Amendment. For commercial speech to come within that provision, it at least must concern lawful activity and not be misleading. Next, we ask whether the asserted governmental interest is substantial. If both inquiries yield positive answers, we must determine whether the regulation directly advances the governmental interest asserted, and whether it is not more extensive than is necessary to serve that interest.

We now apply this four-step analysis for commercial speech to the Commission's arguments in support of its ban on promotional advertising.

The Commission does not claim that the expression at issue either is inaccurate or relates to unlawful activity. Yet the New York Court of Appeals questioned whether Central Hudson's advertising is protected commercial speech. Because appellant holds a monopoly over the sale of electricity in its service area, the state court suggested that the Commission's order restricts no commercial speech of any worth. The court stated that advertising in a "noncompetitive market" could not improve the decisionmaking of consumers. The court saw no constitutional problem with barring commercial speech that it viewed as conveying little useful information.

This reasoning falls short of establishing that appellant's advertising is not commercial speech protected by the First Amendment. Monopoly over the supply of a product provides no protection from competition with substitutes for that product. . . .

The Commission offers two state interests as justifications for the ban on promotional advertising. The first concerns energy conservation. Any increase in demand for electricity—during peak or off-peak periods—means greater consumption of energy. The Commission argues, and the New York court agreed, that the State's interest in conserving energy is sufficient to support suppression of advertising designed to increase consumption of electricity. In view of our country's dependence on energy resources beyond our control, no one can doubt the importance of energy conservation. Plainly, therefore, the state interest asserted is substantial.

The Commission also argues that promotional advertising will aggravate inequities caused by the failure to base the utilities' rates on marginal cost. The utilities argued to the Commission that, if they could promote the use of electricity in periods of low demand, they would improve their utilization of generating capacity. The Commission responded that promotion of off-peak consumption also would increase consumption during peak periods. If peak demand were to rise, the absence of marginal cost rates would mean that the rates charged for the additional power would not reflect the true costs of expanding production. Instead, the extra costs would be borne by all consumers through higher overall rates. Without promotional advertising, the Commission stated, this inequitable turn of events would be less likely to occur. The choice among rate structures involves difficult and important questions of economic supply and distributional fairness. The State's concern that rates be fair and efficient represents a clear and substantial governmental interest.

Next, we focus on the relationship between the State's interests and the advertising ban. Under this criterion, the Commission's laudable concern over the equity and efficiency of appellant's rates does not provide a constitutionally adequate reason for restricting protected speech. The link between the advertising prohibition and appellant's rate structure is, at most, tenuous. The impact of promotional advertising on the equity of appellant's rates is highly speculative. Advertising to increase off-peak usage would have to increase peak usage, while other factors that directly affect the fairness and efficiency of appellant's rates remained constant. Such conditional and remote eventualities simply cannot justify silencing appellant's promotional advertising.

In contrast, the State's interest in energy conservation is directly advanced by the Commission order at issue here. There is an immediate connection between advertising and demand for electricity. Central Hudson would not contest the advertising ban unless it believed that promotion would increase its sales. Thus, we find a direct link between the state interest in conservation and the Commission's order.

We come finally to the critical inquiry in this case: whether the Commission's complete suppression of speech ordinarily protected by the First Amendment is no more extensive than necessary to further the State's interest in energy conservation. The Commission's order reaches all promotional advertising, regardless of the impact of the touted service on overall energy use. But the energy conservation rationale, as important as it is, cannot justify suppressing information about electric devices or services that would cause no net increase in total energy use. In addition, no showing has been made that a more limited restriction on the content of promotional advertising would not serve adequately the State's interests. . . .

The Commission's order prevents appellant from promoting electric services that would reduce energy use by diverting demand from less efficient sources, or that would consume roughly the same amount of energy as do alternative sources. In neither situation would the utility's advertising endanger conservation

or mislead the public. To the extent that the Commission's order suppresses speech that in no way impairs the State's interest in energy conservation, the Commission's order violates the First and Fourteenth Amendments, and must be invalidated.

The Commission also has not demonstrated that its interest in conservation cannot be protected adequately by more limited regulation of appellant's commercial expression. To further its policy of conservation, the Commission could attempt to restrict the format and content of Central Hudson's advertising. It might, for example, require that the advertisements include information about the relative efficiency and expense of the offered service, both under current conditions and for the foreseeable future. In the absence of a showing that more limited speech regulation would be ineffective, we cannot approve the complete suppression of Central Hudson's advertising. . . .

Rehnquist, dissenting:

. . . The Court's analysis, in my view, is wrong in several respects. Initially, I disagree with the Court's conclusion that the speech of a state-created monopoly, which is the subject of a comprehensive regulatory scheme, is entitled to protection under the First Amendment. I also think that the Court errs here in failing to recognize that the state law is most accurately viewed as an economic regulation, and that the speech involved (if it falls within the scope of the First Amendment at all) occupies a significantly more subordinate position in the hierarchy of First Amendment values than the Court gives it today. Finally, the Court, in reaching its decision, improperly substitutes its own judgment for that of the State in deciding how a proper ban on promotional advertising should be drafted. With regard to this latter point, the Court adopts as its final part of a four-part test a "no more extensive than necessary" analysis that will unduly impair a state legislature's ability to adopt legislation reasonably designed to promote interests that have always been rightly thought to be of great importance to the State. . . .

This Court has previously recognized that, although commercial speech may be entitled to First Amendment protection, that protection is not as extensive as that accorded to the advocacy of ideas. . . .

The Court's decision today fails to give due deference to this subordinate position of commercial speech. The Court in so doing returns to the bygone era of *Lochner v. New York,* in which it was common practice for this Court to strike down economic regulations adopted by a State based on the Court's own notions of the most appropriate means for the State to implement its considered policies.

I had thought by now it had become well established that a State has broad discretion in imposing economic regulations. . . .

The Court today holds not only that commercial speech is entitled to First Amendment protection, but also that, when it is protected, a State may not regulate it unless its reason for doing so amounts to a "substantial" governmental interest, its regulation "directly advances" that interest, and its manner of regulation is "not more extensive than necessary" to serve the interest. The test adopted by the Court thus elevates the protection accorded commercial speech that falls within the scope of the First Amendment to a level that is virtually indistinguishable from that of noncommercial speech. . . . New York's order here is . . . more akin to an economic regulation to which virtually complete deference should be accorded by this Court. . . .

I remain of the view that the Court unlocked a Pandora's Box when it "elevated" commercial speech to the level of traditional political speech by according it First Amendment protection in *Virginia Pharmacy Board v. Virginia Citizens Consumer Council*. The line between "commercial speech," and the kind of speech that those who drafted the First Amendment had in mind may not be a technically or intellectually easy one to draw, but it surely produced far fewer problems than has the development of judicial doctrine in this area since *Virginia Pharmacy Board*. For in the world of political advocacy and its marketplace of ideas, there is no such thing as a "fraudulent" idea: there may be useless proposals, totally unworkable schemes, as well as very sound proposals that will receive the imprimatur of the "marketplace of ideas" through our majoritarian system of election and representative government. The free flow of information is important in this context not because it will lead to the discovery of any objective "truth," but because it is essential to our system of self-government. . . .

New York Times v. Sullivan

376 U.S. 254 (1964), 9-0
Opinion of the Court: Bennan (Black, Clark, Douglas, Goldberg, Harlan, Stewart, Warren, White)

Since much more is said and published about public officials than private persons, why does the Court give them less protection against defamation? What is "malice" as the Court uses the term here? How does it differ from negligence? What must be shown to prove malice?

Brennan, for the Court:

We are required in this case to determine for the first time the extent to which the constitutional protections for speech and press limit a State's power to award damages in a libel action brought by a public official against critics of his official conduct.

Respondent L. B. Sullivan is one of the three elected Commissioners of the City of Montgomery, Alabama. . . .

He brought this civil libel action against the four individual petitioners, who are Negroes and Alabama clergymen, and against petitioner the New York Times Company, a New York corporation which publishes the New York Times, a daily newspaper. A jury in the Circuit Court of Montgomery County awarded him damages of $500,000, the full amount claimed, against all the petitioners, and the Supreme Court of Alabama affirmed.

[His] complaint alleged that he had been libeled by statements in a full-page advertisement that was carried in the New York Times on March 29, 1960. Entitled "Heed Their Rising Voices," the advertisement began by stating that,

"As the whole world knows by now, thousands of Southern Negro students are engaged in widespread nonviolent demonstrations in positive affirmation of the right to live in human dignity as guaranteed by the U.S. Constitution and the Bill of Rights."

Of the 10 paragraphs of text in the advertisement, the third and a portion of the sixth were the basis of [Sullivan's] claim of libel. They read as follows:

Third paragraph:

In Montgomery, Alabama, after students sang "My Country, 'Tis of Thee" on the State Capitol steps, their leaders were expelled from school, and truckloads of police armed with shotguns and tear-gas ringed the Alabama State College Campus. When the entire student body protested to state authorities by refusing to reregister, their dining hall was padlocked in an attempt to starve them into submission.

Sixth paragraph:

Again and again, the Southern violators have answered Dr. King's peaceful protests with intimidation and violence. They have bombed his home, almost killing his wife and child. They have assaulted his person. They have arrested him seven times—for "speeding," "loitering" and similar "offenses." And now they have charged him with "perjury"—a felony under which they could imprison him for ten years. . . .

Although neither of these statements mentions [Sullivan] by name, he contended that the word "police" in the third paragraph referred to him as the Montgomery Commissioner who supervised the Police Department, so that he was being accused of "ringing" the campus with police. . . .

It is uncontroverted that some of the statements contained in the two paragraphs were not accurate descriptions of events which occurred in Montgomery. Although Negro students staged a demonstration on the State Capitol steps, they sang the National Anthem and not "My Country, 'Tis of Thee." Although nine students were expelled by the State Board of Education, this was not for leading the demonstration at the Capitol, but for demanding service at a lunch counter in the Montgomery County Courthouse on another day. Not the entire student body, but most of it, had protested the expulsion, not by refusing to register, but by boycotting classes on a single day; virtually all the students did register for the ensuing semester. The campus dining hall was not padlocked on any occasion, and the only students who may have been barred from eating there were the few who had neither signed a preregistration application nor requested temporary meal tickets. Although the police were deployed near the campus in large numbers on three occasions, they did not at any time "ring" the campus, and they were not called to the campus in connection with the demonstration on the State Capitol steps, as the third paragraph implied. Dr. King had not been arrested seven times, but only four, and although he claimed to have been assaulted some years earlier in connection with his arrest for loitering outside a courtroom, one of the officers who made the arrest denied that there was such an assault.

On the premise that the charges in the sixth paragraph could be read as referring to him, [Sullivan] was allowed to prove that he had not participated in the events described. . . .

Under Alabama law, as applied in this case, a publication is "libelous per se" if the words "tend to injure a person . . . in his reputation" or to "bring [him] into public contempt"; the trial court stated that the standard was met if the words are such as to "injure him in his public office, or impute misconduct to him in his office, or want of official integrity, or want of fidelity to a public trust. . . . Once "libel per se" has been established, the defendant has no defense as to stated facts unless he can persuade the jury that they were true in all their particulars. . . . Unless he can discharge the burden of proving truth, general damages are presumed, and may be awarded without proof of pecuniary injury. . . .

The question before us is whether this rule of liability, as applied to an action brought by a public official against critics of his official conduct, abridges the freedom of speech and of the press that is guaranteed by the First and Fourteenth Amendments.

. . . [W]e consider this case against the background of a profound national commitment to the principle that debate on public issues should be uninhibited, robust, and wide-open, and that it may well include vehement, caustic, and sometimes unpleasantly sharp attacks on government and public officials. The present advertisement, as an expression of grievance and protest on one of the major public issues of our time, would seem clearly to qualify for the constitutional protection. The question is whether it forfeits that protection by the falsity of some of its factual statements and by its alleged defamation of [Sullivan].

Authoritative interpretations of the First Amendment guarantees have consistently refused to recognize an exception for any test of truth—whether administered by judges, juries, or administrative officials—and especially one that puts the burden of proving truth on the speaker. The constitutional protection does not turn upon "the truth, popularity, or social utility of the ideas and beliefs which are offered." . . .

. . . [E]rroneous statement is inevitable in free debate, and . . . it must be protected if the freedoms of expression are to have the "breathing space" that they "need . . . to survive. . . .

Injury to official reputation affords no more warrant for repressing speech that would otherwise be free than does factual error. Where judicial officers are involved, this Court has held that concern for the dignity and reputation of the courts does not justify the punishment as criminal contempt of criticism of the judge or his decision. This is true even though the utterance contains "half-truths" and "misinformation." Such repression can be justified, if at all, only by a clear and present danger of the obstruction of justice. If judges are to be treated as "men of fortitude, able to thrive in a hardy climate," surely the same must be true of other government officials, such as elected city commissioners. Criticism of their official conduct does not lose its constitutional protection merely because it is effective criticism, and hence diminishes their official reputations.

If neither factual error nor defamatory content suffices to remove the constitutional shield from criticism of official conduct, the combination of the two elements is no less inadequate. This is the lesson to be drawn from the great controversy over the Sedition Act of 1798, which first crystallized a national awareness of the central meaning of the First Amendment. That statute made it a crime, punishable by a $5,000 fine and five years in prison, "if any person shall write, print, utter or publish . . . any false, scandalous and malicious writing or writings against the government of the United States, or either house of the Congress . . . or the President . . . with intent to defame . . . or to bring them, or either of them, into contempt or disrepute; or to excite against them, or either or any of them, the hatred of the good people of the United States." The Act allowed the defendant the defense of truth, and provided that the jury were to be judges both of the law and the facts. Despite these qualifications, the Act was vigorously condemned as unconstitutional in an attack joined in by Jefferson and Madison. . . .

Although the Sedition Act was never tested in this Court, the attack upon its validity has carried the day in the court of history. Fines levied in its prosecution were repaid by Act of Congress on the ground that it was unconstitutional. . . .

There is no force in [Sullivan's] argument that the constitutional limitations implicit in the history of the Sedition Act apply only to Congress, and not to the States. It is true that the First Amendment was originally addressed only to action by the Federal Government, and that Jefferson, for one, while denying the power of Congress "to controul the freedom of the press," recognized such a power in the States. See the 1804 Letter to Abigail Adams. But this distinction was eliminated with the adoption of the Fourteenth Amendment and the application to the States of the First Amendment's restrictions.

What a State may not constitutionally bring about by means of a criminal statute is likewise beyond the reach of its civil law of libel. The fear of damage awards under a rule such as that invoked by the Alabama courts here may be markedly more inhibiting than the fear of prosecution under a criminal statute. Alabama, for example, has a criminal libel law which subjects to prosecution "any person who speaks, writes, or prints of and concerning another any accusation falsely and maliciously importing the commission by such person of a felony, or any other indictable offense involving moral turpitude," and which allows as punishment upon conviction a fine not exceeding $500 and a prison sentence of six months. Presumably, a person charged with violation of this statute enjoys ordinary criminal law safeguards such as the requirements of an indictment and of proof beyond a reasonable doubt. These safeguards are not available to the defendant in a civil action. The judgment awarded in this case— without the need for any proof of actual pecuniary loss—was one thousand times greater than the maximum fine provided by the Alabama criminal statute, and one hundred times greater than that provided by the Sedition Act. . . . Whether or not a newspaper can survive a succession of such judgments, the pall of fear and timidity imposed upon those who would give voice to public criticism is an atmosphere in which the First Amendment freedoms cannot survive. Plainly the Alabama law of civil libel is "a form of regulation that creates hazards to protected freedoms markedly greater than those that attend reliance upon the criminal law."

The state rule of law is not saved by its allowance of the defense of truth. . . . A rule compelling the critic of official conduct to guarantee the truth of all his factual assertions—and to do so on pain of libel judgments virtually unlimited in amount—leads to a comparable "self-censorship." Allowance of the defense of truth, with the burden of proving it on the defendant, does not mean that only false speech will be deterred. Even courts accepting this defense as an adequate safeguard have recognized the difficulties of adducing legal proofs that the alleged libel was true in all its factual particulars. Under such a rule, would-be critics of official conduct may be deterred from voicing their criticism, even though it is believed to be true and even though it is, in fact, true, because of doubt whether it can be proved in court or fear of the expense of having to do so. They tend to make only statements which "steer far wider of the unlawful zone." The rule thus dampens the vigor and limits the variety of public debate. It is inconsistent with the First and Fourteenth Amendments.

The constitutional guarantees require . . . a federal rule that prohibits a public official from recovering damages for a defamatory falsehood relating to his official conduct unless he proves that the statement was made with "actual malice"—that is, with knowledge that it was false or with reckless disregard of whether it was false or not. . . .

We hold today that the Constitution delimits a State's power to award damages for libel in actions brought by public officials against critics of their official conduct. Since this is such an action, the rule requiring proof of actual malice is applicable. . . .

Applying these standards, we consider that the proof presented to show actual malice lacks the convincing clarity which the constitutional standard demands, and hence that it would not constitutionally sustain the judgment for [Sullivan] under the proper rule of law. The case of the individual petitioners requires little discussion. Even assuming that they could constitutionally be found to have authorized the use of their names on the advertisement, there was no evidence whatever that they were aware of any erroneous statements or were in any way reckless in that regard. The judgment against them is thus without constitutional support.

As to the Times, we similarly conclude that the facts do not support a finding of actual malice. . . .

Black, concurring:

. . . I base my vote to reverse on the belief that the First and Fourteenth Amendments not merely "delimit" a State's power to award damages to "public officials against critics of their official conduct," but completely prohibit a State from exercising such a power. The Court goes on to hold that a State can subject such critics to damages if "actual malice" can be proved against them. "Malice," even as defined by the Court, is an elusive, abstract concept, hard to prove and hard to disprove. . . . and certainly does not measure up to the sturdy safeguard embodied in the First Amendment. Unlike the Court, therefore, I vote to reverse exclusively on the ground that the Times and the individual defendants had an absolute, unconditional constitutional right to publish in the Times advertisement their criticisms of the Montgomery agencies and officials. . . .

. . . An unconditional right to say what one pleases about public affairs is what I consider to be the minimum guarantee of the First Amendment.

I regret that the Court has stopped short of this holding indispensable to preserve our free press from destruction.

Gertz v. Robert Welch, Inc.

418 U.S. 323 (1974), 5-4
Opinion of the Court: Powell (Blackmun, Marshall, Rehnquist, Stewart)
Dissenting: Brennan, Burger, Douglas, White

Is Gertz a "public figure"? How has the public figure doctrine been modified or clarified by this decision? When and for what purpose would a defamation plaintiff like Gertz need to prove "malice"? What is the chief disagreement between the majority justices and the dissenters?

Powell, for the Court:
This Court has struggled for nearly a decade to define the proper accommodation between the law of defamation and the freedoms of speech and press protected by the First Amendment. With this decision we return to that effort. We granted certiorari to reconsider the extent of a publisher's constitutional privilege against liability for defamation of a private citizen.

In 1968, a Chicago policeman named Nuccio shot and killed a youth named Nelson. The state authorities prosecuted Nuccio for the homicide and ultimately obtained a conviction for murder in the second degree. The Nelson family retained petitioner Elmer Gertz, a reputable attorney, to represent them in civil litigation against Nuccio.

Respondent publishes American Opinion, a monthly outlet for the views of the John Birch Society. Early in the 1960s, the magazine began to warn of a nationwide conspiracy to discredit local law enforcement agencies and create in their stead a national police force capable of supporting a Communist dictatorship. As part of the continuing effort to alert the public to this assumed danger, the managing editor of American Opinion commissioned an article on the murder trial of Officer Nuccio. For this purpose, he engaged a regular contributor to the magazine. In March, 1969, respondent published the resulting article under the title "FRAME-UP: Richard Nuccio And The War On Police." The article purports to demonstrate that the testimony against Nuccio at his criminal trial was false, and that his prosecution was part of the Communist campaign against the police.

In his capacity as counsel for the Nelson family in the civil litigation, petitioner attended the coroner's inquest into the boy's death and initiated actions for damages, but he neither discussed Officer Nuccio with the press nor played any part in the criminal proceeding. Notwithstanding petitioner's remote connection with the prosecution of Nuccio, respondent's magazine portrayed him as an architect of the "frame-up." According to the article, the police file on petitioner took "a big, Irish cop to lift." The article stated that petitioner had been an official of the "Marxist League for Industrial Democracy, originally known as the Intercollegiate Socialist Society, which has advocated the violent seizure of our government."

It labeled Gertz a "Leninist" and a "Communist-fronter." It also stated that Gertz had been an officer of the National Lawyers Guild, described as a Communist organization that "probably did more than any other outfit to plan the Communist attack on the Chicago police during the 1968 Democratic Convention."

These statements contained serious inaccuracies. The implication that petitioner had a criminal record was false. Petitioner had been a member and officer of the National Lawyers Guild some 15 years earlier, but there was no evidence that he or that organization had taken any part in planning the 1968 demonstrations in Chicago. There was also no basis for the charge that petitioner was a "Leninist" or a "Communist-fronter." And he had never been a member of the "Marxist League for Industrial Democracy" or the "Intercollegiate Socialist Society." . . .

The New York Times standard defines the level of constitutional protection appropriate to the context of defamation of a public person. Those who, by reason of the notoriety of their achievements or the vigor and success with which they seek the public's attention, are properly classed as public figures and those who hold governmental office may recover for injury to reputation only on clear and convincing proof that the defamatory falsehood was made with knowledge of its falsity or with reckless disregard for the truth. This standard administers an extremely powerful antidote to the inducement to media self-censorship of the common law rule of strict liability for libel and slander. And it exacts a correspondingly high price from the victims of defamatory falsehood. Plainly, many deserving plaintiffs, including some intentionally subjected to injury, will be unable to surmount the barrier of the New York Times test. Despite this substantial abridgment of the state law right to compensation for wrongful hurt to one's reputation, the Court has concluded that the protection of the New York Times privilege should be available to publishers and broadcasters of defamatory falsehood concerning public officials and public figures. We think that these decisions are correct, but we do not find their holdings justified solely by reference to the interest of the press and broadcast media in immunity from liability. Rather, we believe that the New York Times rule states an accommodation between this concern and the limited state interest present in the context of libel actions brought by public persons. For the reasons stated below, we conclude that the state interest in compensating injury to the reputation of private individuals requires that a different rule should obtain with respect to them. . . .

. . . [W]e have no difficulty in distinguishing among defamation plaintiffs. The first remedy of any victim of defamation is self-help—using available opportunities to contradict the lie or correct the error, and thereby to minimize its adverse impact on reputation. Public officials and public figures usually enjoy significantly greater access to the channels of effective communication, and hence have a more realistic opportunity to counteract false statements than private individuals normally enjoy. Private individuals are therefore more vulnerable to injury, and the state interest in protecting them is correspondingly greater.

More important than the likelihood that private individuals will lack effective opportunities for rebuttal, there is a compelling normative consideration underlying the distinction between public and private defamation plaintiffs. An individual who decides to seek governmental office must accept certain necessary consequences of that involvement in public affairs. He runs the risk of closer public scrutiny than might otherwise be the case. And society's interest in the officers of government is not strictly limited to the formal discharge of official duties. . . .

Those classed as public figures stand in a similar position. Hypothetically, it may be possible for someone to become a public figure through no purposeful action of his own, but the instances of truly involuntary public figures must be exceedingly rare. For the most part, those who attain this status have assumed roles of especial prominence in the affairs of society. Some occupy positions of such persuasive power and influence that they are deemed public figures for all purposes. More commonly, those classed as public figures have thrust themselves to the forefront of particular public controversies in order to influence the resolution of the issues involved. In either event, they invite attention and comment.

Even if the foregoing generalities do not obtain in every instance, the communications media are entitled to act on the assumption that public officials and public figures have voluntarily exposed themselves to increased risk of injury from defamatory falsehood concerning them. No such assumption is justified with respect to a private individual. He has not accepted public office or assumed an "influential role in ordering society." He has relinquished no part of his interest in the protection of his own good name, and consequently he has a more compelling call on the courts for redress of injury inflicted by defamatory falsehood. Thus, private individuals are not only more vulnerable to injury than public officials and public figures; they are also more deserving of recovery.

For these reasons, we conclude that the States should retain substantial latitude in their efforts to enforce a legal remedy for defamatory falsehood injurious to the reputation of a private individual. The extension of the New York Times test proposed by the *Rosenbloom* plurality would abridge this legitimate state interest to a degree that we find unacceptable. . . .

We hold that, so long as they do not impose liability without fault, the States may define for themselves the appropriate standard of liability for a publisher or broadcaster of defamatory falsehood injurious to a private individual. This approach provides a more equitable boundary between the competing concerns involved here. It recognizes the strength of the legitimate state interest in compensating private individuals for wrongful injury to reputation, yet shields the press and broadcast media from the rigors of strict liability for defamation. At least this conclusion obtains where, as here, the substance of the defamatory statement "makes substantial danger to reputation apparent." This phrase places in perspective the conclusion we announce today. Our inquiry would involve considerations somewhat different from those discussed above if a State purported to condition civil liability on a factual misstatement whose content did not warn a reasonably prudent editor or broadcaster of its defamatory potential. Such a case is not now before us, and we intimate no view as to its proper resolution.

Our accommodation of the competing values at stake in defamation suits by private individuals allows the States to impose liability on the publisher or broadcaster of defamatory falsehood on a less demanding showing than that required by New York Times. This conclusion is not based on a belief that the considerations which prompted the adoption of the New York Times privilege for defamation of public officials and its extension to public figures are

wholly inapplicable to the context of private individuals. Rather, we endorse this approach in recognition of the strong and legitimate state interest in compensating private individuals for injury to reputation. But this countervailing state interest extends no further than compensation for actual injury. For the reasons stated below, we hold that the States may not permit recovery of presumed or punitive damages, at least when liability is not based on a showing of knowledge of falsity or reckless disregard for the truth.

The common law of defamation is an oddity of tort law, for it allows recovery of purportedly compensatory damages without evidence of actual loss. Under the traditional rules pertaining to actions for libel, the existence of injury is presumed from the fact of publication. Juries may award substantial sums as compensation for supposed damage to reputation without any proof that such harm actually occurred. The largely uncontrolled discretion of juries to award damages where there is no loss unnecessarily compounds the potential of any system of liability for defamatory falsehood to inhibit the vigorous exercise of First Amendment freedoms. Additionally, the doctrine of presumed damages invites juries to punish unpopular opinion, rather than to compensate individuals for injury sustained by the publication of a false fact. More to the point, the States have no substantial interest in securing for plaintiffs such as this petitioner gratuitous awards of money damages far in excess of any actual injury.

We would not, of course, invalidate state law simply because we doubt its wisdom, but here we are attempting to reconcile state law with a competing interest grounded in the constitutional command of the First Amendment. It is therefore appropriate to require that state remedies for defamatory falsehood reach no farther than is necessary to protect the legitimate interest involved. It is necessary to restrict defamation plaintiffs who do not prove knowledge of falsity or reckless disregard for the truth to compensation for actual injury. We need not define "actual injury," as trial courts have wide experience in framing appropriate jury instructions in tort actions. Suffice it to say that actual injury is not limited to out-of-pocket loss. Indeed, the more customary types of actual harm inflicted by defamatory falsehood include impairment of reputation and standing in the community, personal humiliation, and mental anguish and suffering. Of course, juries must be limited by appropriate instructions, and all awards must be supported by competent evidence concerning the injury, although there need be no evidence which assigns an actual dollar value to the injury.

We also find no justification for allowing awards of punitive damages against publishers and broadcasters held liable under state-defined standards of liability for defamation. In most jurisdictions jury discretion over the amounts awarded is limited only by the gentle rule that they not be excessive. Consequently, juries assess punitive damages in wholly unpredictable amounts bearing no necessary relation to the actual harm caused. And they remain free to use their discretion selectively to punish expressions of unpopular views. Like the doctrine of presumed damages, jury discretion to award punitive damages unnecessarily exacerbates the danger of media self-censorship, but, unlike the former rule, punitive damages are wholly irrelevant to the state interest that justifies a negligence standard for private defamation actions. They are not compensation for injury. Instead, they are private fines levied by civil juries to punish reprehensible conduct and to deter its future occurrence. In short, the private defamation plaintiff who establishes liability under a less demanding standard than that stated by New York Times may recover only such damages as are sufficient to compensate him for actual injury.

Notwithstanding our refusal to extend the New York Times privilege to defamation of private individuals, respondent contends that we should affirm the judgment below on the ground that petitioner is either a public official or a public figure. There is little basis for the former assertion. Several years prior to the present incident, petitioner had served briefly on housing committees appointed by the mayor of Chicago, but, at the time of publication, he had never held any remunerative governmental position. Respondent admits this, but argues that petitioner's appearance at the coroner's inquest rendered him a "de facto public official." Our cases recognize no such concept. Respondent's suggestion would sweep all lawyers under the New York Times rule as officers of the court, and distort the plain meaning of the "public official" category beyond all recognition. We decline to follow it.

Respondent's characterization of petitioner as a public figure raises a different question. That designation may rest on either of two alternative bases. In some instances an individual may achieve such pervasive fame or notoriety that he becomes a public figure for all purposes and in all contexts. More commonly, an individual voluntarily injects himself or is drawn into a particular public controversy, and thereby becomes a public figure for a limited range of issues. In either case, such persons assume special prominence in the resolution of public questions.

Petitioner has long been active in community and professional affairs. He has served as an officer of local civic groups and of various professional organizations, and he has published several books and articles on legal subjects. Although petitioner was consequently well known in some circles, he had achieved no general fame or notoriety in the community. None of the prospective jurors called at the trial had ever heard of petitioner prior to this litigation, and respondent offered no proof that this response was atypical of the local population. We would not lightly assume that a citizen's participation in community and professional affairs rendered him a public figure for all purposes. Absent clear evidence of general fame or notoriety in the community, and pervasive involvement in the affairs of society, an individual should not be deemed a public personality for all aspects of his life. It is preferable to reduce the public figure question to a more meaningful context by looking to the nature and extent of an individual's participation in the particular controversy giving rise to the defamation.

In this context, it is plain that petitioner was not a public figure. He played a minimal role at the coroner's inquest, and his participation related solely to his representation of a private client. He took no part in the criminal prosecution of Officer Nuccio. Moreover, he never discussed either the criminal or civil litigation with the press, and was never quoted as having done so. He plainly did not thrust himself into the vortex of this public issue, nor did he engage the public's attention in an attempt to influence its outcome. We are persuaded that the trial court did not err in refusing to characterize petitioner as a public figure for the purpose of this litigation.

We therefore conclude that the New York Times standard is inapplicable to this case, and that the trial court erred in entering judgment for respondent. Because the jury was allowed to impose liability without fault and was permitted to presume damages without proof of injury, a new trial is necessary. . . .

Blackmun, concurring:
The Court . . . seeks today to strike a balance between competing values where necessarily uncertain assumptions about human behavior color the result. Although

the Court's opinion in the present case departs from the rationale of the *Rosenbloom* [*v. Metromedia*] plurality, in that the Court now conditions a libel action by a private person upon a showing of negligence, as contrasted with a showing of willful or reckless disregard, I . . . join, the Court's opinion and its judgment for two reasons:

1. By removing the specters of presumed and punitive damages in the absence of New York Times malice, the Court eliminates significant and powerful motives for self-censorship that otherwise are present in the traditional libel action. By so doing, the Court leaves what should prove to be sufficient and adequate breathing space for a vigorous press. . . .

2. The Court was sadly fractionated in *Rosenbloom*. A result of that kind inevitably leads to uncertainty. I feel that it is of profound importance for the Court to come to rest in the defamation area and to have a clearly defined majority position that eliminates the unsureness engendered by *Rosenbloom's* diversity. If my vote were not needed to create a majority, I would adhere to my prior view. A definitive ruling, however, is paramount.

Burger, dissenting:

. . . Agreement or disagreement with the law as it has evolved to this time does not alter the fact that it has been orderly development with a consistent basic rationale. In today's opinion, the Court abandons the traditional thread so far as the ordinary private citizen is concerned, and introduces the concept that the media will be liable for negligence in publishing defamatory statements with respect to such persons. Although I agree with much of what Mr. Justice White states, I do not read the Court's new doctrinal approach in quite the way he does. I am frank to say I do not know the parameters of a "negligence" doctrine as applied to the news media. Conceivably this new doctrine could inhibit some editors, as the dissents of Mr. Justice Douglas and Mr. Justice Brennan suggest. But I would prefer to allow this area of law to continue to evolve as it has up to now with respect to private citizens, rather than embark on a new doctrinal theory which has no jurisprudential ancestry.

The petitioner here was performing a professional representative role as an advocate in the highest tradition of the law, and, under that tradition, the advocate is not to be invidiously identified with his client. The important public policy which underlies this tradition— the right to counsel—would be gravely jeopardized if

every lawyer who takes an "unpopular" case, civil or criminal, would automatically become fair game for irresponsible reporters and editors who might, for example, describe the lawyer as a "mob mouthpiece" for representing a client with a serious prior criminal record, or as an "ambulance chaser" for representing a claimant in a personal injury action. . . .

Douglas, dissenting:

. . . Unlike the right of privacy which, by the terms of the Fourth Amendment, must be accommodated with reasonable searches and seizures and warrants issued by magistrates, the rights of free speech and of a free press were protected by the Framers in verbiage whose proscription seems clear. I have stated before my view that the First Amendment would bar Congress from passing any libel law. . . .

With the First Amendment made applicable to the States through the Fourteenth, I do not see how States have any more ability to "accommodate" freedoms of speech or of the press than does Congress. . . .

White, dissenting:

For some 200 years—from the very founding of the Nation—the law of defamation and right of the ordinary citizen to recover for false publication injurious to his reputation have been almost exclusively the business of state courts and legislatures. Under typical state defamation law, the defamed private citizen had to prove only a false publication that would subject him to hatred, contempt, or ridicule. Given such publication, general damage to reputation was presumed, while punitive damages required proof of additional facts. The law governing the defamation of private citizens remained untouched by the First Amendment, because, until relatively recently, the consistent view of the Court was that libelous words constitute a class of speech wholly unprotected by the First Amendment, subject only to limited exceptions carved out since 1964.

But now, using that Amendment as the chosen instrument, the Court, in a few printed pages, has federalized major aspects of libel law by declaring unconstitutional in important respects the prevailing defamation law in all or most of the 50 States. That result is accomplished by requiring the plaintiff in each and every defamation action to prove not only the defendant's culpability beyond his act of publishing defamatory material, but also actual damage to reputation resulting from the publication. Moreover, punitive damages may not be recovered by showing malice in the traditional sense of ill will; knowing falsehood or reckless disregard of the truth will now be required. . . .

It is difficult for me to understand why the ordinary citizen should himself carry the risk of damage and suffer the injury in order to vindicate First Amendment values by protecting the press and others from liability for circulating false information. This is particularly true because such statements serve no purpose whatsoever in furthering the public interest or the search for truth, but, on the contrary, may frustrate that search, and, at the same time, inflict great injury on the defenseless individual. The owners of the press and the stockholders of the communications enterprises can much better bear the burden. And if they cannot, the public at large should somehow pay for what is essentially a public benefit derived at private expense. . . .

The impact of today's decision on the traditional law of libel is immediately obvious and indisputable. No longer will the plaintiff be able to rest his case with proof of a libel defamatory on its face or proof of a slander historically actionable *per se*. In addition he must prove some further degree of culpable conduct on the part of the publisher, such as intentional or reckless falsehood or negligence. . . . The Court rejects the judgment of experience that some publications are so inherently capable of injury, and actual injury so difficult to prove, that the risk of falsehood should be borne by the publisher, not the victim. . . . Under the new rule the plaintiff can lose, not because the statement is true, but because it was not negligently made. . . .

Hustler Magazine, Inc. v. Falwell

485 U.S. 46 (1988), 8-0
Opinion of the Court: Rehnquist (Blackmun, Brennan, Marshall, O'Connor, Scalia, Stevens, White)
Not participating: Kennedy

What injury did Falwell claim? Why did the Court reject the claim? Is publication of outright and "outrageous" falsities not "actual malice" as long as they are labeled a parody or lampoon? Should public figures have any protection from such publication? Would it make any difference in this case if there was evidence some readers of Hustler *believed the statements to be true? How many readers? Who gains from*

this decision besides publishers, writers, and artists? What is gained? Why is this not an obscenity case?

Rehnquist, for the Court:
Petitioner Hustler Magazine, Inc., is a magazine of nationwide circulation. Respondent Jerry Falwell, a nationally known minister who has been active as a commentator on politics and public affairs, sued petitioner and its publisher, petitioner Larry Flynt, to recover damages for invasion of privacy, libel, and intentional infliction of emotional distress. The District Court directed a verdict against respondent on the privacy claim, and submitted the other two claims to a jury. The jury found for petitioners on the defamation claim, but found for respondent on the claim for intentional infliction of emotional distress and awarded damages. We now consider whether this award is consistent with the First and Fourteenth Amendments of the United States Constitution.

The inside front cover of the November, 1983, issue of Hustler Magazine featured a "parody" of an advertisement for Campari Liqueur that contained the name and picture of respondent and was entitled "Jerry Falwell talks about his first time." This parody was modeled after actual Campari ads that included interviews with various celebrities about their "first times." Although it was apparent by the end of each interview that this meant the first time they sampled Campari, the ads clearly played on the sexual double entendre of the general subject of "first times." Copying the form and layout of these Campari ads, *Hustler's* editors chose respondent as the featured celebrity and drafted an alleged "interview" with him in which he states that his "first time" was during a drunken incestuous rendezvous with his mother in an outhouse. The Hustler parody portrays respondent and his mother as drunk and immoral, and suggests that respondent is a hypocrite who preaches only when he is drunk. In small print at the bottom of the page, the ad contains the disclaimer, "ad parody—not to be taken seriously." The magazine's table of contents also lists the ad as "Fiction; Ad and Personality Parody." . . .

. . . Respondent would have us find that a State's interest in protecting public figures from emotional distress is sufficient to deny First Amendment protection to speech that is patently offensive and is intended to inflict emotional injury, even when that speech could not reasonably have been interpreted as stating actual facts about the public figure involved. This we decline to do.

At the heart of the First Amendment is the recognition of the fundamental importance of the free flow of ideas and opinions on matters of public interest and concern. . . .

The sort of robust political debate encouraged by the First Amendment is bound to produce speech that is critical of those who hold public office or those public figures who are "intimately involved in the resolution of important public questions or, by reason of their fame, shape events in areas of concern to society at large." *Associated Press v. Walker,* decided with *Curtis Publishing Co. v. Butts.* . . . Such criticism, inevitably, will not always be reasoned or moderate; public figures as well as public officials will be subject to "vehement, caustic, and sometimes unpleasantly sharp attacks," *New York Times* [v. *Sullivan*]. . . .

Of course, this does not mean that any speech about a public figure is immune from sanction in the form of damages. Since *New York Times Co. v. Sullivan,* we have consistently ruled that a public figure may hold a speaker liable for the damage to reputation caused by publication of a defamatory falsehood, but only if the statement was made "with knowledge that it was false or with reckless disregard of whether it was false or not." False statements of fact are particularly valueless; they interfere with the truthseeking function of the marketplace of ideas, and they cause damage to an individual's reputation that cannot easily be repaired by counterspeech, however persuasive or effective. But even though falsehoods have little value in and of themselves, they are "nevertheless inevitable in free debate," and a rule that would impose strict liability on a publisher for false factual assertions would have an undoubted "chilling" effect on speech relating to public figures that does have constitutional value. . . .

Respondent argues, however, that a different standard should apply in this case because, here, the State seeks to prevent not reputational damage, but the severe emotional distress suffered by the person who is the subject of an offensive publication. In respondent's view, and in the view of the Court of Appeals, so long as the utterance was intended to inflict emotional distress, was outrageous, and did in fact inflict serious emotional distress, it is of no constitutional import whether the statement was a fact or an opinion, or whether it was true or false. It is the intent to cause injury that is the gravamen of the tort, and the State's interest in preventing emotional harm simply outweighs whatever interest a speaker may have in speech of this type.

Generally speaking, the law does not regard the intent to inflict emotional distress as one which should receive much solicitude, and it is quite understandable that most, if not all, jurisdictions have chosen to make it civilly culpable where the conduct in question is sufficiently "outrageous." But in the world of debate about public affairs, many things done with motives that are less than admirable are protected by the First Amendment. In *Garrison v. Louisiana,* we held that, even when a speaker or writer is motivated by hatred or ill-will, his expression was protected by the First Amendment . . . Thus, while such a bad motive may be deemed controlling for purposes of tort liability in other areas of the law, we think the First Amendment prohibits such a result in the area of public debate about public figures.

Were we to hold otherwise, there can be little doubt that political cartoonists and satirists would be subjected to damages awards without any showing that their work falsely defamed its subject. Webster's defines a caricature as "the deliberately distorted picturing or imitating of a person, literary style, etc. by exaggerating features or mannerisms for satirical effect." The appeal of the political cartoon or caricature is often based on exploitation of unfortunate physical traits or politically embarrassing events—an exploitation often calculated to injure the feelings of the subject of the portrayal. The art of the cartoonist is often not reasoned or evenhanded, but slashing and one-sided. . . .

Despite their sometimes caustic nature, from the early cartoon portraying George Washington as an ass down to the present day, graphic depictions and satirical cartoons have played a prominent role in public and political debate. Nast's castigation of the Tweed Ring, Walt McDougall's characterization of Presidential candidate James G. Blaine's banquet with the millionaires at Delmonico's as "The Royal Feast of Belshazzar," and numerous other efforts have undoubtedly had an effect on the course and outcome of contemporaneous debate. Lincoln's tall, gangling posture, Teddy Roosevelt's glasses and teeth, and Franklin D. Roosevelt's jutting jaw and cigarette holder have been memorialized by political cartoons with an effect that could not have been obtained by the photographer or the portrait artist. From the viewpoint of history, it is clear that our political discourse would have been considerably poorer without them.

Respondent contends, however, that the caricature in question here was so "outrageous" as to distinguish it from more traditional political cartoons. There is no doubt that the caricature of respondent and his mother published in *Hustler* is at best a distant cousin of the political cartoons described above, and a rather poor relation at that. If it were possible by laying down a principled standard to separate the one from the other, public discourse would probably suffer little or no harm. But we doubt that there is any such standard, and we are quite sure that the pejorative description "outrageous" does not supply one. "Outrageousness" in the area of political and social discourse has an inherent subjectiveness about it which would allow a jury to impose liability on the basis of the jurors' tastes or views, or perhaps on the basis of their dislike of a particular expression. An "outrageousness" standard thus runs afoul of our longstanding refusal to allow damages to be awarded because the speech in question may have an adverse emotional impact on the audience. And, as we stated in *FCC v. Pacifica Foundation*:

> [T]he fact that society may find speech offensive is not a sufficient reason for suppressing it. Indeed, if it is the speaker's opinion that gives offense, that consequence is a reason for according it constitutional protection. For it is a central tenet of the First Amendment that the government must remain neutral in the marketplace of ideas.

Admittedly, these oft-repeated First Amendment principles, like other principles, are subject to limitations. We recognized in *Pacifica Foundation* that speech that is "'vulgar,' 'offensive,' and 'shocking'" is "not entitled to absolute constitutional protection under all circumstances." In *Chaplinsky v. New Hampshire*, we held that a State could lawfully punish an individual for the use of insulting "'fighting' words—those which by their very utterance inflict injury or tend to incite an immediate breach of the peace." These limitations are but recognition of the observation in *Dun & Bradstreet, Inc. v. Greenmoss Builders, Inc.* that this Court has "long recognized that not all speech is of equal First Amendment importance." But the sort of expression involved in this case does not seem to us to be governed by any exception to the general First Amendment principles stated above.

We conclude that public figures and public officials may not recover for the tort of intentional infliction of emotional distress by reason of publications such as the one here at issue without showing, in addition, that the publication contains a false statement of fact which was made with "actual malice," i.e., with knowledge that the statement was false or with reckless disregard as to whether or not it was true. This is not merely a "blind application" of the New York Times standard, it reflects our considered judgment that such a standard is necessary to give adequate "breathing space" to the freedoms protected by the First Amendment. . . .

Time, Inc. v. Hill

385 U.S. 374 (1967), 5-4
Opinion of the Court: Brennan (Black, Douglas, Stewart, White)
Dissenting (Clark, Fortas, Harlan, in part, Warren)

Why specifically did the New York Right of Privacy Act fail in this case? Under what circumstances may private persons recover against the media for loss of privacy? What is the point of disagreement between Justices Brennan and Harlan? It is clear what the Hills lost and the media gained by this decision, but are there other interests who benefit or lose? Why is this not a defamation case?

Brennan, for the Court:
The question in this case is whether appellant [Time, Inc.], publisher of *Life Magazine*, was denied constitutional protections of speech and press by the application by the New York courts of §§551 of the New York Civil Rights Law to award appellee [Hill] damages on allegations that *Life* falsely reported that a new play portrayed an experience suffered by [him] and his family.

The article appeared in *Life* in February, 1955. It was entitled "True Crime Inspires Tense Play," with the subtitle, "The ordeal of a family trapped by convicts gives Broadway a new thriller, 'The Desperate Hours.'" The text of the article reads as follows:

> Three years ago, Americans all over the country read about the desperate ordeal of the James Hill family, who were held prisoners in their home outside Philadelphia by three escaped convicts. Later, they read about it in Joseph Hayes' novel, *The Desperate Hours*, inspired by the family's experience. Now they can see the story reenacted in Hayes' Broadway play based on the book, and next year will see it in his movie,

which has been filmed but is being held up until the play has a chance to pay off.

The play, directed by Robert Montgomery and expertly acted, is a heart-stopping account of how a family rose to heroism in a crisis. LIFE photographed the play during its Philadelphia tryout, transported some of the actors to the actual house where the Hills were besieged. On the next page, scenes from the play are reenacted on the site of the crime.

The pictures on the ensuing two pages included an enactment of the son being "roughed up" by one of the convicts, entitled "brutish convict," a picture of the daughter biting the hand of a convict to make him drop a gun, entitled "daring daughter," and one of the father throwing his gun through the door after a "brave try" to save his family is foiled.

The James Hill referred to in the article is the plaintiff. He and his wife and five children involuntarily became the subjects of a front-page news story after being held hostage by three escaped convicts in their suburban Whitemarsh, Pennsylvania, home for 19 hours on September 11-12, 1952. The family was released unharmed. . . . The convicts were thereafter apprehended in a widely publicized encounter with the police which resulted in the killing of two of the convicts. Shortly thereafter, the family moved to Connecticut. [Hill] discouraged all efforts to keep them in the public spotlight through magazine articles or appearances on television.

In the spring of 1953, Joseph Hayes' novel, *The Desperate Hours*, was published. The story depicted the experience of a family of four held hostage by three escaped convicts in the family's suburban home. But, unlike Hill's experience, the family of the story suffer violence at the hands of the convicts; the father and son are beaten and the daughter subjected to a verbal sexual insult.

The book was made into a play, also entitled *The Desperate Hours*, and it is *Life's* article about the play which is the subject of [Hill]'s action. The complaint sought damages under §§551 on allegations that the Life article was intended to, and did, give the impression that the play mirrored the Hill family's experience, which, to the knowledge of defendant ". . . was false and untrue." [Time, Inc.]'s defense was that the article was "a subject of legitimate news interest," "a subject of general interest and of value and concern to the public" at the time of publication, and that it was "published in good faith without any malice whatsoever. . . . "

The jury awarded [Hill] $50,000 compensatory and $25,000 punitive damages. On appeal, the Appellate Division of the Supreme Court ordered a new trial as to damages, but sustained the jury verdict of liability. . . .

Although "Right of Privacy" is the caption of §§50–51, the term nowhere appears in the text of the statute itself. The text of the statute appears to proscribe only conduct of the kind involved in Roberson, that is, the appropriation and use in advertising or to promote the sale of goods, of another's name, portrait or picture without his consent. An application of that limited scope would present different questions of violation of the constitutional protections for speech and press.

The New York courts have, however, construed the statute to operate much more broadly. The Court of Appeals stated that "over the years since the statute's enactment in 1903, its social desirability and remedial nature have led to its being given a liberal construction consonant with its over-all purpose. . . . "

Specifically, it has been held in some circumstances to authorize a remedy against the press and other communications media which publish the names, pictures, or portraits of people without their consent. Reflecting the fact, however, that such applications may raise serious questions of conflict with the constitutional protections for speech and press, decisions under the statute have tended to limit the statute's application. "[E]ver mindful that the written word or picture is involved, courts have engrafted exceptions and restrictions onto the statute to avoid any conflict with the free dissemination of thoughts, ideas, newsworthy events, and matters of public interest.

In the light of questions that counsel were asked to argue on reargument, it is particularly relevant that the Court of Appeals made crystal clear in the Spahn opinion that truth is a complete defense in actions under the statute based upon reports of newsworthy people or events. . . .

But although the New York statue affords "little protection" to the "privacy" of a newsworthy person, "whether he be such by choice or involuntarily," the statute gives him a right of action when his name, picture, or portrait is the subject of a "fictitious" report or article. *Spahn* points up the distinction. *Spahn* was an action under the statute brought by the well known professional baseball pitcher, Warren Spahn. He sought an injunction and damages against the unauthorized publication of what purported to be a biography of his life. The trial judge had found that "the record unequivocally establishes that the book publicizes areas of Warren Spahn's personal and private life, albeit inaccurate and distorted, and consists of a host, a preponderant percentage, of factual errors, distortions and fanciful passages. . . .

"The Court of Appeals sustained the holding that, in these circumstances, the publication was proscribed by §51 of the Civil Rights Law, and was not within the exceptions and restrictions for newsworthy events engrafted onto the statute. The Court of Appeals said:

> But it is erroneous to confuse privacy with "personality," or to assume that privacy, though lost for a certain time or in a certain context, goes forever unprotected. . . . Thus, it may be appropriate to say that the plaintiff here, Warren Spahn, is a public personality and that, insofar as his professional career is involved, he is substantially without a right to privacy. That is not to say, however, that his "personality" may be fictionalized and that, as fictionalized, it may be exploited for the defendants' commercial benefit through the medium of an unauthorized biography.

As the instant case went to the jury, [Hill], too, was regarded to be a newsworthy person "substantially without a right to privacy" insofar as his hostage experience was involved, but to be entitled to his action insofar as that experience was "fictionalized" and "exploited for the defendants' commercial benefit." "Fictionalization," the Spahn opinion states, "is the heart of the cases in point."

The opinion goes on to say that the "establishment of minor errors in an otherwise accurate" report does not prove "fictionalization." Material and substantial falsification is the test. However, it is not clear whether proof of knowledge of the falsity or that the article was prepared with reckless disregard for the truth is also required. In *New York Times Co. v. Sullivan,* we held that the Constitution delimits a State's power to award damages for libel in actions brought by public officials against critics of their official conduct. Factual error, content defamatory of official reputation, or both, are insufficient for an award of damages for false statements unless actual malice—knowledge that the statements are false or in reckless disregard of the truth—is alleged and proved. The Spahn opinion reveals that the defendant in that case relied on *New York Times* as the basis of an argument that application of the statute to the publication of a substantially fictitious biography would run afoul of the constitutional guarantees. The Court of Appeals held that *New York Times* had no application. The court, after distinguishing the cases on the ground that Spahn did not deal with public officials or official conduct, then says, "The free speech which is encouraged and essential to the operation of a healthy government is something quite different from an individual's attempt to enjoin the publication of a fictitious biography of him. No public interest is served by protecting the dissemination of the latter. We perceive no constitutional infirmities in this respect."

If this is meant to imply that proof of knowing or reckless falsity is not essential to a constitutional application of the statute in these cases, we disagree with the Court of Appeals. We hold that the constitutional protections for speech and press preclude the application of the New York statute to redress false reports of matters of public interest in the absence of proof that the defendant published the report with knowledge of its falsity or in reckless disregard of the truth.

The guarantees for speech and press are not the preserve of political expression or comment upon public affairs, essential as those are to healthy government. One need only pick up any newspaper or magazine to comprehend the vast range of published matter which exposes persons to public view, both private citizens and public officials. Exposure of the self to others in varying degrees is a concomitant of life in a civilized community. The risk of this exposure is an essential incident of life in a society which places a primary value on freedom of speech and of press.

"Freedom of discussion, if it would fulfill its historic function in this nation, must embrace all issues about which information is needed or appropriate to enable the members of society to cope with the exigencies of their period." . . . We have no doubt that the subject of the Life article, the opening of a new play linked to an actual incident, is a matter of public interest. . . .

In this context, sanctions against either innocent or negligent misstatement would present a grave hazard of discouraging the press from exercising the constitutional guarantees. Those guarantees are not for the benefit of the press so much as for the benefit of all of us. A broadly defined freedom of the press assures the maintenance of our political system and an open society. Fear of large verdicts in damage suits for innocent or merely negligent misstatement, even fear of the expense involved in their defense, must inevitably cause publishers to "steer . . . wider of the unlawful zone." . . .

But the constitutional guarantees can tolerate sanctions against calculated falsehood without significant impairment of their essential function. We held in *New York Times* that calculated falsehood enjoyed no immunity in the case of alleged defamation of a public official concerning his official conduct. Similarly, calculated falsehood should enjoy no immunity in the situation here presented us. . . .

We find applicable here the standard of knowing or reckless falsehood, not through blind application of *New York Times Co. v. Sullivan,* relating solely to libel actions by public officials, but only upon consideration of the factors which arise in the particular context of the application of the New York statute in cases involving private individuals. This is neither a libel action by a private individual nor a statutory action by a public official. Therefore, although the First Amendment principles pronounced in *New York Times* guide our conclusion, we reach that conclusion only by applying these principles in this discrete context. It therefore serves no purpose to distinguish the facts here from those in *New York Times.* Were this a libel action, the distinction which has been suggested between the relative opportunities of the public official and the private individual to rebut defamatory charges might be germane. And the additional state interest in the protection of the individual against damage to his reputation would be involved. Moreover, a different test might be required in a statutory action by a public official, as opposed to a libel action by a public official or a statutory action by a private individual. Different considerations might arise concerning the degree of "waiver" of the protection the State might afford. But the question whether the same standard should be applicable both to persons voluntarily and involuntarily thrust into the public limelight is not here before us.

Turning to the facts of the present case, the proofs reasonably would support either a jury finding of innocent or merely negligent misstatement by Life, or a finding that Life portrayed the play as a reenactment of the Hill family's experience reckless of the truth or with actual knowledge that the portrayal was false. . . .

[Hill] argues that the instructions to determine whether Life "altered or changed" the true facts, and whether, apart from incidental errors, the article was a "substantial fiction" or a "fictionalized version" were tantamount to instructions that the jury must find that Life knowingly falsified the facts. We do not think that the instructions bear that interpretation, particularly in light of the marked contrast in the instructions on compensatory and punitive damages. The element of "knowingly" is mentioned only in the instruction that punitive damages must be supported by a finding that Life falsely connected the Hill family with the play "knowingly or through failure to make a reasonable investigation." Moreover, even as to punitive damages, the instruction that such damages were justified on the basis of "failure to make a reasonable investigation" is an instruction that proof of negligent misstatement is enough, and we have rejected the test of negligent misstatement as inadequate. Next, the trial judge plainly did not regard his instructions as limiting the jury to a verdict of liability based on a finding of knowing or reckless falsity; he denied [Time, Inc.]'s motion to dismiss after the close of the evidence because he perceived that it was for the jury to find "whether the Life article was true, or whether an inference could be obtained from reading it that it was not true." This implies a view that "fictionalization" was synonymous with "falsity" without regard to knowledge or even negligence, except for the purpose of an award of punitive damages. Finally, nothing in the New York cases decided at the time of trial limited liability to cases of knowing or reckless falsity, and Spahn, decided since, has left the question in doubt. . . .

The [Time, Inc.] argues that the statute should be declared unconstitutional on its face if construed by the New York courts to impose liability without proof of knowing or reckless falsity. Such a declaration would not be warranted even if it were entirely clear that this had previously been the view of the New York courts. The New York Court of Appeals, as the Spahn opinion demonstrates, has been assiduous in construing the statute to avoid invasion of the constitutional protections of speech and press. We, therefore, confidently expect that the New York courts will apply the statute consistently with the constitutional command. Any possible difference with us as to the thrust of the constitutional command is narrowly limited in this case to the failure of the trial judge to instruct the jury that a verdict of liability could be predicated only on a finding of knowing or reckless falsity in the publication of the *Life* article.

The judgment of the Court of Appeals is set aside, and the case is remanded for further proceedings not inconsistent with this opinion.

Harlan, concurring in part and dissenting in part:

. . . It would be unreasonable to assume that Mr. Hill could find a forum for making a successful refutation of the Life material, or that the public's interest in it would be sufficient for the truth to win out by comparison, as it might in that area of discussion central to a free society. Thus, the state interest in encouraging careful checking and preparation of published material is far stronger than in *New York Times*. The dangers of unchallengeable untruth are far too well documented to be summarily dismissed.

Second, there is a vast difference in the state interest in protecting individuals like Mr. Hill from irresponsibly prepared publicity and the state interest in similar protection for a public official. In *New York Times*, we acknowledged public officials to be a breed from whom hardiness to exposure to charges, innuendoes, and criticisms might be demanded and who voluntarily assumed the risk of such things by entry into the public arena. But Mr. Hill came to public attention through an unfortunate circumstance not of his making, rather than his voluntary actions, and he can in no sense be considered to have "waived" any protection the State might justifiably afford him from irresponsible publicity. Not being inured to the vicissitudes of journalistic scrutiny, such an individual is more easily injured, and his means of self-defense are more limited. The public is less likely to view with normal skepticism what is written about him, because it is not accustomed to seeing his name in the press and expects only a disinterested report.

The coincidence of these factors in this situation leads me to the view that a State should be free to hold the press to a duty of making a reasonable investigation of the underlying facts and limiting itself to "fair comment" on the materials so gathered. Theoretically, of course, such a rule might slightly limit press discussion of matters touching individuals like Mr Hill. But, from a pragmatic standpoint, until now, the press, at least in New York, labored under the more exacting handicap of the existing New York pri-

vacy law and has certainly remained robust. Other professional activity of great social value is carried on under a duty of reasonable care, and there is no reason to suspect the press would be less hardy than medical practitioners or attorneys. . . .

Bartnicki v. Vopper

532 U.S. 514 (2001), 6-3
Opinion of the Court: Stevens (Breyer, Ginsburg, Kennedy, O'Connor, Souter)
Dissenting: Rehnquist, Scalia, Thomas

Does the First Amendment provide protection for speech that discloses the contents of an illegally intercepted communication? What are the interests served by Title III of the Omnibus Crime Control and Safe Streets Act of 1968? How do these interests balance against each other? When does a matter of "public concern" outweigh privacy considerations? What is Chief Justice Rehnquist's reasoning for advocating application of the privacy right?

Stevens, for the Court:

These cases raise an important question concerning what degree of protection, if any, the First Amendment provides to speech that discloses the contents of an illegally intercepted communication. That question is both novel and narrow. Despite the fact that federal law has prohibited such disclosures since 1934, this is the first time that we have confronted such an issue.

The suit at hand involves the repeated intentional disclosure of an illegally intercepted cellular telephone conversation about a public issue. The persons who made the disclosures did not participate in the interception, but they did know—or at least had reason to know—that the interception was unlawful. Accordingly, these cases present a conflict between interests of the highest order—on the one hand, the interest in the full and free dissemination of information concerning public issues, and, on the other hand, the interest in individual privacy and, more specifically, in fostering private speech. The Framers of the First Amendment surely did not foresee the advances in science that produced the conversation, the interception, or the conflict that gave rise to this action. It is therefore not surprising that Circuit judges, as well as the Members of this Court, have come to differing conclusions about the First Amendment's application to this issue. Nevertheless, having considered the interests at stake, we are firmly convinced that the disclosures made by respondents in this suit are protected by the First Amendment.

During 1992 and most of 1993, the Pennsylvania State Education Association, a union representing the teachers at the Wyoming Valley West High School, engaged in collective-bargaining negotiations with the school board. Petitioner Kane, then the president of the local union, testified that the negotiations were "'contentious'" and received "a lot of media attention." In May 1993, petitioner Bartnicki, who was acting as the union's "chief negotiator," used the cellular phone in her car to call Kane and engage in a lengthy conversation about the status of the negotiations. An unidentified person intercepted and recorded that call.

In their conversation, Kane and Bartnicki discussed the timing of a proposed strike, difficulties created by public comment on the negotiations, and the need for a dramatic response to the board's intransigence. At one point, Kane said: "'If they're not gonna move for three percent, we're gonna have to go to their, their homes . . . To blow off their front porches, we'll have to do some work on some of those guys. (PAUSES). Really, uh, really and truthfully because this is, you know, this is bad news. (UNDECIPHERABLE).'"

In the early fall of 1993, the parties accepted a non-binding arbitration proposal that was generally favorable to the teachers. In connection with news reports about the settlement, respondent Vopper, a radio commentator who had been critical of the union in the past, played a tape of the intercepted conversation on his public affairs talk show. Another station also broadcast the tape, and local newspapers published its contents. After filing suit against Vopper and other representatives of the media, Bartnicki and Kane (hereinafter petitioners) learned through discovery that Vopper had obtained the tape from Jack Yocum, the head of a local taxpayers' organization that had opposed the union's demands throughout the negotiations. Yocum, who was added as a defendant, testified that he had found the tape in his mailbox shortly after the interception and recognized the voices of Bartnicki and Kane. . . .

. . . Relying on both federal and Pennsylvania statutory provisions, petitioners sought actual damages, statutory damages, punitive damages, and attorney's fees and costs. After the parties completed their discovery, they filed cross-motions for summary judgment.

. . . [T]he District Court rejected respondents' First Amendment defense because the statutes were content-neutral laws of general applicability that contained "no indicia of prior restraint or the chilling of free speech." . . .

As we pointed out in *Berger v. New York,* sophisticated methods of eavesdropping on oral conversations and intercepting telephone calls have been practiced for decades, primarily by law enforcement authorities. In *Berger,* we held that New York's broadly written statute authorizing the police to conduct wiretaps violated the Fourth Amendment. Largely in response to that decision, and to our holding in *Katz v. United States,* that the attachment of a listening and recording device to the outside of a telephone booth constituted a search, "Congress undertook to draft comprehensive legislation both authorizing the use of evidence obtained by electronic surveillance on specified conditions, and prohibiting its use otherwise. The ultimate result of those efforts was Title III of the Omnibus Crime Control and Safe Streets Act of 1968, entitled Wiretapping and Electronic Surveillance.

One of the stated purposes of that title was "to protect effectively the privacy of wire and oral communications." In addition to authorizing and regulating electronic surveillance for law enforcement purposes, Title III also regulated private conduct. One part of those regulations, §2511(1), defined five offenses punishable by a fine of not more than $10,000, by imprisonment for not more than five years, or by both. Subsection (a) applied to any person who "willfully intercepts . . . any wire or oral communication." Subsection (b) applied to the intentional use of devices designed to intercept oral conversations; subsection (d) applied to the use of the contents of illegally intercepted wire or oral communications; and subsection (e) prohibited the unauthorized disclosure of the contents of interceptions that were authorized for law enforcement purposes. Subsection (c), the original version of the provision most directly at issue in this case, applied to any person who "willfully discloses, or endeavors to disclose, to any other person the contents of any wire or oral communication, knowing or having reason to know that the information was obtained through the interception of a wire or oral communication in violation of this subsection." The oral communications protected by the Act were only those "uttered by a person exhibiting an expectation that such communication is not subject to interception under circumstances justifying such expectation."

As enacted in 1968, Title III did not apply to the monitoring of radio transmissions. In the Electronic Communications Privacy Act of 1986, however, Congress enlarged the coverage of Title III to prohibit the interception of "electronic" as well as oral and wire communications. . . .

. . . The [constitutional] question is whether the application of these statutes in [the] circumstances violates the First Amendment. . . .

In answering that question, we accept respondents' submission on three factual matters that serve to distinguish most of the cases that have arisen under §2511. First, respondents played no part in the illegal interception. Rather, they found out about the interception only after it occurred, and in fact never learned the identity of the person or persons who made the interception. Second, their access to the information on the tapes was obtained lawfully, even though the information itself was intercepted unlawfully by someone else. Third, the subject matter of the conversation was a matter of public concern. If the statements about the labor negotiations had been made in a public arena—during a bargaining session, for example—they would have been newsworthy. . . . .

We agree with petitioners that §2511(1)(c), as well as its Pennsylvania analog, is in fact a content-neutral law of general applicability. . . . In determining whether a regulation is content based or content neutral, we look to the purpose behind the regulation; typically, "[g]overnment regulation of expressive activity is content neutral so long as it is 'justified without reference to the content of the regulated speech.'"

In this case, the basic purpose of the statute at issue is to "protec[t] the privacy of wire[, electronic,] and oral communications." The statute does not distinguish based on the content of the intercepted conversations, nor is it justified by reference to the content of those conversations. Rather, the communications at issue are singled out by virtue of the fact that they were illegally intercepted—by virtue of the source, rather than the subject matter. . . .

As a general matter, "state action to punish the publication of truthful information seldom can satisfy constitutional standards." More specifically, this Court has repeatedly held that "if a newspaper lawfully obtains

truthful information about a matter of public significance then state officials may not constitutionally punish publication of the information, absent a need . . . of the highest order." *Smith v. Daily Mail Publishing Co.* . . .

. . . Accordingly, we consider whether, given the facts of this case, the interests served by §2511(1) can justify its restrictions on speech.

The Government identifies two interests served by the statute-first, the interest in removing an incentive for parties to intercept private conversations, and second, the interest in minimizing the harm to persons whose conversations have been illegally intercepted. We assume that those interests adequately justify the prohibition in §2511(1)(d) against the interceptor's own use of information that he or she acquired by violating §2511(1)(a), but it by no means follows that punishing disclosures of lawfully obtained information of public interest by one not involved in the initial illegality is an acceptable means of serving those ends.

The normal method of deterring unlawful conduct is to impose an appropriate punishment on the person who engages in it. . . . But it would be quite remarkable to hold that speech by a law-abiding possessor of information can be suppressed in order to deter conduct by a non-law-abiding third party. . . .

The Government's second argument, however, is considerably stronger. Privacy of communication is an important interest, and Title III's restrictions are intended to protect that interest, thereby "encouraging the uninhibited exchange of ideas and information among private parties . . . "

Accordingly, it seems to us that there are important interests to be considered on both sides of the constitutional calculus. . . .

In this case, privacy concerns give way when balanced against the interest in publishing matters of public importance. As Warren and Brandeis stated in their classic law review article: "The right of privacy does not prohibit any publication of matter which is of public or general interest." . . .

We think it clear that parallel reasoning requires the conclusion that a stranger's illegal conduct does not suffice to remove the First Amendment shield from speech about a matter of public concern. The months of negotiations over the proper level of compensation for teachers at the Wyoming Valley West High School were unquestionably a matter of public concern, and respondents were clearly engaged in debate about that concern.

Breyer, concurring:

I join the Court's opinion because I agree with its "narrow" holding, limited to the special circumstances present here: (1) the radio broadcasters acted lawfully (up to the time of final public disclosure); and (2) the information publicized involved a matter of unusual public concern, namely a threat of potential physical harm to others. I write separately to explain why, in my view, the Court's holding does not imply a significantly broader constitutional immunity for the media.

As the Court recognizes, the question before us—a question of immunity from statutorily imposed civil liability—implicates competing constitutional concerns. The statutes directly interfere with free expression in that they prevent the media from publishing information. At the same time, they help to protect personal privacy—an interest here that includes not only the "right to be let alone," but also "the interest . . . in fostering private speech." Given these competing interests "on both sides of the equation, the key question becomes one of proper fit."

I would ask whether the statutes strike a reasonable balance between their speech-restricting and speech-enhancing consequences. . . .

The statutory restrictions before us directly enhance private speech. . . . [They] ensure the privacy of telephone conversations. . . .

At the same time, these statutes restrict public speech directly, deliberately, and of necessity. They include media publication within their scope not simply as a means, say, to deter interception, but also as an end. Media dissemination of an intimate conversation to an entire community will often cause the speakers serious harm over and above the harm caused by an initial disclosure to the person who intercepted the phone call. And the threat of that widespread dissemination can create a far more powerful disincentive to speak privately than the comparatively minor threat of disclosure to an interceptor and perhaps to a handful of others. . . .

As a general matter, despite the statutes' direct restrictions on speech, the Federal Constitution must tolerate laws of this kind because of the importance of these privacy and speech-related objectives. . . .

Nonetheless, looked at more specifically, the statutes, as applied in these circumstances, do not reasonably reconcile the competing constitutional objectives. Rather, they disproportionately interfere with media freedom. For one thing, the broadcasters here engaged in no unlawful activity other than the ultimate publication of the information another had previously obtained. They

"neither encouraged nor participated directly or indirectly in the interception." . . .

For another thing, the speakers had little or no legitimate interest in maintaining the privacy of the particular conversation. . . . Where publication of private information constitutes a wrongful act, the law recognizes a privilege allowing the reporting of threats to public safety. . . .

Further, the speakers themselves, the president of a teacher's union and the union's chief negotiator, were "limited public figures," for they voluntarily engaged in a public controversy. They thereby subjected themselves to somewhat greater public scrutiny and had a lesser interest in privacy than an individual engaged in purely private affairs. . . .

Thus, in finding a constitutional privilege to publish unlawfully intercepted conversations of the kind here at issue, the Court does not create a "public interest" exception that swallows up the statutes' privacy-protecting general rule. Rather, it finds constitutional protection for publication of intercepted information of a special kind. Here, the speakers' legitimate privacy expectations are unusually low, and the public interest in defeating those expectations is unusually high. Given these circumstances, along with the lawful nature of respondents' behavior, the statutes' enforcement would disproportionately harm media freedom. . . .

For these reasons, we should avoid adopting overly broad or rigid constitutional rules, which would unnecessarily restrict legislative flexibility. I consequently agree with the Court's holding that the statutes as applied here violate the Constitution, but I would not extend that holding beyond these present circumstances.

Rehnquist, dissenting:

Technology now permits millions of important and confidential conversations to occur through a vast system of electronic networks. . . . In an attempt to prevent some of the most egregious violations of privacy, the United States, the District of Columbia, and 40 States have enacted laws prohibiting the intentional interception and knowing disclosure of electronic communications. The Court holds that all of these statutes violate the First Amendment insofar as the illegally intercepted conversation touches upon a matter of "public concern," an amorphous concept that the Court does not even attempt to define. But the Court's decision diminishes, rather than enhances, the purposes of the First Amendment: chilling the speech of the millions of Americans who rely upon electronic technology to communicate each day. . . .

To effectuate important privacy and speech interests, Congress and the vast majority of States have proscribed the intentional interception and knowing disclosure of the contents of electronic communications. . . .

The Court correctly observes that these are "content-neutral law[s] of general applicability" which serve recognized interests of the "highest order": "the interest in individual privacy and . . . in fostering private speech." It nonetheless subjects these laws to the strict scrutiny normally reserved for governmental attempts to censor different viewpoints or ideas. There is scant support, either in precedent or in reason, for the Court's tacit application of strict scrutiny. . . .

. . . Congress and the Pennsylvania Legislature have acted "'without reference to the content of the regulated speech.'" There is no intimation that these laws seek "to suppress unpopular ideas or information or manipulate the public debate" or that they "distinguish favored speech from disfavored speech on the basis of the ideas or views expressed." The antidisclosure provision is based solely upon the manner in which the conversation was acquired, not the subject matter of the conversation or the viewpoints of the speakers. . . . As the concerns motivating strict scrutiny are absent, these content-neutral restrictions upon speech need pass only intermediate scrutiny. . . .

Undaunted, the Court places an inordinate amount of weight upon the fact that the receipt of an illegally intercepted communication has not been criminalized. . . . Congress and the overwhelming majority of States reasonably have concluded that sanctioning the knowing disclosure of illegally intercepted communications will deter the initial interception itself, a crime which is extremely difficult to detect. . . .

The same logic applies here and demonstrates that the incidental restriction on alleged First Amendment freedoms is no greater than essential to further the interest of protecting the privacy of individual communications. Were there no prohibition on disclosure, an unlawful eavesdropper who wanted to disclose the conversation could anonymously launder the interception through a third party and thereby avoid detection. Indeed, demand for illegally obtained private information would only increase if it could be disclosed without repercussion. The law against interceptions, which the Court agrees is valid, would be utterly ineffectual without these antidisclosure provisions. . . .

The statutes undeniably protect [the] venerable right of privacy. Concomitantly, they further the First Amendment rights of the parties to the conversation. . . .

Although the Court recognizes and even extols the virtues of this right to privacy, these are. . . . overridden by the Court's newfound right to publish unlawfully acquired information of "public concern." The Court concludes that the private conversation between petitioners is somehow a "debate . . . worthy of constitutional protection." Perhaps the Court is correct that "[i]f the statements about the labor negotiations had been made in a public arena—during a bargaining session, for example—they would have been newsworthy." The point, however, is that Bartnicki and Kane had no intention of contributing to a public "debate" at all, and it is perverse to hold that another's unlawful interception and knowing disclosure of their conversation is speech "worthy of constitutional protection." . . .

Surely "the interest in individual privacy," at its narrowest must embrace the right to be free from surreptitious eavesdropping on, and involuntary broadcast of, our cellular telephone conversations. The Court subordinates that right, not to the claims of those who themselves wish to speak, but to the claims of those who wish to publish the intercepted conversations of others. Congress' effort to balance the above claim to privacy against a marginal claim to speak freely is thereby set at naught.

Roth v. United States

354 U.S. 476 (1957), 7-2
Opinion of the Court: Brennan (6-3)
Concurring: Harlan
Dissenting: (Black, Douglas)

This case, a federal prosecution, was heard and decided with a companion case, Alberts v. California, *a state prosecution. Justice Harlan dissented in the Court's opinion in* Roth, *but concurred in* Alberts. *The two cases and the rule the Court propounds are sometimes simply referred to as* Roth-Alberts.

How did the Court change the test for obscenity? How does each part of the test expand protection for sexual expression or representation? What is or is not "utterly without redeeming social importance"? What questions has the Court left unanswered? Does obscenity still remain outside First Amendment protection? Why did the Court find it necessary to develop an elaborate test for obscenity instead of simply embracing one Justice Stewart was to suggest in a later case: "I know it when I see it."

Brennan, for the Court:

The constitutionality of a criminal obscenity statute is the question in each of these cases. In Roth, the primary constitutional question is whether the federal obscenity statute violates the provision of the First Amendment that "Congress shall make no law . . . abridging the freedom of speech, or of the press. . . . " In Alberts, the primary constitutional question is whether the obscenity provisions of the California Penal Code invade the freedoms of speech and press as they may be incorporated in the liberty protected from state action by the Due Process Clause of the Fourteenth Amendment. . . .

Roth conducted a business in New York in the publication and sale of books, photographs and magazines. He used circulars and advertising matter to solicit sales. He was convicted by a jury in the District Court for the Southern District of New York upon 4 counts of a 26-count indictment charging him with mailing obscene circulars and advertising, and an obscene book, in violation of the federal obscenity statute. . . .

Alberts conducted a mail-order business from Los Angeles. He was convicted by the Judge of the Municipal Court of the Beverly Hills Judicial District (having waived a jury trial) under a misdemeanor complaint which charged him with lewdly keeping for sale obscene and indecent books, and with writing, composing and publishing an obscene advertisement of them, in violation of the California Penal Code. . . .

The dispositive question is whether obscenity is utterance within the area of protected speech and press. Although this is the first time the question has been squarely presented to this Court, either under the First Amendment or under the Fourteenth Amendment, expressions found in numerous opinions indicate that this Court has always assumed that obscenity is not protected by the freedoms of speech and press. . . .

In light of this history, it is apparent that the unconditional phrasing of the First Amendment was not intended to protect every utterance. This phrasing did not prevent this Court from concluding that libelous utterances are not within the area of constitutionally protected speech. At the time of the adoption of the First Amendment, obscenity law was not as fully developed as libel law, but there is sufficiently contemporaneous evidence to show that obscenity, too, was outside the protection intended for speech and press. . . .

All ideas having even the slightest redeeming social importance—unorthodox ideas, controversial ideas, even ideas hateful to the prevailing climate of opinion—have the full protection of the guaranties, unless excludable because they encroach upon the limited area of more important interests. But implicit in the history of the First Amendment is the rejection of obscenity as utterly without redeeming social importance. . . . This is the same judgment expressed by this Court in *Chaplinsky v. New Hampshire:*

> . . . There are certain well defined and narrowly limited classes of speech, the prevention and punishment of which have never been thought to raise any Constitutional problem. These include the lewd and obscene. . . . It has been well observed that such utterances are no essential part of any exposition of ideas, and are of such slight social value as a step to truth that any benefit that may be derived from them is clearly outweighed by the social interest in order and morality. . . . (emphasis added)

We hold that obscenity is not within the area of constitutionally protected speech or press.

It is strenuously urged that these obscenity statutes offend the constitutional guaranties because they punish incitation to impure sexual thoughts, not shown to be related to any overt antisocial conduct which is or may be incited in the persons stimulated to such thoughts. . . .

. . . It is insisted that the constitutional guaranties are violated because convictions may be had without proof either that obscene material will perceptibly create a clear and present danger of anti-social conduct, or will probably induce its recipients to such conduct. But, in light of our holding that obscenity is not protected speech, the complete answer to this argument is in the holding of this Court in *Beauharnais v. Illinois:*

> Libelous utterances not being within the area of constitutionally protected speech, it is unnecessary, either for us or for the State courts, to consider the issues behind the phrase "clear and present danger." Certainly no one would contend

that obscene speech, for example, may be punished only upon a showing of such circumstances. Libel, as we have seen, is in the same class.

However, sex and obscenity are not synonymous. Obscene material is material which deals with sex in a manner appealing to prurient interest. The portrayal of sex, e.g., in art, literature and scientific works, is not itself sufficient reason to deny material the constitutional protection of freedom of speech and press. Sex, a great and mysterious motive force in human life, has indisputably been a subject of absorbing interest to mankind through the ages; it is one of the vital problems of human interest and public concern. . . .

The early leading standard of obscenity allowed material to be judged merely by the effect of an isolated excerpt upon particularly susceptible persons. *Regina v. Hicklin,* (1868). Some American courts adopted this standard, but later decisions have rejected it and substituted this test: whether, to the average person, applying contemporary community standards, the dominant theme of the material, taken as a whole, appeals to prurient interest. The Hicklin test, judging obscenity by the effect of isolated passages upon the most susceptible persons, might well encompass material legitimately treating with sex, and so it must be rejected as unconstitutionally restrictive of the freedoms of speech and press. On the other hand, the substituted standard provides safeguards adequate to withstand the charge of constitutional infirmity. . . .

Many decisions have recognized that these terms of obscenity statutes are not precise. This Court, however, has consistently held that lack of precision is not itself offensive to the requirements of due process. " . . . [T]he Constitution does not require impossible standards"; all that is required is that the language "conveys sufficiently definite warning as to the proscribed conduct when measured by common understanding and practices. . . . "

In summary, then, we hold that these statutes, applied according to the proper standard for judging obscenity, do not offend constitutional safeguards against convictions based upon protected material, or fail to give men in acting adequate notice of what is prohibited. . . .

Harlan, concurrring in *Alberts,* dissenting in *Roth:*
The question in [*Alberts*] is whether the defendant was deprived of liberty without due process of law when he was convicted for selling certain materials found by the judge to be obscene because they would have a "tendency to deprave or corrupt its readers by exciting lascivious thoughts or arousing lustful desire."

In judging the constitutionality of this conviction, we should remember that our function in reviewing state judgments under the Fourteenth Amendment is a narrow one. We do not decide whether the policy of the State is wise, or whether it is based on assumptions scientifically substantiated. We can inquire only whether the state action so subverts the fundamental liberties implicit in the Due Process Clause that it cannot be sustained as a rational exercise of power. The States' power to make printed words criminal is, of course, confined by the Fourteenth Amendment, but only insofar as such power is inconsistent with our concepts of "ordered liberty."

What, then, is the purpose of this California statute? Clearly the state legislature has made the judgment that printed words can "deprave or corrupt" the reader—that words can incite to antisocial or immoral action. The assumption seems to be that the distribution of certain types of literature will induce criminal or immoral sexual conduct. It is well known, of course, that the validity of this assumption is a matter of dispute among critics, sociologists, psychiatrists, and penologists. There is a large school of thought, particularly in the scientific community, which denies any causal connection between the reading of pornography and immorality, crime, or delinquency. Others disagree. Clearly it is not our function to decide this question. That function belongs to the state legislature. Nothing in the Constitution requires California to accept as truth the most advanced and sophisticated psychiatric opinion. It seems to me clear that it is not irrational, in our present state of knowledge, to consider that pornography can induce a type of sexual conduct which a State may deem obnoxious to the moral fabric of society. In fact, the very division of opinion on the subject counsels us to respect the choice made by the State. . . .

What has been said, however, does not dispose of the case. It still remains for us to decide whether the state court's determination that this material should be suppressed is consistent with the Fourteenth Amendment, and that, of course, presents a federal question as to which we, and not the state court, have the ultimate responsibility. And so, in the final analysis, I concur in the judgment because, upon an independent perusal of the material involved, and in light of the considerations discussed above, I cannot say that its suppression would so interfere with the communication of "ideas" in any proper sense of that term that it would offend the Due Process Clause. I therefore agree with the Court that appellant's conviction must be affirmed. . . .

We are faced [in *Roth*] with the question whether the federal obscenity statute, as construed and applied in this case, violates the First Amendment to the Constitution. To me, this question is of quite a different order than one where we are dealing with state legislation under the Fourteenth Amendment. I do not think it follows that state and federal powers in this area are the same, and that, just because the State may suppress a particular utterance, it is automatically permissible for the Federal Government to do the same. . . .

Not only is the federal interest in protecting the Nation against pornography attenuated, but the dangers of federal censorship in this field are far greater than anything the States may do. It has often been said that one of the great strengths of our federal system is that we have, in the forty-eight States, forty-eight experimental social laboratories. "State statutory law reflects predominantly this capacity of a legislature to introduce novel techniques of social control. The federal system has the immense advantage of providing forty-eight separate centers for such experimentation."

Different States will have different attitudes toward the same work of literature. The same book which is freely read in one State might be classed as obscene in another. And it seems to me that no overwhelming danger to our freedom to experiment and to gratify our tastes in literature is likely to result from the suppression of a borderline book in one of the States so long as there is no uniform nationwide suppression of the book, and so long as other States are free to experiment with the same or bolder books. . . .

I judge this case, then, in view of what I think is the attenuated federal interest in this field, in view of the very real danger of a deadening uniformity which can result from nationwide federal censorship, and in view of the fact that the constitutionality of this conviction must be weighed against the First, and not the Fourteenth, Amendment. So viewed, I do not think that this conviction can be upheld. . . .

Douglas, dissenting:
When we sustain these convictions, we make the legality of a publication turn on the purity of thought which a book or tract instills in the mind of the reader. I do not think we can approve that standard and be faithful to the command of the First Amendment, which, by its terms, is a restraint on Congress and which by the Fourteenth is a restraint on the States. . . .

The absence of dependable information on the effect of obscene literature on human conduct should make us wary. It should put us on the side of protecting society's interest in literature, except and unless it can be said that the particular publication has an impact on action that the government can control. . . .

Any test that turns on what is offensive to the community's standards is too loose, too capricious, too destructive of freedom of expression to be squared with the First Amendment. Under that test, juries can censor, suppress, and punish what they don't like, provided the matter relates to "sexual impurity" or has a tendency "to excite lustful thoughts." This is community censorship in one of its worst forms. . . .

. . . Unlike the law of libel, wrongfully relied on in *Beauharnais*, there is no special historical evidence that literature dealing with sex was intended to be treated in a special manner by those who drafted the First Amendment. In fact, the first reported court decision in this country involving obscene literature was in 1821. I reject too the implication that problems of freedom of speech and of the press are to be resolved by weighing against the values of free expression the judgment of the Court that a particular form of that expression has "no redeeming social importance." The First Amendment, its prohibition in terms absolute, was designed to preclude courts as well as legislatures from weighing the values of speech against silence. The First Amendment puts free speech in the preferred position.

Freedom of expression can be suppressed if, and to the extent that, it is so closely brigaded with illegal action as to be an inseparable part of it. As a people, we cannot afford to relax that standard. For the test that suppresses a cheap tract today can suppress a literary gem tomorrow. All it need do is to incite a lascivious thought or arouse a lustful desire. The list of books that judges or juries can place in that category is endless.

I would give the broad sweep of the First Amendment full support. I have the same confidence in the ability of our people to reject noxious literature as I have in their capacity to sort out the true from the false in theology, economics, politics, or any other field.

Miller v. California

413 U.S. 15 (1973), 5-4

Opinion of the Court: Burger (Blackmun, Powell, Rehnquist, White)

Dissenting: Brennan, Douglas, Marshall, Stewart

What elements of the obscenity test are changed by this decision? Do the changes narrow or widen what may be obscene? To what extent do they create or restore a "variable" obscenity? Should the First Amendment require national uniform standards or should it accommodate diversity where community values are asserted? Does the decision now allow the Court to avoid deciding itself whether specific expression is obscene or not? Or is the Court inevitably destined to become the "Supreme Board of Censors" Justice Black feared?

Burger, for the Court:

. . . [Miller] conducted a mass mailing campaign to advertise the sale of illustrated books, euphemistically called "adult" material. After a jury trial, he was convicted of violating California Penal Code §311.2(a), a misdemeanor, by knowingly distributing obscene matter. . . . [His] conviction was specifically based on his conduct in causing five unsolicited advertising brochures to be sent through the mail in an envelope addressed to a restaurant in Newport Beach, California. The envelope was opened by the manager of the restaurant and his mother. They had not requested the brochures; they complained to the police.

The brochures advertise four books entitled "Intercourse," "Man-Woman," "Sex Orgies Illustrated," and "An Illustrated History of Pornography," and a film entitled "Marital Intercourse." While the brochures contain some descriptive printed material, primarily they consist of pictures and drawings very explicitly depicting men and women in groups of two or more engaging in a variety of sexual activities, with genitals often prominently displayed.

This case involves the application of a State's criminal obscenity statute to a situation in which sexually explicit materials have been thrust by aggressive sales action upon unwilling recipients who had in no way indicated any desire to receive such materials. . . .

This much has been categorically settled by the Court, that obscene material is unprotected by the First Amendment. "The First and Fourteenth Amendments have never been treated as absolutes. We acknowledge, however, the inherent dangers of undertaking to regulate any form of expression. State statutes designed to regulate obscene materials must be carefully limited. As a result, we now confine the permissible scope of such regulation to works which depict or describe sexual conduct. That conduct must be specifically defined by the applicable state law, as written or authoritatively construed. A state offense must also be limited to works which, taken as a whole, appeal to the prurient interest in sex, which portray sexual conduct in a patently offensive way, and which, taken as a whole, do not have serious literary, artistic, political, or scientific value.

The basic guidelines for the trier of fact must be: (a) whether "the average person, applying contemporary community standards" would find that the work, taken as a whole, appeals to the prurient interest, (b) whether the work depicts or describes, in a patently offensive way, sexual conduct specifically defined by the applicable state law; and (c) whether the work, taken as a whole, lacks serious literary, artistic, political, or scientific value. We do not adopt as a constitutional standard the "utterly without redeeming social value" test of *Memoirs v. Massachusetts*, that concept has never commanded the adherence of more than three Justices at one time. If a state law that regulates obscene material is thus limited, as written or construed, the First Amendment values applicable to the States through the Fourteenth Amendment are adequately protected by the ultimate power of appellate courts to conduct an independent review of constitutional claims when necessary.

We emphasize that it is not our function to propose regulatory schemes for the States. That must await their concrete legislative efforts. It is possible, however, to give a few plain examples of what a state statute could define for regulation under part (b) of the standard announced in this opinion, supra:

(a) Patently offensive representations or descriptions of ultimate sexual acts, normal or perverted, actual or simulated.

(b) Patently offensive representations or descriptions of masturbation, excretory functions, and lewd exhibition of the genitals.

Sex and nudity may not be exploited without limit by films or pictures exhibited or sold in places of public accommodation any more than live sex and nudity can be exhibited or sold without limit in such public places. At a minimum, prurient, patently offensive depiction or description of sexual conduct must have serious literary, artistic, political, or scientific value to merit First Amendment protection. For example, medical books for the education of physicians and related personnel necessarily use graphic illustrations and descriptions of human anatomy. In resolving the inevitably sensitive questions of fact and law, we must continue to rely on the jury system, accompanied by the safeguards that judges, rules of evidence, presumption of innocence, and other protective features provide, as we do with rape, murder, and a host of other offenses against society and its individual members.

Justice Brennan, author of the opinion of the Court . . . *Roth v. United States,* has abandoned his former position and now maintains that no formulation of this Court, the Congress, or the States can adequately distinguish obscene material unprotected by the First Amendment from protected expression. Paradoxically, [he] indicates that suppression of unprotected obscene material is permissible to avoid exposure to unconsenting adults, as in this case, and to juveniles, although he gives no indication of how the division between protected and nonprotected materials may be drawn with greater precision for these purposes than for regulation of commercial exposure to consenting adults only. Nor does he indicate where in the Constitution he finds the authority to distinguish between a willing "adult" one month past the state law age of majority and a willing "juvenile" one month younger.

Under the holdings announced today, no one will be subject to prosecution for the sale or exposure of obscene materials unless these materials depict or describe patently offensive "hard core" sexual conduct specifically defined by the regulating state law, as written or construed. We are satisfied that these specific prerequisites will provide fair notice to a dealer in such materials that his public and commercial activities may bring prosecution. The inability to define regulated materials with ultimate, god-like precision altogether removes the power of the States or the Congress to regulate, then "hard core" pornography may be exposed without limit to the juvenile, the passerby, and the consenting adult alike, as, indeed, Mr. Justice Douglas contends. In this belief, however, Mr. Justice Douglas now stands alone. . . .

Under a National Constitution, fundamental First Amendment limitations on the powers of the States do not vary from community to community, but this does not mean that there are, or should or can be, fixed, uniform national standards of precisely what appeals to the "prurient interest" or is "patently offensive." These are essentially questions of fact, and our Nation is simply too big and too diverse for this Court

to reasonably expect that such standards could be articulated for all 50 States in a single formulation, even assuming the prerequisite consensus exists. When triers of fact are asked to decide whether "the average person, applying contemporary community standards" would consider certain materials "prurient," it would be unrealistic to require that the answer be based on some abstract formulation. The adversary system, with lay jurors as the usual ultimate factfinders in criminal prosecutions, has historically permitted triers of fact to draw on the standards of their community, guided always by limiting instructions on the law. To require a State to structure obscenity proceedings around evidence of a national "community standard" would be an exercise in futility. . . .

We conclude that neither the State's alleged failure to offer evidence of "national standards," nor the trial court's charge that the jury consider state community standards, were constitutional errors. Nothing in the First Amendment requires that a jury must consider hypothetical and unascertainable "national standards" when attempting to determine whether certain materials are obscene as a matter of fact. . . .

It is neither realistic nor constitutionally sound to read the First Amendment as requiring that the people of Maine or Mississippi accept public depiction of conduct found tolerable in Las Vegas, or New York City. People in different States vary in their tastes and attitudes, and this diversity is not to be strangled by the absolutism of imposed uniformity. . . . [T]he primary concern with requiring a jury to apply the standard of "the average person, applying contemporary community standards" is to be certain that, so far as material is not aimed at a deviant group, it will be judged by its impact on an average person, rather than a particularly susceptible or sensitive person—or indeed a totally insensitive one. We hold that the requirement that the jury evaluate the materials with reference to "contemporary standards of the State of California" serves this protective purpose and is constitutionally adequate. . . .

Douglas, dissenting:

Today we leave open the way for California to send a man to prison for distributing brochures that advertise books and a movie under freshly written standards defining obscenity which until today is decision were never the part of any law. . . .

Today the Court retreats from the earlier formulations of the constitutional test and undertakes to make new definitions. This effort, like the earlier ones, is earnest and well intentioned. The difficulty is that we do not deal with constitutional terms, since "obscenity" is not mentioned in the Constitution or Bill of Rights. And the First Amendment makes no such exception from "the press" which it undertakes to protect nor, as I have said on other occasions, is an exception necessarily implied, for there was no recognized exception to the free press at the time the Bill of Rights was adopted which treated "obscene" publications differently from other types of papers, magazines, and books. So there are no constitutional guidelines for deciding what is and what is not "obscene." The Court is at large because we deal with tastes and standards of literature. What shocks me may be sustenance for my neighbor. What causes one person to boil up in rage over one pamphlet or movie may reflect only his neurosis, not shared by others. We deal here with a regime of censorship which, if adopted, should be done by constitutional amendment after full debate by the people. . . .

The idea that the First Amendment permits government to ban publications that are "offensive" to some people puts an ominous gloss on freedom of the press. That test would make it possible to ban any paper or any journal or magazine in some benighted place. The First Amendment was designed "to invite dispute," to induce "a condition of unrest," to "create dissatisfaction with conditions as they are," and even to stir "people to anger." The idea that the First Amendment permits punishment for ideas that are "offensive" to the particular judge or jury sitting in judgment is astounding. No greater leveler of speech or literature has ever been designed. To give the power to the censor, as we do today, is to make a sharp and radical break with the traditions of a free society. The First Amendment was not fashioned as a vehicle for dispensing tranquilizers to the people. Its prime function was to keep debate open to "offensive" as well as to "staid" people. The tendency throughout history has been to subdue the individual and to exalt the power of government. The use of the standard "offensive" gives authority to government that cuts the very vitals out of the First Amendment. As is intimated by the Court's opinion, the materials before us may be garbage. But so is much of what is said in political campaigns, in the daily press, on TV, or over the radio. By reason of the First Amendment—and solely because of it—speakers and publishers have not been threatened or subdued because their thoughts and ideas may be "offensive" to some. . . .

Brennan, dissenting:

[*Justice Brennan dissented in both* Miller v. California *and its companion case* Paris Adult Theatre I v. Slaton. *This excerpt is from his more elaborate dissent in the latter case in which the Court upheld a civil complaint against a theatre for showing an obscene film, even though the theatre admitted only adults.*]

Our experience with the Roth approach has certainly taught us that the outright suppression of obscenity cannot be reconciled with the fundamental principles of the First and Fourteenth Amendments. For we have failed to formulate a standard that sharply distinguishes protected from unprotected speech, and out of necessity, we have resorted to the Redrup approach, which resolves cases as between the parties, but offers only the most obscure guidance to legislation, adjudication by other courts, and primary conduct. By disposing of cases through summary reversal or denial of certiorari, we have deliberately and effectively obscured the rationale underlying the decisions. It comes as no surprise that judicial attempts to follow our lead conscientiously have often ended in hopeless confusion. . . .

As a result of our failure to define standards with predictable application to any given piece of material, there is no probability of regularity in obscenity decisions by state and lower federal courts. That is not to say that these courts have performed badly in this area or paid insufficient attention to the principles we have established. The problem is, rather, that one cannot say with certainty that material is obscene until at least five members of this Court, applying inevitably obscure standards, have pronounced it so. The number of obscenity cases on our docket gives ample testimony to the burden that has been placed upon this Court. . . .

. . . More important, the practice effectively censors protected expression by leaving lower court determinations of obscenity intact even though the status of the allegedly obscene material is entirely unsettled until final review here. In addition, the uncertainty of the standards creates a continuing source of tension between state and federal courts, since the need for an independent determination by this Court seems to render superfluous even the most conscientious analysis by state tribunals. And our inability to justify our decisions with a persuasive rationale—or indeed, any rationale at all—necessarily creates the impression that we are merely second-guessing state court judges. . . .

In short, while I cannot say that the interests of the State apart from the question of juveniles and unconsenting adults—are trivial or nonexistent, I am compelled to conclude that these interests cannot justify the substantial damage to constitutional rights and to this Nation's judicial machinery that inevitably results from state efforts to bar the distribution even of unprotected material to consenting adults. I would hold, therefore, that, at least in the absence of distribution to juveniles or obtrusive exposure to unconsenting adults, the First and Fourteenth Amendments prohibit the State and Federal Governments from attempting wholly to suppress sexually oriented materials on the basis of their allegedly "obscene" contents. . . .

Reno v. American Civil Liberties Union

521 U.S. 844 (1997), 7-2
Opinion of the Court: Stevens (Breyer, Ginsburg, Kennedy, Scalia, Souter, Thomas)
Dissenting: O'Connor, Rehnquist

In the Communications Decency Act (CDA), part of the Telecommunications Act of 1996, Congress made it a crime for anyone to knowingly transmit, including on the Internet, "any comment, request, suggestion, proposal, image or other communication" to anyone under 18 that was "obscene," "indecent," or "patently offensive." A three-judge district court found the provisions to be unconstitutionally vague and overbroad. That finding was appealed by the attorney general in this case.

How did the act fail to meet First Amendment standards? How did the Court distinguish earlier holdings that allowed restriction of sexually explicit material directed at underage persons where that material was not obscene for adults? On what points do Stevens and O'Connor disagree? Does the First Amendment require that all communications media be treated equally? Why didn't Congress pay more attention to the Supreme Court's established obscenity test?

Stevens, for the Court:

At issue is the constitutionality of two statutory provisions enacted to protect minors from "indecent" and "patently offensive" communications on the Internet. Notwithstanding the legitimacy and importance of the congressional goal of protecting children from harmful materials, we agree with the three judge District Court that the statute abridges "the freedom of speech" protected by the First Amendment. . . .

Regardless of whether the CDA is so vague that it violates the Fifth Amendment, the many ambiguities concerning the scope of its coverage render it problematic for purposes of the First Amendment. For instance, each of the two parts of the CDA uses a different linguistic form. The first uses the word "indecent," while the second speaks of material that "in context, depicts or describes, in terms patently offensive as measured by contemporary community standards, sexual or excretory activities or organs." Given the absence of a definition of either term, this difference in language will provoke uncertainty among speakers about how the two standards relate to each other and just what they mean. Could a speaker confidently assume that a serious discussion about birth control practices, homosexuality, the First Amendment issues raised by the Appendix to our [*F.C.C. v.*] *Pacifica* [*Foundation*] opinion, or the consequences of prison rape would not violate the CDA? This uncertainty undermines the likelihood that the CDA has been carefully tailored to the congressional goal of protecting minors from potentially harmful materials.

The vagueness of the CDA is a matter of special concern for two reasons. First, the CDA is a content based regulation of speech. The vagueness of such a regulation raises special First Amendment concerns because of its obvious chilling effect on free speech. Second, the CDA is a criminal statute. In addition to the opprobrium and stigma of a criminal conviction, the CDA threatens violators with penalties including up to two years in prison for each act of violation. The severity of criminal sanctions may well cause speakers to remain silent rather than communicate even arguably unlawful words, ideas, and images. . . .

The Government argues that the statute is no more vague than the obscenity standard this Court established in *Miller v. California*. But that is not so. In *Miller*, this Court reviewed a criminal conviction against a commercial vendor who mailed brochures containing pictures of sexually explicit activities to individuals who had not requested such materials. Having struggled for some time to establish a definition of obscenity, we set forth in Miller the test for obscenity that controls to this day: "(a) whether the average person, applying contemporary community standards would find that the work, taken as a whole, appeals to the prurient interest; (b) whether the work depicts or describes, in a patently offensive way, sexual conduct specifically defined by the applicable state law; and (c) whether the work, taken as a whole, lacks serious literary, artistic, political, or scientific value."

Because the CDA's "patently offensive" standard (and, we assume arguendo, its synonymous "indecent" standard) is one part of the three prong Miller test, the Government reasons, it cannot be unconstitutionally vague.

The Government's assertion is incorrect as a matter of fact. The second prong of the Miller test—the purportedly analogous standard—contains a critical requirement that is omitted from the CDA: that the proscribed material be "specifically defined by the applicable state law." This requirement reduces the vagueness inherent in the open ended term "patently offensive" as used in the CDA. Moreover, the Miller definition is limited to "sexual conduct," whereas the CDA extends also to include (1) "excretory activities" as well as (2) "organs" of both a sexual and excretory nature.

The Government's reasoning is also flawed. Just because a definition including three limitations is not vague, it does not follow that one of those limitations, standing by itself, is not vague. Each of *Miller's* additional two prongs—(1) that, taken as a whole, the material appeal to the "prurient" interest, and (2) that it "lac[k] serious literary, artistic, political, or scientific value"—critically limits the uncertain sweep of the obscenity definition. The second requirement is particularly important because, unlike the "patently offensive" and "prurient interest" criteria, it is not judged by contemporary community standards. This "societal value" requirement, absent in the CDA, allows appellate courts to impose some limitations and regularity on the definition by setting, as a matter of law, a national floor for socially redeeming value. The Government's contention that courts will be able to give such legal limitations to the CDA's standards is belied by *Miller's* own rationale for having juries determine whether material is "patently offensive" according to community standards: that such questions are essentially ones of fact.

In contrast to *Miller* and our other previous cases, the CDA thus presents a greater threat of censoring speech that, in fact, falls outside the statute's scope. Given the vague contours of the coverage of the statute, it unquestionably silences some speakers whose messages would be entitled to constitutional protection. That danger provides further reason for insisting that the statute not be overly broad. The CDA's burden on protected speech cannot be justified if it could be avoided by a more carefully drafted statute.

We are persuaded that the CDA lacks the precision that the First Amendment requires when a statute regulates the content of speech. In order to deny minors access to potentially harmful speech, the CDA effectively suppresses a large amount of speech that adults have a constitutional right to receive and to address to one another. That burden on adult speech is unacceptable if less restrictive alternatives would be at least as effective in achieving the legitimate purpose that the statute was enacted to serve.

In evaluating the free speech rights of adults, we have made it perfectly clear that "[s]exual expression which is indecent but not obscene is protected by the First Amendment." . . . Indeed, *Pacifica* itself admonished that "the fact that society may find speech offensive is not a sufficient reason for suppressing it."

It is true that we have repeatedly recognized the governmental interest in protecting children from harmful materials. But that interest does not justify an unnecessarily broad suppression of speech addressed to adults. . . .

In arguing that the CDA does not so diminish adult communication, the Government relies on the incorrect factual premise that prohibiting a transmission whenever it is known that one of its recipients is a minor would not interfere with adult to adult communication. The findings of the District Court make clear that this premise is untenable. . . .

The breadth of the CDA's coverage is wholly unprecedented. Unlike the regulations upheld in *Ginsberg* [v. *New York*] and *Pacifica*, the scope of the CDA is not limited to commercial speech or commercial entities. Its open ended prohibitions embrace all nonprofit entities and individuals posting indecent messages or displaying them on their own computers in the presence of minors. The general, undefined terms "indecent" and "patently offensive" cover large amounts of nonpornographic material with serious educational or other value. Moreover, the "community standards" criterion as applied to the Internet means that any communication available to a nation wide audience will be judged by the standards of the community most likely to be offended by the message. The regulated subject matter includes any of the seven "dirty words" used in the *Pacifica* monologue, the use of which the Government's expert acknowledged could constitute a felony.

It may also extend to discussions about prison rape or safe sexual practices, artistic images that include nude subjects, and arguably the card catalogue of the Carnegie Library. . . .

In this Court, though not in the District Court, the Government asserts that—in addition to its interest in protecting children—its "[e]qually significant" interest in fostering the growth of the Internet provides an independent basis for upholding the constitutionality of the CDA. The Government apparently assumes that the unregulated availability of "indecent" and "patently offensive" material on the Internet is driving countless citizens away from the medium because of the risk of exposing themselves or their children to harmful material.

We find this argument singularly unpersuasive. The dramatic expansion of this new marketplace of ideas contradicts the factual basis of this contention. The record demonstrates that the growth of the Internet has been and continues to be phenomenal. As a matter of constitutional tradition, in the absence of evidence to the contrary, we presume that governmental regulation of the content of speech is more likely to interfere with the free exchange of ideas than to encourage it. The interest in encouraging freedom of expression in a democratic society outweighs any theoretical but unproven benefit of censorship.

For the foregoing reasons, the judgment of the district court is affirmed.

O'Connor, concurring in part, dissenting in part:

I write separately to explain why I view the Communications Decency Act of 1996 (CDA) as little more than an attempt by Congress to create "adult zones" on the Internet. Our precedent indicates that the creation of such zones can be constitutionally sound. Despite the soundness of its purpose, however, portions of the CDA are unconstitutional because they stray from the blueprint our prior cases have developed for constructing a "zoning law" that passes constitutional muster. . . .

The creation of "adult zones" is by no means a novel concept. States have long denied minors access to certain establishments frequented by adults. State shave also denied minors access to speech deemed to be "harmful to minors." The Court has previously sustained such zoning laws, but only if they respect the First Amendment rights of adults and minors. That is to say, a zoning law is valid if (i) it does not unduly restrict adult access to the material; and (ii) minors have no First Amendment right to read or view the

banned material. As applied to the Internet as it exists in 1997, the "display" provision and some applications of the "indecency transmission" and "specific person" provisions fail to adhere to the first of these limiting principles by restricting adults' access to protected materials in certain circumstances. Unlike the Court, however, I would invalidate the provisions only in those circumstances. . . .

Cyberspace differs from the physical world in another basic way: Cyberspace is malleable. Thus, it is possible to construct barriers in cyberspace and use them to screen for identity, making cyberspace more like the physical world and, consequently, more amenable to zoning laws. This transformation of cyberspace is already underway. Internet speakers (users who post-material on the Internet) have begun to zone cyberspace itself through the use of "gateway" technology. Such technology requires Internet users to enter information about themselves—perhaps an adult identification number or a credit card number—before they can access certain areas of cyberspace, much like a bouncer checks a person's driver's license before admitting him to a nightclub. Internet users who access information have not attempted to zone cyberspace itself, but have tried to limit their own power to access information in cyberspace, much as a parent controls what her children watch on television by installing a lock box. This user based zoning is accomplished through the use of screening software (such as Cyber Patrol or SurfWatch) or browsers with screening capabilities, both of which search addresses and text for keywords that are associated with "adult" sites and, if the user wishes, blocks access to such sites. The Platform for Internet Content Selection (PICS) project is designed to facilitate user based zoning by encouraging Internet speakers to rate the content of their speech using codes recognized by all screening programs. . . .

Although the prospects for the eventual zoning of the Internet appear promising, I agree with the Court that we must evaluate the constitutionality of the CDA as it applies to the Internet as it exists today. Given the present state of cyberspace, I agree with the Court that the "display" provision cannot pass muster. Until gateway technology is available throughout cyberspace, and it is not in 1997, a speaker cannot be reasonably assured that the speech he displays will reach only adults because it is impossible to confine speech to an "adult zone." Thus, the only way for a speaker to avoid liability under the CDA is to refrain completely from using indecent speech. But this forced silence impinges on the First Amendment right of adults to make and obtain this speech and, for all intents and purposes, "reduce[s] the adult population [on the Internet] to reading only what is fit for children." As a result, the "display" provision cannot withstand scrutiny.

The "indecency transmission" and "specific person" provisions present a closer issue, for they are not unconstitutional in all of their applications. As discussed above, the "indecency transmission" provision makes it a crime to transmit knowingly an indecent message to a person the sender knows is under 18 years of age. The "specific person" provision proscribes the same conduct, although it does not as explicitly require the sender to know that the intended recipient of his indecent message is a minor. Appellant urges the Court to construe the provision to impose such a knowledge requirement, and I would do so.

So construed, both provisions are constitutional as applied to a conversation involving only an adult and one or more minors—e.g., when an adult speaker sends an e mail knowing the addressee is a minor, or when an adult and minor converse by themselves or with other minors in a chat room. In this context, these provisions are no different from the law we sustained in *Ginsberg*. Restricting what the adult may say to the minors in no way restricts the adult's ability to communicate with other adults. He is not prevented from speaking indecently to other adults in a chat room (because there are no other adults participating in the conversation) and he remains free to send indecent e mails to other adults. The relevant universe contains only one adult, and the adult in that universe has the power to refrain from using indecent speech and consequently to keep all such speech within the room in an "adult" zone. . . .

Thus, the constitutionality of the CDA as a zoning law hinges on the extent to which it substantially interferes with the First Amendment rights of adults. Because the rights of adults are infringed only by the "display" provision and by the "indecency transmission" and "specific person" provisions as applied to communications involving more than one adult, I would invalidate the CDA only to that extent. Insofar as the "indecency transmission" and "specific person" provisions prohibit the use of indecent speech in communications between an adult and one or more minors, however, they can and should be sustained. The Court reaches a contrary conclusion, and from that holding I respectfully dissent.

Ashcroft v. Free Speech Coalition

535 U.S. ___ (2002), 6-3
Opinion of the Court: Kennedy (Breyer, Ginsburg, Souter, Stevens)
Concurring: Thomas
Concurring in part, dissenting in part: O'Connor
Dissenting: Rehnquist, Scalia

Does the Child Pornography Prevention Act abridge freedom of speech? What kind of pornography does it prohibit? Can the government suppress lawful speech as a means of suppressing unlawful behavior? How does the statute go beyond those designed to prevent the abuse and exploitation of children? Why does Chief Justice Rehnquist believe the statute is constitutional?

We consider in this case whether the Child Pornography Prevention Act of 1996, 18 U.S.C. §2251, abridges the freedom of speech. The CPPA extends the federal prohibition against child pornography to sexually explicit images that appear to depict minors but were produced without using any real children. The statute prohibits, in specific circumstances, possessing or distributing these images, which may be created by using adults who look like minors or by using computer imaging. The new technology, according to Congress, makes it possible to create realistic images of children who do not exist.

By prohibiting child pornography that does not depict an actual child, the statute goes beyond *New York v. Ferber,* which distinguished child pornography from other sexually explicit speech because of the State's interest in protecting the children exploited by the production process. As a general rule, pornography can be banned only if obscene, but under *Ferber,* pornography showing minors can be proscribed whether or not the images are obscene under the definition set forth in *Miller v. California. Ferber* recognized that "[t]he Miller standard, like all general definitions of what may be banned as obscene, does not reflect the State's particular and more compelling interest in prosecuting those who promote the sexual exploitation of children." . . .

The principal question to be resolved, then, is whether the CPPA is constitutional where it proscribes a significant universe of speech that is neither obscene under *Miller* nor child pornography under *Ferber.*

Before 1996, Congress defined child pornography as the type of depictions at issue in *Ferber,* images made using actual minors. The CPPA retains that prohibition at 18 U.S.C. §2256(8)(A) and adds three other prohibited categories of speech, of which the first, §2256(8)(B), and the third, §2256(8)(D), are at issue in this case. Section 2256(8)(B) prohibits "any visual depiction, including any photograph, film, video, picture, or computer or computer-generated image or picture" that "is, or appears to be, of a minor engaging in sexually explicit conduct." . . .

Respondents . . . challenge §2256(8)(D). Like the text of the "appears to be" provision, the sweep of this provision is quite broad. Section 2256(8)(D) defines child pornography to include any sexually explicit image that was "advertised, promoted, presented, described, or distributed in such a manner that conveys the impression" it depicts "a minor engaging in sexually explicit conduct." . . .

Fearing that the CPPA threatened the activities of its members, respondent Free Speech Coalition and others challenged the statute in the United States District Court for the Northern District of California. The Coalition, a California trade association for the adult-entertainment industry, alleged that its members did not use minors in their sexually explicit works, but they believed some of these materials might fall within the CPPA's expanded definition of child pornography. The other respondents are Bold Type, Inc., the publisher of a book advocating the nudist lifestyle; Jim Gingerich, a painter of nudes; and Ron Raffaelli, a photographer specializing in erotic images. Respondents alleged that the "appears to be" and "conveys the impression" provisions are overbroad and vague, chilling them from producing works protected by the First Amendment. . . .

The First Amendment commands, "Congress shall make no law . . . abridging the freedom of speech." The government may violate this mandate in many ways, but a law imposing criminal penalties on protected speech is a stark example of speech suppression. The CPPA's penalties are indeed severe. A first offender may be imprisoned for 15 years. A repeat offender faces a prison sentence of not less than 5 years and not more than 30 years in prison. While even minor punishments can chill protected speech, this case provides a textbook example of why we permit facial challenges to statutes that burden expression. With these severe penalties in force, few legitimate movie producers or book publishers, or few other speakers in any capacity, would risk distributing images in or near the uncertain reach of this law. The Constitution

gives significant protection from overbroad laws that chill speech within the First Amendment's vast and privileged sphere. Under this principle, the CPPA is unconstitutional on its face if it prohibits a substantial amount of protected expression. . . .

. . . [T]he CPPA is much more than a supplement to the existing federal prohibition on obscenity. Under *Miller v. California*, the Government must prove that the work, taken as a whole, appeals to the prurient interest, is patently offensive in light of community standards, and lacks serious literary, artistic, political, or scientific value. The CPPA, however, extends to images that appear to depict a minor engaging in sexually explicit activity without regard to the *Miller* requirements. The materials need not appeal to the prurient interest. Any depiction of sexually explicit activity, no matter how it is presented, is proscribed. The CPPA applies to a picture in a psychology manual, as well as a movie depicting the horrors of sexual abuse. It is not necessary, moreover, that the image be patently offensive. Pictures of what appear to be 17-year-olds engaging in sexually explicit activity do not in every case contravene community standards.

The CPPA prohibits speech despite its serious literary, artistic, political, or scientific value. The statute proscribes the visual depiction of an idea—that of teenagers engaging in sexual activity—that is a fact of modern society and has been a theme in art and literature throughout the ages. . . .

Our society, like other cultures, has empathy and enduring fascination with the lives and destinies of the young. Art and literature express the vital interest we all have in the formative years we ourselves once knew, when wounds can be so grievous, disappointment so profound, and mistaken choices so tragic, but when moral acts and self-fulfillment are still in reach. Whether or not the [artistic works] we mention violate the CPPA, they explore themes within the wide sweep of the statute's prohibitions. If these [works] contain a single graphic depiction of sexual activity within the statutory definition, the possessor of the [work] would be subject to severe punishment without inquiry into the work's redeeming value. This is inconsistent with an essential First Amendment rule: The artistic merit of a work does not depend on the presence of a single explicit scene. Under *Miller*, the First Amendment requires that redeeming value be judged by considering the work as a whole. Where the scene is part of the narrative, the work itself does not for this reason become obscene, even though the scene in isolation might be offensive. For this reason, and the others we have noted, the CPPA cannot be read to prohibit obscenity, because it lacks the required link between its prohibitions and the affront to community standards prohibited by the definition of obscenity.

The Government seeks to address this deficiency by arguing that speech prohibited by the CPPA is virtually indistinguishable from child pornography, which may be banned without regard to whether it depicts works of value. . . . The production of the work, not its content, [is] the target of the statute. The fact that a work contain[s] serious literary, artistic, or other value [does] not excuse the harm it cause[s] to its child participants.

In contrast to the speech in *Ferber*, speech that itself is the record of sexual abuse, the CPPA prohibits speech that records no crime and creates no victims by its production. Virtual child pornography is not "intrinsically related" to the sexual abuse of children, as were the materials in *Ferber*. While the Government asserts that the images can lead to actual instances of child abuse, the causal link is contingent and indirect. The harm does not necessarily follow from the speech, but depends upon some unquantified potential for subsequent criminal acts.

The CPPA, for reasons we have explored, is inconsistent with *Miller* and finds no support in *Ferber*. The Government seeks to justify its prohibitions in other ways. It argues that the CPPA is necessary because pedophiles may use virtual child pornography to seduce children. There are many things innocent in themselves, however, such as cartoons, video games, and candy, that might be used for immoral purposes, yet we would not expect those to be prohibited because they can be misused. The Government, of course, may punish adults who provide unsuitable materials to children, and it may enforce criminal penalties for unlawful solicitation. The precedents establish, however, that speech within the rights of adults to hear may not be silenced completely in an attempt to shield children from it. . . .

Here, the Government wants to keep speech from children not to protect them from its content but to protect them from those who would commit other crimes. The principle, however, remains the same: The Government cannot ban speech fit for adults simply because it may fall into the hands of children. The evil in question depends upon the actor's unlawful conduct, conduct defined as criminal quite apart

from any link to the speech in question. This establishes that the speech ban is not narrowly drawn. The objective is to prohibit illegal conduct, but this restriction goes well beyond that interest by restricting the speech available to law-abiding adults.

The Government submits further that virtual child pornography whets the appetites of pedophiles and encourages them to engage in illegal conduct. This rationale cannot sustain the provision in question. The mere tendency of speech to encourage unlawful acts is not a sufficient reason for banning it. The government "cannot constitutionally premise legislation on the desirability of controlling a person's private thoughts." First Amendment freedoms are most in danger when the government seeks to control thought or to justify its laws for that impermissible end. The right to think is the beginning of freedom, and speech must be protected from the government because speech is the beginning of thought.

To preserve these freedoms, and to protect speech for its own sake, the Court's First Amendment cases draw vital distinctions between words and deeds, between ideas and conduct. The government may not prohibit speech because it increases the chance an unlawful act will be committed "at some indefinite future time." The government may suppress speech for advocating the use of force or a violation of law only if "such advocacy is directed to inciting or producing imminent lawless action and is likely to incite or produce such action." There is here no attempt, incitement, solicitation, or conspiracy. The Government has shown no more than a remote connection between speech that might encourage thoughts or impulses and any resulting child abuse. . . .

Finally, the Government says that the possibility of producing images by using computer imaging makes it very difficult for it to prosecute those who produce pornography by using real children. Experts, we are told, may have difficulty in saying whether the pictures were made by using real children or by using computer imaging. The necessary solution, the argument runs, is to prohibit both kinds of images. The argument, in essence, is that protected speech may be banned as a means to ban unprotected speech. This analysis turns the First Amendment upside down.

The Government may not suppress lawful speech as the means to suppress unlawful speech. Protected speech does not become unprotected merely because it resembles the latter. The Constitution requires the reverse. "[T]he possible harm to society in permitting some unprotected speech to go unpunished is out-weighed by the possibility that protected speech of others may be muted. . . . " The overbreadth doctrine prohibits the Government from banning unprotected speech if a substantial amount of protected speech is prohibited or chilled in the process. . . .

In sum, §2256(8)(B) covers materials beyond the categories recognized in *Ferber* and *Miller*. The provision abridges the freedom to engage in a substantial amount of law-ful speech. For this reason, it is over-broad and unconstitutional.

Respondents challenge §2256(8)(D) as well. This provision bans depictions of sexually explicit conduct that are "advertised, promoted, presented, described, or distributed in such a manner that conveys the impression that the material is or contains a visual depiction of a minor engaging in sexually explicit conduct." The parties treat the section as nearly identical to the provision prohibiting materials that appear to be child pornography. In the Government's view, the difference between the two is that "the 'conveys the impression' provision requires the jury to assess the material at issue in light of the manner in which it is promoted." The Government's assumption, however, is that the determination would still depend principally upon the content of the prohibited work.

We disagree with this view. The CPPA prohibits sexually explicit materials that "conve[y] the impression" they depict minors. While that phrase may sound like the "appears to be" prohibition in §2256(8)(B), it requires little judgment about the content of the image. Under §2256(8)(D), the work must be sexually explicit, but otherwise the content is irrelevant. Even if a film contains no sexually explicit scenes involving minors, it could be treated as child pornography if the title and trailers convey the impression that the scenes would be found in the movie. . . .

Section 2256(8)(D), however, prohibits a substantial amount of speech. . . . Materials falling within the proscription are tainted and unlawful in the hands of all who receive it, though they bear no responsibility for how it was marketed, sold, or described. . . . [T]he CPPA does more than prohibit pandering. It prohibits possession of material described, or pandered, as child pornography by someone earlier in the distribution chain. The provision prohibits a sexually explicit film containing no youthful actors, just because it is placed in a box suggesting a prohibited movie. Possession is a crime even when the possessor knows the movie was mislabeled. The First Amendment requires a more precise restriction. For this reason, §2256(8)(D) is substantially overbroad and in violation of the First Amendment.

For the reasons we have set forth, the prohibitions of §§2256(8)(B) and 2256(8)(D) are overbroad and unconstitutional. Having reached this conclusion, we need not address respondents' further contention that the provisions are unconstitutional because of vague statutory language. . . .

O'Connor, concurring in part, dissenting in part:

The Child Pornography Prevention Act of 1996 (CPPA), proscribes the "knowin[g]" reproduction, distribution, sale, reception, or possession of images that fall under the statute's definition of child pornography, §2252A(a). Possession is punishable by up to 5 years in prison for a first offense, §2252A(b), and all other transgressions are punishable by up to 15 years in prison for a first offense, §2252A(a). The CPPA defines child pornography to include "any visual depiction . . . of sexually explicit conduct" where "such visual depiction is, or appears to be, of a minor engaging in sexually explicit conduct," §2256(8)(B), or "such visual depiction is advertised, promoted, presented, described, or distributed in such a manner that conveys the impression that the material is or contains a visual depiction of a minor engaging in sexually explicit conduct," §2256(8)(D). . . .

The CPPA provides for two affirmative defenses. First, a defendant is not liable for possession if the defendant possesses less than three proscribed images and promptly destroys such images or reports the matter to law enforcement. Second, a defendant is not liable for the remaining acts proscribed in §2252A(a) if the images involved were produced using only adult subjects and are not presented in such a manner as to "convey the impression" they contain depictions of minors engaging in sexually explicit conduct. §2252A(c).

This litigation involves a facial challenge to the CPPA's prohibitions of pornographic images that "appea[r] to be . . . of a minor" and of material that "conveys the impression" that it contains pornographic images of minors. While I agree with the Court's judgment that the First Amendment requires that the latter prohibition be struck down, I disagree with its decision to strike down the former prohibition in its entirety. The "appears to be . . . of a minor" language in §2256(8)(B) covers two categories of speech: pornographic images of adults that look like children ("youthful-adult pornography") and pornographic images of children created wholly on a computer, without using any actual children ("virtual-child pornography"). The Court concludes, correctly, that the CPPA's ban on youthful-adult pornography is overbroad. In my view, however, respondents fail to present sufficient evidence to demonstrate that the ban on virtual-child pornography is overbroad. . . .

. . . The basis for this holding is unclear. Although a content-based regulation may serve a compelling state interest, and be as narrowly tailored as possible while substantially serving that interest, the regulation may unintentionally ensnare speech that has serious literary, artistic, political, or scientific value or that does not threaten the harms sought to be combated by the Government. If so, litigants may challenge the regulation on its face as overbroad, but in doing so they bear the heavy burden of demonstrating that the regulation forbids a substantial amount of valuable or harmless speech. Respondents have not made such a demonstration. Respondents provide no examples of films or other materials that are wholly computer-generated and contain images that "appea[r] to be . . . of minors" engaging in indecent conduct, but that have serious value or do not facilitate child abuse. Their overbreadth challenge therefore fails. . . .

Rehnquist, dissenting:

. . . I agree with Justice O'Connor that serious First Amendment concerns would arise were the Government ever to prosecute someone for simple distribution or possession of a film with literary or artistic value. . . . I write separately, however, because the Child Pornography Prevention Act of 1996 need not be construed to reach such materials. We normally do not strike down a statute on First Amendment grounds "when a limiting instruction has been or could be placed on the challenged statute." This case should be treated no differently.

Other than computer generated images that are virtually indistinguishable from real children engaged in sexually explicitly conduct, the CPPA can be limited so as not to reach any material that was not already unprotected before the CPPA. The CPPA's definition of "sexually explicit conduct" is quite explicit in this regard. It makes clear that the statute only reaches "visual depictions" of: "[A]ctual or simulated . . . sexual intercourse, including genital-genital, oral-genital, anal-genital, or oral-anal, whether between persons of the same or opposite sex; . . . bestiality; . . . masturbation; . . . sadistic or masochistic abuse; . . . or lascivious exhibition of the genitals or pubic area of any person."

The Court and Justice O'Connor suggest that this very graphic definition reaches the depiction of youthful looking adult actors engaged in suggestive sexual activity, presumably because the definition extends to "simulated" intercourse. Read as a whole, however, I think the definition reaches only the sort of "hard core of child pornography" that we found without protection in *Ferber*. So construed, the CPPA bans visual depictions of youthful looking adult actors engaged in actual sexual activity; mere suggestions of sexual activity, such as youthful looking adult actors squirming under a blanket, are more akin to written descriptions than visual depictions, and thus fall outside the purview of the statute.

The reference to "simulated" has been part of the definition of "sexually explicit conduct" since the statute was first passed. But the inclusion of "simulated" conduct, alongside "actual" conduct, does not change the "hard core" nature of the image banned. The reference to "simulated" conduct simply brings within the statute's reach depictions of hard core pornography that are "made to look genuine." . . .

To the extent the CPPA prohibits possession or distribution of materials that "convey the impression" of a child engaged in sexually explicit conduct, that prohibition can and should be limited to reach "the sordid business of pandering" which lies outside the bounds of First Amendment protection. . . .

. . . [M]aterials promoted as conveying the impression that they depict actual minors engaged in sexually explicit conduct do not escape regulation merely because they might warrant First Amendment protection if promoted in a different manner. . . . The Court's concern is that an individual who merely possesses protected materials might offend the CPPA regardless of whether the individual actually intended to possess materials containing unprotected images.

. . . [C]onsistent with the narrow class of images the CPPA is intended to prohibit, the CPPA can be construed to prohibit only the knowing possession of materials actually containing visual depictions of real minors engaged in sexually explicit conduct, or computer generated images virtually indistinguishable from real minors engaged in sexually explicit conduct. The mere possession of materials containing only suggestive depictions of youthful looking adult actors need not be so included.

In sum, while potentially impermissible applications of the CPPA may exist, I doubt that they would be "substantial . . . in relation to the statute's plainly legitimate sweep." The aim of ensuring the enforceability of our Nation's child pornography laws is a compelling one. The CPPA is targeted to this aim by extending the definition of child pornography to reach computer-generated images that are virtually indistinguishable from real children engaged in sexually explicit conduct. The statute need not be read to do any more than precisely this, which is not offensive to the First Amendment.

I would construe the CPPA in a manner consistent with the First Amendment, and uphold the statute in its entirety.

III

SOCIAL CON

5

PRIVACY AND PUBLIC MORALITY

Autonomous privacy refers to the right to make decisions about intimate or highly personal matters—procreation, death, willing sexual partners, bodily intrusions or constraints, mind-altering substances—without interference or control by government. Weighed against such a right are the interests of public health and safety, and public morality. The last, an ancient community interest, is hardly less amorphous or better defined than the privacy it may compromise.

Public morality refers to prevailing and collectively determined standards of right and wrong behavior. Where these are based on general agreement or very broad consensus and deal with behavior obviously harmful to others—the condemnation of homicide, incest, rape, theft, for example—they have become criminal law, violation of which may be punishable by fines, imprisonment, or even death. But on many other questions, there may be less agreement about whether a rule is desirable at all and whether its violation should be met with criminal penalties or simply left to exhortation and social sanction.

These less well-settled issues may lead to struggles over moral hegemony—whose ideas of right and wrong are to be "in force." Such disputes are every bit as political as those about taxation or the regulation of commerce, because partisans on one side or the other may try to enlist government in realizing their preferences. When large majorities support particular views, there is a good chance these views may become embodied in laws and official policies.

Struggles over morality issues are more likely to have important symbolic meaning than those over property and other economic matters. The commitment to one side or another is apt to have emotional valence far greater than that evident in material disputes.

Today, gains in tolerance and a greater sensitivity to diversity may moderate public morality conflict. At the same time, advances in communication may stoke such conflict by shrinking the cultural "space" that, in the past, often put distance between dominant majorities and nonconforming groups and individuals. Defenders of a given rule of public morality may argue that it contributes to public health, safety, order, and stability, conserving public resources, or is simply justified by "ancient wisdom." Critics may reply that the rule interferes with what is "no one's business" or, worse, represents moral oppression.

The individual has claims on and rights against the community, but the community has claims on and rights against individuals who want to live in it and benefit from its resources. Though few would dispute this reciprocity, conflict lies in the details and over where lines are to be drawn. The questions that arise are about balancing government authority and individual rights, majority views and nonconforming ones, interests of the community and those of persons. These issues are among the oldest in organized society and the most difficult in democratic politics.

In several early decisions the Court identified an element of privacy in the freedom to make personal choices that did not adversely affect important government interests. It had upheld, for example, the wartime right to have German taught in a private school (*Meyer v. Nebraska*, 1923), the right to send one's children to a religious school (*Pierce v. Society of Sisters*, 1925), the right to protection against certain bodily intrusions (*Rochin v. California*, 1952). It recognized "the inviolability of privacy" including the right to join and be a member of an organization short of the government's proven "significant need" to have membership information. (*NAACP v. Alabama*, 1958). These decisions were based on rights other than privacy, but all recognized an element of personal autonomy that could not be violated by government except for the most important of reasons.

Important as autonomous privacy was in these cases, the Court did not hold it to be an independent right protected by the Constitution and rooted in its text until its historic 1965 decision *Griswold v. Connecticut* (p. 301). The executive director of the state's Planned Parenthood League and a doctor at its New Haven center were convicted of advising a married couple on the use of contraceptives. The state's anticontraception law made giving such information to anyone a misdemeanor. Voting 7-2, the justices

had little difficulty in striking down the law (even the dissenters were in disdain, one calling it an "uncommonly silly" enactment). Writing for five members of the majority, Justice William O. Douglas held the law to violate a constitutional right to privacy of married persons. He argued that certain rights were implicit in others enumerated in the Bill of Rights. Express guarantees have "penumbras formed by emanations from those guarantees that help give them life and substance." The First, Third, Fourth, Fifth, and Ninth Amendments imply "zones of privacy" that form the basis for the constitutional right of privacy.

For many critics of the decision, including the two dissenters, Black and Stewart, the stretch to find a textual basis for an unmentioned right was little more than a resurrection of substantive due process by which the Court had once read nonenumerated rights, like liberty of contract, into the Constitution and then used them to strike down government regulation of property and business. It is noteworthy that two concurring justices, Harlan and White, were straightforwardly willing to make the right of privacy a substantive part of due process, interference with which would earn the Court's closest scrutiny. For Harlan, deciding if legislation violated "basic values implicit in the concept of ordered liberty" was a different substantive due process than the discredited one that held certain nonenumerated economic rights to be enshrined in the Constitution.

Whether the protection of autonomous privacy was implied from textual rights or was an element of "natural justice" included by the Court in due process, the value of privacy had long been recognized in American legal philosophy and, at the time of *Griswold*, in American case and statutory law as well. This value was eloquently stated by Justice Brandeis dissenting in the early wiretap case of *Olmstead v. United States*, 1928:

> The makers of our Constitution undertook to secure conditions favorable to the pursuit of happiness. They recognized the significance of

Officers of the Planned Parenthood League of Connecticut, Estelle Griswold, left, executive director, and Mrs. Ernest Jahncke, president, celebrate the Supreme Court's decision in *Griswold v. Connecticut* overturning the state's anti-contraception law and establishing a constitutional right of privacy for the first time.

man's spiritual nature, his feelings and of his intellect. They knew that only part of the pain, pleasures and satisfactions of life are to be found in material things. They sought to protect Americans in their beliefs, their thoughts, their emotions and their sensations. They conferred, as against the Government, the right to be let alone—the most comprehensive of rights and the right most valued by civilized men. (277 U.S. 438 at 478)

The autonomous privacy protected in *Griswold* differs from the informational privacy we saw Brandeis and Warren describing in the last chapter, which seeks to protect personal life from public glare. Both privacies deal with the right to be "left alone," but the first rests on intimacy and personal decision, the second on seclusion and control of information. In the first, the intruder is government, in the second it is usually the media, though other nongovernmental commercial interests may also be active. The first is counterpoised against public morality, the second against public information. The first is now firmly based in the Constitution, the second is rooted in tort law and may collide with

constitutionally protected freedom of the press. Unsurprisingly, the first form of privacy, to which we now turn, has fared better in the Supreme Court than the second.

Reproductive Freedom

The Supreme Court's decision in *Griswold* upholding the right of married persons to receive contraceptives and be given birth control information was soon extended to unmarried women. The grounds for doing so, however, were equal protection rather than privacy. In *Eisenstadt v. Baird*, 1972, the Court struck down a Massachusetts law that made it illegal for unmarried persons to obtain contraceptives because it discriminated against a class of persons without being reasonably related to the state's interest in deterring premarital sex or controlling harmful products. In a dictum, however, Justice William Brennan left little doubt that privacy was also on the Court's mind. "If the right to privacy means anything, it is the right of the *individual*, married or single, to be free from unwarranted governmental intrusion into matters so fundamentally affecting a person as the decision whether to bear or beget a child." (405 U.S. 438 at 453)

A year after *Eisenstadt,* the Court extended the *Griswold* constitutional right of privacy to termination of pregnancy in one of the most debated decisions in its history, *Roe v. Wade* (p. 304). At issue was a Texas law that barred abortions except if needed to save the woman's life. "Jane Roe," who later revealed herself to be Norma McCorvey, claimed, falsely as it later turned out, that her pregnancy followed from a gang rape. Because the pregnancy did not endanger her life, she could not get an abortion in Texas without breaking the law. In a companion case, *Doe v. Bolton,* a married woman wanting an abortion challenged a Georgia law that required that such procedures—allowable only if the woman's life was in danger, the fetus was massively defective, or pregnancy resulted from rape—be performed in hospitals and have approval of a staff committee.

Abortion had long been regulated by law. For several centuries in England and through the first half of the nineteenth in the United States it was subject to common law rules. Generally these permitted abortions before quickening—the perceivable movement of the fetus in the womb, usually not occurring before the fourth or fifth month of pregnancy—but not afterward. By the turn of the century, however, many states, at the urging of doctors' organizations and to more closely supervise medical practice, enacted abortion laws that abandoned the quickening standard and barred interruption of pregnancy at anytime. Despite reforms in the 1960s in which some states permitted abortions to protect a woman's health, most still had more restrictive laws when the Roe and Doe cases were appealed to the Supreme Court. Texas's dated to 1859.

The Court's 7-2 decision in the two cases, reasoned in Justice Harry Blackmun's majority opinion, struck down the state laws and established a largely unrestricted privacy right for a woman to have an abortion in the first three months of pregnancy and a qualified right during the middle three months. Only in the last three months when the fetus was viable—presumed capable of "meaningful life" outside the womb—was the state's interest in the "potentiality of life" compelling enough to impose general restrictions. But even these had to give way if a woman's life was at stake. Constitutionally, the decision was based on a right to privacy rooted in the due process clause of the Fourteenth Amendment. Justices White and Rehnquist dissented arguing, as the dissenters in *Griswold* had, that the Court had read its own preferences into the Constitution rather than leaving choices between competing values to elected legislatures.

The decision produced strong public responses in support and opposition. It was widely hailed by feminists and many moderates who believed anti-abortion statutes were unfair to women and needed to be revisited or repealed. It was to be attacked by many religious and conservative groups, some members of which saw it as coming close to permitting murder. It spurred formation of the "Right to Life" movement, which began to lobby Congress and state legislatures to impose new restrictions, even to amend the Constitution. These efforts spurred a no less active "pro-choice" movement in opposition urging preservation and extension of the newly won constitutional right. *Roe v. Wade* did not create the abortion controversy that confronts us to this day, but it did raise it to new and sharper levels. Its pragmatic "middle ground" of offering something to both sides, so often successful in resolving other conflict, did not satisfy those on either side who viewed the issue as one of absolute right and wrong.

The abortion question remains a salient issue in American political life, affecting elections and judicial nominations, producing scores of new laws, and calling forth marches and demonstrations. Norma McCorvey herself continued to live in the middle of the fire. After *Roe,* she worked many years in abortion clinics, had bouts with alcohol abuse and drug addiction, and attempted suicide. In 1995, she joined Operation Rescue, a right-to-life group, and later started an organization of her own called Roe No More.

Since *Roe* in 1973, the Supreme Court has heard more than 30 abortion appeals. Most of these have been challenges to state or federal regulations enacted since *Roe* and because of *Roe*. These decisions, some expanding freedom of choice, some sustaining restrictions, have put the Court in the center of a moral maelstrom and repeatedly forced it to make legal decisions on medical issues. Like it or not, the justices have become medical ethicists. Moreover, the Court has been sharply divided. Almost all the cases have been decided by votes of 5-4 or 6-3.

In *Roe*, the Court held that abortion regulations would be constitutional only if they were narrowly tailored to further a compelling governmental interest. These interests were apparently two: protection of the life and health of the woman and protection of the fetus in the last trimester of pregnancy if not endangering the life or health of the woman. Regulations could not be justified as attempts to deter abortions. In one of its more important decisions, *Webster v. Reproductive Health Services*, 1989, a majority of the Court, without expressly saying so, appeared to move away from the rigid trimester analysis of *Roe*. We turn to several issues the Court has addressed in the post-*Roe* appeals.

Procedures

States may require that persons performing abortions be licensed medical doctors (*Planned Parenthood of Central Missouri v. Danforth*, 1983), but not that all abortions, including those in the first trimester, be performed in hospitals as opposed to outpatient clinics (*Akron v. Akron Center for Reproductive Health*, 1983). Though states may require that a report on each abortion performed be made to public health authorities, the Court held in *Planned Parenthood of Southeastern Pennsylvania v. Casey*, 1992, (p. 309) they may not require record-keeping be open to the public if that would identify women who had abortions (*Planned Parenthood of Central Missouri v. Danforth*, 1983).

State laws may require that doctors tell the woman of the risks and medical consequences of abortion, get her written consent to the procedure, and wait 24 hours after consent before it is performed (*Planned Parenthood of Southeastern Pennsylvania v. Casey*, 1992). But the Court has struck down requirements that a woman be given materials describing a fetus, information on alternatives to abortion including availability of medical assistance benefits for prenatal care, childbirth, and neonatal care, or be told the father is liable for assisting in child support. These, the Court said, would coercively affect the woman's right to choose.

It is not clear to what extent states can bar the aborting of viable fetuses and exactly what determines viability. The Court has upheld a law that called for a doctor to use such measures as fetal weight and lung capacity when pregnancy had reached the twentieth week (*Webster v. Reproductive Health Services*, 1989). But doctors who abort viable fetuses may not be required to exercise the care normally taken to preserve the life and health of an unborn child if the law fails to state that the woman's health must have first consideration (*Thornburgh v. American College of Obstetricians and Gynecologists*, 1986).

Because states have an interest in preserving the life of a viable fetus, they may require for abortions in the last trimester the presence of a second doctor who could care for the fetus should it be viable (*Planned Parenthood Association of Kansas City v. Ashcroft*, 1983). Such regulation may not call for the doctor to save the fetus unless it also makes clear the life and health of the woman is paramount. To be valid, second-physician requirements must also make exceptions for emergencies in which getting a second doctor might be impracticable (*Thornburgh v. American College of Obstetricians and Gynecologists*, 1986).

In the 1980s and 1990s more than 30 states passed laws banning a procedure known as "partial birth" abortions used to terminate pregnancies after four months. Though the method has several variations, it causes the fetus to be vaginally delivered or partly delivered at which point

A Journey on the Court

When Justice Blackmun retired from the Supreme Court in 1994 at 85, the third oldest justice to serve, he was arguably the Court's most liberal member. This could not have been predicted on the June day 24 years earlier when the diminutive federal judge with a conservative record took his seat. Blackmun liked to maintain that he had remained constant but the Court around him had become more conservative. Though the last is true, it is also true that Blackmun became increasingly concerned with personal rights and, doing so, left an indelible mark on constitutional jurisprudence. His name will be forever linked with *Roe v. Wade*, but his influence was important in other areas of civil liberties as well.

Born in Nashville, Ill., Blackmun grew up in middle-class circumstances in St. Paul, Minn., where his father owned a hardware store. He was a boyhood friend of Warren Burger, later to precede him to the Supreme Court as its chief justice, and was best man at Burger's wedding. An excellent student, Blackmun won a scholarship to Harvard, though there he also had to work as a janitor and deliver milk to help pay expenses. Graduating summa cum laude in mathematics, he thought briefly about becoming a doctor but chose law instead, receiving an LL.B., also from Harvard. Returning to Minnesota, he served briefly as a law clerk for a judge on the federal Eighth Circuit Court of Appeals and then entered private practice in Minneapolis. Eventually, he became general counsel at the renowned Mayo Clinic in Rochester, Minn., where his work often dealt with the interplay of legal and medical issues, a subject of lifelong interest.

In 1959, he was appointed to the Eighth Circuit Court, replacing Judge John Sanborn for whom he had clerked 27 years before. At his swearing in, Sanborn called him "the best legal scholar I have ever known." In 11 years on that court he developed a reputation for diligence and excelled in writing taxation opinions. He might have served out a career as one of that court's leaders had President Richard Nixon succeeded in appointing a Southerner to the Supreme Court in 1970 to replace Justice Abe Fortas who had resigned.

Nixon had promised during his 1968 presidential campaign to appoint "strict constructionists," meaning conservatives, to the Court. He also wanted to acknowledge the Southern electoral support he had received by appointing the first Southerner in 20 years. But two successive nominees, federal judges Clement Haynsworth of South Car-

---

it is killed. In *Stenberg v. Carhart*, 2000, the Court struck down a Nebraska law that barred such procedures and made doctors who perform them subject to criminal punishment. Though the law made an exception if the woman's life might be in danger, it failed to make one if only her health was threatened. It also, the Court said, imposed an "undue burden" on a woman's choice of procedure and so her right to choose abortion itself.

Consent and Notification

State consent statutes have required that the father of the fetus or one or both parents of the mother consent to the abortion before it can be performed. The Supreme Court has invalidated father consent requirements, rejecting the argument that a father had a controlling legal interest in the pregnancy. A state may not give power

olina and G. Harrold Carswell of Florida, were rejected by a Democratic Senate, mainly because of their records and views on civil rights issues. When Warren Burger, whom Nixon had appointed chief justice the year before, suggested his old friend on the Eighth Circuit, the president nominated the 61-year-old Minnesotan to become the Court's ninety-eighth Justice. He was confirmed, 94-0.

Though the seat he filled had an illustrious lineage that included Oliver Wendell Holmes, Benjamin Cardozo, and Felix Frankfurter, the self-effacing Blackmun never seemed to acquire a sense of self-importance. Alluding to the two failed nominations that preceded his, he often referred to himself as "old number three." Where other Washington figures routinely rode in limousines or drove large, impressive cars, Blackmun was delighted with the attention his old blue Volkswagen "beetle" attracted. He dressed modestly and rarely wore a suit to work.

Partly because of their lifelong friendship, it was widely expected that Blackmun would be a close echo of his generally conservative chief, Burger. Journalists, unable to resist, dubbed them "the Minnesota twins." And many of Blackmun's early opinions and votes upheld "law and order" and other conservative legal positions. But it slowly became apparent that he would march to his own drummer and be an independent force on the Court.

The case that set him this path, of course, was *Roe v. Wade*, decided in his third year on the Court. Assigned to write the opinion rationalizing the Court's controversial ruling, Blackmun went about doing so with characteristic diligence. Because the case was argued twice and took more than a year to decide, Blackmun had time during the Court's summer recess in 1972 to do research at the Mayo Clinic on the legal and medical questions of pregnancy and abortion, eventually developing his trimester analysis. His opinion in January 1973, which commanded the support of six other justices, extended the new constitutional right of privacy announced in *Griswold v. Connecticut* and fueled one of the most persistent and deeply rooted moral debates in American politics.

Blackmun continued to move further away from Burger, personally and ideologically. On civil liberties issues, he began voting often with the Court's two established liberals, Brennan and Thurgood Marshall. He wrote important majority opinions expanding protection for commercial speech, the rights of aliens, and reinforcing the wall of separation between church and state. His dissents in *Bowers v. Hardwick* and the abortion funding cases showed a long-standing commitment to privacy-as-autonomy that began with his Roe opinion.

His scholarship notwithstanding, Blackmun was a slow writer who often had difficulty making up his mind, a quality that caused him to agonize over many of his decisions. Critics, though respecting his jurisprudential abilities, believe his legal reasoning in later years too often veered off into sentimentality. True or not, he remains a shaping figure of the late twentieth-century Supreme Court.

Blackmun was succeeded by Stephen G. Breyer in 1994. In retirement, he had more time for the two passions in his life that rivaled the law—music and baseball. He also embarked on a new career—movie acting—with a cameo role in *Amistad* based on the 1830s capture of a Spanish slave ship, in which, fittingly, he portrayed Supreme Court Justice Joseph Story. He died on March 4, 1999, at 90.

over reproductive functions of an adult woman to anyone but the woman alone (*Planned Parenthood of Central Missouri v. Danforth*, 1983; *Planned Parenthood of Southeastern Pennsylvania v. Casey*, 1992).

However, parental consent and notification requirements where the woman is an unemancipated minor (an unmarried person under majority age still dependent on one or both parents) have given the Court more difficulty. Recognizing that the state has a special interest in regulating abortions for minors, it reaffirmed the well-settled principle that the rights of minors are not necessarily coextensive with those of adults. But in its wariness about giving anyone but the pregnant female a veto over abortion, it has held notification of one or both parents, though possibly helpful in counseling the daughter, might also lead to the minor's right being overborne.

The justices have been far from united in the matter, however, and both majority and plurality decisions have turned on whether consent or notification requirements also provide for a "judicial by-pass." This procedure allows the minor to avoid required consent or notification by asking that the matter be put before a court or other designated adjudicatory body. The Court has upheld one-parent consent requirements if they include such a proceeding (*Bellotti v. Baird*, 1979, plurality opinion; *Planned Parenthood Association of Kansas City v. Ashcroft*, 1983; *Planned Parenthood of Southeastern Pennsylvania v. Casey*, 1992). It has not yet sustained a requirement that both parents consent or be notified, but has upheld a 48-hour waiting period after notification of one parent (*Hodgson v. Minnesota*, 1990).

The judicial by-pass must allow the female minor to show that she has the maturity to make the decision to have the abortion. If she cannot demonstrate such maturity, the adjudicatory body must have authority to by-pass parental notification if it concludes abortion is still in the best interest of the minor (*Baird v. Bellotti*, 1979, plurality opinion; *Ohio v. Akron Center for Reproductive Health*, 1990).

Access to Public Medical Resources

The Court has consistently rejected claims that indigent women to have a right to an abortion at public expense, reasoning that the right of privacy is a right to be free of government interference, not one to government support. Thus in *Maher v. Roe*, 1977, it upheld Connecticut's refusal to reimburse Medicaid recipients for abortion expenses unless the abortion was medically or psychologically necessary. That the state provided benefits for childbirth was not a denial of equal protection of women having elective abortions, because the state has "a strong interest in encouraging normal childbirth."

In 1976, Congress passed the first in a series of "Hyde Amendments" (named after their chief sponsor, Representative Henry Hyde), that barred the use of federal funds for abortions except when the life of the woman was in danger or when pregnancy was the result of rape or incest. These provisions were upheld in *Harris v. McRae*, 1980 (p. 313), the Court stating that though government may not put obstacles in the path of a woman's freedom of choice, it was not required to remove those it did not create. Federal subsidization of the constitutionally protected freedom of choice was not a matter of constitutional entitlement but a question for Congress to decide.

In the 1970 Public Health Service Act, Congress appropriated federal money to help support family planning services but barred funds from programs in which abortion was a method of family planning. In 1988, the Secretary of Health and Human Services interpreted this provision to mean that clinics receiving federal support could not counsel pregnant women about the possibility of an abortion. This "gag" rule was challenged by several doctors who worked at such clinics in *Rust v. Sullivan*, 1991. The Supreme Court found no abuse of discretion by the Secretary in interpreting the law nor denial of a constitutional right. A woman's right to choose an abortion did not require the government to "distort the scope of its mandated program" or financially support an activity because it is constitutionally protected. Nor did the "gag" rule abridge the doctors' freedom of speech. They were free to counsel women about abortions outside the federally supported programs. The rule was rescinded by the Clinton administration in 1993.

A city's policy of denying indigent women abortions at public hospitals was upheld (*Poelker v. Doe*, 1972), as have state regulations barring the use of public facilities or the aid of public employees in abortions not needed to save the woman's life (*Webster v. Reproductive Health Services*, 1989).

None of the Court's rulings on access to public funds, resources, or facilities prevent states from paying for or otherwise subsidizing abortions; they hold only that the Constitution does not require they do so.

Sexual Conduct

Sexual behavior and reproduction have been centerpieces of social control in every known human society. Though specific norms and standards may be different, no society has been free of regulation. Rape and statutory rape (consensual intercourse of an adult with a minor), incest, bestiality, sodomy, and prostitution, for example, have been commonly addressed by law and usually made criminal. Yet perhaps no activity except eating or elimination is considered more personal and private than sexual activity. Except for issues of reproductive choice, the Supreme Court has drawn the constitutional line between collective moral standards and individual autonomy in only one other realm of sexual behavior—homosexual acts—and that in but one decision.

When the Constitution was ratified, each of the 13 original states had criminal laws against sodomy, usually defined, as it is today by Georgia, for example, as "any sexual act involving the sex organs of one person and the mouth or anus of another." [Official Code of Georgia, Section 16-6-2] At ratification of the Fourteenth Amendment in 1868, 32 of 37 states had antisodomy laws, as did every state to enter the Union after that. But, starting with Illinois in 1962, more than half have now repealed such laws or have had them struck down by their state courts as violating the state constitution. In other states, sexual acts between consenting adults of the same sex remain felonies or misdemeanors.

The Supreme Court ruled on sodomy in *Bowers v. Hardwick*, 1986 (p. 316), a case growing out of a challenge to the Georgia law, quoted earlier. Hardwick was arrested by a police officer who witnessed a homosexual act when he walked into Hardwick's bedroom. He had been sent to Hardwick's address with a warrant stemming from an earlier incident of public drinking and had been admitted to the rented house by another tenant. Though the local prosecutor decided not to bring charges, Hardwick filed a suit challenging the constitutionality of the antisodomy law. Divided 5-4, the Court sustained the law, Justice Byron White holding that the Court's earlier right of privacy decisions had dealt with matters of "family, marriage, and procreation." He rejected the argument that all private sexual conduct between consenting adults is constitutionally protected from state regulation. He distinguished the 1969 case of *Stanley v. Georgia*, in which the Court overturned a conviction for possession of obscene materials that had been found in the defendant's home, as based on a First Amendment right and so not controlling the case at hand.

The Bowers opinion expressly declined to rule whether a state might constitutionally regulate heterosexual sodomy between unmarried persons, or whether a criminal penalty for sodomy might be a cruel and unusual punishment that would violate the Eighth Amendment. The closeness of the decision and the fact that one member of the majority, Justice Powell, admitted shortly after retiring from the Court that he had come to believe the case was wrongly decided, raise doubt whether a similar result would obtain today. Nonetheless, the Court has not returned to the question. One reason, no doubt, is that there are few prosecutions. Gains in tolerance and awareness, due in part at least to the AIDS epidemic and the gay rights movement, are evident. Opinion polls continue to show that most Americans believe consensual homosexual sexual acts are wrong, but the percentage holding such a view has been declining, particularly for the proposition that such acts should be made criminal. Issues of discrimination based on sexual orientation are taken up in Chapter 9.

Death

No decision is more personal or important than one not to go on living. Yet suicide is declaimed by public morality in most societies. All states in the United States have laws that forbid or try to deter it, though many states have decriminalized the act. With these laws go others making it a punishable offense to assist a person in ending

The Right to Have Offspring

In *Griswold v. Connecticut*, the Court decided there was a constitutional right of privacy to be free of state interference with birth control, and in *Roe v. Wade*, to end a pregnancy. But is there a reciprocal constitutional right to conceive and have a child free of state intervention?

In an early twentieth-century case, the Supreme Court held that a person had no absolute autonomy over the integrity of his or her own body. Sustaining a Massachusetts statute that required smallpox vaccinations, against objections based on religious beliefs, Justice John Marshall Harlan held for the Court that bodily privacy might be intruded on in the name of a valid and important public interest.

> There are manifold restraints to which every person is necessarily subject for the common good. . . . Real liberty for all could not exist under the operation of a principle which recognizes the right of each individual person to use his own, whether in respect to his person or his property, regardless of the injury that may be done to others . . . Even liberty itself, the greatest of all rights, is not unrestricted license to act according to one's own will.
> [*Jacobson v. Massachusetts*, 197 U.S. 11 (1905) at 3]

The issue of bodily violability came before the Court again in a case growing out of the eugenics movement. Eugenicists believed that the human race, like other species, could be improved by guided propagation, particularly by avoiding breeding by those "unfit." Though hardly a new idea—it was advocated by Plato in *The Republic*—it fitted nicely with Progressivism, the country's dominant political philosophy in the first two decades of the twentieth century. The Progressives, who elected three presidents, Theodore Roosevelt, Taft, and Wilson, championed "good government" reforms, the application of administrative "science" to government, and generally the making of government more rationally respon-

sive to human needs, especially those of public health and safety. Though many of the reforms, like women's suffrage, broadened democratic participation, Progressivism carried with it a high-minded, mildly paternalistic public morality in its determined opposition to drinking, gambling, and prostitution. Eugenics reform, with its appeal to rational efficiency and improvement, scored several successes during the Progressive period. By the 1920s, more than half the states had laws providing for the sexual sterilization of the inmates of public mental asylums.

Caught up in these large events was Carrie Buck, an 18-year-old Virginia woman with an IQ-tested mental age of nine. She had been committed to a state asylum for the "feeble-minded" after she became pregnant through a rape. Her mother, with a mental age of seven, was a resident of the same institution. After Buck gave birth to a daughter, alleged also to be mentally retarded, authorities asked that she be sterilized under the state's eugenics law that allowed, with certain procedural safeguards, sterilization in cases of hereditary insanity, idiocy, imbecility, and epilepsy. If Buck were sterilized, they argued, she could be released; if not, she faced spending her procreative years in confinement.

The matter was constructed as a test case of state eugenics laws and was eventually appealed to the Supreme Court as *Buck v. Bell* in 1927. There, by a vote of 8-1, the state law and the sterilization order were sustained. Justice Holmes's opinion, troubling to those who have seen him as a champion of civil liberties, accepted the eugenic arguments and found no violation of due process right or denial of equal protection. Broadening the principle of *Jacobson v. Massachusetts*, he concluded with characteristic terseness,

> We have seen more than once that the public welfare may call upon the best citizens for their lives. It would be strange if it could not call upon those who already sap the strength of the State for these lesser sacrifices, often not felt to be such by those concerned, in order to prevent our being

their life. Though many of these reflect conservative religious or social values, they also rest on important concerns about the mental stability of the would-be suicide and the motives of those who might give assistance.

Difficult questions arise when a gravely ill or injured person refuses life-sustaining medical intervention. Even more difficult are those when such a person is comatose and not capable of decision. In recent years, many states have permitted relatives

swamped with incompetence. Is it better for all the world, if instead of waiting to execute degenerate offspring for crime, or let them starve for their imbecility, society can prevent those who are manifestly unfit from continuing their kind. The principle that sustains compulsory vaccination is broad enough to cover cutting the Fallopian tubes . . . Three generations of imbeciles are enough. [274 U.S. 200 at 207]

Though the decision encouraged other states to enact and apply eugenics laws, eugenic "science" gradually fell into disfavor with events in Germany in the late 1930s. In the name of improving the Aryan race, Nazi laws authorized sterilization of the mentally retarded and others with debilitating or disfavored characteristics thought to be inheritable, including epilepsy, schizophrenia, drug addiction, homosexuality, and some forms of blindness. Later these laws were supplemented by others authorizing euthanasia for certain persons judged to be medically "unfit." In our own time, several nations have tried to limit population growth. India, for example, has encouraged birth control including voluntary sterilization. In the Communist People's Republic of China, strict limits on family size have been enforced with penalties.

At the outset of World War II, most American states had laws authorizing sterilization of the "feeble-minded," and some, "habitual criminals." The constitutionality of the last came before the Court in *Skinner v. Oklahoma* in 1942. The state's enactment defined an habitual criminal as anyone convicted of three or more "felonies involving moral turpitude." Skinner, who was ordered sterilized, had been convicted once for stealing chickens and twice for armed robbery. The Court was unanimous in striking down the law, though its reasoning was based on Fourteenth Amendment equal protection rather than on due process of law. Because the law assumed that a tendency to commit larceny was habitual, but one to commit "white collar" crimes such as embezzlement was not, it denied equal protection of the law. Though the holding was narrow, Justice Douglas's opinion left little doubt that the Court had much broader concerns in mind.

> We are dealing here with legislation which involves one of the basic civil rights of man. Marriage and procreation are fundamental to the very existence and survival of the race. The power to sterilize, if exercised, may have subtle, far-reaching and devastating effects. In evil or reckless hands it can cause races or types which are inimical to the dominant group to wither and disappear. There is no redemption for the individual whom the law touches. Any experiment which the state conducts is to his irreparable injury. He is forever deprived of a basic liberty. [316 U.S. 535 at 551]

By 1942, the United States was at war with Japan and Nazi Germany, and the latter's genocidal policies had become evident. By this time also, eugenics theory that criminal traits were inheritable was largely discredited. Not so, however, the incidence of mental retardation or "feeble-mindedness." Thus the decision in *Skinner* did not overrule *Buck v. Bell*. That case, in fact, has never been overruled, though the expansion of due process and equal protection rights make it an improbable precedent today.

Skinner was decided just five years after the Court had abandoned substantive due process as a check on economic regulation in *West Coast Hotel Company v. Parrish*. Yet the Court created an unwritten "fundamental right" not to have one's ability to conceive taken away by questionable classifying schemes such as *Oklahoma* had used. Such classification, Douglas said, called for the Court's "strict scrutiny." This rule was an important constitutional step to a substantive equal protection jurisprudence in which certain other "fundamental" but unwritten rights would be protected against government regulation, a matter we will deal with in later chapters. It also established a right to have offspring, limited only by a compelling public interest free of invidious classifications.

or guardians of permanently comatose patients or those terminally ill but unable to make decisions on their own behalf, to decide if continuation of life-prolonging medical intervention is in the patient's "best interest." In the widely publicized New Jersey case of *In re Quinlan*, 1976, the state's supreme court sustained the right of two parents to have a life-sustaining respirator removed from their 22-year old daughter, long comatose and medically "brain dead" from an overdose of drugs, as the only way to prevent the destruction of her right to privacy.

The Supreme Court's first encounter with "the right to die" as a constitutional issue was in *Cruzan v. Director, Missouri Department of Mental Health*, 1990 (p. 321). At stake was the fate of a 32-year-old comatose woman judged "brain dead" after suffering severe injuries in a car accident and kept alive through artificial feeding. Her parents asked that the feeding tubes be removed and she be allowed to die. When the hospital refused to do so without a court order, the Cruzans petitioned for a directive, arguing that their daughter would not have wanted to live in a vegetative state.

On appeal from a ruling against the Cruzans, the Supreme Court assumed that a competent person would have a constitutional right to reject life-sustaining medical treatment, but held that a state could require at least some evidence that a comatose person had clearly expressed such a preference. The demand for clear sign was reasonable given the state's interest in preventing abuses in surrogate decisions. (Following the ruling, the Cruzans petitioned for a new lower court hearing at which several of their daughter's coworkers and friends testified they heard her say several times she would not want to live in a vegetative state. On this evidence, the judge ruled the feeding tube could be removed.)

Cruzan did nothing to disturb laws such as New Jersey's, or decisions such as *In re Quinlan* that allow surrogate decisions by guardians or family members for the permanently comatose or the incompetent terminally ill. It held only that a state could demand clear and convincing evidence of the patient's wishes. Such situations now arise more frequently because of heroic advances in life-sustaining medical technology, such as artificial feeding and hydration, respirators, and resuscitation techniques that may delay death in the permanently comatose or terminally ill. For this reason many states, starting with California in 1976, have enacted "living will" or "natural death"

laws. These typically allow anyone at any time in life to execute a witnessed statement that should they be in a permanently comatose condition or terminally incompetent, they do not want "life-prolonging" procedures to be applied, and to designate a named person to make that decision for them.

A different problem arises when a competent terminally ill person not on life support wants to hasten death by affirmative acts that need the assistance of others, especially doctors. In every state but Oregon, giving such help is illegal and even criminal. The Supreme Court dealt with this matter for the first time in *Washington v. Glucksberg*, 1997 (p. 325), in which five doctors on behalf of several terminally ill but competent patients challenged the constitutionality of the state's antisuicide law. They argued that the law, dating to 1854, violated a fundamental liberty to make intimate decisions that was protected by due process. In a companion case, *Vacco v. Quill*, a similar law in New York State was challenged as a denial of equal protection because it treated terminally ill patients not on life-support systems differently than those who were. The Court unanimously rejected these challenges, citing long-standing traditions against suicide and a state's interest in preserving life and overseeing ethics of the medical profession. But, it made the unusual extrajudicial observation that "throughout the Nation, Americans are engaged in an earnest and profound debate about the morality, legality, and practicality of physician-assisted suicide," noting that the Court's decision "permits this debate to continue."

So far, the debate has resulted in only one state—Oregon—acting to allow doctor-assisted suicide. Its Death With Dignity Act of 1994 permits doctors to prescribe lethal dosages of certain drugs to terminally ill but competent patients who ask for them. In *Lee v. Oregon*, 1997, the Supreme Court refused to hear an appeal from a lower federal court that had constitutionally sustained the law. Voters in Washington and California in the 1990s, how-

James Romney, suffering from amyotrophic lateral schlerosis (Lou Gehrig's disease), was a plaintiff in a successful 2002 suit to block the Justice Department from prosecuting Oregon doctors who prescribed lethal drugs for terminally ill patients under the state's physician-assisted suicide law. With Romney are attorney Kathryn Tucker and Eli Stutsman, left, coauthor of the law. In 49 other states, assisting in a suicide is a statutory or common law crime.

ever, rejected initiative proposals to make doctor-assisted suicide legal.

Autonomy Revisited

After boldly finding a right to privacy in the Constitution and even more boldly applying it to protect a woman's decision to have an abortion in *Roe v. Wade,* the Supreme Court has been modest in extending it further. In fact, it has increasingly phrased the issue as one of a "fundamental liberty" of due process and used the phrase "privacy" less often. As a matter of nomenclature, this may be useful because autonomy issues—for example, a decision to terminate a pregnancy or end one's life—though highly personal, are not "private" in the usual meaning of that term. They are also difficult to fit under the same conceptual tent as those of "informational privacy," one reason the "right to privacy" remains ambiguous and not well defined.

Many proponents of an expansive right to privacy-as-autonomy, liberals and conservatives alike, urge the right be extended not only to adult consensual sex, suicide, and assisted suicide, but to a range of public health and safety laws that require vaccinations, the wearing of car seat belts, motorcycle helmets, and the like, and also to a range of "lifestyle" regulations such as those governing the length of police and firefighters hair. Weighed against these arguments is the fact that no human society has ever permitted the complete private personal autonomy of individual members. Even in the United States with a well-established constitutional freedom of speech, the right to communicate is not absolute. American courts have regularly upheld laws designed in part to protect the individual from him or herself, including the regulation of drinking and drug use. The rationale for such restrictions also rests on the safeguarding of public health and safety and the conserving of society's medical resources.

Autonomy's main quarrel is with public morality. A strong tradition of civil liberties and individual freedom carries with it concern that restrictions enforcing moral standards may be rooted in intolerance or insensitivity to those with nonconforming lifestyles. In any society, dominant groups may be able to use government to enforce social and moral values they find congenial and interfere with those they do not. In a democracy, the dominant group may be a majority and, at times, a very large majority. Still many would argue that public morality, like the criminal law to which it is closely related, reflects not only rules about which there is wide agreement but an enduring wisdom human beings have acquired by living in community for thousands of years.

Whichever the case, it is fair to say that the Framers of the Constitution, the Bill of Rights and the Fourteenth Amendment gave little thought to questions of public morality in the looming constituent acts that occupied them. As issues have arisen, it has fallen to the Supreme Court to decide to what degree the Constitution protects autonomous privacy. Where the Court has sustained the right after *Griswold,* it has tended to do so less by deriving it from expressly enumerated rights than by discovering it to be a "fundamental liberty" protected by the due process clause of the Fifth and Fourteenth Amendments. This exercise of substantive due process opens the Court to both the praise and the criticism that attends judicial activism. Is such reading of the Constitution simply "judicial legislation" in which a handful of unelected men and women put their own values into the Constitution? Or is it a means by which an eighteenth- and nineteenth-century document is kept up to date in an era of increasing sensitivity to individual rights? This, of course, is a question we meet many times in this book and one that may be objectively unanswerable in the end because whatever answer is given is itself a judgment of value rather than of fact.

FURTHER READING

General

Allen, Anita, *Uneasy Access: Privacy for Women in a Free Society* (1988)

Dionisopoulos, P. Alan, and Craig R. Ducat, *The Right to Privacy: Essays and Cases* (1976)

Etzioni, Amatai, *The Limits of Privacy* (1999)

Hixson, Richard F., *Privacy in a Public Society: Human Rights in Conflict* (1987)

Lieberman, Jethro K., *Privacy and the Law* (1978)

McWhirter, Darlken A., and Jon D. Bible, *Privacy as a Constitutional Right: Sex, Drugs, and the Right to Life* (1992)

O'Brien, David, *Privacy, Law, and Public Policy* (1979)

Pennock, J. Roland, and John W. Chapman, eds., *Privacy, Nomos XIII* (1971)

———, *Due Process, Nomos XVIII* (1977)

Placencia, Madeline, and Paul Finkelman, eds., *Right to Privacy and the Constitution* (1999)

Schoemann, Ferdinand D., ed., *Philosophical Dimensions of Privacy* (1984)

Strum, Philippa, *Privacy: The Debate in the United States Since 1945* (1998)

Abortion Rights

Burgess, Susan R., *Contest for Constitutional Authority: The Abortion and War Powers Debate* (1992)

Craig, Barbara Hinkson, and David M. O'Brien, *Abortion and American Politics* (1993)

Critchlow, Donald T., ed., *The Politics of Abortion and Birth Control in Historical Perspective* (1996)

Devins, Neal E., *Shaping Constitutional Values: Elected Government, the Supreme Court, and the Abortion Debate* (1996)

Devins, Neal E., and Wendy L. Watson, eds., *Federal Abortion Politics: A Documentary History* (1995)

Dworkin, Ronald, *Life's Dominion: An Argument about Abortion, Euthanasia, and Individual Freedom* (1993)

Epstein, Lee, and Joseph F. Kobylka, *The Supreme Court and Legal Change: Abortion and the Death Penalty* (1992)

Faux, Marion, Roe v. Wade: *The Untold Story of the Landmark Supreme Court Decision that Made Abortion Legal* (1988)

Glendon, Mary Ann, *Abortion and Divorce in Western Law* (1987)

Gordon, Linda, *Woman's Body, Women's Right: Birth Control in America,* rev. ed. (1990)

Graber, Mark A., *Rethinking Abortion: Equal Choice, the Constitution, and Reproductive Politics* (1996)

Judges, Donald P., *Hard Choices, Lost Voices: How the Abortion Conflict Has Divided America, Distorted Constitutional Law, and Damaged the Courts* (1993)

Lee, Ellie, *Abortion Law and Politics Today* (1998)

Luker, Kristen, *Abortion and the Politics of Motherhood* (1984)

McDonagh, Eileen L., *Breaking the Abortion Deadlock* (1996)

Mohr, James C., *Abortion in America* (1978)

Noonan, John T., Jr., *A Private Choice: Abortion in America in the Seventies* (1979)

Nossiff, Rosemary, *Before Roe: Abortion Policy in the States* (2001)

O'Connor, Karen, *No Neutral Ground? Abortion Politics in an Age of Absolutes* (1996)

Posner, Richard, *Sex and Reason* (1992)

Presser, Stephen B., *Recapturing the Constitution: Race, Religion, and Abortion Reconsidered* (1994)

Reagan, Leslie J., *When Abortion Was a Crime: Women, Medicine, and the Law in the United States, 1867–1973* (1997)

Rubin, Eva R., *Abortion, Politics, and the Courts:* Roe v. Wade *and Its Aftermath* (1987)

———, *The Abortion Controversy: A Documentary History* (1994)

Scheidler, Joseph M., *Closed: 99 Ways to Stop Abortion* (1985)

Tribe, Laurence H., *Abortion: The Clash of Absolutes* (1990)

Yarnold, Barbara M., *Abortion Politics in the Federal Courts: Rights Versus Right* (1995)

The Right to Die

Behuniak, Susan M., *A Caring Jurisprudence: Listening to Patient at the Supreme Court* (1999)

Glick, Henry R., *The Right to Die: Policy Innovation and Its Consequences* (1992)

Humphrey, Derek, *Lawful Exit: The Limits of Freedom for Help in Dying* (1993)

Humphrey, Derek, and Mary Clement, *Freedom to Die: People, Politics, and the Right-to-Die Movement* (1998)

Meisel, Alan, *The Right to Die* (1989)

Neeley, G. Steven, *The Constitutional Right to Suicide: A Legal and Philosophical Examination* (1994)

Scherer, Jennifer M., and Rita J. Simon, *Euthanasia and the Right to Die: A Comparative View* (1999)

Uhlmann, Michael M, ed., *Last Rights? Assisted Suicide and Euthanasia Debated* (1998)

Urofsky, Melvin I., *Letting Go: Death, Dying, and the Law* (1993)

———, *Lethal Judgments: Assisted Suicide and American Law* (2000)

Zucker, Marjorie B., *The Right to Die Debate: A Documentary History* (1999)

On Leading Cases

Friedman, Leon, ed., *The Supreme Court Confronts Abortion: The Briefs, Argument, and Decision in Planned Parenthood v. Casey* (1993)

Garrow, David J., *Liberty and Sexuality: The Right of Privacy and the Making of* Roe v. Wade (1998)

Krason, Stephen M., *Abortion Politics, Morality, and the Constitution: A Critical Study of* Roe v. Wade *and* Doe v. Bolton *and a Basis for Change* (1984)

Smith, David J., *The Sterilization of Carrie Buck* (1989)

Additional works are listed in General and Supplementary bibliography.

CASES

Griswold v. Connecticut

381 U.S. 479 (1965), 7-2

Opinion of the Court: Douglas (Brennan, Clark, Goldberg, Harlan, Warren, White)

Dissenting: Black, Stewart

Where in the Constitution is the right of privacy located? How do Justices Douglas and Goldberg differ on this question? What privacy is recognized by the Court and why is it violated by the state law? Why was Justice Black willing to uphold the law? How would he interpret the Ninth Amendment? Has a majority of the Court here "invented" a new constitutional right based on their own sensibilities or have they made a reasonable extrapolation of rights in the Bill of Rights to circumstances its framers could not have easily foreseen? If the latter, why wasn't such extrapolation made earlier?

Douglas, for the Court:

Appellant Griswold is Executive Director of the Planned Parenthood League of Connecticut. Appellant Buxton is a licensed physician and a professor at the Yale Medical School who served as Medical Director for the League at its Center in New Haven—a center open and operating from November 1 to November 10, 1961, when appellants were arrested.

They gave information, instruction, and medical advice to *married persons* as to the means of preventing conception. They examined the wife and prescribed the best contraceptive device or material for her use. Fees were usually charged, although some couples were serviced free.

The statutes whose constitutionality is involved in this appeal are §§53-32 and 54-196 of the General Statutes of Connecticut (1958 rev.). The former provides:

> Any person who uses any drug, medicinal article or instrument for the purpose of preventing conception shall be fined not less than fifty dollars or imprisoned not less than sixty days nor more than one year or be both fined and imprisoned.
>
> Section 54-196 provides:
>
> Any person who assists, abets, counsels, causes, hires or commands another to commit any offense may be prosecuted and punished as if he were the principal offender.

The appellants were found guilty as accessories and fined $100 each, against the claim that the accessory statute, as so applied, violated the Fourteenth Amendment. . . .

. . . We do not sit as a super-legislature to determine the wisdom, need, and propriety of laws that touch economic problems, business affairs, or social conditions. This law, however, operates directly on an intimate relation of husband and wife and their physician's role in one aspect of that relation.

The association of people is not mentioned in the Constitution nor in the Bill of Rights. The right to educate a child in a school of the parents' choice—whether public or private or parochial—is also not mentioned. Nor is the right to study any particular subject or any foreign language. Yet the First Amendment has been construed to include certain of those rights.

By *Pierce v. Society of Sisters*, the right to educate one's children as one chooses is made applicable to the States by the force of the First and Fourteenth Amendments. By *Meyer v. Nebraska* the same dignity is given the right to study the German language in a private school. In other words, the State may not, consistently with the spirit of the First Amendment, contract the spectrum of available knowledge. The right of freedom of speech and press includes not only the right to utter or to print, but the right to distribute, the right to receive, the right to read and freedom of inquiry, freedom of thought, and freedom to teach—indeed, the freedom of the entire university community. Without those peripheral rights, the specific rights would be less secure. And so we reaffirm the principle of the Pierce and the Meyer cases.

In *NAACP v. Alabama,* we protected the "freedom to associate and privacy in one's associations," noting that freedom of association was a peripheral First Amendment right. Disclosure of membership lists of a constitutionally valid association, we held, was invalid "as entailing the likelihood of a substantial restraint upon the exercise by petitioner's members of their right to freedom of association." In other words, the First Amendment has a penumbra where privacy is protected from governmental intrusion. In like context, we have protected forms of "association" that are not political in the customary sense, but pertain to the social, legal, and economic benefit of the members.. In *Schware v. Board of Bar Examiners,* we held it not permissible to bar a lawyer from practice because he had once been a member of the Communist Party. The man's "association with that Party" was not shown to be "anything more than a political faith in a political party" and was not action of a kind proving bad moral character.

Those cases involved more than the "right of assembly"—a right that extends to all, irrespective of their race or ideology. The right of "association," like the right of belief, is more than the right to attend a meeting; it includes the right to express one's attitudes or philosophies by membership in a group or by affiliation with it or by other lawful means. Association in that context is a form of expression of opinion, and, while it is not expressly included in the First Amendment, its existence is necessary in making the express guarantees fully meaningful.

The . . . cases suggest that specific guarantees in the Bill of Rights have penumbras, formed by emanations from those guarantees that help give them life and substance. Various guarantees create zones of privacy. The right of association contained in the penumbra of the

First Amendment is one, as we have seen. The Third Amendment, in its prohibition against the quartering of soldiers "in any house" in time of peace without the consent of the owner, is another facet of that privacy. The Fourth Amendment explicitly affirms the "right of the people to be secure in their persons, houses, papers, and effects, against unreasonable searches and seizures." The Fifth Amendment, in its Self-Incrimination Clause, enables the citizen to create a zone of privacy which government may not force him to surrender to his detriment. The Ninth Amendment provides: "The enumeration in the Constitution, of certain rights, shall not be construed to deny or disparage others retained by the people." . . .

The present case, then, concerns a relationship lying within the zone of privacy created by several fundamental constitutional guarantees. And it concerns a law which, in forbidding the use of contraceptives, rather than regulating their manufacture or sale, seeks to achieve its goals by means having a maximum destructive impact upon that relationship. Such a law cannot stand in light of the familiar principle, so often applied by this Court, that a "governmental purpose to control or prevent activities constitutionally subject to state regulation may not be achieved by means which sweep unnecessarily broadly and thereby invade the area of protected freedoms." *NAACP v. Alabama*. Would we allow the police to search the sacred precincts of marital bedrooms for telltale signs of the use of contraceptives? The very idea is repulsive to the notions of privacy surrounding the marriage relationship.

We deal with a right of privacy older than the Bill of Rights—older than our political parties, older than our school system. Marriage is a coming together for better or for worse, hopefully enduring, and intimate to the degree of being sacred. It is an association that promotes a way of life, not causes; a harmony in living, not political faiths; a bilateral loyalty, not commercial or social projects. Yet it is an association for as noble a purpose as any involved in our prior decisions.

Goldberg, concurring:

While this Court has had little occasion to interpret the Ninth Amendment, "[i]t cannot be presumed that any clause in the constitution is intended to be without effect." *Marbury v. Madison*. In interpreting the Constitution, "real effect should be given to all the words it uses." *Myers v. United States*. The Ninth Amendment to the Constitution may be regarded by

some as a recent discovery, and may be forgotten by others, but, since 1791, it has been a basic part of the Constitution which we are sworn to uphold. To hold that a right so basic and fundamental and so deep-rooted in our society as the right of privacy in marriage may be infringed because that right is not guaranteed in so many words by the first eight amendments to the Constitution is to ignore the Ninth Amendment, and to give it no effect whatsoever. Moreover, a judicial construction that this fundamental right is not protected by the Constitution because it is not mentioned in explicit terms by one of the first eight amendments or elsewhere in the Constitution would violate the Ninth Amendment, which specifically states that "[t]he enumeration in the Constitution, of certain rights, shall not be construed to deny or disparage others retained by the people." (Emphasis added.)

. . . I do not take the position of my Brother Black in his dissent in *Adamson v. California* that the entire Bill of Rights is incorporated in the Fourteenth Amendment, and I do not mean to imply that the Ninth Amendment is applied against the States by the Fourteenth. Nor do I mean to state that the Ninth Amendment constitutes an independent source of rights protected from infringement by either the States or the Federal Government. Rather, the Ninth Amendment shows a belief of the Constitution's authors that fundamental rights exist that are not expressly enumerated in the first eight amendments, and an intent that the list of rights included there not be deemed exhaustive. . . .

. . . In sum, the Ninth Amendment simply lends strong support to the view that the "liberty" protected by the Fifth and Fourteenth Amendments from infringement by the Federal Government or the States is not restricted to rights specifically mentioned in the first eight amendments. . . .

Black, dissenting:

. . . The Court talks about a constitutional "right of privacy" as though there is some constitutional provision or provisions forbidding any law ever to be passed which might abridge the "privacy" of individuals. But there is not. There are, of course, guarantees in certain specific constitutional provisions which are designed in part to protect privacy at certain times and places with respect to certain activities. Such, for example, is the Fourth Amendment's guarantee against "unreasonable searches and seizures." But I think it belittles that Amendment to talk about it as though it protects nothing but "privacy." To treat it that way is to give it a niggardly interpretation, not the kind of liberal reading I think any Bill of Rights provision should be given. The average man would very likely not have his feelings soothed any more by having his property seized openly than by having it seized privately and by stealth. He simply wants his property left alone. And a person can be just as much, if not more, irritated, annoyed and injured by an unceremonious public arrest by a policeman as he is by a seizure in the privacy of his office or home.

One of the most effective ways of diluting or expanding a constitutionally guaranteed right is to substitute for the crucial word or words of a constitutional guarantee another word or words, more or less flexible and more or less restricted in meaning. This fact is well illustrated by the use of the term "right of privacy" as a comprehensive substitute for the Fourth Amendment's guarantee against "unreasonable searches and seizures." "Privacy" is a broad, abstract and ambiguous concept which can easily be shrunken in meaning but which can also, on the other hand, easily be interpreted as a constitutional ban against many things other than searches and seizures. I have expressed the view many times that First Amendment freedoms, for example, have suffered from a failure of the courts to stick to the simple language of the First Amendment in construing it, instead of invoking multitudes of words substituted for those the Framers used. . . .

I realize that many good and able men have eloquently spoken and written, sometimes in rhapsodical strains, about the duty of this Court to keep the Constitution in tune with the times. The idea is that the Constitution must be changed from time to time, and that this Court is charged with a duty to make those changes. For myself, I must, with all deference, reject that philosophy. The Constitution makers knew the need for change, and provided for it. Amendments suggested by the people's elected representatives can be submitted to the people or their selected agents for ratification. That method of change was good for our Fathers, and, being somewhat old-fashioned, I must add it is good enough for me. And so I cannot rely on the Due Process Clause or the Ninth Amendment or any mysterious and uncertain natural law concept as a reason for striking down this state law. The Due Process Clause, with an "arbitrary and capricious" or "shocking to the conscience" formula, was liberally used by this Court to strike down economic

legislation in the early decades of this century, threatening, many people thought, the tranquility and stability of the Nation. That formula, based on subjective considerations of "natural justice," is no less dangerous when used to enforce this Court's views about personal rights than those about economic rights. I had thought that we had laid that formula, as a means for striking down state legislation, to rest once and for all in cases like *West Coast Hotel Co. v. Parrish.* . . .

Roe v. Wade

410 U.S. 113 (1973), 7-2
Opinion of the Court: Blackmun (Brennan, Burger, Douglas, Marshall, Powell, Stewart)
Dissenting: Rehnquist, White

What right to terminate pregnancy is recognized by the Court? Why is such a right protected by the Constitution? What is the basis for Justice Blackmun's trimester analysis? Is his justification reasonable? How are the state's interests phrased? Which interests are recognized? Is Justice Rehnquist's dissent based on opposition to abortion? How do he and Blackmun differ on what is acceptable interpretation of the Constitution?

Blackmun, for the Court:

This Texas federal appeal and its Georgia companion, *Doe v. Bolton*, present constitutional challenges to state criminal abortion legislation. The Texas statutes under attack here are typical of those that have been in effect in many States for approximately a century. . . .

Our task, of course, is to resolve the issue by constitutional measurement, free of emotion and of predilection. We seek earnestly to do this, and, because we do, we have inquired into, and in this opinion place some emphasis upon, medical and medical-legal history and what that history reveals about man's attitudes toward the abortion procedure over the centuries. . . .

The Texas statutes . . . make it a crime to "procure an abortion," as therein defined, or to attempt one, except with respect to "an abortion procured or attempted by medical advice for the purpose of saving the life of the mother.". . .

Jane Roe, a single woman . . . sought a declaratory judgment that the Texas criminal abortion statutes were unconstitutional on their face, and an injunction restraining the defendant from enforcing the statutes.

Norma McCorvey, the "Jane Roe" of *Roe v. Wade,* who successfully challenged Texas's anti-abortion law in 1973, was transformed into something of a public figure. Shown here 15 years after the decision, McCorvey later became a right-to-life activist.

Roe alleged that she was unmarried and pregnant; that she wished to terminate her pregnancy by an abortion "performed by a competent, licensed physician, under safe, clinical conditions"; that she was unable to get a "legal" abortion in Texas because her life did not appear to be threatened by the continuation of her pregnancy; and that she could not afford to travel to another jurisdiction in order to secure a legal abortion under safe conditions. . . .

It perhaps is not generally appreciated that the restrictive criminal abortion laws in effect in a majority of States today are of relatively recent vintage. Those laws, generally proscribing abortion or its attempt at any time during pregnancy except when necessary to preserve the pregnant woman's life, are not of ancient or even of common law origin. Instead, they derive from statutory changes effected, for the most part, in the latter half of the 19th century. . . .

Three reasons have been advanced to explain historically the enactment of criminal abortion laws in the 19th century and to justify their continued existence.

It has been argued occasionally that these laws were the product of a Victorian social concern to discourage illicit sexual conduct. Texas, however, does not advance this justification in the present case, and it appears that no court or commentator has taken the argument seriously. The appellant and amici contend, moreover, that this is not a proper state purpose, at all and suggest that, if it were, the Texas statutes are overbroad in protecting it, since the law fails to distinguish between married and unwed mothers.

A second reason is concerned with abortion as a medical procedure. When most criminal abortion laws were first enacted, the procedure was a hazardous one for the woman. . . .

Modern medical techniques have altered this situation. [Roe] and various amici refer to medical data indicating that abortion in early pregnancy, that is, prior to the end of the first trimester, although not without its risk, is now relatively safe. Mortality rates for women undergoing early abortions, where the procedure is legal, appear to be as low as or lower than the rates for normal childbirth. Consequently, any interest of the State in protecting the woman from an inherently hazardous procedure, except when it would be equally dangerous for her to forgo it, has largely disappeared. Of course, important state interests in the areas of health and medical standards do remain.

The State has a legitimate interest in seeing to it that abortion, like any other medical procedure, is performed under circumstances that insure maximum safety for the patient. This interest obviously extends at least to the performing physician and his staff, to the facilities involved, to the availability of after-care, and to adequate provision for any complication or emergency that might arise. The prevalence of high mortality rates at illegal "abortion mills" strengthens, rather than weakens, the State's interest in regulating the conditions under which abortions are performed. Moreover, the risk to the woman increases as her pregnancy continues. Thus, the State retains a definite interest in protecting the woman's own health and safety when an abortion is proposed at a late stage of pregnancy.

The third reason is the State's interest—some phrase it in terms of duty—in protecting prenatal life. Some of the argument for this justification rests on the theory that a new human life is present from the moment of conception. The State's interest and general obligation to protect life then extends, it is argued, to prenatal life. Only when the life of the pregnant mother herself is at stake, balanced against the life she carries within her, should the interest of the embryo or fetus not prevail. Logically, of course, a legitimate state interest in this area need not stand or fall on acceptance of the belief that life begins at conception or at some other point prior to live birth. In assessing the State's interest, recognition may be given to the less rigid claim that as long as at least potential life is involved, the State may assert interests beyond the protection of the pregnant woman alone.

Parties challenging state abortion laws have sharply disputed in some courts the contention that a purpose of these laws, when enacted, was to protect prenatal life. ... [T]hey claim that most state laws were designed solely to protect the woman. Because medical advances have lessened this concern, at least with respect to abortion in early pregnancy, they argue that with respect to such abortions the laws can no longer be justified by any state interest. . . .

It is with these interests, and the eight to be attached to them, that this case is concerned.

The Constitution does not explicitly mention any right of privacy. In a line of decisions. . . . the Court has recognized that a right of personal privacy, or a guarantee of certain areas or zones of privacy, does exist under the Constitution. . . .

This right of privacy, whether it be founded in the Fourteenth Amendment's concept of personal liberty and restrictions upon state action, as we feel it is, or, as the District Court determined, in the Ninth Amendment's reservation of rights to the people, is broad enough to encompass a woman's decision whether or not to terminate her pregnancy. The detriment that the State would impose upon the pregnant woman by denying this choice altogether is apparent. Specific and direct harm medically diagnosable even in early pregnancy may be involved. Maternity, or additional offspring, may force upon

the woman a distressful life and future. Psychological harm may be imminent. Mental and physical health may be taxed by child care. There is also the distress, for all concerned, associated with the unwanted child, and there is the problem of bringing a child into a family already unable, psychologically and otherwise, to care for it. In other cases, as in this one, the additional difficulties and continuing stigma of unwed motherhood may be involved. All these are factors the woman and her responsible physician necessarily will consider in consultation.

On the basis of elements such as these, [Roe] and some amici argue that the woman's right is absolute and that she is entitled to terminate her pregnancy at whatever time, in whatever way, and for whatever reason she alone chooses. With this we do not agree. [Roe]'s arguments that Texas either has no valid interest at all in regulating the abortion decision, or no interest strong enough to support any limitation upon the woman's sole determination, are unpersuasive. The Court's decisions recognizing a right of privacy also acknowledge that some state regulation in areas protected by that right is appropriate. As noted above, a State may properly assert important interests in safeguarding health, in maintaining medical standards, and in protecting potential life. At some point in pregnancy, these respective interests become sufficiently compelling to sustain regulation of the factors that govern the abortion decision. The privacy right involved, therefore, cannot be said to be absolute. In fact, it is not clear to us that the claim asserted by some amici that one has an unlimited right to do with one's body as one pleases bears a close relationship to the right of privacy previously articulated in the Court's decisions. The Court has refused to recognize an unlimited right of this kind in the past.

We, therefore, conclude that the right of personal privacy includes the abortion decision, but that this right is not unqualified, and must be considered against important state interests in regulation. . . .

Where certain "fundamental rights" are involved, the Court has held that regulation limiting these rights may be justified only by a "compelling state interest," and that legislative enactments must be narrowly drawn to express only the legitimate state interests at stake. . . .

The appellee and certain amici argue that the fetus is a "person" within the language and meaning of the Fourteenth Amendment. In support of this, they outline at length and in detail the well known facts of fetal development. If this suggestion of personhood is established, the [Roe]'s case, of course, collapses, for the fetus' right to life would then be guaranteed specifically by the Amendment. [Roe] conceded as much on reargument. On the other hand, the appellee conceded on reargument that no case could be cited that holds that a fetus is a person within the meaning of the Fourteenth Amendment.

The Constitution does not define "person" in so many words. [Here, Justice Blackmun notes the various references to "person" in the Constitution.] But in nearly all these instances, the use of the word is such that it has application only post-natally. None indicates, with any assurance, that it has any possible pre-natal application.

All this, together with our observation, supra, that, throughout the major portion of the 19th century, prevailing legal abortion practices were far freer than they are today, persuades us that the word "person," as used in the Fourteenth Amendment, does not include the unborn. . . .

This conclusion, however, does not of itself fully answer the contentions raised by Texas, and we pass on to other considerations.

The pregnant woman cannot be isolated in her privacy. She carries an embryo and, later, a fetus, if one accepts the medical definitions of the developing young in the human uterus. The situation therefore is inherently different from marital intimacy, or bedroom possession of obscene material, or marriage, or procreation, or education. . . .

Texas urges that, apart from the Fourteenth Amendment, life begins at conception and is present throughout pregnancy, and that, therefore, the State has a compelling interest in protecting that life from and after conception. We need not resolve the difficult question of when life begins. When those trained in the respective disciplines of medicine, philosophy, and theology are unable to arrive at any consensus, the judiciary, at this point in the development of man's knowledge, is not in a position to speculate as to the answer. . . .

In view of all this, we do not agree that, by adopting one theory of life, Texas may override the rights of the pregnant woman that are at stake. We repeat, however, that the State does have an important and legitimate interest in preserving and protecting the health of the pregnant woman, whether she be a resident of the State or a nonresident who seeks medical consultation and treatment there, and that it has still another important and legitimate interest in protecting the potentiality of human life. These interests are separate and distinct. Each grows in substantiality as the woman approaches term and, at a point during pregnancy, each becomes "compelling."

With respect to the State's important and legitimate interest in the health of the mother, the "compelling" point, in the light of present medical knowledge, is at approximately the end of the first trimester. This is so because of the now-established medical fact . . . that, until the end of the first trimester mortality in abortion may be less than mortality in normal childbirth. It follows that, from and after this point, a State may regulate the abortion procedure to the extent that the regulation reasonably relates to the preservation and protection of maternal health. Examples of permissible state regulation in this area are requirements as to the qualifications of the person who is to perform the abortion; as to the licensure of that person; as to the facility in which the procedure is to be performed, that is, whether it must be a hospital or may be a clinic or some other place of less-than-hospital status; as to the licensing of the facility; and the like.

This means, on the other hand, that, for the period of pregnancy prior to this "compelling" point, the attending physician, in consultation with his patient, is free to determine, without regulation by the State, that, in his medical judgment, the patient's pregnancy should be terminated. If that decision is reached, the judgment may be effectuated by an abortion free of interference by the State.

With respect to the State's important and legitimate interest in potential life, the "compelling" point is at viability. This is so because the fetus then presumably has the capability of meaningful life outside the mother's womb. State regulation protective of fetal life after viability thus has both logical and biological justifications. If the State is interested in protecting fetal life after viability, it may go so far as to proscribe abortion during that period, except when it is necessary to preserve the life or health of the mother.

Measured against these standards, the Texas Penal Code, in restricting legal abortions to those "procured or attempted by medical advice for the purpose of saving the life of the mother," sweeps too broadly. The statute makes no distinction between abortions performed early in pregnancy and those performed later, and it limits to a single reason, "saving" the mother's life, the legal justification for the procedure. The statute, therefore, cannot survive the constitutional attack made upon it here. . . .

To summarize and to repeat:

A state criminal abortion statute of the current Texas type, that excepts from criminality only a life-saving procedure on behalf of the mother, without regard to pregnancy stage and without recognition of the other interests involved, is violative of the Due Process Clause of the Fourteenth Amendment.

(a) For the stage prior to approximately the end of the first trimester, the abortion decision and its effectuation must be left to the medical judgment of the pregnant woman's attending physician.

(b) For the stage subsequent to approximately the end of the first trimester, the State, in promoting its interest in the health of the mother, may, if it chooses, regulate the abortion procedure in ways that are reasonably related to maternal health.

(c) For the stage subsequent to viability, the State in promoting its interest in the potentiality of human life may, if it chooses, regulate, and even proscribe, abortion except where it is necessary, in appropriate medical judgment, for the preservation of the life or health of the mother. . . .

This holding, we feel, is consistent with the relative weights of the respective interests involved, with the lessons and examples of medical and legal history, with the lenity of the common law, and with the demands of the profound problems of the present day. The decision leaves the State free to place increasing restrictions on abortion as the period of pregnancy lengthens, so long as those restrictions are tailored to the recognized state interests. The decision vindicates the right of the physician to administer medical treatment according to his professional judgment up to the points where important state interests provide compelling justifications for intervention. Up to those points, the abortion decision in all its aspects is inherently, and primarily, a medical decision, and basic responsibility for it must rest with the physician. If an individual practitioner abuses the privilege of exercising proper medical judgment, the usual remedies, judicial and intra-professional, are available. . . .

Rehnquist, dissenting:

. . . I have difficulty in concluding, as the Court does, that the right of "privacy" is involved in this case. Texas, by the statute here challenged, bars the performance of a medical abortion by a licensed physician on a plaintiff such as Roe. A transaction resulting in an operation such as this is not "private" in the ordinary usage of that word. Nor is the "privacy" that the Court finds here even a distant relative of the freedom from searches and seizures protected by the Fourth Amendment to the Constitution, which the Court has referred to as embodying a right to privacy.

If the Court means by the term "privacy" no more than that the claim of a person to be free from unwanted state regulation of consensual transactions may be a form of "liberty" protected by the Fourteenth Amendment, there is no doubt that similar claims have been upheld in our earlier decisions on the basis of that liberty. I agree with the statement of Mr. Justice Stewart in his concurring opinion that the "liberty," against deprivation of which without due process the Fourteenth Amendment protects, embraces more than the rights found in the Bill of Rights. But that liberty is not guaranteed absolutely against deprivation, only against deprivation without due process of law. The test traditionally applied in the area of social and economic legislation is whether or not a law such as that challenged has a rational relation to a valid state objective. The Due Process Clause of the Fourteenth Amendment undoubtedly does place a limit, albeit a broad one, on legislative power to enact laws such as this. If the Texas statute were to prohibit an abortion even where the mother's life is in jeopardy, . . . such a statute would lack a rational relation to a valid state objective. . . . But the Court's sweeping invalidation of any restrictions on abortion during the first trimester is impossible to justify under that standard, and the conscious weighing of competing factors that the Court's opinion apparently substitutes for the established test is far more appropriate to a legislative judgment than to a judicial one.

The Court eschews the history of the Fourteenth Amendment in its reliance on the "compelling state interest" test. But the Court adds a new wrinkle to this test by transposing it from the legal considerations associated with the Equal Protection Clause of the Fourteenth Amendment to this case arising under the Due Process Clause of the Fourteenth Amendment. Unless I misapprehend the consequences of this transplanting of the "compelling state interest test," the Court's opinion will accomplish the seemingly impossible feat of leaving this area of the law more confused than it found it.

While the Court's opinion quotes from the dissent of Mr. Justice Holmes in *Lochner v. New York,* the result it reaches is more closely attuned to the majority opinion of Mr. Justice Peckham in that case. As in *Lochner* and similar cases applying substantive due process standards to economic and social welfare legislation, the adoption of the compelling state interest standard will inevitably require this Court to examine the legislative policies and pass on the wisdom of these policies in the very process of deciding whether a particular state interest put forward may or may not be "compelling." The decision here to break pregnancy into three distinct terms and to outline the permissible restrictions the State may impose in each one, for example, partakes more of judicial legislation than it does of a determination of the intent of the drafters of the Fourteenth Amendment.

The fact that a majority of the States reflecting, after all, the majority sentiment in those States, have had restrictions on abortions for at least a century is a strong indication, it seems to me, that the asserted right to an abortion is not "so rooted in the traditions and conscience of our people as to be ranked as fundamental," *Snyder v. Massachusetts.* Even today, when society's views on abortion are changing, the very existence of the debate is evidence that the "right" to an abortion is not so universally accepted as the [Roe] would have us believe. . . .

Planned Parenthood of Southeastern Pennsylvania v. Casey

505 U.S. 833 (1992), 5-4
Opinion of the Court: Kennedy, O'Connor, Souter
Concurring in part: Blackmun, Rehnquist, Scalia, Stevens, Thomas, White
Dissenting in part: Blackmun, Rehnquist, Scalia, Stevens, Thomas, White

The Supreme Court was fragmented in this important case. There was no overall majority opinion. Three justices announced the judgment of the Court and collaborated in writing the Opinion of the Court in which other justices joined on various points. Six justices dissented on various points. In all, eight statements were filed, totaling more than 100 pages. Excerpted here are main parts of the O'Connor-Kennedy-Souter opinion. Parts of other opinions are briefly summarized following. Several provisions of the Pennsylvania Abortion Control Act were challenged. These included: s.3205, requiring that a woman seeking an abortion give her informed consent after she has been given certain information at least 24 hours before the procedure; s.3206, requiring the informed consent of one parent if the woman is a minor but also providing for a judicial bypass; s.3209, requiring, with certain exceptions, that a married woman seeking an abortion sign a statement that she has notified her husband of her intention. Another provision, s.3203, defines a "medical emergency" that would excuse compliance with

the requirements. Other provisions impose reporting requirements on facilities providing abortion services. Plaintiffs in the case, five abortion clinics and a doctor representing a class of doctors who perform abortions, sued for a declaratory judgment that each of the provisions was unconstitutional and for injunctive relief.

Which state regulations were held to violate the Constitution and which were not? Why is the right of privacy compromised by some of them and not by others? Or does the Court merely give greater weight to some than to others? How does this decision modify Roe v. Wade *(p. 304)? Is* Roe v. Wade *stronger or weaker as a result? Is this decision a compromise between pro- and anti-abortion rights positions?*

O'Connor, Kennedy, Souter, for the Court:

I

Liberty finds no refuge in a jurisprudence of doubt. Yet, 19 years after our holding that the Constitution protects a woman's right to terminate her pregnancy in its early stages, *Roe v. Wade,* that definition of liberty is still questioned. Joining the respondents as amicus curiae, the United States, as it has done in five other cases in the last decade, again asks us to overrule *Roe.* . . .

After considering the fundamental constitutional questions resolved by *Roe,* principles of institutional integrity, and the rule of stare decisis, we are led to conclude this: the essential holding of *Roe v. Wade* should be retained and once again reaffirmed. . . .

II

. . . Neither the Bill of Rights nor the specific practices of States at the time of the adoption of the Fourteenth Amendment marks the outer limits of the substantive sphere of liberty which the Fourteenth Amendment protects. . . .

The inescapable fact is that adjudication of substantive due process claims may call upon the Court in interpreting the Constitution to exercise that same capacity which, by tradition, courts always have exercised: reasoned judgment. Its boundaries are not susceptible of expression as a simple rule. That does not mean we are free to invalidate state policy choices with which we disagree; yet neither does it permit us to shrink from the duties of our office. . . .

Our law affords constitutional protection to personal decisions relating to marriage, procreation, contraception, family relationships, child rearing, and education. . . . These matters, involving the most intimate and personal choices a person may make in a lifetime, choices central to personal dignity and autonomy, are central to the liberty protected by the Fourteenth Amendment. At the heart of liberty is the right to define one's own concept of existence, of meaning, of the universe, and of the mystery of human life. Beliefs about these matters could not define the attributes of personhood were they formed under compulsion of the State. . . .

. . . Abortion is a unique act. It is an act fraught with consequences for others: for the woman who must live with the implications of her decision; for the persons who perform and assist in the procedure; for the spouse, family, and society which must confront the knowledge that these procedures exist, procedures some deem nothing short of an act of violence against innocent human life; and, depending on one's beliefs, for the life or potential life that is aborted. Though abortion is conduct, it does not follow that the State is entitled to proscribe it in all instances. That is because the liberty of the woman is at stake in a sense unique to the human condition, and so, unique to the law. The mother who carries a child to full term is subject to anxieties, to physical constraints, to pain that only she must bear. That these sacrifices have from the beginning of the human race been endured by woman with a pride that ennobles her in the eyes of others and gives to the infant a bond of love cannot alone be grounds for the State to insist she make the sacrifice. Her suffering is too intimate and personal for the State to insist, without more, upon its own vision of the woman's role, however dominant that vision has been in the course of our history and our culture. The destiny of the woman must be shaped to a large extent on her own conception of her spiritual imperatives and her place in society. . . .

It was this dimension of personal liberty that *Roe* sought to protect. . . .

III

. . . The sum of the . . . inquiry to this point shows *Roe's* underpinnings unweakened in any way affecting its central holding. While it has engendered disapproval, it has not been unworkable. An entire generation has come of age free to assume *Roe's* concept of liberty in defining the capacity of women to act in society, and to make reproductive decisions; no erosion of principle going to liberty or personal autonomy has left *Roe's* central holding a doctrinal remnant; *Roe* portends no developments at odds with other precedent for the analysis of personal liberty; and no

changes of fact have rendered viability more or less appropriate as the point at which the balance of interests tips. Within the bounds of normal stare decisis analysis, then, and subject to the considerations on which it customarily turns, the stronger argument is for affirming *Roe's* central holding, with whatever degree of personal reluctance any of us may have, not for overruling it. . . .

. . . Our analysis would not be complete, however, without explaining why overruling *Roe's* central holding would not only reach an unjustifiable result under principles of stare decisis, but would seriously weaken the Court's capacity to exercise the judicial power and to function as the Supreme Court of a Nation dedicated to the rule of law. To understand why this would be so, it is necessary to understand the source of this Court's authority, the conditions necessary for its preservation, and its relationship to the country's understanding of itself as a constitutional Republic.

The root of American governmental power is revealed most clearly in the instance of the power conferred by the Constitution upon the Judiciary of the United States, and specifically upon this Court. As Americans of each succeeding generation are rightly told, the Court cannot buy support for its decisions by spending money, and, except to a minor degree, it cannot independently coerce obedience to its decrees. The Court's power lies, rather, in its legitimacy, a product of substance and perception that shows itself in the people's acceptance of the Judiciary as fit to determine what the Nation's law means, and to declare what it demands.

The underlying substance of this legitimacy is of course the warrant for the Court's decisions in the Constitution and the lesser sources of legal principle on which the Court draws. That substance is expressed in the Court's opinions, and our contemporary understanding is such that a decision without principled justification would be no judicial act at all. But even when justification is furnished by apposite legal principle, something more is required. Because not every conscientious claim of principled justification will be accepted as such, the justification claimed must be beyond dispute. The Court must take care to speak and act in ways that allow people to accept its decisions on the terms the Court claims for them, as grounded truly in principle, not as compromises with social and political pressures having, as such, no bearing on the principled choices that the Court is obliged to make. Thus, the Court's legitimacy depends on making legally principled decisions under circumstances in which their principled character is sufficiently plausible to be accepted by the Nation. . . .

In two circumstances, however, the Court would almost certainly fail to receive the benefit of the doubt in overruling prior cases. There is, first, a point beyond which frequent overruling would overtax the country's belief in the Court's good faith. . . .

That first circumstance can be described as hypothetical; the second is to the point here and now. Where, in the performance of its judicial duties, the Court decides a case in such a way as to resolve the sort of intensely divisive controversy reflected in *Roe* and those rare, comparable cases, its decision has a dimension that the resolution of the normal case does not carry. It is the dimension present whenever the Court's interpretation of the Constitution calls the contending sides of a national controversy to end their national division by accepting a common mandate rooted in the Constitution.

The Court is not asked to do this very often, having thus addressed the Nation only twice in our lifetime, in the decisions of *Brown* [v. *Board of Education*] and *Roe*. But when the Court does act in this way, its decision requires an equally rare precedential force to counter the inevitable efforts to overturn it and to thwart its implementation. Some of those efforts may be mere unprincipled emotional reactions; others may proceed from principles worthy of profound respect. But whatever the premises of opposition may be, only the most convincing justification under accepted standards of precedent could suffice to demonstrate that a later decision overruling the first was anything but a surrender to political pressure and an unjustified repudiation of the principle on which the Court staked its authority in the first instance. So to overrule under fire in the absence of the most compelling reason to reexamine a watershed decision would subvert the Court's legitimacy beyond any serious question. . . .

The Court's duty in the present case is clear. In 1973, it confronted the already-divisive issue of governmental power to limit personal choice to undergo abortion, for which it provided a new resolution based on the due process guaranteed by the Fourteenth Amendment. Whether or not a new social consensus is developing on that issue, its divisiveness is no less today than in 1973, and pressure to overrule the decision, like pressure to retain it, has grown only more intense. A decision to overrule *Roe's* essential holding

under the existing circumstances would address error, if error there was, at the cost of both profound and unnecessary damage to the Court's legitimacy, and to the Nation's commitment to the rule of law. It is therefore imperative to adhere to the essence of *Roe's* original decision, and we do so today. . . .

IV

From what we have said so far, it follows that it is a constitutional liberty of the woman to have some freedom to terminate her pregnancy. We conclude that the basic decision in *Roe* was based on a constitutional analysis which we cannot now repudiate. The woman's liberty is not so unlimited, however, that, from the outset, the State cannot show its concern for the life of the unborn and, at a later point in fetal development, the State's interest in life has sufficient force so that the right of the woman to terminate the pregnancy can be restricted.

That brings us, of course, to the point where much criticism has been directed at *Roe*, a criticism that always inheres when the Court draws a specific rule from what in the Constitution is but a general standard. We conclude, however, that the urgent claims of the woman to retain the ultimate control over her destiny and her body, claims implicit in the meaning of liberty, require us to perform that function. Liberty must not be extinguished for want of a line that is clear. And it falls to us to give some real substance to the woman's liberty to determine whether to carry her pregnancy to full term.

We conclude the line should be drawn at viability, so that, before that time, the woman has a right to choose to terminate her pregnancy. . . .

. . . [V]iability, as we noted in *Roe*, is the time at which there is a realistic possibility of maintaining and nourishing a life outside the womb, so that the independent existence of the second life can, in reason and all fairness, be the object of state protection that now overrides the rights of the woman. Consistent with other constitutional norms, legislatures may draw lines which appear arbitrary without the necessity of offering a justification. But courts may not. We must justify the lines we draw. And there is no line other than viability which is more workable. To be sure, as we have said, there may be some medical developments that affect the precise point of viability, but this is an imprecision within tolerable limits, given that the medical community and all those who must apply its discoveries will continue to explore the matter. The viability line also has, as a practical matter, an element of fairness. In some broad sense, it might be said that a woman who fails to act before viability has consented to the State's intervention on behalf of the developing child.

The woman's right to terminate her pregnancy before viability is the most central principle of *Roe v. Wade*. It is a rule of law and a component of liberty we cannot renounce.

On the other side of the equation is the interest of the State in the protection of potential life. . . .

. . . *Roe v. Wade* speaks with clarity in establishing not only the woman's liberty but also the State's "important and legitimate interest in potential life." . . .

Roe established a trimester framework to govern abortion regulations. Under this elaborate but rigid construct, almost no regulation at all is permitted during the first trimester of pregnancy; regulations designed to protect the woman's health, but not to further the State's interest in potential life, are permitted during the second trimester; and, during the third trimester, when the fetus is viable, prohibitions are permitted provided the life or health of the mother is not at stake. . . .

The trimester framework no doubt was erected to ensure that the woman's right to choose not become so subordinate to the State's interest in promoting fetal life that her choice exists in theory, but not in fact. We do not agree, however, that the trimester approach is necessary to accomplish this objective. A framework of this rigidity was unnecessary, and, in its later interpretation, sometimes contradicted the State's permissible exercise of its powers.

Though the woman has a right to choose to terminate or continue her pregnancy before viability, it does not at all follow that the State is prohibited from taking steps to ensure that this choice is thoughtful and informed. Even in the earliest stages of pregnancy, the State may enact rules and regulations designed to encourage her to know that there are philosophic and social arguments of great weight that can be brought to bear in favor of continuing the pregnancy to full term, and that there are procedures and institutions to allow adoption of unwanted children as well as a certain degree of state assistance if the mother chooses to raise the child herself. . . .

. . . We give this summary:

(a) To protect the central right recognized by *Roe v. Wade* while at the same time accommodating the State's profound interest in potential life, we will employ the undue burden analysis as explained in this opinion. An undue burden exists, and therefore a provision of law is invalid, if its purpose or effect is to place a substantial obstacle in the path of a woman seeking an abortion before the fetus attains viability.

(b) We reject the rigid trimester framework of *Roe v. Wade*. To promote the State's profound interest in potential life, throughout pregnancy, the State may take measures to ensure that the woman's choice is informed, and measures designed to advance this interest will not be invalidated as long as their purpose is to persuade the woman to choose childbirth over abortion. These measures must not be an undue burden on the right.

(c) As with any medical procedure, the State may enact regulations to further the health or safety of a woman seeking an abortion. Unnecessary health regulations that have the purpose or effect of presenting a substantial obstacle to a woman seeking an abortion impose an undue burden on the right.

(d) Our adoption of the undue burden analysis does not disturb the central holding of *Roe v. Wade,* and we reaffirm that holding. Regardless of whether exceptions are made for particular circumstances, a State may not prohibit any woman from making the ultimate decision to terminate her pregnancy before viability.

(e) We also reaffirm *Roe's* holding that "subsequent to viability, the State, in promoting its interest in the potentiality of human life, may, if it chooses, regulate, and even proscribe, abortion except where it is necessary, in appropriate medical judgment, for the preservation of the life or health of the mother."

These principles control our assessment of the Pennsylvania statute, and we now turn to the issue of the validity of its challenged provisions. [On this issue, Justices O'Connor, Kennedy, and Souter hold that the "undue burden" test is violated only by the spousal consent requirement.]

* * *

[Justice Blackmun argued that the strict scrutiny standard of review required by the Court's abortion case precedents leaves all challenged sections of the Pennsylvania law unconstitutional. He concurred in that part of the Opinion of the Court holding the requirement of spousal notification unconstitutional.]

[Chief Justice Rehnquist, joined by Justices Scalia, Thomas, and White, concluded that "historical traditions of the American people," reflected in English common law and in American abortion statutes in effect when the Fourteenth Amendment was ratified, do not support the view that the right to terminate pregnancy is "fundamental." Thus, laws regulating that right need not be subjected to strict scrutiny review. The "undue burden" standard adopted by the Opinion of the Court has no basis in constitutional law and is less workable than the trimester framework the Opinion discards. The new standard will allow the Court to impose its own preferences on the states in the form of a complex abortion code. A woman's interest in having an abortion is a form of liberty protected by the due process clause, but states may regulate abortion procedures in ways "rationally related to a legitimate state interest." The requirement that a doctor give information about the abortion procedure and its risks and alternatives is not a large burden and is clearly related to maternal health and a state's interest in informed consent. For the same reason, the mandatory 24-hour waiting period should be upheld. This delay helps ensure the woman's decision to abort is well considered, in addition to rationally furthering the state's interest in maternal health and unborn life.]

[Justice Scalia, joined by Justices Rehnquist, Thomas, and White, concluded that a woman's decision to terminate her pregnancy is not a constitutionally protected "liberty" because first, it is not addressed in the Constitution, and second, "longstanding traditions of American society" have permitted it to be legally proscribed.]

Harris v. McRae

448 U.S. 297 (1980), 5-4
Opinion of the Court: Stewart (Burger, Powell, Rehnquist, White)
Dissenting: Blackmun, Brennan, Marshall, Stevens

On what ground does the Court uphold the Hyde Amendment? As a result of this decision can it be said that women have a right to abortion or that they have a right to prevent the government from interfering with obtaining an abortion? For nonindigent women, is there any difference? On what points do the dissenters take issue with Justice Stewart's analysis? Does the Court's decision prevent the public funding of abortions?

Stewart, for the Court:
This case presents statutory and constitutional questions concerning the public funding of abortions under Title XIX of the Social Security Act, commonly known as the "Medicaid" Act, and recent annual Appropriations Acts containing the so-called "Hyde Amendment." The statutory question is whether Title XIX requires a State that participates in the Medicaid program to fund the cost of medically necessary abortions for which federal reimbursement is unavailable under the Hyde Amendment. The constitutional question, which arises only if Title XIX imposes no such requirement, is whether the Hyde Amendment, by denying public funding for certain medically necessary abortions, contravenes the liberty or equal protection guarantees of the Due Process Clause of the Fifth Amendment, or either of the Religion Clauses of the First Amendment.

The Medicaid program was created in 1965, when Congress added Title XIX to the Social Security Act for the purpose of providing federal financial assistance to States that choose to reimburse certain costs of medical treatment for needy persons. Although participation in the Medicaid program is entirely optional, once a State elects to participate, it must comply with the requirements of Title XIX. . . .

Since September, 1976, Congress has prohibited—either by an amendment to the annual appropriations bill for the Department of Health, Education, and Welfare or by a joint resolution—the use of any federal funds to reimburse the cost of abortions under the Medicaid program except under certain specified circumstances. This funding restriction is commonly known as the "Hyde Amendment," after its original congressional sponsor, Representative Hyde. The current version of the Hyde Amendment, applicable for fiscal year 1980, provides:

> [N]one of the funds provided by this joint resolution shall be used to perform abortions except where the life of the mother would be endangered if the fetus were carried to term; or except for such medical procedures necessary for the victims of rape or incest when such rape or incest has been reported promptly to a law enforcement agency or public health service. . . .

On September 30, 1976, the day on which Congress enacted the initial version of the Hyde Amendment, these consolidated cases were filed in the District Court for the Eastern District of New York. The plaintiffs—Cora McRae, a New York Medicaid recipient then in the first trimester of a pregnancy that she wished to terminate, the New York City Health and Hospitals Corp., a public benefit corporation that operates 16 hospitals, 12 of which provide abortion services, and others—sought to enjoin the enforcement of the funding restriction on abortions. . . .

It is well settled that, quite apart from the guarantee of equal protection, if a law "impinges upon a fundamental right explicitly or implicitly secured by the Constitution, [it] is presumptively unconstitutional." Accordingly, before turning to the equal protection issue in this case, we examine whether the Hyde Amendment violates any substantive rights secured by the Constitution.

We address first the appellees' argument that the Hyde Amendment, by restricting the availability of certain medically necessary abortions under Medicaid, impinges on the "liberty" protected by the Due Process Clause . . . of the Fourteenth Amendment [which] includes not only the freedoms explicitly mentioned in the Bill of Rights, but also a freedom of personal choice in certain matters of marriage and family life. This implicit constitutional liberty, the Court in [*Roe v.*] *Wade* held, includes the freedom of a woman to decide whether to terminate a pregnancy.

But the Court in *Wade* also recognized that a State has legitimate interests during a pregnancy in both ensuring the health of the mother and protecting potential human life. These state interests, which were found to be "separate and distinct" and to "gro[w] in substantiality as the woman approaches term," pose a conflict with a woman's untrammeled freedom of choice. . . .

The Hyde Amendment, like the Connecticut welfare regulation at issue in *Maher* [*v. Roe*], places no governmental obstacle in the path of a woman who chooses to terminate her pregnancy, but rather, by means of unequal subsidization of abortion and other medical services, encourages alternative activity deemed in the public interest. The present case does differ factually from *Maher* insofar as that case involved a failure to fund nontherapeutic abortions, whereas the Hyde Amendment withholds funding of certain medically necessary abortions. Accordingly, the appellees argue that, because the Hyde Amendment affects a significant interest not present or asserted in *Maher*—the interest of a woman in protecting her health during pregnancy—and because that interest lies at the core of the personal constitutional freedom recognized in *Wade*, the present case is constitutionally different from *Maher*. . . .

. . . But, regardless of whether the freedom of a woman to choose to terminate her pregnancy for health reasons lies at the core or the periphery of the due process liberty recognized in *Wade*, it simply does not follow that a woman's freedom of choice carries with it a constitutional entitlement to the financial resources to avail herself of the full range of protected choices. The reason why was explained in *Maher*: although government may not place obstacles in the path of a woman's exercise of her freedom of choice, it need not remove those not of its own creation. Indigency falls in the latter category. The financial constraints that restrict an indigent woman's ability to enjoy the full range of constitutionally protected freedom of choice are the product not of governmental restrictions on access to abortions, but rather of her indigency. Although Congress has opted to subsidize medically necessary services generally, but not certain medically necessary abortions, the fact remains that the Hyde Amendment leaves an indigent woman with at least the same range of choice in deciding whether to obtain a medically necessary abortion as she would have had if Congress had chosen to subsidize no health care costs at all. We are thus not persuaded that the Hyde Amendment impinges on the constitutionally protected freedom of choice recognized in *Wade*.

Although the liberty protected by the Due Process Clause affords protection against unwarranted government interference with freedom of choice in the context of certain personal decisions, it does not confer an entitlement to such funds as may be necessary to realize all the advantages of that freedom. To hold otherwise would mark a drastic change in our understanding of the Constitution. It cannot be that, because government may not prohibit the use of contraceptives, *Griswold v. Connecticut,* or prevent parents from sending their child to a private school, *Pierce v. Society of Sisters,* government therefore has an affirmative constitutional obligation to ensure that all persons have the financial resources to obtain contraceptives or send their children to private schools. To translate the limitation on governmental power implicit in the Due Process Clause into an affirmative funding obligation would require Congress to subsidize the medically necessary abortion of an indigent woman even if Congress had not enacted a Medicaid program to subsidize other medically necessary services. Nothing in the Due Process Clause supports such an extraordinary result. Whether freedom of choice that is constitutionally protected warrants federal subsidization is a question for Congress to answer, not a matter of constitutional entitlement. Accordingly, we conclude that the Hyde Amendment does not impinge on the due process liberty recognized in *Wade.*

The appellees also argue that the Hyde Amendment contravenes rights secured by the Religion Clauses of the First Amendment. It is the appellees' view that the Hyde Amendment violates the Establishment Clause because it incorporates into law the doctrines of the Roman Catholic Church concerning the sinfulness of abortion and the time at which life commences. Moreover, insofar as a woman's decision to seek a medically necessary abortion may be a product of her religious beliefs under certain Protestant and Jewish tenets, the appellees assert that the funding limitations of the Hyde Amendment impinge on the freedom of religion guaranteed by the Free Exercise Clause.

It is well settled that "a legislative enactment does not contravene the Establishment Clause if it has a secular legislative purpose, if its principal or primary effect neither advances nor inhibits religion, and if it does not foster an excessive governmental entanglement with religion." Applying this standard, the District Court properly concluded that the Hyde Amendment does not run afoul of the Establishment Clause. Although neither a State nor the Federal Government can constitutionally "pass laws which aid one religion, aid all religions, or prefer one religion over another," *Everson v. Board of Education,* it does not follow that a statute violates the Establishment Clause because it "happens to coincide or harmonize with the tenets of some or all religions." *McGowan v. Maryland.* . . .

We need not address the merits of the appellees' arguments concerning the Free Exercise Clause, because the appellees lack standing to raise a free exercise challenge to the Hyde Amendment. The named appellees fall into three categories: (1) the indigent pregnant women who sued on behalf of other women similarly situated, (2) the two officers of the Women's Division, and (3) the Women's Division itself. The named appellees in the first category lack standing to challenge tie Hyde Amendment on free exercise grounds because none alleged, much less proved, that she sought an abortion under compulsion of religious belief. Although the named appellees in the second category did provide a detailed description of their religious beliefs, they failed to allege either that they are or expect to be pregnant or that they are eligible to receive Medicaid. These named appellees,

therefore, lack the personal stake in the controversy needed to confer standing to raise such a challenge to the Hyde Amendment. . . .

It remains to be determined whether the Hyde Amendment violates the equal protection component of the Fifth Amendment. This challenge is premised on the fact that, although federal reimbursement is available under Medicaid for medically necessary services generally, the Hyde Amendment does not permit federal reimbursement of all medically necessary abortions. The District Court held, and the appellees argue here, that this selective subsidization violates the constitutional guarantee of equal protection

The guarantee of equal protection under the Fifth Amendment is not a source of substantive rights or liberties, but rather a right to be free from invidious discrimination in statutory classifications and other governmental activity. It is well settled that where a statutory classification does not itself impinge on a right or liberty protected by the Constitution, the validity of classification must be sustained unless "the classification rests on grounds wholly irrelevant to the achievement of [any legitimate governmental] objective." *McGowan v. Maryland.* This presumption of constitutional validity, however, disappears if a statutory classification is predicated on criteria that are, in a constitutional sense, "suspect," the principal example of which is a classification based on race.

For the reasons stated above, we have already concluded that the Hyde Amendment violates no constitutionally protected substantive rights. We now conclude as well that it is not predicated on a constitutionally suspect classification. In reaching this conclusion, we again draw guidance from the Court's decision in *Maher v. Roe.* . . .

It is our view that the present case is indistinguishable from *Maher* in this respect. Here, as in *Maher,* the principal impact of the Hyde Amendment falls on the indigent. But that fact does not itself render the funding restriction constitutionally invalid, for this Court has held repeatedly that poverty, standing alone, is not a suspect classification. That *Maher* involved the refusal to fund nontherapeutic abortions, whereas the present case involves the refusal to fund medically necessary abortions, has no bearing on the factors that render a classification "suspect" within the meaning of the constitutional guarantee of equal protection.

The remaining question then is whether the Hyde Amendment is rationally related to a legitimate governmental objective. It is the Government's position that the Hyde Amendment bears a rational relationship to its legitimate interest in protecting the potential life of the fetus. We agree....

Where, as here, the Congress has neither invaded a substantive constitutional right or freedom nor enacted legislation that purposefully operates to the detriment of a suspect class, the only requirement of equal protection is that congressional action be rationally related to a legitimate governmental interest. The Hyde Amendment satisfies that standard. It is not the mission of this Court or any other to decide whether the balance of competing interests reflected in the Hyde Amendment is wise social policy. If that were our mission, not every Justice who has subscribed to the judgment of the Court today could have done so. But we cannot, in the name of the Constitution, overturn duly enacted statutes simply "because they may be unwise, improvident, or out of harmony with a particular school of thought." *Williamson v. Lee Optical Co....*

For the reasons stated in this opinion, we hold that a State that participates in the Medicaid program is not obligated under Title XIX to continue to fund those medically necessary abortions for which federal reimbursement is unavailable under the Hyde Amendment. We further hold that the funding restrictions of the Hyde Amendment violate neither the Fifth Amendment nor the Establishment Clause of the First Amendment. It is also our view that the appellees lack standing to raise a challenge to the Hyde Amendment under the Free Exercise Clause of the First Amendment....

Brennan, dissenting:

... [T]he State's interest in protecting the potential life of the fetus cannot justify the exclusion of financially and medically needy women from the benefits to which they would otherwise be entitled solely because the treatment that a doctor has concluded is medically necessary involves an abortion. I write separately to express my continuing disagreement with the Court's mischaracterization of the nature of the fundamental right recognized in *Roe v. Wade,* and its misconception of the manner in which that right is infringed by federal and state legislation withdrawing all funding for medically necessary abortions.... The proposition for which [*Roe v. Wade*] stands thus is not that the State is under an affirmative obligation to ensure access to abortions for all who may desire them; it is that the State must refrain from wielding its enor-

mous power and influence in a manner that might burden the pregnant woman's freedom to choose whether to have an abortion....

Marshall, dissenting:

... The Court's opinion studiously avoids recognizing the undeniable fact that, for women eligible for Medicaid—poor women—denial of a Medicaid-funded abortion is equivalent to denial of legal abortion altogether. By definition, these women do not have the money to pay for an abortion themselves. If abortion is medically necessary and a funded abortion is unavailable, they must resort to back-alley butchers, attempt to induce an abortion themselves by crude and dangerous methods, or suffer the serious medical consequences of attempting to carry the fetus to term. Because legal abortion is not a realistic option for such women, the predictable result of the Hyde Amendment will be a significant increase in the number of poor women who will die or suffer significant health damage because of an inability to procure necessary medical services....

Bowers v. Hardwick

478 U.S. 186 (1986), 5-4
Opinion of the Court: White (Burger, O'Connor, Powell, Rehnquist)
Dissenting: Blackmun, Brennan, Marshall, Stevens

Why has a "fundamental" right not been violated by the Florida law? How did Justice White distinguish the Court's privacy decisions? To what extent is his decision based on historical grounds? What state interests are recognized? Is the decision best understood as one carefully refraining from "leading" public opinion on a controversial issue and thus deferring to the political process? As a determination not to read another "fundamental" right into the Constitution? As one essentially reflecting the value preferences of the justices? Hardwick brought this case to challenge a law that was not used against him. Was that a high-risk gamble? Is it likely that gay rights have been strengthened, weakened, or not much affected by that strategy and the decision in this case? What may explain why the Court has not heard another case on the issue?

White, for the Court:

In August, 1982, [Michael] Hardwick ... was charged with violating the Georgia statute criminalizing sodomy by committing that act with another adult male in the bedroom of [his] home. After a preliminary hearing, the District Attorney decided not to present the matter to the grand jury unless further evidence developed.

[Hardwick] then brought suit in the Federal District Court, challenging the constitutionality of the statute insofar as it criminalized consensual sodomy. He asserted that he was a practicing homosexual, that the Georgia sodomy statute, as administered by the defendants, placed him in imminent danger of arrest, and that the statute for several reasons violates the Federal Constitution. . . . This case does not require a judgment on whether laws against sodomy between consenting adults in general, or between homosexuals in particular, are wise or desirable. It raises no question about the right or propriety of state legislative decisions to repeal their laws that criminalize homosexual sodomy, or of state court decisions invalidating those laws on state constitutional grounds. The issue presented is whether the Federal Constitution confers a fundamental right upon homosexuals to engage in sodomy, and hence invalidates the laws of the many States that still make such conduct illegal, and have done so for a very long time. The case also calls for some judgment about the limits of the Court's role in carrying out its constitutional mandate.

We first register our disagreement with the Court of Appeals and with [Hardwick] that the Court's prior cases have construed the Constitution to confer a right of privacy that extends to homosexual sodomy and, for all intents and purposes, have decided this case. The reach of this line of cases was sketched in *Carey v. Population Services International. Pierce v. Society of Sisters,* and *Meyer v. Nebraska* were described as dealing with childrearing and education; Prince v. Massachusetts with family relationships; *Skinner v. Oklahoma ex rel. Williamson,* with procreation; *Loving v. Virginia,* with marriage; *Griswold v. Connecticut,* supra, and *Eisenstadt v. Baird,* with contraception; and Roe v. Wade, with abortion. The latter three cases were interpreted as construing the Due Process Clause of the Fourteenth Amendment to confer a fundamental individual right to decide whether or not to beget or bear a child.

Accepting the decisions in these cases and the above description of them, we think it evident that none of the rights announced in those cases bears any resemblance to the claimed constitutional right of homosexuals to engage in acts of sodomy that is asserted in this case. No connection between family, marriage, or procreation, on the one hand, and homosexual ac-

tivity, on the other, has been demonstrated, either by the Court of Appeals or by [Hardwick]. Moreover, any claim that these cases nevertheless stand for the proposition that any kind of private sexual conduct between consenting adults is constitutionally insulated from state proscription is unsupportable. Indeed, the Court's opinion in *Carey* twice asserted that the privacy right, which the *Griswold* line of cases found to be one of the protections provided by the Due Process Clause, did not reach so far.

Precedent aside, however, [Hardwick] would have us announce, as the Court of Appeals did, a fundamental right to engage in homosexual sodomy. This we are quite unwilling to do. It is true that, despite the language of the Due Process Clauses of the Fifth and Fourteenth Amendments, which appears to focus only on the processes by which life, liberty, or property is taken, the cases are legion in which those Clauses have been interpreted to have substantive content, subsuming rights that to a great extent are immune from federal or state regulation or proscription. Among such cases are those recognizing rights that have little or no textual support in the constitutional language. *Meyer, Prince, and Pierce* fall in this category, as do the privacy cases from *Griswold* to *Carey.*

Striving to assure itself and the public that announcing rights not readily identifiable in the Constitution's text involves much more than the imposition of the Justices' own choice of values on the States and the Federal Government, the Court has sought to identify the nature of the rights qualifying for heightened judicial protection. In *Palko v. Connecticut,* it was said that this category includes those fundamental liberties that are "implicit in the concept of ordered liberty," such that "neither liberty nor justice would exist if [they] were sacrificed." A different description of fundamental liberties appeared in *Moore v. East Cleveland,* where they are characterized as those liberties that are "deeply rooted in this Nation's history and tradition."

It is obvious to us that neither of these formulations would extend a fundamental right to homosexuals to engage in acts of consensual sodomy. Proscriptions against that conduct have ancient roots. Sodomy was a criminal offense at common law, and was forbidden by the laws of the original 13 States when they ratified the Bill of Rights. In 1868, when the Fourteenth Amendment was ratified, all but 5 of the 37 States in the Union had criminal sodomy laws. In fact, until 1961, all 50 States outlawed sodomy, and today, 24 States and the District of Columbia continue to provide criminal penalties for sodomy performed in private and between consenting adults. Against this background, to claim that a right to engage in such conduct is "deeply rooted in this Nation's history and tradition" or "implicit in the concept of ordered liberty" is, at best, facetious.

Nor are we inclined to take a more expansive view of our authority to discover new fundamental rights imbedded in the Due Process Clause. The Court is most vulnerable and comes nearest to illegitimacy when it deals with judge-made constitutional law having little or no cognizable roots in the language or design of the Constitution. That this is so was painfully demonstrated by the faceoff between the Executive and the Court in the 1930s, which resulted in the repudiation of much of the substantive gloss that the Court had placed on the Due Process Clauses of the Fifth and Fourteenth Amendments. There should be, therefore, great resistance to expand the substantive reach of those Clauses, particularly if it requires redefining the category of rights deemed to be fundamental. Otherwise, the Judiciary necessarily takes to itself further authority to govern the country without express constitutional authority. The claimed right pressed on us today falls far short of overcoming this resistance.

[Hardwick], however, asserts that the result should be different where the homosexual conduct occurs in the privacy of the home. He relies on *Stanley v. Georgia*, where the Court held that the First Amendment prevents conviction for possessing and reading obscene material in the privacy of one's home:

If the First Amendment means anything, it means that a State has no business telling a man, sitting alone in his house, what books he may read or what films he may watch.

Stanley did protect conduct that would not have been protected outside the home, and it partially prevented the enforcement of state obscenity laws; but the decision was firmly grounded in the First Amendment. The right pressed upon us here has no similar support in the text of the Constitution, and it does not qualify for recognition under the prevailing principles for construing the Fourteenth Amendment. Its limits are also difficult to discern. Plainly enough, otherwise illegal conduct is not always immunized whenever it occurs in the home. Victimless crimes, such as the possession and use of illegal drugs, do not escape the law where they are committed at home. *Stanley* itself recognized that its holding offered no protection for the possession in the home of drugs, firearms, or stolen goods. And if [Hardwick's] submission is limited to the voluntary sexual conduct between consenting adults, it would be difficult, except by fiat, to limit the claimed right to homosexual conduct while leaving exposed to prosecution adultery, incest, and other sexual crimes even though they are committed in the home. We are unwilling to start down that road.

Even if the conduct at issue here is not a fundamental right, [Hardwick] asserts that there must be a rational basis for the law, and that there is none in this case other than the presumed belief of a majority of the electorate in Georgia that homosexual sodomy is immoral and unacceptable. This is said to be an inadequate rationale to support the law. The law, however, is constantly based on notions of morality, and if all laws representing essentially moral choices are to be invalidated under the Due Process Clause, the courts will be very busy indeed. Even [Hardwick] makes no such claim, but insists that majority sentiments about the morality of homosexuality should be declared inadequate. We do not agree, and are unpersuaded that the sodomy laws of some 25 States should be invalidated on this basis.

Burger, concurring:

I join the Court's opinion, but I write separately to underscore my view that, in constitutional terms, there is no such thing as a fundamental right to commit homosexual sodomy.

As the Court notes, the proscriptions against sodomy have very "ancient roots." Decisions of individuals relating to homosexual conduct have been subject to state intervention throughout the history of Western civilization. Condemnation of those practices is firmly rooted in Judeo-Christian moral and ethical standards. Homosexual sodomy was a capital crime under Roman law. During the English Reformation, when powers of the ecclesiastical courts were transferred to the King's Courts, the first English statute criminalizing sodomy was passed. Blackstone described "the infamous crime against nature" as an offense of "deeper malignity" than rape, a heinous act "the very mention of which is a disgrace to human nature," and "a crime not fit to be named." The common law of England, including its prohibition of sodomy, became the received law of Georgia and the other Colonies. In 1816, the Georgia Legislature passed the statute at issue here, and that statute has been continuously in force in one form or another since that time. To hold that the act of homosexual sodomy is somehow protected as a fundamental right would be to cast aside millennia of moral teaching.

This is essentially not a question of personal "preferences," but rather of the legislative authority of the State. I find nothing in the Constitution depriving a State of the power to enact the statute challenged here.

Powell, concurring:

. . . I agree with the Court that there is no fundamental right—i.e., no substantive right under the Due Process Clause—such as that claimed by Hardwick, and found to exist by the Court of Appeals. This is not to suggest, however, that [he] may not be protected by the Eighth Amendment of the Constitution. The Georgia statute at issue in this case, authorizes a court to imprison a person for up to 20 years for a single private, consensual act of sodomy. In my view, a prison sentence for such conduct—certainly a sentence of long duration—would create a serious Eighth Amendment issue. Under the Georgia statute, a single act of sodomy, even in the private setting of a home, is a felony comparable in terms of the possible sentence imposed to serious felonies such as aggravated battery, first-degree arson, and robbery.

In this case, however, [Hardwick] has not been tried, much less convicted and sentenced. Moreover, [he] has not raised the Eighth Amendment issue below. For these reasons this constitutional argument is not before us.

Blackmun, dissenting:

This case is no more about "a fundamental right to engage in homosexual sodomy," as the Court purports to declare than *Stanley v. Georgia* was about a fundamental right to watch obscene movies, or *Katz v. United States* was about a fundamental right to place interstate bets from a telephone booth. Rather, this case is about "the most comprehensive of rights and the right most valued by civilized men," namely, "the right to be let alone."

The statute at issue, denies individuals the right to decide for themselves whether to engage in particular forms of private, consensual sexual activity. The Court concludes that [it] is valid essentially because "the laws of . . . many States . . . still make such conduct illegal and have done so for a very long time." But the

fact that the moral judgments expressed by statutes like [this one] may be "natural and familiar . . . ought not to conclude our judgment upon the question whether statutes embodying them conflict with the Constitution of the United States."

. . . Like Justice Holmes, I believe that [i]t is revolting to have no better reason for a rule of law than that so it was laid down in the time of Henry IV. It is still more revolting if the grounds upon which it was laid down have vanished long since, and the rule simply persists from blind imitation of the past. I believe we must analyze Hardwick's claim in the light of the values that underlie the constitutional right to privacy. If that right means anything, it means that, before Georgia can prosecute its citizens for making choices about the most intimate aspects of their lives, it must do more than assert that the choice they have made is an "'abominable crime not fit to be named among Christians.'"

In its haste to reverse the Court of Appeals and hold that the Constitution does not "confe[r] a fundamental right upon homosexuals to engage in sodomy," the Court relegates the actual statute being challenged to a footnote, and ignores the procedural posture of the case before it. A fair reading of the statute and of the complaint clearly reveals that the majority has distorted the question this case presents.

First, the Court's almost obsessive focus on homosexual activity is particularly hard to justify in light of the broad language Georgia has used. Unlike the Court, the Georgia Legislature has not proceeded on the assumption that homosexuals are so different from other citizens that their lives may be controlled in a way that would not be tolerated if it limited the choices of those other citizens. Rather, Georgia has provided that "[a] person commits the offense of sodomy when he performs or submits to any sexual act involving the sex organs of one person and the mouth or anus of another."

The sex or status of the persons who engage in the act is irrelevant as a matter of state law. In fact, to the extent I can discern a legislative purpose for Georgia's 1968 enactment of §16-6-2, that purpose seems to have been to broaden the coverage of the law to reach heterosexual as well as homosexual activity. I therefore see no basis for the Court's decision to treat this case as an "as applied" challenge to §16-6-2, or for Georgia's attempt, both in its brief and at oral argument, to defend §16-6-2 solely on the grounds that it prohibits homosexual activity. Michael Hardwick's standing may rest in significant part on Georgia's apparent willingness to enforce against homosexuals a law it seems not to have any desire to enforce against heterosexuals. But his claim that §16-6-2 involves an unconstitutional intrusion into his privacy and his right of intimate association does not depend in any way on his sexual orientation.

Second, I disagree with the Court's refusal to consider whether §16-6-2 runs afoul of the Eighth or Ninth Amendments or the Equal Protection Clause of the Fourteenth Amendment. [Hardwick]'s complaint expressly invoked the Ninth Amendment, and he relied heavily before this Court on *Griswold v. Connecticut,* which identifies that Amendment as one of the specific constitutional provisions giving "life and substance" to our understanding of privacy. More importantly, the procedural posture of the case requires that we affirm the Court of Appeals' judgment if there is any ground on which [Hardwick] may be entitled to relief. . . .

Our cases long have recognized that the Constitution embodies a promise that a certain private sphere of individual liberty will be kept largely beyond the reach of government. In construing the right to privacy, the Court has proceeded along two somewhat distinct, albeit complementary, lines. First, it has recognized a privacy interest with reference to certain decisions that are properly for the individual to make. Second, it has recognized a privacy interest with reference to certain places without regard for the particular activities in which the individuals who occupy them are engaged. The case before us implicates both the decisional and the spatial aspects of the right to privacy.

The Court concludes today that none of our prior cases dealing with various decisions that individuals are entitled to make free of governmental interference "bears any resemblance to the claimed constitutional right of homosexuals to engage in acts of sodomy that is asserted in this case." While it is true that these cases may be characterized by their connection to protection of the family, the Court's conclusion that they extend no further than this boundary ignores the warning in *Moore v. East Cleveland* against clos[ing] our eyes to the basic reasons why certain rights associated with the family have been accorded shelter under the Fourteenth Amendment's Due Process Clause.

We protect those rights not because they contribute, in some direct and material way, to the general public welfare, but because they form so central

a part of an individual's life. "[T]he concept of privacy embodies the 'moral fact that a person belongs to himself, and not others nor to society as a whole'" . . .

In a variety of circumstances, we have recognized that a necessary corollary of giving individuals freedom to choose how to conduct their lives is acceptance of the fact that different individuals will make different choices. For example, in holding that the clearly important state interest in public education should give way to a competing claim by the Amish to the effect that extended formal schooling threatened their way of life, the Court declared

"There can be no assumption that today's majority is 'right' and the Amish and others like them are 'wrong.' A way of life that is odd or even erratic, but interferes with no rights or interests of others, is not to be condemned because it is different." *Wisconsin v. Yoder*

The behavior for which Hardwick faces prosecution occurred in his own home, a place to which the Fourth Amendment attaches special significance. The Court's treatment of this aspect of the case is symptomatic of its overall refusal to consider the broad principles that have informed our treatment of privacy in specific cases. Just as the right to privacy is more than the mere aggregation of a number of entitlements to engage in specific behavior, so too protecting the physical integrity of the home is more than merely a means of protecting specific activities that often take place there. Even when our understanding of the contours of the right to privacy depends on "reference to a 'place,'" *Katz v. United States,* "the essence of a Fourth Amendment violation is "not the breaking of [a person's] doors, and the rummaging of his drawers," but rather is "the invasion of his indefeasible right of personal security, personal liberty and private property." *California v. Ciraolo*

The Court's interpretation of the pivotal case of *Stanley v. Georgia* is entirely unconvincing. *Stanley* held that Georgia's undoubted power to punish the public distribution of constitutionally unprotected, obscene material did not permit the State to punish the private possession of such material. According to the majority here, Stanley relied entirely on the First Amendment, and thus, it is claimed, sheds no light on cases not involving printed materials. But that is not what *Stanley* said. Rather, the Stanley Court anchored its holding in the Fourth Amendment's special protection for the individual in his home. . . .

... Indeed, the right of an individual to conduct intimate relationships in the intimacy of his or her own home seems to me to be the heart of the Constitution's protection of privacy. ...

Cruzan v. Director, Missouri Department of Health

497 U.S. 261 (1990), 5-4

Opinion of the Court: Rephnquist (Kennedy, O'Connor, Scalia, White)

Dissenting: Blackmun, Brennan, Marshall, Stevens

Did the Court decide for or against the Cruzans? What are the interests of the state? Are they reasonable ones? What kind of evidence would overcome them? Is it fair to describe the issue in this case as "the right to die"? How could it be more precisely phrased?

Rehnquist, for the Court:

Petitioner Nancy Beth Cruzan was rendered incompetent as a result of severe injuries sustained during an automobile accident. Copetitioners Lester and Joyce Cruzan, Nancy's parents and coguardians, sought a court order directing the withdrawal of their daughter's artificial feeding and hydration equipment after it became apparent that she had virtually no chance of recovering her cognitive faculties. The Supreme Court of Missouri held that, because there was no clear and convincing evidence of Nancy's desire to have life-sustaining treatment withdrawn under such circumstances, her parents lacked authority to effectuate such a request. ...

We granted certiorari to consider the question of whether Cruzan has a right under the United States Constitution which would require the hospital to withdraw life-sustaining treatment from her under these circumstances. ...

... This is the first case in which we have been squarely presented with the issue of whether the United States Constitution grants what is in common parlance referred to as a "right to die." ... The Fourteenth Amendment provides that no State shall "deprive any person of life, liberty, or property, without due process of law." The principle that a competent person has a constitutionally protected liberty interest in refusing unwanted medical treatment may be inferred from our prior decisions. In *Jacobson v. Massachusetts,* for instance, the Court balanced an individual's liberty interest in declining an unwanted smallpox vaccine against the State's interest in preventing disease. Decisions prior to the incorporation of the Fourth Amendment into the Fourteenth Amendment analyzed searches and seizures involving the body under the Due Process Clause and were thought to implicate substantial liberty interests. ...

But determining that a person has a "liberty interest" under the Due Process Clause does not end the inquiry; "whether respondent's constitutional rights have been violated must be determined by balancing his liberty interests against the relevant state interests." *Youngberg v. Romeo*

Petitioners insist that, under the general holdings of our cases, the forced administration of life-sustaining medical treatment, and even of artificially-delivered food and water essential to life, would implicate a competent person's liberty interest. Although we think the logic of the cases discussed above would embrace such a liberty interest, the dramatic consequences involved in refusal of such treatment would inform the inquiry as to whether the deprivation of that interest is constitutionally permissible. But for purposes of this case, we assume that the United States Constitution would grant a competent person a constitutionally protected right to refuse lifesaving hydration and nutrition.

Petitioners go on to assert that an incompetent person should possess the same right in this respect as is possessed by a competent person. ...

The difficulty with petitioners' claim is that, in a sense, it begs the question: an incompetent person is not able to make an informed and voluntary choice to exercise a hypothetical right to refuse treatment or any other right. Such a "right" must be exercised for her, if at all, by some sort of surrogate. Here, Missouri has in effect recognized that, under certain circumstances, a surrogate may act for the patient in electing to have hydration and nutrition withdrawn in such a way as to cause death, but it has established a procedural safeguard to assure that the action of the surrogate conforms as best it may to the wishes expressed by the patient while competent. Missouri requires that evidence of the incompetent's wishes as to the withdrawal of treatment be proved by clear and convincing evidence. The question, then, is whether the United States Constitution forbids the establishment of this procedural requirement by the State. We hold that it does not.

Whether or not Missouri's clear and convincing evidence requirement comports with the United States Constitution depends in part on what interests the State may properly seek to protect in this situation. Missouri relies on its interest in the protection and preservation of human life, and there can be no gainsaying this interest. As a general matter, the States—indeed, all civilized nations—demonstrate their commitment to life by treating homicide as serious crime. Moreover, the majority of States in this country have laws imposing criminal penalties on one who assists another to commit suicide. We do not think a State is required to remain neutral in the face of an informed and voluntary decision by a physically able adult to starve to death.

But in the context presented here, a State has more particular interests at stake. The choice between life and death is a deeply personal decision of obvious and overwhelming finality. We believe Missouri may legitimately seek to safeguard the personal element of this choice through the imposition of heightened evidentiary requirements. It cannot be disputed that the Due Process Clause protects an interest in life as well as an interest in refusing life-sustaining medical treatment. Not all incompetent patients will have loved ones available to serve as surrogate decisionmakers. And even where family members are present, "[t]here will, of course, be some unfortunate situations in which family members will not act to protect a patient." *In re Jobes* A State is entitled to guard against potential abuses in such situations. Similarly, a State is entitled to consider that a judicial proceeding to make a determination regarding an incompetent's wishes may very well not be an adversarial one, with the added guarantee of accurate factfinding that the adversary process brings with it. Finally, we think a State may properly decline to make judgments about the "quality" of life that a particular individual may enjoy, and simply assert an unqualified interest in the preservation of human life to be weighed against the constitutionally protected interests of the individual.

In our view, Missouri has permissibly sought to advance these interests through the adoption of a "clear and convincing" standard of proof to govern such proceedings. . . .

We think it self-evident that the interests at stake in the instant proceedings are more substantial, both on an individual and societal level, than those involved in a run-of-the-mine civil dispute. But not only does the standard of proof reflect the importance of a particular adjudication, it also serves as "a societal judgment about how the risk of error should be distributed between the litigants." The more stringent the burden of proof a party must bear, the more that party bears the risk of an erroneous decision. We believe that Missouri may permissibly place an increased risk of an erroneous decision on those seeking to terminate an incompetent individual's life-sustaining treatment. An erroneous decision not to terminate results in a maintenance of the status quo; the possibility of subsequent developments such as advancements in medical science, the discovery of new evidence regarding the patient's intent, changes in the law, or simply the unexpected death of the patient despite the administration of life-sustaining treatment, at least create the potential that a wrong decision will eventually be corrected or its impact mitigated. An erroneous decision to withdraw life-sustaining treatment, however, is not susceptible of correction. . . .

. . . There is no doubt that statutes requiring wills to be in writing, and statutes of frauds which require that a contract to make a will be in writing, on occasion frustrate the effectuation of the intent of a particular decedent, just as Missouri's requirement of proof in this case may have frustrated the effectuation of the not-fully-expressed desires of Nancy Cruzan. But the Constitution does not require general rules to work faultlessly; no general rule can.

In sum, we conclude that a State may apply a clear and convincing evidence standard in proceedings where a guardian seeks to discontinue nutrition and hydration of a person diagnosed to be in a persistent vegetative state. We note that many courts which have adopted some sort of substituted judgment procedure in situations like this, whether they limit consideration of evidence to the prior expressed wishes of the incompetent individual, or whether they allow more general proof of what the individual's decision would have been, require a clear and convincing standard of proof for such evidence.

The Supreme Court of Missouri held that . . . the testimony adduced at trial did not amount to clear and convincing proof of the patient's desire to have hydration and nutrition withdrawn. In so doing, it reversed a decision of the Missouri trial court, which had found that the evidence "suggest[ed]" Nancy Cruzan would not have desired to continue such measures, but which had not adopted the standard of "clear and convincing evidence" enunciated by the Supreme Court. The testimony adduced at trial consisted primarily of Nancy Cruzan's statements, made to a housemate about a year before her accident, that she would not want to live should she face life as a "vegetable," and other observations to the same effect. The observations did not deal in terms with withdrawal of medical treatment or of hydration and nutrition. We cannot say that the Supreme Court of Missouri committed constitutional error in reaching the conclusion that it did.

Petitioners alternatively contend that Missouri must accept the "substituted judgment" of close family members even in the absence of substantial proof that their views reflect the views of the patient. They rely primarily upon our decisions in *Michael H. v. Gerald D.* and *Parham v. J.R.* But we do not think these cases support their claim. In *Michael H.*, we upheld the constitutionality of California's favored treatment of traditional family relationships; such a holding may not be turned around into a constitutional requirement that a State must recognize the primacy of those relationships in a situation like this. And in *Parham*, where the patient was a minor, we also upheld the constitutionality of a state scheme in which parents made certain decisions for mentally ill minors. Here again, petitioners would seek to turn a decision which allowed a State to rely on family decisionmaking into a constitutional requirement that the State recognize such decisionmaking. But constitutional law does not work that way.

No doubt is engendered by anything in this record but that Nancy Cruzan's mother and father are loving and caring parents. If the State were required by the United States Constitution to repose a right of "substituted judgment" with anyone, the Cruzans would surely qualify. But we do not think the Due Process Clause requires the State to repose judgment on these matters with anyone but the patient herself. Close family members may have a strong feeling—a feeling not at all ignoble or unworthy, but not entirely disinterested, either—that they do not wish to witness the continuation of the life of a loved one which they regard as hopeless, meaningless, and even degrading. But there is no automatic assurance that the view of close family members will necessarily be the same as the patient's would have been had she been confronted with the prospect of her situation while competent. All of the reasons previously discussed for allowing Missouri to require clear and convincing evidence of the patient's wishes lead us to conclude that the State may choose to defer only to

those wishes, rather than confide the decision to close family members.

O'Connor, concurring:

I agree that a protected liberty interest in refusing unwanted medical treatment may be inferred from our prior decisions, and that the refusal of artificially delivered food and water is encompassed within that liberty interest. I write separately to clarify why I believe this to be so.

As the Court notes, the liberty interest in refusing medical treatment flows from decisions involving the State's invasions into the body. Because our notions of liberty are inextricably entwined with our idea of physical freedom and self-determination, the Court has often deemed state incursions into the body repugnant to the interests protected by the Due Process Clause. . . .

The State's imposition of medical treatment on an unwilling competent adult necessarily involves some form of restraint and intrusion. . . .

. . . Artificial feeding cannot readily be distinguished from other forms of medical treatment. . . . Requiring a competent adult to endure such procedures against her will burdens the patient's liberty, dignity, and freedom to determine the course of her own treatment. Accordingly, the liberty guaranteed by the Due Process Clause must protect, if it protects anything, an individual's deeply personal decision to reject medical treatment, including the artificial delivery of food and water. . . .

Today's decision, holding only that the Constitution permits a State to require clear and convincing evidence of Nancy Cruzan's desire to have artificial hydration and nutrition withdrawn, does not preclude a future determination that the Constitution requires the States to implement the decisions of a patient's duly appointed surrogate. Nor does it prevent States from developing other approaches for protecting an incompetent individual's liberty interest in refusing medical treatment. As is evident from the Court's survey of state court decisions, no national consensus has yet emerged on the best solution for this difficult and sensitive problem. Today we decide only that one State's practice does not violate the Constitution; the more challenging task of crafting appropriate procedures for safeguarding incompetents' liberty interests is entrusted to the "laboratory" of the States . . .

Brennan, dissenting:

. . . Because I believe that Nancy Cruzan has a fundamental right to be free of unwanted artificial nutrition and hydration, which right is not outweighed by any interests of the State, and because I find that the improperly biased procedural obstacles imposed by the Missouri Supreme Court impermissibly burden that right, I respectfully dissent. Nancy Cruzan is entitled to choose to die with dignity . . .

. . . Nor does the fact that Nancy Cruzan is now incompetent deprive her of her fundamental rights. . . . As the majority recognizes, the question is not whether an incompetent has constitutional rights, but how such rights may be exercised. . . .

Although the right to be free of unwanted medical intervention, like other constitutionally protected interests, may not be absolute, no State interest could outweigh the rights of an individual in Nancy Cruzan's position. Whatever a State's possible interests in mandating life-support treatment under other circumstances, there is no good to be obtained here by Missouri's insistence that Nancy Cruzan remain on life-support systems if it is indeed her wish not to do so. Missouri does not claim, nor could it, that society as a whole will be benefited by Nancy's receiving medical treatment. No third party's situation will be improved, and no harm to others will be averted.

The only state interest asserted here is a general interest in the preservation of life. But the State has no legitimate general interest in someone's life, completely abstracted from the interest of the person living that life, that could outweigh the person's choice to avoid medical treatment. . . .

This is not to say that the State has no legitimate interests to assert here. As the majority recognizes, Missouri has a parens patriae interest in providing Nancy Cruzan, now incompetent, with as accurate as possible a determination of how she would exercise her rights under these circumstances. Second, if and when it is determined that Nancy Cruzan would want to continue treatment, the State may legitimately assert an interest in providing that treatment. But until Nancy's wishes have been determined, the only state interest that may be asserted is an interest in safeguarding the accuracy of that determination.

Accuracy, therefore, must be our touchstone. Missouri may constitutionally impose only those procedural requirements that serve to enhance the accuracy of a determination of Nancy Cruzan's wishes or are at least consistent with an accurate determination. The

Missouri "safeguard" that the Court upholds today does not meet that standard. The determination needed in this context is whether the incompetent person would choose to live in a persistent vegetative state on life-support or to avoid this medical treatment.

Missouri's rule of decision imposes a markedly asymmetrical evidentiary burden. Only evidence of specific statements of treatment choice made by the patient when competent is admissible to support a finding that the patient, now in a persistent vegetative state, would wish to avoid further medical treatment. Moreover, this evidence must be clear and convincing. No proof is required to support a finding that the incompetent person would wish to continue treatment. . . .

. . . The new medical technology can reclaim those who would have been irretrievably lost a few decades ago and restore them to active lives. For Nancy Cruzan, it failed, and for others with wasting incurable disease it may be doomed to failure. In these unfortunate situations, the bodies and preferences and memories of the victims do not escheat to the State; nor does our Constitution permit the State or any other government to commandeer them. No singularity of feeling exists upon which such a government might confidently rely as parens patriae. . . .

. . . Yet Missouri and this Court have displaced Nancy's own assessment of the processes associated with dying. They have discarded evidence of her will, ignored her values, and deprived her of the right to a decision as closely approximating her own choice as humanly possible. They have done so disingenuously in her name, and openly in Missouri's own. That Missouri and this Court may truly be motivated only by concern for incompetent patients makes no matter. As one of our most prominent jurists warned us decades ago: "Experience should teach us to be most on our guard to protect liberty when the government's purposes are beneficent. . . . The greatest dangers to liberty lurk in insidious encroachment by men of zeal, well meaning but without understanding." *Olmstead v. United States*, Brandeis, dissenting.

Stevens, dissenting:

Our Constitution is born of the proposition that all legitimate governments must secure the equal right of every person to "Life, Liberty, and the pursuit of Happiness." In the ordinary case, we quite naturally assume that these three ends are compatible, mutually enhancing, and perhaps even coincident. The Court would make an exception here. It permits the State's abstract, undifferentiated interest in the preservation of life to overwhelm the best interests of Nancy Beth Cruzan, interests which would, according to an undisputed finding, be served by allowing her guardians to exercise her constitutional right to discontinue medical treatment. Ironically, the Court reaches this conclusion despite endorsing three significant propositions which should save it from any such dilemma. First, a competent individual's decision to refuse life-sustaining medical procedures is an aspect of liberty protected by the Due Process Clause of the Fourteenth Amendment. Second, upon a proper evidentiary showing, a qualified guardian may make that decision on behalf of an incompetent ward. Third, in answering the important question presented by this tragic case, it is wise "not to attempt by any general statement, to cover every possible phase of the subject." Together, these considerations suggest that Nancy Cruzan's liberty to be free from medical treatment must be understood in light of the facts and circumstances particular to her.

I would so hold: in my view, the Constitution requires the State to care for Nancy Cruzan's life in a way that gives appropriate respect to her own best interests. . . .

In this case, as is no doubt true in many others, the predicament confronted by the healthy members of the Cruzan family merely adds emphasis to the best interests finding made by the trial judge. Each of us has an interest in the kind of memories that will survive after death. To that end, individual decisions are often motivated by their impact on others. A member of the kind of family identified in the trial court's findings in this case would likely have not only a normal interest in minimizing the burden that her own illness imposes on others but also an interest in having their memories of her filled predominantly with thoughts about her past vitality rather than her current condition. The meaning and completion of her life should be controlled by persons who have her best interests at heart—not by a state legislature concerned only with the "preservation of human life."

The Cruzan family's continuing concern provides a concrete reminder that Nancy Cruzan's interests did not disappear with her vitality or her consciousness. However commendable may be the State's interest in human life, it cannot pursue that interest by appropriating Nancy Cruzan's life as a symbol for its own purposes. Lives do not exist in abstraction from persons, and to pretend otherwise is not to honor but to desecrate the State's responsibility for protecting life. A State that seeks to demonstrate its commitment to life may do so by aiding those who are actively struggling for life and health. In this endeavor, unfortunately, no State can lack for opportunities: there can be no need to make an example of tragic cases like that of Nancy Cruzan.

Washington v. Glucksberg

521 U.S. 702 (1997), 9-0
Opinion of the Court: Rehnquist (Kennedy, O'Connor, Scalia, Thomas)
Concurring: Breyer, Ginsberg, O'Connor, Souter, Stevens

What constitutional right or rights are claimed in this case? What state interests does the Court address? Is the decision consistent with the Cruzan *case (p. 321)? Why have dissenting justices in* Cruzan *joined the majority or concurred with it in this case? Does the decision here prevent either a state from conferring a right to commit suicide or a right of a doctor to assist a patient in committing suicide?*

Rehnquist, for the Court:

. . . It has always been a crime to assist a suicide in the State of Washington. . . . Today, Washington law provides: "A person is guilty of promoting a suicide attempt when he knowingly causes or aids another person to attempt suicide." . . . "Promoting a suicide attempt" is a felony, punishable by up to five years' imprisonment and up to a $10,000 fine. At the same time, Washington's Natural Death Act, enacted in 1979, states that the "withholding or withdrawal of life sustaining treatment" at a patient's direction "shall not, for any purpose, constitute a suicide."

Petitioners in this case are the State of Washington and its Attorney General. Respondents . . . are physicians who practice in Washington. These doctors occasionally treat terminally ill, suffering patients, and declare that they would assist these patients in ending their lives if not for Washington's assisted suicide ban. In January 1994, respondents, along with three gravely ill, pseudonymous plaintiffs who have since died and Compassion in Dying, a nonprofit organization that counsels people considering physician assisted suicide, sued in the United States District Court, seeking a declaration that Wash Rev. Code 9A.36.060(1) (1994) is, on its face, unconstitutional. The plaintiffs asserted "the existence of a liberty interest protected by the Fourteenth Amendment which extends to a personal choice by a mentally competent, terminally ill adult to commit physician assisted suicide."...

We begin, as we do in all due process cases, by examining our Nation's history, legal traditions, and practices. In almost every State—indeed, in almost every western democracy—it is a crime to assist a suicide. The States' assisted suicide bans are not innovations. Rather, they are longstanding expressions of the States' commitment to the protection and preservation of all human life....

More specifically, for over 700 years, the Anglo American common law tradition has punished or otherwise disapproved of both suicide and assisting suicide....

Though deeply rooted, the States' assisted suicide bans have in recent years been reexamined and, generally, reaffirmed. Because of advances in medicine and technology, Americans today are increasingly likely to die in institutions, from chronic illnesses. Public concern and democratic action are therefore sharply focused on how best to protect dignity and independence at the end of life, with the result that there have been many significant changes in state laws and in the attitudes these laws reflect. Many States, for example, now permit "living wills," surrogate health care decisionmaking, and the withdrawal or refusal of life sustaining medical treatment. At the same time, however, voters and legislators continue for the most part to reaffirm their States' prohibitions on assisting suicide.

The Washington statute at issue in this case, Wash. Rev. Code §9A.36.060 (1994), was enacted in 1975 as part of a revision of that State's criminal code. Four years later, Washington passed its Natural Death Act, which specifically stated that the "withholding or withdrawal of life sustaining treatment... shall not, for any purpose, constitute a suicide" and that "[n]othing in this chapter shall be construed to condone, authorize, or approve mercy killing...." In 1991, Washington voters rejected a ballot initiative which, had it passed, would have permitted a form of physician assisted suicide. Washington then added a provision to the Natural Death Act expressly excluding physician assisted suicide.

California voters rejected an assisted suicide initiative similar to Washington's in 1993. On the other hand, in 1994, voters in Oregon enacted, also through ballot initiative, that State's "Death With Dignity Act,"

which legalized physician assisted suicide for competent, terminally ill adults. Since the Oregon vote, many proposals to legalize assisted suicide have been and continue to be introduced in the States' legislatures, but none has been enacted. And just last year, Iowa and Rhode Island joined the overwhelming majority of States explicitly prohibiting assisted suicide. Also, on April 30, 1997, President Clinton signed the Federal Assisted Suicide Funding Restriction Act of 1997, which prohibits the use of federal funds in support of physician assisted suicide.

Thus, the States are currently engaged in serious, thoughtful examinations of physician assisted suicide and other similar issues....

... [O]ur laws have consistently condemned, and continue to prohibit, assisting suicide. Despite changes in medical technology and notwithstanding an increased emphasis on the importance of end of life decisionmaking, we have not retreated from this prohibition. Against this backdrop of history, tradition, and practice, we now turn to respondents' constitutional claim.

The Due Process Clause guarantees more than fair process, and the "liberty" it protects includes more than the absence of physical restraint.... The Clause also provides heightened protection against government interference with certain fundamental rights and liberty interests. In a long line of cases, we have held that, in addition to the specific freedoms protected by the Bill of Rights, the "liberty" specially protected by the Due Process Clause includes the rights to marry, *Loving v. Virginia;* to have children, *Skinner v. Oklahoma ex rel. Williamson,;* to direct the education and upbringing of one's children, *Meyer v. Nebraska, Pierce v. Society of Sisters;* to marital privacy, *Griswold v. Connecticut;* to use contraception, *Eisenstadt v. Baird;* to bodily integrity, *Rochin v. California;* and to abortion, [*Planned Parenthood of Southeastern Pennsylvania* v.] *Casey.* We have also assumed, and strongly suggested, that the Due Process Clause protects the traditional right to refuse unwanted lifesaving medical treatment. *Cruzan* [v. *Director, Missouri Department of Health*].

But we "ha[ve] always been reluctant to expand the concept of substantive due process because guideposts for responsible decisionmaking in this unchartered area are scarce and open ended." By extending constitutional protection to an asserted right or liberty interest, we, to a great extent, place the matter outside the arena of public debate and legislative action. We must therefore "exercise the utmost care whenever we are asked to break new ground in this field," lest the liberty protected by the Due Process Clause be subtly transformed into the policy preferences of the members of this Court.

Our established method of substantive due process analysis has two primary features: First, we have regularly observed that the Due Process Clause specially protects those fundamental rights and liberties which are, objectively, "deeply rooted in this Nation's history and tradition," Second, we have required in substantive due process cases a "careful description" of the asserted fundamental liberty interest. . . .

. . . This approach tends to rein in the subjective elements that are necessarily present in due process judicial review. In addition, by establishing a threshold requirement—that a challenged state action implicate a fundamental right—before requiring more than a reasonable relation to a legitimate state interest to justify the action, it avoids the need for complex balancing of competing interests in every case.

. . . [R]espondents assert a "liberty to choose how to die" and a right to "control of one's final days," and describe the asserted liberty as "the right to choose a humane, dignified death," and "the liberty to shape death." . . .

We now inquire whether this asserted right has any place in our Nation's traditions. Here, we are confronted with a consistent and almost universal tradition that has long rejected the asserted right, and continues explicitly to reject it today, even for terminally ill, mentally competent adults. To hold for respondents, we would have to reverse centuries of legal doctrine and practice, and strike down the considered policy choice of almost every State.

Respondents contend, however, that the liberty interest they assert is consistent with this Court's substantive due process line of cases, if not with this Nation's history and practice. Pointing to *Casey* and *Cruzan*, respondents read our jurisprudence in this area as reflecting a general tradition of "self sovereignty," and as teaching that the "liberty" protected by the Due Process Clause includes "basic and intimate exercises of personal autonomy." According to respondents, our liberty jurisprudence, and the broad, individualistic principles it reflects, protects the "liberty of competent, terminally ill adults to make end of life decisions free of undue government interference." The question presented in this case, however, is whether the protections of the Due

Process Clause include a right to commit suicide with another's assistance. With this "careful description" of respondents' claim in mind, we turn to *Casey* and *Cruzan*.

In *Cruzan*, we considered whether Nancy Beth Cruzan, who had been severely injured in an automobile accident and was in a persistive vegetative state, "ha[d] a right under the United States Constitution which would require the hospital to withdraw life sustaining treatment" at her parents' request. . . . "[F]or purposes of [that] case, we assume[d] that the United States Constitution would grant a competent person a constitutionally protected right to refuse lifesaving hydration and nutrition." We concluded that, notwithstanding this right, the Constitution permitted Missouri to require clear and convincing evidence of an incompetent patient's wishes concerning the withdrawal of life sustaining treatment. . . .

. . . In *Cruzan* itself, we recognized that most States outlawed assisted suicide—and even more do today—and we certainly gave no intimation that the right to refuse unwanted medical treatment could be somehow transmuted into a right to assistance in committing suicide. . . .

. . . That many of the rights and liberties protected by the Due Process Clause sound in personal autonomy does not warrant the sweeping conclusion that any and all important, intimate, and personal decisions are so protected.

The history of the law's treatment of assisted suicide in this country has been and continues to be one of the rejection of nearly all efforts to permit it. That being the case, our decisions lead us to conclude that the asserted "right" to assistance in committing suicide is not a fundamental liberty interest protected by the Due Process Clause. The Constitution also requires, however, that Washington's assisted suicide ban be rationally related to legitimate government interests. This requirement is unquestionably met here. As the court below recognized, Washington's assisted suicide ban implicates a number of state interests.

First, Washington has an "unqualified interest in the preservation of human life." . . .

The State also has an interest in protecting the integrity and ethics of the medical profession. In contrast to the Court of Appeals' conclusion that "the integrity of the medical profession would [not] be threatened in any way by [physician assisted suicide]," the American Medical Association, like many other medical and physicians' groups, has concluded that "[p]hysician assisted suicide is fundamentally incompatible with the physician's role as healer." . . .

Next, the State has an interest in protecting vulnerable groups—including the poor, the elderly, and disabled persons—from abuse, neglect, and mistakes. The Court of Appeals dismissed the State's concern that disadvantaged persons might be pressured into physician assisted suicide as "ludicrous on its face." We have recognized, however, the real risk of subtle coercion and undue influence in end of life situations. . . .

Finally, the State may fear that permitting assisted suicide will start it down the path to voluntary and perhaps even involuntary euthanasia. . . . [W]hat is couched as a limited right to "physician assisted suicide" is likely, in effect, a much broader license, which could prove extremely difficult to police and contain. . . .

We therefore hold that Wash. Rev. Code §9A.36.060(1) does not violate the Fourteenth Amendment, either on its face or "as applied to competent, terminally ill adults who wish to hasten their deaths by obtaining medication prescribed by their doctors."

Throughout the Nation, Americans are engaged in an earnest and profound debate about the morality, legality, and practicality of physician assisted suicide. Our holding permits this debate to continue, as it should in a democratic society. . . .

O'Connor, concurring:

. . . I join the Court's opinions because I agree that there is no generalized right to "commit suicide." But respondents urge us to address the narrower question whether a mentally competent person who is experiencing great suffering has a constitutionally cognizable interest in controlling the circumstances of his or her imminent death. I see no need to reach that question in the context of the facial challenges to the New York and Washington laws at issue here. . . .

. . . There is no dispute that dying patients in Washington and New York can obtain palliative care, even when doing so would hasten their deaths. The difficulty in defining terminal illness and the risk that a dying patient's request for assistance in ending his or her life might not be truly voluntary justifies the prohibitions on assisted suicide we uphold here.

Stevens, concurring:

. . . I write separately to make it clear that there is also room for further debate about the limits that the

Constitution places on the power of the States to punish the practice [of physician assisted suicide]. . . .

. . . Although as a general matter the State's interest in the contributions each person may make to society outweighs the person's interest in ending her life, this interest does not have the same force for a terminally ill patient faced not with the choice of whether to live, only of how to die. . . .

Similarly, the State's legitimate interests in preventing suicide, protecting the vulnerable from coercion and abuse, and preventing euthanasia are less significant in this context. I agree that the State has a compelling interest in preventing persons from committing suicide because of depression, or coercion by third parties. But the State's legitimate interest in preventing abuse does not apply to an individual who is not victimized by abuse, who is not suffering from depression, and who makes a rational and voluntary decision to seek assistance in dying. . . .

Relatedly, the State and amici express the concern that patients whose physical pain is inadequately treated will be more likely to request assisted suicide. Encouraging the development and ensuring the availability of adequate pain treatment is of utmost importance; palliative care, however, cannot alleviate all pain and suffering. . . .

The final major interest asserted by the State is its interest in preserving the traditional integrity of the medical profession. The fear is that a rule permitting physicians to assist in suicide is inconsistent with the perception that they serve their patients solely as healers. But for some patients, it would be a physician's refusal to dispense medication to ease their suffering and make their death tolerable and dignified that would be inconsistent with the healing role . . .

Souter, concurring:

. . . The argument supporting respondents' position thus progresses through three steps of increasing forcefulness. First, it emphasizes the decriminalization of suicide. Reliance on this fact is sanctioned under the standard that looks not only to the tradition retained, but to society's occasional choices to reject traditions of the legal past. While the common law prohibited both suicide and aiding a suicide, with the prohibition on aiding largely justified by the primary prohibition on self inflicted death itself, the State's rejection of the traditional treatment of the one leaves the criminality of the other open to questioning that previously would not have been appropriate. The second step in the argument is to emphasize that the State's own act of decriminalization gives a freedom of choice much like the individual's option in recognized instances of bodily autonomy. One of these, abortion, is a legal right to choose in spite of the interest a State may legitimately invoke in discouraging the practice, just as suicide is now subject to choice, despite a state interest in discouraging it. The third step is to emphasize that respondents claim a right to assistance not on the basis of some broad principle that would be subject to exceptions if that continuing interest of the State's in discouraging suicide were to be recognized at all. Respondents base their claim on the traditional right to medical care and counsel, subject to the limiting conditions of informed, responsible choice when death is imminent, conditions that support a strong analogy to rights of care in other sit-

uations in which medical counsel and assistance have been available as a matter of course. There can be no stronger claim to a physician's assistance than at the time when death is imminent, a moral judgment implied by the State's own recognition of the legitimacy of medical procedures necessarily hastening the moment of impending death.

In my judgment, the importance of the individual interest here, as within that class of "certain interests" demanding careful scrutiny of the State's contrary claim, cannot be gainsaid. Whether that interest might in some circumstances, or at some time, be seen as "fundamental" to the degree entitled to prevail is not, however, a conclusion that I need draw here, for I am satisfied that the State's interests . . . are sufficiently serious to defeat the present claim that its law is arbitrary or purposeless. . . .

6

CRIME AND PUNISHMENT

Due process of law ranks with freedom and equality in the American trinity of civil liberties. It is an ancient legal right designed to ensure fundamental fairness for anyone in an adverse relationship to government authority. In the United States, government may not take life, liberty, or property without observing due process. This means that governmental acts must not be arbitrary or unreasonable. Though due process applies to legislative and administrative hearings and to civil actions in courts, the most important constitutional issues have arisen in its application to criminal law enforcement.

Because civilized societies no longer rely on private justice, a criminal act is an offense against the state as well as the victim. Government rather than family, friends, or vigilante groups serves as society's agent of social control for dealing with criminal acts. This role may include investigation, seizure of evidence, arrest of suspected persons, their interrogation, accusation, trial, and, if convicted, punishment. Due process is designed to assure that all stages in this adverse relationship will be fair, particularly that fact-finding will be impartial and that decisions on the facts will convict and justly punish the guilty and free the innocent.

Procedural rights are not designed to acquit the accused or coddle the convicted but rather to make sure that police, prosecutors, courts, and prisons act within well-settled and long-established rules of fairness. Only with such assurances can a community in good conscience arrest, try, and punish persons for harmful acts. Though most persons accused of crimes may have, as a factual matter, committed them or even worse ones, due process demands that anyone accused or suspected of a crime be presumed innocent until proved otherwise, that government rather than the accused carry the burden of proof, and that it be met by evidence leaving no reasonable doubt.

The importance of due process is made clear in a striking comparison offered by Justice Robert Jackson at the height of the Cold War, a half-century ago:

> Procedural fairness and regularity are of the indispensable essence of liberty. Severe substantive laws can be endured if they are fairly and

impartially applied. Indeed, if put to the choice, one might well prefer to live under Soviet substantive law applied in good faith by our common-law procedures than under our substantive law enforced by Soviet procedural practices. Let it not be overlooked that due process of law is not for the sole benefit of the accused. It is the best insurance for the Government itself against those blunders which leave lasting stains on a system of justice. [*Shaunghnessy v. United States* ex rel. *Mezei*, 345 U.S. 206 at 224 (1953) (dissenting opinion)]

To be caught up in an adverse government proceeding is to be in jeopardy. A criminal case by its nature is an unequal contest. Few defendants are as wealthy as, say, O. J. Simpson and able to hire lawyers who can overmatch the state's attorneys. Prosecutor's offices have limited budgets like other government agencies, but the resources they command in a given case are apt to be greater than those of the defendant.

The idea of a legal or formal government process that was "due" is traceable in English common law to the twelfth-century reigns of Henry I and Henry II, and an element of it appears in the Magna Carta in 1215. As a collection of well-settled fair procedures of the common law, due process was brought to the New World by the English settlers and became rooted in colonial law in the seventeenth century.

The Bill of Rights, added to the new federal constitution in 1791, gave constitutional status to many of these common-law protections including, in the Fifth Amendment, a due process clause itself. These procedural rights include:

- freedom from unreasonable searches and seizures
- the requirement that no warrants be issued without probable cause
- the requirement that a criminal charge be by indictment of a grand jury
- freedom from double jeopardy
- the right to a speedy trial by an impartial jury in the district where the crime was committed
- the right to be informed of the accusation

- the right to confront witnesses
- the right to subpoena witnesses
- the right to have the aid of counsel
- the right to a jury trial in civil suits in which the claim is more than $20
- freedom from excessive bail
- freedom from cruel and unusual punishments

It is important to distinguish procedural due process from its substantive version. The first deals with the ways and means by which government treats persons with whom it has an adverse relationship. In contrast, substantive due process deals not with "how" but "what" and holds there are certain things government may not do, no matter what procedures it uses. Put another way, substantive due process refers to the content or subject matter of a law and whether it violates a protected liberty; procedural due process deals with the way in which a law is applied and whether it violates established fairness.

Rights in the First Amendment—the freedoms of speech, press, assembly, and religion—and the derived right of privacy from the First, Third, Fourth, and Fifth Amendments are substantive. As we have seen, all have been held to apply to the states through the Fourteenth Amendment. Most of the remaining rights in the Bill of Rights are procedural and most but not all have now been held applicable to the states.

Procedural due process rights can also be found in each of the state constitutions, mainly in their bills of rights, which in the case of the original 13 states, antedated the Constitution and its Bill of Rights.

Search

The search for, discovery, and "seizure" of evidence is an important, often essential, part of solving crimes and protecting public safety. But this extraordinary power, which by its nature invades privacy, can easily be abused. In colonial times, citizens had little or no protection if their property were the object of government forays.

The open-ended writs of assistance, the general search warrant created by Parliament to counter rampant American smuggling and evasion of imperial trade laws, contributed to the grievances that led to the Revolution.

Inclusion of the Fourth Amendment and its protection against "unreasonable searches and seizures" in the Bill of Rights was in direct response to abuses of these free-wheeling searches. By requiring that warrants be based on "probable cause" and that they describe the places to be searched and things to be seized, the Amendment weighs society's interest in solving crimes and punishing the wrongdoers against the individual's interest in privacy and security of home and property.

Unfortunately, the Amendment does not define its most important terms: "searches," "unreasonable," and "probable cause." And it says nothing at all about how it is to be enforced. The courts have had to clarify and give specific meaning to these matters in cases over many years.

At first, the Amendment's protection was limited to physical intrusions of one's person or property and did not include surveillance by eavesdropping or wiretapping. But in *Katz v. United States*, 1967 (p. 374), the Court, recognizing advances in communications technology, broadened the meaning of "search" and thus the Amendment's protection. It held that attaching a listening device to the outside of a public telephone booth to get incriminating information on a suspected bookie was a search within terms of the Amendment. More important, the Amendment protected not just property but a "reasonable expectation of privacy," in this case, that which the user of a closed telephone booth might expect to have.

This expectation of privacy extends to curtilage—the outdoor area immediately surrounding a house or dwelling. But in *California v. Ciraolo*, 1986, the Supreme Court held it was not violated by police who discovered an illegal crop of marijuana through aerial observation of a backyard that was otherwise shielded from public streets by a fence. Outside areas beyond curtilage

are "open fields" and do not cross the Fourth Amendment's protective threshold. (*Oliver v. United States*, 1984)

Protection against unreasonable searches is not limited to acts of police and other law enforcement agents but extends to searches by any employees of government including fire and building inspectors and public school teachers. But because the Amendment, like others in the Bill of Rights, checks only government, it does not protect against searches by private parties no matter how unreasonable they may be, unless such persons are shown to have acted at the request or direction of government officers.

Warrants and Probable Cause

Search without a warrant, that is, without an authorizing legal writ, is generally considered "unreasonable," but this rule has several important exceptions noted in the next section. A valid warrant allows entry on private property to look for and seize incriminating evidence. It must be based on "probable cause supported by oath or affirmation." The standard defies exact definition, but generally requires police to show something more than mere belief or suspicion that incriminating evidence will be found though this may be well short of absolute certainty. This belief may rest on earlier investigative work or on credible information from third parties including informants. At one time, anonymous tips did not satisfy probable cause, but in *Illinois v. Gates*, 1983, in which police got an unsigned letter describing a drug operation, the Court held that in deciding probable cause, the credibility of such tips must be judged by the "totality of the circumstances," in which anonymity was only one element.

Probable cause is decided by the judicial officer asked to issue the warrant. By interposing the judiciary between the police and criminal suspects, the warrant requirement tries to insure "neutrality and detachment" in weighing applications for searches. In *Coolidge v. New Hampshire*, 1971, the Supreme Court held that it was not satisfied where the warrant was issued by an executive officer, in this case, the state attorney general acting as a justice of the peace. However, the Court has upheld issuance of warrants by municipal court clerks, on the theory that these officials are enough removed and detached from law enforcement. (*Shadwick v. Tampa,* 1972)

Requirements of the Fourth Amendment notwithstanding, in practice about 90 percent of police applications for search warrants are approved, most in a matter of minutes.*

Searches without Warrants

The Fourth Amendment does not require that a search be with a warrant, only that a warranted search be based on probable cause and that no search be "unreasonable." Most searches, in fact, are made without warrants. Unsurprisingly, these have led to more controversy and constitutional challenges than those with warrants. What kind of search without a warrant is reasonable? The immediate answer is one made with probable cause in exigent circumstances that would make getting a warrant impractical, or where the search was conducted with consent. Accordingly there are several kinds of searches without warrants that are not "unreasonable" if based on probable cause. As we shall see, however, there are exceptions to these exceptions.

Incident to a Valid Arrest. The main reasons for searching at the point of arrest are protection of the arresting officer from concealed weapons the suspect may have and preventing incriminating evidence from being destroyed. The person and clothing of the suspect may be searched along with bags or containers he or she may be carrying. Where an arrest is made in the home, early cases upheld search of the suspect's entire house or apartment. But in *Chimel v. California,* 1969 (p. 376), in which police arrested a burglary suspect at home, the Supreme Court narrowed the scope to areas within his immediate control. This is usually interpreted to mean the space within the suspect's reach or lunge.

A search incident to arrest for one offense may yield incriminating evidence of another. In *United States v. Robinson,* 1973, a police officer who had probable cause to stop Robinson for driving without a license (he knew the license had been suspended several days earlier) discovered a packet of heroin in a pat-down search. The evidence was held validly seized and admissible in a prosecution for drug possession, even though the officer had no probable cause to believe Robinson had heroin when he was stopped.

Where evidence may deteriorate or be lost, the Court has sustained searches internal to the body. In *Schmerber v. California,* 1966, a police officer followed the defendant to a hospital after a minor car accident and arrested him for drunk driving. At the officer's request, a doctor took a blood sample that showed the presence of an incriminating amount of alcohol. Because evidence would have been lost had time been taken to get a warrant, the search was not unreasonable. Moreover, the blood sampling, though a bodily intrusion, was done by a qualified person and was only a minor inconvenience.

The Court has not spoken definitively about what strip or bodily cavity searches would be reasonable incidents to arrest under the Fourth Amendment. But it has found extraordinary bodily intrusion to violate due process of law. In *Rochin v. California,* 1952, police entering Rochin's apartment in search of drugs saw him hurriedly swallow several capsules. When they failed to forcibly extract them from his mouth, they took him to a hospital and ordered that his stomach be pumped out. The contents yielded illegal morphine. The Court disallowed use of the evidence because the conduct of the police was such as to "shock the conscience" and thus exceed government acts permitted by due process.

Hot Pursuit and Plain View. Two exceptions are associated with arrests or valid searches already under way. In *Warden v. Hayden,* 1967, for example,

---

* Richard Van Duizend, Sutton, L., and Carter, C., *The Search Warrant Process: Preconceptions, Perceptions, and Practices* (Washington, D.C.: National Center for State Courts, 1994), 25–32.

several police officers responding to a bank robbery call were told that the fleeing suspect had entered a house. They knocked on the door and were admitted by Ms. Hayden. Telling her why they were there, they starting looking through the house. One discovered Hayden feigning sleep in an upstairs bedroom and arrested him. At nearly the same time, other officers found two guns, the apparent robbery weapons, in a flush tank and clothes resembling those the robber wore in a washing machine. Though police had not chased Hayden into the house, the Supreme Court held that exigent circumstances justified the warrantless search. In *United States v. Santana,* 1976, police, who had probable cause but no warrant to arrest Santana on drug charges, arrived at her house and found her standing outside. When she saw the police she went inside but left the door open. The officers followed her and in making the arrest seized a quantity of heroin. The Court held the warrantless search reasonable.

Police are not required to overlook incriminating evidence they discover in "plain view" even if they had no probable cause to believe it was there. Reasonableness depends on whether the officers had good reason to be where they were when the discovery was made, as they would be, say, in making an arrest, being in hot pursuit, or otherwise making a valid search. Like many terms in the law, "plain view" is one of art, and the line between what is in plain view and what is not may be fine. For example, in *Arizona v. Hicks,* 1987, police lawfully entered an apartment to look for weapons after someone shot through the floor to the apartment below. They noted expensive stereo equipment in otherwise shabby surroundings. One of the officers moved the equipment to locate the serial number and then phoned police headquarters for confirmation the equipment was stolen. The Supreme Court held that the search for the serial number was unreasonable because it had not been in plain view when police made an otherwise valid entry.

Searches without Probable Cause. The Supreme Court has sustained some narrow-purpose, minimally intrusive searches without requiring warrants or probable cause. In the oft-cited *Terry v. Ohio,* (p. 379), 1968, it upheld a "stop and frisk" search to find out whether a person was armed. A police officer who suspected that two men were "casing" a store intending to rob it, stopped them and made a pat-down search that produced illegal concealed weapons. The Court held that such a search could be made on an experienced officer's "reasonable suspicion" and did not need probable cause. But in the companion case of *Sibron v. New York,* a stop-and-frisk search was unreasonable where, without any suspicion that a suspect was armed or dangerous, an officer reached into the suspect's pocket to find illegal drugs. Validity of the *Terry* search has been extended to seizure of drugs found in protective frisks for weapons, but police may not continue tactile examination of an unidentified object in a suspect's pockets once it is clear that it is not a weapon. (*Minnesota v. Dickerson,* 1993)

That a person runs at the sight of police may be an element in creating reasonable suspicion to justify a stop-and-frisk search. In *Illinois v. Wardlow,* 1999, the defendant, standing on a sidewalk at mid-day in a high crime neighborhood, turned and ran down an alley when four police cars on narcotics patrol drove up. After chase and capture, a pat-down search yielded a concealed gun. "Headlong flight," the Court said, "is not necessarily indication of wrongdoing, but it is certainly suggestive of such." Determination of reasonable suspicion, it added, must be "based on commonsense judgments and inferences about human behavior."

The *Terry* principle also applies to the detention of property. In *United States v. Place,* 1983, for example, federal agents had reasonable suspicion to think that Place, who was getting off a plane, might have narcotics in his luggage. They seized his bags and allowed them to be sniffed by a trained drug-detection dog. When the dog's behavior appeared to confirm their suspicion, they got a warrant for a full search of the bags. Though sustaining the reasonableness of the search, the Court noted the importance of brevity in intrusions not based on probable cause and held that a 90-minute detention of the bags was excessive.

Can police detain a person by stopping him from entering his home while they get a warrant to search the home based on probable cause to believe that a quantity of marijuana is inside? This was the issue in *Illinois v. McArthur*, 2001, in which the Court upheld the "stop" of the defendant who had been sitting on his porch. Expressly balancing privacy and law enforcement interests, it held there was need to prevent the defendant from destroying evidence and noted that he was merely prevented from going back inside unaccompanied and that detention was brief, no longer than reasonably necessary to get a warrant.

Automobiles. Because of their mobility, cars and other vehicles present special problems in deciding the reasonableness of a search. In the early case of *Carroll v. United States*, 1925, the Supreme Court upheld a warrantless search of a car by federal agents who had probable cause to believe it contained bootleg liquor in violation of national prohibition law. The Court laid the groundwork for an extensive exception to the warrant requirement, based on the impracticality of getting warrants in most car situations and less expectation of privacy in a car than at home. Normally such warrantless searches must be incident to a valid arrest or because police have probable cause to believe they will discover evidence of a crime. A warrantless search made after a car has been impounded and the driver taken in police custody is not unreasonable because the car is still considered mobile. (*Chambers v. Maroney*, 1970)

Do reasonable searches include the opening of closed containers found in a car? After first upholding searches of the passenger compartment, including the zipped pockets of items of clothing not being worn, though not of luggage or opaquely wrapped packages in the trunk of the car, the Court resolved much of the uncertainty in *United States v. Ross*, 1982 (p. 382). Police found closed packages containing heroin in the car's trunk. Even though the drugs were not in plain view, the Court held that if probable cause was present, police "may conduct a search of the vehicle that is as thorough as a magistrate could authorize in a warrant." The Ross rule got

further clarification in *California v. Acevedo*, 1991, in which police were held not to need a warrant to search all closed containers if they had probable cause that one or more held contraband (items it is illegal to possess).

In several recent decisions, the Court has given police more discretion to search for illegal drugs under the guise of traffic enforcement and protection of officer safety. In *Whren v. United States*, 1996, for example, it held unanimously that though a traffic stop by officers on a drug patrol was a pretext, they had probable cause to make it when the driver failed to give a turn signal. Seizure of two bags of crack cocaine in plain view in a passenger's hands was then reasonable. A year later, in *Maryland v. Wilson*, the Court cited federal statistics showing that nearly 6,000 police officers had been assaulted and 11 killed in traffic stops in one year, to support its holding that officers making even routine stops may order the driver and passengers out of the car without reason to believe they had committed any crimes. In this case, a passenger getting out dropped a bag of cocaine on the ground. The Court went a step further in *Wyoming v. Houghton*, 1999, holding that officers who made a stop for speeding and then had probable cause to believe the car contained drugs by seeing a hypodermic syringe sticking out of the driver's shirt pocket, could search the personal belongings of the passengers and driver.

But in *Knowles v. Iowa*, 1998, it ruled unanimously that a stop for speeding, for which a ticket was issued, did not justify full search of the car absent probable cause to believe incriminating evidence, in this case marijuana, would be found. A traffic citation, the Court said, does not authorize the same kind of search that would be permissible with a full custodial arrest.

When a car is impounded because its driver has been arrested or because it has been towed away for being parked in a tow-away zone, or simply abandoned, police in most jurisdictions routinely make an inventory of its contents. This safeguards valuables, protects the police against later claims of lost property, and removes possibly dangerous items that may be in the car. In *South Dakota v. Opperman*, 1976, such an inventory search of a towed car uncovered marijuana in an unlocked glove compartment. The Supreme Court held routine inventory of a lawfully seized car to be reasonable. Though there was no probable cause that criminal evidence would be discovered, the officer taking the inventory had a right to be where he was and could seize such evidence under the plain view doctrine.

Consensual Searches. Just as most searches are made without warrants, most warrantless searches, perhaps as many as 98 percent are made with consent.* Such voluntary cooperation is an important part of investigatory work. Consent itself makes a search reasonable under the Fourth Amendment; no probable cause need be shown.

But consent must truly be voluntary, a question of fact to be tested by the totality of the circumstances. Relevant circumstances include the age and competence of the person consenting, how much display of force was made by the police, and how persistent they were in their demand. Knowledge of a right to refuse consent is not necessary. (*Schneckloth v. Bustamonte,* 1973) Police who make a traffic stop may get permission to search the car without telling the driver that the stop is over. In *Ohio v. Robinette,* 1996, a motorist given a warning for speeding and handed back his license was asked, "Before you get going, are you carrying any illegal contraband in your car?" Robinette said he was not and gave permission to make a search, which produced a small quantity of illegal drugs. However, outright deception is a different matter. A search made with agreement of the driver after police falsely told him they had a warrant, is nonconsensual. (*Bumper v. North Carolina,* 1968)

The Court has upheld random police searches for drugs and weapons on buses where passengers were advised they could refuse to give consent (*Florida v. Bostick,* 1991), and more recently upheld such searches even though passengers were not told they could refuse permission. Applying a "totality of the circumstances" analysis in *United States v. Drayton,* 2002, it held there was no overbearing intimidation where three officers

boarding a bus did not make threats, block exits, or brandish weapons. The defendant had given consent when one asked, "Do you mind if I check your person?"

Consent by third parties presents a special problem. It arises in situations where the same living or working space is shared, as by spouses or roommates. After several years in which it wavered, the Court in 1974 held that a person may validly consent to a search of premises "to which they have joint access or control for most purposes." (*United States v. Matlock*) It has since ruled that a search is consensual even if a third party did not have authority to give it but appeared to police as though they did. In *Illinois v. Rodriguez,* a woman with whom the defendant had earlier shared an apartment several weeks earlier let police into the apartment she referred to as "our place" with a key that she kept without the defendant's knowledge.

Administrative and General Safety Searches. Several other kinds of searches or inspections may be made without a warrant and generally without probable cause. Many have to do with general public safety rather than criminal investigation and many are made by government inspectors or investigators who are not police officers. Instead of criminal suspects, it is often a segment or class of the general population that is subject to such searches.

All municipalities have fire, health, building, and other safety codes that may call for inspections, routine and otherwise. Generally, these administrative searches require warrants but the warrants need not meet the strict standards of probable cause required for those in criminal investigations. In companion cases in 1967, *Camara v. Municipal Court* and *See v. Seattle,* the Court invalidated warrantless building inspections of a private apartment and the nonpublic area of a commercial building. The administrative version of probable cause does not require suspicion of criminal activity, only that the proposed search is "reasonable," a matter decided by balancing public safety against the loss of privacy. But there are a few businesses—liquor

---

* Ibid., 21

stores, gun shops, pawnshops, and auto junk-yards, for example—that have traditionally had close government oversight and thus less expectation of privacy for those who own or work in them. They may be inspected without warrants. (*Colonnade Catering Corp. v. United States*, 1970)

Property damaged by fire is a special problem. The Court held in *Michigan v. Tyler*, 1978, that a fire official may inspect a fire scene immediately after the fire has been put out and remain there for a reasonable time to investigate its cause, all without a warrant. But if later entries are made, they must be with a warrant. If the purpose is to gather criminal evidence rather than to find out the origin of the fire, a traditional warrant supported by probable cause must be obtained.

Schools are also a special case. Students in public schools are entitled to protection against unreasonable searches, but a teacher or administrator may make warrantless searches of students and their property if they have reasonable suspicion they will find evidence that school rules have been violated. In *New Jersey v. T. L. O.*, 1985, the Court upheld search of a student's purse on suspicion of smoking where the search produced evidence of drug dealing. It rejected the warrant requirement as interfering with "the maintenance of the swift and informal disciplinary proceedings needed in the schools."

General administrative searches in the interest of public safety were upheld in two 1989 decisions applying to railway workers and to certain Customs Service employees. In the first, *Skinner v. Railway Labor Executives Association*, railway workers who had accidents or violated safety rules were required to take blood, breath, or urine tests for alcohol and drugs. In *National Treasury Employees Union v. Von Raab*, the Customs Service used similar tests on employees who carried firearms or were applying for promotions to jobs dealing with drug seizures. Citing the "safety-sensitive" nature of the work (studies, for example, suggested drug and alcohol use were important factors in railway accidents) and the slight intrusion on privacy, the Court held it not necessary to show probable cause for discovering

drug or alcohol use in a particular person. Nor were warrants required because evidence of alcohol or drug use is passed from the body quickly.

The Court's approval of suspicionless testing in special circumstances was carried a step further in *Vernonia School District 47J v. Acton*, 1995, in which the schools required a urine test for drugs as a condition for being on sports teams. It found the intrusion on privacy to be minor and outweighed by the schools' interest in deterring drug use. Application of the ruling was extended in the Court's 2002 decision *Pottawatamie Board of Education v. Earls* to students participating in extracurricular activities. A rural school district in Tecumseh, Okla., required that all students in "competitive" extracurricular activites, which included participating in the choir, the cheerleading squad, the Spanish club, and a chapter of Future Farmers of America, be subject to random testing for drugs. Justice Clarence Thomas based the majority's 5-4 decision not on the school district's need to deal with a pressing problem of drug use, as was the case in *Vernonia*, but on the broader ground of a public school system's "custodial responsibilities" to its students. Under the program, students testing positive were referred to counselling but were not reported to police or subject to school discipline. The Court's reasoning appeared to open the possibility that it might eventually sustain random testing of *all* students. At the time of the decision, only about 5 percent of all schools tested student athletes for drugs and only about 2 percent, students in other extracurricular activities.

In an earlier case, the Court was unwilling to sustain a Georgia law requiring drug testing for all candidates for statewide political office (*Chandler v. Miller*, 1997). *Vernonia* was distinguished because here the state had made no showing that there was a thriving "drug culture" among electoral candidates or that drug users were more likely to be candidates.

A public hospital's urine drug testing of maternity patients and women receiving prenatal care was held unconstitutional by the Court because information on those who tested positive was used not just for counseling but also given to police as possible ground for arrest and prosecution for drug offenses and child neglect. In *Ferguson v. Charleston,* 2001 (p. 385), the Court distinguished the testing from that in *Skinner, Von Raab,* and *Vernonia School District* because it was done partly for criminal investigation and without the knowledge or consent of persons "searched." This outweighed the state's interest in protection of the unborn from drug use by mothers-to-be. The Court was not moved that the possibility of prosecution served less to punish wrongdoing than to be another tool in modifying harmful behavior.

Nor has the Court been willing to sustain general, indiscriminate tactile searches for drugs. It held that Border Patrol agents, boarding a bus to make routine immigration checks, conducted an unconstitutional search when they walked down the aisle squeezing passengers' overhead luggage, where there was neither probable cause nor reasonable suspicion that drugs would be found. (*Bonds v. United States,* 2000)

Far more general and routine are x-ray searches of luggage at airports to scan for metallic objects that may be weapons or bombs. Such searches are likely to be considered reasonable, particularly after the September 11, 2001, terrorist attacks and because of reduced expectation of privacy at airports, even though few are made with probable cause or even reasonable suspicion and almost none turns up objects of the search.

Use of New Technology

Advances in communications technology allow searching to be done through wiretaps, sensitive microphones, and other devices the framers of the Fourth Amendment could not have foreseen. When the Supreme Court first dealt with such new instruments in *Olmstead v. United States,* 1928, it held that telephone wiretaps used to get evidence of bootlegging did not violate the Fourth Amendment. It reasoned that conversations were not the "persons, houses, papers or effects" the Amendment expressly protects. Because they were on phone lines away from the suspect's house, they did not physically intrude or trespass on his property. In a notable dissent, Justice Louis Brandeis argued that the Fourth Amendment was intended to protect "the privacies of life"; it needed to be read with awareness that "discovery and invention have made it possible for government . . . to obtain disclosure in court of what is whispered in a closet." [277 U.S. 438 at 473]

Yet for more than 40 years the Court stuck to the physical intrusion or trespass doctrine in dealing with new technologies, holding, for example, that use of searchlights, aerial surveillance, or hidden tape recorders on undercover agents who were on the suspect's property with permission, were not searches, but that use of a "spike" microphone in a wall shared with the suspect's premises was. It was not until *Katz v. United States,* the telephone booth case discussed earlier, that the Court abandoned its trespass analysis for one based on expectation of privacy, close to Brandeis's dissenting view in *Olmstead.*

Growing concern about federal electronic surveillance was one of the reasons Congress passed the Omnibus Crime Control and Safe Streets Act of 1968. Title III bars wiretapping or other interception of electronic communication without a warrant, unless one party to the conversation has given consent. It has since been broadened to cover new devices such as cellular telephones. Before a wiretap order can be issued, the government must show probable cause that the suspect has committed or is committing one of the federal crimes enumerated in the statute and that less intrusive means would not uncover the incriminating evidence. Wiretaps are issued for 30 days after which recordings must be delivered to the court issuing the warrant, where they are put under seal.

The Supreme Court upheld the warrant requirement in the act in *United States v. United States District Court,* 1972, in which the government argued the U.S. attorney general could authorize wiretaps in internal security investigations without judicial approval. The Court said the decision did not limit executive-ordered wiretaps of foreign agents or foreign powers where the president's powers to conduct foreign affairs might permit taps without warrants.

Use of certain other electronic devices for surveillance and monitoring is not searching within the meaning of the Fourth Amendment. In *Smith v. Maryland,* 1979, for example, the Court upheld use of a "pen register" at a central telephone office to record numbers dialed. It observed that a phone user had reason to know the phone company must record dialed calls for billing and repair and thus had low expectation of privacy about the identity of such calls. Similarly, the attachment of "beepers" to a suspect's car or some other item he or she may be carrying has been upheld as long as monitoring is limited to nonprivate areas. (*United States v. Knotts,* 1983; *United States v. Karo,* 1984)

But in *Kyllo v. United States,* 2001 (p. 389), the Court held that external scanning of a home with a thermal imaging device to detect high sources of heat coming from inside was an unconstitutional search. The scan helped give police probable cause to believe Kyllo had high-intensity lamps typically used for growing marijuana indoors. With this information they got a warrant to search the house and found marijuana. The Court held that where police use a device, not in general use, to get details of the interior of a private home they could not otherwise get without entry, the surveillance was a Fourth Amendment "search" and unreasonable without a warrant.

The unique communication opportunities of the Internet are likely to raise new search issues. Because of the expectation-of-privacy complexities of the new medium, these may call for the Court to apply different standards of probable cause and reasonable suspicion than it has in other areas. The chief privacy questions that have arisen are those of protecting intrusion from private parties rather than government.

The Exclusionary Rule

The evidentiary requirement known as the exclusionary rule is the chief remedy where a search has violated the Fourth Amendment. It bars evidence from being admitted in a criminal

"See through" high technology can create Fourth Amendment search and seizure issues when used by police in investigative work. Here a firefighter demonstrates a thermal-imaging device similar to the one at issue in *Kyllo v. United States.* In firefighting, the instrument can be used to locate persons trapped in burning buildings.

trial of the person whose right was compromised. The rule penalizes the prosecutor who, it is assumed, will then police the police. The remedy is controversial because it may suppress otherwise reliable evidence of the defendant's guilt.

The rule is entirely judge-made and was first used by the Supreme Court in the federal case of *Weeks v. United States,* 1914 to stop federal prosecutors from using evidence obtained from unreasonable searches by federal authorities. Because the Fourth Amendment did not yet apply as a limit on states, *Weeks* did not prevent federal prosecutors from using evidence obtained in state searches that would be unreasonable by the amendment's standards. Even after the Court held the amendment to be part of due process, it did not hold the exclusionary rule to be other than a supervisory one for the federal courts. (*Wolf v. Colorado,* 1949)

Not until *Mapp v. Ohio,* 1961 (p. 393), was the rule held to be a constitutional requirement of the Fourth Amendment thus governing state courts as well as federal. Looking for evidence in connection with a bombing, Cleveland police made an all-out search of Mapp's apartment without a warrant. They found no evidence of bombing, but did discover obscene materials for which Mapp was later prosecuted. The Court overturned the conviction, holding that the evidence was the product of an unreasonable search and so could not be admitted against Mapp.

Because many justices in the post-Warren Court years have had misgivings about the exclusionary rule, its status, at least as a constitutional requirement, is now in doubt. The Court has moved away from one of the two rationales for the rule, that it protects the integrity of the courts by not making them "accomplices in the willful disobedience of the Constitution," (*Elkins v. United States,* 1960) and has relied mainly on the other, deterrence of unlawful acts by the police.

In *United States v. Calandria,* 1974, for example, the Court held that the rule did not apply to a prosecutor's use of evidence obtained in an unreasonable search, when he questioned witnesses before a grand jury. The rule was aimed "to deter future unlawful police conduct," not redress an injury to the privacy of the search victim. The reasoning has allowed the Court to expressly balance the deterrent benefit of the rule against the cost of its use. Thus, in *United States v. Leon,* 1984, it set out the "good faith" exception, which means that evidence gathered by police who believed they were acting with a valid warrant could not be suppressed even though the warrant was later found to be lacking probable cause. Nor does the exclusionary rule apply where a courthouse computer error led a police officer to believe that a search warrant under which he acted was valid, where in fact it had been quashed. (*Arizona v. Hicks,* 1995)

Other remedies may apply to Fourth Amendment violations. These include a civil tort action by the search victim against the wrongdoing officers, criminal prosecutions of the officers, or administrative discipline by civilian police review boards where they exist or by police departments. But none has been effective except in the most flagrant cases of police misconduct. Civil suits for damages have proved difficult to win, and prosecutors, who must work closely with the police, are often reluctant to bring charges against officers.

Arrest

For anyone who is later a defendant in a criminal case, arrest is often the first encounter with law enforcement. Though the definition of arrest varies greatly in the statutory and common law of the 50 states, "traditional" arrest usually means taking of a person into custody or at least preventing him or her from leaving within a reasonable time. In this sense, not all encounters with police are arrests. For example, an officer stopping a person to ask questions or see identification is usually not an arrest. Nor is a stop for an apparent traffic offense or issuance of a ticket or summons. As we saw in *Terry v. Ohio,* stopping and "frisking" on reasonable suspicion that a concealed weapon may be found is a temporary investigatory detention rather than a traditional arrest.

Constitutionally, traditional arrests are "seizures" and, like searches, are subject to the warrant and probable cause requirements of the Fourth Amendment. An arrest warrant, like one for searching, is issued by a magistrate and interposes judicial authority between police and suspected persons. Warrants must be based on probable cause, meaning that police must furnish trustworthy information that links the suspect to a crime. That evidence sworn to in an affidavit need not show the conclusive guilt required in a courtroom proof, but must be a probable indication of it. It may be based on direct discoveries or on information from victims, eyewitnesses, or reliable informers.

Despite these Fourth Amendment requirements, most arrests are made without warrants because exigencies of the situation leave no time for getting them. But the rule of probable cause still applies. For example, most states allow a warrantless arrest to be made in a public place if police have probable cause to believe the suspect has committed a felony (the most serious class of crimes). The constitutionality of such arrests was affirmed by the Supreme Court in *United States v. Watson,* 1976. Rules for warrantless arrests for misdemeanors (a less serious class of crimes) are sometimes stricter, often requiring police to have observed the criminal act.

But the Fourth Amendment does not bar a warrantless custodial arrest for a minor offense, such as not wearing a seatbelt. In *Atwater v. Lago Vista,* 2001, the Court upheld the arrest, handcuffing, and removal to the police station of a driver whom a police officer saw not to be wearing a seatbelt as required by Texas law. After being detained in a jail cell for an hour, Atwater was taken before a magistrate and released on bond. She challenged the arrest in an action against the city. Examining English and American statutory and common law, the intent behind the Fourth Amendment, and the years of practice since its ratification, the Court was not persuaded that warrantless misdemeanor arrests were limited to

breaches of the peace, as Atwater argued. Noting that the police officer had probable cause to believe Atwater had committed a crime, he was not stopped from a custodial arrest even though the offense was minor and punishable only by fine.

A special problem arises if a warrantless arrest is made in the home. In *Payton v. New York,* 1980, the Supreme Court held that a nonconsensual entry into the suspect's home to make a "routine" felony arrest violated the Fourth Amendment if it was without a warrant. The Court took note of the Amendment's historic concern for the sanctity of the home. But even here there are exceptions, such as when police are in "hot pursuit," or have good reason to believe the suspect is armed and dangerous, will flee, or destroy evidence if not arrested immediately. (*Minnesota v. Olson,* 1990) With less serious offenses, the Court is less likely to find exigencies that justify a warrantless arrest in the home. For example, a warrantless entry into the suspect's home was not justified where the offense was drunk driving, a misdemeanor, even though the chief evidence— alcohol in the suspect's bloodstream—might be lost if police first took time to get a warrant. (*Welsh v. Wisconsin,* 1984)

In special locations, such as airports and borders, the Court has upheld warrantless stops and detentions on suspicion alone. In *United States v. Montoya de Hernandez,* 1985, for example, a person whom agents had reason to believe was a drug courier was held incommunicado in an airport security room for 16 hours while a warrant was obtained authorizing an x-ray and rectal examination, which revealed several plastic balloons filled with cocaine. Many law enforcement agencies have developed drug courier "profiles" based on characteristics of clothing, luggage, and personal behavior as reason for stopping and detaining. But fitting such a profile alone is not enough to create the reasonable suspicion needed for a stop. (*Reid v. Georgia,* 1980) Whether the Supreme Court will relax this standard in the case of new terrorist profiles developed after Sept. 11, 2001, remains to be seen. Widespread use of racial profiles, particularly for stopping vehicles, has come under severe criticism in recent years, and may raise equal protection clause issues as well as those under the Fourth Amendment. The Supreme Court has also yet to rule on the constitutionality of such stops.

The nation's interest in protecting its borders against drug smuggling and entry of illegal aliens or terrorists justifies stops of vehicles at fixed border checkpoints without suspicion of individualized wrongdoing. But in *Brignoni-Ponce v. United States,* 1975, the Court required there be at least reasonable suspicion for stops by roving border patrols in areas away from checkpoints. Such suspicion is not met solely by the occupants of the vehicle appearing to be of foreign ancestry.

In *Delaware v. Prouse,* 1979, the Court disallowed random stops of individual motorists to check license and registration if there was no suspicion of wrongdoing. However in *Michigan Department of State Police v. Sitz,* 1990, it upheld use of sobriety checkpoints where all cars were stopped and the average detention was 25 seconds. The Court weighed the state's interest in deterring drunk driving against the intrusion on the motorists that it described as "slight."

The Court drew a line in checkpoint stops in *Indianapolis v. Edmond,* 2000 (p. 396). It held the city's policy of setting up stops to interdict illegal drugs unconstitutional because its purpose was the discovery of "ordinary criminal wrongdoing," unlike the permissable checkpoint stops at border crossings to discover smuggling or entry of illegal aliens, or those in the Sitz case aimed at ensuring highway safety by removing drunk drivers. Despite the gravity of the drug problem, the Indianapolis program, if sustained, could justify road checkpoints for almost any law enforcement purpose.

Police must often use force in making arrests, and state laws typically allow as much force to be used as needed to secure custody or prevent escape, according greater discretion in the case of felonies than lesser crimes. But how much force is too much? A common-law rule, made statu-

tory in many states, allowed deadly force to be used to subdue a fleeing felon. But in *Tennessee v. Garner,* 1985, the Supreme Court held this rule subject to the Fourth Amendment's standard of reasonableness. A police officer shot and killed an unarmed house burglar who was fleeing over a backyard fence. Such deadly force is excessive unless the arresting officer has probable cause that the resisting suspect might harm the officer or others or had committed a felony by using or threatening to use deadly force. The Court broadened the *Garner* principle by holding that force used in an investigatory stop must also meet the Fourth Amendment standard of reasonableness. What is reasonable and what is excessive vary greatly with the seriousness of the apparent crime, the danger posed by the suspect, and other circumstantial matters of the moment. (*Graham v. Connor,* 1989)

Illegal or unreasonable arrests, which may number in the millions each year, have remedies. These include criminal prosecution of the arresting officers, civil suit against them for damages, department disciplinary action, and the imposing of an evidentiary penalty on the prosecution if the arrested person is brought to trial. Only the last—exclusion from trial of incriminating evidence against the defendant gained from the invalid arrest—has proved consistently effective.

Interrogation

Questioning a suspect who has been taken into custody is a basic part of police work. Information obtained may lead to other evidence, in turn, to solution of the crime. Where the suspect admits guilt, the confession may be the best and sometimes only evidence of guilt. For society, a confession may bring psychic closure to a troubling event and allow just punishment. For the wrongdoer, it may be a first step toward repentance and possibly eventual rehabilitation.

But interrogation often takes place in intimidating, highly stressful circumstances in which there may be few immediate limits on the police. The temptation to solve crimes by getting confessions, antipathy toward the suspect, or simple professional zeal has sometimes led to "third degree" methods including physical abuse, psychological coercion, and outright trickery. Such overreaching violates a basic sense of fairness and the presumption of innocence. It may also compromise the reliability of confessions or incriminating statements that are made. For these reasons, confessions and damaging statements by persons in custody get close scrutiny when offered as evidence in court. Besides certain supervisory rules set out for the federal courts, the Supreme Court has imposed constitutional requirements on police interrogation that are based on due process and the privilege against self-incrimination in the Fifth Amendment, and the right to counsel in the Sixth. Their application is similar to that for unreasonable searches—inadmissibility. Evidence obtained in violation of the Constitution is excluded from the prosecutor's case at trial.

Though inadmissibility of confessions extracted by torture or threat of force was well established in English common law by the end of the eighteenth century, exclusion had been less strictly practiced in American courts. When the Supreme Court first addressed the matter in *Bram v. United States*, 1897, it held admission of a coerced confession violated the privilege against self-incrimination. But because the privilege was not yet part of due process and thus part of the Fourteenth Amendment, *Bram* did not apply to the states, where most police work takes place. Not until *Brown v. Mississippi*, 1936, did the court check the use of coerced confessions in state courts, holding that incriminating statements gotten by "brutality and violence" violated the due process. The "voluntariness" principle was extended to confessions obtained through psychological coercion (*Chambers v. Florida*, 1940) and reaffirmed in many later cases (*Fikes v. Alabama*, 1953, for example).

In applying a federal statute that called for a suspect in custody to be brought before a magistrate "without unnecessary delay" for a hearing and possible arraignment, the Court in *McNabb v. United States*, 1943, moved beyond traditional notions of voluntariness to hold that confessions during a prolonged period, even if voluntary, could not be used in the federal courts. This was reaffirmed in the controversial *Mallory v. United States*, 1957, in which the Court overturned conviction of a rapist who confessed voluntarily during an 18-hour period between arrest and arraignment. Widespread criticism of the McNabb-Mallory rule, as it came to be called, resulted in Congress including a provision in the Omnibus Crime Control and Safe Streets Act of 1968, making voluntary confessions within six hours of arrest admissible notwithstanding delay, and delay beyond six hours not an absolute bar to admissability.

Ambiguity surrounding the notion of voluntariness eventually led the Warren Court to recast the constitutional limits on police interrogation in the 1960s and dramatically expand a suspect's rights in both federal and state jurisdictions. The way was paved by two important decisions not directly bearing on custodial questioning. In *Gideon v. Wainwright*, 1963, discussed in the next section, a criminal defendant's Sixth Amendment right to have "assistance of counsel" was held applicable to the states through the due process clause of the Fourteenth Amendment and gave indigent defendants charged with serious offenses the right to court-appointed counsel. The following year in *Malloy v. Hogan*, discussed in a later section, the Court held the Fifth Amendment's privilege against self-incrimination also applied to the states through the Fourteenth Amendment.

A year after *Gideon*, the Court ruled that a person under indictment could not be interrogated or otherwise induced to make incriminating statements without the presence of their lawyer (*Massiah v. United States*, 1964). In *Escobedo v. Illinois* (p. 400), the same year, it expanded the rule to preindictment custodial interrogation when police work had shifted from an "investigatory" to an "accusatory" stage focusing on the arrested person as the "prime suspect." After his arrest for murder, Escobedo had several times asked to see his lawyer who, in turn, had asked to see him, but police kept them apart until Escobedo had made incriminating statements and then confessed to the crime. The Sixth Amendment right to counsel would be seriously impaired, the Court said, if it applied only after a confession was obtained.

Two years later, in *Miranda v. Arizona* (p. 402), the most controversial of all Warren-era criminal justice decisions, the Court went yet further and set out constitutional rules for custodial interrogation. It shifted from the right-to-counsel principle in *Escobedo* and the voluntariness and totality-of-the-circumstances methods of other cases, to a reasoning based on the Fifth Amendment's privilege against self-incrimination. Building on *Malloy v. Hogan,* it applied the new guidelines to state and local police. Miranda's conviction for kidnapping and rape was based largely on a confession made during interrogation. In reversing, the Court, divided 5-4 as in *Escobedo,* held the privilege against self-incrimination, once assumed to apply mainly to situations of compelled testimony under oath in a formal proceeding, now applied to a custodial suspect. That person must be informed of a right to remain silent, that anything said might be used adversely in court, that there was a right to have the presence of counsel, and if the suspect was indigent, to have counsel appointed by the court.

Though stoutly defended by civil libertarians, the Miranda decision, coming on the heels of several other Warren Court holdings expanding rights of criminal suspects and defendants, was widely criticized as undermining police work and the battle against crime. Trying to counter the new requirements, Congress added a provision to the Crime Control Act making the admissibility of confessions in federal courts depend on whether they were voluntary as measured by the "totality of the circumstances." Failure to give the Miranda warnings would be only one factor in these circumstances. The law was largely ignored by the Justice Department, which assumed it was unconstitutional.

Meanwhile, *Miranda* became an issue in the 1968 presidential election when Richard Nixon, the eventual winner, made "law and order" a main campaign theme and promised to appoint justices who would be less solicitous of criminal defendants and more responsive to law enforcement needs. His four appointments to the Court, Chief Justice Warren Burger and Associate Justices Harry Blackmun, Lewis Powell, and William

Ernesto Miranda, whose rape conviction was overturned by the U.S. Supreme Court in *Miranda v. Arizona* because he had not been told at his arrest and questioning that he had a right to remain silent. Miranda was retried and convicted without the use of his unwarned incriminating statements. Paroled after serving nine years, he sold autographed cards carrying a printed statement of the Supreme Court's "Miranda warning." In 1976, he was stabbed to death in an argument in a bar. Two Miranda cards were found on his person. His alleged killer was informed of his Miranda rights on arrest.

Rehnquist, the nucleus of the "Nixon Court," all had judicial or political records generally conservative on criminal justice issues.

Though the post-Warren Courts under Burger and later Rehnquist as chief justices did not overrule *Miranda,* as many observers thought they might, they did narrow its scope significantly. The later Courts have upheld certain derivative use of confessions made without the Miranda warnings. In *Michigan v. Tucker,* 1974, for example, the defendant, without benefit of the Miranda warning, told police he had been with another person far from the scene when the crime was committed. Police questioned the witness who did not corroborate the story. The Court upheld admission of the witness's testimony on the ground that its reliability was not affected by the defendant not having had the Miranda warning. In another case, in which a suspect made incriminating statements without the warning, was then given the warning and made further, more damaging statements, the Court ruled that though the first statements were not admissible, those given after the warning were. (*Oregon v. Elstad,* 1985)

In *Harris v. New York,* 1971, the defendant had made unwarned incriminating statements to police that the prosecutor was not permitted to introduce in presenting his case against the defendant. But, later, when the defendant took the witness stand and contradicted what he had told the police, the trial judge allowed the prosecutor to introduce the statements to impeach the defendant's credibility. In affirming, the Supreme Court reasoned that the unwarned statements were not used to prove the defendant's guilt on the criminal charge but only to show his lack of truthfulness on the witness stand.

Though the Court has held that interrogation is not limited to simple direct questioning but may include its "functional equivalent" in other acts of the police, it is the suspect's perception not the intent or motives of the police that decides whether a questioning actually took place. For example, in *Rhode Island v. Innis,* 1980, police, told by a murder suspect they had arrested that he wanted to see a lawyer, refrained from questioning him. Nonetheless, while being taken to the police station in a squad car, Innis voluntarily revealed where the missing murder weapon could be found. He did so after the squad car passed a school for handicapped children near the murder site and one of the escorting officers said to another, "God forbid . . . if a little girl would pick up the gun and maybe kill herself." The Court held the conversation between the officers did not constitute an interrogation.

The suspect's perception has also been held to be salient in cases of covert interrogation. Where an undercover police agent posed as a fellow prisoner and elicited incriminating statements about a murder, the Court had held the Miranda warnings were not required because the suspect was not in the kind of coercive circumstances the Miranda rule was designed to address. (*Illinois v. Perkins,* 1980)

The Court has also set out a so-called public safety exception to the Miranda requirement. In *New York v. Quarles,* 1984, police caught a suspected rapist after a chase through a supermarket. When they saw he had an empty holster, one of the officers asked, "Where's the gun?" The suspect pointed to where he had thrown it away. The Court held the unwarned statement about the gun was admissible because the danger that a discarded and possibly loaded weapon posed for the police and the public outweighed the merits of giving the Miranda warning.

Miranda was weakened still further in *Arizona v. Fulminante,* 1991, in which the Court held that the "harmless error" test should apply to the admission of a coerced confession just as it does to other evidentiary questions. If other evidence in the trial was enough to convict, admission of the confession would not call for a reversal.

These and several other post-*Miranda* decisions narrowed both the theoretical scope and practical application of *Miranda.* To many observers it seemed only a matter of time before the court overturned the case entirely. That opportunity came dramatically in *Dickerson v. United States,* 2000 (p. 405), in which a lower federal appeals court had ruled that unwarned statements could be admitted at trial under Section 3501 of the United States Code, embodying the provision of the Crime Control Act mentioned earlier. The now 30-year-old law, embracing a voluntariness standard tested by the "totality of the circumstances," was not defended by the Justice Department in the case. In a 7-2 decision, the Court held that the Miranda warning was not simply a step in a rule of evidence, but a constitutional requirement that could not be legislatively superseded by Congress. It then expressly declined to overrule *Miranda* itself, saying that after nearly 35 years, the required warnings "have become part of our national culture."

Thus *Miranda* was saved, but the rule itself, chipped away by exceptions and qualifications, is a narrower one today than that anticipated by the justices of the Warren Court who issued it. Nor has *Dickerson* ended the controversy over the rule's effect. Opponents continue to maintain that it undermines the solution of many crimes and allows wrongdoers, confessed or otherwise, to go unpunished. Supporters argue that by being a check on police abuse, the rule is basic to a civilized system of criminal justice. Still others argue that the rule needs to be strengthened, not weakened, because police, with some help from the Court, have found many ways to circumvent it. Empirical studies are inconclusive, but several suggest that the rate of confessions obtained by the police has not appreciably diminished in the post-*Miranda* years.*

Counsel

An adversarial criminal justice system in which two sides—government and defendant—present contrasting evidence and argue before an impartial trier of fact in conformity with complex, often highly technical procedures, puts a premium on skilled professional representation. Defense lawyers in a criminal case help to even what is, institutionally at least, an unequal contest in which government can call on experienced attorneys, ample resources, and the formidable investigatory arm of the police. Counsel are, as the Supreme Court said in *Gideon v. Wainwright* (p. 408), "necessities not luxuries." The importance of representation in criminal cases was recognized in eighteenth century English common law and in many colonial statutes and later revolutionary state constitutions. In drafting the Bill of Rights, the first Congress included among the Sixth Amendment's different trial rights that an accused person "have the assistance of counsel for his own defense."

The right, like others in the Bill of Rights, was designed to apply only to the federal government. For nearly 150 years, even in the federal courts, it meant only that a criminal defendant could *employ* and be represented by a lawyer, not that an indigent defendant had right to an appointed one. This understanding was evident in the first Congress, which in 1790 mandated that counsel be assigned an indigent defendant charged with a capital offense, but said nothing about other criminal cases.

The Supreme Court abandoned this interpretation in *Johnson v. Zerbst,* a 1938 counterfeiting case in which an indigent defendant was convicted without counsel. In reversing, the Court ruled that federal courts could not deprive a defendant of life or liberty without having had counsel unless that assistance was intelligently waived. Based on the Sixth Amendment, the decision gave indigent defendants the right to a lawyer in all federal cases where imprisonment was a possibility.

The issue in state trials was taken up in the first of the Court's two celebrated "Scottsboro" decisions, *Powell v. Alabama,* 1932. Eight illiterate, itinerant, and indigent black youths 13 to 21 had been convicted and sentenced to death for raping two white women on a freight train passing through Scottsboro, Ala. When no lawyer showed up for the defendants on the day of the trial, the

---

* Marvin Zlaman and Siegal, Larry, *Criminal Procedure,* 2nd ed., p. 518. Review of the studies in Welsh S. White, "Defending Miranda: A Reply to Professor Caplan," *Vanderbilt Law Review* 39 (1968), 1–22.

The nine "Scottsboro boys" are shown here with famed defense attorney Samuel Leibowitz in 1933. The Scottsboro incident gave rise to several legal actions, including U.S. Supreme Court decisions in *Powell v. Alabama* in 1932 and *Norris v. Alabama,* 1935. Leibowitz, later a judge, was hired by International Labor Defense, a Communist-backed group that struggled with the NAACP for control of the case after the youths' first convictions were overturned in *Powell.*

judge appointed "all members of the bar" present in the courtroom to represent them. This resulted in two attorneys unenthusiastically appearing for the defendants. They had no chance to investigate the case and only 30 minutes to consult the defendants. The Supreme Court overturned the convictions, not because they violated the Sixth Amendment, which did not yet apply to the states, but because they offended the due process standard of the Fourteenth Amendment. The importance of having counsel was set out by Justice George Sutherland:

> "Even the intelligent and educated layman has small and sometimes no skill in the science of the law. If charged with a crime, he is incapable, generally, of determining for himself whether the indictment is good or bad. He is unfamiliar with the rules of evidence . . . [H]e may be put on trial without a proper charge and convicted on incompetent evidence, or evidence irrelevant to the issue or otherwise inadmissible. He lacks both the skill and knowledge adequately to prepare his defense, even though he have a perfect one. He requires the guiding hand of counsel at every step in the proceedings against him. Without it, though he be not guilty, he faces the danger of conviction because he does not know how to establish his innocence. If that be true of men of intelligence, how much more true is it of the ignorant and illiterate, or those of feeble intellect." [287 U.S. 45 at 68-69 (1932)]

The Court's method in *Powell* was similar to the one it was to use in *Brown v. Mississippi,* four years later, for dealing with state admissibility of coerced confessions. A procedural due process protection was discovered where a substantive right in the Bill of Rights was not applicable to the states. It soon became clear, however, that the Powell ruling would be largely limited to trials for capital crimes. In refusing to overturn a state robbery conviction of an indigent defendant without counsel in *Betts v. Brady,* 1942, the Court held that due process was violated not by the absence of counsel per se but by the absence having led to an unfair result. *Powell* was distinguished because its defendants were illiterate and uneducated, its issues more complex, and that it was a capital case. In the years following *Betts,* the Court heard appeals from scores of state convictions in which defendants were not represented. In most, it found the presence of "special circumstances" that it said made fair trial impossible without counsel. These included cases in which there was a capital charge (*Tomkins v. Missouri,* 1945), the defendant was young or handicapped (*DeMeerleer v. Michigan,* 1947), the legal issues were too complex or technical for a lay person to grasp (*Rice v. Olsen,* 1945), and the trial judge's conduct seemed questionable. (*Townsend v. Burke,* 1948) These cases, of course, were but a tiny fraction of convictions in state courts without counsel.

In its 1963 landmark decision *Gideon v. Wainwright,* the Warren Court abandoned the case-by-case "special circumstances" method, declaring that counsel was required in all state felony cases. Clarence Earl Gideon, who was to become one of the most celebrated convicts in American history thanks partly to Anthony Lewis's equally celebrated account of the case, *Gideon's Trumpet,* could not afford a lawyer and represented himself at his Florida trial for burglary. Convicted and sentenced to five years, Gideon, then 51, with little formal education and other jail terms behind him, had filed a handwritten petition from his cell asking the Supreme Court for review. The Court accepted the case and appointed the experienced Washington attorney Abe Fortas, later to be a justice himself, to represent Gideon on appeal. It held unanimously,

Prisoner Clarence Earl Gideon's handwritten petition to the Supreme Court for a writ of certiorari to review his conviction.

that representation by counsel in felony cases was a basic requirement of due process and no longer dependent on a showing that its absence would lead to an unfair trial. Thus the federal Sixth Amendment right was applied to the states.

As noted in the preceding section, the Warren Court quickly extended the right to suspects interrogated by the police in _Escobedo v. Illinois,_ 1964, and to postindictment interrogation in _Massiah v. United States,_ 1964, besides mandating it as an informational element in the Miranda warning.

Gideon itself was limited to felonies, but in _Argersinger v. Hamlin,_ 1972, the Court, unanimously reversing a concealed weapons misdemeanor conviction and six-month sentence, appeared to give the right to counsel to any indigent criminal defendant. But in _Scott v. Illinois,_ 1979, it qualified that reach by holding that defendants charged with crimes for which imprisonment could be imposed but was not, did not have a right to appointed counsel. Scott, an indigent had been fined $50 on a theft conviction for which the maximum punishment was a year in prison, a $500 fine, or both.

In the decade following _Gideon,_ the Court turned its attention to stages of criminal justice other than police interrogation and trial that it said constitutionally required the presence of counsel. The right was held applicable to preindictment preliminary hearings (_Coleman v. Alabama,_ 1970) and to the placement of indicted defendants in police lineups. (_United States v. Wade,_ 1967 and its state counterpart, _Gilbert v. California,_ 1967) It was held not applicable to the placement of an unindicted suspect in a lineup (_Kirby v. Illinois,_ 1972) or to police identification sessions in which photographs of the defendant were shown to witnesses (_United States v. Ash,_ 1973) In posttrial stages, the right was held to apply to a first appeal of conviction (_Douglas v. California,_ 1963) but not to later, discretionary appeals. (_Ross v. Moffit,_ 1974) It applies to probation hearings (_Mempa v. Rhay,_ 1967) and those on revocation of probation or parole. (_Gagnon v. Scarpelli,_ 1973)

Yet questions remain. For example, does the right to counsel imply a right to effective counsel? Indigent defendants who have appointed counsel are not apt to have the expert defense from a battery of lawyers that well-heeled criminal defendants such as O.J. Simpson might afford. In states and counties with public defender systems, an indigent may have the help of an experienced and able attorney, yet many public defender offices are understaffed and underfinanced, and the lawyers in them harried. In most other states and counties an indigent defendant is assigned a lawyer in private practice, usually from a segment of the legal profession specializing in criminal defense on an assigned fee basis. Though many attorneys in this group are able, dedicated, and hard-working, others occupy a marginal place in the profession and are often unable to sustain a higher-rewarding practice.

The Supreme Court has said that the right to counsel cannot leave defendants to "the mercies of incompetent counsel." (_McMann v. Richardson,_ 1970) Yet much representational work calls for subjective judgment, and courts have traditionally given great benefit of doubt to practicing attorneys. In 1984, the Court, for the first time, set a general standard for evaluating claims of ineffective representation in criminal cases: "whether counsel's conduct so undermined the proper functioning of the adversarial process that the trial cannot be relied on as having produced a just result." [_Strickland v. Washington,_ 466 U.S. 688 at 689] This proof is not easily met. For example, that assigned counsel had no criminal law experience and only a brief time to prepare for trial, did not alone show that the defendant had not gotten a fair trial. (_United States v. Cronic,_ 1984) Instances of constitutionally ineffective counsel include an attorney's failure to file an appeal by the legal deadline (_Evitts. v. Lucey,_ 1985) and another's failure to move to suppress highly incriminating prosecution evidence from an illegal search because he mistakenly believed the prosecutor was required on his own initiative to share all evidence with the defense. (_Kimmelman v. Morrison,_ 1986)

Conflict of interest may be ground for finding ineffective representation that would violate the Sixth Amendment. These situations may arise where a single attorney has been assigned to represent codefendants. In *Holloway v. Arkansas,* 1978, for example, the trial judge's refusal to appoint separate counsel for codefendants after the appointed counsel asserted a conflict of interest existed, was held to be a reversible error.

May an indigent defendant waive the right to appointed counsel and represent him or herself? The importance of counsel and the old adage that "he who is his own lawyer has a fool for a client," would seem to imply a negative answer. Yet the Supreme Court has held otherwise. In *Faretta v. California,* 1975, it drew a right of self-representation from the Sixth Amendment's collection of trial rights. At his trial for theft, Faretta asked for but was denied permission to conduct his own defense. Represented by a public defender, he was convicted. In reversing, the Supreme Court held that a mentally competent defendant cannot be compelled "to accept a lawyer he does not want."

Self-Incrimination

Protection against compulsory self-incrimination is embodied in the Fifth Amendment provision that "no person . . . shall be compelled in any criminal case to be a witness himself." Though only one of several criminal defense rights in amendment, it has become synonymous with the amendment as a whole. Thus "taking the Fifth" refers to the exercise of the privilege against self-incrimination. Those who invoke the privilege may, of course, be guilty parties trying not to give damaging information, but innocent persons, afraid of being entrapped in a web of statements that may make them appear guilty, also have reason to call on the protection. In either case, the privilege is designed to avoid "the cruel trilemma of self-accusation, perjury, or contempt," in which a person testifying under oath might admit incriminating truth that could lead to punishment,

or lie and be open to a perjury charge, or refuse to answer at all and be held in contempt. (*Pennsylvania v. Muniz,* 1990)

The idea that incriminating statements should not be compelled has roots in early English common law. The privilege was spurred by excesses of ecclesiastical courts and the Star Chamber, whose inquisitorial procedures were used to investigate heresy and political subversion in the sixteenth and seventeenth centuries. Opposition to compulsory self-incrimination was well established in the American colonies, and protection was recognized in the constitutional and common law of each of the 13 original states. It is not surprising that it was included in the federal Bill of Rights. Nearly 175 years later, the Supreme Court in *Malloy v. Hogan* (p. 412) found the protection to be part of Fourteenth Amendment due process and thus a uniform constitutional requirement in both state and federal jurisdictions. The defendant Malloy, a convicted gambler, had been imprisoned by Connecticut for contempt for invoking the Fifth Amendment privilege in refusing to answer questions about his earlier arrest and conviction.

Though the Fifth Amendment privilege speaks of "criminal case," it may be invoked before grand juries, legislative committees, and in administrative hearings and other official proceedings where a person testifies under oath. The Supreme Court has cited the privilege as a constitutional basis for holding coerced confessions inadmissible and mandating the Miranda warning for suspects in custody, but most issues surrounding it have to do with the testimonial role of witnesses under oath. In such proceedings a person thought to have important information must give it if summoned. Invoking the privilege in response to specific questions is an exception that allows a witness not to answer without the threat of being cited and punished for contempt.

Because the exception is designed to protect only against statements that might lead to a criminal charge, it cannot be used to avoid speaking about matters that are embarrassing or disreputable but not criminal. The privilege is also personal; it may not be used to protect friends. Nor may it be invoked to avoid giving information about criminal acts for which one has already been tried or on which the statute of limitations has run. The privilege is individual and cannot be used by corporations or other collective entities. Finally, it should not be confused with so-called privileged relationships, such as doctor-patient, lawyer-client, clergyman-confessor, or husband-wife, the parties to which cannot usually be compelled to testify about communications between them. The special treatment of these relationships is based on common or statutory law rather than constitutional requirements and is not limited to statements that may incriminate.

A special group to whom the privilege applies are defendants in criminal cases. They cannot be compelled to take the witness stand by the prosecution or to testify at all. However, a defendant who testifies voluntarily has waived the privilege, at least on matters of the criminal charge, and may be cross-examined. In the sensational 1997 O.J. Simpson murder trial, for example, the defendant chose not to testify about the slashing deaths of his wife and her friend. But in a later wrongful death civil action arising from the same events, he could not avoid taking the witness stand and, having been acquitted on the homicide charges, could not refuse to answer questions about the deaths, which he was eventually found to have caused.

Though the privilege is important in maintaining basic fairness between government and individual, its use, like the silence permitted for privileged relationships, is not without social cost. Individuals often have valuable information needed for larger public ends but which might incriminate them if they gave it. This is particularly true in the investigation of large-scale, conspiratorial wrongdoing. For this reason, Congress and most state legislatures have enacted so-called immunity statutes, which trade prosecution for testimony. A witness given immunity from prosecution is then forced to testify under pain of being held in contempt and possibly imprisoned for not doing so. The constitu-

tionality of overcoming the privilege through immunity grants was upheld in *Brown v. Walker*, 1896. Justice Felix Frankfurter put the matter starkly in a later case, "once the reason for the privilege ceases, the privilege ceases." [*Ullmann v. United States*, 350 U.S. 422, 438, (1952)]

Immunized testimony obtained in one jurisdiction, federal or state, cannot be used for prosecution in the other. In *Murphy v. Waterfront Commission of New York Harbor*, 1964, a union official called before the commission was given immunity to testify about a work stoppage. He was cited for contempt after he invoked the privilege fearing his testimony might subject him to a federal prosecution. In lifting the citation, the Supreme Court held that a grant of immunity by one jurisdiction prevents the other from prosecuting on the testimony given.

For many years, immunity was "transactional," barring prosecution for any matter or transaction about which the witness testified. But to preserve the public's right to have wrongdoers prosecuted and avoid giving witnesses "immunity baths," Congress in the Organized Crime Control Act of 1970 authorized the grant of a more limited "use" immunity, barring only prosecution on the witness's testimony or evidence derived from it. Independently gathered evidence against the witness may be used in a criminal indictment. "Use" immunity does not violate the Fifth Amendment but the government must carry the burden of showing that its evidence was "derived from a legitimate source wholly independent of the compelled testimony." [*Kastigar v. United States* (1972) 406 U.S. 441 at 446]

Invoking the privilege against self-incrimination cannot be reason for imposing noncriminal penalties or disabilities, nor can inferences officially be drawn from use of the privilege. Many states once permitted criminal trial judges or prosecutors to comment to the jury on the defendant's refusal to take the witness stand. The Supreme Court, which had refused to strike down this practice because the Fifth Amendment privilege did not apply to the states (*Twining v. New Jersey*, 1908, *Adamson v. California*, 1947), did find a constitutional violation once the privilege was incorporated into Fourteenth Amendment due process. In *Griffin v. California,* 1965, it held that permitting inferences of guilt to be drawn from the defendant's failure to testify penalized the exercise of a constitutional right.

Invoking of the privilege cannot be automatic grounds for dismissal from public employment. In *Slochower v. Board of Higher Education of New York City,* 1956, a Brooklyn College professor who had "taken the Fifth" before a House UnAmerican Activities Committee hearing to avoid speaking about past political affiliations, was fired under a city charter provision that required dismissal of anyone invoking the privilege. In ordering reinstatement, the Supreme Court said the privilege "would be reduced to a hollow mockery if its exercise could be taken as an equivalent of a confession of guilt." [350 U.S. 551 at 557] Nor may a lawyer be disbarred for using the privilege in a disciplinary hearing (*Spevack v. Klein,* 1967) nor a party official be divested of state party offices for refusing to waive the privilege before a grand jury (*Lefkowitz. v. Cunningham,* 1977). In *Garrity v. New Jersey,* 1967, the Court found coercion present where two police officers confessed to fixing traffic tickets after they were told they would lose their pension benefits if they invoked the privilege.

Asserting the privilege for nontestimonial statements or information has raised separate issues. A provision of the Internal Security Act of 1950, a centerpiece of Congress's domestic anti-Communist efforts in the 1950s, required that all "communist front" and "communist action" organizations register with the attorney general. When officers of the Communist Party refused to register the party arguing the provision violated their individual Fifth Amendment protection, a unanimous Court in *Albertson v. United States,* 1965, held unanimously that registration required giving information that could be personally incriminating. It rejected the government's argument that the registration forms were no different from tax returns, observing that the tax reporting requirements were "neutral on their face and directed at the public at large." [382 U.S. 70 at 79]

However, the Court has held the privilege does not apply to personally held private business records if the record-keeping was itself required by law. (*Shapiro v. United States,* 1948) Nor, given the personal nature of the privilege, can it be invoked by a taxpayer to block an Internal Revenue Service summons on an accountant for records the taxpayer had given him. (*Couch v. United States,* 1973) When the federal gambler's occupational tax, which required persons "in the business of accepting wagers," to register with the Internal Revenue Service was first challenged, it was upheld. Though admitting that accepting wagers was widely illegal, the Court held that the privilege against self-incrimination applied only to past acts while registration addressed only prospective ones. (*United States v. Kahriger,* 1953) This strained reasoning was abandoned in *Marchetti v. United States,* 1968, in which the Court ruled that the registration compelled self-incrimination. But in *California v. Byers,* 1971, the Court held the privilege could not be invoked to avoid compliance with a state law that required motorists in car accidents to give their names and addresses to other parties affected.

Accusation and Plea Bargaining

Formal charges against a criminal suspect are initiated by a prosecutor on information gathered by police or in a private complaint. Prosecutors have great discretion in deciding whether to bring charges, though the equal protection clause of the Fourteenth Amendment prevents them from basing this decision on race, religion, or other invidious classifications. (*Oyler v. Boles,* 1962) Because the resources of their offices are limited, they must be selective; not all police investigations or private complaints may be acted upon. Selection of cases most likely to be won, usually those in which guilt is clearest, or which have gotten the most public attention, is compelling.

The prosecutor's evidence must be examined by a magistrate or grand jury to decide whether it is enough to warrant a criminal trial. In slightly more than half the states, it is presented to a magistrate in a formal accusatory document called an *information,* which outlines the case against the suspect. The magistrate schedules a hearing, usually open, at which the suspect's counsel has opportunity to look at the evidence. Unlike a trial, however, the hearing is not a full adversarial proceeding.

In the remaining states—mostly older ones east of the Mississippi—formal accusation is by indictment of a grand jury, a body of 12 to 24 persons, impaneled, usually for a fixed term, to examine prosecution evidence. Though this procedure is a Fifth Amendment requirement of criminal accusation in the federal courts, it is one of the few rights in the Bill of Rights still not applied to the states. As we saw in *Hurtado v. California,* 1884 (p. 36), one of the Supreme Court's earliest Fourteenth Amendment cases, it sustained a murder conviction where the defendant had been accused by the process of information allowable under state law. Though of long common law standing, grand jury indictment was not essential to due process and is thus not a limit on the states.

In keeping with its common-law heritage, grand jury proceedings are closed and considered nonadversarial. This protects suspects who may not be indicted from adverse publicity and presumably encourages less inhibited testimony from witnesses. However, witnesses, whether suspects or not, have no right to the presence of counsel (*United States v. Mandujaro,* 1976), to confront other witnesses, challenge evidence, or have exculpatory evidence presented. (*United States v. Williams,* 1992) They do retain the Fifth Amendment's privilege against self-incrimination unless given immunity (*Lefkowitz v. Turley,* 1973). Most grand juries are empowered to call witnesses, subpoena documents, and grant immunity, though usually their work is limited to reviewing evidence presented by the prosecutor. When a grand jury finds that evidence, if true or uncontroverted, would probably support a criminal conviction, it

returns an indictment or *true bill.* If the evidence is insufficient, it reports a *no bill,* and the matter against the suspect is dropped. Neither result is a determination of guilt or innocence.

Historically, grand juries were checks against weakly supported charges and overzealous prosecution. Though this may still be true today, modern grand juries typically follow the prosecutor's lead. Perhaps for this reason, the Supreme Court has not found the Fifth Amendment right to be an essential element of fair procedure. Also, as a practical matter, the alternative of accusation by information has the advantage being cheaper and saving time.

If a formal accusation is made by information or grand jury indictment, the suspect—now the defendant—is arraigned. This is an appearance before a judge at which the specific charge or charges are read and the defendant is asked to plead. His or her response is "guilty," "not guilty," or "*nolo contendere*" (no contest, which for most purposes is treated as a guilty plea). Unless the plea is not guilty, no trial is needed, and the defendant is sentenced or has other penalty imposed by the court.

More than 90 percent of felony defendants and an even higher rate of those accused of misdemeanors plead guilty or no contest. About a third of the guilty pleas are bargained, that is, negotiated between prosecutor and defendant or defendant's counsel. In such agreements, the defendant typically pleads guilty to a lesser charge (for example, carrying a concealed weapon rather than armed robbery) and the prosecutor drops or asks the court to drop a more serious one ("charge bargaining"), or pleads guilty and the prosecutor recommends that a lighter sentence be imposed ("sentence bargaining"). The advantage of such bargains for the government is clear: saving time and expense of not conducting trials. If all criminal cases went to trial, the criminal justice system would quickly jam to a halt. Relief would call for vastly greater numbers of prosecutors, defense lawyers, judges, jurors, and courtrooms. Work productivity lost to jury service and significantly higher taxes would be part of the social cost.

Nonetheless, plea bargains remain controversial. Some critics argue that in "copping a plea," a defendant, benefiting from leniency, escapes full punishment for criminal acts. Others, including many civil libertarians, say that a plea bargain precludes a definitive finding of guilt in open court with the government carrying the burden of proof before an impartial trier of fact. More to the point, the defendant waives important constitutional rights including the privilege against self-incrimination, a jury trial, and the chance to confront witnesses, leaving the prosecutor and defense attorney, who is often an appointed counsel with his or her own economic interest in avoiding trial, as deciders of the case.

The Supreme Court has repeatedly denied constitutional challenges to plea bargaining, emphasizing its pragmatic advantages: "The defendant avoids extended pretrial incarceration and the anxieties and uncertainties of a trial; he gains a speedy disposition of his case, the chance to acknowledge his guilt, and a prompt start in realizing whatever potential there may be for rehabilitation. Judges and prosecutors conserve vital and scarce resources. The public is protected from the risks posed by those charged with criminal offenses who are at large on bail while awaiting completion of criminal proceedings." [*Blackledge v. Allison,* 431 U.S. 63 (1977) at 71]

A bargained plea of guilty must be voluntary (*Brady v. United States,* 1969), made with full knowledge of its implications (*Henderson v. Morgan,* 1976), and the prosecutor must have kept the bargain. (*Santobello v. New York,* 1971) However in *Bordenkircher v. Hayes,* 1977, the Court rejected a due process challenge that a prosecutor's plea bargaining tactics were vindictive. The defendant Hayes had first been indicted for forgery, carrying a 2–10-year sentence. In plea negotiations, the prosecutor offered to recommend a five-year sentence if Hayes pleaded guilty. If he did not, the prosecutor would rein-

dict him under a "habitual offender" law that would make Hayes, who had two previous felony convictions, subject to a mandatory life sentence if convicted. Hayes rejected the offer, was reindicted, found guilty by a jury, and sentenced to life. Though recognizing that discretion could be abused, the Court upheld the conviction, reasoning that the prosecutor had merely engaged in the "give and take of negotiation common to plea bargaining" and had not acted vindictively in such a way as to violate due process.

Bail and Detention

A suspect arrested and formally accused may be released on bail until trial. Bail is property or a sum of money pledged by the defendant that he or she will appear for trial. The amount is set by a judge but in certain cases may be denied. If a defendant does not have the means or cannot borrow money for bail, he or she may be held in custody until the trial starts and while it continues. "Jumping" bail—not appearing for trial—is a criminal offense itself and usually results in forfeiture of the money or property pledged.

In a phrase drawn from the English Bill of Rights in 1689, the Eighth Amendment to the federal Constitution directs that "excessive bail shall not be required." The provision honors the presumption that an accused person is innocent until proved guilty. Being free before trial also allows the defendant to better prepare a defense. Weighed against this is the possibility that he or she will not appear or may commit crimes while awaiting trial.

The Eighth Amendment provision leads to two constitutional questions: What amount of bail is "excessive"? And under what circumstances, if any, may it be denied altogether? Bail set extremely high, of course, may be the equivalent of no bail at all. In an early definitive ruling, the Supreme Court held that "the right to release before trial is conditioned on the accused's giving adequate assurance that he will stand trial and submit to sentence if found guilty . . . Bail set at a figure higher than an amount reasonably calculated to fulfill the purpose is 'excessive' under the Eighth Amendment." [*Stack v. Boyle,* 342 U.S. 1 (1951), at 5] The amount at issue was $50,000, a considerable sum at the time, but the Court's standard is one fit to individual circumstances rather than tied to a fixed sum. The following year, it ruled the right to bail was not absolute, that the Eighth Amendment guaranteed only "that bail shall not be excessive in those cases where it is proper to grant bail." [*Carlson v. Landon,* 342 U.S. 524 (1952), at 545]

The Federal Rules of Criminal Procedure list several considerations in setting bail in federal cases: the circumstances of the offense, the weight of the evidence against the defendant, the defendant's financial ability to raise bail, and his or her "character." Federal courts are also governed by the Bail Reform Acts of 1966 and 1984. The first, passed amid concern about a large number of persons held while awaiting trial, authorizes release of defendants in non-capital cases on their own recognizance or on unsecured signature bonds unless release would not "reasonably assure" the defendant would appear at trial. The 1984 act, passed after growing evidence that many crimes, especially drug dealing, were committed by persons on bail awaiting trial, authorizes federal judges and magistrates to refuse bail if the defendant appears to be a danger to other persons.

This preventive detention was challenged in *United States v. Salerno,* 1987, in which bail had been denied to an organized crime figure indicted on racketeering charges who prosecutors showed was likely to commit a murder if released. The Supreme Court sustained the detention, holding that though appearance for trial was the main purpose in setting bail, the Eighth Amendment did not bar refusal of bail if the defendant in remaining free would be a "demonstrable danger to the community."

Protection against excessive bail, like the requirement of indictment by a grand jury, is one of the few rights in the Bill of Rights not incorporated into the Fourteenth Amendment and made applicable to the states. Every state, however, has a body of statutory and case law that defines bail rights. The Supreme Court has sustained state preventive detention of juvenile defendants against a due process challenge, where there was substantial risk that a serious crime would be committed before trial. (*Schall v. Martin; Abrams v. Martin*)

Trial

Though only a small percentage of criminal cases go to trial, that proceeding is the most formal, visible, and definitive stratum of criminal justice. The accused's guilt of an offense is proved or not proved in open court. Trials have had potential for drama throughout the long history of Anglo-American law and the law of other nations as well. It is not surprising that they have inspired countless stories, novels, and plays, as well as movie and television dramatizations. They are also the chief means by which the public participates—in this instance as an attentive audience—in the criminal justice process.

In Anglo-American law, trials are adversarial events in which contending parties argue legal issues and present one-sided versions of facts to an impartial and largely passive arbiter. As one observer has put it, a trial is "a regulated storytelling contest between champions of competing interpretive stories."* The only neutral parties in a criminal trial are the judge and jury. The judge chairs the proceeding and makes rulings on questions of law that arise. The jury—petit in contrast to grand—is the finder of fact and presumably discovers "truth" by sifting and weigh-

---

* Richard Goodpaster, "On the Theory of the American Adversary Criminal Trial," 78 *Journal of Criminal Law and Criminology* 118 (1987) at 120.

ing evidence presented by partisan agents. In a "bench" trial—one without a jury—the judge is the trier of fact.

Technically, the finder of fact does not decide the guilt or innocence of the defendant but whether the prosecution has proved guilt *beyond reasonable doubt*. Innocence is presumed. This is an important distinction and reflects a much heavier burden of proof than is borne in a civil case, where each side carries an equal share. In a civil case, the party having a *preponderance* of the evidence—the better and weightier evidence—wins. In a criminal case, the prosecution may have the preponderance of the evidence but that evidence may fall short of showing the defendant guilty beyond reasonable doubt. If it does, the law calls for acquittal, that is, a verdict of "not guilty." This is not a finding of the defendant factually innocent of the charge, though of course he or she may be. Thus it is possible that a defendant may be factually guilty but legally not guilty. In the O.J. Simpson cases, the defendant was acquitted of murder where the government needed to prove guilt beyond reasonable doubt, but was found to have committed the killings in a civil suit in which the plaintiffs needed only a preponderance of the evidence. The heavy burden of proof on the government in a criminal case also means that the defendant, theoretically at least, need not prove anything, though the defense of course will try to make as many favorable points as possible.

The prosecution's burden of proving guilt beyond reasonable doubt is required by due process and is "a prime instrument for reducing the risk of convictions resting on factual error. The standard also provides concrete substance for the presumption of innocence." [*In re Winship*, 397 U.S. 362 (1970), at 363] Attempts to shift part of the burden to the defendant have been struck down. In *Mullaney v. Wilber*, 1975, for example, the Supreme Court invalidated a Maine statute under which a defendant charged with premeditated homicide could have the charge reduced during trial to manslaughter (unpremedi-

tated homicide) if he or she proved they acted in the "heat of passion" or on "sudden provocation." The Court held due process required the prosecution prove every element of the charged crime beyond reasonable doubt, which for premeditated homicide included the absence of heated passion or sudden provocation.

By Jury

Americans are often surprised to learn that the use of juries in criminal cases is far from universal. In Britain, with which the United States shares a common legal heritage, juries are used in only about 1 percent of criminal cases; there is no right to a jury in most cases. By comparison, Article III of the Constitution requires in federal cases "the trial of all crimes, except in cases of impeachment, shall be by jury." Many of those who opposed the Constitution at the time of ratification argued this provision did not go far enough. Further assurances were added in the Sixth Amendment's requirement that "In all criminal prosecutions, the accused shall enjoy the right to a speedy and public trail by an impartial jury." As we have seen, this provision was first applied to the states in *Duncan v. Louisiana*, 1968 (p. 41), in which the Supreme Court reversed the conviction of a misdeamnor defendant who had had a bench trial. The jury was "an inestimable safeguard against the corrupt or overzealous prosecutor and against the compliant, biased, or eccentric judge." But it made clear this new application to the states did not apply to trials for petty offenses, which it later held to be those carrying a maximum penalty of six months. (*Baldwin v. New York*, 1970)

Because jury trials are expensive and require citizens give much time to jury service, several states have experimented with the size of the trial jury, historically standing at 12, and with its decision rule, historically unanimity. In *Williams v. Florida*, 1970, the Supreme Court upheld the state's use of six-person juries in noncapital cases. In *Johnson v. Louisiana* and

The Highest Crime

Treason calls to mind images of betrayal, treachery, disloyalty—a "selling out" of one's country—an act so heinous that it is punishable by death in most countries, even today. Yet the charge of treason had a checkered history in England and other European countries of colonial and precolonial times, where it was sometimes used indiscriminately against persons otherwise loyal but who were merely critics or political opponents of the government. Besides death, conviction often led to seizure of the defendant's property—another temptation to bring the charge—and "corruption of blood," meaning disqualification of his heirs from inheritance.

Treason is one of four crimes mentioned in the Constitution but the only one defined. Its terms, occupying an entire section of Article III, are deliberately narrow. It consists only of "levying war" against the United States or "adhering" to its "enemies, giving them aid and comfort." Conviction requires the testimony of "two witnesses to the same overt act, or on confession in open court." Also, there may be no "corruption of blood, or forfeiture except during the life of the person attainted." Not only were the Framers well aware the treason charge had been abused in the past, they knew the United States owed its independence to a collectively disloyal act and that almost every leading revolutionary, starting with George Washington, could have been charged with treason had they been taken captive.

The constitutional limits were narrowed further by Chief Justice John Marshall in the 1807 treason charge against former vice president Aaron Burr. Presiding at the trial in Richmond as part of his circuit-riding duties, Marshall rejected the government's reasoning that the constitutional definition included "constructive" treason. Burr was said to have arranged a meeting, which he did not attend, for the purpose of planning war against the United States. Marshall said the government would need to show Burr had engaged in an "overt" act of war, which merely calling a meeting was not.

The Civil War created different and far more serious issues of loyalty and disloyalty. The North's theory of the conflict, that it was not a war between two nations but an insurrection by a part against the whole, held that war-making by the rebels was treasonous. Captured Confederate soldiers could be tried and, if convicted, executed. This position was soon abandoned when the South threatened to retaliate by executing captured Union soldiers. Though at odds with its war theory, the North treated captured Confederate soldiers as prisoners of war.

A second issue was how to deal with various disloyal acts of civilians, ranging from mere denouncements of President Lincoln and circulation of pro-Southern literature to espionage and sabotage. Many of these acts, which engaged perhaps thousands or even tens of thousands of persons in the Northern states, were surely the "adhering to enemies, giving them aid and comfort." Because of their number and the strict evidentiary limits in the constitutional definition that now excluded "constructive" treason, Congress passed several laws declaring that aiding the rebellion was a crime distinct from treason and punishable by fine and imprisonment. These laws and the wartime suspension of the writ of habeas corpus allowed many suspects to be held for indefinite periods and some to be tried by military commissions. After the war, in *Ex parte Milligan*, the Supreme Court held military trials of civilians in areas where civil courts were open and operating to violate the right to grand jury indictment in the Fifth Amendment, and to a public jury trial in the Sixth.

A presidentially created military commission was used to try eight German saboteurs who had been landed by submarine on Long Island and in Florida in the early days of World War II. All were captured or turned themselves in within a few days. All were convicted under the Fifteenth Article of War, an international law authorizing trials of foreign nationals by military tribunals, and six were executed. In

Apodaca v. Oregon, both 1972, it upheld statutes that allowing nonunanimous verdicts of 11-1, 10-2, or 9-3. The Court thought these reforms, which reduce the number of deadlocked or "hung" juries, did not favor prosecution or defense. Yet, because the government carries the

Ex parte Quirin, 1942, the Supreme Court upheld the military procedure and ruling, denying the defendants were entitled to the constitutional guarantees of the Fifth and Sixth Amendments. Because the Constitution does not require grand jury indictment or a jury trial for American military personnel charged with offenses, the Court said it was untenable that those rights apply to members of a foreign military.

Out of the saboteurs incident came the Court's first treason cases. (Because the jury in the Burr trial acquitted the defendant, Marshall's ruling on the treason clause in that case did not reach the Court.) While at large, several of the saboteurs had met publicly with a naturalized citizen of German birth who had befriended them and offered to hold their money in safekeeping. In *Cramer v. United States*, 1945, the Supreme Court overturned the friend's conviction for treason, holding that absent specific proof of intent to commit treason, his one witnessed overt act—the meeting—was not enough to make out the crime.

In the second case, *Haupt v. United States*, 1947, the defendant was the father of one of the saboteurs, who lived in the United States. He had given shelter to his son and tried to get him a job in a defense plant manufacturing a sensitive bombsight. Retreating from *Cramer's* narrow ruling on what made an "overt act," it upheld Haupt's conviction and rejected the claim that his actions were merely those of a father concerned about the welfare of his son.

After *Haupt*, the government prosecuted several American nationals for treasonous acts committed in foreign countries during World War II, including making radio propaganda broadcasts for Germany and Japan. In *Kawakita v. United States*, 1952, the Court held that treason against the United States by American citizens was not limited to acts committed in the United States.

Despite the rulings in *Haupt* and *Kawakita*, the crime remains, as intended, difficult to prove. That it took 150 years before the Supreme Court even

heard a treason appeal is testimony to the rarity of the charge. Government prosecutors have preferred to use criminal statutes to deal with disloyal acts. The convicted atomic spies Julius and Ethel Rosenberg, for example, were charged under the Espionage Act, which sets out capital offenses not bearing the evidentiary limits the Constitution places on treason.

Treason charges appear to have limited utility in the American war on terrorism. Theoretically, they could have been brought against John Walker Lindh, an American captured while fighting for the Taliban in Afghanistan. There were clearly overt acts in his case, but would fighting against the Afghan Northern Alliance, which only later became an ally of the United States, be the "levying war" the Constitution requires? Were the Taliban the "enemy" within the meaning of the treason clause when he joined them? It is not surprising the government chose to forego a treason indictment in favor of several other charges, including those under a 1994 law making it a crime to give material support to a terrorist organization. None of these offenses is punishable by death.

As in *Haupt*, treason charges can be brought against disloyal aliens within the United States because they owe the country temporary allegiance while in its jurisdiction. But in the case of Zacarias Moussaoui, alleged to have been the missing twentieth hijacker in the September 11, 2001, airliner terrorist attacks, the government chose not to indict for treason, which would have required two witnesses to an overt treasonous act. Instead, it charged Moussaoui with conspiracy to commit deadly terrorism and to kill American government employees, capital crimes that allow circumstantial proof. Though such charges might have been brought before a presidentially created military commission, as were those against the World War II saboteurs, the government chose to try the case in federal court.

Treason charges would have no applicability to captured Taliban or al Queda fighters in Afghanistan or other foreign countries who are not American citizens because they owe no allegiance to the United States.

burden of proof in a criminal case, it can be argued that persuading six persons of something is easier than persuading nine, ten, eleven, or

twelve. In later cases, the Court drew the line at six persons, rejecting Georgia's use of a jury of five (*Ballew v. Georgia*, 1978) and has disallowed the reaching of less than unanimous verdicts by six-person juries. (*Burch v. Louisiana,* 1979)

External Pressure and Prejudice

For a criminal trial to be a search for truth through deliberate procedures that honor the presumption of innocence, it must be held in an environment free of external pressures and local "passion." Many trials generate high public interest and excite emotion, particularly if the crime was heinous, the defendant or victim well-known, or the defendant a member of a group subject to local prejudice. Collective bias may be ingrained and even institutionalized as it was against many black defendants in the once-segregated South.

The intrusion of blatant external pressure on criminal justice proceedings has been fairly rare in the annals of American courts. One of the few cases to reach the Supreme Court, *Moore v. Dempsey,* 1923, showed the Court's determination not to allow such bias to affect judicial result. Five black men had been convicted of killing a white man following a racial disturbance in Arkansas. Public anger, at least among local whites, kept defense witnesses from being called. The trial lasted only 45 minutes. The jury deliberated only five. A threatening mob surrounded the courthouse making it unlikely that the defendants, had they been acquitted, could have left the building unharmed. The Supreme Court held these unfortunate facts violated the defendants' right to due process. In Justice Oliver Wendell Holmes's memorable statement, "If . . . the whole proceeding is a mask—that counsel, jury, and judge were swept to the fatal end by an irresistible wave of public passion . . . the possibility that the trial court and counsel saw no other way of avoiding an immediate outbreak of the mob can prevent this Court from securing to the petitioners their constitutional rights." [261 U.S. 86 (1923) at 91]

Though the circumstances of *Moore v. Dempsey* were unusual, there is no denying that local prej-udice because of race or other factors is often a reality. One way courts deal with such conditions is through a change of venue, that is, the relocation of the trial to another and presumably more neutral area. In state cases, however, such transfers are limited to areas within the state. Another alternative is sequestration of the jury, the attempt to insulate it from local contact and publicity for duration of the trial. Such isolation, however, often works a hardship on jurors and is apt to be porous.

Community passions and prejudices are often made worse by pretrial publicity. As we saw in Chapter 4, the problem may be greater today because media coverage of trials and pretrial hearings is more extensive and because new technology allows more graphic and immediate reporting. In *Sheppard v. Maxwell,* 1996, the Court held the due process right to a fair trial was violated in the "circus-like" environment of the defendant's trial and the court's failure to control prejudicial publicity and insulate the jury. The matter of trial coverage is complex because the media have First Amendment rights and an important professional obligation to report public and governmental proceedings. Courts have usually tried to deal with prejudicial publicity by maintaining rigorous procedures within the judicial system that would counter the effect of local "passions" against the defendant. These efforts have focused mainly on insuring that the trial be conducted by an unbiased judge and decided by an unbiased finding of fact.

Impartial Judge and Jury

Complete objectivity and disinterest is an improbable reach for most lay persons, perhaps even most judges. But professional legal training and the obligation to be fair that is part of judging means that most judges will strive to be impartial. Perhaps, for this reason, the Supreme Court has given less attention to possibility of personal bias than to the problem that built-in structural factors may work to compromise disinterest. Thus in *Tumey v. Ohio,* 1927, it invalidated a bootlegging conviction under a small town's ordinance that required part of any fine imposed go to the judge. This arrangement violated the defendant's due process rights because it put him on trial before someone who had "a direct, personal substantial pecuniary interest" in the conviction. The principle was later extended to an arrangement in which a village mayor sat as traffic court judge and the fines imposed were an important part of the village's income. (*Ward v. Village of Monroeville,* 1973)

Insuring impartiality in juries is more complex. Jurors are not likely to have pecuniary interests in conviction or acquittal, but they are lay persons of the community without legal training and often with little or no experience as jurors. In well-publicized cases, they are apt to have been exposed to information that might be prejudicial. For these reasons and because the Sixth Amendment expressly guarantees a criminal defendant the right to "an impartial jury," all jurisdictions have procedures to discover lack of impartiality and exclude prospective jurors who display it.

The chief mechanism for this is this is the voir dire ("to speak the truth") examination of prospective jurors, at which each person called for impaneling is questioned individually by the judge or, in some jurisdictions, by prosecutor and defense counsel. Its purpose is to find out whether the prospective juror has already formed an opinion of the defendant's guilt or innocence or has views, attitudes, or associations that might bias his or her judgment in the case. Prospective jurors whose impartiality is in doubt may be challenged and dismissed for cause, at the judge's discretion. Most jurisdictions also allow both sides a small number of peremptory challenges to individual prospective jurors, for which no reason need be given. A defendant has a constitutional right to have a prospective juror dismissed where cause is shown, but has no constitutional right to peremptory challenges, which are created and governed by statute or

rules of the court. (*Stilson v. United States,* 1919) When the voir dire process fails, as in a case where eight of the twelve impaneled jurors admitted believing the defendant guilty before any evidence was presented, a conviction may be overturned on due process grounds. (*Irvin v. Dowd,* 1961)

The Supreme Court has been reluctant to impute lack of impartiality to any particular category of persons. The issue came up in a challenge to impaneling federal workers as jurors in federal criminal trials, where, of course, the government is a party. The Court ruled that government employees must be questioned individually for bias and not dismissed for cause simply because they hold government jobs. (*United States v. Wood,* 1936) The issue arose again and perhaps more keenly in the contempt of Congress trial of Eugene Dennis, secretary of the American Communist Party, at the peak of the Cold War. The Court rejected Dennis's argument that the seven federal employees who served on his jury should have been dismissed, reiterating that proof of individual bias was the constitutional standard. (*Dennis v. United States,* 1950)

Would a prospective juror's opposition to the death penalty be cause to dismiss him or her from serving on a jury hearing a capital case? When the Court first took the matter up in *Witherspoon v. Illinois,* 1968, it held the general practice of excluding such persons to be unconstitutional. A jury drawn only from those not opposed to capital punishment would be "a hanging jury," Justice Potter Stewart said, thus imputing lack of impartiality to a class of persons, which the Court had expressly refrained from doing in other cases. Later, concerned that the rule made it harder to get convictions in murder cases where the death sentence might be imposed, it moved away from this Warren-era decision. Excluding a prospective juror who admitted that scruples about capital punishment would interfere with judging the guilt or innocence of the defendant was constitutionally permissible. (*Wainwright v. Witt,* 1985) Correspondingly, a prospective juror who said he would automatically vote to impose the death penalty if the defendant were found guilty could be dismissed for lacking impartiality. (*Morgan v. Illinois*, 1992)

Representative Jury

"Jury of one's peers" is the historic phrase that describes a jury drawn from fellow citizens rather than, say, government officials or a selected elite. The expectation is that juries will represent or at least reflect a cross-section of the community. But even under the best of circumstances that ideal is only approximated because most communities have diverse groups and classes while each jury has only 12 or fewer persons. Neither "peers" nor "cross-section" are terms mentioned in the Constitution, but the Supreme Court has long accepted the principle that juries be representative of the community. This is illustrated in *Thiel v. Southern Pacific*, 1946, in which a trial judge had excluded all persons who worked for hourly wages so they would not suffer financial hardship by losing wages while gaining only the pittance fee that jury service paid. In finding such exclusion unacceptable, the Supreme Court held the cross-section principle does not mean that 'every jury must contain representatives of all the social, religious, racial, political, and geographical groups of the community . . . but it does mean that prospective jurors shall be selected by court officials without systematic or intentional exclusion of any of these groups." [328 U.S. 217 at 224] In 1975, the Court expressly held that a 'fair cross-section" was a requirement of the Sixth Amendment's right to a jury trial in criminal cases. (*Taylor v. Louisiana*)

The chief "systematic or intended" exclusion was the effort to keep black persons from serving on juries. As far back as 1880, the Supreme Court had struck down a state statute that expressly barred blacks, as a violation of equal protection (*Strauder v. West Virginia*), but it did not address more widespread, covert administrative discrimination until *Norris v. Alabama* in 1935, the second of the celebrated Scottsboro

cases. The black youths whose earlier rape conviction had been overturned for lack of counsel in *Powell v. Alabama*, had been retried and convicted again. This verdict was appealed on the ground that black persons had been systematically excluded from jury service in the county where the trial was held. Evidence showed that though nearly 8 percent of the county's population was black, no black person had served on a jury within the memory of the county's oldest residents. These facts, the Court said, created a presumption of intentional discrimination that would require the state to prove discrimination had not occurred, a difficult burden to carry in this case and others like it. The equal protection principle and the inference of discrimination were later applied to circumstances where no person of Mexican descent in a county having a large Mexican-American population had served on a jury in 25 years. (*Hernandez v. Texas*, 1954)

When the Court first considered a prosecutor's use of peremptory challenges to exclude persons because of race, it refused to interfere with them (*Swain v. Alabama*, 1965), only to overrule itself 20 years later in *Batson v. Kentucky*, 1986 (p. 414). The Court held that where the defense made a prima facie case that peremptory challenges were used to keep a person of the defendant's race off the jury, the prosecution would need to prove that they were not based on racial discrimination. The Batson rule, was later applied where defense counsel used peremptory challenges for a racially discriminating purpose (*Georgia v. McCollum*, 1992), and to both sides in civil trials (*Edmonson v. Leesville Concrete Co.*, 1991). These rulings do not mean that a defendant has a right to have at least one person of his or her race on the jury, rather that a defendant of any race has the right not to have persons excluded for racial reasons. All-white juries of course are common, and in Washington, D. C., and many other large cities today, all-black juries are not uncommon. In either case, the occurrence must be by chance, not design.

Exclusion or exemption of women from juries has raised similar issues, though the reason for such practice is usually benign. The Supreme Court at first upheld an arrangement where women could voluntarily serve on juries but were not in the normal juror "draft" because, as it said, "woman is still regarded as the center of home and family life." [*Hoyt v. Florida,* 368 U.S. 57 at 62 (1961)] But 14 years later, in *Taylor v. Louisiana,* it held that giving women a voluntary exemption violated the defendant's Sixth Amendment right to an impartial jury drawn from a cross-section of the community. Later, the Batson rule on peremptory challenges was extended to include those to women as women. (*J.E.B. v. Alabama ex. rel. T.B.,* 1994) The fair cross-section principle is also embodied in the Federal Jury Selection and Service Act of 1974, which bars exclusion because of race, religion, gender, national origin, or economic status. The judge at voir dire, of course, retains discretion to excuse a person from jury service for personal hardship.

The use of specially qualified "blue ribbon" juries to hear cases that have particularly important or complex issues, raises cross-section issues. A New York statute, now repealed, gave the trial judge discretion to impanel such juries. Persons were chosen by measures of learning and intelligence from the general jury pool. There were no qualifications of race, gender, religion, occupational or economic status. The law was challenged by two union officials convicted of conspiracy and extortion by such a blue ribbon jury. In *Fay v. New York,* 1947, the Court narrowly rejected the contention that such juries discriminate against manual and service workers and favor those in the higher economic and social strata. The mere absence of a particular class from a jury was not a constitutional violation. For that, purposeful discrimination would need to be shown.

Speedy and Public Trial

The phrase "justice delayed is justice denied" is a familiar one in American law. Long delays may lead to deterioration of physical evidence and the death or disappearance of witnesses. Delay in resolving a criminal case can force a defendant or suspect, yet to be proved guilty, to live with uncertainty and, if being held, spend a long time in pretrial detention. One way the law deals with these issues is through limitations statutes that specify a time—usually a number of years—after occurrence of the crime in which the government must bring formal accusation if it is going to proceed at all. Another is the provision in the Sixth Amendment and in almost every state constitution giving the defendant a right to a speedy trial. The right got little attention from the Supreme Court until the 1960s when it was applied to the states (*Klopfer v. North Carolina*), at a time when state criminal justice systems had unusually large backlogs of cases.

The requirement of "speedy" called for clarification. To what stages of criminal justice did it apply? What delay was too long? Could long delay ever be justified? In *United States v. Marion,* 1971, in which three years elapsed between offense and indictment, the Court held unanimously that the Sixth Amendment right did not apply to the period before indictment if the defendants had not been arrested or held. The following year in *Barker v. Wingo,* in which the defendant was brought to trial five years after indictment, a unanimous Court spoke definitively. It rejected both the defendant's argument that the Sixth Amendment required a trial within a fixed, specified period, and the government's that the defendant had automatically waived the right by not objecting to the delay earlier. It then devised a balancing test of four elements: how long the delay, the government's reason for it, whether the defendant failed to object, and the prejudicial effect of delay on the defense. Though the five-year lapse was unusually long, the Court noted that it was caused by an important prosecution witness not being available rather than a deliberate effort to hinder the defense and that the delay did the defense no harm.

Negative response to the decision resulted in Congress passing the Speedy Trial Act in 1974, over objections of the Justice Department and against the advice of many federal judges. The law, which applies only to federal cases, sets a limit of 100 days between arrest and trial: 30 after arrest, 10 after indictment, and 60 after arraignment to start of the trial.

Inclusion of the right to a public trial in the Sixth Amendment reflected long-standing Anglo-American antipathy to secret trials and the excesses of the sixteenth- and seventeenth-century Courts of Star Chamber. Openness of criminal justice proceedings was thought to be a safeguard for the defendant. As we have seen, however, local sentiment may run strongly against a defendant and, in today's hyper-media age, highly publicized proceedings may work to a defendant's disfavor. Nonetheless, the Sixth Amendment right is a defendant's to have, and the Supreme Court has held it important enough to include it in due process and thus apply to the states. It did this in striking down Michigan's single-judge grand jury system in which a judge, sitting in an accusatory role in closed session, could find a witness believed to be lying, to be in contempt and, with no break in the proceedings, pronounce guilt and impose sentence. (*In re Oliver,* 1948)

As we have already seen, the First Amendment guarantees the press and public the right to attend trials though access to certain pretrial proceedings may be limited. The right to a public trial prevents the closing of pretrial hearings over the defendant's objection, unless it is shown that open hearings would prejudice a fair trial. (*Walker v. Georgia,* 1984) A trial judge retains great discretion to exclude particular persons from the courtroom, for example those who are disorderly, those who cannot be comfortably seated, and, in certain cases, minors.

Confronting and Obtaining Witnesses

A rule of common law dating to the early seventeenth century gave a criminal defendant opportunity to face and question accusing witnesses. This right was included in the Sixth Amendment's so-called confrontation clause. As a practical matter, it means that the prosecution may not use testimonial evidence against the defendant unless the witness giving it does so in open court and can be cross-examined.

Though most states have similar provisions in their constitutions or statutory law, the Supreme Court has held the confrontation right basic to a fair trial and thus part of due process and constitutionally applicable to the states. The case was *Pointer v. Texas,* 1965, in which a chief witness against the defendant had moved to another state and was not able to testify in person. The prosecution introduced, instead, a transcript of the witness's statements made during a pretrial hearing. The Court held that such use violated the confrontation clause.

A more common issue arises when the prosecutor tries to protect the identity of police informants. The Court has ruled that unwillingness to disclose identity violates the defendant's confrontation right. (*Jencks v. United States,* 1957) In such cases, the government is faced with the hard choice of producing the witness for cross-examination or foregoing his or her testimonial role.

In other cases, the Court has held the confrontation clause to be violated if an edited confession of a codefendant was admitted but no opportunity was given to question the codefendant (*Gray v. Maryland,* 1998), and if the trial judge refused to allow questioning of a juvenile who was a prosecution witness about past criminal behavior that might affect his credibility. (*Davis v. Alaska,* 1974) Though the Court has not ruled on the matter directly, lower courts have allowed the declarations of dying persons and the testimony of deceased persons given at earlier trials to be admitted.

An important question arises with the testimony of children in sexual abuse cases. In 1988, the Court struck down an Iowa law that permitted child accusers to testify behind a screen. (*Coy v. Iowa*) But two years later, in *Maryland v.*

Craig (p. 416), it expressly modified the Sixth Amendment guarantee by holding that a state may permit a child to testify on closed circuit television though the defendant's counsel retained the right to cross-examine. Justice Sandra Day O'Connor said that "a state's interests in the physical and psychological well-being of child abuse victims may be sufficiently important to outweigh . . . a defendant's right to face his or her accusers in court." [497 U.S. 836 at 844]

Though a rape defendant has the right to confront his accuser in court, the Supreme Court has upheld the constitutionality of state "rape shield" laws. Typically these protect an accusing witness from being questioned about her previous sexual behavior with persons other than the defendant or require the defendant to give several days notice of his intent to undertake such questioning. (*Michigan v. Lucas,* 1991)

The Sixth Amendment also guarantees a defendant the right "to have compulsory process for obtaining witnesses in his favor," which gives the defense the same subpoena power as the prosecution. The provision rejected the earlier English practice of not permitting accused felons or traitors to call witnesses in their defense. In *Washington v. Texas,* 1967, the Supreme Court unanimously held the right was basic enough to be part of due process and binding on the states when it struck down a Texas law that barred codefendants from testifying for one another.

A defendant's right to be present at trial, though not mentioned in the Sixth Amendment or elsewhere in the Constitution, is implicit in the right to confront witnesses. (*Lewis v. United States,* 1892) Nonetheless, a defendant may not thwart progress of the trial by refusing to be present or by disruptive behavior. Noisy outbursts, abusive language, or disorderly acts may be disciplined by a contempt citation. If that does not work, the trial judge may order the defendant to be bound and gagged or removed from the courtroom. As Justice William Brennan put it a concurring opinion, "Due process does not require the presence of the defendant if his presence means that there will be no orderly process at all." [*Illinois v. Allen,* 397 U.S. 337 at 350 (1970)]

Double Jeopardy

The right against double jeopardy finds American embodiment in the Fifth Amendment's quaintly stated provision that no one may be "subject for the same offense to be twice put in jeopardy of life or limb." Like most other rights in the Bill of Rights, it begs for elaboration. Several Rehnquist Court decisions in the 1990s have clarified some but not all aspects of it.

The clearest and most certain protection is the bar to prosecution for a crime for which there has already been an acquittal. This means the government may not appeal a not guilty verdict and the defendant is forever free from prosecution for the crime charged in the case. In this sense, double jeopardy parallels the rule of *res judicata* ("the thing adjudicated") in civil cases, which holds that an issue between parties once decided on its merits in a court of competent jurisdiction cannot be relitigated between those parties.

The double jeopardy clause also protects against a second prosecution for an offense to which the defendant has already pleaded or been found guilty. But a second trial is not precluded if the defendant's conviction in the first was overturned on appeal. (*United States v. Ball,* 1896) Nor is it barred if the jury was deadlocked in the first (*United States v. Perez,* 1824) or the trial judge, on the defendant's motion, dismissed the charges. (*United States v. Scott,* 1978) But a defendant convicted in a new trial may not be given a harsher sentence than one imposed in the first unless it is based on harmful conduct after the time of the original sentencing. (*North Carolina v. Pearce,* 1969)

Exactly what constitutes a "same offense"? The Court has held that it is not double jeopardy for a defendant to be tried by both federal and state governments if his or her alleged acts were crimes under the laws of each (*United States v. Lanza,* 1922) or be tried by two states if the acts violated the laws of each. Thus in *Heath v. Alabama,* 1985, in which the defendant had earlier pleaded guilty to arranging the murder of his wife in Georgia, there was no double jeopardy for Alabama to try him for kidnapping and murder where she had been taken to that state and killed. The "two sovereignty" principle applied to prosecution of Los Angeles police officers for the notorious Rodney King beating, which was captured on videotape and nationally publicized. The officers, acquitted of aggravated assault in a state trial, were convicted in a later federal prosecution for violating a federal law that makes it a crime to deprive a person of a civil right.

In *Ashe v. Swenson,* 1970, the Supreme Court held that when there were multiple victims of the same offense, multiple trials would subject the defendant to double jeopardy. Ashe, alleged to have robbed six men who were playing poker, was acquitted on a charge of robbing one of the players. Because later prosecutions would rely on the same evidence as the first, Ashe could not be tried for robbing any of the others. Prosecutions for distinct crimes growing out of the same incident, however, are not double jeopardy. Manufacturing illegal drugs and conspiring to manufacture and distribute the same are separate offenses even though some of the same evidence is used in proof of each. "[A] substantive crime and a conspiracy to commit that crime are not the 'same offense' for double jeopardy purposes . . . because the essence of a conspiracy offense is in the agreement or confederation to commit the crime." [*United States v. Felix,* 503 U.S. 378 at 388 (1992)] Whether a second prosecution is double jeopardy depends not on whether it uses the same proof of the defendant's conduct but whether the two offenses have the same "elements." (*United States v. Dixon,* 1993)

Do civil liabilities or noncriminal disabilities constitute double jeopardy if imposed after a criminal conviction? Civil tort actions are not precluded by a criminal acquittal because they do not put the defendant in jeopardy of "life or limb," even though the cases may arise from the same incident as they did in the O. J. Simpson trials. But in *Department of Revenue of Montana v. Kurth Ranch,* 1994, the Court struck down a state law imposing a $100 per ounce tax on confiscated illegal drugs, in this instance $181,000 in all, as applied to a family convicted of growing marijuana. It held the tax to be "unmistakably punitive" in being so high and imposed only after a criminal conviction and on material the government had already destroyed. The Court took a different position two years later in upholding civil forfeiture proceedings brought by the government after a criminal conviction, to seize property used in the crime and purchased with the fruits of the crime. (*United States v. Ursery,* 1996)

Finally, in *Kansas v. Hendricks,* 1997, the Court continued to apply a narrow double jeopardy standard when it sustained the state's practice of committing certain convicted sex offenders to mental hospitals for treatment *after* they had served their prison sentences. The commitment of those who have shown they are not able to control their behavior, the Court said, was not a second punishment but a civil proceeding to protect the public.

Punishment

The principle that cruel and unusual punishments should not be imposed on those convicted of crimes is traceable in Anglo-American law back through the English Bill of Rights in 1689 to the Magna Carta of 1215. It appears in early colonial law, and its phrasing in the Eighth Amendment in the Bill of Rights was taken verbatim from Virginia's Declaration of Rights in 1776. The amendment was clearly aimed to bar such barbarous and degrading practices as burning at the stake, drawing and quartering, crucifixion, disembowelment, amputation, branding, use of the rack and wheel, and dragging through the streets, all used at one time or other in human penal history. As Chief Justice Earl Warren phrased it, "The basic concept underlying the Eighth Amendment is nothing less than the dignity of man. Though the

State has the power to punish, the Amendment stands to assure that this power be exercised within the limits of civilized standards." [*Trop v. Dulles*, 356 U.S. 86 at 100 (1958)]

Methods and Severity

Two main questions of interpretation have arisen. What methods of punishment are acceptable? Is the severity of punishment disproportionate to the crime? The Supreme Court's earliest cases had to do with the forms of execution. In 1878, it upheld use of the firing squad (*Wilkerson v. Utah*) and, in 1890, electrocution. (In *re Kemmler*) The second, clearly unusual at the time, was held to be more "humane" than hanging, then the most common method of capital punishment. In 1947, a closely divided Court refused to hold a second attempt to execute a condemned prisoner to be a cruel and unusual punishment after the electric chair failed to work in the first attempt. (*Louisiana ex. rel. Francis v. Resweber*) The Court has not had to rule on the constitutionality of traditional corporal punishments, such as flogging, because almost all have been repealed by statute.

In *Trop v. Dulles*, 1954, a plurality of the Court held that expatriation—removal of citizenship—violated the Eighth Amendment when used as punishment for wartime desertion because it meant "the total destruction of the individual's status in organized society." The case is noteworthy less for this exaggerated statement than for Warren's additional observation that protection against cruel and unusual punishment, "must draw its meaning from the evolving standards of decency that mark the progress of a maturing society." [356 U.S. 86 at 101]

Questions of severity mainly arise about length of sentence and conditions of confinement. In its earliest case on the issue, *Weems v. United States*, 1910, the Court invalidated a territorial statute in the Philippines under which a defendant was sentenced to 12 years at hard labor in chains, as a cruel and unusual punishment for the crime of falsifying a public document. In *Robinson v. California*, 1962, the Warren Court applied the

Eighth Amendment provision to the states, striking down a law that made narcotics addiction a criminal offense alone without proof of purchase or possession. It held addiction to be an illness and thus a sentence of 90 days a cruel and unusual punishment. But six years later, it narrowly refused to extend this analysis to jail time for public drunkenness, as imposed on a chronic alcoholic. [*Powell v. Texas*, 1968]

The Burger and Rehnquist Courts have been reluctant to strike down heavy and often mandatory penalties for drug trafficking that have been legislated by Congress and many states. Thus no Eighth Amendment violation was found in a 40-year sentence for possessing and distributing 9 ounces of marijuana (*Hutto v. Davis*, 1982) or in a life sentence without possibility of parole for possessing 650 grams of cocaine. (*Harmelin v. Michigan*, 1991)

Habitual offender laws, enacted in many states in recent years, have led to Eighth Amendment challenges. Typically, these are "three-strike" laws that impose mandatory life sentences for a third conviction of certain types of crimes. In *Rummel v. Estelle*, 1980, the Court, 5-4, upheld a life sentence for a third theft conviction where the total stolen in the three offenses was $289. But three years later, with Justice Blackmun, a member of the majority in *Rummel* now joining its dissenters, the Court held, again 5-4, that a life sentence for passing a $100 bad check was cruel and unusual punishment where the defendant's six previous convictions were for nonviolent offenses. (*Solem v. Helm*, 1983)

Though prison conditions are subject to Eighth Amendment scrutiny, the Court has tended to defer to prison authorities where security was at issue. (*Whitley v. Albers*, 1986) It has also refused to find a violation where conditions were merely restrictive or harsh because "they are part of the penalty that criminal offenders pay for their offense against society." (*Rhoades v. Chapman*, 1981) In *Hudson v. McMillian*, 1992, in which injurious force had been used to quell a nonviolent dispute between two inmates, the Court held the test of an Eighth

Amendment conditions-of-confinement violation was not whether a prisoner was injured but whether authorities "maliciously or sadistically" caused harm in restoring discipline or showed "deliberate indifference" to the physical health or medical needs of inmates. In later cases, the Court found constitutional violations where a prisoner was able to prove "deliberate indifference" to his objection of being placed in a cell with another prisoner who was a chain smoker (*Helling v. McKinney*, 1993), and where a transsexual prisoner, born male, was raped after being housed with male prisoners. "Being violently assaulted in prison," Justice David Souter said, "is . . . not part of the penalty that criminal offenders pay for their offenses against society." [*Farmer v. Brennan*, 511 U.S. 825 at 840 (1994)] More recently in *Hope v. Pelzer*, 2002, the Court held that prison guards who had allegedly handcuffed an inmate to a hitching post for two hours in hot sun as punishment for disruptive behavior, were not immune from a civil suit brought against them by the inmate. The Court found the punishment, if proven, was cruel and unusual in violation of the Eighth Amendment.

The Death Penalty

Capital punishment is of ancient origin and is still used in many countries today. In the United States it has usually been a punishment for premeditated or "first degree" homicide, though it has also been authorized for treason, kidnapping, and certain other felonies. All 13 states had death penalty laws at the time the Constitution was ratified, and though capital punishment is not mentioned specifically in the Constitution, several clauses recognize it implicitly. The Fifth and Fourteenth Amendments, for example, bar the taking of "life, liberty, or property" without due process of law, and the Fifth also bars prosecution for "a capital or otherwise infamous crime" without indictment by a grand jury and provides no one may be put twice in jeopardy of "life or limb."

As already noted, the Supreme Court when first asked to rule on the constitutionality of cap-

ital punishment in the late nineteenth century, sustained the penalty. (*Wilkerson v. Utah*, 1879) Later, holding that execution by electrocution was not a cruel or unusual, Chief Justice Melville Fuller said, "punishments are cruel when they involve torture or lingering death; but the punishment of death is not cruel, within the meaning of that word . . . in the Constitution. It implies that there is something inhuman and barbarous, something more than the mere extinguishment of life." [In *re Kemmler*, 136 U.S. 436 at 47 (1890)] Executions in the United States reached a peak in the early 1930s then declined to none in 1968 as the issue of capital punishment came to be widely debated, with strong arguments made for and against its abolition. When the Supreme Court heard a challenge to the penalty in *Furman v. Georgia*, 1972, more than 600 prisoners were on "death row," almost all in state prisons. Many opponents of capital punishment expected the Court to hold the death penalty unconstitutional.

Though its position was badly fragmented in the case, the Court struck down capital punishment procedures for the first time. The 5-4 decision, per curium, was accompanied by nine separate opinions. A majority of the justices found Georgia's jury-imposed death penalty to be a cruel and unusual punishment because juries had no guidelines and imposition of the penalty appeared to be random and unpredictable. Some justices also noted that it was imposed disproportionately on black defendants. But only two in the majority, Brennan and Marshall, found the death penalty to be unconstitutional per se. After the decision, all 38 states retaining death penalty statutes revised their procedures. Twenty-five required a separate sentencing hearing for those found guilty of homicide and specified particular aggravating and mitigating circumstances that were to be taken into account. The other states, electing to deal with the issue of randomness by removing discretion altogether, made the death penalty mandatory for certain types of homicide. Though a few states abolished the penalty, *Furman's* effect was reform of capital punishment rather than its abolition.

The Court soon heard cases that challenged both kinds of reform. In *Gregg v. Georgia,* 1976 (p. 420), with only Brennan and Marshall dissenting, it upheld the state's revised procedures that now required a separate sentencing hearing governed by specific guidelines before the death penalty could be imposed, and was emphatic on upholding the constitutionality of capital punishment. But in two other cases decided the same day, laws requiring mandatory death sentences for certain crimes were struck down for not allowing the defendant's character and behavior or circumstances of the crime to be taken into account. (*Woodson v. North Carolina* and *Roberts v. Louisiana,* both 1976) Thus acceptable capital punishment procedures would need to avoid the pre-*Furman* tolerance of completely unguided discretion and the post-*Furman* total removal of discretion.

Since *Gregg,* the Court has heard more than 60 capital punishment cases. It has held the death penalty disproportionate punishment for rape (*Coker v. Georgia,* 1977); that it may not be imposed on someone who aided in a robbery by driving the getaway car but did not take part in or witness a murder that took place (*Enmund v. Florida,* 1982); but that it might be imposed on a felony accomplice who played an important role in a crime resulting in murder and was shown to be "reckless and indifferent" to human life. (*Tison v. Arizona,* 1987)

The issue of who might impose the death sentence, absent from *Furman* and *Gregg,* was not directly addressed by the Court until *Ring v. Arizona,* 2002. The state's law allowed a judge to make factual findings after the jury verdict, to support a death sentence where the maximum penalty was otherwise life imprisonment. This was struck down as violating the defendant's Sixth Amendment right to a trial by jury. That right was diminished, said Justice Ruth Ginsburg for a majority of the justices, if it included a jury's fact finding to convict the defendant, "but not the fact finding necessary to put him to death." The decision voided the death sentencing procedures in five states where a single judge or a panel of judges,

alone, could impose the death penalty. It did not directly affect the law of four others where the jury advises the judge on whether a capital sentence should be imposed. Nor, of course, does it affect at all the procedures of 29 other states with capital punishment where the sentence of life or death lies with the jury entirely.

Can characteristics of the defendant bearing on his or her ability to be responsible make the death penalty a cruel and unusual punishment? The Court has held that murderers who were 15 or younger at the time of their crimes may not later be executed (*Thompson v. Oklahoma,* 1988), but that those who were 16 or older may be. (*Stanford v. Kentucky,* 1989) The Eighth Amendment bars execution of a convicted murderer who is insane or has become insane while on death row and cannot understand the reason for his execution. (*Ford v. Wainwright,* 1986) At first the Court held that it does not prevent the execution of a mildly retarded murderer who had been found competent to stand trial, as long as the sentencing jury had opportunity to weigh mitigating evidence. (*Penry v. Lynaugh,* 1989) But in a dramatic reversal in *Atkins v. Virginia,* 2002, involving a death row inmate with an IQ of 59, the Court, 6-3, overruled the earlier decision to hold execution of a retarded person unconstitutional. For the Court, Justice John Paul Stevens, citing a growing "national consensus," observed that "today our society views mentally retarded offenders as less culpable than the average criminal." Despite this social finding, he did not elaborate on how the new legal status was to be determined. The dissenters, who challenged the existence of any such consensus, argued that retardation was not a discrete mental health category with well-defined lines.

Racial disparities, which underlay the Furman decision, were directly at issue in *McCleskey v. Kemp,* 1987 (p. 424), in which the defendant cited studies showing that blacks who murder whites were more likely to receive the death penalty than whites who murder blacks. The Court held that the studies failed to prove that those who decided the defendant's sentence were racially biased in imposing the death penalty.

The Demographics of Death Row

Though capital punishment for murder and certain other crimes is as old as organized society, it has been abolished in many countries and its use in the United States has declined. From 25 to 30 executions a year in the first decade of independence, the number grew steadily with the nation's population, reaching a peak of 199 in 1935. But in ratio to population, it actually fell from one per 160,000 persons in the 1780s to one per 650,000 in 1935. Today it is about one per 4,250,000.

After 1935, the number of executions dropped almost annually until there were none by 1968. For the next eight years there was a de facto moratorium, largely because of *Furman v. Georgia* in 1972, which raised constitutional doubts about the death penalty and the legal procedures for imposing it. Many convicted defendants in capital cases continued to receive the death sentence, however, and the Supreme Court's later decision in *Gregg v. Georgia*, 1976 (p. 420), upholding the constitutionality of capital punishment under reformed procedures, allowed executions to be resumed. From 1977 through 2001, 762 persons were executed in 32 states (more than a third in Texas) and two others by the federal government. The national average has been 30 a year, but in the period 1992–2001, it rose to nearly 60.

In 2002, more than 3,800 persons were under sentence of death, that is, were on "death row," 28 percent in California and Texas. But as many as 400 of these prisoners may be affected by the Supreme Court's 2002 death penalty decisions (p. 369). The great disparity between the death row population and the numbers of persons executed is accounted for by appeals, stays, commutations, resentencing, and new trials. Since 1990, the ratio of executions to death row inmates was one in 78, though it has been steadily declining since *McCleskey v. Zant* in 1991.

Today, 12 states—Alaska, Connecticut, Hawaii, Iowa, Maine, Michigan, Minnesota, North Dakota, Rhode Island, Vermont, West Virginia, and Wisconsin, and the District of Columbia no longer impose the death penalty. In other states only homicide remains a capital crime and in many, proof of aggravating circumstances must be shown before a sentence of death can be imposed. There have been no executions for rape or other crimes in the states since 1964.

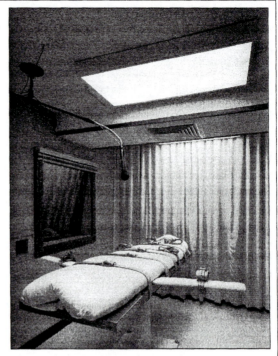

The lethal injection chamber at Texas state prison in Huntsville.

Congress, however, has made 60 specific federal crimes subject to the death penalty. Almost all have to do with homicide, such as murder of the president, a member of Congress, other government employees, foreign officials, or jurors, or murder committed in the smuggling of illegal immigrants. The exceptions include treason (see "The Highest Crime"), espionage, and drug trafficking in large amounts. In 1996, a year after the Oklahoma City bombing, Congress passed the Anti-Terrorism and Effective Death Penalty Act, adding conspiracy to commit "deadly terrorism," air piracy, and use of weapons of mass destruction to crimes other than homicide for which the death sentence could be imposed.

Methods of execution have varied over the years. Before the twentieth century, hanging was the most common until replaced in most states by electrocution. Today, 36 states and the federal government authorize lethal injection, which is generally regarded as the most humane way to extinguish life. Since 1976, according to the Justice Department's Bureau of Justice Statistics, three-fourths of the executions in the United States have been by this method. Electrocution is still authorized by 10 states, cyanide gas by 11, hanging by 3, and the firing squad by 2. Except for Alabama and Nebraska, which rely solely on the electric chair, these methods are now used only as alternatives to lethal injection.

Persons on death row are not a cross-section of the country. They are more closely representative of its prison population. A recent study by the Death Penalty Information Center shows they are overwhelmingly male—more than 98 percent—and more than half are in prisons of the 11 Southern states of the old Confederacy. Fifty-six percent are white, 35 percent black, 7 percent Hispanic, and 2 percent Native American, Asian, or of other racial background. Their ages range from 18 to 65, the average being 37. Because many have been on death row for several years, their average age at conviction was considerably less. Only 10 percent attended college. More than half did not finish high school, and 14 percent had an eighth-grade education or less. As many as 10 percent may be mentally retarded. More than half had never married; 20 percent were divorced or separated. Nearly two-thirds had previous felony convictions, 9 percent for homicide. At the time of their capital offense, 7 percent had other charges pending against them; nearly 30 percent were on probation or parole.

Capital punishment remains a controversial and polarizing public issue, having important symbolic meaning for many supporters and opponents alike. The chief arguments favoring the penalty are that it is a deterrent, particularly to murder, and that it is retributive and thus psychologically indemnifying for the anger, sense of loss, and other negative emotions that crimes like murder often stir. The deterrent effect is hard to prove or disprove because evidence is often anecdotal or based on simple correlations of aggregates that do not of themselves demonstrate causal effect and must compete with scores of intervening factors for explanatory power. For example, homicide rates have not dramatically risen in states that no longer impose the death penalty, but this does not prove the penalty had no effect on the murder rate. Since 1976 when the brief national moratorium ended and executions resumed, the number of murders in the country first rose, then declined, then rose again, and has now declined again, while the number of death sentences and executions has risen almost annually.

The retributive effect of the death penalty touches an elemental "an eye for and eye" sense of justice that appears to lie deep within the human breast. But that a quarter of the states and many foreign industrialized nations have abolished capital punishment suggests this primordial response may not be unyielding. Support for the death penalty in polled public opinion in the United States, long at 70 percent or higher, has declined to 50 in recent years when respondents were asked to consider life imprisonment without possibility of parole as an alternative.

Opposition to capital punishment rests on many grounds but two of the most important are humaneness and the possibility of exoneration. Though the use of lethal injection has removed much of the violence and suffering associated with other methods of execution, opponents of the death penalty argue that the deliberate extinguishing of life by the state has a brutalizing effect on society itself.

The possibility that a condemned person may later be shown to be innocent by discovery of new evidence has always been a strong argument against capital punishment. Since 1973, 98 condemned persons have been exonerated, according to a Death Penalty Information Center compilation. Though this figure is only a small percentage of all persons who have been on death row during those years, it is disturbingly high as an absolute number. Because exonerating evidence in these cases happened to come to light, their number no doubt understates the true incidence of innocence.

After first ruling the other way, the Court has held that so-called victim-impact statements, describing the effect of the murder on the victim's family, may be introduced at sentencing hearings. (*Payne v. Tennessee*, 1991, overruling *Booth v. Maryland*, 1987) But if a prosecutor asking for the death penalty argues that the defendant is likely to be dangerous in the future, the defendant has a right to have the sentencing jury be told that a life sentence would carry no possibility of parole. (*Simmons v. South Carolina*, 1994)

Finally, in *McCleskey v. Zant*, 1991, a second appeal by the defendant in *McCleskey v. Kemp*, the Court held that claims omitted from a first appeal intentionally or through "inexcusable neglect" would not be considered in a later petition. The decision countered the practice of some death row inmates and their lawyers of stringing out claims in successive appeals, which often took years to run their course. The Court held that second appeals could be taken up only if there was cause—factors beyond the defendant's control—for not earlier raising errors that harmed the defendant at trial or but for which innocence might have been proved. The decision dramatically reduced the number of death row petitions and shortened the period between sentence and execution.

FURTHER READING

General

Acker, James R., and David C. Brody, *Criminal Procedure: A Contemporary Perspective* (1999)

Amar, Akhil Reed, *The Constitution and Criminal Procedure: First Principles* (1997)

Barnett, Randy E., and John Hagel, III., eds., *Assessing the Criminal: Restitution, Retribution, and the Legal Process* (1977)

Bodenhamer, David J., *Fair Trial: Rights of the Accused in American History* (1992)

Bradley Craig M., *The Failure of the Criminal Procedure Revolution* (1993)

Casper, Jonathan D., *American Criminal Justice: The Defendant's Perspective* (1972)

Cole, George F., ed., *Criminal Justice: Law and Politics* (1993)

Eisenstein, James, Roy B. Flemming, and Peter F. Narduli, *The Contours of Justice: Communities and Their Courts* (1988)

Fellman, David, *The Defendant's Rights* (1976)

Flicker, Barbara, *Standards for Juvenile Justice: A Summary and Analysis* (1982)

Friedman, Lawrence M., *Crime and Punishment in American History* (1993)

Kennedy, Randall, *Race, Crime, and the Law* (1997)

Levy, Leonard, *The Origins of the Fifth Amendment* (1968)
———, *Against the Law: The Nixon Court and Criminal Justice* (1974)

Loewy, Arthur H., ed., *A Criminal Law Anthology* (1992)

Mann, Coramae Richey, *Unequal Justice: A Question of Color* (1993)

Neubauer, David W., *Debating Crime: Rhetoric and Reality* (2001)

Packer, Herbert L., *The Limits of the Criminal Sanction* (1968)

Pestritto, Ronald J., *Founding the Criminal Law: Punishment and Political Thought in the Origins of America* (2000)

Schwartz, Martin D., and Dragan Milovanovic, *Race, Gender, and Class in Criminology: The Intersections* (1999)

Silberman, Charles E., *Criminal Violence, Criminal Justice* (1978)

Skolnick, Jerome, *Justice without Trial: Law Enforcement in Democratic Society*, 3rd ed. (1994)

Wilbanks, William, *The Myth of a Racist Criminal Justice System* (1987)

Wilson, James C., ed., *Crime and Public Policy*, 2nd ed. (1994)

Arrest, Search, and Interrogation

Baker, Liva, *Miranda: Crime, Law, and Politics* (1985)

Carr, James G., *The Law of Electronic Surveillance*, 2nd ed. (1986)

Creamer, Shane J., *The Law of Arrest, Search, and Seizure* (1980)

Gilliom, John, *Surveillance, Privacy, and the Law: Employee Drug Testing and the Politics of Social Control* (1994)

Griswold, Erwin N., *Search and Seizure: A Dilemma for the Supreme Court* (1975)

Kamisar, Yale, *Police Interrogation and Confessions: Essays in Law and Policy* (1980)

LaFave, Wayne R., *Arrest: The Decision to Take a Suspect into Custody* (1965)

———, *Search and Seizure: A Treatise on the Fourth Amendment*, 2 vols. (1987)

———, *A Treatise on the Fourth Amendment*, 3rd ed. (1995)

Landynski, Jacob W., *Search and Seizure and the Supreme Court* (1966)

Myren, Richard A., *Law and Justice* (1987)

Neubauer, David W., *America's Courts and the Criminal Justice System* (1988)

Rossum, Ralph A., *The Politics of the Criminal Justice System: An Organizational Analysis* (1978)

Scheingold, Stuart, *The Politics of Law and Order* (1984)

Schlesinger, Steven R., *Exclusionary Injustice* (1977)

Schwartz, Herman, *Taps, Bugs, and Fooling the People* (1977)

Stephens, Otis, *The Supreme Court and Confessions of Guilt* (1973)

Self-Incrimination

Berger, Mark, *Taking the Fifth: The Supreme Court and the Privilege against Self-Incrimination* (1980)

Helmholz, R.H., et al., *The Privilege Against Self-Incrimination: Its Origins and Development* (1997)

Trial Rights

Abramson, Jeffrey, *We the Jury: The Jury System and the Ideal of Democracy* (1994)

Adler, Stephen, J., *The Jury: Disorder in the Court* (1994)

Eisenstein, James, and Herbert Jacob, *Felony Justice* (1977)

Finkel, Norman J., *Commonsense Justice: Jurors Notions of the Law* (1995)

Hastie, Reid, Steven D. Penrod, and Nancy Pennington, *Inside the Jury* (1983)

Heumann, Milton, *Plea Bargaining* (1978)

Kalven, Harry, and Hans Zeisel, *The American Jury* (1966)

Levine, James P., *Juries and Politics* (1992)

Shapiro, Barbara J., *Beyond Reasonable Doubt and Probable Cause: Historical Perspectives on the Anglo-American Law of Evidence* (1991)

Thaler, Paul, *The Watchful Eye: American Justice in the Age of the Television Trial* (1994)

Walker, Sam, Cassia Spohn, and Miriam DeLone, *The Color of Justice* (1996)

Double Jeopardy

Friedland, Martin, *Double Jeopardy* (1969)

Sigler, Jay A., *Double Jeopardy: The Development of a Legal and Social Policy* (1969)

Punishment

Acker, James R., Robert M. Bohm, and Charles Lanier, eds., *America's Experiment with Capital Punishment: Reflections on the Past, Present, and Future of the Ultimate Penal Sanction* (1998)

Baldus, David C., George Woodworth, Charles A. Pulaski, Jr., *Equal Justice and the Death Penalty: Legal and Empirical Analysis* (1990)

Baldus, David C., George Woodworth, Charles A. Pulaski, Jr., and James W. L. Cole, *Statistical Proof of Discrimination* (1980)

Bedau, Hugo Adam, ed., *The Death Penalty in America*, 3rd ed. (1982)

———, *Death Is Different: Studies in the Morality, Law, and Politics of Capital Punishment* (1987)

———, *The Death Penalty in America: Current Controversies* (1997)

Berger, Raoul, *Death Penalties: The Supreme Court's Obstacle Course* (1982)

Berkson, Larry C., *The Concept of Cruel and Unusual Punishment* (1975)

Berns, Walter, *For Capital Punishment: Crime and the Morality of the Death Penalty* (1979)

Black, Charles L., *Capital Punishment: The Inevitability of Caprice and Mistake* (1974)

Bowers, William J., and Glenn L. Pierce, *Legal Homicide: Death as Punishment in America, 1864–1982* (1984)

Epstein, Lee, and Joseph F. Kobylka, *The Supreme Court and Legal Change: Abortion and the Death Penalty* (1992)

Gerber, Rudolph J., *Cruel and Usual: Our Criminal Justice System* (1999)

Gross, Samuel R., *Death and Discrimination: Racial Disparities in Capital Sentencing* (1989)

Haines, Herbert H., *Against Capital Punishment: The Anti-Death Penalty Movement in America, 1972–1994* (1996)

Marquart, James W., Sheldon Ekland-Olson, and Jonathan R. Sorenson, *The Rope, the Chair, and the Needle: Capital Punishment in Texas, 1923–1990* (1994)

Meltsner, Michael, *Cruel and Unusual: The Supreme Court and Capital Punishment* (1973)

Miller, Kent S., and Michael L. Radelet, *Executing the Mentally Ill: The Criminal Justice System and the Case of Alvin Ford* (1993)

Nakell, Barry, and Kenneth A. Hardy, *The Arbitrariness of the Death Penalty* (1987)

Prejean, Sister Helen, *Dead Man Walking* (1994)

Radelet, Michael L., Hugo Adam Bedau, and Constance E. Putnam, *In Spite of Innocence: The Ordeal of 400 Americans Wrongly Convicted of Crimes Punishable by Death* (1992)

Russell, Gregory D., *The Death Penalty and Racial Bias: Overturning Supreme Court Assumptions* (1994)

Sellin, Thorsten, *The Penalty of Death* (1980)

Smith, Christopher E., *The Rehnquist Court and Criminal Punishment* (1997)

Tonry, Michael, *Malign Neglect: Race, Crime, and Punishment* (2000)

Van den Haag, Ernest, *Punishing Criminals: Concerning a Very Old and Painful Question* (1975)

Van den Haag, Ernest, and John P. Conrad, *The Death Penalty: A Debate* (1983)

Vila, Bryan, and Cynthia Morris, ed., *Capital Punishment in the United States: A Documentary History* (1997)

White, Welsh S., *The Death Penalty in the Nineties: An Examination of the Modern System of Capital Punishment* (1991)

Yackle, Larry W., *Postconviction Remedies* (1981)

———, *Reform and Regret: The Story of Federal Judicial Involvement in the Alabama Prison System* (1989)

On Leading Cases

Carter, Dan T., *Scottsboro: A Tragedy of the American South* (1969)

Goodman, James, *Stories of Scottsboro: The Rape Case That Shocked 1930's America and Revived the Struggle for Equality* (1994)

Lewis, Anthony, *Gideon's Trumpet* (1964)

Additional works are listed in General and Supplemental Bibliography.

CASES

Katz v. United States

389 U.S. 347 (1967), 7-1
Opinion of the Court: Stewart (Brennan, Douglas, Fortas, Harlan, Warren, White)
Dissenting: Black
Not participating: Marshall

How does the Court clarify the meaning of the Fourth Amendment? What is an "expectation of privacy"? On what does it depend? Do persons engaged in illegal acts have the same expectation of privacy as other persons? Should they?

Stewart, for the Court:

The petitioner [Katz] was convicted . . . [of] transmitting wagering information by telephone from Los Angeles to Miami and Boston, in violation of a federal statute. At trial, the Government was permitted, over [Katz's] objection, to introduce evidence of the [his] end of telephone conversations, overheard by FBI agents who had attached an electronic listening and recording device to the outside of the public telephone booth from which he had placed his calls. . . .

. . . [Katz] has strenuously argued that the booth was a "constitutionally protected area." The Government has maintained with equal vigor that it was not. But this effort to decide whether or not a given "area," viewed in the abstract, is "constitutionally protected" deflects attention from the problem presented by this case. For the Fourth Amendment protects people, not places. What a person knowingly exposes to the public, even in his own home or office, is not a subject of Fourth Amendment protection. But what he seeks to preserve as private, even in an area accessible to the public, may be constitutionally protected.

The Government stresses the fact that the telephone booth from which [Katz] made his calls was constructed partly of glass, so that he was as visible after he entered it as he would have been if he had remained outside. But what he sought to exclude when he entered the booth was not the intruding eye—it was the uninvited ear. He did not shed his right to do so simply because he made his calls from a place where he might be seen. No less than an individual in a business office, in a friend's apartment, or in a taxicab, a person in a telephone booth may rely upon the protection of the Fourth Amendment. One who occupies it, shuts the door behind him, and pays the toll that permits him to place a call is surely entitled to assume that the words he utters into the mouthpiece will not be broadcast to the world. To read the Constitution more narrowly is to ignore the vital role that the public telephone has come to play in private communication.

The Government contends, however, that the activities of its agents in this case should not be tested by Fourth Amendment requirements, for the surveillance technique they employed involved no physical penetration of the telephone booth from which [Katz] placed his calls. It is true that the absence of such penetration was at one time thought to foreclose further Fourth Amendment inquiry, for that Amendment was thought to limit only searches and seizures of tangible property. But "[t]he premise that property interests control the right of the Government to search and seize has been discredited." *Warden v. Hayden* Thus, although a closely divided Court supposed in Olmstead [*v. United States*] that surveillance without any trespass and without the seizure of any material object fell outside the ambit of the Constitution, we have since departed from the narrow view on which that decision rested. Indeed, we have expressly held that the Fourth Amendment governs not only the seizure of tangible items, but extends as well to the recording of oral statements, overheard without any "technical trespass under . . . local property law." *Silverman v. United States* Once this much is acknowledged, and once it is recognized that the Fourth Amendment protects people—and not simply "areas"—against unreasonable searches and seizures, it becomes clear that the reach of that Amendment cannot turn upon the presence or absence of a physical intrusion into any given enclosure.

We conclude that the underpinnings of *Olmstead* and *Goldman* [v. *United States*] have been so eroded by our subsequent decisions that the "trespass" doctrine there enunciated can no longer be regarded as controlling. The Government's activities in electronically listening to and recording [Katz's] words violated the privacy upon which he justifiably relied while using the telephone booth, and thus constituted a "search and seizure" within the meaning of the Fourth Amend-

ment. The fact that the electronic device employed to achieve that end did not happen to penetrate the wall of the booth can have no constitutional significance.

The question remaining for decision, then, is whether the search and seizure conducted in this case complied with constitutional standards. In that regard, the Government's position is that its agents acted in an entirely defensible manner: they did not begin their electronic surveillance until investigation of [Katz's] activities had established a strong probability that he was using the telephone in question to transmit gambling information to persons in other States, in violation of federal law. Moreover, the surveillance was limited, both in scope and in duration, to the specific purpose of establishing the contents of [his] unlawful telephonic communications. The agents confined their surveillance to the brief periods during which he used the telephone booth, and they took great care to overhear only the conversations of the [Katz] himself.

Accepting this account of the Government's actions as accurate, it is clear that this surveillance was so narrowly circumscribed that a duly authorized magistrate, properly notified of the need for such investigation, specifically informed of the basis on which it was to proceed, and clearly apprised of the precise intrusion it would entail, could constitutionally have authorized, with appropriate safeguards, the very limited search and seizure that the Government asserts, in fact, took place. Only last Term we sustained the validity of such an authorization, holding that, under sufficiently "precise and discriminate circumstances," a federal court may empower government agents to employ a concealed electronic device "for the narrow and particularized purpose of ascertaining the truth of the . . . allegations" of a "detailed factual affidavit alleging the commission of a specific criminal offense." *Osborn v. United States* Discussing that holding, the Court in *Berger v. New York*, said that "the order authorizing the use of the electronic device" in *Osborn* "afforded similar protections to those . . . of conventional warrants authorizing the seizure of tangible evidence." Through those protections, "no greater invasion of privacy was permitted than was necessary under the circumstances." Here, too, a similar judicial order could have accommodated "the legitimate needs of law enforcement" by authorizing the carefully limited use of electronic surveillance.

The Government urges that, because its agents relied upon the decisions in *Olmstead* and *Goldman*, and because they did no more here than they might properly have done with prior judicial sanction, we should retroactively validate their conduct. That we cannot do. It is apparent that the agents in this case acted with restraint. Yet the inescapable fact is that this restraint was imposed by the agents themselves, not by a judicial officer. They were not required, before commencing the search, to present their estimate of probable cause for detached scrutiny by a neutral magistrate. They were not compelled, during the conduct of the search itself, to observe precise limits established in advance by a specific court order. Nor were they directed, after the search had been completed, to notify the authorizing magistrate in detail of all that had been seized. In the absence of such safeguards, this Court has never sustained a search upon the sole ground that officers reasonably expected to find evidence of a particular crime and voluntarily confined their activities to the least intrusive means consistent with that end. Searches conducted without warrants have been held unlawful "notwithstanding facts unquestionably showing probable cause," *Agnello v. United States,* for the Constitution requires "that the deliberate, impartial judgment of a judicial officer . . . be interposed between the citizen and the police. . . ." *Wong Sun v. United States . . .*

These considerations do not vanish when the search in question is transferred from the setting of a home, an office, or a hotel room to that of a telephone booth. Wherever a man may be, he is entitled to know that he will remain free from unreasonable searches and seizures. The government agents here ignored "the procedure of antecedent justification . . . that is central to the Fourth Amendment," a procedure that we hold to be a constitutional precondition of the kind of electronic surveillance involved in this case. . . .

Black, dissenting:

If I could agree with the Court that eavesdropping carried on by electronic means (equivalent to wiretapping) constitutes a "search" or "seizure," I would be happy to join the Court's opinion For on that premise, my Brother Stewart sets out methods in accord with the Fourth Amendment to guide States in the enactment and enforcement of laws passed to regulate wiretapping by government. In this respect, today's opinion differs sharply from *Berger v. New York,* . . . which held void on its face a New York statute authorizing wiretapping on warrants issued by magistrates on showings of

probable cause. The Berger case also set up what appeared to be insuperable obstacles to the valid passage of such wiretapping laws by States. The Court's opinion in this case, however, removes the doubts about state power in this field and abates to a large extent the confusion and near-paralyzing effect of the Berger holding. Notwithstanding these good efforts of the Court, I am still unable to agree with its interpretation of the Fourth Amendment.

My basic objection is two-fold: (1) I do not believe that the words of the Amendment will bear the meaning given them by today's decision, and (2) I do not believe that it is the proper role of this Court to rewrite the Amendment in order "to bring it into harmony with the times," and thus reach a result that many people believe to be desirable. . . .

Chimel v. California

395 U.S. 752 (1969), 6-2
Opinion of the Court: Stewart (Brennan, Douglas, Harlan, Marshall, Warren)
Dissenting: Black, White

What area surrounding an arrested person may be searched without violating the Fourth Amendment? How does this change the rule that had been in effect before? What is the Court's rationale for the change? Why does Justice White believe the search in this case was reasonable? If the Court can say what the Fourth Amendment requires in one case and, a few years later, in another case involving similar circumstances say that it requires something quite different, what does that say about the meaning of the Fourth Amendment?

Stewart, for the Court:

. . . Late in the afternoon of September 13, 1965, three police officers arrived at the . . . home of the petitioner with a warrant authorizing his arrest for the burglary of a coin shop. The officers knocked on the door, identified themselves to the petitioner's wife . . . [who] ushered them into the house, where they waited 10 or 15 minutes until the petitioner returned home from work . . . [and then] . . . handed him the arrest warrant and asked for permission to "look around." [He] objected, but was advised that, "on the basis of the lawful arrest," the officers would nonetheless conduct a search. No search warrant had been issued.

Accompanied by [his] wife, the officers then looked through the entire three-bedroom house, including the attic, the garage, and a small workshop. In some rooms, the search was relatively cursory. In the master bedroom and sewing room, however, the officers directed the petitioner's wife to open drawers and "to physically move contents of the drawers from side to side so that [they] might view any items that would have come from [the] burglary."

After completing the search, they seized numerous items—primarily coins, but also several medals, tokens, and a few other objects. The entire search took between 45 minutes and an hour.

At the petitioner's subsequent state trial on two charges of burglary, the items taken from his house were admitted into evidence against him over his objection that they had been unconstitutionally seized. He was convicted. . . .

. . . [W]e proceed on the hypothesis that the California courts were correct in holding that the arrest of the petitioner was valid under the Constitution. This brings us directly to the question whether the warrantless search of the petitioner's entire house can be constitutionally justified as incident to that arrest. The decisions of this Court bearing upon that question have been far from consistent, as even the most cursory review makes evident. . . .

[I]n *Harris v. United States* . . . officers had obtained a warrant for Harris' arrest on the basis of his alleged involvement with the cashing and interstate transportation of a forged check. He was arrested in the living room of his four-room apartment, and, in an attempt to recover two canceled checks thought to have been used in effecting the forgery, the officers undertook a thorough search of the entire apartment. Inside a desk drawer, they found a sealed envelope marked "George Harris, personal papers." The envelope, which was then torn open, was found to contain altered Selective Service documents, and those documents were used to secure Harris' conviction for violating the Selective Training and Service Act of 1940. The Court rejected *Harris'* Fourth Amendment claim, sustaining the search as "incident to arrest."

Only a year after *Harris,* however, the pendulum swung again. In *Trupiano v. United States* agents raided the site of an illicit distillery, saw one of several conspirators operating the still, and arrested him, contemporaneously "seiz[ing] the illicit distillery." The Court held that the arrest and others made subsequently had been valid, but that the unexplained failure of the agents to procure a search warrant—in spite of the fact that they had had more than enough time before the raid to do so—rendered the search unlawful. The opinion stated:

> It is a cardinal rule that, in seizing goods and articles, law enforcement agents must secure and use search warrants wherever reasonably practicable. . . .
>
> A search or seizure without a warrant as an incident to a lawful arrest has always been considered to be a strictly limited right. It grows out of the inherent necessities of the situation at the time of the arrest. But there must be something more in the way of necessity than merely a lawful arrest.

In 1950, two years after *Trupiano,* came *United States v. Rabinowitz,* the decision upon which California primarily relies in the case now before us. . . .

Rabinowitz has come to stand for the proposition, inter alia, that a warrantless search "incident to a lawful arrest" may generally extend to the area that is considered to be in the "possession" or under the "control" of the person arrested. And it was on the basis of that proposition that the California courts upheld the search of the petitioner's entire house in this case. That doctrine, however, at least in the broad sense in which it was applied by the California courts in this case, can withstand neither historical nor rational analysis. . . .

Only last Term, in *Terry Ohio,* we emphasized that "the police must, whenever practicable, obtain advance judicial approval of searches and seizures through the warrant procedure," and that "[t]he scope of [a] search must be 'strictly tied to and justified by' the circumstances which rendered its initiation permissible." . . .

A similar analysis underlies the "search incident to arrest" principle, and marks its proper extent. When an arrest is made, it is reasonable for the arresting officer to search the person arrested in order to remove any weapons that the latter might seek to use in order to resist arrest or effect his escape. Otherwise, the officer's safety might well be endangered, and the arrest itself frustrated. In addition, it is entirely reasonable for the arresting officer to search for and seize any evidence on the arrestee's person in order to prevent its concealment or destruction. And the area into which an arrestee might reach in order to grab a weapon or evidentiary items must, of course, be governed by a like rule. A gun on a table or in a drawer in front of one who is arrested can be as dangerous to the arresting officer as one concealed in the clothing of the person arrested. There is ample justification, therefore, for a search of the arrestee's person and the area "within his immediate control"—construing that phrase to mean the area from within which he might gain possession of a weapon or destructible evidence.

There is no comparable justification, however, for routinely searching any room other than that in which an arrest occurs—or, for that matter, for searching through all the desk drawers or other closed or concealed areas in that room itself. Such searches, in the absence of well recognized exceptions, may be made only under the authority of a search warrant. The "adherence to judicial processes" mandated by the Fourth Amendment requires no less. . . .

It is argued in the present case that it is "reasonable" to search a man's house when he is arrested in it. But that argument is founded on little more than a subjective view regarding the acceptability of certain sorts of police conduct, and not on considerations relevant to Fourth Amendment interests. Under such an unconfined analysis, Fourth Amendment protection in this area would approach the evaporation point. It is not easy to explain why, for instance, it is less subjectively "reasonable" to search a man's house when he is arrested on his front lawn—or just down the street—than it is when he happens to be in the house at the time of arrest. . . .

It would be possible, of course, to draw a line between *Rabinowitz* and *Harris,* on the one hand, and this case, on the other. For *Rabinowitz* involved a single room, and *Harris* a four-room apartment, while, in the case before us, an entire house was searched. But such a distinction would be highly artificial. The rationale that allowed the searches and seizures in *Rabinowitz* and *Harris* would allow the searches and seizures in this case. No consideration relevant to the Fourth Amendment suggests any point of rational limitation once the search is allowed to go beyond the area from which the person arrested might obtain weapons or evidentiary items. The only reasoned distinction is one between a search of the person arrested and the area within his reach, on the one hand, and more extensive searches, on the other.

The petitioner correctly points out that one result of decisions such as *Rabinowitz* and *Harris* is to give law enforcement officials the opportunity to engage in searches not justified by probable cause, by the simple expedient of arranging to arrest suspects at home, rather than elsewhere. We do not suggest that

the petitioner is necessarily correct in his assertion that such a strategy was utilized here, but the fact remains that, had he been arrested earlier in the day, at his place of employment, rather than at home, no search of his house could have been made without a search warrant. . . .

Application of sound Fourth Amendment principles to the facts of this case produces a clear result. The search here went far beyond the petitioner's person and the area from within which he might have obtained either a weapon or something that could have been used as evidence against him. There was no constitutional justification, in the absence of a search warrant, for extending the search beyond that area. The scope of the search was, therefore, "unreasonable" under the Fourth and Fourteenth Amendments, and petitioner's conviction cannot stand.

White, dissenting:

. . . The issue in this case is not the breadth of the search, since there was clearly probable cause for the search which was carried out. No broader search than if the officers had a warrant would be permitted. The only issue is whether a search warrant was required as a precondition to that search. It is agreed that such a warrant would be required absent exigent circumstances. I would hold that the fact of arrest supplies such an exigent circumstance, since the police had lawfully gained entry to the premises to effect the arrest and since delaying the search to secure a warrant would have involved the risk of not recovering the fruits of the crime.

The majority today proscribes searches for which there is probable cause and which may prove fruitless unless carried out immediately. This rule will have no added effect whatsoever in protecting the rights of the criminal accused at trial against introduction of evidence seized without probable cause. Such evidence could not be introduced under the old rule. Nor does the majority today give any added protection to the right of privacy of those whose houses there is probable cause to search. A warrant would still be sworn out for those houses, and the privacy of their owners invaded. The only possible justification for the majority's rule is that, in some instances, arresting officers may search when they have no probable cause to do so, and that such unlawful searches might be prevented if the officers first sought a warrant from a magistrate. Against the possible protection of privacy in that class of cases, in which the privacy of the house has already been invaded by entry to make the arrest—an entry for which the majority does not assert that any warrant is necessary—must be weighed the risk of destruction of evidence for which there is probable cause to search, as a result of delays in obtaining a search warrant. Without more basis for radical change than the Court's opinion reveals, I would not upset the balance of these interests which has been struck by the former decisions of this Court.

In considering searches incident to arrest, it must be remembered that there will be immediate opportunity to challenge the probable cause for the search in an adversary proceeding. The suspect has been apprised of the search by his very presence at the scene, and, having been arrested, he will soon be brought into contact with people who can explain his rights. . . . [A] search contemporaneous with a warrantless arrest is specially safeguarded, since "[s]uch an arrest may constitutionally be made only upon probable cause, the existence of which is subject to judicial examination, and such an arrest demands the prompt bringing of the person arrested before a judicial officer, where the existence of probable cause is to be inquired into." *Mallory v. United States* . . .

An arrested man, by definition conscious of the police interest in him, and provided almost immediately with a lawyer and a judge, is in an excellent position to dispute the reasonableness of his arrest and contemporaneous search in a full adversary proceeding. I would uphold the constitutionality of this search contemporaneous with an arrest, since there were probable cause both for the search and for the arrest, exigent circumstances involving the removal or destruction of evidence, and satisfactory opportunity to dispute the issues of probable cause shortly thereafter. In this case, the search was reasonable.

Terry v. Ohio

392 U.S. 1 (1968), 8-1
Opinion of the Court: Warren (Black, Brennan, Fortas, Harlan, Marshall, Stewart, White)
Dissenting: Douglas

How does this case change the rule that the Fourth Amendment requires probable cause to make a search without a warrant? What are the limits to the type of search upheld in this case? What is the difference between probable cause and mere suspicion? Is the previous experience of the searching officer relevant in the Court's analysis? Is this case better understood as one allowing a greater number of limited searches based on lesser cause or as allowing a greater number of searches but for more limited purpose?

Warren, for the Court:

. . . Petitioner Terry was convicted of carrying a concealed weapon . . . [T]he prosecution introduced in evidence two revolvers and a number of bullets seized from Terry and a codefendant, Richard Chilton, by Cleveland Police Detective Martin McFadden, [who] testified that, while . . . patrolling in plain clothes in downtown Cleveland . . . his attention was attracted by two men, Chilton and Terry, standing on the corner of Huron Road and Euclid Avenue. He had never seen the two men before, and he was unable to say precisely what first drew his eye to them. However, he testified that he had been a policeman for 39 years and a detective for 35, and that he had been assigned to patrol this vicinity of downtown Cleveland for shoplifters and pickpockets for 30 years. . . .

. . . [A]fter observing their elaborately casual and oft-repeated reconnaissance of [a] store window on Huron Road, he suspected the two men [now joined by a third] of "casing a job, a stick-up" . . . [He] approached, . . . identified himself as a police officer and asked for their names. . . . [He then] patted down the outside of [Terry's] clothing. In the left breast pocket of [his] overcoat, . . . McFadden felt a pistol. He reached inside the overcoat pocket, but was unable to remove the gun. At this point, keeping Terry between himself and the others . . . he removed Terry's overcoat completely, removed a .38 caliber revolver from the pocket and ordered all three men to face the wall with their hands raised. Officer McFadden proceeded to pat down the outer clothing of Chilton and the third man, Katz. He discovered another revolver in the outer pocket of Chilton's overcoat, but no weapons were found on Katz. The officer testified that he only patted the men down to see whether they had weapons, and that he did not put his hands beneath the outer garments of either Terry or Chilton until he felt their guns. So far as appears from the record, he never placed his hands beneath Katz's outer garments. . . .

. . . We have recently held that "the Fourth Amendment protects people, not places," *Katz v. United States*, and wherever an individual may harbor a reasonable "expectation of privacy," he is entitled to be free from unreasonable governmental intrusion. Of course, the specific content and incidents of this right must be shaped by the context in which it is asserted. For "what the Constitution forbids is not all searches and seizures, but unreasonable searches and seizures." *Elkins v. United States.* Unquestionably petitioner was entitled to the protection of the Fourth Amendment as he walked down the street in Cleveland. The question is whether, in all the circumstances of this on-the-street encounter, his right to personal security was violated by an unreasonable search and seizure....

Our first task is to establish at what point in this encounter the Fourth Amendment becomes relevant. That is, we must decide whether and when Officer McFadden "seized" Terry, and whether and when he conducted a "search." There is some suggestion in the use of such terms as "stop" and "frisk" that such police conduct is outside the purview of the Fourth Amendment because neither action rises to the level of a "search" or "seizure" within the meaning of the Constitution. We emphatically reject this notion. It is quite plain that the Fourth Amendment governs "seizures" of the person which do not eventuate in a trip to the stationhouse and prosecution for crime—"arrests" in traditional terminology. It must be recognized that, whenever a police officer accosts an individual and restrains his freedom to walk away, he has "seized" that person. And it is nothing less than sheer torture of the English language to suggest that a careful exploration of the outer surfaces of a person's clothing all over his or her body in an attempt to find weapons is not a "search." Moreover, it is simply fantastic to urge that such a procedure performed in public by a policeman while the citizen stands helpless, perhaps facing a wall with his hands raised, is a "petty indignity." It is a serious intrusion upon the sanctity of the person, which may inflict great indignity and arouse strong resentment, and it is not to be undertaken lightly.

The danger in the logic which proceeds upon distinctions between a "stop" and an "arrest," or "seizure" of the person, and between a "frisk" and a "search," is twofold. It seeks to isolate from constitutional scrutiny the initial stages of the contact between the policeman and the citizen. And, by suggesting a rigid all-or-nothing model of justification and regulation under the Amendment, it obscures the utility of limitations upon the scope, as well as the initiation, of police action as a means of constitutional regulation. This Court has held, in the past that a search which is reasonable at its inception may violate the Fourth Amendment by virtue of its intolerable intensity and scope. The scope of the search must be "strictly tied to and justified by" the circumstances which rendered its initiation permissible.

The distinctions of classical "stop-and-frisk" theory thus serve to divert attention from the central inquiry under the Fourth Amendment—the reasonableness in all the circumstances of the particular governmental invasion of a citizen's personal security. "Search" and "seizure" are not talismans. We therefore reject the notions that the Fourth Amendment does not come into play at all as a limitation upon police conduct if the officers stop short of something called a "technical arrest" or a "full-blown search."

In this case, there can be no question, then, that Officer McFadden "seized" petitioner and subjected him to a "search" when he took hold of him and patted down the outer surfaces of his clothing. We must decide whether, at that point, it was reasonable for Officer McFadden to have interfered with petitioner's personal security as he did....

... Certainly it would be unreasonable to require that police officers take unnecessary risks in the performance of their duties. American criminals have a long tradition of armed violence, and every year in this country many law enforcement officers are killed in the line of duty, and thousands more are wounded. Virtually all of these deaths and a substantial portion of the injuries are inflicted with guns and knives.

In view of these facts, we cannot blind ourselves to the need for law enforcement officers to protect themselves and other prospective victims of violence in situations where they may lack probable cause for an arrest. When an officer is justified in believing that the individual whose suspicious behavior he is investigating at close range is armed and presently dangerous to the officer or to others, it would appear to be clearly unreasonable to deny the officer the power to take necessary measures to determine whether the person is, in fact, carrying a weapon and to neutralize the threat of physical harm....

We must now examine the conduct of Officer McFadden in this case to determine whether his search and seizure of petitioner were reasonable, both at their inception and as conducted.... [W]hen Officer McFadden approached the three men gathered before the display window at Zucker's store, he had observed enough to make it quite reasonable to fear that they were armed, and nothing in their response to his hailing them, identifying himself as a police officer, and asking their names served to dispel that reasonable belief. We cannot say his decision at that point to seize Terry and pat his clothing for weapons was the product of a volatile or inventive imagination, or was undertaken simply as an act of harassment; the record evidences the tempered act of a policeman who, in the course of an investigation, had to make a quick decision as to how to protect himself and others from possible danger, and took limited steps to do so.

The manner in which the seizure and search were conducted is, of course, as vital a part of the inquiry as whether they were warranted at all. The Fourth Amendment proceeds as much by limitations upon the scope of governmental action as by imposing preconditions upon its initiation. . . .

We need not develop at length in this case, however, the limitations which the Fourth Amendment places upon a protective seizure and search for weapons. These limitations will have to be developed in the concrete factual circumstances of individual cases. Suffice it to note that such a search, unlike a search without a warrant incident to a lawful arrest, is not justified by any need to prevent the disappearance or destruction of evidence of crime. The sole justification of the search in the present situation is the protection of the police officer and others nearby, and it must therefore be confined in scope to an intrusion reasonably designed to discover guns, knives, clubs, or other hidden instruments for the assault of the police officer.

The scope of the search in this case presents no serious problem in light of these standards. Officer McFadden patted down the outer clothing of petitioner and his two companions. He did not place his hands in their pockets or under the outer surface of their garments until he had felt weapons, and then he merely reached for and removed the guns. . . . Officer McFadden confined his search strictly to what was minimally necessary to learn whether the men were armed and to disarm them once he discovered the weapons. He did not conduct a general exploratory search for whatever evidence of criminal activity he might find.

We conclude that the revolver seized from Terry was properly admitted in evidence against him. At the time he seized petitioner and searched him for weapons, Officer McFadden had reasonable grounds to believe that petitioner was armed and dangerous, and it was necessary for the protection of himself and others to take swift measures to discover the true facts and neutralize the threat of harm if it materialized.

The policeman carefully restricted his search to what was appropriate to the discovery of the particular items which he sought. Each case of this sort will, of course, have to be decided on its own facts. We merely hold today that, where a police officer observes unusual conduct which leads him reasonably to conclude in light of his experience that criminal activity may be afoot and that the persons with whom he is dealing may be armed and presently dangerous, where, in the course of investigating this behavior, he identifies himself as a policeman and makes reasonable inquiries, and where nothing in the initial stages of the encounter serves to dispel his reasonable fear for his own or others' safety, he is entitled for the protection of himself and others in the area to conduct a carefully limited search of the outer clothing of such persons in an attempt to discover weapons which might be used to assault him. Such a search is a reasonable search under the Fourth Amendment, and any weapons seized may properly be introduced in evidence against the person from whom they were taken.

Douglas, dissenting:

I agree that petitioner was "seized" within the meaning of the Fourth Amendment. I also agree that frisking petitioner and his companions for guns was a "search." But it is a mystery how that "search" and that "seizure" can be constitutional by Fourth Amendment standards unless there was "probable cause" to believe that (1) a crime had been committed or (2) a crime was in the process of being committed or (3) a crime was about to be committed.

The opinion of the Court disclaims the existence of "probable cause." If loitering were in issue and that was the offense charged, there would be "probable cause" shown. But the crime here is carrying concealed weapons; and there is no basis for concluding that the officer had "probable cause" for believing that that crime was being committed. Had a warrant been sought, a magistrate would, therefore, have been unauthorized to issue one, for he can act only if there is a showing of "probable cause." We hold today that the police have greater authority to make a "seizure" and conduct a "search" than a judge has to authorize such action. We have said precisely the opposite over and over again. . . .

To give the police greater power than a magistrate is to take a long step down the totalitarian path. Perhaps such a step is desirable to cope with modern forms of lawlessness. But if it is taken, it should be the deliberate choice of the people through a constitutional amendment. . . .

There have been powerful hydraulic pressures throughout our history that bear heavily on the Court to water down constitutional guarantees and give the police the upper hand. That hydraulic pressure has probably never been greater than it is today.

Yet if the individual is no longer to be sovereign, if the police can pick him up whenever they do not like the cut of his jib, if they can "seize" and "search" him in their discretion, we enter a new regime. The decision to enter it should be made only after a full debate by the people of this country. . . .

United States v. Ross

456 U.S. 798 (1982), 6-3
Opinion of the Court: Stevens (Blackmun, Burger,
 Powell, Rehnquist, O'Connor)
Dissenting: Brennan, Marshall, White

On information from an informant describing sales of narcotics from the trunk of a car parked at a certain location, District of Columbia police officers drove to the location, found the car, and arrested the driver, Ross, who matched the description given by the informant. Opening the car's trunk, one of the officers found a closed brown paper bag and, after opening it, discovered plastic bags containing white powder (later determined to be heroin). The officer drove the car to headquarters, where a second warrantless search of the trunk turned up a zippered leather pouch containing cash. Ross was later convicted of possession of heroin with intent to distribute. The heroin and currency found in the searches were admitted as evidence over Ross's objection.

What are the Court's reasons for holding that the constitutional rules for searching cars are different from those for searching homes or buildings? How does the Court rely on or move away from its previous holdings on searches of cars? How does it reason that the search in this case was conducted with probable cause? Is this decision consistent with Katz v. United States *(p. 374)?*

Stevens, for the Court:

In *Carroll v. United States*, the Court held that a warrantless search of an automobile stopped by police officers who had probable cause to believe the vehicle contained contraband was not unreasonable within the meaning of the Fourth Amendment. The Court in *Carroll* did not explicitly address the scope of the search that is permissible. In this case, we consider the extent to which police officers—who have legitimately stopped an automobile and who have probable cause to believe that contraband is concealed somewhere within it—may conduct a probing search of compartments and containers within the vehicle whose contents are not in plain view. We hold that they may conduct a search of the vehicle that is as thorough as a magistrate could authorize in a warrant "particularly describing the place to be searched." . . .

We begin with a review of the decision in Carroll itself. . . .

. . . [S]ince its earliest days Congress had recognized the impracticability of securing a warrant in cases involving the transportation of contraband goods. It is this impracticability, viewed in historical perspective, that provided the basis for the Carroll decision. Given the nature of an automobile in transit, the Court recognized that an immediate intrusion is necessary if police officers are to secure the illicit substance. In this class of cases, the Court held that a warrantless search of an automobile is not unreasonable. . . .

In defining the nature of this "exception" to the general rule that, "[i]n cases where the securing of a warrant is reasonably practicable, it must be used," the Court in *Carroll* emphasized the importance of the requirement that officers have probable cause to believe that the vehicle contains contraband. . . .

In short, the exception to the warrant requirement established in *Carroll*—the scope of which we consider in this case—applies only to searches of vehicles that are supported by probable cause. In this class of cases, a search is not unreasonable if based on facts that would justify the issuance of a warrant, even though a warrant has not actually been obtained.

The rationale justifying a warrantless search of an automobile that is believed to be transporting contraband arguably applies with equal force to any movable container that is believed to be carrying an illicit substance. That argument, however, was squarely rejected in *United States v. Chadwick*.

Chadwick involved the warrantless search of a 200-pound footlocker secured with two padlocks. Federal railroad officials in San Diego became suspicious when they noticed that a brown footlocker loaded onto a train bound for Boston was unusually heavy and leaking talcum powder, a substance often used to mask the odor of marihuana. Narcotics agents met the train in Boston and a trained police dog signaled the presence of a controlled substance inside the footlocker. The agents did not seize the footlocker, however, at this time; they waited until respondent Chadwick arrived and the footlocker was placed in the trunk of Chadwick's automobile. Before the engine was started, the officers arrested Chadwick and his two companions. The agents then removed the footlocker to a secured place, opened it without a warrant, and discovered a large quantity of marihuana [sic]. . . .

The Court in *Chadwick* specifically rejected the argument that the warrantless search was "reasonable" because a footlocker has some of the mobile characteristics that support warrantless searches of automobiles. The Court recognized that "a person's expectations of privacy in personal luggage are substantially greater than in an automobile," and noted that the practical problems associated with the temporary detention of a piece of luggage during the period of time necessary to obtain a warrant are significantly less than those associated with the detention of an automobile. In ruling that the warrantless search of the footlocker was unjustified, the Court reaffirmed the general principle that closed packages and containers may not be searched without a warrant. In sum, the Court in *Chadwick* declined to extend the rationale of the "automobile exception" to permit a warrantless search of any movable container found in a public place.

The facts in *Arkansas v. Sanders,* were similar to those in *Chadwick.* In *Sanders,* a Little Rock police officer received information from a reliable informant that Sanders would arrive at the local airport on a specified flight that afternoon carrying a green suitcase containing marihuana. The officer went to the airport. Sanders arrived on schedule, and retrieved a green suitcase from the airline baggage service. Sanders gave the suitcase to a waiting companion, who placed it in the trunk of a taxi. Sanders and his companion drove off in the cab; police officers followed and stopped the taxi several blocks from the airport. The officers opened the trunk, seized the suitcase, and searched it on the scene without a warrant. As predicted, the suitcase contained marihuana.

The Arkansas Supreme Court ruled that the warrantless search of the suitcase was impermissible under the Fourth Amendment, and this Court affirmed. As in *Chadwick,* the mere fact that the suitcase had been placed in the trunk of the vehicle did not render the automobile exception of *Carroll* applicable; the police had probable cause to seize the suitcase before it was placed in the trunk of the cab, and did not have

probable cause to search the taxi itself. Since the suitcase had been placed in the trunk, no danger existed that its contents could have been secreted elsewhere in the vehicle. As the Chief Justice noted in his opinion concurring in the judgment: "Because the police officers had probable cause to believe that respondent's green suitcase contained marihuana before it was placed in the trunk of the taxicab, their duty to obtain a search warrant before opening it is clear under *United States v. Chadwick.* . . . "

Robbins v. California . . . was a case in which suspicion was not directed at a specific container. In that case, the Court for the first time was forced to consider whether police officers who are entitled to conduct a warrantless search of an automobile stopped on a public roadway may open a container found within the vehicle. In the early morning of January 5, 1975, police officers stopped Robbins' station wagon because he was driving erratically. Robbins got out of the car, but later returned to obtain the vehicle's registration papers. When he opened the car door, the officers smelled marihuana smoke. One of the officers searched Robbins and discovered a vial of liquid; in a search of the interior of the car the officer found marihuana. The police officers then opened the tailgate of the station wagon and raised the cover of a recessed luggage compartment. In the compartment, they found two packages wrapped in green opaque plastic. The police unwrapped the packages and discovered a large amount of marihuana in each. . . .

. . . The California Court of Appeal held that "[s]earch of the automobile was proper when the officers learned that appellant was smoking marijuana when they stopped him," and that the warrantless search of the packages was justified because "the contents of the packages could have been inferred from their outward appearance, so that appellant could not have held a reasonable expectation of privacy with respect to the contents."

This Court reversed [Robbins's conviction]. Writing for a plurality, Justice Stewart rejected the argument that the outward appearance of the packages precluded Robbins from having a reasonable expectation of privacy in their contents. He also squarely rejected the argument that there is a constitutional distinction between searches of luggage and searches of "less worthy" containers. Justice Stewart reasoned that all containers are equally protected by the Fourth Amendment unless their contents are in plain view. The plurality concluded that the warrantless search was impermissible because *Chadwick* and *Sanders* had established that "a closed piece of luggage found in a lawfully searched car is constitutionally protected to the same extent as are closed pieces of luggage found anywhere else."

In an opinion concurring in the judgment, Justice Powell, the author of the Court's opinion in *Sanders*, stated that "[t]he plurality's approach strains the rationales of our prior cases, and imposes substantial burdens on law enforcement without vindicating any significant values of privacy." . . .

. . . Justice Powell concluded that institutional constraints made it inappropriate to reexamine basic doctrine without full adversary presentation. He concurred in the judgment, since it was supported—although not compelled—by the Court's opinion in *Sanders*, and stated that a future case might present a better opportunity for thorough consideration of the basic principles in this troubled area.

That case has arrived. Unlike *Chadwick* and *Sanders*, in this case, police officers had probable cause to search respondent's entire vehicle. Unlike *Robbins*, in this case, the parties have squarely addressed the question whether, in the course of a legitimate warrantless search of an automobile, police are entitled to open containers found within the vehicle. We now address that question. Its answer is determined by the scope of the search that is authorized by the exception to the warrant requirement set forth in Carroll. . . .

. . . [T]he practical consequences of the Carroll decision would be largely nullified if the permissible scope of a warrantless search of an automobile did not include containers and packages found inside the vehicle. Contraband goods rarely are strewn across the trunk or floor of a car; since, by their very nature, such goods must be withheld from public view, they rarely can be placed in an automobile unless they are enclosed within some form of container. The Court in *Carroll* held that "contraband goods concealed and illegally transported in an automobile or other vehicle may be searched for without a warrant." As we noted in *Henry v. United States*, the decision in *Carroll* "merely relaxed the requirements for a warrant on grounds of practicability." It neither broadened nor limited the scope of a lawful search based on probable cause. . . .

In the same manner, an individual's expectation of privacy in a vehicle and its contents may not survive if probable cause is given to believe that the vehicle is transporting contraband. Certainly the privacy interests in a car's trunk or glove compartment may be no less than those in a movable container. An individual undoubtedly has a significant interest that the upholstery of his automobile will not be ripped or a hidden compartment within it opened. These interests must yield to the authority of a search, however, which—in light of *Carroll*—does not itself require the prior approval of a magistrate. The scope of a warrantless search based on probable cause is no narrower—and no broader—than the scope of a search authorized by a warrant supported by probable cause. Only the prior approval of the magistrate is waived; the search otherwise is as the magistrate could authorize.

The scope of a warrantless search of an automobile thus is not defined by the nature of the container in which the contraband is secreted. Rather, it is defined by the object of the search and the places in which there is probable cause to believe that it may be found. Just as probable cause to believe that a stolen lawnmower may be found in a garage will not support a warrant to search an upstairs bedroom, probable cause to believe that undocumented aliens are being transported in a van will not justify a warrantless search of a suitcase. Probable cause to believe that a container placed in the trunk of a taxi contains contraband or evidence does not justify a search of the entire cab.

Our decision today is inconsistent with the disposition in *Robbins v. California* and with the portion of the opinion in *Arkansas v. Sanders* on which the plurality in *Robbins* relied. Nevertheless, the doctrine of stare decisis does not preclude this action. Although we have rejected some of the reasoning in Sanders, we adhere to our holding in that case; although we reject the precise holding in *Robbins*, there was no Court opinion supporting a single rationale for its judgment, and the reasoning we adopt today was not presented by the parties in that case. Moreover, it is clear that no legitimate reliance interest can be frustrated by our decision today. Of greatest importance, we are convinced that the rule we apply in this case is faithful to the interpretation of the Fourth Amendment that the Court has followed with substantial consistency throughout our history.

Marshall, dissenting:
The majority today not only repeals all realistic limits on warrantless automobile searches, it repeals the Fourth Amendment warrant requirement itself. By equating a police officer's estimation of probable cause with a magistrate's, the Court utterly disregards the value of a neutral and detached magistrate. . . .

According to the majority, whenever police have probable cause to believe that contraband may be found within an automobile that they have stopped on the highway, they may search not only the automobile but also any container found inside it, without obtaining a warrant. The scope of the search, we are told, is as broad as a magistrate could authorize in a warrant to search the automobile. The majority makes little attempt to justify this rule in terms of recognized Fourth Amendment values. The Court simply ignores the critical function that a magistrate serves. And although the Court purports to rely on the mobility of an automobile and the impracticability of obtaining a warrant, it never explains why these concerns permit the warrantless search of a container, which can easily be seized and immobilized while police are obtaining a warrant.

The new rule adopted by the Court today is completely incompatible with established Fourth Amendment principles, and takes a first step toward an unprecedented "probable cause" exception to the warrant requirement. In my view, under accepted standards, the warrantless search of the containers in this case clearly violates the Fourth Amendment....

The majority's rule is flatly inconsistent with these established Fourth Amendment principles concerning the scope of the automobile exception and the importance of the warrant requirement. Historically, the automobile exception has been limited to those situations where its application is compelled by the justifications described above. Today, the majority makes no attempt to base its decision on these justifications. This failure is not surprising, since the traditional rationales for the automobile exception plainly do not support extending it to the search of a container found inside a vehicle.

The practical mobility problem—deciding what to do with both the car and the occupants if an immediate search is not conducted—is simply not present in the case of movable containers, which can easily be seized and brought to the magistrate. The "lesser expectation of privacy" rationale also has little force. A container, as opposed to the car itself, does not reflect diminished privacy interests. Moreover, the practical corollary that this Court has recognized—that depriving occupants of the use of a car may be a greater intrusion than an immediate search—is of doubtful relevance here, since the owner of a container will rarely suffer significant inconvenience by being deprived of its use while a warrant is being obtained.

Ultimately, the majority, unable to rely on the justifications underlying the automobile exception, simply creates a new "probable cause" exception to the warrant requirement for automobiles. We have soundly rejected attempts to create such an exception in the past, and we should do so again today....

The only convincing explanation I discern for the majority's broad rule is expediency: it assists police in conducting automobile searches, ensuring that the private containers into which criminal suspects often place goods will no longer be a Fourth Amendment shield....

This case will have profound implications for the privacy of citizens traveling in automobiles, as the Court well understands. "For countless vehicles are stopped on highways and public streets every day, and our cases demonstrate that it is not uncommon for police officers to have probable cause to believe that contraband may be found in a stopped vehicle."

A closed paper bag, a toolbox, a knapsack, a suitcase, and an attache case can alike be searched without the protection of the judgment of a neutral magistrate, based only on the rarely disturbed decision of a police officer that he has probable cause to search for contraband in the vehicle. The Court derives satisfaction from the fact that its rule does not exalt the rights of the wealthy over the rights of the poor. A rule so broad that all citizens lose vital Fourth Amendment protection is no cause for celebration.

Ferguson v. Charleston

532 U.S. 67 (2001), 7-2
Opinion of the Court: Stevens (Breyer, Ginsburg, Kennedy, O'Connor, Rehnquist, Souter)
Dissenting: Scalia, Thomas

What are the Court's reasons for holding drug-testing unconstitutional in this case? Which are most important? Why is this case different from those in which it upheld the testing of school athletes, railway workers, and narcotic agents? What special need did the M-7 policy serve? How did the immediate objectives of the searches interfere with the ultimate purpose of the M-7 policy? How could the Charleston program be made constitutional?

Stevens, for the Court:
In this case, we must decide whether a state hospital's performance of a diagnostic test to obtain evidence of a patient's criminal conduct for law enforcement purposes is an unreasonable search if the patient has not consented to the procedure. More narrowly, the

question is whether the interest in using the threat of criminal sanctions to deter pregnant women from using cocaine can justify a departure from the general rule that an official nonconsensual search is unconstitutional if not authorized by a valid warrant.

In the fall of 1988, staff members at the public hospital operated in the city of Charleston by the Medical University of South Carolina (MUSC) became concerned about an apparent increase in the use of cocaine by patients who were receiving prenatal treatment. In response to this perceived increase, as of April 1989, MUSC began to order drug screens to be performed on urine samples from maternity patients who were suspected of using cocaine. If a patient tested positive, she was then referred by MUSC staff to the county substance abuse commission for counseling and treatment. . . .

. . . [Charleston Solicitor Charles] Condon took first steps in developing the policy at issue in this case. He organized the initial meetings, decided who would participate, and issued the invitations, in which he described his plan to prosecute women who tested positive for cocaine while pregnant. The task force that Condon formed included representatives of MUSC, the police, the County Substance Abuse Commission and the Department of Social Services. Their deliberations led to MUSC's adoption of a 12-page document entitled "POLICY M-7," dealing with the subject of "Management of Drug Abuse During Pregnancy."

The first three pages of Policy M-7 set forth the procedure to be followed by the hospital staff to "identify/assist pregnant patients suspected of drug abuse." The first section, entitled the "Identification of Drug Abusers," provided that . . . a chain of custody should be followed when obtaining and testing urine samples, presumably to make sure that the results could be used in subsequent criminal proceedings. The policy also provided for education and referral to a substance abuse clinic for patients who tested positive. Most important, it added the threat of law enforcement intervention that "provided the necessary 'leverage' to make the [p]olicy effective." . . .

. . . The policy also prescribed in detail the precise offenses with which a woman could be charged, depending on the stage of her pregnancy. If the pregnancy was weeks or less, the patient was to be charged with simple possession. If it was 28 weeks or more, she was to be charged with possession and distribution to a person under the age of 18—in this case, the fetus. If she delivered "while testing positive for illegal drugs,"

she was also to be charged with unlawful neglect of a child. Under the policy, the police were instructed to interrogate the arrestee in order "to ascertain the identity of the subject who provided illegal drugs to the suspect." Other than the provisions describing the substance abuse treatment to be offered to women who tested positive, the policy made no mention of any change in the prenatal care of such patients, nor did it prescribe any special treatment for the newborns.

Petitioners are 10 women who received obstetrical care at MUSC and who were arrested after testing positive for cocaine. . . . Respondents include the city of Charleston, law enforcement officials who helped develop and enforce the policy, and representatives of MUSC.

Petitioners' complaint challenged the validity of the policy under various theories, including the claim that warrantless and nonconsensual drug tests conducted for criminal investigatory purposes were unconstitutional searches. Respondents advanced two principal defenses to the constitutional claim: (1) that, as a matter of fact, petitioners had consented to the searches; and (2) that, as a matter of law, the searches were reasonable, even absent consent, because they were justified by special non-law-enforcement purposes. . . .

We granted certiorari. . . . Because we do not reach the question of the sufficiency of the evidence with respect to consent, we necessarily assume for purposes of our decision that the searches were conducted without the informed consent of the patients. We conclude that the judgment should be reversed and the case remanded for a decision on the consent issue.

Because MUSC is a state hospital, the members of its staff are government actors, subject to the strictures of the Fourth Amendment. Moreover, the urine tests conducted by those staff members were indisputably searches within the meaning of the Fourth Amendment. . . .

Because the hospital seeks to justify its authority to conduct drug tests and to turn the results over to law enforcement agents without the knowledge or consent of the patients, this case differs from the four previous cases in which we have considered whether comparable drug tests "fit within the closely guarded category of constitutionally permissible suspicionless searches." In three of those cases, we sustained drug tests for railway employees involved in train accidents, *Skinner v. Railway Labor Executives' Assn.*, for United States Customs Service employees seeking promotion to certain sensitive positions, *Treasury Employees v. Von*

Raab, and for high school students participating in interscholastic sports, *Vernonia School District 47J v. Acton.* In a fourth case, we struck down such testing for candidates for designated state offices as unreasonable. *Chandler v. Miller.*

In each of those cases, we employed a balancing test that weighed the intrusion on the individual's interest in privacy against the "special needs" that supported the program. As an initial matter, we note that the invasion of privacy in this case is far more substantial than in those cases. In the previous four cases, there was no misunderstanding about the purpose of the test or the potential use of the test results, and there were protections against the dissemination of the results to third parties. . . . The reasonable expectation of privacy enjoyed by the typical patient undergoing diagnostic tests in a hospital is that the results of those tests will not be shared with nonmedical personnel without her consent.

The critical difference between those four drug-testing cases and this one, however, lies in the nature of the "special need" asserted as justification for the warrantless searches. In each of those earlier cases, the "special need" that was advanced as a justification for the absence of a warrant or individualized suspicion was one divorced from the State's general interest in law enforcement. . . . In this case, however, the central and indispensable feature of the policy from its inception was the use of law enforcement to coerce the patients into substance abuse treatment. . . .

Respondents argue in essence that their ultimate purpose-namely, protecting the health of both mother and child-is a benificent one. . . . In this case, a review of the M-7 policy plainly reveals that the purpose actually served by the MUSC searches "is ultimately indistinguishable from the general interest in crime control."

In looking to the programmatic purpose, we consider all the available evidence in order to determine the relevant primary purpose. In this case, as Judge Blake put it in her dissent below, "it . . . is clear from the record that an initial and continuing focus of the policy was on the arrest and prosecution of drug-abusing mothers. . . ." Tellingly, the document codifying the policy incorporates the police's operational guidelines. It devotes its attention to the chain of custody, the range of possible criminal charges, and the logistics of police notification and arrests. Nowhere, however, does the document discuss different courses of medical treatment for either mother or infant, aside from treatment for the mother's addiction.

Moreover, throughout the development and application of the policy, the Charleston prosecutors and police were extensively involved in the day-to-day administration of the policy. Police and prosecutors decided who would receive the reports of positive drug screens and what information would be included with those reports. . . . They had access to . . . medical files on the women who tested positive, routinely attended the substance abuse team's meetings, and regularly received copies of team documents discussing the women's progress. . . .

While the ultimate goal of the program may well have been to get the women in question into substance abuse treatment and off of drugs, the immediate objective of the searches was to generate evidence for law enforcement purposes in order to reach that goal. . . . Because law enforcement involvement always serves some broader social purpose or objective, under respondents' view, virtually any nonconsensual suspicionless search could be immunized under the special needs doctrine by defining the search solely in terms of its ultimate, rather than immediate, purpose. Such an approach is inconsistent with the Fourth Amendment. Given the primary purpose of the Charleston program, which was to use the threat of arrest and prosecution in order to force women into treatment, and given the extensive involvement of law enforcement officials at every stage of the policy, this case simply does not fit within the closely guarded category of "special needs."

The fact that positive test results were turned over to the police does not merely provide a basis for distinguishing our prior cases applying the "special needs" balancing approach to the determination of drug use. It also provides an affirmative reason for enforcing the strictures of the Fourth Amendment. While state hospital employees, like other citizens, may have a duty to provide the police with evidence of criminal conduct from their patients *for the specific purpose of incriminating those patients* [emphasis in original], they have a special obligation to make sure that the patients are fully informed about their constitutional rights, as standards of knowing waiver require.

As respondents have repeatedly insisted, their motive was benign rather than punitive. Such a motive, however, cannot justify a departure from Fourth Amendment protections, given the pervasive involvement of law enforcement with the development and application of the MUSC policy. The stark and unique fact that characterizes this case is that Policy M-7 was designed to obtain evidence of criminal conduct by the tested patients that would be turned over to the police and that could be admissible in subsequent criminal prosecutions. While respondents are correct that drug abuse both was and is a serious problem, "the gravity of the threat alone cannot be dispositive of questions concerning what means law enforcement officers may employ to pursue a given purpose." *Indianapolis v. Edmond.* The Fourth Amendment's general prohibition against nonconsensual, warrantless, and suspicionless searches necessarily applies to such a policy. . . .

Scalia, dissenting:

The first step in Fourth Amendment analysis is to identify the search or seizure at issue. What petitioners [and] the Court . . . really object to is not the urine testing, but the hospital's reporting of positive drug-test results to police. But the latter is obviously not a search. At most it may be a "derivative use of the product of a past unlawful search," which, of course, "work[s] no new Fourth Amendment wrong" and "presents a question, not of rights, but of remedies." There is only one act that could conceivably be regarded as a search of petitioners in the present case: the taking of the urine sample. . . . Some would argue . . . that testing of the urine is prohibited by some generalized privacy right, . . . but it is not even arguable that the testing of urine that has been lawfully obtained is a Fourth Amendment search. . . .

It is rudimentary Fourth Amendment law that a search which has been consented to is not unreasonable. There is no contention in the present case that the urine samples were extracted forcibly. . . .

Until today, we have never held-or even suggested-that material which a person voluntarily entrusts to someone else cannot be given by that person to the police, and used for whatever evidence it may contain. Without so much as discussing the point, the Court today opens a hole in our Fourth Amendment jurisprudence, the size and shape of which is entirely indeterminate. Today's holding would be remarkable enough if the confidential relationship violated by the police conduct were at least one protected by state law. . . . Since the Court declines even to discuss the issue, it leaves law enforcement officials entirely in the dark as to when they can use incriminating evidence obtained from "trusted" sources. Presumably the lines will be drawn [on a] case-by-case [basis], taking [a] social judgment . . . out of democratic control, and confiding it to the . . . judgment of this Court—uncontrolled be-

cause there is no common-law precedent to guide it. I would adhere to our established law, which says that information obtained through violation of a relationship of trust is obtained consensually, and is hence not a search. . . .

. . . [T]here is no basis for saying that obtaining of the urine sample was unconstitutional. The special-needs doctrine is thus quite irrelevant, since it operates only to validate searches and seizures that are otherwise unlawful. In the ensuing discussion, however, I shall assume that the taking of the urine sample was . . . coerced. Indeed, I shall even assume that the testing of the urine constituted an unconsented search of the patients' effects. On those assumptions, the special-needs doctrine would become relevant; and, properly applied, would validate what was done here.

The conclusion of the Court that the special-needs doctrine is inapplicable rests upon its contention that respondents "undert[ook] to obtain [drug] evidence from their patients" not for any medical purpose, but "for the specific purpose of incriminating those patients." In other words, the purported medical rationale was merely a pretext; there was no special need. . . .

The cocaine tests started in April 1989, *neither at police suggestion nor with police involvement* [emphasis in original]. Expectant mothers who tested positive were referred by hospital staff for substance-abuse treatment, an obvious health benefit to both mother and child. And, since "[i]nfants whose mothers abuse cocaine during pregnancy are born with a wide variety of physical and neurological abnormalities,", which require medical attention, the tests were of additional medical benefit in predicting needed postnatal treatment for the child. Thus, in their origin—before the police were in any way involved—the tests had an immediate, not merely an "ultimate," purpose of improving maternal and infant health. . . .

[T]here can be no basis for the Court's purported ability to "distinguis[h] this case from circumstances in which physicians or psychologists, in the course of ordinary medical procedures aimed at helping the patient herself, come across information that . . . is subject to reporting requirements," unless it is this: That the addition of a law-enforcement-related purpose to a legitimate medical purpose destroys applicability of the "special-needs" doctrine. But that is quite impossible, since the special-needs doctrine was developed, and is ordinarily employed, precisely to enable searches by law enforcement officials who, of course, ordinarily have a law enforcement objective. . . .

... [I]t is not the function of this Court—at least not in Fourth Amendment cases—to weigh petitioners' privacy interest against the State's interest in meeting the crisis of "crack babies" that developed in the late 1980's. . . . [T]he outcome of a wise weighing of those interests is by no means clear. The initial goal of the doctors and nurses who conducted cocaine-testing in this case was to refer pregnant drug addicts to treatment centers, and to prepare for necessary treatment of their possibly affected children. When the doctors and nurses agreed to the program providing test results to the police, they did so because they wanted to use the sanction of arrest as a strong incentive for their addicted patients to undertake drug-addiction treatment. And the police themselves used it for that benign purpose, as is shown by the fact that only 30 of 253 women testing positive for cocaine were ever arrested, and only 2 of those prosecuted. . . .

There was no unconsented search in this case. And if there was, it would have been validated by the special-needs doctrine. . . .

Kyllo v. United States

533 U.S. 27 (2001), 5-4
Opinion of the Court: Scalia (Breyer, Ginsburg, Souter, Thomas)
Dissenting: Kennedy, O'Connor, Rehnquist, Stevens

Is use of a thermal-imaging device aimed at a private home from a public street a search within the meaning of the Fourth Amendment? Has the government violated a subjective expectation of privacy that society recognizes as legitimate? Should the degree of privacy secured by the Fourth Amendment be affected by advances in technology? How do Justices Scalia and Stevens disagree on the intrusiveness of the search? How does each deal with the "expectation of privacy"?

Scalia, for the Court:
This case presents the question whether the use of a thermal-imaging device aimed at a private home from a public street to detect relative amounts of heat within the home constitutes a "search" within the meaning of the Fourth Amendment.

In 1991 Agent William Elliott of the United States Department of the Interior came to suspect that marijuana was being grown in the home belonging to petitioner Danny Kyllo. Indoor marijuana growth typically requires high-intensity lamps. In order to determine whether an amount of heat was emanating from petitioner's home consistent with the use of such lamps. Agent Elliott and Dan Haas used an Agema Thermovision 210 thermal imager to scan the triplex. Thermal imagers detect infrared radiation, which virtually all objects emit but which is not visible to the naked eye. The imager converts radiation into images based on relative warmth-black is cool, white is hot, shades of gray connote relative differences; in that respect, it operates somewhat like a video camera showing heat images. The scan of Kyllo's home took only a few minutes and was performed from the passenger seat of Agent Elliott's vehicle across the street from the front of the house and also from the street in back of the house. The scan showed that the roof over the garage and a side wall of Kyllo's home were relatively hot compared to the rest of the home and substantially warmer than neighboring homes in the triplex. Agent Elliott concluded that Kyllo was using halide lights to grow marijuana in his house, which indeed he was. Based on tips from informants, utility bills, and the thermal imaging, a Federal Magistrate Judge issued a warrant authorizing a search of Kyllo's home, and the agents found an indoor growing operation involving more than 100 plants. Petitioner was indicted on one count of manufacturing marijuana, in violation of 21 U.S.C. §841(a).

The Fourth Amendment provides that "[t]he right of the people to be secure in their persons, houses, papers, and effects, against unreasonable searches and seizures, shall not be violated." "At the very core" of the Fourth Amendment "stands the right of a man to retreat into his own home and there be free from unreasonable governmental intrusion." With few exceptions, the question whether a warrantless search of a home is reasonable and hence constitutional must be answered no.

On the other hand, the antecedent question of whether or not a Fourth Amendment "search" has occurred is not so simple under our precedent. The permissibility of ordinary visual surveillance of a home used to be clear because, well into the 20th century, our Fourth Amendment jurisprudence was tied to common-law trespass. Visual surveillance was unquestionably lawful because "'the eye cannot by the laws of England be guilty of a trespass.'" We have since decoupled violation of a person's Fourth Amendment rights from trespassory violation of his property, but the lawfulness of warrantless visual surveillance of a home has still been preserved. As we observed in *California v.*

Ciraolo, "[t]he Fourth Amendment protection of the home has never been extended to require law enforcement officers to shield their eyes when passing by a home on public thoroughfares."

... In assessing when a search is not a search, we have applied somewhat in reverse the principle first enunciated in *Katz v. United States. Katz* involved eavesdropping by means of an electronic listening device placed on the outside of a telephone booth-a location not within the catalog ("persons, houses, papers, and effects") that the Fourth Amendment protects against unreasonable searches. We held that the Fourth Amendment nonetheless protected Katz from the warrantless eavesdropping because he "justifiably relied" upon the privacy of the telephone booth. As Justice Harlan's oft-quoted concurrence described it, a Fourth Amendment search occurs when the government violates a subjective expectation of privacy that society recognizes as reasonable. We have subsequently applied this principle to hold that a Fourth Amendment search does not occur-even when the explicitly protected location of a house is concerned-unless "the individual manifested a subjective expectation of privacy in the object of the challenged search," and "society [is] willing to recognize that expectation as reasonable." We have applied this test in holding that it is not a search for the police to use a pen register at the phone company to determine what numbers were dialed in a private home, and we have applied the test on two different occasions in holding that aerial surveillance of private homes and surrounding areas does not constitute a search. ...

It would be foolish to contend that the degree of privacy secured to citizens by the Fourth Amendment has been entirely unaffected by the advance of technology. For example, the technology enabling human flight has exposed to public view (and hence, we have said, to official observation) uncovered portions of the house and its curtilage that once were private. The question we confront today is what limits there are upon this power of technology to shrink the realm of guaranteed privacy.

The Katz test-whether the individual has an expectation of privacy that society is prepared to recognize as reasonable-has often been criticized as circular, and hence subjective and unpredictable. While it may be difficult to refine *Katz* when the search of areas such as telephone booths, automobiles, or even the curtilage and uncovered portions of residences are at issue, in the case of the search of the interior of

homes-the prototypical and hence most commonly litigated area of protected privacy-there is a ready criterion, with roots deep in the common law, of the minimal expectation of privacy that exists, and that is acknowledged to be reasonable. To withdraw protection of this minimum expectation would be to permit police technology to erode the privacy guaranteed by the Fourth Amendment. We think that obtaining by sense-enhancing technology any information regarding the interior of the home that could not otherwise have been obtained without physical "intrusion into a constitutionally protected area," constitutes a search-at least where (as here) the technology in question is not in general public use. This assures preservation of that degree of privacy against government that existed when the Fourth Amendment was adopted. On the basis of this criterion, the information obtained by the thermal imager in this case was the product of a search.

The Government maintains, however, that the thermal imaging must be upheld because it detected "only heat radiating from the external surface of the house." The dissent makes this its leading point, contending that there is a fundamental difference between what it calls "off-the-wall" observations and "through-the-wall surveillance." ... We rejected such a mechanical interpretation of the Fourth Amendment in *Katz,* where the eavesdropping device picked up only sound waves that reached the exterior of the phone booth. Reversing that approach would leave the homeowner at the mercy of advancing technology—including imaging technology that could discern all human activity in the home. While the technology used in the present case was relatively crude, the rule we adopt must take account of more sophisticated systems that are already in use or in development. ...

... The Government also contends that the thermal imaging was constitutional because it did not "detect private activities occurring in private areas." It points out that in *Dow Chemical* [*v. United States*] we observed that the enhanced aerial photography did not reveal any "intimate details." Dow Chemical, however, involved enhanced aerial photography of an industrial complex, which does not share the Fourth Amendment sanctity of the home. The Fourth Amendment's protection of the home has never been tied to measurement of the quality or quantity of information obtained. ... In the home, all details are intimate details, because the entire area is held safe from prying government eyes. ...

Limiting the prohibition of thermal imaging to "intimate details" would not only be wrong in principle; it would be impractical in application, failing to provide "a workable accommodation between the needs of law enforcement and the interests protected by the Fourth Amendment." To begin with, there is no necessary connection between the sophistication of the surveillance equipment and the "intimacy" of the details that it observes—which means that one cannot say (and the police cannot be assured that use of the relatively crude equipment at issue here will always be lawful. The Agema Thermovision 210 might disclose, for example, at what hour each night the lady of the house takes her daily sauna and bath—a detail that many would consider "intimate'; and a much more sophisticated system might detect nothing more intimate than the fact that someone left the closet light on. We could not, in other words, develop a rule approving only that through-the-wall surveillance which identifies objects no smaller than 36 by 36 inches, but would have to develop a jurisprudence specifying which home activities are "intimate" and which are not. And even when (if ever) that jurisprudence were fully developed, no police officer would be able to know in advance whether his through-the-wall surveillance picks up "intimate" details—and thus would be unable to know in advance whether it is constitutional. . . .

We have said that the Fourth Amendment draws "a firm line at the entrance to the house." That line, we think, must be not only firm but also bright—which requires clear specification of those methods of surveillance that require a warrant. While it is certainly possible to conclude from the videotape of the thermal imaging that occurred in this case that no "significant" compromise of the homeowner's privacy has occurred, we must take the long view, from the original meaning of the Fourth Amendment forward. "The Fourth Amendment is to be construed in the light of what was deemed an unreasonable search and seizure when it was adopted, and in a manner which will conserve public interests as well as the interests and rights of individual citizens." Where, as here, the Government uses a device that is not in general public use, to explore details of the home that would previously have been unknowable without physical intrusion, the surveillance is a "search" and is presumptively unreasonable without a warrant.

Since we hold the Thermovision imaging to have been an unlawful search, it will remain for the District Court to determine whether, without the evidence it provided, the search warrant issued in this case was supported by probable cause-and if not, whether there is any other basis for supporting admission of the evidence that the search pursuant to the warrant produced. . . .

Stevens, dissenting:

There is, in my judgment, a distinction of constitutional magnitude between "through-the-wall surveillance" that gives the observer or listener direct access to information in a private area, and the thought processes used to draw inferences from information in the public domain. . . .

Moreover, I believe that the supposedly "bright-line" rule the Court has created in response to its concerns about future technological developments is unnecessary, unwise, and inconsistent with the Fourth Amendment.

There is no need for the Court to craft a new rule to decide this case, as it is controlled by established principles from our Fourth Amendment jurisprudence. One of those core principles, of course, is that "searches and seizures inside a home without a warrant are presumptively unreasonable." But it is equally well settled that searches and seizures of property in plain view are presumptively reasonable. Whether that property is residential or commercial, the basic principle is the same: "What a person knowingly exposes to the public, even in his own home or office, is not a subject of Fourth Amendment protection." *Katz v. United States.* . . .

Indeed, the ordinary use of the senses might enable a neighbor or passerby to notice the heat emanating from a building, particularly if it is vented, as was the case here. Additionally, any member of the public might notice that one part of a house is warmer than another part or a nearby building if, for example, rainwater evaporates or snow melts at different rates across its surfaces. . . .

Thus, the notion that heat emissions from the outside of a dwelling is a private matter implicating the protections of the Fourth Amendment (the text of which guarantees the right of people "to be secure in their . . . houses" against unreasonable searches and seizures (emphasis added) is not only unprecedented but also quite difficult to take seriously. . . .

. . . In the Court's own words, based on what the thermal imager "showed" regarding the outside of petitioner's home, the officers "concluded" that Kyllo was engaging in illegal activity inside the home. It would be quite absurd to characterize their thought processes as "searches," regardless of whether they inferred (rightly) that Kyllo was growing marijuana in his house, or (wrongly) that "the lady of the house [was taking] her daily sauna and bath." . . .

Instead of trying to answer the question whether the use of the thermal imager in this case was even arguably unreasonable, the Court has fashioned a rule that is intended to provide essential guidance for the day when "more sophisticated systems" gain the "ability to 'see' through walls and other opaque barriers." The newly minted rule encompasses "obtaining by sense-enhancing technology any information regarding the interior of the home that could not otherwise have been obtained without physical intrusion into a constitutionally protected area . . . at least where (as here) the technology in question is not in general public use." . . . [T]he Court's new rule is at once too broad and too narrow, and is not justified by the Court's explanation for its adoption . . . I would not erect a constitutional impediment to the use of sense-enhancing technology unless it provides its user with the functional equivalent of actual presence in the area being searched.

Despite the Court's attempt to draw a line that is "not only firm but also bright," the contours of its new rule are uncertain because its protection apparently dissipates as soon as the relevant technology is "in general public use." Yet how much use is general public use is not even hinted at by the Court's opinion, which makes the somewhat doubtful assumption that the thermal imager used in this case does not satisfy that criterion. . . .

. . . It is clear, however, that the category of "sense-enhancing technology" covered by the new rule, is far too broad. It would, for example, embrace potential mechanical substitutes for dogs trained to react when they sniff narcotics. . . .

. . . The application of the Court's new rule to "any information regarding the interior of the home," is also unnecessarily broad. If it takes sensitive equipment to detect an odor that identifies criminal conduct and nothing else, the fact that the odor emanates from the interior of a home should not provide it with constitutional protection. . . .

. . . The final requirement of the Court's new rule, that the information "could not otherwise have been obtained without physical intrusion into a constitutionally protected area," also extends too far as the

Court applies it. As noted, the Court effectively treats the mental process of analyzing data obtained from external sources as the equivalent of a physical intrusion into the home. As I have explained, however, the process of drawing inferences from data in the public domain should not be characterized as a search.

The two reasons advanced by the Court as justifications for the adoption of its new rule are both unpersuasive. First, the Court suggests that its rule is compelled by our holding in *Katz*, because in that case, as in this, the surveillance consisted of nothing more than the monitoring of waves emanating from a private area into the public domain. Yet there are critical differences between the cases. In *Katz*, the electronic listening device attached to the outside of the phone booth allowed the officers to pick up the content of the conversation inside the booth, making them the functional equivalent of intruders because they gathered information that was otherwise available only to someone inside the private area. . . . By contrast, the thermal imager here disclosed only the relative amounts of heat radiating from the house. . . . Surely, there is a significant difference between the general and well-settled expectation that strangers will not have direct access to the contents of private communications, on the one hand, and the rather theoretical expectation that an occasional home-owner would even care if anybody noticed the relative amounts of heat emanating from the walls of his house, on the other. . . .

. . . Second, the Court argues that the permissibility of "through-the-wall surveillance" cannot depend on a distinction between observing "intimate details" such as "the lady of the house [taking] her daily sauna and bath," and noticing only "the nonintimate rug on the vestibule floor" or "objects no smaller than 36 by 36 inches." This entire argument assumes, of course, that the thermal imager in this case could or did perform "through-the-wall surveillance" that could identify any detail "that would previously have been unknowable without physical intrusion." In fact, the device could not, and did not, enable its user to identify either the lady of the house, the rug on the vestibule floor, or anything else inside the house, whether smaller or larger than 36 by 36 inches. . . .

Although the Court is properly and commendably concerned about the threats to privacy that may flow from advances in the technology available to the law enforcement profession, it has unfortunately failed to heed the tried and true counsel of judicial restraint.

Instead of concentrating on the rather mundane issue that is actually presented by the case before it, the Court has endeavored to craft an all-encompassing rule for the future. It would be far wiser to give legislators an unimpeded opportunity to grapple with these emerging issues rather than to shackle them with prematurely devised constitutional constraints. . . .

Mapp v. Ohio

367 U.S. 643 (1961), 6-3
Opinion of the Court: Clark (Black, Brennan, Douglas, Stewart, Warren)
Dissenting: Frankfurter, Harlan, Whittaker

What is the Court's reasoning for holding the search unconstitutional? For applying the Fourth Amendment's protection against unreasonable searches to the states? What is the exclusionary rule? Is it required by the Constitution or is it simply a judicial control the Court imposes on other courts as a rule of evidence? The exclusionary rule penalizes the prosecutor rather than the police. Does this make sense? Are there other ways the Court could give effect to the Fourth Amendment's protection against unreasonable searches? Are they practical? Is this case consistent with Chimel v. California *(p. 376)?*

Clark, for the Court:

Appellant stands convicted of knowingly having had in her possession and under her control certain lewd and lascivious books, pictures, and photographs in violation of §2905.34 of Ohio's Revised Code. . . .

On May 23, 1957, three Cleveland police officers arrived at appellant's residence in that city pursuant to information that a person [was] hiding out in the home, who was wanted for questioning in connection with a recent bombing, and that there was a large amount of policy paraphernalia being hidden in the home. . . .

. . . [A]ppellant, after telephoning her attorney, refused to admit them without a search warrant. They advised their headquarters of the situation and undertook a surveillance of the house.

The officers again sought entrance some three hours later when four or more additional officers arrived on the scene. . . . [A]t least one of the several doors to the house was forcibly opened and the policemen gained admittance. Meanwhile Miss Mapp's attorney arrived, but the officers, having secured their own

entry . . . would permit him neither to see Miss Mapp nor to enter the house. It appears that Miss Mapp was halfway down the stairs from the upper floor to the front door when the officers . . . broke into the hall. She demanded to see the search warrant. A paper, claimed to be a warrant, was held up by one of the officers. She grabbed the "warrant" and placed it in her bosom. A struggle ensued in which the officers recovered the piece of paper and as a result of which they handcuffed appellant . . . Appellant, in handcuffs, was then forcibly taken upstairs to her bedroom where the officers searched a dresser, a chest of drawers, a closet and some suitcases. They also looked into a photo album and . . . personal papers. . . . The search spread to the rest of the second floor including the . . . bedroom, the living room, the kitchen and a dinette. The basement of the building and a trunk . . . were also searched. The obscene materials for possession of which she was ultimately convicted were discovered in the course of [the] search. . . .

The State says that, even if the search were made without authority, or otherwise unreasonably, it is not prevented from using the unconstitutionally seized evidence at trial, citing *Wolf v. Colorado,* in which this Court did indeed hold "that, in a prosecution in a State court for a State crime, the Fourteenth Amendment does not forbid the admission of evidence obtained by an unreasonable search and seizure." On this appeal, of which we have noted probable jurisdiction, it is urged once again that we review that holding.

Seventy-five years ago, in *Boyd v. United States,* considering the Fourth and Fifth Amendments as running "almost into each other" on the facts before it, this Court held that the doctrines of those Amendments

apply to all invasions on the part of the government and its employes of the sanctity of a man's home and the privacies of life. It is not the breaking of his doors, and the rummaging of his drawers, that constitutes the essence of the offence; but it is the invasion of his indefeasible right of personal security, personal liberty and private property. . . . Breaking into a house and opening boxes and drawers are circumstances of aggravation; but any forcible and compulsory extortion of a man's own testimony or of his private papers to be used as evidence to convict him of crime or to forfeit his goods, is within the condemnation . . . [of those Amendments] . . .

... Less than 30 years after *Boyd,* this Court, in *Weeks v. United States,* stated that the Fourth Amendment ... put the courts of the United States and Federal officials, in the exercise of their power and authority, under limitations and restraints [and] ... forever secure[d] the people, their persons, houses, papers and effects against all unreasonable searches and seizures under the guise of law ... , and the duty of giving to it force and effect is obligatory upon all entrusted under our Federal system with the enforcement of the laws. ...

In 1949, 35 years after *Weeks* was announced, this Court, in *Wolf v. Colorado,* again for the first time, discussed the effect of the Fourth Amendment upon the States through the operation of the Due Process Clause of the Fourteenth Amendment. ...

The Court in Wolf first stated that "[t]he contrariety of views of the States" on the adoption of the exclusionary rule of Weeks was "particularly impressive" and, in this connection, that it could not "brush aside the experience of States which deem the incidence of such conduct by the police too slight to call for a deterrent remedy ... by overriding the [States'] relevant rules of evidence."

While, in 1949, prior to the Wolf case, almost two-thirds of the States were opposed to the use of the exclusionary rule, now, despite the Wolf case, more than half of those since passing upon it, by their own legislative or judicial decision, have wholly or partly adopted or adhered to the Weeks rule. ...

It therefore plainly appears that the factual considerations supporting the failure of the Wolf Court to include the Weeks exclusionary rule when it recognized the enforceability of the right to privacy against the States in 1949, while not basically relevant to the constitutional consideration, could not, in any analysis, now be deemed controlling. ...

... Today we once again examine *Wolf's* constitutional documentation of the right to privacy free from unreasonable state intrusion, and, after its dozen years on our books, are led by it to close the only courtroom door remaining open to evidence secured by official lawlessness in flagrant abuse of that basic right, reserved to all persons as a specific guarantee against that very same unlawful conduct. We hold that all evidence obtained by searches and seizures in violation of the Constitution is, by that same authority, inadmissible in a state court. ...

Since the Fourth Amendment's right of privacy has been declared enforceable against the States through the Due Process Clause of the Fourteenth, it is enforceable against them by the same sanction of exclusion as is used against the Federal Government. Were it otherwise, then, just as without the Weeks rule the assurance against unreasonable federal searches and seizures would be "a form of words," valueless and undeserving of mention in a perpetual charter of inestimable human liberties, so too, without that rule, the freedom from state invasions of privacy would be so ephemeral and so neatly severed from its conceptual nexus with the freedom from all brutish means of coercing evidence as not to merit this Court's high regard as a freedom "implicit in the concept of ordered liberty." At the time that the Court held in *Wolf* that the Amendment was applicable to the States through the Due Process Clause, the cases of this Court, as we have seen, had steadfastly held that as to federal officers the Fourth Amendment included the exclusion of the evidence seized in violation of its provisions. Even *Wolf* "stoutly adhered" to that proposition. The right to privacy, when conceded operatively enforceable against the States, was not susceptible of destruction by avulsion of the sanction upon which its protection and enjoyment had always been deemed dependent under the Boyd, Weeks and Silverthorne cases. Therefore, in extending the substantive protections of due process to all constitutionally unreasonable searches—state or federal—it was logically and constitutionally necessary that the exclusion doctrine—an essential part of the right to privacy—be also insisted upon as an essential ingredient of the right newly recognized by the Wolf case. In short, the admission of the new constitutional right by *Wolf* could not consistently tolerate denial of its most important constitutional privilege, namely, the exclusion of the evidence which an accused had been forced to give by reason of the unlawful seizure. To hold otherwise is to grant the right but, in reality, to withhold its privilege and enjoyment. Only last year, the Court itself recognized that the purpose of the exclusionary rule "is to deter—to compel respect for the constitutional guaranty in the only effectively available way—by removing the incentive to disregard it." *Elkins v. United States* ...

Moreover, our holding that the exclusionary rule is an essential part of both the Fourth and Fourteenth Amendments is not only the logical dictate of prior cases, but it also makes very good sense. There is no war between the Constitution and common sense. Presently, a federal prosecutor may make no use of evidence illegally seized, but a State's attorney across the street may, although he supposedly is operating under the enforceable prohibitions of the same Amendment. Thus, the State, by admitting evidence unlawfully seized, serves to encourage disobedience to the Federal Constitution which it is bound to uphold. . . .

Federal-state cooperation in the solution of crime under constitutional standards will be promoted, if only by recognition of their now mutual obligation to respect the same fundamental criteria in their approaches. . . .

Nor can it lightly be assumed that, as a practical matter, adoption of the exclusionary rule fetters law enforcement. Only last year, this Court expressly considered that contention and found that "pragmatic evidence of a sort" to the contrary was not wanting. . . .

The ignoble shortcut to conviction left open to the State tends to destroy the entire system of constitutional restraints on which the liberties of the people rest. Having once recognized that the right to privacy embodied in the Fourth Amendment is enforceable against the States, and that the right to be secure against rude invasions of privacy by state officers is, therefore, constitutional in origin, we can no longer permit that right to remain an empty promise. . . .

Black, concurring.:

. . . I am still not persuaded that the Fourth Amendment, standing alone, would be enough to bar the introduction into evidence against an accused of papers and effects seized from him in violation of its commands. For the Fourth Amendment does not itself contain any provision expressly precluding the use of such evidence, and I am extremely doubtful that such a provision could properly be inferred from nothing more than the basic command against unreasonable searches and seizures. Reflection on the problem, however, in the light of cases coming before the Court since *Wolf,* has led me to conclude that, when the Fourth Amendment's ban against unreasonable searches and seizures is considered together with the Fifth Amendment's ban against compelled self-incrimination, a constitutional basis emerges which not only justifies, but actually requires, the exclusionary rule. . . .

Harlan, dissenting:

In overruling the Wolf case, the Court, in my opinion, has forgotten the sense of judicial restraint which,

with due regard for stare decisis, is one element that should enter into deciding whether a past decision of this Court should be overruled. Apart from that, I also believe that the Wolf rule represents sounder Constitutional doctrine than the new rule which now replaces it. . . .

The occasion which the Court has taken here is in the context of a case where the question was briefed not at all and argued only extremely tangentially. The unwisdom of overruling *Wolf* without full-dress argument is aggravated by the circumstance that that decision is a comparatively recent one (1949) to which three members of the present majority have at one time or other expressly subscribed, one, to be sure, with explicit misgivings. I would think that our obligation to the States, on whom we impose this new rule, as well as the obligation of orderly adherence to our own processes would demand that we seek that aid which adequate briefing and argument lends to the determination of an important issue. It certainly has never been a postulate of judicial power that mere altered disposition, or subsequent membership on the Court, is sufficient warrant for overturning a deliberately decided rule of Constitutional law. . . .

At the heart of the majority's opinion in this case is the following syllogism: (1) the rule excluding in federal criminal trials evidence which is the product of an illegal search and seizure is "part and parcel" of the Fourth Amendment; (2) Wolf held that the "privacy" assured against federal action by the Fourth Amendment is also protected against state action by the Fourteenth Amendment, and (3) it is therefore "logically and constitutionally necessary" that the Weeks exclusionary rule should also be enforced against the States. . . .

. . . [W]hat the Court is now doing is to impose upon the States not only federal substantive standards of "search and seizure", but also the basic federal remedy for violation of those standards. For I think it entirely clear that the Weeks exclusionary rule is but a remedy which, by penalizing past official misconduct, is aimed at deterring such conduct in the future.

I would not impose upon the States this federal exclusionary remedy. The reasons given by the majority for now suddenly turning its back on *Wolf* seem to me notably unconvincing.

First, it is said that "the factual grounds upon which *Wolf* was based" have since changed, in that more States now follow the Weeks exclusionary rule than was so at the time Wolf was decided. While that is true, a recent survey indicates that, at present, one-half of the States still adhere to the common law non-exclusionary rule. . . .

The preservation of a proper balance between state and federal responsibility in the administration of criminal justice demands patience on the part of those who might like to see things move faster among the States in this respect. Problems of criminal law enforcement vary widely from State to State. One State, in considering the totality of its legal picture, may conclude that the need for embracing the Weeks rule is pressing because other remedies are unavailable or inadequate to secure compliance with the substantive Constitutional principle involved. Another, though equally solicitous of Constitutional rights, may choose to pursue one purpose at a time, allowing all evidence relevant to guilt to be brought into a criminal trial, and dealing with Constitutional infractions by other means. Still another may consider the exclusionary rule too rough-and-ready a remedy, in that it reaches only unconstitutional intrusions which eventuate in criminal prosecution of the victims. Further, a State after experimenting with the Weeks rule for a time may, because of unsatisfactory experience with it, decide to revert to a non-exclusionary rule. And so on. From the standpoint of Constitutional permissibility in pointing a State in one direction or another, I do not see at all why "time has set its face against" the considerations which led Mr. Justice Cardozo, then chief judge of the New York Court of Appeals, to reject for New York in *People v. Defore*, the Weeks exclusionary rule. For us, the question remains, as it has always been, one of state power, not one of passing judgment on the wisdom of one state course or another. In my view, this Court should continue to forbear from fettering the States with an adamant rule which may embarrass them in coping with their own peculiar problems in criminal law enforcement. . . .

Indianapolis v. Edmond

531 U.S. 32 (2000), 6-3
Opinion of the Court: O'Connor (Stevens, Kennedy, Scalia, in part, Souter, Ginsburg, Breyer)
Dissenting: Rehnquist, Scalia, in part, Thomas

*The Court has upheld checkpoint stops as a way of combating drunk driving, an offense many persons might consider less serious or at least no more serious than drug use or drug traf-*ficking. *Why did the Court not uphold checkpoint stops for the latter? When would a search be reasonable in the absence of individualized suspicion of wrongdoing? What is the primary purpose of the Indianapolis checkpoint program? Can the Court inquire into this purpose? What does Justice O'Connor mean by saying that in checkpoint cases, the Court will not "approve a program whose primary purpose is ultimately indistinguishable from the general interest in crime control"? Why is this not a problem for Chief Justice Rehnquist?*

O'Connor, for the Court:

In *Michigan Dept. of State Police v. Sitz,* and *United States v. Martinez-Fuerte,* we held that brief, suspicionless seizures at highway checkpoints for the purposes of combating drunk driving and intercepting illegal immigrants were constitutional. We now consider the constitutionality of a highway checkpoint program whose primary purpose is the discovery and interdiction of illegal narcotics.

In August 1998, the city of Indianapolis began to operate vehicle checkpoints on Indianapolis roads in an effort to interdict unlawful drugs. The city conducted six such roadblocks between August and November that year, stopping 1,161 vehicles and arresting 104 motorists. Fifty-five arrests were for drug-related crimes, while 49 were for offenses unrelated to drugs. The overall "hit rate" of the program was thus approximately nine percent.

. . . At each checkpoint location, the police stop a predetermined number of vehicles. Pursuant to written directives issued by the chief of police, at least one officer approaches the vehicle, advises the driver that he or she is being stopped briefly at a drug checkpoint, and asks the driver to produce a license and registration. The officer also looks for signs of impairment and conducts an open-view examination of the vehicle from the outside. A narcotics-detection dog walks around the outside of each stopped vehicle.

The directives instruct the officers that they may conduct a search only by consent or based on the appropriate quantum of particularized suspicion. The officers must conduct each stop in the same manner until particularized suspicion develops, and the officers have no discretion to stop any vehicle out of sequence. The city agreed in the stipulation to operate the checkpoints in such a way as to ensure that the total duration of each stop, absent reasonable suspicion or probable cause, would be five minutes or less. . . .

Respondents James Edmond and Joell Palmer were each stopped at a narcotics checkpoint in late

September 1998. Respondents then filed a lawsuit on behalf of themselves and the class of all motorists who had been stopped or were subject to being stopped in the future at the Indianapolis drug checkpoints. Respondents claimed that the roadblocks violated the Fourth Amendment of the United States Constitution and the search and seizure provision of the Indiana Constitution. Respondents requested declaratory and injunctive relief for the class, as well as damages and attorney's fees for themselves. . . .

The Fourth Amendment requires that searches and seizures be reasonable. A search or seizure is ordinarily unreasonable in the absence of individualized suspicion of wrongdoing. While such suspicion is not an "irreducible" component of reasonableness, we have recognized only limited circumstances in which the usual rule does not apply. For example, we have upheld certain regimes of suspicionless searches where the program was designed to serve "special needs, beyond the normal need for law enforcement." . . . We have also allowed searches for certain administrative purposes without particularized suspicion of misconduct, provided that those searches are appropriately limited.

We have also upheld brief, suspicionless seizures of motorists at a fixed Border Patrol checkpoint designed to intercept illegal aliens, and at a sobriety checkpoint aimed at removing drunk drivers from the Road. In addition, in *Delaware v. Prouse,* we suggested that a similar type of roadblock with the purpose of verifying drivers' licenses and vehicle registrations would be permissible. In none of these cases, however, did we indicate approval of a checkpoint program whose primary purpose was to detect evidence of ordinary criminal wrongdoing.

In *Martinez-Fuerte,* we entertained Fourth Amendment challenges to stops at two permanent immigration checkpoints located on major United States highways less than 100 miles from the Mexican border. We noted at the outset the particular context in which the constitutional question arose, describing in some detail the "formidable law enforcement problems" posed by the northbound tide of illegal entrants into the United States. [W]e found that the balance tipped in favor of the Government's interests in policing the Nation's borders. . . .

In *Sitz,* we evaluated the constitutionality of a Michigan highway sobriety checkpoint program. The *Sitz* checkpoint involved brief suspicionless stops of motorists so that police officers could detect signs of intox-

ication and remove impaired drivers from the road. Motorists who exhibited signs of intoxication were diverted for a license and registration check and, if warranted, further sobriety tests. This checkpoint program was clearly aimed at reducing the immediate hazard posed by the presence of drunk drivers on the highways, and there was an obvious connection between the imperative of highway safety and the law enforcement practice at issue. The gravity of the drunk driving problem and the magnitude of the State's interest in getting drunk drivers off the road weighed heavily in our determination that the program was constitutional.

In *Prouse,* we invalidated a discretionary, suspicionless stop for a spot check of a motorist's driver's license and vehicle registration. The officer's conduct in that case was unconstitutional primarily on account of his exercise of "standardless and unconstrained discretion." We nonetheless acknowledged the States' "vital interest in ensuring that only those qualified to do so are permitted to operate motor vehicles, that these vehicles are fit for safe operation, and hence that licensing, registration, and vehicle inspection requirements are being observed." Accordingly, we suggested that "[q]uestioning of all oncoming traffic at roadblock-type stops" would be a lawful means of serving this interest in highway safety.

We further indicated in *Prouse* that we considered the purposes of such a hypothetical roadblock to be distinct from a general purpose of investigating crime. The State proffered the additional interests of "the apprehension of stolen motor vehicles and of drivers under the influence of alcohol or narcotics" in its effort to justify the discretionary spot check. We attributed the entirety of the latter interest to the State's interest in roadway safety. We also noted that the interest in apprehending stolen vehicles may be partly subsumed by the interest in roadway safety. . . . Not only does the common thread of highway safety thus run through *Sitz* and *Prouse,* but *Prouse* itself reveals a difference in the Fourth Amendment significance of highway safety interests and the general interest in crime control.

It is well established that a vehicle stop at a highway checkpoint effectuates a seizure within the meaning of the Fourth Amendment. The fact that officers walk a narcotics-detection dog around the exterior of each car at the Indianapolis checkpoints does not transform the seizure into a search. . . . [A] sniff by a dog that simply walks around a car is "much less intrusive than a typical search." Rather, what principally distinguishes these checkpoints from those we have previously approved is their primary purpose.

As petitioners concede, the Indianapolis checkpoint program unquestionably has the primary purpose of interdicting illegal narcotics. In their stipulation of facts, the parties repeatedly refer to the checkpoints as "drug checkpoints" and describe them as "being operated by the City of Indianapolis in an effort to interdict unlawful drugs in Indianapolis." . . .

We have never approved a checkpoint program whose primary purpose was to detect evidence of ordinary criminal wrongdoing. Rather, our checkpoint cases have recognized only limited exceptions to the general rule that a seizure must be accompanied by some measure of individualized suspicion. . . . [E]ach of the checkpoint programs that we have approved was designed primarily to serve purposes closely related to the problems of policing the border or the necessity of ensuring roadway safety. Because the primary purpose of the Indianapolis narcotics checkpoint program is to uncover evidence of ordinary criminal wrongdoing, the program contravenes the Fourth Amendment.

Petitioners propose several ways in which the narcotics-detection purpose of the instant checkpoint program may instead resemble the primary purposes of the checkpoints in *Sitz* and *Martinez-Fuerte.* Petitioners state that the checkpoints in those cases had the same ultimate purpose of arresting those suspected of committing crimes. . . . If we were to rest the case at this high level of generality, there would be little check on the ability of the authorities to construct roadblocks for almost any conceivable law enforcement purpose. Without drawing the line at roadblocks designed primarily to serve the general interest in crime control, the Fourth Amendment would do little to prevent such intrusions from becoming a routine part of American life. Petitioners also emphasize the severe and intractable nature of the drug problem as justification for the checkpoint program. There is no doubt that traffic in illegal narcotics creates social harms of the first magnitude. . . . But the gravity of the threat alone cannot be dispositive of questions concerning what means law enforcement officers may employ to pursue a given purpose. Rather, in determining whether individualized suspicion is required, we must consider the nature of the interests threatened and their connection to the particular law enforcement practices at issue. We are particularly reluctant to recognize exceptions to the general rule

of individualized suspicion where governmental authorities primarily pursue their general crime control ends. . . .

Nor can the narcotics—interdiction purpose of the checkpoints be rationalized in terms of a highway safety concern similar to that present in *Sitz.* The detection and punishment of almost any criminal offense serves broadly the safety of the community, and our streets would no doubt be safer but for the scourge of illegal drugs. Only with respect to a smaller class of offenses, however, is society confronted with the type of immediate, vehicle-bound threat to life and limb that the sobriety checkpoint in *Sitz* was designed to eliminate. . . .

The primary purpose of the Indianapolis narcotics checkpoints is in the end to advance "the general interest in crime control." We decline to suspend the usual requirement of individualized suspicion where the police seek to employ a checkpoint primarily for the ordinary enterprise of investigating crimes. We cannot sanction stops justified only by the generalized and ever-present possibility that interrogation may reveal that any given motorist has committed some crime.

Of course, there are circumstances that may justify a law enforcement checkpoint where the primary purpose would otherwise, but for some emergency, relate to ordinary crime control. For example, as the Court of Appeals noted, the Fourth Amendment would almost certainly permit an appropriately tailored roadblock set up to thwart an imminent terrorist attack or to catch a dangerous criminal who is likely to flee by way of a particular route. The exigencies created by these scenarios are far removed from the circumstances under which authorities might simply stop cars as a matter of course to see if there just happens to be a felon leaving the jurisdiction. While we do not limit the purposes that may justify a checkpoint program to any rigid set of categories, we decline to approve a program whose primary purpose is ultimately indistinguishable from the general interest in crime control.

Petitioners argue that our prior cases preclude an inquiry into the purposes of the checkpoint program. For example, they cite *Whren v. United States* and *Bond v. United States* to support the proposition that "where the government articulates and pursues a legitimate interest for a suspicionless stop, courts should not look behind that interest to determine whether the government's 'primary purpose' is valid." These cases, however, do not control the instant situation. In

Whren, we held that an individual officer's subjective intentions are irrelevant to the Fourth Amendment validity of a traffic stop that is justified objectively by probable cause to believe that a traffic violation has occurred. We observed that our prior cases "foreclose any argument that the constitutional reasonableness of traffic stops depends on the actual motivations of the individual officers involved." . . .

[I]n *Bond,* we addressed the question whether a law enforcement officer violated a reasonable expectation of privacy in conducting a tactile examination of carry-on luggage in the overhead compartment of a bus. In doing so, we simply noted that the principle of *Whren* rendered the subjective intent of an officer irrelevant to this analysis. . . . [S]ubjective intent was irrelevant in *Bond* because the inquiry that our precedents required focused on the objective effects of the actions of an individual officer. By contrast, our cases dealing with intrusions that occur pursuant to a general scheme absent individualized suspicion have often required an inquiry into purpose at the programmatic level.

Petitioners argue that the Indianapolis checkpoint program is justified by its lawful secondary purposes of keeping impaired motorists off the road and verifying licenses and registrations. If this were the case, however, law enforcement authorities would be able to establish checkpoints for virtually any purpose so long as they also included a license or sobriety check. For this reason, we examine the available evidence to determine the primary purpose of the checkpoint program. . . .

Because the primary purpose of the Indianapolis checkpoint program is ultimately indistinguishable from the general interest in crime control, the checkpoints violate the Fourth Amendment. . . .

Rehnquist, dissenting:
The State's use of a drug-sniffing dog, according to the Court's holding, annuls what is otherwise plainly constitutional under our Fourth Amendment jurisprudence: brief, standardized, discretionless, roadblock seizures of automobiles, seizures which effectively serve a weighty state interest with only minimal intrusion on the privacy of their occupants. Because these seizures serve the State's accepted and significant interests of preventing drunken driving and checking for driver's licenses and vehicle registrations, and because there is nothing in the record to indicate that the addition of the dog sniff lengthens these otherwise legitimate seizures, I dissent.

As it is nowhere to be found in the Court's opinion, I begin with blackletter roadblock seizure law. "The principal protection of Fourth Amendment rights at checkpoints lies in appropriate limitations on the scope of the stop." Roadblock seizures are consistent with the Fourth Amendment if they are "carried out pursuant to a plan embodying explicit, neutral limitations on the conduct of individual officers." Specifically, the constitutionality of a seizure turns upon "a weighing of the gravity of the public concerns served by the seizure, the degree to which the seizure advances the public interest, and the severity of the interference with individual liberty."

We first applied these principles in *Martinez-Fuerte,* which approved highway checkpoints for detecting illegal aliens. [W]e balanced the United States' formidable interest in checking the flow of illegal immigrants against the limited "objective" and "subjective" intrusion on the motorists. The objective intrusion—the stop itself, the brief questioning of the occupants, and the visual inspection of the car—was considered "limited" because "[n]either the vehicle nor its occupants [were] searched." . . .

In *Michigan Dept. of State Police v. Sitz,* we upheld the State's use of a highway sobriety checkpoint after applying the framework set out in Martinez-Fuerte. There, we recognized the gravity of the State's interest in curbing drunken driving and found the objective intrusion of the approximately 25-second seizure to be "slight." . . .

Because of the valid reasons for conducting these roadblock seizures, it is constitutionally irrelevant that petitioners also hoped to interdict drugs. In *Whren v. United States,* we held that an officer's subjective intent would not invalidate an otherwise objectively justifiable stop of an automobile. The reasonableness of an officer's discretionary decision to stop an automobile, at issue in *Whren,* turns on whether there is probable cause to believe that a traffic violation has occurred. . . .

Once the constitutional requirements for a particular seizure are satisfied, the subjective expectations of those responsible for it, be it police officers or members of a city council, are irrelevant. . . . It is the objective effect of the State's actions on the privacy of the individual that animates the Fourth Amendment. . . .

With these checkpoints serving two important state interests, the remaining prongs of the *Brown v. Texas* balancing test are easily met. The seizure is objectively reasonable as it lasts, on average, two to three minutes and does not involve a search. The subjective intrusion is likewise limited as the checkpoints are clearly marked and operated by uniformed officers who are directed to stop every vehicle in the same manner. The only difference between this case and *Sitz* is the presence of the dog. We have already held, however, that a "sniff test" by a trained narcotics dog is not a "search" within the meaning of the Fourth Amendment because it does not require physical intrusion of the object being sniffed and it does not expose anything other than the contraband items. And there is nothing in the record to indicate that the dog sniff lengthens the stop. Finally, the checkpoints' success rate—49 arrests for offenses unrelated to drugs—only confirms the State's legitimate interests in preventing drunken driving and ensuring the proper licensing of drivers and registration of their vehicles. . . .

These stops effectively serve the State's legitimate interests; they are executed in a regularized and neutral manner; and they only minimally intrude upon the privacy of the motorists. They should therefore be constitutional.

The Court . . . adds a new non-law-enforcement primary purpose test lifted from a distinct area of Fourth Amendment jurisprudence relating to the searches of homes and businesses. . . .

We have already rejected an invitation to apply the non-law-enforcement primary purpose test that the Court now finds so indispensable. The respondents in *Sitz* argued that the *Brown v. Texas* balancing test was not the "proper method of analysis" with regards to roadblock seizures: "Respondents argue that there must be a showing of some special governmental need 'beyond the normal need' for criminal law enforcement before a balancing analysis is appropriate, and that [the State] ha[s] demonstrated no such special need." . . .

The "special needs" doctrine, which has been used to uphold certain suspicionless searches performed for reasons unrelated to law enforcement, is an exception to the general rule that a search must be based on individualized suspicion of wrongdoing. . . . The doctrine permits intrusions into a person's body and home, areas afforded the greatest Fourth Amendment protection. But there were no such intrusions here.

Because of these extrinsic limitations upon roadblock seizures, the Court's newfound non-law-enforcement primary purpose test is both unnecessary to secure Fourth Amendment rights and bound to produce wide-ranging litigation over the "purpose" of any given seizure. . . .

Petitioners' program complies with our decisions regarding roadblock seizures of automobiles, and the addition of a dog sniff does not add to the length or the intrusion of the stop. . . . [S]uch stops are consistent with the Fourth Amendment. . . .

Escobedo v. Illinois

378 U.S. 478 (1964), 5-4
Opinion of the Court: Goldberg (Black, Brennan, Douglas, Warren)
Dissenting: Clark, Harlan, Stewart, White

Escobedo was arrested and taken to police headquarters for interrogation about the fatal shooting of his brother-in-law. He asked several times to see his lawyer, who, though present in the building, was not allowed to consult his client. Escobedo was not told by police of his right to remain silent and, after persistent questioning, made a damaging statement that was admitted at trial in which he was convicted of the murder.

Since Escobedo was not mistreated or coerced during interrogation, why was it necessary for him to see his lawyer, according the the Court? Is this case essentially about police interrogation or about the right to counsel? Does the Court make clear which? What constitutional difference does it make? Does the Court discuss retroactive application of this decision? Why does Justice White believe the Court's decision is not required by the Constitution? Why does he believe it is a bad one?

Goldberg for the Court:
The critical question in this case is whether, under the circumstances, the refusal by the police to honor [Escobedo's] request to consult with his lawyer during the course of an interrogation constitutes a denial of "the Assistance of Counsel" in violation of the Sixth Amendment to the Constitution as "made obligatory upon the States by the Fourteenth Amendment," *Gideon v. Wainwright,* and thereby renders inadmissible in a state criminal trial any incriminating statement elicited by the police during the interrogation. . . .

The interrogation here was conducted before [Escobedo] was formally indicted. But in the context of this case, that fact should make no difference. When [he] requested, and was denied, an opportunity to consult with his lawyer, the investigation had ceased to be a general investigation of "an unsolved crime." [He] had become the accused, and the purpose of the interrogation was to "get him" to confess his guilt despite his constitutional right not to do so. At the time of his arrest and throughout the course of the interrogation, the police told [him] that they had convincing evidence that he had fired the fatal shots. Without informing him of his absolute right to remain silent in the face of this accusation, the police urged him to make a statement. . . .

In *Gideon v. Wainwright*, we held that every person accused of a crime, whether state or federal, is entitled to a lawyer at trial. The rule sought by the State here, however, would make the trial no more than an appeal from the interrogation, and the "right to use counsel at the formal trial [would be] a very hollow thing [if], for all practical purposes, the conviction is already assured by pretrial examination." In *re Groban*. . . .

We have learned the lesson of history, ancient and modern, that a system of criminal law enforcement which comes to depend on the "confession" will, in the long run, be less reliable and more subject to abuses than a system which depends on extrinsic evidence independently secured through skillful investigation. . . .

We have also learned the companion lesson of history that no system of criminal justice can, or should, survive if it comes to depend for its continued effectiveness on the citizens' abdication through unawareness of their constitutional rights. No system worth preserving should have to fear that, if an accused is permitted to consult with a lawyer, he will become aware of, and exercise, these rights. If the exercise of constitutional rights will thwart the effectiveness of a system of law enforcement, then there is something very wrong with that system.

We hold, therefore, that where, as here, the investigation is no longer a general inquiry into an unsolved crime, but has begun to focus on a particular suspect, the suspect has been taken into police custody, the police carry out a process of interrogations that lends itself to eliciting incriminating statements, the suspect has requested and been denied an opportunity to consult with his lawyer, and the police have not effectively warned him of his absolute constitutional right to remain silent, the accused has been denied "the Assistance of Counsel" in violation of the Sixth Amendment to the Constitution as "made obligatory upon the States by the Fourteenth Amendment," *Gideon v. Wainwright*, and that no statement elicited by the police during the interrogation may be used against him at a criminal trial.

Crooker v. California does not compel a contrary result. In that case, the Court merely rejected the absolute rule sought by [Escobedo], that "every state denial of a request to contact counsel [is] an infringement of the constitutional right without regard to the circumstances of the case." . . .

. . . The Court's opinion in *Cicenia v. Lagay*, decided the same day, merely said that the "contention that petitioner had a constitutional right to confer with counsel is disposed of by *Crooker v. California*. . . ." That case adds nothing, therefore, to Crooker. In any event, to the extent that *Cicenia* or *Crooker* may be inconsistent with the principles announced today, they are not to be regarded as controlling.

Nothing we have said today affects the powers of the police to investigate "an unsolved crime," by gathering information from witnesses and by other "proper investigative efforts." We hold only that, when the process shifts from investigatory to accusatory—when its focus is on the accused and its purpose is to elicit a confession—our adversary system begins to operate, and, under the circumstances here, the accused must be permitted to consult with his lawyer.

White, dissenting:

In *Massiah v. United States*, the Court held that, as of the date of the indictment, the prosecution is dissentitled to secure admissions from the accused. The Court now moves that date back to the time when the prosecution begins to "focus" on the accused. Although the opinion purports to be limited to the facts of this case, it would be naive to think that the new constitutional right announced will depend upon whether the accused has retained his own counsel, or has asked to consult with counsel in the course of interrogation. At the very least, the Court holds that, once the accused becomes a suspect and, presumably, is arrested, any admission made to the police thereafter is inadmissible in evidence unless the accused has waived his right to counsel. The decision is thus another major step in the direction of the goal which the Court seemingly has in mind—to bar from evidence all admissions obtained from an individual suspected of crime, whether involuntarily made or not. . . .

By abandoning the voluntary-involuntary test for admissibility of confessions, the Court seems driven by the notion that it is uncivilized law enforcement to use an accused's own admissions against him at his trial. It attempts to find a home for this new and nebulous rule of due process by attaching it to the right to counsel guaranteed in the federal system by the Sixth Amendment and binding upon the States by virtue of the due process guarantee of the Fourteenth Amendment. The right to counsel now not only entitles the accused to counsel's advice and aid in preparing for trial, but stands as an impenetrable barrier to any interrogation once the accused has become a suspect. From that very moment, apparently his right to counsel attaches, a rule wholly unworkable and impossible to administer unless police cars are equipped with public defenders and undercover agents and police informants have defense counsel at their side. . . .

. . . The only "inquisitions" the Constitution forbids are those which compel incrimination. Escobedo's statements were not compelled, and the Court does not hold that they were.

This new American judges' rule, which is to be applied in both federal and state courts, is perhaps thought to be a necessary safeguard against the possibility of extorted confessions. To this extent, it reflects a deep-seated distrust of law enforcement officers everywhere, unsupported by relevant data or current material based upon our own experience. Obviously law enforcement officers can make mistakes and exceed their authority, as today's decision shows that even judges can do, but I have somewhat more faith than the Court evidently has in the ability and desire of prosecutors and of the power of the appellate courts to discern and correct such violations of the law. . . .

Miranda v. Arizona

384 U.S. 436 (1966), 5-4
Opinion of the Court: Warren (Black, Brennan, Douglas, Fortas)
Dissenting: Clark, Harlan, Stewart, White

Miranda was one of four cases the Supreme Court heard and decided together. In each, the defendant, in police custody, was questioned by officers, detectives, or a prosecuting attorney in an isolated room. None was given a full and effective warning of his rights at the start of interrogation. In all four cases, the questioning drew incriminating oral admissions and, in three, signed statements as well, which were admitted at the trials. All defendants were convicted.

What is the "Miranda" warning? What does it consist of? At what point must it be given? On what right or rights in the Constitution is it based? Is this case a logical progres-
sion from Gideon v. Wainwright, p. 408, and Escobedo v. Illinois (p. 400) or has the Court struck a new path? What important questions are left unanswered?

Warren, for the Court:

. . . We start here, as we did in Escobedo, with the premise that our holding is not an innovation in our jurisprudence, but is an application of principles long recognized and applied in other settings. We have undertaken a thorough reexamination of the Escobedo decision and the principles it announced, and we reaffirm it. That case was but an explication of basic rights that are enshrined in our Constitution—that "No person . . . shall be compelled in any criminal case to be a witness against himself," and that "the accused shall . . . have the Assistance of Counsel"—rights which were put in jeopardy in that case through official overbearing. These precious rights were fixed in our Constitution only after centuries of persecution and struggle. . . .

The constitutional issue we decide in each of these cases is the admissibility of statements obtained from a defendant questioned while in custody or otherwise deprived of his freedom of action in any significant way. . . .

An understanding of the nature and setting of this in-custody interrogation is essential to our decisions today. The difficulty in depicting what transpires at such interrogations stems from the fact that, in this country, they have largely taken place incommunicado. From extensive factual studies undertaken in the early 1930's, including the famous Wickersham Report . . . it is clear that police violence and the "third degree" flourished at that time. In a series of cases decided by this Court long after these studies, the police resorted to physical brutality—beating, hanging, whipping—and to sustained and protracted questioning incommunicado in order to extort confessions. The Commission on Civil Rights in 1961 found much evidence to indicate that "some policemen still resort to physical force to obtain confessions," The use of physical brutality and violence is not, unfortunately, relegated to the past or to any part of the country. . . .

The examples given above are undoubtedly the exception now, but they are sufficiently widespread to be the object of concern. Unless a proper limitation upon custodial interrogation is achieved—such as these decisions will advance—there can be no assurance that practices of this nature will be eradicated in the foreseeable future. . . .

Again we stress that the modern practice of in-custody interrogation is psychologically, rather than physically, oriented. As we have stated before, "Since *Chambers v. Florida*, this Court has recognized that coercion can be mental as well as physical, and that the blood of the accused is not the only hallmark of an unconstitutional inquisition." *Blackburn v. Alabama*

Interrogation still takes place in privacy. Privacy results in secrecy, and this, in turn, results in a gap in our knowledge as to what, in fact, goes on in the interrogation rooms. A valuable source of information about present police practices, however, may be found in various police manuals and texts which document procedures employed with success in the past, and which recommend various other effective tactics. These texts are used by law enforcement agencies themselves as guides. It should be noted that these texts professedly present the most enlightened and effective means presently used to obtain statements through custodial interrogation. By considering these texts and other data, it is possible to describe procedures observed and noted around the country.

The officers are told by the manuals that the "principal psychological factor contributing to a successful interrogation is privacy—being alone with the person under interrogation." . . .

The manuals suggest that the suspect be offered legal excuses for his actions in order to obtain an initial admission of guilt. Where there is a suspected revenge killing, for example, the interrogator may say:

> Joe, you probably didn't go out looking for this fellow with the purpose of shooting him. My guess is, however, that you expected something from him, and that's why you carried a gun—for your own protection. You knew him for what he was, no good. Then when you met him, he probably started using foul, abusive language and he gave some indication that he was about to pull a gun on you, and that's when you had to act to save your own life. That's about it, isn't it, Joe? . . .

When the techniques . . . prove unavailing, the texts recommend they be alternated with a show of some hostility. . . .

It is obvious that such an interrogation environment is created for no purpose other than to subjugate the individual to the will of his examiner. This atmosphere carries its own badge of intimidation. To be sure, this is not physical intimidation, but it is equally destructive of human dignity. . . .

From the foregoing, we can readily perceive an intimate connection between the privilege against self-incrimination and police custodial questioning. . . .

We . . . conclude that, without proper safeguards, the process of in-custody interrogation of persons suspected or accused of crime contains inherently compelling pressures which work to undermine the individual's will to resist and to compel him to speak where he would not otherwise do so freely. In order to combat these pressures and to permit a full opportunity to exercise the privilege against self-incrimination, the accused must be adequately and effectively apprised of his rights, and the exercise of those rights must be fully honored. . . .

At the outset, if a person in custody is to be subjected to interrogation, he must first be informed in clear and unequivocal terms that he has the right to remain silent. For those unaware of the privilege, the warning is needed simply to make them aware of it—the threshold requirement for an intelligent decision as to its exercise. . . .

The warning of the right to remain silent must be accompanied by the explanation that anything said can and will be used against the individual in court. This warning is needed in order to make him aware not only of the privilege, but also of the consequences of forgoing it. . . .

The circumstances surrounding in-custody interrogation can operate very quickly to overbear the will of one merely made aware of his privilege by his interrogators. Therefore, the right to have counsel present at the interrogation is indispensable to the protection of the Fifth Amendment privilege under the system we delineate today. . . .

An individual need not make a pre-interrogation request for a lawyer. While such request affirmatively secures his right to have one, his failure to ask for a lawyer does not constitute a waiver. No effective waiver of the right to counsel during interrogation can be recognized unless specifically made after the warnings we here delineate have been given. . . .

In order fully to apprise a person interrogated of the extent of his rights under this system, then, it is necessary to warn him not only that he has the right to consult with an attorney, but also that, if he is indigent, a lawyer will be appointed to represent him. Without this additional warning, the admonition of the right to consult with counsel would often be understood as meaning only that he can consult with a lawyer if he has one or has the funds to obtain one. The warning of a right to counsel would be hollow if not couched in terms that would convey to the indigent—the person most often subjected to interrogation—the knowledge that he too has a right to have counsel present. . . .

Once warnings have been given, the subsequent procedure is clear. If the individual indicates in any manner, at any time prior to or during questioning, that he wishes to remain silent, the interrogation must cease. At this point, he has shown that he intends to exercise his Fifth Amendment privilege; any statement taken after the person invokes his privilege cannot be other than the product of compulsion, subtle or otherwise. Without the right to cut off questioning, the setting of in-custody interrogation operates on the individual to overcome free choice in producing a statement after the privilege has been once invoked. If the individual states that he wants an attorney, the interrogation must cease until an attorney is present. At that time, the individual must have an opportunity to confer with the attorney and to have him present during any subsequent questioning. If the individual cannot obtain an attorney and he indicates that he wants one before speaking to police, they must respect his decision to remain silent.

This does not mean, as some have suggested, that each police station must have a "station house lawyer" present at all times to advise prisoners. It does mean, however, that, if police propose to interrogate a person, they must make known to him that he is entitled to a lawyer and that, if he cannot afford one, a lawyer will be provided for him prior to any interrogation. If authorities conclude that they will not provide counsel during a reasonable period of time in which investigation in the field is carried out, they may refrain from doing so without violating the person's Fifth Amendment privilege so long as they do not question him during that time.

If the interrogation continues without the presence of an attorney and a statement is taken, a heavy burden rests on the government to demonstrate that the defendant knowingly and intelligently waived his privilege against self-incrimination and his right to retained or appointed counsel. . . .

In dealing with statements obtained through interrogation, we do not purport to find all confessions inadmissible. Confessions remain a proper element in law enforcement. Any statement given freely and voluntarily without any compelling influences is, of course, admissible in evidence. The fundamental import of the privilege while an individual is in custody

is not whether he is allowed to talk to the police without the benefit of warnings and counsel, but whether he can be interrogated. There is no requirement that police stop a person who enters a police station and states that he wishes to confess to a crime, or a person who calls the police to offer a confession or any other statement he desires to make. Volunteered statements of any kind are not barred by the Fifth Amendment, and their admissibility is not affected by our holding today. . . .

White, dissenting:

. . . The obvious underpinning of the Court's decision is a deep-seated distrust of all confessions. As the Court declares that the accused may not be interrogated without counsel present, absent a waiver of the right to counsel, and as the Court all but admonishes the lawyer to advise the accused to remain silent, the result adds up to a judicial judgment that evidence from the accused should not be used against him in any way, whether compelled or not. This is the not so subtle overtone of the opinion—that it is inherently wrong for the police to gather evidence from the accused himself. And this is precisely the nub of this dissent. I see nothing wrong or immoral, and certainly nothing unconstitutional, in the police's asking a suspect whom they have reasonable cause to arrest whether or not he killed his wife, or in confronting him with the evidence on which the arrest was based, at least where he has been plainly advised that he may remain completely silent. Until today, "the admissions or confessions of the prisoner, when voluntarily and freely made, have always ranked high in the scale of incriminating evidence." *Brown v. Walker* Particularly when corroborated, as where the police have confirmed the accused's disclosure of the hiding place of implements or fruits of the crime, such confessions have the highest reliability, and significantly contribute to the certitude with which we may believe the accused is guilty. Moreover, it is by no means certain that the process of confessing is injurious to the accused. To the contrary, it may provide psychological relief, and enhance the prospects for rehabilitation. This is not to say that the value of respect for the inviolability of the accused's individual personality should be accorded no weight, or that all confessions should be indiscriminately admitted. This Court has long read the Constitution to proscribe compelled confessions, a salutary rule from which there should be no retreat. But I see no sound basis, factual or otherwise, and the Court gives none, for concluding that the present rule against the receipt of coerced confessions is inadequate for the task of sorting out inadmissible evidence, and must be replaced by the per se rule which is now imposed. Even if the new concept can be said to have advantages of some sort over the present law, they are far outweighed by its likely undesirable impact on other very relevant and important interests.

The most basic function of any government is to provide for the security of the individual and of his property. These ends of society are served by the criminal laws which for the most part are aimed at the prevention of crime. Without the reasonably effective performance of the task of preventing private violence and retaliation, it is idle to talk about human dignity and civilized values.

The modes by which the criminal laws serve the interest in general security are many. First, the murderer who has taken the life of another is removed from the streets, deprived of his liberty, and thereby prevented from repeating his offense. In view of the statistics on recidivism in this country, and of the number of instances in which apprehension occurs only after repeated offenses, no one can sensibly claim that this aspect of the criminal law does not prevent crime or contribute significantly to the personal security of the ordinary citizen.

Secondly, the swift and sure apprehension of those who refuse to respect the personal security and dignity of their neighbor unquestionably has its impact on others who might be similarly tempted. That the criminal law is wholly or partly ineffective with a segment of the population or with many of those who have been apprehended and convicted is a very faulty basis for concluding that it is not effective with respect to the great bulk of our citizens, or for thinking that, without the criminal laws, or in the absence of their enforcement, there would be no increase in crime. Arguments of this nature are not borne out by any kind of reliable evidence that I have seen to this date.

Thirdly, the law concerns itself with those whom it has confined. The hope and aim of modern penology, fortunately, is as soon as possible to return the convict to society a better and more law-abiding man than when he left. Sometimes there is success, sometimes failure. But at least the effort is made, and it should be made to the very maximum extent of our present and future capabilities.

The rule announced today will measurably weaken the ability of the criminal law to perform these tasks. It is a deliberate calculus to prevent interrogations, to reduce the incidence of confessions and pleas of guilty, and to increase the number of trials. Criminal trials, no matter how efficient the police are, are not sure bets for the prosecution, nor should they be if the evidence is not forthcoming. Under the present law, the prosecution fails to prove its case in about 30% of the criminal cases actually tried in the federal courts. But it is something else again to remove from the ordinary criminal case all those confessions which heretofore have been held to be free and voluntary acts of the accused, and to thus establish a new constitutional barrier to the ascertainment of truth by the judicial process. There is, in my view, every reason to believe that a good many criminal defendants who otherwise would have been convicted on what this Court has previously thought to be the most satisfactory kind of evidence will now, under this new version of the Fifth Amendment, either not be tried at all or will be acquitted if the State's evidence, minus the confession, is put to the test of litigation. . . .

Dickerson v. United States

530 U.S. 428 (2000), 7-2
Opinion of the Court: Rehnquist (Breyer, Ginsburg, Kennedy, O'Connor, Souter, Stevens)
Dissenting: Scalia, Thomas

What does the Crime Control and Safe Streets Act provide that is inconsistent with the Miranda decision? Was it necessary to hold that the Miranda warning was a constitutional requirement rather than simply a Court-imposed rule of evidence for the courts? Congress passed the act in 1968, two years after the Miranda decision and §3501 was considered, in part at least, an attempt to weaken the decision. Why do you suppose it took the Court more than 30 years to hear a case raising the issue of the constitutionality of §3501? Chief Justice Rehnquist has often voted to narrow the scope and applicability of Miranda and was a chief critic of the decision among the justices. Why does he now write an opinion to uphold the decision? Is it a tacit admission that Miranda *was correctly decided, an honoring of it now as precedent, or a reluctance to disturb settled law enforcement practices?*

Rehnquist, for the Court:

In *Miranda v. Arizona,* we held that certain warnings must be given before a suspect's statement made during custodial interrogation could be admitted in evidence. In the wake of that decision, Congress enacted 18 U.S.C. §3501 which in essence laid down a rule that the admissibility of such statements should turn only on whether or not they were voluntarily made. We hold that *Miranda*, being a constitutional decision of this Court, may not be in effect overruled by an Act of Congress, and we decline to overrule *Miranda* ourselves. We therefore hold that *Miranda* and its progeny in this Court govern the admissibility of statements made during custodial interrogation in both state and federal courts.

Petitioner Dickerson was indicted for bank robbery, conspiracy to commit bank robbery, and using a firearm in the course of committing a crime of violence, all in violation of the applicable provisions of Title 18 of the United States Code. Before trial, Dickerson moved to suppress a statement he had made at a Federal Bureau of Investigation field office, on the grounds that he had not received "Miranda warnings" before being interrogated. The District Court granted his motion to suppress, and the Government took an interlocutory appeal to the United States Court of Appeals for the Fourth Circuit. That court, by a divided vote, reversed the District Court's suppression order. It agreed with the District Court's conclusion that petitioner had not received Miranda warnings before making his statement. But it went on to hold that §3501, which in effect makes the admissibility of statements such as Dickerson's turn solely on whether they were made voluntarily, was satisfied in this case. It then concluded that our decision in *Miranda* was not a constitutional holding, and that therefore Congress could by statute have the final say on the question of admissibility....

Given §3501's express designation of voluntariness as the touchstone of admissibility, its omission of any warning requirement, and the instruction for trial courts to consider a nonexclusive list of factors relevant to the circumstances of a confession, we agree with the Court of Appeals that Congress intended by its enactment to overrule *Miranda*. Because of the obvious conflict between our decision in *Miranda* and §3501, we must address whether Congress has constitutional authority to thus supersede *Miranda*. If Congress has such authority, §3501's totality-of-the-circumstances approach must prevail over *Miranda's* requirement of warnings; if not, that section must yield to *Miranda's* more specific requirements.

The law in this area is clear. This Court has supervisory authority over the federal courts, and we may use that authority to prescribe rules of evidence and procedure that are binding in those tribunals. However, the power to judicially create and enforce non-constitutional "rules of procedure and evidence for the federal courts exists only in the absence of a relevant Act of Congress." *Palermo v. United States.* Congress retains the ultimate authority to modify or set aside any judicially created rules of evidence and procedure that are not required by the Constitution.

But Congress may not legislatively supersede our decisions interpreting and applying the Constitution. This case therefore turns on whether the Miranda Court announced a constitutional rule or merely exercised its supervisory authority to regulate evidence in the absence of congressional direction. Recognizing this point, the Court of Appeals surveyed *Miranda* and its progeny to determine the constitutional status of the Miranda decision. Relying on the fact that we have created several exceptions to *Miranda's* warnings requirement and that we have repeatedly referred to the Miranda warnings as "prophylactic," and "not themselves rights protected by the Constitution," *Michigan v. Tucker,* the Court of Appeals concluded that the protections announced in *Miranda* are not constitutionally required.

We disagree with the Court of Appeals' conclusion, although we concede that there is language in some of our opinions that supports the view taken by that court. But first and foremost of the factors on the other side—that *Miranda* is a constitutional decision— is that both *Miranda* and two of its companion cases applied the rule to proceedings in state courts—to wit, Arizona, California, and New York. Since that time, we have consistently applied *Miranda's* rule to prosecutions arising in state courts. It is beyond dispute that we do not hold a supervisory power over the courts of the several States. With respect to proceedings in state courts, our "authority is limited to enforcing the commands of the United States Constitution." *Mu'Min v. Virginia.*

The Miranda opinion itself begins by stating that the Court granted certiorari "to explore some facets of the problems . . . of applying the privilege against self-incrimination to in-custody interrogation, and to give concrete constitutional guidelines for law enforcement agencies and courts to follow." In fact, the majority opinion is replete with statements indicating that the majority thought it was announcing a constitutional rule.4 Indeed, the Court's ultimate conclusion was that the unwarned confessions obtained in the four cases before the Court in *Miranda* "were obtained from the defendant under circumstances that did not meet constitutional standards for protection of the privilege."

Additional support for our conclusion that *Miranda* is constitutionally based is found in the *Miranda* Court's invitation for legislative action to protect the constitutional right against coerced self-incrimination. After discussing the "compelling pressures" inherent in custodial police interrogation, the *Miranda* Court concluded that, "[i]n order to combat these pressures and to permit a full opportunity to exercise the privilege against self-incrimination, the accused must be adequately and effectively appraised of his rights and the exercise of those rights must be fully honored." However, the Court emphasized that it could not foresee "the potential alternatives for protecting the privilege which might be devised by Congress or the States," and it accordingly opined that the Constitution would not preclude legislative solutions that differed from the prescribed *Miranda* warnings but which were "at least as effective in apprising accused persons of their right of silence and in assuring a continuous opportunity to exercise it."

Whether or not we would agree with *Miranda's* reasoning and its resulting rule, were we addressing the issue in the first instance, the principles of stare decisis weigh heavily against overruling it now. While "'stare decisis is not an inexorable command,' *Payne v. Tennessee*, particularly when we are interpreting the Constitution, even in constitutional cases, the doctrine carries such persuasive force that we have always required a departure from precedent to be supported by some 'special justification.'"

We do not think there is such justification for overruling *Miranda*. *Miranda* has become embedded in routine police practice to the point where the warnings have become part of our national culture. While we have overruled our precedents when subsequent cases have undermined their doctrinal underpinnings, we do not believe that this has happened to the *Miranda* decision. If anything, our subsequent cases have reduced the impact of the *Miranda* rule on legitimate law enforcement while reaffirming the decision's core ruling that unwarned statements may not be used as evidence in the prosecution's case in chief.

The disadvantage of the *Miranda* rule is that statements which may be by no means involuntary, made by a defendant who is aware of his "rights," may nonetheless be excluded and a guilty defendant go free as a result. But experience suggests that the totality-of-the-circumstances test which §3501 seeks to revive is more difficult than *Miranda* for law enforcement officers to conform to, and for courts to apply in a consistent manner. The requirement that *Miranda* warnings be given does not, of course, dispense with the voluntariness inquiry. But as we said in *Berkemer v. McCarty*, "[c]ases in which a defendant can make a colorable argument that a self-incriminating statement was 'compelled' despite the fact that the law enforcement authorities adhered to the dictates of *Miranda* are rare."

In sum, we conclude that *Miranda* announced a constitutional rule that Congress may not supersede legislatively. Following the rule of stare decisis, we decline to overrule *Miranda* ourselves.

Scalia, dissenting:

Those to whom judicial decisions are an unconnected series of judgments that produce either favored or disfavored results will doubtless greet today's decision as a paragon of moderation, since it declines to overrule *Miranda v. Arizona*. Those who understand the judicial process will appreciate that today's decision is not a reaffirmation of *Miranda*, but a radical revision of the most significant element of *Miranda* (as of all cases): the rationale that gives it a permanent place in our jurisprudence. . . .

It takes only a small step to bring today's opinion out of the realm of power-judging and into the mainstream of legal reasoning: The Court need only go beyond its carefully couched iterations that "*Miranda* is a constitutional decision," that "*Miranda* is constitutionally based," that *Miranda* has "constitutional underpinnings," and come out and say quite clearly: "We reaffirm today that custodial interrogation that is not preceded by *Miranda* warnings or their equivalent violates the Constitution of the United States." It cannot say that, because a majority of the Court does not believe it. The Court therefore acts in plain violation of the Constitution when it denies effect to this Act of Congress. . . .

. . . [T]he Court asserts that *Miranda* must be a "constitutional decision" announcing a "constitutional rule," and thus immune to congressional modification, because we have since its inception applied it to the States. If this argument is meant as an invocation of *stare decisis*, it fails because, though it is true that our cases applying *Miranda* against the States must be reconsidered if *Miranda* is not required by the Constitution, it is likewise true that our cases . . . based on the principle that *Miranda* is *not* required by the Constitution will have to be reconsidered if it *is*. . . . Congress's attempt to set aside *Miranda*, since it represents an assertion that violation of *Miranda* is not a violation of the Constitution, *also* represents an assertion that the Court has no power to impose *Miranda* on the States.... [O]ur continued application of the *Miranda* code to the States despite our consistent statements that running afoul of its dictates does not necessarily—or even usually—result in an actual constitutional violation, represents not the source of *Miranda*'s salvation but rather evidence of its ultimate illegitimacy....

[W]hile I agree with the Court that §3501 cannot be upheld without also concluding that *Miranda* represents an illegitimate exercise of our authority to review state-court judgments, I do not share the Court's hesitation in reaching that conclusion. For while the Court is also correct that the doctrine of *stare decisis* demands some "special justification" for a departure from longstanding precedent—even precedent of the constitutional variety—that criterion is more than met here.... Despite the Court's Orwellian assertion to the contrary, it is undeniable that later cases... have "undermined [*Miranda*'s] doctrinal underpinnings," denying constitutional violation and thus stripping the holding of its only constitutionally legitimate support. *Miranda*'s critics and supporters alike have long made this point....

[Nor] am I persuaded by the argument for retaining *Miranda* that touts its supposed workability as compared with the totality-of-the-circumstances test it purported to replace. *Miranda*'s proponents cite *ad nauseam* the fact that the Court was called upon to make difficult and subtle distinctions in applying the "voluntariness" test in some 30-odd due process "coerced confessions" cases in the 30 years between *Brown* v. *Mississippi*, and *Miranda*. It is not immediately apparent, however, that the judicial burden has been eased by the "bright-line" rules adopted in *Miranda*. In fact, in the 34 years since *Miranda* was decided, this Court has been called upon to decide nearly 60 cases involving a host of *Miranda* issues, most of them predicted with remarkable prescience by Justice White in his *Miranda* dissent....

Finally, I am not convinced by petitioner's argument that *Miranda* should be preserved because the decision occupies a special place in the "public's consciousness." As far as I am aware, the public is not under the illusion that we are infallible. I see little harm in admitting that we made a mistake in taking away from the people the ability to decide for themselves what protections (beyond those required by the Constitution) are reasonably affordable in the criminal in-

vestigatory process. And I see much to be gained by reaffirming for the people the wonderful reality that they govern themselves—which means that "[t]he powers not delegated to the United States by the Constitution" that the people adopted, "nor prohibited ... to the States" by that Constitution, "are reserved to the States respectively, or to the people."

... In imposing its Court-made code upon the States, the original opinion at least *asserted* that it was demanded by the Constitution. Today's decision does not pretend that it is—and yet *still* asserts the right to impose it against the will of the people's representatives in Congress. Far from believing that *stare decisis* compels this result, I believe we cannot allow to remain on the books even a celebrated decision—*especially* a celebrated decision—that has come to stand for the proposition that the Supreme Court has power to impose extraconstitutional constraints upon Congress and the States. This is not the system that was established by the Framers, or that would be established by any sane supporter of government by the people.....

Gideon v. Wainwright

372 U.S. 335 (1963), 9-0
Opinion of the
Court: Black (Brennan, Clark, Douglas, Goldberg, Harlan, Stewart, Warren, White)

Did the Court find that Gideon did not have a fair trial? Where a defendant is convicted, does not having had a lawyer necessarily mean that the trial was unfair? Did this decision build on the doctrinal development of earlier cases or did it completely break new ground? What problems does it present for state criminal justice systems? Did the Court take these into account? What questions are left unanswered?

Black, for the Court:

Petitioner was charged in a Florida state court with having broken and entered a poolroom with intent to commit a misdemeanor. This offense is a felony under Florida law. Appearing in court without funds and without a lawyer, petitioner asked the court to appoint counsel for him, [but was told] "the only time the Court can appoint counsel to represent a defendant is when that person is charged with a capital offense." ...

Put to trial before a jury, Gideon conducted his defense about as well as could be expected from a lay-

Clarence Earl Gideon in a law library.

man. He made an opening statement to the jury, cross-examined the State's witnesses, presented witnesses in his own defense, declined to testify himself, and made a short argument "emphasizing his innocence to the charge contained in the Information filed in this case." The jury returned a verdict of guilty, and petitioner was sentenced to serve five years in the state prison. . . .

. . . Since 1942, when *Betts v. Brady* was decided by a divided Court, the problem of a defendant's federal constitutional right to counsel in a state court has been a continuing source of controversy and litigation in both state and federal courts. To give this problem another review here, we granted certiorari. Since Gideon was proceeding in forma pauperis, we appointed counsel to represent him and requested both sides to discuss in their briefs and oral arguments the following: "Should this Court's holding in *Betts v. Brady* be reconsidered?"

The facts upon which Betts claimed that he had been unconstitutionally denied the right to have counsel appointed to assist him are strikingly like the facts upon which Gideon here bases his federal constitutional claim. Betts was indicted for robbery in a Maryland state court. On arraignment, he told the trial judge of his lack of funds to hire a lawyer and asked the court to appoint one for him. Betts was ad-

vised that it was not the practice in that county to appoint counsel for indigent defendants except in murder and rape cases. He then pleaded not guilty, had witnesses summoned, cross-examined the State's witnesses, examined his own, and chose not to testify himself. He was found guilty by the judge, sitting without a jury, and sentenced to eight years in prison. Like Gideon, Betts sought release by habeas corpus, alleging that he had been denied the right to assistance of counsel in violation of the Fourteenth Amendment. Betts was denied any relief, and, on review, this Court affirmed. It was held that a refusal to appoint counsel for an indigent defendant charged with a felony did not necessarily violate the Due Process Clause of the Fourteenth Amendment, which, for reasons given, the Court deemed to be the only applicable federal constitutional provision. The Court said:

> Asserted denial [of due process] is to be tested by an appraisal of the totality of facts in a given case. That which may, in one setting, constitute a denial of fundamental fairness, shocking to the universal sense of justice, may, in other circumstances, and in the light of other considerations, fall short of such denial.

Treating due process as "a concept less rigid and more fluid than those envisaged in other specific and particular provisions of the Bill of Rights," the Court held that refusal to appoint counsel under the particular facts and circumstances in the Betts case was not so "offensive to the common and fundamental ideas of fairness" as to amount to a denial of due process. Since the facts and circumstances of the two cases are so nearly indistinguishable, we think the *Betts v. Brady* holding, if left standing, would require us to reject Gideon's claim that the Constitution guarantees him the assistance of counsel. Upon full reconsideration, we conclude that *Betts v. Brady* should be overruled.

The Sixth Amendment provides, "In all criminal prosecutions, the accused shall enjoy the right ... to have the Assistance of Counsel for his defence." We have construed this to mean that, in federal courts, counsel must be provided for defendants unable to employ counsel unless the right is competently and intelligently waived. Betts argued that this right is extended to indigent defendants in state courts by the Fourteenth Amendment. In response, the Court stated that, while the Sixth Amendment laid down "no rule for the conduct of the States, the question recurs whether the constraint laid by the Amendment upon the national courts expresses a rule so fundamental and essential to a fair trial, and so, to due process of law, that it is made obligatory upon the States by the Fourteenth Amendment."

In order to decide whether the Sixth Amendment's guarantee of counsel is of this fundamental nature, the Court in *Betts* set out and considered "[r]elevant data on the subject ... afforded by constitutional and statutory provisions subsisting in the colonies and the States prior to the inclusion of the Bill of Rights in the national Constitution, and in the constitutional, legislative, and judicial history of the States to the present date." On the basis of this historical data, the Court concluded that "appointment of counsel is not a fundamental right, essential to a fair trial." ...

We accept *Betts v. Brady's* assumption, based as it was on our prior cases, that a provision of the Bill of Rights which is "fundamental and essential to a fair trial" is made obligatory upon the States by the Fourteenth Amendment. We think the Court in *Betts* was wrong, however, in concluding that the Sixth Amendment's guarantee of counsel is not one of these fundamental rights. Ten years before *Betts v. Brady,* this Court, after full consideration of all the historical data examined in *Betts,* had unequivocally declared that "the right to the aid of counsel is of this fundamental character." *Powell v. Alabama.* While the Court,

at the close of its *Powell* opinion, did, by its language, as this Court frequently does, limit its holding to the particular facts and circumstances of that case, its conclusions about the fundamental nature of the right to counsel are unmistakable. Several years later, in 1936, the Court reemphasized what it had said about the fundamental nature of the right to counsel in this language:

> We concluded that certain fundamental rights, safeguarded by the first eight amendments against federal action, were also safeguarded against state action by the due process of law clause of the Fourteenth Amendment, and among them the fundamental right of the accused to the aid of counsel in a criminal prosecution. *Grosjean v. American Press Co.* . . .

. . . In light of these and many other prior decisions of this Court, it is not surprising that the *Betts* Court, when faced with the contention that "one charged with crime, who is unable to obtain counsel, must be furnished counsel by the State," conceded that "[e]xpressions in the opinions of this court lend color to the argument. . . ." The fact is that, in deciding as it did—that "appointment of counsel is not a fundamental right, essential to a fair trial"—the Court in *Betts v. Brady* made an abrupt break with its own well considered precedents. In returning to these old precedents, sounder, we believe, than the new, we but restore constitutional principles established to achieve a fair system of justice. Not only these precedents, but also reason and reflection, require us to recognize that, in our adversary system of criminal justice, any person haled into court, who is too poor to hire a lawyer, cannot be assured a fair trial unless counsel is provided for him. This seems to us to be an obvious truth. Governments, both state and federal, quite properly spend vast sums of money to establish machinery to try defendants accused of crime. Lawyers to prosecute are everywhere deemed essential to protect the public's interest in an orderly society. Similarly, there are few defendants charged with crime, few indeed, who fail to hire the best lawyers they can get to prepare and present their defenses. That government hires lawyers to prosecute and defendants who have the money hire lawyers to defend are the strongest indications of the widespread belief that lawyers in criminal courts are necessities, not luxuries. The right of one charged with crime to counsel may not be deemed fundamental and essential to fair trials in some countries, but it is in ours. From the very beginning, our state and national constitutions and laws have laid great emphasis on procedural and substantive safeguards designed to assure fair trials before impartial tribunals in which every defendant stands equal before the law. This noble ideal cannot be realized if the poor man charged with crime has to face his accusers without a lawyer to assist him. A defendant's need for a lawyer is nowhere better stated than in the moving words of Mr. Justice Sutherland in *Powell v. Alabama*:

> The right to be heard would be, in many cases, of little avail if it did not comprehend the right to be heard by counsel. Even the intelligent and educated layman has small and sometimes no skill in the science of law. If charged with crime, he is incapable, generally, of determining for himself whether the indictment is good or bad. He is unfamiliar with the rules of evidence. Left without the aid of counsel, he may be put on trial without a proper charge, and convicted upon incompetent evidence, or evidence irrelevant to the issue or otherwise inadmissible. He lacks both the skill and knowledge adequately to prepare his defense, even though he have a perfect one. He requires the guiding hand of counsel at every step in the proceedings against him. Without it, though he be not guilty, he faces the danger of conviction because he does not know how to establish his innocence.

The Court in *Betts v. Brady* departed from the sound wisdom upon which the Court's holding in *Powell v. Alabama* rested. Florida, supported by two other States, has asked that *Betts v. Brady* be left intact. Twenty-two States, as friends of the Court, argue that *Betts* was "an anachronism when handed down," and that it should now be overruled. We agree. . . .

Harlan, concurring:

I agree that *Betts v. Brady* should be overruled, but consider it entitled to a more respectful burial than has been accorded, at least on the part of those of us who were not on the Court when that case was decided.

I cannot subscribe to the view that *Betts v. Brady* represented "an abrupt break with its own well considered precedents." In 1932, in *Powell v. Alabama*, a capital case, this Court declared that, under the particular facts there presented—"the ignorance and illiteracy of the defendants, their youth, the circumstances of public hostility . . . and, above all, that they stood in deadly peril of their lives"—the state court had a duty to assign counsel for the trial as a necessary requisite of due process of law. It is evident that these limiting facts were not added to the opinion as an afterthought; they were repeatedly emphasized and were clearly regarded as important to the result.

Thus, when this Court, a decade later, decided *Betts v. Brady*, it did no more than to admit of the possible existence of special circumstances in noncapital, as well as capital, trials, while at the same time insisting that such circumstances be shown in order to establish a denial of due process. The right to appointed counsel had been recognized as being considerably broader in federal prosecutions, but to have imposed these requirements on the States would indeed have been "an abrupt break" with the almost immediate past. The declaration that the right to appointed counsel in state prosecutions, as established in *Powell v. Alabama*, was not limited to capital cases was, in truth, not a departure from, but an extension of, existing precedent. . . .

. . . The Court has come to recognize, in other words, that the mere existence of a serious criminal charge constituted, in itself, special circumstances requiring the services of counsel at trial. In truth, the *Betts v. Brady* rule is no longer a reality.

This evolution, however, appears not to have been fully recognized by many state courts, in this instance charged with the front-line responsibility for the enforcement of constitutional rights. To continue a rule which is honored by this Court only with lip service is not a healthy thing, and, in the long run, will do disservice to the federal system. . . .

In agreeing with the Court that the right to counsel in a case such as this should now be expressly recognized as a fundamental right embraced in the Fourteenth Amendment, I wish to make a further observation. When we hold a right or immunity, valid against the Federal Government, to be "implicit in the concept of ordered liberty" and thus valid against the States, I do not read our past decisions to suggest that, by so holding, we automatically carry over an entire body of federal law and apply it in full sweep to the States. Any such concept would disregard the frequently wide disparity between the legitimate interests of the States and of the Federal Government, the divergent problems that they face, and the significantly different consequences of their actions. United States, In what is done today, I do not understand the Court to depart from the principles laid down in

Palko v. Connecticut or to embrace the concept that the Fourteenth Amendment "incorporates" the Sixth Amendment as such. . . .

Malloy v. Hogan

378 U.S. 1 (1964), 5-4
Opinion of the Court: Brennan (Black, Douglas, Goldberg, Warren)
Dissenting: Clark, Harlan, Stewart, White

How were the defendant's constitutional rights violated? What questions of federalism appear in this case? Why did the Court say it was necessary that the federal and state government's be held to the same standard with regard to the privilege against self-incrimination?

Brennan, for the Court:

. . . The petitioner was arrested during a gambling raid in 1959 by Hartford, Connecticut, police. He pleaded guilty to the crime of pool selling, a misdemeanor, and was sentenced to one year in jail and fined $500. The sentence was ordered to be suspended after 90 days, at which time he was to be placed on probation for two years. About 16 months after his guilty plea, [he] was ordered to testify before a referee appointed by the Superior Court of Hartford County to conduct an inquiry into alleged gambling and other criminal activities in the county. [He] was asked a number of questions related to events surrounding his arrest and conviction. He refused to answer any question "on the grounds it may tend to incriminate me." The Superior Court adjudged him in contempt, and committed him to prison until he was willing to answer the questions. . . .

The Court has not hesitated to reexamine past decisions according the Fourteenth Amendment a less central role in the preservation of basic liberties than that which was contemplated by its Framers when they added the Amendment to our constitutional scheme. Thus, . . . *Palko v. Connecticut* suggested that the rights secured by the Fourth Amendment were not protected against state action, citing, the statement of the Court in 1914 in *Weeks v. United States,* that "the Fourth Amendment is not directed to individual misconduct of [state] officials." In 1961, however, the Court held that, in the light of later decisions, it was taken as settled that ". . . the Fourth Amendment's right of privacy has been declared en-

forceable against the States through the Due Process Clause of the Fourteenth. . . ." *Mapp v. Ohio* Again, although the Court held in 1942 that, in a state prosecution for a noncapital offense, "appointment of counsel is not a fundamental right," *Betts v. Brady,* only last Term, this decision was reexamined and it was held that provision of counsel in all criminal cases was "a fundamental right, essential to a fair trial," and thus was made obligatory on the States by the Fourteenth Amendment. *Gideon v. Wainwright*

We hold today that the Fifth Amendment's exception from compulsory self-incrimination is also protected by the Fourteenth Amendment against abridgment by the States. Decisions of the Court since *Twining* [*v. New Jersey*] and *Adamson* [*v. California*] have departed from the contrary view expressed in those cases. We discuss first the decisions which forbid the use of coerced confessions in state criminal prosecutions.

Brown v. Mississippi was the first case in which the Court held that the Due Process Clause prohibited the States from using the accused's coerced confessions against him. The Court in Brown felt impelled, in light of Twining, to say that its conclusion did not involve the privilege against self-incrimination. "Compulsion by torture to extort a confession is a different matter." But this distinction was soon abandoned, and today the admissibility of a confession in a state criminal prosecution is tested by the same standard applied in federal prosecutions since 1897, when, in *Bram v. United States,* the Court held that "[i]n criminal trials in the courts of the United States, wherever a question arises whether a confession is incompetent because not voluntary, the issue is controlled by that portion of the Fifth Amendment to the Constitution of the United States commanding that no person shall be compelled in any criminal case to be a witness against himself." . . .

The marked shift to the federal standard in state cases began with *Lisenba v. California,* where the Court spoke of the accused's "free choice to admit, to deny or to refuse to answer." The shift reflects recognition that the American system of criminal prosecution is accusatorial, not inquisitorial, and that the Fifth Amendment privilege is its essential mainstay Governments, state and federal, are thus constitutionally compelled to establish guilt by evidence independently and freely secured, and may not, by coercion, prove a charge against an accused out of his own mouth. Since the Fourteenth Amendment prohibits the States from inducing a person to confess through "sympathy falsely aroused," or other like inducement far short of "compulsion by torture," it follows . . . that it also forbids the States to resort to imprisonment, as here, to compel him to answer questions that might incriminate him. The Fourteenth Amendment secures against state invasion the same privilege that the Fifth Amendment guarantees against federal infringement—the right of a person to remain silent unless he chooses to speak in the unfettered exercise of his own will, and to suffer no penalty, as held in *Twining*, for such silence.

This conclusion is fortified by our recent decision in *Mapp v. Ohio* [which] held that the Fifth Amendment privilege against self-incrimination implemented the Fourth Amendment in such cases, and that the two guarantees of personal security conjoined in the Fourteenth Amendment to make the exclusionary rule obligatory upon the States. We relied upon the great case of *Boyd v. United States,* which . . . held that "Breaking into a house and opening boxes and drawers are circumstances of aggravation; but any forcible and compulsory extortion of a man's own testimony or of his private papers to be used as evidence to convict him of crime or to forfeit his goods is within the condemnation of [those Amendments]. . . ."

In thus returning to the *Boyd* view that the privilege is one of the "principles of a free government," *Mapp* necessarily repudiated the *Twining* concept of the privilege as a mere rule of evidence "best defended not as an unchangeable principle of universal justice, but as a law proved by experience to be expedient." . . .

. . . The State urges, however, that the availability of the federal privilege to a witness in a state inquiry is to be determined according to a less stringent standard than is applicable in a federal proceeding. We disagree. We have held that the guarantees of the First Amendment, the prohibition of unreasonable searches and seizures of the Fourth Amendment, and the right to counsel guaranteed by the Sixth Amendment, are all to be enforced against the States under the Fourteenth Amendment according to the same standards that protect those personal rights against federal encroachment. . . . The Court thus has rejected the notion that the Fourteenth Amendment applies to the States only a "watered-down, subjective version of the individual guarantees of the Bill of Rights," If *Cohen v. Hurley,* and *Adamson v. California* suggest such an application of the privilege against

self-incrimination, that suggestion cannot survive recognition of the degree to which the *Twining* view of the privilege has been eroded. What is accorded is a privilege of refusing to incriminate one's self, and the feared prosecution may be by either federal or state authorities. It would be incongruous to have different standards determine the validity of a claim of privilege based on the same feared prosecution depending on whether the claim was asserted in a state or federal court. Therefore, the same standards must determine whether an accused's silence in either a federal or state proceeding is justified. . . .

. . . It was admitted on behalf of the State at oral argument—and indeed it is obvious from the questions themselves—that the State desired to elicit from the petitioner the identity of the person who ran the pool-selling operation in connection with which he had been arrested in 1959. It was apparent that petitioner might apprehend that, if this person were still engaged in unlawful activity, disclosure of his name might furnish a link in a chain of evidence sufficient to connect the petitioner with a more recent crime for which he might still be prosecuted. . . .

. . . We conclude therefore that, as to each of the questions, it was "evident from the implications of the question, in the setting in which it [was] asked, that a responsive answer to the question or an explanation of why it [could not] be answered might be dangerous because injurious disclosure could result" *Hoffman v. United States*

Harlan, dissenting:

. . . I can only read the Court's opinion as accepting in fact what it rejects in theory: the application to the States, via the Fourteenth Amendment, of the forms of federal criminal procedure embodied within the first eight Amendments to the Constitution. While it is true that the Court deals today with only one aspect of state criminal procedure, and rejects the wholesale "incorporation" of such federal constitutional requirements, the logical gap between the Court's premises and its novel constitutional conclusion can, I submit, be bridged only by the additional premise that the Due Process Clause of the Fourteenth Amendment is a shorthand directive to this Court to pick and choose among the provisions of the first eight Amendments and apply those chosen, freighted with their entire accompanying body of federal doctrine, to law enforcement in the States. . . .

Batson v. Kentucky

476 U.S. 79 (1986), 7-2
Opinion of the Court: Powell (Blackmun, Brennan,
 Marshall, O'Connor, Stevens, White)
Dissenting: Burger, Rehnquist

*What is the function of peremptory challenges? Normally, de-
fense objections to jury selection procedures must reference
their effect on fairness of the defendant's trial. Has that been
changed by this decision? Who is making assumptions about
race affecting partiality? The prosecutor? The defense? The
Court? The dissenters? Everyone? In the light of this decision, what other discriminatory use of peremptory challenges
might be held invalid?*

Powell, for the Court:

This case requires us to reexamine that portion of
Swain v. Alabama, concerning the evidentiary burden
placed on a criminal defendant who claims that he
has been denied equal protection through the State's
use of peremptory challenges to exclude members of
his race from the petit jury.

Petitioner [Batson], a black man, was indicted in
Kentucky on charges of second-degree burglary and
receipt of stolen goods. On the first day of trial in Jefferson Circuit Court, the judge conducted voir dire examination of the venire, excused certain jurors for
cause, and permitted the parties to exercise peremptory challenges. The prosecutor used his peremptory
challenges to strike all four black persons on the
venire, and a jury composed only of white persons was
selected. Defense counsel moved to discharge the jury
before it was sworn on the ground that the prosecutor's removal of the black veniremen violated petitioner's rights under the Sixth and Fourteenth
Amendments to a jury drawn from a cross-section of
the community, and under the Fourteenth Amendment to equal protection of the laws. Counsel requested a hearing on his motion. Without expressly
ruling on the request for a hearing, the trial judge observed that the parties were entitled to use their
peremptory challenges to "strike anybody they want
to." The judge then denied petitioner's motion, reasoning that the cross-section requirement applies only
to selection of the venire, and not to selection of the
petit jury itself.

The jury convicted petitioner on both counts. . . .

In *Swain v. Alabama,* this Court recognized that a
"State's purposeful or deliberate denial to Negroes on
account of race of participation as jurors in the administration of justice violates the Equal Protection
Clause." This principle has been "consistently and repeatedly" reaffirmed, in numerous decisions of this
Court both preceding and following *Swain.* We reaffirm the principle today.

More than a century ago, the Court decided that
the State denies a black defendant equal protection
of the laws when it puts him on trial before a jury
from which members of his race have been purposefully excluded. *Strauder v. West Virginia.* That decision
laid the foundation for the Court's unceasing efforts
to eradicate racial discrimination in the procedures
used to select the venire from which individual jurors
are drawn. In *Strauder,* the Court explained that the
central concern of the recently ratified Fourteenth
Amendment was to put an end to governmental discrimination on account of race. Exclusion of black citizens from service as jurors constitutes a primary
example of the evil the Fourteenth Amendment was
designed to cure. . . .

The harm from discriminatory jury selection extends beyond that inflicted on the defendant and the
excluded juror to touch the entire community. Selection procedures that purposefully exclude black persons from juries undermine public confidence in the
fairness of our system of justice. . . .

In *Strauder,* the Court invalidated a state statute that
provided that only white men could serve as jurors. We
can be confident that no State now has such a law. The
Constitution requires, however, that we look beyond
the face of the statute defining juror qualifications,
and also consider challenged selection practices to afford "protection against action of the State through its
administrative officers in effecting the prohibited discrimination." *Norris v. Alabama* Thus, the Court has
found a denial of equal protection where the procedures implementing a neutral statute operated to exclude persons from the venire on racial grounds, and
has made clear that the Constitution prohibits all
forms of purposeful racial discrimination in selection
of jurors. While decisions of this Court have been concerned largely with discrimination during selection of
the venire, the principles announced there also forbid
discrimination on account of race in selection of the
petit jury. Since the Fourteenth Amendment protects
an accused throughout the proceedings bringing him
to justice, the State may not draw up its jury lists pursuant to neutral procedures, but then resort to discrimination at "other stages in the selection process."

Accordingly, the component of the jury selection process at issue here, the State's privilege to strike individual jurors through peremptory challenges, is subject to the commands of the Equal Protection Clause. Although a prosecutor ordinarily is entitled to exercise permitted peremptory challenges "for any reason at all, as long as that reason is related to his view concerning the outcome" of the case to be tried, mandamus granted sub nom. the Equal Protection Clause forbids the prosecutor to challenge potential jurors solely on account of their race or on the assumption that black jurors as a group will be unable impartially to consider the State's case against a black defendant.

The principles announced in *Strauder* never have been questioned in any subsequent decision of this Court. Rather, the Court has been called upon repeatedly to review the application of those principles to particular facts. A recurring question in these cases, as in any case alleging a violation of the Equal Protection Clause, was whether the defendant had met his burden of proving purposeful discrimination on the part of the State. That question also was at the heart of the portion of *Swain v. Alabama* we reexamine today. . . .

A number of lower courts following the teaching of *Swain* reasoned that proof of repeated striking of blacks over a number of cases was necessary to establish a violation of the Equal Protection Clause. Since this interpretation of *Swain* has placed on defendants a crippling burden of proof, prosecutors' peremptory challenges are now largely immune from constitutional scrutiny. For reasons that follow, we reject this evidentiary formulation as inconsistent with standards that have been developed since *Swain* for assessing a prima facie case under the Equal Protection Clause. . . .

The showing necessary to establish a prima facie case of purposeful discrimination in selection of the venire may be discerned in this Court's decisions. The defendant initially must show that he is a member of a racial group capable of being singled out for different treatment. In combination with that evidence, a defendant may then make a prima facie case by proving that, in the particular jurisdiction, members of his race have not been summoned for jury service over an extended period of time. Proof of systematic exclusion from the venire raises an inference of purposeful discrimination, because the "result bespeaks discrimination." . . .

Since the ultimate issue is whether the State has discriminated in selecting the defendant's venire, however, the defendant may establish a prima facie case "in other ways than by evidence of long-continued unexplained absence" of members of his race "from many panels." In cases involving the venire, this Court has found a prima facie case on proof that members of the defendant's race were substantially underrepresented on the venire from which his jury was drawn, and that the venire was selected under a practice providing "the opportunity for discrimination." This combination of factors raises the necessary inference of purposeful discrimination because the Court has declined to attribute to chance the absence of black citizens on a particular jury array where the selection mechanism is subject to abuse. When circumstances suggest the need, the trial court must undertake a "factual inquiry" that "takes into account all possible explanatory factors" in the particular case. . . .

In deciding whether the defendant has made the requisite showing, the trial court should consider all relevant circumstances. For example, a "pattern" of strikes against black jurors included in the particular venire might give rise to an inference of discrimination. Similarly, the prosecutor's questions and statements during voir dire examination and in exercising his challenges may support or refute an inference of discriminatory purpose. These examples are merely illustrative. We have confidence that trial judges, experienced in supervising voir dire, will be able to decide if the circumstances concerning the prosecutor's use of peremptory challenges creates a prima facie case of discrimination against black jurors. . . .

While we recognize, of course, that the peremptory challenge occupies an important position in our trial procedures, we do not agree that our decision today will undermine the contribution the challenge generally makes to the administration of justice. The reality of practice, amply reflected in many state and federal court opinions, shows that the challenge may be, and unfortunately at times has been, used to discriminate against black jurors. By requiring trial courts to be sensitive to the racially discriminatory use of peremptory challenges, our decision enforces the mandate of equal protection and furthers the ends of justice. In view of the heterogeneous population of our Nation, public respect for our criminal justice system and the rule of law will be strengthened if we ensure that no citizen is disqualified from jury service because of his race. . . .

In this case, petitioner made a timely objection to the prosecutor's removal of all black persons on the venire. Because the trial court flatly rejected the objection without requiring the prosecutor to give an explanation for his action, we remand this case for further proceedings. If the trial court decides that the facts establish, prima facie, purposeful discrimination and the prosecutor does not come forward with a neutral explanation for his action, our precedents require that petitioner's conviction be reversed.

Rehnquist, dissenting:

. . . I cannot subscribe to the Court's unprecedented use of the Equal Protection Clause to restrict the historic scope of the peremptory challenge, which has been described as "a necessary part of trial by jury." *Swain* In my view, there is simply nothing "unequal" about the State's using its peremptory challenges to strike blacks from the jury in cases involving black defendants, so long as such challenges are also used to exclude whites in cases involving white defendants, Hispanics in cases involving Hispanic defendants, Asians in cases involving Asian defendants, and so on. This case-specific use of peremptory challenges by the State does not single out blacks, or members of any other race for that matter, for discriminatory treatment. Such use of peremptories is, at best, based upon seat-of-the-pants instincts, which are undoubtedly crudely stereotypical and may in many cases be hopelessly mistaken. But as long as they are applied across-the-board to jurors of all races and nationalities, I do not see—and the Court most certainly has not explained—how their use violates the Equal Protection Clause.

Nor does such use of peremptory challenges by the State infringe upon any other constitutional interests. The Court does not suggest that exclusion of blacks from the jury through the State's use of peremptory challenges results in a violation of either the fair-cross-section or impartiality component of the Sixth Amendment. And because the case-specific use of peremptory challenges by the State does not deny blacks the right to serve as jurors in cases involving nonblack defendants, it harms neither the excluded jurors nor the remainder of the community.

The use of group affiliations, such as age, race, or occupation, as a "proxy" for potential juror partiality, based on the assumption or belief that members of one group are more likely to favor defendants who belong to the same group, has long been accepted as a legitimate basis for the State's exercise of peremptory challenges. Indeed, given the need for reasonable limitations on the time devoted to voir dire, the use of such "proxies" by both the State and the defendant may be extremely useful in eliminating from the jury persons who might be biased in one way or another. The Court today holds that the State may not use its peremptory challenges to strike black prospective jurors on this basis without violating the Constitution. But I do not believe there is anything in the Equal Protection Clause, or any other constitutional provision, that justifies such a departure from the substantive holding contained in Part II of *Swain.* Petitioner in the instant case failed to make a sufficient showing to overcome the presumption announced in *Swain* that the State's use of peremptory challenges was related to the context of the case. . . .

Maryland v. Craig

497 U.S. 836 (1990), 5-4
Opinion of the Court: O'Connor (Blackmun, Kennedy, Rehnquist, White)
Dissenting: Brennan, Marshall, Scalia, Stevens

Why is the confrontation of witnesses an important enough criminal justice right to be included in the Bill of Rights? What does it cover? Was the right satisfied in this case? What other means might be used to protect child witnesses who may be terrified by the defendant? Suppose the defendant acted as his own attorney in the case? Can the spectacle of shielding a child from the defendant be damaging to the defendant in the eyes of the jury?

O'Connor, for the Court:

In October, 1986, a Howard County grand jury charged respondent, Sandra Ann Craig, with child abuse, first and second degree sexual offenses, perverted sexual practice, assault, and battery. The named victim in each count was Brooke Etze, a six-year-old child who, from August, 1984, to June, 1986, had attended a kindergarten and prekindergarten center owned and operated by Craig.

In March, 1987, before the case went to trial, the State sought to invoke a Maryland statutory procedure that permits a judge to receive, by one-way closed circuit television, the testimony of a child witness who is alleged to be a victim of child abuse. To invoke the procedure, the trial judge must first determin[e] that testimony by the child victim in the courtroom will result in the child suffering serious emotional distress such that the child cannot reasonably communicate."

Once the procedure is invoked, the child witness, prosecutor, and defense counsel withdraw to a separate room; the judge, jury, and defendant remain in the courtroom. The child witness is then examined and cross-examined in the separate room, while a video monitor records and displays the witness' testimony to those in the courtroom. During this time, the witness cannot see the defendant. The defendant remains in electronic communication with defense counsel, and objections may be made and ruled on as if the witness were testifying in the courtroom.

In support of its motion invoking the one-way closed circuit television procedure, the State presented expert testimony that Brooke, as well as a number of other children who were alleged to have been sexually abused by Craig, would suffer "serious emotional distress such that [they could not] reasonably communicate," if required to testify in the courtroom. The Maryland Court of Appeals characterized the evidence as follows:

> The expert testimony in each case suggested that each child would have some or considerable difficulty in testifying in Craig's presence. For example, as to one child, the expert said that what "would cause him the most anxiety would be to testify in front of Mrs. Craig. . . ." The child "wouldn't be able to communicate effectively." As to another, an expert said she "would probably stop talking and she would withdraw and curl up." With respect to two others, the testimony was that one would "become highly agitated, that he may refuse to talk, or, if he did talk, that he would choose his subject regardless of the questions," while the other would "become extremely timid and unwilling to talk."

Craig objected to the use of the procedure on Confrontation Clause grounds, but the trial court rejected that contention. . . . The trial court then found Brooke and three other children competent to testify, and accordingly permitted them to testify against Craig via the one-way closed circuit television procedure. The jury convicted Craig on all counts. . . .

The Confrontation Clause of the Sixth Amendment, made applicable to the States through the Fourteenth Amendment, provides: "In all criminal prosecutions, the accused shall enjoy the right . . . to be confronted with the witnesses against him."

We observed in *Coy v. Iowa* that "the Confrontation Clause guarantees the defendant a face-to-face meeting with witnesses appearing before the trier of fact." . . .

We have never held, however, that the Confrontation Clause guarantees criminal defendants the absolute right to a face-to-face meeting with witnesses against them at trial. Indeed, in *Coy v. Iowa*, we expressly "le[ft] for another day . . . the question whether any exceptions exist" to the "irreducible literal meaning of the Clause: "a right to meet face to face all those who appear and give evidence at trial." . . .

The central concern of the Confrontation Clause is to ensure the reliability of the evidence against a criminal defendant by subjecting it to rigorous testing in the, context of an adversary proceeding before the trier of fact. The word "confront," after all, also means a clashing of forces or ideas, thus carrying with it the notion of adversariness. . . . [T]he right guaranteed by the Confrontation Clause includes not only a "personal examination,"but also" "1) insures that the witness will give his statements under oath—thus impressing him with the seriousness of the matter and guarding against the lie by the possibility of a penalty for perjury; (2) forces the witness to submit to cross-examination, the "greatest legal engine ever invented for the discovery of truth;" [and] (3) permits the jury that is to decide the defendant's fate to observe the demeanor of the witness in making his statement, thus aiding the jury in assessing his credibility." *California v. Green*

The combined effect of these elements of confrontation—physical presence, oath, cross-examination, and observation of demeanor by the trier of fact—serves the purposes of the Confrontation Clause by ensuring that evidence admitted against an accused is reliable and subject to the rigorous adversarial testing that is the norm of Anglo-American criminal proceedings. . . .

We have recognized, for example, that face-to-face confrontation enhances the accuracy of factfinding by reducing the risk that a witness will wrongfully implicate an innocent person. . . .

Although face-to-face confrontation forms "the core of the values furthered by the Confrontation Clause," we have nevertheless recognized that it is not the sine qua non of the confrontation right. . . .

For this reason, we have never insisted on an actual face-to-face encounter at trial in every instance in which testimony is admitted against a defendant. . . .

In sum, our precedents establish that "the Confrontation Clause reflects a preference for face-to-face confrontation at trial, "a preference that "must occasionally give way to considerations of public policy and the necessities of the case."" . . .

That the face-to-face confrontation requirement is not absolute does not, of course, mean that it may easily be dispensed with. As we suggested in *Coy,* our precedents confirm that a defendant's right to confront accusatory witnesses may be satisfied absent a physical, face-to-face confrontation at trial only where denial of such confrontation is necessary to further an important public policy and only where the reliability of the testimony is otherwise assured.

Maryland's statutory procedure, when invoked, prevents a child witness from seeing the defendant as he or she testifies against the defendant at trial. We find it significant, however, that Maryland's procedure preserves all of the other elements of the confrontation right: the child witness must be competent to testify and must testify under oath; the defendant retains full opportunity for contemporaneous cross-examination; and the judge, jury, and defendant are able to view (albeit by video monitor) the demeanor (and body) of the witness as he or she testifies. Although we are mindful of the many subtle effects face-to-face confrontation may have on an adversary criminal proceeding, the presence of these other elements of confrontation—oath, cross-examination, and observation of the witness' demeanor—adequately ensures that the testimony is both reliable and subject to rigorous adversarial testing in a manner functionally equivalent to that accorded live, in-person testimony. These safeguards of reliability and adversariness render the use of such a procedure a far cry from the undisputed prohibition of the Confrontation Clause: trial by ex parte affidavit or inquisition. Rather, we think these elements of effective confrontation not only permit a defendant to "confound and undo the false accuser, or reveal the child coached by a malevolent adult," but may well aid a defendant in eliciting favorable testimony from the child witness. Indeed, to the extent the child witness' testimony may be said to be technically given out-of-court (though we do not so hold), these assurances of reliability and adversariness are far greater than those required for admission of hearsay testimony under the Confrontation Clause. We are therefore confident that use of the one-way closed-circuit television procedure, where necessary to further an important state interest, does not impinge upon the truth-seeking or symbolic purposes of the Confrontation Clause. . . .

The critical inquiry in this case, therefore, is whether use of the procedure is necessary to further an important state interest. The State contends that it has a substantial interest in protecting children who are allegedly victims of child abuse from the trauma of testifying against the alleged perpetrator, and that its statutory procedure for receiving testimony from such witnesses is necessary to further that interest. . . .

We . . . conclude today that a State's interest in the physical and psychological wellbeing of child abuse victims may be sufficiently important to outweigh, at least in some cases, a defendant's right to face his or her accusers in court. That a significant majority of States has enacted statutes to protect child witnesses from the trauma of giving testimony in child abuse cases attests to the wide-spread belief in the importance of such a public policy. Thirty-seven States, for example, permit the use of videotaped testimony of sexually abused children; 24 States have authorized the use of one-way closed circuit television testimony in child abuse cases; and 8 States authorize the use of a two-way system in which the child-witness is permitted to see the courtroom and the defendant on a video monitor and in which the jury and judge is permitted to view the child during the testimony. . . .

The requisite finding of necessity must, of course, be a case-specific one: the trial court must hear evidence and determine whether use of the one-way closed circuit television procedure is necessary to protect the welfare of the particular child witness who seeks to testify. The trial court must also find that the child witness would be traumatized, not by the courtroom generally, but by the presence of the defendant. Denial of face-to-face confrontation is not needed to further the state interest in protecting the child witness from trauma unless it is the presence of the defendant that causes the trauma. In other words, if the state interest were merely the interest in protecting child witnesses from courtroom trauma generally, denial of face-to-face confrontation would be unnecessary, because the child could be permitted to testify in less intimidating surroundings, albeit with the defendant present. Finally, the trial court must find that the emotional distress suffered by the child witness in the presence of the defendant is more than de minimis, i.e., more than "mere nervousness or excitement or some reluctance to testify.". . .

In sum, we conclude that, where necessary to protect a child witness from trauma that would be caused by testifying in the physical presence of the defendant, at least where such trauma would impair the child's ability to communicate, the Confrontation Clause does not prohibit use of a procedure that, despite the absence of face-to-face confrontation, ensures the reliability of the evidence by subjecting it to rigorous adversarial testing and thereby preserves the essence of effective confrontation. Because there is no dispute that the child witnesses in this case testified under oath, were subject to full cross-examination, and were able to be observed by the judge, jury, and defendant as they testified, we conclude that, to the extent that a proper finding of necessity has been made, the admission of such testimony would be consonant with the Confrontation Clause. . . .

Scalia, dissenting:

Seldom has this Court failed so conspicuously to sustain a categorical guarantee of the Constitution against the tide of prevailing current opinion. The Sixth Amendment provides, with unmistakable clarity, that "[i]n all criminal prosecutions, the accused shall enjoy the right . . . to be confronted with the witnesses against him." The purpose of enshrining this protection in the Constitution was to assure that none of the many policy interests from time to time pursued by statutory law could overcome a defendant's right to face his or her accusers in court. The Court, however, says:

> We . . . conclude today that a State's interest in the physical and psychological wellbeing of child abuse victims may be sufficiently important to outweigh, at least in some cases, a defendant's right to face his or her accusers in court. That a significant majority of States has enacted statutes to protect child witnesses from the trauma of giving testimony in child abuse cases attests to the wide-spread belief in the importance of such a public policy.

Because of this subordination of explicit constitutional text to currently favored public policy, the following scene can be played out in an American courtroom for the first time in two centuries: A father whose young daughter has been given over to the exclusive custody of his estranged wife, or a mother whose young son has been taken into custody by the State's child welfare department, is sentenced to prison for sexual abuse on the basis of testimony by a child the parent has not seen or spoken to for many months, and the guilty verdict is rendered without giving the parent so much as the opportunity to sit in the presence of the child, and to ask, personally or through counsel, "it is really not true, is it, that I— your father (or mother) whom you see before you— did these terrible things?" Perhaps that is a procedure today's society desires; perhaps (though I doubt it) it is even a fair procedure; but it is assuredly not a procedure permitted by the Constitution.

Because the text of the Sixth Amendment is clear, and because the Constitution is meant to protect against, rather than conform to, current "widespread belief," I respectfully dissent. . . .

In the last analysis, however, this debate is not an appropriate one. I have no need to defend the value of confrontation, because the Court has no authority to question it. It is not within our charge to speculate that, "where face-to-face confrontation causes significant emotional distress in a child witness," confrontation might "in fact disserve the Confrontation Clause's truth-seeking goal." If so, that is a defect in the Constitution—which should be amended by the procedures provided for such an eventuality, but cannot be corrected by judicial pronouncement that it is archaic, contrary to "widespread belief" and thus null and void. For good or bad, the Sixth Amendment requires confrontation, and we are not at liberty to ignore it. To quote the document one last time (for it plainly says all that need be said): "In all criminal prosecutions, the accused shall enjoy the right . . . to be confronted with the witnesses against him" (emphasis added).

The Court today has applied "interest-balancing" analysis where the text of the Constitution simply does not permit it. We are not free to conduct a cost-benefit analysis of clear and explicit constitutional guarantees, and then to adjust their meaning to comport with our findings. The Court has convincingly proved that the Maryland procedure serves a valid interest, and gives the defendant virtually everything the Confrontation Clause guarantees (everything, that is, except confrontation). I am persuaded, therefore, that the Maryland procedure is virtually constitutional. Since it is not, however, actually constitutional, I would affirm the judgment of the Maryland Court of Appeals reversing the judgment of conviction.

Gregg v. Georgia

428 U.S. 153 (1976), 7-2
Opinion announcing the judgment of the Court:
  Stewart (Powell, Stevens)
Concurring: Blackmun, Burger, Rehnquist, White
Dissenting: Brennan, Marshall

After Georgia's death penalty laws were struck down in Furman v. Georgia, *1972, the state revised its capital crimes trial and sentencing procedures to meet the Court's qualified objections. Under the new arrangements, which separate trial and penalty stages, Gregg was convicted of the armed robbery and murder of two men. At the penalty stage under the new law, the jury was instructed that it could recommend either a death sentence or a life prison sentence on the capital counts; that it was free to consider mitigating or aggravating circumstances, and that it could not recommend the death sentence unless it first found beyond a reasonable doubt (1) that the murder was committed while the offender was engaged in the commission of other capital felonies—armed robberies of the victims; (2) that he committed the murder for the purpose of receiving the victims' money and automobile; or (3) that the murder was "outrageously and wantonly vile, horrible and inhuman" in that it "involved the depravity of [the] mind of the defendant." The jury found the first and second of these aggravating circumstances, and returned a sentence of death.*

How did the state reform and recast its death sentence procedures to meet the Court's objections in the Furman *case? Do the new provisions make it less likely that capital punishment will be imposed arbitrarily or with racial bias? Do these new procedures make execution less of a cruel and unusual punishment constitutionally? Morally?*

Stewart, announcing the judgement of the Court:

. . . We address initially the basic contention that the punishment of death for the crime of murder is, under all circumstances, "cruel and unusual" in violation of the Eighth and Fourteenth Amendments of the Constitution. . . .

. . . [U]ntil *Furman v. Georgia,* the Court never confronted squarely the fundamental claim that the punishment of death always, regardless of the enormity of the offense or the procedure followed in imposing the sentence, is cruel and unusual punishment in violation of the Constitution. Although this issue was presented and addressed in *Furman,* it was not resolved by the Court. Four Justices would have held that capital punishment is not unconstitutional per se; two Justices

would have reached the opposite conclusion; and three Justices, while agreeing that the statutes then before the Court were invalid as applied, left open the question whether such punishment may ever be imposed. We now hold that the punishment of death does not invariably violate the Constitution. . . .

. . . [T]he Eighth Amendment has not been regarded as a static concept. As Mr. Chief Justice Warren said, in an oft-quoted phrase, "[t]he Amendment must draw its meaning from the evolving standards of decency that mark the progress of a maturing society." *Trop v. Dulles* Thus, an assessment of contemporary values concerning the infliction of a challenged sanction is relevant to the application of the Eighth Amendment. As we develop below more fully, see infra at, this assessment does not call for a subjective judgment. It requires, rather, that we look to objective indicia that reflect the public attitude toward a given sanction.

But our cases also make clear that public perceptions of standards of decency with respect to criminal sanctions are not conclusive. A penalty also must accord with "the dignity of man," which is the "basic concept underlying the Eighth Amendment." *Trop v. Dulles* This means, at least, that the punishment not be "excessive." When a form of punishment in the abstract (in this case, whether capital punishment may ever be imposed as a sanction for murder), rather than in the particular (the propriety of death as a penalty to be applied to a specific defendant for a specific crime), is under consideration, the inquiry into "excessiveness" has two aspects. First, the punishment must not involve the unnecessary and wanton infliction of pain. Second, the punishment must not be grossly out of proportion to the severity of the crime. . . .

Of course, the requirements of the Eighth Amendment must be applied with an awareness of the limited role to be played by the courts. . . . This does not mean that judges have no role to play, for the Eighth Amendment is a restraint upon the exercise of legislative power.

. . . [I]n assessing a punishment selected by a democratically elected legislature against the constitutional measure, we presume its validity. We may not require the legislature to select the least severe penalty possible so long as the penalty selected is not cruelly inhumane or disproportionate to the crime involved. And a heavy burden rests on those who would attack the judgment of the representatives of the people. . . .

... We now consider specifically whether the sentence of death for the crime of murder is a per se violation of the Eighth and Fourteenth Amendments to the Constitution. We note first that history and precedent strongly support a negative answer to this question.

The imposition of the death penalty for the crime of murder has a long history of acceptance both in the United States and in England. The common law rule imposed a mandatory death sentence on all convicted murderers. And the penalty continued to be used into the 20th century by most American States, although the breadth of the common law rule was diminished, initially by narrowing the class of murders to be punished by death and subsequently by widespread adoption of laws expressly granting juries the discretion to recommend mercy.

It is apparent from the text of the Constitution itself that the existence of capital punishment was accepted by the Framers. At the time the Eighth Amendment was ratified, capital punishment was a common sanction in every State. Indeed, the First Congress of the United States enacted legislation providing death as the penalty for specified crimes. The Fifth Amendment, adopted at the same time as the Eighth, contemplated the continued existence of the capital sanction by imposing certain limits on the prosecution of capital cases: "No person shall be held to answer for a capital, or otherwise infamous crime, unless on a presentment or indictment of a Grand Jury . . . ; nor shall any person be subject for the same offense to be twice put in jeopardy of life or limb; . . . nor be deprived of life, liberty, or property, without due process of law." . . .

And the Fourteenth Amendment, adopted over three-quarters of a century later, similarly contemplates the existence of the capital sanction in providing that no State shall deprive any person of "life, liberty, or property" without due process of law.

For nearly two centuries, this Court, repeatedly and often expressly, has recognized that capital punishment is not invalid per se. . . .

Four years ago, the petitioners in *Furman* and its companion cases predicated their argument primarily upon the asserted proposition that standards of decency had evolved to the point where capital punishment no longer could be tolerated. The petitioners in those cases said, in effect, that the evolutionary process had come to an end, and that standards of decency required that the Eighth Amendment be construed finally as prohibiting capital punishment for any crime, regardless of its depravity and impact on society. This view was accepted by two Justices. Three other Justices were unwilling to go so far; focusing on the procedures by which convicted defendants were selected for the death penalty, rather than on the actual punishment inflicted, they joined in the conclusion that the statutes before the Court were constitutionally invalid.

The petitioners in the capital cases before the Court today renew the "standards of decency" argument, but developments during the four years since *Furman* have undercut substantially the assumptions upon which their argument rested. Despite the continuing debate, dating back to the 19th century, over the morality and utility of capital punishment, it is now evident that a large proportion of American society continues to regard it as an appropriate and necessary criminal sanction.

The most marked indication of society's endorsement of the death penalty for murder is the legislative response to *Furman*. The legislatures of at least 35 States have enacted new statutes that provide for the death penalty for at least some crimes that result in the death of another person. And the Congress of the United States, in 1974, enacted a statute providing the death penalty for aircraft piracy that results in death. These recently adopted statutes have attempted to address the concerns expressed by the Court in *Furman* primarily (i) by specifying the factors to be weighed and the procedures to be followed in deciding when to impose a capital sentence, or (ii) by making the death penalty mandatory for specified crimes. But all of the post-*Furman* statutes make clear that capital punishment itself has not been rejected by the elected representatives of the people.

In the only state-wide referendum occurring since *Furman* and brought to our attention, the people of California adopted a constitutional amendment that authorized capital punishment, in effect negating a prior ruling by the Supreme Court of California . . . that the death penalty violated the California Constitution.

The jury also is a significant and reliable objective index of contemporary values, because it is so directly involved. . . .

. . . [T]he actions of juries in many States since *Furman* are fully compatible with the legislative judgments, reflected in the new statutes, as to the continued utility and necessity of capital punishment in appropriate cases. At the close of 1974, at least 254 persons had been sentenced to death since *Furman,* and, by the end of March, 1976, more than 460 persons were subject to death sentences.

As we have seen, however, the Eighth Amendment demands more than that a challenged punishment be acceptable to contemporary society. The Court also must ask whether it comports with the basic concept of human dignity at the core of the Amendment. Although we cannot "invalidate a category of penalties because we deem less severe penalties adequate to serve the ends of the sanction imposed cannot be so totally without penological justification that it results in the gratuitous infliction of suffering.

The death penalty is said to serve two principal social purposes: retribution and deterrence of capital crimes by prospective offenders.

In part, capital punishment is an expression of society's moral outrage at particularly offensive conduct. This function may be unappealing to many, but it is essential in an ordered society that asks its citizens to rely on legal processes, rather than self-help, to vindicate their wrongs. . . .

"Retribution is no longer the dominant objective of the criminal law," but neither is it a forbidden objective, nor one inconsistent with our respect for the dignity of men. Indeed, the decision that capital punishment may be the appropriate sanction in extreme cases is an expression of the community's belief that certain crimes are themselves so grievous an affront to humanity that the only adequate response may be the penalty of death.

Statistical attempts to evaluate the worth of the death penalty as a deterrent to crimes by potential offenders have occasioned a great deal of debate. The result simply have been inconclusive. . . .

Although some of the studies suggest that the death penalty may not function as a significantly greater deterrent than lesser penalties, there is no convincing empirical evidence either supporting or refuting this view. We may nevertheless assume safely that there are murderers, such as those who act in passion, for whom the threat of death has little or no deterrent effect. But for many others, the death penalty undoubtedly is a significant deterrent. There are carefully contemplated murders, such as murder for hire, where the possible penalty of death may well enter into the cold calculus that precedes the decision to act. And there are some categories of murder, such as murder by a life prisoner, where other sanctions may not be adequate.

The value of capital punishment as a deterrent of crime is a complex factual issue the resolution of which properly rests with the legislatures, which can evaluate the results of statistical studies in terms of their own local conditions and with a flexibility of approach that is not available to the courts. Indeed, many of the post-*Furman* statutes reflect just such a responsible effort to define those crimes and those criminals for which capital punishment is most probably an effective deterrent.

In sum, we cannot say that the judgment of the Georgia Legislature that capital punishment may be necessary in some cases is clearly wrong. Considerations of federalism, as well as respect for the ability of a legislature to evaluate, in terms of its particular State, the moral consensus concerning the death penalty and its social utility as a sanction, require us to conclude, in the absence of more convincing evidence, that the infliction of death as a punishment for murder is not without justification, and thus is not unconstitutionally severe.

Finally, we must consider whether the punishment of death is disproportionate in relation to the crime for which it is imposed. There is no question that death, as a punishment, is unique in its severity and irrevocability. When a defendant's life is at stake, the Court has been particularly sensitive to insure that every safeguard is observed. But we are concerned here only with the imposition of capital punishment for the crime of murder, and, when a life has been taken deliberately by the offender, we cannot say that the punishment is invariably disproportionate to the crime. It is an extreme sanction, suitable to the most extreme of crimes.

We hold that the death penalty is not a form of punishment that may never be imposed, regardless of the circumstances of the offense, regardless of the character of the offender, and regardless of the procedure followed in reaching the decision to impose it.

We now consider whether Georgia may impose the death penalty on the petitioner in this case.

While *Furman* did not hold that the infliction of the death penalty per se violates the Constitution's ban on cruel and unusual punishments, it did recognize that the penalty of death is different in kind from any other punishment imposed under our system of criminal justice. Because of the uniqueness of the death penalty, *Furman* held that it could not be imposed under sentencing procedures that created a substantial risk that it would be inflicted in an arbitrary and capricious manner. . . .

. . . [T]he concerns expressed in *Furman* that the penalty of death not be imposed in an arbitrary or capricious manner can be met by a carefully drafted statute that ensures that the sentencing authority is given adequate information and guidance. As a general proposition, these concerns are best met by a system that provides for a bifurcated proceeding at which the sentencing authority is apprised of the information relevant to the imposition of sentence and provided with standards to guide its use of the information. . . .

. . . Georgia's new sentencing procedures require, as a prerequisite to the imposition of the death penalty, specific jury findings as to the circumstances of the crime or the character of the defendant. Moreover, to guard further against a situation comparable to that presented in *Furman,* the Supreme Court of Georgia compares each death sentence with the sentences imposed on similarly situated defendants to ensure that the sentence of death in a particular case is not disproportionate. On their face, these procedures seem to satisfy the concerns of *Furman.* No longer should there be "no meaningful basis for distinguishing the few cases in which [the death penalty] is imposed from the many cases in which it is not." . . .

The basic concern of *Furman* centered on those defendants who were being condemned to death capriciously and arbitrarily. Under the procedures before the Court in that case, sentencing authorities were not directed to give attention to the nature or circumstances of the crime committed or to the character or record of the defendant. Left unguided, juries imposed the death sentence in a way that could only be called freakish. The new Georgia sentencing procedures, by contrast, focus the jury's attention on the particularized nature of the crime and the particularized characteristics of the individual defendant. While the jury is permitted to consider any aggravating or mitigating circumstances, it must find and identify at least one statutory aggravating factor before it may impose a penalty of death. In this way, the jury's discretion is channeled. No longer can a jury wantonly and freakishly impose the death sentence; it is always circumscribed by the legislative guidelines. In addition, the review function of the Supreme Court of Georgia affords additional assurance that the concerns that prompted our decision in *Furman* are not present to any significant degree in the Georgia procedure applied here.

For the reasons expressed in this opinion, we hold that the statutory system under which Gregg was sentenced to death does not violate the Constitution.

White, concurring:

. . . Petitioner's argument that there is an unconstitutional amount of discretion in the system which separates those suspects who receive the death penalty from those who receive life imprisonment, a lesser penalty, or are acquitted or never charged, seems to be, in final analysis, an indictment of our entire system of justice. Petitioner has argued, in effect, that no matter how effective the death penalty may be as a punishment, government, created and run as it must be by humans, is inevitably incompetent to administer it. This cannot be accepted as a proposition of constitutional law. Imposition of the death penalty is surely an awesome responsibility for any system of justice and those who participate in it. Mistakes will be made, and discriminations will occur which will be difficult to explain. However, one of society's most basic tasks is that of protecting the lives of its citizens, and one of the most basic ways in which it achieves the task is through criminal laws against murder. I decline to interfere with the manner in which Georgia has chosen to enforce such laws on what is simply an assertion of lack of faith in the ability of the system of justice to operate in a fundamentally fair manner. . . .

Brennan, dissenting:

. . . .Death, for whatever crime and under all circumstances, "is truly an awesome punishment. The calculated killing of a human being by the State involves, by its very nature, a denial of the executed person's humanity. . . . An executed person has indeed 'lost the right to have rights'." *Trop v. Dulles* Death is not only an unusually severe punishment, unusual in its pain, in its finality, and in its enormity, but it serves no penal purpose more effectively than a less severe punishment; therefore the principle inherent in the Clause that prohibits pointless infliction of excessive punishment when less severe punishment can adequately achieve the same purposes invalidates punishment.

The fatal constitutional infirmity in the punishment of death is that it treats "members of the human race as nonhumans, as objects to be toyed with and discarded. [It is] thus inconsistent with the fundamental premise of the Clause that even the vilest criminal remains a human being possessed of common human dignity." . . .

. . . I therefore would hold on that ground alone, that death is today a cruel and unusual punishment prohibited by the Clause . . .

Marshall, dissenting:

. . . In *Furman,* I concluded that the death penalty is constitutionally invalid for two reasons. First, the death penalty is excessive. And second, the American people, fully informed as to the purposes of the death penalty and its liabilities, would, in my view, reject it as morally unacceptable.

Since the decision in *Furman,* the legislatures of 35 States have enacted new statutes authorizing the imposition of the death sentence for certain crimes, and Congress has enacted a law providing the death penalty for air piracy resulting in death. I would be less than candid if I did not acknowledge that these developments have a significant bearing on a realistic assessment of the moral acceptability of the death penalty to the American people. But if the constitutionality of the death penalty turns, as I have urged, on the opinion of an informed citizenry, then even the enactment of new death statutes cannot be viewed as conclusive. . . . .

Even assuming, however, that the post-*Furman* enactment of statutes authorizing the death penalty renders the prediction of the views of an informed citizenry an uncertain basis for a constitutional decision, the enactment of those statutes has no bearing whatsoever on the conclusion that the death penalty is unconstitutional because it is excessive. . . .

. . . The evidence I reviewed in *Furman* remains convincing, in my view, that "capital punishment is not necessary as a deterrent to crime in our society." The justification for the death penalty must be found elsewhere.

The other principal purpose said to be served by the death penalty is retribution. The notion that retribution can serve as a moral justification for the sanction of death finds credence in the opinion of my Brothers Stewart, Powell, and Stevens. . . . It is this notion that I find to be the most disturbing aspect of today's unfortunate decisions. . . .

McCleskey v. Kemp

481 U.S. 279 (1987), 5-4
Opinion of the Court: Powell (O'Connor, Rehnquist, Scalia, White)
Dissenting: Blackmun, Brennan, Marshall, Stevens

What constitutional claim did McCleskey make? Did the studies the Supreme Court examined support it? Was McCleskey's death sentence free of racial bias? To what extent can or

should proof of bias against a group or class of persons substitute for proof of bias against an individual member of that group or class? Though the criminal justice issues are different in the two cases, is the Court's approach in this case consistent with its approach in Batson v. Kentucky *(p. 414)?*

Powell, for the Court:

This case presents the question whether a complex statistical study that indicates a risk that racial considerations enter into capital sentencing determinations proves that petitioner McCleskey's capital sentence is unconstitutional under the Eighth or Fourteenth Amendment.

McCleskey, a black man, was convicted of two counts of armed robbery and one count of murder . . . [The] convictions arose out of the robbery of a furniture store and the killing of a white police officer during the course of the robbery. . . .

Several weeks later, McCleskey was arrested in connection with an unrelated offense. He confessed that he had participated in the furniture store robbery, but denied that he had shot the police officer. . . .

The jury convicted McCleskey of murder. At the penalty hearing, [it] heard arguments as to the appropriate sentence. Under Georgia law, [it] could not consider imposing the death penalty unless it found beyond a reasonable doubt that the murder was accompanied by one of the statutory aggravating circumstances. The jury in this case found two aggravating circumstances to exist beyond a reasonable doubt: the murder was committed during the course of an armed robbery, and the murder was committed upon a peace officer engaged in the performance of his duties. In making its decision whether to impose the death sentence, the jury considered the mitigating and aggravating circumstances of McCleskey's conduct. McCleskey offered no mitigating evidence. The jury recommended that he be sentenced to death on the murder charge . . . The court followed the jury's recommendation and sentenced McCleskey to death.

On appeal, the Supreme Court of Georgia affirmed the convictions and the sentences. . . .

McCleskey next filed a petition for a writ of habeas corpus [claiming] . . . that the Georgia capital sentencing process is administered in a racially discriminatory manner in violation of the Eighth and Fourteenth Amendments to the United States Constitution. . . . [He] proffered a statistical study performed by Professors David C. Baldus, Charles Pulaski, and George Woodworth (the Baldus study) that purports to show a disparity in the imposition of the death sentence in Georgia based on the race of the murder victim and, to a lesser extent, the race of the defendant. The Baldus study is actually two sophisticated statistical studies that examine over 2,000 murder cases that occurred in Georgia during the 1970's. The raw numbers collected by Professor Baldus indicate that defendants charged with killing white persons received the death penalty in 11% of the cases, but defendants charged with killing blacks received the death penalty in only 1% of the cases. The raw numbers also indicate a reverse racial disparity according to the race of the defendant: 4% of the black defendants received the death penalty, as opposed to 7% of the white defendants.

Baldus also divided the cases according to the combination of the race of the defendant and the race of the victim. He found that the death penalty was assessed in 22% of the cases involving black defendants and white victims; 8% of the cases involving white defendants and white victims; 1% of the cases involving black defendants and black victims; and 3% of the cases involving white defendants and black victims. Similarly, Baldus found that prosecutors sought the death penalty in 70% of the cases involving black defendants and white victims; 32% of the cases involving white defendants and white victims; 15% of the cases involving black defendants and black victims; and 19% of the cases involving white defendants and black victims.

Baldus subjected his data to an extensive analysis, taking account of 230 variables that could have explained the disparities on nonracial grounds. One of his models concludes that, even after taking account of 39 nonracial variables, defendants charged with killing white victims were 4.3 times as likely to receive a death sentence as defendants charged with killing blacks. According to this model, black defendants were 1.1 times as likely to receive a death sentence as other defendants. Thus, the Baldus study indicates that black defendants, such as McCleskey, who kill white victims have the greatest likelihood of receiving the death penalty. . . .

McCleskey's first claim is that the Georgia capital punishment statute violates the Equal Protection Clause of the Fourteenth Amendment. He argues that race has infected the administration of Georgia's statute in two ways: persons who murder whites are more likely to be sentenced to death than persons who murder blacks, and black murderers are more likely to be sentenced to death than white murderers.

As a black defendant who killed a white victim, McCleskey claims that the Baldus study demonstrates that he was discriminated against because of his race and because of the race of his victim. In its broadest form, McCleskey's claim of discrimination extends to every actor in the Georgia capital sentencing process, from the prosecutor who sought the death penalty and the jury that imposed the sentence to the State itself that enacted the capital punishment statute and allows it to remain in effect despite its allegedly discriminatory application. We agree with the Court of Appeals, and every other court that has considered such a challenge, that this claim must fail.

Our analysis begins with the basic principle that a defendant who alleges an equal protection violation has the burden of proving "the existence of purposeful discrimination." A corollary to this principle is that a criminal defendant must prove that the purposeful discrimination "had a discriminatory effect" on him. Thus, to prevail under the Equal Protection Clause, McCleskey must prove that the decisionmakers in his case acted with discriminatory purpose. He offers no evidence specific to his own case that would support an inference that racial considerations played a part in his sentence. Instead, he relies solely on the Baldus study. McCleskey argues that the Baldus study compels an inference that his sentence rests on purposeful discrimination. McCleskey's claim that these statistics are sufficient proof of discrimination, without regard to the facts of a particular case, would extend to all capital cases in Georgia, at least where the victim was white and the defendant is black. . . .

McCleskey also suggests that the Baldus study proves that the State as a whole has acted with a discriminatory purpose. He appears to argue that the State has violated the Equal Protection Clause by adopting the capital punishment statute and allowing it to remain in force despite its allegedly discriminatory application. But "'[d]iscriminatory purpose' . . . implies more than intent as volition or intent as awareness of consequences. It implies that the decisionmaker, in this case a state legislature, selected or reaffirmed a particular course of action at least in part "because of," not merely "in spite of," its adverse effects upon an identifiable group." *Personnel Administrator of Massachusetts v. Feeney*

For this claim to prevail, McCleskey would have to prove that the Georgia Legislature enacted or maintained the death penalty statute because of an anticipated racially discriminatory effect. In *Gregg v.*

Georgia this Court found that the Georgia capital sentencing system could operate in a fair and neutral manner. There was no evidence then, and there is none now, that the Georgia Legislature enacted the capital punishment statute to further a racially discriminatory purpose. Nor has McCleskey demonstrated that the legislature maintains the capital punishment statute because of the racially disproportionate impact suggested by the Baldus study. As legislatures necessarily have wide discretion in the choice of criminal laws and penalties, and as there were legitimate reasons for the Georgia Legislature to adopt and maintain capital punishment, we will not infer a discriminatory purpose on the part of the State of Georgia. Accordingly, we reject McCleskey's equal protection claims.

McCleskey also argues that the Baldus study demonstrates that the Georgia capital sentencing system violates the Eighth Amendment. . . .

. . . [O]ur decisions since Furman have identified a constitutionally permissible range of discretion in imposing the death penalty. First, there is a required threshold below which the death penalty cannot be imposed. In this context, the State must establish rational criteria that narrow the decisionmaker's judgment as to whether the circumstances of a particular defendant's case meet the threshold. Moreover, a societal consensus that the death penalty is disproportionate to a particular offense prevents a State from imposing the death penalty for that offense. Second, States cannot limit the sentencer's consideration of any relevant circumstance that could cause it to decline to impose the penalty. In this respect, the State cannot channel the sentencer's discretion, but must allow it to consider any relevant information offered by the defendant.

In light of our precedents under the Eighth Amendment, McCleskey cannot argue successfully that his sentence is "disproportionate to the crime in the traditional sense." He does not deny that he committed a murder in the course of a planned robbery, a crime for which this Court has determined that the death penalty constitutionally may be imposed. His disproportionality claim "is of a different sort." McCleskey argues that the sentence in his case is disproportionate to the sentences in other murder cases.

On the one hand, he cannot base a constitutional claim on an argument that his case differs from other cases in which defendants did receive the death penalty. On automatic appeal, the Georgia Supreme Court found that McCleskey's death sentence was not disproportionate to other death sentences imposed in the State. The court supported this conclusion with an appendix containing citations to 13 cases involving generally similar murders. Moreover,where the statutory procedures adequately channel the sentencer's discretion, such proportionality review is not constitutionally required. . . .

Two additional concerns inform our decision in this case. First, McCleskey's claim, taken to its logical conclusion, throws into serious question the principles that underlie our entire criminal justice system. The Eighth Amendment is not limited in application to capital punishment, but applies to all penalties. Thus, if we accepted McCleskey's claim that racial bias has impermissibly tainted the capital sentencing decision, we could soon be faced with similar claims as to other types of penalty. Moreover, the claim that his sentence rests on the irrelevant factor of race easily could be extended to apply to claims based on unexplained discrepancies that correlate to membership in other minority groups, and even to gender. Similarly, since McCleskey's claim relates to the race of his victim, other claims could apply with equally logical force to statistical disparities that correlate with the race or sex of other actors in the criminal justice system, such as defense attorneys or judges. Also, there is no logical reason that such a claim need be limited to racial or sexual bias. If arbitrary and capricious punishment is the touchstone under the Eighth Amendment, such a claim could—at least in theory—be based upon any arbitrary variable, such as the defendant's facial characteristics, or the physical attractiveness of the defendant or the victim, that some statistical study indicates may be influential in jury decisionmaking. As these examples illustrate, there is no limiting principle to the type of challenge brought by McCleskey. The Constitution does not require that a State eliminate any demonstrable disparity that correlates with a potentially irrelevant factor in order to operate a criminal justice system that includes capital punishment. . . .

Second, McCleskey's arguments are best presented to the legislative bodies. It is not the responsibility— or indeed even the right—of this Court to determine the appropriate punishment for particular crimes. It is the legislatures, the elected representatives of the people, that are "constituted to respond to the will and consequently the moral values of the people." *Furman v. Georgia,* (Burger, dissenting). Legislatures also are better qualified to weigh and "evaluate the results of statistical studies in terms of their own local conditions and with a flexibility of approach that is not available to the courts." *Gregg v. Georgia*

Capital punishment is now the law in more than two-thirds of our States. It is the ultimate duty of courts to determine on a case-by-case basis whether these laws are applied consistently with the Constitution. Despite McCleskey's wide-ranging arguments that basically challenge the validity of capital punishment in our multiracial society, the only question before us is whether, in his case, see supra, at 283-285, the law of Georgia was properly applied. We agree with the District Court and the Court of Appealsf or the Eleventh Circuit that this was carefully and correctly done in this case. . . .

Brennan, dissenting:

. . . .It is important to emphasize at the outset that the Court's observation that McCleskey cannot prove the influence of race on any particular sentencing decision is irrelevant in evaluating his Eighth Amendment claim. Since *Furman v. Georgia* the Court has been concerned with the risk of the imposition of an arbitrary sentence, rather than the proven fact of one. *Furman* held that the death penalty "may not be imposed under sentencing procedures that create a substantial risk that the punishment will be inflicted in an arbitrary and capricious manner." . . . This emphasis on risk acknowledges the difficulty of divining the jury's motivation in an individual case. In addition, it reflects the fact that concern for arbitrariness focuses on the rationality of the system as a whole, and that a system that features a significant probability that sentencing decisions are influenced by impermissible considerations cannot be regarded as rational. . . .

Defendants challenging their death sentences thus never have had to prove that impermissible considerations have actually infected sentencing decisions. We have required instead that they establish that the system under which they were sentenced posed a significant risk of such an occurrence. McCleskey's claim does differ, however, in one respect from these earlier cases: it is the first to base a challenge not on speculation about how a system might operate, but on empirical documentation of how it does operate.

The Court assumes the statistical validity of the Baldus study, and acknowledges that McCleskey has demonstrated a risk that racial prejudice plays a role in capital sentencing in Georgia. Nonetheless, it finds the probability of prejudice insufficient to create constitutional concern. Close analysis of the Baldus study, however, in light of both statistical principles and human experience, reveals that the risk that race influenced McCleskey's sentence is intolerable by any imaginable standard. . . .

Evaluation of McCleskey's evidence cannot rest solely on the numbers themselves. We must also ask whether the conclusion suggested by those numbers is consonant with our understanding of history and human experience. Georgia's legacy of a race-conscious criminal justice system, as well as this Court's own recognition of the persistent danger that racial attitudes may affect criminal proceedings, indicates that McCleskey's claim is not a fanciful product of mere statistical artifice. . . .

The Court cites four reasons for shrinking from the implications of McCleskey's evidence: the desirability of discretion for actors in the criminal justice system, the existence of statutory safeguards against abuse of that discretion, the potential consequences for broader challenges to criminal sentencing, and an understanding of the contours of the judicial role. While these concerns underscore the need for sober deliberation, they do not justify rejecting evidence as convincing as McCleskey has presented. . . .

Furthermore, the Court's fear of the expansive ramifications of a holding for McCleskey in this case is unfounded, because it fails to recognize the uniquely sophisticated nature of the Baldus study. McCleskey presents evidence that is far and away the most refined data ever assembled on any system of punishment, data not readily replicated through casual effort. Moreover, that evidence depicts not merely arguable tendencies, but striking correlations, all the more powerful because nonracial explanations have been eliminated. Acceptance of petitioner's evidence would therefore establish are markedly stringent standard of statistical evidence unlikely to be satisfied with any frequency.

The Court's projection of apocalyptic consequences for criminal sentencing is thus greatly exaggerated. The Court can indulge in such speculation only by ignoring its own jurisprudence demanding the highest scrutiny on issues of death and race. As a result, it fails to do justice to a claim in which both those elements are intertwined—an occasion calling for the most sensitive inquiry a court can conduct. Despite its acceptance of the validity of Warren McCleskey's evidence, the Court is willing to let his death sentence stand because it fears that we cannot successfully define a different standard for lesser punishments. This fear is baseless. . . .

. . . [I]t has been scarcely a generation since this Court's first decision striking down racial segregation, and barely two decades since the legislative prohibition of racial discrimination in major domains of national life. These have been honorable steps, but we cannot pretend that, in three decades, we have completely escaped the grip of a historical legacy spanning centuries. Warren McCleskey's evidence confronts us with the subtle and persistent influence of the past. His message is a disturbing one to a society that has formally repudiated racism, and a frustrating one to a Nation accustomed to regarding its destiny as the product of its own will. Nonetheless, we ignore him at our peril, for we remain imprisoned by the past as long as we deny its influence in the present.

It is tempting to pretend that minorities on death row share a fate in no way connected to our own, that our treatment of them sounds no echoes beyond the chambers in which they die. Such an illusion is ultimately corrosive, for the reverberations of injustice are not so easily confined. . . .

IV

EQUALITY INEQUAL

7

RACIAL INTEGRATION AND DISCRIMINATION

Equality is one of the oldest American ideals, sharing an elemental place with liberty and opportunity in the American creed. It may refer to civil, political, or social rights. Civil equality is essentially that before the law and has been historically important in asserting one's status in business relations and in the private economy. It includes the equal right to hold property, make contracts, and enforce civil obligations through law, and the right to due process to defend oneself and one's interests before the law. Political equality refers to the right to vote, hold office, and be represented, in short, the right of access to political power on roughly the same footing as everyone else. Social equality refers to one's right to equal status in the myriad personal interactions that take place in public and quasi-public space.

With a few glaring exceptions—slavery and its latter-day legacy of race discrimination being the most obvious—the American record among nations has been enviable. Political and legal institutions inherited from Great Britain, recast for conditions of the New World, were a big help. No less important was the nation's continuous economic growth and short supply of labor. Economic conditions friendly to ambitious newcomers made progress toward the three equalities easier than it might have been otherwise.

At the same time, racial, religious and ethnic diversity made the United States the most heterogeneous of societies. Since equality is constantly tested by differences, diversity has meant that a *goal* of equality with its moral exhortation was vital if the nation's economic prosperity were to continue and its political and social systems remain open and free. As with all nations, the goal has been imperfectly realized. Though regrettable, this fact may be less significant than that of the goal itself and the nation's continued, renewable dedication to it. We may recall Lincoln's description of the Declaration of Independence, our chief philosophical statement of the equality ideal:

> [It was] meant to set up a standard maxim for free society which should be familiar to all, and revered by all; constantly looked to, constantly labored for, and even though never perfectly attained, constantly approximated, and thereby

431

constantly spreading and deepening its influence and augmenting the happiness and value
of life to all people of all colors everywhere.*

Inequality—the absence or failure of equality—
is manifest in discrimination, random or systematic, intended or unintended. In the American
past this has included segregation and, regionally,
because of the earlier social gulf of slavery, a caste
system.

Despite equality's settled place in American
beliefs, remedying inequality has often proved
difficult. Simple human imperfection clearly
plays a part, as it does in the failure to reach any
collective ideal. But equality/inequality also bears
some zero-sum characteristics. One person's gain
may be another's loss and one person's loss, another's gain. To accord equal status to someone
who did not have it before usually calls for others
to move over and make room. Some may gladly
do this in the name of the ideal; others, however,
for reasons of calculated self-interest or unreason-
ing bias, may be much less inclined. They may
not see or not care about the collective, long-
term benefits that equality promises.

The matter is further complicated because
programs and laws aimed at remedying inequality may contend with other desirable goals, such
as the reward of merit and performance and the
freedom to organize one's individual life. Thus
the pursuit of equality has at least the potential
of creating new inequalities and promoting discrimination in a different form.

Important constitutional questions arise about
the role of government. Inequality has often had
the backing, if not command, of law and authority. Removing government as a perpetrator of inequality has been one task. Using government to
end discrimination originating outside government, has been another.

* "The Founding Fathers," speech, Springfield, Ill., 1857,
in John G. Nicolay and John Hay, eds., *Complete Works of
Abraham Lincoln*, Vol. II (Lincoln Memorial Library, 1894).
p. 236.

This chapter deals with the long struggle of
African-Americans against civil, political, and
social inequality and how that struggle has affected and been affected by constitutional development. It deals with the gap between the
ideal of equality and what many black Americans have actually experienced, a gap the
Swedish economist Gunnar Myrdal 50 years ago
called "an American dilemma" in the title of a
classic study of race relations.

The Antebellum Period

Persons of African descent lived in each of the
pre-Revolutionary English colonies almost from
their founding. Nearly all had arrived as slaves.
By the 1760s, black persons numbered nearly
400,000, about 18 percent of the entire colonial
population. Slavery had been present in all
colonies, but it had never taken much hold in
the North where, for moral and economic reasons, it had either been ended or was fast disap-
pearing when independence was declared. The
egalitarian thrust of the Revolution ended its
last elements in the New England states, New
York, New Jersey, and Pennsylvania. It hastened
manumissions—the voluntary freeing of slaves
by their owners—in Delaware, Maryland, and
Virginia. Even in the states of the deep South,
where slavery had been tied to growing tobacco
and rice, its future economic utility seemed limited. But the invention of the cotton "gin"—an
ingenious device for separating cotton fiber and
seed—radically changed the economy of slavery. Cotton became unusually profitable and
soon became the country's leading export. This
led to more cotton planting and new demand
for field labor, ending whatever chance that
slavery in the South would gradually collapse
under its own weight. It also ensured that the
slave question would become a great divisive issue in the country.

By fact and definition, the slave had no equality and few rights. The law in slave states treated
slaves as persons and as valuable property. Its

chief aim was preserving the slave system against threats of rebellion or disintegration and protecting of the slaveholder's assets. In these slave codes, a slave's movement and freedom to communicate with others was severely restricted and near-absolute obedience was owed to master or owner. Slaves could not testify in court and had almost no access to the legal system except as defendants accused of breaking slave codes or general laws. The law did impose obligations on slaveowners—not to abuse or mistreat, not to abandon the aged or infirm, and to feed, house, and clothe. Masters who violated these provisions were subject to punishment, including the death penalty for murder of a slave. The personal security these laws afforded would have been greater had they been vigorously enforced or had slaves themselves had standing in court.

The status of free black persons in and outside the South was different. But in no sense did it approximate the full civil, political, and social equality of most whites. By the time of the Civil War, free persons of African descent numbered about 500,000, nearly 10 percent of the black population. About half lived in free states. These black persons usually led segregated lives and were often denied political rights. But freedom meant the right to travel, to form institutions, to publish newspapers, to organize to represent themselves, and to protest slavery. Though most Northern free blacks remained unskilled workers—in part because of the hostility of many European immigrants who often competed with them—they played important leadership roles among all blacks after slavery ended.

Most free blacks in the slave states were manumitted or were descendants of those who had been. This road to freedom was highly selective and usually open only to privileged and better-educated slaves. It meant that the free black population in the South was more highly skilled than that in the North. Because few European immigrants entered the South, many free blacks became artisans and even dominated certain trades. Some became wealthy and a few even bought slaves. But the presence of slavery put

social equality for free blacks beyond reach. Seen by whites as potential disrupters of the slave system, they were denied political freedom and power.

In the years before the Civil War, race relations was entirely a matter of state and local law. No federal delegated powers dealt directly with race or with civil or social relations having to do with individuals or groups. Congress had ended the importation of slaves in 1808, as the Constitution allowed it to do under Article I-9. But it also passed the Fugitive Slave Acts in 1793 and 1850 to give effect to Article IV-2 that required runaway slaves be returned to their owners. The chief legal and constitutional focus of the slavery issue was whether slaveholding was to be recognized in the new territories from which new states would eventually be admitted. Though the matter divided the nation and brought on the Civil War, it did not directly affect the rights of free black persons or slaves. The constitutional question that did was the sojourner issue—did a slave become free by once having been in a free state or territory?

The Supreme Court first considered the matter in *Strader v. Graham,* 1851. The underlying issue was whether three Kentucky slaves, allowed by their master to go to Ohio, a free state, to take part in minstrel shows, were still slaves when they returned to Kentucky. In refusing jurisdiction in the case, the Court, dominated by Southerners, held that the status of slaves was a matter of state law alone. As such, it had to be decided by state courts, which in this case had rejected the "once free, always free" principle that sojourning conferred emancipation.

When the Court heard the question again six years later in *Dred Scott v. Sanford,* its decision was the same but based on broader grounds that made the case a grave political and moral misjudgment and hastened the Civil War. As a young man, Scott accompanied his master, a Missouri army doctor, to Fort Snelling in what is now Minnesota but then territory declared free from slavery in the Missouri Compromise of 1820. Years later, having returned to Missouri, a slave state, after his former owner died, Scott sued his new master, John Sanford, for his freedom. (The case was contrived by those sympathetic to getting a declaration of freedom, including Sanford whose name was misspelled as Sandford in the Supreme Court's official record.) Since Sanford lived in New York and Scott in Missouri, the case was brought in federal court in Missouri.

The Court might have decided it simply on the precedent of *Strader v. Graham*, but Chief Justice Roger Taney's opinion for a majority of seven went well beyond that holding. He ruled that Scott had never been free, even in the Minnesota Territory, because Congress had no power to bar slavery in the territories. Thus the Missouri Compromise was unconstitutional, a politically calamitous ruling because it apparently removed Congress and the national government from dealing with the country's leading domestic issue—slavery in the territories. Not stopping there, Taney held that a black person could not be a citizen of the United States or have the right to sue in federal courts. On this technical but morally reprehensible point, the Court dismissed the case. The damage was done. The decision ended whatever chance there was for a political solution to the slavery question and denied black persons the status of national citizenship.

Reconstruction Gains and Losses

Early in the Civil War, Congress abolished slavery in the District of Columbia and freed the few slaves who were in the territories. Abolition of slavery in the South, though it came to underlay the war, had not been an official Union aim at the start, in the hope that secession could be stopped at low cost. After Union military reverses in 1862, President Lincoln, in an act of great strategic and moral force, issued the Emancipation Proclamation on New Year's Day 1863. It declared those slaves in states or parts of states still in rebellion to be "thenceforward and forever free." The order also took the radical step of authorizing recruitment of freed slaves

and free black persons into the Union army and navy. More than 200,000 served in the last two years of the war, making an important contribution to final victory.

Defeat of the South meant the end of slavery and the start of a long and often painful social revolution in that region and later in the nation itself. To ratify the outcome of the war constitutionally and address the status of former slaves, now called Freedmen, three amendments were added to the highest law. The Thirteenth, in 1865, declared simply that "neither slavery nor involuntary servitude . . . shall exist within the United States or any place subject to its jurisdiction." The Fourteenth, in 1868, though not mentioning slavery directly, corrected the Dred Scott decision in its first sentence: "All persons born or nationalized in the United States . . . are citizens of the United States and of the state wherein they reside." The amendment then set out three important limits on the powers of states, in doing so, conferring several individual rights:

> No State shall make or enforce any law which shall abridge the privileges or immunities of citizens of the United States; nor shall any State deprive any person of life, liberty, or property, without due process of law; nor deny to any person within its jurisdiction the equal protection of the laws.

The Fifteenth Amendment, in 1870, dealt directly with the Freedmen. It provided that the right of citizens of the United States to vote "shall not be denied or abridged . . . on account of race, color, or previous condition of servitude."

The decade-long period of Reconstruction, 1865–1876, began with a vying between Lincoln's successor, Democrat Andrew Johnson, and a Congress dominated by so-called Radical Republicans. The president favored a generous peace for the South and quick readmission of the secessionist states. The Republicans, Lincoln's party, demanded harder terms and the protection of Freedmen's rights. Congress delayed readmission of former Confederate states until acceptable reconstructed governments were set up, which meant that many were run by Freedmen and their white "carpetbagger" allies from the North. These governments depended on political support from Congress and the presence of federal military forces. They were doomed when the strength and determination of Congressional Republicans ebbed in the mid-1870s.

In every Southern state, the old white leadership reasserted itself with wide local support. Though forced to recognize freedom of the former slaves, they were determined that little else would change. The chance for first, if halting, steps toward equality for the Freedmen, most of whom had little or no education and few material assets, was lost, and a caste system succeeded slavery. In it, the races were extensively segregated in public life and space. Southern state and local governments succeeded in denying or greatly limiting voting by black persons, despite the Fifteenth Amendment. A thoroughgoing "Jim Crow" discrimination came to pervade Southern life. That this racism hurt whites as well by ensuring that the war-devastated South would lag behind the rest of the nation economically for nearly a century is ironic but almost beside the point. Civil, political, and social equality for black persons was not at hand and would be long in coming.

Not-So-Benign Neglect

The 75 years following the end of Reconstruction was a period in which government, with a few exceptions, did little to ameliorate racial inequality. The caste system imposed in the South remained largely intact. Though most of the descendants of the Freedmen got a rudimentary education and some prospered, moving into the middle class, their progress was slow and seldom encouraged. Advances were against a humiliating tide of segregation and discrimination. Political power was almost totally denied. Even by mid-twentieth century, only a small fraction of black persons voted in Southern states and almost none held public office. Starting in the early decades of the century, large numbers of blacks migrated from the South to large North-

ern cities, looking for jobs or better jobs, and at least a semblance of political equality.

But what of the Civil War amendments, supposedly designed to protect rights of the Freedmen and their descendants? In three important decisions in the last quarter of the nineteenth century, the Supreme Court gave two of the amendments a constricted reading that undercut much of their utility for equal rights. In the first, a set of appeals known as the Slaughterhouse Cases, in 1873, the Court considered the Fourteenth Amendment for the first time. Ironically, the cases were not about rights of black persons but white butchers in New Orleans. At issue was a government regulation that, under the guise of a public health measure, created a near-monopoly for one of their competitors. The butchers contended that the regulation denied them a privilege of citizenship—the right to operate an otherwise lawful business—supposedly protected by the privileges and immunities clause of the amendment.

In rejecting the claim, the Court said the amendment was aimed at protecting the Freedmen, but the grounds for its decision actually weakened the entire clause. A majority held that the privileges the amendment secured from state abridgment were those of national rather than state citizenship. The former had to do with an individual's relation to the national government, such as the right to vote in federal elections or to travel to Washington to petition the government. Other aspects of citizenship, including the right to conduct a business, were subject to state law and not safeguarded by the amendment. The interpretation greatly weakened the privileges and immunities clause as a source for protection of any civil rights.

The second decision, a group of appeals collectively known as the Civil Rights Cases, in 1883, grew out of enforcement of the Civil Rights Act of 1875. Enacted near the end of Reconstruction, the law was Congress's most ambitious attempt to give effect to the Civil War amendments and protect Freedmen's rights. In it, Congress barred racial discrimination in a

range of public settings and accommodations including transport, hotels, restaurants, and other
facilities, almost all privately owned. But a majority of the Court, speaking through Justice Joseph
Bradley, held that the Civil War amendments
did not give Congress the power to pass such a
law. The Fourteenth, as a limit on actions by
states, did not reach discriminatory acts by private owners. Though the Thirteenth, outlawing
slavery, did address private parties (almost all
slaves had been privately owned), discrimination
was not the equivalent of slavery.

The lone dissenter in the case, Justice John
Marshall Harlan, argued that the Civil Rights Act
could be sustained under either amendment. The
Thirteenth, he said, abolished not only slavery
but the "badges" of slavery. Facilities accommodating the public, even if privately owned, were
"affected with a public interest." As such, private
discrimination had the tacit approval of state and
local government and was thus barred by the
Fourteenth Amendment. Though Harlan's interpretation would eventually prevail generations
later, Bradley's majority opinion was closer to the
constitutional understanding of the day. It had the
long-standing effect of preventing Congress from
legislating against local, private discrimination.

The third decision was *Plessy v. Ferguson*, 1896
(p. 467), in which the Court, interpreted the
Fourteenth Amendment's equal protection
clause not to bar state-imposed separation of the
races, in this instance, in railway travel. The case
was brought as a test of the South's Jim Crow
laws, and the Court met it by propounding the
"separate but equal" doctrine: Segregation was
constitutionally permissible as long as the separate facilities were equal. The decision did not
simply sustain segregation, it encouraged it. Increasingly, Southern state and local laws separated the races—in transport, schools, parks,
theaters, hospitals, prisons, and almost all other
important institutions. The effect on civil rights
would have been less pernicious had "equal"
been given as much weight as "separate." But,
overwhelmingly throughout the South, separate
facilities were not equal; those reserved for black
persons were almost always inferior.

The Court's interpretations of the Thirteenth
and Fourteenth Amendments, popular in the
white South, did not shock public opinion in the
nation. They seemed reasonable given the sensibilities of the day. There was no strong social
movement to morally dramatize the unfairness of
inequality, as abolition had done with slavery or
as the later civil rights movement would do with
segregation and discrimination in the 1950s and
60s. The National Association for the Advancement of Colored People (NAACP) would not be
founded until 1909, the National Urban League,
not until 1911.

Not all the Court's few racial discrimination
cases were unfriendly to civil rights. Where the issue was not segregation but exclusion and state
involvement was direct, the Court might sustain a
right. In *Strauder v. West Virginia* and three other
cases in 1880, for example, it held that exclusion
of otherwise qualified black persons from juries
by statutory requirement or official administrative practice violated the equal protection clause.

Only in *Buchanan v. Warley*, 1917, was a form of
segregation successfully challenged. The Court
struck down a Louisville, Ky., ordinance that required residential segregation by barring whites
or blacks from buying houses on blocks where
the majority of houses were occupied by members of the other race. The case was contrived by
a white seller and a black buyer who wanted to
challenge the law. The Court was unanimous in
finding the law violated the Fourteenth Amendment's due process clause, but its decision was
based on a property right, that of buying or selling real property. On these grounds, it distinguished the case from *Plessy v. Ferguson*.

The decision put an end to laws requiring residential segregation that had begun to appear in
many communities of the upper South. But it
also led to greater use of so-called restrictive
covenants—agreements among groups of white
neighbors not to sell or rent their houses to
black persons and sometimes to those of other
specified groups. The Court weakened *Buchanan
v. Warley* in its 1926 decision *Corrigan v. Buckley*,
upholding the legality of such covenants. Ignoring that restrictive covenants were enforceable

only through court orders and thus through state action, it held the Fourteenth Amendment did not bar private discriminatory acts. Such covenants would be recognized by law for another 20 years, until *Shelley v. Kraemer*, 1948 (p. 470), discussed next.

In contrast to Jim Crow laws of the South, some Northern states passed civil rights acts barring mandated segregation in schools, public accommodations, and other places. Others repealed miscegenation statutes (laws barring marriage between persons of different races). Despite such laws, segregated conditions prevailed in many areas of public life in the North because of private white discrimination or avoidance or, to a lesser extent, black choice.

What of the national government? Race relations was an important domestic issue in the country throughout the period between Reconstruction and World War II, yet Congress passed almost no civil rights laws. Though its Fourteenth Amendment powers were narrowed in the Civil Rights Cases, Congress had others, including that over interstate commerce, through which it might have addressed civil rights. That it did not at first may be attributed to a lack of political will, that is, to a lack of perceived popular support. But the legislative draught continued through the Thirties, Forties, and into the Fifties, when national public support for some kinds of civil rights legislation may have risen to majority levels.

But here, two institutions of Congress—the filibuster in the Senate and the seniority system in both houses—worked to the advantage of Southern segregationists. The Senate's rules of debate allow a member once having the floor, to hold it or yield it only to a friendly, that is, a like-minded member. This allowed a small group of Southerners to "talk to death" any civil rights legislation that might be introduced. A filibuster could be broken, but this needed a two-thirds vote (reduced to 60 percent in 1975), which usually meant that Southerners and a few allies could block attempts at closure. The seniority system awarded committee chairmanships to members of the majority party who had the longest continuous service. When the South became essentially a one-party region—Democratic—after Reconstruction, Southern Congressmen and women ran virtually unopposed in general elections. Since defeat of incumbents was unlikely, they were apt to accrue greater seniority than members from other regions in which two-party competition was alive and well. In time, an unusual number of powerful committees in the two houses became chaired by Southerners. Since the most important work on bills is done in committee, the chairs had great power to influence the course of legislation, often being able to block bills entirely if they chose.

New Initiatives

Black migration from the South, stimulated by the mechanization of cotton growing and the lure of new industrial jobs, developed into one of the most important demographic shifts in American history. Though most black persons continued to live in the South, by the 1940s several million had relocated in New York, Chicago, Detroit, St. Louis, Los Angeles, and other large cities of the North and West. At first they augmented and then diluted such thriving black communities as New York City's Harlem and Chicago's South Side. Eventually, a combination of sheer numbers, "white flight," and discriminatory housing patterns turned many areas of the big Northern cities into crowded ghettos with substandard conditions. Racial tensions increased and led to sporadic outbreaks of violence. The periods during and after both World Wars were marked by a spate of racial riots. More than 200 black persons died and hundreds more were injured in a 1917 riot in East St. Louis. In 1919 there were at least 25 riots, including ones in Charleston, Knoxville, and Omaha. In 1943 alone, 270 riots occurred in 50 cities, including Detroit and New York.

Concentrated black populations in large Northern cities were eventually translated into political power. Blacks, such as William Dawson in Chicago and Adam Clayton Powell in New York, were elected and repeatedly reelected to

Congress, becoming powerful legislative figures. Blacks were among the hardest hit groups by the Depression of the 1930s, and large numbers gave up their long-time allegiance to the Republican Party to support Franklin Roosevelt and the New Deal. Black votes became important in many large Northern states. The development became a source of tension in the national Democratic Party, one of whose other main constituencies was the "Solid South," dominated by white segregationists.

The early decades of the twentieth century also witnessed a rise in black militancy and organizational activity. The National Association of Colored People was founded in 1909 by a group of black and white intellectuals, partly in opposition to the "gradualism" of Booker T. Washington, who had been a leading black spokesman. Concentrating its early efforts on lobbying and publicizing issues of racial inequality, the NAACP became the dominant civil rights group in the country, leading the legal and constitutional attack on segregation. The National Urban League was founded by blacks in 1911 to combat racial segregation in Northern cities and to promote community services. In 1925, A. Philip Randolph organized the militant black Brotherhood of Sleeping Car Porters. In the 1930s W.D. Fard and Elijah Poole, later Elijah Muhammad, organized the separatist Black Muslims in Detroit. And in 1942, the Congress on Racial Equality (CORE), aiming to end segregation and discrimination through nonviolence, was founded by James Farmer in Chicago.

Two early Southern aims of organized civil rights groups were voting rights and passage of a federal antilynching law. For many years, Southern states had found ways to nullify the Fifteenth Amendment's explicit protection of the right to vote. These efforts, often blatantly unconstitutional, were successfully attacked in court. The Supreme Court had already held the so-called grandfather clause in voting laws to be unconstitutional in *Guinn v. United States,* 1915. Oklahoma had made literacy a test for voting, but so

not to disenfranchise illiterate whites, excepted anyone descended from a person eligible to vote in 1867, before the Fifteenth Amendment was ratified. The Court was unanimous in striking down this transparent attempt to evade the command of the amendment.

In 1927, the Court found the Fourteenth Amendment's equal protection clause violated by a Texas law that barred black persons from voting in primaries, which in Democratic one-party Texas and most other Southern states were tantamount to election. After the decision, Texas and several other Southern states repealed all primary election laws and allowed the Democratic Party to organize the primaries "privately." This presumably put them beyond reach of both the Fourteenth and Fifteenth Amendments, which protect only against discriminatory state action. But in *Smith v. Allwright,* 1944, a case sponsored by the NAACP, the Court held the Texas "white primary" to violate the Fifteenth Amendment. In conducting the primary, the Court said, the Democratic Party was acting as an agent for the state, which had responsibility for elections.

Because of these rulings and growing determination of Southern blacks to get political rights, eligible black persons registered to vote rose from 5 percent in 1940 to 28 by 1952. Continued efforts by Southern states to hold down black voting by using literacy tests, poll taxes, and a range of questionable administrative practices intensified calls for national legislation to enforce the Fifteenth Amendment's mandate.

Violence and the threat of violence, either of which might go unopposed and unpunished, was an ever-present form of social control in many parts of the white supremacist South. Lynching—the killing of a person suspected of wrongdoing by private persons taking law into their own hands—was the most horrific form of such intimidation. (The name is owed to a Revolutionary War colonel, Charles Lynch, who with associates meted out his own version of justice to Tories suspected of wrongdoing.) Although blacks were not the only victims of lynchings—immigrants, Jews, and other locally unpopular or supposedly threatening figures had also been occasional targets of mob violence—they were its chief objects. Between 1882 and 1968, the date of the last recorded lynching, 4,743 persons, 3,446 of them black, had died in these outrages. Since the figures are only for *recorded* lynchings, the true number is no doubt higher. Summary justice administered by vigilantes had had a long history on the frontier where it had often been the only "law and order." But Southern lynchings in every case took place where courts were open and operating. Many went uninvestigated or were looked into half-heartedly by authorities. Few persons in the mobs were ever tried or punished. Some victims may have committed crimes they were suspected of, but others were clearly falsely accused or simply misunderstood. In some cases, their offense was simply being "uppity" or outspoken in trying to assert rights.

Because state and local authorities were unable or unwilling to prevent lynchings or punish those guilty of them, organized black groups and large numbers of whites outside the South called for federal intervention through new national laws. Different antilynching measures were introduced between 1920 and 1960. All failed in the Senate because of filibusters or threat of them by Southern Senators, who it is fair to say were opposed to lynching but were more opposed to federal legislation on what they saw as matters of state law exclusively.

Most black persons accused or suspected of crimes were, of course, brought into the criminal justice system of their states. But this was no guarantee that justice, which calls for proof of guilt beyond reasonable doubt and for those not guilty to go free, would be done. Black defendants often had no lawyers and few black persons served on juries. In well-publicized crimes, defendants could also expect to face an aroused white community. The Supreme Court decided several notable cases involving "legal lynchings." In *Moore v. Dempsey,* 1923, as

noted in the last chapter, it overturned convictions of black defendants accused of murdering a white farmer, where a raging white mob had surrounded the courthouse and would probably have lynched the defendants had they been acquitted.

As we have already seen, the Court overturned convictions in two cases growing out of the notorious 1931 Scottsboro affair. In *Powell v. Alabama,* the following year, the Court held that these convictions of nine black youths raping of two white girls violated the due process clause of the Fourteenth Amendment because the defendants had not been adequately represented by counsel. In an appeal from convictions in a second trial, *Norris v. Alabama,* 1935, the Court again found a denial of due process, this time because black persons had been systematically excluded from juries in the Alabama county in which the trial took place. We saw in the last chapter that the Scottsboro decisions had far-reaching consequence for the development of rights of accused persons, but in the matter of black civil rights, their effect was more symbolic than substantial. As part of a *cause celebre,* they dramatized the plight of the indigent black defendant in Southern criminal justice systems, but did little to change the everyday workings of those systems.

No twentieth-century event did more to advance equality for black Americans than World War II, which changed perceptions, habits, and folkways throughout American life. The war and the sacrifices it called for were a great disruption of settled status. More than a million black men served in the armed forces, largely in segregated units. The contrast between being asked to fight and perhaps die to end an evil like Nazi racism, the denial of racial equality at home was not lost on them or on many white Americans. A. Philip Randolph's threatened march on Washington in 1941 led President Roosevelt to issue a wartime executive order banning discrimination in federal employment and in defense industries. Randolph

and other black leaders also urged desegregation in the military. This controversial goal was
met when President Harry Truman issued an
executive order to that effect in 1948.

Black veterans returned to a nation that was
different from the prewar one their parents and
grandparents knew. In fact, many important
changes had been long in progress. Years of segregation had forced blacks to develop institutions
of their own, including churches, schools, community, and fraternal organizations, which were a
source of pride and solidarity. Black schools, for
example, had reduced illiteracy rates from 70
percent in 1880 to about 10 percent by 1945.*
Nationally, segregation itself was cracking in important ways. The "color line" was repeatedly broken as reports of the "first black person to . . ."
appeared with a monotony almost as regular as
separation and exclusion had been before. Crystal Bird Fauset from Pennsylvania became the
first black woman to serve in a state legislature, in
1938; Jackie Robinson, the first black major
league baseball player, in 1947; William Hastie,
the first black federal judge, in 1949, were a few
of the better-known examples. Symptomatic of
the postwar age was membership in the NAACP,
which rose from about 50,000 before the war to
nearly a half-million by 1950.

In two areas—education and housing—civil
rights efforts produced important constitutional victories that laid groundwork for later,
broader gains. As far back as 1938, in *Missouri
ex.rel. Gaines v. Canada* the Supreme Court
ruled that exclusion of blacks from a state law
school violated the equal protection cause of
the Fourteenth Amendment if comparable separate legal education was not offered to them.
The decision did not directly challenge the separate but equal doctrine, but enforced its
"equal" command. Missouri's offer to pay the
expense of black applicants if they went to law
schools in neighboring states that admitted

blacks did not meet the "equal" requirement.
The decision was the first crack in the constitutional wall of segregation in education. Though
many saw it as limited to higher education, it
led several Southern states to make efforts to
improve the conditions of black secondary
schools.

After the war, the NAACP, through sponsorship and support, launched a legal attack on
Southern school segregation. In two 1950 cases,
Sweatt v. Painter and *McLaurin v. Oklahoma Board
of Regents,* the Court indicated how difficult it
would be for states to satisfy the "equal" requirement in the doctrine. In the first, it held that in
quality of faculty, library resources, and prestige,
the separate law school Texas had set up for black
students fell short of giving them equal professional training. In the second, the Court held
that Oklahoma in admitting blacks to its state
graduate school yet keeping them segregated in
the classrooms, libraries, and other facilities also
violated the equal protection clause. Though the
decisions again dealt only with higher education,
they contained no constitutional reasons why the
same principles would not apply to the much
larger field of elementary and secondary education in the South. By raising the standards of what
was "equal," the days of the separate but equal
doctrine appeared to be numbered. Another sign
was the Court's unanimity in the cases.

In *Shelley v. Kraemer,* 1948, (p. 470) an important constitutional blow was struck against segregation in housing. Though the Court had ruled
against legalized apartheid in *Buchanan v. Warley*
in 1917, as we have seen, it later held restrictive
housing covenants to be merely private agreements and thus constitutional under the Fourteenth Amendment. In *Shelley,* again unanimous, it
held that though the covenants themselves were
not state action, their enforcement in courts would
be. The decision left them without legal effect.

The postwar triumphs in the Supreme Court
made an important fact increasingly clear: gains
in civil, political, and social equality did not require changes in the Constitution so much as an
accurate reading of its Civil War amendments—

---

* James T. Patterson, *Grand Expectations: The United States,
1945–1974* (New York, Oxford University Press, 1996),
25–26.

the Thirteenth, Fourteenth, and Fifteenth—in the spirit in which they were ratified. At the same time, another fact was also clear: there would be no underestimating white intransigence in the South. The early postwar decisions, though establishing important constitutional principles, did not change much on the ground. Segregation in public schools and in housing and residential patterns was largely unchanged, even in the border states of the South.

The Brown Case

Brown v. Board of Education of Topeka, Kansas (p. 473), the school desegregation case, was only one of four school cases the Court heard together—others were from Delaware, South Carolina, and Virginia. A fifth case, *Bolling v. Sharpe*, challenged segregation in a federal jurisdiction, the District of Columbia, was decided with them. When the Court's opinion was handed down, May 1954, *Brown* took its place with *Marbury v. Madison, McCulloch v. Maryland, Dred Scott v. Sanford,* and a few other cases as the most consequential in American constitutional development.

The cases were financed and guided through the courts by the NAACP and, together, were the strongest and most concerted legal challenge to segregation to date. Local plaintiffs were parents of black children who were forced to attend all-black schools. In *Brown,* eight-year-old Linda Brown attended a black school more than a mile from her home rather than the all-white school seven blocks away. At the time, almost every child, black and white, in states of the Deep South attended racially segregated schools. A vast majority in the border states did so as well. In most instances, this arrangement had the sanction of law. A decision upsetting it would have radical local consequences.

The cases were first argued during the Court's 1952–1953 term, but it became clear that the justices were divided and would move

Eight-year-old Linda Brown, whose name is forever associated with the Supreme Court's historic school desegregation decision in 1954, lived near a public school in Topeka, Kan., that she was not able to attend because of her race.

ahead cautiously. Though none supported segregation, they were not totally agreed on what the Court, able to wield only judicial power, could or should do about it. Genuine concerns about the rights of states were also evident. The most doubtful were Justices Felix Frankfurter, Robert Jackson and Stanley Reed, and Chief Justice Fred Vinson. Unable to agree on the chief issues, the Court scheduled the cases for reargument early the next term. Weeks before that was to take place, Vinson died of a heart attack and President Eisenhower appointed Earl Warren, the Republican governor of California, as the new chief. This change proved of great consequence not only in the school desegregation cases but in a range of other issues that were to come before the Court. Warren had no judicial experience, but he had been an astute and highly successful political figure.

Rather than the usual one or two hours of oral argument, the Court allowed ten over three days. The cases had now become a great set-piece struggle. Thurgood Marshall, chief counsel for the NAACP and later the nation's first black member of the Court, argued the case against segregation. John W. Davis, a leading constitutional lawyer who had once been the Democratic Party's candidate for president, contended for states rights. When the decision was handed down on May 17, the *New York Times* reported it the next day with an eight-column, three-line banner, typography usually reserved for presidential elections or the outbreak of war. The decision's revolutionary significance for race relations in the South was immediately and widely recognized.

The Court was unanimous. It was later learned this was largely from Warren's leadership in overcoming remaining reservations among the justices. The chief wrote the opinion himself. He later said that he wanted it to be short so that it could be printed in full in the newspapers, nontechnical and so more readily understood by the general public, and nonaccusatory so not to stir needless reaction. In the 11-page, carefully worded presentation, citing few legal precedents, he succeeded in all three aims.

A decision against segregation could have rested on established precedent, even the separate but equal doctrine, that black schools in the cases were far from equal. Instead, it struck a new path: "separate educational facilities are inherently unequal" and thus the separate but equal doctrine had no place in public education. To support this conclusion, Warren cited social science studies appearing to show that legally mandated segregation, as he put it, "generate[s] a feeling of inferiority [among black students] as to their status in the community that may affect their hearts and minds in a way unlikely ever to be undone." Straightforward simplicity such as this gave the opinion much of its moral power.

Constitutionally, *Plessy v. Ferguson* was overruled and the equal protection clause of the Fourteenth Amendment was given a new and broader meaning. Though the opinion did not mention segregation in other public institutions and places, it placed the constitutionality of all Jim Crow laws in doubt. In the companion case of *Bolling v. Sharpe,* school segregation in the District of Columbia was held unconstitutional as a violation of the due process clause of the Fifth Amendment. That clause, a limit on the federal government, was now held to contain an implicit equal protection component similar to the Fourteenth Amendment's clause limiting state power.

Amid wide and general praise for the decision among most black persons as well as many whites outside the South, there were critical and even reactive voices as well. A few Southern leaders seemed resigned to the decision, but others vowed resistance to merging of the races in the public schools. More reasoned doubts were also raised. Some constitutional lawyers and scholars criticized Warren for ignoring the original and historical understanding of the Fourteenth Amendment, that it protects and promotes black equality rather than requiring integration.

Others found fault with what they saw as the Court's excessive activism, that in overruling a 50-year-old doctrine, it cited almost no legal precedents (in fact few existed). For them, this was law or policy-making, normally the reserve of the legislative and executive branches. Many found the Court's Fifth Amendment "leap" in *Bolling v. Sharpe* to be even greater than its Fourteenth Amendment one, since the Fifth Amendment's due process clause placing limits on federal power had never been thought to bar racial segregation. Still others questioned the apparent reliance on debatable social science studies of the effects of school segregation. Many, including many black persons, were not convinced that segregated black schools necessarily generated feelings of inferiority, as Warren claimed.

Whatever merit these criticisms may have, they do not diminish what *Brown* had done. It set out a basic constitutional right of equal access to public education. Legally mandated segregation was unconstitutional. It set in motion a desegregation of Southern schools and gave legitimacy and thus an enormous boost to a civil rights movement already underway in Southern states. Ninety-seven years after *Dred Scott* and 86 after the last of the Civil War amendments, it was a main step toward the long-delayed realization of racial equality in the United States.

Missing from Warren's opinion was a specific enforcement order. A great right had been declared, but the Court was silent about its application. Instead, it asked for later reargument on how the decision might be given effect. This resulted in a second Brown decision, known as *Brown II* (p. 475), a year later. This time the Court struck a cautious note. Perhaps fearful of violence, it rejected the NAACP's urging that full integration go ahead immediately. Instead, the Court said that states with segregated schools must make "a prompt and reasonable start toward full compliance." The cases were remanded to lower federal courts with instructions that the plaintiffs be admitted to all-white neighborhood schools "with all deliberate speed."

The court's gradualism was meant to allow good faith time to work out sensible integration plans and make needed adjustments. As it turned out, it was seen by many recalcitrant Southern officials as an invitation to delay and even massively resist desegregation.

A Decade of Deliberate Speed

Even before *Brown II* was decided, segregated schools in Baltimore, Louisville, St. Louis, and Wilmington, Del., and other districts in border states began to admit black children to formerly all-white schools. Response to *Brown I* and *II* in most districts in the Deep South was otherwise. Though a few began to draw up plans for desegregation with a heavy emphasis on gradualism, for example, one grade a year, most did nothing. Reactive opposition whipped energies of most of the white South; in one community after another, White Citizens Councils formed to organize resistance. In elections, candidates urging moderation, if not compliance, were defeated. In several states—Alabama, Georgia, Mississippi, North and South Carolina—legislatures adopted interpositionist resolutions, echoing nullification acts a century and a quarter before. They held that *Brown* had usurped states rights and thus had no lawful effect within their borders. Some, such as Georgia, went further, making it a criminal act for public officials to put school desegregation into effect.

Several states adopted pupil placement laws authorizing local school boards to shift students within their district to keep the races separate. Some of these imaginative plans were little more than insulting ruses, for example, the use of biased psychological tests as the basis for assigning students. In several communities, the public schools were simply closed or abolished, being replaced by private ones that admitted only white students but were underwritten by public grants or tax credits. In Prince Edward County, Va. this resulted in black children having no schools at all for three years before a case

The Super Chief

Justice William O. Douglas ranked Earl Warren with John Marshall and Charles Evans Hughes as the three greatest chief justices in the Supreme Court's history. Few would disagree that Warren was among the most effective and influential justices to sit on the Court. Though not an accomplished legal thinker, he was perfectly suited to be the Court's leader. It was a role in which he could use formidable political skill and personal charm to gain a working consensus within the Court and move it toward an expansive constitutional jurisprudence of civil rights and liberties.

Born in Los Angeles in 1891, the son of Scandinavian immigrants, Warren grew up in the rough and tumble Bakersfield where his father worked for a railroad. He graduated from the University of California at Berkeley and later from its law school. In 1920, after jobs in a law firm and as a legislative aide, he joined the Alameda County prosecutor's office, one of the largest in the state. He would spend the next 50 years in politics and public service, his steady rise seeming almost ordained. When the chief prosecutor's job, an elective office, became vacant in mid-term, Warren with just five years experience was given a temporary appointment. He ran and won a full term in the office in 1926, won reelection in 1930 and again in 1934, establishing a reputation as an uncompromising fighter of violent crime and civic corruption. In a 1931 survey of district attorneys, he was ranked the best in the country. He was elected state attorney general as a Republican in 1938, receiving wide Democratic support. In that position, he played an important part in carrying out the presidential security order to remove nearly 100,000 Japanese Americans from their California homes to interior

relocation camps in the months after Pearl Harbor. It was a role he later came much to regret.

He was elected governor in 1942, again in 1946 when he also won the Democratic nomination, and for an unprecedented third term in 1950. Starting with a conservative agenda, Warren developed an innovative record that included prison and correctional reform, modernization of hospitals, expansion of unemployment and old-age benefits, and highway building. In this, he proved an able administrator. Nationally he became a leader in the liberal wing of the Republican Party and a chief contender for its presidential nomination in 1948 and 1952. After losing to New York's Governor Thomas E. Dewey in 1948, he joined the national ticket as Dewey's running mate. They were narrowly defeated by the incumbent Harry Truman. The 1952 contest eventually narrowed to a close race between the moderate Dwight Eisenhower and the conservative Ohio Senator Robert

---

challenging the arrangement, *Griffin v. Prince Edward County School Board* was won in the Supreme Court in 1964.

In the years following *Brown*, the burden of putting school desegregation into effect fell on lower federal courts in Southern states and on the determination of black parents to challenge

attempts at evasion. In many communities, this took unusual courage. Plaintiffs could face loss of jobs, bank credit, and other economic reprisal, besides being subject to insult and even assault. In most cases, the plaintiffs had the support and encouragement of the NAACP, which offered important legal counsel at trial and ap-

Taft. Realizing his own chances were slim, Warren threw his support to Eisenhower. For this help in winning the nomination, Eisenhower promised to appoint him to the first vacancy on the Supreme Court.

With the unexpected death of Chief Justice Fred Vinson in September 1953, the new president nominated Warren to succeed him. (It was an appointment he would later regret as Warren's liberal activism and that of the Court he led became clear.) The school desegregation case, held over from the preceding term, was by far the most important the Court faced in Warren's first year. His success in getting unanimity of the justices and writing the opinion himself firmly established him as leader of the Court. Having been the most successful politician in California's history, Warren's political and administrative skills were formidable. This coupled with a warmth and suppleness of personality allowed him to excel as leader of a small, intimate group of diverse and sometimes difficult personalities.

The liberal activism of the Warren Court signified the continued transition from a Court that, until a generation before, had dealt mainly with economic questions. Though it had taken an important interest in individual rights, it lacked clear direction. The Warren Court's agenda of civil liberties and equal rights was the work of several justices beside the chief. Most notably, they included Hugo Black and William O. Douglas, holdovers from the earlier Court; William Brennan, like Warren, an Eisenhower appointee; Arthur Goldberg, appointed by John Kennedy; and Thurgood Marshall and Abe Fortas, appointed by Lyndon Johnson. Three other justices, Tom Clark, another holdover; Potter Stewart, an Eisenhower appointee; and Byron White, appointed by Kennedy; often supported the majority's activism. Only Felix Frankfurter, a holdover, and John Marshall Harlan, II, another Eisenhower appointee, both advocates of judicial self-restraint, were apt to be consistent dissenters.

Besides its breakthrough decisions on school segregation and racial discrimination, the Warren Court issued landmark and often highly controversial rulings in almost every area of individual rights. *Baker v. Carr*, 1963, redefining the "political question" doctrine, led to reform of malapportioned legislatures and eventually to the "one person, one vote" standard for representation. *Engel v. Vitale*, 1962, held prayers in the public schools unconstitutional. In *New York Times v. Sullivan*, 1964, the Court widened free speech protection for comment about public officials. In *Gideon v. Wainwright*, 1963, it created a right to counsel for indigent defendants, and in *Miranda v. Arizona*, 1965, required that suspects in police custody must be told that they could remain silent. *Griswold v. Connecticut*, 1965, established a new constitutional right of privacy, opening the door for later Courts to include in it a right to abortion. Between 1958 and 1969, the Court incorporated no fewer than a dozen rights of the Bill of Rights into the Fourteenth Amendment's due process clause, thus extending their reach to acts of state government. These and other cases led Justice Fortas to call the work of the Court "the most profound and pervasive revolution ever achieved by substantially peaceful means."

Despite the innovative record of his Court, Warren himself could hardly be called an original legal mind or even a first-rate constitutional craftsman. More interested in result than theory or doctrinal consistency, he often paid less attention to matters of precedent. The tidy, careful niceties of judicial self-restraint held no independent fascination for him. His accomplishments as a constitutional lawyer lay in the strength of his beliefs in fairness, equality, and individual liberty, and an ability to argue them with simple moral clarity. It was this quality and his natural leadership that seem to make him worthy of Douglas's accolade.

pellate levels. Because of its "instigating" role, the organization became a target for retaliation. As noted in Chapter 3, it successfully resisted Alabama's attempt to get its rank-and-file membership lists and other records to prevent the state from publicizing the names, thus inviting reprisals against its members. The Supreme Court's unanimous decision in *NAACP v. Alabama*, 1958, established an important right of association as an integral part of the First Amendment's freedom of speech.

Lower federal courts consistently upheld the Brown decisions, though most of the judges were local Southerners. In the first year and a

Troops of the 101st Airborne Division escort nine black high school seniors into Little Rock Central High School in Little Rock, Ark., to begin implementation of a desegregation plan, September 25, 1957. The soldiers remained for the entire school year.

half after *Brown I*, they heard 19 cases challenging locally segregated schools. Since delay was part of the Southern strategy of resistance, appeals of the trial decisions were taken in most of the cases, further postponing final court orders. The federal district court judges in the South often found themselves socially ostracized for their rulings. They were "fifty-eight lonely men" in the apt title of a study of legal resistance school desegregation after *Brown.**

The most dramatic of all local struggles over school desegregation was the one in Little Rock, Ark. The school board formulated a plan to desegregate its system one grade a year starting with the twelfth grade at Central High School, and in September 1957, nine black students were admitted. The day before classes started, the state's governor, Orval Faubus, proclaiming his intention of averting public disorder, directed the state national guard to prevent admission of the students. He withdrew the troops under a court order, but the next day an unruly white mob outside the school prevented entry of the black students.

The day following, President Eisenhower sent 1,000 federal soldiers to the school area and federalized the state national guard to keep it from be-

ing used by the governor. It was a difficult decision for the president, who though opposed to segregation, had been conspicuously unenthusiastic about the Brown decision. He believed that progress in race relations could not come through court orders and had already come to regret his appointment of Earl Warren as chief justice. But defiance of federal authority was another matter. Eisenhower saw his Southern popularity, manifest in two presidential elections, plummet as he became the first president since Reconstruction to use federal troops to protect civil rights in the region.

After a year of tension and distraction during which soldiers occupied the high school campus, the school board asked for and got a court order granting it a two-and-a-half-year delay in implementing its desegregation plan. This ruling was quickly appealed to the Supreme Court, which in the notable decision of *Cooper v. Aaron* (p. 476), held the postponement unconstitutional. The justices returned early from summer recess so they could reach a decision before opening of the new school year. They were unanimous and emphatic: granting a delay would allow the threat of mob violence to abridge Fourteenth Amendment rights. Further, in a sharp criticism of state officials, the Court reminded them of federal supremacy and of their own constitutional responsibility to enforce the laws of the nation.

---

* Jack Peltason, *Fifty-Eight Lonely Men* (Urbana, Ill., University of Illinois Press, 1971).

Though the decision, like the stationing of federal troops, stiffened rather than weakened Southern resistance in the immediate, it removed any doubt about what the final outcome of state-mandated school segregation would be. In 1964, 10 years after *Brown,* such segregation had all but ended in the border states. But in those of the former Confederacy, only 2 percent of black students were attending integrated schools. Though the low figure is partly accounted for by residential patterns, most was attributable to official intransigence. Important changes took place in the Deep South as court challenges were exhausted, attitudes softened, and presidential directives withheld federal support money from school districts that had not made substantial progress toward desegregation. No less important in the collapse of segregation were the pressures brought by the civil rights movement.

The Civil Rights Movement

Though organized mobilization in the cause of black equality dates to the abolitionist movement, the modern civil rights movement is associated with the period from the mid-1950s to about 1970. It was perhaps the most successful social movement in American history, yet had no one leader or central organization. The most active groups were the NAACP, led by Roy Wilkens and Thurgood Marshall; Congress on Racial Equality (CORE), led by James Farmer and, later, Floyd McKissick; the Southern Christian Leadership Conference (SCLC), led by Martin Luther King, Fred Shuttlesworth, and Ralph Abernathy; and the Student Non-Violent Coordinating Committee (SNCC), led by John Lewis and, later, Stokeley Carmichael. Many persons, white and black, who worked in the movement had no formal affiliation with any group.

Though the movement pressed for legal rights in court and lobbied for new laws, it was dramatically effective through direct protest and demonstration at the grass-roots level. These efforts often met determined resistance and sometimes violence. The movement contained diverse views, especially on tactics, and clashing personalities, both of which generated great internal tension. It was united, however, on the need, even urgency, to move toward full civil, political, and social equality for black Americans.

The movement is sometimes said to have begun in December 1955 when Rosa Parks, a black woman riding a local bus in Montgomery, Ala., refused to move to the back, in accord with the local practice of segregation. When Parks was arrested, aroused local black leaders filed suit against the bus company and organized a boycott of all city buses by black riders. The protest showed the importance of black churches in promoting solidarity and saw the emergence of a young minister as its leader, the 26-year-old Martin Luther King, Jr. The boycott, which lasted 381 days, was economically punishing, and ended with a victory in court.

In the wake of the boycott, King and 60 other black ministers in Southern states organized the Southern Christian Leadership Conference to press for civil rights in the region. A charismatic figure with exceptional oratorical gifts, King urged nonviolent protest and civil disobedience to challenge Jim Crow laws and practices. He eventually became the civil rights movement's most important figure and a symbol of the activist quest for equality. (See Freedom's Apostle)

Early in 1960, four black college students in Greensboro, N.C., staged a sit-in to protest refusal of service at a campus luncheonette. The demonstration, which ended in a negotiated settlement, led to the formation of the Student Non-Violent Coordinating Committee and sparked hundreds of other sit-ins across the South as segregation in public facilities began to come under siege. The protesters were usually students, often in the hundreds, including many whites from the North. They were often met with heckling and arrest, sometimes assault. Hundreds of these demonstrators were charged with trespass, breach of the peace, and other violations of local laws.

In May 1961, CORE organized a small group of blacks and whites traveling in two buses to challenge segregation in waiting rooms, restrooms, and restaurants in terminals between Washington, D.C. and New Orleans. Known as the Freedom Ride, the demonstrators were attacked by a mob near Anniston, Ala. One bus was burned and several riders beaten. The incident drew national attention, and U.S. Attorney General Robert Kennedy assigned federal marshals to escort the riders for the remainder of the trip. Scores of other Freedom Rides, involving more than 1,000 persons, took place that summer, helping to desegregate public transportation facilities.

In August 1963, civil rights leaders organized the March on Washington, a day of mass gathering for speeches, songs, and prayer to reaffirm solidarity and increase pressure for federal civil rights legislation. Civil rights groups, now often at odds with one another, put aside their differences. More than 200,000 blacks and whites from all parts of the country attended. The climax was Martin Luther King's now famous "I Have a Dream" speech before the Lincoln Memorial.

Increasingly, civil rights groups turned attention directly to the political arena and to efforts to increase black voter registration, now seen as the surest path to long-term gains. The following year, CORE, SNCC, and other groups organized Freedom Summer to increase registration. The main effort focused on Mississippi, a state with proportionally the largest black population in the country but the lowest black voting rate. Several hundred white college students from the North joined local black civil rights workers. In June 1964, three workers—two whites and a black—were murdered. The crimes caused a national uproar and helped spur passage of civil rights legislation pending in Congress. But they also had negative consequences for the movement. Though Freedom Summer continued, it registered only 1,200 new voters, and many in the movement began to doubt the efficacy of turn-the-other-cheek tactics. Failure of the Democratic Party to seat the rump Mississippi Freedom Democratic Party, made up of protesting

blacks, over the white segregationist delegation at its 1964 presidential nominating convention, was a further blow.

Early in 1965, a planned march from Selma, Ala., to Montgomery, the state capital, was broken up by police using tear gas and clubs. News of the incident brought hundreds of civil rights supporters to Selma. Amid growing tension, a group of local whites killed a Northern white minister who had joined the Selma demonstrators. The march, led by Martin Luther King, eventually took place and shortly afterward Congress passed the pending Voting Rights Act of 1965.

Besides their local successes and their effect on national legislation, the civil rights confrontations led to several important Supreme Court decisions and a broader constitutional protection for civil rights. The chief theoretical problem the Court faced in hearing appeals of convictions of sit-in demonstrators and others challenging segregation was the distinction between public and private discrimination. Overturning convictions for violating state-mandated segregation was one thing, overturning them where the discrimination was private in origin was quite another.

The Fourteenth Amendment gave protection against state acts but, as interpreted in the Civil Rights Cases of 1883, did not reach discrimination by private parties. In *Burton v. Wilmington Parking Authority,* 1961, a majority of the Court stretched the concept of state action. Segregation imposed by a privately owned restaurant that leased its space in a facility owned by the State of Delaware was held to violate the Fourteenth Amendment. The Court found the connection between the restaurant and the state was close enough that the restaurant's discriminatory policy could be considered "state action."

Where local laws had mandated segregation in privately owned restaurants and other facilities, convictions of sit-in demonstrators for trespass or breach of the peace were routinely reversed, as in *Peterson v. Greenville,* a 1963 case in which the Court found state action to be present even though the discrimination was initiated by private owners. The definition was broadened further in *Lombard v. Louisiana,* the same year. Though there was no local ordinance requiring segregation in privately owned establishments serving the public, the Court held "state action" was present when local officials denounced the sit-ins and pressured private owners not to give in.

In other cases, the Court found that breach of the peace convictions of protesters demonstrating peacefully on state property violated First Amendment rights of speech and petition. In *Edwards v. South Carolina,* 1963, noted in Chapter 3, the Supreme Court overturned convictions of high school and college students who, protesting racial discrimination and asking repeal of segregation laws, had assembled on grounds of the state capitol. The First Amendment did not allow a state to criminally punish persons who peacefully assemble to express their views, however unpopular they may be.

All in all, the Court overturned hundreds of convictions arising from local sit-ins and other civil rights demonstrations. Lower federal courts did the same with hundreds more. The federal judiciary showed its determination not to allow the quest for civil rights to be worn down by multifarious local prosecutions based on laws that were now clearly unconstitutional.

Toward the end of the 1960s, segregation was crumbling throughout the South. One of the last bastions to go was state miscegenation statutes, forbidding and punishing interracial marriage. In *Loving v. Virginia,* 1967 (p. 479), a white man who had married a black woman appealed his conviction under Virginia's law. Though the law fell with equal severity on members of each race, a unanimous Court held it to violate the Fourteenth Amendment as a restriction on freedom to marry "solely on the basis of racial classification." For the first time the Court held classifications by race, even if otherwise equal in effect, were "inherently suspect." If they were to be sustained, "compelling" reasons would need to be shown, a rule the Court later developed more fully as an integral part of equal protection rights.

The civil rights movement gradually waned in the late 1960s. In one sense, it was the victim of its own success. Important victories had been

The civil rights movement of the 1960s challenged segregation directly and in many venues. Here, whites pour sugar, ketchup, and mustard on heads of sit-in demonstrators at a segregated lunch counter in Jackson, Miss., June, 1963.

Freedom's Apostle

In his tragically brief life of 39 years, the Rev. Martin Luther King, Jr., became the leader of an enormously successful social movement and the nation's leading spokesman for the ideal of equality. Between emerging as leader of the Montgomery bus boycott in 1955 and his murder by exconvict James Earl Ray in 1968, King helped complete a social revolution begun during Reconstruction and beckoned the entire nation to the cause of civil rights.

King was the well-educated son of the Rev. Martin Luther "Daddy" King, Sr., a highly respected preacher in Atlanta's black community. The younger Martin graduated from Morehouse College in Atlanta, attended Crozier Theological Seminary in Pennsylvania, and got a Ph.D. from Boston University. He was particularly influenced by the nonviolent philosophy and social activism of Gandhi and Thoreau and the Christian realism of the American theologian Reinhold Niebuhr. He developed a powerful oratorical style that combined the cadence of Southern black preachers with a New Testament epigrammaticism. When turned to ideas of simple moral clarity, whether constitutional or Christian, the effect was often compelling, as in the closing passages of his great "I Had a Dream" address at the climax of the 1963 March on Washington:

> With this faith [in the achievement of equality and racial tolerance], we will be able to hew out of the mountain of despair, a stone of hope. With this faith, we will be able to transform the jangling discords of our nation into a beautiful symphony of brotherhood.
>
> With this faith we will be able to work together, to go to jail together, to stand together for freedom together, knowing that we will be free one day . . .
>
> When we let freedom ring, when we let it ring from every village and every hamlet, from every state and every city, we will be able to speed up that day when all of God's children, black men and white men, Jews and Gentiles, Protestants and Catholics, will be able to join hands and sing in the words of the old Negro spiritual, "Free at last! Free at last! Thank God, Almighty, we are free at last!"

As leader of the Southern Christian Leadership Conference, King organized and led a series of marches and protests against Southern racial

More than 200,000 white and black persons attended the March on Washington, August 28, 1963, to protest racial segregation and urge passage of national legislation. The gathering at the Reflecting Pool between the Lincoln Memorial and the Washington Monument heard Martin Luther King deliver his "I Have a Dream" speech.

discrimination. The mode was nonviolent, and though the immediate aim was to win local concessions, the grander one was to dramatize intolerance and inequality on a larger moral and political stage.

In 1963, he chose Birmingham, Ala., at the time perhaps the most determinedly segregated city in the United States, to protest discrimination with a series of boycotts, sit-ins, and marches. It was the equivalent of walking into the lion's den. King and his chief lieutenants were quickly arrested. They were to spend more than a week in jail, but the demonstrations continued. Police, led by the hardline Public Safety Director Eugene "Bull" Connor, were at first disciplined and restrained. When hundreds of demonstrators were arrested, it appeared that the authorities might exhaust the protest. But then King had more than 1,000 children march out from his church headquarters into downtown Birmingham. Police arrested 900. The next day when another 1,000 left the church against Connor's orders, his men lost their restraint and ferociously turned on the marchers, adult and child, with water cannons, night sticks, and attack dogs. A few blacks fought back, mainly by throwing stones, which intensified the official violence. By this time, the demonstrations were being reported live on national television, the first to be so. The police attacks produced outcries around the nation. White moderates in Birmingham eventually made some concessions on segregation, but more importantly, the week of demonstrations and police brutality made civil rights the nation's chief domestic issue.*

Two years later, a similar confrontation was played out in Selma, Ala. chosen as the starting point for a voting rights protest march to the state capitol in Montgomery. Again King had chosen a location known for white recalcitrance and in which he expected stiff resistance. A week after the Selma violence, Congress passed the pending Voting Rights Act.

Not all King's projects were successful. The so-called Albany Movement, a protracted local struggle in Albany, Ga. in 1961 and 1962, in which King was twice arrested and jailed, ended without important gains. An attempt to protest housing discrimination in the North failed when King and several other civil rights leaders were assaulted by white counter-demonstrators during a march in Chicago.

Partly for these reasons and partly because some more radically militant black voices had little faith in nonviolence, King came under increasing criticism from within the movement. He had recognized this, but did not waver. In his memorable "Letter from Birmingham Jail," written while in custody during the 1963 demonstrations, he wrote, "I stand in the middle of two opposing forces in the Negro community. One is the force of complacency, made up of Negroes who, because of long years of oppression have been completely drained of self-respect . . . The other force is one of bitterness and hatred, and comes perilously close to advocating violence." He was eminently successful in dealing with the first; on the second, he consistently counseled against giving way to hatred and bitterness no matter how terrible the provocation.

In recognition of his ideas as much as his acts, he was awarded the Nobel Peace Prize in 1964.

King's assassination in Memphis, where he had gone to help striking black sanitation workers, touched off riots in more than 130 cities, resulting in 40 deaths, more than $100 million in property loss, and 20,000 arrests.†

As in the case of other murdered leaders—Lincoln and John and Robert Kennedy—King seems to loom even larger in death than he did in life. Many of Lincoln's admirers believe he would have found a way to navigate the shoals of Reconstruction. Many of King's admirers, who appear to be legion among white and black Americans, believe he would have prevented further racial polarization, found ways to dramatize discrimination outside the South, and effectively pursued collateral issues that affected millions of white as well as black persons, such as the Vietnam War and poverty. He had already broken with President Johnson on the war and had been planning a "poor people's" march on Washington at the time of his death.

These are high expectations. Realistic though they may be or not, King clearly did not lose faith in the American dream of equality, either in a Constitution that he saw embodying it or in a better human

(Continued)

nature that could be appealed to and touched by it. In the words of one contemporary commentator, "He stood in that line of saints which goes back from Gandhi to Jesus; his violent end, like theirs, reflects the hostility of mankind to those who annoy it by trying hard to pull it one more painful step farther up the ladder from ape to angel."[‡]

* James T. Patterson, *Grand Expectations: The United States, 1945–1974* (New York, Oxford University Press, 1996), 479.
[†] Robert Weisbrot, *Freedom Bound: A History of America's Civil Rights Movement* (New York, Norton, 1990), 270.
[‡] I.F. Stone, "The Fire Has Only Just Begun," in Neil Middleton, ed., *The Best of I.F. Stone.*

won in constitutional law, in the passage of the first federal civil rights legislation since Reconstruction, and in forcing concessions in hundreds of local confrontations in the Deep South and border states. Though no one could pretend that full racial equality had arrived or that de facto segregation stemming from residential patterns had disappeared, legally mandated segregation was ended and important blows had been struck against the most overt forms of discrimination.

But there were other reasons for the movement's decline. As internal tensions and divisions heightened, the peaceful, nonviolent strategies of the early years were challenged by a new combativeness and strident calls for action, even violence. Several of the organizations became dominated by black militants such as Stokeley Carmichael, H. Rap Brown, and Floyd McKissick. New groups, such as the Black Panther Party, advocating "black power" and influenced by the ideas of black nationalism and separatism of Elijah Muhammad and Malcolm X, were organized in Northern cities. Partly for these reasons, massive white participation and support fell away or was no longer welcome. Though some black persons saw "black power" as calling for rebellion, for most it was apt to signify racial pride and black independence and self-reliance. For many whites, it seemed fundamentally opposed to integration. The assassination of Martin Luther King in 1968 removed not only the movement's most visible and influential figure, but also, by then, a voice of moderation. Increasingly, white and some black protest energy went into opposing the Vietnam War.

The election of Richard Nixon in 1968 and retirement of Earl Warren as chief justice the following year made it likely that civil rights progress would not advance at the pace it had earlier in the decade. Nixon's "Southern strategy" allowed him to carry of five of eleven Southern states despite being a Republican and despite the presence of a third-party segregationist candidate, George Wallace, governor of Alabama, on the ballot. Nixon's call for "strict constructionism" in interpreting the Constitution meant that new appointees to the Court would not be judicial activists on civil rights and other civil liberties issues. Nixon's four appointments in three years—those of Warren Burger as chief justice, Harry Blackmun, Lewis Powell, and William Rehnquist—effectively ended the Warren Court. The new Court did not turn the civil rights clock back, in fact, it supported some new initiatives against discrimination, but it was not the emphatically activist body its predecessor had been.

New National Legislation

Though President Harry Truman after World War II issued an executive order ending segregation in the armed forces and had appointed an influential national committee on civil rights, the national government, presidentially and congressionally, was otherwise virtually silent on civil rights from the end of Reconstruction in 1876 until the late 1950s. Truman's proposals for antilynching laws and those to insure fair employment practices and voting rights, in accord with recommendations of the national committee, were blocked by Southerners in the House and Senate. The legislative spell was broken in 1957 with passage of a modest civil rights law that set up a federal investigative agency, the Commission on Civil Rights, and made intimidation of voters a federal offense. The Commission reported three years later that little or no progress had been made toward registering black voters. President Eisenhower then asked for further legislation, which Congress, held up by a Southern filibuster of 125 hours, passed as the Civil Rights Act of 1960. It authorized federal court-appointed referees who, if they found illegal denial of the right to vote, could ask for voter registration through court order. As a further step against violence, it made arson and bombing federal crimes where the suspects were assumed to have crossed state lines.

The 1957 and 1960 Acts were a prelude to much stronger civil rights legislation in 1964 and 1965, besides a constitutional amendment, the Twenty-fourth, ratified in 1964. The 1964 Act, originally proposed by the Kennedy administration and passed after the president's assassination, is the most comprehensive civil rights legislation ever enacted. It was a response to pressures generated by the civil rights movement and events in the South and allowed Northern and Western Democrats and Republicans were able to overcome a Southern filibuster. The act had 11 titles dealing with voting rights, segregation in education, and discrimination in public accommodations and employment. Title II, its most important section, addressed many issues the sit-in demonstrations had dramatized. It declared that access to hotels, motels, restaurants, theaters, sports arenas, and other public facilities could not be denied or otherwise abridged because of "race, color, religion, or national origin." The provisions applied where establishments affected commerce or where discrimination was supported by state action, defined as that carried on under "color of law," or local cus-

tom enforced by state authority. Because Congress, unlike the state governments, had no power to reach private discrimination as such, Title II was based in part on Congress's power to regulate interstate commerce in Article I-8. As interpreted by the Court over the years, that power could be used to regulate private commercial interests shown to affect interstate commerce.

These controversial Title II provisions were quickly challenged. In two cases heard together, later in 1964, *Heart of Atlanta Motel v. United States* and *Katzenbach v. McClung,* the Court was faced with discriminatory practices of a privately owned motel and a small local, privately owned restaurant. Since no state action, direct or indirect, was present, the decisive issue was the businesses were related to interstate commerce. In both cases the Court held they were. The motel served many interstate travelers and, though all customers at the restaurant were local, the Court held that much of the food it served came from out of state. This expansive reading of the scope of interstate commerce, by virtually eliminating the interstate and local distinction, allowed federal power to reach private discrimination that it could not through the Fourteenth Amendment's equal protection clause.

The Voting Rights Act of 1965, the need for which had been so immediately dramatized by King's Selma march, had been proposed by President Lyndon Johnson. Despite other voting rights initiatives, franchise discrimination had not been ended. In Alabama, for example, almost 50 percent of the state's population was black, but only 1 percent of its registered voters were. In more than 100 counties in the Deep South, less than 10 percent of the eligible black population was registered. The 1965 act, based on Congress's Fifteenth Amendment powers to protect voting rights, did not rely on individual complaints of discrimination as past voting measures had, but dealt with registration disparities systemically. In states that had discriminated and in which less than 50 percent of black persons of voting age were registered or voted in the last election, it authorized suspension of literacy and other educational tests that had often been used to disqualify blacks. It also authorized appointment of federal examiners to supervise elections in states where there had been discrimination. The examiners were empowered to propose lists of eligible voters and protect the right to vote at polling places on election day. These sweeping powers over local elections were supplemented by requirement that new state voting laws be approved by the United States attorney general or the federal district court of the District of Columbia.

Provisions of the act were quickly but unsuccessfully challenged. In *South Carolina v. Katzenbach,* the following year, the Supreme Court rejected the state's chief contentions, first, that Congress had gone beyond its Fifteenth Amendment power and encroached on that of the states, and second, that the act, which prescribed the greatest federal intervention in state affairs since Reconstruction, violated a constitutional guarantee that all states be treated equally. Citing the doctrine of implied powers set out in *McCulloch v. Maryland,* 1819, the Court held that Congress possessed "any rational means" to reach constitutional ends, in this case, the Fifteenth Amendment's bar to racial discrimination in voting. On equality of the states, that status referred to their entry into the Union; it did not prevent Congress from dealing with specific local problems where there was long denial of a constitutional right.

Of symbolic value but much less practical consequence than the Voting Rights Act was the Twenty-fourth Amendment, outlawing the poll tax in federal elections. The tax was a levy many Southern states had placed on the right to vote, to keep poor blacks "voluntarily" disenfranchised. The amendment was proposed by Congress in August 1962, but by the time of ratification in January 1964, only five states still imposed the tax. Two years later, the Supreme Court invalidated the poll tax in state elections in *Harper v. Virginia Board of Elections,* as a viola-

tion of the equal protection clause of the Fourteenth Amendment.

Unlike other attempts to end voting discrimination in the South, enforcement of the Voting Rights Act produced swift results. In Selma, Ala., for example, black voter registration soon increased sixfold under the eye of federal examiners. By 1970, black registration in the South more than doubled. With voting power came greater attention and solicitation from white politicians, who found that ignoring the needs and interests of black citizens was now more difficult. "Running against the Negro" was no longer the profitable electoral strategy it had once been. Before long, black voting also led, for the first time since the Reconstruction, to the election of hundreds, later thousands, of black officials including mayors, sheriffs, and legislators.

The Civil Rights Act of 1968, dealing mainly with housing discrimination, was passed after the assassination of Martin Luther King and widespread black riots that followed in several Northern cities. A seven-week Southern filibuster was broken only by including a largely unrelated provision that made it a federal crime to cross a state line to incite a riot. The centerpiece of the act was Title VIII, which barred racial or religious discrimination in the sale or rental of housing in buildings of five or more units.

Only a year before passage, the Supreme Court in *Reitman v. Mulkey,* its first housing discrimination case in nearly 15 years, struck down an amendment to the California Constitution that had been adopted in a statewide referendum and which barred the state from interfering with racial discrimination in housing. The Court held that since the amendment's intended effect was repeal of the state's fair housing law, it violated the Fourteenth Amendment by involving the state in private discrimination.

Shortly after passage of the 1968 act, the Court decided *Jones v. Mayer,* in which it resurrected the Reconstruction-era Civil Rights Act of 1866 and gave new effect to its provision that "all citizens" should have the same right to "inherit, purchase, lease, hold, and convey property . . . enjoyed by white citizens." The case grew out of the refusal of a private owner to sell a home to an interracial couple, a matter not covered in the 1968 act. The chief constitutional question was whether the old act could apply to private discrimination. In answering affirmatively, the Court looked to the Thirteenth Amendment, which, outlawing slavery, applies to all parties, public and private. Echoing Justice Harlan's memorable dissent in the Civil Rights Cases, the Court said, Congress had outlawed not only slavery but the "badges" or incidents of slavery, one of which was being racially discriminated against in the sale of property.

A New Era of Complex Civil Rights

The end of the 1960s, the election of Nixon, and the passing of the Warren Court marked a more conservative turn in the nation's political temper. It also signified transition of the struggle for equal rights from a largely regional one dealing with the unfinished work of Reconstruction to recognition of a nationwide problem, at once more complex and morally less well defined.

The Johnson administration had been the most responsive to civil rights in the nation's history, and the Democratic Congress elected with Johnson in his 1964 landslide victory over Barry Goldwater was the most liberal since the early New Deal, 30 years before. But the president's misguided Vietnam policies, which enlarged and prolonged the war and cost tens of thousands more lives, undermined his domestic initiatives including those on civil rights and the War on Poverty. They eventually drove him from office by making his renomination and election in 1968 all but impossible. The war and widespread protests against it became the chief issue of the campaign.

Except for the 1932 election that brought in Franklin D. Roosevelt and the New Deal in the worst of the Great Depression, the 1968 contest was probably the most important of the twentieth century. The Democrats nominated Vice President Hubert Humphrey at a disastrously disunited convention in Chicago. His percentage of the popular vote in the fall, 42.7, was nearly 19 points lower than Johnson's four years before; except for 1928 to 1932, it was the largest four-year swing in the century. The third-party candidacy of George Wallace, governor of Alabama, polled nearly 10 million votes and carried five Southern states—Georgia, Alabama, Mississippi, Louisiana, and Arkansas. Despite this impressive showing for a third party, it marked the last hurrah for massive Southern protest against desegregation. Humphrey's inability to carry more than one Southern state—Texas—was evidence of the fissure within the Democratic Party on civil rights, a problem that would plague if for many years. In the South, the party would be made up of an uneasy alliance of newly enfranchised blacks and moderate whites. As conservative whites moved into the Republican Party, the South eventually became a competitive two-party region.

Because of the salience of the war issue, it would be incorrect to attribute Nixon's election to a "backlash" against civil rights. Yet there was little doubt massive Northern white support had weakened. The battle for desegregation in the South was being won and now new, strident calls for "black power" were heard from the civil rights movement as attention turned to racial discrimination outside the South. Within three years of the election, three stalwarts of the liberal activist Warren Court had resigned or retired—the chief justice, Associate Justice Abe Fortas in 1969, and Justice Hugo Black in 1971. A fourth, Justice William O. Douglas, retired in 1975. The new Burger Court, though ideologically more balanced than its predecessor, did not move to circumscribe civil rights as many had expected.

But the equal rights issues of the Seventies and Eighties were different from those a generation before and showed how intractable some aspects of racial inequality might be. They were not occupied with breaking up a regional caste system that had succeeded slavery or combating overt, often legally mandated discrimination. Instead, the problems now were apt to be nationwide, stemming from the de facto segregation of residential patterns, themselves often the product of discrimination. They were about more subtle, sometimes deeply institutionalized patterns of discrimination. Compounding matters was that new civil rights claims often adversely affected whites who had not engaged in or benefited from discrimination. Compensatory measures often resulted in charges of "reverse discrimination." New civil rights goals sometimes appeared to conflict with the well-established value of reward by merit.

Schools: Desegregation or Racial Balance?

The "with all deliberate speed" standard propounded in *Brown II* gave Southern states and school districts time to effect desegregation. Though much progress had been made by the end of the Sixties, particularly in the border states, many Southern localities showed little or no change in the racial composition of local schools. In one of the last desegregation cases of the Warren Court, *Green v. County School Board of New Kent County*, 1968, the justices struck down a so-called freedom-of-choice plan. It allowed students in a small rural district to choose which of two schools they wanted to attend, one formerly all black, one formerly all white. None of the white students chose the first and only 15 percent of the black students chose the second.

A variation of this plan in other districts gave students who were attending a school in which their race was a majority, the right to transfer to a school in which their race was a minority. These too resulted in a few black students transferring but almost no whites. The plans ended mandated segregation and allowed access to neighborhood schools, but did little to change racial patterns in the schools. In invalidating them, the Court showed its impatience with the pace of "all deliberate speed." More importantly, it recast the thrust of *Brown* from that of outlawing segregation and thus providing for equality of access to that of achieving some sort of racial proportionality in each school.

The problems of giving effect to this approach were at issue in *Swann v. Charlotte-Mecklenburg Board of Education*, 1971 (p. 484), the first important school case heard by the Burger Court. Unlike the rural school district in *Green*, the board of education was responsible for 84,000 students, 29 percent of whom were black, most living in a section of Charlotte. This demographic pattern left the school district still largely segregated even when mandated segregation was ended. To overcome it, a lower federal court had ordered massive busing of students so that each of the district's 100 schools would more closely reflect the racial composition of the entire district.

In a unanimous opinion—one of the last such on civil rights issues—the Court held that remedies to end "all vestiges of state-imposed segregation" were not limited to "the walk-in school." Busing, racial quotas, the pairing of schools, and even the gerrymandering of school zones were devices that might be used. Two important questions were left for future determination. Were the drastic remedies limited to de jure segregation, that is, to districts that had once required separation of the races, or could they be used where segregation had been merely de facto? Did federal court supervision of desegregation end after a unitary system had been effected or did it continue should districts later become resegregated because of changing residential patterns?

School busing in urban and suburban areas, where attending the neighborhood school was often taken for granted, proved generally unpopular with most white and great many black parents. Not only was it an expensive remedy, since large fleets of buses had to be bought and maintained, it appreciably lengthened the school day for many students.

Court-ordered busing to end racial segregation and bring about racial balance occasionally met with protests in Southern states and elsewhere. Here a police escort accompanies buses leaving South Boston High School in Boston, Mass., September, 1974.

Largely ignored in the wake of *Brown* and the struggle to end systemic segregation in the South, was the fact that racial segregation permeated many Northern and Western school districts as well, particularly in large cities. There was, however, one important difference: most of those districts had either never mandated segregation or had repealed it long before *Brown*.

In *Keyes v. Denver School District No. 1,* 1973, the Court handed down its first important decision on non-Southern school segregation and how it would be affected by *Brown*. Dealing mainly with evidentiary problems, it stressed the difference between de facto and de jure segregation. De jure could include that promoted by

school board policies, even without state laws. But where there was no showing of intent to segregate, there was no constitutional violation.

The following year, the Court elaborated on this distinction in *Milliken v. Bradley* (p. 486) and, set an important limit on the reach of segregation remedies. The case came from the Detroit school district, one of the country's largest, serving nearly 300,000 students, about two-thirds of whom were black. The Detroit metropolitan area included 53 suburban school districts in which about 80 percent of the students were white. There was clear evidence that the Detroit district had practiced deliberate segregation. To the NAACP, which argued the case, and the

From Advocate to Justice

When Thurgood Marshall, the grandson of a freed slave, took his seat on the Supreme Court in October 1967 as the first person of African descent to serve as a justice, the occasion was historic but almost anticlimactic. Marshall's mark on American constitutional development was already extraordinary. He had been chief architect of the legal attack on segregation and on the separate but equal doctrine. More than anyone, he had been responsible for a new expansive reading of the equal protection clause of the Fourteenth Amendment as a chief protection against racial discrimination. He had had more success before the Court than any nominee before or since, winning in 29 of 32 appearances. He would be a justice for nearly a quarter of a century and write many important opinions, but even that service did not surpass his achievements as an advocate.

Marshall's father had worked as a steward in an all-white club in Baltimore; his mother was a teacher in an all-black elementary school. He grew up in a segregated world. He attended Lincoln University in Pennsylvania, then an all-black school with an all-white faculty. As a native Marylander, he looked forward to attending the state law school, but was rejected because of race. The insult had a lasting effect on his outlook and career. He went instead to all-black Howard University Law School and quickly came under the influence of its activist dean Charles Hamilton Houston, who was then making the school the spawning ground of civil rights specialists. Marshall, who excelled as a debater, graduated first in his class in 1933. He opened a law office in Baltimore and was soon volunteering time to the local branch of the NAACP. In 1936, Houston, who had left Howard to become special counsel for the NAACP, brought Marshall to New York as his assistant. One of

their early triumphs was the mounting of a constitutional challenge to Missouri's all-white law school and the state's policy of sending qualified black applicants to study at law schools in other states. The resulting victory in the Supreme Court in *Missouri ex. rel. Gaines v. Canada*, 1938, was the first constitutional crack in the doctrine of the Plessy case.

When Houston resigned in 1938, Marshall, then 30, succeeded him. The following year, the NAACP's Legal Defense and Education Fund was created, with Marshall as its director, to help black persons challenge local discrimination by providing moral support and free legal representation. In the years that followed, Marshall crafted a plan that attacked segregation on several legal fronts. Hundreds of cases were filed. Those that went to appeal Marshall usually argued himself. These resulted in several notable Supreme Court triumphs, including *Smith v. Allwright*, 1944, chal-

federal district court that ruled in its favor, it seemed logical to try an area-wide, multidistrict remedy, even if it called for the largest busing operation yet.

But a narrowly divided Court saw it otherwise. It refused to uphold the lower federal court because there was no evidence the suburban districts had practiced segregation. Since they had neither

caused nor contributed to Detroit's de jure segregation, a multidistrict remedy was not constitutionally required. The decision also marked the first setback for the NAACP in the Supreme Court on a school desegregation issue since well before *Brown*. In holding that the scope of a segregation remedy must not exceed the violation, the Court acknowledged reservations about imposing dis-

lenging the "whites only" primary; *Shelley v. Kramer,* 1948, challenging restrictive covenants; and *Brown v. Board of Education,* 1954, the school desegregation case.

In *Brown,* Marshall considered and rejected the safer position of attacking segregation on the ground that black schools, though separate, were not equal. This would have acknowledged the validity of the separate but equal doctrine. Instead, he chose the riskier argument that segregated schools were *inherently* unequal, that no amount of remedial tinkering could make them otherwise. He cited sociological studies that Chief Justice Warren was later to note in his opinion in the case, appearing to show that mandated segregation in education was emotionally damaging to black children. The Court was persuaded. By this time Marshall had well earned the appellation increasingly applied to him of "Mr. Civil Rights."

In the years following *Brown,* the NAACP was occupied with challenging Southern resistance to the ruling and defending attacks on itself. Other notable Marshall cases were decided by the Supreme Court, including *NAACP v. Alabama,* 1958, which set out an important right of freedom of association. Though Marshall knew the battle against segregation in the South would also need to be fought in the trenches, he was often wary of the direct action strategies of Martin Luther King and others. He felt more comfortable working from the top down.

In 1961, President Kennedy nominated him for the federal Second Circuit Court of Appeals. Opposition of several Southerners on the Senate Judiciary Committee produced protracted, often hostile hearings. Marshall was not confirmed for 11 months. After four years on the court, he was persuaded by President Johnson to become United States solicitor general to represent the federal government in its cases before the Supreme Court. His eventual appointment to the Court was anticipated.

When Johnson made it two years later on the resignation of Justice Tom Clark, it touched off another lengthy series of confirmation hearings, despite Marshall's obvious qualifications for the job.

In the next 24 years, he wrote important Opinions of the Court on a wide range of issues. Among the more notable were those in *Stanley v. Georgia,* 1969, upholding the right to possess pornographic materials in the privacy of the home, and *Benton v. Maryland,* 1969, holding the double jeopardy provision in the Fifth Amendment that bars the federal government from trying a person twice for the same crime, applied also to the states.

Marshall fit in well with the liberal Warren Court. But in the more ideologically balanced Courts of the Burger and Rehnquist eras, his most effective opinions were more apt to be in dissent. He generally opposed government regulations of speech, private sexual conduct, and abortions. He was an unwavering opponent of capital punishment even when public opinion moved the other way on the issue. He dissented in every case in which the Court did not overturn a death sentence. He invariably supported affirmative action and stood ready to constitutionally require government to offer certain basic benefits, including educational opportunity and access to legal services, without regard to ability to pay.

Marshall was an able legal craftsman, but his influence on the Court was also in simply being present and not hesitating to remind his colleagues of the hard "real world" he had known only too well. This and his insistence that the Court think carefully about the practical consequences of the legal formalisms it might apply was what his close colleague Justice William Brennan described as Marshall's "special voice." Declining health forced his retirement from the Court in 1991, at 82. He died June 14, 1993.

---

abilities on those not implicated in racial discrimination.

Where did this leave the mostly black Detroit schools? In Justice Thurgood Marshall's dissenting observation, it left black children with "the same separation and inherently unequal education in the future as they have been unconstitutionally afforded in the past." This prediction

turned out to be at least partly incorrect. The Court ordered the case remanded to the federal district court for creation of a different remedy, countering the effects of segregation in Detroit. The lower court eventually ordered the city and the state to set up comprehensive remedial programs in the city schools, including those for testing, training, guidance, and special education. In a second *Milliken v. Bradley,* 1977, these measures were unanimously upheld by the Court.

But debate continued. Were such programs an important expansion of remedies beyond the one of racial balance or were they a separate-but-equal substitute for integration? Were noninte-grative remedies for the effects of segregation inferior to racial balance? They certainly seemed at odds with Chief Justice Warren's assumptions in *Brown.* But if valid then, were those assumptions still valid? One of the most influential early sociological studies of school integration, the Coleman Report, though concluding home environment was more important in a child's academic performance, also found that disadvantaged students (mainly black) who began to go to school with middle class children (mainly white) had higher achievement levels than those not in mixed classrooms and schools.* Yet, 10 years later, sociologist James Coleman, the highly re-spected director of the study, had different thoughts. Massive court-ordered busing, which often resulted in "white flight" and a resegrega-tion of many schools, had done more harm than good. Fixation on achieving racial balance as though it were a panacea, he concluded, had drawn attention away from the more basic prob-lem: the need to eliminate inferior schools.†

In the 1970s, the Supreme Court began to deal with the limits of federal judicial supervi-sion of segregation remedies. To overcome seg-regation in Pasadena, Calif., a federal trial court had approved a pupil assignment plan that re-quired black and other minority students not be the numerical majority in any school. But within four years of achieving this racial balance, shifts in residential patterns again put several schools in violation of the plan. As a result, the trial court ordered new, annual reassignments to maintain balance. In *Pasadena Board of Education v. Span-gler,* 1976, the Supreme Court held that the sec-ond order exceeded the lower court's authority. Later violation of the racial balance standard did not result from deliberate segregation policies of the school district but from demographic changes, that is, from white flight.

The Court has since held in *Board of Educa-tion of Oklahoma City Public Schools v. Dowell,* 1991, that desegregation orders for busing are not meant to be permanent where a school district can show that it removed segregation's past ef-fects "as far as practicable" in good faith and for a reasonable time. But in *United States v. Fordice,* 1992, it added that states and localities having once had de jure segregation bore a heavy bur-den of proof that vestiges of official discrimina-tion were eliminated. In *Missouri v. Jenkins,* 1990 (p. 491), the Court upheld a lower court order to Kansas City to levy taxes to raise more than half a billion dollars for correction of the effects of past segregation. But five years later, in a sec-ond *Missouri v. Jenkins,* it invalidated the same court's later orders that teacher salaries be in-creased and magnet inner-city schools be cre-ated to attract white students from neighboring suburban districts. These orders, said the Court, dealt with "academic goals unrelated to the ef-fect of legal segregation" once practiced in the school district.

The half-century odyssey of school desegrega-tion has seen the complete elimination of man-dated separation of the races in public education. But realizing the ideal of fully integrated schools, like that of a fully integrated society, North and South, has proved elusive. The Supreme Court in the Burger and Rehnquist pe-riods has generally adhered to two principles in what desegregation remedies are required or permitted by the Constitution. One is the quali-tative distinction between de facto and de jure segregation. The other is that the pattern of or-dered busing, white flight, and resegregation was likely to compromise, at least for the imme-diate, the ideal of racial balance. As a result, the Court has been willing to sustain more extensive remedies for de jure segregation. But where en-forcing the ideal of strict racial balance seemed

---

* U.S. Office of Education, *Equality of Educational Opportunity* (Washington, D.C.: U.S. Government Printing Office, 1966).
† Henry J. Abraham and Barbara A. Perry, *Freedom and the Court,* 7th ed. (New York, Oxford University Press, 1998), 364.

impractical or unfair, it has upheld various, even expensive, compensatory measures to overcome the effects of segregation, past and present.

Clearly, the Warren Court had not fully anticipated the strength of white flight and overestimated the support of black parents for heroic school busing and other plans that made their children a permanent minority everywhere. Also, equalizing educational opportunity in elementary and secondary public schools seemed not to depend as much on racial balance as was once thought. If true, it is probably attributable both to compensatory measures and to increasing black independence and achievement. All this said, American public schools are now vastly more integrated than at the time of *Brown*. They will probably become more so with further residential integration, the movement of more black persons into the middle and upper-middle classes, and greater racial understanding by both white and black Americans.

Discrimination in Employment

Title VII of the 1964 Civil Rights Act barred discrimination by employers of 100 or more workers (reduced later to 15 by amendments) because of race, religion, gender, or national origin. It also set up a federal agency, the Equal Employment Opportunity Commission (EEOC) to hear complaints and to help in gaining redress. Title VII was a big advance in the protection of equal rights and elimination "last to be hired, first to be fired" racial discrimination. Before its passage, a complainant might get redress under state antidiscrimination statutes, but such laws, where they were in force, were often inconsistently applied. Usually no Fourteenth Amendment equal protection right could be claimed against discrimination by private employers or labor unions.

The Court made an important interpretation of Title VII in *Griggs v. Duke Power Co.*, 1971, in which several black employees challenged the company's promotion standards that included having a high school diploma and getting a cer-

tain grade on an aptitude test for most jobs including those of mainly physical labor. These resulted in a rejection of many black workers. In striking down the policy, the Court held that where an employer had discriminated in the past and where present tests caused a "disparate impact" on a group protected by Title VII, it did not matter that they were neutral on their face or in intent. In practice, the Court said, they worked to maintain the effects of past discrimination.

Griggs was applied by lower courts to strike down hiring, promotion, and other work policies that were shown to have a disparate racial effect. In *Albemarle Paper Co. v. Moody*, 1975, the Supreme Court affirmed that under Title VII, tests that excluded more blacks than whites were discriminatory unless shown to be related to jobs to be filled. It also held that the award of back pay could be a remedy when there was evidence of past discrimination. In *Franks v. Bowman Transportation Co.*, 1976, it approved an award of retroactive seniority rights where a worker had been denied promotion because of discriminatory policies.

The Court retreated from the "disparate impact" standard where the issue argued was equal protection rather than interpretation of Title VII. In *Washington v. Davis*, 1976, brought under the Fifth Amendment, which contains an implicit equal protection component, several black Washington, D.C. police officers alleged that intelligence and aptitude tests used in hiring and promotion failed substantially more blacks than whites. In upholding the tests, which the Court found neutral on their face and rationally related to job performance, it distinguished "disparate impact" from discriminatory purpose or intent. The second would need to be proved for there to be a constitutional violation. A "disparate impact" might be one element in proving such intent, but alone it was not enough.

The Court dealt more directly with the proof needed in Title VII cases in *Ward's Cove Packing Co. v. Antonio*, 1989, in which employment discrimination was alleged because many nonwhite workers were in low-paying jobs and few in high-paying jobs. The Court held that the complaining employee must show that such disparity was caused by specific employer practices (and not, say, by differences in the availability of qualified nonwhites in the job pool). The employer might justify the practices if it could show that they served legitimate business goals. Partly in response to this decision, Congress amended Title VII in the Civil Rights Act of 1991 to shift more of the burden of proof to defending employers. *Ward's Cove* was "reversed" to the extent that the decision allowed an employer to justify on grounds of "business necessity" a practice that produced a disparate racial result.

Affirmative Action

Affirmative action is the award of benefits or preferences to individuals solely because of their membership in a group that has been discriminated against in the past. Though affirmative action programs may now include women and members of ethnic groups, their most extensive use has affected African Americans. These programs and policies may be voluntary or mandated by law. They have addressed a wide range of events and conditions including hiring and promotion, exemption from seniority rules, admission to college, and the award of public contracts. Their form may range from simple aggressive recruiting and special training programs to outright preferences and the setting aside of certain places or jobs. The aim of affirmative action is less equality of opportunity than racial balance and equality of distributive result.

Except for school busing, no remedy for racial discrimination has caused more debate, much of it heated and racially divisive. In recent years, the issue has entered electoral politics, with referenda being held in at least one state and several cities. Supporters of affirmative action see it as a natural extension of the constitutional requirement to end discrimination, made necessary by the lingering effects of past discrimination, such as poor schools and racially based poverty. Equality of opportunity, it is argued, is not enough to otherwise overcome long-standing, sometimes entrenched discrimination by race.

Critics, who are often supporters of aggressive efforts to equalize opportunity, usually object to the "double standard" in affirmative action and use of new or "reverse" discrimination to overcome vestiges of old. Basing reward on group attributes, they argue, is antithetical to reward by merit, and substitutes quotas and "balance" for qualifications and performance. They also point to the "stigmatizing" effect of affirmative action—the suggestion that blacks cannot compete with whites on equal terms—and the undermining of respect for the achievement of black persons. As a zero-sum matter—gains and benefits of one person or group are losses or disabilities for others—affirmative action is unfair, it is argued, if many of those receiving preferences are not themselves victims of discrimination and many of those losing out had not practiced discrimination.

Affirmative action can probably be said to have begun with President Johnson's executive order following passage of the 1964 Civil Rights Act, requiring affirmative action principles be used in all federal programs. This was aggressively taken up by most federal departments and agencies. By the 1970s, for example, the Department of Health, Education, and Welfare (now the Department of Education), began withholding federal support money from colleges and universities that failed to meet its guidelines for admission of black students and the hiring of black faculty members and staff.

Because of these pressures or on their own initiative, many colleges and universities set up affirmative action programs, some of which were based on outright racial preferences. Unsuccessful white applicants who believed they had been rejected because of their race, began to bring suits, ironically, under the equal protection clause of the Fourteenth Amendment and the Civil Rights Act of 1964. For a while, the Supreme Court avoided ruling on the substantive elements of this difficult issue. (*DeFunis v. Odegaard,* 1974, for example) When it finally did in *Regents of the University of California v. Bakke,* 1978 (p. 492), the justices were divided and their decision was confusing if not internally contradictory.

GeE, I DUNNO — IF THAT'S THE RESTROOMS, THEN IT'S BLATANT SEGREGATION. IF IT'S THE GOVERNMENT CONTRACTS OFFICE, IT'S AFFIRMATIVE ACTION....

WHITES ONLY

MINORITIES ONLY

An editorial cartoonist's view of the ironies of affirmative action.

Bakke, a white applicant to the University of California Medical School at Davis, was rejected for one of the 100 places in the school's annual entering class. It had set aside 16 of these places for a special admissions program limited to minority applicants in which admission standards, measured by grade point average and aptitude test scores, were more lenient. Bakke showed that his standard qualifications were higher than those of applicants admitted under the special program. The Court's holding was actually two decisions, both 5-4. In one, four justices found refusal to admit Bakke to violate Title VII of the 1964 Civil Rights Act that forbade exclusion for race in publicly funded programs. A fifth justice, Powell, found the admissions program to violate the equal protection clause of the Fourteenth Amendment. In effect, these five votes held racial quotas unacceptable.

But then, also 5-4, the Court held that race could be taken into account in seeking greater diversity in the student body. In effect, affirmative action programs were not unconstitutional per se. Except for Powell, who was the fifth vote on both issues, the four other justices in the majority on the first were different from the four

on the second. In this divergent decision, the Court did not make clear how much space remained between a positive consideration of race and a denial of individual right because of race, that is, between racial preferences and racial quotas. What was clear was that the Court had not definitively resolved the affirmative action issue. Despite the misgivings of many supporters of affirmative action, the decision had little effect on existing programs in higher education.

The following year, in *United Steelworkers of America v. Weber,* the Court dealt with affirmative action in employment for the first time. Weber, a white employee of Kaiser Aluminum Company, challenged a part of the company's collective bargaining agreement with the steelworkers that set up an in-plant craft-training program for unskilled workers. Admission to it was by seniority, but half the places were reserved for blacks, the aim being to raise the proportion of black skilled workers in the company's ranks to the level of blacks in the labor force. Weber was not admitted though he had greater seniority than many blacks who were. Emphasizing that the program was temporary and voluntary (not publicly mandated), the Court held it not to violate Title VII of the Civil Rights Act. Despite the act's wording barring racial discrimination in employment, the training program was consistent with its spirit of ending long-term discrimination.

The next year, in *Fullilove v. Klutznick,* the Court reviewed and upheld still another aspect of affirmative action, the so-called minority set-asides. At issue was a section of the federal Public Works Employment Act of 1977 requiring that 10 percent of a $4 billion construction program be set aside for minority-owned contracting firms, whether they were low bidders or not. A majority of the Court, stressing again that the program was temporary and designed to remedy latter-day effects of past wrongs, held it not to violate the equal protection element of the Fifth Amendment's due process clause, as charged by nonminority contractors. The decision encouraged creation of similar set-aside programs at both state and federal levels.

In two cases in the mid-1980s, the Court held against affirmative action principles as applied to layoffs. In *Firefighters Local Union No. 1784 v. Stotts,* 1984, there had been an earlier consent decree in which the Memphis Fire Department, to overcome effects of past discrimination, agreed that at least half the new hires would be of black persons until blacks made up 40 percent of the fire force. When city budget deficits led to layoffs, the department used its long-standing principle of "last hired first fired" principle. The Supreme Court rejected a challenge to this standard by a newly hired black firefighter who had argued that since the 40 percent level had not been reached, more senior whites should be layed off first. At the center of *Wygant v. Jackson Board of Education,* 1986, was a collective bargaining agreement between a local school board and a teachers union that required preferences be given to less senior black teachers if there were layoffs. In sustaining a challenge to this provision by several layed off white teachers with greater seniority, the Court stressed that the racial preferences had not been related to past discrimination in hiring.

When discrimination has been "long-standing, open, and pervasive," the Court has been willing to uphold, though narrowly, racial quotas for promotion aimed at overcoming effects of the

past. In *United States v. Paradise,* 1987, it sustained an order that half of all promotions among Alabama state troopers go to black officers to overcome the effects of past discrimination by the state Department of Public Safety.

Two more recent cases show the Rehnquist Court's narrowing of some aspects of affirmative action. In *City of Richmond v. Crosan,* 1989, it held a municipal set-aside program requiring the primary contractor on every city construction project to allocate at least 30 percent of the dollar amount of the project to minority-owned subcontracting businesses, to violate the equal protection clause in not being a narrowly tailored remedy for past discrimination. The case marked the first time a majority of the Court was willing to apply the so-called strict scrutiny test to affirmative action programs. It considered whether a program was directed at remedying specific practices of the past rather than effects of general societal discrimination, what effect it had on innocent parties, and whether there were other remedies.

In the 1995 set-aside case of *Adarand Constructors, Inc. v. Pena* (p. 498), the Court narrowly held the strict scrutiny standard to apply to federal affirmative action policies as it did to those of state and local government. It ruled against a program of the Department of Transportation that offered financial incentives to general contractors who awarded subcontracts to minority-owned companies. The decision overruled *Metro Broadcasting, Inc. v. F.C.C.,* decided only five years earlier, in which the Court had upheld preferential treatment of minority-owned businesses in the award of broadcast licenses without showing a clear relation to past discrimination. It did not close the door to all such programs in *Adarand,* but made it clear that strict scrutiny would require classifications based on race reach "a compelling government interest" not met by mere seeking of diversity. A constitutionally sustainable program would need to be narrowly tailored to deal with actual discriminatory practices, past or present, rather than based simply on showing of a disparate impact.

FURTHER READING

General

Bardolf, Richard, ed., *The Civil Rights Record: Black Americans and the Law, 1849–1970* (1970)

Bell, Derrick A., *Race, Racism, and American Law* (1980)

———, *Are We Not Saved: The Elusive Quest for Racial Justice* (1987)

Blaustein, Albert P., and Robert L. Zangrando, eds., *Civil Rights and the Black American: A Documentary History* (1970)

Bullock, Charles S., and Charles M. Lamb, eds., *Implementation of Civil Rights Policy* (1984)

Carter, Stephen, *Reflections of an Affirmative Action Baby* (1991)

Chafe, William, *Civilities and Civil Rights* (1980)

Cook, Anthony E., *The Least of These: Race, Law, and Religion in American Culture* (1997)

Davis, Abraham L., *The United States Supreme Court and the Uses of Social Science Data* (1973)

———, *Blacks in the Federal Judiciary: Neutral Arbiters or Judicial Activists?* (1989)

Davis, Abraham L., and Barbara Luck Graham, *The Supreme Court, Race, and Civil Rights from Marshall to Rehnquist* (1995)

Graham, Hugh Davis, *Civil Rights and the Presidency* (1992)

Grofman, Bernard, *The Legacies of the 1964 Civil Rights Act* (2000)

Higham, John, *Shades of Freedom: Racial Politics and the Presumptions of the American Legal Process* (1996)

Klinker, Philip A., *The Unsteady March: The Rise and Decline of Racial Equality in America* (1999)

Kull, Andrew, *The Color-Blind Constitution* (1992)

Lively, Donald E., *The Constitution and Race* (1992)

McCord, John H., *With All Deliberate Speed: Civil Rights Theory and Reality* (1969)

McDonald, Laughlin, and John A. Powell, *The Rights of Racial Minorities* (1998)

Morgan, Richard E., *Disabling America: The "Rights Industry" in Our Time* (1984)

Myrdal, Gunnar, *The American Dilemma: The Negro Problem and Modern Democracy*, 2 vols. (1944)

Nieman, Donald G., *Promises to Keep: African Americans and the Constitutional Order, 1976 to the Present* (1991)

Presser, Stephen B., *Recapturing the Constitution: Race, Religion, and Abortion Reconsidered* (1974)

Riddlesperger, James W., Jr., and Donald W. Jackson, eds., *Presidential Leadership and Civil Rights Policy* (1995)

Riley, Russell L., *The Presidency and the Politics of Racial Inequality: Nation-Keeping from 1831 to 1965* (1990)

Rosenberg, Gerald N., *The Hollow Hope: Can Courts Bring About Social Change* (1991)

Smolla, Rodney A., Federal Civil Rights Acts (1994)

Sowell, Thomas, *Black Education, Myths and Tragedies* (1972)

Spann, Girardeau A., *Race Against the Court: The Supreme Court and Minorities in Contemporary America* (1993)

TenBroek, Jacobus, *Equal under Law* (1965)

Thernstrom, Stephen and Abigail, *America in Black and White: One Nation Indivisible*

Tushnet, Mark V., *Making Civil Rights Law: Thurgood Marshall and the Supreme Court, 1936–1961* (1994)

Tushnet, Mark V., ed., *Thurgood Marshall: His Speeches, Writings, Arguments, Opinions, and Reminiscences* (2001)

Viteritti, Joseph, *Choosing Equality: School Choice, The Constitution, and Civil Society* (1999)

West, Thomas G., *Vindicating the Founders: Race, Class, Sex, and Justice in the Origins of America* (1997)

Before Brown v. Board of Education

Cohen, William, *At Freedom's Edge: Black Mobility and the Southern Quest for Racial Control, 1861–1915* (1991)

Higginbotham, A. Leon, Jr., *In the Matter Color: The Colonial Period* (1978)

Kaczorowski, Robert J., *The Politics of Judicial Interpretation: The Federal Courts, the Department of Justice, and Civil Rights, 1866–1876* (1985)

———, *The Nationalization of Civil Rights: Constitutional Theory and Practice in a Racist Society, 1866–1883* (1987)

Kryder, David, *Divided Arsenal: Race and the American State During World War II* (2000)

Tushnet, Mark, *The American Law of Slavery: 1810–1860: Considerations of Humanity and Interest* (1981)

Wiecek, William M., *The Sources of Antislavery Constitutionalism in American, 1760–1848* (1977)

Woodward, C. Vann, *The Strange Career of Jim Crow*, 3rd rev. ed. (1974)

The Civil Rights Movement

Ball, Howard, Dale Krane, and Thomas P. Lauth, *Compromised Compliance: Implementation of the 1965 Voting Rights Act* (1982)

Belknap, Michal R., *Federal Law and Southern Order: Racial Violence and Constitutional Conflict in the Post-Brown South* (1887)

Friedman, Leon, ed., *Southern Justice* (1967)

——, *The Civil Rights Reader: Basic Documents of the Civil Rights Movement* (1967)

Garrow, David J., *Time on the Cross: Martin Luther King, Jr. and the Southern Christian Leadership Conference* (1988)

Graham, Hugh Davis, *The Civil Rights Era: Origins and Development of National Policy* (1990)

——, *Crusaders in the Courts: How a Dedicated Band of Lawyers Fought for the Civil Rights Revolution (1994)*

Halpern, Stephen C., *On the Limits of the Law: the Ironic Legacy of Title VI of the 1964 Civil Rights Act* (1995)

King, Donald B., and Charles W. Quick, eds., *Legal Aspects of the Civil Rights Movements* (1965)

Krislov, Samuel, *The Negro in Federal Employment: The Quest for Equal Opportunity* (1967)

Lewis, Anthony, *Portrayal of a Decade: The Second American Revolution* (1964)

Miller, Loren, The Petitioners: *The Story of the Supreme Court of the United States and the Negro* (1966)

Muse, Benjamin, *Virginia's Massive Resistance* (1961)

Read, Frank T., and Lucy S. McGough, *Let Them Be Judged: The Judicial Integration of the Deep South* (1978)

Rodgers, Harrell R., Jr., and Charles S. Bullock, III, *Law and Social Change: Civil Rights Laws and Their Consequences* (1972)

Williams, Juan, *Eyes on the Prize: America's Civil Rights Years, 1954–1965* (1988)

Yarbrough, Tinsley E., *A Passion for Justice: J. Waties Waring and Civil Rights* (1987)

School Desegregation

Armor, David, *Forced Justice: School Desegregation and the Law* (1995)

Berman, Daniel H., *It Is So Ordered: The Supreme Court Rules on School Desegregation* (1966)

Blaustein, Albert P., and Clarence Clyde Ferguson, Jr., *Desegregation and the Law: The Meaning and Effect of the School Desegregation Cases* (1962)

Buell, Emmett H., and Richard A. Brisbin, *School Desegregation and Defended Neighborhoods: The Boston Controversy* (1982)

Graglia, Lino A., *Disaster by Decree: The Supreme Court, Race and the Schools* (1976)

Mauney, Connie Pat, *Evolving Equality: The Courts and Desegregation in Tennessee* (1979)

Orfield, Gary, *Must We Bus? Segregated Schools and National Policy* (1978)

Peltason, Jack, *Fifty-Eight Lonely Men: Southern Federal Judges and School Desegregation* (1961)

Wilkinson, J. Harve, *From* Brown *to* Bakke*: The Supreme Court and School Desegregation, 1954–1978* (1979)

Wolters, Raymond, *The Burden of* Brown*: Thirty Years of School Desegregation* (1984)

Affirmative Action and Complex Civil Rights

Belz, Herman, *Equality Transformed: A Quarter-Century of Affirmative Action (1991)*

Bergmann, Barbara, *In Defense of Affirmative Action* (1996)

Bok, Derek, and William Bowen, *The Shape of the River: Long Term Consequences of Considering Raced in College and University Admissions* (1998)

Eastland, Terry, *Ending Affirmative Action: The Case for Colorblind Justice* (1996)

——, and William J. Bennett, *Counting by Race: Equality from the Founding Fathers to* Bakke *and* Weber (1979)

Epstein, Richard A., *Forbidden Grounds: The Case Against Employment Discrimination Laws* (1992)

Foster, James C., and Mary C. Segers, et al., *Elusive Equality: Liberalism, Affirmative Action, and Social Change in America* (1983)

Glazer, Nathan, *Affirmative Discrimination* (1976)

Haar, Charles M., *Suburbs under Seige: Race, Space, and Audacious Judges* (1996)

Jones, Augustus J., Jr., *Affirmative Talk, Affirmative Action: A Comparative Study of the Politics of Affirmative Action* (1991)

Livingston, John C., *Fair Game? Inequality and Affirmative Action* (1979)

Moreno, Paul D., *From Direct Action to Affirmative Action: Fair Employment Law and Policy in America, 1933–1972* (1977)

O'Neill, Timothy, Bakke *and the Politics of Equality: Friends and Foes in the Classroom of Litigation* (1985)

O'Neill, Robert M., *Discriminating against Discrimination* (1975)

Peterson, Paul E., ed., *Classifying by Race* (1996)

Roche, George C., III, *The Balancing Act: Quota Hiring in Higher Education* (1974)

Rosenfeld, Michel, *Affirmative Action and Justice: A Philosophical and Constitutional Inquiry* (1991)

Rossum, Ralph A., *Reverse Discrimination: The Constitution Debate* (1980)

Schwartz, Bernard, *Behind* Bakke: *Affirmative Action and the Supreme Court* (1988)

Sindler, Allan P., Bakke, Defunis, *and Minority Admissions* (1978)

Smith, Robert C., *Racism in the Post-Civil Rights Era* (1997)

Sullivan, Charles A., Michael J. Zimmer, and Richard F. Richards, *Federal Statutory Law of Employment Discrimination* (1980

Urofsky, Melvin, *A Conflict of Rights: The Supreme Court and Affirmative Action* (1991)

Wasby, Stephen, *Race Relations Litigation in an Age of Complexity* (1995)

Zimmer, Michael J., et al., *Employment Discrimination: Selected Statutes* (1997)

———, *Cases and Material on Employment Discrimination* (2000)

On Leading Cases

Balkin, Jack M., ed., *What* Brown v. Board of Education *Should Have Said: The Nation's Top Legal Experts Rewrite America's Landmark Civil Rights Decision* (2001)

Ball, Howard, *The Bakke Case: Race, Education, and Affirmative Action* (2000)

Cortner, Richard C., *The "Scottsboro" Case in Mississippi: The Supreme Court and* Brown v. Mississippi (1986)

———, *A Mob Intent on Death: The NAACP and the Arkansas Riot Cases* (1988)

———, *Civil Rights and Public Accommodations: The Heart of Atlanta Motel and McClung Cases* (2001)

Friedman, Leon, ed., *Argument: The Oral Argument Before the Supreme Court in* Board v. Board of Education of Topeka, *1952–1955* (1983)

Kluger, Richard, *Simple Justice: The History of* Brown v. Board of Education *and Black America's Struggle for Total Equality* (1975)

Kluger, Richard, *Simple Justice: The History of* Brown v. Board of Education *and Black America's Struggle for Equality* (1977)

Lofgren, Charles A., *The Plessy Case: A Study in Legal-Historical Interpretation* (1987)

Sarat, Austin, ed., *Race, Law and Culture: Reflections on* Brown v. Board of Education (1996)

Schwartz, Bernard, *Swann's Way: The School Busing Case and the Supreme Court* (1986)

Tushnet, Mark V., Brown v. Board of Education: *The Battle for Integration* (1995)

Vose, Clement, *Caucasians Only: The Supreme Court, the NAACP, and the Restrictive Covenant Cases* (1959)

Wolf, Eleanor P., *Trial and Error: The Detroit School Desegregation Case* (1981)

Additional works are listed in the General and Supplementary Bibliography.

CASES

Plessy v. Ferguson

163 U.S. 537 (1896), 7-1
Opinion of the Court: Brown (Field, Fuller, Gray, Peckham, Shiras, White)
Dissenting: Harlan
Not participating: Brewer

Why did the Fourteenth Amendment not bar racial segregation according to the Court? What doctrinal interpretation did the Court give to the amendment's equal protection clause? What is Justice Harlan's understanding of the equal protection clause? Is his understanding closer than Justice Brown's to the intention of the framers of the amendment? Closer to opinion of the day? How equal were racially segregated facilities likely to be? Might the doctrine of this case have been used to advance racial equality had "but equal" been fully implemented?

Would racial integration then have been dictated by economic necessity rather than moral imperative?

Brown, for the Court:

This case turns upon the constitutionality of an act of the General Assembly of the State of Louisiana, passed in 1890, providing for separate railway carriages for the white and colored races.

The first section of the statute enacts:

> that all railway companies carrying passengers in their coaches in this State shall provide equal but separate accommodations for the white and colored races by providing two or more passenger coaches for each passenger train, or by dividing the passenger coaches by a partition so as to secure separate accommodations: Provided,

That this section shall not be construed to apply to street railroads. No person or persons, shall be admitted to occupy seats in coaches other than the ones assigned to them on account of the race they belong to. . . .

. . . Plessy, being a passenger between two stations within the State of Louisiana, was assigned by officers of the company to the coach used for the race to which he belonged, but he insisted upon going into a coach used by the race to which he did not belong. Neither in the information nor plea was his particular race or color averred. The petition for the writ of prohibition averred that petitioner was seven-eighths Caucasian and one eighth African blood; that the mixture of colored blood was not discernible in him, and that he was entitled to every right, privilege and immunity secured to citizens of the United States of the white race; and that, upon such theory, he took possession of a vacant seat in a coach where passengers of the white race were accommodated, and was ordered by the conductor to vacate said coach and take a seat in another assigned to persons of the colored race, and, having refused to comply with such demand, he was forcibly ejected with the aid of a police officer, and imprisoned in the parish jail to answer a charge of having violated the above act.

The constitutionality of this act is attacked upon the ground that it conflicts both with the Thirteenth Amendment of the Constitution, abolishing slavery, and the Fourteenth Amendment, which prohibits certain restrictive legislation on the part of the States. . . .

The object of the [Fourteenth] amendment was undoubtedly to enforce the absolute equality of the two races before the law, but, in the nature of things, it could not have been intended to abolish distinctions based upon color, or to enforce social, as distinguished from political, equality, or a commingling of the two races upon terms unsatisfactory to either. Laws permitting, and even requiring, their separation in places where they are liable to be brought into contact do not necessarily imply the inferiority of either race to the other, and have been generally, if not universally, recognized as within the competency of the state legislatures in the exercise of their police power. The most common instance of this is connected with the establishment of separate schools for white and colored children, which has been held to be a valid exercise of the legislative power even by courts of States where the political rights of the colored race have been longest and most earnestly enforced.

One of the earliest of these cases is that of *Roberts v. City of Boston,* in which the Supreme Judicial Court of Massachusetts held that the general school committee of Boston had power to make provision for the instruction of colored children in separate schools established exclusively for them, and to prohibit their attendance upon the other schools. . . .

. . . Similar laws have been enacted by Congress under its general power of legislation over the District of Columbia, as well as by the legislatures of many of the States, and have been generally, if not uniformly, sustained by the courts.

Laws forbidding the intermarriage of the two races may be said in a technical sense to interfere with the freedom of contract, and yet have been universally recognized as within the police power of the State.

The distinction between laws interfering with the political equality of the Negro and those requiring the separation of the two races in schools, theatres and railway carriages has been frequently drawn by this court. . . .

In this connection, it is also suggested by the learned counsel for the plaintiff in error that the same argument that will justify the state legislature in requiring railways to provide separate accommodations for the two races will also authorize them to require separate cars to be provided for people whose hair is of a certain color, or who are aliens, or who belong to certain nationalities, or to enact laws requiring colored people to walk upon one side of the street and white people upon the other, or requiring white men's houses to be painted white and colored men's black, or their vehicles or business signs to be of different colors, upon the theory that one side of the street is as good as the other, or that a house or vehicle of one color is as good as one of another color. The reply to all this is that every exercise of the police power must be reasonable, and extend only to such laws as are enacted in good faith for the promotion for the public good, and not for the annoyance or oppression of a particular class. . . .

So far, then, as a conflict with the Fourteenth Amendment is concerned, the case reduces itself to the question whether the statute of Louisiana is a reasonable regulation, and, with respect to this, there must necessarily be a large discretion on the part of the legislature. In determining the question of reasonableness, it is at liberty to act with reference to the established usages, customs, and traditions of the people, and with a view to the promotion of their comfort and the preservation of the public peace and good order. Gauged by this standard, we cannot say that a law which authorizes or even requires the separation of the two races in public conveyances is unreasonable, or more obnoxious to the Fourteenth Amendment than the acts of Congress requiring separate schools for colored children in the District of Columbia, the constitutionality of which does not seem to have been questioned, or the corresponding acts of state legislatures.

We consider the underlying fallacy of the plaintiff's argument to consist in the assumption that the enforced separation of the two races stamps the colored race with a badge of inferiority. If this be so, it is not by reason of anything found in the act, but solely because the colored race chooses to put that construction upon it. The argument necessarily assumes that if, as has been more than once the case and is not unlikely to be so again, the colored race should become the dominant power in the state legislature, and should enact a law in precisely similar terms, it would thereby relegate the white race to an inferior position. We imagine that the white race, at least, would not acquiesce in this assumption. The argument also assumes that social prejudices may be overcome by legislation, and that equal rights cannot be secured to the Negro except by an enforced commingling of the two races. We cannot accept this proposition. If the two races are to meet upon terms of social equality, it must be the result of natural affinities, a mutual appreciation of each other's merits, and a voluntary consent of individuals. . . .

Legislation is powerless to eradicate racial instincts or to abolish distinctions based upon physical differences, and the attempt to do so can only result in accentuating the difficulties of the present situation. If the civil and political rights of both races be equal, one cannot be inferior to the other civilly or politically. If one race be inferior to the other socially, the Constitution of the United States cannot put them upon the same plane. . . .

Harlan, dissenting:

. . . In respect of civil rights common to all citizens, the Constitution of the United States does not, I think, permit any public authority to know the race of those entitled to be protected in the enjoyment of such rights. Every true man has pride of race, and, under appropriate circumstances, when the rights of others, his equals before the law, are not to be affected, it is his privilege to express such pride and to take such action based upon it as to him seems proper. But I deny that any legislative body or judicial tribunal may have regard to the race of citizens when the civil rights of those citizens are involved. Indeed, such legislation as that here in question is inconsistent not only with that equality of rights which pertains to citizenship, National and State, but with the personal liberty enjoyed by everyone within the United States.

The Thirteenth Amendment does not permit the withholding or the deprivation of any right necessarily inhering in freedom. It not only struck down the institution of slavery as previously existing in the United States, but it prevents the imposition of any burdens or disabilities that constitute badges of slavery or servitude. It decreed universal civil freedom in this country. This court has so adjudged. But that amendment having been found inadequate to the protection of the rights of those who had been in slavery, it was followed by the Fourteenth Amendment, which added greatly to the dignity and glory of American citizenship and to the security of personal liberty. . . .

. . . These two amendments, if enforced according to their true intent and meaning, will protect all the civil rights that pertain to freedom and citizenship. Finally, and to the end that no citizen should be denied, on account of his race, the privilege of participating in the political control of his country, it as declared by the Fifteenth Amendment that "the right of citizens of the United States to vote shall not be denied or abridged by the United States or by any State on account of race, color or previous condition of servitude."

These notable additions to the fundamental law were welcomed by the friends of liberty throughout the world. They removed the race line from our governmental systems. They had, as this court has said, a common purpose, namely to secure "to a race recently emancipated, a race that through many generations have been held in slavery, all the civil rights that the superior race enjoy." . . .

. . . If a State can prescribe, as a rule of civil conduct, that whites and blacks shall not travel as passengers in the same railroad coach, why may it not so regulate the use of the streets of its cities and towns as to compel white citizens to keep on one side of a street and black citizens to keep on the other? Why may it not, upon like grounds, punish whites and blacks who ride together in streetcars or in open vehicles on a public road or street? Why may it not require sheriffs to assign whites to one side of a courtroom and blacks to the other? And why may it not also prohibit the commingling of the two races in the galleries of legislative halls or in public assemblages convened for the consideration of the political questions of the day? Further, if this statute of Louisiana is consistent with the personal liberty of citizens, why may not the State require the separation in railroad coaches of native and naturalized citizens of the United States, or of Protestants and Roman Catholics? . . .

The white race deems itself to be the dominant race in this country. And so it is in prestige, in achievements, in education, in wealth and in power. So, I doubt not, it will continue to be for all time if it remains true to its great heritage and holds fast to the principles of constitutional liberty. But in view of the Constitution, in the eye of the law, there is in this country no superior, dominant, ruling class of citizens. There is no caste here. Our Constitution is color-blind, and neither knows nor tolerates classes among citizens. In respect of civil rights, all citizens are equal before the law. The humblest is the peer of the most powerful. The law regards man as man, and takes no account of his surroundings or of his color when his civil rights as guaranteed by the supreme law of the land are involved. It is therefore to be regretted that this high tribunal, the final expositor of the fundamental law of the land, has reached the conclusion that it is competent for a State to regulate the enjoyment by citizens of their civil rights solely upon the basis of race.

In my opinion, the judgment this day rendered will, in time, prove to be quite as pernicious as the decision made by this tribunal in the Dred Scott Case. . . .

I am of opinion that the statute of Louisiana is inconsistent with the personal liberty of citizens, white and black, in that State, and hostile to both the spirit and letter of the Constitution of the United States. If laws of like character should be enacted in the several States of the Union, the effect would be in the highest degree mischievous. Slavery, as an institution tolerated by law would, it is true, have disappeared from our country, but there would remain a power in the States, by sinister legislation, to interfere with the full enjoyment of the blessings of freedom to regulate civil rights, common to all citizens, upon the basis of race, and to place in a condition of legal inferiority a large body of American citizens now constituting a part of the political community called the People of the United States, for whom and by whom, through representatives, our government is administered. Such a system is inconsistent with the guarantee given by the Constitution to each State of a republican form

of government, and may be stricken down by Congressional action, or by the courts in the discharge of their solemn duty to maintain the supreme law of the land, anything in the constitution or laws of any State to the contrary notwithstanding. . . .

Shelley v. Kraemer

334 U.S. 1 (1948), 6-0
Opinion of the Court: Vinson (Black, Burton, Douglas, Frankfurter, Murphy)
Not participating: Jackson, Reed, Rutledge

Why was a finding of state action necessary to this decision? In addition to making contracts, what other kinds of private acts or actions depend for their effect on state support, tacit or otherwise, or at least on state toleration? Can state inaction—for example, failure to ban private discrimination—be considered "state action"? Would this obliterate the distinction between public and private action? How can this case be reconciled with Plessy v. Ferguson *(p. 467)?*

Vinson, for the Court:

. . . [In] 1911, thirty out of a total of thirty-nine owners of property fronting both sides of Labadie Avenue between Taylor Avenue and Cora Avenue in the city of St. Louis, signed an agreement, which was subsequently recorded, providing in part:

> . . . the said property is hereby restricted to the use and occupancy for the term of Fifty years from this date, so that it shall be a condition all the time and whether recited and referred to as [sic] not in subsequent conveyances and shall attach to the land as a condition precedent to the sale of the same, that hereafter no part of said property or any portion thereof shall be, for said term of Fifty-years, occupied by any person not of the Caucasian race, it being intended hereby to restrict the use of said property for said period of time against the occupancy as owners or tenants of any portion of said property for resident or other purpose by people of the Negro or Mongolian Race. . . .

On August 11, 1945 . . . petitioners Shelley, who are Negroes, [bought one of] the parcel[s] in question. The trial court found that petitioners had no actual knowledge of the restrictive agreement at the time of the purchase.

Charles H. Houston, former chief counsel for the National Association for the Advancement of Colored People, successfully argued the case against restrictive covenants before the Supreme Court. As dean of the Howard University Law School, he trained many civil rights lawyers, including his successor at the NAACP, Thurgood Marshall, who was co-counsel in *Shelley v. Kraemer.*

On October 9, 1945, respondents, as owners of other property subject to the terms of the restrictive covenant, brought suit in the Circuit Court of the city of St. Louis praying that petitioners Shelley be restrained from taking possession of the property and that judgment be entered divesting title out of petitioners Shelley and revesting title in the immediate grantor or in such other person as the court should direct. The trial court denied the requested relief on the ground that the restrictive agreement, upon which respondents based their action, had never become final and complete because it was the intention of the parties to that agreement that it was not to become effective until signed by all property owners in the district, and signatures of all the owners had never been obtained.

The Supreme Court of Missouri, sitting en banc, reversed and directed the trial court to grant the relief for which respondents had prayed. That court held the agreement effective and concluded that enforcement of its provisions violated no rights guaranteed to petitioners by the Federal Constitution. . . .

Whether the equal protection clause of the Fourteenth Amendment inhibits judicial enforcement by state courts of restrictive covenants based on race or color is a question which this Court has not heretofore been called upon to consider. . . .

It cannot be doubted that among the civil rights intended to be protected from discriminatory state action by the Fourteenth Amendment are the rights to acquire, enjoy, own and dispose of property . . . Thus . . . the Civil Rights Act of 1866 which was enacted by Congress while the Fourteenth Amendment was also under consideration, provides: "All citizens of the United States shall have the same right, in every State and Territory, as is enjoyed by white citizens thereof to inherit, purchase, lease, sell, hold, and convey real and personal property."

This Court has given specific recognition to the same principle.

It is likewise clear that restrictions on the right of occupancy of the sort sought to be created by the private agreements in these cases could not be squared with the requirements of the Fourteenth Amendment if imposed by state statute or local ordinance. We do not understand respondents to urge the contrary. In the case of *Buchanan v. Warley,* a unanimous Court declared unconstitutional the provisions of a city ordinance which denied to colored persons the right to occupy houses in blocks in which the greater number of houses were occupied by white persons, and imposed similar restrictions on white persons with respect to blocks in which the greater number of houses were occupied by colored persons. During the course of the opinion in that case, this Court stated: "The Fourteenth Amendment and these statutes enacted in furtherance of its purpose operate to qualify and entitle a colored man to acquire property without state legislation discriminating against him solely because of color." . . .

Since the decision of this Court in the Civil Rights Cases, the principle has become firmly embedded in our constitutional law that the action inhibited by the first section of the Fourteenth Amendment is only such action as may fairly be said to be that of the States. That Amendment erects no shield against merely private conduct, however discriminatory or wrongful.

We conclude, therefore, that the restrictive agreements, standing alone, cannot be regarded as violative of any rights guaranteed to petitioners by the Fourteenth Amendment. So long as the purposes of those agreements are effectuated by voluntary adherence to their terms, it would appear clear that there has been no action by the State, and the provisions of the Amendment have not been violated.

But here there was more. These are cases in which the purposes of the agreements were secured only by judicial enforcement by state courts of the restrictive terms of the agreements. . . .

That the action of state courts and judicial officers in their official capacities is to be regarded as action of the State within the meaning of the Fourteenth Amendment is a proposition which has long been established . . . That principle was given expression in the earliest cases involving the construction of the terms of the Fourteenth Amendment. Thus, in *Virginia v. Rives,* this Court stated: "It is doubtless true that a State may act through different agencies, either by its legislative, its executive, or its judicial authorities, and the prohibitions of the amendment extend to all action of the State denying equal protection of the laws, whether it be action by one of these agencies or by another." . . .

But the examples of state judicial action which have been held by this Court to violate the Amendment's commands are not restricted to situations in which the judicial proceedings were found in some manner to be procedurally unfair. It has been recognized that the action of state courts in enforcing a substantive common law rule formulated by those courts, may result in the denial of rights guaranteed by the Fourteenth Amendment, even though the judicial proceedings in such cases may have been in complete accord with the most rigorous conceptions of procedural due process. . . .

Against this background of judicial construction, extending over a period of some three-quarters of a century, we are called upon to consider whether enforcement by state courts of the restrictive agreements in these cases may be deemed to be the acts of those States, and, if so, whether that action has denied these petitioners the equal protection of the laws which the Amendment was intended to insure.

We have no doubt that there has been state action in these cases in the full and complete sense of the phrase. The undisputed facts disclose that petitioners were willing purchasers of properties upon which they desired to establish homes. The owners of the properties were willing sellers, and contracts of sale were accordingly consummated. It is clear that, but for the active intervention of the state courts, supported by the full panoply of state power, petitioners would have been free to occupy the properties in question without restraint.

These are not cases, as has been suggested, in which the States have merely abstained from action, leaving private individuals free to impose such discriminations as they see fit. Rather, these are cases in which the States have made available to such individuals the full coercive power of government to deny to petitioners, on the grounds of race or color, the enjoyment of property rights in premises which petitioners are willing and financially able to acquire and which the grantors are willing to sell. . . .

The enforcement of the restrictive agreements by the state courts in these cases was directed pursuant to the common law policy of the States as formulated by those courts in earlier decisions. In the Missouri case, enforcement of the covenant was directed in the first instance by the highest court of the State after the trial court had determined the agreement to be invalid for want of the requisite number of signatures. In the Michigan case, the order of enforcement by the trial court was affirmed by the highest state court. The judicial action in each case bears the clear and unmistakable imprimatur of the State. We have noted that previous decisions of this Court have established the proposition that judicial action is not immunized from the operation of the Fourteenth Amendment simply because it is taken pursuant to the state's common law policy. . . .

. . . We have noted that freedom from discrimination by the States in the enjoyment of property rights was among the basic objectives sought to be effectuated by the framers of the Fourteenth Amendment. That such discrimination has occurred in these cases is clear. . . .

Respondents urge, however, that, since the state courts stand ready to enforce restrictive covenants excluding white persons from the ownership or occupancy of property covered by such agreements, enforcement of covenants excluding colored persons may not be deemed a denial of equal protection of the laws to the colored persons who are thereby affected. This contention does not bear scrutiny.... The rights created by the first section of the Fourteenth Amendment are, by its terms, guaranteed to the individual. The rights established are personal rights. It is, therefore, no answer to these petitioners to say that the courts may also be induced to deny white persons rights of ownership and occupancy on grounds of race or color. Equal protection of the laws is not achieved through indiscriminate imposition of inequalities....

The historical context in which the Fourteenth Amendment became a part of the Constitution should not be forgotten. Whatever else the framers sought to achieve, it is clear that the matter of primary concern was the establishment of equality in the enjoyment of basic civil and political rights and the preservation of those rights from discriminatory action on the part of the States based on considerations of race or color. Seventy-five years ago, this Court announced that the provisions of the Amendment are to be construed with this fundamental purpose in mind. Upon full consideration, we have concluded that, in these cases, the States have acted to deny petitioners the equal protection of the laws guaranteed by the Fourteenth Amendment. Having so decided, we find it unnecessary to consider whether petitioners have also been deprived of property without due process of law or denied privileges and immunities of citizens of the United States....

Brown v. Board of Education of Topeka (I)

347 U.S. 483 (1954), 9-0

Opinion of the Court: Warren (Black, Burton, Clark, Douglas, Franfurter, Jackson, Minton, Reed)

Under the title of Brown, the Court heard and decided four cases challenging racial segregation in the public schools in Kansas, South Carolina, Virginia, and Delaware.

Does the Court's decision rest on any legal or constitutional precedent or is it an entire break with precedent? What psychological assumptions underlie the decision? What specific questions are left for later resolution? If the social science studies Chief Justice Warren cites to support the decision were shown to be methodologically flawed or their conclusions unfounded, how much would that damage the decision? Should he have tried to develop a broader justification than one based on educational opportunity and self-esteem before making an important reinterpretation of one of the Constitution's premier clauses? Might he have profitably borrowed here from Harlan's dissent in Plessy v. Ferguson (p. 467)? Is he unwittingly condescending toward black schools and black teachers in assuming that the education of black students can improve only through contact with white students? Is the goal of a fully integrated society that seems to underlie the decision as valid today as it seemed in 1954?

Warren, for the Court:

... In each of the cases, minors of the Negro race, through their legal representatives, seek the aid of the courts in obtaining admission to the public schools of their community on a nonsegregated basis. In each instance, they had been denied admission to schools attended by white children under laws requiring or permitting segregation according to race. This segregation was alleged to deprive the plaintiffs of the equal protection of the laws under the Fourteenth Amendment. In each of the cases other than the Delaware case, a three-judge federal district court denied relief to the plaintiffs on the so-called "separate but equal" doctrine announced by this Court in *Plessy v. Fergson.* Under that doctrine, equality of treatment is accorded when the races are provided substantially equal facilities, even though these facilities be separate. In the Delaware case, the Supreme Court of Delaware adhered to that doctrine, but ordered that the plaintiffs be admitted to the white schools because of their superiority to the Negro schools.

The plaintiffs contend that segregated public schools are not "equal" and cannot be made "equal," and that hence they are deprived of the equal protection of the laws. Because of the obvious importance of the question presented, the Court took jurisdiction. Argument was heard in the 1952 Term, and reargument was heard this Term on certain questions propounded by the Court.

Reargument was largely devoted to the circumstances surrounding the adoption of the Fourteenth Amendment in 1868. It covered exhaustively consideration of the Amendment in Congress, ratification by the states, then-existing practices in racial segregation, and the views of proponents and opponents of the Amendment. This discussion and our own investigation convince us that, although these sources cast some light, it is not enough to resolve the problem with which we are faced. At best, they are inconclusive. The most avid proponents of the post-War Amendments undoubtedly intended them to remove all legal distinctions among "all persons born or naturalized in the United States." Their opponents, just as certainly, were antagonistic to both the letter and the spirit of the Amendments and wished them to have the most limited effect. What others in Congress and the state legislatures had in mind cannot be determined with any degree of certainty.

An additional reason for the inconclusive nature of the Amendment's history with respect to segregated schools is the status of public education at that time. In the South, the movement toward free common schools, supported by general taxation, had not yet taken hold. Education of white children was largely in the hands of private groups. Education of Negroes was almost nonexistent, and practically all of the race were illiterate. In fact, any education of Negroes was forbidden by law in some states. Today, in contrast, many Negroes have achieved outstanding success in the arts and sciences, as well as in the business and professional world. It is true that public school education at the time of the Amendment had advanced further in the North, but the effect of the Amendment on Northern States was generally ignored in the congressional debates. Even in the North, the conditions of public education did not approximate those existing today. The curriculum was usually rudimentary; ungraded schools were common in rural areas; the school term was but three months a year in many states, and compulsory school attendance was virtually unknown. As a consequence, it is not surprising that there should be so little in the history of the Fourteenth Amendment relating to its intended effect on public education.

In the first cases in this Court construing the Fourteenth Amendment, decided shortly after its adoption, the Court interpreted it as proscribing all state-imposed discriminations against the Negro race. The doctrine of "separate but equal" did not make its appearance in this Court until 1896 in the case of *Plessy v. Ferguson*, involving not education but transportation. American courts have since labored with the doctrine for over half a century. In this Court, there have been six cases involving the "separate but equal" doctrine in the field of public education. In *Cumming v. County Board of Education* and *Gong Lum v. Rice*, the validity of the doctrine itself was not challenged. In more recent cases, all on the graduate

school level, inequality was found in that specific benefits enjoyed by white students were denied to Negro students of the same educational qualifications. *Missouri ex rel. Gaines v. Canada, Sipuel v. Oklahoma, Sweatt v. Painter, McLaurin v. Oklahoma State Regents*. In none of these cases was it necessary to reexamine the doctrine to grant relief to the Negro plaintiff. And in *Sweatt v. Painter*, the Court expressly reserved decision on the question whether *Plessy v. Ferguson* should be held inapplicable to public education.

In the instant cases, that question is directly presented. Here, unlike *Sweatt v. Painter*, there are findings below that the Negro and white schools involved have been equalized, or are being equalized, with respect to buildings, curricula, qualifications and salaries of teachers, and other "tangible" factors. Our decision, therefore, cannot turn on merely a comparison of these tangible factors in the Negro and white schools involved in each of the cases. We must look instead to the effect of segregation itself on public education.

In approaching this problem, we cannot turn the clock back to 1868, when the Amendment was adopted, or even to 1896, when *Plessy v. Ferguson* was written. We must consider public education in the light of its full development and its present place in American life throughout the Nation. Only in this way can it be determined if segregation in public schools deprives these plaintiffs of the equal protection of the laws.

Today, education is perhaps the most important function of state and local governments. Compulsory school attendance laws and the great expenditures for education both demonstrate our recognition of the importance of education to our democratic society. It is required in the performance of our most basic public responsibilities, even service in the armed forces. It is the very foundation of good citizenship. Today it is a principal instrument in awakening the child to cultural values, in preparing him for later professional training, and in helping him to adjust normally to his environment. In these days, it is doubtful that any child may reasonably be expected to succeed in life if he is denied the opportunity of an education. Such an opportunity, where the state has undertaken to provide it, is a right which must be made available to all on equal terms.

We come then to the question presented: Does segregation of children in public schools solely on the basis of race, even though the physical facilities and other "tangible" factors may be equal, deprive the children of the minority group of equal educational opportunities? We believe that it does.

In *Sweatt v. Painter* in finding that a segregated law school for Negroes could not provide them equal educational opportunities, this Court relied in large part on "those qualities which are incapable of objective measurement but which make for greatness in a law school." In *McLaurin v. Oklahoma State Regents*, the Court, in requiring that a Negro admitted to a white graduate school be treated like all other students, again resorted to intangible considerations:" . . . his ability to study, to engage in discussions and exchange views with other students, and, in general, to learn his profession." Such considerations apply with added force to children in grade and high schools. To separate them from others of similar age and qualifications solely because of their race generates a feeling of inferiority as to their status in the community that may affect their hearts and minds in a way unlikely ever to be undone. The effect of this separation on their educational opportunities was well stated by a finding in the Kansas case by a court which nevertheless felt compelled to rule against the Negro plaintiffs:

Segregation of white and colored children in public schools has a detrimental effect upon the colored children. The impact is greater when it has the sanction of the law, for the policy of separating the races is usually interpreted as denoting the inferiority of the Negro group. A sense of inferiority affects the motivation of a child to learn. Segregation with the sanction of law, therefore, has a tendency to [retard] the educational and mental development of Negro children and to deprive them of some of the benefits they would receive in a racial[ly] integrated school system.

Whatever may have been the extent of psychological knowledge at the time of *Plessy v. Ferguson*, this finding is amply supported by modern authority. Any language in *Plessy v. Ferguson* contrary to this finding is rejected.

We conclude that, in the field of public education, the doctrine of "separate but equal" has no place. Separate educational facilities are inherently unequal. Therefore, we hold that the plaintiffs and others similarly situated for whom the actions have been brought are, by reason of the segregation complained of, deprived of the equal protection of the laws guaranteed by the Fourteenth Amendment. This disposition makes unnecessary any discussion whether such segregation also violates the Due Process Clause of the Fourteenth Amendment.

Because these are class actions, because of the wide applicability of this decision, and because of the great variety of local conditions, the formulation of decrees in these cases presents problems of considerable complexity. On reargument, the consideration of appropriate relief was necessarily subordinated to the primary question—the constitutionality of segregation in public education. We have now announced that such segregation is a denial of the equal protection of the laws. In order that we may have the full assistance of the parties in formulating decrees, the cases will be restored to the docket, and the parties are requested to present further argument on Questions 4 and 5 previously propounded by the Court for the reargument this Term. The Attorney General of the United States is again invited to participate. The Attorneys General of the states requiring or permitting segregation in public education will also be permitted to appear as amici curiae upon request to do so by September 15, 1954, and submission of briefs by October 1, 1954.

Brown v. Board of Education of Topeka II

349 U.S. 294 (1955), 9-0
Opinion of the Court: Warren (Black, Burton, Clark, Douglas, Frankfurter, Harlan, Minton, Reed)

Why did the Court defer the question of implementation of its ruling in Brown I? *Was it a sound strategy? A partial retreat from* Brown I? *Is "with all deliberate speed" essentially a general statement and exhortation or does the Court give it more specific meaning? Are not most, if not all, court decisions, especially those of the Supreme Court, expected to be implement with all deliberate speed? Who gains and loses by this decision?*

Warren, for the Court:

These cases were decided on May 17, 1954. The opinions of that date, declaring the fundamental principle that racial discrimination in public education is unconstitutional, are incorporated herein by reference. All provisions of federal, state, or local law requiring or permitting such discrimination must yield to this principle. There remains for consideration the manner in which relief is to be accorded.

Because these cases arose under different local conditions and their disposition will involve a variety of local problems, we requested further argument on the question of relief. In view of the nationwide importance of the decision, we invited the Attorney General of the United States and the Attorneys General of all states requiring or permitting racial discrimination in public education to present their views on that question. The parties, the United States, and the States of Florida, North Carolina, Arkansas, Oklahoma, Maryland, and Texas filed briefs and participated in the oral argument.

These presentations were informative and helpful to the Court in its consideration of the complexities arising from the transition to a system of public education freed of racial discrimination. The presentations also demonstrated that substantial steps to eliminate racial discrimination in public schools have already been taken, not only in some of the communities in which these cases arose, but in some of the states appearing as amici curiae, and in other states as well. Substantial progress has been made in the District of Columbia and in the communities in Kansas and Delaware involved in this litigation. The defendants in the cases coming to us from South Carolina and Virginia are awaiting the decision of this Court concerning relief.

Full implementation of these constitutional principles may require solution of varied local school problems. School authorities have the primary responsibility for elucidating, assessing, and solving these problems; courts will have to consider whether the action of school authorities constitutes good faith implementation of the governing constitutional principles. Because of their proximity to local conditions and the possible need for further hearings, the courts which originally heard these cases can best perform this judicial appraisal. Accordingly, we believe it appropriate to remand the cases to those courts. In fashioning and effectuating the decrees, the courts will be guided by equitable principles. Traditionally, equity has been characterized by a practical flexibility in shaping its remedies and by a facility for adjusting and reconciling public and private needs. These cases call for the exercise of these traditional attributes of equity power. At stake is the personal interest of the plaintiffs in admission to public schools as soon as practicable on a nondiscriminatory basis. To effectuate this interest may call for elimination of a variety of obstacles in making the transition to school systems operated in accordance with the constitutional principles set forth in our May 17, 1954, decision. Courts of equity may properly take into account the public interest in the elimination of such obstacles in a systematic and effective manner. But it should go without saying that the vitality of these consti-

tutional principles cannot be allowed to yield simply because of disagreement with them.

While giving weight to these public and private considerations, the courts will require that the defendants make a prompt and reasonable start toward full compliance with our May 17, 1954, ruling. Once such a start has been made, the courts may find that additional time is necessary to carry out the ruling in an effective manner. The burden rests upon the defendants to establish that such time is necessary in the public interest and is consistent with good faith compliance at the earliest practicable date. To that end, the courts may consider problems related to administration, arising from the physical condition of the school plant, the school transportation system, personnel, revision of school districts and attendance areas into compact units to achieve a system of determining admission to the public schools on a nonracial basis, and revision of local laws and regulations which may be necessary in solving the foregoing problems. They will also consider the adequacy of any plans the defendants may propose to meet these problems and to effectuate a transition to a racially nondiscriminatory school system. During this period of transition, the courts will retain jurisdiction of these cases.

The judgments below, except that, in the Delaware case, are accordingly reversed, and the cases are remanded to the District Courts to take such proceedings and enter such orders and decrees consistent with this opinion as are necessary and proper to admit to public schools on a racially nondiscriminatory basis with all deliberate speed the parties to these cases. The judgment in the Delaware case—ordering the immediate admission of the plaintiffs to schools previously attended only by white children—is affirmed on the basis of the principles stated in our May 17, 1954, opinion, but the case is remanded to the Supreme Court of Delaware for such further proceedings as that Court may deem necessary in light of this opinion.

Cooper v. Aaron

358 U.S. 1 (1958), 9-0

Opinion of the Court: Warren, Black, Brennan, Burton, Clark, Douglas, Frankfurter, Harlan, Whittaker

Under the Little Rock School Board's plan to desegregate the city's public schools one grade a year, nine black high school seniors, the respondents in this case, were admitted to the pre-

viously all-white Central High School in September 1957. Opposition of the Arkansas governor, legislature, and local authorities, as well as threats of mob violence, kept the black students from attending school until President Eisenhower sent federal troops to the high school campus and surrounding neighborhood to maintain order. The troops were kept in place for the entire school year. In June 1958, after finding that these events had produced "tensions, bedlam, chaos and turmoil in the school," a federal district court granted the school board's request that desegregation be suspended for two-and-a-half years. The Eighth Circuit Court of Appeals reversed this ruling and the school board appealed to the U.S. Supreme Court. The justices returned from their summer vacation in August to hear and decide the case before the new school year began. On September 12, the Court issued a per curiam opinion, affirming the Court of Appeals. The fuller opinion was written later when the Court began its October term. To emphasize the importance of the issue in this case, the justices took the unusual step of each signing the Court's opinion individually.

What argument is made for a delay in implementing the school desegregation plan? Was it a reasonable one? What would have been the effect of the Court granting a delay? The Court says "the controlling legal precedents are plain." What are they? Why did the Court cite Marbury v. Madison? Who gains and who loses as a result of this decision?

For the Court, Warran, Black, Brennan, Burton, Clark, Douglas, Frankfurter, Harlan, Whittaker:

. . . In affirming the judgment of the Court of Appeals which reversed the District Court, we have accepted without reservation the position of the School Board, the Superintendent of Schools, and their counsel that they displayed entire good faith in the conduct of these proceedings and in dealing with the unfortunate and distressing sequence of events which has been outlined. We likewise have accepted the findings of the District Court as to the conditions at Central High School during the 1957–1958 school year, and also the findings that the educational progress of all the students, white and colored, of that school has suffered, and will continue to suffer if the conditions which prevailed last year are permitted to continue.

The significance of these findings, however, is to be considered in light of the fact, indisputably revealed by the record before us, that the conditions they depict are directly traceable to the actions of legislators and executive officials of the State of Arkansas, taken in their official capacities, which reflect their own determination to resist this Court's decision in the

Brown case and which have brought about violent resistance to that decision in Arkansas. In its petition for certiorari filed in this Court, the School Board itself describes the situation in this language: "The legislative, executive, and judicial departments of the state government opposed the desegregation of Little Rock schools by enacting laws, calling out troops, making statements villifying federal law and federal courts, and failing to utilize state law enforcement agencies and judicial processes to maintain public peace."

One may well sympathize with the position of the Board in the face of the frustrating conditions which have confronted it, but, regardless of the Board's good faith, the actions of the other state agencies responsible for those conditions compel us to reject the Board's legal position. Had Central High School been under the direct management of the State itself, it could hardly be suggested that those immediately in charge of the school should be heard to assert their own good faith as a legal excuse for delay in implementing the constitutional rights of these respondents, when vindication of those rights was rendered difficult or impossible by the actions of other state officials. The situation here is in no different posture because the members of the School Board and the Superintendent of Schools are local officials; from the point of view of the Fourteenth Amendment, they stand in this litigation as the agents of the State.

The constitutional rights of respondents are not to be sacrificed or yielded to the violence and disorder which have followed upon the actions of the Governor and Legislature. As this Court said some 41 years ago in a unanimous opinion in a case involving another aspect of racial segregation: "It is urged that this proposed segregation will promote the public peace by preventing race conflicts. Desirable as this is, and important as is the preservation of the public peace, this aim cannot be accomplished by laws or ordinances which deny rights created or protected by the federal Constitution." *Buchanan v. Warley* Thus, law and order are not here to be preserved by depriving the Negro children of their constitutional rights. The record before us clearly establishes that the growth of the Board's difficulties to a magnitude beyond its unaided power to control is the product of state action. Those difficulties, as counsel for the Board forthrightly conceded on the oral argument in this Court, can also be brought under control by state action.

The controlling legal principles are plain. The command of the Fourteenth Amendment is that no

"State" shall deny to any person within its jurisdiction the equal protection of the laws.

A State acts by its legislative, its executive, or its judicial authorities. It can act in no other way. The constitutional provision, therefore, must mean that no agency of the State, or of the officers or agents by whom its powers are exerted, shall deny to any person within its jurisdiction the equal protection of the laws. Whoever, by virtue of public position under a State government, . . . denies or takes away the equal protection of the laws violates the constitutional inhibition; and, as he acts in the name and for the State, and is clothed with the State's power, his act is that of the State. This must be so, or the constitutional prohibition has no meaning. *Ex parte Virginia*

Thus, the prohibitions of the Fourteenth Amendment extend to all action of the State denying equal protection of the laws; whatever the agency of the State taking the action, or whatever the guise in which it is taken. In short, the constitutional rights of children not to be discriminated against in school admission on grounds of race or color declared by this Court in the Brown case can neither be nullified openly and directly by state legislators or state executive or judicial officers nor nullified indirectly by them through evasive schemes for segregation whether attempted "ingeniously or ingenuously."

What has been said, in the light of the facts developed, is enough to dispose of the case. However, we should answer the premise of the actions of the Governor and Legislature that they are not bound by our holding in the Brown case. It is necessary only to recall some basic constitutional propositions which are settled doctrine.

Article VI of the Constitution makes the Constitution the "supreme Law of the Land." In 1803, Chief Justice Marshall, speaking for a unanimous Court, referring to the Constitution as "the fundamental and paramount law of the nation," declared in the notable case of *Marbury v. Madison* that "It is emphatically the province and duty of the judicial department to say what the law is." This decision declared the basic principle that the federal judiciary is supreme in the exposition of the law of the Constitution, and that principle has ever since been respected by this Court and the Country as a permanent and indispensable feature of our constitutional system. It follows that the interpretation of the Fourteenth Amendment enunciated by this Court in the Brown case is the supreme law of the land, and Art. VI of the Constitution makes it of binding effect on the States "any Thing in the Constitution or Laws of any State to the Contrary notwithstanding." Every state legislator and executive and judicial officer is solemnly committed by oath taken pursuant to Art. VI, cl. 3 "to support this Constitution." Chief Justice Taney, speaking for a unanimous Court in 1859, said that this requirement reflected the framers' "anxiety to preserve it [the Constitution] in full force, in all its powers, and to guard against resistance to or evasion of its authority, on the part of a State. . . ." *Ableman v. Booth*

No state legislator or executive or judicial officer can war against the Constitution without violating his undertaking to support it. Chief Justice Marshall spoke for a unanimous Court in saying that: "If the legislatures of the several states may at will, annul the judgments of the courts of the United States, and destroy the rights acquired under those judgments, the constitution itself becomes a solemn mockery. . . ." A Governor who asserts a power to nullify a federal court order is similarly restrained. If he had such power, said Chief Justice Hughes, in 1932, also for a unanimous Court, "it is manifest that the fiat of a state Governor, and not the Constitution of the United States, would be the supreme law of the land; that the restrictions of the Federal Constitution upon the exercise of state power would be but impotent phrases. . . ." *Sterling v. Constantin*

It is, of course, quite true that the responsibility for public education is primarily the concern of the States, but it is equally true that such responsibilities, like all other state activity, must be exercised consistently with federal constitutional requirements as they apply to state action. The Constitution created a government dedicated to equal justice under law. The Fourteenth Amendment embodied and emphasized that ideal. State support of segregated schools through any arrangement, management, funds, or property cannot be squared with the Amendment's command that no State shall deny to any person within its jurisdiction the equal protection of the laws. The right of a student not to be segregated on racial grounds in schools so maintained is indeed so fundamental and pervasive that it is embraced in the concept of due process of law. The basic decision in Brown was unanimously reached by this Court only after the case had been briefed and twice argued and the issues had been given the most serious consideration. Since the first Brown opinion, three new Justices have come to the Court. They are at one with the Justices still on the Court who participated in that basic decision as to its correctness, and that decision is now unanimously reaffirmed. The principles announced in that decision and the obedience of the States to them, according to the command of the Constitution, are indispensable for the protection of the freedoms guaranteed by our fundamental charter for all of us. Our constitutional ideal of equal justice under law is thus made a living truth.

Frankfurter, concurring:
While unreservedly participating with my brethren in our joint opinion, I deem it appropriate also to deal individually with the great issue here at stake. . . .

> The conception of a government by laws dominated the thoughts of those who founded this Nation and designed its Constitution, although they knew as well as the belittlers of the conception that laws have to be made, interpreted and enforced by men. To that end, they set apart a body of men who were to be the depositories of law, who, by their disciplined training and character and by withdrawal from the usual temptations of private interest, may reasonably be expected to be "as free, impartial, and independent as the lot of humanity will admit." So strongly were the framers of the Constitution bent on securing a reign of law that they endowed the judicial office with extraordinary safeguards and prestige. No one, no matter how exalted his public office or how righteous his private motive, can be judge in his own case. That is what courts are for. *United States v. United Mine Workers* (concurring opinion)

The duty to abstain from resistance to "the supreme Law of the Land," U.S. Const., Art. VI, §2, as declared by the organ of our Government for ascertaining it, does not require immediate approval of it, nor does it deny the right of dissent. Criticism need not be stilled. Active obstruction or defiance is barred. Our kind of society cannot endure if the controlling authority of the Law as derived from the Constitution is not to be the tribunal specially charged with the duty of ascertaining and declaring what is "the supreme Law of the Land." Particularly is this so where the declaration of what "the supreme Law" commands on an underlying moral issue is not the dubious pronouncement of a gravely divided Court,

but is the unanimous conclusion of a long-matured deliberative process. The Constitution is not the formulation of the merely personal views of the members of this Court, nor can its authority be reduced to the claim that state officials are its controlling interpreters. Local customs, however hardened by time, are not decreed in heaven. Habits and feelings they engender may be counteracted and moderated. Experience attests that such local habits and feelings will yield, gradually though this be, to law and education. And educational influences are exerted not only by explicit teaching. They vigorously flow from the fruitful exercise of the responsibility of those charged with political official power, and from the almost unconsciously transforming actualities of living under law. . . .

Loving v. Virginia

388 U.S. 1 (1967), 9-0
Opinion of the Court: Warren (Black, Brennan, Clark, Douglas, Fortas, Harlan, Stewart, White)

What did the Virginia law prohibit? On what grounds did Virginia deny there was a violation of equal protection or that the law racially discriminatory? What state interest is asserted? Why did the Court find the law unconstitutional?

Warren, for the Court:
This case presents a constitutional question never addressed by this Court: whether a statutory scheme adopted by the State of Virginia to prevent marriages between persons solely on the basis of racial classifications violates the Equal Protection and Due Process Clauses of the Fourteenth Amendment. . . .

In June, 1958, two residents of Virginia, Mildred Jeter, a Negro woman, and Richard Loving, a white man, were married in the District of Columbia pursuant to its laws. Shortly after their marriage, the Lovings returned to Virginia and established their marital abode in Caroline County. At the October Term, 1958, of the Circuit Court of Caroline County, a grand jury issued an indictment charging the Lovings with violating Virginia's ban on interracial marriages. On January 6, 1959, the Lovings pleaded guilty to the charge, and were sentenced to one year in jail; however, the trial judge suspended the sentence for a period of 25 years on the condition that the Lovings leave the State and not return to Virginia together for 25 years. . . .

After their convictions, the Lovings took up residence in the District of Columbia. On November 6, 1963, they filed a motion in the state trial court to vacate the judgment and set aside the sentence on the ground that the statutes which they had violated were repugnant to the Fourteenth Amendment....

The two statutes under which appellants were convicted and sentenced are part of a comprehensive statutory scheme aimed at prohibiting and punishing interracial marriages. The Lovings were convicted of violating §258 of the Virginia Code:

> Leaving State to evade law.—If any white person and colored person shall go out of this State, for the purpose of being married, and with the intention of returning, and be married out of it, and afterwards return to and reside in it, cohabiting as man and wife, they shall be punished as provided in §20-59, and the marriage shall be governed by the same law as if it had been solemnized in this State. The fact of their cohabitation here as man and wife shall be evidence of their marriage.
>
> Section 259, which defines the penalty for miscegenation, provides:
>
> Punishment for marriage.—If any white person intermarry with a colored person, or any colored person intermarry with a white person, he shall be guilty of a felony and shall be punished by confinement in the penitentiary for not less than one nor more than five years....

In upholding the constitutionality of these provisions in the decision below, the Supreme Court of Appeals of Virginia referred to its 1965 decision in *Naim v. Naim* ... that the State's legitimate purposes were "to preserve the racial integrity of its citizens," and to prevent "the corruption of blood," "a mongrel breed of citizens," and "the obliteration of racial pride," obviously an endorsement of the doctrine of White Supremacy. The court also reasoned that marriage has traditionally been subject to state regulation without federal intervention, and, consequently, the regulation of marriage should be left to exclusive state control by the Tenth Amendment.

While the state court is no doubt correct in asserting that marriage is a social relation subject to the State's police power, the State does not contend in its argument before this Court that its powers to regulate marriage are unlimited notwithstanding the commands of the Fourteenth Amendment....

Because we reject the notion that the mere "equal application" of a statute containing racial classifications is enough to remove the classifications from the Fourteenth Amendment's proscription of all invidious racial discriminations, we do not accept the State's contention that these statutes should be upheld if there is any possible basis for concluding that they serve a rational purpose. The mere fact of equal application does not mean that our analysis of these statutes should follow the approach we have taken in cases involving no racial discrimination.... In these cases, involving distinctions not drawn according to race, the Court has merely asked whether there is any rational foundation for the discriminations, and has deferred to the wisdom of the state legislatures. In the case at bar, however, we deal with statutes containing racial classifications, and the fact of equal application does not immunize the statute from the very heavy burden of justification which the Fourteenth Amendment has traditionally required of state statutes drawn according to race....

... We have rejected the proposition that the debates in the Thirty-ninth Congress or in the state legislatures which ratified the Fourteenth Amendment supported the theory advanced by the State, that the requirement of equal protection of the laws is satisfied by penal laws defining offenses based on racial classifications so long as white and Negro participants in the offense were similarly punished....

There can be no question but that Virginia's miscegenation statutes rest solely upon distinctions drawn according to race. The statutes proscribe generally accepted conduct if engaged in by members of different races. Over the years, this Court has consistently repudiated "[d]istinctions between citizens solely because of their ancestry" as being "odious to a free people whose institutions are founded upon the doctrine of equality." At the very least, the Equal Protection Clause demands that racial classifications, especially suspect in criminal statutes, be subjected to the "most rigid scrutiny," and, if they are ever to be upheld, they must be shown to be necessary to the accomplishment of some permissible state objective, independent of the racial discrimination which it was the object of the Fourteenth Amendment to eliminate. Indeed, two members of this Court have already stated that they "cannot conceive of a valid legislative purpose ... which makes the color of a person's skin the test of whether his conduct is a criminal offense." *McLaughlin v. Florida,* (Stewart, concurring).

There is patently no legitimate overriding purpose independent of invidious racial discrimination which justifies this classification. The fact that Virginia prohibits only interracial marriages involving white persons demonstrates that the racial classifications must stand on their own justification, as measures designed to maintain White Supremacy. We have consistently denied the constitutionality of measures which restrict the rights of citizens on account of race. There can be no doubt that restricting the freedom to marry solely because of racial classifications violates the central meaning of the Equal Protection Clause.

These statutes also deprive the Lovings of liberty without due process of law in violation of the Due Process Clause of the Fourteenth Amendment. The freedom to marry has long been recognized as one of the vital personal rights essential to the orderly pursuit of happiness by free men.

Marriage is one of the "basic civil rights of man," fundamental to our very existence and survival. To deny this fundamental freedom on so unsupportable a basis as the racial classifications embodied in these statutes, classifications so directly subversive of the principle of equality at the heart of the Fourteenth Amendment, is surely to deprive all the State's citizens of liberty without due process of law. The Fourteenth Amendment requires that the freedom of choice to marry not be restricted by invidious racial discriminations. Under our Constitution, the freedom to marry, or not marry, a person of another race resides with the individual, and cannot be infringed by the State.

These convictions must be reversed.

Moose Lodge No. 107 v. Irvis

407 U.S. 163 (1972), 6-3
Opinion of the Court: Rehnquist (Blackmun, Burger, Powell, Stewart, White)
Dissenting: Brennan, Douglas, Marshall

What argument did Irvis make that his constitutional rights were violated? Why was it rejected by the Court? Does Douglas persuasively make a case that Irvis is correct? How does this case clarify what "state action" is? What is the remedy for private discrimination? Should there be one? Why isn't this a freedom of association case?

Rehnquist, for the Court:

Appellee Irvis, a Negro ... was refused service by appellant Moose Lodge, a local branch of the national fraternal organization located in Harrisburg, Pennsylvania. [He] then brought this action ... for injunctive relief. ... He claimed that, because the Pennsylvania liquor board had issued ... Moose Lodge a private club license that authorized the sale of alcoholic beverages on its premises, the refusal of service to him was "state action" for the purposes of the Equal Protection Clause of the Fourteenth Amendment. He named both Moose Lodge and the Pennsylvania Liquor Authority as defendants, seeking injunctive relief that would have required the defendant liquor board to revoke Moose Lodge's license so long as it continued its discriminatory practices. [H]e sought no damages. ...

Moose Lodge is a private club in the ordinary meaning of that term. It is a local chapter of a national fraternal organization having well defined requirements for membership. It conducts all of its activities in a building that is owned by it. It is not publicly funded. Only members and guests are permitted in any lodge of the order; one may become a guest only by invitation of a member or upon invitation of the house committee.

[Irvis], while conceding the right of private clubs to choose members upon a discriminatory basis, asserts that the licensing of Moose Lodge to serve liquor by the Pennsylvania Liquor Control Board amounts to such state involvement with the club's activities as to make its discriminatory practices forbidden by the Equal Protection Clause of the Fourteenth Amendment. The relief sought and obtained by [him] in the District Court was an injunction forbidding the licensing by the liquor authority of Moose Lodge until it ceased its discriminatory practices. We conclude that Moose Lodge's refusal to serve food and beverages to a guest by reason of the fact that he was a Negro does not, under the circumstances here presented, violate the Fourteenth Amendment.

In 1883, this Court, in The Civil Rights Cases set forth the essential dichotomy between discriminatory action by the State, which is prohibited by the Equal Protection Clause, and private conduct, "however discriminatory or wrongful," against which that clause "erects no shield." That dichotomy has been subsequently reaffirmed in *Shelley v. Kraemer* and in *Burton v. Wilmington Parking Authority.*

While the principle is easily stated, the question of whether particular discriminatory conduct is private, on the one hand, or amounts to "state action," on the other hand, frequently admits of no easy answer. "Only by sifting facts and weighing circumstances can the nonobvious involvement of the State in private conduct be attributed its true significance." *Burton v. Wilmington Parking Authority.*

Our cases make clear that the impetus for the forbidden discrimination need not originate with the State if it is state action that enforces privately originated discrimination. The Court held in *Burton v. Wilmington Parking Authority* that a private restaurant owner who refused service because of a customer's race violated the Fourteenth Amendment where the restaurant was located in a building owned by a state-created parking authority and leased from the authority. The Court, after a comprehensive review of the relationship between the lessee and the parking authority, concluded that the latter had "so far insinuated itself into a position of interdependence with Eagle [the restaurant owner] that it must be recognized as a joint participant in the challenged activity, which, on that account, cannot be considered to have been so "purely private" as to fall without the scope of the Fourteenth Amendment."

The Court has never held, of course, that discrimination by an otherwise private entity would be violative of the Equal Protection Clause if the private entity receives any sort of benefit or service at all from the State, or if it is subject to state regulation in any degree whatever. Since state-furnished services include such necessities of life as electricity, water, and police and fire protection, such a holding would utterly emasculate the distinction between private, as distinguished from state, conduct set forth in The Civil Rights Cases and adhered to in subsequent decisions. Our holdings indicate that, where the impetus for the discrimination is private, the State must have "significantly involved itself with invidious discriminations," *Reitman v. Mulkey,* in order for the discriminatory action to fall within the ambit of the constitutional prohibition.

Our prior decisions dealing with discriminatory refusal of service in public eating places are significantly different factually from the case now before us. *Peterson v. City of Greenville* dealt with the trespass prosecution of persons who "sat in" at a restaurant to protest its refusal of service to Negroes. There, the Court held that, although the ostensible initiative for the trespass prosecution came from the proprietor, the existence of a local ordinance requiring segregation of races in such places was tantamount to the State's

having "commanded a particular result." With one exception . . . there is no suggestion in this record that the Pennsylvania statutes and regulations governing the sale of liquor are intended either overtly or covertly to encourage discrimination.

In *Burton* the Court's full discussion of the facts in its opinion indicates the significant differences between that case and this. . . .

Here, there is nothing approaching the symbiotic relationship between lessor and lessee that was present in *Burton,* where the private lessee obtained the benefit of locating in a building owned by the state-created parking authority, and the parking authority was enabled to carry out its primarily public purpose of furnishing parking space by advantageously leasing portions of the building constructed for that purpose to commercial lessees such as the owner of the Eagle Restaurant. Unlike *Burton,* the Moose Lodge building is located on land owned by it, not by any public authority. Far from apparently holding itself out as a place of public accommodation, Moose Lodge quite ostentatiously proclaims the fact that it is not open to the public at large. Nor is it located and operated in such surroundings that, although private in name, it discharges a function or performs a service that would otherwise in all likelihood be performed by the State. In short, while Eagle was a public restaurant in a public building, Moose Lodge is a private social club in a private building.

With the exception hereafter noted, the Pennsylvania Liquor Control Board plays absolutely no part in establishing or enforcing the membership or guest policies of the club that it licenses to serve liquor. There is no suggestion in this record that Pennsylvania law, either as written or as applied, discriminates against minority groups either in their right to apply for club licenses themselves or in their right to purchase and be served liquor in places of public accommodation. The only effect that the state licensing of Moose Lodge to serve liquor can be said to have on the right of any other Pennsylvanian to buy or be served liquor on premises other than those of Moose Lodge is that, for some purposes, club licenses are counted in the maximum number of licenses that may be issued in a given municipality. . . .

The District Court was at pains to point out in its opinion what it considered to be the "pervasive" nature of the regulation of private clubs by the Pennsylvania Liquor Control Board. As that court noted, an applicant for a club license must make such physical alterations in its premises as the board may require, must file a list of the names and addresses of its members and employees, and must keep extensive financial records. . . .

However detailed this type of regulation may be in some particulars, it cannot be said to in any way foster or encourage racial discrimination. Nor can it be said to make the State in any realistic sense a partner or even a joint venturer in the club's enterprise. The limited effect of the prohibition against obtaining additional club licenses when the maximum number of retail licenses allotted to a municipality has been issued, when considered together with the availability of liquor from hotel, restaurant, and retail licensees, falls far short of conferring upon club licensees a monopoly in the dispensing of liquor in any given municipality or in the State as a whole. We therefore hold that, with the exception hereafter noted, the operation of the regulatory scheme enforced by the Pennsylvania Liquor Control Board does not sufficiently implicate the State in the discriminatory guest policies of Moose Lodge to make the latter "state action" within the ambit of the Equal Protection Clause of the Fourteenth Amendment.

The District Court found that the regulations of the Liquor Control Board adopted pursuant to statute affirmatively require that "[e]very club licensee shall adhere to all of the provisions of its Constitution and By-Laws." . . .

Even though the Liquor Control Board regulation in question is neutral in its terms, the result of its application in a case where the constitution and bylaws of a club required racial discrimination would be to invoke the sanctions of the State to enforce a concededly discriminatory private rule. State action, for purposes of the Equal Protection Clause, may emanate from rulings of administrative and regulatory agencies, as well as from legislative or judicial action. *Shelley v. Kraemer* makes it clear that the application of state sanctions to enforce such a rule would violate the Fourteenth Amendment. Although the record before us is not as clear as one would like, [Moose Lodge] has not persuaded us that the District Court should have denied any and all relief.

[Irvis] was entitled to a decree enjoining the enforcement of §113.09 of the regulations promulgated by the Pennsylvania Liquor Control Board insofar as that regulation requires compliance by Moose Lodge with provisions of its constitution and bylaws containing racially discriminatory provisions. He was entitled to no more. . . .

Douglas, dissenting:

. . . [T]he fact that a private club gets some kind of permit from the State or municipality does not make it ipso facto a public enterprise or undertaking, any more than the grant to a householder of a permit to operate an incinerator puts the householder in the public domain. We must, therefore, examine whether there are special circumstances involved in the Pennsylvania scheme which differentiate the liquor license possessed by Moose Lodge from the incinerator permit.

Pennsylvania has a state store system of alcohol distribution. Resale is permitted by hotels, restaurants, and private clubs which all must obtain licenses from the Liquor Control Board. The scheme of regulation is complete and pervasive, and the state courts have sustained many restrictions on the licensees. Once a license is issued, the licensee must comply with many detailed requirements or risk suspension or revocation of the license. Among these requirements is Regulation §113.09 which says: "Every club licensee shall adhere to all of the provisions of its Constitution and By laws." This regulation means, as applied to Moose Lodge, that it must adhere to the racially discriminatory provision of the Constitution of its Supreme Lodge. . . .

. . . The result . . . is the same as though Pennsylvania had put into its liquor licenses a provision that the license may not be used to dispense liquor to blacks, browns, yellows—or atheists or agnostics. Regulation §113.09 is thus an invidious form of state action.

Were this regulation the only infirmity in Pennsylvania's licensing scheme, I would perhaps agree with the majority that the appropriate relief would be a decree enjoining its enforcement. But there is another flaw in the scheme not so easily cured. Liquor licenses in Pennsylvania, unlike driver's licenses, or marriage licenses, are not freely available to those who meet racially neutral qualifications. There is a complex quota system, which the majority accurately describes. What the majority neglects to say is that the quota for Harrisburg, where Moose Lodge No. 107 is located, has been full for many years. No more club licenses may be issued in that city.

This state-enforced scarcity of licenses restricts the ability of blacks to obtain liquor, for liquor is commercially available only at private clubs for a significant portion of each week. Access by blacks to places that serve liquor is further limited by the fact that the state quota is filled. A group desiring to form a nondiscriminatory club which would serve blacks must purchase a license held by an existing club, which can exact a monopoly price for the transfer. The availability of such a license is speculative, at best, however, for, as Moose Lodge itself concedes, without a liquor license, a fraternal organization would be hard-pressed to survive.

Thus, the State of Pennsylvania is putting the weight of its liquor license, concededly a valued and important adjunct to a private club, behind racial discrimination. . . .

Swann v. Charlotte-Mecklenburg Board of Education

402 U.S. 1 (1971), 9-0
Opinion of the Court: Burger (Black, Blackmun, Brennan, Douglas, Harlan, Marshall, Stewart, White)

A school desegregation plan for the Charlotte-Mecklenburg school system in North Carolina, approved by a federal district court in 1965 and based on geographic zoning and free transfers, failed to achieve much integration. In the 1968–1969 school year, the system, which includes the city of Charlotte, had more than 84,000 students—60,000 white, 24,000 black in 107 schools. Of the black students, 14,000 still attended schools that were at least 99 percent black. In 1969, the District Court ordered the school board to come up with a more effective plan. When it found the board's new plan unsatisfactory, it appointed an expert who drew up a desegregation plan requiring extensive busing of students to get greater racial balance among the system's schools. The plan was challenged in this case.

Was the district court's pupil assignment scheme based on the race of the student? Why did the Court not find racial quotas violated the equal protection clause? What is the difference between de jure and de facto segregation? If effects of the former had not been present, would the Court have sustained the district court's plan? What means other than busing might be used to effect greater racial integration within a school district?

Burger, for the Court:

We granted certiorari in this case to review important issues as to the duties of school authorities and the scope of powers of federal courts under this Court's mandates to eliminate racially separate public schools established and maintained by state action.

This case and those argued with it arose in States having a long history of maintaining two sets of schools in a single school system deliberately oper-

ated to carry out a governmental policy to separate pupils in schools solely on the basis of race. That was what *Brown v. Board of Education* was all about. These cases present us with the problem of defining in more precise terms than heretofore the scope of the duty of school authorities and district courts in implementing *Brown I* and the mandate to eliminate dual systems and establish unitary systems at once. Meanwhile, district courts and courts of appeals have struggled in hundreds of cases with a multitude and variety of problems under this Court's general directive. Understandably, in an area of evolving remedies, those courts had to improvise and experiment without detailed or specific guidelines. This Court, in *Brown I,* appropriately dealt with the large constitutional principles; other federal courts had to grapple with the flinty, intractable realities of day-to-day implementation of those constitutional commands. Their efforts, of necessity, embraced a process of "trial and error," and our effort to formulate guidelines must take into account their experience. . . .

The central issue in this case is that of student assignment, and there are essentially four problem areas: (1) to what extent racial balance or racial quotas may be used as an implement in a remedial order to correct a previously segregated system; (2) whether every all-Negro and all-white school must be eliminated as an indispensable part of a remedial process of desegregation; (3) what the limits are, if any, on the rearrangement of school districts and attendance zones, as a remedial measure; and (4) what the limits are, if any, on the use of transportation facilities to correct state-enforced racial school segregation.

(1) Racial Balances or Racial Quotas.

The constant theme and thrust of every holding from *Brown I* to date is that state-enforced separation of races in public schools is discrimination that violates the Equal Protection Clause. The remedy commanded was to dismantle dual school systems.

We are concerned in these cases with the elimination of the discrimination inherent in the dual school systems, not with myriad factors of human existence which can cause discrimination in a multitude of ways on racial, religious, or ethnic grounds. The target of the cases from *Brown I* to the present was the dual school system. The elimination of racial discrimination in public schools is a large task, and one that should not be retarded by efforts to achieve broader purposes lying beyond the jurisdiction of school authorities. One vehicle can carry only a limited amount of baggage. . . .

Our objective in dealing with the issues presented by these cases is to see that school authorities exclude no pupil of a racial minority from any school, directly or indirectly, on account of race; it does not and cannot embrace all the problems of racial prejudice, even when those problems contribute to disproportionate racial concentrations in some schools.

In this case, it is urged that the District Court has imposed a racial balance requirement of 71%–29% on individual schools. . . .

. . . If we were to read the holding of the District Court to require, as a matter of substantive constitutional right, any particular degree of racial balance or mixing, that approach would be disapproved and we would be obliged to reverse. The constitutional command to desegregate schools does not mean that every school in every community must always reflect the racial composition of the school system as a whole. . . .

. . . [T]he use made of mathematical ratios was no more than a starting point in the process of shaping a remedy, rather than an inflexible requirement. From that starting point, the District Court proceeded to frame a decree that was within its discretionary powers, as an equitable remedy for the particular circumstances. As we said in *Green* [*v. School Board of New Kent County*], a school authority's remedial plan or a district court's remedial decree is to be judged by its effectiveness. Awareness of the racial composition of the whole school system is likely to be a useful starting point in shaping a remedy to correct past constitutional violations. In sum, the very limited use made of mathematical ratios was within the equitable remedial discretion of the District Court.

(2) One-race Schools.

The record in this case reveals the familiar phenomenon that, in metropolitan areas, minority groups are often found concentrated in one part of the city. In some circumstances, certain schools may remain all or largely of one race until new schools can be provided or neighborhood patterns change. Schools all or predominately of one race in a district of mixed population will require close scrutiny to determine that school assignments are not part of state-enforced segregation.

In light of the above, it should be clear that the existence of some small number of one-race, or virtually one-race, schools within a district is not, in and of itself, the mark of a system that still practices segregation by law. The district judge or school authorities should make every effort to achieve the greatest possible degree of actual desegregation, and will thus necessarily be concerned with the elimination of one-race schools. No per se rule can adequately embrace all the difficulties of reconciling the competing interests involved; but, in a system with a history of segregation, the need for remedial criteria of sufficient specificity to assure a school authority's compliance with its constitutional duty warrants a presumption against schools that are substantially disproportionate in their racial composition. Where the school authority's proposed plan for conversion from a dual to a unitary system contemplates the continued existence of some schools that are all or predominately of one race, they have the burden of showing that such school assignments are genuinely nondiscriminatory. The court should scrutinize such schools, and the burden upon the school authorities will be to satisfy the court that their racial composition is not the result of present or past discriminatory action on their part.

An optional majority-to-minority transfer provision has long been recognized as a useful part of every desegregation plan. Provision for optional transfer of those in the majority racial group of a particular school to other schools where they will be in the minority is an indispensable remedy for those students willing to transfer to other schools in order to lessen the impact on them of the state-imposed stigma of segregation. In order to be effective, such a transfer arrangement must grant the transferring student free transportation and space must be made available in the school to which he desires to move. The court orders in this and the companion Davis case now provide such an option.

(3) Remedial Altering of Attendance Zones.

The maps submitted in these cases graphically demonstrate that one of the principal tools employed by school planners and by courts to break up the dual school system has been a frank—and sometimes drastic—gerrymandering of school districts and attendance zones. An additional step was pairing, "clustering," or "grouping" of schools with attendance assignments made deliberately to accomplish the transfer of Negro students out of formerly segregated Negro schools and transfer of white students to formerly all-Negro schools. More often than not, these zones are neither compact nor contiguous; indeed they may be on opposite ends of the city. As an interim corrective measure, this cannot be said to be beyond the broad remedial powers of a court.

Absent a constitutional violation, there would be no basis for judicially ordering assignment of students on a racial basis. All things being equal, with no history of discrimination, it might well be desirable to assign pupils to schools nearest their homes. But all things are not equal in a system that has been deliberately constructed and maintained to enforce racial segregation. The remedy for such segregation may be administratively awkward, inconvenient, and even bizarre in some situations, and may impose burdens on some; but all awkwardness and inconvenience cannot be avoided in the interim period when remedial adjustments are being made to eliminate the dual school systems.

No fixed or even substantially fixed guidelines can be established as to how far a court can go, but it must be recognized that there are limits. The objective is to dismantle the dual school system. "Racially neutral" assignment plans proposed by school authorities to a district court may be inadequate; such plans may fail to counteract the continuing effects of past school segregation resulting from discriminatory location of school sites or distortion of school size in order to achieve or maintain an artificial racial separation. When school authorities present a district court with a "loaded game board," affirmative action in the form of remedial altering of attendance zones is proper to achieve truly nondiscriminatory assignments. In short, an assignment plan is not acceptable simply because it appears to be neutral. . . .

We hold that the pairing and grouping of noncontiguous school zones is a permissible tool, and such action is to be considered in light of the objectives sought. . . .

(4) Transportation of Students.

The scope of permissible transportation of students as an implement of a remedial decree has never been defined by this Court, and, by the very nature of the problem, it cannot be defined with precision. . . .

The importance of bus transportation as a normal and accepted tool of educational policy is readily discernible in this. . . . The Charlotte school authorities did not purport to assign students on the basis of geographically drawn zones until 1965, and then they allowed almost unlimited transfer privileges. The District Court's conclusion that assignment of children to the school nearest their home serving their grade would not produce an effective dismantling of the dual system is supported by the record.

Thus, the remedial techniques used in the District Court's order were within that court's power to pro-

vide equitable relief; implementation of the decree is well within the capacity of the school authority.

The decree provided that the buses used to implement the plan would operate on direct routes. Students would be picked up at schools near their homes and transported to the schools they were to attend. The trips for elementary school pupils average about seven miles, and the District Court found that they would take "not over 35 minutes, at the most." This system compares favorably with the transportation plan previously operated in Charlotte, under which, each day, 23,600 students on all grade levels were transported an average of 15 miles one way for an average trip requiring over an hour. In these circumstances, we find no basis for holding that the local school authorities may not be required to employ bus transportation as one tool of school desegregation. Desegregation plans cannot be limited to the walk-in school. . . .

. . . At some point, these school authorities and others like them should have achieved full compliance with this Court's decision in *Brown I.* The systems would then be "unitary" in the sense required by our decisions in *Green* and *Alexander* [v. *Holmes County Board of Education*]

It does not follow that the communities served by such systems will remain demographically stable, for, in a growing, mobile society, few will do so. Neither school authorities nor district courts are constitutionally required to make year-by-year adjustments of the racial composition of student bodies once the affirmative duty to desegregate has been accomplished and racial discrimination through official action is eliminated from the system. This does not mean that federal courts are without power to deal with future problems; but, in the absence of a showing that either the school authorities or some other agency of the State has deliberately attempted to fix or alter demographic patterns to affect the racial composition of the schools, further intervention by a district court should not be necessary. . . .

Milliken v. Bradley

418 U.S. 717 (1974), 5-4

Opinion of the Court: Burger (Blackmun, Powell, Rehnquist, Stewart)

Dissenting: Brennan, Douglas, Marshall, White

After finding that the Detroit Board of Education had helped bring about racial segregation in the city's schools and that a

Detroit-only desegregation plan would not be able to end segregation, a federal district court appointed a panel to draw up a desegregation plan encompassing the three-county metropolitan area including 53 suburban school districts. There was no evidence that any of the suburban districts had policies or programs that perpetrated school segregation. As drawn up, the plan, which required extensive busing of students, was affirmed by the Court of Appeals.

How is this case different from Swann v. Charlotte-Mecklenburg Board of Education *(p. 484)? How much of this decision is based on the absence of de jure segregation in the suburban school districts and how much on the ideal and tradition of local control of the public schools? Should the differences between this case and* Swann *result in a different decision? Why did Douglas and Marshall think not? In a later case, the Court suggested that the state make more effort to improve the quality of the mostly all-black schools in Detroit in lieu of an area-wide, cross-district integration plan based on massive busing. Would that be a good trade-off? Would it be a retreat to a version of "separate but equal" but with a greater emphasis on "equal"? Are all-white or nearly all-white schools now constitutional as long as black students have not been excluded and all-black or nearly all-black schools are not allowed to become inferior?*

Burger, for the Court:

We granted certiorari in these consolidated cases to determine whether a federal court may impose a multi-district, area-wide remedy to a single-district de jure segregation problem absent any finding that the other included school district have failed to operate unitary school systems within their districts, absent any claim or finding that the boundary lines of any affected school district were established with the purpose of fostering racial segregation in public schools, absent any finding that the included districts committed acts which effected segregation within the other districts, and absent a meaningful opportunity for the included neighboring school districts to present evidence or be heard on the propriety of a multi-district remedy or on the question of constitutional violations by those neighboring districts. . . .

Viewing the record as a whole, it seems clear that the District Court and the Court of Appeals shifted the primary focus from a Detroit remedy to the metropolitan area only because of their conclusion that total desegregation of Detroit would not produce the racial balance which they perceived as desirable. Both courts proceeded on an assumption that the Detroit schools could not be truly desegregated—in their

view of what constituted desegregation—unless the racial composition of the student body of each school substantially reflected the racial composition of the population of the metropolitan area as a whole. The metropolitan area was then defined as Detroit plus 53 of the outlying school districts. . . .

Here, the District Court's approach to what constituted "actual desegregation" raises the fundamental question, not presented in *Swann* [v. *Charlotte-Mecklenburg Board of Education*], as to the circumstances in which a federal court may order desegregation relief that embraces more than a single school district. The court's analytical starting point was its conclusion that school district lines are no more than arbitrary lines on a map drawn "for political convenience." Boundary lines may be bridged where there has been a constitutional violation calling for inter-district relief, but the notion that school district lines may be casually ignored or treated as a mere administrative convenience is contrary to the history of public education in our country. No single tradition in public education is more deeply rooted than local control over the operation of schools; local autonomy has long been thought essential both to the maintenance of community concern and support for public schools and to quality of the educational process. . . .

The Michigan educational structure involved in this case, in common with most States, provides for a large measure of local control, and a review of the scope and character of these local powers indicates the extent to which the inter-district remedy approved by the two courts could disrupt and alter the structure of public education in Michigan. The metropolitan remedy would require, in effect, consolidation of 54 independent school districts historically administered as separate units into a vast new super school district. Entirely apart from the logistical and other serious problems attending large-scale transportation of students, the consolidation would give rise to an array of other problems in financing and operating this new school system. Some of the more obvious questions would be: what would be the status and authority of the present popularly elected school boards? would the children of Detroit be within the jurisdiction and operating control of a school board elected by the parents and residents of other districts? what board or boards would levy taxes for school operations in these 54 districts constituting the consolidated metropolitan area? what provisions could be made for assuring substantial equality in tax levies among the 54 districts, if this were deemed requisite? what provisions would be made for financing? would the validity of long-term bonds be jeopardized unless approved by all of the component districts as well as the State? what body would determine that portion of the curricula now left to the discretion of local school boards? who would establish attendance zones, purchase school equipment, locate and construct new schools, and indeed attend to all the myriad day-to-day decisions that are necessary to school operations affecting potentially more than three-quarters of a million pupils?

It may be suggested that all of these vital operational problems are yet to be resolved by the District Court, and that this is the purpose of the Court of Appeals' proposed remand. But it is obvious from the scope of the inter-district remedy itself that, absent a complete restructuring of the laws of Michigan relating to school districts, the District Court will become first, a de facto "legislative authority" to resolve these complex questions, and then the "school superintendent" for the entire area. This is a task which few, if any, judges are qualified to perform and one which would deprive the people of control of schools through their elected representatives.

Of course, no state law is above the Constitution. School district lines and the present laws with respect to local control are not sacrosanct, and, if they conflict with the Fourteenth Amendment, federal courts have a duty to prescribe appropriate remedies. But our prior holdings have been confined to violations and remedies within a single school district. We therefore turn to address, for the first time, the validity of a remedy mandating cross-district or inter-district consolidation to remedy a condition of segregation found to exist in only one district.

The controlling principle consistently expounded in our holdings is that the scope of the remedy is determined by the nature and extent of the constitutional violation. Before the boundaries of separate and autonomous school districts may be set aside by consolidating the separate units for remedial purposes or by imposing a cross-district remedy, it must first be shown that there has been a constitutional violation within one district that produces a significant segregative effect in another district. Specifically, it must be shown that racially discriminatory acts of the state or local school districts, or of a single school district have been a substantial cause of inter-district segregation. Thus, an inter-district remedy might be in order where the racially

discriminatory acts of one or more school districts caused racial segregation in an adjacent district, or where district lines have been deliberately drawn on the basis of race. In such circumstances, an inter-district remedy would be appropriate to eliminate the inter-district segregation directly caused by the constitutional violation. Conversely, without an inter-district violation and inter-district effect, there is no constitutional wrong calling for an inter-district remedy.

The record before us, voluminous as it is, contains evidence of de jure segregated conditions only in the Detroit schools; indeed, that was the theory on which the litigation was initially based, and on which the District Court took evidence. With no showing of significant violation by the 53 outlying school districts and no evidence of any inter-district violation or effect, the court went beyond the original theory of the case as framed by the pleadings and mandated a metropolitan area remedy. To approve the remedy ordered by the court would impose on the outlying districts, not shown to have committed any constitutional violation, a wholly impermissible remedy based on a standard not hinted at in *Brown I* and *II* or any holding of this Court.

In dissent, Mr. Justice White and Mr. Justice Marshall undertake to demonstrate that agencies having state-wide authority participated in maintaining the dual school system found to exist in Detroit. They are apparently of the view that, once such participation is shown, the District Court should have a relatively free hand to reconstruct school districts outside of Detroit in fashioning relief. Our assumption, arguendo, that state agencies did participate in the maintenance of the Detroit system, should make it clear that it is not on this point that we part company. The difference between us arises, instead, from established doctrine laid down by our cases. [E]ach addressed the issue of constitutional wrong in terms of an established geographic and administrative school system populated by both Negro and white children. In such a context, terms such as "unitary" and "dual" systems, and "racially identifiable schools," have meaning, and the necessary federal authority to remedy the constitutional wrong is firmly established. But the remedy is necessarily designed, as all remedies are, to restore the victims of discriminatory conduct to the position they would have occupied in the absence of such conduct. Disparate treatment of white and Negro students occurred within the Detroit school system, and not elsewhere, and, on this record, the remedy must be limited to that system.

The constitutional right of the Negro respondents residing in Detroit is to attend a unitary school system in that district. Unless petitioners drew the district lines in a discriminatory fashion, or arranged for white students residing in the Detroit District to attend schools in Oakland and Macomb Counties, they were under no constitutional duty to make provisions for Negro students to do so. The view of the dissenters, that the existence of a dual system in Detroit can be made the basis for a decree requiring cross-district transportation of pupils, cannot be supported on the grounds that it represents merely the devising of a suitably flexible remedy for the violation of rights already established by our prior decisions. It can be supported only by drastic expansion of the constitutional right itself, an expansion without any support in either constitutional principle or precedent....

We conclude that the relief ordered by the District Court and affirmed by the Court of Appeals was based upon an erroneous standard and was unsupported by record evidence that acts of the outlying districts effected the discrimination found to exist in the schools of Detroit. Accordingly, the judgment of the Court of Appeals is reversed and the case is remanded for further proceedings consistent with this opinion leading to prompt formulation of a decree directed to eliminating the segregation found to exist in Detroit city schools, a remedy which has been delayed since 1970.

Douglas, dissenting:
... When we rule against the metropolitan area remedy, we take a step that will likely put the problems of the blacks and our society back to the period that antedated the "separate but equal" regime of *Plessy v. Ferguson.* The reason is simple.

The inner core of Detroit is now rather solidly black; and the blacks, we know, in many instances are likely to be poorer, just as were the Chicanos in *San Antonio School District v. Rodriguez.* By that decision, the poorer school districts must pay their own way. It is therefore a foregone conclusion that we have now given the States a formula whereby the poor must pay their own way.

Today's decision, given *Rodriguez*, means that there is no violation of the Equal Protection Clause though the schools are segregated by race and though the black schools are not only "separate" but "inferior."

So far as equal protection is concerned, we are now in a dramatic retreat from the 7-to-1 decision in

1896 that blacks could be segregated in public facilities, provided they received equal treatment.

... [T]here is, so far as the school cases go, no constitutional difference between de facto and de jure segregation. Each school board performs state action for Fourteenth Amendment purposes when it draws the lines that confine it to a given area, when it builds schools at particular sites, or when it allocates students. The creation of the school districts in Metropolitan Detroit either maintained existing segregation or caused additional segregation. Restrictive covenants maintained by state action or inaction build black ghettos. It is state action when public funds are dispensed by housing agencies to build racial ghettos. Where a community is racially mixed and school authorities segregate schools, or assign black teachers to black schools or close schools in fringe areas and build new schools in black areas and in more distant white areas, the State creates and nurtures a segregated school system just as surely as did those States involved in *Brown v. Board of Education* when they maintained dual school systems.

All these conditions and more were found by the District Court to exist. The issue is not whether there should be racial balance, but whether the State's use of various devices that end up with black schools and white schools brought the Equal Protection Clause into effect. Given the State's control over the educational system in Michigan, the fact that the black schools are in one district and the white schools are in another is not controlling—either constitutionally or equitably. No specific plan has yet been adopted. We are still at an interlocutory stage of a long drawn-out judicial effort at school desegregation. It is conceivable that ghettos develop on their own, without any hint of state action. But since Michigan, by one device or another, has, over the years, created black school districts and white school districts, the task of equity is to provide a unitary system for the affected area where, as here, the State washes its hands of its own creations.

Marshall, dissenting:
In *Brown v. Board of Education,* this Court held that segregation of children in public schools on the basis of race deprives minority group children of equal educational opportunities, and therefore denies them the equal protection of the laws under the Fourteenth Amendment. This Court recognized then that remedying decades of segregation in public education

would not be an easy task. Subsequent events, unfortunately, have seen that prediction bear bitter fruit. But however imbedded old ways, however ingrained old prejudices, this Court has not been diverted from its appointed task of making "a living truth" of our constitutional ideal of equal justice under law.

After 20 years of small, often difficult steps toward that great end, the Court today takes a giant step backwards. Notwithstanding a record showing widespread and pervasive racial segregation in the educational system provided by the State of Michigan for children in Detroit, this Court holds that the District Court was powerless to require the State to remedy its constitutional violation in any meaningful fashion. Ironically purporting to base its result on the principle that the scope of the remedy in a desegregation case should be determined by the nature and the extent of the constitutional violation, the Court's answer is to provide no remedy at all for the violation proved in this case, thereby guaranteeing that Negro children in Detroit will receive the same separate and inherently unequal education in the future as they have been unconstitutionally afforded in the past.

I cannot subscribe to this emasculation of our constitutional guarantee of equal protection of the laws, and must respectfully dissent. Our precedents, in my view, firmly establish that where, as here, state-imposed segregation has been demonstrated, it becomes the duty of the State to eliminate root and branch all vestiges of racial discrimination and to achieve the greatest possible degree of actual desegregation. I agree with both the District Court and the Court of Appeals that, under the facts of this case, this duty cannot be fulfilled unless the State of Michigan involves outlying metropolitan area school districts in its desegregation remedy. Furthermore, I perceive no basis either in law or in the practicalities of the situation justifying the State's interposition of school district boundaries as absolute barriers to the implementation of an effective desegregation remedy. . . .

The rights at issue in this case are too fundamental to be abridged on grounds as superficial as those relied on by the majority today. We deal here with the right of all of our children, whatever their race, to an equal start in life and to an equal opportunity to reach their full potential as citizens. Those children who have been denied that right in the past deserve better than to see fences thrown up to deny them that right in the future. Our Nation, I fear, will be ill-served by the Court's refusal to remedy separate and

unequal education, for unless our children begin to learn together, there is little hope that our people will ever learn to live together.

The great irony of the Court's opinion and, in my view, its most serious analytical flaw, may be gleaned from its concluding sentence, in which the Court remands for "prompt formulation of a decree directed to eliminating the segregation found to exist in Detroit city schools, a remedy which has been delayed since 1970." The majority, however, seems to have forgotten the District Court's explicit finding that a Detroit-only decree, the only remedy permitted under today's decision, "would not accomplish desegregation." . . .

We cautioned in *Swann*, of course, that the dismantling of a segregated school system does not mandate any particular racial balance. We also concluded that a remedy under which there would remain a small number of racially identifiable schools was only presumptively inadequate and might be justified. But this is a totally different case. The flaw of a Detroit-only decree is not that it does not reach some ideal degree of racial balance or mixing. It simply does not promise to achieve actual desegregation at all. It is one thing to have a system where a small number of students remain in racially identifiable schools. It is something else entirely to have a system where all students continue to attend such schools.

The continued racial identifiability of the Detroit schools under a Detroit-only remedy is not simply a reflection of their high percentage of Negro students. What is or is not a racially identifiable vestige of de jure segregation must necessarily depend on several factors. Foremost among these should be the relationship between the schools in question and the neighboring community. . . .

Desegregation is not and was never expected to be an easy task. Racial attitudes ingrained in our Nation's childhood and adolescence are not quickly thrown aside in its middle years. But just as the inconvenience of some cannot be allowed to stand in the way of the rights of others, so public opposition, no matter how strident, cannot be permitted to divert this Court from the enforcement of the constitutional principles at issue in this case. Today's holding, I fear, is more a reflection of a perceived public mood that we have gone far enough in enforcing the Constitution's guarantee of equal justice than it is the product of neutral principle of law. In the short run, it may seem to be the easier course to allow our great metropolitan areas to be divided up each into two cities—

one white, the other black—but it is a course, I predict, our people will ultimately regret. I dissent.

Missouri v. Jenkins

495 U.S. 33 (1990), 9-0
Opinion of the Court: White (Blackmun, Brennan, Kennedy, Marshall, O'Connor, Rehnquist, Scalia, Stevens)

This case grew out of lengthy litigation over segregation in Kansas City, Mo., schools. A federal district court concluded that the city's school district operated a segregated school system. But instead of ordering extensive busing in connection with suburban school districts in which there had also been de jure segregation, the Court approved an expensive "magnet school" plan to attract white students. To help pay for the plan, it ordered an increase in local property taxes, nearly doubling the rate. Though the Supreme Court was unanimous, four justices, Blackmun, Brennan, Marshall, and Stevens, dissented on specific points omitted from the excerpt here.

What desegregation plans had been implemented? Did the district court in ordering that taxes should be raised to pay for desegregation go beyond the modern requirements of the equal protection clause? Was it a judicial usurpation of legislative power? Who gains and who loses as a result of this decision?

White, for the Court:

The United States District Court for the Western District of Missouri imposed an increase in the property taxes levied by the Kansas City, Missouri, School District (KCMSD) to ensure funding for the desegregation of KCMSD's public schools. We granted certiorari to consider the State of Missouri's argument that the District Court lacked the power to raise local property taxes. For the reasons given below, we hold that the District Court abused its discretion in imposing the tax increase. We also hold, however, that the modifications of the District Court's order made by the Court of Appeals do satisfy equitable and constitutional principles governing the District Court's power....

The State urges us to hold that the tax increase violated Article III, the Tenth Amendment, and principles of federal/state comity. We find it unnecessary to reach the difficult constitutional issues, for we agree with the State that the tax increase contravened the

principles of comity that must govern the exercise of the District Court's equitable discretion in this area.

It is accepted by all the parties, as it was by the courts below, that the imposition of a tax increase by a federal court was an extraordinary event. In assuming for itself the fundamental and delicate power of taxation, the District Court not only intruded on local authority but circumvented it altogether. Before taking such a drastic step, the District Court was obliged to assure itself that no permissible alternative would have accomplished the required task. We have emphasized that, although the "remedial powers of an equity court must be adequate to the task, . . . they are not unlimited," and one of the most important considerations governing the exercise of equitable power is a proper respect for the integrity and function of local government institutions. Especially is this true where, as here, those institutions are ready, willing, and—but for the operation of state law curtailing their powers—able to remedy the deprivation of constitutional rights themselves.

The District Court believed that it had no alternative to imposing a tax increase. But there was an alternative, the very one outlined by the Court of Appeals: it could have authorized or required KCMSD to levy property taxes at a rate adequate to fund the desegregation remedy, and could have enjoined the operation of state laws that would have prevented KCMSD from exercising this power. The difference between the two approaches is far more than a matter of form. Authorizing and directing local government institutions to devise and implement remedies not only protects the function of those institutions but, to the extent possible, also places the responsibility for solutions to the problems of segregation upon those who have themselves created the problems.

As *Brown v. Board of Education II* observed, local authorities have the "primary responsibility for elucidating, assessing, and solving" the problems of desegregation. This is true as well of the problems of financing desegregation, for no matter has been more consistently placed upon the shoulders of local government than that of financing public schools. . . .

. . . By no means should a district court grant local government carte blanche, but local officials should at least have the opportunity to devise their own solutions to these problems.

The District Court therefore abused its discretion in imposing the tax itself. The Court of Appeals should not have allowed the tax increase to stand, and should have reversed the District Court in this respect. . . .

. . . The modifications ordered by the Court of Appeals cannot be assailed as invalid under the Tenth Amendment. "The Tenth Amendment's reservation of nondelegated powers to the States is not implicated by a federal court judgment enforcing the express prohibitions of unlawful state conduct enacted by the Fourteenth Amendment." *Millikin v. Bradley.* . . .

The State maintains, however, that . . . the federal judicial power can go no further than to require local governments to levy taxes as authorized under state law. In other words, the State argues that federal courts cannot set aside state-imposed limitations on local taxing authority, because to do so is to do more than to require the local government "to exercise the power that is theirs." We disagree. . . .

It is . . . clear that a local government with taxing authority may be ordered to levy taxes in excess of the limit set by state statute where there is reason based in the Constitution for not observing the statutory limitation. . . . Here the KCMSD may be ordered to levy taxes despite the statutory limitations on its authority in order to compel the discharge of an obligation imposed on KCMSD by the Fourteenth Amendment. To hold otherwise would fail to take account of the obligations of local governments, under the Supremacy Clause, to fulfill the requirements that the Constitution imposes on them. However wide the discretion of local authorities in fashioning desegregation remedies may be, "if a state-imposed limitation on a school authority's discretion operates to inhibit or obstruct the operation of a unitary school system or impede the disestablishing of a dual school system, it must fall; state policy must give way when it operates to hinder vindication of federal constitutional guarantees." *North Carolina State Bd of Education v. Swann* Even though a particular remedy may not be required in every case to vindicate constitutional guarantees, where (as here) it has been found that a particular remedy is required, the State cannot hinder the process by preventing a local government from implementing that remedy.

Accordingly, the judgment of the Court of Appeals is affirmed insofar as it required the District Court to modify its funding order, and reversed insofar as it allowed the tax increase imposed by the District Court to stand. The case is remanded for further proceedings consistent with this opinion.

Regents of the University of California v. Bakke

438 U.S. 265 (1978), 5-4
Opinion of the Court: Powell

The voting in this case was complex. Three issues were decided by 5-4 votes, but only Justice Powell was in the majority on all three. On whether Bakke was denied equal protection and whether the Regents had used improper racial "quotas," Burger, Rehnquist, Stevens, and Stewart concurred while Blackmun, Brennan, Marshall, and White dissented. On the third issue, whether race could be taken into account in a university's admissions policy, Blackmun, Brennan, Marshall, and White concurred while Burger, Rehnquist, Stevens, and Stewart dissented.

The medical school of the University of California at Davis had two admissions programs—general and special—for the entering class of 100 students. In the general, candidates with overall undergraduate grade point averages below 2.5 on a scale of 4.0 were summarily rejected. A separate admissions committee, a majority of whom were members of minority groups, administered the special program. "Economically and/or educationally disadvantaged" applicants and members of a "minority group" (blacks, Chicanos, Asians, American Indians) could ask to be considered under the special program. These special candidates were not subject to the 2.5 grade point cutoff and were not ranked against candidates in the general admissions process. During a four-year period, 63 minority students were admitted to the medical school under the special program and 44 under the general program. No disadvantaged whites were admitted under the special program, though many applied. Allan Bakke, a white male, applied in 1973 and 1974 under the general admissions program. Though he had a score of 468 out of 500 on the Medical College Admissions Test in 1973, he was rejected because no general applicants with scores less than 470 were accepted after a certain date. At that time, four special admission seats were still unfilled. In 1974, Bakke applied early and though he had a score of 549 out of 600, he was rejected again. In neither year was his name placed on the discretionary waiting list. In both years, special applicants were admitted with significantly lower scores.

Was Bakke denied equal protection of the law? Were racial admissions quotas held unconstitutional? Was affirmative action held unconstitutional? How might a university take race into account in its admissions policies without establishing racial quotas or practicing "reverse discrimination"? Is the Court clear on this point? How did the justices differ on the standard of scrutiny the Court should use in the

Allan Bakke received his medical degree from the Medical School of the University of California at Davis, June 4, 1982.

case? Does the equal protection clause protect individual rights or group rights? Does this question help to explain Powell's pivotal role in this case? Are policies that consistently benefit members of one race more than another racially discriminating in a constitutional sense? Does the intent or motivation behind the policies matter or should effect be their chief constitutional measure?

Powell, for the Court:
. . . The guarantees of the Fourteenth Amendment extend to all persons. Its language is explicit: "No State shall . . . deny to any person within its jurisdiction the equal protection of the laws." It is settled beyond question that the "rights created by the first section of the Fourteenth Amendment are, by its terms, guaranteed to the individual. The rights established are personal rights" *Shelley v. Kraemer* The guarantee of equal protection cannot mean one thing when applied to one individual and something else when applied to a person of another color. If both are not accorded the same protection, then it is not equal.

Nevertheless, petitioner argues that the court below erred in applying strict scrutiny to the special admissions program because white males, such as respondent, are not a "discrete and insular minority" requiring extraordinary protection from the majoritarian political process. This rationale, however, has never been invoked in our decisions as a prerequisite

to subjecting racial or ethnic distinctions to strict scrutiny. Nor has this Court held that discreteness and insularity constitute necessary preconditions to a holding that a particular classification is invidious. These characteristics may be relevant in deciding whether or not to add new types of classifications to the list of "suspect" categories or whether a particular classification survives close examination. Racial and ethnic classifications, however, are subject to stringent examination . . .

This perception of racial and ethnic distinctions is rooted in our Nation's constitutional and demographic history. The Court's initial view of the Fourteenth Amendment was that its "one pervading purpose" was "the freedom of the slave race, the security and firm establishment of that freedom, and the protection of the newly-made freeman and citizen from the oppressions of those who had formerly exercised dominion over him." *Slaughter-House Cases.* . . .

Although many of the Framers of the Fourteenth Amendment conceived of its primary function as bridging the vast distance between members of the Negro race and the white "majority," Slaughter-House Cases, supra, the Amendment itself was framed in universal terms, without reference to color, ethnic origin, or condition of prior servitude. . . .

Petitioner urges us to adopt for the first time a more restrictive view of the Equal Protection Clause, and hold that discrimination against members of the white "majority" cannot be suspect if its purpose can be characterized as "benign." The clock of our liberties, however, cannot be turned back to 1868. It is far too late to argue that the guarantee of equal protection to all persons permits the recognition of special wards entitled to a degree of protection greater than that accorded others.

The Fourteenth Amendment is not directed solely against discrimination due to a "two-class theory"—that is, bad upon differences between "white" and Negro.

Once the artificial line of a "two-class theory" of the Fourteenth Amendment is put aside, the difficulties entailed in varying the level of judicial review according to a perceived "preferred" status of a particular racial or ethnic minority are intractable. The concepts of "majority" and "minority" necessarily reflect temporary arrangements and political judgments. As observed above, the white "majority" itself is composed of various minority groups, most of which can lay claim to a history of prior discrimination at the hands of the State and private individuals. Not all of these groups can receive preferential treatment and corresponding judicial tolerance of distinctions drawn in terms of race and nationality, for then the only "majority" left would be a new minority of white Anglo-Saxon Protestants. There is no principled basis for deciding which groups would merit "heightened judicial solicitude" and which would not. Courts would be asked to evaluate the extent of the prejudice and consequent harm suffered by various minority groups. Those whose societal injury is thought to exceed some arbitrary level of tolerability then would be entitled to preferential classifications at the expense of individuals belonging to other groups. Those classifications would be free from exacting judicial scrutiny. As these preferences began to have their desired effect, and the consequences of past discrimination were undone, new judicial rankings would be necessary. The kind of variable sociological and political analysis necessary to produce such rankings simply does not lie within the judicial competence—even if they otherwise were politically feasible and socially desirable.

Moreover, there are serious problems of justice connected with the idea of preference itself. First, it may not always be clear that a so-called preference is, in fact, benign. Courts may be asked to validate burdens imposed upon individual members of a particular group in order to advance the group's general interest. Nothing in the Constitution supports the notion that individuals may be asked to suffer otherwise impermissible burdens in order to enhance the societal standing of their ethnic groups. Second, preferential programs may only reinforce common stereotypes holding that certain groups are unable to achieve success without special protection based on a factor having no relationship to individual worth. Third, there is a measure of inequity in forcing innocent persons in respondent's position to bear the burdens of redressing grievances not of their making.

By hitching the meaning of the Equal Protection Clause to these transitory considerations, we would be holding, as a constitutional principle, that judicial scrutiny of classifications touching on racial and ethnic background may vary with the ebb and flow of political forces. Disparate constitutional tolerance of such classifications well may serve to exacerbate racial and ethnic antagonisms, rather than alleviate them. Also, the mutability of a constitutional principle, based upon shifting political and social judgments, undermines the chances for consistent application of the Constitution from one generation to the next, a critical feature of its coherent interpretation. In expounding the Constitution, the Court's role is to discern "principles sufficiently absolute to give them roots throughout the community and continuity over significant periods of time, and to lift them above the level of the pragmatic political judgments of a particular time and place."

... The special admissions program purports to serve the purposes of: (i) "reducing the historic deficit of traditionally disfavored minorities in medical schools and in the medical profession," (ii) countering the effects of societal discrimination, (iii) increasing the number of physicians who will practice in communities currently underserved; and (iv) obtaining the educational benefits that flow from an ethnically diverse student body. It is necessary to decide which, if any, of these purposes is substantial enough to support the use of a suspect classification. ...

... [T]he attainment of a diverse student body. This clearly is a constitutionally permissible goal for an institution of higher education. Academic freedom, though not a specifically enumerated constitutional right, long has been viewed as a special concern of the First Amendment. The freedom of a university to make its own judgments as to education includes the selection of its student body. Mr. Justice Frankfurter summarized the "four essential freedoms" that constitute academic freedom: "It is the business of a university to provide that atmosphere which is most conducive to speculation, experiment and creation. It is an atmosphere in which there prevail "the four essential freedoms" of a university—to determine for itself on academic grounds who may teach, what may be taught, how it shall be taught, and who may be admitted to study." *Sweezy v. New Hampshire . . .*

The atmosphere of "speculation, experiment and creation"—so essential to the quality of higher education—is widely believed to be promoted by a diverse student body. . . . [I]t is not too much to say that the "nation's future depends upon leaders trained through wide exposure" to the ideas and mores of students as diverse as this Nation of many peoples.

Thus, in arguing that its universities must be accorded the right to select those students who will contribute the most to the "robust exchange of ideas," petitioner invokes a countervailing constitutional interest, that of the First Amendment. In this light, petitioner must be viewed as seeking to achieve a goal that is of paramount importance in the fulfillment of its mission. . . .

Ethnic diversity, however, is only one element in a range of factors a university properly may consider in attaining the goal of a heterogeneous student body. Although a university must have wide discretion in making the sensitive judgments as to who should be admitted, constitutional limitations protecting individual rights may not be disregarded. Respondent urges—and the courts below have held—that petitioner's dual admissions program is a racial classification that impermissibly infringes his rights under the Fourteenth Amendment. As the interest of diversity is compelling in the context of a university's admissions program, the question remains whether the program's racial classification is necessary to promote this interest.

It may be assumed that the reservation of a specified number of seats in each class for individuals from the preferred ethnic groups would contribute to the attainment of considerable ethnic diversity in the student body. But petitioner's argument that this is the only effective means of serving the interest of diversity is seriously flawed. In a most fundamental sense, the argument misconceives the nature of the state interest that would justify consideration of race or ethnic background. It is not an interest in simple ethnic diversity, in which a specified percentage of the student

body is in effect guaranteed to be members of selected ethnic groups, with the remaining percentage an undifferentiated aggregation of students. The diversity that furthers a compelling state interest encompasses a far broader array of qualifications and characteristics, of which racial or ethnic origin is but a single, though important, element. Petitioner's special admissions program, focused solely on ethnic diversity, would hinder, rather than further, attainment of genuine diversity. . . .

The experience of other university admissions programs, which take race into account in achieving the educational diversity valued by the First Amendment, demonstrates that the assignment of a fixed number of places to a minority group is not a necessary means toward that end. An illuminating example is found in the Harvard College program. . . .

In [Harvard's] admissions program, race or ethnic background may be deemed a "plus" in a particular applicant's file, yet it does not insulate the individual from comparison with all other candidates for the available seats. The file of a particular black applicant may be examined for his potential contribution to diversity without the factor of race being decisive when compared, for example, with that of an applicant identified as an Italian-American if the latter is thought to exhibit qualities more likely to promote beneficial educational pluralism. Such qualities could include exceptional personal talents, unique work or service experience, leadership potential, maturity, demonstrated compassion, a history of overcoming disadvantage, ability to communicate with the poor, or other qualifications deemed important. In short, an admissions program operated in this way is flexible enough to consider all pertinent elements of diversity in light of the particular qualifications of each applicant, and to place them on the same footing for consideration, although not necessarily according them the same weight. Indeed, the weight attributed to a particular quality may vary from year to year depending upon the "mix" both of the student body and the applicants for the incoming class.

This kind of program treats each applicant as an individual in the admissions process. The applicant who loses out on the last available seat to another candidate receiving a "plus" on the basis of ethnic background will not have been foreclosed from all consideration for that seat simply because he was not the right color or had the wrong surname. It would mean only that his combined qualifications, which may have included similar nonobjective factors, did not outweigh those of the other applicant. His qualifications would have been weighed fairly and competitively, and he would have no basis to complain of unequal treatment under the Fourteenth Amendment.

It has been suggested that an admissions program which considers race only as one factor is simply a subtle and more sophisticated—but no less effective— means of according racial preference than the Davis program. A facial intent to discriminate, however, is evident in petitioner's preference program, and not denied in this case. No such facial infirmity exists in an admissions program where race or ethnic background is simply one element—to be weighed fairly against other elements—in the selection process. "A boundary line," as Mr. Justice Frankfurter remarked in another connection, "is none the worse for being narrow." And a court would not assume that a university, professing to employ a facially nondiscriminatory admissions policy, would operate it as a cover for the functional equivalent of a quota system. In short, good faith would be presumed in the absence of a showing to the contrary in the manner permitted by our cases.

In summary, it is evident that the Davis special admissions program involves the use of an explicit racial classification never before countenanced by this Court. It tells applicants who are not Negro, Asian, or Chicano that they are totally excluded from a specific percentage of the seats in an entering class. No matter how strong their qualifications, quantitative and extracurricular, including their own potential for contribution to educational diversity, they are never afforded the chance to compete with applicants from the preferred groups for the special admissions seats. At the same time, the preferred applicants have the opportunity to compete for every seat in the class.

The fatal flaw in petitioner's preferential program is its disregard of individual rights as guaranteed by the Fourteenth Amendment. Such rights are not absolute. But when a State's distribution of benefits or imposition of burdens hinges on ancestry or the color of a person's skin, that individual is entitled to a demonstration that the challenged classification is necessary to promote a substantial state interest. Petitioner has failed to carry this burden. For this reason, that portion of the California court's judgment holding petitioner's special admissions program invalid under the Fourteenth Amendment must be affirmed.

In enjoining petitioner from ever considering the race of any applicant, however, the courts below failed to recognize that the State has a substantial interest that legitimately may be served by a properly devised admissions program involving the competitive consideration of race and ethnic origin. For this reason, so much of the California court's judgment as enjoins petitioner from any consideration of the race of any applicant must be reversed. . . .

Brennan, White, Marshall, and Blackmun, concurring in part and dissenting in part:

The assertion of human equality is closely associated with the proposition that differences in color or creed, birth or status, are neither significant nor relevant to the way in which persons should be treated. Nonetheless, the position that such factors must be "constitutionally an irrelevance," summed up by the shorthand phrase "[o]ur Constitution is colorblind," *Plessy v. Ferguson,* (Harlan, J., dissenting), has never been adopted by this Court as the proper meaning of the Equal Protection Clause. Indeed, we have expressly rejected this proposition on a number of occasions. . . .

Respondent argues that racial classifications are always suspect, and, consequently, that this Court should weigh the importance of the objectives served by Davis' special admissions program to see if they are compelling. In addition, he asserts that this Court must inquire whether, in its judgment, there are alternatives to racial classifications which would suit Davis' purposes. Petitioner, on the other hand, states that our proper role is simply to accept petitioner's determination that the racial classifications used by its program are reasonably related to what it tells us are its benign purposes. We reject petitioner's view, but, because our prior cases are in many respects inapposite to that before us now, we find it necessary to define with precision the meaning of that inexact term, "strict scrutiny."

Unquestionably we have held that a government practice or statute which restricts "fundamental rights" or which contains "suspect classifications" is to be subjected to "strict scrutiny," and can be justified only if it furthers a compelling government purpose and, even then, only if no less restrictive alternative is available. Nor do whites, as a class, have any of the "traditional indicia of suspectness: the class is not saddled with such disabilities, or subjected to such a history of purposeful unequal treatment, or relegated to such a position of political powerlessness as to command extraordinary protection from the majoritarian political process." *San Antonio Independent School District v. Rodriguez.* . . .

On the other hand, the fact that this case does not fit neatly into our prior analytic framework for race cases does not mean that it should be analyzed by applying the very loose rational basis standard of review that is the very least that is always applied in equal protection cases. . . . Instead, a number of considerations—developed in gender discrimination cases but which carry even more force when applied to racial classifications—lead us to conclude that racial classifications designed to further remedial purposes "'must serve important governmental objectives, and must be substantially related to achievement of those objectives.'" *Craig v. Boren*

First, race, like, "gender-based classifications, too often [has] been inexcusably utilized to stereotype and stigmatize politically powerless segments of society." *Kahn v. Shevin* Second, race, like gender and illegitimacy, is an immutable characteristic which its possessors are powerless to escape or set aside. . . .

Because this principle is so deeply rooted, it might be supposed that it would be considered in the legislative process and weighed against the benefits of programs preferring individuals because of their race. But this is not necessarily so. . . . Moreover, it is clear from our cases that there are limits beyond which majorities may not go when they classify on the basis of immutable characteristics. Thus, even if the concern for individualism is weighed by the political process, that weighing cannot waive the personal rights of individuals under the Fourteenth Amendment.

In sum, because of the significant risk that racial classifications established for ostensibly benign purposes can be misused, causing effects not unlike those created by invidious classifications, it is inappropriate to inquire only whether there is any conceivable basis that might sustain such a classification. Instead, to justify such a classification, an important and articulated purpose for its use must be shown. In addition, any statute must be stricken that stigmatizes any group or that singles out those least well represented in the political process to bear the brunt of a benign program. Thus, our review under the Fourteenth Amendment should be strict—not "'strict' in theory and fatal in fact," because it is stigma that causes fatality—but strict and searching nonetheless.

Davis' articulated purpose of remedying the effects of past societal discrimination is, under our cases, sufficiently important to justify the use of race-conscious admissions programs where there is a sound basis for concluding that minority underrepresentation is substantial and chronic, and that the handicap of past discrimination is impeding access of minorities to the Medical School. . . .

Certainly, on the basis of the undisputed factual submissions before this Court, Davis had a sound basis for believing that the problem of underrepresentation of minorities was substantial and chronic, and that the problem was attributable to handicaps imposed on minority applicants by past and present racial discrimination. Until at least 1973, the practice of medicine in this country was, in fact, if not in law, largely the prerogative of whites. In 1950, for example, while Negroes constituted 10% of the total population, Negro physicians constituted only 2.2% of the total number of physicians. The overwhelming majority of these, moreover, were educated in two predominantly Negro medical schools. By 1970, the gap between the proportion of Negroes in medicine and their proportion in the population had widened: the number of Negroes employed in medicine remained frozen at 2.2% while the Negro population had increased to 11.1%. The number of Negro admittees to predominantly white medical schools, moreover, had declined in absolute numbers during the years 1955 to 1964.

The second prong of our test—whether the Davis program stigmatizes any discrete group or individual and whether race is reasonably used in light of the program's objectives—is clearly satisfied by the Davis program.

It is not even claimed that Davis' program in any way operates to stigmatize or single out any discrete and insular, or even any identifiable, nonminority group. . . . True, whites are excluded from participation in the special admissions program, but this fact only operates to reduce the number of whites to be admitted in the regular admissions program in order to permit admission of a reasonable percentage—less than their proportion of the California population—of otherwise underrepresented qualified minority applicants. . . .

. . . With respect to any factor (such as poverty or family educational background) that may be used as a substitute for race as an indicator of past discrimination, whites greatly outnumber racial minorities simply because whites make up a far larger percentage of the total population, and therefore far outnumber minorities in absolute terms at every socioeconomic level. For example, of a class of recent medical school applicants from families with less than $10,000 income, at least 71% were white. Of all 1970 families headed by a person not a high school graduate which included related children under 18, 80% were white and 20% were racial minorities. Moreover, while race is positively correlated with differences in GPA and MCAT scores, economic disadvantage is not. Thus, it appears that economically disadvantaged whites do not score less well than economically advantaged whites, while economically advantaged blacks score less well than do disadvantaged whites. These statistics graphically illustrate that the University's purpose to integrate its classes by compensating for past discrimination could not be achieved by a general preference for the economically disadvantaged or the children of parents of limited education unless such groups were to make up the entire class. . . .

Finally, Davis' special admissions program cannot be said to violate the Constitution simply because it has set aside a predetermined number of places for qualified minority applicants, rather than using minority status as a positive factor to be considered in evaluating the applications of disadvantaged minority applicants. For purposes of constitutional adjudication, there is no difference between the two approaches. In any admissions program which accords special consideration to disadvantaged racial minorities, a determination of the degree of preference to be given is unavoidable, and any given preference that results in the exclusion of a white candidate is no more or less constitutionally acceptable than a program such as that at Davis. . . .

Adarand Constructors, Inc. v. Pena

515 U.S. 200 (1995), 5-4
Opinion of the Court: O'Connor (Kennedy, Rehnquist, Scalia, Thomas)
Dissenting: Breyer, Ginsburg, Souter, Stevens

What did the federal law in this case require? Why did its application deny Adarand equal protection? What standard of scrutiny does O'Connor apply? Does the Court offer any guidance for when affirmative action plans violate equal protection and when they merely promote it? What is the difference between "invidious" and "benign" discrimination? Do the justices agree that both are equally repugnant to the Constitution? Is affirmative action a form of reparations?

O'Connor, for the Court:

Petitioner Adarand Constructors, Inc., claims that the Federal Government's practice of giving general contractors on government projects a financial incentive to hire subcontractors controlled by "socially and economically disadvantaged individuals," and, in particular, the Government's use of race-based presumptions in identifying such individuals, violates the equal protection component of the Fifth Amendment's Due Process Clause. . . .

In 1989, the Central Federal Lands Highway Division (CFLHD), which is part of the United States Department of Transportation (DOT), awarded the prime contract for a highway construction project in Colorado to Mountain Gravel & Construction Company. Mountain Gravel then solicited bids from subcontractors for the guardrail portion of the contract. Adarand, a Colorado-based highway construction company specializing in guardrail work, submitted the low bid. Gonzales Construction Company also submitted a bid.

The prime contract's terms provide that Mountain Gravel would receive additional compensation if it hired subcontractors certified as small businesses controlled by "socially and economically disadvantaged individuals," Gonzales is certified as such a business; Adarand is not. Mountain Gravel awarded the subcontract to Gonzales, despite Adarand's low bid, and Mountain Gravel's Chief Estimator has submitted an affidavit stating that Mountain Gravel would have accepted Adarand's bid had it not been for the additional payment it received by hiring Gonzales instead. . . .

. . . Although this Court has always understood that Clause to provide some measure of protection against arbitrary treatment by the Federal Government, it is not as explicit a guarantee of equal treatment as the Fourteenth Amendment, which provides that "No State shall . . . deny to any person within its jurisdiction the equal protection of the laws" (emphasis added). Our cases have accorded varying degrees of significance to the difference in the language of those two Clauses. We think it necessary to revisit the issue here. . . .

Cases decided after *McLaughlin* [v. *Florida*, 1964, have treated] the equal protection obligations imposed by the Fifth and the Fourteenth Amendments as indistinguishable. . . .

Most. . . . involved classifications burdening groups that have suffered discrimination in our society. In 1978, the Court confronted the question whether race-based governmental action designed to benefit such groups should also be subject to "the most rigid scrutiny." *Regents of Univ. of California v. Bakke* involved an equal protection challenge to a state-run medical school's practice of reserving a number of spaces in its entering class for minority students. The petitioners argued that "strict scrutiny" should apply only to "classifications that disadvantage 'discrete and insular minorities.'"

Two years after *Bakke*, the Court faced another challenge to remedial race-based action, this time involving action undertaken by the Federal Government. In *Fullilove v. Klutznick*, the Court upheld Congress' inclusion of a 10% set-aside for minority-owned businesses in the Public Works Employment Act of 1977. As in *Bakke*, there was no opinion for the Court. . . .

In *Wygant v. Jackson Board of Ed.*, the Court considered a Fourteenth Amendment challenge to another form of remedial racial classification. The issue in *Wygant* was whether a school board could adopt race-based preferences in determining which teachers to lay off. Justice Powell's plurality opinion observed that "the level of scrutiny does not change merely because the challenged classification operates against a group that historically has not been subject to governmental discrimination," and stated the two-part inquiry as "whether the layoff provision is supported by a compelling state purpose and whether the means chosen to accomplish that purpose are narrowly tailored." . . .

The Court's failure to produce a majority opinion in *Bakke*, *Fullilove*, and *Wygant* left unresolved the proper analysis for remedial race-based governmental action. . . .

The Court resolved the issue at least in part, in 1989. *Richmond v. J.A. Croson Co.* concerned a city's determination that 30% of its contracting work should go to minority-owned businesses. A majority of the Court in *Croson* held that "the standard of review under the Equal Protection Clause is not dependent on the race of those burdened or benefited by a particular classification," and that the single standard of review for racial classifications should be "strict scrutiny." . . .

With *Croson*, the Court finally agreed that the Fourteenth Amendment requires strict scrutiny of all race-based action by state and local governments. But *Croson* of course had no occasion to declare what standard of review the Fifth Amendment requires for such action taken by the Federal Government. *Croson* observed simply that the Court's "treatment of an exercise of congressional power in *Fullilove* cannot be dispositive here," because *Croson's* facts did not implicate Congress' broad power under §5 of the Fourteenth Amendment. . . .

Despite lingering uncertainty in the details, however, the Court's cases through *Croson* had established three general propositions with respect to governmental racial classifications. First, skepticism: "'[a]ny preference based on racial or ethnic criteria must necessarily receive a most searching examination,'" Second, consistency: "the standard of review under the Equal Protection Clause is not dependent on the race of those burdened or benefited by a particular classification." And third, congruence: "[e]qual protection analysis in the Fifth Amendment area is the same as that under the Fourteenth Amendment." Taken together, these three propositions lead to the conclusion that any person, of whatever race, has the right to demand that any governmental actor subject to the Constitution justify any racial classification subjecting that person to unequal treatment under the strictest judicial scrutiny. . . .

A year later, however, the Court took a surprising turn. *Metro Broadcasting, Inc. v. FCC* involved a Fifth Amendment challenge to two race-based policies of the Federal Communications Commission. In *Metro Broadcasting*, the Court repudiated the long-held notion that "it would be unthinkable that the same Constitution would impose a lesser duty on the Federal Government" than it does on a State to afford equal protection of the laws. It did so by holding that "benign" federal racial classifications need only satisfy intermediate scrutiny, even though *Croson* had recently concluded that such classifications enacted by a State must satisfy strict scrutiny. "[B]enign" federal racial classifications, the Court said, "—even if those measures are not "remedial" in the sense of being designed to compensate victims of past governmental or societal discrimination—are constitutionally permissible to the extent that they serve important governmental objectives within the power of Congress and are substantially related to achievement of those objectives." The Court did not explain how to tell whether a racial classification should be deemed "benign," other than to express "confiden[ce] that an "examination of the legislative scheme and its history" will separate benign measures from other types of racial classifications."

Applying this test, the Court first noted that the FCC policies at issue did not serve as a remedy for past discrimination. Id. at 566. Proceeding on the assumption that the policies were nonetheless "benign," it concluded that they served the "important governmental objective" of "enhancing broadcast diversity," and that they were "substantially related" to that objective. It therefore upheld the policies.

By adopting intermediate scrutiny as the standard of review for congressionally mandated "benign" racial classifications, Metro Broadcasting departed from prior cases in two significant respects. First, it turned its back on *Croson's* explanation of why strict scrutiny of all governmental racial classifications is essential:

> Absent searching judicial inquiry into the justification for such race-based measures, there is simply no way of determining what classifications are "benign" or "remedial" and what classifications are in fact motivated by illegitimate notions of racial inferiority or simple racial politics. Indeed, the purpose of strict scrutiny is to "smoke out" illegitimate uses of race by assuring that the legislative body is pursuing a goal important enough to warrant use of a highly suspect tool. The test also ensures that the means chosen "fit" this compelling goal so closely that there is little or no possibility that the motive for the classification was illegitimate racial prejudice or stereotype.

We adhere to that view today, despite the surface appeal of holding "benign" racial classifications to a lower standard. . . .

Second, *Metro Broadcasting* squarely rejected one of the three propositions established by the Court's earlier equal protection cases, namely, congruence between the standards applicable to federal and state racial classifications, and in so doing also undermined the other two—skepticism of all racial classifications and consistency of treatment irrespective of the race of the burdened or benefited group. . . .

The three propositions undermined by *Metro Broadcasting* all derive from the basic principle that the Fifth and Fourteenth Amendments to the Constitution protect persons, not groups. It follows from that principle that all governmental action based on race—a group classification long recognized as "in most circumstances irrelevant and therefore prohibited,"—should be subjected to detailed judicial inquiry to ensure that the personal right to equal protection of the laws has not been infringed. These ideas have long been central to this Court's understanding of equal protection, and holding "benign" state and federal racial classifications to different standards does not square with them. "[A] free people

whose institutions are founded upon the doctrine of equality," ibid., should tolerate no retreat from the principle that government may treat people differently because of their race only for the most compelling reasons. Accordingly, we hold today that all racial classifications, imposed by whatever federal, state, or local governmental actor, must be analyzed by a reviewing court under strict scrutiny. In other words, such classifications are constitutional only if they are narrowly tailored measures that further compelling governmental interests. To the extent that *Metro Broadcasting* is inconsistent with that holding, it is overruled. . . .

Because our decision today alters the playing field in some important respects, we think it best to remand the case to the lower courts for further consideration in light of the principles we have announced. The Court of Appeals, following *Metro Broadcasting* and *Fullilove,* analyzed the case in terms of intermediate scrutiny. It upheld the challenged statutes and regulations because it found them to be "narrowly tailored to achieve [their] significant governmental purpose of providing subcontracting opportunities for small disadvantaged business enterprises."

The Court of Appeals did not decide the question whether the interests served by the use of subcontractor compensation clauses are properly described as "compelling." It also did not address the question of narrow tailoring in terms of our strict scrutiny cases, by asking, for example, whether there was "any consideration of the use of race-neutral means to increase minority business participation" in government contracting, or whether the program was appropriately limited such that it "will not last longer than the discriminatory effects it is designed to eliminate." . . .

Scalia, concurring in part and concurring in the judgment:

I join the opinion of the Court . . . except insofar as it may be inconsistent with the following: in my view, government can never have a "compelling interest" in discriminating on the basis of race in order to "make up" for past racial discrimination in the opposite direction. Individuals who have been wronged by unlawful racial discrimination should be made whole, but, under our Constitution, there can be no such thing as either a creditor or a debtor race. That concept is alien to the Constitution's focus upon the individual. . . . To pursue the concept of racial entitlement—even for the most admirable and benign of purposes—is to reinforce and preserve for future mischief the way of thinking that produced race slavery, race privilege and race hatred. In the eyes of government, we are just one race here. It is American.

It is unlikely, if not impossible, that the challenged program would survive under this understanding of strict scrutiny, but I am content to leave that to be decided on remand.

Thomas, concurring in part and concurring in the judgment:

I agree with the majority's conclusion that strict scrutiny applies to all government classifications based on race. I write separately, however, to express my disagreement with the premise underlying Justice Stevens' and Justice Ginsburg's dissents: that there is a racial paternalism exception to the principle of equal protection. I believe that there is a "moral [and] constitutional equivalence," between laws designed to subjugate a race and those that distribute benefits on the basis of race in order to foster some current notion of equality. Government cannot make us equal; it can only recognize, respect, and protect us as equal before the law.

That these programs may have been motivated, in part, by good intentions cannot provide refuge from the principle that under our Constitution, the government may not make distinctions on the basis of race. As far as the Constitution is concerned, it is irrelevant whether a government's racial classifications are drawn by those who wish to oppress a race or by those who have a sincere desire to help those thought to be disadvantaged. There can be no doubt that the paternalism that appears to lie at the heart of this program is at war with the principle of inherent equality that underlies and infuses our Constitution.

These programs not only raise grave constitutional questions, they also undermine the moral basis of the equal protection principle. Purchased at the price of immeasurable human suffering, the equal protection principle reflects our Nation's understanding that such classifications ultimately have a destructive impact on the individual and our society. Unquestionably, "[i]nvidious [racial] discrimination is an engine of oppression." It is also true that "[r]emedial" racial preferences may reflect "a desire to foster equality in society." But there can be no doubt that racial paternalism and its unintended consequences can be as poisonous and pernicious as any other form of discrimination. So-called "benign"

discrimination teaches many that because of chronic and apparently immutable handicaps, minorities cannot compete with them without their patronizing indulgence. Inevitably, such programs engender attitudes of superiority or, alternatively, provoke resentment among those who believe that they have been wronged by the government's use of race. These programs stamp minorities with a badge of inferiority and may cause them to develop dependencies or to adopt an attitude that they are "entitled" to preferences. . . .

In my mind, government-sponsored racial discrimination based on benign prejudice is just as noxious as discrimination inspired by malicious prejudice. In each instance, it is racial discrimination, plain and simple. . . .

Stevens, dissenting:

Instead of deciding this case in accordance with controlling precedent, the Court today delivers a disconcerting lecture about the evils of governmental racial classifications. . . .

The Court's concept of "consistency" assumes that there is no significant difference between a decision by the majority to impose a special burden on the members of a minority race and a decision by the majority to provide a benefit to certain members of that minority notwithstanding its incidental burden on some members of the majority. In my opinion that assumption is untenable. There is no moral or constitutional equivalence between a policy that is designed to perpetuate a caste system and one that seeks to eradicate racial subordination. Invidious discrimination is an engine of oppression, subjugating a disfavored group to enhance or maintain the power of the majority. Remedial race-based preferences reflect the opposite impulse: a desire to foster equality in society. No sensible conception of the Government's constitutional obligation to "govern impartially," should ignore this distinction. . . .

The consistency that the Court espouses would disregard the difference between a "No Trespassing" sign and a welcome mat. It would treat a Dixiecrat Senator's decision to vote against Thurgood Marshall's confirmation in order to keep African Americans off the Supreme Court as on a par with President Johnson's evaluation of his nominee's race as a positive factor. It would equate a law that made black citizens ineligible for military service with a program aimed at recruiting black soldiers. An attempt by the majority to exclude members of a minority race from a regulated market is fundamentally different from a subsidy that enables a relatively small group of newcomers to enter that market. An interest in "consistency" does not justify treating differences as though they were similarities.

The Court's explanation for treating dissimilar race-based decisions as though they were equally objectionable is a supposed inability to differentiate between "invidious" and "benign" discrimination. But the term "affirmative action" is common and well understood. Its presence in everyday parlance shows that people understand the difference between good intentions and bad. As with any legal concept, some cases may be difficult to classify, but our equal protection jurisprudence has identified a critical difference between state action that imposes burdens on a disfavored few and state action that benefits the few "in spite of" its adverse effects on the many. . . .

Moreover, the Court may find that its new "consistency" approach to race-based classifications is difficult to square with its insistence upon rigidly separate categories for discrimination against different classes of individuals. For example, as the law currently stands, the Court will apply "intermediate scrutiny" to cases of invidious gender discrimination and "strict scrutiny" to cases of invidious race discrimination, while applying the same standard for benign classifications as for invidious ones. If this remains the law, then today's lecture about "consistency" will produce the anomalous result that the Government can more easily enact affirmative action programs to remedy discrimination against women than it can enact affirmative action programs to remedy discrimination against African Americans— even though the primary purpose of the Equal Protection Clause was to end discrimination against the former slaves. When a court becomes preoccupied with abstract standards, it risks sacrificing common sense at the altar of formal consistency. . . .

The Court's concept of "congruence" assumes that there is no significant difference between a decision by the Congress of the United States to adopt an affirmative action program and such a decision by a State or a municipality. In my opinion, that assumption is untenable. It ignores important practical and legal differences between federal and state or local decisionmakers. . . .

. . . [A] reason for giving greater deference to the National Legislature than to a local law-making body is that federal affirmative action programs represent the will of our entire Nation's elected representatives, whereas a state or local program may have an impact on nonresident entities who played no part in the decision to enact it. Thus, in the state or local context, individuals who were unable to vote for the local representatives who enacted a race-conscious program may nonetheless feel the effects of that program. . . .

Presumably, the majority is now satisfied that its theory of "congruence" between the substantive rights provided by the Fifth and Fourteenth Amendments disposes of the objection based upon divided constitutional powers. But it is one thing to say (as no one seems to dispute) that the Fifth Amendment encompasses a general guarantee of equal protection as broad as that contained within the Fourteenth Amendment. It is another thing entirely to say that Congress' institutional competence and constitutional authority entitles it to no greater deference when it enacts a program designed to foster equality than the deference due a State legislature. The latter is an extraordinary proposition; and, as the foregoing discussion demonstrates, our precedents have rejected it explicitly and repeatedly. . . .

The Court's holding in *Fullilove* surely governs the result in this case. The Public Works Employment Act of 1977, which this Court upheld in *Fullilove*, is different in several critical respects from the portions of the Small Business Act (SBA), and the Surface Transportation and Uniform Relocation Assistance Act of 1987 (STURAA), challenged in this case. Each of those differences makes the current program designed to provide assistance to disadvantaged business enterprises (DBE's) significantly less objectionable than the 1977 categorical grant of $400 million in exchange for a 10% set-aside in public contracts to "a class of investors defined solely by racial characteristics." In no meaningful respect is the current scheme more objectionable than the 1977 Act. Thus, if the 1977 Act was constitutional, then so must be the SBA and STURAA. Indeed, even if my dissenting views in *Fullilove* had prevailed, this program would be valid. . . .

. . . The majority's concept of "consistency" ignores a difference, fundamental to the idea of equal protection, between oppression and assistance. The majority's concept of "congruence" ignores a difference, fundamental to our constitutional system, between the Federal Government and the States. And the majority's concept of stare decisis ignores the force of binding precedent. I would affirm the judgment of the Court of Appeals.

8

ALIENAGE AND CITIZENSHIP

The American population today—nearly 300 million—is more than a hundred times greater than that of 1776. This extraordinary gain is largely attributable to a steady influx of newcomers. Added to white, black, and Native Americans already in place, immigrants have made the United States in race, religion, ethnicity, and cultural origins the world's most heterogeneous nation. Today this diversity is celebrated, even glorified, as images of the "melting pot" seem out of fashion. Yet that this heightened awareness has occurred may be a tribute to the success of assimilating forces: very likely the stronger the cement of a common culture, the greater the tolerance for accentuating differences. American society has been enriched by the contributions of persons of different ways, languages, religions, and national origins. But the encounter of differences may also threaten and be stressful and, as such, challenge the ideal of equality, just as assimilation, despite its dangers of conformity, may help to realize equality.

The image of the United States as a "nation of immigrants" is accurate in the sense that ge-

nealogically all Americans, even Native Americans, originated elsewhere than the Western Hemisphere. But it is probably more accurate to think of the United States as a continuously receiving culture, incorporating newcomers and itself being endlessly changed in the process. No other great immigrant-receiving nations of the last 200 years—Canada, Argentina, Brazil, Australia, for example—has drawn nearly as many nor nearly as diverse a body of newcomers as the United States. Those who entered have often differed more from each than from the receiving culture.

This chapter deals with the constitutional aspects of this development. Included are matters of alienage, citizenship, civil rights, and in the case of Native Americans, treaty and tribal rights.

Those Who Were Here First

Native Americans, mistaken for inhabitants of India by fifteenth-century Spanish explorers, were themselves descended from peoples who crossed into Alaska from Asia over a land bridge tens of thousands of years before. There is no ev-idence that human beings evolved on their own in the Western Hemisphere. First occupants of the Americas were, if not immigrants, migrants, probably hunter bands following animal herds. At the time of European explorations hundreds of centuries later, millions of "Indians" occu-pied, thinly in many places, all North and South America. In many areas, particularly in South and Central America, they built complex civiliza-tions based on agriculture.

Encounters with a European culture techno-logically and administratively more advanced were dramatic and tragic. Relations with the whites, which ranged from friendly to hostile, were always problematic with misunderstand-ings and cruelty to spare on both sides. Unlike the French and Spanish, who at first came to prospect or trade, the English came to settle. Their extensive and continuously reinforced colonies along the Atlantic coast established a pattern in which Indians who were not assimi-lated or did not accept European culture were pushed westward until finally enveloped and confined to small enclaves or "reservations." They were no match for the steady stream of settlers who brought with them superior tech-nology and military force.

In some cases, Indians relinquished land through negotiation and received payment, in others they were simply forced out. In the 1830s, for example, more than 17,000 Cherokees were rounded up by Georgia and removed to Okla-homa along the "Trail of Tears," a trek on which several thousand died. Tribes allied with one white side or another in the French and Indian War, the American Revolution, and the Civil War, gained or suffered accordingly. Acquisition of guns and horses, which allowed some Plains Indians to remain "hostiles" almost to the 1890s, was a mixed blessing. Alcohol and European dis-eases from which most Indians had little natural immunity, proved disastrous.

Intermarriage and wide individual assimilation led to population estimates understating Indian ancestry. Tribal population, thought to have been

at least a million in the early nineteenth century in the area of what is now the present United States, fell to a low of 228,000 in 1890. Indian birthrate rose in the twentieth century with im-provement in health conditions and new political stability. Since the 1930s, federal policy has en-couraged the reassertion of tribal authority. Yet the reservations, well-springs of traditional cul-ture, often battle poverty and lag educationally behind norms for the rest of the country.

The legal and constitutional status of Indian tribes and tribal Indians as individuals is unique and complicated. The federal government may as-sert jurisdiction over Indian affairs through the so-called Indian commerce clause, the power of Congress in Article I-8 to "regulate commerce . . . with the Indian tribes." More often, it has used its treaty power to deal with the tribes as semi-sovereign political entities. This unusual status was affirmed by the Supreme Court in *Cherokee Nation v. Georgia,* 1831, in which Chief Justice John Marshall held tribes to be "domestic dependent nations" under the protection of the United States. The following year in *Worcester v. Georgia,* he elaborated, holding that state laws had no force within Indian territory possessed through treaty. Though these decisions did not stop Georgia, with the tacit support of President Andrew Jack-son, from removing the Cherokees under a fraud-ulent treaty, the quasi-sovereignty of Indian tribes remains well established in constitutional law.

The semi-independent status of the tribes has greatly complicated legal relations with the states over such matters as taxation, water rights, hunt-ing and fishing, environmental regulation, and gambling. Though state and local authority over reservation activity is limited unless addressed in treaty provisions, questions of individual liberty and application of the equal protection clause still arise.

The Supreme Court has made a distinction be-tween federal acts regulating tribal Indians as members of quasi-sovereign entities and classify-ing them for special treatment because of their Indian ancestry. The latter would be considered race based and fall under the Court's "strict scrutiny" equal protection review. Governmental acts based on the political status of the tribes, however, are held to the lesser "mere rationality" test. Thus in *Morton v. Mancari*, 1974, the Court upheld employment preferences for tribal members in the federal Bureau of Indian Affairs. In *Washington v. Washington State Commercial Passenger Fishing Vessel Association*, 1979, it held that granting of preferential fishing rights to Indians as tribal members was not a form of benign racial classification that might otherwise violate equal protection principles.

Though tribal Indians are now full citizens of the United States, the Supreme Court at first held in *Talton v. Mayes*, 1896, that the rights in the Bill of Rights did not apply in Indian tribal courts. But in 1968, Congress enacted the so-called Indian Bill of Rights as Title II of the Civil Rights Act of that year. It made most rights in the Bill of Rights and others elsewhere in the Constitution applicable to Indian tribal governments. Specifically omitted was the ban on religious establishment, the right to a jury trial in civil cases, the right of indigent criminal defendants to free legal counsel, and the guarantee of a republican form of government.

Congress's authority to impose these rights was upheld in *Santa Clara Pueblo v. Martinez* in 1978. But the Court ruled that federal judicial authority was limited mainly to granting writs of habeas corpus to persons in tribal custody who claimed violation of a federal right. The Court held that the Indian Bill of Rights did not take away tribal immunity from suits by individuals nor create a cause of action against tribal officers. Thus enforcement of the Indian Bill of Rights is primarily left to tribal courts.

To have allowed federal courts general jurisdiction in these civil liberties matters would almost certainly have compromised tribal sovereign and the opportunity of members to follow traditional Indian lifestyle. However, it would have given greater security and protection for individual tribal members.

Jurisdiction of tribal courts is limited to members of the tribe. In *Duro v. Reina*, 1990, the Court held that a tribal court did not have jurisdiction over an Indian who was a member of another tribe for criminal acts committed on the reservation. The Court observed that "the retained sovereign of the tribe is but a recognition of certain additional authority the tribes maintain over Indians who consent to be tribal members." Tribal members, of course, are subject to all federal, state, and local laws when outside the reservation.

Immigration as National Policy

Given its importance in American development, it is paradoxical that immigration receives almost no mention in the Constitution. Article I-9 barred Congress until the year 1808 from interfering with the "migration or importation" of persons the states wanted to admit. This oblique reference to the slave trade was a price the Framers paid to keep the slave-trading states from breaking up the Constitutional Convention. Congress ended the slave trade as soon as the moratorium expired. The only other reference remotely connected with immigration is the power of Congress in Article I-8 to "establish a uniform rule of naturalization." By not addressing immigration, the Framers left the matter to the individual states. Most of them assumed that entry would remain open and free, a generosity of policy their leading member, James Madison, called the "luster of our country."

By the 1820s, coastal states with major ports— Massachusetts, New York, Pennsylvania, Maryland, and South Carolina—concerned about the ever-increasing flow of newcomers and entry of the indigent and medically infirm, had begun to regulate immigration. New York's requirement that ship captains give background information and pay a small head tax for each passenger was challenged in *New York v. Miln*, 1837. Against an argument that the regulation obstructed interstate and foreign commerce, the Supreme Court sustained it as a public health measure within the power of the states. Twelve years later in two appeals known as the Passenger Cases, a closely

From Many Streams

Migration to the United States has been one of the most important demographic events of modern times. Since 1820, when reliable figures were first compiled, more than 60 million persons have emigrated to the United States. They have come from every country of the world, from every background, holding every religious belief, and speaking every language. Before the Civil War, they came at the rate of 125,000 a year; between 1865 and 1930, more than 460,000 a year. At its peak, 1905–1914, the immigration level averaged more than a million annually. In 1910, for example, one American in seven was foreign born and one in ten had been in the country less than 10 years.

Because of the Depression, World War II, and new restrictions on entry, the rate of immigration fell to less than 50,000 a year between 1930 and 1945. Since then it has steadily risen, and now averages about 900,000 a year, mainly persons from Latin America and Asia. Today, nearly 8 percent of Americans are foreign born, one of the highest national figures in the world.

The national and continental origins of all American immigrants since 1820 are as follows:

Europe	38,000,000
Canada	6,000,000
Mexico	5,000,000
Asia	4,500,000
Other Americas	4,000,000
Africa, (excluding slaves)	250,000
Australia and New Zealand	150,000*

Massive immigration has both a "push" and a "pull." Most people left their homelands to escape outright poverty. Others have come because of religious or political persecution or were war refugees. The Mayflower pilgrims at Plymouth Rock in 1620 were only the first in a long line of those seeking religious freedom and tolerance. They have included the Quakers and German Mennonites in seventeenth-century Pennsylvania, Roman Catholics in Maryland, and French Protestant Huguenots in colonial New York.

Scottish royalists who came to Boston in 1650 were among the first political refugees. French royalists, exiled after the French Revolution, settled along the Ohio River in 1790. Germans sought refuge after failed revolutions on the Continent in 1830 and 1848. Mexicans came during the Mexican Revolution in 1910. Jews and other Europeans fled Nazism in the 1930s. After World War II and during much of the Cold War, immigrants included many admitted under the Displaced Persons Act. Twenty thousand Cubans fled the Castro regime in 1959 and more than 120,000 others left the island in the 1980s for political reasons. Tens of thousands of Vietnamese and other Southeast Asians entered the United States following the Vietnam War.

However, the chief reason for emigrating has been economic. Almost half of white immigrants to the colonies before the Revolution came as indentured servants, hoping that independence after a term of labor would open the door to opportunity.

*Leonard Dinnerstein, Roger L. Nichols, and David M. Reimers, *Natives and Strangers: A Multicultural History of Americans* (New York, Oxford University Press, 1996), 124.

divided Court reversed itself. It held a state tax on entering immigrants interfered with Congress's power over foreign commerce, even where the levy was used to pay the hospital care for the infirm. Though the decision made immigration a matter of national regulation, Congress produced no national policy. This remarkable void is attributable to the long shadow of the slavery issue. Southern states, wary that federal power might be used to interfere with slavery, opposed almost any national legislation dealing with entry or egress of persons. See "From Many Streams."

After the Civil War, the Supreme Court went further and in *Henderson v. Mayor of New York*, 1875, held all state immigration laws unconstitutional as interfering with Congress's exclusive power. The task of receiving, monitoring, and orienting newcomers then fell to private charities. As the influx of foreigners reached half a million a year, resources of these groups were overwhelmed and pressure mounted for a na-

In the nineteenth century a dramatic rise in European population and a growing commercialization of agriculture that cut farm work left many in rural areas impoverished. Agricultural disasters, like the Irish potato famine in the 1840s that brought more than a million immigrants to the United States in the decade following, were periodic. Craft workers, such as Scottish weavers, German clock-makers, and Swedish potters, found themselves displaced by machines. Others less skilled faced subsistence-level factory work in increasingly crowded cities.

It is no surprise that many saw hope for a better life in the New World. Stories of fortune, sometimes outrageously embellished, found their way back to Europe. America became a magnet. Yet, despite the lure, emigration remained a hard, serious decision, often resulting in a break-up of families; few undertook it for the sake of high adventure. Though a bit romantic perhaps, Emma Lazarus's eloquent welcoming lines inscribed at the base of the Statue of Liberty in New York harbor catch the forces of push and pull for many who emigrated: "Give me your tired, your poor, your huddled masses yearning to be free. The wretched refuse of your teeming shore. Send these, the homeless, tempest-tost to me. I lift my lamp beside the golden door!"

The United States, in the midst of the greatest territorial and economic expansion in history, had an almost constant need for settlers to farm and mine the West and for labor, mostly unskilled, to move the wheels of new industry. Many newcomers prospered, if not, their children or grandchildren did. Some, such as the Scotsman Andrew Carnegie, the Austro-Hungarian Joseph Pulitzer, and the Italian A.P. Giannini, did so beyond wildest dreams. But the more typical experience was one of years of hardship, perhaps living in tenements or company towns, a struggle to learn a new language and new ways, and often meeting prejudice and discrimination. Yet starting at the bottom or not, the social contract of American immigration was that the "golden door" of opportunity would open and remain open once one became an American.

However difficult the experience, few immigrants gave up and returned to the "old" country. More likely, friends and relatives there were urged to come over, and many did. Emigration is, in effect, voting with one's feet. As such, it is a more powerful statement than a ballot cast on election day or an opinion given in a poll. That more than 60 million have voted "yea" and only a negligible few "nay" may be the greatest endorsement a country has ever had.

Massive immigration, however economically beneficial, has never stopped being a political issue. Newcomers, often with a different language and different ways and beliefs, have not always been as welcome as Emma Lazarus's inscription would have it. Hard times have sometimes led to keen competition for jobs, especially among unskilled workers. The immigrant's claim to public resources may sometimes obscure the subsidizing role newcomers often play by working for low wages and filling jobs others want to avoid.

The diversity newcomers represent can also be a source of tension and, at times, challenge commitment of the native born to the ideal of equality. These difficulties are not new nor are they peculiar the United States among heterogeneous, immigrant-receiving nations.

tional policy. In 1891, Congress finally set up an administrative unit in the Justice Department to deal with immigration. By the early twentieth century, it passed several laws restricting entry, and the era of largely free, unlimited immigration was over.

In the Emergency Quota Act in 1921, Congress introduced proportional quotas as the basis of immigration policy. An annual maximum of 375,000 persons was set, but no more than 3 percent of those of any nationality, measured by the census of 1910, could enter. In the Johnson-Reed Immigration Act of 1924, the overall quota was cut in half and a 2 percent limit for any nationality as measured by the census of 1890 became the proportional standard. This reduced the numbers of immigrants entering from Eastern and Southern Europe and Asia. No restrictions were placed on those entering from Canada or Latin America. After World War II, Congress made a temporary exception to the quota policy in the Displaced Persons Act, which permitted special entry to 450,000 European war refugees. The Immigration and Nationality Act of 1951, also known as the McCarran-Walter Act, excepted spouses and minor children from the national-origin quotas.

Such quotas were ended in the Immigration Act of 1965, which set an overall limit, not counting immediate family members, of 120,000 persons from Western Hemisphere countries and 170,000 from other nations. Preferences were given to relatives of U.S. citizens and persons with special skill or education. In the Immigration Control and Reform Act of 1986, the Simpson-Rodino Act, Congress turned its attention to the problem of illegal immigrants, who were thought to number more than 3 million, mainly from Mexico. The law allowed such aliens to legalize their status on proof they had lived continuously in the United States since 1982. It also put sanctions on employers who hired undocumented foreign workers. The Immigration Act of 1990 set an annual resident visa limit of 675,000, about 20 percent reserved for persons sponsored by employers for specified jobs. Lobbying by ethnic groups led to an increase in these provisions in the interest of family unification.

Nationalities making up the largest immigrant groups have shifted continuously, depending on the presence or absence of quotas and on economic and political conditions in countries of origin. In recent years, about 40 percent of entrants have been from Asia, including the Middle East, about 7.5 percent from Europe, and about 3 percent from Africa, including North Africa.

Opposition and Conflict

There is no constitutional right of entry into the United States. As an attribute of sovereignty, the federal government, through Congress, has the right to control and, if it chooses, bar immigration altogether. That the United States permitted, even encouraged, virtually unlimited immigration for more than a century is almost unique in the history of nations.

The great, steady influx of persons brought with it social and economic gains and costs. Differences in class, religion, language, cultural values, and complexion between newcomers and native born created stress of adjustment for both sides. The more immigrants and the sharper the differences, the more probable this stress would produce outright conflict, discrimination, and calls for restrictions on entry. Tensions were apt to be eased in good economic times but made worse during downturns, when jobs were fewer and the willingness of immigrants to work for lower wages was more resented than appreciated.

Violence was not uncommon. Immigrant groups often clashed with native born and with each other. In Philadelphia in 1842, widespread rioting among Irish immigrants was directed mainly at free blacks. Two years later clashes of the Irish with other native born left 20 persons dead. In 1877, anti-Chinese riots swept San Francisco. Events such as these overshadowed countless small-scale hostilities that occurred with regularity among individuals throughout the nineteenth century and into the twentieth. They were more frequent in large coastal cities where large numbers of immigrants often lived cheek and jowl with native born with whom they competed for jobs and facilities.

Nativism, as anti-immigrant sentiment came to be called, began to take organized form before the Civil War. The Native-American Association, formed in Washington, D.C. in 1837, reflected concern that the Catholicism of most Irish and many German immigrants, supposedly dominated by priests, posed a threat to American democratic principles. In the 1850s, with immigration rising to new levels, the American Party was formed, advocating severe restrictions on entry. It had grown out of a secret fraternal organization whose members, denying knowledge of it, were called "Know Nothings," a name that stuck on the party. Despite early popularity in which it attracted more than a million members and won 40 House seats in the 1854 midterm elections, the party soon split on the even more profound issue of slavery. It nominated former president Millard Fillmore in 1856, and though he won 22 percent of the vote, carried only one state. Another upstart third party, the Republican, formed on the slavery question, did much better; it, rather than the Know Nothing became the nation's second major party.

Though the Know Nothings had completely disappeared from the political scene by 1860, opposition to unlimited mass immigration did not. Agitation was particularly strong on the West Coast in response to the influx of Chinese. When entrants reached 40,000 in 1882 alone, pressure mounted and Congress passed the Chinese Exclusion Act, barring the immigration of Chinese laborers for 10 years. It was the nation's first immigrant exclusion law and was repeatedly renewed until World War II. Congress also barred the entry of convicts, paupers, and the insane of any nationality. In 1885 the importation of all contract laborers was proscribed.

The Chinese Exclusion Act was challenged in *Chae Chan Ping v. United States,* 1889. A unanimous Supreme Court made it emphatically clear that the United States could exclude foreign nationals as an attribute of its national sovereignty. "If it could not," Justice Stephen Field wrote, "it would be to that extent subject to the control of another power." Though the principle of exclusion may be constitutionally unobjectionable, it has often been applied in a discriminatory way. The same year Congress excluded the Chinese, for example, two-and-one-half times as many Scandinavians and six times as many Germans entered the country.

The anti-Chinese law did not mean there was no other opposition to mass immigration. Agitation continued as the number of entrants rose almost annually to new heights. The Immigration Restriction League, founded in Boston in 1894, urged that immigrants be required to take literacy tests for entry. When Congress passed such a law in 1897, it was vetoed by President Grover Cleveland. A similar law in 1917 was enacted over the veto of President Wilson. The quota system set up in the 1920s was a partial victory for anti-immigration forces.

That system and later regulations are probably best understood not as pro- or anti-immigration but the brokered results of different interests and forces coming into play from time to time. Opposition came not just from those warning of Catholicism and the "Yellow peril" or made anxious by diversity, but also from labor groups concerned about jobs and localities faced with the high cost of receiving large groups of newcomers. Immigration has traditionally been supported by employers with big labor needs and certain entrepreneurial interests, and by the foreign born and their families.

Any regulation almost certainly favors certain individuals and groups to the disadvantage of others. The quota system, first pegged to nationality distribution in 1910, favored groups that had already arrived in large numbers. When it was repegged to the nationality distribution of 1890, it hurt those coming from Eastern and Southern Europe. When nation quotas were ended and family unification exceptions were made to the overall quota, it benefited those coming from countries with high birth rates. When preferences were given to those possessing certain skill and training, it favored countries with highly developed education systems and Westernized economies. The Chinese Exclusion Act itself was soon a boon to Japanese and Filipino immigrants, who were welcomed when it became clear that many jobs the Chinese had filled were disdained by the native born.

The controversy over immigration—how much and who and what the gains and costs are—will probably continue as long as the United States is an independent nation. Its resolution in law and policy today may be different from what it was in the past or may be in the future. In the remainder of the chapter we turn to the rights of aliens in American society and questions of citizenship, denaturalization, deportation, and access to jobs and public resources. These matters have tested the ideal of equality, finding it triumphant at times, wanting at others.

Citizenship and Naturalization

Though the term "citizen" is used more than a dozen times in the Constitution, including in seven amendments, citizenship itself was not constitutionally defined until after the Civil War. This curious omission by the Framers may be partly understood as an attempt to avoid additional breaches at the convention over the status of the slaves. But it is also true that the Framers and their compatriots did not attach unusual importance to the idea as a definer of status or source of rights. The Bill of Rights, for example, speaks of "persons" rather than "citizens." Where the Framers did attend to citizenship it was to set out one of several criteria for holding national office and to prevent states from discriminating against persons who were from other states. Except for granting Congress power to "establish a uniform rule of naturalization," in Article I-8, they said nothing about citizenship as opposed to alienage or how citizenship was acquired.

In the Dred Scott Case in 1857, the Supreme Court, stepping in where the Framers had not, defined citizenship negatively. In a misguided attempt to resolve the slavery question on terms favorable to the South, the Court through Chief Justice Roger Taney held that black persons, including free blacks, could not be citizens. This decision was undone after the Civil War in ratification of the Fourteenth Amendment. The first sentence gives citizenship its long missing constitutional definition: "All persons born or naturalized in the United States, and subject to the jurisdiction thereof, are citizens of the United States and of the state wherein they reside."

Phrased this way, the amendment adopted the English common law principle of *jus soli*—"the law of the soil"—as the basis of citizenship rather than the Roman civil law rule of *jus sanguinis*—the law of blood relationship—that prevailed in much of the rest of Europe. Citizenship results

from birth within a territory rather than by descent. Children born in the United States of resident alien parents are citizens of the United States and can never be deported. The *jus soli* principle headed off many jurisdictional conflicts and promoted immigration.

It was affirmed by the Supreme Court in *Wong United States v. Kim Ark*, 1898, in which the complainant, born in the United States to Chinese immigrant parents, had been denied readmission after traveling to China. The government argued that the Chinese exclusion law in effect at the time and Congress's decision to bar citizenship to Chinese resident aliens meant that Wong Kim Ark was not a citizen and could not reenter. The Court rejected this *jus sanguinis* position, holding that the Fourteenth Amendment conferred citizenship on all native-born persons regardless of parental nationality. The decision was an important victory for Asian Americans at a time of great anti-Asian feeling on the West Coast.

Citizenship may also be gained by achievement, that is, through naturalization, a process by which resident aliens may qualify. Congress has power in Article I-8 to establish rules for naturalization, yet even without this grant, it would have the right to set the conditions of citizenship as an attribute of national sovereignty.

After ratification of the Fourteenth Amendment, Congress conferred alien eligibility for naturalization on "white persons and persons of African nativity or descent." In 1943, it extended it to resident aliens born in the Western Hemisphere and to persons of Chinese nationality or descent. Final racial and ethnic barriers to naturalization were removed by the Immigration and Nationality Act of 1952, which provided that "the right of a person to become a naturalized citizen . . . shall not be denied or abridged because of race or sex or because such person is married." This right is statutory not constitutional. It is conferred by Congress and, presumably, could be withdrawn by it.

As an individual matter, naturalization requires a period of legal residence in the United States, moral fitness, and an oath of allegiance. In

More than 7,000 new citizens are sworn in at the Convention Center in Los Angeles in 1995. One man, front center, has fashioned an outfit from the American flag in honor of the day.

the last, the citizen-to-be pledges to uphold the Constitution, defend and protect it against all enemies foreign and domestic, and renounce allegiance to foreign powers. These requirements have been grounds for denying naturalization to aliens shown to be alcoholics, polygamists, advocates of violent overthrow of the government or engaged in illegal gambling, prostitution, or other criminal activity. Denial of naturalization to pacifists because of their unwillingness to bear arms to defend the United States, first upheld by the Supreme Court in *United States v. MacIntosh,* 1931, was later disallowed in *Girouard v. United States,* 1946. The latter decision rests statutory rather than constitutional grounds. The Court held that Congress did not intend to bar a religious pacifist who, though refusing to bear arms, was willing to serve in a noncombatant military position. In 1952, largely because of *Girouard,* Congress expressly permitted religious pacifists applying for naturalization to swear a willingness to perform noncombatant military service or "work of national importance under civilian direction," rather than bear arms.

Besides acquiring citizenship through birth or naturalization, several groups have had it conferred or thrust upon them. Such collective naturalization occurs where Congress has declared certain populations to be American citizens. American Indians having tribal allegiance, for example, were declared to be citizens in 1887. In 1952, certain persons in territories under American jurisdiction—Alaska and Hawaii, both not yet states, Puerto Rico, the Panama Canal Zone, Guam, and the Virgin Islands, were declared to be U.S. citizens. Unless granted statutory amnesty, resident aliens who have entered the country illegally are not eligible for naturalization.

Denaturalization and Expatriation

Apart from being ineligible for the presidency under Article II-1, naturalized citizens are on the same constitutional footing and have the same rights, privileges, and responsibilities as those native born. They may not be denaturalized, that is, have their citizenship involuntarily removed, except when naturalization has been obtained by fraud or conditions placed on citizenship have not been met. For example, in *Fedorenko v. United States,* 1981, denaturalization was upheld where the former alien had not admitted on a visa application that he had been a concentration camp guard during World War II, a fact that would have barred him from entry. But the government's proof of fraud or bad faith must be "clear, unequivocal, and convincing." In *Schneiderman v. United States,* 1943, the Supreme Court overturned a denaturalization order where it was shown only that Schneiderman had been a member of a Communist organization within five years of his naturalization. Though naturalization could be denied those advocating violent overthrow of the government, the Court held the Justice Department had not proved that Schneiderman had done more than abstractly discuss such an end.

The Court has upheld reasonable conditions on maintaining citizenship but not ones clearly discriminatory against naturalized citizens. In *Schneider v. Rusk,* 1964, it invalidated a section of the Nationality Act of 1952 that revoked citizenship of naturalized citizens who later lived in their native land for three consecutive years. Holding the rights of naturalized and native-born citizens to be coextensive, the Court found the act drastically limited the right of naturalized citizens to "live and work abroad in a way that other citizens have." Where a person has been naturalized *outside* the United States, the Court has upheld limited conditions. At issue in *Rogers v. Bellei,* 1971, was a 1953 naturalization provision conferring citizenship on children born abroad to one parent with U.S. citizenship. Such citizenship could be retained only if the conferee later spent five consecutive years in the United States between ages 14 and 28. Divided five to four, the Court held that because persons born outside the United States did not fall under the *jus soli* definition of citizenship in the Fourteenth Amendment, Congress could impose reasonable conditions on citizenship conferred *jus sanguinis.*

In defining citizenship, the Fourteenth Amendment makes no provision for its termination. In *Perkins v. Elg,* 1939, the Supreme Court held that any citizen, native born or naturalized, may relinquish citizenship. What may constitute this voluntary act—expatriation—however, has raised difficult questions. In the Immigration and Natu-

ralization Act of 1952, Congressional made several voluntary acts expatriating as a matter of law. They include voting in a foreign election, military desertion during wartime, and leaving the country to avoid military service. The Court was sharply divided when it first dealt with these provisions in 1958. In *Perez v. Brownell,* it upheld the foreign elections provision, but in *Trop v. Dulles,* decided the same day, struck down the one on military desertion. The first was within the power of Congress to avoid embarrassment in its conduct of foreign affairs, but use of expatriation as a penalty for desertion, according to four of five justices in the majority, exceeded its power to raise and maintain military forces.

Five years later, in *Kennedy v. Mendoza-Martinez,* decided during the early stages of the Vietnam War, the Court struck down the provision on leaving the country to avoid military service. Revoking citizenship as punishment (rather than as an adjunct power to conducting foreign affairs) violated procedural safeguards of the Fifth and Sixth Amendments. In 1967, in *Afroyim v. Rusk,* the Court overturned *Perez v. Brownell,* holding that a naturalized citizen who had voted in an Israeli election had not by that fact alone expatriated himself. The ruling and broader statement that Congress had no power to revoke Fourteenth Amendment citizenship except when obtained by fraud, meant that the government would need to prove not only that a citizen had performed an act Congress made expatriating but that in doing so, *intended* to renounce citizenship. Thus in *Vance v. Terrazo,* 1980, the Court held that an American citizen who took an oath of Mexican citizenship that included renunciation of citizenship in all other governments, had not expatriated himself unless that was his proven intention in taking the Mexican oath.

Deportation

The same delegated and inherent powers Congress has over immigration and naturalization gives it authority to deport—to send back to country of origin—aliens in the United States. Among the reasons Congress has prescribed are illegal entry, conviction of a serious crime within five years of entry, and membership in certain organizations, such as the Communist Party, that advocate violent overthrow of the government. As long as deportation conforms to a reason Congress has set out, the Supreme Court will usually not interfere. No constitutional right stands in the way of Congressional policy on deportation.

However, because resident aliens are "persons" entitled to protection of the Bill of Rights, deportation must meet certain procedural requirements. Thus in *Ng Fung Ho v. White*, 1922, the Court ruled that a resident alien held for deportation was entitled to an administrative hearing at which the statutory basis for deportation and the subject's violation of applicable provisions had to be set out. Deportation does not require a court order nor, if based on a valid administrative hearing is it normally reviewable by the courts.

During the Cold War, deportation of aliens who were Communists or former Communists led to a series of Supreme Court decisions. Congress provided for such deportation in three important laws, the Alien Registration Act of 1940, the Internal Security Act of 1950, and the Immigration and Naturalization Act of 1952. In *Harisiades v. Shaughnessey*, 1952, the Court upheld deportation of a resident alien who had left the party even before the 1940 law took effect. Two years later in *Galvan v. Press*, deportation was upheld even against an alien who was not aware of the party's advocacy of violent overthrow of the government. But in later cases, the Court interpreted the statutory provisions to require the Justice Department prove the alien, as a party member, understood the party's illegal aim. (*Rowoldt v. Perfetto*, 1957; *Gastelum-Quinones v. Kennedy*, 1963)

Alien status cannot justify indefinite detention where deportation has been ordered but cannot be effected. In *Zadvydas v. Davis*, 2001, the government tried to deport Zadvydas because of a criminal record, but the two countries that might have received him refused, claiming he was not their citizen. The Court held that in these circumstances six months was a reasonable limit under Congress's deportation detention statute, without violating due process. But it conceded this constitutional objection could be overcome were Congress to expressly grant the attorney general power of indefinite detention or, absent that, the government could show special justification for such detention. This dictum, only six weeks before the September 11 terrorist attacks, may come to have special import in the nation's efforts to counter terrorism.

Alienage and Equal Protection

The equal protection clause of the Fourteenth Amendment, that no state shall "deny to any person within is jurisdiction the equal protection of the laws," requires that government treat similarly situated persons similarly. It protects against arbitrary classification of persons and against the government making invidious distinctions among them as individuals, that is, distinctions based on attributes rather than behavior. The Fifth Amendment's due process clause, speaking to the federal government, has been held to contain an implicit equal protection limit on federal power. Weighed against these individual rights are valid police power interests of state and local government and the federal government's power to conduct foreign affairs.

Because the equal protection clause is phrased as protecting "persons" rather than "citizens," its shield extends to aliens. This was the Supreme Court's conclusion in the early case of *Yick Wo v. Hopkins* 1888, (p. 523). Ostensibly as a fire law, San Francisco enacted an ordinance requiring operators of laundries housed in wooden buildings to obtain licenses. Yick Wo, a Chinese alien, who operated a laundry in a wooden building that had passed a fire inspection was denied a license. Almost all laundries in San Francisco were housed in wooden buildings and all but one operated by Chinese-Americans had been denied licenses while most white establishments were granted them. Discrimination because of attribute seemed apparent. When the city offered no reasonable explanation for the disparate licensing, the Court concluded that Chinese owners had been singled out, thus violating the equal protection clause. A law fair on its face, the Court said, may be administered with "an unequal hand."

With few exceptions, the Court did not build on the constitutional principle set out in *Yick Wo* until the mid-twentieth century. As we saw in the previous chapter, an expansive equal protection doctrine would await the Court's racial desegregation cases in the 1950s and 1960s. One exception was *Truax v. Raich*, 1915, in which the Court struck down an Arizona law that required 80 percent of workforce in businesses with five or more employees to be U.S. citizens. It found the law discriminatory in serving no public or governmental interest. More typical, however, was *Patsone v. Pennsylvania*, decided the year before, in which the Court sustained a state law that forbade aliens to shoot wild game. A "public interest" was present because wild game was a natural resource that a state could maintain for its citizens.

The public interest test required only that there be some public or governmental purpose to laws distinguishing aliens and citizens. Thus the Court upheld a state barring aliens from hire on public works projects (*Heim v. McCall*, 1915), and from operating pool halls (*Clarke v. Deckebach*, 1927). The last rested on the stretched reasoning that because such places were frequented by criminals and because aliens were less familiar with the law than citizens, there was a public interest in barring their proprietorship.

Also upheld were laws in several Western states that disqualified aliens not eligible for citizenship under Congressional statutes—then mainly Asians—from owning land or having indirect control of land. In *Terrace v. Thompson*, 1923, the Court, acknowledging a state's interest in regulating its territory, found that Congress's distinction between aliens eligible for citizenship and those not, provided a "reasonable basis for classification in state law." This kind of reasoning and the limited judicial scrutiny that accompanied it allowed laws with underlying discriminatory purpose—in this case the discouragement of Japanese immigrant farmers—to stand. They

were, of course, but one legal reflection of widespread concern about immigration and its possible dislocating effects.

Expanding Protection

As the Court moved toward a more expansive theory of equal protection in the late 1940s, it began taking a different position on state and local laws singling out aliens. Following the evacuation of Japanese Americans from the West Coast during World War II, California barred coastal fishing licenses to any "person ineligible for citizenship." Takahashi, a Japanese resident alien returning to California after the war, was denied a license even though he had held one for 25 years before the war. In *Takahashi v. Fish and Game Commission*, 1948, the Supreme Court held that distinctions Congress made in regulating eligibility for citizenship could not be used by a state to prevent aliens from earning a living in the same way that citizens might. The question was soon moot because Congress, in 1952, removed the last racial and ethnic restrictions to naturalization. See "Removal."

But it was not until 1971 in *Graham v. Richardson* (p. 524) that the Court adopted a radically different standard of judicial review for alienage classifications. Arizona, along with several other states, limited eligibility for welfare benefits to citizens and resident aliens who had lived in the United States a certain number of years, in its case, 15. The Court unanimously held that classifications based on alienage, like those of race or national origin, were "inherently suspect" under the Fourteenth Amendment and subject to "strict" judicial scrutiny. To be upheld, they must be closely related to a "compelling governmental interest." Conservation of public resources, such as welfare benefits, was not such an interest, thus such laws unconstitutionally discriminated against aliens, who like citizens, pay taxes. The Court also found the law invalid on grounds of national supremacy. Because the federal government has exclusive authority to admit aliens and set out conditions on which they may stay in the United States, state laws disabling aliens interfered with national policy.

The Court soon applied the new standard of review to protect the opportunity of aliens to practice a profession or obtain education. In *In re Griffiths*, 1973, it overturned a Connecticut law that denied aliens admission to the bar. Because alienage was now a suspect classification, the state needed to show a compelling interest in keeping aliens from practicing law. Using the same reasoning, it struck down a New York law that made aliens who were not intending to become citizens ineligible for state scholarships and other educational support.(*Nyquist v. Mauclet*, 1977)

Employment or participation in state government itself has presented a more complex problem. In *Sugarman v. Dougall*, 1973, applying strict scrutiny, the Court held invalid a New York law that barred aliens from all state civil service positions filled by competitive examination. It rejected the state's contention that the law was needed so that policymaking positions would be held by persons of undivided loyalty. However valid that need, the law's sweeping disqualification of aliens was not narrowly confined to it and thus served as an arbitrary preference for those who were citizens. Nonetheless, in a dictum, the Court allowed that a state might require citizenship for the participation in the work of "representative government," such as voting or the formation and administration of policy.

This exception was the basis for the Court's decision in *Foley v. Connelie*, 1978, in which it upheld a New York statute barring aliens from serving as state police officers. Because officers play a role in the enforcement of policy and have wide discretionary powers, they are a part of self-governance that a state, in its constitutional prerogative, may reserve to citizens. In such matters, the Court said, it need only be shown that exclusion has a rational basis rather than it meeting a "compelling interest."

In other cases, the Court has widened the scope of employment that might fall under the self-governance exception to strict scrutiny. Thus in *Ambach v. Norwick*, 1979 (p. 526), it upheld 5-4 a New York law barring aliens not intending to become citizens from teaching in the public schools. Teachers, the Court said, play an important role in preparing young persons for eventual participation in governing. On this finding, the Court held the exclusion of aliens was rationally related to self-governance. (The New York law, it should be noted, did not bar aliens from teaching in private schools or public higher education.) The Court extended the self-governance analysis to uphold a California law barring aliens from working as state probation officers.(*Cabell v. Chavez-Salido*, 1982)

However, the Court has held the work of a notary public to be mainly clerical and ministerial, not the "responsibilities that go to the heart of representative government." In applying the strict scrutiny test then in *Bernal v. Fainter*, 1984, it invalidated a Texas law that barred aliens from

Table 8.1 Judicial Review of Alienage Regulations

Standard of review	Rational relationship	"Heightened scrutiny"	"Strict scrutiny"
Required government interest:	Almost any	"Substantial"	"Compelling"
State regulation of:			
the governmental process	X		
illegal aliens		X	
other interests			X
Federal regulation:			
related to foreign affairs	X		
not related to foreign affairs			X

Removal

The Japanese attack on Pearl Harbor, December 7, 1941, marking American entry into World War II, found the nation militarily unprepared and having given little thought to matters of internal security. It also turned attention to 127,000 Americans of Japanese birth or descent in the country, most of whom lived in California. When the early months of the war went badly and a Japanese attack on the West Coast seemed possible, increasing calls were heard for a roundup and containment of Japanese Americans, some of whom it was thought might engage in sabotage. These anxieties ranged from the hysterical to the not totally unreasonable. That they were to prove unfounded did not make them less real. They were fed and made worse by long-standing bias against Japanese and many other Asians in California and other far Western states.

In early 1942, President Franklin Roosevelt issued an evacuation order, later supported by Congress, by which 112,000 Issei, (persons of Japanese birth) and Nissei, (Americans born of Japanese descent) on the West Coast were to be relocated in camps mainly in six interior states. Seventy thousand were native-born American citizens, and not

one case of sabotage or attempted sabotage had been proved. Despite these facts, the Issei and Nissei remained in the camps, which were cramped and enormously depriving, until the end of the war. A few were allowed to leave to fill jobs where there were labor shortages. More than 1,200 joined the United States Army where they were organized into the much decorated 442nd Regimental Combat Unit that fought with distinction in Italy.

Aspects of the Relocation Program, as internment was called, were challenged in cases before the Supreme Court, the two most important of which were *Hirabayashi v. United States,* 1943, involving a curfew order, and *Koramatsu v. United States,* 1944, involving a refusal to report to a detention center as a first step in relocation. In both, a majority of the Court sustained the government's position. In neither did it reach the constitutional issue of equal protection.

The program clearly singled out Japanese Americans solely because of ethnicity. No criminal acts were shown and no similar wartime treatment was accorded German Americans or Italian Americans. But in *Koramatsu,* Justice Hugo Black, writing for a majority of six, largely ignored the equal protection issue, preferring to base the decision on the president's war power and authority to protect national and internal security. For Black and the majority, the program was a justifiable measure to help deal with

---

serving as notaries, as unnecessary to any compelling government interest.

Having entered the country wrongly, illegal aliens can be classified differently from resident aliens, but they may still have equal protection rights. This was the Court's 5-4 ruling in *Plyler v. Doe,* 1982, (p. 529), overturning a Texas law that withheld state money for the education of children of illegal aliens and allowed local school districts to deny them enrollment. The Court rejected the state's argument that illegal aliens were not persons "within its jurisdiction" to whom it owed equal protection under the Fourteenth Amendment. But because illegal alienage is based not on an attribute but on conscious behavior—entering the country illegally—it was not a suspect classification, and the Court did not apply its strict scrutiny standard of

review. Instead, it used an intermediate or "heightened scrutiny" standard for circumstances where a state denied an important benefit and could not show that its restriction furthered "some substantial goal." Such an interest was not met simply by the saving of public money.

In a 2001 class action suit under Title VI of the Civil Rights Act of 1964 to enjoin Alabama from giving driver's license exams only in English, the Court held that private parties lacked the right to enforce the act's regulations. Though the state's practice may have had a "disparate impact" on persons because of their national origin, any private rights of action to enforce federal law must be created by Congress. In *Alexander v. Sandoval,* the Court did not interpret Title VI as having created such a right.

an overriding national emergency. Three dissenting justices, Owen Roberts, Robert Jackson, and Frank Murphy, less willing to ignore the well-established prejudice against Japanese Americans in the West, found internment where no criminal acts were shown to violate equal protection guarantees.

In 1988, Congress voted to make some financial restitution for the forced deprivation of internment. Sixty thousand former internees still living received an average of $20,000 each for property losses sustained, small compensation for actual financial losses, to say nothing of intangible injuries suffered.

Longstanding anti-Japanese sentiment on the West Coast reached a peak during World War II. Here, a barbershop proprietor in Kent, Wash., in 1944, points to a sign indicating his feeling about the return of interned Japanese-Americans after the war.

Federal Power

Though the federal government is held to equal protection standards implicit in the Fifth Amendment's due process clause, it has powers over aliens the states do not. These derive, as do its authority over immigration and naturalization, from its inherent power to conduct foreign affairs. The Supreme Court acknowledged this in two 1976 cases decided the same day. In *Matthews v. Diaz*, it unanimously held that Congress could exclude aliens from federal medical insurance until they had lived in the United States continuously for five years. It was classification of the sort the Court had found unconstitutional at the hands of a state in *Graham v. Richardson* under the strict scrutiny test. But, here, basing the decision on the federal government's responsibilities in foreign affairs, the Court found it reasonable for Congress to tie eligibility for benefits to length of residence. Aliens do not have a permanent commitment to the United States and they continue to have obligations and benefits of citizenship in another nation. They (and American citizens living abroad) may be the subject of negotiations and agreements between the United States and other nations. The decision also makes clear that the federal government can use alienage as a classification in ways it could not use race, religion, or national origin.

In the second case, *Hampton v. Mow Sun Wong*, the Court, 5-4, invalidated a regulation of the Federal Civil Service Commission that excluded aliens from competitive civil service jobs. But it did not hold that Congress was powerless to make such distinctions, only that it appeared not to have authorized the Commission to do so. Since it was not clear that the regulation had to do with foreign policy matters rather than work efficiency, it was invalid for reasons the Court had set out in *Sugarman v. Dougall*. Presumably, if Congress had made it clear that such civil service restrictions were related to foreign affairs, they would be upheld.

The standards the Court has used in reviewing aïienage regulations are given tabular summary in Table 8.1. The Court has often been narrowly and sharply divided and, perhaps for that reason, not always clear about the standards used.

FURTHER READING

Native Americans

Bailyn, Bernard, *The Peopling of North America: An Introduction* (1986)

Price, Monroe E., and Robert N. Clinton, *Law and the American Indian: Readings, Notes, Cases* (1983)

Prucha, Rancis P., *The Great Father: the United States Government and the American Indians*, 2 vols. (1984)

Washburn, Wilcomb E., *The Indian in America* (1975)

Immigration

Archdeacon, Thomas J., *Becoming American: An Ethnic History* (1983)

Axtell, James, *The European and the Indian: Essays on the Ethnic History of Colonial North America* (1981)

Bodnar, John, *The Transplanted: A History of Immigration in Urban America* (1985)

Chin, Gabriel J., Victor C. Romero, and Michael A. Scaperlanda, eds., *Immigration and the Constitution* (2001)

Cornelius, Wayne A., *America in the Era of Limits: Migrants, Nativists, and the Future of U.S.-Mexican Relations* (1982)

Daniels, Roger, *Coming to America: A History of Immigration and Ethnicity in American Life* (1991)

Dinnerstein, Leonard, Roger L. Nichols, and David M. Reimers, *Natives and Strangers: A Multicultural History of Americans* (1996)

Glazer, Nathan, *Clamor at the Gates: The New American Immigration* (1985)

Higham, John, *Send These to Me: Immigrants in Urban America* (1975)

King, Desmond, *Making Americans: Immigration, Race, and the Origins of Diverse Democracy* (2000)

Reimers, David M., ed., *Still the Golden Door: the Third World Comes to America* (1985)

Alienage and Citizenship

Carlinger, David, *The Rights of Aliens*, 2nd ed. (1990)

Hull, Elizabeth, *Without Justice for All: The Constitutional Rights of Aliens* (1985)

Neuman, Gerald L., *Strangers to the Constitution: Immigrants, Borders, and Fundamental Law* (1996)

Shuck, Peter H., and Rogers M. Smith, *Citizenship without Consent: Illegal Aliens in the American Polity* (1985)

Equal Protection

Billington, Ray Allen, *The Origins of Nativism in the United States, 1800–1844* (1974)

Chuman, Frank F., *The Bamboo People: The Law and Japanese-Americans* (1976)

Gyory, Andrew, *Closing the Gate: Race, Politics, and the Chinese Exclusion Act* (1998)

Irons, Peter, ed., *Justice Delayed: The Record of the Japanese-American Internment Cases* (1989)

Jackson, Donald W., *Even the Children of Strangers: Equality Under the U.S. Constitution* (1992)

Karst, Kenneth L., *Belonging to America: Equal Citizenship and the Constitution* (1989)

Sandmeyer, Elmer C., *The Anti-Chinese Movement in California* (1939)

Wollenberg, Charles, *All Deliberate Speed, Segregation and Exclusion in California Schools, 1885–1975* (1978)

Additional works are listed in the General and Supplementary Bibliography.

CASES

Zadvydas v. Davis

533 U.S. 678 (2001), 5-4

Opinion of the Court: Breyer (Ginsburg, O'Connor, Souter, Stevens)

Dissenting: Kennedy, Rehnquist, Scalia, Thomas (in part)

What detention provisions does the Immigration and Nationality Act (INA) contain? At what point would detaining a deportable alien violate due process of law? Why is due process not violated from day one of detention? What procedural protections are available to the alien? Could Congress authorize longer detention without violating due process?

Breyer, for the Court:

When an alien has been found to be unlawfully present in the United States and a final order of removal has been entered, the Government ordinarily secures the alien's removal during a subsequent 90-day statutory "removal period," during which time the alien normally is held in custody.

A special statute authorizes further detention if the Government fails to remove the alien during those 90 days. It says:

> "An alien ordered removed who is inadmissible ... [or] removable [as a result of violations of status requirements or entry conditions, violations of criminal law, or reasons of security or foreign policy] or who has been determined by the Attorney General to be a risk to the community or unlikely to comply with the order of removal, may be detained beyond the removal period and, if released, shall be subject to [certain] terms of supervision. . . ." 8 U.S.C. §1231(a)(6).

In these cases, we must decide whether this post-removal-period statute authorizes the Attorney General to detain a removable alien indefinitely beyond the removal period or only for a period reasonably necessary to secure the alien's removal. We deal here with aliens who were admitted to the United States but subsequently ordered removed. . . . [W]e construe the statute to contain an implicit "reasonable time" limitation. . . .

We consider two separate instances of detention. The first concerns Kestutis Zadvydas, a resident alien who was born, apparently of Lithuanian parents, in a displaced persons camp in Germany in 1948. When he was eight years old, Zadvydas immigrated to the United States with his parents and other family members, and he has lived here ever since.

Zadvydas has a long criminal record, involving drug crimes, attempted robbery, attempted burglary, and theft. He has a history of flight, from both criminal and deportation proceedings. Most recently, he was convicted of possessing, with intent to distribute, cocaine; sentenced to 16 years' imprisonment; released on parole after two years; taken into INS custody; and, in 1994, ordered deported to Germany.

In 1994, Germany told the INS that it would not accept Zadvydas because he was not a German citizen. Shortly thereafter, Lithuania refused to accept Zadvydas because he was neither a Lithuanian citizen nor a permanent resident. In 1996, the INS asked the Dominican Republic (Zadvydas' wife's country) to accept him, but this effort proved unsuccessful. In 1998, Lithuania rejected, as inadequately documented, Zadvydas' effort to obtain Lithuanian citizenship based on his parents' citizenship; Zadvydas' reapplication is apparently still pending.

The INS kept Zadvydas in custody after expiration of the removal period. . . .

The second case is that of Kim Ho Ma. Ma was born in Cambodia in 1977. When he was two, his family fled, taking him to refugee camps in Thailand and the Philippines and eventually to the United States, where he has lived as a resident alien since the age of seven. In 1995, at age 17, Ma was involved in a gang-related shooting, convicted of manslaughter, and sentenced to 38 months' imprisonment. He served two years, after which he was released into INS custody.

In light of his conviction of an "aggravated felony," Ma was ordered removed. The 90-day removal period expired in early 1999, but the INS continued to keep Ma in custody, because, in light of his former gang membership, the nature of his crime, and his planned participation in a prison hunger strike, it was "unable to conclude that Mr. Ma would remain nonviolent and not violate the conditions of release." . . .

We consolidated the two cases for argument; and we now decide them together. . . .

The Government argues that the statute means what it literally says. It sets no "limit on the length of time beyond the removal period that an alien who falls within one of the Section 1231(a)(6) categories may be detained." . . .

. . . [W]e read an implicit limitation into the statute before us. In our view, the statute, read in light of the Constitution's demands, limits an alien's post-removal-period detention to a period reasonably necessary to bring about that alien's removal from the United States. It does not permit indefinite detention.

A statute permitting indefinite detention of an alien would raise a serious constitutional problem. The Fifth Amendment's Due Process Clause forbids the Government to "depriv[e]" any "person . . . of . . . liberty . . . without due process of law." Freedom from imprisonment from government custody, detentioin, or other forms of physical restraint—lies at the heart of the liberty that Clause protects. And this Court has said that government detention violates that Clause unless the detention is ordered in a *criminal* proceeding with adequate procedural protections. . . . The proceedings at issue here are civil, not criminal, and we assume that they are nonpunitive in purpose and effect. There is no sufficiently strong special justification here for indefinite civil detention. . . . The statute, says the Government, has two regulatory goals: "ensuring the appearance of aliens at future immigration proceedings" and "[p]reventing danger to the community." But by definition the first justification—preventing flight—is weak or nonexistent where removal seems a remote possibility at best. As this Court said in *Jackson v. Indiana,* where detention's goal is no longer practically attainable, detention no longer "bear[s] [a] reasonable relation to the purpose for which the individual [was] committed."

The second justification—protecting the community—does not necessarily diminish in force over time. But we have upheld preventive detention based on dangerousness only when limited to specially dangerous individuals and subject to strong procedural protections. . . . In cases in which preventive detention is of potentially *indefinite* duration, we have also demanded that the dangerousness rationale be accompanied by some other special circumstance, such as mental illness, that helps to create the danger.

The civil confinement here at issue is not limited, but potentially permanent. The provision authorizing detention does not apply narrowly to "a small segment of particularly dangerous individuals," say, suspected terrorists, but broadly to aliens ordered removed for many and various reasons, including tourist visa violations. And, once the flight risk justification evaporates, the only special circumstance present is the alien's removable status itself, which bears no relation to a detainee's dangerousness.

Moreover, the sole procedural protections available to the alien are found in administrative proceedings, where the alien bears the burden of proving he is not dangerous, without significant later judicial review. This Court has suggested, however, that the Constitution may well preclude granting "an administrative body the unreviewable authority to make determinations implicating fundamental rights." The serious constitutional problem arising out of a statute that, in these circumstances, permits an indefinite, perhaps permanent, deprivation of human liberty without any such protection is obvious. . . .

Despite this constitutional problem, if "Congress has made its intent" in the statute "clear," 'we must give effect to that intent.' We cannot find here, however, any clear indication of congressional intent to grant the Attorney General the power to hold indefinitely in confinement an alien ordered removed. . . .

The Government points to the statute's word "may." But while "may" suggests discretion, it does not necessarily suggest unlimited discretion. In that respect the word "may" is ambiguous. Indeed, if Congress had meant to authorize long-term detention of unremovable aliens, it certainly could have spoken in clearer terms. ("If no country is willing to receive" a terrorist alien ordered removed, "the Attorney General may, notwithstanding any other provision of law, retain the alien in custody" and must review the detention determination every six months). . . .

The Government also points to the statute's history. That history catalogs a series of changes, from an initial period (before 1952) when lower courts had interpreted statutory silence, to mean that deportation-related detention must end within a reasonable time, to a period (from the early 1950's through the late 1980's) when the statutes permitted, but did not require, post-deportation-order detention for up to six months, to more recent statutes that have at times mandated and at other times permitted the post-deportation-order detention of aliens falling into certain categories such as aggravated felons. . . .

We have found nothing in the history of these statutes that clearly demonstrates a congressional intent to authorize indefinite, perhaps permanent, detention. Consequently, interpreting the statute to avoid a serious constitutional threat, we conclude that, once removal is no longer reasonably foreseeable, continued detention is no longer authorized by statute. . . .

. . . Whether a set of particular circumstances amounts to detention within, or beyond, a period reasonably necessary to secure removal is determinative of whether the detention is, or is not, pursuant to statutory authority. The basic federal habeas corpus statute grants the federal courts authority to answer that question.

In answering [it], the habeas court must ask whether the detention in question exceeds a period reasonably necessary to secure removal. It should measure reasonableness primarily in terms of the statute's basic purpose, namely assuring the alien's presence at the moment of removal. Thus, if removal is not reasonably foreseeable, the court should hold continued detention unreasonable and no longer authorized by statute. In that case, of course, the alien's release may and should be conditioned on any of the various forms of supervised release that are appropriate in the circumstances, and the alien may no doubt be returned to custody upon a violation of those conditions. And if removal is reasonably foreseeable, the habeas court should consider the risk of the alien's committing further crimes as a factor potentially justifying confinement within that reasonable removal period.

Ordinary principles of judicial review in this area recognize primary Executive Branch responsibility. They counsel judges to give expert agencies decision-making leeway in matters that invoke their expertise. They recognize Executive Branch primacy in foreign policy matters. And they consequently require courts to listen with care when the Government's foreign policy judgments, including, for example, the status of repatriation negotiations, are at issue, and to grant the Government appropriate leeway when its judgments rest upon foreign policy expertise.

We realize that recognizing this necessary Executive leeway will often call for difficult judgments. In order to limit the occasions when courts will need to make them, we think it practically necessary to recognize some presumptively reasonable period of detention. . . .

While an argument can be made for confining any presumption to 90 days, we doubt that when Congress shortened the removal period to 90 days in 1996 it believed that all reasonably foreseeable removals could be accomplished in that time. We do have reason to believe, however, that Congress previously doubted the constitutionality of detention for more than six months. Consequently, for the sake of uniform administration in the federal courts, we recognize that period . . . This six-month presumption, of course, does not mean that every alien not removed must be released after six months. To the contrary, an alien may be held in confinement until it has been determined that there is no significant likelihood of removal in the reasonably foreseeable future. . . .

Kennedy, dissenting:

The Court says its duty is to avoid a constitutional question. It deems the duty performed by interpreting a statute in obvious disregard of congressional intent. . . . Far from avoiding a constitutional question, the Court's ruling causes systemic dislocation in the balance of powers, thus raising serious constitutional concerns not just for the cases at hand but for the Court's own view of its proper authority. . . .

The Immigration and Nationality Act (INA) is straightforward enough. It provides:

"An alien ordered removed who is inadmissible under section 1182 of this title, removable under section 1227(a)(1)(C), 1227(a)(2), or 1227(a)(4) of this title or who has been determined by the Attorney General to be a risk to the community or unlikely to comply with the order of removal, may be detained beyond the removal period and, if released, shall be subject to the terms of supervision in paragraph (3)."

By this statute, Congress confers upon the Attorney General discretion to detain an alien ordered removed. It gives express authorization to detain "beyond the removal period." . . .

The majority's reading of the statutory authorization to "detai[n] beyond the removal period," however, is not plausible. An interpretation which defeats the stated congressional purpose does not suffice to invoke the constitutional doubt rule, for it is "plainly contrary to the intent of Congress." The majority announces it will reject the Government's argument "that the statute means what it literally says," but then declines to offer any other acceptable textual interpretation. The majority does not demonstrate an ambiguity in the delegation of the detention power to the Attorney General. It simply amends the statute to impose a time limit tied to the progress of negotiations to effect the aliens' removal. The statute cannot be so construed. The requirement the majority reads into the law simply bears no relation to the text; and in fact it defeats the statutory purpose and design. . . .

Congress' power to detain aliens in connection with removal or exclusion, the Court has said, is part of the Legislature's considerable authority over immigration matters. ("Proceedings to exclude or expel would be vain if those accused could not be held in custody pending the inquiry into their true character, and while arrangements were being made for their deportation"). It is reasonable to assume, then, and it is the proper interpretation of the INA and §1231(a)(6), that when Congress provided for detention "beyond the removal period," it exercised its considerable power over immigration and delegated to the Attorney General the discretion to detain inadmissible and other removable aliens for as long as they are determined to be either a flight risk or a danger to the Nation.

The majority's interpretation, moreover, defeats the very repatriation goal in which it professes such interest. The Court rushes to substitute a judicial judgment for the Executive's discretion and authority.... The result of the Court's rule is that, by refusing to accept repatriation of their own nationals, other countries can effect the release of these individuals back into the American community....

The risk to the community posed by the mandatory release of aliens who are dangerous or a flight risk is far from insubstantial; the motivation to protect the citizenry from aliens determined to be dangerous is central to the immigration power itself....

The Court today assumes a role in foreign relations which is unprecedented, unfortunate, and unwise. Its misstep results in part from a misunderstanding of the liberty interests these aliens retain, an issue next to be discussed.

The aliens' claims are substantial; their plight is real. They face continued detention, perhaps for life, unless it is shown they no longer present a flight risk or a danger to the community....

As persons within our jurisdiction, the aliens are entitled to the protection of the Due Process Clause. Liberty under the Due Process Clause includes protection against unlawful or arbitrary personal restraint or detention. The liberty rights of the aliens before us here are subject to limitations and conditions not applicable to citizens, however. No party to this proceeding contests the initial premise that the aliens have been determined to be removable after a fair hearing under lawful and proper procedures. Aliens ordered removed are given notice of their right to appeal the decision, may move the immigration judge to reconsider, can seek discretionary cancellation of removal, and can obtain habeas review

of the Attorney General's decision not to consider waiver of deportation. As a result, aliens like Zadvydas and Ma do not arrive at their removable status without thorough, substantial procedural safeguards....

That said, it must be made clear that these aliens are in a position far different from aliens with a lawful right to remain here. They are removable, and their rights must be defined in accordance with that status. The due process analysis must begin with a "careful description of the asserted right." We have "long held that an alien seeking initial admission to the United States requests a privilege and has no constitutional rights regarding his application, for the power to admit or exclude aliens is a sovereign prerogative." The same is true for those aliens like Zadvydas and Ma, who face a final order of removal. When an alien is removable, he or she has no right under the basic immigration laws to remain in this country. The removal orders reflect the determination that the aliens' ties to this community are insufficient to justify their continued presence in the United States. An alien's admission to this country is conditioned upon compliance with our laws, and removal is the consequence of a breach of that understanding....

Whether a due process right is denied when removable aliens who are flight risks or dangers to the community are detained turns, then, not on the substantive right to be free, but on whether there are adequate procedures to review their cases, allowing persons once subject to detention to show that through rehabilitation, new appreciation of their responsibilities, or under other standards, they no longer present special risks or danger if put at large. The procedures to determine and to review the status-required detention go far toward this objective.

By regulations, promulgated after notice and comment, the Attorney General has given structure to the discretion delegated by the INA in order to ensure fairness and regularity in INS detention decisions....

[But] [t]he majority instead would have the Judiciary review the status of repatriation negotiations, which, one would have thought, are the paradigmatic examples of nonjusticiable inquiry. The inquiry would require the Executive Branch to surrender its primacy in foreign affairs and submit reports to the courts respecting its ongoing negotiations in the international sphere.... The Court's rule is a serious misconception of the proper judicial function, and it is not what Congress enacted....

Yick Wo v. Hopkins

118 U.S. 356 (1886), 9-0
Opinion of the Court: Matthews (Blatchford, Bradley,
Field, Gray, Harlan, Miller, Waite, Woods)

*A San Francisco ordinance barred operation of laundries in
buildings that were not made of brick or stone, without special
permission. Special permission was granted in all of more
than 300 applications filed by Caucasians, but was denied in
all of 200 applications filed by Chinese aliens. Yick Wo and
other aliens continued to operate laundries in wooden buildings and were arrested and convicted under the ordinance.*

*Citizens are mentioned specifically in the Fourteenth
Amendment. Are aliens? How does Yick Wo qualify for the
amendment's protection? What theory of fundamental rights
does Justice Matthews develop? On its face, what public interest
or interests did the San Francisco ordinance regulating laundry buildings serve? In the way the law was administered,
what interest did it serve? Did the city have an explanation for
denying a permit in this case? Did the Court examine administrative motives by inferring them from administrative results? Is
this consistent with its approach in modern civil rights cases?*

Matthews, for the Court:

The rights of the petitioners . . . are not less because
they are aliens and subjects of the Emperor of
China. . . .

The Fourteenth Amendment to the Constitution is
not confined to the protection of citizens. It says:
"Nor shall any State deprive any person of life, liberty,
or property without due process of law; nor deny to
any person within its jurisdiction the equal protection
of the laws."

These provisions are universal in their application
to all persons within the territorial jurisdiction, without regard to any differences of race, of color, or of
nationality, and the equal protection of the laws is a
pledge of the protection of equal laws. . . .

It is contended on the part of the petitioners that
the ordinances for violations of which they are sever-
ally sentenced to imprisonment are void on their face
as being within the prohibitions of the Fourteenth
Amendment, and, in the alternative, if not so, that
they are void by reason of their administration, operating unequally so as to punish in the present petitioners what is permitted to others as lawful, without
any distinction of circumstances—an unjust and illegal discrimination, it is claimed, which, though not

made expressly by the ordinances, is made possible
by them.

When we consider the nature and the theory of our
institutions of government, the principles upon which
they are supposed to rest, and review the history of their
development, we are constrained to conclude that they
do not mean to leave room for the play and action of
purely personal and arbitrary power. Sovereignty itself
is, of course, not subject to law, for it is the author and
source of law; but, in our system, while sovereign powers are delegated to the agencies of government, sovereignty itself remains with the people, by whom and for
whom all government exists and acts. And the law is the
definition and limitation of power. It is, indeed, quite
true that there must always be lodged somewhere, and
in some person or body, the authority of final decision,
and in many cases of mere administration, the responsibility is purely political, no appeal lying except to the ultimate tribunal of the public judgment, exercised either
in the pressure of opinion or by means of the suffrage.
But the fundamental rights to life, liberty, and the pursuit of happiness, considered as individual possessions,
are secured by those maxims of constitutional law
which are the monuments showing the victorious
progress of the race in securing to men the blessings of
civilization under the reign of just and equal laws, so
that, in the famous language of the Massachusetts Bill
of Rights, the government of the commonwealth "may
be a government of laws, and not of men." For the very
idea that one man may be compelled to hold his life, or
the means of living, or any material right essential to
the enjoyment of life at the mere will of another seems
to be intolerable in any country where freedom pre-
vails, as being the essence of slavery itself.

There are many illustrations that might be given of
this truth, which would make manifest that it was self-
evident in the light of our system of jurisprudence.
The case of the political franchise of voting is one.
Though not regarded strictly as a natural right, but as
a privilege merely conceded by society according to
its will under certain conditions, nevertheless it is regarded as a fundamental political right, because
preservative of all rights. . . .

. . . In the present cases, we are not obliged to reason
from the probable to the actual. . . . For [they] present
the ordinances in actual operation, and the facts shown
establish an administration directed so exclusively
against a particular class of persons as to warrant and require the conclusion that, whatever may have been the

intent of the ordinances as adopted, they are applied by the public authorities charged with their administration, and thus representing the State itself, with a mind so unequal and oppressive as to amount to a practical denial by the State of that equal protection of the laws which is secured to the petitioners, as to all other persons, by the broad and benign provisions of the Fourteenth Amendment to the Constitution of the United States. Though the law itself be fair on its face and impartial in appearance, yet, if it is applied and administered by public authority with an evil eye and an unequal hand, so as practically to make unjust and illegal discriminations between persons in similar circumstances, material to their rights, the denial of equal justice is still within the prohibition of the Constitution. . . .

The present cases . . . are within this class. It appears that both petitioners have complied with every requisite deemed by the law or by the public officers charged with its administration necessary for the protection of neighboring property from fire or as a precaution against injury to the public health. No reason whatever, except the will of the supervisors, is assigned why they should not be permitted to carry on, in the accustomed manner, their harmless and useful occupation, on which they depend for a livelihood. And while this consent of the supervisors is withheld from them and from two hundred others who have also petitioned, all of whom happen to be Chinese subjects, eighty others, not Chinese subjects, are permitted to carry on the same business under similar conditions. The fact of this discrimination is admitted. No reason for it is shown, and the conclusion cannot be resisted that no reason for it exists except hostility to the race and nationality to which the petitioners belong, and which, in the eye of the law, is not justified. The discrimination is, therefore, illegal, and the public administration which enforces it is a denial of the equal protection of the laws and a violation of the Fourteenth Amendment of the Constitution. The imprisonment of the petitioners is, therefore, illegal, and they must be discharged. . . .

Graham v. Richardson

403 U.S. 365 (1971), 9-0
Opinion of the Court: Blackmun (Black, Brennan, Burger, Douglas, Harlan, Marshall, Stewart, White)

To be eligible for welfare benefits, Arizona required that a recipient be a citizen or have lived in the United States 15 years.

The case was heard and decided with a similar one from Pennsylvania Sailer v. Leer.

Was the state's interest here reasonable? Substantial? Compelling? Why are classifications based on alienage "inherently suspect," according to the Court? What kind of scrutiny did the Court apply? On what grounds besides equal protection is the Arizona law unconstitutional? What difference does it make which grounds are used? Might the national government pass laws disabling aliens or restricting their benefits that the states cannot?

Blackmun, for the Court:

. . . The issue here is whether the Equal Protection Clause of the Fourteenth Amendment prevents a State from conditioning welfare benefits either (a) upon the beneficiary's possession of United States citizenship, or (b) if the beneficiary is an alien, upon his having resided in this country for a specified number of years. . . .

Appellee Carmen Richardson, at the institution of this suit in July, 1969, was 64 years of age. She is a lawfully admitted resident alien. She emigrated from Mexico in 1956, and, since then, has resided continuously in Arizona. She became permanently and totally disabled. She also met all other requirements for eligibility for . . . benefits except the 15-year residency specified for aliens. She applied for benefits, but was denied relief solely because of the residency provision. . . .

It has long been settled, and it is not disputed here, that the term "person" in this context encompasses lawfully admitted resident aliens, as well as citizens of the United States, and entitles both citizens and aliens to the equal protection of the laws of the State in which they reside. . . .

Under traditional equal protection principles, a State retains broad discretion to classify as long as its classification has a reasonable basis. . . . But the Court's decisions have established that classifications based on alienage, like those based on nationality or race, are inherently suspect and subject to close judicial scrutiny. Aliens as a class are a prime example of a "discrete and insular" minority for whom such heightened judicial solicitude is appropriate. . . .

Arizona and Pennsylvania seek to justify their restrictions on the eligibility of aliens for public assistance solely on the basis of a State's "special public interest" in favoring its own citizens over aliens in the distribution of limited resources such as welfare benefits. It is true that this Court on occasion has upheld state statutes that treat citizens and noncitizens differently, the ground for distinction having been that such laws were necessary to protect special interests of the State or its citizens. Thus, in *Truax v. Raich* the Court, in striking down an Arizona statute restricting the employment of aliens, emphasized that "[t]he discrimination defined by the act does not pertain to the regulation or distribution of the public domain, or of the common property or resources of the people of the State, the enjoyment of which may be limited to its citizens as against both aliens and the citizens of other States." And in *Crane v. New York* the Court affirmed . . . a New York statute prohibiting the employment of aliens on public works projects. The New York court's opinion contained Mr. Justice Cardozo's well known observation:

> To disqualify aliens is discrimination indeed, but not arbitrary discrimination, for the principle of exclusion is the restriction of the resources of the state to the advancement and profit of the members of the state. Ungenerous and unwise such discrimination may be. It is not for that reason unlawful. . . . The state, in determining what use shall be made of its own moneys, may legitimately consult the welfare of its own citizens, rather than that of aliens. Whatever is a privilege, rather than a right, may be made dependent upon citizenship. In its war against poverty, the state is not required to dedicate its own resources to citizens and aliens alike. . . .

Whatever may be the contemporary vitality of the special public interest doctrine . . . a State's desire to preserve limited welfare benefits for its own citizens is inadequate to justify Pennsylvania's making noncitizens ineligible for public assistance, and Arizona's restricting benefits to citizens and longtime resident aliens. First, the special public interest doctrine was heavily grounded on the notion that "[w]hatever is a privilege, rather than a right, may be made dependent upon citizenship." Second, as the Court recognized in *Shapiro* [v. *Thompson*]:

> [A] State has a valid interest in preserving the fiscal integrity of its programs. It may legitimately attempt to limit its expenditures, whether for public assistance, public education, or any other program. But a State may not accomplish such a purpose by invidious distinctions between classes of its citizens. . . . The saving of welfare costs cannot justify an otherwise invidious classification.

Since an alien, as well as a citizen, is a "person" for equal protection purposes, a concern for fiscal integrity is no more compelling a justification for the questioned classification in these cases than it was in *Shapiro*.

Appellants, however, would narrow the application of *Shapiro* to citizens by arguing that the right to travel, relied upon in that decision, extends only to citizens and not to aliens. . . . The Court has never decided whether the right applies specifically to aliens, and it is unnecessary to reach that question here. It is enough to say that the classification involved in Shapiro was subjected to strict scrutiny under the compelling state interest test, not because it was based on any suspect criterion such as race, nationality, or alienage, but because it impinged upon the fundamental right of interstate movement. . . . The classifications involved in the instant cases, on the other hand, are inherently suspect, and are therefore subject to strict judicial scrutiny whether or not a fundamental right is impaired. . . .

We agree with the three-judge court in the Pennsylvania case that the "justification of limiting expenses is particularly inappropriate and unreasonable when the discriminated class consists of aliens. Aliens, like citizens, pay taxes, and may be called into the armed forces. Unlike the short-term residents in Shapiro, aliens may live within a state for many years, work in the state and contribute to the economic growth of the state."

There can be no "special public interest" in tax revenues to which aliens have contributed on an equal basis with the residents of the State.

Accordingly, we hold that a state statute that denies welfare benefits to resident aliens and one that denies them to aliens who have not resided in the United States for a specified number of years violate the Equal Protection Clause.

An additional reason why the state statutes at issue in these cases do not withstand constitutional scrutiny emerges from the area of federal state relations. The National Government has "broad constitutional powers in determining what aliens shall be admitted to the United States, the period they may remain, regulation of their conduct before naturalization, and the terms and conditions of their naturalization." *Takahashi v. Fish & Game Comm'n* Pursuant to that power, Congress has provided, as part of a comprehensive plan for the regulation of immigration and naturalization, that "[a]liens who are paupers, professional beggars, or vagrants," or aliens who "are likely at any time to become public charges," shall be excluded from admission into the United States, and that any alien lawfully admitted shall be deported who "has within five years after entry become a public charge from causes not affirmatively shown to have arisen after entry. . . ." Admission of aliens likely to become public charges may be conditioned upon the posting of a bond or cash deposit. But Congress has not seen fit to impose any burden or restriction on aliens who become indigent after their entry into the United States. . . .

State laws that restrict the eligibility of aliens for welfare benefits merely because of their alienage conflict with these overriding national policies in an area constitutionally entrusted to the Federal Government. . . . Congress has broadly declared as federal policy that lawfully admitted resident aliens who become public charges for causes arising after their entry are not subject to deportation, and that, as long as they are here, they are entitled to the full and equal benefit of all state laws for the security of persons and property. The state statutes at issue in the instant cases impose auxiliary burdens upon the entrance or residence of aliens who suffer the distress, after entry, of economic dependency or public assistance. Alien residency requirements for welfare benefits necessarily operate, as did the residency requirements in *Shapiro*, to discourage entry into or continued residency in the State. . . .

In *Truax*, the Court considered the "reasonableness" of a state restriction on the employment of aliens in terms of its effect on the right of a lawfully admitted alien to live where he chooses:

> . . . [R]easonable classification implies action consistent with the legitimate interests of the State, and . . . these cannot be so broadly conceived as to bring them into hostility to exclusive Federal power. The authority to control immigration—to admit or exclude aliens—is vested solely in the Federal Government. . . . The assertion of an authority to deny to aliens the opportunity of earning a livelihood when lawfully admitted to the State would be tantamount to the assertion of the right to deny them entrance and abode, for, in ordinary cases, they cannot live where they cannot work. And, if such a policy were permissible, the practical result would be that those lawfully admitted to the country under the authority of the acts of Congress, instead of enjoying in a substantial sense and in their full scope the privileges conferred by the admission, would be seg-

regated in such of the States as chose to offer hospitality.

The same is true here, for, in the ordinary case, an alien, becoming indigent and unable to work, will be unable to live where, because of discriminatory denial of public assistance, he cannot "secure the necessities of life, including food, clothing and shelter." State alien residency requirements that either deny welfare benefits to noncitizens or condition them on longtime residency, equate with the assertion of a right, inconsistent with federal policy, to deny entrance and abode. Since such laws encroach upon exclusive federal power, they are constitutionally impermissible. . . .

Ambach v. Norwick

441 U.S. 68 (1979), 5-4
Opinion of the Court: Powell (Burger, Rehnquist, Stewart, White)
Dissenting: Blackmun, Brennan, Marshall, Stevens

What is the rationale for the New York law? On what grounds does the Court uphold it? What is its standard of review? This case deals with the conferral (or nonconferral) of opportunities rather than material benefits, but can it be distinguished otherwise from Graham v. Richardson *(p. 524)? How is teaching related to "self-governance"? Does it make sense for aliens to be barred from teaching in public secondary schools when they are free to teach in colleges and universities and in private secondary schools? What is the significance of the New York law excepting aliens who intend to become citizens?*

Powell, for the Court:

This case presents the question whether a State, consistently with the Equal Protection Clause of the Fourteenth Amendment, may refuse to employ as elementary and secondary school teachers aliens who are eligible for United States citizenship but who refuse to seek naturalization.

New York Education Law §3001(3) forbids certification as a public school teacher of any person who is not a citizen of the United States, unless that person has manifested an intention to apply for citizenship. The Commissioner of Education is authorized to create exemptions from this prohibition, and has done so with respect to aliens who are not yet eligible for citizenship. Unless a teacher obtains certification, he may not work in a public elementary or secondary school in New York.

Appellee Norwick was born in Scotland, and is a subject of Great Britain. She has resided in this country since 1965, and is married to a United States citizen. Appellee Dachinger is a Finnish subject who came to this country in 1966, and also is married to a United States citizen. Both . . . currently meet all of the educational requirements New York has set for certification as a public school teacher, but they consistently have refused to seek citizenship in spite of their eligibility to do so. Norwick applied in 1973 for a teaching certificate covering nursery school through sixth grade, and Dachinger sought a certificate covering the same grades in 1975. Both applications were denied because of appellees' failure to meet the requirements of §3001(3). . . .

The decisions of this Court regarding the permissibility of statutory classifications involving aliens have not formed an unwavering line over the years. State regulation of the employment of aliens long has been subject to constitutional constraints. In *Yick Wo v. Hopkins,* the Court struck down an ordinance which was applied to prevent aliens from running laundries, and in *Truax v. Raich,* a law requiring at least 80% of the employees of certain businesses to be citizens was held to be an unconstitutional infringement of an alien's "right to work for a living in the common occupations of the community. . . ." At the same time, however, the Court also has recognized a greater degree of latitude for the States when aliens were sought to be excluded from public employment. At the time *Truax* was decided, the governing doctrine permitted States to exclude aliens from various activities when the restriction pertained to "the regulation or distribution of the public domain, or of the common property or resources of the people of the State. . . ." Hence, as part of a larger authority to forbid aliens from owning land, harvesting wildlife, or maintaining an inherently dangerous enterprise, States permissibly could exclude aliens from working on public construction projects, and, it appears, from engaging in any form of public employment at all.

Over time, the Court's decisions gradually have restricted the activities from which States are free to exclude aliens. The first sign that the Court would question the constitutionality of discrimination against aliens even in areas affected with a "public interest" appeared in *Oyama v. California,* 1948. The Court there held that statutory presumptions designed to discourage evasion of California's ban on alien landholding discriminated against the citizen children of aliens. The same Term, the Court held that the "ownership" a

State exercises over fish found in its territorial waters "is inadequate to justify California in excluding any or all aliens who are lawful residents of the State from making a living by fishing in the ocean off its shores while permitting all others to do so." *Takahashi v. Fish & Game Comm'n.*

This process of withdrawal from the former doctrine culminated in *Graham v. Richardson,* which, for the first time, treated classifications based on alienage as "inherently suspect and subject to close judicial scrutiny." Applying *Graham,* this Court has held invalid statutes that prevented aliens from entering a State's classified civil service, practicing law, working as an engineer, and receiving state educational benefits.

Although our more recent decisions have departed substantially from the public interest doctrine of *Truax's* day, they have not abandoned the general principle that some state functions are so bound up with the operation of the State as a governmental entity as to permit the exclusion from those functions of all persons who have not become part of the process of self-government. In *Sugarman v. Dougall,* we recognized that a State could, "in an appropriately defined class of positions, require citizenship as a qualification for office." . . . The exclusion of aliens from such governmental positions would not invite as demanding scrutiny from this Court.

Applying the rational basis standard, we held last Term that New York could exclude aliens from the ranks of its police force. *Foley v. Connelie.* Because the police function fulfilled "a most fundamental obligation of government to its constituency," and, by necessity, cloaked policemen with substantial discretionary powers, we viewed the police force as being one of those appropriately defined classes of positions for which a citizenship requirement could be imposed. Accordingly, the State was required to justify its classification only "by a showing of some rational relationship between the interest sought to be protected and the limiting classification."

The rule for governmental functions, which is an exception to the general standard applicable to classifications based on alienage, rests on important principles inherent in the Constitution. The distinction between citizens and aliens, though ordinarily irrelevant to private activity, is fundamental to the definition and government of a State. The Constitution itself refers to the distinction no less than 11 times, indicating that the status of citizenship was meant to have significance in the structure of our government. The assumption of that status, whether by birth or naturalization, denotes

an association with the polity which, in a democratic republic, exercises the powers of governance. The form of
this association is important: an oath of allegiance or
similar ceremony cannot substitute for the unequivocal
legal bond citizenship represents. It is because of this
special significance of citizenship that governmental entities, when exercising the functions of government,
have wider latitude in limiting the participation of
noncitizens.

In determining whether, for purposes of equal
protection analysis, teaching in public schools constitutes a governmental function, we look to the role of
public education and to the degree of responsibility
and discretion teachers possess in fulfilling that role.
Each of these considerations supports the conclusion
that public school teachers may be regarded as performing a task "that go[es] to the heart of representative government."

Public education, like the police function, "fulfills a
most fundamental obligation of government to its constituency." The importance of public schools in the
preparation of individuals for participation as citizens,
and in the preservation of the values on which our society rests, long has been recognized by our decisions. . . .

. . . [A] State properly may regard all teachers as
having an obligation to promote civic virtues and understanding in their classes, regardless of the subject
taught. Certainly a State also may take account of a
teacher's function as an example for students, which
exists independently of particular classroom subjects.
In light of the foregoing considerations, we think it
clear that public school teachers come well within the
"governmental function" principle recognized in *Sugarman* and *Foley*. Accordingly, the Constitution requires
only that a citizenship requirement applicable to teaching in the public schools bear a rational relationship to
a legitimate state interest.

As the legitimacy of the State's interest in furthering
the educational goals outlined above is undoubted, it
remains only to consider whether §3001(3) bears a rational relationship to this interest. The restriction is
carefully framed to serve its purpose, as it bars from
teaching only those aliens who have demonstrated
their unwillingness to obtain United States citizenship.
Appellees, and aliens similarly situated, in effect have
chosen to classify themselves. They prefer to retain citizenship in a foreign country, with the obligations it entails of primary duty and loyalty. They have rejected the
open invitation extended to qualify for eligibility to
teach by applying for citizenship in this country. The

people of New York, acting through their elected representatives, have made a judgment that citizenship
should be a qualification for teaching the young of the
State in the public schools, and §3001(3) furthers that
judgment.

Blackmun, dissenting:
Once again the Court is asked to rule upon the constitutionality of one of New York's many statutes that impose a requirement of citizenship upon a person
before that person may earn his living in a specified occupation. These New York statutes, for the most part,
have their origin in the frantic and over-reactive days of
the First World War when attitudes of parochialism
and fear of the foreigner were the order of the day.
This time we are concerned with the right to teach in
the public schools of the State, at the elementary and
secondary levels, and with the citizenship requirement
that N.Y.Educ.Law §3001(3)

As the Court acknowledges, its decisions regarding
the permissibility of statutory classifications concerning
aliens "have not formed an unwavering line over the
years." Thus, just last Term, in *Foley v. Connelie*, the Court
upheld against equal protection challenge the New York
statute limiting appointment of members of the state
police force to citizens of the United States. The touchstone, the Court indicated, was that citizenship may be
a relevant qualification for fulfilling "important non-
elective executive, legislative, and judicial positions"
held by "officers who participate directly in the formulation, execution, or review of broad public policy."

For such positions, a State need show only some rational relationship between the interest sought to be
protected and the limiting classification. Police, it then
was felt, were clothed with authority to exercise an almost infinite variety of discretionary powers that could
seriously affect members of the public. They thus fell
within the category of important officers who participate directly in the execution of "broad public policy."
The Court was persuaded that citizenship bore a rational relationship to the special demands of police positions, and that a State therefore could constitutionally
confine that public responsibility to citizens of the
United States. . . .

On the other hand, the Court frequently has invalidated a state provision that denies a resident alien the
right to engage in specified occupational activity: *Yick
Wo v. Hopkins* (ordinance applied so as to prevent Chinese subjects from engaging in the laundry business);
Truax v. Raich (statute requiring an employer's work-

force to be composed of not less than 80% "qualified electors or native-born citizens"); *Takahashi v. Fish & Game Comm'n* (limitation of commercial fishing licenses to persons not "ineligible to citizenship"); *Sugarman v. Dougall* (New York statute relating to permanent positions in the "competitive class" of the state civil service); *In re Griffiths* (the practice of law); *Nelson v. Miranda* (social service worker and teacher); *Examining Board v. Flores de Otero* (the practice of civil engineering). See also *Nyquist v. Mauclet* (New York statute barring certain resident aliens from state financial assistance for higher education).

. . . [T]he Court has held more than once that state classifications based on alienage are "inherently suspect and subject to close judicial scrutiny." *Graham v. Richardson* And "[a]lienage classifications by a State that do not withstand this stringent examination cannot stand."

There is thus a line, most recently recognized in *Foley v. Connelie*, between those employments that a State, in its wisdom, constitutionally may restrict to United States citizens, on the one hand, and those employments, on the other, that the State may not deny to resident aliens. For me, the present case falls on the *Sugarman-Griffiths-Flores de Otero-Mauclet* side of that line, rather than on the narrowly isolated *Foley* side. . . .

But the Court, to the disadvantage of appellees, crosses the line from *Griffiths* to *Foley* by saying, that the "distinction between citizens and aliens, though ordinarily irrelevant to private activity, is fundamental to the definition and government of a State." It then concludes that public school teaching "constitutes a governmental function," ibid., and that public school teachers may be regarded as performing a task that goes "to the heart of representative government." The Court speaks of the importance of public schools in the preparation of individuals for participation as citizens, and in the preservation of the values on which our society rests. After then observing that teachers play a critical part in all this, the Court holds that New York's citizenship requirement is constitutional because it bears a rational relationship to the State's interest in furthering these educational goals.

I perceive a number of difficulties along the easy road the Court takes to this conclusion:

First, the New York statutory structure itself refutes the argument. . . . The State, apparently under §3001(3), would not hesitate to employ an alien teacher while he waits to attain citizenship, even though he may fail ever to attain it. And the stark fact that the State permits some aliens to sit on certain local school boards, reveals how shallow and indistinct is New York's line of demarcation between citizenship and noncitizenship. . . .

Second, the New York statute is all-inclusive in its disqualifying provisions: "No person shall be employed or authorized to teach in the public schools of the state who is . . . [n]ot a citizen." It sweeps indiscriminately. . . .

Third, the New York classification is irrational. Is it better to employ a poor citizen teacher than an excellent resident alien teacher? Is it preferable to have a citizen who has never seen Spain or a Latin American country teach Spanish to eighth graders and to deny that opportunity to a resident alien who may have lived for 20 years in the culture of Spain or Latin America? The State will know how to select its teachers responsibly, wholly apart from citizenship, and can do so selectively and intelligently. That is the way to accomplish the desired result. An artificial citizenship bar is not a rational way. . . .

Fourth, it is logically impossible to differentiate between this case, concerning teachers, and *In re Griffiths*, concerning attorneys. . . . [An attorney] represents us in our critical courtroom controversies even when citizenship and loyalty may be questioned. He stands as an officer of every court in which he practices. . . . [H]e, too, is an influence in legislation, in the community, and in the role-model figure that the professional person enjoys.

If an attorney has a constitutional right to take a bar examination and practice law, despite his being a resident alien, it is impossible for me to see why a resident alien otherwise completely competent and qualified, as these appellees concededly are, is constitutionally disqualified from teaching in the public schools of the great State of New York. The District Court expressed it well and forcefully when it observed that New York's exclusion "seems repugnant to the very heritage the State is seeking to inculcate." . . .

Plyler v. Doe

457 U.S. 202 (1982), 5-4
Opinion of the Court: Brennan (Blackmun, Marshall, Powell, Stevens)
Dissenting: Burger (O'Connor, Rehnquist, White)

On what grounds did Texas argue that withholding funds for the education of the children of illegal aliens was not a

violation of equal protection? Why is alienage a suspect clas-
sification? What standard of review did the Court use in this
case? What kind of state interest would be required to uphold
the state law? Why isn't saving public money such an inter-
est? What might be? Is educating the children of illegal
aliens likely to save public money in the long run? Is the
Court's rationale in this case limited to education or does it
include other services and opportunities that might be denied
to illegal aliens and their children? Could Congress in estab-
lishing rules for entering the country and declaring illegal
entrants unwelcome, authorize the states to deny education
and other public services to illegal aliens? Would this be a
matter of one part of the Constitution colliding with an-
other? If so, what would be constitutional?

Brennan, for the Court:
The question presented by these cases is whether, consistent with the Equal Protection Clause of the Fourteenth Amendment, Texas may deny to undocumented school-age children the free public education that it provides to children who are citizens of the United States or legally admitted aliens.

Since the late 19th century, the United States has restricted immigration into this country. Unsanctioned entry into the United States is a crime, and those who have entered unlawfully are subject to deportation. But despite the existence of these legal restrictions, a substantial number of persons have succeeded in unlawfully entering the United States, and now live within various States, including the State of Texas.

In May, 1975, the Texas Legislature revised its education laws to withhold from local school districts any state funds for the education of children who were not "legally admitted" into the United States. The 1975 revision also authorized local school districts to deny enrollment in their public schools to children not "legally admitted" to the country. These cases involve constitutional challenges to those provisions.

This is a class action, filed in the United States District Court for the Eastern District of Texas in September, 1977, on behalf of certain school-age children of Mexican origin residing in Smith County, Tex., who could not establish that they had been legally admitted into the United States. The action complained of the exclusion of plaintiff children from the public schools of the Tyler Independent School District. . . .

The Fourteenth Amendment provides that "[n]o State shall . . . deprive any person of life, liberty, or property, without due process of law; nor deny to any person within its jurisdiction the equal protection of

the laws." . . . Aliens, even aliens whose presence in this country is unlawful, have long been recognized as "persons" guaranteed due process of law by the Fifth and Fourteenth Amendments. Indeed, we have clearly held that the Fifth Amendment protects aliens whose presence in this country is unlawful from invidious discrimination by the Federal Government. . . .

Our conclusion that the illegal aliens who are plaintiffs in these cases may claim the benefit of the Fourteenth Amendment's guarantee of equal protection only begins the inquiry. The more difficult question is whether the Equal Protection Clause has been violated by the refusal of the State of Texas to reimburse local school boards for the education of children who cannot demonstrate that their presence within the United States is lawful, or by the imposition by those school boards of the burden of tuition on those children. . . .

Sheer incapability or lax enforcement of the laws barring entry into this country, coupled with the failure to establish an effective bar to the employment of undocumented aliens, has resulted in the creation of a substantial "shadow population" of illegal migrants—numbering in the millions—within our borders. This situation raises the specter of a permanent caste of undocumented resident aliens, encouraged by some to remain here as a source of cheap labor, but nevertheless denied the benefits that our society makes available to citizens and lawful residents. The existence of such an underclass presents most difficult problems for a Nation that prides itself on adherence to principles of equality under law.

The children who are plaintiffs in these cases are special members of this underclass. Persuasive arguments support the view that a State may withhold its beneficence from those whose very presence within the United States is the product of their own unlawful conduct. These arguments do not apply with the same force to classifications imposing disabilities on the minor children of such illegal entrants. . . .

Of course, undocumented status is not irrelevant to any proper legislative goal. Nor is undocumented status an absolutely immutable characteristic, since it is the product of conscious, indeed unlawful, action. But §21.031 is directed against children, and imposes its discriminatory burden on the basis of a legal characteristic over which children can have little control. It is thus difficult to conceive of a rational justification for penalizing these children for their presence within the United States. Yet that appears to be precisely the effect of §21.031.

Public education is not a "right" granted to individuals by the Constitution. But neither is it merely some governmental "benefit" indistinguishable from other forms of social welfare legislation. Both the importance of education in maintaining our basic institutions and the lasting impact of its deprivation on the life of the child mark the distinction. . . .

. . . In addition, education provides the basic tools by which individuals might lead economically productive lives to the benefit of us all. In sum, education has a fundamental role in maintaining the fabric of our society. We cannot ignore the significant social costs borne by our Nation when select groups are denied the means to absorb the values and skills upon which our social order rests.

In addition to the pivotal role of education in sustaining our political and cultural heritage, denial of education to some isolated group of children poses an affront to one of the goals of the Equal Protection Clause: the abolition of governmental barriers presenting unreasonable obstacles to advancement on the basis of individual merit. Paradoxically, by depriving the children of any disfavored group of an education, we foreclose the means by which that group might raise the level of esteem in which it is held by the majority. But more directly, "education prepares individuals to be self-reliant and self-sufficient participants in society." *Wisconsin v. Yoder* Illiteracy is an enduring disability. The inability to read and write will handicap the individual deprived of a basic education each and every day of his life. The inestimable toll of that deprivation on the social, economic, intellectual, and psychological wellbeing of the individual, and the obstacle it poses to individual achievement, make it most difficult to reconcile the cost or the principle of a status-based denial of basic education with the framework of equality embodied in the Equal Protection Clause. . . .

These well-settled principles allow us to determine the proper level of deference to be afforded §21.031. Undocumented aliens cannot be treated as a suspect class, because their presence in this country in violation of federal law is not a "constitutional irrelevancy." Nor is education a fundamental right; a State need not justify by compelling necessity every variation in the manner in which education is provided to its population. But more is involved in these cases than the abstract question whether §21.031 discriminates against a suspect class, or whether education is a fundamental right. Section 21.031 imposes a lifetime hardship on a discrete class of children not accountable for their dis-

abling status. The stigma of illiteracy will mark them for the rest of their lives. By denying these children a basic education, we deny them the ability to live within the structure of our civic institutions, and foreclose any realistic possibility that they will contribute in even the smallest way to the progress of our Nation. In determining the rationality of §21.031, we may appropriately take into account its costs to the Nation and to the innocent children who are its victims. In light of these countervailing costs, the discrimination contained in §21.031 can hardly be considered rational unless it furthers some substantial goal of the State. . . .

Appellants argue that the classification at issue furthers an interest in the "preservation of the state's limited resources for the education of its lawful residents." Of course, a concern for the preservation of resources, standing alone, can hardly justify the classification used in allocating those resources. The State must do more than justify its classification with a concise expression of an intention to discriminate. Apart from the asserted state prerogative to act against undocumented children solely on the basis of their undocumented status—an asserted prerogative that carries only minimal force in the circumstances of these cases—we discern three colorable state interests that might support §21.031.

First, appellants appear to suggest that the State may seek to protect itself from an influx of illegal immigrants. While a State might have an interest in mitigating the potentially harsh economic effects of sudden shifts in population, §21.031 hardly offers an effective method of dealing with an urgent demographic or economic problem. There is no evidence in the record suggesting that illegal entrants impose any significant burden on the State's economy. To the contrary, the available evidence suggests that illegal aliens underutilize public services, while contributing their labor to the local economy and tax money to the state fisc. The dominant incentive for illegal entry into the State of Texas is the availability of employment; few if any illegal immigrants come to this country, or presumably to the State of Texas, in order to avail themselves of a free education. Thus, even making the doubtful assumption that the net impact of illegal aliens on the economy of the State is negative, we think it clear that "[c]harging tuition to undocumented children constitutes a ludicrously ineffectual attempt to stem the tide of illegal immigration," at least when compared with the alternative of prohibiting the employment of illegal aliens.

Second, while it is apparent that a State may "not . . . reduce expenditures for education by barring [some arbitrarily chosen class of] children from its schools," *Shapiro v. Thompson,* appellants suggest that undocumented children are appropriately singled out for exclusion because of the special burdens they impose on the State's ability to provide high-quality public education. But the record in no way supports the claim that exclusion of undocumented children is likely to improve the overall quality of education in the State. . . .

. . . Of course, even if improvement in the quality of education were a likely result of barring some number of children from the schools of the State, the State must support its selection of this group as the appropriate target for exclusion. In terms of educational cost and need, however, undocumented children are "basically indistinguishable" from legally resident alien children.

Finally, appellants suggest that undocumented children are appropriately singled out because their unlawful presence within the United States renders them less likely than other children to remain within the boundaries of the State, and to put their education to productive social or political use within the State. Even assuming that such an interest is legitimate, it is an interest that is most difficult to quantify. The State has no assurance that any child, citizen or not, will employ the education provided by the State within the confines of the State's borders. . . .

If the State is to deny a discrete group of innocent children the free public education that it offers to other children residing within its borders, that denial must be justified by a showing that it furthers some substantial state interest. No such showing was made here. . . .

Burger, dissenting:

Were it our business to set the Nation's social policy, I would agree without hesitation that it is senseless for an enlightened society to deprive any children— including illegal aliens—of an elementary education. I fully agree that it would be folly—and wrong—to tolerate creation of a segment of society made up of illiterate persons, many having a limited or no command of our language. However, the Constitution does not constitute us as "Platonic Guardians," nor does it vest in this Court the authority to strike down laws because they do not meet our standards of desirable social policy, "wisdom," or "common sense." We trespass on the assigned function of the political branches under our structure of limited and separated powers when we assume a policymaking role as the Court does today.

The Court makes no attempt to disguise that it is acting to make up for Congress' lack of "effective leadership" in dealing with the serious national problems caused by the influx of uncountable millions of illegal aliens across our borders. The failure of enforcement of the immigration laws over more than a decade and the inherent difficulty and expense of sealing our vast borders have combined to create a grave socioeconomic dilemma. It is a dilemma that has not yet even been fully assessed, let alone addressed. However, it is not the function of the Judiciary to provide "effective leadership" simply because the political branches of government fail to do so. . . .

In a sense, the Court's opinion rests on such a unique confluence of theories and rationales that it will likely stand for little beyond the results in these particular cases. Yet the extent to which the Court departs from principled constitutional adjudication is nonetheless disturbing. . . .

The Equal Protection Clause does not mandate identical treatment of different categories of persons. The dispositive issue in these cases, simply put, is whether, for purposes of allocating its finite resources, a state has a legitimate reason to differentiate between persons who are lawfully within the state and those who are unlawfully there. The distinction the State of Texas has drawn—based not only upon its own legitimate interests but on classifications established by the Federal Government in its immigration laws and policies—is not unconstitutional. . . .

. . . [T]he Equal Protection Clause does not preclude legislators from classifying among persons on the basis of factors and characteristics over which individuals may be said to lack "control." Indeed, in some circumstances, persons generally, and children in particular, may have little control over or responsibility for such things as their ill health, need for public assistance, or place of residence. Yet a state legislature is not barred from considering, for example, relevant differences between the mentally healthy and the mentally ill, or between the residents of different counties simply because these may be factors unrelated to individual choice or to any "wrongdoing." The Equal Protection Clause protects against arbitrary and irrational classifications, and against invidious discrimination stemming from prejudice and hostility; it is not an all-encompassing "equalizer" designed to eradicate every distinction for which persons are not "responsible."

... This Court has recognized that, in allocating governmental benefits to a given class of aliens, one "may take into account the character of the relationship between the alien and this country." When that "relationship" is a federally prohibited one, there can, of course, be no presumption that a state has a constitutional duty to include illegal aliens among the recipients of its governmental benefits. ...

Once it is conceded—as the Court does—that illegal aliens are not a suspect class, and that education is not a fundamental right, our inquiry should focus on and be limited to whether the legislative classification at issue bears a rational relationship to a legitimate state purpose. ...

Without laboring what will undoubtedly seem obvious to many, it simply is not "irrational" for a state to conclude that it does not have the same responsibility to provide benefits for persons whose very presence in the state and this country is illegal as it does to provide for persons lawfully present. By definition, illegal aliens have no right whatever to be here, and the state may reasonably, and constitutionally, elect not to provide them with governmental services at the expense of those who are lawfully in the state. ... The Court has failed to offer even a plausible explanation why illegality of residence in this country is not a factor that may legitimately bear upon the bona fides of state residence and entitlement to the benefits of lawful residence.

It is significant that the Federal Government has seen fit to exclude illegal aliens from numerous social welfare programs, such as the food stamp program, the old-age assistance, aid to families with dependent children, aid to the blind, aid to the permanently and totally disabled, and supplemental security income programs, the Medicare hospital insurance benefits program, and the Medicaid hospital insurance benefits for the aged and disabled program. Although these exclusions do not conclusively demonstrate the constitutionality of the State's use of the same classification for comparable purposes, at the very least they tend to support the rationality of excluding illegal alien residents of a state from such programs so as to preserve the state's finite revenues for the benefit of lawful residents. ...

Congress, "vested by the Constitution with the responsibility of protecting our borders and legislating with respect to aliens," bears primary responsibility for addressing the problems occasioned by the millions of illegal aliens flooding across our southern border. Similarly, it is for Congress, and not this Court, to assess the "social costs borne by our Nation when select groups are denied the means to absorb the values and skills upon which our social order rests." While the "specter of a permanent caste" of illegal Mexican residents of the United States is indeed a disturbing one, it is but one segment of a larger problem, which is for the political branches to solve. I find it difficult to believe that Congress would long tolerate such a self-destructive result—that it would fail to deport these illegal alien families or to provide for the education of their children. Yet instead of allowing the political processes to run their course—albeit with some delay—the Court seeks to do Congress' job for it, compensating for congressional inaction. It is not unreasonable to think that this encourages the political branches to pass their problems to the Judiciary.

The solution to this seemingly intractable problem is to defer to the political processes, unpalatable as that may be to some. ...

9

GENDER AND OTHER DISCRIMINATION

Though race discrimination presents the most profound challenge to the ideal of equality, the failing is not the only one in our social domain in which practice has fallen short of ideal. The struggle of women for equal status before the law and equal opportunity in the workplace dates to the early nineteenth century; less formally, it may be as old as the human community itself. Invidious distinctions based on age, birth status, sexual orientation, and economic means are also matters of long standing that have only recently gotten statutory and constitutional attention.

Most Americans subscribe to the ideal of equality, but equalizing unequal status is often, as we have seen, a zero-sum project. For some persons to gain something they do not have, others may need to make room or give up something they already have. This may not be true in some matters, such as gaining even-handed treatment from the police, but it may often be in others where material resources or economic and social opportunities is at stake in circumstances of scarcity.

The equality principle can also clash with another premier value in the American ethos: the reward of merit. As long as talent, skill, and achievement are unevenly distributed among individuals, unequal gains and rewards are likely to follow. In fact the prospect of unequal rewards or advantages may be a chief incentive for achievement. But when rewards or advantages are based even in part on race, gender, national origin, and other "natural" attributes, they are today constitutionally suspect. Determining which rewards and advantages are those of merit and which may be unduly affected by unacceptable distinctions is often factually complex. Persuading those who believe their gains are based on achievement to make room for those with fewer advantages can be politically difficult.

Gender

From earliest colonial times women played an important role in the settlement and building of the country. Hard conditions and

535

unusual economic opportunity blunted but did not do away with many traditional role differences between the sexes. That American women may have had more freedom than women in other countries and many privileges men lacked, does not diminish the stark fact that they did not have equality as that ideal is understood today.

The Right to Vote

Organized efforts to improve women's lot—a women's movement, in modern terms—long antedated issues of equality under the Constitution. Though activists were often allied with the antislavery movement, their early efforts focused on family and moral concerns such as spousal abuse, abandonment, prostitution, and temperance rather than on political rights. The first national women's rights meeting, at Seneca Falls, N.Y., in 1848, produced a memorable declaration calling for equal rights not merely in marriage but in education, work, and political life. In the years after the Civil War, two competing women's organizations, headed by early champions of women's rights, Susan B. Anthony, Elizabeth Cady Stanton, Lucy Stone, and Julia Ward Howe, each demanded that women be given the right to vote. This early suffragist

endeavor met with limited success—by 1890 only two states, Utah and Wyoming, had enfranchised women.

Most feminist efforts to get the vote were directed to persuading legislatures and the general public. Forays into the courts were few and generally proved disappointing. One test case, *Minor v. Happersett,* did reach the Supreme Court in 1875, but its prospects were not promising. Only two years before, in *Bradwell v. Illinois,* the Court, in its first holding on a gender issue, had refused to overturn a state court ruling that barred women from practicing law. The Fourteenth Amendment's privileges and immunities clause, protecting the attributes of national rather than state citizenship, did not embrace the right to practice a profession. The narrow ruling was consistent with the Court's first pronouncement on the clause in the Slaughterhouse Cases two years before on the right to be in a certain business. The two decisions made it easy for the Court in *Minor,* to hold unanimously that suffrage was not a privilege and immunity of national citizenship either. States, if they chose, were free to give "that important trust to men alone."

The drive for the vote and for other advances in equality gained new and stronger impetus as it became part of the general and broader

Anna Shaw, in black, and Carrie Chapmen Catt, founders of the League of Women Voters, lead an estimated 20,000 supporters down New York's Fifth Avenue in a 1918 women's suffrage march. A year later, Congress proposed the Nineteenth Amendment, giving women the right to vote.

agenda of Progressive reform after the turn of the century and as the ranks of feminists grew substantially. Suffragist groups campaigned widely and made voting a spearhead for progress toward all rights. These efforts eventually won wide support among men as well as women and resulted in Congress proposing the Nineteenth Amendment in 1919 forbidding denial or abridgment of the right to vote on the basis of gender. It was ratified the following year. What could not be won through constitutional interpretation was gained through amendment.

Women in Need of Protection

Many broad Progressive reforms affecting women called attention to differences between the sexes and the need to give women special help, especially in the workplace. Though many of these may seem paternalistic today when gender differences are played down, they were well-intentioned at the beginning of the twentieth century and were widely supported by women's organizations.

Oregon's limit of the workday of women to 10 hours was an early example and was motivated by concern for women's health. The law was challenged by an employer and brought before the Supreme Court in *Muller v. Oregon*, 1908. The Court sustained the law as a valid use of state police power to protect the health of women workers, rejecting the employer's argument that it interfered with the liberty to contract. It was a formidable and unexpected victory for reform, attributable in part to an extraordinary brief filed by Louis Brandeis, a leading attorney of the day (and later to be a member of the Court), who had been hired by the state to defend the law. Because the Court had often found state regulation of working conditions to lack factual support, at least as the Court saw the facts, Brandeis gave 98 pages of his 102-page brief to a summary and analysis of women's working conditions and their effect on health. This was based on studies his law firm had collected in the United States and other countries. (The "Brandeis brief," as such empirical displays

became known, impressed not only the justices but reform lawyers and was widely imitated in later cases.)

When workplace reform was extended from concerns about health to those of reward, however, the result was different. In *Adkins v. Children's Hospital*, 1923, a more conservative Taft Court struck down federal legislation that established a minimum wage for women in the District of Columbia. The law was designed to protect women against exploitation by employers, but the Court, bent on reviving its liberty of contract theory, ignored the grossly unequal bargaining positions of the average worker and her employer.

The debate the case produced also widened the old fissure among women's groups between those of a more radical—modern is perhaps a better term—persuasion who argued for equality in all matters and more traditional reformers who, fearing loss of important gains made against exploitative and unscrupulous employers, stressed the differences between the genders in social and economic circumstances. In a different form perhaps, it is a debate heard in the women's movement even to the present day. Conservative Justice George Sutherland, who wrote the Court's opinion in *Adkins* and was himself married to a feminist, phrased the matter as one of not putting greater restrictions on the liberty of contract of women than men.

Minimum wage laws for women were finally upheld by the Court in *West Coast Hotel Co. v. Parrish*, 1937, a decision that also marked the end of the Supreme Court's resistance to the New Deal, in the face of President Franklin Roosevelt's controversial "court-packing" plan. But the Court's about-face came less from having a different view of women than a different view of government intervention in the labor marketplace and abandonment of its liberty of contract doctrine.

In later cases on other issues, the Court upheld protective laws based on gender distinction that modern critics might label sex-role stereotyping. Typical was the statute sustained in *Goesaert v. Cleary*, 1948, barring women from serving drinks behind a bar unless they were the wife or daughter of the bar owner. In *Hoyt v. Florida*,

1961, the Warren Court upheld gender distinctions in a state law that required males to serve on juries but made service by women voluntary. As Justice John Marshall Harlan II put it in what would be the Court's last echo of distinctions once assumed to be gender-given:

> Despite the enlightened emancipation of women from the restrictions and protections of bygone years, and their entry into many parts of the community life formerly considered to be reserved to men, woman is still regarded as the center of home and family life. [368 U.S. 57 at 61-62]

Modern Issues of Opportunity

The modern-day women's movement can probably be said to have started in the 1960s. The National Organization of Women, (NOW) was founded in 1966 about the same time that a number of other women's organizations came into being. Their goals have always been broader and more comprehensive than simply winning legal rights. Successes and failures, like those in the struggle against race discrimination, cannot be measured by laws and court decisions alone. Even so, a basic aim of modern activists has been to gain constitutional condemnation of gender-based discrimination, less because women needed social protection than that they were excluded from important opportunity. Because feminist arguments had had mixed success in the courts, organized women's groups revived an old idea: amend the Constitution to insure equal treatment, as the Constitution had been amended to protect the rights of former slaves after the Civil War and to secure women the right to vote in 1920. A national lobbying effort resulted in Congress proposing the Equal Rights Amendment, (ERA) in 1972. Encouraged by success civil rights groups winning court rulings against racial discrimination, a concurrent effort was made to win constitutionally based rights through litigation that would persuade courts to interpret or reinterpret existing Constitutional provisions. The first of these efforts failed, the second has largely succeeded.

The ERA, which declared simply that "equality of rights under the laws shall not be denied or

Phyllis Schlafly, national leader of the "Stop the Equal Rights Amendment," speaks with reporters at a rally at the Illinois State Capitol in 1975.

abridged in the United States or any state on account of sex," was approved by the required two-thirds of the House and Senate and sent to the states for ratification in 1972. The feminist revival of the 1970s spurred expectations that the amendment would win swift approval in the states and, indeed, 30 states ratified within a year. But as opposition led by several religious groups and Phyllis Schafly's organization Stop ERA—the amendment had touched the old schism in the women's movement—mounted, support in most of the remaining states waned. When the amendment's original seven-year deadline expired in 1979 without ratification, Congress controversially extended it by 39 months to June 30, 1982. But not much new support was gained and as the new deadline expired, 15 states had voted against ratification and five others that had ratified rescinded approval. Some opponents argued that the ERA would jeopardize hard-won protections of women in the workplace: laws requiring child support from divorced husbands, and the exemption of women from conscripted military service. Ironically, one of the telling arguments against the amendment was that the increasing number of court decisions enhancing equality for wo-men, discussed next, made the amendment unnecessary.

One of the first of these decisions was *Reed v. Reed,* 1971 (p. 549), in which the early Burger Court reviewed an Idaho law that required preference be given to male relatives in appointing executors of estates of persons who had died intestate, that is, without wills. The law's reasoning was that because men tended to be more experienced in financial matters, their appointment would make work of the probate courts easier. In holding the law to violate the equal protection clause of the Fourteenth Amendment, the Court applied that constitutional requirement to a gender distinction for the first time. Different treatment of the sexes was sustainable only if it was "reasonable, not arbitrary." Arguing the case against Idaho law was Ruth Bader Ginsburg, a feminist lawyer, who 22 years later would herself be a member of the Court.

Three years later in *Frontiero v. Richardson* (p. 550), the issue was how allowances for military dependents were to be computed. The Court struck down a federal law that called for female members of the armed forces to show they paid more than half their dependent spouse's support but put no such burden of proof on male members who had dependent spouses. The law failed because it allowed potentially greater benefits for males than females similarly situated. The majority of eight justices was divided, however, on whether the standard of review in gender discrimination should be the "strict scrutiny" applied to racial distinctions or merely the one of "rational basis" in which a law might be upheld if the gender distinctions were simply "reasonable."

The Court's review of gender discrimination was further defined when it held that sex-based distinction against males might also violate equal protection. In *Craig v. Boren,* 1976 (p. 553), it invalidated an Oklahoma law that permitted women 18 or older to buy beer having an alcohol content of 3.2 percent but required men to be 21. The state cited studies that men 18–20 were much more likely to be arrested for drunk driving and public drunkenness than women in the same age group. The gender distinction presented the Court with a problem because the law obviously had a rational basis.

Justice William Brennan, speaking for a majority, held that sex-based classifications were subject to greater scrutiny than that of the rational basis test. To be upheld, such distinctions "must serve important governmental objectives and must be substantially related to those objectives." This standard of review fell somewhere between the "strict scrutiny" applied to racial classifications that demanded proof of a "compelling" government interest and rational basis requiring only that a law not be arbitrary. Though admitting Oklahoma had an important government interest in traffic safety, the law did not, at least in the Court's view, "substantially" further that goal.

Three decisions in the early 1980s show the Court's uncertain application of this intermediate standard of scrutiny. After the Vietnam War,

Congress ended the military draft, but in 1980 its registration provisions were reinstated by President Jimmy Carter. These, applied only to males because only males would be conscripted if selective service were ever reinstated. This gender distinction was challenged as a violation of equal protection by several men required to register. In *Rostker v. Goldberg,* 1981 (p. 556), the Court rejected their argument and sustained male-only registration because of the military's need for flexibility in rotating soldiers in and out of combat positions and because women did not then serve in combat. (The Court did not consider the combat restriction.) So gender-based registration bore a substantial relationship to an important government end.

A California law making heterosexual intercourse between persons ages 14–17 a crime of statutory rape for the male but no offense for the female was challenged in *Michael M. v. Superior Court of Sonoma County,* 1981. A plurality of the justices accepted the state's reasoning that the law helped discourage teenage pregnancy and that because only females could become pregnant, the gender distinction was substantially related to that end. Though the decision reflects the Court's greater willingness to accept gender distinctions based on physical differences between the sexes, the decision may rest as well on an unacknowledged acceptance of long-standing gender roles.

In *Mississippi University for Women v. Hogan,* 1982, the Court dealt with the controversial issue of single-sex schools in higher education. Mississippi's policy of limiting enrollment in one of its nursing schools only to women was challenged by a man denied admission. In her first opinion, the Court's first woman justice, Sandra Day O'Connor, held that excluding men was not closely enough related to Mississippi's stated goal of compensating women for discriminatory barriers they might face. To succeed academically, women did not need an environment protected from men.

The Court has been increasingly willing to strike down gender distinctions that once may have had rational basis but today appear simply stereotypical. For example, it has held that states may not give husbands the right to dispose of jointly owned spousal property without the wife's consent. (*Kirchberg v. Fennstra,* 1981) Nor may husbands but not wives be required to pay alimony in a divorce (*Orr v. Orr,* 1979), or an unwed mother be allowed to withhold consent to the adoption of her child without the father having the same right. (*Caban v. Mohammed,* 1979) Similarly, the Court has struck down provisions of the Social Security Act that denied survivors benefits to widowers but gave them to widows (*Weinberger v. Wiesenfeld,* 1975), or denied benefits to families with dependent children where the mother rather than the father as the chief breadwinner became unemployed. (*Califano v. Wescott,* 1979)

But the Court was willing to uphold gender distinction where Congress imposed more rigorous requirements for establishing parentage (and thus citizenship) of a child born abroad out of wedlock, where the father rather than the mother was the American citizen. In *Tuan Anh Nguyen v. Immigration and Naturalization Service,* 2001, it found no violation of equal protection. The gender distinction was based on the "significant difference" between a mother's and a father's relationship to a child at the time of birth and was justified by two important government interests: ensuring there was a biological relationship and that the child and citizen parent have had a chance to form "real everyday ties providing connection between child and citizen parent and, in turn, the United States."

Pregnancy and the ability to become pregnant are fundamental gender differences that have given rise to work discrimination issues under Title VII of the Civil Rights Act of 1964. When the Supreme Court in *General Electric Co. v. Gilbert,* 1976, interpreted the act not to prevent employers from refusing women workers disability benefits for pregnancy leave, Congress amended the law to include such benefits. The Court has since held that pregnancy leave may not adversely affect a woman's seniority rights. (*Nashville Gas Co. v. Satty,* 1979)

In a controversial ruling, again reflecting the collision of protection and opportunity, the Court held in *International Union, American Workers, Aerospace Agricultural Implement Workers of America, U.A.W. v. Johnson Controls, Inc.,* 1991, that the company's "fetal protection" policy violated Title VII as amended by the Pregnancy Discrimination Act of 1978. As a battery manufacturer, the company had barred fertile women from jobs, many high-paying, that would expose them to lead. Because the protection of fetuses was not essential to battery manufacture, the Court said, the gender distinction was not a "bona fide occupational qualification" under the federal law.

The well-established gender difference in life expectancy cannot justify under Title VII a government insurance plan requiring women make higher contributions to a pension fund than men. (*Los Angeles Department of Water and Power v. Manhart,* 1978) Nor may such expected longevity justify women receiving a lower monthly retirement benefit. (*Arizona Governing Committee for Tax Annuity and Deferred Compensation Plans v. Norris,* 1983) Statistical

differences about a class, even if true, do not support a policy that treats "individuals simply as components" of a racial, religious, sexual, or national class." (*Manhart,* 1978)

In 1996, the Court's earlier ruling against gender exclusion in higher education came into conflict with historic gender distinctions based, partly at least, on physical differences, in the admissions policy of the all-male, state-supported Virginia Military Institute, (VMI). The school, most of whose graduating cadets go on to careers as military officers, is celebrated for its Spartan "adversative" model of education featuring physical rigor, emotional stress, and absence of privacy. To meet an earlier challenge to the exclusion policy, Virginia had set up a parallel program for women called the Virginia Women's Institute for Leadership (VWIL) on another campus. In *United States v. Virginia* (p. 559), this "solution" was held unconstitutional by the Supreme Court, which called attention to the many differences between VMI and VWIL. The second program was but "a pale shadow" of the first and so denied equal protection to women wanting to attend VMI and who otherwise qualified for admission. The state had

Justices Ruth Bader Ginsburg and Sandra Day O'Connor. Justice O'Connor, appointed by President Ronald Reagan in 1981, was the first woman to sit on the Supreme Court. Justice Ginsburg was second, appointed by President Bill Clinton in 1993.

given no "exceedingly persuasive justification" for excluding all women.

Sexual Harassment

Though the line between simple unwanted attention and sex-based pressure may often be a thin one, the Burger and Rehnquist Courts have been increasingly responsive to women's complaints about hostile workplace environments and have extended protection against gender discrimination and sexually harassing behavior. Though many state laws forbid harassment, the Court's chief decisions have come through interpretation of Title VII of the Pregnancy Discrimination Act outlawing employer discrimination not only in hiring and firing but in "the privileges and conditions of employment."

In *Meritor Savings Bank v. Vinson*, 1986, in which a bank employee alleged she was sexually harassed by a supervisor during a four-year period, the Court unanimously held that sexual harassment was sexual discrimination under Title VII. Victims did not need to prove tangible or economic loss. Nor did it matter that a sexual relationship that developed may have been voluntary.

The Court was again unanimous in *Harris v. Forklift Systems*, 1993, holding that a complainant-employee need not prove even psychological injury when the discriminating behavior was severe and pervasive enough to create a "hostile or abusive" work environment. Judges and juries may weigh the frequency of abusive behavior, its severity, whether it was physically intimidating, and whether it interfered with the complainant's work in determining if such an environment existed.

In later cases, the Court has ruled that actionable workplace harassment extends to that which has a same-sex origin (*Oncale v. Sundowner Offshore Services*, 1998) and that employers are liable in sexual harassment suits unless they can show they took reasonable care to prevent or promptly correct the abusive behavior or that the complainant-employee acted unrea-

sonably in not taking advantage of grievance procedures. (*Burlington Industries, Inc. v. Ellerth*, 1998)

Age

Many laws discriminate among persons by age, usually by imposing disabilities on those thought to be too young for certain activities or responsibilities, such as driving a car, buying alcoholic drinks, or getting married. Restrictions because of immaturity can simply be outgrown and seldom raise an equal protection question. However, laws imposing a disability—usually forced retirement—upon someone only because they have reached a certain age do raise equality issues. Ousting older workers ostensibly because of diminishing skill has been a practice of long standing, justified to prevent the harm or inefficiency that sub-par performance can produce. But it is also true that retirement, forced or otherwise, redistributes employment and usually allows replacement of higher paid workers with lower paid. That both employers and younger workers benefit from mandatory retirements, shows again that on many equality issues, a gain or protection for one person may impose a cost or loss of opportunity on another. Complicating the picture is that most persons today enjoy longer life and better health in their late years than past generations have. Traditional retirement ages, such as 65 that is still the centerpiece of the social security system and many private pension programs, are increasingly out of step with gains in life expectancy. Blanket classification applying to everyone in an age group also ignores that aging is marked by great individual differences including those in work performance.

Responding to some of these issues, Congress passed age discrimination acts in 1967, 1975, and 1979, barring some but not all employers from firing or otherwise discriminating against employees between 40 and 70 because of their age. The Supreme Court has heard few age discrimination cases, but one of its first, *Massachusetts Board of Retirement v. Murgia*, 1976 (p. 564), before the last federal legislation, dealt with the constitutionality of retirement classifications. At issue was a Massachusetts statute mandating retirement of state police officers at 50. In sustaining the law, the Court held that age was not a "suspect" classification like that of race or national origin where there is "a history of purposeful unequal treatment." So the state law was subject only to the "rational basis" test that, in the Court's view, was easily met. It was not irrational for Massachusetts to conclude that age, after a certain point, was reasonably related to the job performance of state police officers.

Under the new federal age discrimination laws, the Court held that a 59-year-old test pilot dismissed because of age had to be restored to his job with back pay. (*McDonnell Douglas v. Houghton*, 1977) But in *Vance v. Bradley*, 1979, it applied its *Murgia* reasoning to sustain a federal regulation that required members of the U.S. Foreign Service to retire at 60. The mandate was reasonably related to the risk and rigors of overseas service. In a more recent application of the rational basis test in *Gregory v. Ashcroft*, 1990, it upheld a provision of the Missouri constitution forcing public officials to retire at 70, against a challenge by a state judge. Speaking for the Court, Justice O'Connor observed,

> The Missouri mandatory retirement provision, like all legal classifications, is founded on a generalization. It is far from true that all judges suffer significant deterioration in performance at age 70. It is probably not true that most do. It may not be true at all. But a State "does not violate the Equal Protection Clause merely because the classifications made by its laws are imperfect." [501 U.S. 452 at 472]

Her comment reflects the limited judicial review and considerable deference to legislative judgment called for by the rational basis test, especially compared with the Court's "heightened"

review of gender pension classifications that were reasonably based on life expectancy statistics, noted earlier.

Birth Status

Distinctions between legitimate and illegitimate children have had long standing in law and policy, and only in recent years has the Supreme Court brought them under equal protection review. Illegitimate children have faced barriers in receiving government benefits in the death or disability of a parent, in gaining standing to sue for the wrongful death of a parent, and in inheriting from the estate of a deceased parent. The last, aimed at discouraging birth out of wedlock and protecting established and legally recognized families, has given the Court the most difficulty. It is also an area in which the gain of a right puts a burden not on government or an insurance company and thus on taxpayers or policyholders in general, but on specific other persons, namely the legitimate children in a family.

After some initial ambivalence in which the Court applied a simple rationality test to laws classifying legitimate and illegitimate children, it has largely settled on a more demanding review though one falling short of "strict scrutiny." For example, having held that dependent illegitimate children could sue for damages in the wrongful death of their mother because not letting them do so lacked rational basis (*Levy v. Louisiana*, 1968), the Court upheld a state law that barred them from suing to share equally in the estate of their father who had died without a will. (*Labine v. Vincent*, 1971) But it struck down as serving "no legitimate state interest" a state workman's compensation statute that denied benefits to dependent unacknowledged illegitimate children (*Weber v. Aetna Casualty Co.*, 1972) and similar federal social security provisions. (*Jimenez v. Weinberger*, 1974) It also invalidated a state law that gave legitimate but not illegitimate children a right to enforce support payments from their father. (*Gomez v. Perez*, 1973)

The Court returned to the inheritance question in *Trimble v. Gordon,* 1977, in which it struck down an Illinois law that gave illegitimate children a right to inherit from a mother dying without a will but allowed legitimate children to inherit from either parent dying intestate. The Court appeared to be moving toward subjecting distinctions between legitimate and illegitimate children to a more rigorous review, but the following year in *Lalli v. Lalli,* it upheld a state law that barred illegitimate children from inheriting from a deceased father who died intestate unless there was an earlier judicial finding of his paternity. Here the Court was obviously sensitive to the state's interest of protecting against fraudulent claims.

It was not until *Clark v. Jeter,* 1988, that the Court formally adopted an intermediate standard of review, similar to that for gender distinctions. It held that birth status discrimination must be not only be reasonable but also bear "a substantial relationship to an important state interest."

In a collateral line of cases, some also touching on gender-based distinctions, the Court has dealt with the rights of the fathers of illegitimate children. For example, in *Stanley v. Illinois,* 1972, a father who had lived with the mother and illegitimate child until the mother's death could not be denied a hearing on his fitness to retain custody of the child simply because the child was illegitimate. But in *Quilloin v. Walcott,* 1978, the claim of an illegitimate child's natural father to veto an adoption by the husband of the natural mother was rejected where the father had neither acknowledged his paternity nor established a relationship with the child. In a decision noted earlier, the Court struck down a New York law that allowed the mother of an illegitimate child to withhold consent to its adoption but not giving an equal right to the father. (*Caban v. Mohammed,* 1979)

Sexual Orientation

Discrimination against homosexuality has a long history and consistently wide, if somewhat diminishing, support in public opinion. There is no general agreement about whether a homosexual orientation is a natural attribute and, like race, national origin, gender, age, or birth status, and thus a "given" about which a person has no choice or is simply an acquired preference in complex environmental circumstances. If it is the first, the case for constitutional protection similar to that for the other classifications would be strengthened.

Law and policy on the issue are now in great flux, partly because of the greater visibility of the discrimination issue brought about by the lobbying and litigating of gay rights groups and the public awareness of the toll taken by AIDS. Many states and municipalities have removed disabilities on gays, by decriminalizing homosexual acts in private. Others, however, have reinforced existing distinctions. There is no federal law barring discrimination because of sexual orientation as there is for that based on race, national origin, gender, and age. In 1966, Congress pointedly omitted sexual orientation from distinctions it outlawed in the workplace. In the Defense of Marriage Act, 1996, it withheld federal recognition of same-sex marriages now legal in certain states and released other states from giving them "full faith and credit." Even though the armed forces has modified its policy of excluding gays by not asking about sexual orientation in its "don't ask, don't tell" policy, members may still be discharged for homosexual conduct.

To date, the Supreme Court has had little to say in all of this. We have already seen that it has sustained state antisodomy laws in *Bowers v. Hardwick,* 1986, and the right of a private organization to exclude homosexuals as leaders in *Boy Scouts of America v. Dale,* 2000. But these decisions dealt with privacy and association issues, respectively. The Court did not see them as discrimination cases subject to equal protection analysis.

Romer v. Evans, 1996 (p. 567), was the first and so far only sexual orientation case in which the Court defined the central issue as one of a Fourteenth Amendment claim. After several cities in Colorado passed laws forbidding discrimination

Standards of Review in Equal Protection Analysis

Extent of review:
Tier one: greatest or "strict scrutiny"
Tier two: intermediate or "heightened" scrutiny
Tier three: least scrutiny, greatest deference to the "political" branches

Classification or distinctions based on:
Tier one: race, certain aspects of national origin
Tier two: gender, birth status, illegal alienage (state regulation of)
Tier three: age, sexual orientation, economic status

Government's need to justify the law or policy:
Tier one: must further a "compelling" government interest such as protecting public health or safety, in the least restrictive way possible
Tier two: must importantly further a "substantial" government interest

Tier three: must have a "rational basis," be reasonably related to a "legitimate" government interest, and not be arbitrary

Rights:
Tier one: "fundamental," derived from the Constitution, for example, speech, voting, interstate travel, access to the courts
Tier two: mainly statutory, for example, freedom from discrimination in the workplace
Tier three: mainly statutory and due process, for example, freedom from arbitrary or unreasonable laws or policies

Examples of leading cases:
Tier one: *Brown v. Board of Education, Graham v. Richardson*
Tier two: *Craig v. Boren*
Tier three: *Romer v. Evans, San Antonio Independent School District v. Rodriquez*

---

because of sexual orientation, voters used the statewide initiative process to amend the state's constitution to make such protective laws unconstitutional. Finding an equal protection violation, the Court said that by "imposing a broad and undifferentiated disability on a single named group," the amendment removed rights that everyone else in the state had. In reaching this conclusion, it did not go further than the rational basis test to find that the amendment was not "directed to any identifiable legitimate purpose or discrete objective."

Romer v. Evans will probably not be the Court's last word on distinctions of sexual orientation. Changes in state laws and policies, especially on same-sex marriages, gay domestic partnerships, and discrimination in the workplace almost guarantee that other constitutional questions will be addressed. Whether the Court will use a test more rigorous than rational basis remains to be seen, though the historic status of homosexuals

as a class of persons subject to discrimination may argue for it.

Economic Discrimination

Most laws and government policies have some economic affect and some even classify persons by their economic means. Almost every law or policy with economic effect has unequal effect. For example, those with greater income pay greater income taxes, those owning homes with greater assessed valuation pay higher property taxes, and where a tax is designed to be progressive, those with greater means also pay at higher rates. When there is no classification by means, such as with a fixed fee or charge, the economic burden still falls unequally—it is felt more heavily by persons with fewer means than by those with more. Unlike race, national origin, gender, age, etc., economic inequality is not an innate

A group of University of Colorado students in Boulder celebrate the Supreme Court's decision in *Romer v. Evans* that held Colorado's Amendment 2 unconstitutional, May 20, 1996.

characteristic. But does economic discrimination, intended or otherwise, impermissibly violate the exercise of a constitutional right?

When the post-New Deal "Roosevelt" Court addressed this issue for the first time in 1941, it was over a challenge to California's Depression-era "anti-Okie" law that made it unlawful to bring a known indigent into the state. In *Edwards v. California*, the Court held the law unconstitutional not for discriminating against indigency but for impeding the right of interstate travel that, the Court said, was sanctioned by the commerce clause.

In *Shapiro v. Thompson*, 1969 (p. 571), the Warren Court relied on the right to travel to find a discriminatory effect in the administration of Connecticut's welfare laws. To conserve resources for in-state welfare recipients, many states in the 1960s applied residency restrictions to welfare applicants. Connecticut's were typical in requiring a one-year residence before an indigent from another state could get benefits. Calling the right to move interstate "fundamental," the Court held the state's policy, though reasonable, did not serve a "compelling state interest" needed to pass strict scrutiny.

The decision was an important extension of *Edwards* not because welfare residency laws made an indigent's entry into a state illegal, as California's had, but because impeding a fundamental right for some persons but not for others violated equal protection of the law. Thus it opened such laws to the scrutiny analysis the Court used in discrimination cases. In this, as we have seen, the Court applies "strict" scrutiny to "suspect" classifications or distinctions and sustains them only when they further a "compelling government interest." Other classifications or distinctions not "suspect" may also come under strict scrutiny if they affect fundamental rights—those expressly protected by the Constitution, such as freedom of speech, or held by the Court to be derived from the Constitution, such as the right of interstate travel.

In *Shapiro*, Connecticut's distinction between indigent residents and indigent nonresidents was reasonable and not suspect, but because it affected a fundamental right, it had to further a compelling state interest that the Court said it did not. Besides the right to travel, the Court has held voting and access to the courts to be fundamental rights that indigents may not be deprived of by laws or policies that discriminate economically (for example, *Harper v. Virginia Board of Elections*, 1966, striking down a poll tax.) The Shapiro decision raised but left unanswered two important questions: whether poverty or indigency alone could make economic classifications "suspect" and whether other fundamental rights might be seen as impeded by economic classifications. When the answers began to come they did little to extend the Shapiro doctrine.

In *Dandridge v. Williams*, 1970, in which there was no right to travel issue, the Court upheld a state law that put an upper limit on the number of children for which a family could get welfare support. The Court held that welfare was merely a right created by legislation not a fundamental one derived from the Constitution. As such, classifications like the one at issue were subject only to the rational basis test, which was easily met. The law was reasonably aimed at conserving state resources and did not use suspect criteria such as race or national origin.

Three years later the Court heard a class action suit that challenged the financing of public schools in Texas. Like almost every other state at the time, Texas relied heavily on local property taxes to support local schools. Because school districts with high property evaluations could generate more revenue and at lower rates than those with lower valuations, there were large disparities in spending per student and, arguably, in the quality of education between richer and poorer districts. In *San Antonio Independent School District v. Rodriguez* (p. 574), the Court, 5-4, refused to find the financing arrangement violated equal protection. Like welfare, education was not a fundamental right derived from the Constitution even though it might be important to the exercise of fundamental rights such as freedom of speech or voting. Nor did the Court find the state school financing arrangements to disadvantage an identifiable group. Hence, only the rational basis test used in review of most other social and economic legislation and policy would apply. It was reasonable for Texas to finance public schools mainly through local property taxes. "Where wealth is involved, the equal protection clause does not require absolute equality or precisely equal advantages." The poor, in effect, were not a suspect class. Laws and policies rooted in economic distinctions did not merit the same strict judicial review as those based on race, national origin, or even gender and birth status.

Had the Court reached the opposite conclusion in *Rodriguez* the result, for better or worse, would have revolutionized public school financing in the United States because most states had arrangements similar to Texas's. Yet, in the years since, extensive revisions have indeed taken place in school financing. The courts of New Jersey, Ohio, and a few other states, for example, have found funding disparities to violate the state constitution. In several other states, legislatures have restructured public school financing to rely less on property taxes and to more extensively underwrite schools in poorer districts.

Invalidating a law or policy because it discriminates among persons economically has obvious redistributive effect. Gains or benefits won by some are paid for by others, even if the others are the general tax-paying public or special groups of taxpayers. Such redistribution is not called for by the Constitution except when distinctions or classifications impede fundamental rights or are from suspect criteria such as race. But neither is it constitutionally forbidden. Carried far enough or imposed pervasively enough, redistribution would have a leveling effect that, in the past at least, would be politically unacceptable. But great, harmful disparities in wealth and means may not have been politically acceptable either when they seem to be reinforced, perpetuated, or even made worse by law or policy. Where the balance is to be drawn, the Supreme Court has said, is an issue that is less constitutional than political.

FURTHER READING

General

Baer, Judith A., _Equality under the Constitution: Reclaiming the Fourteenth Amendment_ (1983)

Mezey, Susan Gluck, _In Pursuit of Equality_ (1992)

Posner, Richard A., _Sex and Reason_ (1992)

———, _Overcoming Law_ (1995)

Richards, David A.J., _Conscience and the Constitution_ (1993)

Gender

Baer, Judith A., _Women in American Law: The Struggle toward Equality from the New Deal to the Present_ (1996)

———, _Our Lives Before the Law: Constructing a Feminist Jurisprudence_ (1999)

———, ed., _Historical and Multicultural Encyclopedia of Women's Reproductive Rights in the United States_ (2002)

Chester, Ronald, _Equal Access: Women Lawyers in a Changing American_ (1985)

Epstein, Cynthia Fuchs, _Women in Law_ (1983)

Epstein, Richard A., _Forbidden Grounds: The Case against Employment Discrimination Laws_ (1992)

Sara Evans, Personal Politics: _The Roots of Women's Liberation in the Civil Rights Movement and the New Left_ (1980)

Flexner, Eleanor, _Century of Struggle_, rev. ed. (1975)

Frug, Mary Jo, _Post-Modern Legal Feminism_ (1992)

Goldstein, Joel H., _The Effects of the Adoption of Woman Suffrage: Sex Difference in Voting Behavior_ (1984)

Goldstein, Leslie Friedman, _The Constitutional Rights of Women_, 2nd ed. (1988)

———, ed., _Feminist Jurisprudence: The Difference Debate_ (1992)

Hagan, John, and Fiona Kay, _Gender in Practice: A Study of Lawyers' Lives_ (1995)

Hartmann, Susan M., _From Margin to Mainstream: American Women and Politics Since 1960_ (1989)

Hoff, Joan, _Law, Gender, and Injustice: A Legal History of U.S. Women_ (1991)

Kirp, David L., Mark G. Yudof, and Marlene Strong Franks, _Gender Justice_ (1986)

Lentz, Bernard F., and David M. Laband, _Sex Discrimination in the Legal Profession_ (1995)

MacKinnon, Catherine, _Feminism Unmodified: Discourses on Life and Law_ (1987)

Mansbridge, Jane J., _Why We Lost the ERA_ (1986)

McGlen, Nancy E., and Karen O'Connor, _Women's Rights: The Struggle for Equality in the 19th and 20th Centuries_ (1983)

Minow, Martha, _Making All the Difference: Inclusion, Exclusion, and American Law_ (1990)

Morello, Karen Berger, _The Invisible Bar: The Woman Lawyer in America_ (1986)

Moss, Kary L., _The Rights of Women and Girls_ (1998)

Otten, Laura, _Women's Rights and the Law_ (1993)

Pierce, Jennifer L., _Gender Trials: Emotional Lives in Contemporary Law Firms_ (1995)

Rhode, Deborah L., _Justice and Gender: Sex Discrimination and the Law_ (1989)

———, _Speaking of Sex: The Denial of Gender Inequality_ (1997)

Ross, Susan Deller, and Ann Barcher, _The Rights of Women_ (1984)

Smith, Patricia, ed., _Feminist Jurisprudence_ (1993)

Sullivan, Charles A., Michael J. Zimmer, and Richard F. Richards, _Federal Statutory Law of Employment Discrimination_ (1980)

Weisberg, Kelly D., ed., _Feminist Legal Theory: Foundations_ (1993)

Zimmer, Michael J., et al., _Employment Discrimination: Selected Statutes_ (1997)

———, _Cases and Material on Employment Discrimination_ (2000)

Sexual Orientation

Gerstmann, Evan, _The Constitutional Underclass: Gays, Lesbians and the Failure of Class-Based Equal Protection_ (1999)

Rimmerman, Craig A., Kenneth D. Wald, and Clyde Wilcox, eds., _The Politics of Gay Rights_ (2000)

Strasser, Mark, _Legally Wed: Same-Sex Marriage and the Constitution_ (1998)

———, _The Challenge of Same-Sex Marriage: Federalist Principles and Constitutional Protections_ (1999)

Wealth and Poverty

Bussiere, Elizabeth, _(Dis)entitling the Poor: The Warren Court, Welfare Rights, and the American Political Tradition_ (1997)

Harrington, Michael, _The New American Poverty_ (1984)

King, Michael, and Judith Trowell, *Children's Welfare and the Law: The Limits of Legal Intervention* (1992)

Lawrence, Susan E., *The Poor in Court: The Legal Services Program and Supreme Court Decision Making* (1990)

Piven, Frances Fox, and Richard A. Cloward, *Regulating the Poor: The Function of Public Welfare* (1972)

Reed, Douglas S., *On Equal Terms: The Constitutional Politics of Educational Opportunity* (2001)

Smith, Christopher E., *The Courts and the Poor* (1991)

Soss, Joe, *Unwanted Claims: The Politics of Participation in the U.S. Welfare System* (2000)

Additional works listed in General and Supplementary Bibliography.

CASES

Reed v. Reed

404 U.S. 71 (1971), 7-0

Opinion of the Court: Burger (Blackmun, Brennan, Douglas, Marshall, Stewart, White)

What state interest or interests were served by the law in question? How did the Court characterize them? How did it characterize the right violated? Did the Court reject the state's interest because it was not legitimate or because it was overcome by the right asserted against it? Did the Court supply any general guidelines for deciding future cases where gender discrimination is alleged?

Burger, for the Court:

Richard Lynn Reed, a minor, died intestate in Ada County, Idaho, on March 29, 1967. His adoptive parents, who had separated sometime prior to his death, are the parties to this appeal. Approximately seven months after Richard's death, his mother, appellant Sally Reed, filed a petition in the Probate Court of Ada County, seeking appointment as administratrix of her son's estate. Prior to the date set for a hearing on the mother's petition, appellee Cecil Reed, the father of the decedent, filed a competing petition seeking to have himself appointed administrator of the son's estate. The probate court . . . ordered that letters of administration be issued to appellee Cecil Reed. . . . The court treated §§15-312 and 15-314 of the Idaho Code as the controlling statutes, and read those sections as compelling a preference for Cecil Reed because he was a male.

Section 15-312 designates the persons who are entitled to administer the estate of one who dies intestate. [It] lists 11 classes of persons . . . one [of which] is "[t]he father or mother" of the person dying intestate. Under this section, then, appellant and appellee, being members of the same entitlement class, would seem to have been equally entitled to administer their son's estate. Section 1314 provides, however, that "[o]f several persons claiming and equally entitled [under §1312] to administer, males must be preferred to females, and relatives of the whole to those of the half blood."

In issuing its order, the probate court implicitly recognized the equality of entitlement of the two applicants under §15-312, and noted that neither of the applicants was under any legal disability. . . .

Idaho does not, of course, deny letters of administration to women altogether. Indeed, under §15-312, a woman whose spouse dies intestate has a preference over a son, father, brother, or any other male relative of the decedent. Moreover, we can judicially notice that, in this country, presumably due to the greater longevity of women, a large proportion of estates, both intestate and under wills of decedents, are administered by surviving widows.

Section 15-314 is restricted in its operation to those situations where competing applications for letters of administration have been filed by both male and female members of the same entitlement class established by §15-312. In such situations, §15-314 provides that different treatment be accorded to the applicants on the basis of their sex; it thus establishes a classification subject to scrutiny under the Equal Protection Clause.

In applying that clause, this Court has consistently recognized that the Fourteenth Amendment does not deny to States the power to treat different classes of persons in different ways. The Equal Protection Clause of that amendment does, however, deny to States the power to legislate that different treatment be accorded to persons placed by a statute into different classes on the basis of criteria wholly unrelated to the objective of that statute. A classification "must be reasonable, not arbitrary, and must rest upon some ground of difference having a fair and substantial relation to the object of the legislation, so that all persons similarly circumstances shall be treated alike." *Royster Guano Co. v. Virginia.* The question presented by this case, then, is whether a difference in the sex of competing applicants for letters of administration bears a rational relationship to a state objective that is sought to be advanced by the operation of §§15-312 and 15-314.

In upholding the latter section, the Idaho Supreme Court concluded that its objective was to eliminate one area of controversy when two or more persons, equally entitled under §15-312, seek letters of administration, and thereby present the probate court "with the issue of which one should be named." The court also concluded that, where such persons are not of the same sex, the elimination of females from consideration "is neither an illogical nor arbitrary method devised by the legislature to resolve an issue that would otherwise require a hearing as to the relative merits . . . of the two or more petitioning relatives. . . ."

Clearly the objective of reducing the workload on probate courts by eliminating one class of contests is not without some legitimacy. The crucial question, however, is whether §15-314 advances that objective in a manner consistent with the command of the Equal Protection Clause. We hold that it does not. To give a mandatory preference to members of either sex over members of the other, merely to accomplish the elimination of hearings on the merits, is to make the very kind of arbitrary legislative choice forbidden by the Equal Protection Clause of the Fourteenth Amendment; and whatever may be said as to the positive values of avoiding intrafamily controversy, the choice in this context may not lawfully be mandated solely on the basis of sex.

We note finally that, if §15-314 is viewed merely as a modifying appendage to §15-312 and as aimed at the same objective, its constitutionality is not thereby saved. The objective of §15-312 clearly is to establish degrees of entitlement of various classes of persons in accordance with their varying degrees and kinds of relationship to the intestate. Regardless of their sex, persons within any one of the enumerated classes of that section are similarly situated with respect to that objective. By providing dissimilar treatment for men and women who are thus similarly situated, the challenged section violates the Equal Protection Clause.

Frontiero v. Richardson

411 U.S. 677 (1973), 8-1
Opinion of the Court: Brennan (Douglas, Marshall, Stewart, White)
Concurring: Powell, Burger, Blackmun
Dissenting: Rehnquist

What interest did the federal regulation serve? Was it a reasonable one? Was it in or out of touch with existing economic and family realities? Why did it fail here? Would even the slightest gender distinction ever be justified by administrative convenience, however great that convenience might be? How do Brennan and Powell differ on the standard of review to be used? How do they differ on the significance of the Equal Rights Amendment? Why is the federal government bound by equal protection principles if the Fourteenth Amendment limits only the states?

Brennan, for the Court:

The question before us concerns the right of a female member of the uniformed services to claim her spouse as a "dependent" for the purposes of obtaining increased quarters allowances and medical and dental benefits under 37 U.S.C. §§401, 403, and 10 U.S.C. §§1072, 1076, on an equal footing with male members. Under these statutes, a serviceman may claim his wife as a "dependent" without regard to whether she is in fact, dependent upon him for any part of her support. A servicewoman, on the other hand, may not claim her husband as a "dependent" under these programs unless he is in fact, dependent upon her for over one-half of his support. Thus, the question for decision is whether this difference in treatment constitutes an unconstitutional discrimination against servicewomen in violation of the Due Process Clause of the Fifth Amendment. . . .

Appellant Sharron Frontiero, a lieutenant in the United States Air Force, sought increased quarters allowances, and housing and medical benefits for her husband, appellant Joseph Frontiero, on the ground that he was her "dependent." Although such benefits would automatically have been granted with respect to the wife of a male member of the uniformed services, appellant's application was denied because she failed to demonstrate that her husband was dependent on her for more than one-half of his support. . . .

At the outset, appellants contend that classifications based upon sex, like classifications based upon race, alienage, and national origin, are inherently suspect, and must therefore be subjected to close judicial scrutiny. We agree, and, indeed, find at least implicit support for such an approach in our unanimous decision only last Term in *Reed v. Reed*. . . .

The Court noted that the Idaho statute "provides that different treatment be accorded to the applicants on the basis of their sex; it thus establishes a classification subject to scrutiny under the Equal Protection Clause." Under "traditional" equal protection analysis, a legislative classification must be sustained unless it is "patently arbitrary" and bears no rational relationship to a legitimate governmental interest.

In an effort to meet this standard, appellee contended that the statutory scheme was a reasonable measure designed to reduce the workload on probate courts by eliminating one class of contests. Moreover, appellee argued that the mandatory preference for male applicants was, in itself, reasonable, since "men [are], as a rule, more conversant with business affairs than . . . women." Indeed, appellee maintained that "it is a matter of common knowledge that women still are not engaged in politics, the professions, business or industry to the extent that men are." And the Idaho Supreme Court, in upholding the constitutionality of this statute, suggested that the Idaho Legislature might reasonably have "concluded that, in general, men are better qualified to act as an administrator than are women."

Despite these contentions, however, the Court held the statutory preference for male applicants unconstitutional. In reaching this result, the Court implicitly rejected appellee's apparently rational explanation of the statutory scheme, and concluded that, by ignoring the individual qualifications of particular applicants, the challenged statute provided "dissimilar treatment for men and women who are . . . similarly situated." The Court therefore held that, even though the State's interest in achieving administrative efficiency "is not without some legitimacy . . . [t]o give a mandatory preference to members of either sex over members of the other merely to accomplish the elimination of hearings on the merits is to make the very kind of arbitrary legislative choice forbidden by the [Constitution]. . . ." This departure from "traditional" rational basis analysis with respect to sex-based classifications is clearly justified.

There can be no doubt that our Nation has had a long and unfortunate history of sex discrimination. Traditionally, such discrimination was rationalized by an attitude of "romantic paternalism" which, in practical effect, put women not on a pedestal, but in a cage. . . .

. . . [O]ur statute books gradually became laden with gross, stereotyped distinctions between the sexes, and, indeed, throughout much of the 19th century, the position of women in our society was, in many respects, comparable to that of blacks under the pre-Civil War slave codes. Neither slaves nor women could hold office, serve on juries, or bring suit in their own names, and married women traditionally were denied the legal capacity to hold or convey property or to serve as legal guardians of their own children. And although blacks were guaranteed the right to vote in 1870, women were denied even that right—which is itself "preservative of other basic civil and political rights"—until adoption of the Nineteenth Amendment half a century later.

It is true, of course, that the position of women in America has improved markedly in recent decades. Nevertheless, it can hardly be doubted that, in part because of the high visibility of the sex characteristic, women still face pervasive, although at times more subtle, discrimination in our educational institutions, in the job market and, perhaps most conspicuously, in the political arena.

Moreover, since sex, like race and national origin, is an immutable characteristic determined solely by the accident of birth, the imposition of special disabilities upon the members of a particular sex because of their sex would seem to violate "the basic concept of our system that legal burdens should bear some relationship to individual responsibility. . . ." And what differentiates sex from such nonsuspect statuses as intelligence or physical disability, and aligns it with the recognized suspect criteria, is that the sex characteristic frequently bears no relation to ability to perform or contribute to society. As a result, statutory distinctions between the sexes often have the effect of invidiously relegating the entire class of females to inferior legal status without regard to the actual capabilities of its individual members.

We might also note that, over the past decade, Congress has itself manifested an increasing sensitivity to sex-based classifications. In Tit. VII of the Civil Rights Act of 1964, for example, Congress expressly declared that no employer, labor union, or other organization subject to the provisions of the Act shall discriminate against any individual on the basis of "race, color, religion, sex, or national origin." Similarly, the Equal Pay Act of 1963 provides that no employer covered by the

Act "shall discriminate . . . between employees on the basis of sex." And §1 of the Equal Rights Amendment, passed by Congress on March 22, 1972, and submitted to the legislatures of the States for ratification, declares that "[e]quality of rights under the law shall not be denied or abridged by the United States or by any State on account of sex." Thus, Congress itself has concluded that classifications based upon sex are inherently invidious, and this conclusion of a coequal branch of Government is not without significance to the question presently under consideration.

With these considerations in mind, we can only conclude that classifications based upon sex, like classifications based upon race, alienage, or national origin, are inherently suspect, and must therefore be subjected to strict judicial scrutiny. Applying the analysis mandated by that stricter standard of review, it is clear that the statutory scheme now before us is constitutionally invalid.

The sole basis of the classification established in the challenged statutes is the sex of the individuals involved. . . .

Moreover, the Government concedes that the differential treatment accorded men and women under these statutes serves no purpose other than mere "administrative convenience." In essence, the Government maintains that, as an empirical matter, wives in our society frequently are dependent upon their husbands, while husbands rarely are dependent upon their wives. Thus, the Government argues that Congress might reasonably have concluded that it would be both cheaper and easier simply conclusively to presume that wives of male members are financially dependent upon their husbands, while burdening female members with the task of establishing dependency in fact.

The Government offers no concrete evidence, however, tending to support its view that such differential treatment in fact saves the Government any money. In order to satisfy the demands of strict judicial scrutiny, the Government must demonstrate, for example, that it is actually cheaper to grant increased benefits with respect to all male members than it is to determine which male members are, in fact, entitled to such benefits, and to grant increased benefits only to those members whose wives actually meet the dependency requirement. Here, however, there is substantial evidence that, if put to the test, many of the wives of male members would fail to qualify for benefits. And in light of the fact that the dependency de-

termination with respect to the husbands of female members is presently made solely on the basis of affidavits, rather than through the more costly hearing process, the Government's explanation of the statutory scheme is, to say the least, questionable.

In any case, our prior decisions make clear that, although efficacious administration of governmental programs is not without some importance, "the Constitution recognizes higher values than speed and efficiency." And when we enter the realm of "strict judicial scrutiny," there can be no doubt that "administrative convenience" is not a shibboleth, the mere recitation of which dictates constitutionality. On the contrary, any statutory scheme which draws a sharp line between the sexes, solely for the purpose of achieving administrative convenience, necessarily commands "dissimilar treatment for men and women who are . . . similarly situated," and therefore involves the "very kind of arbitrary legislative choice forbidden by the [Constitution]. . . ." *Reed v. Reed* We therefore conclude that, by according differential treatment to male and female members of the uniformed services for the sole purpose of achieving administrative convenience, the challenged statutes violate the Due Process Clause of the Fifth Amendment insofar as they require a female member to prove the dependency of her husband.

Powell, concurring:

I agree that the challenged statutes constitute an unconstitutional discrimination against servicewomen in violation of the Due Process Clause of the Fifth Amendment, but I cannot join the opinion of Mr. Justice Brennan, which would hold that all classifications based upon sex, "like classifications based upon race, alienage, and national origin," are "inherently suspect, and must therefore be subjected to close judicial scrutiny." It is unnecessary for the Court in this case to characterize sex as a suspect classification, with all of the far-reaching implications of such a holding. which abundantly supports our decision today, did not add sex to the narrowly limited group of classifications which are inherently suspect. In my view, we can and should decide this case on the authority of *Reed*, and reserve for the future any expansion of its rationale.

There is another, and I find compelling, reason for deferring a general categorizing of sex classifications as invoking the strictest test of judicial scrutiny. The Equal Rights Amendment, which if adopted will resolve the substance of this precise question, has been approved by the Congress and submitted for ratification by the States. If this Amendment is duly adopted, it will represent the will of the people accomplished in the manner prescribed by the Constitution. By acting prematurely and unnecessarily, as I view it, the Court has assumed a decisional responsibility at the very time when state legislatures, functioning within the traditional democratic process, are debating the proposed Amendment. It seems to me that this reaching out to preempt by judicial action a major political decision which is currently in process of resolution does not reflect appropriate respect for duly prescribed legislative processes.

There are times when this Court, under our system, cannot avoid a constitutional decision on issues which normally should be resolved by the elected representatives of the people. But democratic institutions are weakened, and confidence in the restraint of the Court is impaired, when we appear unnecessarily to decide sensitive issues of broad social and political importance at the very time they are under consideration within the prescribed constitutional processes.

Craig v. Boren

429 U.S. 190 (1976), 7-2
Opinion of the Court: Brennan (Blackmun, Marshall, Powell, Stevens, White)
Concurring: Stewart
Dissenting: Burger, Rehnquist

What was the state's interest in this case? Was it stronger or weaker than government interests asserted in Reed v. Reed *(p. 549) and* Frontiero v. Richardson *(p. 550)? What is the Court's standard of review? How does it differ from that used in previous gender discrimination cases? Did Oklahoma's law penalize the vast majority of males in the age group for the transgressions of a few? Is there any way to avoid this possibility that would be practical and not financially exorbitant? Are Brennan's comments about relying on statistical conclusions of social science studies consistent with his dissent in* McCleskey v. Kemp *(p. 424)? With* Brown v. Board of Education *(p. 473)? Should a different level of review be used for laws that discriminate against men than against women? Would that itself be a form of gender discrimination? Might the equal protection defect in the Oklahoma law be resolved by removing a benefit rather than conferring a right, that is, by the state barring all persons under 21 from drinking 3.2% beer?*

Brennan, for the Court:

The interaction of two sections of an Oklahoma statute, Okla.Stat., Tit. 37, §241 and 245 prohibits the sale of "nonintoxicating" 3.2% beer to males under the age of 21 and to females under the age of 18. The question to be decided is whether such a gender-based differential constitutes a denial to males 18–20 years of age of the equal protection of the laws in violation of the Fourteenth Amendment.

This action was brought . . . by appellant Craig, a male then between 18 and 21 years of age, and by appellant Whitener, a licensed vendor of 3.2% beer. The complaint sought declaratory and injunctive relief against enforcement of the gender-based differential on the ground that it constituted invidious discrimination against males 18–20 years of age. . . .

We first address a preliminary question of standing. Appellant Craig attained the age of 21 after we noted probable jurisdiction. Therefore, since only declaratory and injunctive relief against enforcement of the gender-based differential is sought, the controversy has been rendered moot as to Craig. The question thus arises whether appellant Whitener, the licensed vendor of 3.2% beer, who has a live controversy against enforcement of the statute, may rely upon the equal protection objections of males 18–20 years of age to establish her claim of unconstitutionality of the age-sex differential. We conclude that she may. . . .

. . . The operation of §§241 and 245 plainly has inflicted "injury in fact" upon appellant sufficient to guarantee her "concrete adverseness," and to satisfy the constitutionally based standing requirements imposed by Art. III. The legal duties created by the statutory sections under challenge are addressed directly to vendors such as appellant. She is obliged either to heed the statutory discrimination, thereby incurring a direct economic injury through the constriction of her buyers' market, or to disobey the statutory command and suffer, in the words of Oklahoma's Assistant Attorney General, "sanctions and perhaps loss of license." This Court repeatedly has recognized that such injuries establish the threshold requirements of a "case or controversy" mandated by Art. III. . . .

. . . [V]endors and those in like positions have been uniformly permitted to resist efforts at restricting their operations by acting as advocates of the rights of third parties who seek access to their market or function. . . .

Analysis may appropriately begin with the reminder that *Reed* emphasized that statutory classifications that distinguish between males and females are "subject to scrutiny under the Equal Protection Clause." To withstand constitutional challenge, previous cases establish that classifications by gender must serve important governmental objectives and must be substantially related to achievement of those objectives. . . .

We accept for purposes of discussion the District Court's identification of the objective underlying §§241 and 245 as the enhancement of traffic safety. Clearly, the protection of public health and safety represents an important function of state and local governments. However, appellees' statistics, in our view, cannot support the conclusion that the gender-based distinction closely serves to achieve that objective, and therefore the distinction cannot, under *Reed*, withstand equal protection challenge. . . .

Even were this statistical evidence accepted as accurate, it nevertheless offers only a weak answer to the equal protection question presented here. The most focused and relevant of the statistical surveys, arrests of 18–20-year-olds for alcohol-related driving offenses, exemplifies the ultimate unpersuasiveness of this evidentiary record. Viewed in terms of the correlation between sex and the actual activity that Oklahoma seeks to regulate—driving while under the influence of alcohol—the statistics broadly establish that .18% of females and 2% of males in that age group were arrested for that offense. While such a disparity is not trivial in a statistical sense, it hardly can form the basis for employment of a gender line as a classifying device. Certainly if maleness is to serves a proxy for drinking and driving, a correlation of 2% must be considered an unduly tenuous "fit." Indeed, prior cases have consistently rejected the use of sex as a decisionmaking factor even though the statutes in question certainly rested on far more predictive empirical relationships than this.

Moreover, the statistics exhibit a variety of other shortcomings that seriously impugn their value to equal protection analysis. Setting aside the obvious methodological problems, the surveys do not adequately justify the salient features of Oklahoma's gender-based traffic safety law. None purports to measure the use and dangerousness of 3.2% beer, as opposed to alcohol generally, a detail that is of particular importance since, in light of its low alcohol level, Oklahoma apparently considers the 3.2% beverage to be "nonintoxicating." Moreover, many of the studies, while graphically documenting the unfortunate increase in driving while under the influence of alco-

hol, make no effort to relate their findings to age-sex differentials as involved here. . . .

There is no reason to belabor this line of analysis. It is unrealistic to expect either members of the judiciary or state officials to be well versed in the rigors of experimental or statistical technique. But this merely illustrates that proving broad sociological propositions by statistics is a dubious business, and one that inevitably is in tension with the normative philosophy that underlies the Equal Protection Clause. Suffice to say that the showing offered by the appellees does not satisfy us that sex represents a legitimate, accurate proxy for the regulation of drinking and driving. In fact, when it is further recognized that Oklahoma's statute prohibits only the selling of 3.2% beer to young males, and not their drinking the beverage once acquired (even after purchase by their 18–20-year-old female companions), the relationship between gender and traffic safety becomes far too tenuous to satisfy [*Reed v.*] *Reed's* requirement that the gender-based difference be substantially related to achievement of the statutory objective.

We hold, therefore, that under *Reed*, Oklahoma's 3.2% beer statute invidiously discriminates against males 18–20 years of age.

Appellees argue, however, that §§241 and 245 enforce state policies concerning the sale and distribution of alcohol and by force of the Twenty-first Amendment should therefore be held to withstand the equal protection challenge. . . . Our view is, and we hold, that the Twenty-first Amendment does not save the invidious gender-based discrimination from invalidation as a denial of equal protection of the laws in violation of the Fourteenth Amendment. . . .

. . . [B]oth federal and state courts uniformly have declared the unconstitutionality of gender lines that restrain the activities of customers of state-regulated liquor establishments irrespective of the operation of the Twenty-first Amendment. Even when state officials have posited sociological or empirical justifications for these gender-based differentiations, the courts have struck down discriminations aimed at an entire class under the guise of alcohol regulation. In fact, social science studies that have uncovered quantifiable differences in drinking tendencies dividing along both racial and ethnic lines strongly suggest the need for application of the Equal Protection Clause in preventing discriminatory treatment that almost certainly would be perceived as invidious. In sum, the principles embodied in the Equal Protection. Clause are not to be rendered inapplicable by statistically measured but loose-fitting generalities concerning the drinking tendencies of aggregate groups. We thus hold that the operation of the Twenty-first Amendment does not alter the application of equal protection standards that otherwise govern this case.

We conclude that the gender-based differential contained in Okla.Stat., Tit. 37, §45 constitutes a denial of the equal protection of the laws to males aged 18–20. . . .

Rehnquist, dissenting:

The Court's disposition of this case is objectionable on two grounds. First is its conclusion that men challenging a gender-based statute which treats them less favorably than women may invoke a more stringent standard of judicial review than pertains to most other types of classifications. Second is the Court's enunciation of this standard, without citation to any source, as being that "classifications by gender must serve important governmental objectives, and must be substantially related to achievement of those objectives." The only redeeming feature of the Court's opinion, to my mind, is that it apparently signals a retreat by those who joined the plurality opinion in *Frontiero v. Richardson*, from their view that sex is a "suspect" classification for purposes of equal protection analysis. I think the Oklahoma statute challenged here need pass only the "rational basis" equal protection analysis . . . and I believe that it is constitutional under that analysis.

In *Frontiero v. Richardson*, the opinion for the plurality sets forth the reasons of four Justices for concluding that sex should be regarded as a suspect classification for purposes of equal protection analysis. These reasons center on our Nation's "long and unfortunate history of sex discrimination," which has been reflected in a whole range of restrictions on the legal rights of women, not the least of which have concerned the ownership of property and participation in the electoral process. Noting that the pervasive and persistent nature of the discrimination experienced by women is in part the result of their ready identifiability, the plurality rested its invocation of strict scrutiny largely upon the fact that "statutory distinctions between the sexes often have the effect of invidiously relegating the entire class of females to inferior legal status without regard to the actual capabilities of its individual members."

Subsequent to *Frontiero*, the Court has declined to hold that sex is a suspect class, and no such holding is imported by the Court's resolution of this case. However, the Court's application here of an elevated or "intermediate" level scrutiny, like that invoked in cases dealing with discrimination against females, raises the question of why the statute here should be treated any differently from counties legislative classifications unrelated to sex which have been upheld under a minimum rationality standard.

Most obviously unavailable to support any kind of special scrutiny in this case is a history or pattern of past discrimination, such as was relied on by the plurality in *Frontiero* to support its invocation of strict scrutiny. There is no suggestion in the Court's opinion that males in this age group are in any way peculiarly disadvantaged, subject to systematic discriminatory treatment, or otherwise in need of special solicitude from the courts.

The Court does not discuss the nature of the right involved, and there is no reason to believe that it sees the purchase of 3.2% beer as implicating any important interest, let alone one that is "fundamental" in the constitutional sense of invoking strict scrutiny. Indeed, the Court's accurate observation that the statute affects the selling, but not the drinking, of 3.2% beer, further emphasizes the limited effect that it has on even those persons in the age group involved. There is, in sum, nothing about the statutory classification involved here to suggest that it affects an interest, or works against a group, which can claim under the Equal Protection Clause that it is entitled to special judicial protection.

It is true that a number of our opinions contain broadly phrased dicta implying that the same test should be applied to all classifications based on sex, whether affecting females or males. However, before today, no decision of this Court has applied an elevated level of scrutiny to invalidate a statutory discrimination harmful to males, except where the statute impaired an important personal interest protected by the Constitution. There being no such interest here, and there being no plausible argument that this is a discrimination against females, the Court's reliance on our previous sex discrimination cases is ill-founded. It treats gender classification as a talisman which—without regard to the rights involved or the persons affected—calls into effect a heavier burden of judicial review.

The Court's conclusion that a law which treats males less favorably than females "must serve important governmental objectives and must be substantially related to achievement of those objectives" apparently comes out of thin air. The Equal Protection Clause contains no such language, and none of our previous cases adopt that standard. I would think we have had enough difficulty with the two standards of review which our cases have recognized—the norm of "rational basis," and the "compelling state interest" required where a "suspect classification" is involved—so as to counsel weightily against the insertion of still another "standard" between those two. How is this Court to divine what objectives are important? How is it to determine whether a particular law is "substantially" related to the achievement of such objective, rather than related in some other way to its achievement? Both of the phrases used are so diaphanous and elastic as to invite subjective judicial preferences or prejudices relating to particular types of legislation, masquerading as judgments whether such legislation is directed at "important" objectives or, whether the relationship to those objectives is "substantial" enough.

I would have thought that, if this Court were to leave anything to decision by the popularly elected branches of the Government, where no constitutional claim other than that of equal protection is invoked, it would be the decision as to what governmental objectives to be achieved by law are "important," and which are not. As for the second part of the Court's new test, the Judicial Branch is probably in no worse position than the Legislative or Executive Branches to determine if there is any rational relationship between a classification and the purpose which it might be thought to serve. But the introduction of the adverb "substantially" requires courts to make subjective judgments as to operational effects, for which neither their expertise nor their access to data fits them. And even if we manage to avoid both confusion and the mirroring of our own preferences in the development of this new doctrine, the thousands of judges in other courts who must interpret the Equal Protection Clause may not be so fortunate. . . .

Rostker v. Goldberg

453 U.S. 57 (1981), 6-3
Opinion of the Court: Rehnquist (Blackmun, Burger, Powell, Stevens, Stewart)
Dissenting: Brennan, Marshall, White

This case was brought by several men required to register under the Military Selective Service Act. Though actual conscription had been discontinued in 1975 by presidential order, President Carter reactivated the registration process in 1980.

How does the Court phrase the government's interest? Does that interest have a close or rational connection with the gender discrimination of the requirement? What is Marshall's approach to this question? Has the Court retreated from its analysis in Craig v. Boren *(p. 553)? Would it have been possible for a woman to challenge this law? Would it be possible after* United States v. Virginia *(p. 559)?*

Rehnquist, for the Court:
The question presented is whether the Military Selective Service Act, [MSSA] violates the Fifth Amendment to the United States Constitution in authorizing the President to require the registration of males, and not females.

Congress is given the power under the Constitution "To raise and support Armies," "To provide and maintain a Navy," and "To make Rules for the Government and Regulation of the land and naval Forces." Pursuant to this grant of authority, Congress has enacted the Military Selective Service Act. Section 3 of the Act empowers the President, by proclamation, to require the registration of "every male citizen" and male resident aliens between the ages of 18 and 26. The purpose of this registration is to facilitate any eventual conscription. . . . The MSSA registration provision serves no other purpose beyond providing a pool for subsequent induction.

Registration for the draft . . . was discontinued in 1975. . . . In early 1980, President Carter determined that it was necessary to reactivate the draft registration process. The immediate impetus for this decision was the Soviet armed invasion of Afghanistan. . . . He also recommended that Congress take action to amend the MSSA to permit the registration and conscription of women as well as men. . . .

Congress agreed that it was necessary to reactivate the registration process and allocated funds for that purpose. . . .

. . . [T]hree days before registration was to commence, the District Court issued an opinion finding that the Act violated the Due Process Clause of the Fifth Amendment and permanently enjoined the Government from requiring registration under the Act. . . .

Whenever called upon to judge the constitutionality of an Act of Congress—"the gravest and most delicate duty that this Court is called upon to perform," the Court accords "great weight to the decisions of

Congress." The Congress is a coequal branch of government whose Members take the same oath we do to uphold the Constitution of the United States. As Justice Frankfurter noted in *Joint Anti-Fascist Refugee Committee v. McGrath,* we must have "due regard to the fact that this Court is not exercising a primary judgment, but is sitting in judgment upon those who also have taken the oath to observe the Constitution and who have the responsibility for carrying on government." The customary deference accorded the judgments of Congress is certainly appropriate when, as here, Congress specifically considered the question of the Act's constitutionality.

This is not, however, merely a case involving the customary deference accorded congressional decisions. The case arises in the context of Congress' authority over national defense and military affairs, and perhaps in no other area has the Court accorded Congress greater deference. In rejecting the registration of women, Congress explicitly relied upon its constitutional powers under Art. I, §8. The "specific findings" section of the Report of the Senate Armed Services Committee, later adopted by both Houses of Congress, began by stating:

> Article I, section 8 of the Constitution commits exclusively to the Congress the powers to raise and support armies, provide and maintain a Navy, and make rules for Government and regulation of the land and naval forces, and pursuant to these powers it lies within the discretion of the Congress to determine the occasions for expansion of our Armed Forces, and the means best suited to such expansion, should it prove necessary.

This Court has consistently recognized Congress' "broad constitutional power" to raise and regulate armies and navies. . . .

Not only is the scope of Congress' constitutional power in this area broad, but the lack of competence on the part of the courts is marked. . . .

This case is quite different from several of the gender-based discrimination cases we have considered in that, despite appellees' assertions, Congress did not act "unthinkingly" or "reflexively and not for any considered reason." The question of registering women for the draft not only received considerable national attention and was the subject of wide-ranging public debate, but also was extensively considered by

Congress in hearings, floor debate, and in committee. Hearings held by both Houses of Congress in response to the President's request for authorization to register women adduced extensive testimony and evidence concerning the issue. These hearings built on other hearings held the previous year addressed to the same question. . . .

While proposals to register women were being rejected in the course of transferring funds to register males, Committees in both Houses which had conducted hearings on the issue were also rejecting the registration of women. . . .

The foregoing clearly establishes that the decision to exempt women from registration was not the "'accidental byproduct of a traditional way of thinking about females.'" . . . Congress determined that any future draft, which would be facilitated by the registration scheme, would be characterized by a need for combat troops. The Senate Report explained, in a specific finding later adopted by both Houses, that, "[i]f mobilization were to be ordered in a wartime scenario, the primary manpower need would be for combat replacements.'" . . . The purpose of registration, therefore, was to prepare for a draft of combat troops.

Women as a group, however, unlike men as a group, are not eligible for combat. The restrictions on the participation of women in combat in the Navy and Air Force are statutory. . . . The Army and Marine Corps preclude the use of women in combat as a matter of established policy. Congress specifically recognized and endorsed the exclusion of women from combat in exempting women from registration. In the words of the Senate Report:

> The principle that women should not intentionally and routinely engage in combat is fundamental, and enjoys wide support among our people. It is universally supported by military leaders who have testified before the Committee . . . .Current law and policy exclude women from being assigned to combat in our military forces, and the Committee reaffirms this policy.

. . . The existence of the combat restrictions clearly indicates the basis for Congress' decision to exempt women from registration. The purpose of registration was to prepare for a draft of combat troops. Since women are excluded from combat, Congress concluded that they would not be needed in the event of a draft, and therefore decided not to register them.

... The reason women are exempt from registration is not because military needs can be met by drafting men. This is not a case of Congress arbitrarily choosing to burden one of two similarly situated groups, such as would be the case with an all-black or all-white, or an all-Catholic or all-Lutheran, or an all-Republican or all-Democratic registration. Men and women, because of the combat restrictions on women, are simply not similarly situated for purposes of a draft or registration for a draft.

Congress' decision to authorize the registration of only men, therefore, does not violate the Due Process Clause. The exemption of women from registration is not only sufficiently, but also closely, related to Congress' purpose in authorizing registration. The fact that Congress and the Executive have decided that women should not serve in combat fully justifies Congress in not authorizing their registration, since the purpose of registration is to develop a pool of potential combat troops. . . . The Constitution requires that Congress treat similarly situated persons similarly, not that it engage in gestures of superficial equality. . . .

... In sum, Congress carefully evaluated the testimony that 80,000 women conscripts could be usefully employed in the event of a draft, and rejected it in the permissible exercise of its constitutional responsibility. . . .

Marshall, dissenting:

The Court today places its imprimatur on one of the most potent remaining public expressions of "ancient canards about the proper role of women." It upholds a statute that requires males, but not females, to register for the draft, and which thereby categorically excludes women from a fundamental civic obligation. Because I believe the Court's decision is inconsistent with the Constitution's guarantee of equal protection of the laws, I dissent. . . .

By now it should be clear that statutes like the MSSA, which discriminate on the basis of gender, must be examined under the "heightened" scrutiny mandated by *Craig v. Boren*. Under this test, a gender-based classification cannot withstand constitutional challenge unless the classification is substantially related to the achievement of an important governmental objective. This test applies whether the classification discriminates against males or females. The party defending the challenged classification carries the burden of demonstrating both the importance of the governmental objective it serves and the substantial relationship

between the discriminatory means and the asserted end. Consequently, before we can sustain the MSSA, the Government must demonstrate that the gender-based classification it employs bears "a close and substantial relationship to [the achievement of] important governmental objectives." . . .

... I agree with the majority, that "[n]o one could deny that . . . the Government's interest in raising and supporting armies is an 'important governmental interest.'" Consequently, the first part of the *Craig v. Boren* test is satisfied. But the question remains whether the discriminatory means employed itself substantially serves the statutory end. . . .

... When, as here, a federal law that classifies on the basis of gender is challenged as violating this constitutional guarantee, it is ultimately for this Court, not Congress, to decide whether there exists the constitutionally required "close and substantial relationship" between the discriminatory means employed and the asserted governmental objective. In my judgment, there simply is no basis for concluding in this case that excluding women from registration is substantially related to the achievement of a concededly important governmental interest in maintaining an effective defense. . . .

In the first place, although the Court purports to apply the *Craig v. Boren* test, the "similarly situated" analysis the Court employs is in fact significantly different from the *Craig v. Boren* approach. The Court essentially reasons that the gender classification employed by the MSSA is constitutionally permissible because nondiscrimination is not necessary to achieve the purpose of registration to prepare for a draft of combat troops. In other words, the majority concludes that women may be excluded from registration because they will not be needed in the event of a draft.

This analysis, however, focuses on the wrong question. The relevant inquiry under the *Craig v. Boren* test is not whether a gender-neutral classification would substantially advance important governmental interests. Rather, the question is whether the gender-based classification is itself substantially related to the achievement of the asserted governmental interest. Thus, the Government's task in this case is to demonstrate that excluding women from registration substantially furthers the goal of preparing for a draft of combat troops. Or to put it another way, the Government must show that registering women would substantially impede its efforts to prepare for such a draft. Under our precedents, the Government cannot meet this burden without showing that a gender-neutral statute would be a less effective means of attaining this end. . . .

In this case, the Government makes no claim that preparing for a draft of combat troops cannot be accomplished just as effectively by registering both men and women but drafting only men if only men turn out to be needed. Nor can the Government argue that this alternative entails the additional cost and administrative inconvenience of registering women. This Court has repeatedly stated that the administrative convenience of employing a gender classification is not an adequate constitutional justification under the *Craig v. Boren* test.

The fact that registering women in no way obstructs the governmental interest in preparing for a draft of combat troops points up a second flaw in the Court's analysis. The Court essentially reduces the question of the constitutionality of male-only registration to the validity of a hypothetical program for conscripting only men. The Court posits a draft in which all conscripts are either assigned to those specific combat posts presently closed to women or must be available for rotation into such positions. By so doing, the Court is able to conclude that registering women would be no more than a "gestur[e] of superficial equality," since women are necessarily ineligible for every position to be filled in its hypothetical draft. If it could indeed be guaranteed in advance that conscription would be reimposed by Congress only in circumstances where, and in a form under which, all conscripts would have to be trained for and assigned to combat or combat rotation positions from which women are categorically excluded, then it could be argued that registration of women would be pointless.

But, of course, no such guarantee is possible. Certainly, nothing about the MSSA limits Congress to reinstituting the draft only in such circumstances. . . .

. . . [T]he discussion and findings in the Senate Report do not enable the Government to carry its burden of demonstrating that completely excluding women from the draft by excluding them from registration substantially furthers important governmental objectives. . . .

. . . Congressional enactments in the area of military affairs must, like all other laws, be judged by the standards of the Constitution. For the Constitution is the supreme law of the land, and all legislation must conform to the principles it lays down. . . .

Furthermore, "[w]hen it appears that an Act of Congress conflicts with [a constitutional] provisio[n], we have no choice but to enforce the paramount commands of the Constitution. We are sworn to do no less. We cannot push back the limits of the Constitution merely to accommodate challenged legislation." *Trop v. Dulles.* In some 106 instances since this Court was established, it has determined that congressional action exceeded the bounds of the Constitution. I believe the same is true of this statute. In an attempt to avoid its constitutional obligation, the Court today "pushes back the limits of the Constitution" to accommodate an Act of Congress. . . .

United States v. Virginia

518 U.S. 515 (1996), 7-1
Opinion of the Court: Ginsburg (Breyer, Kennedy, O'Connor, Souter, Stevens)
Concurring: Rehnquist
Dissenting: Scalia   Not participating: Thomas

This case was brought against Virginia Military Institute (VMI) by the Justice Department, which alleged that the school's policy of admitting only men violated the equal protection clause of the Fourteenth Amendment. After a federal district court ruled in VMI's favor, the Fourth Circuit Court of Appeals reversed and ordered Virginia to remedy the constitutional violation. The state then set up a parallel program for women, the Virginia Women's Institute for Leadership (VWIL), at Mary Baldwin College, a private liberal arts school for women. Both the district and appeals courts found the arrangement satisfied the Constitution's equal protection requirement. Though acknowledging the VWIL degree lacked the historical prestige of a VMI degree, the court of appeals found the educational benefits at the two schools comparable.

How did the Supreme Court phrase what the state would need to prove to justify this or any other gender distinction? Does Justice Ginsburg employ the intermediate scrutiny or has she introduced a new one? Was the setting up of a leadership school for women a return to the "separate but equal" understanding of equal protection? How can a new institution ever be "equal" to a highly successful established one? Suppose Virginia had made certain physical characteristics or skills, such as minimum height or weight-lifting strength, a requirement for admission to VMI. Would they be constitutional if they disqualified all women? Most women? Scalia, dissenting, argues that the Court should

Erin Claunch was one of the first group of women to enroll at Virginia Military Academy after the Supreme Court ruled the school's male-only admissions policy unconstitutional. Though some women dropped out, Claunch, shown here in March 2000, rose to the rank of battalion commander, the second-highest student military post at the school. Behind her is a statute of Gen. Stonewall Jackson on the school's campus at Lexington, Va.

"preserve *our society's values regarding (among other things) equal protection, not to* revise *them." What might those values be and are they self-evident? Embracing such a role for the Court, how would Scalia have decided* Brown v. Board of Education *(p. 473)? Is this case consistent with* Rostker v. Goldberg *(p. 556)?*

Ginsburg, for the Court:

... [T]his case present[s] two ultimate issues. First, does Virginia's exclusion of women from the educational opportunities provided by VMI—extraordinary opportunities for military training and civilian leadership development—deny to women "capable of all of the individual activities required of VMI cadets," the equal protection of the laws guaranteed by the Fourteenth Amendment? Second, if VMI's "unique" situation, as Virginia's sole single sex public institution of higher education—offends the Constitution's equal protection principle, what is the remedial requirement? ...

To summarize the Court's current directions for cases of official, classification based on gender: Focusing on the differential treatment or denial of opportu-

nity for which relief is sought, the reviewing court must determine whether the proffered justification is demanding and it rests entirely on the State. The State must show "at least that the [challenged] classification serves 'important governmental objectives and that the discriminatory means employed' are 'substantially related to the achievement of those objectives.'" *Wengler v. Druggists Mutual Ins. Co* The justification must be genuine, not hypothesized or invented post hoc in response to litigation. And it must not rely on overbroad generalizations about the different talents, capacities, or preferences of males and females.

The heightened review standard our precedent establishes does not make sex a proscribed classification. Supposed "inherent differences" are no longer accepted as a ground for race or national origin classifications. Physical differences between men and women, however, are enduring: "[T]he two sexes are not fungible; a community made up exclusively of one [sex] is different from a community composed of both." *Ballard v. United States*

"Inherent differences" between men and women, we have come to appreciate, remain cause for celebration, but not for denigration of the members of either sex or for artificial constraints on an individual's opportunity. Sex classifications may be used to compensate women "for particular economic disabilities [they have] suffered," *Califano v. Webster,* to "promot[e] equal employment opportunity," to advance full development of the talent and capacities of our Nation's people. But such classifications may not be used, as they once were, to create or perpetuate the legal, social, and economic inferiority of women.

Measuring the record in this case against the review standard just described, we conclude that Virginia has shown no "exceedingly persuasive justification" for excluding all women from the citizen soldier training afforded by VMI. We therefore affirm the Fourth Circuit's initial judgment, which held that Virginia had violated the Fourteenth Amendment's Equal Protection Clause. Because the remedy proffered by Virginia—the Mary Baldwin VWIL program—does not cure the constitutional violation, it does not provide equal opportunity, we reverse the Fourth Circuit's final judgment in this case.

The Fourth Circuit initially held that Virginia had advanced no state policy by which it could justify, under equal protection principles, its determination "to afford VMI's unique type of program to men and not to women." Virginia challenges that "liability" ruling and asserts two justifications in defense of VMI's exclusion of women. First, the Commonwealth contends, "single sex education provides important educational benefits," and the option of single sex education contributes to "diversity in educational approaches." Second, the Commonwealth argues, "the unique VMI method of character development and leadership training," the school's adversative approach, would have to be modified were VMI to admit women. We consider these two justifications in turn.

Single sex education affords pedagogical benefits to at least some students, Virginia emphasizes, and that reality is uncontested in this litigation. Similarly, it is not disputed that diversity among public educational institutions can serve the public good. But Virginia has not shown that VMI was established, or has been maintained, with a view to diversifying, by its categorical exclusion of women, educational opportunities within the State. . . .

. . . A purpose genuinely to advance an array of educational options, as the Court of Appeals recognized, is not served by VMI's historic and constant plan—a plan to "affor[d] a unique educational benefit only to males." However "liberally" this plan serves the State's sons, it makes no provision whatever for her daughters. That is not equal protection.

Virginia next argues that VMI's adversative method of training provides educational benefits that cannot be made available, unmodified, to women. Alterations to accommodate women would necessarily be "radical," so "drastic," Virginia asserts, as to transform, indeed "destroy," VMI's program. Neither sex would be favored by the transformation, Virginia maintains: Men would be deprived of the unique opportunity currently available to them; women would not gain that opportunity because their participation would "eliminat[e] the very aspects of [the] program that distinguish [VMI] from . . . other institutions of higher education in Virginia." . . .

The United States does not challenge any expert witness estimation on average capacities or preferences of men and women. Instead, the United States emphasizes that time and again since this Court's turning point decision in *Reed v. Reed,* we have cautioned reviewing courts to take a "hard look" at generalizations or "tendencies" of the kind pressed by Virginia, and relied upon by the District Court. . . .

The notion that admission of women would downgrade VMI's stature, destroy the adversative system and, with it, even the school, is a judgment hardly proved, a prediction hardly different from other "self fulfilling prophec[ies]," once routinely used to deny rights or opportunities. . . .

Women's successful entry into the federal military academies and their participation in the Nation's military forces indicate that Virginia's fears for the future of VMI may not be solidly grounded. The State's justification for excluding all women from "citizen soldier" training for which some are qualified, in any event, cannot rank as "exceedingly persuasive," as we have explained and applied that standard. . . .

In the second phase of the litigation, Virginia presented its remedial plan—maintain VMI as a male only college and create VWIL as a separate program for women. The plan met District Court approval. The Fourth Circuit, in turn, deferentially reviewed the State's proposal and decided that the two single sex programs directly served Virginia's reasserted purposes: single gender education, and "achieving the results of an adversative method in a military environment." Inspecting the VMI and VWIL educational programs to determine whether they "afford[ed] to both genders benefits comparable in substance, [if] not in form and detail," the Court of Appeals concluded that Virginia had arranged for men and women opportunities "sufficiently comparable" to survive equal protection evaluation. The United States challenges this "remedial" ruling as pervasively misguided. . . .

Virginia chose not to eliminate, but to leave untouched, VMI's exclusionary policy. For women only, however, Virginia proposed a separate program, different in kind from VMI and unequal in tangible and intangible facilities. Having violated the Constitution's equal protection requirement, Virginia was obliged to show that its remedial proposal "directly address[ed] and relate[d] to" the violation, the equal protection denied to women ready, willing, and able to benefit from educational opportunities of the kind VMI offers. . . .

VWIL affords women no opportunity to experience the rigorous military training for which VMI is famed. . . . Instead, the VWIL program "deemphasize[s]" military education, and uses a "cooperative method" of education "which reinforces self esteem," VWIL students participate in ROTC and a "largely ceremonial" Virginia Corps of Cadets, but Virginia deliberately did not make VWIL a military institute. The VWIL House is not a military style residence and VWIL students need not live together throughout the 4 year program, eat meals together, or wear uniforms during the school day. VWIL students thus do not experience the "barracks" life "crucial to the VMI experience," the spartan living arrangements designed to foster an "egalitarian ethic." "[T]he most important aspects of the VMI educational experience occur in the barracks," the District Court found, yet Virginia deemed that core experience nonessential, indeed inappropriate, for training its female citizen soldiers.

VWIL students receive their "leadership training" in seminars, externships, and speaker series, episodes and encounters lacking the "[p]hysical rigor, mental stress, . . . minute regulation of behavior, and indoctrination in desirable values" made hallmarks of VMI's citizen soldier training. Kept away from the pressures, hazards, and psychological bonding characteristic of VMI's adversative training, VWIL students will not know the "feeling of tremendous accomplishment" commonly experienced by VMI's successful cadets.

Virginia maintains that these methodological differences are "justified pedagogically," based on "important differences between men and women in learning and developmental needs," "psychological and sociological differences" Virginia describes as "real" and "not stereotypes." . . .

In contrast to the generalizations about women on which Virginia rests, we note again these dispositive realities: VMI's "implementing methodology" is not "inherently unsuitable to women," "some women . . . do well under [the] adversative model," "some women, at least, would want to attend [VMI] if they had the opportunity," "some women are capable of all of the individual activities required of VMI cadets," and "can meet the physical standards [VMI] now impose[s] on men." It is on behalf of these women that the United States has instituted this suit, and it is for them that a remedy must be crafted, a remedy that will end their exclusion from a state supplied educational opportunity for which they are fit, a decree that will "bar like discrimination in the future."

In myriad respects other than military training, VWIL does not qualify as VMI's equal. VWIL's student body, faculty, course offerings, and facilities hardly match VMI's. Nor can the VWIL graduate anticipate the benefits associated with VMI's 157-year history, the school's prestige, and its influential alumni network. . . .

Virginia's VWIL solution is reminiscent of the remedy Texas proposed 50 years ago, in response to a state trial court's 1946 ruling that, given the equal protection guarantee, African Americans could not be denied a legal education at a state facility. Reluctant to admit African Americans to its flagship University of Texas Law School, the State set up a separate school for Herman Sweatt and other black law students. . . .

This Court contrasted resources at the new school with those at the school from which Sweatt (in *Sweatt v. Painter*) had been excluded. . . . More important than the tangible features, the Court emphasized, are "those qualities which are incapable of objective measurement but which make for greatness" in a school, including "reputation of the faculty, experience of the administration, position and influence of the alumni, standing in the community, traditions and prestige." Facing the marked differences reported in the Sweatt opinion, the Court unanimously ruled that Texas had not shown "substantial equality in the [separate] educational opportunities" the State offered. Accordingly, the Court held, the Equal Protection Clause required Texas to admit African Americans to the University of Texas Law School. In line with *Sweatt*, we rule here that Virginia has not shown substantial equality in the separate educational opportunities the State supports at VWIL and VMI.

When Virginia tendered its VWIL plan, the Fourth Circuit did not inquire whether the proposed remedy, approved by the District Court, placed women denied the VMI advantage in "the position they would have occupied in the absence of [discrimination]." Instead, the Court of Appeals considered whether the State could provide, with fidelity to the equal protection principle, separate and unequal educational programs for men and women. . . .

The Fourth Circuit plainly erred in exposing Virginia's VWIL plan to a deferential analysis, for "all gender based classifications today" warrant "heightened scrutiny." Valuable as VWIL may prove for students who seek the program offered, Virginia's remedy affords no cure at all for the opportunities and advantages withheld from women who want a VMI education and can make the grade. In sum, Virginia's remedy does not match the constitutional violation; the State has shown no "exceedingly persuasive justification" for withholding from women qualified for the experience premier training of the kind VMI affords. . . .

For the reasons stated, the initial judgment of the Court of Appeals is affirmed, the final judgment of the Court of Appeals, is reversed, and the case is remanded for further proceedings consistent with this opinion.

Rehnquist, concurring:
The Court defines the constitutional violation in this case as "the categorical exclusion of women from an extraordinary educational opportunity afforded to men." By defining the violation in this way, and by emphasizing that a remedy for a constitutional violation must place the victims of discrimination in "'the position they would have occupied in the absence of [discrimination],'" the Court necessarily implies that the only adequate remedy would be the admission of women to the all male institution. As the foregoing discussion suggests, I would not define the violation in this way; it is not the "exclusion of women" that violates the Equal Protection Clause, but the maintenance of an all men school without providing any—much less a comparable—institution for women.

Accordingly, the remedy should not necessarily require either the admission of women to VMI, or the creation of a VMI clone for women. An adequate remedy in my opinion might be a demonstration by Virginia that its interest in educating men in a single sex environment is matched by its interest in educating women in a single sex institution. To demonstrate such, the State does not need to create two institutions with the same number of faculty PhD's, similar SAT scores, or comparable athletic fields. Nor would it necessarily require that the women's institution offer the same curriculum as the men's; one could be strong in computer science, the other could be strong in liberal arts. It would be a sufficient remedy, I think, if the two institutions offered the same quality of education and were of the same overall calibre. . . .

In the end, the women's institution Virginia proposes, VWIL, fails as a remedy, because it is distinctly inferior to the existing men's institution and will continue to be for the foreseeable future. VWIL simply is not, in any sense, the institution that VMI is. In particular, VWIL is a program appended to a private college, not a self standing institution; and VWIL is substantially underfunded as compared to VMI. I therefore ultimately agree with the Court that Virginia has not provided an adequate remedy.

In the end, the women's institution Virginia proposes, VWIL, fails as a remedy, because it is distinctly inferior to the existing men's institution and will continue to be for the foreseeable future. VWIL simply is not, in any sense, the institution that VMI is. In particular, VWIL is a program appended to a private college, not a self standing institution; and VWIL is substantially underfunded as compared to VMI. I therefore ultimately agree with the Court that Virginia has not provided an adequate remedy

Scalia, dissenting:
I have no problem with a system of abstract tests such as rational basis, intermediate, and strict scrutiny (though I think we can do better than applying strict scrutiny and intermediate scrutiny whenever we feel like it). Such formulas are essential to evaluating whether the new restrictions that a changing society constantly imposes upon private conduct comport with that "equal protection" our society has always accorded in the past. But in my view the function of this Court is to *preserve* our society's values regarding (among other things) equal protection, not to *revise* them; to prevent backsliding from the degree of restriction the Constitution imposed upon democratic government, not to prescribe, on our own authority, progressively higher degrees. For that reason it is my view that, whatever abstract tests we may choose to devise, they

cannot supersede—and indeed ought to be crafted *so as to reflect*—those constant and unbroken national traditions that embody the people's understanding of ambiguous constitutional texts. More specifically, it is my view that "when a practice not expressly prohibited by the text of the Bill of Rights bears the endorsement of a long tradition of open, widespread, and unchallenged use that dates back to the beginning of the Republic, we have no proper basis for striking it down." *Rutan* v. *Republican Party of Ill.* . . . .

Today, however, change is forced upon Virginia, and reversion to single sex education is prohibited nationwide, not by democratic processes but by order of this Court. Even while bemoaning the sorry, bygone days of "fixed notions" concerning women's education, see *ante*, at 18-19, and n. 10, 20-21, 25-27, the Court favors current notions so fixedly that it is willing to write them into the Constitution of the United States by application of custom built "tests." This is not the interpretation of a Constitution, but the creation of one. . . .

Not content to execute a *de facto* abandonment of the intermediate scrutiny that has been our standard for sex based classifications for some two decades, the Court purports to reserve the question whether, even in principle, a higher standard (*i.e.*, strict scrutiny) should apply. . . .

The Court's intimations are particularly out of place because it is perfectly clear that, if the question of the applicable standard of review for sex based classifications were to be regarded as an appropriate subject for reconsideration, the stronger argument would be not for elevating the standard to strict scrutiny, but for reducing it to rational basis review. . . .

It is hard to consider women a "discrete and insular minorit[y]" unable to employ the "political processes ordinarily to be relied upon," when they constitute a majority of the electorate. And the suggestion that they are incapable of exerting that political power smacks of the same paternalism that the Court so roundly condemns. . . .

As is frequently true, the Court's decision today will have consequences that extend far beyond the parties to the case. What I take to be the Court's unease with these consequences, and its resulting unwillingness to acknowledge them, cannot alter the reality.

Under the constitutional principles announced and applied today, single sex public education is unconstitutional. By going through the motions of applying a balancing test—asking whether the State has

adduced an "exceedingly persuasive justification" for its sex based classification—the Court creates the illusion that government officials in some future case will have a clear shot at justifying some sort of single sex public education. Indeed, the Court seeks to create even a greater illusion than that: It purports to have said nothing of relevance to *other* public schools at all. . . .

There are few extant single sex public educational programs. The potential of today's decision for widespread disruption of existing institutions lies in its application to *private* single sex education. Government support is immensely important to private educational institutions. . . .

The only hope for state assisted single sex private schools is that the Court will not apply in the future the principles of law it has applied today. That is a substantial hope, I am happy and ashamed to say. After all, did not the Court today abandon the principles of law it has applied in our earlier sex classification cases? And does not the Court positively invite private colleges to rely upon our ad hocery by assuring them this case is "unique"? I would not advise the foundation of any new single sex college (especially an all male one) with the expectation of being allowed to receive any government support; but it is too soon to abandon in despair those single sex colleges already in existence. It will certainly be possible for this Court to write a future opinion that ignores the broad principles of law set forth today, and that characterizes as utterly dispositive the opinion's perceptions that VMI was a uniquely prestigious all male institution, conceived in chauvinism, etc., etc. I will not join that opinion.

Massachusetts Board of Retirement v. Murgia

427 U.S. 307 (1976), 8-1
Per Curium Opinion
Dissenting: Marshall
Not participating: Stevens

Why is age not a "suspect" classification? Should an age-mandated retirement rule be limited to assessing each individual's competence to continue working rather than being a blanket requirement for an entire group? Would such a limitation be cumbersome administratively? Would that be sufficient reason to uphold a blanket classification?

Per curiam:

This case presents the question whether the provision of Mass.Gen.Laws Ann. c. 32, §26(3)(a) that a uniformed state police officer "shall be retired . . . upon his attaining age fifty," denies appellee police officer equal protection of the laws in violation of the Fourteenth Amendment.

Appellee Robert Murgia was an officer in the Uniformed Branch of the Massachusetts State Police. The Massachusetts Board of Retirement retired him upon his 50th birthday. Appellee brought this civil action . . . alleging that the operation of §26(3)(a) denied him equal protection of the laws. . . .

We need state only briefly our reasons for agreeing that strict scrutiny is not the proper test for determining whether the mandatory retirement provision denies appellee equal protection. *San Antonio School District v. Rodriguez* reaffirmed that equal protection analysis requires strict scrutiny of a legislative classification only when the classification impermissibly interferes with the exercise of a fundamental right or operates to the peculiar disadvantage of a suspect class. Mandatory retirement at age 50 under the Massachusetts statute involves neither situation.

This Court's decisions give no support to the proposition that a right of governmental employment per se is fundamental. Accordingly, we have expressly stated that a standard less than strict scrutiny "has consistently been applied to state legislation restricting the availability of employment opportunities."

Nor does the class of uniformed state police officers over 50 constitute a suspect class for purposes of equal protection analysis. *Rodriguez,* observed that a suspect class is one "saddled with such disabilities, or subjected to such a history of purposeful unequal treatment, or relegated to such a position of political powerlessness as to command extraordinary protection from the majoritarian political process."

While the treatment of the aged in this Nation has not been wholly free of discrimination, such persons, unlike, say, those who have been discriminated against on the basis of race or national origin, have not experienced a "history of purposeful unequal treatment" or been subjected to unique disabilities on the basis of stereotyped characteristics not truly indicative of their abilities. The class subject to the compulsory retirement feature of the Massachusetts statute consists of uniformed state police officers over the age of 50. It cannot be said to discriminate only against the elderly. Rather, it draws the line at a certain age

in middle life. But even old age does not define a "discrete and insular" group, in need of "extraordinary protection from the majoritarian political process." Instead, it marks a stage that each of us will reach if we live out our normal span. Even if the statute could be said to impose a penalty upon a class defined as the aged, it would not impose a distinction sufficiently akin to those classifications that we have found suspect to call for strict judicial scrutiny.

Under the circumstances, it is unnecessary to subject the State's resolution of competing interests in this case to the degree of critical examination that our cases under the Equal Protection Clause recently have characterized as "strict judicial scrutiny."

We turn then to examine this state classification under the rational basis standard. This inquiry employs a relatively relaxed standard reflecting the Court's awareness that the drawing of lines that create distinctions is peculiarly a legislative task and an unavoidable one. Perfection in making the necessary classifications is neither possible nor necessary. Such action by a legislature is presumed to be valid.

In this case, the Massachusetts statute clearly meets the requirements of the Equal Protection Clause, for the State's classification rationally furthers the purpose identified by the State: through mandatory retirement at age 50, the legislature seeks to protect the public by assuring physical preparedness of its uniformed police. Since physical ability generally declines with age, mandatory retirement at 50 serves to remove from police service those whose fitness for uniformed work presumptively has diminished with age. This clearly is rationally related to the State's objective. There is no indication that §26(3)(a) has the effect of excluding from service so few officers who are in fact unqualified as to render age 50 a criterion wholly unrelated to the objective of the statute.

That the State chooses not to determine fitness more precisely through individualized testing after age 50 is not to say that the objective of assuring physical fitness is not rationally furthered by a maximum age limitation. It is only to say that, with regard to the interest of all concerned, the State perhaps has not chosen the best means to accomplish this purpose. But where rationality is the test, a State "does not violate the Equal Protection Clause merely because the classifications made by its laws are imperfect." *Dandridge v. Williams.*

We do not make light of the substantial economic and psychological effects premature and compulsory retirement can have on an individual; nor do we denigrate the ability of elderly citizens to continue to contribute to society. The problems of retirement have been well documented and are beyond serious dispute. But "[w]e do not decide today that the [Massachusetts statute] is wise, that it best fulfills the relevant social and economic objectives that [Massachusetts] might ideally espouse, or that a more just and humane system could not be devised." *Dandridge v. Williams* We decide only that the system enacted by the Massachusetts Legislature does not deny appellee equal protection of the laws.

Marshall, dissenting:

. . . Although there are signs that its grasp on the law is weakening, the rigid two-tier model still holds sway as the Court's articulated description of the equal protection test. Again, I must object to its perpetuation. The model's two fixed modes of analysis, strict scrutiny and mere rationality, simply do not describe the inquiry the Court has undertaken—or should undertake in equal protection cases. Rather, the inquiry has been much more sophisticated, and the Court should admit as much. It has focused upon the character of the classification in question, the relative importance to individuals in the class discriminated against of the governmental benefits that they do not receive, and the state interests asserted in support of the classification.

Although the Court outwardly adheres to the two-tier model, it has apparently lost interest in recognizing further "fundamental" rights and "suspect" classes. In my view, this result is the natural consequence of the limitations of the Court's traditional equal protection analysis. If a statute invades a "fundamental" right or discriminates against a "suspect" class, it is subject to strict scrutiny. If a statute is subject to strict scrutiny, the statute always, or nearly always, is struck down. Quite obviously, the only critical decision is whether strict scrutiny should be invoked at all. It should be no surprise, then, that the Court is hesitant to expand the number of categories of rights and classes subject to strict scrutiny, when each expansion involves the invalidation of virtually every classification bearing upon a newly covered category.

But however understandable the Court's hesitancy to invoke strict scrutiny, all remaining legislation should not drop into the bottom tier, and be measured by the mere rationality test. For that test, too, when applied as articulated, leaves little doubt about the outcome; the challenged legislation is always upheld. It cannot be gainsaid that there remain rights, not now classified as "fundamental," that remain vital to the flourishing of a free society, and classes, not now classified as "suspect," that are unfairly burdened by invidious discrimination unrelated to the individual worth of their members. Whatever we call these rights and classes, we simply cannot forgo all judicial protection against discriminatory legislation bearing upon them, but for the rare instances when the legislative choice can be termed "wholly irrelevant" to the legislative goal. . . .

The danger of the Court's verbal adherence to the rigid two-tier test, despite its effective repudiation of that test in the cases, is demonstrated by its efforts here. There is simply no reason why a statute that tells able-bodied police officers, ready and willing to work, that they no longer have the right to earn a living in their chosen profession merely because they are 50 years old should be judged by the same minimal standards of rationality that we use to test economic legislation that discriminates against business interests. Yet, the Court today not only invokes the minimal level of scrutiny, it wrongly adheres to it. Analysis of the three factors I have identified above—the importance of the governmental benefits denied, the character of the class, and the asserted state interests—demonstrates the Court's error.

Whether "fundamental" or not, "'the right of the individual . . . to engage in any of the common occupations of life'" has been repeatedly recognized by this Court as falling within the concept of liberty guaranteed by the Fourteenth Amendment. . . .

While depriving any government employee of his job is a significant deprivation, it is particularly burdensome when the person deprived is an older citizen. Once terminated, the elderly cannot readily find alternative employment. The lack of work is not only economically damaging, but emotionally and physically draining. Deprived of his status in the community and of the opportunity for meaningful activity, fearful of becoming dependent on others for his support, and lonely in his new-found isolation, the involuntarily retired person is susceptible to physical and emotional ailments as a direct consequence of his enforced idleness. Ample clinical evidence supports the conclusion that mandatory retirement poses a direct threat to the health and life expectancy of the retired person, and these consequences of termination for age are not disputed by appellants. . . .

Of course, the Court is quite right in suggesting that distinctions exist between the elderly and traditional suspect classes such as Negroes, and between the elderly and "quasi-suspect" classes such as women or illegitimates. The elderly are protected not only by certain anti discrimination legislation, but by legislation that provides them with positive benefits not enjoyed by the public at large. Moreover, the elderly are not isolated in society, and discrimination against them is not pervasive but is centered primarily in employment. The advantage of a flexible equal protection standard, however, is that it can readily accommodate such variables. The elderly are undoubtedly discriminated against, and when legislation denies them an important benefit—employment—I conclude that, to sustain the legislation, appellants must show a reasonably substantial interest and a scheme reasonably closely tailored to achieving that interest. This inquiry, ultimately, is not markedly different from that undertaken by the Court in *Reed v. Reed.*

Turning, then, to appellants' arguments, I agree that the purpose of the mandatory retirement law is legitimate, and indeed compelling. The Commonwealth has every reason to assure that its state police officers are of sufficient physical strength and health to perform their jobs. In my view, however, the means chosen, the forced retirement of officers at age 50, is so overinclusive that it must fall.

All potential officers must pass a rigorous physical examination. Until age 40, this same examination must be passed every two years—when the officer reenlists—and, after age 40, every year. Appellants have conceded that "[w]hen a member passes his reenlistment or annual physical, he is found to be qualified to perform all of the duties of the Uniformed Branch of the Massachusetts State Police."

If a member fails the examination, he is immediately terminated or refused reenlistment. Thus, the only members of the state police still on the force at age 50 are those who have been determined—repeatedly—by the Commonwealth to be physically fit for the job. Yet all of these physically fit officers are automatically terminated at age 50. Appellants do not seriously assert that their testing is no longer effective at age 50, nor do they claim that continued testing would serve no purpose because officers over 50 are no longer physically able to perform their. Thus, the Commonwealth is in the position of already individually testing its police officers for physical fitness, conceding that such testing is adequate to determine the physical ability of an officer to continue on the job, and conceding that that ability may continue after age 50. In these circumstances, I see no reason at all for automatically terminating those officers who reach the age of 50; indeed, that action seems the height of irrationality.

Accordingly, I conclude that the Commonwealth's mandatory retirement law cannot stand when measured against the significant deprivation the Commonwealth's action works upon the terminated employees. . . .

Romer v. Evans

517 U.S. 620 (1996), 6-3
Opinion of the Court: Kennedy (Breyer, Ginsburg, O'Connor, Souter, Stevens)
Dissenting: Rehnquist, Scalia, Thomas

The plaintiffs (respondents) in this case were several gay persons and three Colorado municipalities who challenged the federal constitutionality of an amendment to the Colorado Constitution. The nominal defendant (petitioner) Romer was governor of the state.

Normally, a constitutional amendment overcoming "errant" local laws and practices is an important exercise of the democratic process, as the Fourteenth Amendment was itself. What does the Court say about this element of popular government? Is barring a city or town from passing laws protecting against discrimination that is based on sexual orientation the same as taking rights away on the basis of sexual orientation? If so, what rights have been taken away? According to Scalia, what state interest or interests are reflected in the amendment? Are they reasonable? Who gains and loses through this decision and what is gained and lost? Is this decision consistent with Bowers v. Hardwick *(p. 316)?*

Kennedy, for the Court:

. . . The enactment challenged in this case is an amendment to the Constitution of the State of Colorado, adopted in a 1992 statewide referendum. The parties and the state courts refer to it as "Amendment 2," its designation when submitted to the voters. The impetus for the amendment and the contentious campaign that preceded its adoption came in large part from ordinances that had been passed in various Colorado municipalities. For example, the cities of

Aspen and Boulder and the City and County of Denver each had enacted ordinances which banned discrimination in many transactions and activities, including housing, employment, education, public accommodations, and health and welfare services. What gave rise to the statewide controversy was the protection the ordinances afforded to persons discriminated against by reason of their sexual orientation. Amendment 2 repeals these ordinances to the extent they prohibit discrimination on the basis of "homosexual, lesbian or bisexual orientation, conduct, practices or relationships."

Yet Amendment 2, in explicit terms, does more than repeal or rescind these provisions. It prohibits all legislative, executive or judicial action at any level of state or local government designed to protect the named class, a class we shall refer to as homosexual persons or gays and lesbians. The amendment reads:

> "No Protected Status Based on Homosexual, Lesbian, or Bisexual Orientation. Neither the State of Colorado, through any of its branches or departments, nor any of its agencies, political subdivisions, municipalities or school districts, shall enact, adopt or enforce any statute, regulation, ordinance or policy whereby homosexual, lesbian or bisexual orientation, conduct, practices or relationships shall constitute or otherwise be the basis of or entitle any person or class of persons to have or claim any minority status, quota preferences, protected status or claim of discrimination. This Section of the Constitution shall be in all respects self-executing." . . .

The State's principal argument in defense of Amendment 2 is that it puts gays and lesbians in the same position as all other persons. So, the State says, the measure does no more than deny homosexuals special rights. This reading of the amendment's language is implausible. . . .

Sweeping and comprehensive is the change in legal status effected by this law. So much is evident from the ordinances that the Colorado Supreme Court declared would be void by operation of Amendment 2. Homosexuals, by state decree, are put in a solitary class with respect to transactions and relations in both the private and governmental spheres. The amendment withdraws from homosexuals, but no others, specific legal protection from the injuries caused by discrimination, and it forbids reinstatement of these laws and policies. . . .

Amendment 2 bars homosexuals from securing protection against the injuries that . . . public-accommodations laws address. That in itself is a severe consequence, but there is more. Amendment 2, in addition, nullifies specific legal protections for this targeted class in all transactions in housing, sale of real estate, insurance, health and welfare services, private education, and employment. . . .

Amendment 2's reach may not be limited to specific laws passed for the benefit of gays and lesbians. It is a fair, if not necessary, inference from the broad language of the amendment that it deprives gays and lesbians even of the protection of general laws and policies that prohibit arbitrary discrimination in governmental and private settings. . . . At some point in the systematic administration of these laws, an official must determine whether homosexuality is an arbitrary and thus forbidden basis for decision. Yet a decision to that effect would itself amount to a policy prohibiting discrimination on the basis of homosexuality, and so would appear to be no more valid under Amendment 2 than the specific prohibitions against discrimination the state court held invalid.

If this consequence follows from Amendment 2, as its broad language suggests, it would compound the constitutional difficulties the law creates. The state court did not decide whether the amendment has this effect, however, and neither need we. In the course of rejecting the argument that Amendment 2 is intended to conserve resources to fight discrimination against suspect classes, the Colorado Supreme Court made the limited observation that the amendment is not intended to affect many anti-discrimination laws protecting non-suspect classes. In our view that does not resolve the issue. In any event, even if, as we doubt, homosexuals could find some safe harbor in laws of general application, we cannot accept the view that Amendment 2's prohibition on specific legal protections does no more than deprive homosexuals of special rights. To the contrary, the amendment imposes a special disability upon those persons alone. Homosexuals are forbidden the safeguards that others enjoy or may seek without constraint. They can obtain specific protection against discrimination only by enlisting the citizenry of Colorado to amend the state constitution or perhaps, on the State's view, by trying to pass helpful laws of general applicability. This is so no matter how local or discrete the harm, no matter how public and widespread the injury. We find nothing special in the protections Amendment 2 withholds. These are protections taken for granted by most people either because they already have them or do not need them; these are protections against exclusion from an almost limitless number of transactions and endeavors that constitute ordinary civic life in a free society.

The Fourteenth Amendment's promise that no person shall be denied the equal protection of the laws must co-exist with the practical necessity that most legislation classifies for one purpose or another, with resulting disadvantage to various groups or persons. We have attempted to reconcile the principle with the reality by stating that, if a law neither burdens a fundamental right nor targets a suspect class, we will uphold the legislative classification so long as it bears a rational relation to some legitimate end.

Amendment 2 fails, indeed defies, even this conventional inquiry. First, the amendment has the peculiar property of imposing a broad and undifferentiated disability on a single named group, an exceptional and, as we shall explain, invalid form of legislation. Second, its sheer breadth is so discontinuous with the reasons offered for it that the amendment seems inexplicable by anything but animus toward the class that it affects; it lacks a rational relationship to legitimate state interests.

Taking the first point, even in the ordinary equal protection case calling for the most deferential of standards, we insist on knowing the relation between the classification adopted and the object to be attained.... By requiring that the classification bear a rational relationship to an independent and legitimate legislative end, we ensure that classifications are not drawn for the purpose of disadvantaging the group burdened by the law.

Amendment 2 confounds this normal process of judicial review. It is at once too narrow and too broad. It identifies persons by a single trait and then denies them protection across the board. The resulting disqualification of a class of persons from the right to seek specific protection from the law is unprecedented in our jurisprudence....

It is not within our constitutional tradition to enact laws of this sort. Central both to the idea of the rule of law and to our own Constitution's guarantee of equal protection is the principle that government and each of its parts remain open on impartial terms to all who seek its assistance.... Respect for this principle explains why laws singling out a certain class of citizens for disfavored legal status or general hardships are rare. A law declaring that in general it shall be more difficult for one group of citizens than for all others to seek aid from the government is itself a denial of equal protection of the laws in the most literal sense....

A second and related point is that laws of the kind now before us raise the inevitable inference that the disadvantage imposed is born of animosity toward the class of persons affected.... Even laws enacted for broad and ambitious purposes often can be explained by reference to legitimate public policies which justify the incidental disadvantages they impose on certain persons. Amendment 2, however, in making a general announcement that gays and lesbians shall not have any particular protections from the law, inflicts on them immediate, continuing, and real injuries that outrun and belie any legitimate justifications that may be claimed for it. We conclude that, in addition to the far-reaching deficiencies of Amendment 2 that we have noted, the principles it offends, in another sense, are conventional and venerable; a law must bear a rational relationship to a legitimate governmental purpose, and Amendment 2 does not.

The primary rationale the State offers for Amendment 2 is respect for other citizens' freedom of association, and in particular the liberties of landlords or employers who have personal or religious objections to homosexuality. Colorado also cites its interest in conserving resources to fight discrimination against other groups. The breadth of the Amendment is so far removed from these particular justifications that we find it impossible to credit them. We cannot say that Amendment 2 is directed to any identifiable legitimate purpose or discrete objective. It is a status-based enactment divorced from any factual context from which we could discern a relationship to legitimate state interests; it is a classification of persons undertaken for its own sake, something the Equal Protection Clause does not permit.

We must conclude that Amendment 2 classifies homosexuals not to further a proper legislative end but to make them unequal to everyone else. This Colorado cannot do. A State cannot so deem a class of persons a stranger to its laws. Amendment 2 violates the Equal Protection Clause, and the judgment of the Supreme Court of Colorado is affirmed.

Scalia, dissenting:

... The constitutional amendment before us here is not the manifestation of a "'bare ... desire to harm'" homosexuals, but is rather a modest attempt by seemingly tolerant Coloradans to preserve traditional sexual mores against the efforts of a politically powerful minority to revise those mores through use of the laws. That objective, and the means chosen to achieve it, are not only unimpeachable under any constitutional doctrine hitherto pronounced (hence the opinion's heavy reliance upon principles of righteousness rather than judicial holdings); they have been specifically approved by the Congress of the United States and by this Court. . . .

. . . The amendment prohibits special treatment of homosexuals, and nothing more. It would not affect, for example, a requirement of state law that pensions be paid to all retiring state employees with a certain length of service; homosexual employees, as well as others, would be entitled to that benefit. But it would prevent the State or any municipality from making death-benefit payments to the "life partner" of a homosexual when it does not make such payments to the long-time roommate of a nonhomosexual employee. Or again, it does not affect the requirement of the State's general insurance laws that customers be afforded coverage without discrimination unrelated to anticipated risk. Thus, homosexuals could not be denied coverage, or charged a greater premium, with respect to auto collision insurance; but neither the State nor any municipality could require that distinctive health insurance risks associated with homosexuality (if there are any) be ignored.

Despite all of its hand-wringing about the potential effect of Amendment 2 on general antidiscrimination laws, the Court's opinion ultimately does not dispute all this, but assumes it to be true. The only denial of equal treatment it contends homosexuals have suffered is this: They may not obtain preferential treatment without amending the state constitution. That is to say, the principle underlying the Court's opinion is that one who is accorded equal treatment under the laws, but cannot as readily as others obtain preferential treatment under the laws, has been denied equal protection of the laws. . . .

The central thesis of the Court's reasoning is that any group is denied equal protection when, to obtain advantage (or, presumably, to avoid disadvantage), it must have recourse to a more general and hence more difficult level of political decisionmaking than others. The world has never heard of such a principle, which is why the Court's opinion is so long on emotive utterance and so short on relevant legal citation.

And it seems to me most unlikely that any multilevel democracy can function under such a principle. For whenever a disadvantage is imposed, or conferral of a benefit is prohibited, at one of the higher levels of democratic decisionmaking (i.e., by the state legislature rather than local government, or by the people at large in the state constitution rather than the legislature), the affected group has (under this theory) been denied equal protection. To take the simplest of examples, consider a state law prohibiting the award of municipal contracts to relatives of mayors or city councilmen. Once such a law is passed, the group composed of such relatives must, in order to get the benefit of city contracts, persuade the state legislature—unlike all other citizens, who need only persuade the municipality. It is ridiculous to consider this a denial of equal protection, which is why the Court's theory is unheard-of. . . .

I turn next to whether there was a legitimate rational basis for the substance of the constitutional amendment—for the prohibition of special protection for homosexuals. It is unsurprising that the Court avoids discussion of this question, since the answer is so obviously yes. The case most relevant to the issue before us today is . . . *Bowers v. Hardwick,* [in which] we held that the Constitution does not prohibit what virtually all States had done from the founding of the Republic until very recent years—making homosexual conduct a crime. . . . If it is constitutionally permissible for a State to make homosexual conduct criminal, surely it is constitutionally permissible for a State to enact other laws merely disfavoring homosexual conduct. . . . [I]t is constitutionally permissible for a State to adopt a provision not even disfavoring homosexual conduct, but merely prohibiting all levels of state government from bestowing special protections upon homosexual conduct. . . .

. . . The Colorado amendment does not, to speak entirely precisely, prohibit giving favored status to people who are homosexuals; they can be favored for many reasons—for example, because they are senior citizens or members of racial minorities. But it prohibits giving them favored status because of their homosexual conduct—that is, it prohibits favored status for homosexuality.

But though Coloradans are . . . entitled to be hostile toward homosexual conduct, the fact is that the degree of hostility reflected by Amendment 2 is the smallest conceivable. The Court's portrayal of Coloradans as a society fallen victim to pointless, hate-filled "gay-bashing" is so false as to be comical. Colorado not only is one of the 25 States that have repealed their antisodomy laws, but was among the first to do so. But the society that eliminates criminal punishment for homosexual acts does not necessarily abandon the view that homosexuality is morally wrong and socially harmful; often, abolition simply reflects the view that enforcement of such criminal laws involves unseemly intrusion into the intimate lives of citizens. . . .

There is a problem, however, which arises when criminal sanction of homosexuality is eliminated but moral and social disapprobation of homosexuality is meant to be retained. The Court cannot be unaware of that problem; it is evident in many cities of the country, and occasionally bubbles to the surface of the news, in heated political disputes over such matters as the introduction into local schools of books teaching that homosexuality is an optional and fully acceptable "alternate life style." The problem (a problem, that is, for those who wish to retain social disapprobation of homosexuality) is that, because those who engage in homosexual conduct tend to reside in disproportionate numbers in certain communities, and of course care about homosexual-rights issues much more ardently than the public at large, they possess political power much greater than their numbers, both locally and statewide. Quite understandably, they devote this political power to achieving not merely a grudging social toleration, but full social acceptance, of homosexuality.

By the time Coloradans were asked to vote on Amendment 2, their exposure to homosexuals' quest for social endorsement was not limited to newspaper accounts of happenings in places such as New York, Los Angeles, San Francisco, and Key West. Three Colorado cities—Aspen, Boulder, and Denver—had enacted ordinances that listed "sexual orientation" as an impermissible ground for discrimination, equating the moral disapproval of homosexual conduct with racial and religious bigotry. The phenomenon had even appeared statewide: the Governor of Colorado had signed an executive order pronouncing that "in the State of Colorado we recognize the diversity in our pluralistic society and strive to bring an end to discrimination in any form," and directing state agency-heads to "ensure non-discrimination" in hiring and promotion based on, among other things, "sexual orientation." I do not mean to be critical of these legislative successes; homosexuals are as enti-

tled to use the legal system for reinforcement of their moral sentiments as are the rest of society. But they are subject to being countered by lawful, democratic countermeasures as well. . . .

Shapiro v. Thompson

394 U.S. 618 (1969), 6-3
Opinion of the Court: Brennan (Douglas, Fortas, Marshall, Stewart, White)
Dissenting: Black, Harlan,

This Connecticut case was heard and decided with two others, from Pennsylvania and the District of Columbia. At issue in all three were statutory provisions denying welfare assistance to otherwise eligible persons because they did not reside in the jurisdiction for one year.

Does this decision rest on a "right to travel" or on traditional equal protection principles? What, if any, difference does it make? Where is the right to travel located in the Constitution? Can it be derived from the Constitution? Should it be rephrased as "the right to travel among the states"?

Brennan, for the Court:

Primarily, appellants justify the waiting period requirement as a protective device to preserve the fiscal integrity of state public assistance programs. It is asserted that people who require welfare assistance during their first year of residence in a State are likely to become continuing burdens on state welfare programs. Therefore, the argument runs, if such people can be deterred from entering the jurisdiction by denying them welfare benefits during the first year, state programs to assist long-time residents will not be impaired by a substantial influx of indigent newcomers.

There is weighty evidence that exclusion from the jurisdiction of the poor who need or may need relief was the specific objective of these provisions. In the Congress, sponsors of federal legislation to eliminate all residence requirements have been consistently opposed by representatives of state and local welfare agencies who have stressed the fears of the States that elimination of the requirements would result in a heavy influx of individuals into States providing the most generous benefits. . . .

We do not doubt that the one-year waiting period device is well suited to discourage the influx of poor families in need of assistance. An indigent who desires to migrate, resettle, find a new job, and start a new life will doubtless hesitate if he knows that he must risk making the move without the possibility of falling back on state welfare assistance during his first year of residence, when his need may be most acute. But the purpose of inhibiting migration by needy persons into the State is constitutionally impermissible.

This Court long ago recognized that the nature of our Federal Union and our constitutional concepts of personal liberty unite to require that all citizens be free to travel throughout the length and breadth of our land uninhibited by statutes, rules, or regulations which unreasonably burden or restrict this movement. That proposition was early stated by Chief Justice Taney in the Passenger Cases, "For all the great purposes for which the Federal government was formed, we are one people, with one common country. We are all citizens of the United States; and, as members of the same community, must have the right to pass and repass through every part of it without interruption, as freely as in our own States."

We have no occasion to ascribe the source of this right to travel interstate to a particular constitutional provision. It suffices that, as Mr. Justice Stewart said for the Court in *United States v. Guest:*

> "The constitutional right to travel from one State to another . . . occupies a position fundamental to the concept of our Federal Union. It is a right that has been firmly established and repeatedly recognized. . . . [T]he right finds no explicit mention in the Constitution. The reason, it has been suggested, is that a right so elementary was conceived from the beginning to be a necessary concomitant of the stronger Union the Constitution created. In any event, freedom to travel throughout the United States has long been recognized as a basic right under the Constitution.

Thus, the purpose of deterring the in-migration of indigents cannot serve as justification for the classification created by the one-year waiting period, since that purpose is constitutionally impermissible. If a law has "no other purpose . . . than to chill the assertion of constitutional rights by penalizing those who choose to exercise them, then it [is] patently unconstitutional." *United States v. Jackson*

Alternatively, appellants argue that, even if it is impermissible for a State to attempt to deter the entry of all indigents, the challenged classification may be justified as a permissible state attempt to discourage those indigents who would enter the State solely to obtain larger benefits. We observe first that none of the statutes before us is tailored to serve that objective. Rather, the class of barred newcomers is all-inclusive, lumping the great majority who come to the State for other purposes with those who come for the sole purpose of collecting higher benefits. In actual operation, therefore, the three statutes enact what, in effect, are nonrebuttable presumptions that every applicant for assistance in his first year of residence came to the jurisdiction solely to obtain higher benefits. Nothing whatever in any of these records supplies any basis in fact for such a presumption.

More fundamentally, a State may no more try to fence out those indigents who seek higher welfare benefits than it may try to fence out indigents generally. Implicit in any such distinction is the notion that indigents who enter a State with the hope of securing higher welfare benefits are somehow less deserving than indigents who do not take this consideration into account. But we do not perceive why a mother who is seeking to make a new life for herself and her children should be regarded as less deserving because she considers, among others factors, the level of a State's public assistance. Surely such a mother is no less deserving than a mother who moves into a particular State in order to take advantage of its better educational facilities. . . .

We recognize that a State has a valid interest in preserving the fiscal integrity of its programs. It may legitimately attempt to limit its expenditures, whether for public assistance, public education, or any other program. But a State may not accomplish such a purpose by invidious distinctions between classes of its citizens. It could not, for example, reduce expenditures for education by barring indigent children from its schools. Similarly, in the cases before us, appellants must do more than show that denying welfare benefits to new residents saves money. The saving of welfare costs cannot justify an otherwise invidious classification. . . .

Appellants next advance as justification certain administrative and related governmental objectives allegedly served by the waiting period requirement. They argue that the requirement (1) facilitates the planning of the welfare budget; (2) provides an objective test of residency; (3) minimizes the opportunity for recipients fraudulently to receive payments from more than one Jurisdiction, and (4) encourages early entry of new residents into the labor force.

... [W]e reject appellants' argument that a mere showing of a rational relationship between the waiting period and these four admittedly permissible state objectives will suffice to justify the classification. . . .

We conclude therefore that appellants in these cases do not use and have no need to use the one-year requirement for the governmental purposes suggested. Thus, even under traditional equal protection tests, a classification of welfare applicants according to whether they have lived in the State for one year would seem irrational and unconstitutional. But, of course, the traditional criteria do not apply in these cases. Since the classification here touches on the fundamental right of interstate movement, its constitutionality must be judged by the stricter standard of whether it promotes a compelling state interest. Under this standard, the waiting period requirement clearly violates the Equal Protection Clause. . . .

Harlan, dissenting:

... The "compelling interest" doctrine, which today is articulated more explicitly than ever before, constitutes an increasingly significant exception to the long-established rule that a statute does not deny equal protection if it is rationally related to a legitimate governmental objective. The "compelling interest" doctrine has two branches. The branch which requires that classifications based upon "suspect" criteria be supported by a compelling interest apparently had its genesis in cases involving racial classifications, which have, at least since been regarded as inherently "suspect." The criterion of "wealth" apparently was added to the list of "suspects" as an alternative justification for the rationale in which Virginia's poll tax was struck down. The criterion of political allegiance may have been added in *Williams v. Rhodes.* Today the list apparently has been further enlarged to include classifications based upon recent interstate movement, and perhaps those based upon the exercise of any constitutional right. . . .

I think that this branch of the "compelling interest" doctrine is sound when applied to racial classifications, for, historically, the Equal Protection Clause was largely a product of the desire to eradicate legal distinctions founded upon race. However, I believe that the more recent extensions have been unwise. . . . I do not consider wealth a "suspect" statutory criterion. And when, as in *Williams v. Rhodes,* supra, and the present case, a classification is based upon the exercise of rights guaranteed against state infringement by the

Federal Constitution, then there is no need for any resort to the Equal Protection Clause; in such instances, this Court may properly and straightforwardly invalidate any undue burden upon those rights under the Fourteenth Amendment's Due Process Clause.

The second branch of the "compelling interest" principle is even more troublesome. For it has been held that a statutory classification is subject to the "compelling interest" test if the result of the classification may be to affect a "fundamental right," regardless of the basis of the classification. This rule . . . has reappeared today in the Court's cryptic suggestion that the "compelling interest" test is applicable merely because the result of the classification may be to deny the appellees "food, shelter, and other necessities of life," as well as in the Court's statement that, "[s]ince the classification here touches on the fundamental right of interstate movement, its constitutionality must be judged by the stricter standard of whether it promotes a compelling state interest."

I think this branch of the "compelling interest" doctrine particularly unfortunate and unnecessary. It is unfortunate because it creates an exception which threatens to swallow the standard equal protection rule. Virtually every state statute affects important rights. This Court has repeatedly held, for example, that the traditional equal protection standard is applicable to statutory classifications affecting such fundamental matters as the right to pursue a particular occupation, the right to receive greater or smaller wages or to work more or less hours, and the right to inherit property. Rights such as these are, in principle, indistinguishable from those involved here, and to extend the "compelling interest" rule to all cases in which such rights are affected would go far toward making this Court a "super-legislature." This branch of the doctrine is also unnecessary. When the right affected is one assured by the Federal Constitution, any infringement can be dealt with under the Due Process Clause. But when a statute affects only matters not mentioned in the Federal Constitution and is not arbitrary or irrational, I must reiterate that I know of nothing which entitles this Court to pick out particular human activities, characterize them as "fundamental," and give them added protection under an unusually stringent equal protection test. . . .

... If the issue is regarded purely as one of equal protection, then, for the reasons just set forth, this nonracial classification should be judged by ordinary equal protection standards. . . .

... Today's decision, it seems to me, reflects to an unusual degree the current notion that this Court possesses a peculiar wisdom all its own whose capacity to lead this Nation out of its present troubles is contained only by the limits of judicial ingenuity in contriving new constitutional principles to meet each problem as it arises. For anyone who, like myself, believes that it is an essential function of this Court to maintain the constitutional divisions between state and federal authority and among the three branches of the Federal Government, today's decision is a step in the wrong direction. This resurgence of the expansive view of "equal protection" carries the seeds of more judicial interference with the state and federal legislative process, much more indeed than does the judicial application of "due process" according to traditional concepts about which some members of this Court have expressed fears as to its potentialities for setting us judges "at large." I consider it particularly unfortunate that this judicial roadblock to the powers of Congress in this field should occur at the very threshold of the current discussions regarding the "federalizing" of these aspects of welfare relief.

San Antonio Independent School District v. Rodriguez

411 U.S. 1 (1973), 5-4
Opinion of the Court: Powell (Blackmun, Burger, Rehnquist)
Concurring: Stewart
Dissenting: Brennan, Douglas, Marshall, White

This was a class action on behalf of schoolchildren who were members of minority groups or were of poor families and lived in school districts that had low property tax bases. Texas financed its public schools through a combination of state and local sources. Nearly half the revenues came from a state program that provided basic minimum payments to all school districts. Each district supplemented this state aid through local property taxes. The class action alleged that reliance on local property taxation created substantial disparities among districts in per pupil expenditures because of the differences in the value of taxable property among the districts. A federal district court found that wealth was a "suspect" classification, that education was a "fundamental" right, and that the state made neither a showing of a compelling state interest in the system nor a rational basis for it.

What denial of a right is claimed in this case? Since financial means presumably affect educational opportunity,

why isn't classification by such means a "suspect" classification? How do Powell and Marshall disagree on the standard of review that should be applied to a "wealth classification"? Does anything in the Constitution or in the Court's previous interpretations of it impose an affirmative obligation on government to provide educational services or other basic public goods? If a state were to abolish its public schools, would that be discrimination based on relative wealth? Would it be constitutional?

Powell, for the Court:

... Texas virtually concedes that its historically rooted dual system of financing education could not withstand the strict judicial scrutiny that this Court has found appropriate in reviewing legislative judgments that interfere with fundamental constitutional rights or that involve suspect classifications. If, as previous decisions have indicated, strict scrutiny means that the State's system is not entitled to the usual presumption of validity, that the State, rather than the complainants, must carry a "heavy burden of justification," that the State must demonstrate that its educational system has been structured with "precision," and is "tailored" narrowly to serve legitimate objectives, and that it has selected the "less drastic means" for effectuating its objectives, the Texas financing system and its counterpart in virtually every other State will not pass muster. The State candidly admits that "[n]o one familiar with the Texas system would contend that it has yet achieved perfection." Apart from its concession that educational financing in Texas has "defects" and "imperfections," the State defends the system's rationality with vigor, and disputes the District Court's finding that it lacks a "reasonable basis."

This, then, establishes the framework for our analysis. We must decide, first, whether the Texas system of financing public education operates to the disadvantage of some suspect class or impinges upon a fundamental right explicitly or implicitly protected by the Constitution, thereby requiring strict judicial scrutiny. If so, the judgment of the District Court should be affirmed. If not, the Texas scheme must still be examined to determine whether it rationally furthers some legitimate, articulated state purpose, and therefore does not constitute an invidious discrimination in violation of the Equal Protection Clause of the Fourteenth Amendment.

The District Court's opinion does not reflect the novelty and complexity of the constitutional questions posed by appellees' challenge to Texas' system of school financing. In concluding that strict judicial scrutiny was required, that court relied on decisions dealing with the rights of indigents to equal treatment in the criminal trial and appellate processes, and on cases disapproving wealth restrictions on the right to vote. Those cases, the District Court concluded, established wealth as a suspect classification. Finding that the local property tax system discriminated on the basis of wealth, it regarded those precedents as controlling. It then reasoned, based on decisions of this Court affirming the undeniable importance of education, that there is a fundamental right to education, and that, absent some compelling state justification, the Texas system could not stand.

We are unable to agree that this case, which in significant aspects is sui generis, may be so neatly fitted into the conventional mosaic of constitutional analysis under the Equal Protection Clause. Indeed, for the several reasons that follow, we find neither the suspect classification nor the fundamental interest analysis persuasive.

The wealth discrimination discovered by the District Court in this case, and by several other courts that have recently struck down school financing laws in other States, is quite unlike any of the forms of wealth discrimination heretofore reviewed by this Court. Rather than focusing on the unique features of the alleged discrimination, the courts in these cases have virtually assumed their findings of a suspect classification through a simplistic process of analysis: since, under the traditional systems of financing public schools, some poorer people receive less expensive educations than other more affluent people, these systems discriminate on the basis of wealth. This approach largely ignores the hard threshold questions, including whether it makes a difference, for purposes of consideration under the Constitution, that the class of disadvantaged "poor" cannot be identified or defined in customary equal protection terms, and whether the relative—rather than absolute—nature of the asserted deprivation is of significant consequence. Before a State's laws and the justifications for the classifications they create are subjected to strict judicial scrutiny, we think these threshold considerations must be analyzed more closely than they were in the court below....

... First, in support of their charge that the system discriminates against the "poor," appellees have made no effort to demonstrate that it operates to the peculiar disadvantage of any class fairly definable as indigent, or as composed of persons whose incomes are beneath any designated poverty level. Indeed,

there is reason to believe that the poorest families are not necessarily clustered in the poorest property districts....

Second, neither appellees nor the District Court addressed the fact that, unlike each of the foregoing cases, lack of personal resources has not occasioned an absolute deprivation of the desired benefit. The argument here is not that the children in districts having relatively low assessable property values are receiving no public education; rather, it is that they are receiving a poorer quality education than that available to children in districts having more assessable wealth. Apart from the unsettled and disputed question whether the quality of education may be determined by the amount of money expended for it, a sufficient answer to appellees' argument is that, at least where wealth is involved, the Equal Protection Clause does not require absolute equality or precisely equal advantages....

For these two reasons—the absence of any evidence that the financing system discriminates against any definable category of "poor" people or that it results in the absolute deprivation of education—the disadvantaged class is not susceptible of identification in traditional terms....

... [I]t is clear that appellees' suit asks this Court to extend its most exacting scrutiny to review a system that allegedly discriminates against a large, diverse, and amorphous class, unified only by the common factor of residence in districts that happen to have less taxable wealth than other districts. The system of alleged discrimination and the class it defines have none of the traditional indicia of suspectness: the class is not saddled with such disabilities, or subjected to such a history of purposeful unequal treatment, or relegated to such a position of political powerlessness as to command extraordinary protection from the majoritarian political process.

We thus conclude that the Texas system does not operate to the peculiar disadvantage of any suspect class....

Nothing this Court holds today in any way detracts from our historic dedication to public education. We are in complete agreement with the conclusion of the three-judge panel below that "the grave significance of education both to the individual and to our society" cannot be doubted. But the importance of a service performed by the State does not determine whether it must be regarded as fundamental for purposes of examination under the Equal Protection Clause....

... It is not the province of this Court to create substantive constitutional rights in the name of guaranteeing equal protection of the laws. ...

Education, of course, is not among the rights afforded explicit protection under our Federal Constitution. Nor do we find any basis for saying it is implicitly so protected. ...

Even if it were conceded that some identifiable quantum of education is a constitutionally protected prerequisite to the meaningful exercise of [the freedoms of speech and press, and the right to vote], we have no indication that the present levels of educational expenditures in Texas provide an education that falls short. Whatever merit appellees' argument might have if a State's financing system occasioned an absolute denial of educational opportunities to any of its children, that argument provides no basis for finding an interference with fundamental rights where only relative differences in spending levels are involved and where—as is true in the present case—no charge fairly could be made that the system fails to provide each child with an opportunity to acquire the basic minimal skills necessary for the enjoyment of the rights of speech and of full participation in the political process. ...

Appellees further urge that the Texas system is unconstitutionally arbitrary because it allows the availability of local taxable resources to turn on "happenstance." ... But any scheme of local taxation—indeed the very existence of identifiable local governmental units—requires the establishment of jurisdictional boundaries that are inevitably arbitrary. It is equally inevitable that some localities are going to be blessed with more taxable assets than others. Nor is local wealth a static quantity. Changes in the level of taxable wealth within any district may result from any number of events, some of which local residents can and do influence. For instance, commercial and industrial enterprises may be encouraged to locate within a district by various actions—public and private.

Moreover, if local taxation for local expenditures were an unconstitutional method of providing for education, then it might be an equally impermissible means of providing other necessary services customarily financed largely from local property taxes, including local police and fire protection, public health and hospitals, and public utility facilities of various kinds. We perceive no justification for such a severe denigration of local property taxation and control as

would follow from appellees' contentions. It has simply never been within the constitutional prerogative of this Court to nullify state-wide measures for financing public services merely because the burdens or benefits thereof fall unevenly depending upon the relative wealth of the political subdivisions in which citizens live.

In sum, to the extent that the Texas system of school financing results in unequal expenditures between children who happen to reside in different districts, we cannot say that such disparities are the product of a system that is so irrational as to be invidiously discriminatory. ... We are unwilling to assume for ourselves a level of wisdom superior to that of legislators, scholars, and educational authorities in 50 States, especially where the alternatives proposed are only recently conceived and nowhere yet tested. The constitutional standard under the Equal Protection Clause is whether the challenged state action rationally furthers a legitimate state purpose or interest. We hold that the Texas plan abundantly satisfies this standard. ...

... We hardly need add that this Court's action today is not to be viewed as placing its judicial imprimatur on the status quo. The need is apparent for reform in tax systems which may well have relied too long and too heavily on the local property tax. And certainly innovative thinking as to public education, its methods, and its funding is necessary to assure both a higher level of quality and greater uniformity of opportunity. These matters merit the continued attention of the scholars who already have contributed much by their challenges. But the ultimate solutions must come from the lawmakers and from the democratic pressures of those who elect them.

Stewart, concurring:

... Unlike other provisions of the Constitution, the Equal Protection Clause confers no substantive rights and creates no substantive liberties. The function of the Equal Protection Clause, rather, is simply to measure the validity of classifications created by state laws.

There is hardly a law on the books that does not affect some people differently from others. But the basic concern of the Equal Protection Clause is with state legislation whose purpose or effect is to create discrete and objectively identifiable classes. And, with respect to such legislation, it has long been settled that the Equal Protection Clause is offended only by laws that are invidiously discriminatory—

only by classifications that are wholly arbitrary or capricious. . . .

Marshall, dissenting:

. . . [In the Court's] view, the Texas scheme must be tested by nothing more than that lenient standard of rationality which we have traditionally applied to discriminatory state action in the context of economic and commercial matters. By so doing, the Court avoids the telling task of searching for a substantial state interest which the Texas financing scheme, with its variations in taxable district property wealth, is necessary to further. I cannot accept such an emasculation of the Equal Protection Clause in the context of this case.

To begin, I must once more voice my disagreement with the Court's rigidified approach to equal protection analysis. The Court apparently seeks to establish today that equal protection cases fall into one of two neat categories which dictate the appropriate standard of review—strict scrutiny or mere rationality. But this Court's decisions in the field of equal protection defy such easy categorization. A principled reading of what this Court has done reveals that it has applied a spectrum of standards in reviewing discrimination allegedly violative of the Equal Protection Clause. This spectrum clearly comprehends variations in the degree of care with which the Court will scrutinize particular classifications, depending, I believe, on the constitutional and societal importance of the interest adversely affected and the recognized invidiousness of the basis upon which the particular classification is drawn. I find, in fact, that many of the Court's recent decisions embody the very sort of reasoned approach to equal protection analysis for which I previously argued—that is, an approach in which "concentration [is] placed upon the character of the classification in question, the relative importance to individuals in the class discriminated against of the governmental benefits that they do not receive, and the asserted state interests in support of the classification." *Dandridge v. Williams* (dissenting opinion).

I therefore cannot accept the majority's labored efforts to demonstrate that fundamental interests, which call for strict scrutiny of the challenged classification, encompass only established rights which we are somehow bound to recognize from the text of the Constitution itself. To be sure, some interests which the Court has deemed to be fundamental for purposes of equal protection analysis are themselves constitutionally protected rights. . . . But it will not do to suggest that the "answer" to whether an interest is fundamental for purposes of equal protection analysis is always determined by whether that interest "is a right . . . explicitly or implicitly guaranteed by the Constitution." . . .

The majority is, of course, correct when it suggests that the process of determining which interests are fundamental is a difficult one. But I do not think the problem is insurmountable. And I certainly do not accept the view that the process need necessarily degenerate into an unprincipled, subjective "picking-and-choosing" between various interests, or that it must involve this Court in creating "substantive constitutional rights in the name of guaranteeing equal protection of the laws." Although not all fundamental interests are constitutionally guaranteed, the determination of which interests are fundamental should be firmly rooted in the text of the Constitution. The task in every case should be to determine the extent to which constitutionally guaranteed rights are dependent on interests not mentioned in the Constitution. As the nexus between the specific constitutional guarantee and the nonconstitutional interest draws closer, the nonconstitutional interest becomes more fundamental and the degree of judicial scrutiny applied when the interest is infringed on a discriminatory basis must be adjusted accordingly. Thus, it cannot be denied that interests such as procreation, the exercise of the state franchise, and access to criminal appellate processes are not fully guaranteed to the citizen by our Constitution. But these interests have nonetheless been afforded special judicial consideration in the face of discrimination because they are, to some extent, interrelated with constitutional guarantees. Procreation is now understood to be important because of its interaction with the established constitutional right of privacy. The exercise of the state franchise is closely tied to basic civil and political rights inherent in the First Amendment. And access to criminal appellate processes enhances the integrity of the range of rights implicit in the Fourteenth Amendment guarantee of due process of law. Only if we closely protect the related interests from state discrimination do we ultimately ensure the integrity of the constitutional guarantee itself. This is the real lesson that must be taken from our previous decisions involving interests deemed to be fundamental. . . .

In summary, it seems to me inescapably clear that this Court has consistently adjusted the care with which it will review state discrimination in light of the constitutional significance of the interests affected and the invidiousness of the particular classification. . . .

. . . The majority suggests, however, that a variable standard of review would give this Court the appearance of a "super-legislature." I cannot agree. Such an approach seems to me a part of the guarantees of our Constitution and of the historic experiences with oppression of and discrimination against discrete, powerless minorities which underlie that document. In truth, the Court itself will be open to the criticism raised by the majority so long as it continues on its present course of effectively selecting in private which cases will be afforded special consideration without acknowledging the true basis of its action. . . .

As the Court points out, no previous decision has deemed the presence of just a wealth classification to be sufficient basis to call forth rigorous judicial scrutiny of allegedly discriminatory state action. That wealth classifications alone have not necessarily been considered to bear the same high degree of suspectness as have classifications based on, for instance, race or alienage may be explainable on a number of grounds. The "poor" may not be seen as politically powerless as certain discrete and insular minority groups. Personal poverty may entail much the same social stigma as historically attached to certain racial or ethnic groups. But personal poverty is not a permanent disability; its shackles may be escaped. Perhaps most importantly, though, personal wealth may not necessarily share the general irrelevance as a basis for legislative action that race or nationality is recognized to have. While the "poor" have frequently been a legally disadvantaged group, it cannot be ignored that social legislation must frequently take cognizance of the economic status of our citizens. Thus, we have generally gauged the invidiousness of wealth classifications with an awareness of the importance of the interests being affected and the relevance of personal wealth to those interests.

When evaluated with these considerations in mind, it seems to me that discrimination on the basis of group wealth in this case likewise calls for careful judicial scrutiny. . . .

10

VOTING AND REPRESENTATION

Democracy refers to popularly accountable government in which the will, choices, and preferences of the governed—"the people"—inform and control laws, policies, and programs. The chief means for this is representation. Except for such unusual devices as initiative, referendum, and the "town meeting," the people do not govern directly. For them to do so in any but the smallest body politic would be unwieldy and probably chaotic. Instead, democratic government is republican democracy in which the people are represented in government. This is mainly through elections, in which representatives—legislators, chief executives, and some judges—are chosen by popular vote among candidates offering competing views. For most citizens, the ballot is the chief way of participating in politics and government and for holding those in power accountable. Because of the importance of this popular check, constitutional democracies are usually careful to describe in their highest laws the mechanisms of voting, elections, and representation. In the United States, the individual's participatory rights rank as civil liberties secured by the First Amendment and subject to equal protection of the law.

The Right to Vote

As framed and ratified, the Constitution said little about voting and nowhere defined a right to vote. Though elective offices were created—senators, representatives, the president and vice president—only members of the House of Representatives were to be chosen by "the people of the several states," (Article I-2) that is, by popular vote. Senators were to be chosen by the legislature of each state, thus only indirectly by the people. The president was to be chosen by electors who alone were selected in each state "in such manner as the legislature thereof may direct." (Article II-1) Of voting for members of the House, the framers said only that eligibility should be the same as for members of the "most numerous branch of the state legislature." (Article I-2) Because the new Constitution shifted great power from the states to the national government, leaving voter qualifications to the states allowed the framers to avoid another contentious issue of states' rights. But it also meant there would be no constitutional or national definition of the right to vote and no uniform qualifications for voting in federal elections.

In the early years under the new government, the franchise—eligibility to vote—in the states was limited to a fraction of the adult population, mainly white males and, in many states, to only those holding property. Though unacceptable in a modern democracy, this attenuated eligibility still made the United States the most democratic nation of its time.

Property qualifications, never very exacting in most states and communities, were gradually dropped and all but disappeared by the Jacksonian era of the 1830s and 1840s. But it was not until after the Civil War that the Constitution was amended to address the right to vote for the first time. The Fifteenth Amendment expressly enfranchised former slaves and other black persons by declaring that the right to vote "shall not be denied or abridged . . . on account of race, color, or previous condition of servitude." The Fourteenth Amendment, ratified 18 months earlier, arguably guaranteed the right to those already enfranchised in declaring that no state "shall make or enforce any law which shall abridge the privileges and immunities of citizens of the US" or deny to anyone equal protection of the law.

During the next 100 years, the Constitution was amended three other times to extend the franchise. The Nineteenth Amendment, in 1920, gave women the right to vote. The Twenty-fourth, in 1964, outlawed the poll tax in federal elections, a device that had been used in many states to discourage poor black persons from voting. And the Twenty-sixth, in 1971, lowered the minimum voting age in all elections to 18.

As we have already seen, the Supreme Court in the Slaughterhouse Cases, 1873, quickly gave the privileges and immunities clause of the Fourteenth Amendment a narrow reading limiting its protection to the privileges and immunities of federal as opposed to state citizenship.

Two years later, in *Minor v. Happersett,* on the issue of a state's denial of the vote to women, it expressly held that the right to vote was not a privilege of federal citizenship.

Race Discrimination

Though the Fifteenth Amendment appeared straightforward in its guarantee of voting rights free of racial discrimination, the Supreme Court soon gave it a narrow interpretation as well. In *United States v. Reese,* 1876, its first reading of the amendment, it held it not to confer voting rights but only the right to be free of discrimination in voting. The Court declined to sustain an indictment of a local election official who had refused to count a black person's vote, because the charge failed to allege his action had been racially motivated. The decision sent the Court down a path of cramped interpretation of the amendment and of legislation designed to give it effect. This let the former Confederate states hold down black voting through such devices as white-only primaries, poll taxes, and literacy tests that were often fraudulently administered, besides the resort to intimidation and violence. Eventually, in *Smith v. Allwright,* 1944, the Court held that in conducting white-only primaries in one-party Southern states, the Democratic party acted not simply as a private organization but as an agent for the state; in such role, it violated the Fifteenth Amendment. The ruling, however, did little to dent widespread Southern disenfranchisement of black persons.

Not until the Voting Rights Act of 1965, passed during the civil rights movement, was substantial headway made against voting discrimination. Rather than relying on individual complaints of voter discrimination as earlier legislation had, the act dealt with discrimination systemically. For Southern states in which less than half the voting age population was registered, it authorized appointment of federal election supervisors and required that any new voting laws enacted in those states be first approved by the U. S. Attorney General or the U. S. District Court for the District of Columbia. These provisions were upheld by the Court in *South Carolina v. Katzenbach,* 1966.

A year before the Voting Rights Act, ratification of the Twenty-fourth Amendment had outlawed poll taxes in federal elections. In *Harper v. Virginia Board of Education,* 1966, the Supreme Court carried the amendment's principle to state and local elections, ruling that Virginia's annual $1.50 fee violated the equal protection clause of the Fourteenth Amendment.

The Voting Rights Act was amended in 1970 to suspend literacy tests throughout the nation for seven years. This was upheld by the Supreme Court in *Oregon v. Mitchell,* the same year, on Congress's power to enforce the Fifteenth Amendment. In 1975, the act was amended to make ban on such tests permanent. The 1975 changes enlarged the definition of disenfranchisement to include use of English-only ballots in areas with large non-English speaking populations. The Voting Rights Act has been one of the most effective civil rights laws in history. Within four years of its passage almost a million black persons not before registered became eligible to vote in the eight Southern states to which it originally applied.

Other Issues

The Court has long held that states can set residency requirements for voting (*Lassiter v. Northampton County Board of Elections,* 1959), but states may not disenfranchise newcomers indefinitely as Texas tried to do with military personnel who had moved to the state, without violating equal protection. (*Carrington v. Rash,* 1965) In the 1970 Voting Rights Act amendment, all voter residency requirements in presidential elections were abolished. In *Dunn v. Blumstein* two years later, the Court invalidated a Tennessee law that had placed a one-year residency requirement before a newcomer could vote in a state election. It found the rule an unreasonable impairment of the rights to vote and of interstate travel. Shorter requirements, such as 50 days, have been upheld as a reasonable way to verify voter lists and prevent fraud. (*Marston v. Lewis* and *Burns v. Fortson,* both 1973)

The Court has looked closely at voting qualifications based on property. In *Kramer v. Union Free School District,* 1979, it struck down a New York law

President Lyndon Johnson signs the Voting Rights Act, August 6, 1965.

The Right to Have One's Vote *Re*counted Equally

The one-person, one-vote principle that votes be weighed equally received a dramatic new application from the Supreme Court in *Bush v. Gore,* the Florida recount case that effectively ended the drawn-out 2000 presidential election. The national contest between George W. Bush, the Republican candidate, and Albert Gore, the Democrat, was so closely divided in the electoral vote that the outcome on election night, November 7, depended on who had won Florida's 25 electors. But the popular vote in that state was virtually even, though official returns based on machine counting of ballots showed Bush held a paper-thin lead.

Gore contested the count. In the days following the election he succeeded in getting full or partial recounts in three counties, though the results did not have much effect on Bush's lead. Eventually Gore won an order from the Florida Supreme Court on December 8 that all "undervotes" be manually recounted throughout the state. Virtually all votes in Florida had been cast by voters perforating punch cards with a stylus. The cards were "read" by machines on election night and those not clearly perforated for either Bush or Gore or any other presidential candidate—undervotes—or appearing to be perforated for two or more candidates—overvotes—were routinely rejected. In many instances, the punched out part of the card—a "chad"—was still attached by one or more of its corners; in other instances, that part of the card was merely indented, that is, not punched through at all. Normally, such votes are considered ambiguous or "spoiled" and are not included in election night tallies.

In its decision, the Florida Supreme Court, divided 4-3, ordered that undervotes—approximately 50,000—be manually counted in 60 of the state's 67 counties (hand recounting already done in seven was ordered accepted) to determine "the intent of the voter." More exact standards for determining this intent were left to each of the county canvassing boards to develop. Bush immediately appealed to the United States Supreme Court, which heard oral argument on December 11 and handed down an unsigned per curiam decision the following night (p. 593).

Voting 7-2, it found the recount order to violate the equal protection clause. The majority opinion, very likely written by Justice O'Connor or Justice Kennedy, held that it did not "satisfy the minimum requirement for non-arbitrary treatment of voters necessary to secure a fundamental right." The Court objected not to the "intent of the voter" standard but to its application. By allowing each county board to decide how it was to be applied, the recount order failed to provide a uniform standard. It was also faulty in failing to include overvotes and in accepting the recounted votes already made in counties using different standards. "When a court orders a statewide remedy," the Court said, "there must be at least some assurance that the rudimentary requirements of equal treatment and fundamental fairness are satisfied."

The case was complicated throughout by urgency. Not only did the nation not know for certain who the next president would be five weeks after the election, there were also two looming federal statutory deadlines. One was December 12 itself, the last day given to state legislatures for resolving disputes over state electors if a state's electoral vote was to be counted in the national tally without constitutional challenge (the so-called safe harbor provision). The other was December 18, the day elected presidential electors in the nation meet in their state capitals to formally cast their ballots.

Five justices in the majority—Rehnquist, O'Connor, Scalia, Kennedy, and Thomas—noting that only hours remained before the December 12 deadline passed, voted simply to reverse the Florida Supreme Court, leaving Bush the winner of the election by roughly his election night margin. Two others—David Souter and Stephen Breyer—citing the December 18 deadline, voted to remand the case to the state court with instructions to continue the recount under uniform standards. They admitted that completing a laborious statewide manual recount of more than 150,000 votes in six days, however, would be "a tall order."

Three justices in the majority—Rehnquist, Scalia, and Thomas—argued in a concurring opinion that by ordering a hand recount and by earlier changing the deadline for certification of the state's vote, the Florida Supreme Court had also violated Article II-1 of the Constitution which specifies that it is the state legislature, not the judiciary, that decides "the manner" of choosing electors.

Justices John Paul Stevens and Ruth Ginsberg, who joined the dissenting views of Souter and Breyer on the remand question, also dissented on the constitutional issue, finding no violation of equal protection in the lack of uniform standards, the procedures for recounting, or acceptance of recounting already completed. Noting that in the past

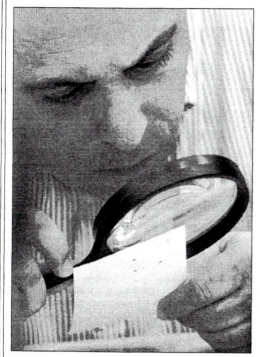

Looking for the president.

the Court found equal protection violations where individual votes were weighed unequally, Stevens observed, "But we have never before called into question the substantive standard by which a state determines that a vote has been legally cast." The majority opinion, he said, ordered "the disenfranchisement of an unknown number of voters whose ballots reveal their intent . . . but were for some reason rejected by the ballot counting machines."

Full implications of the decision for the election process are not yet clear. Though the majority opinion said it was "limited to the present circumstances," it extends equal protection principles to a new area. How far this may carry will await new elections and the challenges that may arise from them. If given wide application, the decision could change the mechanics of voting and give the federal courts a supervisory role in the state and local ballot counting.

An independent audit of all undervotes, commissioned by a media consortium in the weeks following the decision, produced some surprising results. Had the Florida Supreme Court's recount order been allowed to stand and had the recounting applied the most liberal standards, that is, the most inclusive for counting hanging chads and indentations—favored by Gore but opposed by Bush—the result would have produced net gains for Bush, increasing his certified 537 vote lead to 1,665. But if the most restrictive and least inclusive standards were applied, Gore would have had a net lead of three votes. The findings, which attest to the importance of uniform standards, are a final, ironic twist to the closest presidential election in history and to one of the Supreme Court's most controversial decisions.

that required residents of a school district to have children in the district's schools or own or lease taxable property before being eligible to vote for school board members. Applying strict scrutiny to the restriction of a fundamental right, it ruled the law denied equal protection by excluding some persons who might have an interest in school affairs but including others whose interest might be only "remote and indirect." Though the Court has not completely ruled out property requirements in special interest elections, for example,

that of landowning in a water storage district election (*Sayler Land Company v. Tulare Lake Basin Water Storage District,* 1973), it struck down such requirement for voting on local bond issues because the state failed to show a compelling interest in the limitation. (*Hill v. Stone,* 1975)

The Court has upheld state laws denying the right to vote to convicted, unpardoned felons even if their jail term has been served. (*Green v. New York City Board of Elections,* 1968) However, such laws cannot be sustained if shown to be motivated by racial discrimination. (*Hunter v. Underwood,* 1985)

Representation

The right to vote gives rise to another constitutional issue: the right to have one's vote weighed equally on the electoral scales. In representative government it is possible for certain sectors of the population or electorate to become over- or underrepresented. This can happen because of the electoral structure used or because population shifts are ignored in apportioning seats. Before examining how these circumstances may confound the equality principle, two observations are in order.

First, the Constitution itself recognizes unequal representation in its creation of the Senate. Because each state has two Senators, voters in small states are overrepresented and those in large, underrepresented. The difference in population between, for example, California, the most populous state, and Wyoming, the least, is 70 to 1. Yet they are represented equally in the Senate. This constitutional recognition of unequal representation was part of the grand compromise between the small states and the large states that probably kept the Constitutional Convention from breaking up and, later, essential to gaining ratification for the Constitution. Important though it was, it was a product of pragmatic politics, not political theory or philosophy.

Second, though some states had used factors other than population for representation in their upper legislative house, all popularly apportioned their lower house (Nebraska, the only state with a unicameral legislature, based apportionment of seats on population). Yet districts that may once have had roughly equal numbers of voters could become the source of unequal representation as population shifted from some areas of a state to others or, with new entrants, simply grew more rapidly in some areas than others.

In the late nineteenth and early twentieth centuries, social and economic changes resulted in urban areas growing faster than rural and, in the late twentieth century, suburban areas growing faster than either. The solution to such recurrent inequality is reapportionment—the periodic redrawing of legislative districts to reflect demographic changes and so maintain the general equality principle in representation. Usually this meant a loss of some legislative seats by rural areas and gains for urban and suburban ones. Several states undertook periodic reapportioning (as did Congress at the federal level for the House of Representatives). Some states, however, had only weak provisions or none at all, and many state legislatures did not act to reapportion periodically. Incumbent legislators from rural areas that stood to lose seats understandably had little enthusiasm for redrawing district lines. In many states, years of failing to reapportion produced egregious malapportionment as population disparities among legislative districts worsened.

The Path to One Person, One Vote

When the Supreme Court first ruled on apportionment in *Colegrove v. Green,* 1946, it held Illinois's failure to redraw its Congressional districts was a "political question," not suited for judicial determination and best left to the legislature alone, even though the districts had a nine to one population disparity between largest and smallest and had not been reapportioned in more than 40 years.

Sixteen years later in *Baker v. Carr,* the Court took a different view. Malapportionment claims were held to raise constitutionally justiciable issues of equal protection and thus were not intrinsically political questions. The case grew out of a challenge to Tennessee's failure to reapportion since 1901, even though the state's constitution called for the legislature redraw its districts after each decennial census. A majority of six justices rejected Justice Felix Frankfurter's dissenting view that the remedy for legislative inaction lay not in the courts but in an aroused "public conscience." Nor did the majority think the courts would be forced to choose, as Frankfurter contended, "among competing bases of representation—

ultimately . . . among competing theories of political philosophy." Though Justice William Brennan's majority opinion did not reach the merits of the challenge to Tennessee's inaction—that question was returned to the lower courts—it opened legislative districting to constitutional attack and judicial review in nearly every state because in few was it free of substantial population disparity. Within a year, in an astonishing spate of litigation, 36 states were defendants in apportionment lawsuits.

The issue quickly returned to the Supreme Court on its merits. In *Gray v. Sanders,* a year after *Baker,* the Court invalidated Georgia's use of a county-unit system in primary elections. Requiring that a winning candidate carry a certain number of counties, the system worked to give votes in thinly populated counties greater weight than those from more populous ones, making it possible that a candidate might win the popular vote yet not be elected. The Court rejected analogies to the electoral college system in presidential voting and held that all votes in a statewide election must be given equal effect. The general standard under the equal protection clause, Justice William O. Douglas said, in a phrase that was to become a household term, was "one person, one vote."

But how strictly should such a standard to be applied? And would it hold for congressional districts and those of state legislatures? The Court began to answer these questions in three cases decided the following year. *Wesberry v. Sanders* (p. 598) held that a 3-1 population disparity among Georgia's 10 congressional districts, the result of failure to reapportion in more than 30 years violated Article I-2. That provision, requiring the House of Representatives "be composed of members chosen every second year by the people of the several states," could be satisfied, the Court said, only if every person's vote in a congressional election was "worth as much as another's." As nearly as practicable, districts must be equal in population, though there is little evidence this was the framers' intent in drafting Article I-2 and though Congress point-

edly omitted the requirement in its apportioning of seats among the 50 states after each decennial census.

The second 1964 case, *Reynolds v. Sims* (p. 602), was more controversial still and its impact more far-reaching. To meet the requirements of equal protection, both houses of bicameral state legislatures must be based on general numerical equality. Though specifically rejecting the analogy of the U.S. Senate, Chief Justice Earl Warren held that some departure from precisely equal districts might be made if it rested on "legitimate considerations incident to the effectuation of a rational state policy." Because more than 40 state legislatures had substantial population disparity in the apportionment of one or both houses, the Reynolds decision called for extensive redistricting and sealed a shift in power from rural toward urban areas.

In the third case, the Court made it clear that it would require application of the one-person, one-vote standard even if voters in a state overwhelmingly chose to have a different one. Two years before, Colorado, amending its constitution through a popular initiative that won a majority in every county in the state, created a lower legislative house based on population and an upper mainly on population but also giving weight to geographical considerations. In *Lucas v. Forty-fourth General Assembly of Colorado,* the Court struck it down as a violation of equal protection.

These cases left new unanswered questions in the "political thicket" the Court had entered. What, if anything, would allow departure from a strict population standard? What would be an acceptable statistical deviation from precise mathematical equality? Would the Court continue to make a distinction between congressional districts and those of the state legislatures? And, finally, would the one-person, one-vote principle apply to local government?

Though refusing to embrace an exact mathematical standard of equality in *Kirkpatrick v. Preisler,* 1969, the Court struck down Missouri's reapportioned congressional districts that had only a 1.6 percent population deviation because the state had not made a "good faith" effort to draw more equally. In the later 1983 case of *Karcher v. Daggett,* it reaffirmed an exacting standard for congressional redistricting, invalidating New Jersey's plan that had only seven-tenths of 1 percent disparity between largest and smallest districts. The plan did not meet the good faith test because the state failed to show why it rejected a different plan effecting for even greater equality.

The Court has shown greater tolerance for disparity in state legislative districts, upholding variations much larger than those found wanting in *Kirkpatrick* and *Karcher.* In *White v. Regester,* 1973, a variance of 9.9 percent was upheld as *de minimus,* that is, the largest needing no state justification and shifting the burden of proof to the plaintiffs that equal protection principles were violated. In unusual circumstances, the Court has been willing to tolerate variations well beyond the 10 percent rationale. In *Mahan v. Howell,* 1973, for example, it sustained a Virginia plan with a variation of 16.4 percent, because of the state's preference for following city and county boundaries. Wyoming's redistricting plan after the 1980 census had a variation of 89 percent, mainly the result of representation being given to an isolated and thinly populated county that would otherwise have had no voice in the state legislature. It was upheld in *Brown v. Thomson,* 1983, decided the same day that the Karcher case had rejected a 1 percent *de minimus* standard for congressional redistricting.

The Court applied the one-person, one-vote principle to school board and other local elections in which persons are popularly chosen "to perform government functions." (*Hadley v. Junior College District of Metropolitan Kansas City, Missouri,* 1970) Under this rule, it struck down New York City's system for choosing members of its Board of Estimate in which each of the city's five boroughs had equal representation though they had substantially unequal populations.

(*Board of Estimate of New York City v. Morris,* 1989) The Court has made a narrow exception for certain special purpose elections, such as those for water district boards whose decisions disproportionately affect landowners. (*Salyer Land Company v. Tulare Lake Basin Water Storage District,* 1973)

The one-person, one-vote principle now results in routine redistricting after each decennial census if population shifts have created inequalities. This "revolution" led Chief Justice Warren to say in retirement that he believed *Baker v. Carr,* which opened the door to judicial review of malapportionment, to be the most important decision of his tenure, a striking testament given that the Court he led left a record of unparalleled expansion in almost all areas of civil liberties and civil rights.

Multimember Districts

The one-person, one-vote prescription requiring voting districts be largely equal in population, says nothing about the structure of those districts. Voting strength, measured by party, race, ethnic group, or other collective identification, can be diluted or concentrated even though election districts are substantially equal in population.

Where multimember districts are used, districts tend to be fewer but larger even though the seats each has depends on population. All seats are filled in an "at-large" election within the district, in the same way that each of a state's two U.S. senators are elected by voters statewide though at different times. The at-large election may allow a dominant majority in the district to win all the seats and keep an opposed minority from winning any, even though the minority might have been able to elect at least some representatives had the district been broken down into several smaller single-member units. If the important majority/minority division rests, at least in part, on inherent characteristics such as race or ethnicity rather than one simply fluctuating on issues, equal protection questions may arise.

The Supreme Court has held multimember districts not to violate equal protection per se (*Whitcomb v. Chavis*, 1971), but it has struck them down where plaintiffs could show the arrangement was intended to disadvantage black or Mexican-American voters. (*White v. Regester*, 1973) Yet in *Mobile v. Bolden*, 1980, in which an Alabama city used multimember districts and an at-large election to choose the city's governing commission, the Court held that merely showing the scheme reduced electoral strength of the city's black voters did not establish a constitutional violation without proof of discriminatory intent.

Because such intent is often difficult to prove, Congress amended the 1965 Voting Rights Act, two years later, to change the evidentiary standard to the much easier one of effect, for plaintiffs who challenge redistricting plans as racially biased. Under the new provision, the Court struck down a North Carolina plan in *Thornburg v. Gingles* but, in doing so, gave the standard a complex turn. Plaintiffs would need to prove that substantial racial bloc voting existed and that a bloc-voting majority was usually able to "defeat candidates supported by a politically cohesive, geographically insular minority group." [478 U.S. 30 at 49, 1986]

Gerrymanders

The population equality requirement of equal protection does not say which persons are to be included in which districts. Drawing district boundaries to concentrate opposition party strength in as few districts as possible and so spread one's own strength to win more seats is one of the oldest stratagems in American electoral politics. In its most egregious form it has produced districts of bizarre shapes often having little or no geographical contiguity. Such districts are gerrymanders, named for a salamander-shaped electoral district drawn up in Massachusetts in 1812, the inspiration of the state's governor Elbridge Gerry.

In its historical avoidance of electoral issues, the Supreme Court did not rule on the constitutionality of district shaping until *Gomillion v. Lightfoot,* 1960 (p. 605), in which it unanimously struck down a recasting of the city lines of Tuskegee, Ala., that had produced "an uncouth 28-sided figure." The new lines excluded all but a half dozen black voters and the prestigious all-black Tuskegee Institute but included almost every white voter. Though the ruling was based on the Fifteenth Amendment, the voiding of the law singling out "a readily isolated segment of a racial minority for special discriminatory treatment," opened the door for *Baker v. Carr,* two years later, and the use of the equal protection clause of the Fourteenth Amendment to gauge the fairness of electoral districting.

Still, the Court remained cautious in its Fourteenth Amendment review of district shaping for good reason. First, unlike the simple one-person, one-vote principle that required population equality, there is no ready simple standard to judge the fairness of district shape. Second, even the most fair-minded redrawing of districts probably puts some groups of voters in a weaker position than they were before and others in a stronger. For example, to create two largely black state assembly districts, a New York redistricting plan divided a sizable Hasidic Jewish community, formerly a powerful voting group living mainly in one district, almost evenly between the two new districts. In *United Jewish Organizations of Williamsburgh v. Carey,* 1977, the Court rejected the plaintiffs' claim that the express creation of black-majority districts and the resulting weakening of Hasidim voting power rose to a constitutional violation of the rights of voters in the Jewish community.

Caution was evident again in *Davis v. Bandemer,* 1986, in which the Court dealt with the more typical gerrymandering resulting from the reapportionment jockeying of Republicans and Democrats for partisan political advantage that follows each decennial census. Democrats in Indiana objected to a redistricting plan drawn up by the Republican-controlled legislature that had put Democratic voting strength at a disadvantage by creation of several stretched districts. Though the Court held political gerrymandering a justiciable issue, it did not find that the state's plan had been drawn up against a background of "continued frustration of the will of a majority of the voters or a denial to a minority of voters of a fair chance to influence the political process." [478 U.S. 109 at 133]

In the reapportioning that followed the 1990 census, many states tried to increase the number of elected black representatives by creating districts in which there were majorities of black voters. These "majority-minority" districts were generally favored by an unusual alliance of black groups and Republicans. The last, though possibly believing more black legislators was desirable, also saw that by concentrating black voters, who have voted heavily Democratic since the days of the New Deal, Democratic strength would be diluted in the other districts. These plans were generally opposed by white Democratic interests.

The matter first came to the Court in *Shaw v. Reno*, 1993 (p. 667), a challenge to North Carolina's reapportioning of its congressional districts that created two majority-minority districts supposedly to ensure that two of the state's representatives would be African Americans. But the two districts were among the most egregiously shaped in the history of gerrymandering. The 1st encompassed 8 counties starting in the northeastern part of the state and then spreading out into parts of 20 others. The 12th was mainly a narrow, twisting line, 160 miles long and in many places less than three or four miles wide, winding through parts of 10 counties. The plaintiffs in the case, Shaw and five other white voters, argued that such racial redistricting violated equal protection. The Supreme Court, 5-4, decided only that the case, which had been dis-

missed by a lower court, presented a justiciable issue. It then remanded it with instructions that a strict scrutiny standard be applied, meaning the state would need to show a compelling interest for drawing the two districts the way it had.

It did not take long for the issue to return to the Court on its merits. The case was *Miller v. Johnson*, 1995 (p. 610), brought by five white voters in Georgia's new 11th Congressional district that had been redrawn after the 1990 census to have a 60 percent black majority. Though not so extremely shaped as North Carolina's 12th district, it did stretch across the middle of the state from a part of Atlanta in the northwest to the South Carolina border in the east, dividing several counties and cities along the way, so that many mostly black rural and urban areas could be included. The same five-member majority of *Shaw v. Reno*—Justices Rehnquist, O'Connor, Scalia, Kennedy, and Thomas—held such districting was not needed to comply with the intent of the Voting Rights Act to safeguard the right of minorities to vote. That being so, the state had no compelling reason for "carving electorates into racial blocs." (Rep. Cynthia McKinney, an African American, who was elected in the 11th district before the decision, easily won reelection in the same district when it was redrawn and became 58 percent white.)

A year after the Georgia decision, the North Carolina districting of *Shaw v. Reno* returned to the Court on its merits in *Shaw v. Hunt* and was struck down by the same 5-4 division of the Court. The state did not show that past discrimination against blacks gave it a compelling interest now to segregate voters by race and ignore compactness, contiguity, and the traditional boundaries of political subdivisions.

In the last 20 years, with or without majority-minority districts, the number of black representatives in the House has risen more than 85 percent and Hispanic representatives more than 70 percent.

Candidacies and Terms

Because the Constitution makes no mention of candidacy for federal elective office beyond setting out qualifications of age, residence, and citizenship and, for the president, native birth, and says nothing whatever about a right to be a candidate, the states are left free to regulate most aspects of elections. Accordingly they have imposed various restrictions on running for office including those of residency, property ownership, filing fee payment, and a showing of minimum voter support. Different state interests are evident in these regulations, including preventing fragmentation of the vote that might keep winning candidates from getting a majority, discouraging frivolous candidacies, minimizing voter confusion, and generally maintaining electoral stability and integrity.

Starting in the late 1960s, however, the Supreme Court began applying its expansive equal protection principles and First Amendment protections to electoral matters to review restrictions on candidacies. Though the Court has not declared the right of candidacy to be "fundamental," it has sometimes applied a strict scrutiny review to have states show a compelling interest to justify their restrictions. In other cases, it has used a balancing test, insisting only that states have a rational basis for what they do.

The most burdensome requirement is the showing of minimum voter support. This restriction, of course, also works to favor candidates of the two major parties. The matter first came to the Court in *Williams v. Rhodes*, 1968, in which members of a minor party challenged Ohio's requirement that a party offering candidates first get petition signatures equal to 15 percent of voters in the last gubernatorial election—at the time, about 400,000—unless it got 10 percent of the vote in the last election. Applying the strict scrutiny standard, the Court held the regulations hindered the fundamental rights to vote and associate and also violated the equal protection clause by putting a heavier burden on third parties than on Republicans and Democrats. A

year later in *Moore v. Ogilvie*, the Court struck down an Illinois law that required independent candidates for president to file petitions with the signatures of 25,000 qualified voters, at least 200 of which had to come from each of 50 of the state's 102 counties. The Court held that the law, earlier sustained in the pre-*Baker v. Carr* era (*MacDougall v. Green*, 1948), discriminated against more populous counties and thus violated the one-person, one vote principle.

But not all demonstrated support requirements are unconstitutional. In *Jenness v. Fortson*, 1971, the Court sustained a Georgia rule that candidates not winning a primary election get signatures of 5 percent of the qualified voters in the last election. Observing the requirement did not "freeze the status quo," it distinguished it from the more "suffocating" 15 percent provision struck down in *Williams v. Rhodes*. But demonstrated support requirements may not narrowly limit the time allowed for getting petition signatures, for example, to 24 days. [*Storer v. Brown*, 1974] Nor may a state set a filing deadline eight months before the general election for candidates not belonging to a major party. [*Anderson v. Celebrezze*, 1983]

Financial means or property ownership generally may not be used to qualify candidacies. In *Bullock v. Carter*, 1972, the Court sustained a challenge to Texas's requirement that candidates for local office pay filing fees up to $8,900 to run. Because the fee might keep indigent candidates off the ballot, it narrowed the choices that voters had and thus their fundamental right to vote. The Court acknowledged the rational basis for fees as a way of offsetting the cost of elections, but found them not necessary to that end, that is, not a compelling interest called for by a strict scrutiny review. Unless the state had a different way for otherwise qualified candidates to get on the ballot, unusually high fees violated the equal protection. Similarly, the Court found a California filing fee equal to 2 percent of the annual salary of the office sought—here, $701.60 for Los Angeles county commissioner—though reasonable, was a denial of equal protection if applied to indigent candidates. (*Lubin v. Panish*, 1974)

Requirements that candidates be property owners to run for a local school board or be eligible for appointment to an advisory agency of local government, have been invalidated. (*Turner v. Fouche*, 1970; *Quinn v. Millsap*, 1989) Strict scrutiny did not need to be applied in these cases because the Court found no rational relation of property ownership and knowledge of local or community issues.

Except for the Twenty-second Amendment limiting presidential eligibility to two elected terms, the Constitution is silent about how often an incumbent may run for reelection. However, concern about long and entrenched holding of power by individual elected officials was the force behind the term limits movement of the 1990s. The electoral advantages of incumbency have often led to legislative reelection rates of 90 percent or more. As a result, several states imposed limits on the terms state legislators and members of the House of Representatives might serve (a few states had already set term limits for their governors). A challenge to efforts to limit the terms of House members came to the Court in *United States Term Limits v. Thornton*, 1995. The Court held that Article I-4 allowing states to prescribe the "times, places, and manner" of congressional elections did not empower them—Arkansas, in this case—to add qualifications for membership in the House to the ones of age, citizenship, and residence already set out in Article I-2. The decision, which did not address equal protection issues, did not affect a state's power to set term limits for state and local offices.

Campaigns

Voting and candidacy are not the only ways of participating in elections. Promoting candidates or generally trying to influence voters in the choices they make—campaigning—is an important part of democratic politics. Restrictions on campaigns may raise First Amendment issues of the freedoms of speech, press, and association.

This was evident, for example, in *Talley v. California*, 1960, in which the Court struck down a Los Angeles ordinance requiring that campaign pamphlets bear the name and address of the person preparing, sponsoring, or distributing them, as a violation of freedom of expression. Similarly, in the more recent *McIntyre v. Ohio Elections Commission*, 1995, it held unconstitutional the state's ban on anonymous campaign literature, a restriction in effect in 48 other states. "Anonymous pamphleteering," the Court said, "is not a pernicious, fraudulent practice, but an honorable tradition of advocacy and dissent . . . a shield from the tyranny of the majority." On the other hand, the Court has recognized a state's interest in conducting orderly elections and has routinely upheld restrictions on the display or distribution of campaign materials or the solicitation of voters at or near polling places on election day. (*Burson v. Freeman*, 1992)

Many states in which some or all judges are elected have placed limits on what judicial candidates can say about current issues during their campaigns. Typical of these was a canon of judicial conduct adopted by the Minnesota Supreme Court that barred a judicial candidate from "announcing his or her views on disputed legal or political issues." Known as the "announce rule," it was held to violate a candidate's freedom of speech in *Republican Party of Minnesota v. White*, 2002. In writing for a majority of five, Justice Antonin Scalia held the rule not "narrowly tailored" enough to serve the state's interest of promoting impartiality or the appearance of impartiality of the judiciary. If that impartiality meant "having no views on the law," it was not a compelling state interest at all. In a dissenting opinion, Justice Ginsburg argued that judicial elections were different from those of the legislature and executive. Judges "do not sit as representatives of particular persons, communities or parties; they serve no faction or constituency." (Another part of the "announce rule" that barred judicial candidates from pledging to decide a legal issue in a certain way was not at issue in the case.)

The most important issues to arise about campaigns and ones most difficult for the Court are those of campaign finance. The matter has become acute in recent years as the cost of campaigning, particularly the use of the media as the chief campaign vehicle, has skyrocketed. High costs not only give well-financed candidates important advantages, they compel almost perpetual fund-raising by those who are elected, often distracting them from the tasks of their office, to say nothing of creating "debts" to big contributors.

After several half-hearted efforts to rein in campaign spending, Congress enacted bold measures in the Federal Election Campaign Act of 1971, amended further in 1974, placing limits on both contributions and spending. Individuals and groups could not contribute more than $1,000 to a candidate and political committees not more than $5,000. Annual contributions by an individual were limited to $25,000. Individuals and groups were also limited to $1,000 in what they could spend on behalf of a candidate. Candidates were limited in what they might spend on their own campaigns. The act also called for political committees to disclose the identity of contributors.

These provisions were at issue in *Buckley v. Valeo*, 1976 (p. 614), a fragmented decision issued per curiam in which five concurring and dissenting opinions were written. The Court upheld the campaign act's limits on contributions and its disclosure requirements, but struck down the spending provisions. Restricting the amount a person or group could spend on political communication during a campaign violated the First Amendment by reducing "the quantity of expression by restricting the number of issues discussed, the depth of their explication and the size of the audience reached." The Court acknowledged that contribution limits and the disclosure requirement also raised First Amendment issues, but found the infringements justified by the government's interest in preventing corruption and the appearance of undue influence.

In later cases, the Court has generally maintained the distinction between contributions and spending and has not applied the equality principle to either. Spending by political parties on their own for individual candidates cannot be restricted (*Colorado Republican Party v. Federal Elections Commission*, 1996), but contributions by individuals and groups to candidates for state offices can. (*Nixon v. Shrink Missouri Government Political Action Committee*, 2000)

In *Federal Election Commission v. National Conservative Political Action Committee*, 1985, the Court held invalid a section of the Presidential Election Campaign Fund Act that barred independent PACs from spending more than $1,000 on behalf of presidential candidates who chose to receive public campaign funding. Independent PAC spending was not "contributions" and thus not protected by the First Amendment. Limiting spending to $1,000, the Court said, was "much like allowing a speaker in a public hall to express his views while denying him use of an amplifying system." [470 U.S. 480 at 493]

The Court has also made a distinction between contributions to a candidate and contributions to advance an issue. In *Citizens Against Rent Control/Coalition for Fair Housing v. Berkeley*, 1981, it held that a city's attempt to place a $250 limit on individual contributions to groups taking a position on a referendum issue, violated contributors' First Amendment rights. Similarly on First Amendment grounds, the Court struck down a state law that made it illegal to pay persons for circulating petitions to get an issue on the ballot. (*Meyer v. Grant*, 1988)

Corporate campaign activity presents special problems, but the Court has continued to apply the contribution/spending distinction. In *First National Bank of Boston v. Bellotti*, 1978, it held that a state may not bar corporations from spending to influence the outcome of a referendum, in this case one proposing a graduated income tax. The Court affirmed that corporations have free speech rights, noting that "the inherent worth of the speech in terms of its capacity for informing the public does not depend on the identify of its source." [435 U.S. 765 at 777] Similarly, the

Court has upheld the right of a "pro life" organization to publish a newsletter urging voters to support an anti-abortion candidate in an upcoming primary election. (*Federal Elections Commission v. Massachusetts Citizens for Life, Inc.,* 1986) But a state may bar an organization, such as a local chamber of commerce, from spending for a candidate unless the money was voluntarily contributed for political use rather than taken from the organization's general treasury. (*Austin v. Michigan Chamber of Commerce,* 1990)

Campaign financing presents a clash of democratic values and the equality principle, on the one side, and free expression and unrestricted political debate on the other. The Court's equation of money and speech in political campaigns means that few limits can be constitutionally placed on the spending of individual candidates or that by independent groups, that is, so-called soft money. This, in turn, has made today's salient issue of campaign finance reform more difficult for elected legislators, who may be considered parties of interest, to resolve.

FURTHER READING

The Right to Vote

Ball, Howard, Dale Krane, and Thomas P. Lauth, *Compromised Compliance: Implementation of the 1965 Voting Rights Act* (1982)

Bartley, Numan V., and Hugh Davis Graham, *Southern Politics and the Second Reconstruction* (1975)

Chute, Marchette G., *First Liberty: A History of the Right to Vote in America, 1619–1850* (1969)

Davidson, Chander, and Bernard Grofman, eds., *Quiet Revolution in the South: The Impact of the Voting Rights Act, 1965–1990* (1994)

Elliott, Ward E.Y., *The Rise of Guardian Democracy: The Supreme Court's Role in Voting Rights Disputes, 1845–1969* (1974)

Garrow, David J., *Protest at Selma: Martin Luther King, Jr. and the Voting Rights Act of 1965* (1978)

Gelfand, M. David, and Terry E. Allbritton, *Recent Developments on Voting Rights in the United States* (1988)

Gillette, William, *The Right to Vote: Politics and the Passage of the Fifteenth Amendment* (1969)

Hamilton, Charles V., *The Bench and the Ballot: Southern Federal Judges and Black Voters* (1973)

Kousser, J. Morgan, *Colorblind Justice: Minority Voting Rights and the Undoing of the Second Reconstruction* (1999)

Lawson, Stephen, *Black Ballots: Voting Rights in the South, 1944–1969* (1976)

Lewinson, Paul, *Race, Class, and Party: A History of Negro Suffrage and White Politics in the South* (1959)

Norell, Robert J., *Reaping the Whirlwind: The Civil Rights Movement in Tuskegee* (1998)

Parker, Frank R., *Black Votes Count: Political Empowerment in Mississippi After 1965* (1990)

Williamson, Chilton, *American Suffrage from Property to Democracy, 1760–1860* (1960)

Apportionment and Redistricting

Baker, Gordon E., *The Reapportionment Revolution: Representation, Political Power and the Supreme Court* (1966)

Ball, Howard, *The Warren Court's Conception of Democracy: An Evaluation of the Supreme Court's Reapportionment Decisions* (1971)

Boyd, Wiiliam J.D., *Apportionment in the Nineteen Sixties: State Legislature, Congressional Districts* (1967)

Butler, David, and Bruce Can, *Congressional Redistricting: Comparative and Theoretical Perspectives* (1992)

Claude, Richard, *The Supreme Court and the Electoral Process* (1970)

Dixon, Robert G., Jr., *Democratic Representation: Reapportionment in Law and Politics* (1968)

De Grazia, Alfred, *Apportionment and Representative Government* (1963)

Hanson, Royce, *The Political Thicket* (1966)

Maveety, Nancy, *Representation Rights and the Burger Court Years* (1991)

McKay, Robert B., *Reapportionment: The Law and Politics of Equal Representation* (1965)

O'Rourke, Timothy G., *The Impact of Reapportionment* (1980)

Rush, Mark E., *Does Districting Make a Difference: Partisan Representation and Electoral Behavior* (1993)

Race and Representation

Bybee, Keith J., *Mistaken Identity: The Supreme Court and the Politics of Minority Representation* (1998)

Cannon, David T., *Race, Redistricting, and Representation: The Unintended Consequences of Black Majority Districts* (1999)

Cunningham, Maurice T., *Maximization Whatever the Cost: Race, Redistricting, and the Department of Justice* (2001)

Grofman, Bernard, *Political Gerrymandering and the Courts* (1990)

Grofman, Bernard, Lisa Handley, and Richard G. Niemi, *Minority Representation and the Quest for Voting Equality* (1992)

Guinier, Lani, *The Tyranny of the Majority: Fundamental Fairness in Representative Democracy* (1994)

Hudson, David Michael, *Along Racial Lilnes: Consequences of the Voting Rights Act* (1998)

Kinder, Donald R., and Lynn M. Sanders, *Divided by Color: Racial Politics and Democratic Ideals* (1997)

Lublin, David, *The Paradox of Representation* (1997)

Reeves, Keith, *Voting Hopes or Fears? White Voters, Black Candidates, and Racial Politics in America* (1997)

Ryden, David K., *The United States Supreme Court and the Electoral Process* (2000)

Scher, Richard K., Jon L. Mills, and John J. Hotaling, *Voting Rights and Democracy: The Law and Politics of Districting* (1997)

Swain, Carol M., *Black Faces, Black Interests: Representation of African-Americans in Congress* (1993)

Thernstrom, Abigail, *Whose Votes Count? Affirmative Action and Minority Voting Rights* (1987)

Campaigns

Rosenkranz, E. Joshua, *If Buckley Fell: Designing a First Amendment That Reinforces Democracy* (1999)

Rosenthal, Albert J., *Federal Regulation of Campaign Finance: Some Constitutional Questions* (1972)

Slabach, Frederick G., ed., *The Constitution and Campaign Finance Reform* (1998)

Stevenson, Donald Grier, Jr., *Campaigns and the Court: The United States Supreme Court in Presidential Elections* (1999)

On Leading Cases

Cortner, Richard C., *The Apportionment Cases* (1970)

Gillman, Howard, *The Votes That Counted: How the Court Decided the 2000 Presidential Election* (2001)

Greene, Abner, *Understanding the 2000 Election: A Guide to the Legal Battles That Decided the Presidency* (2001)

Peacock, Anthony A., ed., *Affirmative Action and Representation:* Shaw v. Reno *and the Future of Voting Rights* (1997)

Posner, Richard, *Breaking the Deadlock: The 2000 Elections, the Constitution, and the Courts* (2001)

Sunstein, Cass R., and Richard A. Epstein, eds., *The Vote: Bush, Gore, and the Supreme Court* (2001)

Taper, Bernard, Gomillion v. Lightfoot: *Apartheid in Alabama* (1962)

Additional works listed in General and Supplementary Bibliography.

CASES

Bush v. Gore

531 U.S. 98 (2000), 7-2

Per Curiam: (Rehnquist, C.J., O'Connor, Souter, Scalia, Kennedy, Thomas, Breyer)

Concurring: Rehnquist, Scalia, Thomas

Dissenting in part: Souter, Breyer

Dissenting: Stevens, Ginsberg

Is the disagreement between the majority and the dissenters one about the interpretation of statutes and Constitutional provisions? The weight each should be given? The role of courts and the Court? Who should be president? How did Rehnquist differ from the Per Curiam opinion on the grounds for deciding this case? Did Souter support the Court's decision or not? Is this decision essentially limited to the peculiar facts of this case or has the Court extended equal protection analysis into a new area and, if so, how might it apply in election controversies of the future?

Per Curiam:

The petition presents the following questions: whether the Florida Supreme Court established new standards for resolving Presidential election contests, thereby violating Art. II, §1, cl. 2, of the United States Constitution and failing to comply with 3 U.S.C. Section 5, and whether the use of standardless manual recounts violates the Equal Protection and Due Process Clauses. With respect to the equal protection question, we find a violation of the Equal Protection Clause. . . .

The right to vote is protected in more than the initial allocation of the franchise. Equal protection applies as well to the manner of its exercise. Having once granted the right to vote on equal terms, the State may not, by later arbitrary and disparate treatment, value one person's vote over that of another. . . .

. . . The question before us . . . is whether the recount procedures the Florida Supreme Court has adopted are consistent with its obligation to avoid arbitrary and disparate treatment of the members of its electorate.

Much of the controversy seems to revolve around ballot cards designed to be perforated by a stylus but which, either through error or deliberate omission, have not been perforated with sufficient precision for a machine to count them. In some cases a piece of the card—a chad—is hanging, say by two corners. In other cases there is no separation at all, just an indentation.

The Florida Supreme Court has ordered that the intent of the voter be discerned from such ballots. For purposes of resolving the equal protection challenge, it is not necessary to decide whether the Florida Supreme Court had the authority under the legislative scheme for resolving election disputes to define what a legal vote is and to mandate a manual recount implementing that definition. The recount mechanisms implemented in response to the decisions of the Florida Supreme Court do not satisfy the minimum requirement for non-arbitrary treatment of voters necessary to secure the fundamental right. Florida's basic command for the count of legally cast votes is to consider the "intent of the voter." This is unobjectionable as an abstract proposition and a starting principle. The problem inheres in the absence of specific standards to ensure its equal application. The formulation of uniform rules to determine intent based on these recurring circumstances is practicable and, we conclude, necessary.

The law does not refrain from searching for the intent of the actor in a multitude of circumstances; and in some cases the general command to ascertain intent is not susceptible to much further refinement. In this instance, however, the question is not whether to believe a witness but how to interpret the marks or holes or scratches on an inanimate object, a piece of cardboard or paper which, it is said, might not have registered as a vote during the machine count. The factfinder confronts a thing, not a person. The search for intent can be confined by specific rules designed to ensure uniform treatment.

The want of those rules here has led to unequal evaluation of ballots in various respects. As seems to have been acknowledged at oral argument, the standards for accepting or rejecting contested ballots might vary not only from county to county but indeed within a single county from one recount team to another. . . .

. . . At oral argument, respondents estimated there are as many as 110,000 overvotes statewide. As a result, the citizen whose ballot was not read by a machine because he failed to vote for a candidate in a way readable by a machine may still have his vote counted in a manual recount; on the other hand, the citizen who marks two candidates in a way discernable by the machine will not have the same opportunity to have his vote count, even if a manual examination of the ballot would reveal the requisite indicia of intent. Furthermore, the citizen who marks two candidates, only one of which is discernable by the machine, will have his vote counted even though it should have been read as an invalid ballot. The State Supreme Court's inclusion of vote counts based on these variant standards exemplifies concerns with the remedial processes that were under way.

That brings the analysis to yet a further equal protection problem. The votes certified by the court included a partial total from one county, Miami-Dade. The Florida Supreme Court's decision thus gives no assurance that the recounts included in a final certification must be complete. Indeed, it is respondent's submission that it would be consistent with the rules of the recount procedures to include whatever partial counts are done by the time of final certification, and we interpret the Florida Supreme Court's decision to permit this. This accommodation no doubt results from the truncated contest period established by the Florida Supreme Court in Bush I, at respondents' own urging. The press of time does not diminish the constitutional concern. A desire for speed is not a general excuse for ignoring equal protection guarantees.

In addition to these difficulties the actual process by which the votes were to be counted under the Florida Supreme Court's decision raises further concerns. That order did not specify who would recount the ballots. The county canvassing boards were forced to pull together ad hoc teams comprised of judges from various Circuits who had no previous training in handling and interpreting ballots. Furthermore, while others were permitted to observe, they were prohibited from objecting during the recount.

The recount process, in its features here described, is inconsistent with the minimum procedures necessary to protect the fundamental right of each voter in the special instance of a statewide recount under the authority of a single state judicial officer. . . .

The question before the Court is not whether local entities, in the exercise of their expertise, may develop different systems for implementing elections. Instead, we are presented with a situation where a state court with the power to assure uniformity has ordered a statewide recount with minimal procedural safeguards. When a court orders a statewide remedy, there must be at least some assurance that the rudimentary requirements of equal treatment and fundamental fairness are satisfied.

Given the Court's assessment that the recount process underway was probably being conducted in an unconstitutional manner, the Court stayed the order directing the recount so it could hear this case and render an expedited decision. The contest provision, as it was mandated by the State Supreme Court, is not well calculated to sustain the confidence that all citizens must have in the outcome of elections. The State has not shown that its procedures include the necessary safeguards. The problem, for instance, of the estimated 110,000 overvotes has not been addressed, although [state] Chief Justice Wells called attention to the concern in his dissenting opinion.

Upon due consideration of the difficulties identified to this point, it is obvious that the recount cannot be conducted in compliance with the requirements of equal protection and due process without substantial additional work. It would require not only the adoption (after opportunity for argument) of adequate statewide standards for determining what is a legal

vote, and practicable procedures to implement them, but also orderly judicial review of any disputed matters that might arise. In addition, the Secretary of State has advised that the recount of only a portion of the ballots requires that the vote tabulation equipment be used to screen out undervotes, a function for which the machines were not designed. If a recount of overvotes were also required, perhaps even a second screening would be necessary. Use of the equipment for this purpose, and any new software developed for it, would have to be evaluated for accuracy by the Secretary of State, as required by Fla. Stat. §101.015.

The Supreme Court of Florida has said that the legislature intended the State's electors to "participat[e] fully in the federal electoral process," as provided in 3 U.S.C. s.5. That statute, in turn, requires that any controversy or contest that is designed to lead to a conclusive selection of electors be completed by December 12. That date is upon us, and there is no recount procedure in place under the State Supreme Court's order that comports with minimal constitutional standards. Because it is evident that any recount seeking to meet the December 12 date will be unconstitutional for the reasons we have discussed, we reverse the judgment of the Supreme Court of Florida ordering a recount to proceed.

Seven Justices of the Court agree that there are constitutional problems with the recount ordered by the Florida Supreme Court that demand a remedy. The only disagreement is as to the remedy. Because the Florida Supreme Court has said that the Florida Legislature intended to obtain the safe-harbor benefits of 3 U.S.C. s.5, Justice Breyer's proposed remedy—remanding to the Florida Supreme Court for its ordering of a constitutionally proper contest until December 18—contemplates action in violation of the Florida election code, and hence could not be part of an "appropriate" order authorized by Fla. Stat. §102.168(8).

None are more conscious of the vital limits on judicial authority than are the members of this Court, and none stand more in admiration of the Constitution's design to leave the selection of the President to the people, through their legislatures, and to the political sphere. When contending parties invoke the process of the courts, however, it becomes our unsought responsibility to resolve the federal and constitutional issues the judicial system has been forced to confront.

The judgment of the Supreme Court of Florida is reversed, and the case is remanded for further proceedings not inconsistent with this opinion.

Rehnquist, concurring:

We [with Justices Scalia and Thomas] join the per curiam opinion. We write separately because we believe there are additional grounds that require us to reverse the Florida Supreme Court's decision.

... Article II, §1, cl. 2, provides that "[e]ach State shall appoint, in such Manner as the Legislature thereof may direct," electors for President and Vice President. (emphasis added.) ...

In *McPherson v. Blacker* (1892), we explained that Art. II, §1, cl. 2, "convey[s] the broadest power of determination" and "leaves it to the legislature exclusively to define the method" of appointment. Id., at 27. A significant departure from the legislative scheme for appointing Presidential electors presents a federal constitutional question.

3 U.S.C., s.5 informs our application of Art. II, §1, cl. 2, to the Florida statutory scheme, which, as the Florida Supreme Court acknowledged, took that statute into account. Section 5 provides that the State's selection of electors "shall be conclusive, and shall govern in the counting of the electoral votes" if the electors are chosen under laws enacted prior to election day, and if the selection process is completed six days prior to the meeting of the electoral college. As we noted in Bush v. Palm Beach County Canvassing Board.

"Since §5 contains a principle of federal law that would assure finality of the State's determination if made pursuant to a state law in effect before the election, a legislative wish to take advantage of the 'safe harbor' would counsel against any construction of the Election Code that Congress might deem to be a change in the law."

If we are to respect the legislature's Article II powers, therefore, we must ensure that post-election state court actions do not frustrate the legislative desire to attain the "safe harbor" provided by §5.

In Florida, the legislature has chosen to hold statewide elections to appoint the State's 25 electors. Importantly, the legislature has delegated the authority to run the elections and to oversee election disputes to the Secretary of State and to state circuit courts. ...

Acting pursuant to its constitutional grant of authority, the Florida Legislature has created a detailed, if not perfectly crafted, statutory scheme that provides for appointment of Presidential electors by direct election ...

... [I]n a Presidential election the clearly expressed intent of the legislature must prevail. ...

The scope and nature of the remedy ordered by the Florida Supreme Court jeopardizes the "legislative wish" to take advantage of the safe harbor provided by 3 U.S.C. s.5., December 12, 2000, is the last date for a final determination of the Florida electors that will satisfy §5. Yet in the late afternoon of December 8th—four days before this deadline—the Supreme Court of Florida ordered recounts of tens of thousands of so-called "undervotes" spread through 64 of the State's 67 counties. This was done in a search for elusive—perhaps delusive—certainty as to the exact count of 6 million votes. But no one claims that these ballots have not previously been tabulated; they were initially read by voting machines at the time of the election, and thereafter reread by virtue of Florida's automatic recount provision. No one claims there was any fraud in the election. The Supreme Court of Florida ordered this additional recount under the provision of the election code giving the circuit judge the authority to provide relief that is "appropriate under such circumstances."

Given all these factors, and in light of the legislative intent identified by the Florida Supreme Court to bring Florida within the "safe harbor" provision of 3 U.S.C. s.5, the remedy prescribed by the Supreme Court of Florida cannot be deemed an "appropriate" one as of December 8. It significantly departed from the statutory framework in place on November 7, and authorized open-ended further proceedings which could not be completed by December 12, thereby preventing a final determination by that date.

For these reasons, in addition to those given in the per curiam, we would reverse.

Stevens, dissenting:

The federal questions that ultimately emerged in this case are not substantial. Article II provides that "[e]ach State shall appoint, in such Manner as the Legislature thereof may direct, a Number of Electors." Ibid. (emphasis added). It does not create state legislatures out of whole cloth, but rather takes them as they come—as creatures born of, and constrained by, their state constitutions. Lest there be any doubt, we stated over 100 years ago in *McPherson v. Blacker*, (1892), that "[w]hat is forbidden or required to be done by a State" in the Article II context "is forbidden or required of the legislative power under state constitutions as they exist." In the same vein, we also observed that "[t]he [State's] legislative power is the supreme authority except as limited by the constitution of the State." The legislative power in Florida is subject to judicial review pursuant to Article V of the Florida Constitution, and nothing in Article II of the Federal Constitution frees the state legislature from the constraints in the state constitution that created it. . . .

It hardly needs stating that Congress, pursuant to 3 U.S.C. s.5 did not impose any affirmative duties upon the States that their governmental branches could "violate." . . . Neither §5 nor Article II grants federal judges any special authority to substitute their views for those of the state judiciary on matters of state law.

Nor are petitioners correct in asserting that the failure of the Florida Supreme Court to specify in detail the precise manner in which the "intent of the voter," is to be determined rises to the level of a constitutional violation. We found such a violation when individual votes within the same State were weighted unequally, but we have never before called into question the substantive standard by which a State determines that a vote has been legally cast. . . .

Admittedly, the use of differing substandards for determining voter intent in different counties employing similar voting systems may raise serious concerns. Those concerns are alleviated—if not eliminated—by the fact that a single impartial magistrate will ultimately adjudicate all objections arising from the recount process. . . .

In the interest of finality, however, the majority effectively orders the disenfranchisement of an unknown number of voters whose ballots reveal their intent—and are therefore legal votes under state law—but were for some reason rejected by ballot-counting machines. It does so on the basis of the deadlines set forth in Title 3 of the United States Code. But, as I have already noted, those provisions merely provide rules of decision for Congress to follow when selecting among conflicting slates of electors. They do not prohibit a State from counting what the majority concedes to be legal votes until a bona fide winner is determined. . . .

What must underlie petitioners' entire federal assault on the Florida election procedures is an unstated lack of confidence in the impartiality and capacity of the state judges who would make the critical decisions if the vote count were to proceed. Otherwise, their position is wholly without merit. The endorsement of that position by the majority of this Court can only lend credence to the most cynical appraisal of the work of judges throughout the land. It is confidence in the men and women who administer the judicial system that is the true backbone of the rule of law. Time will one day heal the wound to that confidence that will be inflicted by today's decision. One thing, however, is certain. Although we may never know with complete certainty the identity of the winner of this year's Presidential election, the identity of the loser is perfectly clear. It is the Nation's confidence in the judge as an impartial guardian of the rule of law.

Souter, dissenting in part:

As will be clear, I am in substantial agreement with the dissenting opinions of Justice Stevens, Justice Ginsburg and Justice Breyer. I write separately only to say how straightforward the issues before us really are.

There are three issues: whether the State Supreme Court's interpretation of the statute providing for a contest of the state election results somehow violates 3 U.S.C. s.5 whether that court's construction of the state statutory provisions governing contests impermissibly changes a state law from what the State's legislature has provided, in violation of Article II, §1, cl. 2, of the national Constitution; and whether the manner of interpreting markings on disputed ballots failing to cause machines to register votes for President (the undervote ballots) violates the equal protection or due process guaranteed by the Fourteenth Amendment. None of these issues is difficult to describe or to resolve.

The 3 U.S.C. s.5 issue is not serious. That provision sets certain conditions for treating a State's certification of Presidential electors as conclusive in the event that a dispute over recognizing those electors must be resolved in the Congress under 3 U.S.C. s.15. Conclusiveness requires selection under a legal scheme in place before the election, with results determined at least six days before the date set for casting electoral votes. But no State is required to conform to §5 if it cannot do that (for whatever reason); the sanction for failing to satisfy the conditions of §5 is simply loss of what has been called its "safe harbor."

And even that determination is to be made, if made anywhere, in the Congress.

The second matter here goes to the State Supreme Court's interpretation of certain terms in the state statute governing election "contests." . . . The issue is whether the judgment of the state supreme court has displaced the state legislature's provisions for election contests: is the law as declared by the court different from the provisions made by the legislature, to which the national Constitution commits responsibility for determining how each State's Presidential electors are chosen? . . .

. . . None of the state court's interpretations is unreasonable to the point of displacing the legislative enactment quoted. As I will note below, other interpretations were of course possible, and some might have been better than those adopted by the Florida court's majority; the two dissents from the majority opinion of that court and various briefs submitted to us set out alternatives. But the majority view is in each instance within the bounds of reasonable interpretation, and the law as declared is consistent with Article II.

. . . Whatever people of good will and good sense may argue about the merits of the Florida court's reading, there is no warrant for saying that it transcends the limits of reasonable statutory interpretation to the point of supplanting the statute enacted by the "legislature" within the meaning of Article II.

In sum, the interpretations by the Florida court raise no substantial question under Article II. . . .

It is only on the third issue before us that there is a meritorious argument for relief, as this Court's Per Curiam opinion recognizes. It is an issue that might well have been dealt with adequately by the Florida courts if the state proceedings had not been interrupted, and if not disposed of at the state level it could have been considered by the Congress in any electoral vote dispute. But because the course of state proceedings has been interrupted, time is short, and the issue is before us, I think it sensible for the Court to address it.

Petitioners have raised an equal protection claim (or, alternatively, a due process claim, in the charge that unjustifiably disparate standards are applied in different electoral jurisdictions to otherwise identical facts. It is true that the Equal Protection Clause does not forbid the use of a variety of voting mechanisms within a jurisdiction, even though different mechanisms will have different levels of effectiveness in recording voters' intentions; local variety can be justified by concerns about cost, the potential value of innovation, and so on. But evidence in the record here suggests that a different order of disparity obtains under rules for determining a voter's intent that have been applied (and could continue to be applied) to identical types of ballots used in identical brands of machines and exhibiting identical physical characteristics (such as "hanging" or "dimpled" chads). I can

conceive of no legitimate state interest served by these differing treatments of the expressions of voters' fundamental rights. The differences appear wholly arbitrary.

In deciding what to do about this, we should take account of the fact that electoral votes are due to be cast in six days. I would therefore remand the case to the courts of Florida with instructions to establish uniform standards for evaluating the several types of ballots that have prompted differing treatments, to be applied within and among counties when passing on such identical ballots in any further recounting (or successive recounting) that the courts might order.

Unlike the majority, I see no warrant for this Court to assume that Florida could not possibly comply with this requirement before the date set for the meeting of electors, December 18. Although one of the dissenting justices of the State Supreme Court estimated that disparate standards potentially affected 170,000 votes, the number at issue is significantly smaller. The 170,000 figure apparently represents all uncounted votes, both undervotes (those for which no Presidential choice was recorded by a machine) and overvotes (those rejected because of votes for more than one candidate). But as Justice Breyer has pointed out, no showing has been made of legal overvotes uncounted, and counsel for Gore made an uncontradicted representation to the Court that the statewide total of undervotes is about 60,000. To recount these manually would be a tall order, but before this Court stayed the effort to do that the courts of Florida were ready to do their best to get that job done. There is no justification for denying the State the opportunity to try to count all disputed ballots now.

Wesberry v. Sanders

376 U.S. 1 (1964), 8-1
Opinion of the Court: Black (Brennan, Douglas, Goldberg, Warren, White)
Concurring in the judgment but dissenting in part: Clark, Stewart
Dissenting: Harlan

How has a "one person, one vote" standard been applied in this case? What part of the Constitution was violated by the apportionment circumstances in Georgia? Is a one-person, one-vote standard based on the text of the Constitution or what may be implied from it? On an extrapolation of the intent of the framers to modern conditions? On something in-

Rural areas lost political heft in the Supreme Court's "one person, one vote" apportionment doctrine.

herent in the history of the nation? On the political philosophy of the justices themselves? Does the decision enhance the democratic character of American government? If so, what view of that democratic character?

Black, for the Court:

Appellants are citizens and qualified voters of Fulton County, Georgia, and as such are entitled to vote in congressional elections in Georgia's Fifth Congressional District. That district, one of ten created by a 1931 Georgia statute, includes Fulton, DeKalb, and Rockdale Counties, and has a population, according to the 1960 census, of 823,680. The average population of the ten districts is 394,312, less than half that of the Fifth. One district, the Ninth, has only 272,154 people, less than one-third as many as the Fifth. Since there is only one Congressman for each district, this inequality of population means that the Fifth District's Congressman has to represent from two to three times as many people as do Congressmen from some of the other Georgia districts.

Claiming that these population disparities deprived them and voters similarly situated of a right under the Federal Constitution to have their votes for Congressmen given the same weight as the votes of other Georgians, the appellants brought this action under 42 U.S.C. §§1983 and 1988 and 28 U.S.C. §1343(3), asking that the Georgia statute be declared invalid and that the appellees, the Governor and Secretary of State of Georgia, be enjoined from conducting elections under it. The complaint alleged that appellants were deprived of the full benefit of their right to vote, in violation of (1) Art. I, §2, of the Constitution of the United States, which provides that "The House of Representatives shall be composed of Members chosen every second Year by the People of the several States . . . "; (2) the Due Process, Equal Protection, and Privileges and Immunities Clauses of the Fourteenth Amendment, and (3) that part of Section 2 of the Fourteenth Amendment which provides that "Representatives shall be apportioned among the several States according to their respective numbers. . . ."

The case was heard by a three-judge District Court, which found unanimously, from facts not disputed, that:

> It is clear by any standard . . . that the population of the Fifth District is grossly out of balance with that of the other nine congressional districts of Georgia, and, in fact, so much so that the removal of DeKalb and Rockdale Counties from the District, leaving only Fulton with a population of 556,326, would leave it exceeding the average by slightly more than forty percent.

Notwithstanding these findings, a majority of the court dismissed the complaint, citing as their guide Mr. Justice Frankfurter's minority opinion in *Colegrove v. Green,* an opinion stating that challenges to apportionment of congressional districts raised only "political" questions, which were not justiciable. Although the majority below said that the dismissal here was based on "want of equity," and not on nonjusticiability, they relied on no circumstances which were peculiar to the present case; instead, they adopted the language and reasoning of Mr Justice Frankfurter's *Colegrove* opinion in concluding that the appellants had presented a wholly "political" question. . . .

. . . The right to vote is too important in our free society to be stripped of judicial protection by such an interpretation of Article I. This dismissal can no more be justified on the ground of "want of equity" than on the ground of "nonjusticiability." We therefore hold that the District Court erred in dismissing the complaint.

This brings us to the merits. We agree with the District Court that the 1931 Georgia apportionment grossly discriminates against voters in the Fifth Congressional District. A single Congressman represents from two to three times as many Fifth District voters as are represented by each of the Congressmen from the other Georgia congressional districts. The apportionment statute thus contracts the value of some votes and expands that of others. If the Federal Constitution intends that, when qualified voters elect members of Congress, each vote be given as much weight as any other vote, then this statute cannot stand.

We hold that, construed in its historical context, the command of Art. I, §2 that Representatives be chosen "by the People of the several States" means that, as nearly as is practicable, one man's vote in a congressional election is to be worth as much as another's. This rule is followed automatically, of course, when Representatives are chosen as a group on a statewide basis, as was a widespread practice in the first 50 years of our Nation's history. It would be extraordinary to suggest that, in such statewide elections, the votes of inhabitants of some parts of a State, for example, Georgia's thinly populated Ninth District, could be weighted at two or three times the value of the votes of people living in more populous parts of the State, for example, the Fifth District around Atlanta. We do not believe that the Framers of the Constitution intended to permit the same vote-diluting discrimination to be accomplished through the device of districts containing widely varied numbers of inhabitants. To say that a vote is worth more in one district than in another would not only run counter to our fundamental ideas of democratic government, it would cast aside the principle of a House of Representatives elected "by the People," a principle tenaciously fought for and established at the Constitutional Convention. The history of the Constitution, particularly that part of it relating to the adoption of Art. I, §2, reveals that those who framed the Constitution meant that, no matter what the mechanics of an election, whether statewide or by districts, it was population which was to be the basis of the Hose of Representatives. . . .

The . . . Constitutional Convention of 1787 [was] called for "the sole and express purpose of revising the Articles of Confederation. . . ." When the Convention met in May, this modest purpose was soon abandoned for the greater challenge of creating a new and closer form of government than was possible under the Confederation. Soon after the Convention assembled, Edmund Randolph of Virginia presented a plan not merely to amend the Articles of Confederation, but to create an entirely new National Government with a National Executive, National Judiciary, and a National Legislature of two Houses, one house to be elected by "the people," the second house to be elected by the first.

The question of how the legislature should be constituted precipitated the most bitter controversy of the Convention. One principle was uppermost in the minds of many delegates: that, no matter where he lived, each voter should have a voice equal to that of every other in electing members of Congress. . . .

The delegates who wanted every man's vote to count alike were sharp in their criticism of giving each State, regardless of population, the same voice in the National Legislature. Madison entreated the

Convention "to renounce a principle which. was confessedly unjust," and Rufus King of Massachusetts "was prepared for every event rather than sit down under a Govt. founded in a vicious principle of representation and which must be as short-lived as it would be unjust." . . .

The debates at the Convention make at least one fact abundantly clear: that, when the delegates agreed that the House should represent "people," they intended that, in allocating Congressmen, the number assigned to each State should be determined solely by the number of the State's inhabitants. The Constitution embodied Edmund Randolph's proposal for a periodic census to ensure "fair representation of the people," an idea endorsed by Mason as assuring that "numbers of inhabitants" should always be the measure of representation in the House of Representatives. The Convention also overwhelmingly agreed to a resolution offered by Randolph to base future apportionment squarely on numbers and to delete any reference to wealth. And the delegates defeated a motion made by Elbridge Gerry to limit the number of Representatives from newer Western States so that it would never exceed the number from the original States.

It would defeat the principle solemnly embodied in the Great Compromise—equal representation in the House for equal numbers of people—for us to hold that, within the States, legislatures may draw the lines of congressional districts in such a way as to give some voters a greater voice in choosing a Congressman than others. . . .

It is in the light of such history that we must construe Art. I, §2, of the Constitution, which, carrying out the ideas of Madison and those of like views, provides that Representatives shall be chosen "by the People of the several States," and shall be "apportioned among the several States . . . according to their respective Numbers." It is not surprising that our Court has held that this Article gives persons qualified to vote a constitutional right to vote and to have their votes counted. Not only can this right to vote not be denied outright, it cannot, consistently with Article I, be destroyed by alteration of ballots. No right is more precious in a free country than that of having a voice in the election of those who make the laws under which, as good citizens, we must live. Other rights, even the most basic, are illusory if the right to vote is undermined. Our Constitution leaves no room for classification of people in a way that unnecessarily abridges this right. . . .

While it may not be possible to draw congressional districts with mathematical precision, that is no excuse for ignoring our Constitution's plain objective of making equal representation for equal numbers of people the fundamental goal for the House of Representatives. That is the high standard of justice and common sense which the Founders set for us.

Harlan, dissenting:

I had not expected to witness the day when the Supreme Court of the United States would render a decision which casts grave doubt on the constitutionality of the composition of the House of Representatives. It is not an exaggeration to say that such is the effect of today's decision. The Court's holding that the Constitution requires States to select Representatives either by elections at large or by elections in districts composed "as nearly as is practicable" of equal population places in jeopardy the seats of almost all the members of the present House of Representatives.

In the last congressional election, in 1962, Representatives from 42 States were elected from congressional districts. In all but five of those States, the difference between the populations of the largest and smallest districts exceeded 100,000 persons. A difference of this magnitude in the size of districts, the average population of which in each State is less than 500,000, is presumably not equality among districts "as nearly as is practicable," although the Court does not reveal its definition of that phrase. Thus, today's decision impugns the validity of the election of 398 Representatives from 37 States, leaving a "constitutional" House of 37 members now sitting.

Only a demonstration which could not be avoided would justify this Court in rendering a decision the effect of which, inescapably, as I see it, is to declare constitutionally defective the very composition of a coordinate branch of the Federal Government. The Court's opinion not only fails to make such a demonstration, it is unsound logically on its face, and demonstrably unsound historically. . . .

The . . . language of Art. I, §§2 and 4, the surrounding text, and the relevant history are all in strong and consistent direct contradiction of the Court's holding. The constitutional scheme vests in the States plenary power to regulate the conduct of elections for Representatives, and, in order to protect the Federal Government, provides for congressional supervision of the States' exercise of their power. Within this scheme, the appellants do not have the right which they assert, in the absence of provision for equal districts by the Georgia Legislature or the Congress. The constitutional right which the Court creates is manufactured out of whole cloth.

The unstated premise of the Court's conclusion quite obviously is that the Congress has not dealt, and the Court believes it will not deal, with the problem of congressional apportionment in accordance with what the Court believes to be sound political principles. Laying aside for the moment the validity of such a consideration as a factor in constitutional interpretation, it becomes relevant to examine the history of congressional action under Art. I, §4. This history reveals that the Court is not simply undertaking to exercise a power which the Constitution reserves to the Congress; it is also overruling congressional judgment. . . .

Today's decision has portents for our society and the Court itself which should be recognized. This is not a case in which the Court vindicates the kind of individual rights that are assured by the Due Process Clause of the Fourteenth Amendment, whose "vague contours," of course, leave much room for constitutional developments necessitated by changing conditions in a dynamic society. Nor is this a case in which an emergent set of facts requires the Court to frame new principles to protect recognized constitutional rights. The claim for judicial relief in this case strikes at one of the fundamental doctrines of our system of government, the separation of powers. In upholding that claim, the Court attempts to effect reforms in a field which the Constitution, as plainly as can be, has committed exclusively to the political process.

This Court, no less than all other branches of the Government, is bound by the Constitution. The Constitution does not confer on the Court blanket authority to step into every situation where the political branch may be thought to have fallen short. The stability of this institution ultimately depends not only upon its being alert to keep the other branches of government within constitutional bounds, but equally upon recognition of the limitations on the Court's own functions in the constitutional system.

What is done today saps the political process. The promise of judicial intervention in matters of this sort cannot but encourage popular inertia in efforts for political reform through the political process, with the inevitable result that the process is itself weakened. By yielding to the demand for a judicial remedy in this instance, the Court, in my view, does a disservice both to itself and to the broader values of our system of government.

Reynolds v. Sims

377 U.S. 533 (1964), 8-1
Opinion of the Court: Warren (Black, Brennan, Clark, Douglas, Goldberg, Stewart, White)
Dissenting: Harlan

Voters in several Alabama counties brought this case against state election officials, alleging that malapportionment of the state legislature denied them rights under the equal protection clause of the Fourteenth Amendment. A three-judge federal district court ruled for the plaintiffs and ordered a reapportionment of the legislature. The defendant officials appealed to the Supreme Court.

Must the apportionment of both houses of a state legislature be based on population? On precise equality of population? What does Justice Warren mean by saying that departures from an equality standard must rest on "legitimate considerations incident to the effectuation of a rational state policy"? Does he give any examples? On what grounds does he reject the analogy of the U.S. Senate? Is there any point to having a two-house legislature if both houses are based entirely or almost entirely on population? In a democratic age, what other defensible grounds for apportionment might there be? To what extent is the disagreement between Justices Warren and Harlan one of differing political philosophies? How do they differ on their concept of judicial review? If mathematical precision is required in apportionment, would it not be undermined almost immediately by population changes? If it is not required, would not a cutoff line for variation inevitably be arbitrary, for example, a 3 percent tolerance but not a 2 or 4?

Warren, for the Court:

On July 21, 1962, the District Court held that the inequality of the existing representation in the Alabama Legislature violated the Equal Protection Clause of the Fourteenth Amendment, a finding which the Court noted had been "generally conceded" by the parties to the litigation, since population growth and shifts had converted the 1901 scheme, as perpetuated some 60 years later, into an invidiously discriminatory plan completely lacking in rationality. Under the existing provisions, applying 1960 census figures, only 25.1% of the State's total population resided in districts represented by a majority of the members of the Senate, and only 25.7% lived in counties which could elect a majority of the members of the House of Representatives. Population variance ratios of up to about 41-to-1 existed in the Senate, and up to about 16-to-1 in the House. Bullock County, with a population of only 13,462, and Henry County, with a population of only 15,286, each were allocated two seats in the Alabama House, whereas Mobile County, with a population of 314,301, was given only three seats, and Jefferson County, with 634,864 people, had only seven representatives. With respect to senatorial apportionment, since the pertinent Alabama constitutional provisions had been consistently construed as prohibiting the giving of more than one Senate seat to any one county, Jefferson County, with over 600,000 people, was given only one senator, as was Lowndes County, with a 1960 population of only 15,417, and Wilcox County, with only 18,739 people. . . .

Undeniably, the Constitution of the United States protects the right of all qualified citizens to vote, in state as well as in federal, elections. . . .

. . . The right to vote freely for the candidate of one's choice is of the essence of a democratic society, and any restrictions on that right strike at the heart of representative government. And the right of suffrage can be denied by a debasement or dilution of the weight of a citizen's vote just as effectively as by wholly prohibiting the free exercise of the franchise.

In *Baker v. Carr,* we held that a claim asserted under the Equal Protection Clause challenging the constitutionality of a State's apportionment of seats in its legislature, on the ground that the right to vote of certain citizens was effectively impaired, since debased and diluted, in effect presented a justiciable controversy subject to adjudication by federal courts. . . .

In *Gray v. Sanders,* we held that the Georgia county unit system, applicable in statewide primary elections, was unconstitutional, since it resulted in a dilution of the weight of the votes of certain Georgia voters merely because of where they resided. . . .

In *Wesberry v. Sanders,* decided earlier this Term, we held that attacks on the constitutionality of congressional districting plans enacted by state legislatures do not present nonjusticiable questions, and should not be dismissed generally for "want of equity." We determined that the constitutional test for the validity of congressional districting schemes was one of substantial equality of population among the various districts established by a state legislature for the election of members of the Federal House of Representatives. . . .

Gray and *Wesberry* are, of course, not dispositive of or directly controlling on our decision in these cases involving state legislative apportionment controversies. Admittedly, those decisions, in which we held that, in statewide and in congressional elections, one person's vote must be counted equally with those of all other voters in a State, were based on different constitutional considerations, and were addressed to rather distinct problems. But neither are they wholly inapposite. *Gray,* though not determinative here, since involving the weighting of votes in statewide elections, established the basic principle of equality among voters within a State, and held that voters cannot be classified, constitutionally, on the basis of where they live, at least with respect to voting in statewide elections. And our decision in *Wesberry* was, of course, grounded on that language of the Constitution which prescribes that members of the Federal House of Representatives are to be chosen "by the People," while attacks on state legislative apportionment schemes, such as that involved in the instant cases, are principally based on the Equal Protection Clause of the Fourteenth Amendment. Nevertheless, *Wesberry* clearly established that the fundamental principle of representative government in this country is one of equal representation for equal numbers of people, without regard to race, sex, economic status, or place of residence within a State. Our problem, then, is to ascertain, in the instant cases, whether there are any constitutionally cognizable principles which would justify departures from the basic standard of equality among voters in the apportionment of seats in state legislatures.

A predominant consideration in determining whether a State's legislative apportionment scheme constitutes an invidious discrimination violative of rights asserted under the Equal Protection Clause is that the rights allegedly impaired are individual and personal in nature. . . .

Legislators represent people, not trees or acres. Legislators are elected by voters, not farms or cities or economic interests. As long as ours is a representative form of government, and our legislatures are those instruments of government elected directly by and directly representative of the people, the right to elect legislators in a free and unimpaired fashion is a bedrock of our political system. . . .

. . . With respect to the allocation of legislative representation, all voters, as citizens of a State, stand in the same relation regardless of where they live. Any suggested criteria for the differentiation of citizens are insufficient to justify any discrimination, as to the weight of their votes, unless relevant to the permissible purposes of legislative apportionment. Since the achieving of fair and effective representation for all citizens is concededly the basic aim of legislative apportionment, we conclude that the Equal Protection

Clause guarantees the opportunity for equal participation by all voters in the election of state legislators. Diluting the weight of votes because of place of residence impairs basic constitutional rights under the Fourteenth Amendment just as much as invidious discriminations based upon factors such as race....

We hold that, as a basic constitutional standard, the Equal Protection Clause requires that the seats in both houses of a bicameral state legislature must be apportioned on a population basis. Simply stated, an individual's right to vote for state legislators is unconstitutionally impaired when its weight is in a substantial fashion diluted when compared with votes of citizens living in other parts of the State. Since under neither the existing apportionment provisions nor either of the proposed plans was either of the houses of the Alabama Legislature apportioned on a population basis, the District Court correctly held that all three of these schemes were constitutionally invalid....

By holding that, as a federal constitutional requisite, both houses of a state legislature must be apportioned on a population basis, we mean that the Equal Protection Clause requires that a State make an honest and good faith effort to construct districts, in both houses of its legislature, as nearly of equal population as is practicable. We realize that it is a practical impossibility to arrange legislative districts so that each one has an identical number of residents, or citizens, or voters. Mathematical exactness or precision is hardly a workable constitutional requirement.

In *Wesberry v. Sanders* the Court stated that congressional representation must be based on population as nearly as is practicable. In implementing the basic constitutional principle of representative government as enunciated by the Court in *Wesberry*—equality of population among districts—some distinctions may well be made between congressional and state legislative representation. Since, almost invariably, there is a significantly larger number of seats in state legislative bodies to be distributed within a State than congressional seats, it may be feasible to use political subdivision lines to a greater extent in establishing state legislative districts than in congressional districting while still affording adequate representation to all parts of the State. To do so would be constitutionally valid so long as the resulting apportionment was one based substantially on population and the equal population principle was not diluted in any significant way....

History indicates, however, that many States have deviated, to a greater or lesser degree, from the equal population principle in the apportionment of seats in at least one house of their legislatures. So long as the divergences from a strict population standard are based on legitimate considerations incident to the effectuation of a rational state policy, some deviations from the equal population principle are constitutionally permissible with respect to the apportionment of seats in either or both of the two houses of a bicameral state legislature. But neither history alone, nor economic or other sorts of group interests, are permissible factors in attempting to justify disparities from population-based representation. Citizens, not history or economic interests, cast votes. Considerations of area alone provide an insufficient justification for deviations from the equal population principle. Again, people, not land or trees or pastures, vote. Modern developments and improvements in transportation and communications make rather hollow, in the mid-1960's, most claims that deviations from population-based representation can validly be based solely on geographical considerations. Arguments for allowing such deviations in order to insure effective representation for sparsely settled areas and to prevent legislative districts from becoming so large that the availability of access of citizens to their representatives is impaired are today, for the most part, unconvincing....

Although general provisions of the Alabama Constitution provide that the apportionment of seats in both houses of the Alabama Legislature should be on a population basis, other more detailed provisions clearly make compliance with both sets of requirements impossible. With respect to the operation of the Equal Protection Clause, it makes no difference whether a State's apportionment scheme is embodied in its constitution or in statutory provisions. In those States where the alleged malapportionment has resulted from noncompliance with state constitutional provisions which, if complied with, would result in an apportionment valid under the Equal Protection Clause, the judicial task of providing effective relief would appear to be rather simple. We agree with the view of the District Court that state constitutional provisions should be deemed violative of the Federal Constitution only when validly asserted constitutional rights could not otherwise be protected and effectuated. Clearly, courts should attempt to accommodate the relief ordered to the apportionment provisions of state constitutions insofar as is possible. But it is also quite clear that a state legislative apportionment scheme is no less violative of the Federal Constitution when it is based on state constitutional provisions which have been consistently complied with than when resulting from a noncompliance with state constitutional requirements. When there is an unavoidable conflict between the Federal and a State Constitution, the Supremacy Clause, of course, controls.

Harlan, dissenting:

In these cases, the Court holds that seats in the legislatures of six States are apportioned in ways that violate the Federal Constitution. Under the Court's ruling, it is bound to follow that the legislatures in all but a few of the other 44 States will meet the same fate. These decisions, with *Wesberry v. Sanders,* involving congressional districting by the States, and *Gray v. Sanders,* relating to elections for statewide office, have the effect of placing basic aspects of state political systems under the pervasive overlordship of the federal judiciary. . . .

Today's holding is that the Equal Protection Clause of the Fourteenth Amendment requires every State to structure its legislature so that all the members of each house represent substantially the same number of people; other factors may be given play only to the extent that they do not significantly encroach on this basic "population" principle. Whatever may be thought of this holding as a piece of political ideology—and even on that score, the political history and practices of this country from its earliest beginnings leave wide room for debate—I think it demonstrable that the Fourteenth Amendment does not impose this political tenet on the States or authorize this Court to do so.

The Court's constitutional discussion . . . is remarkable . . . for its failure to address itself at all to the Fourteenth Amendment as a whole or to the legislative history of the Amendment pertinent to the matter at hand. Stripped of aphorisms, the Court's argument boils down to the assertion that appellees' right to vote has been invidiously "debased" or "diluted" by systems of apportionment which entitle them to vote for fewer legislators than other voters, an assertion which is tied to the Equal Protection Clause only by the constitutionally frail tautology that "equal" means "equal."

Had the Court paused to probe more deeply into the matter, it would have found that the Equal Protection Clause was never intended to inhibit the States in choosing any democratic method they pleased for the apportionment of their legislatures. This is shown by the language of the Fourteenth Amendment taken as a whole, by the understanding of those who proposed and ratified it, and by the political practices of the States at the time the Amendment was adopted. It is confirmed by numerous state and congressional actions since the adoption of the Fourteenth Amendment, and by the common understanding of the Amendment as evidenced by subsequent constitutional amendments and decisions of this Court before *Baker v. Carr,* supra, made an abrupt break with the past in 1962.

The failure of the Court to consider any of these matters cannot be excused or explained by any concept of "developing" constitutionalism. It is meaningless to speak of constitutional "development" when both the language and history of the controlling provisions of the Constitution are wholly ignored. Since it can, I think, be shown beyond doubt that state legislative apportionments, as such, are wholly free of constitutional limitations, save such as may be imposed by the Republican Form of Government Clause the Court's action now bringing them within the purview of the Fourteenth Amendment amounts to nothing less than an exercise of the amending power by this Court.

So far as the Federal Constitution is concerned, the complaints in these cases should all have been dismissed below for failure to state a cause of action, because what has been alleged or proved shows no violation of any constitutional right. . . .

Gomillion v. Lightfoot

364 U.S. 339 (1960), 9-0

Opinion of the Court: Frankfurter (Black, Brennan, Clark, Douglas, Harlan, Stewart, Warren, Whittaker)

What constitutional violation did the Court find in this case? Why was the decision not based on the equal protection clause? The gerrymander in this case was egregious and blatantly racist, but did the Court develop any guidelines for future cases where representational unfairness might be less clear?

Frankfurter, for the Court:

This litigation challenges the validity, under the United States Constitution, of Local Act No. 140, passed by the Legislature of Alabama in 1957, redefining the boundaries of the City of Tuskegee. Petitioners, Negro citizens of Alabama who were, at the time of this redistricting measure, residents of the City of Tuskegee, brought an action in the United States District Court for the Middle District of Alabama for a declaratory judgment that Act 140 is unconstitutional, and for an injunction to restrain the Mayor and officers of Tuskegee and the officials of Macon County, Alabama, from enforcing the Act against them and other Negroes similarly situated. Petitioners' claim is that enforcement of the statute, which alters the shape of Tuskegee from a square to an uncouth twenty-eight-sided figure, will constitute a discrimination against them in violation of the Due Process and Equal Protection Clauses of the Fourteenth Amendment to the Constitution and will deny them the right to vote in defiance of the Fifteenth Amendment. . . .

At this stage of the litigation, we are not concerned with the truth of the allegations, that is, the ability of petitioners to sustain their allegations by proof. The sole question is whether the allegations entitle them to make good on their claim that they are being denied rights under the United States Constitution. . . .

These allegations, if proven, would abundantly establish that Act 140 was not an ordinary geographic redistricting measure, even within familiar abuses of gerrymandering. If these allegations, upon a trial, remained uncontradicted or unqualified, the conclusion would be irresistible, tantamount for all practical purposes to a mathematical demonstration, that the legislation is solely concerned with segregating white and colored voters by fencing Negro citizens out of town so as to deprive them of their pre-existing municipal vote.

It is difficult to appreciate what stands in the way of adjudging a statute having this inevitable effect invalid in light of the principles by which this Court must judge, and uniformly has judged, statutes that, howsoever speciously defined, obviously discriminate against colored citizens. "The [Fifteenth] Amendment nullifies sophisticated as well as simple-minded modes of discrimination" (*Lane v. Wilson*).

The complaint amply alleges a claim of racial discrimination. Against this claim the respondents have never suggested, either in their brief or in oral argument, any countervailing municipal function which Act 140 is designed to serve. The respondents invoke generalities expressing the State's unrestricted power—unlimited, that is, by the United States Constitution—to establish, destroy, or reorganize by contraction or expansion its political subdivisions, to-wit: cities, counties, and other local units. We freely recognize the breadth and importance of this aspect of the State's political power. . . .

. . . [T]he Court acknowledged that the States have power to do as they will with municipal corporations regardless of consequences. Legislative control of municipalities, no less than other state power, lies within the scope of relevant limitations imposed by the United States Constitution. . . .

. . . [S]uch power, extensive though it is, is met and overcome . . . by the Fifteenth Amendment to the Constitution of the United States, which forbids a State from passing any law which deprives a citizen of his vote because of his race. The opposite conclusion, urged upon us by respondents, would sanction the achievement by a State of any impairment of voting rights whatever, so long as it was cloaked in the garb of the realignment of political subdivisions. . . .

The decisive facts in this case, which at this stage must be taken as proved, are wholly different from the considerations found controlling in *Colegrove* [*v. Green*]. . . .

. . . When a legislature thus singles out a readily isolated segment of a racial minority for special discriminatory treatment, it violates the Fifteenth Amendment. In no case involving unequal weight in voting distribution that has come before the Court did the decision sanction a differentiation on racial lines whereby approval was given to unequivocal withdrawal of the vote solely from colored citizens. Apart from all else, these considerations lift this controversy out of the so-called "political" arena and into the conventional sphere of constitutional litigation. . . .

. . . A statute which is alleged to have worked unconstitutional deprivations of petitioners' rights is not immune to attack simply because the mechanism employed by the legislature is a redefinition of municipal boundaries. According to the allegations here made, the Alabama Legislature has not merely redrawn the Tuskegee city limits with incidental inconvenience to the petitioners; it is more accurate to say that it has deprived the petitioners of the municipal franchise and consequent rights and, to that end, it has incidentally changed the city's boundaries. While in form this is merely an act redefining metes and bounds, if the allegations are established, the inescapable human effect of this essay in geometry and geography is to despoil colored citizens, and only colored citizens, of their theretofore enjoyed voting rights. That was no *Colegrove v. Green.*

When a State exercises power wholly within the domain of state interest, it is insulated from federal judicial review. But such insulation is not carried over when state power is used as an instrument for circumventing a federally protected right. This principle has had many applications. It has long been recognized in cases which have prohibited a State from exploiting a power acknowledged to be absolute in an isolated context to justify the imposition of an "unconstitutional condition." . . . The petitioners are entitled to prove their allegations at trial.

For these reasons, the principal conclusions of the District Court and the Court of Appeals are clearly erroneous, and the decision below must be reversed.

Shaw v. Reno

509 U.S. 630 (1993), 5-4
Opinion of the Court: O'Connor (Kennedy, Rehnquist, Scalia, Thomas)
Dissenting: Blackmun, Souter, Stevens, White

After the 1990 census, the North Carolina legislature redrew the boundaries of its congressional election districts to accommodate assignment to the state of a twelfth seat in the House of Representatives. In doing so, the state created one district that contained a majority of black persons. Because of past racial discrimination in voting, the state was required under the Civil Rights Act of 1965 to have reapportionment plans approved either by a federal court or by the U.S. attorney general. The state submitted the plan to the attorney general, who refused to approve it unless a second "black majority" district was included. The legislature then revised its plan to create a second such district. The revised plan was challenged in this case by white voters who alleged that it had the effect of segregating voters on the basis of race and thus violated the equal protection clause of the Fourteenth Amendment.

Did the Court rule the districting plan unconstitutional? What exactly did it decide? What standard of review did it prescribe? What right was claimed by the plaintiffs? What was White's view of this claim? Besides being visually counterintuitive on a map, is there anything wrong with gerrymanders? Anything unconstitutional per se? In this case, the state used race as a criterion. Twenty years earlier in another North Carolina case, Swann v. Charlotte-Mecklenburg Board of Education *(p. 484), race was also used as a criterion. How was the purpose different? Can the underlying political philosophies of the two cases be reconciled?*

O'Connor, for the Court:

The voting age population of North Carolina is approximately 78% white, 20% black, and 1% Native American; the remaining 1% is predominantly Asian. The black population is relatively dispersed; blacks constitute a majority of the general population in only 5 of the State's 100 counties. . . .

This case involves two of the most complex and sensitive issues this Court has faced in recent years: the means of the constitutional "right" to vote, and the propriety of race-based state legislation designed to benefit members of historically disadvantaged racial minority groups. . . .

An understanding of the nature of appellants' claim is critical to our resolution of the case. In their complaint, appellants did not claim that the General Assembly's reapportionment plan unconstitutionally "diluted" white voting strength. They did not even claim to be white. Rather, appellants' complaint alleged that the deliberate segregation of voters into separate districts on the basis of race violated their constitutional right to participate in a "color blind" electoral process.

Despite their invocation of the ideal of a "color blind" Constitution, appellants appear to concede that race conscious redistricting is not always unconstitutional. That concession is wise: this Court never has held that race conscious state decisionmaking is impermissible in all circumstances. What appellants object to is redistricting legislation that is so extremely irregular on its face that it rationally can be viewed only as an effort to segregate the races for purposes of voting, without regard for traditional districting principles and without sufficiently compelling justification. For the reasons that follow, we conclude that appellants have stated a claim upon which relief can be granted under the Equal Protection Clause. . . .

Appellants contend that redistricting legislation that is so bizarre on its face that it is "unexplainable on grounds other than race," demands the same close scrutiny that we give other state laws that classify citizens by race. Our voting rights precedents support that conclusion. . . .

. . . A reapportionment statute typically does not classify persons at all; it classifies tracts of land, or addresses. Moreover, redistricting differs from other kinds of state decisionmaking in that the legislature always is aware of race when it draws district lines, just as it is aware of age, economic status, religious and political persuasion, and a variety of other demographic factors. That sort of race consciousness does not lead inevitably to impermissible race discrimination. . . . [W]hen members of a racial group live together in one community, a reapportionment plan that concentrates members of the group in one district and excludes them from others may reflect wholly legitimate purposes. The district lines may be drawn, for example, to provide for compact districts of contiguous territory, or to maintain the integrity of political subdivisions.

The difficulty of proof, of course, does not mean that a racial gerrymander, once established, should receive less scrutiny under the Equal Protection Clause than other state legislation classifying citizens by race. Moreover, it seems clear to us that proof sometimes will not be difficult at all. In some exceptional cases, a reapportionment plan may be so highly irregular that, on its face, it rationally cannot be understood as anything other than an effort to "segregat[e] . . . voters" on the basis of race. *Gomillion* [*v. Lightfoot*], in which a tortured municipal boundary line was drawn to exclude black voters, was such a case. So, too, would be a case in which a State concentrated a dispersed minority population in a single district by disregarding traditional districting principles such as compactness, contiguity, and respect for political subdivisions. We emphasize that these criteria are important not because they are constitutionally required—they are not—but because they are objective factors that may serve to defeat a claim that a district has been gerrymandered on racial lines. . . .

Put differently, we believe that reapportionment is one area in which appearances do matter. A reapportionment plan that includes in one district individuals who belong to the same race, but who are otherwise widely separated by geographical and political boundaries, and who may have little in common with one another but the color of their skin, bears an uncomfortable resemblance to political apartheid. It reinforces the perception that members of the same racial group—regardless of their age, education, economic status, or the community in which the live—think alike, share the same political interests, and will prefer the same candidates at the polls. We have rejected such perceptions elsewhere as impermissible racial stereotypes. By perpetuating such notions, a racial gerrymander may exacerbate the very patterns of racial bloc voting that majority minority districting is sometimes said to counteract.

The message that such districting sends to elected representatives is equally pernicious. When a district obviously is created solely to effectuate the perceived common interests of one racial group, elected officials are more likely to believe that their primary obligation is to represent only the members of that group, rather than their constituency as a whole. This is altogether antithetical to our system of representative democracy. . . .

For these reasons, we conclude that a plaintiff challenging a reapportionment statute under the Equal Protection Clause may state a claim by alleging that the legislation, though race neutral on its face, rationally cannot be understood as anything other than an effort to separate voters into different districts on the basis of race, and that the separation lacks sufficient justification. It is unnecessary for us to decide whether or how a reapportionment plan that, on its face, can be explained in nonracial terms successfully could be challenged. Thus, we express no view as to whether "the intentional creation of majority minority districts, without more" always gives rise to an equal protection claim. We hold only that, on the facts of this case, plaintiffs have stated a claim sufficient to defeat the state appellees' motion to dismiss. . . .

Racial classifications of any sort pose the risk of lasting harm to our society. They reinforce the belief, held by too many for too much of our history, that individuals should be judged by the color of their skin. Racial classifications with respect to voting carry particular dangers. Racial gerrymandering, even for remedial purposes, may balkanize us into competing racial factions; it threatens to carry us further from the goal of a political system in which race no longer matters—a goal that the Fourteenth and Fifteenth Amendments embody, and to which the Nation continues to aspire. It is for these reasons that race based districting by our state legislatures demands close judicial scrutiny.

. . . Today we hold only that appellants have stated a claim under the Equal Protection Clause by alleging that the North Carolina General Assembly adopted a reapportionment scheme so irrational on its face that it can be understood only as an effort to segregate voters into separate voting districts because of their race, and that the separation lacks sufficient justification. If the allegation of racial gerrymandering remains un-contradicted, the District Court further must determine whether the North Carolina plan is narrowly tailored to further a compelling governmental interest. Accordingly, we reverse the judgment of the District Court and remand the case for further proceedings consistent with this opinion. . . .

White, dissenting:

. . . The grounds for my disagreement with the majority are simply stated: Appellants have not presented a cognizable claim, because they have not alleged a cognizable injury. To date, we have held that only two types of state voting practices could give rise to a constitutional claim. The first involves direct and outright deprivation of the right to vote, for example by means of a poll tax or literacy test. Plainly, this variety is not implicated by appellants' allegations and need not detain us further. The second type of unconstitutional practice is that which "affects the political strength of various groups," *Mobile v. Bolden,* in violation of the Equal Protection Clause. As for this latter category, we have insisted that members of the political or racial group demonstrate that the challenged action have the intent and effect of unduly diminishing their influence on the political process. Although this severe burden has limited the number of successful suits, it was adopted for sound reasons. . . .

Redistricting plans . . . reflect group interests and inevitably are conceived with partisan aims in mind. To allow judicial interference whenever this occurs would be to invite constant and unmanageable intrusion. Moreover, a group's power to affect the political process does not automatically dissipate by virtue of an electoral loss. Accordingly, we have asked that an identifiable group demonstrate more than mere lack of success at the polls to make out a successful gerrymandering claim. . . .

Racial gerrymanders come in various shades: At large voting schemes, the fragmentation of a minority group among various districts "so that it is a majority in none," the "stacking" of "a large minority population concentration . . . with a larger white population," and finally, the "concentration of [minority voters] into districts where they constitute an excessive majority," also called "packing." In each instance, race is consciously utilized by the legislature for electoral purposes; in each instance, we have put the plaintiff challenging the district lines to the burden of demonstrating that the plan was meant to, and did in

fact, exclude an identifiable racial group from participation in the political process.

Not so, apparently, when the districting "segregates" by drawing odd shaped lines. In that case, we are told, such proof no longer is needed. . . . A plan that "segregates" being functionally indistinguishable from any of the other varieties of gerrymandering, we should be consistent in what we require from a claimant: Proof of discriminatory purpose and effect.

The other part of the majority's explanation of its holding is related to its simultaneous discomfort and fascination with irregularly shaped districts. Lack of compactness or contiguity, like uncouth district lines, certainly is a helpful indicator that some form of gerrymandering (racial or other) might have taken place and that "something may be amiss." Disregard for geographic divisions and compactness often goes hand in hand with partisan gerrymandering.

But while district irregularities may provide strong indicia of a potential gerrymander, they do no more than that. In particular, they have no bearing on whether the plan ultimately is found to violate the Constitution.

Souter, dissenting:

Today, the Court recognizes a new cause of action under which a State's electoral redistricting plan that includes a configuration "so bizarre" that it "rationally cannot be understood as anything other than an effort to separate voters into different districts on the basis of race [without] sufficient justification" will be subjected to strict scrutiny . . . There is no justification for the Court's determination to depart from our prior decisions by carving out this narrow group of cases for strict scrutiny in place of the review customarily applied in cases dealing with discrimination in electoral districting on the basis of race. . . .

There is . . . no theoretical inconsistency in having two distinct approaches to equal protection analysis, one for cases of electoral districting and one for most other types of state governmental decisions. Nor, because of the distinctions between the two categories, is there any risk that Fourteenth Amendment districting law as such will be taken to imply anything for purposes of general Fourteenth Amendment scrutiny about "benign" racial discrimination, or about group entitlement as distinct from individual protection, or about the appropriateness of stricter other heightened scrutiny. . . .

The Court offers no adequate justification for treating the narrow category of bizarrely shaped district claims differently from other districting claims. The only justification I can imagine would be the preservation of sound districting principles," such as compactness and contiguity. But . . . we have held that such principles are not constitutionally required, with the consequence that their absence cannot justify the distinct constitutional regime put in place by the Court today. Since there is no justification for the departure here from the principles that continue to govern electoral districting cases generally in accordance with our prior decisions, I would not respond to the seeming egregiousness of the redistricting now before us by untethering the concept of racial gerrymander in such a case from the concept of harm exemplified by dilution. In the absence of an allegation of such harm, I would affirm the judgment of the District Court. . . .

Miller v. Johnson

512 U.S. 622 (1995), 5-4
Opinion of the Court: Kennedy (O'Connor, Rehnquist, Scalia, Thomas)
Dissenting: Breyer, Ginsburg, Souter, Stevens

Why was Georgia's creation of one or more black-majority districts not required by the Voting Rights Act? What would the state need to show in order to justify them? How does creation of a black-majority district differ from creation of a virtually all-white district as in Gomillion v. Lightfoot *(p. 605)? Are black-majority districts merely a new form of segregation? Are they compatible with the goal of a racially integrated society? Is that goal as valid today as in much of the recent past or is it less urgent because of progress toward it? Is the creation of black-majority districts based on the assumption that white voters will not vote for black candidates? Is that assumption valid? Does a constituent have fair representation only when his or her representative is a member of the same race? If so, what difficulties does that present for electoral districting and apportionment? For an integrated society?*

Kennedy, for the Court:

The constitutionality of Georgia's congressional redistricting plan is at issue here. In *Shaw v. Reno*, we held that a plaintiff states a claim under the Equal Protection Clause by alleging that a state redistricting plan,

on its face, has no rational explanation save as an effort to separate voters on the basis of race. The question we now decide is whether Georgia's new Eleventh District gives rise to a valid equal protection claim under the principles announced in *Shaw*, and, if so, whether it can be sustained nonetheless as narrowly tailored to serve a compelling governmental interest.

The Equal Protection Clause['s] . . . Its central mandate is racial neutrality in governmental decisionmaking. . . . This rule obtains with equal force regardless of "the race of those burdened or benefited by a particular classification." . . . Laws classifying citizens on the basis of race cannot be upheld unless they are narrowly tailored to achieving a compelling state interest.

In *Shaw v. Reno* we recognized that these equal protection principles govern a State's drawing of congressional districts, though, as our cautious approach there discloses, application of these principles to electoral districting is a most delicate task. . . .

This case requires us to apply the principles articulated in *Shaw* to the most recent congressional redistricting plan enacted by the State of Georgia.

In 1965, the Attorney General designated Georgia a covered jurisdiction under §4(b) of the Voting Rights Act In consequence, §5 of the Act requires Georgia to obtain either administrative preclearance by the Attorney General or approval by the United States District Court for the District of Columbia of any change in a "standard, practice, or procedure with respect to voting" made after November 1, 1964. The preclearance mechanism applies to congressional redistricting plans and requires that the proposed change "not have the purpose and will not have the effect of denying or abridging the right to vote on account of race or color." "[T]he purpose of §5 has always been to insure that no voting procedure changes would be made that would lead to a retrogression in the position of racial minorities with respect to their effective exercise of the electoral franchise." . . .

Twice spurned, the General Assembly set out to create three majority minority districts to gain preclearance. Using the ACLU's "max black" plan as its benchmark, the General Assembly enacted a plan that "bore all the signs of [the Justice Department's] involvement: . . .

The new plan also enacted the Macon/Savannah swap necessary to create a third majority black district. The Eleventh District lost the black population of Macon, but picked up Savannah, thereby connecting the black neighborhoods of metropolitan Atlanta and the poor black populace of coastal Chatham County, though 260 miles apart in distance and worlds apart in culture. . . .

. . . Appellents . . . contend that evidence of a legislature's deliberate classification of voters on the basis of race cannot alone suffice to state a claim under *Shaw*. They argue that, regardless of the legislature's purposes, a plaintiff must demonstrate that a district's shape is so bizarre that it is unexplainable other than on the basis of race, and that appellees failed to make that showing here. Appellants' conception of the constitutional violation misapprehends our holding in *Shaw*. . . .

Our observation in *Shaw* of the consequences of racial stereotyping was not meant to suggest that a district must be bizarre on its face before there is a constitutional violation. Nor was our conclusion in *Shaw* that in certain instances a district's appearance (or, to be more precise, its appearance in combination with certain demographic evidence) can give rise to an equal protection claim, a holding that bizarreness was a threshold showing, as appellants believe it to be. Our circumspect approach and narrow holding in *Shaw* did not erect an artificial rule barring accepted equal protection analysis in other redistricting cases. Shape is relevant not because bizarreness is a necessary element of the constitutional wrong or a threshold requirement of proof, but because it may be persuasive circumstantial evidence that race for its own sake, and not other districting principles, was the legislature's dominant and controlling rationale in drawing its district lines. The logical implication, as courts applying *Shaw* have recognized, is that parties may rely on evidence other than bizarreness to establish race based districting. . . .

In sum, we make clear that parties alleging that a State has assigned voters on the basis of race are neither confined in their proof to evidence regarding the district's geometry and makeup nor required to make a threshold showing of bizarreness. Today's case requires us further to consider the requirements of the proof necessary to sustain this equal protection challenge.

Federal court review of districting legislation represents a serious intrusion on the most vital of local functions. . . . Redistricting legislatures will, for example, almost always be aware of racial demographics; but it does not follow that race predominates in the redistricting process. The distinction between being aware of racial considerations and being motivated by them may be difficult to make. This evidentiary difficulty, together with the sensitive nature of redistricting and the presumption of good faith that must be accorded legislative enactments, requires courts to exercise extraordinary caution in adjudicating claims that a state has drawn district lines on the basis of race. The plaintiff's burden is to show, either through circumstantial evidence of a district's shape and demographics or more direct evidence going to legislative purpose, that race was the predominant factor motivating the legislature's decision to place a significant number of voters within or without a particular district. To make this showing, a plaintiff must prove that the legislature subordinated traditional race neutral districting principles, including but not limited to compactness, contiguity, respect for political subdivisions or communities defined by actual shared interests, to racial considerations. Where these or other race neutral considerations are the basis for redistricting legislation, and are not subordinated to race, a state can "defeat a claim that a district has been gerrymandered on racial lines." . . .

In our view, the District Court applied the correct analysis, and its finding that race was the predominant factor motivating the drawing of the Eleventh District was not clearly erroneous. The court found it was "exceedingly obvious" from the shape of the Eleventh District, together with the relevant racial demographics, that the drawing of narrow land bridges to incorporate within the District outlying appendages containing nearly 80% of the district's total black population was a deliberate attempt to bring black populations into the district. . . .

As a result, Georgia's congressional redistricting plan cannot be upheld unless it satisfies strict scrutiny, our most rigorous and exacting standard of constitutional review.

To satisfy strict scrutiny, the State must demonstrate that its districting legislation is narrowly tailored to achieve a compelling interest. There is a "significant state interest in eradicating the effects of past racial discrimination." The State does not argue, however, that it created the Eleventh District to remedy past discrimination, and with good reason: there is little doubt that the State's true interest in designing the Eleventh District was creating a third majority black district to satisfy the Justice Department's preclearance demands. Whether or not in some cases compliance with the Voting Rights Act, standing alone, can provide a compelling interest independent of any interest in remedying past discrimination, it cannot do so here. As we suggested in *Shaw,* compliance with federal antidiscrimination laws cannot justify race based districting where the challenged district was not reasonably necessary under a constitutional reading and application of those laws. The congressional plan challenged here was not required by the Voting Rights Act under a correct reading of the statute. . . .

Georgia's drawing of the Eleventh District was not required under the Act because there was no reasonable basis to believe that Georgia's earlier enacted plans violated §5. Wherever a plan is "ameliorative," a term we have used to describe plans increasing the number of majority minority districts, it "cannot violate §5 unless the new apportionment itself so discriminates on the basis of race or color as to violate the Constitution." Georgia's first and second proposed plans increased the number of majority black districts from 1 out of 10 (10%) to 2 out of 11 (18.18%). These plans were "ameliorative" and could not have violated §5's non retrogression principle. Acknowledging as much, the United States now relies on the fact that the Justice Department may object to a state proposal either on the ground that it has a prohibited purpose or a prohibited effect. The Government justifies its preclearance objections on the ground that the submitted plans violated §5's purpose element. The key to the Government's position, which is plain from its objection letters if not from its briefs to this Court, is and always has been that Georgia failed to proffer a nondiscriminatory purpose for its refusal in the first two submissions to take the steps necessary to create a third majority minority district.

The Government's position is insupportable. . . . The State's policy of adhering to other districting principles instead of creating as many majority minority districts as possible does not support an inference that the plan "so discriminates on the basis of race or color as to violate the Constitution," and thus cannot provide any basis under §5 for the Justice Department's objection.

Instead of grounding its objections on evidence of a discriminatory purpose, it would appear the Government was driven by its policy of maximizing majority black districts. Although the Government now disavows having had that policy, and seems to concede its impropriety, the District Court's well-documented factual finding was that the Department did adopt a maximization policy and followed it in objecting to Georgia's first two plans. . . .

"[T]he purpose of §5 has always been to insure that no voting procedure changes would be made that would lead to a retrogression in the position of racial minorities with respect to their effective exercise of the electoral franchise." The Justice Department's maximization policy seems quite far removed from this purpose. We are especially reluctant to conclude that §5 justifies that policy given the serious constitutional concerns it raises. . . .

The Voting Rights Act, and its grant of authority to the federal courts to uncover official efforts to abridge minorities' right to vote, has been of vital importance in eradicating invidious discrimination from the electoral process and enhancing the legitimacy of our political institutions. Only if our political system and our society cleanse themselves of that discrimination will all members of the polity share an equal opportunity to gain public office regardless of race. As a Nation we share both the obligation and the aspiration of working toward this end. The end is neither assured nor well served, however, by carving electorates into racial blocs. "If our society is to continue to progress as a multiracial democracy, it must recognize that the automatic invocation of race stereotypes retards that progress and causes continued hurt and injury." *Edmondson v. Leesville Concrete Co.* It takes a shortsighted and unauthorized view of the Voting Rights Act to invoke that statute, which has played a decisive role in redressing some of our worst forms of discrimination, to demand the very racial stereotyping the Fourteenth Amendment forbids. . . .

Stevens, dissenting:

. . . I believe the respondents in these cases . . . have not suffered any legally cognizable injury. . . .

In particular instances, of course, members of one race may vote by an overwhelming margin for one candidate, and in some cases that candidate will be of the same race. "Racially polarized voting" is one of the circumstances plaintiffs must prove to advance a vote dilution claim. Such a claim allows voters to allege that gerrymandered district lines have impaired their ability to elect a candidate of their own race. The Court emphasizes, however, that a so called *Shaw* claim is "'analytically distinct' from a vote dilution claim," Neither in *Shaw* . . . nor in the instant cases has the Court answered the question its analytic distinction raises: If the *Shaw* injury does not flow from an increased probability that white candidates will lose, then how can the increased probability that black candidates will win cause white voters, such as respondents, cognizable harm?

The Court attempts an explanation in these cases by equating the injury it imagines respondents have suffered with the injuries African Americans suffered under segregation. The heart of respondents' claim, by the Court's account, is that "a State's assignment of voters on the basis of race," violates the Equal Protection Clause for the same reason a State may not "segregate citizens on the basis of race in its public parks, This equation, however, fails to elucidate the elusive *Shaw* injury. Our desegregation cases redressed the exclusion of black citizens from public facilities reserved for whites. In this case, in contrast, any voter, black or white, may live in the Eleventh District. What respondents contest is the inclusion of too many black voters in the District as drawn. In my view, if respondents allege no vote dilution, that inclusion can cause them no conceivable injury.

The Court's equation of *Shaw* claims with our desegregation decisions is inappropriate for another reason. In each of those cases, legal segregation frustrated the public interest in diversity and tolerance by barring African Americans from joining whites in the activities at issue. The districting plan here, in contrast, serves the interest in diversity and tolerance by increasing the likelihood that a meaningful number of black representatives will add their voices to legislative debates. . . .

Equally distressing is the Court's equation of traditional gerrymanders, designed to maintain or enhance a dominant group's power, with a dominant group's decision to share its power with a previously underrepresented group. In my view, districting plans violate the Equal Protection Clause when they "serve no purpose other than to favor one segment—whether racial, ethnic, religious, economic, or political—that may occupy a position of strength at a particular point in time, or to disadvantage a politically weak segment of the community." In contrast, I do not see how a districting plan that favors a politically weak group can violate equal protection. . . .

The Court's refusal to distinguish an enactment that helps a minority group from enactments that cause it harm is especially unfortunate at the intersection of race and voting, given that African Americans and other disadvantaged groups have struggled so long and so hard for inclusion in that most central exercise of our democracy. I have long believed that treating racial groups differently from other identifiable groups of voters, as the Court does today, is itself an invidious racial classification. Racial minorities should receive neither more nor less protection than other groups against gerrymanders. A fortiori, racial minorities should not be less eligible than other groups to benefit from districting plans the majority designs to aid them.

Ginsburg, dissenting:

. . . Before *Shaw v. Reno*, this Court invoked the Equal Protection Clause to justify intervention in the quintessentially political task of legislative districting in two circumstances: to enforce the one-person, one-vote requirement, and to prevent dilution of a minority group's voting strength.

In *Shaw*, the Court recognized a third basis for an equal protection challenge to a State's apportionment plan. The Court wrote cautiously, emphasizing that judicial intervention is exceptional: "[S]trict [judicial] scrutiny" is in order, the Court declared, if a district is "so extremely irregular on its face that it rationally can be viewed only as an effort to segregate the races for purposes of voting." . . .

The problem in *Shaw* was not the plan architects' consideration of race as relevant in redistricting. Rather, in the Court's estimation, it was the virtual exclusion of other factors from the calculus. Traditional districting practices were cast aside, the Court concluded, with race alone steering placement of district lines.

The record before us does not show that race similarly overwhelmed traditional districting practices in Georgia. . . .

In adopting districting plans, States do not treat people as individuals. Apportionment schemes, by their very nature, assemble people in groups. States do not assign voters to districts based on merit or achievement, standards States might use in hiring employees or engaging contractors. Rather, legislators classify voters in groups—by economic, geographical, political, or social characteristics—and then "reconcile the competing claims of [these] groups." *Davis v. Bandemer*, (O'Connor, J., concurring in judgment).

That ethnicity defines some of these groups is a political reality. Until now, no constitutional infirmity has been seen in districting Irish or Italian voters together, for example, so long as the delineation does not abandon familiar apportionment practices. If

Chinese Americans and Russian Americans may seek and secure group recognition in the delineation of voting districts, then African Americans should not be dissimilarly treated. Otherwise, in the name of equal protection, we would shut out "the very minority group whose history in the United States gave birth to the Equal Protection Clause."

Buckley v. Valeo

424 U.S. 1 (1976), 7-1 (on campaign spending issue), 6-2 (campaign contributions issue)
Per Curiam Opinion
Campaign spending issue: Blackmun, Brennan, Burger, Marshall, Powell, Rehnquist, Stewart
Dissenting: White
Campaign contributions issue: Brennan, Marshall, Powell, Rehnquist, Stewart, White
Dissenting: Blackmun, Burger
Not participating: Stevens

This case, challenging several provisions of the Federal Campaign Election Act of 1971, as amended in 1974, was brought by several plaintiffs, including U.S. Senator James Buckley, a candidate for reelection in New York, and Eugene McCarthy, a candidate for president. Among several government officials named as defendants was U.S. Senate Secretary, Francis Valeo.

On what grounds did the Court hold that campaign contributions are different from campaign spending insofar as each might be limited by law? Are those differences as basic in political reality as the Court makes them out to be constitutionally? What government interests did the Court recognize? What test of review did it apply? In many free speech and press cases, the Court has shown concern about whether persons with little or no means of communicating their ideas have adequate avenues open to them. Has the Court abandoned that concern in this case? Is the underlying philosophy of the decision consistent with the underlying philosophy in Reynolds v. Sims *(p. 602)? In* San Antonio Independent School District v. Rodriguez *(p. 574)?*

Per Curiam Opinion:

. . . The statutes at issue, summarized in broad terms, contain the following provisions: (a) individual political contributions are limited to $1,000 to any single candidate per election, with an over-all annual limitation of $25,000 by any contributor; independent expenditures by individuals and groups "relative to a

clearly identified candidate" are limited to $1,000 a year; campaign spending by candidates for various federal offices and spending for national conventions by political parties are subject to prescribed limits; (b) contributions and expenditures above certain threshold levels must be reported and publicly disclosed; (c) a system for public funding of Presidential campaign activities is established by Subtitle H of the Internal Revenue Code; and (d) a Federal Election Commission is established to administer and enforce the legislation. . . .

A. General Principles

The Act's contribution and expenditure limitations operate in an area of the most fundamental First Amendment activities. Discussion of public issues and debate on the qualifications of candidates are integral to the operation of the system of government established by our Constitution. The First Amendment affords the broadest protection to such political expression in order "to assure [the] unfettered interchange of ideas for the bringing about of political and social changes desired by the people" (*Roth v. United States*). Although First Amendment protections are not confined to "the exposition of ideas," *Winters v. New York* "there is practically universal agreement that a major purpose of that Amendment was to protect the free discussion of governmental affairs, . . . of course includ[ing] discussions of candidates . . ." *Mills v. Alabama* This no more than reflects our "profound national commitment to the principle that debate on public issues should be uninhibited, robust, and wide-open," *New York Times Co. v. Sullivan*. . . .

It is with these principles in mind that we consider the primary contentions of the parties with respect to the Act's limitations upon the giving and spending of money in political campaigns. . . .

B. Contribution Limitations

1. The $1,000 Limitation on Contributions by Individuals and Groups to Candidates and Authorized Campaign Committees

Section 608(b) provides, with certain limited exceptions, that "no person shall make contributions to any candidate with respect to any election for Federal office which, in the aggregate, exceed $1,000." . . .

It is unnecessary to look beyond the Act's primary purpose—to limit the actuality and appearance of corruption resulting from large individual financial contributions—in order to find a constitutionally sufficient justification for the $1,000 contribution limitation. Under a system of private financing of elections, a candidate lacking immense personal or family wealth must depend on financial contributions from others to provide the resources necessary to conduct a successful campaign. The increasing importance of the communications media and sophisticated mass-mailing and polling operations to effective campaigning make the raising of large sums of money an ever more essential ingredient of an effective candidacy. To the extent that large contributions are given to secure a political quid pro quo from current and potential office holders, the integrity of our system of representative democracy is undermined. Although the scope of such pernicious practices can never be reliably ascertained, the deeply disturbing examples surfacing after the 1972 election demonstrate that the problem is not an illusory one.

Of almost equal concern as the danger of actual quid pro quo arrangements is the impact of the appearance of corruption stemming from public awareness of the opportunities for abuse inherent in a regime of large individual financial contributions....

The Act's $1,000 contribution limitation focuses precisely on the problem of large campaign contributions—the narrow aspect of political association where the actuality and potential for corruption have been identified—while leaving persons free to engage in independent political expression, to associate actively through volunteering their services, and to assist to a limited but nonetheless substantial extent in supporting candidates and committees with financial resources. Significantly, the Act's contribution limitations in themselves do not undermine to any material degree the potential for robust and effective discussion of candidates and campaign issues by individual citizens, associations, the institutional press, candidates, and political parties.

We find that, under the rigorous standard of review established by our prior decisions, the weighty interests served by restricting the size of financial contributions to political candidates are sufficient to justify the limited effect upon First Amendment freedoms caused by the $1,000 contribution ceiling....

2. The $5,000 Limitation on Contributions by Political Committees

Section 608(b)(2) permits certain committees, designated as "political committees," to contribute up to $5,000 to any candidate with respect to any election for federal office. In order to qualify for the higher contribution ceiling, a group must have been registered with the Commission as a political committee under 2 U.S.C. §433 for not less than six months, have received contributions from more than 50 persons, and, except for state political party organizations, have contributed to five or more candidates for federal office. Appellants argue that these qualifications unconstitutionally discriminate against ad hoc organizations in favor of established interest groups and impermissibly burden free association. The argument is without merit. Rather than undermining freedom of association, the basic provision enhances the opportunity of bona fide groups to participate in the election process, and the registration, contribution, and candidate conditions serve the permissible purpose of preventing individuals from evading the applicable contribution limitations by labeling themselves committees....

[Limitations on volunteers' incidental expenses, point 3, were upheld on the same reasoning.]

4. The 25,000 Limitation on Total Contributions During any Calendar Year

In addition to the $1,000 limitation on the nonexempt contributions that an individual may make to a particular candidate for any single election, the Act contains an over-all $25,000 limitation on total contributions by an individual during any calendar year.... The over-all $25,000 ceiling does impose an ultimate restriction upon the number of candidates and committees with which an individual may associate himself by means of financial support. But this quite modest restraint upon protected political activity serves to prevent evasion of the $1,000 contribution limitation by a person who might otherwise contribute massive amounts of money to a particular candidate through the use of unearmarked contributions to political committees likely to contribute to that candidate, or huge contributions to the candidate's political party. The limited, additional restriction on associational freedom imposed by the over-all ceiling is thus no more than a corollary of the basic individual contribution limitation that we have found to be constitutionally valid.

C. Expenditure Limitations

The Act's expenditure ceilings impose direct and substantial restraints on the quantity of political speech....

1. The $1,000 Limitation on Expenditures "Relative to a Clearly Identified Candidate"

Section 608(e)(1) provides that "[n]o person may make any expenditure . . . relative to a clearly identified candidate during a calendar year which, when added to all other expenditures made by such person during the year advocating the election or defeat of such candidate, exceeds $1,000." . . .

. . . [T]he constitutionality of §608(e)(1) turns on whether the governmental interests advanced in its support satisfy the exacting scrutiny applicable to limitations on core First Amendment rights of political expression.

We find that the governmental interest in preventing corruption and the appearance of corruption is inadequate to justify §608(e)(1)'s ceiling on independent expenditures. First, assuming . . . that large independent expenditures pose the same dangers of actual or apparent quid pro quo arrangements as do large contributions, §608(e)(1) does not provide an answer that sufficiently relates to the elimination of those dangers. . . .

Second, quite apart from the shortcomings of §608(e)(1) in preventing any abuses generated by large independent expenditures, the independent advocacy restricted by the provision does not presently appear to pose dangers of real or apparent corruption comparable to those identified with large campaign contributions. . . .

While the independent expenditure ceiling thus fails to serve any substantial governmental interest in stemming the reality or appearance of corruption in the electoral process, it heavily burdens core First Amendment expression. For the First Amendment right to "speak one's mind . . . on all public institutions" includes the right to engage in "vigorous advocacy no less than abstract discussion." *New York Times Co. v Sullivan*. . . . Advocacy of the election or defeat of candidates for federal office is no less entitled to protection under the First Amendment than the discussion of political policy generally or advocacy of the passage or defeat of legislation. . . .

For the reasons stated, we conclude that §608(e)(1)'s independent expenditure limitation is unconstitutional under the First Amendment.

2. Limitation on Expenditures by Candidates from Personal or Family Resources

The Act also sets limits on expenditures by a candidate "from his personal funds, or the personal funds of his immediate family, in connection with his campaigns during any calendar year." §608(a)(1). These ceilings vary from $50,000 for Presidential or Vice

Presidential candidates to $35,000 for senatorial candidates, and $25,000 for most candidates for the House of Representatives.

The ceiling on personal expenditures by candidates on their own behalf, like the limitations on independent expenditures contained in §608(e)(1), imposes a substantial restraint on the ability of persons to engage in protected First Amendment expression. The candidate, no less than any other person, has a First Amendment right to engage in the discussion of public issues and vigorously and tirelessly to advocate his own election and the election of other candidates. Indeed, it is of particular importance that candidates have the unfettered opportunity to make their views known so that the electorate may intelligently evaluate the candidates' personal qualities and their positions on vital public issues before choosing among them on election day. Mr. Justice Brandeis' observation that, in our country "public discussion is a political duty," *Whitney v. California*, applies with special force to candidates for public office. Section 608(a)'s ceiling on personal expenditures by a candidate in furtherance of his own candidacy thus clearly and directly interferes with constitutionally protected freedoms.

The primary governmental interest served by the Act—the prevention of actual and apparent corruption of the political process—does not support the limitation on the candidate's expenditure of his own personal funds. . . .

3. Limitations on Campaign Expenditures

Section 608(c) places limitations on over-all campaign expenditures by candidates seeking nomination for election and election to federal office. . . .

No governmental interest that has been suggested is sufficient to justify the restriction on the quantity of political expression imposed by §608(c)'s campaign expenditure limitations. The major evil associated with rapidly increasing campaign expenditures is the danger of candidate dependence on large contributions. The interest in alleviating the corrupting influence of large contributions is served by the Act's contribution limitations and disclosure provisions, rather than by §608(c)'s campaign expenditure ceilings. . . .

The interest in equalizing the financial resources of candidates competing for federal office is no more convincing a justification for restricting the scope of federal election campaigns. Given the limitation on the size of outside contributions, the financial resources available to a candidate's campaign, like the number of volunteers recruited, will normally vary with the size and intensity of the candidate's support. There is nothing invidious, improper, or unhealthy in permitting such funds to be spent to carry the candidate's message to the electorate. . . .

. . . The First Amendment denies government the power to determine that spending to promote one's political views is wasteful, excessive, or unwise. In the free society ordained by our Constitution, it is not the government, but the people—individually, as citizens and candidates, and collectively, as associations and political committees—who must retain control over the quantity and range of debate on public issues in a political campaign.

For these reasons, we hold that §608(c) is constitutionally invalid.

In sum, the provisions of the Act that impose a $1,000 limitation on contributions to a single candidate, §608(b)(1), a $5,000 limitation on contributions by a political committee to a single candidate, §608(b)(2), and a $25,000 limitation on total contributions by an individual during any calendar year, §608(b)(3), are constitutionally valid. These limitations, along with the disclosure provisions, constitute the Act's primary weapons against the reality or appearance of improper influence stemming from the dependence of candidates on large campaign contributions. The contribution ceilings thus serve the basic governmental interest in safeguarding the integrity of the electoral process without directly impinging upon the rights of individual citizens and candidates to engage in political debate and discussion. By contrast, the First Amendment requires the invalidation of the Act's independent expenditure ceiling, §608(e)(1), its limitation on a candidate's expenditures from his own personal funds, §608(a), and its ceilings on overall campaign expenditures, §608(e). These provisions place substantial and direct restrictions on the ability of candidates, citizens, and associations to engage in protected political expression, restrictions that the First Amendment cannot tolerate. . . .

[The Court upheld the recordkeeping, reporting, and disclosure provisions of the Act.]

Conclusion

. . . [W]e sustain the individual contribution limits, the disclosure and reporting provisions, and the public financing scheme. We conclude, however, that the limitations on campaign expenditures, on independent expenditures by individuals and groups, and on

expenditures by a candidate from his personal funds are constitutionally infirm. Finally, we hold that most of the powers conferred by the Act upon the Federal Election Commission can be exercised only by "Officers of the United States," appointed in conformity with Art. II, §2, cl. 2, of the Constitution, and therefore cannot be exercised by the Commission as presently constituted. . . .

Burger, concurring in part, dissenting in part:

. . . [N]o legitimate public interest has been shown in forcing the disclosure of modest contributions that are the prime support of new, unpopular, or unfashionable political causes. There is no realistic possibility that such modest donations will have a corrupting influence, especially on parties that enjoy only "minor" status. . . .

. . . In any event, the dangers to First Amendment rights here are too great. Flushing out the names of supporters of minority parties will plainly have a deterrent effect on potential contributors, a consequence readily admitted by the Court . . .

I agree fully with that part of the Court's opinion that holds unconstitutional the limitations the Act puts on campaign expenditures which "place substantial and direct restrictions on the ability of candidates, citizens, and associations to engage in protected political expression, restrictions that the First Amendment cannot tolerate."

Yet when it approves similarly stringent limitations on contributions, the Court ignores the reasons it finds so persuasive in the context of expenditures. For me, contributions and expenditures are two sides of the same First Amendment coin.

By limiting campaign contributions, the Act restricts the amount of money that will be spent on political activity—and does so directly. . . .

The Court's attempt to distinguish the communication inherent in political contributions from the speech aspects of political expenditures simply "will not wash." We do little but engage in word games unless we recognize that people—candidates and contributors—spend money on political activity because they wish to communicate ideas, and their constitutional interest in doing so is precisely the same whether they or someone else utters the words.

The Court attempts to make the Act seem less restrictive by casting the problem as one that goes to freedom of association, rather than freedom of speech. I have long thought freedom of association and freedom of expression were two peas from the same pod. The contribution limitations of the Act impose a restriction on certain forms of associational activity that are, for the most part, as the Court recognizes, harmless in fact. And the restrictions are hardly incidental in their effect upon particular campaigns. . . .

At any rate, the contribution limits are a far more severe restriction on First Amendment activity than the sort of "chilling" legislation for which the Court has shown such extraordinary concern in the past. . . .

White, concurring in part, dissenting in part:

. . . The disclosure requirements and the limitations on contributions and expenditures are challenged as invalid abridgments of the right of free speech protected by the First Amendment. I would reject these challenges. I agree with the Court's conclusion and much of its opinion with respect to sustaining the disclosure provisions. I am also in agreement with the Court's judgment upholding the limitations on contributions. I dissent, however, from the Court's view that the expenditure limitations of 18 U.S.C. §§608(c) and (e) violate the First Amendment.

Concededly, neither the limitations on contributions nor those on expenditures directly or indirectly purport to control the content of political speech by candidates or by their supporters or detractors. What the Act regulates is giving and spending money, acts that have First Amendment significance not because they are themselves communicative with respect to the qualifications of the candidate, but because money may be used to defray the expenses of speaking or otherwise communicating about the merits or demerits of federal candidates for election. The act of giving money to political candidates, however, may have illegal or other undesirable consequences: it may be used to secure the express or tacit understanding that the giver will enjoy political favor if the candidate is elected. Both Congress and this Court's cases have recognized this as a mortal danger against which effective preventive and curative steps must be taken. . . .

APPENDICES

A. Reading a Supreme Court Decision

When the Supreme Court decides a case it applies political power in the form of judicial authority to resolve or settle a dispute. The Opinion of the Court, unanimous or representing a majority of the justices (in rare instances, a mere plurality), attempts to explain and justify what has been decided. Because opinions are technical legal documents and often deal with complex issues, they require careful yet aggressive reading and rereading. Understanding and mastery of opinions is likely to demand greater time and greater effort than would most text of similar length that students encounter in college study.

For these reasons, most students of law—undergraduate and professional—find it useful to outline a decision and its accompanying opinion(s) in a page or two. This summary is sometimes called a "brief" of a case. It is valuable for two reasons. First, the very process of doing it—of discerning relevant facts, identifying key issues, and grasping the rationale used to decide them—are likely to yield an intellectual mastery of the case that mere conventional reading would not. Second, one's outlines or briefs provide an excellent source of review for research papers and examinations.

In the beginning, briefing may seem difficult and time consuming, but with experience most students become adept and efficient. There is no single correct or universal form for a brief, and many students develop their own idiosyncratic style. A good outline, however, should contain the following features, using the school prayers case as an example:

I.   Title and Other Heading Material
This includes the "name" of the case, the year it was decided, the vote of the justices, and the name of the justice writing the Opinion of the Court. For example:

> *Engel v. Vitale (1962), 6–1, Black*

II. Circumstances of the Case
Who is suing whom about what? Important here are the essential facts that triggered the dispute between the parties and of any larger context—political, economic, or social—in which it arose. Brevity is desirable. Students first starting to make briefs tend to include too much detail. The more concise the statement of relevant facts, the better the Court's opinion has been read. Most constitutional law cases deal with an act of government—a statute, regulation, policy, or other undertaking—that is challenged as not conforming to the Constitution. It is important to identify the specific constitutional provision that is at issue. For example:

> *The New York State Board of Regents, which oversees public education in the state, composed a short nondenominational prayer that it recommended be recited at the beginning of every school day. It read, "Almighty God, we acknowledge our dependence upon Thee, and we beg Thy blessings upon us, our parents, our teachers and our country." Saying the prayer was voluntary; no child was required to join in it. Use of the prayer was challenged by Engel and several other parents of public school children as violating the First Amendment in a suit against their local school board. The lower courts decided in favor of the school board.*

III. The Issue(s) of the Case and the Court's Decision
The issue or issues are the heart of the case. As the Court defined the facts, what question or questions did it resolve? If the issues are stated in question form, the Court's decision can be stated with a simple "yes" or "no." For example:

> *Was reciting the prayer an "establishment" of religion and thus a violation of the First Amendment? Yes.*

IV. The Court's Reasoning
What rationale or explanation did the Court offer to support its decision? Why did the Court uphold or invalidate the challenged government action? What interpretation or meaning did it give to the relevant constitutional provision or

doctrine in the case? (The Court's rendition of the Constitution may be more important than its immediate decision in the case, particularly if the dispute between the parties was relatively inconsequential.) For example:

It is not the business of government to compose official prayers for any group to recite as part of a religious program carried out by government. The First Amendment was added to the Constitution, in part, as a guarantee that the power and prestige of government would not be used to control or influence the kinds of prayers the people might say. The Regents' prayer officially promotes the religious beliefs embodied in it and, doing so, violates the establishment clause of the First Amendment, notwithstanding that the prayer is denominationally neutral and that its observance is voluntary. Violation of the establishment clause, unlike that of the free exercise clause, does not depend on a showing of direct government compulsion. This decision does not imply hostility toward religion, but says that prayers should be left to the people themselves and those to whom they may look to for religious guidance.

V.   Other Voices

In many cases, the justices are not unanimous; they may disagree about the outcome of the dispute before them or, agreeing with the outcome, may differ on the reasons for supporting it. Occasionally, justices who differ may express their views through concurring or dissenting opinions. A concurrence supports the Court's decision but on different grounds. A dissent, which has no force of law, states the reasons why the writer voted against the decision. Though these differing opinions may help illuminate the discussion the justices had in conference before deciding the case, most are of slight long-term consequence. Sometimes, however, points made in a concurrence or dissent help to more fully frame the issues of the case and thus add to our understanding and help us evaluate the majority's reasoning. In unusual circumstances, concurring or dissenting opinions may eventually be transformed from the proverbial "voice in the wilderness" to tomorrow's prevailing theory or doctrine. Many of the latter kinds of concurring and dissenting opinions have been included in the cases in this book. A brief should include a concise statement of how the

views expressed significantly differ from those in the majority opinion. For example:

Justice Douglas concurred: Though it is doubtful the prayer established religion in the strict historic meaning of that term, governmental financing of a religious exercise "inserts a divisive influence into our communities."

Justice Stewart dissented: The Court has "misapplied a great constitutional principle." The establishment clause forbids only governmental establishment of an official church. The prayer does not establish "official religion" any more than do many other invocations of the Deity in public ceremonies. To deny the wish of school children to join in reciting the prayer is to deny their opportunity to share in the spiritual heritage of their nation.

VI.   Developmental Consequences

Why has the case been included in this book? Two lines of inquiry should be pursued. First, how has the meaning of the Constitution been clarified or changed as a result of the Court's decision? For example, what existing doctrine, if any, has been broadened or narrowed? What important cases, if any, are affirmed, overruled, or simply ignored? (Some of these questions may be answered under Part IV.) Second, besides the parties to the case, who are the likely gainers and losers as a result of the decision? What was (or in the future may be) the likely effect of the decision on outstanding political, economic, or social questions or conflict? Since there often may be little or no discussion of nonlegal consequences in the Court's opinion, this part of the brief calls for a contextual analysis and, where consequences may not yet be fully clear, for speculation. For example:

Using the establishment clause's "wall of separation" requirement announced in Everson v. Board of Education, *the decision follows others like* McCollum v. Board of Education *in raising the wall higher and further removing the influence and presence of religion in the public schools. It produced considerable controversy, was widely circumvented, and led to attempts to amend the Constitution. The Court did not retreat, however, as* Abington School District v. Schempp *and other later cases show. Whether the decision reflects judicial independence or judicial arrogance may still be debated.*

B.   Law in the Library and on the Internet

Legal research usually requires access to primary and leading secondary legal sources. Normally these are not fully available in most public or college libraries but may be found in law school libraries, bar association libraries, and of those of some agencies of state and local government. They may also be found, almost completely, on the Internet.

Primary sources are laws themselves and the opinions of courts that apply laws in specific cases and thus interpret and clarify their meaning. Laws include constitutions, treaties, and statutes passed by Congress and state legislatures, ordinances enacted by local government, and regulations issued by federal and state administrative agencies. Legal decisions are those made by federal, state, and local courts at both trial and appellate levels. Most appellate and some trial decisions are accompanied by opinions of the judge or judges in the case, explaining why they decided as they did.

Secondary sources include a variety of books, articles, and reports that supply helpful clarifications of law and commentary on recent trends and developments. These statements do not have the binding effect of judicial opinions, but they are often widely read and influential. They include legal treatises and annotations, legal encyclopedias, scholarly books and articles on the law, jurisprudence, and legal history. Particularly important are law review articles, written by scholars and law students in journals published by law schools.

In the Library

All new laws passed by Congress and state legislatures are collected and published. *Statutes at Large,* for example, contains all acts of Congress including resolutions and joint resolutions. Treaties and diplomatic agreements of the United States are collected and published by the State Department in *United States Treaties and Other International Agreements.* As federal laws are amended, repealed, or supplemented, they are consolidated every six years in the *United States Code,* systematically arranged under 50 subjects called Titles. Since 1936, the administrative regulations of federal agencies as well as executive proclamations and orders appear in the *Federal Register,* published daily. These actions are periodically consolidated in the *Code of Federal Regulations,* organized

under 50 Titles closely paralleling those of the *United States Code.* Each of the 50 states publishes the laws enacted by its legislature and rules issued by its regulatory agencies. Only well-stocked law libraries are likely to have a complete collection of these state volumes. Laws and regulations produced by local government are published but are usually not available beyond the official libraries and records of local government.

Decisions of the United States Supreme Court are published officially by the federal government in *United States Reports.* They are also collected and published by West Publishing Company as *The Supreme Court Reporter* and by the Lawyers Cooperative as *The Lawyer's Edition.* Both include extensive annotations and *The Lawyer's Edition,* excerpts of briefs filed by opposing counsel. All three sources contain all official actions of the Supreme Court and the full text of all opinions written by the justices. Any published opinion in a case may be found through the case's citation, for example, *Baker v. Carr,* 369 U.S.186 (1962) refers to volume 369 of the *United States Reports,* p. 186, the first page of the decision.

Recent decisions of the Supreme Court are given quick but temporary paperbound publication as "advance sheets" or "slip" opinions until they are included in permanent bound volumes. *United States Law Week* contains the full text of decisions announced the previous week as well as a report of recent docket actions taken by the Court. A few newspapers, such as *the New York Times,* publish excerpts of important Supreme Court opinions the day after announcement.

Decisions and opinions of the 12 federal Courts of Appeal are published by West Publishing as *The Federal Reporter,* now in its fourth series. Decisions and opinions of the federal District Courts (the trial level of the federal judiciary), are found in West's *Federal Supplement.* Most states publish the complete rulings of their appellate courts and many of their trial courts. West also publishes regional collections of the decisions and opinions of state supreme courts.

Law review articles are indexed in the *Index to Legal Periodicals* which covers more than 400 publications. Other articles may be located in various periodical indexes, such as Social Sciences Index, Public Affairs Information Service, and Political Abstract.

Relevant books may be located through card catalogs and conventional library research. Many leading reference works on civil liberties, constitutional theory and interpretation, and the Supreme Court are listed in the General Supplementary Bibliography of this book.

On the Internet

Law libraries are expensive to build and maintain and access to them may be limited to law students and legal professionals. Because there are relatively few of these libraries, lack of proximity may also make using them difficult. For this reason the Internet has been a boon not only for lawyers, but for anyone doing legal research, including undergraduate students and members of the general public. The disadvantages to using the Internet lie in the level of accuracy and reliability of information. Electronic errors may occur, and the information presented may not have the editorial quality control usually applied to print publications.

All primary and most secondary legal sources can be found on the Internet though not (at least yet) at a single site. Many of the best sites are oriented toward lawyers in practice, but almost all contain some of the primary and basic secondary sources described earlier. A few of the more useful sites are described next. The list is not exhaustive, and the searcher will easily find links to other sites.

The United States Supreme Court, **http://www. supremecourtus.gov/** The Court's own web site, containing comprehensive information on the Court's docket, rules, and procedures. Also makes available for recent cases the text of slip opinions (those of cases yet to be published in bound volumes).

Legal Information Institute (LII), **http://supct. law.cornell.edu/** A noncommercial site sponsored by Cornell University Law School and oriented mainly toward the Supreme Court. Provides access to nearly all the Court's opinions since 1990 and to more than 600 of its leading decisions since 1793. Tracks current cases as they move through stages of review and makes available synopses of current decisions on the day of announcement. Many links to other sites are included.

Findlaw Resources, **http://www.findlaw.com/** An all-purpose, partly fee-based commercial site. Laws and legal decisions are organized by subject and by court. Contains information on the Supreme Court's calendar, rules, and briefs filed by counsel, and general coverage of legal news. Includes free access to a database of all United States Supreme Court cases

since 1893. The individual cases may be downloaded, **http://www.lawhost.commerce/suprctsrch.html**

FLITE (Federal Legal Information Through Electronics), **http://www.fedworld.gov/supct/** A noncommercial site sponsored by the Technical Administration of the U.S. Department of Commerce. Contains complete text of all 7,407 Supreme Court decisions from 1937 to 1975, any one of which may be downloaded as an ASCII text file. The same data base may be accessed through the Villanova Center for Law and Policy at Villanova University, **http://www.law.vill.edu/**

The Oyez Project, **http://www.court.it-services. nwu.edu/** A noncommercial site sponsored by Northwestern University, offering access to current and many historic Supreme Court decisions. A unique feature is the availability of more than 900 hours of recorded, unedited oral arguments made before the Court. These are delivered by streaming audio or CD.

Jurist, The Legal Education Network, **http://www. jurist.law.pitt.edu/** A noncommercial site sponsored by the University of Pittsburgh School of Law and affiliated law schools in several countries. Oriented toward the teaching and study of law, it allows searching of federal case law and legislation. Contains book reviews of recent legal monographs, news of law schools, conferences, and guides to many legal subjects and current legal issues.

Medill School of Journalism, **http://www.medill. nwu.edu/docket/** Sponsored by Northwestern University and oriented toward journalists, the site offers coverage of Court's docket and brief journalistic descriptions of cases decided during the last two terms of the Court.

The *Washington Post*, **http://www.washington-post.com/wp-srv/national/longterm/supcourt/ supcourt.htm** Reporting on current and past cases by a leading newspaper. Articles can be accessed as written. Also contains general information about the Supreme Court and the justices.

InfoSynthesis, **http://www.usscplus.com/** A partly fee-based site commercial site that contains all Supreme Court decisions from 1907 and leading cases going back to 1793. Makes available the text of the 1,000 cases that have been the most cited by the Court itself, as well as decisions of the Court's current term.

The West Group, Online Legal Services, **http:// www.westgroup.com/** A fully fee-based site of West Publishing that has full coverage of all the Supreme Court's decisions and of others that are reported in the company's print publications mentioned earlier. Access is free to students and faculty at law schools contractually subscribing to the service.

Lexis-Nexus, **http://www.lexis.com/** Like the West Group, a fully fee-based service with comprehensive coverage of the Supreme Court's decisions. Available to law schools and law firms.

Law and Politics Book Review, **http://www.polsci. wvu.edu/lpbr/** Sponsored by the Law and Politics section of the American Political Science Association, it offers reviews of a wide range of books dealing with the law and legal issues.

The Supreme Court Historical Society, **http:// www.supremecourthistory.organization/** Research on the Supreme Court, its work and history.

Administrative Office of the United States Courts, **http://www.uscourt.gov/** Offers general information on the federal courts as well as statistical and other data on caseloads, judicial appointments, and other aspects of the federal judiciary.

National Center for State Courts, **http://www. ncsc.dni.us/** Offers similar information on state courts and links to sites of hundreds of state and local courts in the United States.

C.   Justices of the Supreme Court

	Justice	Year Appt.	Appointing President	Party	State	Previous Position	Age at Appt.	Yrs. on Court	Departure
1	John Jay	1789	Washington	Fed	N.Y.	Diplomat	52	6	1795, res.
2	John Rutledge	1789	Washington	Fed	S.C.	State Judge	43	2	1791, res.
3	William Cushing	1789	Washington	Fed	Mass.	State Judge	50	22	1810, d.
4	James Wilson	1789	Washington	Fed	Pa.	Lawyer	47	9	1798, d.
5	John Blair, Jr.	1789	Washington	Fed	Va.	State Judge	57	6	1796, ret.
6	James Iredell	1790	Washington	Fed	N.C.	Lawyer	38	10	1799, d.
7	Thomas Johnson	1791	Washington	Fed	Md.	State Judge	58	1	1793, ret.
8	William Patterson	1793	Washington	Fed	N.J.	Gov., N.J.	47	13	1806, d.
9	Samuel Chase	1796	Washington	Fed	Md.	State Judge	54	15	1811, d.
10	Oliver Ellsworth	1796	Washington	Fed	Conn.	Senator	50	4	1800, ill.
11	Bushrod Washington	1798	J. Adams	Fed	Va.	Lawyer	36	31	1829, d.
12	Alfred Moore	1799	J. Adams	Fed	N.C.	State Judge	44	4	1804, ret.
13	John Marshall	1801	J. Adams	Fed	Va.	Sec. State	45	34	1835, d.
14	William Johnson	1804	Jefferson	D-Rep	S.C.	State Judge	52	30	1834, d.
15	Henry Livingston	1806	Jefferson	D-Rep	N.Y.	State Judge	49	16	1823, d.
16	Thomas Todd	1807	Jefferson	D-Rep	Ky.	State Judge	42	19	1826, d.
17	Gabriel Duvall	1811	Madison	D-Rep	Md.	Fed. Admin.	58	23	1835, ret.
18	Joseph Story	1811	Madison	D-Rep	Mass.	State Legis.	32	34	1845, d.
19	Smith Thompson	1823	Monroe	D-Rep	N.Y.	Navy Sec.	55	20	1843, d.
20	Robert Trimble	1826	J. Q. Adams	D-Rep	Ky.	Fed. Judge	49	2	1828, d.
21	John McLean	1829	Jackson	Dem	Ohio	Post. Gen.	43	32	1861, d.
22	Henry Baldwin	1830	Jackson	Dem	Pa.	Lawyer	49	14	1844, d.
23	James Wayne	1835	Jackson	Dem	Ga.	Cong. Rep.	45	32	1867, d.
24	Roger Taney	1836	Jackson	Dem	Md.	Lawyer	58	28	1864, d.
25	Philip Barbour	1836	Jackson	Dem	Va.	Fed. Judge	52	5	1841, d.
26	John Catron	1837	Jackson	Dem	Tenn.	Lawyer	51	28	1865, d.
27	John McKinley	1837	Van Buren	Dem	Ala.	Senator	57	15	1852, d.

28	Peter Daniel	1841	Van Buren	Dem	Va.	Fed. Judge	56	19	1860, d.
29	Samuel Nelson	1845	Tyler	Dem	N.Y.	State Judge	52	28	1872, ret.
30	Levi Woodbury	1846	Polk	Dem	N.H.	Senator	56	6	1851, d.
31	Robert Grier	1846	Polk	Dem	Pa.	State Judge	52	23	1870, ill.
32	Benjamin Curtis	1851	Fillmore	Whig	Mass.	Lawyer	42	6	1857, res.
33	John Campbell	1853	Pierce	Dem	Ala.	Lawyer	41	8	1861, res.
34	Nathan Clifford	1858	Buchanan	Dem	Maine	Lawyer	54	23	1881, d.
35	Noah Swayne	1962	Lincoln	Rep	Ohio	Lawyer	57	19	1881, ret.
36	Samuel Miller	1862	Lincoln	Rep	Iowa	Lawyer	46	28	1890, d.
37	David Davis	1862	Lincoln	Rep	Ill.	State Judge	47	14	1877, res.
38	Stephen Field	1863	Lincoln	Dem	Calif.	State Judge	46	35	1897, ill.
39	Salmon Chase	1864	Lincoln	Rep	Ohio	Lawyer	56	8	1873, d.
40	William Strong	1870	Grant	Rep	Pa.	Lawyer	61	11	1880, ret.
41	Joseph Bradley	1870	Grant	Rep	N.J.	Lawyer	56	22	1892, d.
42	Ward Hunt	1872	Grant	Rep	N.Y.	State Judge	62	9	1882, ill.
43	Morrison Waite	1874	Grant	Rep	Ohio	State Govt.	57	14	1888, d.
44	John M. Harlan	1877	Hayes	Rep	Ky.	Lawyer	44	34	1911, d.
45	William Woods	1880	Hayes	Rep	Ga.	Fed. Judge	56	6	1887, d.
46	Stanley Matthews	1881	Garfield	Rep	Ohio	Lawyer	56	8	1889, d.
47	Horace Gray	1881	Arthur	Rep	Mass.	State Judge	53	21	1902, d,
48	Samuel Blatchford	1882	Arthur	Rep	N.Y.	Fed. Judge	62	11	1893, d.
49	Lucius Lamar	1888	Cleveland	Dem	Miss.	Interior Sec.	62	5	1893, d.
50	Melville Fuller	1888	Cleveland	Dem	Ill.	Lawyer	55	22	1910, d.
51	David Brewer	1889	Harrison	Rep	Kans.	Fed. Judge	52	20	1910, d.
52	Henry Brown	1890	Harrison	Rep	Mich.	Fed. Judge	54	15	1906, ill.
53	George Shiras, Jr.	1892	Harrison	Rep	Pa.	Lawyer	60	10	1903, ret.
54	Howell Jackson	1893	Harrison	Dem	Tenn.	Fed. Judge	60	2	1895, d.
55	Edward White	1894	Cleveland	Dem	La.	Senator	48	27	1921, d.
56	Rufus Peckham	1895	Cleveland	Dem	N.Y.	State Judge	57	14	1909, d.
57	Joseph McKenna	1898	McKinley	Rep	Calif.	Atty. Gen.	54	27	1925, ill.
58	Oliver W. Holmes, Jr.	1902	T. Roosevelt	Rep	Mass.	State Judge	61	29	1932, ret.
59	William Day	1903	T. Roosevelt	Rep	Ohio	Fed. Judge	63	20	1922, ret.
60	William Moody	1906	T. Roosevelt	Rep	Mass.	Atty. Gen.	52	4	1910, ill.
61	Horace Lurton	1909	Taft	Dem	Tenn.	Fed. Judge	65	5	1914, d.
62	Chas. Evans Hughes	1910	Taft	Rep	N.Y.	Gov., N.Y.	48	6	1916, res.
63	Willis Van Devanter	1910	Taft	Rep	Wyo.	Fed. Judge	51	26	1937, ret.
64	Joseph Lamar	1910	Taft	Dem	Ga.	State Judge	53	5	1916, d.
65	Mahlon Pitney	1912	Taft	Rep	N.J.	State Judge	54	11	1922, ill.
66	James McReynolds	1914	Wilson	Dem	Tenn.	Atty. Gen.	52	26	1941, ret.
67	Louis Brandeis	1916	Wilson	Rep	Mass.	Lawyer	59	23	1939, ret.
68	John Clarke	1916	Wilson	Dem	Ohio	Fed. Judge	59	6	1922, res.
69	Wm. Howard Taft	1921	Harding	Rep	Ohio	Law Prof.	63	9	1930, ret.
70	George Sutherland	1922	Harding	Rep	Utah	Senator	60	15	1938, ret.

71	Pierce Butler	1922	Harding	Dem	Minn.	Lawyer	56	17	1939, d.
72	Edward Sanford	1923	Harding	Rep	Tenn.	Fed. Judge	57	7	1930, d.
73	Harlan Stone	1925	Coolidge	Rep	N.Y.	Atty. Gen.	52	21	1946, d.
74	Chas. Evans Hughes	1930	Hoover	Rep	N.Y.	Lawyer	68	11	1941, ret.
75	Owen Roberts	1930	Hoover	Rep	Pa.	Law Prof.	55	15	1945, res.
76	Benjamin Cardozo	1932	Hoover	Dem	N.Y.	State Judge	61	6	1938, d.
77	Hugo Black	1937	F. Roosevelt	Dem	Ala.	Senator	51	34	1971, ill.
78	Stanley Reed	1938	F. Roosevelt	Dem	Ky.	Sol. Gen.	53	19	1957, ret.
79	Felix Frankfurter	1939	F. Roosevelt	indp.	Mass.	Law Prof.	56	24	1962, ill.
80	William O. Douglas	1939	F. Roosevelt	Dem	Conn.	SEC Chr.	40	37	1975, ill.
81	Frank Murphy	1940	F. Roosevelt	Dem	Mich.	Atty. Gen.	49	9	1949, d.
82	James Byrnes	1941	F. Roosevelt	Dem	S.C.	Senator	62	1	1942, res.
83	Robert Jackson	1941	F. Roosevelt	Dem	N.Y.	Atty. Gen.	49	13	1954, d.
84	Wiley Rutledge	1943	F. Roosevelt	Dem	Iowa	Fed. Judge	48	7	1949, d.
85	Harold Burton	1945	Truman	Rep	Ohio	Senator	57	13	1958, ill.
86	Fred Vinson	1946	Truman	Dem	Ky.	Treas. Sec.	56	7	1953, d.
87	Tom Clark	1949	Truman	Dem	Tex.	Atty. Gen.	49	18	1967, ret.
88	Sherman Minton	1949	Truman	Dem	Ind.	Fed. Judge	58	7	1956, ill.
89	Earl Warren	1953	Eisenhower	Rep	Calif.	Gov., Calif.	62	16	1969, ret.
90	John M. Harlan II	1955	Eisenhower	Rep	N.Y.	Fed. Judge	55	16	1971, ill.
91	William Brennan	1956	Eisenhower	Dem	N.J.	State Judge	50	34	1990, ret.
92	Charles Whittaker	1957	Eisenhower	Rep	Mo.	Fed. Judge	56	5	1962, ret.
93	Potter Stewart	1958	Eisenhower	Rep	Ohio	Fed. Judge	43	23	1981, ret.
94	Byron White	1962	Kennedy	Dem	Colo.	Dep. A-G	44	31	1993, ret.
95	Arthur Goldberg	1962	Kennedy	Dem	Ill.	Labor Sec.	54	3	1965, res.
96	Abe Fortas	1965	Johnson	Dem	Tenn.	Fed. Admin.	55	4	1969, res.
97	Thurgood Marshall	1967	Johnson	Dem	N.Y.	Fed. Judge	58	24	1991, ret.
98	Warren Burger	1969	Nixon	Rep	Minn.	Fed. Judge	61	17	1986, ret.
99	Harry Blackmun	1970	Nixon	Rep	Minn.	Fed. Judge	61	24	1994, ret.
100	Lewis Powell, Jr.	1971	Nixon	Dem	Va.	Lawyer	64	15	1987, ret.
101	William Rehnquist	1971	Nixon	Rep	Ariz.	Asst. A-G	47		
102	John Paul Stevens	1975	Ford	Rep	Ill.	Fed. Judge	55		
103	Sandra D. O'Connor	1981	Reagan	Rep	Ariz.	State Judge	51		
104	Antonin Scalia	1986	Reagan	Rep	Va.	Fed. Judge	50		
105	Arthur Kennedy	1988	Reagan	Rep	Calif.	Fed. Judge	51		
106	David Souter	1990	Bush	Rep	N.H.	Fed. Judge	51		
107	Clarence Thomas	1991	Bush	Rep	Ga.	Fed. Judge	43		
108	Ruth Ginsberg	1993	Clinton	Dem	N.Y.	Fed. Judge	60		
109	Stephen Breyer	1994	Clinton	Dem	Mass.	Fed. Judge	56		

Note: Previous positions are in the federal government unless otherwise stated.

Years on court are rounded to nearest full year.

Departure: d., died in office; ill., resignation because of infirmities; ret., retired; res., resigned.

In some instances retirement was associated with general disability or that of advanced age.

D.   The Historic Supreme Courts

John Jay, C.J., 1789–1795

1789	Rutledge	Cushing	Wilson	Blair	
1790	Rutledge	Cushing	Wilson	Blair	Iredell
1791	**Johnson**	Cushing	Wilson	Blair	Iredell
1793	**Paterson**	Cushing	Wilson	Blair	Iredell

John Rutledge, C.J., 1795

1795	Paterson	Cushing	Wilson	Blair	Iredell

Oliver Ellsworth, C.J., 1796–1800

1796	Paterson	Cushing	Wilson	**Chase**	Iredell
1798	Paterson	Cushing	**Washington**	Chase	Iredell
1799	Paterson	Cushing	Washington	Chase	**Moore**

John Marshall, C.J., 1801–1835

1801	Paterson	Cushing	Washington	Chase	Moore	
1804	Paterson	Cushing	Washington	Chase	**Johnson**	
1806	**Livingston**	Cushing	Washington	Chase	Johnson	
1807	Livingston	Cushing	Washington	Chase	Johnson	**Todd**
1811	Livingston	**Story**	Washington	**Duvall**	Johnson	Todd
1823	**Thompson**	Story	Washington	Duvall	Johnson	Todd
1826	Thompson	Story	Washington	Duvall	Johnson	**Trimble**
1829	Thompson	Story	Washington	Duvall	Johnson	**McLean**
1830	Thompson	Story	**Baldwin**	Duvall	Johnson	McLean
1835	Thompson	Story	Baldwin	Duvall	**Wayne**	McLean

Roger Taney, C.J., 1836–1864

1836	Thompson	Story	Baldwin	**Barbour**	Wayne	McLean		
1837	Thompson	Story	Baldwin	Barbour	Wayne	McLean	**Catron**	**McKinley**
1841	Thompson	Story	Baldwin	**Daniel**	Wayne	McLean	Catron	McKinley
1845	**Nelson**	**Woodbury**	Baldwin	Daniel	Wayne	McLean	Catron	McKinley
1846	Nelson	Woodbury	**Grier**	Daniel	Wayne	McLean	Catron	McKinley
1851	Nelson	**Curtis**	Grier	Daniel	Wayne	McLean	Catron	McKinley
1863	Nelson	Curtis	Grier	Daniel	Wayne	McLean	Catron	**Campbell**
1858	Nelson	**Clifford**	Grier	Daniel	Wayne	McLean	Catron	Campbell
1862	Nelson	Clifford	Grier	**Miller**	Wayne	**Swayne**	Catron	**Davis**
1863	Nelson	Clifford	Grier	Miller	Wayne	Swayne	Catron	Davis	**Field**

Salmon Chase, C.J., 1864–1873

1864	Nelson	Clifford	Grier	Miller	Wayne	Swayne	Catron	Davis	Field
1865	Nelson	Clifford	Grier	Miller	(vacant)	Swayne	Catron	Davis	Field
1867	Nelson	Clifford	Grier	Miller	(vacant)	Swayne	(vacant)	Davis	Field
1870	Nelson	Clifford	**Strong**	Miller	**Bradley**	Swayne	Davis	Field	
1872	**Hunt**	Clifford	Strong	Miller	Bradley	Swayne	Davis	Field	

Morrison Waite, C.J., 1874–1888

1874	Hunt	Clifford	Strong	Miller	Bradley	Swayne	Davis	Field
1877	Hunt	Clifford	Strong	Miller	Bradley	Swayne	**Harlan**	Field

1880	Hunt	Clifford	**Woods**	Miller	Bradley	Swayne	Harlan	Field
1881	Hunt	**Gray**	Woods	Miller	Bradley	**Matthews**	Harlan	Field
1882	**Blatchford**	Gray	Woods	Miller	Bradley	Matthews	Harlan	Field

Melville Fuller, C.J., 1888–1910

1888	Blatchford	Gray	**L. Lamar**	Miller	Bradley	Matthews	Harlan	Field
1889	Blatchford	Gray	L. Lamar	Miller	Bradley	**Brewer**	Harlan	Field
1890	Blatchford	Gray	L. Lamar	**Brown**	Bradley	Brewer	Harlan	Field
1892	Blatchford	Gray	L. Lamar	Brown	**Shiras**	Brewer	Harlan	Field
1893	Blatchford	Gray	**Jackson**	Brown	Shiras	Brewer	Harlan	Field
1894	**White**	Gray	Jackson	Brown	Shiras	Brewer	Harlan	Field
1895	White	Gray	**Peckham**	Brown	Shiras	Brewer	Harlan	Field
1898	White	Gray	Peckham	Brown	Shiras	Brewer	Harlan	**McKenna**
1902	White	**Holmes**	Peckham	Brown	Shiras	Brewer	Harlan	McKenna
1903	White	Holmes	Peckham	Brown	**Day**	Brewer	Harlan	McKenna
1906	White	Holmes	Peckham	**Moody**	Day	Brewer	Harlan	McKenna
1909	White*	Holmes	**Lurton**	Moody	Day	Brewer	Harlan	McKenna

Edward White, C.J., 1910–1921

1910	**VanD'vanter**	Holmes	Lurton	**J. Lamar**	Day	**Hughes**	Harlan	McKenna
1912	VanD'vanter	Holmes	Lurton	J. Lamar	Day	Hughes	**Pitney**	McKenna
1914	VanD'vanter	Holmes	**McReynolds**	J. Lamar	Day	Hughes	Pitney	McKenna
1916	VanD'vanter	Holmes	McReynolds	**Brandeis**	Day	**Clarke**	Pitney	McKenna

William Howard Taft, C.J., 1921–1930

1921	VanD'vanter	Holmes	McReynolds	Brandeis	Day	Clarke	Pitney	McKenna
1922	VanD'vanter	Holmes	McReynolds	Brandeis	**Butler**	**Sutherland**	Pitney	McKenna
1923	VanD'vanter	Holmes	McReynolds	Brandeis	Butler	Sutherland	**Sanford**	McKenna
1925	VanD'vanter	Holmes	McReynolds	Brandeis	Butler	Sutherland	Sanford	**Stone**

Charles Evans Hughes, C.J., 1930–1941

1930	VanD'vanter	Holmes	McReynolds	Brandeis	Butler	Sutherland	**Roberts**	Stone
1932	VanD'vanter	**Cardozo**	McReynolds	Brandeis	Butler	Sutherland	Roberts	Stone
1937	**Black**	Cardozo	McReynolds	Brandeis	Butler	Sutherland	Roberts	Stone
1938	Black	Cardozo	McReynolds	Brandeis	Butler	**Reed**	Roberts	Stone
1939	Black	**Frankfurter**	McReynolds	**Douglas**	Butler	Reed	Roberts	Stone
1940	Black	Frankfurter	McReynolds	Douglas	**Murphy**	Reed	Roberts	Stone*

Harlan Fiske Stone, C.J., 1941–1946

1941	Black	Frankfurter	**Byrnes**	Douglas	Murphy	Reed	Roberts	**Jackson**
1943	Black	Frankfurter	**Rutledge**	Douglas	Murphy	Reed	Roberts	Jackson
1945	Black	Frankfurter	Rutledge	Douglas	Murphy	Reed	**Burton**	Jackson

Fred Vinson, C.J., 1946–1953

1946	Black	Frankfurter	Rutledge	Douglas	Murphy	Reed	Burton	Jackson
1949	Black	Frankfurter	**Minton**	Douglas	**Clark**	Reed	Burton	Jackson

Earl Warren, C.J., 1953–1969

1953	Black	Frankfurter	Minton	Douglas	Clark	Reed	Burton	Jackson
1955	Black	Frankfurter	Minton	Douglas	Clark	Reed	Burton	**Harlan**

1956	Black	Frankfurter	**Brennan**	Douglas	Clark	Reed	Burton	Harlan
1957	Black	Frankfurter	Brennan	Douglas	Clark	**Whittaker**	Burton	Harlan
1958	Black	Frankfurter	Brennan	Douglas	Clark	Whittaker	**Stewart**	Harlan
1962	Black	**Goldberg**	Brennan	Douglas	Clark	**White**	Stewart	Harlan
1965	Black	**Fortas**	Brennan	Douglas	Clark	White	Stewart	Harlan
1967	Black	Fortas	Brennan	Douglas	**Marshall**	White	Stewart	Harlan

Warren Burger, C.J., 1969–1986

1969	Black	Fortas	Brennan	Douglas	Marshall	White	Stewart	Harlan
1970	Black	**Blackmun**	Brennan	Douglas	Marshall	White	Stewart	**Rehnquist**
1972	**Powell**	Blackmun	Brennan	Douglas	Marshall	White	Stewart	Rehnquist
1975	Powell	Blackmun	Brennan	**Stevens**	Marshall	White	Stewart	Rehnquist
1981	Powell	Blackmun	Brennan	Stevens	Marshall	White	**O'Connor**	Rehnquist*

William Rehnquist, C.J., 1986–

1986	Powell	Blackmun	Brennan	Stevens	Marshall	White	O'Connor	**Scalia**
1988	**Kennedy**	Blackmun	Brennan	Stevens	Marshall	White	O'Connor	Scalia
1990	Kennedy	Blackmun	**Souter**	Stevens	Marshall	White	O'Connor	Scalia
1991	Kennedy	Blackmun	Souter	Stevens	**Thomas**	White	O'Connor	Scalia
1993	Kennedy	Blackmun	Souter	Stevens	Thomas	**Ginsberg**	O'Connor	Scalia
1994	Kennedy	**Breyer**	Souter	Stevens	Thomas	Ginsberg	O'Connor	Scalia

*Elevated to chief justice

GLOSSARY OF LEGAL AND CONSTITUTIONAL TERMS

abstention A doctrine under which federal courts refrain from deciding federal issues in state cases if the case can be decided on state law.

acquittal A verdict in a criminal case that the accused has not been proved guilty.

adjudication The hearing and resolution of issues in a legal case.

administrative law The law dealing with the powers, structure, procedures, and policies of regulatory agencies.

admiralty law The law governing maritime matters including shipping, navigation, and acts on the high seas.

adversary proceeding A legal action in which contending parties with opposing interests frame the issues to be decided.

advisory opinion A judicial opinion on legal issues not arising in an adversarial proceeding. It is usually requested by a legislature or an executive agency.

affidavit A sworn written statement of facts.

affirm To uphold or confirm an earlier judgment, usually that of a lower court.

a fortiori With greater or stronger reason.

allegation A charge or contention of fact that is to be legally proven.

amicus curiae Literally, friend of the court. A person or organization permitted to submit a brief in a lawsuit to which they are not one of the adversarial parties, usually because they have interests to protect that are at issue in the case.

appeal A request that a ruling or decision of a lower court be reviewed by a higher court.

appellant A losing party in a lower court who asks for review of that court's judgment by a higher court.

appellate jurisdiction The power of a higher court to review and correct errors made by a lower court.

appellee The party against whom an appeal is taken to a higher court.

arbitrary Unreasonable, usually referring a governmental act.

arraignment The stage of a criminal case in which the accused appears before the court to hear the charge or charges read, and enters a plea in response.

bill of attainder An act by a legislature directly imposing punishment or legal disability on a person without benefit of trial. It is barred to the federal government and the states under Articles I-9 and I-10 of the Constitution.

brief A written statement of legal arguments submitted by counsel in a lawsuit; the summary of a given case.

case law The law based on judicial decisions, in contrast to that contained in statutes or administrative rules.

case or controversy A legal action based on a claim of actual injury to personal interests in contrast to the raising of merely hypothetical or abstract questions of law; a requirement of Article III-2 for the exercise of the jurisdiction of the federal courts.

cause of action A statement of facts entitling a person to seek judicial relief; a case or complaint.

certification A procedure by which a lower court in a pending case asks a higher court to rule on a specific issue of law that it needs to have clarified or resolved in order to continue the case.

certiorari, **writ of** An order of a higher court to a lower to have the record of a case sent up for review; the chief method by which the United States Supreme Court exercises appellate review.

challenge for cause Dismissal of a perspective juror during the jury selection process, where the juror has been shown to lack impartiality. See also **peremptory challenge.**

civil action A lawsuit in which one party sues another to enforce a right or to redress or prevent a wrong, in contrast to a criminal action brought by government to enforce criminal law.

civil law Law dealing with civil rather than criminal matters, for example, contracts, torts, property.

civil liberties, rights Freedoms of individuals protected by constitutions and certain statutes. Examples include the exercise of religion, the right to speak and publish, to have due process, and the equal protection of law.

class action A lawsuit brought by one or more persons not only for themselves but on behalf of a group or class of others in similar circumstances.

collateral attack An attempt to defeat a judgment by bringing an action, other than an appeal, in another court.

color of law The misuse of power under the guise of legal right. Usually describes illegal or unconstitutional action taken by authorities while purporting to act as authorities, or such action by someone appearing to be clothed with authority.

comity The respect or discretionary courtesy one sovereign gives to the legal actions of another, for example the federal government to the states, the states to each other, or one nation to another.

common law A body of law based on the judgments of courts in which earlier decisions serve as binding precedents for later cases, in contrast to statutes enacted by legislatures. Historically, a system of judge-made law originating in medieval England and based, initially at least, on usage and custom.

complaint A formal statement in which the party bringing a lawsuit states the reasons for the action.

concurring opinion An opinion by an appellate judge or justice agreeing with the decision in the case, but disagreeing with its rationale or offering different or additional reasons for it.

concurrent powers Those exercised by state and federal governments, such as the power to tax.

conspiracy The crime of two or more persons agreeing to commit a criminal act, in contrast to the act itself.

consent decree A court-enforced agreement based on the consent of the parties in a civil case or administrative proceeding.

contempt A punishable act that disobeys a court order or that hinders, embarrasses, or lessens the dignity of a judicial or legislative proceeding.

constitutional courts Federal courts established under Article III-1 of the Constitution, for example the Supreme Court, the 12 Courts of Appeal, and the district courts.

criminal case A judicial action brought by a government prosecutor to enforce a criminal law.

criminal law Law dealing with noncivil matters, for example, robbery, homicide, or the sale or possession of illegal materials.

damages A monetary award in a civil case to compensate for a proven injury or loss; in the case of punitive damages, also to penalize egregious conduct.

declaratory judgment A judicial ruling stating the rights, duties, or status of the parties, but not accompanied by any award of damages.

de facto Actual, in fact. In contrast to *de jure.*

defendant The party who is sued in a civil action or indicted in a criminal case.

de jure Legal, duly authorized. In contrast to *de facto.*

demurrer A motion of the defendant in a civil case asserting that even if the facts alleged in the complaint are true, they are legally insufficient to maintain the suit.

de mininus Minimal, trifling; not sufficiently important for adjudication.

de novo Anew; for a second consideration by a court.

deposition A sworn statement taken out of court from a party or witness in a case, usually during the pretrial discovery process.

dictum (pl: **dicta**) A statement or observation in a court's opinion that is incidental to and not necessary for the decision in the case at hand and thus not binding on future cases. In contrast to holding. Also *obiter dictum.*

discovery The pretrial stage of factual investigation including the taking of testimony in written depositions.

dismissal Termination of a case by court order.

dissenting opinion An opinion by an appellate judge or justice disagreeing with the decision in a case.

distinguish Reasoning by a court that finds an earlier similar case sufficiently different from the case at hand that it does not serve as a controlling precedent.

diversity jurisdiction The authority of federal courts to hear civil cases between citizens of different states.

docket The record of cases to be heard by a court during a given term.

due process of law The fundamentally fair procedures that government must follow before it may deprive any person of life, liberty, or property.

eminent domain The power of government or authorized private parties to take private property for public use. The Fifth Amendment to the Constitution requires that such taking be met with "just compensation."

en banc The sitting of an appellate court with all judges or justices present, rather than hearing by a panel.

entrapment Action of government officers, usually police, inducing a suspect or otherwise innocent person into committing a criminal act.

enjoin Judicially to order that a party do or refrain from doing a specific act; to issue an injunction.

equity A branch of the common law that provides for remedies, such as injunction and specific performance to prevent legal injuries, in contrast to law awarding damages for injuries that have occurred. Historically, equity evolved from flexible rules devised to mitigate the sometimes harsh and rigid requirements of common law, thereby emphasizing the court's basic sense of fairness.

error, writ of An order by an appellate court to a lower court to furnish the records of a case for review; before 1925, the chief method by which cases reached the United States Supreme Court and one over which the Court had little discretion.

ex parte On behalf of one party; a judicial proceeding without the presence an adversary party, for example, a *habeas corpus* hearing.

ex post facto **law** A retroactive criminal law making an act a crime that was not a crime when it was done or making punishment for a crime greater than it was when the crime was committed. Federal and state governments are barred from passing such laws under Articles I-9 and I-10 of the Constitution.

ex rel Literally, on the relation of. Refers to the name of a party on whose behalf an agency of government sues another party.

federal question A legal issue arising under the Constitution, a treaty, federal statute, regulation, or executive order.

felony The most serious category of crimes, including homicide, rape, and robbery, punishable by more than a year in prison.

fiduciary A person in a position of trust; one who handles the property of others, for example a banker or trustee.

franchise The right to vote.

grand jury A group of enpaneled citizens authorized to examine prosecutorial or independently gathered evidence against specific persons and decide whether it is sufficient to support a criminal indictment.

habeas corpus, **writ of** A judicial order to a government officer holding someone in custody to bring the prisoner before the court so the legality of detention may be determined.

harmless error A trial error held by an appellate court not to be important enough to have affected the outcome of the trial or support reversing the trial judgment.

hearsay Testimony of what one person heard another say. Generally not admissible in American courts if the person who spoke the words is available to testify him or herself.

holding The specific legal ruling in a case; that part of the court's opinion considered binding as precedent for future decisions, in contrast to a dictum.

implied powers Authority of the national government that may be reasonably inferred from powers expressly delegated to it in the Constitution; specifically, power derived from the "necessary and proper" clause of Article I-8-18.

immunity Exemption from criminal prosecution or civil suit.

in camera In private; referring to matters taken up in the judge's private chambers or from which the public is excluded.

incorporation In constitutional law, the process by which rights in the Bill of Rights were held to be part of due process of law and thus incorporated into the due process clause of the Fourteenth Amendment as limits on the powers of the states.

indictment A formal criminal charge brought by a grand jury after examination of prosecutorial evidence.

in forma pauperis Literally, in the manner of a pauper; a special status given to indigent persons, particularly in taking appeals, in which they are from certain fees or procedural requirements.

information A criminal charge against a named person brought in a prosecutor's affidavit to a judge. It is used in state jurisdictions that do not indict by grand jury.

inherent powers Authority of the national government not based on delegated or implied powers but inferred from the existence of the United States as a sovereign nation in the international world.

injunction A court order that a party do or refrain from doing a specified act.

in personam A lawsuit brought against a person rather than against property (*in rem*).

in re In the matter of, concerning; refers to a named party about whom a judicial matter has been taken up.

in rem A lawsuit brought against property rather than a person (*in personam*).

inter alia Literally, among other things.

interlocutory decree A temporary judgment before a matter has been conclusively determined.

intervenor A third party who enters a lawsuit to protect an alleged interest.

ipse dixit Asserted but not proved

judicial notice Recognition by a court of certain facts, usually matters of common knowledge, without requiring one side or the other to submit formal proof.

judicial review Appellate examination of lower court proceedings for errors of law; in constitutional law, the power of a court to affirm or strike down governmental acts on constitutional grounds.

jurisdiction The authority of a court to hear a case; the geographical area included in such authority.

jurisprudence Legal philosophy; a body of legal decisions.

justiciable The quality of being suitable for judicial consideration and decision.

legislative courts Federal courts, such as the United States Court of Claims, established by Congress under Article I-8, as distinguished from constitutional courts created under Article III-1.

litigant A party to a lawsuit or legal action.

magistrate A judge of a lower court; in the federal courts, a judicial officer in a district court authorized to handle certain pretrial matters and minor civil and criminal proceedings.

majority opinion The opinion of an appellate court supported by more than half but not all judges or justices, explaining the decision of the court.

mandamus, writ of A court order to a governmental officer to perform a nondiscretionary, ministerial duty.

mandate An order of a court that its decision or ruling in a case be executed.

material Relevant, important, referring to the issues, evidence, or witnesses in a case.

martial law A declared condition under which the military assumes the powers of government in domestic territory during an emergency or crisis; the law prevailing under such circumstances.

merits The substantive issues of a lawsuit in contrast to those having to do with procedure or jurisdiction. A decision "on the merits" is one in which the substantive issues have been heard and decided on the evidence in the case.

ministerial duty A specified duty of a public officer not calling for the discretion or judgment of policy.

misdemeanor A category of crimes less serious than felonies, punishable by fines or imprisonment of not more than a year.

mistrial A trial terminated before completion, usually because procedural error or misconduct prevented a fair trial from continuing, or because a jury has been unable to reach a decision.

mootness Status of a legal issue or question that has resolved itself or, because of changed conditions, is no longer an active controversy between the parties to a case.

motion A formal request by a party to a lawsuit to the court for a specified ruling on an issue in the case or on the case itself.

natural law Principles of human conduct believed to derive from God or nature, applicable to all persons and preceding human law; the law that conforms to a basic desire to act rationally and morally.

nolle prosequi Decision by the prosecutor during a criminal trial to drop charges against the accused.

nolo contendere Literally, "I will not contest." A plea by the accused in a criminal case accepting punishment for an alleged offense without admitting guilt. The plea may lead to lighter punishment or allow denial of the incriminating facts in another proceeding.

obiter dictum See **dictum.**

opinion of the court A statement announcing the judgment of a court explaining its reasoning and supported by at least a majority of the judges or justices participating in the case. In contrast to concurring or dissenting opinions, the opinion of the court is a basis of precedent.

original jurisdiction Authority of a court to originally try a case, in contrast to hearing appeals of cases already tried.

overbreadth, overbroad The quality of a statute or regulation going beyond stated, demonstrated, or legitimate government interest or purpose. Usually refers to such a law impeding a legal or constitutional right.

overrule To nullify or deny, as when a higher court reverses the ruling of a lower court or when it supersedes an earlier decision of its own.

per curiam Literally, by the court. Term given to an unsigned, usually short opinion written collectively by an appellate court. Such opinions may be issued when the legal questions need little explanation or when the court is deeply divided.

per se By itself, inherently.

peremptory challenge The dismissal of a perspective juror by an attorney during the jury selection process, for which no cause or reason need be given. The number of such challenges allowed to each side in a case is limited. See also **challenge for cause.**

petitioner The party bringing a lawsuit; plaintiff in contrast to respondent. In the Supreme Court, the term may refer to the party seeking review.

petit jury Trial jury, as distinguished from grand jury.

plaintiff The party bringing a civil complaint or lawsuit, in contrast to the defendant.

pleading A written statement of facts and argument filed by a party in a lawsuit, for example the plaintiff's complaint or defendant's response.

plenary A reference to power that is full, complete, or exclusive, for example the federal government's in foreign affairs.

plurality opinion An opinion that states the judgment of an appellate court but in its particular reasoning is supported by less than a majority of the judges or justices, and for that reason is not considered binding in future cases.

police power The broad regulatory power of government to protect public health, safety, morals, and welfare.

political question A legal question that a court believes is more appropriately decided by the executive or legislative branches than the judicial, for example, the legality of military hostilities or whether a state has a republican form of government.

precedent An earlier court decision thought to be analogous or so similar to the present case that it cannot be distinguished from it and therefore must guide or control the decision in the present case.

preemption The condition in which an area of policy or authority once open to the states or shared by the states and the federal government has been superseded or occupied exclusively by the federal authority.

preliminary injunction A temporary restraining order issued at the beginning of a lawsuit forbidding one of the parties from carrying out an act that is at issue in the case.

prima facie Literally, at first sight, on its face. Refers to evidence or an entire complaint that is strong enough to be presumptively valid unless refuted.

procedural due process Fundamental fairness in the way and manner in which government deals with the liberty and property of individuals, usually referring to procedural protections, such as the right to notice, to confront witnesses, etc., as distinguished from substantive rights, such as freedom of speech.

prohibition, writ of An order from a higher to a lower court that it cease to hear a particular case, usually on the ground that it belongs in another court.

public law Law dealing with the powers and responsibilities of government, including constitutions and certain statutes, administrative rules, and judicial decisions.

quash To void, vacate, or suppress, as when a court throws out an indictment.

ratio decidendi Literally, the reason for deciding. The holding of a case setting out the court's reasons for what it did, in contrast to statements of dicta.

recuse To disqualify oneself, as where a judge withdraws from hearing a case because of bias or conflict of interest.

remand To send back; the return of a case from a higher court to a lower usually with specific instructions on how to proceed further.

remedy The legal means for preventing or correcting a wrong or enforcing a right.

res judicata Literally, the matter adjudicated. A principle that forecloses further litigation of an issue between the parties to a case, except for an appeal, after the issue has been competently decided.

reserved powers Powers of a government not constitutionally delegated elsewhere or implied from those that are. Under the Tenth Amendment, for example, authority not delegated to the national government nor prohibited to the states is reserved to the states.

respondent The party against whom a suit is filed or an appeal taken.

reverse To overturn, as when an appellate court rules that the trial court should have rendered a decision for the other side in a case.

ripeness Readiness for legal decision or review, which usually means the issues in a case are not hypothetical and the parties have exhausted all other means of remedy or resolution. This prevents the premature hearing of cases.

scienter Knowingly, with knowledge. Usually refers to a criminal defendant's awareness that his or her alleged action was illegal.

sedition The crime of inciting rebellion or advocating violent overthrow of the government.

selective incorporation The case-by-case method the Supreme Court has used to hold that certain rights in the Bill of Rights are part of due process of law and thus serve as limits on state power through the due process clause of the Fourteenth Amendment.

show cause A court order requiring a party to appear and show reason why the court should not take certain action, often the issuance of an injunction.

sovereign immunity Exemption of the government from being sued without its consent.

sovereignty Supremacy of authority or rule; self-governing; the ultimate power of government to make binding decisions and resolve conflicts.

special master An officer appointed by a court to receive evidence and then present findings and conclusions to the court, which rules on them. Almost always used by the Supreme Court in hearing cases under its original jurisdiction.

specific performance A court order that a party perform certain obligations incurred under contract, as distinguished from an award of damages for breach of contract.

standing The requirement that a party bringing a lawsuit allege a direct and sufficiently substantial injury for which there is a legal remedy.

stare decisis Literally, let the decision stand. Reliance on precedent; the principle that rules of law established in earlier cases are binding in later cases that are similar to or cannot be distinguished from the earlier.

state action Conduct or developments for which a state or local government is responsible directly or indirectly rather than being purely a private matter. In constitutional law, the conduct or action that is subject to limits imposed by the Fourteenth or Fifteenth Amendments or by Article I-10 of the Constitution.

states rights Powers reserved to the states under the Tenth Amendment. In constitutional doctrine, opposition to increasing the power of the national government at the expense of the states; emphasis on state power and responsibility within the federal system.

statute of limitations A law setting a time limit for bringing specified types of lawsuits or criminal prosecutions. Most statutes defining crimes have a statute of limitations provision.

statutory law Laws enacted by legislatures, in contrast to case law established in binding judicial decisions.

stay A court order halting the execution of a judgment, usually temporary until further legal consideration can be given to an issue.

strict construction A narrow interpretation of the text of a law or legal document. In constitutional doctrine, the view that the Constitution, particularly in its grant of powers to the national government, should be interpreted in terms of its exact language rather than broadly or liberally.

sua sponte Literally, of its own will. Voluntary, without prompting or suggestion.

subpoena Literally, under penalty. A legal order directing a person to appear in court or other official proceeding to give testimony.

subpoena duces tecum Literally, under penalty bring with you. An order that a person under subpoena bring with him or her certain records, documents, or other material, or to turn these over to a court.

sub silentio Literally, under silence. A court action without express acknowledgment, as when, for example, a precedent is abandoned without the case or cases on which it was based being overruled.

substantive due process The inclusion of certain concrete, nonprocedural rights, such as freedom of speech or, at one time, freedom to make contracts, in the requirements of due process of law—thus generally putting them beyond the power of government to abridge.

summary judgment A court decision resolving a case or legal dispute where it becomes clear that opposing parties do not disagree about the facts; a decision based on a ruling of law rather than a finding of fact.

temporary restraining order See **preliminary injunction**.

three-judge court A special federal panel of district and appellate court judges invoked to expedite the hearing of certain cases or issues. Normally appeals from the rulings of such courts may be taken directly to the Supreme Court.

tort A civil rather than criminal wrong committed by one person against another, for example injury to person or property through negligence, the remedy for which is an award of damages.

ultra vires Literally, beyond powers. Action of a government officer or agency that exceeds vested legal authority.

vacate To set aside or annul, as when a higher court rescinds the judgment of a lower.

vagueness Lack of clarity; a defect in a law that violates the due process requirement that clear notice be given of what is lawful and unlawful.

venire A panel or pool of perspective jurors from which juries are chosen.

venue The geographical area of a court's jurisdiction; the location of a trial.

vested rights Rights believed to be so basic that they may not be interfered with by government. Historically, certain rights to property.

voir dire A pretrial process in which perspective jurors are examined to determine their fitness to serve on the jury that will hear the case.

warrant A court order allowing a competent authority to carry out a specified act, for example a search or an arrest.

writ A court order requiring that something be done or not done.

GENERAL AND SUPPLEMENTAL BIBLIOGRAPHY

(Works specific to individual chapters are found at the ends of chapters)

General and Major Reference Works

Biskupic, Joan, and Elder Witt, *Guide to the United States Supreme Court*, 3rd ed., 2 vols (1997)

Chase, Harold W., and Craig R. Ducat, *The Constitution and What It Means Today* (1978)

Corwin, Edward S., *The Constitution of the United States: Analysis and Interpretation* (1973)

Cushman, Clare, *The Supreme Court Justices: Illustrated Biographies* (1993)

Epstein, Lee, Jeffrey A. Segal, Harold J. Spaeth, and Thomas G. Walker, *The Supreme Court Compendium: Data, Decisions, and Development* (1994)

Friedman, Leon, and Fred I. Israel, *Justices of the United States Supreme Court, 1789–1991*, 5 vols. (1992)

Hall, Kermit L., ed., *The Oxford Companion to the Supreme Court of the United States* (1992)

———, *United States Constitutional and Legal History: Major Historical Essays*, 20 vols. (1987)

———, (compiler), *A Comprehensive Bibliography of American Constitutional and Legal History*, 5 vols., (1984)

———, *The Oxford Guide to United States Supreme Court Opinions* (1999)

Johnson, John W., ed., *Historic United States Court Cases, 1690–1990: An Encyclopedia* (1992)

Levy, Leonard, Kenneth W. Karst, and Dennis J. Mahoney, eds., *The Encyclopedia of the American Constitution*, 4 vols. (1986)

Nelson, William E., and John P. Reid, *The Literature of American Legal History* (1985)

Nowak, John E., and Ronald D. Rotunda, *Constitutional Law*, 4th ed. (1991)

Peltason, J. W., *Understanding the Constitution* (1994)

Pritchett, C. Herman, *The American Constitution*, 3rd ed. (1977)

Tribe, Laurence H., *American Constitutional Law*, 2nd ed. (1988)

Urofsky, Melvin I., and Paul Finkelman, eds., *Documents of American Legal and Constitutional History*, 2 vols. (2001)

Vile, John R., *Encyclopedia of Constitutional Amendments, Proposed Amendments, and Amending Issues, 1789–1995* (1996)

Constitutional Theory and Interpretation

Ackerman, Bruce, *We the People: Foundations* (1991)

———, *We the People: Transformations* (1998)

Agresto, John, *The Supreme Court and Constitutional Democracy* (1984)

Anastaplo, George, *The Amendments to the Constitution: An Interpretation* (1995)

Arkes, Hadley, *The Return of George Sutherland: Restoring a Jurisprudence of Natural Rights* (1994)

———, *Beyond the Constitution* (1990)

Baker, Thomas E., *The Most Wonderful Work . . . : Our Constitution Interpreted* (1996)

Barber, Sotirios A., *On What the Constitution Means* (1984)

———, *The Constitution of Judicial Power* (1993)

Berger, Raoul, *Government by Judiciary* (1977)

Berns, Walter, *Taking the Constitution Seriously* (1987)

Bickel, Alexander M., *The Least Dangerous Branch* (1962)

———, *The Morality of Consent* (1975)

Black, Hugo, *A Constitutional Faith* (1968)

Bobbit, Philip, *Constitutional Fate* (1984)

Bork, Robert, *The Tempting of America* (1989)

Brandon, Mark E., *Free in the World: American Slavery and Constitutional Failure* (1998)

Brisbin, Richard A., Jr., *Justice Antonin Scalia and the Conservative Revival* (1997)

Burgess, Susan A., *Contest for Constitutional Authority* (1992)

Carter, Lief, *Contemporary Constitutional Lawmaking: The Supreme Court and the Art of Politics* (1985)

Choper, Jesse H., *The Supreme Court and the Political Branches: Judicial Review in the National Political Process: A Functional Reconsideration of the Role of the Supreme Court* (1980)

Clayton, Cornell W., and Howard Gilman, eds., *The Supreme Court in American Politics: New Institutionalist Interpretations* (1999)

Conant, Michael, *The Constitution and the Economy: Objective Theory and Critical Commentary* (1991)

Couter, Robert D., *The Strategic Constitution* (2000)

Dworkin, Ronald, *Taking Rights Seriously* (1977)

Edelman, Martin, *Democratic Theories and the Constitution* (1984)

Ely, John Hart, *Democracy and Distrust: A Theory of Judicial Review* (1980)

———, *On Constitutional Ground* (1996)

Franck, Matthew J., *Against the Imperial Judiciary: The Supreme Court v. the Sovereignty of the People* (1996)

Gerber, Scott Douglas, *To Secure These Rights: the Declaration of Independence and Constitutional Interpretation* (1995)

Gerhardt, Michael, et al., *Constitutional Theory: Arguments and Perspectives* (2000)

Goldstein, Leslie Friedman, *In Defense of the Text* (1991)

Goldwin, Robert A., and Robert A. Licht, eds., *The Spirit of the Constitution: Five Conversations* (1990)

Gordon, David, ed., *Secession, State, and Liberty* (1998)

Grasso, Kenneth L., and Cicelia Rodriguez Castillo, eds., *Liberty under Law: American Constitutionalism, Yesterday, Today, and Tomorrow* (1997)

Griffin, Stephen M., *American Constitutionalism: From Theory to Politics* (1996)

Hardin, Russell, *Liberalism, Constitutionalism, and Democracy* (1999)

Harris, William F., II, *The Interpretable Constitution* (1993)

Harwood, Sterling, *Judicial Activism, A Restrained Defense*, rev. ed. (1996)

Hoffman, Daniel N., *Our Elusive Constitution: Silences, Paradoxes, Priorities* (1997)

Jacobson, Gary, *Pragmatism, Statesmanship, and the Supreme Court* (1977)

———, *The Supreme Court and the Decline of Constitutional Aspiration* (1984)

Jaffa, Harry, *Original Intent and the Framers of the Constitution* (1994)

Kahn, Paul W., *The Reign of Law: Marbury v. Madison and the Construction of America* (1997)

———, *Legitimacy and History: Self-Government in American Constitutional Theory* (1993)

Kahn, Ronald, *The Supreme Court and Constitutional Theory, 1953–1993* (1994)

Kalman, Laura, *The Strange Case of Legal Liberalism* (1996)

Ketcham, Ralph, *Framed for Posterity: The Enduring Philosophy of the Constitution* (1993)

Keynes, Edward, *Liberty, Property, and Privacy: Toward a Jurisprudence of Substantive Due Process* (1996)

Kreml, William P., *The Constitutional Divide: The Public and Private Sectors in American Law* (1997)

Lamb, Charles, *Supreme Court Activism and Restraint* (1992)

Levinson, Sanford, *Constitutional Faith* (1988)

Levy, Leonard, *Original Intent and the Framers' Constitution* (1988)

Lewis, Frederick, *The Context of Judicial Activism: Endurance of the Warran Court Legacy in a Conservative Age* (1999)

Lipkin, Robert J., *Constitutional Revolutions: Pragmatism and the Role of Judicial Review in American Constitutionalism* (2000)

Maltz, Earl M., *Rethinking Constitutional Law: Originalism, Interventionism, and the Politics of Judicial Review* (1994)

Mansfield, Harvey C., Jr., *America's Constitutional Soul* (1991)

McCann, Michael W., and Gerald L. Houseman, eds., *Judging the Constitution: Critical Essays on Judicial Lawmaking* (1989)

McClellan, James, *Joseph Story and the American Constitution: A Study in Political and Legal Thought* (1971)

Moore, Wayne D., *Constitutional Rights and the Powers of the People* (1996)

Nagel, Robert F., *Constitutional Cultures: The Mentality and Consequences of Judicial Review* (1989)

———, *Judicial Power and the American Character: Censoring Ourselves in an Anxious Age* (1994)

Peretti, Terri Jennings, *In Defense of a Political Court* (1999)

Perry, Michael, *The Constitution and the Courts: Law or Politics* (1994)

Powe, Lucas A., Jr., *The Warren Court and American Politics* (2000)

Redish, Martin H., *The Constitution as Political Structure* (1995)

Richards, David A.J., *Conscience and the Constitution: History, Theory, and Law of the Reconstruction Amendments* (1993)

Scalia, Antonin, *A Matter of Interpretation: Federal Courts and the Law* (1997)

Schambra, William A., ed., *As Far as Republican Principles Will Admit: Essays by Martin Diamond* (1992)

Schultz, David A., and Christopher E. Smith, *The Jurisprudential Vision of Justice Antonin Scalia* (1996)

Smith, Christopher, *Justice Antonin Scalia and the Supreme Court: The Conservative Moment* (1993)

Smith, Rogers, *Liberalism and American Constitutional Law* (1985)

Smith, Steven D., *The Constitution and the Pride of Reason* (1998)

Snowiss, Sylvia, *Judicial Review and the Law of the Constitution* (1990)

Sosin, J.M., *The Aristocracy of the Long Robe: The Origins of Judicial Review in America* (1989)

Strum, Phillippa, *The Supreme Court and Political Questions* (1974)

Sunderland, Lane V., *Popular Government and the Supreme Court: Securing the Public and Private Rights* (1996)

Sunstein, Cass R., *The Partial Constitution* (1993)

———, *One Case at a Time: Judicial Minimalism on the Supreme Court* (1999)

Tribe, Laurence, *Constitutional Choices* (1985)

Tribe, Laurence H., and Michael C. Dorf, *On Reading the Constitution* (1991)

Tushnet, Mark, *Red, White, and Blue: A Critical Analysis of Constitutional Law* (1988)

———, *Taking the Constitution away from the Courts* (1999)

Van Sickel, Robert W., *Not a Particularly Different Voice: The Jurisprudence of Sandra Day O'Connor* (1998)

Vile, M.J.C., *Constitutionalism and the Separation of Powers* (1967)

Wellington, Harry H., *Interpreting the Constitution: The Supreme Court and the Process of Adjudication* (1990)

Whittington, Keith E., *Constitutional Interpretation: Textual Meaning, Original Intent and Judicial Review*

———, *Constitutional Construction: Divided Powers and Constitutional Meaning* (1999)

Wolfe, Christopher, *The Rise of Judicial Review: From Constitutional Interpretation to Judge-Made Law* (1986)

———, *Judicial Activism* (1991)

The Supreme Court: The Institution and Its Work

Abraham, Henry, *Justices and Presidents: A Political History of Appointments to the Supreme Court*, 3rd ed. (1992)

Atkinson, David N., *Leaving the Bench: Supreme Court Justices at the End* (1999)

Barnum, David G., *The Supreme Court and American Democracy* (1993)

Baum, Lawrence, *The Supreme Court*, 7th ed. (2000)

Brenner, Saul, and Harold J. Spaeth, *Stare Indecisis: The Alteration of Precedent on the Supreme Court, 1946–1992* (1995)

Brigham, John, *The Cult of the Court* (1987)

Casper, Gerhard, and Richard A. Posner, *The Workload of the Supreme Court* (1976)

Clayton, Cornell W., and Howard Gillman, eds., *Supreme Court Decision Making: New Institututional Approaches* (1999)

Cooper, Phillip J., *Battles on the Bench: Conflicts inside the Supreme Court* (1995)

Cooper, Phillip J., and Howard Ball, *The United States Supreme Court: From the Inside Out* (1996)

Danelski, David J., *A Supreme Court Justice Is Appointed* (1964)

Davis, Richard, *Decisions and Images: The Supreme Court and the Press* (1994)

Dickson, Del, ed., *The Supreme Court in Conference* (2001)

Epstein, Lee, *Conservatives in Court* (1985)

Epstein, Lee, and Jack Knight, *The Choices Justices Make* (1998)

Flax, Jane, *The American Dream in Black and White: The Clarence Thomas Hearings* (1998)

Franck, Matthew, and Richard Stevens, eds., *Sober as a Judge: The Supreme Court and Republican Liberty* (1999)

Greenberg, Ellen, *The Supreme Court Explained* (1997)

Halpern, Stephen C., and Charles M. Lamb, eds., *Supreme Court Activism and Restraint* (1982)

Maltese, John Anthony, *The Selling of Supreme Court Nominees* (1995)

Maltzman, Forest, Paul J. Wahlbeck, and James Spriggs, *Crafting Law on the Supreme Court: The Collegial Game* (2000)

Marshall, Thomas, *Public Opinion and the Supreme Court* (1989)

Massaro, John, *Supremely Political: The Role of Ideology and Presidential Management in Unsuccessful Supreme Court Nominations* (1990)

McGuire, Kevin T., *The Supreme Court Bar: Legal Elites in the Washington Community* (1993)

Murphy, Walter L., *Elements of Judicial Strategy* (1964)

O'Brien, David M., *Storm Center: The Supreme Court in American Politics* (1986)

Pacelle, Richard L., Jr. *The Transformation of the Supreme Court's Agenda: From the New Deal to the Reagan Administration* (1991)

Perry, Barbara A., *A "Representative" Court? The Impact of Race, Religion and Gender on Appointments* (1991)

———, *The Priestly Tribe: The Supreme Court's Image in the American Mind* (1999)

Perry, H.W., Jr., *Deciding to Decide: Agenda Setting in the United States Supreme Court* (1991)

Provine, Doris Marie, *Case Selection in the United States Supreme Court* (1980)

Radcliffe, James E., *The Case-or-Controversy Provision* (1978)

Rehnquist, William H., *The Supreme Court: How It Was, How It Is* (1987)

Schwartz, Bernard, *How the Supreme Court Decides Cases* (1996)

Segal, Jeffrey A., and Spaeth, Harold J., *The Supreme Court and the Attitudinal Model* (1993)

Silverstein, Mark, *Judicious Choices: The New Politics of Supreme Court Confirmations* (1994)

Smolla, Rodney, and Neal Devins, eds., *A Year in the Life of the Supreme Court* (1995)

Spaeth, Harold J., and Saul Brenner, eds., *Studies in United States Supreme Court Behavior* (1990)

Spaeth, Harold J., and Jeffrey A. Segal, *Majority Rule or Minority Will: Adherence to Precedent on the U. S. Supreme Court* (1999)

Steamer, Robert J., *Chief Justice: Leadership and the Supreme Court* (1986)

Stearns, Maxwell L., *Constitutional Process: A Social Choice Analysis of Supreme Court Decision Making* (2000)

Stern, Robert L., et al., *Supreme Court Practice*, 7th ed. (1993)

Sunstein, Cass R., *One Case at a Time: Judicial Minimalism on the Supreme Court* (1999)

Tribe, Laurence, *God Save This Honorable Court: How the Choice of Supreme Court Justices Shapes Our History* (1988)

van Geel, T. R., *Understanding Supreme Court Opinions* (1991)

Walker, Thomas G., and Lee Epstein, *The Supreme Court of the United States: An Introduction* (1992)

Wasby, Stephen J., *The Supreme Court in the Federal Judicial System* (1993)

Yalof, David Alistair, *Pursuit of Justices: Presidential Politics and the Selection of Supreme Court Nominees* (1999)

Civil Liberties, General

Abernathy, Glenn M., and Barbara A. Perry, *Civil Liberties under the Constitution* (1993)

Abraham, Henry J., and Barbara A. Perry, *Freedom and the Court*, 7th ed. (1998)

Amar, Akhil Reed, and Alan Hirsch, *For the People: What the Constitution Really Says about Your Rights* (1998)

Baer, Judith A., *Equality under the Constitution: Reclaiming the Fourteenth Amendment* (1983)

Barnett, Randy E., *The Structure of Liberty: Justice and the Rule of Law* (1998)

Bigel, Alan I., *The Supreme Court on Emergency Powers, Foreign Affairs, and the Protection of Civil Liberties, 1935–1975* (1986)

Braveman, Daan, William C. Banks, and Rodney A. Smolla, *Constitutional Law: Structure and Rights in Our Federal System* (2000)

Brigham, John, *Civil Liberties and American Democracy* (1984)

Campbell, Colton C., and John F. Stack, eds., *Congress and the Politics of Emerging Rights* (2001)

Casper, Jonathan, *The Politics of Civil Liberties* (1972)

Cortner, Richard C., *The Supreme Court and Civil Liberties Policy* (1975)

Dorsen, Norman, *Frontiers of Civil Liberties* (1968)

———, ed., *Our Endangered Rights: The ACLU Report on Civil Liberties Today* (1984)

Dworkin, Ronald, *Taking Rights Seriously* (1977)

Epp, Charles, *The Rights Revolution: Lawyers, Activists, and Supreme Courts in Comparative Perspective* (1998)

Epstein, Richard A., *Principles for a Free Society: Reconciling Individual Liberty with the Common Good* (1998)

Finkelman, Paul, and Stephen E. Gottlieb, eds., *Toward a Usable Past: Liberty under State Constitutions* (1991)

Foley, Michael, *American Political Ideas* (1991)

Foner, Eric, *The Story of American Freedom* (1998)

Gardner, Jamers A., ed., *State Expansion of Federal Constitutional Liberties: Individual Rights in a Dual Constitutional System* (1999)

Glendon, Mary Ann, *Rights Talk* (1991)

George, Robert P., *Making Men Moral: Civil Liberties and Public Morality* (1993)

Goldwin, Robert A., and William A. Schambra, eds., *How Does the Constitution Secure Rights?* (1985)

Gottlieb, Stephen E., *Morality Imposed: The Rehnquist Court and Liberty in America* (2000)

Hensley, Thomas R., Christopher E. Smith, and Joyce A. Baugh, *The Changing Supreme Court: Constitutional Rights and Liberties* (1997)

Hickok, Eugene W., Gary L. McDowell, and Philip J. Costopoulos, eds., *Our Peculiar Security: The Written Constitution and Limited Government* (1993)

Katz, Ellis, and G. Alan Tarr, eds., *Federalism and Rights* (1996)

Keller, Robert H., ed., *In Honor of Justice Douglas: A Symposium on Individual Freedom and the Government* (1979)

Kommers, Donald P., *Liberty and Community in American Constitutional Law: Continuing Tensions* (1986)

Landynski, Jacob W., *Individual Rights and Public Police in the New Supreme Court* (1982)

Massey, Calivin R., *Silent Rights: the Ninth Amendment and the Constitution's Unenumerated Rights* (1995)

McClellan, James, *Liberty, Order, and Justice: An Introduction to the Constitutional Principles of Erica Government* (1999)

Moore, Wayne D., *Constitutional Rights and Powers of the People* (1996)

Morgan, Richard E., *The Law and Politics of Civil Rights and Liberties* (1985)

Phelps, Glenn A., and Robert A. Poirier, eds., *Contemporary Debates on Civil Liberties: The Enduring Questions* (1985)

Powe, Lucas A., Jr., *The Warren Court and American Politics* (2000)

Renstrom, Peter, *Constitutional Rights Sourcebook* (1999)

Saari, David J., *Too Much Liberty? Perspectives on Freedom and the American Dream* (1995)

Scheingold, Stuart A., *The Politics of Rights* (1974)

Stephens, Otis H., and John M. Scheb, *American Civil Liberties* (1999)

Tushnet, Mark V., ed., *The Warren Court in Historical Perspective* (1993)

Walker, Samuel, *The Rights Revolution: Rights and Community in Modern American* (1998)

Watson, Bradley C.S., Civil Rights and the Paradox of Liberal Democracy (1999)

———, *Courts and the Culture Wars* (2002)

Wills, Gary, *A Necessary Evil: A History of American Distrust of Government* (1999)

The Bill of Rights: Origins, History, Nationalization

Amar, Akhil Reed, *The Bill of Rights: Creation and Reconstruction* (1998)

Berger, Raoul, *Government by Judiciary: Transformation of the Fourteenth Amendment* (1977)

———, *The Fourteenth Amendment and the Bill of Rights* (1989)

Barnett, Randy E., ed., *The Rights Retained by the People: The History and Means of the Ninth Amendment* (1989)

Cohen, Wiilliiam, Murray Schwartz, and DeAnne Sobul, *The Bill of Rights: A Source Book* (1976)

Cortner, Richard C., *The Supreme Court and the Second Bill of Rights* (1981)

Curtis, Michael Kent, *No State Shall Abridge: The Fourteenth Amendment and the Bill of Rights* (1990)

DeRosa, Marshall, *The Ninth Amendment and the Politics of Creative Jurisprudence: Disparaging the Fundamental Right for Popular Control* (1996)

Dorsen, Norman, *The Evolving Constitution: Essays on the Bill of Rights and the United States Supreme Court* (1987)

Goldman, Roger L., *Individual Rights: The Universal Challenge: 1791–1991, Bicentenniel Celebration of the Bill of Rights* (1991)

Goldwin, Robert A., *From Parchment to Power: How James Madison Used the Bill of Rights to Save the Constitution* (1997)

Hickok, Eugene W., ed., *The Bill of Rights: Original Meaning Current Understanding* (1991)

Levy, Leonard W., *Introduction to the Fourteenth Amendment and the Bill of Rights: Incorporation Theory* (1970)

———, *Origins of the Bill of Rights* (1999)

Lewis, Frederick P., *The Dilemma of the Congressional Power to Enforce the Fourteenth Amendment* (1980)

———, *The Nationalization of Liberty* (1990)

Nelson, Michael, *The Fourteenth Amendment: From Political Principle to Judicial Doctrine* (1988)

Rutland, Robert A., *Birth of the Bill of Rights, 1776-1791* (1955)

Schlam, Lawrence, *The Bill of Rights: Fundamental Freedom* (1981)

Schwartz, Bernard, *The Great Rights of Mankind: A History of the American Bill of Rights* (1992)

Shaw, Stephen K., *The Ninth Amendment: Preservation of the Constitutional Mind* (1990)

Stone, Georffrey R., Richard A. Epstein, and Cass R. Sunstein, *The Bill of Rights in the Modern State* (1992)

Veit, Helen E., Kenneth R. Bowling, and Charles Bangs Bickford, *Creating the Bill of Rights: The Documentary Record from the First Federal Congress* (1991)

Yarborough, Tinsley E., *Mr. Justice Black and His Critics* (1998)

Religion

Adams, Arlin M., and Charles J. Emmerich, *A Nation Dedicated to Religious Liberty: The Constitutional Heritage of the Religion Clauses* (1990)

Ahlstrom, Sidney E., *A Religious History of the American People* (1972)

Alley, Robert, *The Supreme Court on Church and State* (1988)

Berman, Harold J., *Faith and Order: The Reconciliation of Law and Religion* (1993)

Carter, Leif, *An Introduction to Constitutional Interpretation: Cases in Law and Religion* (1991)

Carter, Stephen, *The Culture of Disbelief* (1993)

Choper, Jesse, *Securing Religious Liberty: Principles for Judicial Interpretation of the Religion Clauses* (1995)

Cord, Robert L., *Separation of Church and State: Historical Fact and Current Fiction* (1982)

Currey, Thomas J., *The First Amendment Freedoms: Church and State in America to the Passage of the First Amendment* (1986)

Dolbeare, Kenneth M., and Phillip E. Hammond, *The School Prayers Decisions: From Court Policy to Local Practice* (1971)

Eidsmoe, John, *Christianity and the Constitution: The Faith of Our Founding Fathers* (1987)

Eldredge, Niles, *The Monkey Business: A Scientist Looks at Creationism* (1992)

Evans, Bette, *Interpreting the Free Exercise of Religion* (1997)

Feldman, Stephen, *Please Don't Wish Me a Merry Christmas: A Critical History of the Separation of Church and State* (1997)

Firmage, Edwin Brown, and Richard Collin Mangrum, *Zion in the Courts: A Legal History of the Church of Jesus Christ of Latter-Day Saints, 1830–1900* (1988)

Gedicks, Frederick Mark, *The Rhetoric of Church and State* (1995)

George, Robert P., *The Clash of Orthodoxies: Law, Religion, and Morality in Crisis* (2001)

Greenawalt, Kent, *Religious Convictions and Political Choice* (1988)

Guliuzza, Frank, *Over the Wall: Protecting Religious Expression in the Public Square* (2000)

Herberg, Will, *Protestant, Catholic, Jew: An Essay in American Religious Sociology* (1960)

Hostetler, John A., *Amish Society*, 4th ed. (1993)

Howe, Mark deWolfe, *The Garden and the Wilderness: Religion and Government in American Constitutional History* (1965)

Hutcheson, Richard G., Jr., *God in the White House: How Religion Has Changed the Modern Presidency* (1989)

Ivers, Gregg, *Redefining the First Freedom* (1993)

———, *To Build a Wall: American Jews and the Separation of Church and State* (1995)

Jelen, Ted G., *To Serve God and Mammon: Church-State Relations in American Politics* (2000)

Katz, Wilbur G., *Religion and American Constitutions* (1964)

Kauper, Paul, *Religion and the Constitution* (1964)

Kelly, Dean M., ed., *Government Intervention in Religious Affairs* (1982)

Keynes, Edward, and Randall K. Miller, *The Court vs. Congress: Prayer, Busing, and Abortion* (1989)

Kurland, Phillip, *Religion and the Law* (1962)

———, *Church and State: The Supreme Court and the First Amendment* (1975)

Larson, Edward, *Summer for the Gods: The Scopes Trial and America's Continuing Debate over Science and Religion* (1997)

Lee, Francis Graham, *Church-State Relations* (2002)

Levy, Leonard, *The Establishment Clause: Religion and the First Amendment* (1986)

Loewy, Arnold H., *Religion and the Constitution: Cases and Materials* (1999)

Long, Carolyn N., *Religious Freedom and Indian Rights: The Case of Oregon v. Smith* (2000)

Malbin, Michael, *Religion and Politics: Intentions of the Authors of the First Amendment* (1978)

Manwaring, David, *Render unto Caesar: The Flag Salute Controversy* (1962)

Marty, Martin E., *A Nation of Believers* (1976)

———, *Pilgrims in Their Own Land: 500 Years of Religion in America* (1984)

Mazur, Eric Michael, *The Americanization of Religious Minorities: Confronting the Constitutional Order* (1999)

Miller, William Lee, *The First Liberty: Religion and the American Republic* (1985)

Monsma, Stephen V., *When Sacred and Secular Mix* (1996)

Monsma, Stephen V., and J. Christopher Soper, *Equal Treatment of Religion in a Pluralistic Society* (1998)

Morgan, Richard E., *The Supreme Court and Religion* (1972)

———, *The Politics of Religious Conflict: Church and State in America* (1980)

Muir, William K., *Prayer in the Public Schools: Law and Attitude Change* (1967)

Noonan, John T., *The Lustre of Our Country: The American Experience of Religious Freedom* (1998)

Oaks, Dallin, ed., *The Wall between Church and State* (1963)

Peters, Shawn Francis, *Judging Jehovah's Witnesses: Religious Persecution and the Dawn of the Rights Revolution* (2000)

Pfeffer, Leo, *God, Caesar, and the Constitution* (1975)

———, *Religion, State, and the Burger Court* (1985)

Ravitch, Frank S., *School Prayer and Discrimination* (1999)

Richards, David A.J., *Toleration and the Constitution* (1975)

Rosenblum, Nancy L., *Obligations of Citizenship and Demands of Faith: Religious Accommodation in Pluralist Democracy* (2000)

Sandoz, Ellis, *A Government of Laws: Political Theory, Religion, and the American Founding* (1990)

Sheffer, Martin S., *God versus Caesar: Belief, Worship, and Proselytization under the First Amendment* (1999)

Smith, Steven, *Foreordained Failure: The Quest for a Constitutional Principle of Religious Freedom* (1995)

Sorouf, Frank J., *The Wall of Separation: The Constitutional Politics of Church and State* (1976)

Spinner-Halev, Jeff, *Surviving Diversity: Religion and Democratic Citizenship* (2000)

Stokes, Anson Phelps, *Church and State in the United States*, 3 vols. (1950)

Sullivan, Winnifred Fallers, *Paying the Words Extra: Religious Discourse in the Supreme Court of the United States* (1995)

Swanson, Wayne R., *The Christ Child Goes to Court* (1990)

Weber, Paul J., ed., *Equal Separation: Understanding the Religion Clauses of the First Amendment* (1990)

Weber, Paul J., and Dennis A. Gilber, *Private Churches and Public Money: Church-Government Fiscal Relations* (1981)

Wilcox, Clyde, God's Warriors: *The Christian Right in Twentieth Century America* (1993)

Wills, Garry, *Under God* (1990)

Speech and Press

Abernathy, M. Glenn, *The Right of Assembly and Association* (1981)

Alexander, Larry, ed., *Freedom of Speech* (1999)

Allen, David, and Robert Jensen, eds., *Freeing the First Amendment: Critical Perspectives on Freedom of Expression* (1995)

Anastaplo, George, *Campus Hate-Speech Codes and Twentieth Century Atrocities* (1997)

Baird, Robert M., and Stuart E. Rosenbaum, eds., *Pornography: Private Right or Public Menace?* (1998)

Baker, C. Edwin, *Human Liberty and Freedom of Speech* (1989)

Barendt, Eric M., Laurence Lustgarten, Kenneth Norrie, and Hugh Stephenson, eds., *Libel and the Media: The Chilling Effect* (1997)

Barron, Jerome, *Freedom of the Press for Whom: The Right of Access to Mass Media* (1973)

Belknap, Michal R., *Cold War Political Justice: The Smith Act, the Communist Party, and American Civil Liberties* (1977)

Bennett, Colin J., and Rebecca Grant, eds., *Visions of Privacy: Policy Choices for the Digital Age* (1999)

Berger, Ronald, *Feminism and Pornography* (1991)

Berns, Walter, *The First Amendment and the Future of American Democracy* (1976)

Blanchard, Margaret, *Revolutionary Sparks: Freedom of Expression in Modern America* (1992)

Bloustein, Edward J., *Individual and Group Privacy* (1978)

Bollinger, Lee C., *Freedom of Speech and Extremist Speech in America* (1986)

———, *Images of a Free Press* (1991)

———, *Eternally Vigilant: Free Speech in the Modern Era* (2002)

Bosmajian, Haig, *The Freedom Not to Speak* (1999)

Caputi, Mary, *Voluptuous Yearnings: A Feminist Theory of the Obscene* (1997)

Carmen, Ira H., *Movies, Censorship, and the Law* (1966)

Carter, T. Barton, *The First Amendment and the Fifth Estate: Regulation of Electronic Mass Media* (1993)

Cate, Fred H., *Privacy in the Information Age* (1997)

Chafee, Zechariah, Jr., *Free Speech in the United States* (1941)

Cleary, Edward J., *Beyond the Burning Cross: The First Amendment and the Landmark R. A. V. Case* (1994)

Clor, Harry M., *Obscenity and Public Morality: Censorship in a Liberal Society* (1969)

———, *Public Morality and Liberal Society: Essays on Decency, Law, and Pornography* (1996)

Copp, David, and Susan Wendell, eds., *Pornography and Censorship* (1983)

Cord, Robert, *Protest, Dissent, and the Supreme Court* (1971)

Cortner, Richard C., *The Kingfish and the Constitution: Huey Long, the First Amendment, and the Emergence of Modern Press Freedom in America* (1966)

Cossman, Brenda, Shannon Bell, Becki Ross, and Lisa Gotell, *Bad Attitudes on Trial: Pornography, Feminism, and the Butler Decision* (1997)

Cox, Archibald, *Freedom of Expression* (1981)

Curtis, Michael Kent, *Free Speech, "The People's Darling Privilege"* (2000)

Daly, John Charles, *The Press and the Courts* (1978)

Decew, Judith Wagner, *In Pursuit of Privacy: Law, Ethics, and the Rise of Technology* (1997)

Delgado, Richard, and Jean Stefancic, *Must We Defend Nazis? Hate Speech, Pornography, and the New First Amendment* (1997)

Dennis, Everette, and Eli Noam, *The Costs of Libel* (1989)

Dionisopoulos, P. Alan, and Craig R. Ducat, *The Right to Privacy: Essays and Cases* (1976)

Dooling, Richard, *Blue Streak: Swearing, Free Speech, and Sexual Harassment* (1996)

Dowell, Eldridge F., *A History of Criminal Syndicalism Laws in the United States* (1939)

Downs, Donald A., *Nazis in Skokie: Freedom, Community, and the First Amendment* (1985)

———, *The New Politics of Pornography* (1989)

Easton, Susan, *The Case for the Right to Silence* (1998)

Emerson, Thomas I, *Toward a General Theory of the First Amendment* (1967)

————, *The System of Freedom of Expression* (1970)

Etzioni, Amatai, *The Limits of Privacy* (1999)

Farber, Daniel A., *The First Amendment* (1998)

Fellman, David, *The Constitutional Right of Association* (1963)

Fish, Stanley, *There's No Such Thing as Free Speech, and It's a Good Thing Too* (1994)

Fiss, Owen, *The Irony of Free Speech* (1996)

————, *Liberalism Divided: Freedom of Speech and the Many Uses of State Power* (1996)

Flink, Stanley E., *Sentinel under Seige: The Triumphs and Troubles of America's Free Press* (1998)

Forer, Louis G., *A Chilling Effect: The Mounting Threat of Libel and Invasion of Privacy Action to the First Amendment* (1987)

Friedman, Leon, ed., *Obscenity: The Complete Oral arguments before the Supreme Court in the Major Obscenity Cases* (1983)

Friendly, Fred, *Minnesota Rag: The Dramatic Story of the Landmark Supreme Court Case That Gave Meaning to Freedom of the Press* (1981)

Garry, Patrick, *Scrambling for Protection: The New Media and the First Amendment* (1994)

Gertz, Elmer, *Gertz v. Robert Welch, Inc.: The Story of a Landmark Libel Case* (1992)

Gillmor, Donald M., *Power, Publicity, and the Abuse of Libel Law* (1992)

Goldstein, Robert Justin, *The Flag: The Great 1989–1990 American Flag Desecration Controversy* (1996)

————, *Flag Burning and Free Speech: The Case of Texas v. Johnson* (2000)

Graber, Mark A., *Transforming Free Speech: The Ambiguous Legacy of Civil Libertarianism* (1991)

Greenawalt, Kent, *Fighting Words: Individuals, Communities, and Liberties of Speech* (1995)

Gubar, Susan, *For Adult Use Only: The Dilemmas of Violent Pornography* (1989)

Gutman, A, *Freedom of Association* (1998)

Haltom, William, *Reporting on the Courts: How the Mass Media Cover Judicial Actions* (1998)

Heins, Margaret, *Sin, Sex, and Blasphemy* (1993)

Hensley, Thomas R., ed, *The Boundaries of Freedom of Expression and Order in American Democracy* (2001)

Heumann, Milton, Thomas Church, with David Redlawsk, eds., *Hate Speech on Campus: Cases, Case Studies, and Commentary* (1997)

Hixson, Richard F., *Pornography and the Justices: The Supreme Court and the Intractable Obscenity Problem* (1996)

————, *Privacy in a Public Society: Human Rights in Conflict* (1987)

Hopkins, W. Wat, *Actual Malice: Twenty-five Years after Times v. Sullivan* (1989)

Horn, Robert A., *Groups and the Constitution* (1956)

Hull, Elizabeth, *Taking Liberties: National Barriers to the Free Flow of Ideas* (1990)

Hunt, Lynn, ed., *The Invention of Pornography* (1993)

Ingelhart, Louis E., ed., *Press and Speech Freedoms in America, 1619–1995: A Chronology* (1997)

Itzin, Catherine, ed., *Pornography: Women, Violence, and Civil Liberties* (1993)

Johnson, John W., *The Struggle for Student Rights: Tinker v. Des Moines and the 1960's* (1997)

Kalven, Harry, *A Worthy Tradition: Freedom of Speech in America* (1988)

————, *The Negro and the First Amendment* (1965)

Kane, Peter E., *Errors, Lies, and Libel* (1992)

Kelly, Sean, *Access Denied: The Politics of Press Censorship* (1978)

Kirby, James, *Fumble: Bear Bryant, Wally Butts, and the Great College Football Scandal* (1986)

Kobylka, Joseph F., *The Politics of Obsenity: Group Litigation in a Time of Legal Change* (1991)

Krattenmaker, Thomas G., and Lucas A. Powe, *Regulating Broadcast Programming* (1994)

Krislov, Samuel, *The Supreme Court and Political Freedom* (1968)

Levy, Leonard W., *Emergence of a Free Press* [revised edition of the author's 1960 work *Legacy of Suppression*] (1985)

————, ed., *Freedom of the Press from Zenger to Jefferson* (1996)

Lewis, Anthony, *Make No Law: The Sullivan Case and the First Amendment* (1991)

Lieberman, Jethro K., *Privacy and the Law* (1978)

Lofton, John, *The Press as Guardian of the First Amendment* (1980)

MacKinnon, Catherine, *Only Words* (1993)

Martin, Charles H., *The Angelo Herndon Case and Southern Justice* (1976)

Matsuda, Mari, Charles Lawrence, Richard Delgado, and Kimberle Crenshaw, *Words That Wound: Critical Race Theory, Assaultive Speech, and the First Amendment* (1993)

McCoy, Ralph E., *Freedom of the Press: An Annotated Bibliography, Second Supplement, 1978–1992* (1994)

Meiklejohn, Alexander, *Free Speech and Its Relation to Self-Government* (1948)

————, *Political Freedom: The Constitutional Powers of the People* (1960)

Murphy, Paul L., *The Meaning of Freedom of Speech: First Amendment Freedoms from Wilson to FDR* (1972)

Neuborne, Burt, *Free Speech, Free Markets, Free Choice: An Essay on Commercial Speech* (1987)

————, *The Fourth Estate and the Constitution* (1991)

O'Neill, Robert M., *Free Speech in the College Community* (1997)

Pennock, J. Roland, and John W. Chapman, eds., *Privacy*, *Nomos XIII* (1971)

Polenberg, Richard, *Fighting Faiths: The Abrams Case, the Supreme Court, and Free Speech* (1989)

Pool, Ithiel de Sola, *Technologies of Freedom* (1983)

Posner, Richard, *Sex and Reason* (1992)

Powe, Lucas A., *American Broadcasting and the First Amendment* (1987)

Rabban, David M., Free Speech in Its Forgotten Years (1997)

Randall, Richard S., *Censorship of the Movies: The Social and Political Control of a Mass Medium* (1970)

————, *Freedom and Taboo: Pornography and the Politics of a Self Divided* (1989)

Reeves, Richard, *What the People Know: Freedom and the Press* (1999)

Regan, Priscilla M., *Legislating Privacy: Technology, Social Values, and Public Policy* (1995)

Rembar, Charles, *The End of Obscenity* (1968)

Rice, Charles, Freedom of Association (1962)

Rosenberg, Norman L., *Protecting the Best Men: An Interpretive History of the Law of Libel* (1986)

Rotunda, Ronald D., *Responding to the Media: the Ethical and Constitutional Parameters* (1994)

Rudenstine, David, *The Day the Presses Stopped: A History of the Pentagon Papers Case* (1996)

Saunders, Kevin W., *Violence as Obscenity: Limiting the Media's First Amendment Protection* (1996)

Schauer, Frederick F., *Free Speech: A Philosophical Enquiry* (1982)

Schauer, Frederick F., *The Law of Obscenity* (1976)

Schoemann, Ferdinand D., ed., *Philosophical Dimensions of Privacy* (1984)

Shapiro, Martin, *The Pentagon Papers and the Courts* (1972)

Shiffren, Steven H., *The First Amendment, Democracy and Romance* (1990)

Smith, James Morton, *Freedom's Fetters: The Alien and Sedition Laws and American Civil Liberties* (1956)

Smith, Jeffrey, *Printers and Press Freedom* (1988)

————, *War and Press Freedom: The Problem of Prerogative Power* (1999)

Smolla, Rodney A., *Free Speech in an Open Society* (1992)

————, *Suing the Press: Libel, the Media, and Power* (1986)

————, *Jerry Falwell v. Larry Flynt: The First Amendment on Trial* (1990)

————, *The Law of Defamation* (1999)

Soifer, Aviam, *Law and the Company We Keep* (1995)

Strossen, Nadine, *Defending Pornography: Free Speech, Sex, and the Fight for Women's Rights* (2000)

Strum, Philippa, *When the Nazis Came to Skokie: Freedom for the Speech We Hate* (1999)

————, *Privacy: The Debate in the United States Since 1945* (1998)

Sunstein, Cass A., *Democracy and the Problem of Free Speech* (1993)

Sutherland, Lane, *Obscenity: The Court, the Congress, and the President's Commission* (1985)

Taylor, Telford, *Grand Inquest* (1955)

Turkington, Richard C., and Anita L. Allen, *Privacy: Cases and Materials* (1999)

Van Alstyne, William W., *Interpretations of the First Amendment* (1984)

Walker, Samuel, *Hate Speech: The History of an American Controversy* (1994)

Warren, Samuel D., and Louis Brandeis, "The Right to Privacy," *Harvard Law Review* 4 (1890)

Washburn, Patrick S., *A Question of Sedition* (1986)

Westin, Alan F., *Privacy and Freedom* (1967)

Wolfson, Nicholas, *Corporate First Amendment Rights and the SEC* (1990)

————, *Hate Speech, Sex Speech, Free Speech* (1997)

Yalof, David, and Kenneth Dautrich, *The First Amendment and the Media in the Court of Public Opinion* (2001)

Zimring, Franklin E., and Gordon J. Hawkins, *Pornography in a Free Society* (1991)

Privacy

Allen, Anita, *Uneasy Access: Privacy for Women in a Free Society* (1988)

Behuniak, Susan M., *A Caring Jurisprudence: Listening to Patients at the Supreme Court* (1999)

————, *Physician-Assisted Suicide: The Anatomy of a Constitutional Law Issue* (2002)

Burgess, Susan R., *Contest for Constitutional Authority: The Abortion and War Powers Debate* (1992)

Craig, Barbara Hinkson, and David M. O'Brien, *Abortion and American Politics* (1993)

Critchlow, Donald T., ed., *The Politics of Abortion and Birth Control in Historical Perspective* (1996)

Devins, Neal E., *Shaping Constitutional Values: Elected Government, the Supreme Court, and the Abortion Debate* (1996)

Devins, Neal E., and Wendy L. Watson, eds., *Federal Abortion Politics: A Documentary History* (1995)

Dworkin, Ronald, *Life's Dominion: An Argument about Abortion, Euthanasia, and Individual Freedom* (1993)

Epstein, Lee, and Joseph F. Kobylka, *The Supreme Court and Legal Change: Abortion and the Death Penalty* (1992)

Faux, Marion, *Roe v. Wade: The Untold Story of the Landmark Supreme Court Decision that Made Abortion Legal* (1988)

Friedman, Leon, ed., *The Supreme Court Confronts Abortion: The Briefs, Argument, and Decision in* Planned Parenthood v. Casey (1993)

Garrow, David J., *Liberty and Sexuality: The Right of Privacy and the Making of* Roe v. Wade (1998)

Glendon, Mary Ann, *Abortion and Divorce in Western Law* (1987)

Glick, Henry R., *The Right to Die: Policy Innovation and Its Consequences* (1992)

Gordon, Linda, *Woman's Body, Women's Right: Birth Control in America,* rev. ed. (1990)

Graber, Mark A., *Rethinking Abortion: Equal Choice, the Constitution, and Reproductive Politics* (1996)

Humphrey, Derek, *Lawful Exit: The Limits of Freedom for Help in Dying* (1993)

Humphrey, Derek, and Mary Clement, *Freedom to Die: People, Politics, and the Right-to-Die Movement* (1998)

Judges, Donald P., *Hard Choices, Lost Voices: How the Abortion Conflict Has Divided America, Distorted Constitutional Law,* and *Damaged the Courts* (1993)

Krason, Stephen M., *Abortion Politics, Morality, and the Constitution: A Critical Study of* Roe v. Wade *and* Doe v. Bolton *and a Basis for Change* (1984)

Lee, Ellie, *Abortion Law and Politics Today* (1998)

Luker, Kristen, *Abortion and the Politics of Motherhood* (1984)

McDonagh, Eileen L., *Breaking the Abortion Deadlock* (1996)

McWhirter, Darien A., and Jon D. Bible, *Privacy as a Constitutional Right: Sex, Drugs, and the Right to Life* (1992)

Meisel, Alan, *The Right to Die* (1989)

Mohr, James C., *Abortion in America* (1978)

Neeley, G. Steven, *The Constitutional Right to Suicide: A Legal and Philosophical Examination* (1994)

Noonan, John T., Jr., *A Private Choice: Abortion in America in the Seventies* (1979)

Nossiff, Rosemary, *Before Roe: Abortion Policy in the States* (2001)

O'Brien, David M., *Privacy, Law, and Public Policy* (1979)

O'Connor, Karen, *No Neutral Ground? Abortion Politics in an Age of Absolutes* (1996)

Placencia, Madeline, and Paul Finkelman, eds., *Right to Privacy and the Constitution* (1999)

Posner, Richard, *Sex and Reason* (1992)

Presser, Stephen B., *Recapturing the Constitution: Race, Religion, and Abortion Reconsidered* (1994)

Reagan, Leslie J., *When Abortion Was a Crime: Women, Medicine, and the Law in the United States, 1867–1973* (1997)

Rubin, Eva R., *Abortion, Politics, and the Courts: Roe v. Wade and Its Aftermath* (1987)

———, *The Abortion Controversy: A Documentary History* (1994)

Scheidler, Joseph M., *Closed: 99 Ways to Stop Abortion* (1985)

Scherer, Jennifer M., and Rita J. Simon, *Euthanasia and the Right to Die: A Comparative View* (1999)

Smith, David J., *The Sterilization of Carrie Buck* (1989)

Tribe, Laurence H., *Abortion: The Clash of Absolutes* (1990)

Uhlmann, Michael M., ed., *Last Rights? Assisted Suicide and Euthanasia Debated* (1998)

Urofsky, Melvin I., *Letting Go: Death, Dying, and the Law* (1993)

———, *Lethal Judgments: Assisted Suicide and American Law* (2000)

Wardle, Lynn D., and Mary A. Wood, *A Lawyer Looks at Abortion* (1982)

Yarnold, Barbara M., *Abortion Politics in the Federal Courts: Rights Versus Right* (1995)

Zucker, Marjorie B., *The Right to Die Debate: A Documentary History* (1999)

Criminal Justice

Abramson, Jeffrey, *We the Jury: The Jury System and the Ideal of Democracy* (1994)

Acker, James R., and David C. Brody, *Criminal Procedure: A Contemporary Perspective* (1999)

Acker, James R., and Richard Irving, *Basic Legal Research for Criminal Justice and the Social Sciences* (1998)

Acker, James R., Robert M. Bohm, and Charles Lanier, eds., *America's Experiment with Capital Punishment: Reflections on the Past, Present, and Future of the Ultimate Penal Sanction* (1998)

Adler, Stephen, J., *The Jury: Disorder in the Court* (1994)

Amar, Akhil Reed, *The Constitution and Criminal Procedure: First Principles* (1997)

Baker, Liva, *Miranda: Crime, Law, and Politics* (1985)

Baldus, David C., George Woodworth, and Charles A. Pulaski, Jr., *Equal Justice and the Death Penalty: Legal and Empirical Analysis* (1990)

Baldus, David C., George Woodworth, Charles A. Pulaski, Jr., and James W.L. Cole, *Statistical Proof of Discrimination* (1980)

Barnett, Randy E., and John Hagel, III, eds., *Assessing the Criminal: Restitution, Retribution, and the Legal Process* (1977)

Bedau, Hugo Adam, ed., *The Death Penalty in America*, 3rd ed. (1982)

——, *Death Is Different: Studies in the Morality, Law, and Politics of Capital Punishment* (1987)

——, *The Death Penalty in America: Current Controversies* (1997)

Berger, Mark, *Taking the Fifth: The Supreme Court and the Privilege Against Self-Incrimination* (1980)

Berger, Raoul, *Death Penalties: The Supreme Court's Obstacle Course* (1982)

Berkson, Larry C., *The Concept of Cruel and Unusual Punishment* (1975)

Berns, Walter, *For Capital Punishment: Crime and the Morality of the Death Penalty* (1979)

Black, Charles L., *Capital Punishment: The Inevitability of Caprice and Mistake* (1974)

Bodenhamer, David J., *Fair Trial: Rights of the Accused in American History* (1992)

Bowers, William J., and Glenn L. Pierce, *Legal Homicide: Death as Punishment in America, 1864–1982* (1984)

Bradley, Craig M., *The Failure of the Criminal Procedure Revolution* (1993)

Brody, David C., James R. Acker, and Wayne A. Logan, *Criminal Law* (2001)

Carr, James G., *The Law of Electronic Surveillance*, 2nd ed. (1986)

Carter, Dan T., *Scottsboro: A Tragedy of the American South* (1969)

Casper, Jonathan D., *American Criminal Justice: The Defendant's Perspective* (1972)

Cole, George F., ed., *Criminal Justice: Law and Politics* (1993)

Creamer, Shane J., *The Law of Arrest, Search, and Seizure* (1980)

Eisenstein, James, Roy B. Flemming, and Peter F. Narduli, *The Contours of Justice: Communities and Their Courts* (1988)

Eisenstein, James and Herbert Jacob, *Felony Justice* (1977)

Epstein, Lee, and Joseph F. Kobylka, *The Supreme Court and Legal Change: Abortion and the Death Penalty* (1992)

Fellman, David, *The Defendant's Rights* (1976)

Finkel, Norman J., *Commonsense Justice: Jurors Notions of the Law* (1995)

Flicker, Barbara, *Standards for Juvenile Justice: A Summary and Analysis* (1982)

Friedland, Martin, *Double Jeopardy* (1969)

Friedman, Lawrence M., *Crime and Punishment in American History* (1993)

Gerber, Rudolph J., *Cruel and Usual: Our Criminal Justice System* (1999)

Gilliom, John, *Surveillance, Privacy, and the Law: Employee Drug Testing and the Politics of Social Control* (1994)

Goodman, James, *Stories of Scottsboro: The Rape Case That Shocked 1930's America and Revived the Struggle for Equality* (1994)

Griswold, Erwin N., *Search and Seizure: A Dilemma for the Supreme Court* (1975)

Gross, Samuel R., *Death and Discrimination: Racial Disparities in Capital Sentencing* (1989)

Haines, Herbert H., *Against Capital Punishment: The Anti-Death Penalty Movement in America, 1972–1994* (1996)

Hastie, Reid, Steven D. Penrod, and Nancy Pennington, *Inside the Jury* (1983)

Helmholz, R.H., et. al., *The Privilege Against Self-Incrimination: Its Origins and Development* (1997)

Heumann, Milton, *Plea Bargaining* (1978)

Kalven, Harry, and Hans Zeisel, *The American Jury* (1966)

Kamisar, Yale, *Police Interrogation and Confessions: Essays in Law and Policy* (1980)

Kennedy, Randall, *Race, Crime, and the Law* (1997)

LaFave, Wayne R., *Arrest: The Decision to Take a Suspect into Custody* (1965)

——, *Search and Seizure: A Treatise on the Fourth Amendment*, 2 vols. (1987)

——, *A Treatise on the Fourth Amendment*, 3rd ed. (1995)

LaFrance, Arthur B., and Arnold H. Loewy, *Criminal Procedure: Trial and Sentencing* (1994)

Landynski, Jacob W., *Search and Seizure and the Supreme Court* (1966)

Levine, James P., *Juries and Politics* (1992)

Levy, Leonard, *The Origins of the Fifth Amendment* (1968)

——, *Against the Law: The Nixon Court and Criminal Justice* (1974)

Lewis, Anthony, *Gideon's Trumpet* (1964)

Loewy, Arthur H., ed., *A Criminal Law Anthology* (1992)

Mann, Coramae Richey, *Unequal Justice: A Question of Color* (1993)

Marquart, James W., Sheldon Ekland-Olson, and Jonathan R. Sorenson, *The Rope, the Chair, and the Needle: Capital Punishment in Texas, 1923–1990* (1994)

Meltsner, Michael, *Cruel and Unusual: The Supreme Court and Capital Punishment* (1973)

Miller, Kent S., and Michael L. Radelet, *Executing the Mentally Ill: The Criminal Justice System and the Case of Alvin Ford* (1993)

Myren, Richard A., *Law and Justice* (1987)

Nakell, Barry, and Kenneth A. Hardy, *The Arbitrariness of the Death Penalty* (1987)

Neubauer, David W., *Debating Crime: Rhetoric and Reality* (2001)

——, *America's Courts and the Criminal Justice System* (1988)

Packer, Herbert L., *The Limits of the Criminal Sanction* (1968)

Pestritto, Ronald J., *Founding the Criminal Law: Punishment and Political Thought in the Origins of America* (2000)

Prejean, Sister Helen, *Dead Man Walking* (1994)

Radelet, Michael L., Hugo Adam Bedau, and Constance E. Putnam, *In Spite of Innocence: The Ordeal of 400 Americans Wrongly Convicted of Crimes Punishable by Death* (1992)

Rossum, Ralph A., *The Politics of the Criminal Justice System: An Organizational Analysis* (1978)

Russell, Gregory D., *The Death Penalty and Racial Bias: Overturning Supreme Court Assumptions* (1994)

Scheb, John M., *Criminal Law and Procedure* (2002)

Scheingold, Stuart, *The Politics of Law and Order* (1984)

Schlesinger, Steven R., *Exclusionary Injustice* (1977)

Schwartz, Martin D., and Dragan Milovanovic, *Race, Gender, and Class in Criminology: The Intersections* (1999)

Schwartz, Herman, *Taps, Bugs, and Fooling the People* (1977)

Sellin, Thorsten, *The Penalty of Death* (1980)

Shapiro, Barbara J., *Beyond Reasonable Doubt and Probable Cause: Historical Perspectives on the Anglo-American Law of Evidence* (1991)

Sigler, Jay A., *Double Jeopardy: The Development of a Legal and Social Policy* (1969)

Silberman, Charles E., *Criminal Violence, Criminal Justice* (1978)

Skolnick, Jerome, *Justice without Trial: Law Enforcement in Democratic Society*, 3rd ed. (1994)

Smith, Christopher E., *The Rehnquist Court and Criminal Punishment* (1997)

Stephens, Otis, *The Supreme Court and Confessions of Guilt* (1973)

Thaler, Paul, *The Watchful Eye: American Justice in the Age of the Television Trial* (1994)

Tonry, Michael, *Malign Neglect: Race, Crime, and Punishment* (2000)

Van den Haag, Ernest, *Punishing Criminals: Concerning a Very Old and Painful Question* (1975)

Van den Haag, Ernest, and John P. Conrad, *The Death Penalty: A Debate* (1983)

Vila, Bryan, and Cynthia Morris, ed., *Capital Punishment in the United States: A Documentary History* (1997)

Walker, Sam, Cassia Spohn, and Miriam DeLone, *The Color of Justice* (1996)

White, Welsh S., *The Death Penalty in the Nineties: An Examination of the Modern System of Capital Punishment* (1991)

Wilbanks, William, *The Myth of a Racist Criminal Justice System* (1987)

Wilson, James C., ed., *Crime and Public Policy*, 2nd ed. (1994)

Yackle, Larry W., *Postconviction Remedies* (1981)

——, *Reform and Regret: The Story of Federal Judicial Involvement in the Alabama Prison System* (1989)

Racial Discrimination

Armor, David, *Forced Justice: School Desegregation and the Law* (1995)

Balkin, Jack M., ed., *What Brown v. Board of Education Should Have Said: The Nation's Top Legal Experts Rewrite America's Landmark Civil Rights Decision* (2001)

Ball, Howard, Dale Krane, and Thomas P. Lauth, *Compromised Compliance: Implementation of the 1965 Voting Rights Act* (1982)

Ball, Howard, *The Bakke Case: Race, Education, and Affirmative Action* (2000)

Bardolf, Richard, ed., *The Civil Rights Record: Black Americans and the Law, 1849–1970* (1970)

Belknap, Michal R., *Federal Law and Southern Order: Racial Violence and Constitutional Conflict in the Post-Brown South* (1887)

Bell, Derrick A., *Race, Racism, and American Law* (1980)

——, *Are We Not Saved: The Elusive Quest for Racial Justice* (1987)

Belz, Herman, *Equality Transformed: A Quarter-Century of Affirmative Action* (1991)

Bergmann, Barbara, *In Defense of Affirmative Action* (1996)

Berman, Daniel H., *It Is So Ordered: The Supreme Court Rules on School Desegregation* (1966)

Blaustein, Albert P., and Clarence Clyde Ferguson, Jr., *Desegregation and the Law: The Meaning and Effect of the School Desegregation Cases* (1962)

Blaustein, Albert P., and Robert L. Zangrando, eds., *Civil Rights and the Black American: A Documentary History* (1970)

Bok, Derek, and William Bowen, *The Shape of the River: Long Term Consequences of Considering Race in College and University Admissions* (1998)

Brooks, Roy L., Gilbert P. Carrasco, and Michael Selmi, *Civil Rights Litigation: Cases and Materials* (2000)

Buell, Emmett H., and Richard A. Brisbin, *School Desegregation and Defended Neighborhoods: The Boston Controversy* (1982)

Bullock, Charles S., and Charles M. Lamb, eds., *Implementation of Civil Rights Policy* (1984)

Carter, Stephen, *Reflections of an Affirmative Action Baby* (1991)

Chafe, William, *Civilities and Civil Rights* (1980)

Cohen, William, *At Freedom's Edge: Black Mobility and the Southern Quest for Racial Control, 1861–1915* (1991)

Cook, Anthony E., *The Least of These: Race, Law, and Religion in American Culture* (1997)

Cortner, Richard C., *The "Scottsboro" Case in Mississippi: The Supreme Court and* Brown v. Mississippi (1986)

———, *A Mob Intent on Death: The NAACP and the Arkansas Riot Cases* (1988)

———, *Civil Rights and Public Accommodations: The Heart of Atlanta Motel and McClung Cases* (2001)

Davis, Abraham L., *The United States Supreme Court and the Uses of Social Science Data* (1973)

———, *Blacks in the Federal Judiciary: Neutral Arbiters or Judicial Activists?* (1989)

Davis, Abraham L., and Barbara Luck Graham, *The Supreme Court, Race, and Civil Rights from Marshall to Rehnquist* (1995)

Eastland, Terry, *Ending Affirmative Action: The Case for Colorblind Justice* (1996)

Eastland, Terry, and William J. Bennett, *Counting by Race: Equality from the Founding Fathers to* Bakke *and* Weber (1979)

Epstein, Richard A., *Forbidden Grounds: The Case Against Employment Discrimination Laws* (1992)

Foster, James C., and Mary C. Segers, et al., *Elusive Equality: Liberalism, Affirmative Action, and Social Change in America* (1983)

Friedman, Leon, ed., *Southern Justice* (1967)

———, *Argument: The Oral Argument before the Supreme Court in* Brown v. Board of Education of Topeka, *1952–1955* (1983)

———, *The Civil Rights Reader: Basic Documents of the Civil Rights Movement* (1967)

Garrow, David J., *Time on the Cross: Martin Luther King, Jr. and the Southern Christian Leadership Conference* (1988)

Glazer, Nathan, *Affirmative Discrimination* (1976)

Graglia, Lino A., *Disaster by Decree: The Supreme Court, Race and the Schools* (1976)

Graham, Hugh Davis, *The Civil Rights Era: Origins and Development of National Policy* (1990)

———, *Civil Rights and the Presidency* (1992)

———, *Crusaders in the Courts: How a Dedicated Band of Lawyers Fought for the Civil Rights Revolution* (1994)

Grofman, Bernard, *The Legacies of the 1964 Civil Rights Act* (2000)

Haar, Charles M., *Suburbs under Seige: Race, Space, and Audacious Judges* (1996)

Halpern, Stephen C., *On the Limits of the Law: the Ironic Legacy of Title VI of the 1964 Civil Rights Act* (1995)

Higginbotham, A. Leon, Jr., *In the Matter Color: The Colonial Period* (1978)

Higham, John, *Shades of Freedom: Racial Politics and the Presumptions of the American Legal Process* (1996)

Jones, Augustus J., Jr., *Affirmative Talk, Affirmative Action: A Comparative Study of the Politics of Affirmative Action* (1991)

Kaczorowski, Robert J., *The Politics of Judicial Interpretation: The Federal Courts, the Department of Justice, and Civil Rights, 1866–1876* (1985)

———, *The Nationalization of Civil Rights: Constitutional Theory and Practice in a Racist Society, 1866–1883* (1987)

King, Donald B., and Quick, Charles W., eds., *Legal Aspects of the Civil Rights Movements* (1965)

Klinker, Philip A., *The Unsteady March: The Rise and Decline of Racial Equality in America* (1999)

Kluger, Richard, *Simple Justice: The History of* Brown v. Board of Education *and Black America's Struggle for Equality* (1977)

Krislov, Samuel, *The Negro in Federal Employment: The Quest for Equal Opportunity* (1967)

Kryder, David, *Divided Arsenal: Race and the American State During World War II* (2000)

Kull, Andrew, *The Color-Blind Constitution* (1992)

Lewis, Anthony, *Portrayal of a Decade: The Second American Revolution* (1964)

Lively, Donald E., *The Constitution and Race* (1992)

Livingston, John C., *Fair Game? Inequality and Affirmative Action* (1979)

Lofgren, Charles A., *The Plessy Case: A Study in Legal-Historical Interpretation* (1987)

Mauney, Connie Pat, *Evolving Equality: The Courts and Desegregation in Tennessee* (1979)

McCord, John H., *With All Deliberate Speed: Civil Rights Theory and Reality* (1969)

McDonald, Laughlin, and John A. Powell, *The Rights of Racial Minorities* (1998)

Miller, Loren, *The Petitioners: The Story of the Supreme Court of the United States and the Negro* (1966)

Moreno, Paul D., *From Direct Action to Affirmative Action: Fair Employment Law and Policy in America, 1933–1972* (1977)

Morgan, Richard E., *Disabling America: The "Rights Industry" in Our Time* (1984)

Muse, Benjamin, *Virginia's Massive Resistance* (1961)

Myrdal, Gunnar, *The American Dilemma: The Negro Problem and Modern Democracy*, 2 vols. (1944)

Nieman, Donald G., *Promises to Keep: African Americans and the Constitutional Order, 1976 to the Present* (1991)

O'Neill, Robert M., *Discriminating against Discrimination* (1975)

O'Neill, Timothy, *Bakke and the Politics of Equality: Friends and Foes in the Classroom of Litigation* (1985)

Orfield, Gary, *Must We Bus? Segregated Schools and National Policy* (1978)

Peltason, Jack, *Fifty-Eight Lonely Men: Southern Federal Judges and School Desegregation* (1961)

Peterson, Paul E., ed., *Classifying by Race* (1996)

Presser, Stephen B., *Recapturing the Constitution: Race, Religion, and Abortion Reconsidered* (1974)

Read, Frank T., and Lucy S. McGough, *Let Them Be Judged: The Judicial Integration of the Deep South* (1978)

Riddlesperger, James W., Jr., and Donald W. Jackson, eds., *Presidential Leadership and Civil Rights Policy* (1995)

Riley, Russell L., *The Presidency and the Politics of Racial Inequality: Nation-Keeping from 1831 to 1965* (1990)

Roche, George C., III, *The Balancing Act: Quota Hiring in Higher Education* (1974)

Rodgers, Harrell R., Jr., and Charles S. Bullock, III, *Law and Social Change: Civil Rights Laws and Their Consequences* (1972)

Rosenberg, Gerald N., *The Hollow Hope: Can Courts Bring about Social Change* (1991)

Rosenfeld, Michel, *Affirmative Action and Justice: A Philsophical and Constitutional Inquiry* (1991)

Rossum, Ralph A., *Reverse Discrimination: The Constitution Debate* (1980)

Sarat, Austin, ed., *Race, Law and Culture: Reflections on Brown v. Board of Education* (1996)

Schwartz, Bernard, *Swann's Way: The School Busing Case and the Supreme Court* (1986)

———, *Behind Bakke: Affirmative Action and the Supreme Court* (1988)

Sindler, Allan P., *Bakke, Defunis, and Minority Admissions* (1978)

Smith, Robert C., *Racism in the Post-Civil Rights Era* (1997)

Smolla, Rodney A., *Federal Civil Rights Acts* (1994)

Sowell, Thomas, *Black Education, Myths and Tragedies* (1972)

Spann, Girardeau A., *Race against the Court: The Supreme Court and Minorities in Contemporary America* (1993)

Sullivan, Charles A., Michael J. Zimmer, and Richard F. Richards, *Federal Statutory Law of Employment Discrimination* (1980)

TenBroek, Jacobus, *Equal under Law* (1965)

Thernstrom, Stephen and Abigail, *America in Black and White: One Nation Indivisible*

Tushnet, Mark V., *The American Law of Slavery, 1810–1860: Considerations of Humanity and Interest* (1981)

———, *Making Civil Rights Law: Thurgood Marshall and the Supreme Court, 1936–1961* (1994)

———, *Brown v. Board of Education: The Battle for Integration* (1995)

———, ed., *Thurgood Marshall: His Speeches, Writings, Arguments, Opinions, and Reminiscences* (2001)

Urofsky, Melvin, *A Conflict of Rights: The Supreme Court and Affirmative Action* (1991)

Viteritti, Joseph, *Choosing Equality: School Choice, The Constitution, and Civil Society* (1999)

Vose, Clement, *Caucasians Only: The Supreme Court, the NAACP, and the Restrictive Covenant Cases* (1959)

Wasby, Stephen, *Race Relations Litigation in an Age of Complexity* (1995)

West, Thomas G., *Vindicating the Founders: Race, Class, Sex, and Justice in the Origins of America* (1997)

Wiecek, William M., *The Sources of Antislavery Constitutionalism in American, 1760–1848* (1977)

Wilkinson, J. Harve, *From Brown to Bakke: The Supreme Court and School Desegregation, 1954–1978* (1979)

Williams, Juan, *Eyes on the Prize: America's Civil Rights Years, 1954–1965* (1988)

Wolf, Eleanor P., *Trial and Error: The Detroit School Desegregation Case* (1981)

Wolters, Raymond, *The Burden of* Brown*: Thirty Years of School Desegregation* (1984)

Woodward, C. Vann, *The Strange Career of Jim Crow*, 3rd rev. ed. (1974)

Yarbrough, Tinsley E., *A Passion for Justice: J. Waties Waring and Civil Rights* (1987)

Zimmer, Michael J., et al., *Employment Discrimination: Selected Statutes* (1997)

———, *Cases and Material on Employment Discrimination* (2000)

Alienage

Archdeacon, Thomas J., *Becoming American: An Ethnic History* (1983)

Axtell, James, *The European and the Indian: Essays on the Ethnic History of Colonial North America* (1981)

Baer, Judith A., *Equality under the Constitution: Reclaiming the Fourteenth Amendment* (1983)

Bailyn, Bernard, *The Peopling of North America: An Introduction* (1986)

Billington, Ray Allen, *The Origins of Nativism in the United States, 1800–1844* (1974)

Bodnar, John, *The Transplanted: A History of Immigration in Urban America* (1985)

Carlinger, David, *The Rights of Aliens*, 2nd ed. (1990)

Chin, Gabriel J., Victor C. Romero, and Michael A. Scaperlanda, eds., *Immigration and the Constitution* (2001)

Chuman, Frank F., *The Bamboo People: The Law and Japanese-Americans* (1976)

Cornelius, Wayne A., *America in the Era of Limits: Migrants, Nativists, and the Future of U.S.-Mexican Relations* (1982)

Daniels, Roger, *Coming to America: A History of Immigration and Ethnicity in American Life* (1991)

Dinnerstein, Leonard, Roger L. Nichols, and David M. Reimers, *Natives and Strangers: A Multicultural History of Americans* (1996)

Glazer, Nathan, *Clamor at the Gates: The New American Immigration* (1985)

Gyory, Andrew, *Closing the Gate: Race, Politics, and the Chinese Exclusion Act* (1998)

Higham, John, *Send These to Me: Immigrants in Urban America* (1975)

Hull, Elizabeth, *Without Justice for All: The Constitutional Rights of Aliens* (1985)

Irons, Peter, ed., *Justice Delayed: The Record of the Japanese-American Internment Cases* (1989)

Jackson, Donald W., *Even the Children of Strangers: Equality Under the U. S. Constitution* (1992)

Karst, Kenneth L., *Belonging to America: Equal Citizenship and the Constitution* (1989)

King, Desmond, *Making Americans: Immigration, Race, and the Origins of Diverse Democracy* (2000)

Neuman, Gerald L., *Strangers to the Constitution: Immigrants, Borders, and Fundamental Law* (1996)

Price, Monroe E., and Robert N. Clinton, *Law and the American Indian: Readings, Notes, Cases* (1983)

Prucha, Rancis P., *The Great Father: the United States Government and the American Indians*, 2 vols. (1984)

Reimers, David M., ed., *Still the Golden Door: the Third World Comes to America* (1985)

Sandmeyer, Elmer C., *The Anti-Chinese Movement in California* (1939)

Shuck, Peter H., and Rogers M. Smith, *Citizenship without Consent: Illegal Aliens in the American Polity* (1985)

Washburn, Wilcomb E., *The Indian in America* (1975)

Wollenberg, Charles, *All Deliberate Speed, Segregation and Exclusion in California Schools, 1885–1975* (1978)

Gender and Other Classification

Baer, Judith A., *Equality under the Constitution: Reclaiming the Fourteenth Amendment* (1983)

———, *Women in American Law: The Struggle Toward Equality from the New Deal to the Present* (1996)

———, *Our Lives Before the Law: Constructing a Feminist Jurisprudence* (1999)

———, ed., *Historical and Multicultural Encyclopedia of Women's Reproductive Rights in the United States* (2002)

Bussiere, Elizabeth, *(Dis)entitling the Poor: The Warren Court, Welfare Rights, and the American Political Tradition* (1997)

Chester, Ronald, *Equal Access: Women Lawyers in a Changing American* (1985)

Epstein, Cynthia Fuchs, *Women in Law* (1983)

Epstein, Richard A., *Forbidden Grounds: The Case Against Employment Discrimination Laws* (1992)

Evans, Sara, *Personal Politics: The Roots of Women's Liberation in the Civil Rights Movement and the New Left* (1980)

Flexner, Eleanor, *Century of Struggle*, rev. ed. (1975)

Frug, Mary Jo, *Post-Modern Legal Feminism* (1992)

Gerstmann, Evan, *The Constitutional Underclass: Gays, Lesbians and the Failure of Class-Based Equal Protection* (1999)

Goldstein, Leslie Friedman, *The Constitutional Rights of Women*, 2nd ed. (1988)

———, ed., *Feminist Jurisprudence: The Difference Debate* (1992)

Hagan, John, and Fiona Kay, *Gender in Practice: A Study of Lawyers' Lives* (1995)

Harrington, Michael, *The New American Poverty* (1984)

Hartmann, Susan M., *From Margin to Mainstream: American Women and Politics Since 1960* (1989)

Hoff, Joan, *Law, Gender, and Injustice: A Legal History of U.S. Women* (1991)

King, Michael, and Judith Trowell, *Children's Welfare and the Law: The Limits of Legal Intervention* (1992)

Kirp, David L., Mark G. Yudof, and Marlene Strong Franks, Gender Justice (1986)

Lawrence, Susan E., *The Poor in Court: The Legal Services Program and Supreme Court Decision Making* (1990)

Lentz, Bernard F., and David M. Laband, *Sex Discrimination in the Legal Profession* (1995)

MacKinnon, Catherine, *Feminism Unmodified: Discourses on Life and Law* (1987)

Mansbridge, Jane J., *Why We Lost the ERA* (1986)

McGlen, Nancy E., and Karen O'Connor, *Women's Rights: The Struggle for Equality in the 19th and 20th Centuries* (1983)

Mezey, Susan Gluck, *In Pursuit of Equality* (1992)

Minow, Martha, Making All the Difference: Inclusion, Exclusion, and American Law (1990)

Morello, Karen Berger, *The Invisible Bar: The Woman Lawyer in America* (1986)

Moss, Kary L., *The Rights of Women and Girls* (1998)

Otten, Laura, *Women's Rights and the Law* (1993)

Pierce, Jennifer L., *Gender Trials: Emotional Lives in Contemporary Law Firms* (1995)

Piven, Frances Fox, and Richard A. Cloward, *Regulating the Poor: The Function of Public Welfare* (1972)

Posner, Richard A., *Sex and Reason* (1992)

———, *Overcoming Law* (1995)

Reed, Douglas S., *On Equal Terms: The Constitutional Politics of Educational Opportunity* (2001)

Rhode, Deborah L., *Justice and Gender: Sex Discrimination and the Law* (1989)

———, *Speaking of Sex: The Denial of Gender Inequality* (1997)

Richards, David A.J., *Conscience and the Constitution* (1993)

Rimmerman, Craig A., Kenneth D. Wald, and Clyde Wilcox, eds., *The Politics of Gay Rights* (2000)

Ross, Susan Deller, and Ann Barcher, *The Rights of Women* (1984)

Smith, Patricia, ed., *Feminist Jurisprudence* (1993)

Smith, Christopher E., *The Courts and the Poor* (1991)

Soss, Joe, *Unwanted Claims: The Politics of Participation in the U.S. Welfare System* (2000)

Strasser, Mark, *Legally Wed: Same-Sex Marriage and the Constitution* (1998)

———, *The Challenge of Same-Sex Marriage: Federalist Principles and Constitutional Protections* (1999)

Sullivan, Charles A., Michael J. Zimmer, and Richard F. Richards, *Federal Statutory Law of Employment Discrimination* (1980)

Weisberg, Kelly D., ed., *Feminist Legal Theory: Foundations* (1993)

Zimmer, Michael J., et al., *Employment Discrimination: Selected Statutes* (1997)

———, *Cases and Material on Employment Discrimination* (2000)

Voting and Representation

Baker, Gordon E., *The Reapportionment Revolution: Representation, Political Power and the Supreme Court* (1966)

Ball, Howard, *The Warren Court's Conception of Democracy: An Evaluation of the Supreme Court's Reapportionment Decisions* (1971)

Ball, Howard, Dale Krane, and Thomas P. Lauth, *Compromised Compliance: Implementation of the 1965 Voting Rights Act* (1982)

Bartley, Numan V., and Hugh Davis Graham, *Southern Politics and the Second Reconstruction* (1975)

Boyd, William J.D., *Apportionment in the Nineteen Sixties: State Legislature, Congressional Districts* (1967)

Butler, David, and Bruce Can, *Congressional Redistricting: Comparative and Theoretical Perspectives* (1992)

Bybee, Keith J., *Mistaken Identity: The Supreme Court and the Politics of Minority Representation* (1998)

Cannon, David T., *Race, Redistricting, and Representation: The Unintended Consequences of Black Majority Districts* (1999)

Chute, Marchette G., *First Liberty: A History of the Right to Vote in America, 1619–1850* (1969)

Claude, Richard, *The Supreme Court and the Electoral Process* (1970)

Cortner, Richard C., *The Apportionment Cases* (1970)

Cunningham, Maurice T., *Maximization Whatever the Cost: Race, Redistricting, and the Department of Justice* (2001)

Davidson, Chander, and Bernard Grofman, eds., *Quiet Revolution in the South: The Impact of the Voting Rights Act, 1965–1990* (1994)

De Grazia, Alfred, *Apportionment and Representative Government* (1963)

Dixon, Robert G., Jr., *Democratic Representation: Reapportionment in Law and Politics* (1968)

Elliott, Ward E.Y., *The Rise of Guardian Democracy: The Supreme Court's Role in Voting Rights Disputes, 1845–1969* (1974)

Garrow, David J., *Protest at Selma: Martin Luther King, Jr. and the Voting Rights Act of 1965* (1978)

Gelfand, M. David, and Terry E. Allbritton, *Recent Developments on Voting Rights in the United States* (1988)

Gillette, William, *The Right to Vote: Politics and the Passage of the Fifteenth Amendment* (1969)

Gillman, Howard, *The Votes That Counted: How the Court Decided the 2000 Presidential Election* (2001)

Goldstein, Joel H., *The Effects of the Adoption of Woman Suffrage: Sex Difference in Voting Behavior* (1984)

Greene, Abner, *Understanding the 2000 Election: A Guide to the Legal Battles That Decided the Presidency* (2001)

Grofman, Bernard, *Political Gerrymandering and the Courts* (1990)

Grofman, Bernard, Lisa Handley, and Richard G. Niemi, *Minority Representation and the Quest for Voting Equality* (1992)

Guinier, Lani, *The Tyranny of the Majority: Fundamental Fairness in Representative Democracy* (1994)

Hamilton, Charles V., *The Bench and the Ballot: Southern Federal Judges and Black Voters* (1973)

Hanson, Royce, *The Political Thicket* (1966)

Hudson, David Michael, *Along Racial Lines: Consequences of the Voting Rights Act* (1998)

Kinder, Donald R., and Lynn M. Sanders, *Divided by Color: Racial Politics and Democratic Ideals* (1997)

Kousser, J. Morgan, *Colorblind Justice: Minority Voting Rights and the Undoing of the Second Reconstruction* (1999)

Lawson, Stephen, *Black Ballots: Voting Rights in the South, 1944–1969* (1976)

Lewinson, Paul, *Race, Class, and Party: A History of Negro Suffrage and White Politics in the South* (1959)

Lublin, David, *The Paradox of Representation* (1997)

Maveety, Nancy, *Representation Rights and the Burger Court Years* (1991)

McKay, Robert B., *Reapportionment: The Law and Politics of Equal Representation* (1965)

Norell, Robert J., *Reaping the Whirlwind: The Civil Rights Movement in Tuskegee* (1998)

O'Rourke, Timothy G., *The Impact of Reapportionment* (1980)

Parker, Frank R., *Black Votes Count: Political Empowerment in Mississippi After 1965* (1990)

Peacock, Anthony A., ed., *Affirmative Action and Representation:* Shaw v. Reno *and the Future of Voting Rights* (1997)

Posner, Richard, *Breaking the Deadlock: The 2000 Elections, the Constitution, and the Courts* (2001)

Reeves, Keith, *Voting Hopes or Fears? White Voters, Black Candidates, and Racial Politics in America* (1997)

Rosenkranz, E. Joshua, *If Buckley Fell: Designing a First Amendment That Reinforces Democracy* (1999)

Rosenthal, Albert J., *Federal Regulation of Campaign Finance: Some Constitutional Questions* (1972)

Rush, Mark E., *Does Districting Make a Difference: Partisan Representation and Electoral Behavior* (1993)

Ryden, David K., *The United States Supreme Court and the Electoral Process* (2000)

Scher, Richard K., Jon L. Mills, and John J. Hotaling, *Voting Rights and Democracy: The Law and Politics of Districting* (1997)

Slabach, Frederick G., ed., *The Constitution and Campaign Finance Reform* (1998)

Stevenson, Donald Grier, Jr., *Campaigns and the Court: The United States Supreme Court in Presidential Elections* (1999)

Sunstein, Cass R., and Richard A. Epstein, eds., *The Vote: Bush, Gore, and the Supreme Court* (2001)

Swain, Carol M., *Black Faces, Black Interests: Representation of African-Americans in Congress* (1993)

Taper, Bernard, Gomillion v. Lightfoot: *Apartheid in Alabama* (1962)

Thernstrom, Abigail, *Whose Votes Count? Affirmative Action and Minority Voting Rights* (1987)

Williamson, Chilton, *American Suffrage from Property to Democracy, 1760–1860* (1960)

On Leading Cases

Balkin, Jack M., ed., *What* Brown v. Board of Education *Should Have Said: The Nation's Top Legal Experts Rewrite America's Landmark Civil Rights Decision* (2001)

Ball, Howard, *The Bakke Case: Race, Education, and Affirmative Action* (2000)

Carter, Dan T., *Scottsboro: A Tragedy of the American South* (1969)

Cleary, Edward J., *Beyond the Burning Cross: The First Amendment and the Landmark R. A. V. Case* (1994)

Cortner, Richard C., *The Apportionment Cases* (1970)

———, *The "Scottsboro" Case in Mississippi: The Supreme Court and* Brown v. Mississippi (1986)

———, *A Mob Intent on Death: The NAACP and the Arkansas Riot Cases* (1988)

———, *Civil Rights and Public Accommodations: The Heart of Atlanta Motel and McClung Cases* (2001)

Friedman, Leon, ed., *Argument: The Oral Argument before the Supreme Court in* Board v. Board of Education of Topeka, *1952–1955* (1983)

Friedman, Leon, ed., *The Supreme Court Confronts Abortion: The Briefs, Argument, and Decision in* Planned Parenthood v. Casey (1993)

Friendly, Fred, *Minnesota Rag: The Dramatic Story of the Landmark Supreme Court Case That Gave Meaning to Freedom of the Press* (1981)

Garrow, David J., *Liberty and Sexuality: The Right of Privacy and the Making of* Roe v. Wade (1998)

Gertz, Elmer, Gertz v. Robert Welch, Inc.: *The Story of a Landmark Libel Case* (1992)

Gillman, Howard, *The Votes That Counted: How the Court Decided the 2000 Presidential Election* (2001)

Goldstein, Robert Justin, *Flag Burning and Free Speech: The Case of* Texas v. Johnson (2000)

Goodman, James, *Stories of Scottsboro: The Rape Case That Shocked 1930's America and Revived the Struggle for Equality* (1994)

Greene, Abner, *Understanding the 2000 Election: A Guide to the Legal Battles That Decided the Presidency* (2001)

Irons, Peter H., *The Courage of Their Convictions: Sixteen Americans Who Fought Their Way to the Supreme Court* (1990)

Kirby, James, *Fumble: Bear Bryant, Wally Butts, and the Great College Football Scandal* (1986)

Kluger, Richard, *Simple Justice: The History of* Brown v. Board of Education *and Black America's Struggle for Equality* (1977)

Krason, Stephen M., *Abortion Politics, Morality, and the Constitution: A Critical Study of* Roe v. Wade *and* Doe v. Bolton *and a Basis for Change* (1984)

Larson, Edward, *Summer for the Gods: The Scopes Trial and America's Continuing Debate over Science and Religion* (1997)

Lewis, Anthony, *Gideon's Trumpet* (1964)

———, *Make No Law: The Sullivan Case and the First Amendment* (1991)

Lofgren, Charles A., *The Plessy Case: A Study in Legal-Historical Interpretation* (1987)

Long, Carolyn N., *Religious Freedom and Indian Rights: The Case of* Oregon v. Smith (2000)

Manwaring, David, *Render unto Caesar: The Flag Salute Controversy* (1962)

Martin, Charles H., *The Angelo Herndon Case and Southern Justice* (1976)

Peacock, Anthony A., ed., *Affirmative Action and Representation:* Shaw v. Reno *and the Future of Voting Rights* (1997)

Polenberg, Richard, *Fighting Faiths: The Abrams Case, the Supreme Court, and Free Speech* (1989)

Posner, Richard, *Breaking the Deadlock: The 2000 Election, the Constitution, and the Courts* (2001)

Rudenstine, David, *The Day the Presses Stopped: A History of the Pentagon Papers Case* (1996)

Sarat, Austin, ed., *Race, Law and Culture: Reflections on* Brown v. Board of Education (1996)

Schwartz, Bernard, *Swann's Way: The School Busing Case and the Supreme Court* (1986)

Shapiro, Martin, *The Pentagon Papers and the Courts* (1972)

Smith, David J., *The Sterilization of Carrie Buck* (1989)

Smolla, Rodney A., Jerry Falwell v. Larry Flynt: *The First Amendment on Trial* (1990)

Sunstein, Cass R., and Richard A. Epstein, eds., *The Vote: Bush, Gore, and the Supreme Court* (2001)

Taper, Bernard, Gomillion v. Lightfoot: *Apartheid in Alabama* (1962)

Tushnet, Mark V., Brown v. Board of Education: *The Battle for Integration* (1995)

Vose, Clement, *Caucasians Only: The Supreme Court, the NAACP, and the Restrictive Covenant Cases* (1959)

Wolf, Eleanor P., *Trial and Error: The Detroit School Desegregation Case* (1981)

Judicial Biography

Hugo L. Black:

Ball, Howard, *Hugo L. Black: Cold Steel Warrior* (1996)

Magee, James, *Mr. Justice Black: Absolutist on the Court* (1980)

Newman, Roger K, *Hugo Black, A Biography* (1994)

Louis D. Brandeis:

Baker, Leonard, *Brandeis and Frankfurter: A Dual Biography* (1986)

Mason, Alpheus T., *Brandeis-A Free Man's Life* (1946)

Paper, Lewis J., *Brandeis* (1983)

Strum, Philippa, *Louis D. Brandeis: Justice for the People* (1984)

Benjamin Cardozo:

Kaufman, Andrew L., *Cardozo* (1998)

Polenberg, Eric, *The World of Benjamin Cardozo* (1997)

Posner, Richard A., *Cardozo: A Study in Reputation* (1990)

Salmon P. Chase:

Blue, Frederick J., *Salmon P. Chase: A Life in Politics* (1987)

Hyman, Harold M., *The Reconstruction Justice of Salmon P. Chase* (1997)

Niven, John, *Salmon P. Chase, A Biography (1995)*

David Davis:

King, William L., *Lincoln's Manager: David Davis* (1960)

William O. Douglas:

Simon, James F., *Independent Journey: The Life of William O. Douglas* (1990)

Stephen J. Field:

Kens, Paul, *Justice Stephen Field: Shaping American Liberty from the Gold Rush to the Gilded Age* (1997)

Swisher, Carl B., *Stephen J. Field: Craftsman of the Law* (1969)

Abe Fortas:

Kalman, Laura, *Abe Fortas: A Biography* (1990)

Murphy, Bruce Allen, *Fortas: The Rise and Ruin of a Supreme Court Justice* (1988)

Felix Frankfurter:

Baker, Leonard, *Brandeis and Frankfurter: A Dual Biography* (1986)

Baker, Liva, *Felix Frankfurter* (1969)

Urofsky, Melvin I., *Felix Frankfurter: Judicial Restraint and Individual Liberties* (1991)

Melville W. Fuller:

King, Willard L., *Melville Weston Fuller: Chief Justice of the United States, 1888–1910* (1967)

Arthur Goldberg:

Stebenne, David, *Arthur J. Goldberg: New Deal Liberal* (1996)

John Marshall Harlan, I:

Beth, Loren P., *John Marshall Harlan: The Last Whig Justice* (1992)

Lathan, F.B., *The Great Dissenter-John Marshall Harlan* (1970)

Yarbrough, Tinsley E., *Judicial Enigma: The First Justice Harlan* (1995)

John Marshall Harlan, II:

Yarbrough, Tinsley E., *John Marshall Harlan: Great Dissenter of the Warren Court* (1992)

Oliver Wendell Holmes, Jr.:

Alschular, Albert, *Law without Values: The Life, Work, and Legacy of Justice Holmes* (2000)

Baker, Liva, *The Justice from Beacon Hill: The Life and Times of Oliver Wendell Holmes* (1991)

Bowen, Catherine Drinker, *A Yankee from Olympus: Justice Holmes and His Family* (1944)

Howe, Mark De Wolfe, *Justice Oliver Wendell Holmes: The Proving Years, 1870–1882* (1963)

———, *Justice Oliver Wendell Holmes: The Shaping Years, 1841–1870* (1957)

Novick, Sheldon, *Honorable Justice: The Life of Oliver Wendell Holmes* (1989)

White, G. Edward, *Justice Oliver Wendell Holmes: Law and the Inner Self* (1993)

Charles Evans Hughes:

Pusey, Merlo J., *Charles Evans Hughes* (1951)

John Jay:

Johnson, Herbert A., *John Jay, 1745–1829* (1970)

William Johnson:

Morgan, Donald G., *Justice William Johnson, the First Dissenter: The Career and Constitutional Philosophy of a Jeffersonian Judge* (1954)

John Marshall:

Baker, Leonard, *John Marshall: A Life in Law* (1974)

Beveridge, Albert J., *The Life of John Marshall* (1916)

Johnson, Herbert A., *The Chief Justiceship of John Marshall, 1801–1835* (1997)

Smith, Jean Edward, *John Marshall: Definer of a Nation* (1996)

Stites, Francis N., *John Marshall, Defender of the Constitution* (1981)

Thurgood Marshall:

Rowan, Carl T., *Dream Makers, Dream Breakers: The World of Justice Thurgood Marshall* (1993)

Tushnet, Mark V., *Making Constitutional Law: Thurgood Marshall and the Supreme Court, 1961–1991* (1997)

Williams, Juan, *Thurgood Marshall: American Revolutionary* (1998)

Samuel F. Miller:

Fairman, Charles, *Mr. Justice Miller and the Supreme Court, 1862–1890* (1939)

Frank Murphy:

Fine, Sidney, *Frank Murphy*, 3 vols. (1974–1985)

Howard, J. Woodford, *Mr. Justice Murphy: A Political Biography* (1968)

Sandra Day O'Connor:

Maveety, Nancy, *Justice Sandra Day O'Connor: Strategist on the Supreme Court* (1996)

Lewis F. Powell:

Jeffries, John C., *Justice Lewis F. Powell, Jr.* (1994)

Harlan F. Stone

Konefsky, S.J., *Chief Justice Stone and the Supreme Court* (1946)

Mason, Alpheus T., *Harlan Fiske Stone: Pillar of the Law* (1956)

Joseph Story:

Dunne, Gerald T., *Justice Joseph Story and the Rise of the Supreme Court* (1970)

Newmyer, R. Kent, *Supreme Court Justice Joseph Story: Statesman of the Old Republic* (1985)

George Sutherland:

Paschal, Joel Francis, *Mr. Justice Sutherland, A Man against the State* (1951)

William Howard Taft:

Anderson, Judith Icke, *William Howard Taft: An Intimate History* (1981)

Mason, Alpheus T., *William Howard Taft: Chief Justice* (1965)

Pringle, H., *The Life and Times of William Howard Taft* (1939)

Roger B. Taney:

Lewis, Walker, *Without Fear of Favor: A Biography of Chief Justice Roger Brooke Taney* (1965)

Swisher, Carl B., *Roger B. Taney* (1935)

Morrison R. Waite:

Magrath, C. Peter, *Morrison R. Waite: The Triumph of Character* (1963)

Earl Warren:

Cray, Ed, *Chief Justice: A Biography of Earl Warren* (1997)

Katcher, L., *Earl Warren: A Political Biography* (1967)

Pollack, J.H., *Earl Warren: The Judge Who Changed America* (1979)

White, G. Edward, *Earl Warren: A Public Life* (1982)

Byron R. White:

Hutchinson, Dennis J., *The Man Who Was Whizzer White* (1998)

Edward D. White:

Highsaw, Robert Baker, *Edward Douglass White: Defender of the Conservative Faith* (1981)

CREDITS

INDEX OF CASES

Cases excerpted are in **boldface**.

INDEX OF SUBJECTS